State Rankings 2010

Other titles in the State Fact Finder series

City Crime Rankings

Crime State Rankings

Education State Rankings

Health Care State Rankings

State Rankings 2010

A Statistical View of America

Kathleen O'Leary Morgan

and

Scott Morgan

Editors

CQ PRESS

A Division of SAGE

Washington, D.C.

CQ Press
2300 N Street, NW, Suite 800
Washington, DC 20037

Phone: 202-729-1900; toll-free, 1-866-4CQ-PRESS (1-866-427-7737)

Web: www.cqpress.com

Cover design: Silverander Communications

♾ The paper used in this publication exceeds the requirements of the American
National Standard for Information Sciences—Permanence of Paper for Printed
Library Materials, ANSI Z39.48-1992.

Printed and bound in the United States of America

14 13 12 11 10   1 2 3 4 5

Library of Congress Cataloging-in-Publication Data

ISBN 978-1-60426-615-3 (cloth)
ISBN 978-1-60426-616-0 (paper)

Contents

Detailed Table of Contents

VI. EMPLOYMENT AND LABOR

VII. ENERGY AND ENVIRONMENT

XI. HEALTH

XII. HOUSEHOLDS AND HOUSING

XIII. POPULATION

Introduction and Methodology

Introduction and Methodology

State Rankings 2010 provides an easily accessible collection of data in a broad range of quality-of-life factors in the United States. In this latest edition, *State Rankings* compares data from the fifty states and the District of Columbia in 567 tables in the following fifteen livability categories: agriculture, crime and law enforcement, defense, economy, education, employment and labor, energy and environment, geography, fed-eral government finances, state and local government finances, health, households and housing, population, social welfare, and transportation.

Purpose of This Book

State Rankings 2010 translates complicated and often convoluted statistics into meaningful, easy-to-understand information. Too often there is an abundance of data but far too little information that places the data into context. This book allows researchers, legislators, policy analysts, journalists, and the general public to access information in a manner that not only provides basic facts about a state's quality of life, but also gives a meaningful framework by comparing individual states to the rest of the country.

These data and rankings can be used in a variety of ways, by a variety of audiences, including the following:

- Policymakers can use the data to help identify areas warranting further study.
- Journalists can find impartial state information that places stories into context.
- The general public can learn how a particular state is faring in relation to to other states.
- Librarians can assist patrons with this quick reference and direct them to the Web sites and additional information sources in the book.

The comparison rankings in *State Rankings 2010* provide an annual snapshot of how the states are doing in the fifteen livability categories mentioned above. There are two principle approaches to using these rankings. The first is to examine how a state is doing compared to all the other states via the rankings in this book. The second approach is to compare a state to itself over a given period of time. Both approaches are critical to understanding how and whether a state is making progress. It is important to keep in mind that the rankings are not a definitive indication of which state is the "best." However, since the discussion of many livability factors in clouded by emotional responses, tracking them by the numbers can help bring the discussion back to a more balanced, unbiased review that ultimately leads to better decisions.

Data and Limitations

The data featured in *State Rankings 2010* were chosen specifically by the editors from a variety of government and private-sector sources. The statistics presented are intended to cover a broad array of quality-of-life subject areas, giving users a solid collection of state information. Nonetheless, the statistics are not inclusive of all the data available.

Previous editions of this book have used the term "most livable" when describing states with the highest livability ranking. This term is no longer used, because it is purely descriptive—at no time do we attempt to explain *why* a particular state is ranking higher or lower in livability factors than other states or against the national average. This explanation—currently sought by social science researchers—is beyond the scope of this book. While our selection of factors clearly affects the rankings, we believe the rankings provide a solid measurement of how the fifty states and Washington, D.C., are faring in terms of quality of life in the United States. Researchers, practitioners, and others can use the data with confidence to understand livability issues and guide policy decisions.

Methodology

The comparison rankings for *State Rankings 2010* are determined using the same methodology we have used for the past twenty years. The editors used the previously mentioned fifteen livability categories to select forty-four quality-of-life factors from a broad range of economic, educational, health-oriented, public safety, and environmental statistics. Overall comparison rankings were determined by averaging each state's ranking for each category. The scale is 1 to 50—the higher the number, the higher the state is in the rankings (that is, 50 is the best score).

Data used are for the most recent year for which comparable numbers are available from most states. All factors are given equal weight.

The information in the tables provided in *State Rankings 2010* then is ranked highest to lowest without any subjective determination as to whether a subject is "positive" or "negative." For the state comparison rankings, the editors do make a subjective determination as to whether something is "positive" or "negative." Twenty-five of the forty-four factors were determined to be negative; the remaining nineteen were viewed as positive.

The reason for this division between positive and negative is that if a state ranks first in crime rate (that is, it has the highest crime rate), its comparison ranking is reduced. However, if a state ranks first in per capita personal income (that is, it has the highest income), its comparison ranking is increased. To account for this, we subtract the rankings for the positive factors from 51 so that a state with the highest ranking in a positive factor ends up with a 50 for that factor (remember, high numbers are best).

Once we have chosen the factors and divided them into positive and negative groupings, we average the ranking for each state in all forty-four factors. If a state is missing data for a given factor, its standing is based on the average ranking for the remaining factors.

As an example, Minnesota ranks 31st in crime rate in 2008 (negative factor), 28th in personal bankruptcy rate in 2009 (negative factor), and first in percent of eligible population reported voting in 2008 (positive factor). The 31st and 28th rankings go straight into the comparison formula, whereas the number 1 ranking in percent of eligible population reported voting is first subtracted from 51, with the resulting 50 going into the ranking. For these three factors for Minnesota, we would average 31, 28, and 50 with the result being 36.33. If these three factors were the only ones we had access to, then the resulting average of 36.33 would be the figure we would use to compare Minnesota to the other forty-nine states. However, for the *State Rankings* comparison rankings, an additional forty-one factors are added into the calculations before the final results are determined.

Designed with the researcher in mind, the numbers shown in *State Rankings* require no additional calculations to convert them from millions, thousands, and so on. All states are ranked from highest to lowest, with any ties among the states for a given ranking listed alphabetically. Negative numbers are shown in parentheses. For tables displaying national totals (as opposed to rates or per capita, for example), a separate column shows what percent of the national total each state's total represents. This column, headed by "% of USA," is particularly interesting when compared to a state's share of the nation's population in a given year.

To further assist readers, source information and footnotes are provided at the bottom of each page, while national totals, rates, and percentages are prominently displayed at the top of each table. Every other line is shaded in gray for easier reading. Numerous information-finding tools are provided: a thorough table of contents, table listings at the beginning of each chapter, and a detailed index. In addition, a roster of sources, with addresses, phone numbers, and Web sites is found in the back of the book.

The 2010 State Rankings

RANK	STATE	AVG	09 RANK	CHANGE
46	Alabama	18.57	46	0
18	Alaska	28.11	21	3
45	Arizona	19.23	39	-6
42	Arkansas	20.14	43	1
34	California	22.93	29	-5
12	Colorado	29.61	14	2
14	Connecticut	29.25	8	-6
29	Delaware	23.45	31	2
44	Florida	19.27	41	-3
43	Georgia	19.50	44	1
17	Hawaii	28.23	20	3
23	Idaho	27.00	16	-7
30	Illinois	23.43	26	-4
33	Indiana	23.18	37	4
2	Iowa	33.18	2	0
10	Kansas	30.61	10	0
48	Kentucky	17.86	48	0
36	Louisiana	21.66	44	8
16	Maine	29.16	19	3
19	Maryland	27.73	17	-2
11	Massachusetts	30.50	12	1
35	Michigan	22.43	33	-2
1	Minnesota	33.32	4	3
49	Mississippi	17.84	50	1
26	Missouri	24.75	32	6
20	Montana	27.52	22	2
3	Nebraska	33.16	5	2
38	Nevada	21.50	35	-3
4	New Hampshire	32.86	3	-1
15	New Jersey	29.23	13	-2
39	New Mexico	21.41	38	-1
24	New York	25.43	24	0
41	North Carolina	20.68	42	1
5	North Dakota	31.84	6	1
40	Ohio	20.93	36	-4
32	Oklahoma	23.41	30	-2
25	Oregon	24.98	25	0
27	Pennsylvania	24.66	28	1
28	Rhode Island	23.75	27	-1
50	South Carolina	17.45	49	-1
7	South Dakota	31.68	11	4
47	Tennessee	18.52	47	0
30	Texas	23.43	34	4
8	Utah	31.64	9	1
9	Vermont	31.00	7	-2
13	Virginia	29.30	15	2
22	Washington	27.16	18	-4
37	West Virginia	21.59	40	3
21	Wisconsin	27.45	23	2
6	Wyoming	31.77	1	-5

RANK	STATE	AVG	09 RANK	CHANGE
1	Minnesota	33.32	4	3
2	Iowa	33.18	2	0
3	Nebraska	33.16	5	2
4	New Hampshire	32.86	3	-1
5	North Dakota	31.84	6	1
6	Wyoming	31.77	1	-5
7	South Dakota	31.68	11	4
8	Utah	31.64	9	1
9	Vermont	31.00	7	-2
10	Kansas	30.61	10	0
11	Massachusetts	30.50	12	1
12	Colorado	29.61	14	2
13	Virginia	29.30	15	2
14	Connecticut	29.25	8	-6
15	New Jersey	29.23	13	-2
16	Maine	29.16	19	3
17	Hawaii	28.23	20	3
18	Alaska	28.11	21	3
19	Maryland	27.73	17	-2
20	Montana	27.52	22	2
21	Wisconsin	27.45	23	2
22	Washington	27.16	18	-4
23	Idaho	27.00	16	-7
24	New York	25.43	24	0
25	Oregon	24.98	25	0
26	Missouri	24.75	32	6
27	Pennsylvania	24.66	28	1
28	Rhode Island	23.75	27	-1
29	Delaware	23.45	31	2
30	Illinois	23.43	26	-4
30	Texas	23.43	34	4
32	Oklahoma	23.41	30	-2
33	Indiana	23.18	37	4
34	California	22.93	29	-5
35	Michigan	22.43	33	-2
36	Louisiana	21.66	44	8
37	West Virginia	21.59	40	3
38	Nevada	21.50	35	-3
39	New Mexico	21.41	38	-1
40	Ohio	20.93	36	-4
41	North Carolina	20.68	42	1
42	Arkansas	20.14	43	1
43	Georgia	19.50	44	1
44	Florida	19.27	41	-3
45	Arizona	19.23	39	-6
46	Alabama	18.57	46	0
47	Tennessee	18.52	47	0
48	Kentucky	17.86	48	0
49	Mississippi	17.84	50	1
50	South Carolina	17.45	49	-1

Date Each State Admitted to Statehood*

ALPHA ORDER

RANK	STATE	DATE OF ADMISSION
22	Alabama	December 14, 1819
49	Alaska	January 3, 1959
48	Arizona	February 14, 1912
25	Arkansas	June 15, 1836
31	California	September 9, 1850
38	Colorado	August 1, 1876
5	Connecticut	January 9, 1788
1	Delaware	December 7, 1787
27	Florida	March 3, 1845
4	Georgia	January 2, 1788
50	Hawaii	August 21, 1959
43	Idaho	July 3, 1890
21	Illinois	December 3, 1818
19	Indiana	December 11, 1816
29	Iowa	December 28, 1846
34	Kansas	January 29, 1861
15	Kentucky	June 1, 1792
18	Louisiana	April 30, 1812
23	Maine	March 15, 1820
7	Maryland	April 28, 1788
6	Massachusetts	February 6, 1788
26	Michigan	January 26, 1837
32	Minnesota	May 11, 1858
20	Mississippi	December 10, 1817
24	Missouri	August 10, 1821
41	Montana	November 8, 1889
37	Nebraska	March 1, 1867
36	Nevada	October 31, 1864
9	New Hampshire	June 21, 1788
3	New Jersey	December 18, 1787
47	New Mexico	January 6, 1912
11	New York	July 26, 1788
12	North Carolina	November 21, 1789
39	North Dakota	November 2, 1889
17	Ohio	March 1, 1803
46	Oklahoma	November 16, 1907
33	Oregon	February 14, 1859
2	Pennsylvania	December 12, 1787
13	Rhode Island	May 29, 1790
8	South Carolina	May 23, 1788
39	South Dakota	November 2, 1889
16	Tennessee	June 1, 1796
28	Texas	December 29, 1845
45	Utah	January 4, 1896
14	Vermont	March 4, 1791
10	Virginia	June 26, 1788
42	Washington	November 11, 1889
35	West Virginia	June 20, 1863
30	Wisconsin	May 29, 1848
44	Wyoming	July 10, 1890

RANK ORDER

RANK	STATE	DATE OF ADMISSION
1	Delaware	December 7, 1787
2	Pennsylvania	December 12, 1787
3	New Jersey	December 18, 1787
4	Georgia	January 2, 1788
5	Connecticut	January 9, 1788
6	Massachusetts	February 6, 1788
7	Maryland	April 28, 1788
8	South Carolina	May 23, 1788
9	New Hampshire	June 21, 1788
10	Virginia	June 26, 1788
11	New York	July 26, 1788
12	North Carolina	November 21, 1789
13	Rhode Island	May 29, 1790
14	Vermont	March 4, 1791
15	Kentucky	June 1, 1792
16	Tennessee	June 1, 1796
17	Ohio	March 1, 1803
18	Louisiana	April 30, 1812
19	Indiana	December 11, 1816
20	Mississippi	December 10, 1817
21	Illinois	December 3, 1818
22	Alabama	December 14, 1819
23	Maine	March 15, 1820
24	Missouri	August 10, 1821
25	Arkansas	June 15, 1836
26	Michigan	January 26, 1837
27	Florida	March 3, 1845
28	Texas	December 29, 1845
29	Iowa	December 28, 1846
30	Wisconsin	May 29, 1848
31	California	September 9, 1850
32	Minnesota	May 11, 1858
33	Oregon	February 14, 1859
34	Kansas	January 29, 1861
35	West Virginia	June 20, 1863
36	Nevada	October 31, 1864
37	Nebraska	March 1, 1867
38	Colorado	August 1, 1876
39	North Dakota	November 2, 1889
39	South Dakota	November 2, 1889
41	Montana	November 8, 1889
42	Washington	November 11, 1889
43	Idaho	July 3, 1890
44	Wyoming	July 10, 1890
45	Utah	January 4, 1896
46	Oklahoma	November 16, 1907
47	New Mexico	January 6, 1912
48	Arizona	February 14, 1912
49	Alaska	January 3, 1959
50	Hawaii	August 21, 1959

Source: U.S. Bureau of the Census
    "1980 Census of Population" (vol. 1, part A, PC80-1-A)
    *First thirteen states show date of ratification of Constitution.

STATE FAST FACTS

STATE	NICKNAME	CAPITAL	POPULATION*	AREA**
Alabama	Heart of Dixie	Montgomery	4,708,708	52,420
Alaska	The Last Frontier	Juneau	698,473	664,988
Arizona	Grand Canyon State	Phoenix	6,595,778	113,990
Arkansas	The Natural State	Little Rock	2,889,450	53,178
California	Golden State	Sacramento	36,961,664	163,694
Colorado	Centennial State	Denver	5,024,748	104,094
Connecticut	Constitution State	Hartford	3,518,288	5,544
Delaware	First State	Dover	885,122	2,489
Florida	Sunshine State	Tallahassee	18,537,969	65,758
Georgia	Peach State	Atlanta	9,829,211	59,425
Hawaii	Aloha State	Honolulu	1,295,178	10,926
Idaho	Gem State	Boise	1,545,801	83,568
Illinois	Land of Lincoln	Springfield	12,910,409	57,916
Indiana	Hoosier State	Indianapolis	6,423,113	36,417
Iowa	Hawkeye State	Des Moines	3,007,856	56,273
Kansas	Sunflower State	Topeka	2,818,747	82,278
Kentucky	Bluegrass State	Frankfort	4,314,113	40,411
Louisiana	Pelican State	Baton Rouge	4,492,076	51,988
Maine	Pine Tree State	Augusta	1,318,301	35,384
Maryland	Free State	Annapolis	5,699,478	12,406
Massachusetts	Bay State	Boston	6,593,587	10,554
Michigan	Great Lake State	Lansing	9,969,727	96,713
Minnesota	North Star State	St. Paul	5,266,214	86,935
Mississippi	Magnolia State	Jackson	2,951,996	48,432
Missouri	Show Me State	Jefferson City	5,987,580	69,702
Montana	Treasure State	Helena	974,989	147,039
Nebraska	Cornhusker State	Lincoln	1,796,619	77,349
Nevada	Silver State	Carson City	2,643,085	110,572
New Hampshire	Granite State	Concord	1,324,575	9,348
New Jersey	Garden State	Trenton	8,707,739	8,723
New Mexico	Land of Enchantment	Santa Fe	2,009,671	121,590
New York	Empire State	Albany	19,541,453	54,555
North Carolina	Tar Heel State	Raleigh	9,380,884	53,819
North Dakota	Peace Garden State	Bismarck	646,844	70,698
Ohio	Buckeye State	Columbus	11,542,645	44,825
Oklahoma	Sooner State	Oklahoma City	3,687,050	69,899
Oregon	Beaver State	Salem	3,825,657	98,379
Pennsylvania	Keystone State	Harrisburg	12,604,767	46,055
Rhode Island	Ocean State	Providence	1,053,209	1,545
South Carolina	Palmetto State	Columbia	4,561,242	32,021
South Dakota	Mount Rushmore State	Pierre	812,383	77,116
Tennessee	Volunteer State	Nashville	6,296,254	42,144
Texas	Lone Star State	Austin	24,782,302	268,597
Utah	Beehive State	Salt Lake City	2,784,572	84,897
Vermont	Green Mountain State	Montpelier	621,760	9,616
Virginia	Old Dominion	Richmond	7,882,590	42,775
Washington	Evergreen State	Olympia	6,664,195	71,298
West Virginia	Mountain State	Charleston	1,819,777	24,230
Wisconsin	Badger State	Madison	5,654,774	65,496
Wyoming	Equality State	Cheyenne	544,270	97,812

*2009 Census resident population estimates.
**Total of land and water area in square miles.

STATE SONG	STATE FLOWER	STATE TREE	STATE BIRD
Alabama	Camellia	Southern Pine	Yellowhammer
Alaska's Flag	Forget-Me-Not	Sitka Spruce	Willow Ptarmigan
Arizona	Saguaro Cactus Blossom	Palo Verde	Cactus Wren
Arkansas	Apple Blossom	Pine	Mockingbird
I Love You, California	Golden Poppy	California Redwood	California Valley Quail
Where the Columbines Grow	Rocky Mountain Columbine	Colorado Blue Spruce	Lark Bunting
Yankee Doodle Dandy	Mountain Laurel	White Oak	American Robin
Our Delaware	Peach Blossom	American Holly	Blue Hen Chicken
Swanee River	Orange Blossom	Sabal Palmetto Palm	Mockingbird
Georgia On My Mind	Cherokee Rose	Live Oak	Brown Thrasher
Hawaii Ponoi	Yellow Hibiscus	Candlenut	Nene
Here We Have Idaho	Syringa	White Pine	Mountain Bluebird
Illinois	Purple Violet	White Oak	Cardinal
On the Banks of the Wabash, Far Away	Peony	Tulip Poplar	Cardinal
The Song of Iowa	Wild Rose	Oak	Eastern Goldfinch
Home on the Range	Sunflower	Cottonwood	Western Meadowlark
My Old Kentucky Home	Goldenrod	Tulip Tree	Cardinal
Give Me Louisiana	Magnolia	Cypress	Eastern Brown Pelican
State of Maine Song	White Pine Cone and Tassel	Eastern White Pine	Chickadee
Maryland, My Maryland	Black-eyed Susan	White Oak	Baltimore Oriole
All Hail to Massachusetts	Mayflower	American Elm	Chickadee
Michigan, My Michigan	Apple Blossom	White Pine	Robin
Hail! Minnesota	Pink and White Lady's Slipper	Red Pine	Common Loon
Go, Mississippi!	Magnolia	Magnolia	Mockingbird
Missouri Waltz	Hawthorn	Dogwood	Bluebird
Montana	Bitterroot	Ponderosa Pine	Western Meadowlark
Beautiful Nebraska	Goldenrod	Cottonwood	Western Meadowlark
Home Means Nevada	Sagebrush	Single-Leaf Pinon	Mountain Bluebird
Old New Hampshire	Purple Lilac	White Birch	Purple Finch
Ode to New Jersey	Purple Violet	Red Oak	Eastern Goldfinch
O Fair New Mexico	Yucca	Pinon	Roadrunner
I Love New York	Rose	Sugar Maple	Bluebird
The Old North State	Dogwood	Pine	Cardinal
North Dakota Hymn	Wild Prairie Rose	American Elm	Western Meadowlark
Beautiful Ohio	Scarlet Carnation	Buckeye	Cardinal
Oklahoma!	Mistletoe	Redbud	Scissortailed Flycatcher
Oregon, My Oregon	Oregon Grape	Douglas Fir	Western Meadowlark
Hail! Pennsylvania	Mountain Laurel	Hemlock	Ruffed Grouse
Rhode Island	Violet	Red Maple	Rhode Island Red
Carolina	Yellow Jessamine	Palmetto	Carolina Wren
Hail, South Dakota	Pasque Flower	Black Hills Spruce	Ringnecked Pheasant
The Tennessee Waltz	Iris	Tulip Poplar	Mockingbird
Texas, Our Texas	Bluebonnet	Pecan	Mockingbird
Utah, We Love Thee	Sego Lily	Blue Spruce	Seagull
Hail, Vermont	Red Clover	Sugar Maple	Hermit Thrush
Carry Me Back to Old Virginia	Dogwood	Dogwood	Cardinal
Washington, My Home	Western Rhododendron	Western Hemlock	Willow Goldfinch
The West Virginia Hills; This Is My West Virginia; and West Virginia, My Home, Sweet Home	Big Rhododendron	Sugar Maple	Cardinal
On Wisconsin!	Wood Violet	Sugar Maple	Robin
Wyoming	Indian Paintbrush	Cottonwood	Meadowlark

I. Agriculture

Number of Farms in 2008

National Total = 2,200,000 Farms*

ALPHA ORDER

RANK	STATE	FARMS	% of USA
18	Alabama	48,500	2.2%
50	Alaska	680	0.0%
37	Arizona	15,600	0.7%
17	Arkansas	49,300	2.2%
6	California	81,500	3.7%
27	Colorado	36,500	1.7%
45	Connecticut	4,900	0.2%
48	Delaware	2,500	0.1%
20	Florida	47,500	2.2%
19	Georgia	47,800	2.2%
43	Hawaii	7,500	0.3%
33	Idaho	25,200	1.1%
10	Illinois	75,900	3.5%
14	Indiana	61,000	2.8%
3	Iowa	92,600	4.2%
12	Kansas	65,500	3.0%
5	Kentucky	85,300	3.9%
30	Louisiana	30,000	1.4%
41	Maine	8,000	0.4%
38	Maryland	12,850	0.6%
42	Massachusetts	7,700	0.4%
15	Michigan	55,000	2.5%
7	Minnesota	81,000	3.7%
23	Mississippi	42,000	1.9%
2	Missouri	108,000	4.9%
31	Montana	29,500	1.3%
21	Nebraska	47,400	2.2%
47	Nevada	3,100	0.1%
46	New Hampshire	4,150	0.2%
40	New Jersey	10,300	0.5%
35	New Mexico	20,600	0.9%
26	New York	36,600	1.7%
16	North Carolina	52,500	2.4%
28	North Dakota	32,000	1.5%
11	Ohio	75,000	3.4%
4	Oklahoma	86,600	3.9%
25	Oregon	38,600	1.8%
13	Pennsylvania	63,200	2.9%
49	Rhode Island	1,220	0.1%
32	South Carolina	26,900	1.2%
29	South Dakota	31,300	1.4%
8	Tennessee	79,000	3.6%
1	Texas	247,500	11.3%
36	Utah	16,500	0.8%
44	Vermont	7,000	0.3%
22	Virginia	47,000	2.1%
24	Washington	39,500	1.8%
34	West Virginia	23,200	1.1%
9	Wisconsin	78,000	3.5%
39	Wyoming	11,000	0.5%

RANK ORDER

RANK	STATE	FARMS	% of USA
1	Texas	247,500	11.3%
2	Missouri	108,000	4.9%
3	Iowa	92,600	4.2%
4	Oklahoma	86,600	3.9%
5	Kentucky	85,300	3.9%
6	California	81,500	3.7%
7	Minnesota	81,000	3.7%
8	Tennessee	79,000	3.6%
9	Wisconsin	78,000	3.5%
10	Illinois	75,900	3.5%
11	Ohio	75,000	3.4%
12	Kansas	65,500	3.0%
13	Pennsylvania	63,200	2.9%
14	Indiana	61,000	2.8%
15	Michigan	55,000	2.5%
16	North Carolina	52,500	2.4%
17	Arkansas	49,300	2.2%
18	Alabama	48,500	2.2%
19	Georgia	47,800	2.2%
20	Florida	47,500	2.2%
21	Nebraska	47,400	2.2%
22	Virginia	47,000	2.1%
23	Mississippi	42,000	1.9%
24	Washington	39,500	1.8%
25	Oregon	38,600	1.8%
26	New York	36,600	1.7%
27	Colorado	36,500	1.7%
28	North Dakota	32,000	1.5%
29	South Dakota	31,300	1.4%
30	Louisiana	30,000	1.4%
31	Montana	29,500	1.3%
32	South Carolina	26,900	1.2%
33	Idaho	25,200	1.1%
34	West Virginia	23,200	1.1%
35	New Mexico	20,600	0.9%
36	Utah	16,500	0.8%
37	Arizona	15,600	0.7%
38	Maryland	12,850	0.6%
39	Wyoming	11,000	0.5%
40	New Jersey	10,300	0.5%
41	Maine	8,000	0.4%
42	Massachusetts	7,700	0.4%
43	Hawaii	7,500	0.3%
44	Vermont	7,000	0.3%
45	Connecticut	4,900	0.2%
46	New Hampshire	4,150	0.2%
47	Nevada	3,100	0.1%
48	Delaware	2,500	0.1%
49	Rhode Island	1,220	0.1%
50	Alaska	680	0.0%
	District of Columbia	0	0.0%

Source: U.S. Department of Agriculture, National Agricultural Statistics Service
"Farms and Land in Farms" (http://usda.mannlib.cornell.edu/MannUsda/viewDocumentInfo.do?documentID=1259)
*A farm is any establishment from which $1,000 or more of agricultural products were sold or would normally be sold during the year. This includes places with five or more horses, except horses in boarding stables or racetracks.

Land in Farms in 2008

National Total = 919,900,000 Acres*

RANK	STATE	ACRES	% of USA		RANK	STATE	ACRES	% of USA
31	Alabama	8,950,000	1.0%		1	Texas	130,400,000	14.2%
44	Alaska	890,000	0.1%		2	Montana	60,800,000	6.6%
15	Arizona	26,100,000	2.8%		3	Kansas	46,200,000	5.0%
23	Arkansas	13,700,000	1.5%		4	Nebraska	45,600,000	5.0%
16	California	25,400,000	2.8%		5	South Dakota	43,700,000	4.8%
9	Colorado	31,300,000	3.4%		6	New Mexico	43,000,000	4.7%
49	Connecticut	400,000	0.0%		7	North Dakota	39,600,000	4.3%
47	Delaware	500,000	0.1%		8	Oklahoma	35,100,000	3.8%
30	Florida	9,250,000	1.0%		9	Colorado	31,300,000	3.4%
28	Georgia	10,400,000	1.1%		10	Iowa	30,800,000	3.3%
43	Hawaii	1,110,000	0.1%		11	Wyoming	30,100,000	3.3%
24	Idaho	11,400,000	1.2%		12	Missouri	29,100,000	3.2%
14	Illinois	26,700,000	2.9%		13	Minnesota	26,900,000	2.9%
19	Indiana	14,800,000	1.6%		14	Illinois	26,700,000	2.9%
10	Iowa	30,800,000	3.3%		15	Arizona	26,100,000	2.8%
3	Kansas	46,200,000	5.0%		16	California	25,400,000	2.8%
21	Kentucky	14,000,000	1.5%		17	Oregon	16,400,000	1.8%
33	Louisiana	8,050,000	0.9%		18	Wisconsin	15,200,000	1.7%
41	Maine	1,350,000	0.1%		19	Indiana	14,800,000	1.6%
40	Maryland	2,050,000	0.2%		19	Washington	14,800,000	1.6%
46	Massachusetts	510,000	0.1%		21	Kentucky	14,000,000	1.5%
29	Michigan	10,000,000	1.1%		22	Ohio	13,900,000	1.5%
13	Minnesota	26,900,000	2.9%		23	Arkansas	13,700,000	1.5%
26	Mississippi	11,000,000	1.2%		24	Idaho	11,400,000	1.2%
12	Missouri	29,100,000	3.2%		25	Utah	11,100,000	1.2%
2	Montana	60,800,000	6.6%		26	Mississippi	11,000,000	1.2%
4	Nebraska	45,600,000	5.0%		27	Tennessee	10,900,000	1.2%
37	Nevada	5,900,000	0.6%		28	Georgia	10,400,000	1.1%
48	New Hampshire	470,000	0.1%		29	Michigan	10,000,000	1.1%
45	New Jersey	730,000	0.1%		30	Florida	9,250,000	1.0%
6	New Mexico	43,000,000	4.7%		31	Alabama	8,950,000	1.0%
36	New York	7,100,000	0.8%		32	North Carolina	8,600,000	0.9%
32	North Carolina	8,600,000	0.9%		33	Louisiana	8,050,000	0.9%
7	North Dakota	39,600,000	4.3%		34	Virginia	8,000,000	0.9%
22	Ohio	13,900,000	1.5%		35	Pennsylvania	7,750,000	0.8%
8	Oklahoma	35,100,000	3.8%		36	New York	7,100,000	0.8%
17	Oregon	16,400,000	1.8%		37	Nevada	5,900,000	0.6%
35	Pennsylvania	7,750,000	0.8%		38	South Carolina	4,900,000	0.5%
50	Rhode Island	70,000	0.0%		39	West Virginia	3,700,000	0.4%
38	South Carolina	4,900,000	0.5%		40	Maryland	2,050,000	0.2%
5	South Dakota	43,700,000	4.8%		41	Maine	1,350,000	0.1%
27	Tennessee	10,900,000	1.2%		42	Vermont	1,220,000	0.1%
1	Texas	130,400,000	14.2%		43	Hawaii	1,110,000	0.1%
25	Utah	11,100,000	1.2%		44	Alaska	890,000	0.1%
42	Vermont	1,220,000	0.1%		45	New Jersey	730,000	0.1%
34	Virginia	8,000,000	0.9%		46	Massachusetts	510,000	0.1%
19	Washington	14,800,000	1.6%		47	Delaware	500,000	0.1%
39	West Virginia	3,700,000	0.4%		48	New Hampshire	470,000	0.1%
18	Wisconsin	15,200,000	1.7%		49	Connecticut	400,000	0.0%
11	Wyoming	30,100,000	3.3%		50	Rhode Island	70,000	0.0%
						District of Columbia	0	0.0%

ALPHA ORDER

RANK ORDER

Source: U.S. Department of Agriculture, National Agricultural Statistics Service
   "Farms and Land in Farms" (http://usda.mannlib.cornell.edu/MannUsda/viewDocumentInfo.do?documentID=1259)
*A farm is any establishment from which $1,000 or more of agricultural products were sold or would normally be sold during the year. This includes places with five or more horses, except horses in boarding stables or racetracks.

Average Number of Acres per Farm in 2008

National Average = 418 Acres*

ALPHA ORDER			RANK ORDER		
RANK	STATE	ACRES	RANK	STATE	ACRES
32	Alabama	185	1	Wyoming	2,736
7	Alaska	1,309	2	New Mexico	2,087
5	Arizona	1,673	3	Montana	2,061
22	Arkansas	278	4	Nevada	1,903
21	California	312	5	Arizona	1,673
10	Colorado	858	6	South Dakota	1,396
47	Connecticut	82	7	Alaska	1,309
28	Delaware	200	8	North Dakota	1,238
29	Florida	195	9	Nebraska	962
27	Georgia	218	10	Colorado	858
43	Hawaii	148	11	Kansas	705
14	Idaho	452	12	Utah	673
18	Illinois	352	13	Texas	527
26	Indiana	243	14	Idaho	452
19	Iowa	333	15	Oregon	425
11	Kansas	705	16	Oklahoma	405
39	Kentucky	164	17	Washington	375
24	Louisiana	268	18	Illinois	352
38	Maine	169	19	Iowa	333
41	Maryland	160	20	Minnesota	332
49	Massachusetts	66	21	California	312
34	Michigan	182	22	Arkansas	278
20	Minnesota	332	23	Missouri	269
25	Mississippi	262	24	Louisiana	268
23	Missouri	269	25	Mississippi	262
3	Montana	2,061	26	Indiana	243
9	Nebraska	962	27	Georgia	218
4	Nevada	1,903	28	Delaware	200
46	New Hampshire	113	29	Florida	195
48	New Jersey	71	29	Wisconsin	195
2	New Mexico	2,087	31	New York	194
31	New York	194	32	Alabama	185
39	North Carolina	164	32	Ohio	185
8	North Dakota	1,238	34	Michigan	182
32	Ohio	185	34	South Carolina	182
16	Oklahoma	405	36	Vermont	174
15	Oregon	425	37	Virginia	170
45	Pennsylvania	123	38	Maine	169
50	Rhode Island	57	39	Kentucky	164
34	South Carolina	182	39	North Carolina	164
6	South Dakota	1,396	41	Maryland	160
44	Tennessee	138	42	West Virginia	159
13	Texas	527	43	Hawaii	148
12	Utah	673	44	Tennessee	138
36	Vermont	174	45	Pennsylvania	123
37	Virginia	170	46	New Hampshire	113
17	Washington	375	47	Connecticut	82
42	West Virginia	159	48	New Jersey	71
29	Wisconsin	195	49	Massachusetts	66
1	Wyoming	2,736	50	Rhode Island	57
				District of Columbia**	NA

Source: U.S. Department of Agriculture, National Agricultural Statistics Service
   "Farms and Land in Farms" (http://usda.mannlib.cornell.edu/MannUsda/viewDocumentInfo.do?documentID=1259)
*A farm is any establishment from which $1,000 or more of agricultural products were sold or would normally be sold during the year. This includes places with five or more horses, except horses in boarding stables or racetracks.
**Not applicable.

Average Per-Acre Value of Farmland in 2009

National Average = $2,100 per Acre*

ALPHA ORDER

RANK	STATE	PER-ACRE VALUE
31	Alabama	$2,150
NA	Alaska**	NA
20	Arizona	3,500
28	Arkansas	2,390
7	California	6,100
41	Colorado	1,100
3	Connecticut	12,000
5	Delaware	8,900
8	Florida	5,150
15	Georgia	4,000
NA	Hawaii**	NA
29	Idaho	2,200
12	Illinois	4,530
14	Indiana	4,020
17	Iowa	3,850
42	Kansas	1,030
24	Kentucky	2,850
34	Louisiana	1,970
32	Maine	2,100
6	Maryland	7,500
3	Massachusetts	12,000
18	Michigan	3,750
23	Minnesota	2,870
33	Mississippi	2,000
29	Missouri	2,200
46	Montana	700
39	Nebraska	1,340
43	Nevada	1,000
10	New Hampshire	4,800
2	New Jersey	13,800
48	New Mexico	480
26	New York	2,400
13	North Carolina	4,250
45	North Dakota	780
16	Ohio	3,880
40	Oklahoma	1,170
36	Oregon	1,800
9	Pennsylvania	5,100
1	Rhode Island	15,300
22	South Carolina	2,900
44	South Dakota	890
21	Tennessee	3,300
38	Texas	1,550
36	Utah	1,800
25	Vermont	2,800
10	Virginia	4,800
35	Washington	1,950
26	West Virginia	2,400
18	Wisconsin	3,750
47	Wyoming	520

RANK ORDER

RANK	STATE	PER-ACRE VALUE
1	Rhode Island	$15,300
2	New Jersey	13,800
3	Connecticut	12,000
3	Massachusetts	12,000
5	Delaware	8,900
6	Maryland	7,500
7	California	6,100
8	Florida	5,150
9	Pennsylvania	5,100
10	New Hampshire	4,800
10	Virginia	4,800
12	Illinois	4,530
13	North Carolina	4,250
14	Indiana	4,020
15	Georgia	4,000
16	Ohio	3,880
17	Iowa	3,850
18	Michigan	3,750
18	Wisconsin	3,750
20	Arizona	3,500
21	Tennessee	3,300
22	South Carolina	2,900
23	Minnesota	2,870
24	Kentucky	2,850
25	Vermont	2,800
26	New York	2,400
26	West Virginia	2,400
28	Arkansas	2,390
29	Idaho	2,200
29	Missouri	2,200
31	Alabama	2,150
32	Maine	2,100
33	Mississippi	2,000
34	Louisiana	1,970
35	Washington	1,950
36	Oregon	1,800
36	Utah	1,800
38	Texas	1,550
39	Nebraska	1,340
40	Oklahoma	1,170
41	Colorado	1,100
42	Kansas	1,030
43	Nevada	1,000
44	South Dakota	890
45	North Dakota	780
46	Montana	700
47	Wyoming	520
48	New Mexico	480
NA	Alaska**	NA
NA	Hawaii**	NA
	District of Columbia**	NA

Source: U.S. Department of Agriculture, National Agricultural Statistics Service
  "Land Values and Cash Rents" (http://usda.mannlib.cornell.edu/MannUsda/viewDocumentInfo.do?documentID=1446)
*As of January 1, 2009. Value of farmland and buildings in nominal dollars.
**Not applicable or available.

Percent Change in Average Per-Acre Value of Farmland: 2008 to 2009

National Percent Change = 3.2% Decrease*

ALPHA ORDER				RANK ORDER		
RANK	STATE	PERCENT CHANGE		RANK	STATE	PERCENT CHANGE
40	Alabama	(6.5)		1	New York	2.1
NA	Alaska**	NA		2	Oklahoma	1.7
6	Arizona	0.0		3	North Dakota	1.3
12	Arkansas	(1.2)		4	Kansas	1.0
36	California	(5.3)		5	Nebraska	0.8
31	Colorado	(4.3)		6	Arizona	0.0
38	Connecticut	(5.5)		6	Kentucky	0.0
47	Delaware	(13.6)		6	Nevada	0.0
43	Florida	(8.7)		6	Texas	0.0
41	Georgia	(7.0)		10	Illinois	(0.4)
NA	Hawaii**	NA		10	Pennsylvania	(0.4)
46	Idaho	(12.0)		12	Arkansas	(1.2)
10	Illinois	(0.4)		13	South Carolina	(1.7)
14	Indiana	(2.0)		14	Indiana	(2.0)
17	Iowa	(2.5)		14	New Hampshire	(2.0)
4	Kansas	1.0		16	Massachusetts	(2.4)
6	Kentucky	0.0		17	Iowa	(2.5)
27	Louisiana	(3.9)		18	Wisconsin	(2.6)
34	Maine	(4.5)		19	Utah	(2.7)
39	Maryland	(6.3)		20	South Dakota	(3.3)
16	Massachusetts	(2.4)		21	Minnesota	(3.4)
25	Michigan	(3.8)		21	Vermont	(3.4)
21	Minnesota	(3.4)		23	Ohio	(3.5)
25	Mississippi	(3.8)		23	Washington	(3.5)
31	Missouri	(4.3)		25	Michigan	(3.8)
48	Montana	(22.2)		25	Mississippi	(3.8)
5	Nebraska	0.8		27	Louisiana	(3.9)
6	Nevada	0.0		28	New Mexico	(4.0)
14	New Hampshire	(2.0)		28	Virginia	(4.0)
45	New Jersey	(9.8)		28	West Virginia	(4.0)
28	New Mexico	(4.0)		31	Colorado	(4.3)
1	New York	2.1		31	Missouri	(4.3)
34	North Carolina	(4.5)		31	Tennessee	(4.3)
3	North Dakota	1.3		34	Maine	(4.5)
23	Ohio	(3.5)		34	North Carolina	(4.5)
2	Oklahoma	1.7		36	California	(5.3)
36	Oregon	(5.3)		36	Oregon	(5.3)
10	Pennsylvania	(0.4)		38	Connecticut	(5.5)
44	Rhode Island	(8.9)		39	Maryland	(6.3)
13	South Carolina	(1.7)		40	Alabama	(6.5)
20	South Dakota	(3.3)		41	Georgia	(7.0)
31	Tennessee	(4.3)		42	Wyoming	(7.1)
6	Texas	0.0		43	Florida	(8.7)
19	Utah	(2.7)		44	Rhode Island	(8.9)
21	Vermont	(3.4)		45	New Jersey	(9.8)
28	Virginia	(4.0)		46	Idaho	(12.0)
23	Washington	(3.5)		47	Delaware	(13.6)
28	West Virginia	(4.0)		48	Montana	(22.2)
18	Wisconsin	(2.6)		NA	Alaska**	NA
42	Wyoming	(7.1)		NA	Hawaii**	NA
					District of Columbia**	NA

Source: U.S. Department of Agriculture, National Agricultural Statistics Service
   "Land Values and Cash Rents" (http://usda.mannlib.cornell.edu/MannUsda/viewDocumentInfo.do?documentID=1446)
*As of January 1, 2009. Value of farmland and buildings in nominal dollars.
**Not applicable or available.

Net Farm Income in 2008

National Total = $87,073,782*

ALPHA ORDER

RANK	STATE	FARM INCOME	% of USA
23	Alabama	$1,391,221,323	1.6%
50	Alaska	5,194,073	0.0%
31	Arizona	751,212,765	0.9%
9	Arkansas	3,091,112,591	3.5%
1	California	7,876,806,049	9.0%
24	Colorado	1,388,609,014	1.6%
41	Connecticut	176,974,635	0.2%
39	Delaware	236,671,234	0.3%
20	Florida	1,741,028,843	2.0%
13	Georgia	2,775,046,000	3.2%
45	Hawaii	144,349,801	0.2%
19	Idaho	1,835,849,521	2.1%
4	Illinois	5,333,209,123	6.1%
8	Indiana	3,172,417,411	3.6%
2	Iowa	7,025,965,271	8.1%
6	Kansas	3,683,666,570	4.2%
21	Kentucky	1,548,689,688	1.8%
30	Louisiana	789,845,756	0.9%
43	Maine	167,232,756	0.2%
36	Maryland	490,751,051	0.6%
40	Massachusetts	178,587,274	0.2%
16	Michigan	2,026,734,719	2.3%
3	Minnesota	5,836,394,874	6.7%
25	Mississippi	1,297,998,847	1.5%
11	Missouri	3,034,803,675	3.5%
32	Montana	688,141,767	0.8%
5	Nebraska	4,026,379,183	4.6%
42	Nevada	169,810,238	0.2%
47	New Hampshire	45,986,809	0.1%
38	New Jersey	363,069,027	0.4%
29	New Mexico	829,834,953	1.0%
26	New York	1,145,740,224	1.3%
12	North Carolina	2,833,983,303	3.3%
15	North Dakota	2,348,962,292	2.7%
18	Ohio	1,951,993,858	2.2%
27	Oklahoma	1,026,782,934	1.2%
28	Oregon	870,869,920	1.0%
22	Pennsylvania	1,457,304,464	1.7%
48	Rhode Island	16,552,768	0.0%
34	South Carolina	619,740,027	0.7%
10	South Dakota	3,058,440,664	3.5%
33	Tennessee	621,073,825	0.7%
7	Texas	3,218,209,696	3.7%
37	Utah	375,958,992	0.4%
44	Vermont	164,743,111	0.2%
35	Virginia	551,928,487	0.6%
17	Washington	1,963,260,726	2.3%
49	West Virginia	12,721,587	0.0%
14	Wisconsin	2,577,220,939	3.0%
46	Wyoming	134,699,760	0.2%

RANK ORDER

RANK	STATE	FARM INCOME	% of USA
1	California	$7,876,806,049	9.0%
2	Iowa	7,025,965,271	8.1%
3	Minnesota	5,836,394,874	6.7%
4	Illinois	5,333,209,123	6.1%
5	Nebraska	4,026,379,183	4.6%
6	Kansas	3,683,666,570	4.2%
7	Texas	3,218,209,696	3.7%
8	Indiana	3,172,417,411	3.6%
9	Arkansas	3,091,112,591	3.5%
10	South Dakota	3,058,440,664	3.5%
11	Missouri	3,034,803,675	3.5%
12	North Carolina	2,833,983,303	3.3%
13	Georgia	2,775,046,000	3.2%
14	Wisconsin	2,577,220,939	3.0%
15	North Dakota	2,348,962,292	2.7%
16	Michigan	2,026,734,719	2.3%
17	Washington	1,963,260,726	2.3%
18	Ohio	1,951,993,858	2.2%
19	Idaho	1,835,849,521	2.1%
20	Florida	1,741,028,843	2.0%
21	Kentucky	1,548,689,688	1.8%
22	Pennsylvania	1,457,304,464	1.7%
23	Alabama	1,391,221,323	1.6%
24	Colorado	1,388,609,014	1.6%
25	Mississippi	1,297,998,847	1.5%
26	New York	1,145,740,224	1.3%
27	Oklahoma	1,026,782,934	1.2%
28	Oregon	870,869,920	1.0%
29	New Mexico	829,834,953	1.0%
30	Louisiana	789,845,756	0.9%
31	Arizona	751,212,765	0.9%
32	Montana	688,141,767	0.8%
33	Tennessee	621,073,825	0.7%
34	South Carolina	619,740,027	0.7%
35	Virginia	551,928,487	0.6%
36	Maryland	490,751,051	0.6%
37	Utah	375,958,992	0.4%
38	New Jersey	363,069,027	0.4%
39	Delaware	236,671,234	0.3%
40	Massachusetts	178,587,274	0.2%
41	Connecticut	176,974,635	0.2%
42	Nevada	169,810,238	0.2%
43	Maine	167,232,756	0.2%
44	Vermont	164,743,111	0.2%
45	Hawaii	144,349,801	0.2%
46	Wyoming	134,699,760	0.2%
47	New Hampshire	45,986,809	0.1%
48	Rhode Island	16,552,768	0.0%
49	West Virginia	12,721,587	0.0%
50	Alaska	5,194,073	0.0%
	District of Columbia	0	0.0%

Source: U.S. Department of Agriculture, Economic Research Service
"Net Farm Income and Value of Production per Acre for States, 2008
(http://www.ers.usda.gov/data/FarmIncome/FinfidmuXls.htm)
*Net farm income is a measure of the net value of production in a given year. It is determined by subtracting total production expenses from gross farm income.

Net Farm Income per Operation in 2008

National Average = $39,579 per Operation

ALPHA ORDER

RANK	STATE	PER OPERATION
28	Alabama	$28,685
49	Alaska	7,638
17	Arizona	48,155
10	Arkansas	62,700
2	California	96,648
20	Colorado	38,044
23	Connecticut	36,117
3	Delaware	94,668
22	Florida	36,653
11	Georgia	58,055
40	Hawaii	19,247
7	Idaho	72,851
9	Illinois	70,266
15	Indiana	52,007
5	Iowa	75,874
12	Kansas	56,239
41	Kentucky	18,156
30	Louisiana	26,328
39	Maine	20,904
19	Maryland	38,191
34	Massachusetts	23,193
21	Michigan	36,850
8	Minnesota	72,054
27	Mississippi	30,905
29	Missouri	28,100
33	Montana	23,327
4	Nebraska	84,945
13	Nevada	54,777
47	New Hampshire	11,081
24	New Jersey	35,249
18	New Mexico	40,283
26	New York	31,304
14	North Carolina	53,981
6	North Dakota	73,405
31	Ohio	26,027
45	Oklahoma	11,857
38	Oregon	22,561
35	Pennsylvania	23,059
42	Rhode Island	13,568
36	South Carolina	23,039
1	South Dakota	97,714
48	Tennessee	7,862
43	Texas	13,003
37	Utah	22,785
32	Vermont	23,535
46	Virginia	11,743
16	Washington	49,703
50	West Virginia	548
25	Wisconsin	33,041
44	Wyoming	12,245

RANK ORDER

RANK	STATE	PER OPERATION
1	South Dakota	$97,714
2	California	96,648
3	Delaware	94,668
4	Nebraska	84,945
5	Iowa	75,874
6	North Dakota	73,405
7	Idaho	72,851
8	Minnesota	72,054
9	Illinois	70,266
10	Arkansas	62,700
11	Georgia	58,055
12	Kansas	56,239
13	Nevada	54,777
14	North Carolina	53,981
15	Indiana	52,007
16	Washington	49,703
17	Arizona	48,155
18	New Mexico	40,283
19	Maryland	38,191
20	Colorado	38,044
21	Michigan	36,850
22	Florida	36,653
23	Connecticut	36,117
24	New Jersey	35,249
25	Wisconsin	33,041
26	New York	31,304
27	Mississippi	30,905
28	Alabama	28,685
29	Missouri	28,100
30	Louisiana	26,328
31	Ohio	26,027
32	Vermont	23,535
33	Montana	23,327
34	Massachusetts	23,193
35	Pennsylvania	23,059
36	South Carolina	23,039
37	Utah	22,785
38	Oregon	22,561
39	Maine	20,904
40	Hawaii	19,247
41	Kentucky	18,156
42	Rhode Island	13,568
43	Texas	13,003
44	Wyoming	12,245
45	Oklahoma	11,857
46	Virginia	11,743
47	New Hampshire	11,081
48	Tennessee	7,862
49	Alaska	7,638
50	West Virginia	548
	District of Columbia*	NA

Source: U.S. Department of Agriculture, Economic Research Service
    "Net Farm Income and Value of Production per Acre for States, 2008
    (http://www.ers.usda.gov/data/FarmIncome/FinfidmuXls.htm)
*Not applicable.

Net Farm Income per Acre in 2008

National Average = $95 per Acre

ALPHA ORDER RANK	STATE	PER ACRE	RANK ORDER RANK	STATE	PER ACRE
21	Alabama	$155	1	New Jersey	$497
48	Alaska	6	2	Delaware	473
42	Arizona	29	3	Connecticut	442
11	Arkansas	226	4	Massachusetts	350
6	California	310	5	North Carolina	330
40	Colorado	44	6	California	310
3	Connecticut	442	7	Georgia	267
2	Delaware	473	8	Maryland	239
16	Florida	188	9	Rhode Island	236
7	Georgia	267	10	Iowa	228
25	Hawaii	130	11	Arkansas	226
19	Idaho	161	12	Minnesota	217
15	Illinois	200	13	Indiana	214
13	Indiana	214	14	Michigan	203
10	Iowa	228	15	Illinois	200
34	Kansas	80	16	Florida	188
29	Kentucky	111	16	Pennsylvania	188
31	Louisiana	98	18	Wisconsin	170
27	Maine	124	19	Idaho	161
8	Maryland	239	19	New York	161
4	Massachusetts	350	21	Alabama	155
14	Michigan	203	22	Ohio	140
12	Minnesota	217	23	Vermont	135
28	Mississippi	118	24	Washington	133
30	Missouri	104	25	Hawaii	130
47	Montana	11	26	South Carolina	126
33	Nebraska	88	27	Maine	124
42	Nevada	29	28	Mississippi	118
31	New Hampshire	98	29	Kentucky	111
1	New Jersey	497	30	Missouri	104
46	New Mexico	19	31	Louisiana	98
19	New York	161	31	New Hampshire	98
5	North Carolina	330	33	Nebraska	88
37	North Dakota	59	34	Kansas	80
22	Ohio	140	35	South Dakota	70
42	Oklahoma	29	36	Virginia	69
39	Oregon	53	37	North Dakota	59
16	Pennsylvania	188	38	Tennessee	57
9	Rhode Island	236	39	Oregon	53
26	South Carolina	126	40	Colorado	44
35	South Dakota	70	41	Utah	34
38	Tennessee	57	42	Arizona	29
45	Texas	25	42	Nevada	29
41	Utah	34	42	Oklahoma	29
23	Vermont	135	45	Texas	25
36	Virginia	69	46	New Mexico	19
24	Washington	133	47	Montana	11
50	West Virginia	3	48	Alaska	6
18	Wisconsin	170	49	Wyoming	4
49	Wyoming	4	50	West Virginia	3
				District of Columbia*	NA

Source: U.S. Department of Agriculture, Economic Research Service
"Net Farm Income and Value of Production per Acre for States, 2008
(http://www.ers.usda.gov/data/FarmIncome/FinfidmuXls.htm)
*Not applicable.

Farm Income: Cash Receipts from Commodities in 2008

National Total = $324,186,534,000*

ALPHA ORDER

RANK	STATE	FARM INCOME	% of USA
27	Alabama	$4,464,047,000	1.4%
50	Alaska	31,243,000	0.0%
29	Arizona	3,464,560,000	1.1%
12	Arkansas	8,347,267,000	2.6%
1	California	36,186,738,000	11.2%
20	Colorado	6,509,475,000	2.0%
43	Connecticut	600,589,000	0.2%
39	Delaware	1,094,632,000	0.3%
16	Florida	7,978,082,000	2.5%
18	Georgia	7,392,985,000	2.3%
44	Hawaii	574,129,000	0.2%
21	Idaho	6,415,352,000	2.0%
5	Illinois	16,356,792,000	5.0%
8	Indiana	9,961,847,000	3.1%
2	Iowa	24,752,867,000	7.6%
7	Kansas	13,967,498,000	4.3%
25	Kentucky	4,837,758,000	1.5%
32	Louisiana	3,034,676,000	0.9%
42	Maine	675,739,000	0.2%
36	Maryland	1,965,060,000	0.6%
46	Massachusetts	569,789,000	0.2%
19	Michigan	6,605,896,000	2.0%
6	Minnesota	15,838,092,000	4.9%
24	Mississippi	4,967,775,000	1.5%
11	Missouri	8,436,098,000	2.6%
34	Montana	2,901,656,000	0.9%
4	Nebraska	17,315,687,000	5.3%
45	Nevada	572,109,000	0.2%
48	New Hampshire	212,892,000	0.1%
38	New Jersey	1,117,636,000	0.3%
30	New Mexico	3,116,892,000	1.0%
26	New York	4,694,088,000	1.4%
10	North Carolina	9,752,797,000	3.0%
17	North Dakota	7,629,358,000	2.4%
15	Ohio	7,979,401,000	2.5%
23	Oklahoma	5,837,796,000	1.8%
28	Oregon	4,374,986,000	1.3%
22	Pennsylvania	6,122,333,000	1.9%
49	Rhode Island	67,545,000	0.0%
35	South Carolina	2,359,507,000	0.7%
14	South Dakota	8,047,577,000	2.5%
31	Tennessee	3,116,047,000	1.0%
3	Texas	19,172,501,000	5.9%
37	Utah	1,514,542,000	0.5%
41	Vermont	687,802,000	0.2%
33	Virginia	2,999,440,000	0.9%
13	Washington	8,180,417,000	2.5%
47	West Virginia	525,040,000	0.2%
9	Wisconsin	9,885,558,000	3.0%
40	Wyoming	973,944,000	0.3%

RANK ORDER

RANK	STATE	FARM INCOME	% of USA
1	California	$36,186,738,000	11.2%
2	Iowa	24,752,867,000	7.6%
3	Texas	19,172,501,000	5.9%
4	Nebraska	17,315,687,000	5.3%
5	Illinois	16,356,792,000	5.0%
6	Minnesota	15,838,092,000	4.9%
7	Kansas	13,967,498,000	4.3%
8	Indiana	9,961,847,000	3.1%
9	Wisconsin	9,885,558,000	3.0%
10	North Carolina	9,752,797,000	3.0%
11	Missouri	8,436,098,000	2.6%
12	Arkansas	8,347,267,000	2.6%
13	Washington	8,180,417,000	2.5%
14	South Dakota	8,047,577,000	2.5%
15	Ohio	7,979,401,000	2.5%
16	Florida	7,978,082,000	2.5%
17	North Dakota	7,629,358,000	2.4%
18	Georgia	7,392,985,000	2.3%
19	Michigan	6,605,896,000	2.0%
20	Colorado	6,509,475,000	2.0%
21	Idaho	6,415,352,000	2.0%
22	Pennsylvania	6,122,333,000	1.9%
23	Oklahoma	5,837,796,000	1.8%
24	Mississippi	4,967,775,000	1.5%
25	Kentucky	4,837,758,000	1.5%
26	New York	4,694,088,000	1.4%
27	Alabama	4,464,047,000	1.4%
28	Oregon	4,374,986,000	1.3%
29	Arizona	3,464,560,000	1.1%
30	New Mexico	3,116,892,000	1.0%
31	Tennessee	3,116,047,000	1.0%
32	Louisiana	3,034,676,000	0.9%
33	Virginia	2,999,440,000	0.9%
34	Montana	2,901,656,000	0.9%
35	South Carolina	2,359,507,000	0.7%
36	Maryland	1,965,060,000	0.6%
37	Utah	1,514,542,000	0.5%
38	New Jersey	1,117,636,000	0.3%
39	Delaware	1,094,632,000	0.3%
40	Wyoming	973,944,000	0.3%
41	Vermont	687,802,000	0.2%
42	Maine	675,739,000	0.2%
43	Connecticut	600,589,000	0.2%
44	Hawaii	574,129,000	0.2%
45	Nevada	572,109,000	0.2%
46	Massachusetts	569,789,000	0.2%
47	West Virginia	525,040,000	0.2%
48	New Hampshire	212,892,000	0.1%
49	Rhode Island	67,545,000	0.0%
50	Alaska	31,243,000	0.0%
	District of Columbia	0	0.0%

Source: U.S. Department of Agriculture, Economic Research Service
    "Farm Marketings" (http://www.ers.usda.gov/data/FarmIncome/firkdmu.htm)
*Commodities include crops and livestock.

Farm Income: Crops in 2008

National Total = $183,096,154,000

ALPHA ORDER				RANK ORDER			
RANK	STATE	FARM INCOME	% of USA	RANK	STATE	FARM INCOME	% of USA
34	Alabama	$962,090,000	0.5%	1	California	$25,554,460,000	14.0%
50	Alaska	24,847,000	0.0%	2	Iowa	14,885,135,000	8.1%
27	Arizona	1,959,073,000	1.1%	3	Illinois	14,232,026,000	7.8%
16	Arkansas	3,996,846,000	2.2%	4	Minnesota	9,751,524,000	5.3%
1	California	25,554,460,000	14.0%	5	Nebraska	8,995,559,000	4.9%
22	Colorado	2,378,962,000	1.3%	6	Texas	8,141,946,000	4.4%
41	Connecticut	412,741,000	0.2%	7	Indiana	7,105,353,000	3.9%
44	Delaware	266,201,000	0.1%	8	Kansas	6,754,709,000	3.7%
10	Florida	6,593,082,000	3.6%	9	North Dakota	6,717,004,000	3.7%
21	Georgia	2,735,270,000	1.5%	10	Florida	6,593,082,000	3.6%
39	Hawaii	510,968,000	0.3%	11	Washington	6,206,640,000	3.4%
20	Idaho	3,010,797,000	1.6%	12	South Dakota	5,366,125,000	2.9%
3	Illinois	14,232,026,000	7.8%	13	Ohio	5,235,504,000	2.9%
7	Indiana	7,105,353,000	3.9%	14	Missouri	4,819,933,000	2.6%
2	Iowa	14,885,135,000	8.1%	15	Michigan	4,077,677,000	2.2%
8	Kansas	6,754,709,000	3.7%	16	Arkansas	3,996,846,000	2.2%
29	Kentucky	1,930,163,000	1.1%	17	Wisconsin	3,574,130,000	2.0%
26	Louisiana	1,984,860,000	1.1%	18	North Carolina	3,291,424,000	1.8%
42	Maine	340,722,000	0.2%	19	Oregon	3,234,147,000	1.8%
36	Maryland	809,539,000	0.4%	20	Idaho	3,010,797,000	1.6%
40	Massachusetts	454,293,000	0.2%	21	Georgia	2,735,270,000	1.5%
15	Michigan	4,077,677,000	2.2%	22	Colorado	2,378,962,000	1.3%
4	Minnesota	9,751,524,000	5.3%	23	Pennsylvania	2,180,061,000	1.2%
24	Mississippi	2,075,972,000	1.1%	24	Mississippi	2,075,972,000	1.1%
14	Missouri	4,819,933,000	2.6%	25	New York	2,011,400,000	1.1%
31	Montana	1,722,068,000	0.9%	26	Louisiana	1,984,860,000	1.1%
5	Nebraska	8,995,559,000	4.9%	27	Arizona	1,959,073,000	1.1%
43	Nevada	272,891,000	0.1%	28	Oklahoma	1,930,408,000	1.1%
46	New Hampshire	119,182,000	0.1%	29	Kentucky	1,930,163,000	1.1%
35	New Jersey	940,463,000	0.5%	30	Tennessee	1,780,255,000	1.0%
37	New Mexico	709,727,000	0.4%	31	Montana	1,722,068,000	0.9%
25	New York	2,011,400,000	1.1%	32	Virginia	1,043,071,000	0.6%
18	North Carolina	3,291,424,000	1.8%	33	South Carolina	974,919,000	0.5%
9	North Dakota	6,717,004,000	3.7%	34	Alabama	962,090,000	0.5%
13	Ohio	5,235,504,000	2.9%	35	New Jersey	940,463,000	0.5%
28	Oklahoma	1,930,408,000	1.1%	36	Maryland	809,539,000	0.4%
19	Oregon	3,234,147,000	1.8%	37	New Mexico	709,727,000	0.4%
23	Pennsylvania	2,180,061,000	1.2%	38	Utah	527,064,000	0.3%
49	Rhode Island	57,156,000	0.0%	39	Hawaii	510,968,000	0.3%
33	South Carolina	974,919,000	0.5%	40	Massachusetts	454,293,000	0.2%
12	South Dakota	5,366,125,000	2.9%	41	Connecticut	412,741,000	0.2%
30	Tennessee	1,780,255,000	1.0%	42	Maine	340,722,000	0.2%
6	Texas	8,141,946,000	4.4%	43	Nevada	272,891,000	0.1%
38	Utah	527,064,000	0.3%	44	Delaware	266,201,000	0.1%
47	Vermont	115,938,000	0.1%	45	Wyoming	225,555,000	0.1%
32	Virginia	1,043,071,000	0.6%	46	New Hampshire	119,182,000	0.1%
11	Washington	6,206,640,000	3.4%	47	Vermont	115,938,000	0.1%
48	West Virginia	96,272,000	0.1%	48	West Virginia	96,272,000	0.1%
17	Wisconsin	3,574,130,000	2.0%	49	Rhode Island	57,156,000	0.0%
45	Wyoming	225,555,000	0.1%	50	Alaska	24,847,000	0.0%
					District of Columbia	0	0.0%

Source: U.S. Department of Agriculture, Economic Research Service
"Farm Marketings" (http://www.ers.usda.gov/data/FarmIncome/firkdmu.htm)

Farm Income: Livestock in 2008

National Total = $141,090,378,000*

ALPHA ORDER

RANK	STATE	FARM INCOME	% of USA
15	Alabama	$3,501,958,000	2.5%
50	Alaska	6,392,000	0.0%
28	Arizona	1,505,487,000	1.1%
10	Arkansas	4,350,422,000	3.1%
2	California	10,632,275,000	7.5%
11	Colorado	4,130,511,000	2.9%
44	Connecticut	187,851,000	0.1%
38	Delaware	828,430,000	0.6%
29	Florida	1,385,000,000	1.0%
9	Georgia	4,657,714,000	3.3%
48	Hawaii	63,161,000	0.0%
16	Idaho	3,404,556,000	2.4%
25	Illinois	2,124,762,000	1.5%
19	Indiana	2,856,496,000	2.0%
3	Iowa	9,867,730,000	7.0%
5	Kansas	7,212,786,000	5.1%
17	Kentucky	2,907,594,000	2.1%
35	Louisiana	1,049,816,000	0.7%
42	Maine	335,019,000	0.2%
33	Maryland	1,155,522,000	0.8%
46	Massachusetts	115,500,000	0.1%
23	Michigan	2,528,221,000	1.8%
8	Minnesota	6,086,568,000	4.3%
18	Mississippi	2,891,801,000	2.0%
14	Missouri	3,616,167,000	2.6%
32	Montana	1,179,590,000	0.8%
4	Nebraska	8,320,130,000	5.9%
43	Nevada	299,219,000	0.2%
47	New Hampshire	93,711,000	0.1%
45	New Jersey	177,172,000	0.1%
24	New Mexico	2,407,164,000	1.7%
21	New York	2,682,688,000	1.9%
6	North Carolina	6,461,372,000	4.6%
37	North Dakota	912,353,000	0.6%
20	Ohio	2,743,897,000	1.9%
13	Oklahoma	3,907,387,000	2.8%
34	Oregon	1,140,835,000	0.8%
12	Pennsylvania	3,942,270,000	2.8%
49	Rhode Island	10,388,000	0.0%
30	South Carolina	1,384,588,000	1.0%
22	South Dakota	2,681,449,000	1.9%
31	Tennessee	1,335,793,000	0.9%
1	Texas	11,030,553,000	7.8%
36	Utah	987,477,000	0.7%
40	Vermont	571,864,000	0.4%
27	Virginia	1,956,366,000	1.4%
26	Washington	1,973,778,000	1.4%
41	West Virginia	428,770,000	0.3%
7	Wisconsin	6,311,426,000	4.5%
39	Wyoming	748,391,000	0.5%

RANK ORDER

RANK	STATE	FARM INCOME	% of USA
1	Texas	$11,030,553,000	7.8%
2	California	10,632,275,000	7.5%
3	Iowa	9,867,730,000	7.0%
4	Nebraska	8,320,130,000	5.9%
5	Kansas	7,212,786,000	5.1%
6	North Carolina	6,461,372,000	4.6%
7	Wisconsin	6,311,426,000	4.5%
8	Minnesota	6,086,568,000	4.3%
9	Georgia	4,657,714,000	3.3%
10	Arkansas	4,350,422,000	3.1%
11	Colorado	4,130,511,000	2.9%
12	Pennsylvania	3,942,270,000	2.8%
13	Oklahoma	3,907,387,000	2.8%
14	Missouri	3,616,167,000	2.6%
15	Alabama	3,501,958,000	2.5%
16	Idaho	3,404,556,000	2.4%
17	Kentucky	2,907,594,000	2.1%
18	Mississippi	2,891,801,000	2.0%
19	Indiana	2,856,496,000	2.0%
20	Ohio	2,743,897,000	1.9%
21	New York	2,682,688,000	1.9%
22	South Dakota	2,681,449,000	1.9%
23	Michigan	2,528,221,000	1.8%
24	New Mexico	2,407,164,000	1.7%
25	Illinois	2,124,762,000	1.5%
26	Washington	1,973,778,000	1.4%
27	Virginia	1,956,366,000	1.4%
28	Arizona	1,505,487,000	1.1%
29	Florida	1,385,000,000	1.0%
30	South Carolina	1,384,588,000	1.0%
31	Tennessee	1,335,793,000	0.9%
32	Montana	1,179,590,000	0.8%
33	Maryland	1,155,522,000	0.8%
34	Oregon	1,140,835,000	0.8%
35	Louisiana	1,049,816,000	0.7%
36	Utah	987,477,000	0.7%
37	North Dakota	912,353,000	0.6%
38	Delaware	828,430,000	0.6%
39	Wyoming	748,391,000	0.5%
40	Vermont	571,864,000	0.4%
41	West Virginia	428,770,000	0.3%
42	Maine	335,019,000	0.2%
43	Nevada	299,219,000	0.2%
44	Connecticut	187,851,000	0.1%
45	New Jersey	177,172,000	0.1%
46	Massachusetts	115,500,000	0.1%
47	New Hampshire	93,711,000	0.1%
48	Hawaii	63,161,000	0.0%
49	Rhode Island	10,388,000	0.0%
50	Alaska	6,392,000	0.0%
	District of Columbia	0	0.0%

Source: U.S. Department of Agriculture, Economic Research Service
"Farm Marketings" (http://www.ers.usda.gov/data/FarmIncome/firkdmu.htm)
*Includes livestock products.

Farm Income: Government Payments in 2008

National Total = $12,237,568,000*

ALPHA ORDER

RANK	STATE	PAYMENTS	% of USA
26	Alabama	$162,025,000	1.3%
49	Alaska	5,013,000	0.0%
32	Arizona	89,978,000	0.7%
13	Arkansas	382,928,000	3.1%
10	California	434,045,000	3.5%
20	Colorado	261,070,000	2.1%
45	Connecticut	13,289,000	0.1%
39	Delaware	24,412,000	0.2%
27	Florida	159,403,000	1.3%
12	Georgia	397,699,000	3.2%
47	Hawaii	8,435,000	0.1%
29	Idaho	150,740,000	1.2%
4	Illinois	635,881,000	5.2%
16	Indiana	321,903,000	2.6%
2	Iowa	803,532,000	6.6%
3	Kansas	647,705,000	5.3%
14	Kentucky	370,523,000	3.0%
23	Louisiana	219,945,000	1.8%
44	Maine	14,568,000	0.1%
36	Maryland	57,431,000	0.5%
43	Massachusetts	14,772,000	0.1%
25	Michigan	166,342,000	1.4%
5	Minnesota	544,269,000	4.4%
15	Mississippi	334,423,000	2.7%
6	Missouri	538,475,000	4.4%
18	Montana	294,459,000	2.4%
8	Nebraska	518,502,000	4.2%
46	Nevada	13,246,000	0.1%
48	New Hampshire	7,834,000	0.1%
40	New Jersey	17,220,000	0.1%
34	New Mexico	74,661,000	0.6%
35	New York	69,106,000	0.6%
7	North Carolina	518,648,000	4.2%
9	North Dakota	510,590,000	4.2%
19	Ohio	275,243,000	2.2%
17	Oklahoma	316,831,000	2.6%
31	Oregon	124,811,000	1.0%
33	Pennsylvania	87,393,000	0.7%
50	Rhode Island	3,631,000	0.0%
28	South Carolina	152,979,000	1.3%
11	South Dakota	400,726,000	3.3%
22	Tennessee	224,572,000	1.8%
1	Texas	1,180,674,000	9.6%
37	Utah	47,473,000	0.4%
41	Vermont	15,604,000	0.1%
30	Virginia	132,774,000	1.1%
24	Washington	200,943,000	1.6%
42	West Virginia	15,168,000	0.1%
21	Wisconsin	229,991,000	1.9%
38	Wyoming	45,684,000	0.4%

RANK ORDER

RANK	STATE	PAYMENTS	% of USA
1	Texas	$1,180,674,000	9.6%
2	Iowa	803,532,000	6.6%
3	Kansas	647,705,000	5.3%
4	Illinois	635,881,000	5.2%
5	Minnesota	544,269,000	4.4%
6	Missouri	538,475,000	4.4%
7	North Carolina	518,648,000	4.2%
8	Nebraska	518,502,000	4.2%
9	North Dakota	510,590,000	4.2%
10	California	434,045,000	3.5%
11	South Dakota	400,726,000	3.3%
12	Georgia	397,699,000	3.2%
13	Arkansas	382,928,000	3.1%
14	Kentucky	370,523,000	3.0%
15	Mississippi	334,423,000	2.7%
16	Indiana	321,903,000	2.6%
17	Oklahoma	316,831,000	2.6%
18	Montana	294,459,000	2.4%
19	Ohio	275,243,000	2.2%
20	Colorado	261,070,000	2.1%
21	Wisconsin	229,991,000	1.9%
22	Tennessee	224,572,000	1.8%
23	Louisiana	219,945,000	1.8%
24	Washington	200,943,000	1.6%
25	Michigan	166,342,000	1.4%
26	Alabama	162,025,000	1.3%
27	Florida	159,403,000	1.3%
28	South Carolina	152,979,000	1.3%
29	Idaho	150,740,000	1.2%
30	Virginia	132,774,000	1.1%
31	Oregon	124,811,000	1.0%
32	Arizona	89,978,000	0.7%
33	Pennsylvania	87,393,000	0.7%
34	New Mexico	74,661,000	0.6%
35	New York	69,106,000	0.6%
36	Maryland	57,431,000	0.5%
37	Utah	47,473,000	0.4%
38	Wyoming	45,684,000	0.4%
39	Delaware	24,412,000	0.2%
40	New Jersey	17,220,000	0.1%
41	Vermont	15,604,000	0.1%
42	West Virginia	15,168,000	0.1%
43	Massachusetts	14,772,000	0.1%
44	Maine	14,568,000	0.1%
45	Connecticut	13,289,000	0.1%
46	Nevada	13,246,000	0.1%
47	Hawaii	8,435,000	0.1%
48	New Hampshire	7,834,000	0.1%
49	Alaska	5,013,000	0.0%
50	Rhode Island	3,631,000	0.0%
	District of Columbia	0	0.0%

Source: U.S. Department of Agriculture, Economic Research Service
   "Farm Income" (http://www.ers.usda.gov/Data/FarmIncome/FinfidmuXls.htm)
*Government payments made directly to farmers in cash.

Acres Planted in 2009

National Total = 319,296,000 Acres*

ALPHA ORDER			
RANK	STATE	ACRES	% of USA
30	Alabama	2,200,000	0.7%
NA	Alaska**	NA	NA
38	Arizona	741,000	0.2%
15	Arkansas	7,751,000	2.4%
23	California	4,106,000	1.3%
17	Colorado	6,061,000	1.9%
46	Connecticut	90,000	0.0%
41	Delaware	472,000	0.1%
36	Florida	1,044,000	0.3%
24	Georgia	3,769,000	1.2%
48	Hawaii	22,000	0.0%
22	Idaho	4,329,000	1.4%
2	Illinois	22,945,000	7.2%
10	Indiana	12,155,000	3.8%
1	Iowa	24,748,000	7.8%
3	Kansas	22,669,000	7.1%
18	Kentucky	5,769,000	1.8%
27	Louisiana	3,410,000	1.1%
43	Maine	281,000	0.1%
34	Maryland	1,452,000	0.5%
45	Massachusetts	102,000	0.0%
16	Michigan	6,426,000	2.0%
6	Minnesota	19,594,000	6.1%
21	Mississippi	4,354,000	1.4%
9	Missouri	13,556,000	4.2%
13	Montana	9,100,000	2.9%
7	Nebraska	19,035,000	6.0%
40	Nevada	519,000	0.2%
47	New Hampshire	72,000	0.0%
42	New Jersey	315,000	0.1%
35	New Mexico	1,045,000	0.3%
28	New York	2,935,000	0.9%
19	North Carolina	4,925,000	1.5%
5	North Dakota	21,583,000	6.8%
12	Ohio	10,021,000	3.1%
11	Oklahoma	10,562,000	3.3%
31	Oregon	2,124,000	0.7%
25	Pennsylvania	3,728,000	1.2%
49	Rhode Island	10,000	0.0%
33	South Carolina	1,654,000	0.5%
8	South Dakota	17,352,000	5.4%
20	Tennessee	4,907,000	1.5%
4	Texas	22,467,000	7.0%
37	Utah	994,000	0.3%
43	Vermont	281,000	0.1%
29	Virginia	2,672,000	0.8%
26	Washington	3,600,000	1.1%
39	West Virginia	701,000	0.2%
14	Wisconsin	8,160,000	2.6%
32	Wyoming	1,704,000	0.5%

RANK ORDER			
RANK	STATE	ACRES	% of USA
1	Iowa	24,748,000	7.8%
2	Illinois	22,945,000	7.2%
3	Kansas	22,669,000	7.1%
4	Texas	22,467,000	7.0%
5	North Dakota	21,583,000	6.8%
6	Minnesota	19,594,000	6.1%
7	Nebraska	19,035,000	6.0%
8	South Dakota	17,352,000	5.4%
9	Missouri	13,556,000	4.2%
10	Indiana	12,155,000	3.8%
11	Oklahoma	10,562,000	3.3%
12	Ohio	10,021,000	3.1%
13	Montana	9,100,000	2.9%
14	Wisconsin	8,160,000	2.6%
15	Arkansas	7,751,000	2.4%
16	Michigan	6,426,000	2.0%
17	Colorado	6,061,000	1.9%
18	Kentucky	5,769,000	1.8%
19	North Carolina	4,925,000	1.5%
20	Tennessee	4,907,000	1.5%
21	Mississippi	4,354,000	1.4%
22	Idaho	4,329,000	1.4%
23	California	4,106,000	1.3%
24	Georgia	3,769,000	1.2%
25	Pennsylvania	3,728,000	1.2%
26	Washington	3,600,000	1.1%
27	Louisiana	3,410,000	1.1%
28	New York	2,935,000	0.9%
29	Virginia	2,672,000	0.8%
30	Alabama	2,200,000	0.7%
31	Oregon	2,124,000	0.7%
32	Wyoming	1,704,000	0.5%
33	South Carolina	1,654,000	0.5%
34	Maryland	1,452,000	0.5%
35	New Mexico	1,045,000	0.3%
36	Florida	1,044,000	0.3%
37	Utah	994,000	0.3%
38	Arizona	741,000	0.2%
39	West Virginia	701,000	0.2%
40	Nevada	519,000	0.2%
41	Delaware	472,000	0.1%
42	New Jersey	315,000	0.1%
43	Maine	281,000	0.1%
43	Vermont	281,000	0.1%
45	Massachusetts	102,000	0.0%
46	Connecticut	90,000	0.0%
47	New Hampshire	72,000	0.0%
48	Hawaii	22,000	0.0%
49	Rhode Island	10,000	0.0%
NA	Alaska**	NA	NA
	District of Columbia**	NA	NA

Source: U.S. Department of Agriculture, National Agricultural Statistics Service
"Crop Production: 2009 Summary" (Cr Pr 2-1 (10), January 2010)
(http://usda.mannlib.cornell.edu/MannUsda/viewDocumentInfo.do?documentID=1047)
*Estimated totals.
**No acreage or not available.

Acres Harvested in 2009

National Total = 301,603,000 Acres*

ALPHA ORDER

RANK	STATE	ACRES	% of USA
30	Alabama	2,082,000	0.7%
NA	Alaska**	NA	NA
37	Arizona	734,000	0.2%
15	Arkansas	7,504,000	2.5%
24	California	3,550,000	1.2%
17	Colorado	5,781,000	1.9%
46	Connecticut	86,000	0.0%
41	Delaware	463,000	0.2%
35	Florida	1,017,000	0.3%
26	Georgia	3,406,000	1.1%
48	Hawaii	22,000	0.0%
21	Idaho	4,186,000	1.4%
2	Illinois	22,747,000	7.5%
10	Indiana	12,087,000	4.0%
1	Iowa	24,487,000	8.1%
3	Kansas	21,876,000	7.3%
18	Kentucky	5,629,000	1.9%
27	Louisiana	3,288,000	1.1%
43	Maine	276,000	0.1%
34	Maryland	1,395,000	0.5%
45	Massachusetts	99,000	0.0%
16	Michigan	6,301,000	2.1%
5	Minnesota	19,255,000	6.4%
22	Mississippi	4,168,000	1.4%
9	Missouri	13,403,000	4.4%
12	Montana	8,689,000	2.9%
6	Nebraska	18,618,000	6.2%
40	Nevada	512,000	0.2%
47	New Hampshire	72,000	0.0%
42	New Jersey	307,000	0.1%
38	New Mexico	714,000	0.2%
28	New York	2,886,000	1.0%
19	North Carolina	4,734,000	1.6%
4	North Dakota	20,926,000	6.9%
11	Ohio	9,911,000	3.3%
13	Oklahoma	8,007,000	2.7%
31	Oregon	2,079,000	0.7%
23	Pennsylvania	3,653,000	1.2%
49	Rhode Island	9,000	0.0%
33	South Carolina	1,596,000	0.5%
7	South Dakota	16,829,000	5.6%
20	Tennessee	4,727,000	1.6%
8	Texas	15,769,000	5.2%
36	Utah	936,000	0.3%
44	Vermont	273,000	0.1%
29	Virginia	2,574,000	0.9%
25	Washington	3,513,000	1.2%
39	West Virginia	695,000	0.2%
14	Wisconsin	7,924,000	2.6%
32	Wyoming	1,611,000	0.5%

RANK ORDER

RANK	STATE	ACRES	% of USA
1	Iowa	24,487,000	8.1%
2	Illinois	22,747,000	7.5%
3	Kansas	21,876,000	7.3%
4	North Dakota	20,926,000	6.9%
5	Minnesota	19,255,000	6.4%
6	Nebraska	18,618,000	6.2%
7	South Dakota	16,829,000	5.6%
8	Texas	15,769,000	5.2%
9	Missouri	13,403,000	4.4%
10	Indiana	12,087,000	4.0%
11	Ohio	9,911,000	3.3%
12	Montana	8,689,000	2.9%
13	Oklahoma	8,007,000	2.7%
14	Wisconsin	7,924,000	2.6%
15	Arkansas	7,504,000	2.5%
16	Michigan	6,301,000	2.1%
17	Colorado	5,781,000	1.9%
18	Kentucky	5,629,000	1.9%
19	North Carolina	4,734,000	1.6%
20	Tennessee	4,727,000	1.6%
21	Idaho	4,186,000	1.4%
22	Mississippi	4,168,000	1.4%
23	Pennsylvania	3,653,000	1.2%
24	California	3,550,000	1.2%
25	Washington	3,513,000	1.2%
26	Georgia	3,406,000	1.1%
27	Louisiana	3,288,000	1.1%
28	New York	2,886,000	1.0%
29	Virginia	2,574,000	0.9%
30	Alabama	2,082,000	0.7%
31	Oregon	2,079,000	0.7%
32	Wyoming	1,611,000	0.5%
33	South Carolina	1,596,000	0.5%
34	Maryland	1,395,000	0.5%
35	Florida	1,017,000	0.3%
36	Utah	936,000	0.3%
37	Arizona	734,000	0.2%
38	New Mexico	714,000	0.2%
39	West Virginia	695,000	0.2%
40	Nevada	512,000	0.2%
41	Delaware	463,000	0.2%
42	New Jersey	307,000	0.1%
43	Maine	276,000	0.1%
44	Vermont	273,000	0.1%
45	Massachusetts	99,000	0.0%
46	Connecticut	86,000	0.0%
47	New Hampshire	72,000	0.0%
48	Hawaii	22,000	0.0%
49	Rhode Island	9,000	0.0%
NA	Alaska**	NA	NA
	District of Columbia**	NA	NA

Source: U.S. Department of Agriculture, National Agricultural Statistics Service
"Crop Production: 2009 Summary" (Cr Pr 2-1 (10), January 2010)
(http://usda.mannlib.cornell.edu/MannUsda/viewDocumentInfo.do?documentID=1047)
*Estimated totals.
**No acreage or not available.

Acres Harvested: Corn in 2009

National Total = 86,482,000 Acres*

<table>
<tr><td colspan="4">ALPHA ORDER</td><td colspan="4">RANK ORDER</td></tr>
<tr><td>RANK</td><td>STATE</td><td>ACRES</td><td>% of USA</td><td>RANK</td><td>STATE</td><td>ACRES</td><td>% of USA</td></tr>
<tr><td>30</td><td>Alabama</td><td>280,000</td><td>0.3%</td><td>1</td><td>Iowa</td><td>13,700,000</td><td>15.8%</td></tr>
<tr><td>NA</td><td>Alaska**</td><td>NA</td><td>NA</td><td>2</td><td>Illinois</td><td>12,000,000</td><td>13.9%</td></tr>
<tr><td>41</td><td>Arizona</td><td>50,000</td><td>0.1%</td><td>3</td><td>Nebraska</td><td>9,150,000</td><td>10.6%</td></tr>
<tr><td>25</td><td>Arkansas</td><td>430,000</td><td>0.5%</td><td>4</td><td>Minnesota</td><td>7,600,000</td><td>8.8%</td></tr>
<tr><td>22</td><td>California</td><td>550,000</td><td>0.6%</td><td>5</td><td>Indiana</td><td>5,600,000</td><td>6.5%</td></tr>
<tr><td>16</td><td>Colorado</td><td>1,100,000</td><td>1.3%</td><td>6</td><td>South Dakota</td><td>5,000,000</td><td>5.8%</td></tr>
<tr><td>44</td><td>Connecticut</td><td>26,000</td><td>0.0%</td><td>7</td><td>Kansas</td><td>4,100,000</td><td>4.7%</td></tr>
<tr><td>31</td><td>Delaware</td><td>170,000</td><td>0.2%</td><td>8</td><td>Wisconsin</td><td>3,850,000</td><td>4.5%</td></tr>
<tr><td>38</td><td>Florida</td><td>70,000</td><td>0.1%</td><td>9</td><td>Ohio</td><td>3,350,000</td><td>3.9%</td></tr>
<tr><td>26</td><td>Georgia</td><td>420,000</td><td>0.5%</td><td>10</td><td>Missouri</td><td>3,000,000</td><td>3.5%</td></tr>
<tr><td>NA</td><td>Hawaii**</td><td>NA</td><td>NA</td><td>11</td><td>Michigan</td><td>2,350,000</td><td>2.7%</td></tr>
<tr><td>29</td><td>Idaho</td><td>300,000</td><td>0.3%</td><td>11</td><td>Texas</td><td>2,350,000</td><td>2.7%</td></tr>
<tr><td>2</td><td>Illinois</td><td>12,000,000</td><td>13.9%</td><td>13</td><td>North Dakota</td><td>1,950,000</td><td>2.3%</td></tr>
<tr><td>5</td><td>Indiana</td><td>5,600,000</td><td>6.5%</td><td>14</td><td>Pennsylvania</td><td>1,350,000</td><td>1.6%</td></tr>
<tr><td>1</td><td>Iowa</td><td>13,700,000</td><td>15.8%</td><td>15</td><td>Kentucky</td><td>1,220,000</td><td>1.4%</td></tr>
<tr><td>7</td><td>Kansas</td><td>4,100,000</td><td>4.7%</td><td>16</td><td>Colorado</td><td>1,100,000</td><td>1.3%</td></tr>
<tr><td>15</td><td>Kentucky</td><td>1,220,000</td><td>1.4%</td><td>17</td><td>New York</td><td>1,070,000</td><td>1.2%</td></tr>
<tr><td>21</td><td>Louisiana</td><td>630,000</td><td>0.7%</td><td>18</td><td>North Carolina</td><td>870,000</td><td>1.0%</td></tr>
<tr><td>43</td><td>Maine</td><td>28,000</td><td>0.0%</td><td>19</td><td>Mississippi</td><td>730,000</td><td>0.8%</td></tr>
<tr><td>24</td><td>Maryland</td><td>470,000</td><td>0.5%</td><td>20</td><td>Tennessee</td><td>670,000</td><td>0.8%</td></tr>
<tr><td>45</td><td>Massachusetts</td><td>17,000</td><td>0.0%</td><td>21</td><td>Louisiana</td><td>630,000</td><td>0.7%</td></tr>
<tr><td>11</td><td>Michigan</td><td>2,350,000</td><td>2.7%</td><td>22</td><td>California</td><td>550,000</td><td>0.6%</td></tr>
<tr><td>4</td><td>Minnesota</td><td>7,600,000</td><td>8.8%</td><td>23</td><td>Virginia</td><td>480,000</td><td>0.6%</td></tr>
<tr><td>19</td><td>Mississippi</td><td>730,000</td><td>0.8%</td><td>24</td><td>Maryland</td><td>470,000</td><td>0.5%</td></tr>
<tr><td>10</td><td>Missouri</td><td>3,000,000</td><td>3.5%</td><td>25</td><td>Arkansas</td><td>430,000</td><td>0.5%</td></tr>
<tr><td>37</td><td>Montana</td><td>72,000</td><td>0.1%</td><td>26</td><td>Georgia</td><td>420,000</td><td>0.5%</td></tr>
<tr><td>3</td><td>Nebraska</td><td>9,150,000</td><td>10.6%</td><td>27</td><td>Oklahoma</td><td>390,000</td><td>0.5%</td></tr>
<tr><td>47</td><td>Nevada</td><td>4,000</td><td>0.0%</td><td>28</td><td>South Carolina</td><td>335,000</td><td>0.4%</td></tr>
<tr><td>46</td><td>New Hampshire</td><td>15,000</td><td>0.0%</td><td>29</td><td>Idaho</td><td>300,000</td><td>0.3%</td></tr>
<tr><td>36</td><td>New Jersey</td><td>80,000</td><td>0.1%</td><td>30</td><td>Alabama</td><td>280,000</td><td>0.3%</td></tr>
<tr><td>33</td><td>New Mexico</td><td>130,000</td><td>0.2%</td><td>31</td><td>Delaware</td><td>170,000</td><td>0.2%</td></tr>
<tr><td>17</td><td>New York</td><td>1,070,000</td><td>1.2%</td><td>31</td><td>Washington</td><td>170,000</td><td>0.2%</td></tr>
<tr><td>18</td><td>North Carolina</td><td>870,000</td><td>1.0%</td><td>33</td><td>New Mexico</td><td>130,000</td><td>0.2%</td></tr>
<tr><td>13</td><td>North Dakota</td><td>1,950,000</td><td>2.3%</td><td>34</td><td>Vermont</td><td>91,000</td><td>0.1%</td></tr>
<tr><td>9</td><td>Ohio</td><td>3,350,000</td><td>3.9%</td><td>35</td><td>Wyoming</td><td>90,000</td><td>0.1%</td></tr>
<tr><td>27</td><td>Oklahoma</td><td>390,000</td><td>0.5%</td><td>36</td><td>New Jersey</td><td>80,000</td><td>0.1%</td></tr>
<tr><td>40</td><td>Oregon</td><td>60,000</td><td>0.1%</td><td>37</td><td>Montana</td><td>72,000</td><td>0.1%</td></tr>
<tr><td>14</td><td>Pennsylvania</td><td>1,350,000</td><td>1.6%</td><td>38</td><td>Florida</td><td>70,000</td><td>0.1%</td></tr>
<tr><td>48</td><td>Rhode Island</td><td>2,000</td><td>0.0%</td><td>39</td><td>Utah</td><td>65,000</td><td>0.1%</td></tr>
<tr><td>28</td><td>South Carolina</td><td>335,000</td><td>0.4%</td><td>40</td><td>Oregon</td><td>60,000</td><td>0.1%</td></tr>
<tr><td>6</td><td>South Dakota</td><td>5,000,000</td><td>5.8%</td><td>41</td><td>Arizona</td><td>50,000</td><td>0.1%</td></tr>
<tr><td>20</td><td>Tennessee</td><td>670,000</td><td>0.8%</td><td>42</td><td>West Virginia</td><td>47,000</td><td>0.1%</td></tr>
<tr><td>11</td><td>Texas</td><td>2,350,000</td><td>2.7%</td><td>43</td><td>Maine</td><td>28,000</td><td>0.0%</td></tr>
<tr><td>39</td><td>Utah</td><td>65,000</td><td>0.1%</td><td>44</td><td>Connecticut</td><td>26,000</td><td>0.0%</td></tr>
<tr><td>34</td><td>Vermont</td><td>91,000</td><td>0.1%</td><td>45</td><td>Massachusetts</td><td>17,000</td><td>0.0%</td></tr>
<tr><td>23</td><td>Virginia</td><td>480,000</td><td>0.6%</td><td>46</td><td>New Hampshire</td><td>15,000</td><td>0.0%</td></tr>
<tr><td>31</td><td>Washington</td><td>170,000</td><td>0.2%</td><td>47</td><td>Nevada</td><td>4,000</td><td>0.0%</td></tr>
<tr><td>42</td><td>West Virginia</td><td>47,000</td><td>0.1%</td><td>48</td><td>Rhode Island</td><td>2,000</td><td>0.0%</td></tr>
<tr><td>8</td><td>Wisconsin</td><td>3,850,000</td><td>4.5%</td><td>NA</td><td>Alaska**</td><td>NA</td><td>NA</td></tr>
<tr><td>35</td><td>Wyoming</td><td>90,000</td><td>0.1%</td><td>NA</td><td>Hawaii**</td><td>NA</td><td>NA</td></tr>
<tr><td></td><td></td><td></td><td></td><td></td><td>District of Columbia**</td><td>NA</td><td>NA</td></tr>
</table>

Source: U.S. Department of Agriculture, National Agricultural Statistics Service
   "Crop Production: 2009 Summary" (Cr Pr 2-1 (10), January 2010)
   (http://usda.mannlib.cornell.edu/MannUsda/viewDocumentInfo.do?documentID=1047)
*Estimated totals. Acres harvested for grain and silage. There were 79,630,000 acres harvested for grain.
**No acreage or not available.

Acres Harvested: Soybeans in 2009

National Total = 76,407,000 Acres*

ALPHA ORDER				RANK ORDER			
RANK	STATE	ACRES	% of USA	RANK	STATE	ACRES	% of USA
24	Alabama	430,000	0.6%	1	Iowa	9,530,000	12.5%
NA	Alaska**	NA	NA	2	Illinois	9,350,000	12.2%
NA	Arizona**	NA	NA	3	Minnesota	7,120,000	9.3%
11	Arkansas	3,270,000	4.3%	4	Indiana	5,440,000	7.1%
NA	California**	NA	NA	5	Missouri	5,300,000	6.9%
NA	Colorado**	NA	NA	6	Nebraska	4,760,000	6.2%
NA	Connecticut**	NA	NA	7	Ohio	4,530,000	5.9%
28	Delaware	183,000	0.2%	8	South Dakota	4,190,000	5.5%
30	Florida	34,000	0.0%	9	North Dakota	3,870,000	5.1%
22	Georgia	450,000	0.6%	10	Kansas	3,650,000	4.8%
NA	Hawaii**	NA	NA	11	Arkansas	3,270,000	4.3%
NA	Idaho**	NA	NA	12	Mississippi	2,030,000	2.7%
2	Illinois	9,350,000	12.2%	13	Michigan	1,990,000	2.6%
4	Indiana	5,440,000	7.1%	14	North Carolina	1,770,000	2.3%
1	Iowa	9,530,000	12.5%	15	Wisconsin	1,620,000	2.1%
10	Kansas	3,650,000	4.8%	16	Tennessee	1,530,000	2.0%
17	Kentucky	1,420,000	1.9%	17	Kentucky	1,420,000	1.9%
18	Louisiana	940,000	1.2%	18	Louisiana	940,000	1.2%
NA	Maine**	NA	NA	19	South Carolina	570,000	0.7%
21	Maryland	475,000	0.6%	19	Virginia	570,000	0.7%
NA	Massachusetts**	NA	NA	21	Maryland	475,000	0.6%
13	Michigan	1,990,000	2.6%	22	Georgia	450,000	0.6%
3	Minnesota	7,120,000	9.3%	23	Pennsylvania	445,000	0.6%
12	Mississippi	2,030,000	2.7%	24	Alabama	430,000	0.6%
5	Missouri	5,300,000	6.9%	25	Oklahoma	390,000	0.5%
NA	Montana**	NA	NA	26	New York	254,000	0.3%
6	Nebraska	4,760,000	6.2%	27	Texas	190,000	0.2%
NA	Nevada**	NA	NA	28	Delaware	183,000	0.2%
NA	New Hampshire**	NA	NA	29	New Jersey	87,000	0.1%
29	New Jersey	87,000	0.1%	30	Florida	34,000	0.0%
NA	New Mexico**	NA	NA	31	West Virginia	19,000	0.0%
26	New York	254,000	0.3%	NA	Alaska**	NA	NA
14	North Carolina	1,770,000	2.3%	NA	Arizona**	NA	NA
9	North Dakota	3,870,000	5.1%	NA	California**	NA	NA
7	Ohio	4,530,000	5.9%	NA	Colorado**	NA	NA
25	Oklahoma	390,000	0.5%	NA	Connecticut**	NA	NA
NA	Oregon**	NA	NA	NA	Hawaii**	NA	NA
23	Pennsylvania	445,000	0.6%	NA	Idaho**	NA	NA
NA	Rhode Island**	NA	NA	NA	Maine**	NA	NA
19	South Carolina	570,000	0.7%	NA	Massachusetts**	NA	NA
8	South Dakota	4,190,000	5.5%	NA	Montana**	NA	NA
16	Tennessee	1,530,000	2.0%	NA	Nevada**	NA	NA
27	Texas	190,000	0.2%	NA	New Hampshire**	NA	NA
NA	Utah**	NA	NA	NA	New Mexico**	NA	NA
NA	Vermont**	NA	NA	NA	Oregon**	NA	NA
19	Virginia	570,000	0.7%	NA	Rhode Island**	NA	NA
NA	Washington**	NA	NA	NA	Utah**	NA	NA
31	West Virginia	19,000	0.0%	NA	Vermont**	NA	NA
15	Wisconsin	1,620,000	2.1%	NA	Washington**	NA	NA
NA	Wyoming**	NA	NA	NA	Wyoming**	NA	NA
					District of Columbia**	NA	NA

Source: U.S. Department of Agriculture, National Agricultural Statistics Service
"Crop Production: 2009 Summary" (Cr Pr 2-1 (10), January 2010)
(http://usda.mannlib.cornell.edu/MannUsda/viewDocumentInfo.do?documentID=1047)
*Estimated totals.
**No acreage or not available.

Acres Harvested: Wheat in 2009

National Total = 49,868,000 Acres*

<table>
<tr><td colspan="4">ALPHA ORDER</td><td colspan="4">RANK ORDER</td></tr>
<tr><td>RANK</td><td>STATE</td><td>ACRES</td><td>% of USA</td><td>RANK</td><td>STATE</td><td>ACRES</td><td>% of USA</td></tr>
<tr><td>27</td><td>Alabama</td><td>180,000</td><td>0.4%</td><td>1</td><td>Kansas</td><td>8,800,000</td><td>17.6%</td></tr>
<tr><td>NA</td><td>Alaska**</td><td>NA</td><td>NA</td><td>2</td><td>North Dakota</td><td>8,415,000</td><td>16.9%</td></tr>
<tr><td>35</td><td>Arizona</td><td>129,000</td><td>0.3%</td><td>3</td><td>Montana</td><td>5,305,000</td><td>10.6%</td></tr>
<tr><td>20</td><td>Arkansas</td><td>390,000</td><td>0.8%</td><td>4</td><td>Oklahoma</td><td>3,500,000</td><td>7.0%</td></tr>
<tr><td>18</td><td>California</td><td>485,000</td><td>1.0%</td><td>5</td><td>South Dakota</td><td>3,009,000</td><td>6.0%</td></tr>
<tr><td>6</td><td>Colorado</td><td>2,479,000</td><td>5.0%</td><td>6</td><td>Colorado</td><td>2,479,000</td><td>5.0%</td></tr>
<tr><td>NA</td><td>Connecticut**</td><td>NA</td><td>NA</td><td>7</td><td>Texas</td><td>2,450,000</td><td>4.9%</td></tr>
<tr><td>37</td><td>Delaware</td><td>67,000</td><td>0.1%</td><td>8</td><td>Washington</td><td>2,225,000</td><td>4.5%</td></tr>
<tr><td>40</td><td>Florida</td><td>14,000</td><td>0.0%</td><td>9</td><td>Nebraska</td><td>1,600,000</td><td>3.2%</td></tr>
<tr><td>24</td><td>Georgia</td><td>250,000</td><td>0.5%</td><td>10</td><td>Minnesota</td><td>1,595,000</td><td>3.2%</td></tr>
<tr><td>NA</td><td>Hawaii**</td><td>NA</td><td>NA</td><td>11</td><td>Idaho</td><td>1,250,000</td><td>2.5%</td></tr>
<tr><td>11</td><td>Idaho</td><td>1,250,000</td><td>2.5%</td><td>12</td><td>Ohio</td><td>980,000</td><td>2.0%</td></tr>
<tr><td>14</td><td>Illinois</td><td>820,000</td><td>1.6%</td><td>13</td><td>Oregon</td><td>877,000</td><td>1.8%</td></tr>
<tr><td>19</td><td>Indiana</td><td>450,000</td><td>0.9%</td><td>14</td><td>Illinois</td><td>820,000</td><td>1.6%</td></tr>
<tr><td>39</td><td>Iowa</td><td>22,000</td><td>0.0%</td><td>15</td><td>Missouri</td><td>730,000</td><td>1.5%</td></tr>
<tr><td>1</td><td>Kansas</td><td>8,800,000</td><td>17.6%</td><td>16</td><td>North Carolina</td><td>600,000</td><td>1.2%</td></tr>
<tr><td>20</td><td>Kentucky</td><td>390,000</td><td>0.8%</td><td>17</td><td>Michigan</td><td>560,000</td><td>1.1%</td></tr>
<tr><td>28</td><td>Louisiana</td><td>175,000</td><td>0.4%</td><td>18</td><td>California</td><td>485,000</td><td>1.0%</td></tr>
<tr><td>NA</td><td>Maine**</td><td>NA</td><td>NA</td><td>19</td><td>Indiana</td><td>450,000</td><td>0.9%</td></tr>
<tr><td>26</td><td>Maryland</td><td>195,000</td><td>0.4%</td><td>20</td><td>Arkansas</td><td>390,000</td><td>0.8%</td></tr>
<tr><td>NA</td><td>Massachusetts**</td><td>NA</td><td>NA</td><td>20</td><td>Kentucky</td><td>390,000</td><td>0.8%</td></tr>
<tr><td>17</td><td>Michigan</td><td>560,000</td><td>1.1%</td><td>22</td><td>Tennessee</td><td>340,000</td><td>0.7%</td></tr>
<tr><td>10</td><td>Minnesota</td><td>1,595,000</td><td>3.2%</td><td>23</td><td>Wisconsin</td><td>315,000</td><td>0.6%</td></tr>
<tr><td>30</td><td>Mississippi</td><td>165,000</td><td>0.3%</td><td>24</td><td>Georgia</td><td>250,000</td><td>0.5%</td></tr>
<tr><td>15</td><td>Missouri</td><td>730,000</td><td>1.5%</td><td>25</td><td>Virginia</td><td>210,000</td><td>0.4%</td></tr>
<tr><td>3</td><td>Montana</td><td>5,305,000</td><td>10.6%</td><td>26</td><td>Maryland</td><td>195,000</td><td>0.4%</td></tr>
<tr><td>9</td><td>Nebraska</td><td>1,600,000</td><td>3.2%</td><td>27</td><td>Alabama</td><td>180,000</td><td>0.4%</td></tr>
<tr><td>41</td><td>Nevada</td><td>13,000</td><td>0.0%</td><td>28</td><td>Louisiana</td><td>175,000</td><td>0.4%</td></tr>
<tr><td>NA</td><td>New Hampshire**</td><td>NA</td><td>NA</td><td>28</td><td>Pennsylvania</td><td>175,000</td><td>0.4%</td></tr>
<tr><td>38</td><td>New Jersey</td><td>29,000</td><td>0.1%</td><td>30</td><td>Mississippi</td><td>165,000</td><td>0.3%</td></tr>
<tr><td>33</td><td>New Mexico</td><td>140,000</td><td>0.3%</td><td>31</td><td>South Carolina</td><td>150,000</td><td>0.3%</td></tr>
<tr><td>36</td><td>New York</td><td>105,000</td><td>0.2%</td><td>32</td><td>Utah</td><td>147,000</td><td>0.3%</td></tr>
<tr><td>16</td><td>North Carolina</td><td>600,000</td><td>1.2%</td><td>33</td><td>New Mexico</td><td>140,000</td><td>0.3%</td></tr>
<tr><td>2</td><td>North Dakota</td><td>8,415,000</td><td>16.9%</td><td>34</td><td>Wyoming</td><td>132,000</td><td>0.3%</td></tr>
<tr><td>12</td><td>Ohio</td><td>980,000</td><td>2.0%</td><td>35</td><td>Arizona</td><td>129,000</td><td>0.3%</td></tr>
<tr><td>4</td><td>Oklahoma</td><td>3,500,000</td><td>7.0%</td><td>36</td><td>New York</td><td>105,000</td><td>0.2%</td></tr>
<tr><td>13</td><td>Oregon</td><td>877,000</td><td>1.8%</td><td>37</td><td>Delaware</td><td>67,000</td><td>0.1%</td></tr>
<tr><td>28</td><td>Pennsylvania</td><td>175,000</td><td>0.4%</td><td>38</td><td>New Jersey</td><td>29,000</td><td>0.1%</td></tr>
<tr><td>NA</td><td>Rhode Island**</td><td>NA</td><td>NA</td><td>39</td><td>Iowa</td><td>22,000</td><td>0.0%</td></tr>
<tr><td>31</td><td>South Carolina</td><td>150,000</td><td>0.3%</td><td>40</td><td>Florida</td><td>14,000</td><td>0.0%</td></tr>
<tr><td>5</td><td>South Dakota</td><td>3,009,000</td><td>6.0%</td><td>41</td><td>Nevada</td><td>13,000</td><td>0.0%</td></tr>
<tr><td>22</td><td>Tennessee</td><td>340,000</td><td>0.7%</td><td>42</td><td>West Virginia</td><td>5,000</td><td>0.0%</td></tr>
<tr><td>7</td><td>Texas</td><td>2,450,000</td><td>4.9%</td><td>NA</td><td>Alaska**</td><td>NA</td><td>NA</td></tr>
<tr><td>32</td><td>Utah</td><td>147,000</td><td>0.3%</td><td>NA</td><td>Connecticut**</td><td>NA</td><td>NA</td></tr>
<tr><td>NA</td><td>Vermont**</td><td>NA</td><td>NA</td><td>NA</td><td>Hawaii**</td><td>NA</td><td>NA</td></tr>
<tr><td>25</td><td>Virginia</td><td>210,000</td><td>0.4%</td><td>NA</td><td>Maine**</td><td>NA</td><td>NA</td></tr>
<tr><td>8</td><td>Washington</td><td>2,225,000</td><td>4.5%</td><td>NA</td><td>Massachusetts**</td><td>NA</td><td>NA</td></tr>
<tr><td>42</td><td>West Virginia</td><td>5,000</td><td>0.0%</td><td>NA</td><td>New Hampshire**</td><td>NA</td><td>NA</td></tr>
<tr><td>23</td><td>Wisconsin</td><td>315,000</td><td>0.6%</td><td>NA</td><td>Rhode Island**</td><td>NA</td><td>NA</td></tr>
<tr><td>34</td><td>Wyoming</td><td>132,000</td><td>0.3%</td><td>NA</td><td>Vermont**</td><td>NA</td><td>NA</td></tr>
<tr><td></td><td></td><td></td><td></td><td></td><td>District of Columbia**</td><td>NA</td><td>NA</td></tr>
</table>

Source: U.S. Department of Agriculture, National Agricultural Statistics Service
"Crop Production: 2009 Summary" (Cr Pr 2-1 (10), January 2010)
(http://usda.mannlib.cornell.edu/MannUsda/viewDocumentInfo.do?documentID=1047)
*Estimated totals.
**No acreage or not available.

Cattle on Farms in 2010

National Total = 93,701,200 Cattle*

ALPHA ORDER

RANK ORDER

RANK	STATE	CATTLE	% of USA
24	Alabama	1,280,000	1.4%
49	Alaska	14,500	0.0%
32	Arizona	930,000	1.0%
16	Arkansas	1,890,000	2.0%
5	California	5,150,000	5.5%
10	Colorado	2,600,000	2.8%
44	Connecticut	48,000	0.1%
48	Delaware	20,000	0.0%
17	Florida	1,720,000	1.8%
29	Georgia	1,060,000	1.1%
42	Hawaii	151,000	0.2%
14	Idaho	2,140,000	2.3%
27	Illinois	1,170,000	1.2%
33	Indiana	870,000	0.9%
7	Iowa	3,850,000	4.1%
3	Kansas	6,000,000	6.4%
13	Kentucky	2,300,000	2.5%
34	Louisiana	840,000	0.9%
43	Maine	87,000	0.1%
41	Maryland	195,000	0.2%
45	Massachusetts	43,000	0.0%
28	Michigan	1,100,000	1.2%
12	Minnesota	2,420,000	2.6%
31	Mississippi	970,000	1.0%
6	Missouri	4,150,000	4.4%
11	Montana	2,550,000	2.7%
2	Nebraska	6,250,000	6.7%
37	Nevada	450,000	0.5%
46	New Hampshire	37,000	0.0%
47	New Jersey	36,000	0.0%
20	New Mexico	1,550,000	1.7%
22	New York	1,410,000	1.5%
35	North Carolina	820,000	0.9%
17	North Dakota	1,720,000	1.8%
24	Ohio	1,280,000	1.4%
4	Oklahoma	5,450,000	5.8%
26	Oregon	1,260,000	1.3%
19	Pennsylvania	1,620,000	1.7%
50	Rhode Island	4,700	0.0%
38	South Carolina	380,000	0.4%
8	South Dakota	3,800,000	4.1%
15	Tennessee	2,040,000	2.2%
1	Texas	13,300,000	14.2%
36	Utah	800,000	0.9%
40	Vermont	265,000	0.3%
20	Virginia	1,550,000	1.7%
30	Washington	1,040,000	1.1%
39	West Virginia	370,000	0.4%
9	Wisconsin	3,400,000	3.6%
23	Wyoming	1,320,000	1.4%

RANK	STATE	CATTLE	% of USA
1	Texas	13,300,000	14.2%
2	Nebraska	6,250,000	6.7%
3	Kansas	6,000,000	6.4%
4	Oklahoma	5,450,000	5.8%
5	California	5,150,000	5.5%
6	Missouri	4,150,000	4.4%
7	Iowa	3,850,000	4.1%
8	South Dakota	3,800,000	4.1%
9	Wisconsin	3,400,000	3.6%
10	Colorado	2,600,000	2.8%
11	Montana	2,550,000	2.7%
12	Minnesota	2,420,000	2.6%
13	Kentucky	2,300,000	2.5%
14	Idaho	2,140,000	2.3%
15	Tennessee	2,040,000	2.2%
16	Arkansas	1,890,000	2.0%
17	Florida	1,720,000	1.8%
17	North Dakota	1,720,000	1.8%
19	Pennsylvania	1,620,000	1.7%
20	New Mexico	1,550,000	1.7%
20	Virginia	1,550,000	1.7%
22	New York	1,410,000	1.5%
23	Wyoming	1,320,000	1.4%
24	Alabama	1,280,000	1.4%
24	Ohio	1,280,000	1.4%
26	Oregon	1,260,000	1.3%
27	Illinois	1,170,000	1.2%
28	Michigan	1,100,000	1.2%
29	Georgia	1,060,000	1.1%
30	Washington	1,040,000	1.1%
31	Mississippi	970,000	1.0%
32	Arizona	930,000	1.0%
33	Indiana	870,000	0.9%
34	Louisiana	840,000	0.9%
35	North Carolina	820,000	0.9%
36	Utah	800,000	0.9%
37	Nevada	450,000	0.5%
38	South Carolina	380,000	0.4%
39	West Virginia	370,000	0.4%
40	Vermont	265,000	0.3%
41	Maryland	195,000	0.2%
42	Hawaii	151,000	0.2%
43	Maine	87,000	0.1%
44	Connecticut	48,000	0.1%
45	Massachusetts	43,000	0.0%
46	New Hampshire	37,000	0.0%
47	New Jersey	36,000	0.0%
48	Delaware	20,000	0.0%
49	Alaska	14,500	0.0%
50	Rhode Island	4,700	0.0%
	District of Columbia	0	0.0%

Source: U.S. Department of Agriculture, National Agricultural Statistics Service
"Cattle" (http://usda.mannlib.cornell.edu/MannUsda/viewDocumentInfo.do?documentID=1017)
*As of January 1, 2010.

Milk Cows on Farms in 2008

National Total = 9,189,000 Milk Cows*

ALPHA ORDER

RANK	STATE	MILK COWS	% of USA
43	Alabama	13,000	0.1%
50	Alaska	600	0.0%
13	Arizona	181,000	2.0%
40	Arkansas	17,000	0.2%
1	California	1,813,000	19.7%
17	Colorado	118,000	1.3%
37	Connecticut	19,000	0.2%
47	Delaware	6,800	0.1%
16	Florida	125,000	1.4%
26	Georgia	77,000	0.8%
48	Hawaii	2,900	0.0%
5	Idaho	513,000	5.6%
21	Illinois	103,000	1.1%
14	Indiana	166,000	1.8%
12	Iowa	213,000	2.3%
20	Kansas	110,000	1.2%
23	Kentucky	90,000	1.0%
33	Louisiana	29,000	0.3%
32	Maine	33,000	0.4%
30	Maryland	58,000	0.6%
41	Massachusetts	15,000	0.2%
8	Michigan	335,000	3.6%
6	Minnesota	460,000	5.0%
36	Mississippi	21,000	0.2%
19	Missouri	112,000	1.2%
38	Montana	18,000	0.2%
29	Nebraska	59,000	0.6%
35	Nevada	27,000	0.3%
41	New Hampshire	15,000	0.2%
45	New Jersey	10,000	0.1%
9	New Mexico	332,000	3.6%
3	New York	627,000	6.8%
31	North Carolina	48,000	0.5%
33	North Dakota	29,000	0.3%
10	Ohio	275,000	3.0%
27	Oklahoma	69,000	0.8%
18	Oregon	115,000	1.3%
4	Pennsylvania	550,000	6.0%
49	Rhode Island	1,100	0.0%
38	South Carolina	18,000	0.2%
24	South Dakota	85,000	0.9%
28	Tennessee	63,000	0.7%
7	Texas	389,000	4.2%
24	Utah	85,000	0.9%
15	Vermont	140,000	1.5%
22	Virginia	100,000	1.1%
11	Washington	238,000	2.6%
43	West Virginia	13,000	0.1%
2	Wisconsin	1,247,000	13.6%
46	Wyoming	7,100	0.1%

RANK ORDER

RANK	STATE	MILK COWS	% of USA
1	California	1,813,000	19.7%
2	Wisconsin	1,247,000	13.6%
3	New York	627,000	6.8%
4	Pennsylvania	550,000	6.0%
5	Idaho	513,000	5.6%
6	Minnesota	460,000	5.0%
7	Texas	389,000	4.2%
8	Michigan	335,000	3.6%
9	New Mexico	332,000	3.6%
10	Ohio	275,000	3.0%
11	Washington	238,000	2.6%
12	Iowa	213,000	2.3%
13	Arizona	181,000	2.0%
14	Indiana	166,000	1.8%
15	Vermont	140,000	1.5%
16	Florida	125,000	1.4%
17	Colorado	118,000	1.3%
18	Oregon	115,000	1.3%
19	Missouri	112,000	1.2%
20	Kansas	110,000	1.2%
21	Illinois	103,000	1.1%
22	Virginia	100,000	1.1%
23	Kentucky	90,000	1.0%
24	South Dakota	85,000	0.9%
24	Utah	85,000	0.9%
26	Georgia	77,000	0.8%
27	Oklahoma	69,000	0.8%
28	Tennessee	63,000	0.7%
29	Nebraska	59,000	0.6%
30	Maryland	58,000	0.6%
31	North Carolina	48,000	0.5%
32	Maine	33,000	0.4%
33	Louisiana	29,000	0.3%
33	North Dakota	29,000	0.3%
35	Nevada	27,000	0.3%
36	Mississippi	21,000	0.2%
37	Connecticut	19,000	0.2%
38	Montana	18,000	0.2%
38	South Carolina	18,000	0.2%
40	Arkansas	17,000	0.2%
41	Massachusetts	15,000	0.2%
41	New Hampshire	15,000	0.2%
43	Alabama	13,000	0.1%
43	West Virginia	13,000	0.1%
45	New Jersey	10,000	0.1%
46	Wyoming	7,100	0.1%
47	Delaware	6,800	0.1%
48	Hawaii	2,900	0.0%
49	Rhode Island	1,100	0.0%
50	Alaska	600	0.0%
	District of Columbia	0	0.0%

Source: U.S. Department of Agriculture, National Agricultural Statistics Service
   "Milk Production, Disposition and Income: 2008 Summary" (May 2009)
   (http://usda.mannlib.cornell.edu/MannUsda/viewDocumentInfo.do?documentID=1105)
*Average number during year. Excludes heifers not yet fresh.

Milk Production in 2008

National Total = 185,654,000,000 Pounds of Milk*

ALPHA ORDER

RANK	STATE	POUNDS	% of USA
43	Alabama	197,000,000	0.1%
50	Alaska	8,800,000	0.0%
13	Arizona	4,210,000,000	2.3%
42	Arkansas	220,000,000	0.1%
1	California	40,683,000,000	21.9%
15	Colorado	2,706,000,000	1.5%
35	Connecticut	365,000,000	0.2%
47	Delaware	113,000,000	0.1%
19	Florida	2,104,000,000	1.1%
25	Georgia	1,399,000,000	0.8%
48	Hawaii	35,500,000	0.0%
4	Idaho	11,549,000,000	6.2%
20	Illinois	1,917,000,000	1.0%
14	Indiana	3,371,000,000	1.8%
12	Iowa	4,278,000,000	2.3%
18	Kansas	2,187,000,000	1.2%
26	Kentucky	1,250,000,000	0.7%
36	Louisiana	349,000,000	0.2%
32	Maine	587,000,000	0.3%
29	Maryland	1,051,000,000	0.6%
41	Massachusetts	255,000,000	0.1%
7	Michigan	7,625,000,000	4.1%
6	Minnesota	8,656,000,000	4.7%
38	Mississippi	324,000,000	0.2%
23	Missouri	1,678,000,000	0.9%
37	Montana	333,000,000	0.2%
28	Nebraska	1,075,000,000	0.6%
33	Nevada	553,000,000	0.3%
40	New Hampshire	290,000,000	0.2%
45	New Jersey	168,000,000	0.1%
9	New Mexico	7,290,000,000	3.9%
3	New York	12,103,000,000	6.5%
31	North Carolina	921,000,000	0.5%
34	North Dakota	444,000,000	0.2%
11	Ohio	4,980,000,000	2.7%
27	Oklahoma	1,144,000,000	0.6%
17	Oregon	2,233,000,000	1.2%
5	Pennsylvania	10,682,000,000	5.8%
49	Rhode Island	18,100,000	0.0%
39	South Carolina	322,000,000	0.2%
24	South Dakota	1,641,000,000	0.9%
30	Tennessee	999,000,000	0.5%
8	Texas	7,384,000,000	4.0%
22	Utah	1,732,000,000	0.9%
16	Vermont	2,531,000,000	1.4%
21	Virginia	1,753,000,000	0.9%
10	Washington	5,531,000,000	3.0%
44	West Virginia	195,000,000	0.1%
2	Wisconsin	24,080,000,000	13.0%
46	Wyoming	133,700,000	0.1%

RANK ORDER

RANK	STATE	POUNDS	% of USA
1	California	40,683,000,000	21.9%
2	Wisconsin	24,080,000,000	13.0%
3	New York	12,103,000,000	6.5%
4	Idaho	11,549,000,000	6.2%
5	Pennsylvania	10,682,000,000	5.8%
6	Minnesota	8,656,000,000	4.7%
7	Michigan	7,625,000,000	4.1%
8	Texas	7,384,000,000	4.0%
9	New Mexico	7,290,000,000	3.9%
10	Washington	5,531,000,000	3.0%
11	Ohio	4,980,000,000	2.7%
12	Iowa	4,278,000,000	2.3%
13	Arizona	4,210,000,000	2.3%
14	Indiana	3,371,000,000	1.8%
15	Colorado	2,706,000,000	1.5%
16	Vermont	2,531,000,000	1.4%
17	Oregon	2,233,000,000	1.2%
18	Kansas	2,187,000,000	1.2%
19	Florida	2,104,000,000	1.1%
20	Illinois	1,917,000,000	1.0%
21	Virginia	1,753,000,000	0.9%
22	Utah	1,732,000,000	0.9%
23	Missouri	1,678,000,000	0.9%
24	South Dakota	1,641,000,000	0.9%
25	Georgia	1,399,000,000	0.8%
26	Kentucky	1,250,000,000	0.7%
27	Oklahoma	1,144,000,000	0.6%
28	Nebraska	1,075,000,000	0.6%
29	Maryland	1,051,000,000	0.6%
30	Tennessee	999,000,000	0.5%
31	North Carolina	921,000,000	0.5%
32	Maine	587,000,000	0.3%
33	Nevada	553,000,000	0.3%
34	North Dakota	444,000,000	0.2%
35	Connecticut	365,000,000	0.2%
36	Louisiana	349,000,000	0.2%
37	Montana	333,000,000	0.2%
38	Mississippi	324,000,000	0.2%
39	South Carolina	322,000,000	0.2%
40	New Hampshire	290,000,000	0.2%
41	Massachusetts	255,000,000	0.1%
42	Arkansas	220,000,000	0.1%
43	Alabama	197,000,000	0.1%
44	West Virginia	195,000,000	0.1%
45	New Jersey	168,000,000	0.1%
46	Wyoming	133,700,000	0.1%
47	Delaware	113,000,000	0.1%
48	Hawaii	35,500,000	0.0%
49	Rhode Island	18,100,000	0.0%
50	Alaska	8,800,000	0.0%
	District of Columbia	0	0.0%

Source: U.S. Department of Agriculture, National Agricultural Statistics Service
"Milk Production, Disposition and Income: 2008 Summary" (May 2009)
(http://usda.mannlib.cornell.edu/MannUsda/viewDocumentInfo.do?documentID=1105)
*Excludes milk suckled by calves.

Milk Production per Milk Cow in 2008

National Average = 20,204 Pounds of Milk per Cow*

ALPHA ORDER

RANK	STATE	POUNDS
43	Alabama	15,154
46	Alaska	14,667
1	Arizona	23,260
48	Arkansas	12,941
6	California	22,440
3	Colorado	22,932
19	Connecticut	19,211
37	Delaware	16,618
35	Florida	16,832
27	Georgia	18,169
49	Hawaii	12,241
5	Idaho	22,513
24	Illinois	18,612
10	Indiana	20,307
11	Iowa	20,085
12	Kansas	19,882
47	Kentucky	13,889
50	Louisiana	12,034
32	Maine	17,788
28	Maryland	18,121
34	Massachusetts	17,000
4	Michigan	22,761
23	Minnesota	18,817
41	Mississippi	15,429
45	Missouri	14,982
25	Montana	18,500
26	Nebraska	18,220
8	Nevada	20,481
15	New Hampshire	19,333
36	New Jersey	16,800
7	New Mexico	21,958
18	New York	19,303
20	North Carolina	19,188
42	North Dakota	15,310
29	Ohio	18,109
38	Oklahoma	16,580
14	Oregon	19,417
13	Pennsylvania	19,422
39	Rhode Island	16,455
31	South Carolina	17,889
17	South Dakota	19,306
40	Tennessee	15,857
21	Texas	18,982
9	Utah	20,376
30	Vermont	18,079
33	Virginia	17,530
2	Washington	23,239
44	West Virginia	15,000
16	Wisconsin	19,310
22	Wyoming	18,831

RANK ORDER

RANK	STATE	POUNDS
1	Arizona	23,260
2	Washington	23,239
3	Colorado	22,932
4	Michigan	22,761
5	Idaho	22,513
6	California	22,440
7	New Mexico	21,958
8	Nevada	20,481
9	Utah	20,376
10	Indiana	20,307
11	Iowa	20,085
12	Kansas	19,882
13	Pennsylvania	19,422
14	Oregon	19,417
15	New Hampshire	19,333
16	Wisconsin	19,310
17	South Dakota	19,306
18	New York	19,303
19	Connecticut	19,211
20	North Carolina	19,188
21	Texas	18,982
22	Wyoming	18,831
23	Minnesota	18,817
24	Illinois	18,612
25	Montana	18,500
26	Nebraska	18,220
27	Georgia	18,169
28	Maryland	18,121
29	Ohio	18,109
30	Vermont	18,079
31	South Carolina	17,889
32	Maine	17,788
33	Virginia	17,530
34	Massachusetts	17,000
35	Florida	16,832
36	New Jersey	16,800
37	Delaware	16,618
38	Oklahoma	16,580
39	Rhode Island	16,455
40	Tennessee	15,857
41	Mississippi	15,429
42	North Dakota	15,310
43	Alabama	15,154
44	West Virginia	15,000
45	Missouri	14,982
46	Alaska	14,667
47	Kentucky	13,889
48	Arkansas	12,941
49	Hawaii	12,241
50	Louisiana	12,034
	District of Columbia**	NA

Source: U.S. Department of Agriculture, National Agricultural Statistics Service
   "Milk Production, Disposition and Income: 2008 Summary" (May 2009)
   (http://usda.mannlib.cornell.edu/MannUsda/viewDocumentInfo.do?documentID=1105)
*Excludes milk suckled by calves.
**Not applicable.

Hogs and Pigs on Farms in 2009

National Total = 65,807,000 Hogs and Pigs*

ALPHA ORDER

RANK	STATE	HOGS AND PIGS	% of USA
28	Alabama	140,000	0.2%
50	Alaska	1,400	0.0%
26	Arizona	167,000	0.3%
23	Arkansas	200,000	0.3%
29	California	100,000	0.2%
16	Colorado	720,000	1.1%
45	Connecticut	2,900	0.0%
41	Delaware	7,500	0.0%
35	Florida	20,000	0.0%
22	Georgia	210,000	0.3%
37	Hawaii	13,000	0.0%
32	Idaho	36,000	0.1%
4	Illinois	4,350,000	6.6%
5	Indiana	3,650,000	5.5%
1	Iowa	19,300,000	29.3%
10	Kansas	1,810,000	2.8%
20	Kentucky	350,000	0.5%
39	Louisiana	10,000	0.0%
43	Maine	4,900	0.0%
33	Maryland	30,000	0.0%
38	Massachusetts	11,000	0.0%
13	Michigan	1,080,000	1.6%
3	Minnesota	7,400,000	11.2%
17	Mississippi	365,000	0.6%
7	Missouri	3,100,000	4.7%
25	Montana	175,000	0.3%
6	Nebraska	3,150,000	4.8%
45	Nevada	2,900	0.0%
47	New Hampshire	2,400	0.0%
40	New Jersey	8,000	0.0%
49	New Mexico	1,500	0.0%
31	New York	77,000	0.1%
2	North Carolina	9,700,000	14.7%
27	North Dakota	160,000	0.2%
9	Ohio	2,020,000	3.1%
8	Oklahoma	2,310,000	3.5%
36	Oregon	17,000	0.0%
11	Pennsylvania	1,180,000	1.8%
48	Rhode Island	1,700	0.0%
21	South Carolina	225,000	0.3%
12	South Dakota	1,170,000	1.8%
24	Tennessee	185,000	0.3%
14	Texas	770,000	1.2%
15	Utah	730,000	1.1%
44	Vermont	3,000	0.0%
17	Virginia	365,000	0.6%
34	Washington	23,000	0.0%
42	West Virginia	5,000	0.0%
19	Wisconsin	360,000	0.5%
30	Wyoming	87,000	0.1%

RANK ORDER

RANK	STATE	HOGS AND PIGS	% of USA
1	Iowa	19,300,000	29.3%
2	North Carolina	9,700,000	14.7%
3	Minnesota	7,400,000	11.2%
4	Illinois	4,350,000	6.6%
5	Indiana	3,650,000	5.5%
6	Nebraska	3,150,000	4.8%
7	Missouri	3,100,000	4.7%
8	Oklahoma	2,310,000	3.5%
9	Ohio	2,020,000	3.1%
10	Kansas	1,810,000	2.8%
11	Pennsylvania	1,180,000	1.8%
12	South Dakota	1,170,000	1.8%
13	Michigan	1,080,000	1.6%
14	Texas	770,000	1.2%
15	Utah	730,000	1.1%
16	Colorado	720,000	1.1%
17	Mississippi	365,000	0.6%
17	Virginia	365,000	0.6%
19	Wisconsin	360,000	0.5%
20	Kentucky	350,000	0.5%
21	South Carolina	225,000	0.3%
22	Georgia	210,000	0.3%
23	Arkansas	200,000	0.3%
24	Tennessee	185,000	0.3%
25	Montana	175,000	0.3%
26	Arizona	167,000	0.3%
27	North Dakota	160,000	0.2%
28	Alabama	140,000	0.2%
29	California	100,000	0.2%
30	Wyoming	87,000	0.1%
31	New York	77,000	0.1%
32	Idaho	36,000	0.1%
33	Maryland	30,000	0.0%
34	Washington	23,000	0.0%
35	Florida	20,000	0.0%
36	Oregon	17,000	0.0%
37	Hawaii	13,000	0.0%
38	Massachusetts	11,000	0.0%
39	Louisiana	10,000	0.0%
40	New Jersey	8,000	0.0%
41	Delaware	7,500	0.0%
42	West Virginia	5,000	0.0%
43	Maine	4,900	0.0%
44	Vermont	3,000	0.0%
45	Connecticut	2,900	0.0%
45	Nevada	2,900	0.0%
47	New Hampshire	2,400	0.0%
48	Rhode Island	1,700	0.0%
49	New Mexico	1,500	0.0%
50	Alaska	1,400	0.0%
	District of Columbia	0	0.0%

Source: U.S. Department of Agriculture, National Agricultural Statistics Service
"Quarterly Hogs and Pigs" (http://usda.mannlib.cornell.edu/MannUsda/viewDocumentInfo.do?documentID=1086)
*As of December 1, 2009.

Chickens in 2008 (Leading States Only)

National Total = 9,009,100,000 Chickens*

<table>
<tr><td colspan="4">ALPHA ORDER</td><td colspan="4">RANK ORDER</td></tr>
<tr><td>RANK</td><td>STATE</td><td>CHICKENS</td><td>% of USA</td><td>RANK</td><td>STATE</td><td>CHICKENS</td><td>% of USA</td></tr>
<tr><td>3</td><td>Alabama</td><td>1,062,900,000</td><td>11.8%</td><td>1</td><td>Georgia</td><td>1,409,200,000</td><td>15.6%</td></tr>
<tr><td>NA</td><td>Alaska***</td><td>NA</td><td>NA</td><td>2</td><td>Arkansas</td><td>1,160,000,000</td><td>12.9%</td></tr>
<tr><td>NA</td><td>Arizona***</td><td>NA</td><td>NA</td><td>3</td><td>Alabama</td><td>1,062,900,000</td><td>11.8%</td></tr>
<tr><td>2</td><td>Arkansas</td><td>1,160,000,000</td><td>12.9%</td><td>4</td><td>Mississippi</td><td>840,700,000</td><td>9.3%</td></tr>
<tr><td>NA</td><td>California**</td><td>NA</td><td>NA</td><td>5</td><td>North Carolina</td><td>796,100,000</td><td>8.8%</td></tr>
<tr><td>NA</td><td>Colorado***</td><td>NA</td><td>NA</td><td>6</td><td>Texas</td><td>640,800,000</td><td>7.1%</td></tr>
<tr><td>NA</td><td>Connecticut**</td><td>NA</td><td>NA</td><td>7</td><td>Kentucky</td><td>306,100,000</td><td>3.4%</td></tr>
<tr><td>10</td><td>Delaware</td><td>242,900,000</td><td>2.7%</td><td>8</td><td>Maryland</td><td>298,600,000</td><td>3.3%</td></tr>
<tr><td>16</td><td>Florida</td><td>63,800,000</td><td>0.7%</td><td>9</td><td>Virginia</td><td>250,300,000</td><td>2.8%</td></tr>
<tr><td>1</td><td>Georgia</td><td>1,409,200,000</td><td>15.6%</td><td>10</td><td>Delaware</td><td>242,900,000</td><td>2.7%</td></tr>
<tr><td>NA</td><td>Hawaii***</td><td>NA</td><td>NA</td><td>11</td><td>Oklahoma</td><td>237,800,000</td><td>2.6%</td></tr>
<tr><td>NA</td><td>Idaho***</td><td>NA</td><td>NA</td><td>12</td><td>South Carolina</td><td>236,900,000</td><td>2.6%</td></tr>
<tr><td>NA</td><td>Illinois***</td><td>NA</td><td>NA</td><td>13</td><td>Tennessee</td><td>199,700,000</td><td>2.2%</td></tr>
<tr><td>NA</td><td>Indiana**</td><td>NA</td><td>NA</td><td>14</td><td>Pennsylvania</td><td>160,900,000</td><td>1.8%</td></tr>
<tr><td>NA</td><td>Iowa**</td><td>NA</td><td>NA</td><td>15</td><td>West Virginia</td><td>85,700,000</td><td>1.0%</td></tr>
<tr><td>NA</td><td>Kansas***</td><td>NA</td><td>NA</td><td>16</td><td>Florida</td><td>63,800,000</td><td>0.7%</td></tr>
<tr><td>7</td><td>Kentucky</td><td>306,100,000</td><td>3.4%</td><td>17</td><td>Ohio</td><td>57,500,000</td><td>0.6%</td></tr>
<tr><td>NA</td><td>Louisiana**</td><td>NA</td><td>NA</td><td>18</td><td>Wisconsin</td><td>51,700,000</td><td>0.6%</td></tr>
<tr><td>NA</td><td>Maine***</td><td>NA</td><td>NA</td><td>19</td><td>Minnesota</td><td>44,900,000</td><td>0.5%</td></tr>
<tr><td>8</td><td>Maryland</td><td>298,600,000</td><td>3.3%</td><td>20</td><td>Nebraska</td><td>6,700,000</td><td>0.1%</td></tr>
<tr><td>NA</td><td>Massachusetts***</td><td>NA</td><td>NA</td><td>NA</td><td>Alaska***</td><td>NA</td><td>NA</td></tr>
<tr><td>NA</td><td>Michigan**</td><td>NA</td><td>NA</td><td>NA</td><td>Arizona***</td><td>NA</td><td>NA</td></tr>
<tr><td>19</td><td>Minnesota</td><td>44,900,000</td><td>0.5%</td><td>NA</td><td>California**</td><td>NA</td><td>NA</td></tr>
<tr><td>4</td><td>Mississippi</td><td>840,700,000</td><td>9.3%</td><td>NA</td><td>Colorado***</td><td>NA</td><td>NA</td></tr>
<tr><td>NA</td><td>Missouri**</td><td>NA</td><td>NA</td><td>NA</td><td>Connecticut**</td><td>NA</td><td>NA</td></tr>
<tr><td>NA</td><td>Montana***</td><td>NA</td><td>NA</td><td>NA</td><td>Hawaii***</td><td>NA</td><td>NA</td></tr>
<tr><td>20</td><td>Nebraska</td><td>6,700,000</td><td>0.1%</td><td>NA</td><td>Idaho***</td><td>NA</td><td>NA</td></tr>
<tr><td>NA</td><td>Nevada***</td><td>NA</td><td>NA</td><td>NA</td><td>Illinois***</td><td>NA</td><td>NA</td></tr>
<tr><td>NA</td><td>New Hampshire***</td><td>NA</td><td>NA</td><td>NA</td><td>Indiana**</td><td>NA</td><td>NA</td></tr>
<tr><td>NA</td><td>New Jersey***</td><td>NA</td><td>NA</td><td>NA</td><td>Iowa**</td><td>NA</td><td>NA</td></tr>
<tr><td>NA</td><td>New Mexico***</td><td>NA</td><td>NA</td><td>NA</td><td>Kansas***</td><td>NA</td><td>NA</td></tr>
<tr><td>NA</td><td>New York**</td><td>NA</td><td>NA</td><td>NA</td><td>Louisiana**</td><td>NA</td><td>NA</td></tr>
<tr><td>5</td><td>North Carolina</td><td>796,100,000</td><td>8.8%</td><td>NA</td><td>Maine***</td><td>NA</td><td>NA</td></tr>
<tr><td>NA</td><td>North Dakota***</td><td>NA</td><td>NA</td><td>NA</td><td>Massachusetts***</td><td>NA</td><td>NA</td></tr>
<tr><td>17</td><td>Ohio</td><td>57,500,000</td><td>0.6%</td><td>NA</td><td>Michigan**</td><td>NA</td><td>NA</td></tr>
<tr><td>11</td><td>Oklahoma</td><td>237,800,000</td><td>2.6%</td><td>NA</td><td>Missouri**</td><td>NA</td><td>NA</td></tr>
<tr><td>NA</td><td>Oregon**</td><td>NA</td><td>NA</td><td>NA</td><td>Montana***</td><td>NA</td><td>NA</td></tr>
<tr><td>14</td><td>Pennsylvania</td><td>160,900,000</td><td>1.8%</td><td>NA</td><td>Nevada***</td><td>NA</td><td>NA</td></tr>
<tr><td>NA</td><td>Rhode Island***</td><td>NA</td><td>NA</td><td>NA</td><td>New Hampshire***</td><td>NA</td><td>NA</td></tr>
<tr><td>12</td><td>South Carolina</td><td>236,900,000</td><td>2.6%</td><td>NA</td><td>New Jersey***</td><td>NA</td><td>NA</td></tr>
<tr><td>NA</td><td>South Dakota***</td><td>NA</td><td>NA</td><td>NA</td><td>New Mexico***</td><td>NA</td><td>NA</td></tr>
<tr><td>13</td><td>Tennessee</td><td>199,700,000</td><td>2.2%</td><td>NA</td><td>New York**</td><td>NA</td><td>NA</td></tr>
<tr><td>6</td><td>Texas</td><td>640,800,000</td><td>7.1%</td><td>NA</td><td>North Dakota***</td><td>NA</td><td>NA</td></tr>
<tr><td>NA</td><td>Utah***</td><td>NA</td><td>NA</td><td>NA</td><td>Oregon**</td><td>NA</td><td>NA</td></tr>
<tr><td>NA</td><td>Vermont***</td><td>NA</td><td>NA</td><td>NA</td><td>Rhode Island***</td><td>NA</td><td>NA</td></tr>
<tr><td>9</td><td>Virginia</td><td>250,300,000</td><td>2.8%</td><td>NA</td><td>South Dakota***</td><td>NA</td><td>NA</td></tr>
<tr><td>NA</td><td>Washington**</td><td>NA</td><td>NA</td><td>NA</td><td>Utah***</td><td>NA</td><td>NA</td></tr>
<tr><td>15</td><td>West Virginia</td><td>85,700,000</td><td>1.0%</td><td>NA</td><td>Vermont***</td><td>NA</td><td>NA</td></tr>
<tr><td>18</td><td>Wisconsin</td><td>51,700,000</td><td>0.6%</td><td>NA</td><td>Washington**</td><td>NA</td><td>NA</td></tr>
<tr><td>NA</td><td>Wyoming***</td><td>NA</td><td>NA</td><td>NA</td><td>Wyoming***</td><td>NA</td><td>NA</td></tr>
<tr><td></td><td></td><td></td><td></td><td></td><td>District of Columbia***</td><td>NA</td><td>NA</td></tr>
</table>

Source: U.S. Department of Agriculture, National Agricultural Statistics Service
   "Poultry - Production and Value: 2008 Summary" (May 2009)
      (http://usda.mannlib.cornell.edu/MannUsda/viewDocumentInfo.do?documentID=1130)
*Broilers. Total includes numbers for states not shown separately but excludes states producing less than 500,000 birds. **These states produced a combined total of 855,900,000 chickens. They are combined to avoid disclosing individual operations. National total does not include chickens used for egg production. ***Not available.

Eggs Produced in 2008

National Total = 90,151,000,000 Eggs

	ALPHA ORDER					RANK ORDER		
RANK	**STATE**	**EGGS**	**% of USA**		**RANK**	**STATE**	**EGGS**	**% of USA**
14	Alabama	2,150,000,000	2.4%		1	Iowa	14,407,000,000	16.0%
NA	Alaska*	NA	NA		2	Ohio	7,168,000,000	8.0%
NA	Arizona*	NA	NA		3	Indiana	6,523,000,000	7.2%
8	Arkansas	3,139,000,000	3.5%		4	Pennsylvania	6,181,000,000	6.9%
5	California	5,272,000,000	5.8%		5	California	5,272,000,000	5.8%
23	Colorado	1,090,000,000	1.2%		6	Texas	4,928,000,000	5.5%
26	Connecticut	780,000,000	0.9%		7	Georgia	4,576,000,000	5.1%
NA	Delaware*	NA	NA		8	Arkansas	3,139,000,000	3.5%
12	Florida	2,749,000,000	3.0%		9	North Carolina	3,063,000,000	3.4%
7	Georgia	4,576,000,000	5.1%		10	Nebraska	2,777,000,000	3.1%
38	Hawaii	73,300,000	0.1%		11	Minnesota	2,767,000,000	3.1%
36	Idaho	150,000,000	0.2%		12	Florida	2,749,000,000	3.0%
18	Illinois	1,453,000,000	1.6%		13	Michigan	2,653,000,000	2.9%
3	Indiana	6,523,000,000	7.2%		14	Alabama	2,150,000,000	2.4%
1	Iowa	14,407,000,000	16.0%		15	Missouri	1,885,000,000	2.1%
NA	Kansas*	NA	NA		16	Washington	1,533,000,000	1.7%
22	Kentucky	1,140,000,000	1.3%		17	Mississippi	1,511,000,000	1.7%
32	Louisiana	479,000,000	0.5%		18	Illinois	1,453,000,000	1.6%
24	Maine	1,028,000,000	1.1%		19	Wisconsin	1,220,000,000	1.4%
31	Maryland	666,000,000	0.7%		20	New York	1,167,000,000	1.3%
41	Massachusetts	36,000,000	0.0%		21	South Carolina	1,143,000,000	1.3%
13	Michigan	2,653,000,000	2.9%		22	Kentucky	1,140,000,000	1.3%
11	Minnesota	2,767,000,000	3.1%		23	Colorado	1,090,000,000	1.2%
17	Mississippi	1,511,000,000	1.7%		24	Maine	1,028,000,000	1.1%
15	Missouri	1,885,000,000	2.1%		25	Utah	914,000,000	1.0%
37	Montana	115,000,000	0.1%		26	Connecticut	780,000,000	0.9%
10	Nebraska	2,777,000,000	3.1%		27	Oklahoma	774,000,000	0.9%
NA	Nevada*	NA	NA		28	Oregon	769,000,000	0.9%
39	New Hampshire	65,000,000	0.1%		29	Virginia	726,000,000	0.8%
33	New Jersey	421,000,000	0.5%		30	South Dakota	691,000,000	0.8%
NA	New Mexico*	NA	NA		31	Maryland	666,000,000	0.7%
20	New York	1,167,000,000	1.3%		32	Louisiana	479,000,000	0.5%
9	North Carolina	3,063,000,000	3.4%		33	New Jersey	421,000,000	0.5%
NA	North Dakota*	NA	NA		34	Tennessee	351,000,000	0.4%
2	Ohio	7,168,000,000	8.0%		35	West Virginia	247,000,000	0.3%
27	Oklahoma	774,000,000	0.9%		36	Idaho	150,000,000	0.2%
28	Oregon	769,000,000	0.9%		37	Montana	115,000,000	0.1%
4	Pennsylvania	6,181,000,000	6.9%		38	Hawaii	73,300,000	0.1%
NA	Rhode Island*	NA	NA		39	New Hampshire	65,000,000	0.1%
21	South Carolina	1,143,000,000	1.3%		40	Vermont	55,000,000	0.1%
30	South Dakota	691,000,000	0.8%		41	Massachusetts	36,000,000	0.0%
34	Tennessee	351,000,000	0.4%		42	Wyoming	2,400,000	0.0%
6	Texas	4,928,000,000	5.5%		NA	Alaska*	NA	NA
25	Utah	914,000,000	1.0%		NA	Arizona*	NA	NA
40	Vermont	55,000,000	0.1%		NA	Delaware*	NA	NA
29	Virginia	726,000,000	0.8%		NA	Kansas*	NA	NA
16	Washington	1,533,000,000	1.7%		NA	Nevada*	NA	NA
35	West Virginia	247,000,000	0.3%		NA	New Mexico*	NA	NA
19	Wisconsin	1,220,000,000	1.4%		NA	North Dakota*	NA	NA
42	Wyoming	2,400,000	0.0%		NA	Rhode Island*	NA	NA
						District of Columbia	0	0.0%

Source: U.S. Department of Agriculture, National Agricultural Statistics Service
    "Poultry - Production and Value: 2008 Summary" (May 2009)
       (http://usda.mannlib.cornell.edu/MannUsda/viewDocumentInfo.do?documentID=1130)
*These states produced a combined 1,315,000,000 eggs. They are combined to avoid disclosing individual operations.

II. Crime and Law Enforcement

Crimes in 2008

National Total = 11,149,927 Crimes*

ALPHA ORDER

RANK	STATE	CRIMES	% of USA
20	Alabama	211,454	1.9%
46	Alaska	24,598	0.2%
11	Arizona	307,979	2.8%
28	Arkansas	123,882	1.1%
1	California	1,265,920	11.4%
25	Colorado	157,671	1.4%
33	Connecticut	96,514	0.9%
40	Delaware	37,444	0.3%
3	Florida	885,199	7.9%
6	Georgia	435,319	3.9%
39	Hawaii	49,516	0.4%
41	Idaho	35,502	0.3%
5	Illinois	446,135	4.0%
15	Indiana	233,998	2.1%
36	Iowa	81,209	0.7%
31	Kansas	106,140	1.0%
29	Kentucky	122,960	1.1%
21	Louisiana	197,574	1.8%
42	Maine	33,832	0.3%
16	Maryland	233,558	2.1%
22	Massachusetts	185,133	1.7%
10	Michigan	343,751	3.1%
24	Minnesota	162,527	1.5%
34	Mississippi	94,781	0.9%
14	Missouri	246,404	2.2%
45	Montana	27,679	0.2%
37	Nebraska	56,754	0.5%
30	Nevada	108,477	1.0%
44	New Hampshire	29,595	0.3%
17	New Jersey	227,477	2.0%
35	New Mexico	90,468	0.8%
4	New York	466,118	4.2%
8	North Carolina	416,060	3.7%
50	North Dakota	13,220	0.1%
7	Ohio	431,859	3.9%
26	Oklahoma	144,568	1.3%
27	Oregon	134,144	1.2%
9	Pennsylvania	351,068	3.1%
43	Rhode Island	32,470	0.3%
18	South Carolina	222,374	2.0%
49	South Dakota	14,854	0.1%
12	Tennessee	296,142	2.7%
2	Texas	1,093,134	9.8%
32	Utah	97,943	0.9%
47	Vermont	16,615	0.1%
19	Virginia	215,516	1.9%
13	Washington	267,839	2.4%
38	West Virginia	51,575	0.5%
23	Wisconsin	170,548	1.5%
48	Wyoming	15,710	0.1%

RANK ORDER

RANK	STATE	CRIMES	% of USA
1	California	1,265,920	11.4%
2	Texas	1,093,134	9.8%
3	Florida	885,199	7.9%
4	New York	466,118	4.2%
5	Illinois	446,135	4.0%
6	Georgia	435,319	3.9%
7	Ohio	431,859	3.9%
8	North Carolina	416,060	3.7%
9	Pennsylvania	351,068	3.1%
10	Michigan	343,751	3.1%
11	Arizona	307,979	2.8%
12	Tennessee	296,142	2.7%
13	Washington	267,839	2.4%
14	Missouri	246,404	2.2%
15	Indiana	233,998	2.1%
16	Maryland	233,558	2.1%
17	New Jersey	227,477	2.0%
18	South Carolina	222,374	2.0%
19	Virginia	215,516	1.9%
20	Alabama	211,454	1.9%
21	Louisiana	197,574	1.8%
22	Massachusetts	185,133	1.7%
23	Wisconsin	170,548	1.5%
24	Minnesota	162,527	1.5%
25	Colorado	157,671	1.4%
26	Oklahoma	144,568	1.3%
27	Oregon	134,144	1.2%
28	Arkansas	123,882	1.1%
29	Kentucky	122,960	1.1%
30	Nevada	108,477	1.0%
31	Kansas	106,140	1.0%
32	Utah	97,943	0.9%
33	Connecticut	96,514	0.9%
34	Mississippi	94,781	0.9%
35	New Mexico	90,468	0.8%
36	Iowa	81,209	0.7%
37	Nebraska	56,754	0.5%
38	West Virginia	51,575	0.5%
39	Hawaii	49,516	0.4%
40	Delaware	37,444	0.3%
41	Idaho	35,502	0.3%
42	Maine	33,832	0.3%
43	Rhode Island	32,470	0.3%
44	New Hampshire	29,595	0.3%
45	Montana	27,679	0.2%
46	Alaska	24,598	0.2%
47	Vermont	16,615	0.1%
48	Wyoming	15,710	0.1%
49	South Dakota	14,854	0.1%
50	North Dakota	13,220	0.1%
	District of Columbia	38,720	0.3%

Source: CQ Press using reported data from the Federal Bureau of Investigation
"Crime in the United States 2008" (Uniform Crime Reports, September 14, 2009, http://www.fbi.gov/ucr/ucr.htm)
*Includes murder, rape, robbery, aggravated assault, burglary, larceny-theft, and motor vehicle theft.

Percent Change in Number of Crimes: 2007 to 2008

National Percent Change = 0.9% Decrease*

ALPHA ORDER

RANK	STATE	PERCENT CHANGE
8	Alabama	3.4
49	Alaska	(10.9)
26	Arizona	(0.8)
32	Arkansas	(2.5)
33	California	(2.6)
36	Colorado	(3.3)
6	Connecticut	3.8
4	Delaware	6.7
20	Florida	0.8
6	Georgia	3.8
50	Hawaii	(14.2)
38	Idaho	(4.8)
22	Illinois	0.1
29	Indiana	(1.1)
44	Iowa	(6.6)
47	Kansas	(7.5)
9	Kentucky	3.0
37	Louisiana	(4.2)
19	Maine	0.9
12	Maryland	2.1
14	Massachusetts	1.7
40	Michigan	(5.2)
42	Minnesota	(6.0)
46	Mississippi	(7.0)
30	Missouri	(1.2)
41	Montana	(5.3)
48	Nebraska	(7.7)
44	Nevada	(6.6)
1	New Hampshire	10.8
9	New Jersey	3.0
5	New Mexico	4.6
18	New York	1.0
20	North Carolina	0.8
14	North Dakota	1.7
27	Ohio	(0.9)
24	Oklahoma	(0.7)
43	Oregon	(6.1)
14	Pennsylvania	1.7
3	Rhode Island	7.7
23	South Carolina	(0.3)
11	South Dakota	2.4
24	Tennessee	(0.7)
31	Texas	(1.3)
27	Utah	(0.9)
2	Vermont	9.3
12	Virginia	2.1
39	Washington	(5.1)
17	West Virginia	1.6
34	Wisconsin	(2.7)
35	Wyoming	(3.2)

RANK ORDER

RANK	STATE	PERCENT CHANGE
1	New Hampshire	10.8
2	Vermont	9.3
3	Rhode Island	7.7
4	Delaware	6.7
5	New Mexico	4.6
6	Connecticut	3.8
6	Georgia	3.8
8	Alabama	3.4
9	Kentucky	3.0
9	New Jersey	3.0
11	South Dakota	2.4
12	Maryland	2.1
12	Virginia	2.1
14	Massachusetts	1.7
14	North Dakota	1.7
14	Pennsylvania	1.7
17	West Virginia	1.6
18	New York	1.0
19	Maine	0.9
20	Florida	0.8
20	North Carolina	0.8
22	Illinois	0.1
23	South Carolina	(0.3)
24	Oklahoma	(0.7)
24	Tennessee	(0.7)
26	Arizona	(0.8)
27	Ohio	(0.9)
27	Utah	(0.9)
29	Indiana	(1.1)
30	Missouri	(1.2)
31	Texas	(1.3)
32	Arkansas	(2.5)
33	California	(2.6)
34	Wisconsin	(2.7)
35	Wyoming	(3.2)
36	Colorado	(3.3)
37	Louisiana	(4.2)
38	Idaho	(4.8)
39	Washington	(5.1)
40	Michigan	(5.2)
41	Montana	(5.3)
42	Minnesota	(6.0)
43	Oregon	(6.1)
44	Iowa	(6.6)
44	Nevada	(6.6)
46	Mississippi	(7.0)
47	Kansas	(7.5)
48	Nebraska	(7.7)
49	Alaska	(10.9)
50	Hawaii	(14.2)

District of Columbia   4.0

Source: CQ Press using reported data from the Federal Bureau of Investigation
   "Crime in the United States 2008" (Uniform Crime Reports, September 14, 2009, http://www.fbi.gov/ucr/ucr.htm)
*Includes murder, rape, robbery, aggravated assault, burglary, larceny-theft, and motor vehicle theft.

Crime Rate in 2008

National Rate = 3,667.0 Crimes per 100,000 Population*

ALPHA ORDER

RANK	STATE	RATE
6	Alabama	4,535.7
22	Alaska	3,584.2
4	Arizona	4,738.0
11	Arkansas	4,338.5
26	California	3,444.1
29	Colorado	3,192.1
41	Connecticut	2,756.5
12	Delaware	4,288.7
2	Florida	4,829.7
8	Georgia	4,494.4
18	Hawaii	3,843.8
47	Idaho	2,329.8
25	Illinois	3,458.0
21	Indiana	3,669.6
42	Iowa	2,704.7
19	Kansas	3,787.8
35	Kentucky	2,880.1
10	Louisiana	4,479.3
45	Maine	2,569.9
15	Maryland	4,145.8
37	Massachusetts	2,849.1
27	Michigan	3,436.3
31	Minnesota	3,113.4
28	Mississippi	3,225.3
14	Missouri	4,168.1
36	Montana	2,861.1
30	Nebraska	3,182.3
13	Nevada	4,172.0
48	New Hampshire	2,249.1
44	New Jersey	2,619.9
5	New Mexico	4,559.1
46	New York	2,391.6
7	North Carolina	4,511.4
49	North Dakota	2,060.9
20	Ohio	3,759.9
17	Oklahoma	3,969.1
24	Oregon	3,539.4
39	Pennsylvania	2,820.2
32	Rhode Island	3,090.0
1	South Carolina	4,963.9
50	South Dakota	1,847.0
3	Tennessee	4,765.0
9	Texas	4,493.5
23	Utah	3,579.2
43	Vermont	2,674.4
40	Virginia	2,774.0
16	Washington	4,089.6
38	West Virginia	2,842.4
33	Wisconsin	3,030.4
34	Wyoming	2,949.3

RANK ORDER

RANK	STATE	RATE
1	South Carolina	4,963.9
2	Florida	4,829.7
3	Tennessee	4,765.0
4	Arizona	4,738.0
5	New Mexico	4,559.1
6	Alabama	4,535.7
7	North Carolina	4,511.4
8	Georgia	4,494.4
9	Texas	4,493.5
10	Louisiana	4,479.3
11	Arkansas	4,338.5
12	Delaware	4,288.7
13	Nevada	4,172.0
14	Missouri	4,168.1
15	Maryland	4,145.8
16	Washington	4,089.6
17	Oklahoma	3,969.1
18	Hawaii	3,843.8
19	Kansas	3,787.8
20	Ohio	3,759.9
21	Indiana	3,669.6
22	Alaska	3,584.2
23	Utah	3,579.2
24	Oregon	3,539.4
25	Illinois	3,458.0
26	California	3,444.1
27	Michigan	3,436.3
28	Mississippi	3,225.3
29	Colorado	3,192.1
30	Nebraska	3,182.3
31	Minnesota	3,113.4
32	Rhode Island	3,090.0
33	Wisconsin	3,030.4
34	Wyoming	2,949.3
35	Kentucky	2,880.1
36	Montana	2,861.1
37	Massachusetts	2,849.1
38	West Virginia	2,842.4
39	Pennsylvania	2,820.2
40	Virginia	2,774.0
41	Connecticut	2,756.5
42	Iowa	2,704.7
43	Vermont	2,674.4
44	New Jersey	2,619.9
45	Maine	2,569.9
46	New York	2,391.6
47	Idaho	2,329.8
48	New Hampshire	2,249.1
49	North Dakota	2,060.9
50	South Dakota	1,847.0

District of Columbia   6,542.3

Source: CQ Press using reported data from the Federal Bureau of Investigation
"Crime in the United States 2008" (Uniform Crime Reports, September 14, 2009, http://www.fbi.gov/ucr/ucr.htm)
*Includes murder, rape, robbery, aggravated assault, burglary, larceny-theft, and motor vehicle theft.

Percent Change in Crime Rate: 2007 to 2008

National Percent Change = 1.7% Decrease*

ALPHA ORDER				RANK ORDER		
RANK	STATE	PERCENT CHANGE		RANK	STATE	PERCENT CHANGE
8	Alabama	2.6		1	New Hampshire	10.8
49	Alaska	(11.3)		2	Vermont	9.3
32	Arizona	(3.2)		3	Rhode Island	8.4
32	Arkansas	(3.2)		4	Delaware	5.7
30	California	(3.1)		5	New Mexico	3.9
36	Colorado	(4.8)		6	Connecticut	3.8
6	Connecticut	3.8		7	New Jersey	3.0
4	Delaware	5.7		8	Alabama	2.6
19	Florida	0.4		9	Kentucky	2.4
10	Georgia	2.3		10	Georgia	2.3
50	Hawaii	(14.5)		11	Maryland	1.8
38	Idaho	(6.3)		12	Pennsylvania	1.5
21	Illinois	(0.3)		12	West Virginia	1.5
25	Indiana	(1.6)		14	North Dakota	1.4
43	Iowa	(7.1)		14	South Dakota	1.4
48	Kansas	(8.3)		14	Virginia	1.4
9	Kentucky	2.4		17	Maine	0.9
42	Louisiana	(6.8)		17	Massachusetts	0.9
17	Maine	0.9		19	Florida	0.4
11	Maryland	1.8		20	New York	0.0
17	Massachusetts	0.9		21	Illinois	(0.3)
35	Michigan	(4.6)		22	North Carolina	(0.9)
41	Minnesota	(6.4)		23	Ohio	(1.0)
45	Mississippi	(7.6)		24	Oklahoma	(1.4)
27	Missouri	(1.8)		25	Indiana	(1.6)
38	Montana	(6.3)		25	Tennessee	(1.6)
47	Nebraska	(8.1)		27	Missouri	(1.8)
46	Nevada	(7.9)		28	South Carolina	(1.9)
1	New Hampshire	10.8		29	Texas	(3.0)
7	New Jersey	3.0		30	California	(3.1)
5	New Mexico	3.9		30	Wisconsin	(3.1)
20	New York	0.0		32	Arizona	(3.2)
22	North Carolina	(0.9)		32	Arkansas	(3.2)
14	North Dakota	1.4		34	Utah	(4.2)
23	Ohio	(1.0)		35	Michigan	(4.6)
24	Oklahoma	(1.4)		36	Colorado	(4.8)
44	Oregon	(7.2)		37	Wyoming	(5.0)
12	Pennsylvania	1.5		38	Idaho	(6.3)
3	Rhode Island	8.4		38	Montana	(6.3)
28	South Carolina	(1.9)		38	Washington	(6.3)
14	South Dakota	1.4		41	Minnesota	(6.4)
25	Tennessee	(1.6)		42	Louisiana	(6.8)
29	Texas	(3.0)		43	Iowa	(7.1)
34	Utah	(4.2)		44	Oregon	(7.2)
2	Vermont	9.3		45	Mississippi	(7.6)
14	Virginia	1.4		46	Nevada	(7.9)
38	Washington	(6.3)		47	Nebraska	(8.1)
12	West Virginia	1.5		48	Kansas	(8.3)
30	Wisconsin	(3.1)		49	Alaska	(11.3)
37	Wyoming	(5.0)		50	Hawaii	(14.5)

District of Columbia   3.4

Source: CQ Press using reported data from the Federal Bureau of Investigation
"Crime in the United States 2008" (Uniform Crime Reports, September 14, 2009, http://www.fbi.gov/ucr/ucr.htm)
*Includes murder, rape, robbery, aggravated assault, burglary, larceny-theft, and motor vehicle theft.

Violent Crimes in 2008

National Total = 1,382,012 Violent Crimes*

ALPHA ORDER

RANK	STATE	CRIMES	% of USA
21	Alabama	21,111	1.5%
40	Alaska	4,474	0.3%
16	Arizona	29,059	2.1%
27	Arkansas	14,374	1.0%
1	California	185,173	13.4%
25	Colorado	16,946	1.2%
32	Connecticut	10,427	0.8%
36	Delaware	6,141	0.4%
2	Florida	126,265	9.1%
8	Georgia	46,384	3.4%
41	Hawaii	3,512	0.3%
42	Idaho	3,483	0.3%
5	Illinois	67,780	4.9%
20	Indiana	21,283	1.5%
34	Iowa	8,520	0.6%
31	Kansas	11,505	0.8%
30	Kentucky	12,646	0.9%
17	Louisiana	28,944	2.1%
47	Maine	1,547	0.1%
12	Maryland	35,393	2.6%
15	Massachusetts	29,174	2.1%
7	Michigan	50,166	3.6%
28	Minnesota	13,717	1.0%
35	Mississippi	8,373	0.6%
14	Missouri	29,819	2.2%
44	Montana	2,497	0.2%
38	Nebraska	5,416	0.4%
24	Nevada	18,837	1.4%
45	New Hampshire	2,069	0.1%
18	New Jersey	28,351	2.1%
29	New Mexico	12,896	0.9%
4	New York	77,585	5.6%
10	North Carolina	43,099	3.1%
49	North Dakota	1,068	0.1%
11	Ohio	39,997	2.9%
23	Oklahoma	19,184	1.4%
33	Oregon	9,747	0.7%
6	Pennsylvania	51,036	3.7%
43	Rhode Island	2,621	0.2%
13	South Carolina	32,691	2.4%
46	South Dakota	1,620	0.1%
9	Tennessee	44,897	3.2%
3	Texas	123,564	8.9%
37	Utah	6,070	0.4%
50	Vermont	844	0.1%
22	Virginia	19,882	1.4%
19	Washington	21,691	1.6%
39	West Virginia	4,968	0.4%
26	Wisconsin	15,421	1.1%
48	Wyoming	1,236	0.1%

RANK ORDER

RANK	STATE	CRIMES	% of USA
1	California	185,173	13.4%
2	Florida	126,265	9.1%
3	Texas	123,564	8.9%
4	New York	77,585	5.6%
5	Illinois	67,780	4.9%
6	Pennsylvania	51,036	3.7%
7	Michigan	50,166	3.6%
8	Georgia	46,384	3.4%
9	Tennessee	44,897	3.2%
10	North Carolina	43,099	3.1%
11	Ohio	39,997	2.9%
12	Maryland	35,393	2.6%
13	South Carolina	32,691	2.4%
14	Missouri	29,819	2.2%
15	Massachusetts	29,174	2.1%
16	Arizona	29,059	2.1%
17	Louisiana	28,944	2.1%
18	New Jersey	28,351	2.1%
19	Washington	21,691	1.6%
20	Indiana	21,283	1.5%
21	Alabama	21,111	1.5%
22	Virginia	19,882	1.4%
23	Oklahoma	19,184	1.4%
24	Nevada	18,837	1.4%
25	Colorado	16,946	1.2%
26	Wisconsin	15,421	1.1%
27	Arkansas	14,374	1.0%
28	Minnesota	13,717	1.0%
29	New Mexico	12,896	0.9%
30	Kentucky	12,646	0.9%
31	Kansas	11,505	0.8%
32	Connecticut	10,427	0.8%
33	Oregon	9,747	0.7%
34	Iowa	8,520	0.6%
35	Mississippi	8,373	0.6%
36	Delaware	6,141	0.4%
37	Utah	6,070	0.4%
38	Nebraska	5,416	0.4%
39	West Virginia	4,968	0.4%
40	Alaska	4,474	0.3%
41	Hawaii	3,512	0.3%
42	Idaho	3,483	0.3%
43	Rhode Island	2,621	0.2%
44	Montana	2,497	0.2%
45	New Hampshire	2,069	0.1%
46	South Dakota	1,620	0.1%
47	Maine	1,547	0.1%
48	Wyoming	1,236	0.1%
49	North Dakota	1,068	0.1%
50	Vermont	844	0.1%
	District of Columbia	8,509	0.6%

Source: Reported data from the Federal Bureau of Investigation
"Crime in the United States 2008" (Uniform Crime Reports, September 14, 2009, http://www.fbi.gov/ucr/ucr.htm)
*Violent crimes are offenses of murder, forcible rape, robbery, and aggravated assault.

Percent Change in Number of Violent Crimes: 2007 to 2008

National Percent Change = 1.9% Decrease*

ALPHA ORDER

RANK	STATE	PERCENT CHANGE
11	Alabama	1.8
24	Alaska	(1.0)
42	Arizona	(5.0)
39	Arkansas	(4.2)
36	California	(3.1)
20	Colorado	0.2
3	Connecticut	16.3
9	Delaware	3.0
40	Florida	(4.3)
29	Georgia	(1.5)
19	Hawaii	0.3
35	Idaho	(3.0)
25	Illinois	(1.1)
17	Indiana	0.6
37	Iowa	(3.2)
47	Kansas	(8.4)
14	Kentucky	1.1
46	Louisiana	(7.6)
22	Maine	(0.5)
31	Maryland	(1.9)
8	Massachusetts	4.8
45	Michigan	(7.1)
48	Minnesota	(8.6)
29	Mississippi	(1.5)
18	Missouri	0.5
49	Montana	(9.3)
15	Nebraska	0.9
32	Nevada	(2.2)
4	New Hampshire	14.5
23	New Jersey	(0.9)
27	New Mexico	(1.4)
34	New York	(2.9)
10	North Carolina	2.0
2	North Dakota	17.2
12	Ohio	1.6
7	Oklahoma	6.2
50	Oregon	(9.6)
27	Pennsylvania	(1.4)
6	Rhode Island	9.0
44	South Carolina	(5.9)
1	South Dakota	20.3
37	Tennessee	(3.2)
13	Texas	1.2
33	Utah	(2.3)
5	Vermont	9.3
41	Virginia	(4.4)
16	Washington	0.7
21	West Virginia	(0.4)
43	Wisconsin	(5.4)
26	Wyoming	(1.2)

RANK ORDER

RANK	STATE	PERCENT CHANGE
1	South Dakota	20.3
2	North Dakota	17.2
3	Connecticut	16.3
4	New Hampshire	14.5
5	Vermont	9.3
6	Rhode Island	9.0
7	Oklahoma	6.2
8	Massachusetts	4.8
9	Delaware	3.0
10	North Carolina	2.0
11	Alabama	1.8
12	Ohio	1.6
13	Texas	1.2
14	Kentucky	1.1
15	Nebraska	0.9
16	Washington	0.7
17	Indiana	0.6
18	Missouri	0.5
19	Hawaii	0.3
20	Colorado	0.2
21	West Virginia	(0.4)
22	Maine	(0.5)
23	New Jersey	(0.9)
24	Alaska	(1.0)
25	Illinois	(1.1)
26	Wyoming	(1.2)
27	New Mexico	(1.4)
27	Pennsylvania	(1.4)
29	Georgia	(1.5)
29	Mississippi	(1.5)
31	Maryland	(1.9)
32	Nevada	(2.2)
33	Utah	(2.3)
34	New York	(2.9)
35	Idaho	(3.0)
36	California	(3.1)
37	Iowa	(3.2)
37	Tennessee	(3.2)
39	Arkansas	(4.2)
40	Florida	(4.3)
41	Virginia	(4.4)
42	Arizona	(5.0)
43	Wisconsin	(5.4)
44	South Carolina	(5.9)
45	Michigan	(7.1)
46	Louisiana	(7.6)
47	Kansas	(8.4)
48	Minnesota	(8.6)
49	Montana	(9.3)
50	Oregon	(9.6)

District of Columbia	2.3

Source: Reported data from the Federal Bureau of Investigation
"Crime in the United States 2008" (Uniform Crime Reports, September 14, 2009, http://www.fbi.gov/ucr/ucr.htm)
*Violent crimes are offenses of murder, forcible rape, robbery, and aggravated assault.

Violent Crime Rate in 2008

National Rate = 454.5 Violent Crimes per 100,000 Population*

ALPHA ORDER

RANK	STATE	RATE
19	Alabama	452.8
7	Alaska	651.9
21	Arizona	447.0
15	Arkansas	503.4
14	California	503.8
26	Colorado	343.1
31	Connecticut	297.8
4	Delaware	703.4
5	Florida	688.9
17	Georgia	478.9
37	Hawaii	272.6
44	Idaho	228.6
11	Illinois	525.4
27	Indiana	333.8
34	Iowa	283.8
22	Kansas	410.6
32	Kentucky	296.2
6	Louisiana	656.2
50	Maine	117.5
9	Maryland	628.2
20	Massachusetts	449.0
16	Michigan	501.5
38	Minnesota	262.8
33	Mississippi	284.9
13	Missouri	504.4
39	Montana	258.1
30	Nebraska	303.7
2	Nevada	724.5
48	New Hampshire	157.2
29	New Jersey	326.5
8	New Mexico	649.9
24	New York	398.1
18	North Carolina	467.3
47	North Dakota	166.5
25	Ohio	348.2
10	Oklahoma	526.7
40	Oregon	257.2
23	Pennsylvania	410.0
42	Rhode Island	249.4
1	South Carolina	729.7
46	South Dakota	201.4
3	Tennessee	722.4
12	Texas	507.9
45	Utah	221.8
49	Vermont	135.9
41	Virginia	255.9
28	Washington	331.2
36	West Virginia	273.8
35	Wisconsin	274.0
43	Wyoming	232.0

RANK ORDER

RANK	STATE	RATE
1	South Carolina	729.7
2	Nevada	724.5
3	Tennessee	722.4
4	Delaware	703.4
5	Florida	688.9
6	Louisiana	656.2
7	Alaska	651.9
8	New Mexico	649.9
9	Maryland	628.2
10	Oklahoma	526.7
11	Illinois	525.4
12	Texas	507.9
13	Missouri	504.4
14	California	503.8
15	Arkansas	503.4
16	Michigan	501.5
17	Georgia	478.9
18	North Carolina	467.3
19	Alabama	452.8
20	Massachusetts	449.0
21	Arizona	447.0
22	Kansas	410.6
23	Pennsylvania	410.0
24	New York	398.1
25	Ohio	348.2
26	Colorado	343.1
27	Indiana	333.8
28	Washington	331.2
29	New Jersey	326.5
30	Nebraska	303.7
31	Connecticut	297.8
32	Kentucky	296.2
33	Mississippi	284.9
34	Iowa	283.8
35	Wisconsin	274.0
36	West Virginia	273.8
37	Hawaii	272.6
38	Minnesota	262.8
39	Montana	258.1
40	Oregon	257.2
41	Virginia	255.9
42	Rhode Island	249.4
43	Wyoming	232.0
44	Idaho	228.6
45	Utah	221.8
46	South Dakota	201.4
47	North Dakota	166.5
48	New Hampshire	157.2
49	Vermont	135.9
50	Maine	117.5

District of Columbia	1,437.7

Source: Reported data from the Federal Bureau of Investigation
"Crime in the United States 2008" (Uniform Crime Reports, September 14, 2009, http://www.fbi.gov/ucr/ucr.htm)
*Violent crimes are offenses of murder, forcible rape, robbery, and aggravated assault.

Percent Change in Violent Crime Rate: 2007 to 2008

National Percent Change = 2.7% Decrease*

ALPHA ORDER

RANK	STATE	PERCENT CHANGE
11	Alabama	1.1
24	Alaska	(1.4)
44	Arizona	(7.4)
39	Arkansas	(4.9)
33	California	(3.6)
23	Colorado	(1.3)
3	Connecticut	16.3
9	Delaware	2.1
38	Florida	(4.7)
30	Georgia	(2.9)
16	Hawaii	(0.1)
37	Idaho	(4.5)
25	Illinois	(1.5)
15	Indiana	0.1
34	Iowa	(3.7)
47	Kansas	(9.3)
12	Kentucky	0.4
48	Louisiana	(10.0)
18	Maine	(0.4)
27	Maryland	(2.1)
8	Massachusetts	4.0
43	Michigan	(6.4)
46	Minnesota	(9.0)
28	Mississippi	(2.2)
16	Missouri	(0.1)
49	Montana	(10.2)
12	Nebraska	0.4
32	Nevada	(3.5)
4	New Hampshire	14.5
22	New Jersey	(0.8)
28	New Mexico	(2.2)
35	New York	(3.9)
14	North Carolina	0.2
2	North Dakota	16.9
10	Ohio	1.5
7	Oklahoma	5.4
50	Oregon	(10.6)
26	Pennsylvania	(1.6)
5	Rhode Island	9.8
44	South Carolina	(7.4)
1	South Dakota	19.1
36	Tennessee	(4.1)
19	Texas	(0.5)
41	Utah	(5.5)
6	Vermont	9.3
40	Virginia	(5.1)
21	Washington	(0.6)
19	West Virginia	(0.5)
42	Wisconsin	(5.8)
31	Wyoming	(3.0)

RANK ORDER

RANK	STATE	PERCENT CHANGE
1	South Dakota	19.1
2	North Dakota	16.9
3	Connecticut	16.3
4	New Hampshire	14.5
5	Rhode Island	9.8
6	Vermont	9.3
7	Oklahoma	5.4
8	Massachusetts	4.0
9	Delaware	2.1
10	Ohio	1.5
11	Alabama	1.1
12	Kentucky	0.4
12	Nebraska	0.4
14	North Carolina	0.2
15	Indiana	0.1
16	Hawaii	(0.1)
16	Missouri	(0.1)
18	Maine	(0.4)
19	Texas	(0.5)
19	West Virginia	(0.5)
21	Washington	(0.6)
22	New Jersey	(0.8)
23	Colorado	(1.3)
24	Alaska	(1.4)
25	Illinois	(1.5)
26	Pennsylvania	(1.6)
27	Maryland	(2.1)
28	Mississippi	(2.2)
28	New Mexico	(2.2)
30	Georgia	(2.9)
31	Wyoming	(3.0)
32	Nevada	(3.5)
33	California	(3.6)
34	Iowa	(3.7)
35	New York	(3.9)
36	Tennessee	(4.1)
37	Idaho	(4.5)
38	Florida	(4.7)
39	Arkansas	(4.9)
40	Virginia	(5.1)
41	Utah	(5.5)
42	Wisconsin	(5.8)
43	Michigan	(6.4)
44	Arizona	(7.4)
44	South Carolina	(7.4)
46	Minnesota	(9.0)
47	Kansas	(9.3)
48	Louisiana	(10.0)
49	Montana	(10.2)
50	Oregon	(10.6)

District of Columbia	1.7

Source: Reported data from the Federal Bureau of Investigation
 "Crime in the United States 2008" (Uniform Crime Reports, September 14, 2009, http://www.fbi.gov/ucr/ucr.htm)
*Violent crimes are offenses of murder, forcible rape, robbery, and aggravated assault.

Murders in 2008

National Total = 16,272 Murders*

ALPHA ORDER

RANK	STATE	MURDERS	% of USA
18	Alabama	353	2.2%
42	Alaska	28	0.2%
15	Arizona	407	2.5%
27	Arkansas	162	1.0%
1	California	2,142	13.2%
28	Colorado	157	1.0%
31	Connecticut	123	0.8%
38	Delaware	57	0.4%
3	Florida	1,168	7.2%
7	Georgia	636	3.9%
44	Hawaii	25	0.2%
45	Idaho	23	0.1%
5	Illinois	790	4.9%
19	Indiana	327	2.0%
35	Iowa	76	0.5%
32	Kansas	113	0.7%
23	Kentucky	198	1.2%
11	Louisiana	527	3.2%
40	Maine	31	0.2%
12	Maryland	493	3.0%
25	Massachusetts	167	1.0%
10	Michigan	542	3.3%
33	Minnesota	109	0.7%
21	Mississippi	237	1.5%
13	Missouri	455	2.8%
45	Montana	23	0.1%
36	Nebraska	68	0.4%
26	Nevada	163	1.0%
48	New Hampshire	13	0.1%
16	New Jersey	376	2.3%
30	New Mexico	142	0.9%
4	New York	836	5.1%
8	North Carolina	604	3.7%
50	North Dakota	3	0.0%
9	Ohio	543	3.3%
22	Oklahoma	212	1.3%
34	Oregon	82	0.5%
6	Pennsylvania	701	4.3%
41	Rhode Island	29	0.2%
20	South Carolina	305	1.9%
43	South Dakota	26	0.2%
14	Tennessee	408	2.5%
2	Texas	1,374	8.4%
39	Utah	39	0.2%
47	Vermont	17	0.1%
17	Virginia	368	2.3%
24	Washington	192	1.2%
37	West Virginia	60	0.4%
29	Wisconsin	146	0.9%
49	Wyoming	10	0.1%

RANK ORDER

RANK	STATE	MURDERS	% of USA
1	California	2,142	13.2%
2	Texas	1,374	8.4%
3	Florida	1,168	7.2%
4	New York	836	5.1%
5	Illinois	790	4.9%
6	Pennsylvania	701	4.3%
7	Georgia	636	3.9%
8	North Carolina	604	3.7%
9	Ohio	543	3.3%
10	Michigan	542	3.3%
11	Louisiana	527	3.2%
12	Maryland	493	3.0%
13	Missouri	455	2.8%
14	Tennessee	408	2.5%
15	Arizona	407	2.5%
16	New Jersey	376	2.3%
17	Virginia	368	2.3%
18	Alabama	353	2.2%
19	Indiana	327	2.0%
20	South Carolina	305	1.9%
21	Mississippi	237	1.5%
22	Oklahoma	212	1.3%
23	Kentucky	198	1.2%
24	Washington	192	1.2%
25	Massachusetts	167	1.0%
26	Nevada	163	1.0%
27	Arkansas	162	1.0%
28	Colorado	157	1.0%
29	Wisconsin	146	0.9%
30	New Mexico	142	0.9%
31	Connecticut	123	0.8%
32	Kansas	113	0.7%
33	Minnesota	109	0.7%
34	Oregon	82	0.5%
35	Iowa	76	0.5%
36	Nebraska	68	0.4%
37	West Virginia	60	0.4%
38	Delaware	57	0.4%
39	Utah	39	0.2%
40	Maine	31	0.2%
41	Rhode Island	29	0.2%
42	Alaska	28	0.2%
43	South Dakota	26	0.2%
44	Hawaii	25	0.2%
45	Idaho	23	0.1%
45	Montana	23	0.1%
47	Vermont	17	0.1%
48	New Hampshire	13	0.1%
49	Wyoming	10	0.1%
50	North Dakota	3	0.0%
	District of Columbia	186	1.1%

Source: Reported data from the Federal Bureau of Investigation
   "Crime in the United States 2008" (Uniform Crime Reports, September 14, 2009, http://www.fbi.gov/ucr/ucr.htm)
*Includes nonnegligent manslaughter.

Murder Rate in 2008

National Rate = 5.4 Murders per 100,000 Population*

ALPHA ORDER

ALPHA ORDER

RANK	STATE	RATE
5	Alabama	7.6
28	Alaska	4.1
13	Arizona	6.3
18	Arkansas	5.7
16	California	5.8
33	Colorado	3.2
31	Connecticut	3.5
10	Delaware	6.5
12	Florida	6.4
8	Georgia	6.6
45	Hawaii	1.9
47	Idaho	1.5
15	Illinois	6.1
22	Indiana	5.1
40	Iowa	2.5
29	Kansas	4.0
25	Kentucky	4.6
1	Louisiana	11.9
41	Maine	2.4
2	Maryland	8.8
38	Massachusetts	2.6
21	Michigan	5.4
44	Minnesota	2.1
3	Mississippi	8.1
4	Missouri	7.7
41	Montana	2.4
30	Nebraska	3.8
13	Nevada	6.3
49	New Hampshire	1.0
26	New Jersey	4.3
6	New Mexico	7.2
26	New York	4.3
10	North Carolina	6.5
50	North Dakota	0.5
23	Ohio	4.7
16	Oklahoma	5.8
43	Oregon	2.2
19	Pennsylvania	5.6
36	Rhode Island	2.8
7	South Carolina	6.8
33	South Dakota	3.2
8	Tennessee	6.6
19	Texas	5.6
48	Utah	1.4
37	Vermont	2.7
23	Virginia	4.7
35	Washington	2.9
32	West Virginia	3.3
38	Wisconsin	2.6
45	Wyoming	1.9

RANK ORDER

RANK	STATE	RATE
1	Louisiana	11.9
2	Maryland	8.8
3	Mississippi	8.1
4	Missouri	7.7
5	Alabama	7.6
6	New Mexico	7.2
7	South Carolina	6.8
8	Georgia	6.6
8	Tennessee	6.6
10	Delaware	6.5
10	North Carolina	6.5
12	Florida	6.4
13	Arizona	6.3
13	Nevada	6.3
15	Illinois	6.1
16	California	5.8
16	Oklahoma	5.8
18	Arkansas	5.7
19	Pennsylvania	5.6
19	Texas	5.6
21	Michigan	5.4
22	Indiana	5.1
23	Ohio	4.7
23	Virginia	4.7
25	Kentucky	4.6
26	New Jersey	4.3
26	New York	4.3
28	Alaska	4.1
29	Kansas	4.0
30	Nebraska	3.8
31	Connecticut	3.5
32	West Virginia	3.3
33	Colorado	3.2
33	South Dakota	3.2
35	Washington	2.9
36	Rhode Island	2.8
37	Vermont	2.7
38	Massachusetts	2.6
38	Wisconsin	2.6
40	Iowa	2.5
41	Maine	2.4
41	Montana	2.4
43	Oregon	2.2
44	Minnesota	2.1
45	Hawaii	1.9
45	Wyoming	1.9
47	Idaho	1.5
48	Utah	1.4
49	New Hampshire	1.0
50	North Dakota	0.5
	District of Columbia	31.4

Source: Reported data from the Federal Bureau of Investigation
"Crime in the United States 2008" (Uniform Crime Reports, September 14, 2009, http://www.fbi.gov/ucr/ucr.htm)
*Includes nonnegligent manslaughter.

Percent of Murders Involving Firearms in 2008

National Percent = 66.9% of Murders*

<table>
<tr><td colspan="3">ALPHA ORDER</td><td colspan="3">RANK ORDER</td></tr>
<tr><td>RANK</td><td>STATE</td><td>PERCENT</td><td>RANK</td><td>STATE</td><td>PERCENT</td></tr>
<tr><td>3</td><td>Alabama</td><td>77.5</td><td>1</td><td>Illinois*</td><td>79.4</td></tr>
<tr><td>39</td><td>Alaska</td><td>48.1</td><td>2</td><td>Louisiana</td><td>79.2</td></tr>
<tr><td>9</td><td>Arizona</td><td>71.6</td><td>3</td><td>Alabama</td><td>77.5</td></tr>
<tr><td>12</td><td>Arkansas</td><td>70.1</td><td>4</td><td>Delaware</td><td>77.2</td></tr>
<tr><td>14</td><td>California</td><td>69.4</td><td>4</td><td>Mississippi</td><td>77.2</td></tr>
<tr><td>33</td><td>Colorado</td><td>57.0</td><td>6</td><td>Missouri</td><td>76.7</td></tr>
<tr><td>21</td><td>Connecticut</td><td>63.4</td><td>7</td><td>Pennsylvania</td><td>74.4</td></tr>
<tr><td>4</td><td>Delaware</td><td>77.2</td><td>8</td><td>Indiana</td><td>71.9</td></tr>
<tr><td>NA</td><td>Florida**</td><td>NA</td><td>9</td><td>Arizona</td><td>71.6</td></tr>
<tr><td>11</td><td>Georgia</td><td>70.8</td><td>9</td><td>Maryland</td><td>71.6</td></tr>
<tr><td>43</td><td>Hawaii</td><td>44.0</td><td>11</td><td>Georgia</td><td>70.8</td></tr>
<tr><td>25</td><td>Idaho</td><td>60.9</td><td>12</td><td>Arkansas</td><td>70.1</td></tr>
<tr><td>1</td><td>Illinois*</td><td>79.4</td><td>13</td><td>Michigan</td><td>70.0</td></tr>
<tr><td>8</td><td>Indiana</td><td>71.9</td><td>14</td><td>California</td><td>69.4</td></tr>
<tr><td>47</td><td>Iowa</td><td>33.8</td><td>15</td><td>South Carolina</td><td>67.8</td></tr>
<tr><td>35</td><td>Kansas</td><td>55.5</td><td>16</td><td>Kentucky</td><td>66.5</td></tr>
<tr><td>16</td><td>Kentucky</td><td>66.5</td><td>17</td><td>New Mexico</td><td>65.7</td></tr>
<tr><td>2</td><td>Louisiana</td><td>79.2</td><td>18</td><td>Virginia</td><td>65.6</td></tr>
<tr><td>46</td><td>Maine</td><td>35.5</td><td>19</td><td>Texas</td><td>65.2</td></tr>
<tr><td>9</td><td>Maryland</td><td>71.6</td><td>20</td><td>Ohio</td><td>63.7</td></tr>
<tr><td>37</td><td>Massachusetts</td><td>54.3</td><td>21</td><td>Connecticut</td><td>63.4</td></tr>
<tr><td>13</td><td>Michigan</td><td>70.0</td><td>22</td><td>New Jersey</td><td>62.8</td></tr>
<tr><td>38</td><td>Minnesota</td><td>50.9</td><td>23</td><td>Rhode Island</td><td>62.1</td></tr>
<tr><td>4</td><td>Mississippi</td><td>77.2</td><td>24</td><td>North Carolina</td><td>61.8</td></tr>
<tr><td>6</td><td>Missouri</td><td>76.7</td><td>25</td><td>Idaho</td><td>60.9</td></tr>
<tr><td>40</td><td>Montana</td><td>47.8</td><td>26</td><td>Oklahoma</td><td>60.4</td></tr>
<tr><td>44</td><td>Nebraska</td><td>40.9</td><td>27</td><td>West Virginia</td><td>60.0</td></tr>
<tr><td>32</td><td>Nevada</td><td>57.1</td><td>28</td><td>South Dakota</td><td>59.1</td></tr>
<tr><td>48</td><td>New Hampshire</td><td>16.7</td><td>29</td><td>Tennessee</td><td>58.8</td></tr>
<tr><td>22</td><td>New Jersey</td><td>62.8</td><td>30</td><td>Washington</td><td>57.9</td></tr>
<tr><td>17</td><td>New Mexico</td><td>65.7</td><td>31</td><td>Oregon</td><td>57.3</td></tr>
<tr><td>34</td><td>New York</td><td>56.9</td><td>32</td><td>Nevada</td><td>57.1</td></tr>
<tr><td>24</td><td>North Carolina</td><td>61.8</td><td>33</td><td>Colorado</td><td>57.0</td></tr>
<tr><td>49</td><td>North Dakota</td><td>0.0</td><td>34</td><td>New York</td><td>56.9</td></tr>
<tr><td>20</td><td>Ohio</td><td>63.7</td><td>35</td><td>Kansas</td><td>55.5</td></tr>
<tr><td>26</td><td>Oklahoma</td><td>60.4</td><td>36</td><td>Wisconsin</td><td>54.8</td></tr>
<tr><td>31</td><td>Oregon</td><td>57.3</td><td>37</td><td>Massachusetts</td><td>54.3</td></tr>
<tr><td>7</td><td>Pennsylvania</td><td>74.4</td><td>38</td><td>Minnesota</td><td>50.9</td></tr>
<tr><td>23</td><td>Rhode Island</td><td>62.1</td><td>39</td><td>Alaska</td><td>48.1</td></tr>
<tr><td>15</td><td>South Carolina</td><td>67.8</td><td>40</td><td>Montana</td><td>47.8</td></tr>
<tr><td>28</td><td>South Dakota</td><td>59.1</td><td>41</td><td>Vermont</td><td>47.1</td></tr>
<tr><td>29</td><td>Tennessee</td><td>58.8</td><td>42</td><td>Utah</td><td>46.3</td></tr>
<tr><td>19</td><td>Texas</td><td>65.2</td><td>43</td><td>Hawaii</td><td>44.0</td></tr>
<tr><td>42</td><td>Utah</td><td>46.3</td><td>44</td><td>Nebraska</td><td>40.9</td></tr>
<tr><td>41</td><td>Vermont</td><td>47.1</td><td>45</td><td>Wyoming</td><td>40.0</td></tr>
<tr><td>18</td><td>Virginia</td><td>65.6</td><td>46</td><td>Maine</td><td>35.5</td></tr>
<tr><td>30</td><td>Washington</td><td>57.9</td><td>47</td><td>Iowa</td><td>33.8</td></tr>
<tr><td>27</td><td>West Virginia</td><td>60.0</td><td>48</td><td>New Hampshire</td><td>16.7</td></tr>
<tr><td>36</td><td>Wisconsin</td><td>54.8</td><td>49</td><td>North Dakota</td><td>0.0</td></tr>
<tr><td>45</td><td>Wyoming</td><td>40.0</td><td>NA</td><td>Florida**</td><td>NA</td></tr>
<tr><td></td><td></td><td></td><td></td><td>District of Columbia**</td><td>NA</td></tr>
</table>

Source: CQ Press using reported data from the Federal Bureau of Investigation
   "Crime in the United States 2008" (Uniform Crime Reports, September 14, 2009, http://www.fbi.gov/ucr/ucr.htm)
*Of the 14,180 murders in 2008 for which supplemental data were received by the F.B.I. There were an additional 2,092 murders
for which the type of murder weapon was not reported to the F.B.I. Includes nonnegligent manslaughter. National and state
percents based on reporting jurisdictions only. Illinois's percent is for Chicago and Rockford only.
**Not available.

Rapes in 2008

National Total = 89,000 Rapes*

ALPHA ORDER				RANK ORDER			
RANK	STATE	RAPES	% of USA	RANK	STATE	RAPES	% of USA
20	Alabama	1,617	1.8%	1	California	8,903	10.0%
39	Alaska	441	0.5%	2	Texas	8,014	9.0%
18	Arizona	1,673	1.9%	3	Florida	5,972	6.7%
24	Arkansas	1,395	1.6%	4	Michigan	4,502	5.1%
1	California	8,903	10.0%	5	Ohio	4,419	5.0%
12	Colorado	2,098	2.4%	6	Illinois	4,118	4.6%
36	Connecticut	674	0.8%	7	Pennsylvania	3,478	3.9%
43	Delaware	366	0.4%	8	New York	2,801	3.1%
3	Florida	5,972	6.7%	9	Washington	2,628	3.0%
11	Georgia	2,195	2.5%	10	North Carolina	2,284	2.6%
44	Hawaii	365	0.4%	11	Georgia	2,195	2.5%
38	Idaho	551	0.6%	12	Colorado	2,098	2.4%
6	Illinois	4,118	4.6%	13	Tennessee	2,062	2.3%
17	Indiana	1,720	1.9%	14	Minnesota	1,805	2.0%
35	Iowa	888	1.0%	15	Virginia	1,758	2.0%
26	Kansas	1,190	1.3%	16	Massachusetts	1,736	2.0%
23	Kentucky	1,408	1.6%	17	Indiana	1,720	1.9%
25	Louisiana	1,232	1.4%	18	Arizona	1,673	1.9%
42	Maine	375	0.4%	19	South Carolina	1,638	1.8%
29	Maryland	1,127	1.3%	20	Alabama	1,617	1.8%
16	Massachusetts	1,736	2.0%	21	Missouri	1,615	1.8%
4	Michigan	4,502	5.1%	22	Oklahoma	1,466	1.6%
14	Minnesota	1,805	2.0%	23	Kentucky	1,408	1.6%
34	Mississippi	890	1.0%	24	Arkansas	1,395	1.6%
21	Missouri	1,615	1.8%	25	Louisiana	1,232	1.4%
46	Montana	294	0.3%	26	Kansas	1,190	1.3%
37	Nebraska	583	0.7%	27	Oregon	1,156	1.3%
32	Nevada	1,102	1.2%	28	New Mexico	1,139	1.3%
41	New Hampshire	391	0.4%	29	Maryland	1,127	1.3%
30	New Jersey	1,122	1.3%	30	New Jersey	1,122	1.3%
28	New Mexico	1,139	1.3%	31	Wisconsin	1,120	1.3%
8	New York	2,801	3.1%	32	Nevada	1,102	1.2%
10	North Carolina	2,284	2.6%	33	Utah	893	1.0%
48	North Dakota	232	0.3%	34	Mississippi	890	1.0%
5	Ohio	4,419	5.0%	35	Iowa	888	1.0%
22	Oklahoma	1,466	1.6%	36	Connecticut	674	0.8%
27	Oregon	1,156	1.3%	37	Nebraska	583	0.7%
7	Pennsylvania	3,478	3.9%	38	Idaho	551	0.6%
47	Rhode Island	277	0.3%	39	Alaska	441	0.5%
19	South Carolina	1,638	1.8%	40	South Dakota	432	0.5%
40	South Dakota	432	0.5%	41	New Hampshire	391	0.4%
13	Tennessee	2,062	2.3%	42	Maine	375	0.4%
2	Texas	8,014	9.0%	43	Delaware	366	0.4%
33	Utah	893	1.0%	44	Hawaii	365	0.4%
50	Vermont	127	0.1%	45	West Virginia	362	0.4%
15	Virginia	1,758	2.0%	46	Montana	294	0.3%
9	Washington	2,628	3.0%	47	Rhode Island	277	0.3%
45	West Virginia	362	0.4%	48	North Dakota	232	0.3%
31	Wisconsin	1,120	1.3%	49	Wyoming	180	0.2%
49	Wyoming	180	0.2%	50	Vermont	127	0.1%
					District of Columbia	186	0.2%

Source: Reported data from the Federal Bureau of Investigation
   "Crime in the United States 2008" (Uniform Crime Reports, September 14, 2009, http://www.fbi.gov/ucr/ucr.htm)
*Forcible rape is the carnal knowledge of a female forcibly and against her will. Assaults or attempts to commit rape by force or threat of force are included. However, statutory rape without force and other sex offenses are excluded.

Rape Rate in 2008

National Rate = 29.3 Rapes per 100,000 Population*

ALPHA ORDER

RANK	STATE	RATE
16	Alabama	34.7
1	Alaska	64.3
39	Arizona	25.7
4	Arkansas	48.9
41	California	24.2
6	Colorado	42.5
48	Connecticut	19.3
9	Delaware	41.9
23	Florida	32.6
42	Georgia	22.7
32	Hawaii	28.3
14	Idaho	36.2
25	Illinois	31.9
36	Indiana	27.0
30	Iowa	29.6
6	Kansas	42.5
20	Kentucky	33.0
33	Louisiana	27.9
31	Maine	28.5
45	Maryland	20.0
37	Massachusetts	26.7
5	Michigan	45.0
17	Minnesota	34.6
28	Mississippi	30.3
35	Missouri	27.3
27	Montana	30.4
22	Nebraska	32.7
8	Nevada	42.4
29	New Hampshire	29.7
50	New Jersey	12.9
2	New Mexico	57.4
49	New York	14.4
40	North Carolina	24.8
14	North Dakota	36.2
12	Ohio	38.5
10	Oklahoma	40.2
26	Oregon	30.5
33	Pennsylvania	27.9
38	Rhode Island	26.4
13	South Carolina	36.6
3	South Dakota	53.7
19	Tennessee	33.2
21	Texas	32.9
23	Utah	32.6
44	Vermont	20.4
43	Virginia	22.6
11	Washington	40.1
45	West Virginia	20.0
47	Wisconsin	19.9
18	Wyoming	33.8

RANK ORDER

RANK	STATE	RATE
1	Alaska	64.3
2	New Mexico	57.4
3	South Dakota	53.7
4	Arkansas	48.9
5	Michigan	45.0
6	Colorado	42.5
6	Kansas	42.5
8	Nevada	42.4
9	Delaware	41.9
10	Oklahoma	40.2
11	Washington	40.1
12	Ohio	38.5
13	South Carolina	36.6
14	Idaho	36.2
14	North Dakota	36.2
16	Alabama	34.7
17	Minnesota	34.6
18	Wyoming	33.8
19	Tennessee	33.2
20	Kentucky	33.0
21	Texas	32.9
22	Nebraska	32.7
23	Florida	32.6
23	Utah	32.6
25	Illinois	31.9
26	Oregon	30.5
27	Montana	30.4
28	Mississippi	30.3
29	New Hampshire	29.7
30	Iowa	29.6
31	Maine	28.5
32	Hawaii	28.3
33	Louisiana	27.9
33	Pennsylvania	27.9
35	Missouri	27.3
36	Indiana	27.0
37	Massachusetts	26.7
38	Rhode Island	26.4
39	Arizona	25.7
40	North Carolina	24.8
41	California	24.2
42	Georgia	22.7
43	Virginia	22.6
44	Vermont	20.4
45	Maryland	20.0
45	West Virginia	20.0
47	Wisconsin	19.9
48	Connecticut	19.3
49	New York	14.4
50	New Jersey	12.9
	District of Columbia	31.4

Source: Reported data from the Federal Bureau of Investigation
   "Crime in the United States 2008" (Uniform Crime Reports, September 14, 2009, http://www.fbi.gov/ucr/ucr.htm)
*Forcible rape is the carnal knowledge of a female forcibly and against her will. Assaults or attempts to commit rape by force or threat of force are included. However, statutory rape without force and other sex offenses are excluded.

Robberies in 2008

National Total = 441,855 Robberies*

RANK	STATE	ROBBERIES	% of USA
18	Alabama	7,346	1.7%
42	Alaska	645	0.1%
14	Arizona	9,697	2.2%
31	Arkansas	2,735	0.6%
1	California	69,385	15.7%
29	Colorado	3,365	0.8%
27	Connecticut	3,907	0.9%
34	Delaware	1,838	0.4%
3	Florida	36,273	8.2%
8	Georgia	17,357	3.9%
39	Hawaii	1,086	0.2%
45	Idaho	241	0.1%
5	Illinois	24,054	5.4%
15	Indiana	7,532	1.7%
38	Iowa	1,248	0.3%
35	Kansas	1,684	0.4%
26	Kentucky	4,004	0.9%
23	Louisiana	5,994	1.4%
44	Maine	333	0.1%
10	Maryland	13,203	3.0%
19	Massachusetts	7,069	1.6%
11	Michigan	12,964	2.9%
25	Minnesota	4,177	0.9%
30	Mississippi	3,016	0.7%
17	Missouri	7,390	1.7%
46	Montana	172	0.0%
37	Nebraska	1,299	0.3%
21	Nevada	6,473	1.5%
43	New Hampshire	419	0.1%
12	New Jersey	12,701	2.9%
33	New Mexico	2,172	0.5%
4	New York	31,778	7.2%
9	North Carolina	14,334	3.2%
50	North Dakota	72	0.0%
7	Ohio	18,719	4.2%
28	Oklahoma	3,683	0.8%
32	Oregon	2,641	0.6%
6	Pennsylvania	18,873	4.3%
41	Rhode Island	879	0.2%
20	South Carolina	6,599	1.5%
47	South Dakota	120	0.0%
13	Tennessee	10,800	2.4%
2	Texas	37,753	8.5%
36	Utah	1,421	0.3%
48	Vermont	89	0.0%
16	Virginia	7,437	1.7%
22	Washington	6,347	1.4%
40	West Virginia	889	0.2%
24	Wisconsin	5,126	1.2%
49	Wyoming	86	0.0%

RANK	STATE	ROBBERIES	% of USA
1	California	69,385	15.7%
2	Texas	37,753	8.5%
3	Florida	36,273	8.2%
4	New York	31,778	7.2%
5	Illinois	24,054	5.4%
6	Pennsylvania	18,873	4.3%
7	Ohio	18,719	4.2%
8	Georgia	17,357	3.9%
9	North Carolina	14,334	3.2%
10	Maryland	13,203	3.0%
11	Michigan	12,964	2.9%
12	New Jersey	12,701	2.9%
13	Tennessee	10,800	2.4%
14	Arizona	9,697	2.2%
15	Indiana	7,532	1.7%
16	Virginia	7,437	1.7%
17	Missouri	7,390	1.7%
18	Alabama	7,346	1.7%
19	Massachusetts	7,069	1.6%
20	South Carolina	6,599	1.5%
21	Nevada	6,473	1.5%
22	Washington	6,347	1.4%
23	Louisiana	5,994	1.4%
24	Wisconsin	5,126	1.2%
25	Minnesota	4,177	0.9%
26	Kentucky	4,004	0.9%
27	Connecticut	3,907	0.9%
28	Oklahoma	3,683	0.8%
29	Colorado	3,365	0.8%
30	Mississippi	3,016	0.7%
31	Arkansas	2,735	0.6%
32	Oregon	2,641	0.6%
33	New Mexico	2,172	0.5%
34	Delaware	1,838	0.4%
35	Kansas	1,684	0.4%
36	Utah	1,421	0.3%
37	Nebraska	1,299	0.3%
38	Iowa	1,248	0.3%
39	Hawaii	1,086	0.2%
40	West Virginia	889	0.2%
41	Rhode Island	879	0.2%
42	Alaska	645	0.1%
43	New Hampshire	419	0.1%
44	Maine	333	0.1%
45	Idaho	241	0.1%
46	Montana	172	0.0%
47	South Dakota	120	0.0%
48	Vermont	89	0.0%
49	Wyoming	86	0.0%
50	North Dakota	72	0.0%
	District of Columbia	4,430	1.0%

Source: Reported data from the Federal Bureau of Investigation
"Crime in the United States 2008" (Uniform Crime Reports, September 14, 2009, http://www.fbi.gov/ucr/ucr.htm)
*Robbery is the taking or attempting to take anything of value by force or threat of force.

Robbery Rate in 2008

National Rate = 145.3 Robberies per 100,000 Population*

ALPHA ORDER

RANK	STATE	RATE
11	Alabama	157.6
30	Alaska	94.0
15	Arizona	149.2
28	Arkansas	95.8
5	California	188.8
38	Colorado	68.1
22	Connecticut	111.6
3	Delaware	210.5
4	Florida	197.9
7	Georgia	179.2
33	Hawaii	84.3
47	Idaho	15.8
6	Illinois	186.4
21	Indiana	118.1
42	Iowa	41.6
39	Kansas	60.1
31	Kentucky	93.8
18	Louisiana	135.9
44	Maine	25.3
2	Maryland	234.4
24	Massachusetts	108.8
19	Michigan	129.6
35	Minnesota	80.0
25	Mississippi	102.6
20	Missouri	125.0
45	Montana	17.8
36	Nebraska	72.8
1	Nevada	248.9
43	New Hampshire	31.8
17	New Jersey	146.3
23	New Mexico	109.5
9	New York	163.0
12	North Carolina	155.4
50	North Dakota	11.2
9	Ohio	163.0
26	Oklahoma	101.1
37	Oregon	69.7
14	Pennsylvania	151.6
34	Rhode Island	83.7
16	South Carolina	147.3
48	South Dakota	14.9
8	Tennessee	173.8
13	Texas	155.2
40	Utah	51.9
49	Vermont	14.3
29	Virginia	95.7
27	Washington	96.9
41	West Virginia	49.0
32	Wisconsin	91.1
46	Wyoming	16.1

RANK ORDER

RANK	STATE	RATE
1	Nevada	248.9
2	Maryland	234.4
3	Delaware	210.5
4	Florida	197.9
5	California	188.8
6	Illinois	186.4
7	Georgia	179.2
8	Tennessee	173.8
9	New York	163.0
9	Ohio	163.0
11	Alabama	157.6
12	North Carolina	155.4
13	Texas	155.2
14	Pennsylvania	151.6
15	Arizona	149.2
16	South Carolina	147.3
17	New Jersey	146.3
18	Louisiana	135.9
19	Michigan	129.6
20	Missouri	125.0
21	Indiana	118.1
22	Connecticut	111.6
23	New Mexico	109.5
24	Massachusetts	108.8
25	Mississippi	102.6
26	Oklahoma	101.1
27	Washington	96.9
28	Arkansas	95.8
29	Virginia	95.7
30	Alaska	94.0
31	Kentucky	93.8
32	Wisconsin	91.1
33	Hawaii	84.3
34	Rhode Island	83.7
35	Minnesota	80.0
36	Nebraska	72.8
37	Oregon	69.7
38	Colorado	68.1
39	Kansas	60.1
40	Utah	51.9
41	West Virginia	49.0
42	Iowa	41.6
43	New Hampshire	31.8
44	Maine	25.3
45	Montana	17.8
46	Wyoming	16.1
47	Idaho	15.8
48	South Dakota	14.9
49	Vermont	14.3
50	North Dakota	11.2
	District of Columbia	748.5

Source: Reported data from the Federal Bureau of Investigation
"Crime in the United States 2008" (Uniform Crime Reports, September 14, 2009, http://www.fbi.gov/ucr/ucr.htm)
*Robbery is the taking or attempting to take anything of value by force or threat of force.

Aggravated Assaults in 2008

National Total = 834,885 Aggravated Assaults*

<table>
<tr><td colspan="4">ALPHA ORDER</td><td colspan="4">RANK ORDER</td></tr>
<tr><th>RANK</th><th>STATE</th><th>ASSAULTS</th><th>% of USA</th><th>RANK</th><th>STATE</th><th>ASSAULTS</th><th>% of USA</th></tr>
<tr><td>21</td><td>Alabama</td><td>11,795</td><td>1.4%</td><td>1</td><td>California</td><td>104,743</td><td>12.5%</td></tr>
<tr><td>40</td><td>Alaska</td><td>3,360</td><td>0.4%</td><td>2</td><td>Florida</td><td>82,852</td><td>9.9%</td></tr>
<tr><td>16</td><td>Arizona</td><td>17,282</td><td>2.1%</td><td>3</td><td>Texas</td><td>76,423</td><td>9.2%</td></tr>
<tr><td>26</td><td>Arkansas</td><td>10,082</td><td>1.2%</td><td>4</td><td>New York</td><td>42,170</td><td>5.1%</td></tr>
<tr><td>1</td><td>California</td><td>104,743</td><td>12.5%</td><td>5</td><td>Illinois</td><td>38,818</td><td>4.6%</td></tr>
<tr><td>23</td><td>Colorado</td><td>11,326</td><td>1.4%</td><td>6</td><td>Michigan</td><td>32,158</td><td>3.9%</td></tr>
<tr><td>34</td><td>Connecticut</td><td>5,723</td><td>0.7%</td><td>7</td><td>Tennessee</td><td>31,627</td><td>3.8%</td></tr>
<tr><td>36</td><td>Delaware</td><td>3,880</td><td>0.5%</td><td>8</td><td>Pennsylvania</td><td>27,984</td><td>3.4%</td></tr>
<tr><td>2</td><td>Florida</td><td>82,852</td><td>9.9%</td><td>9</td><td>Georgia</td><td>26,196</td><td>3.1%</td></tr>
<tr><td>9</td><td>Georgia</td><td>26,196</td><td>3.1%</td><td>10</td><td>North Carolina</td><td>25,877</td><td>3.1%</td></tr>
<tr><td>42</td><td>Hawaii</td><td>2,036</td><td>0.2%</td><td>11</td><td>South Carolina</td><td>24,149</td><td>2.9%</td></tr>
<tr><td>41</td><td>Idaho</td><td>2,668</td><td>0.3%</td><td>12</td><td>Louisiana</td><td>21,191</td><td>2.5%</td></tr>
<tr><td>5</td><td>Illinois</td><td>38,818</td><td>4.6%</td><td>13</td><td>Maryland</td><td>20,570</td><td>2.5%</td></tr>
<tr><td>22</td><td>Indiana</td><td>11,704</td><td>1.4%</td><td>14</td><td>Missouri</td><td>20,359</td><td>2.4%</td></tr>
<tr><td>32</td><td>Iowa</td><td>6,308</td><td>0.8%</td><td>15</td><td>Massachusetts</td><td>20,202</td><td>2.4%</td></tr>
<tr><td>29</td><td>Kansas</td><td>8,518</td><td>1.0%</td><td>16</td><td>Arizona</td><td>17,282</td><td>2.1%</td></tr>
<tr><td>31</td><td>Kentucky</td><td>7,036</td><td>0.8%</td><td>17</td><td>Ohio</td><td>16,316</td><td>2.0%</td></tr>
<tr><td>12</td><td>Louisiana</td><td>21,191</td><td>2.5%</td><td>18</td><td>New Jersey</td><td>14,152</td><td>1.7%</td></tr>
<tr><td>48</td><td>Maine</td><td>808</td><td>0.1%</td><td>19</td><td>Oklahoma</td><td>13,823</td><td>1.7%</td></tr>
<tr><td>13</td><td>Maryland</td><td>20,570</td><td>2.5%</td><td>20</td><td>Washington</td><td>12,524</td><td>1.5%</td></tr>
<tr><td>15</td><td>Massachusetts</td><td>20,202</td><td>2.4%</td><td>21</td><td>Alabama</td><td>11,795</td><td>1.4%</td></tr>
<tr><td>6</td><td>Michigan</td><td>32,158</td><td>3.9%</td><td>22</td><td>Indiana</td><td>11,704</td><td>1.4%</td></tr>
<tr><td>30</td><td>Minnesota</td><td>7,626</td><td>0.9%</td><td>23</td><td>Colorado</td><td>11,326</td><td>1.4%</td></tr>
<tr><td>35</td><td>Mississippi</td><td>4,230</td><td>0.5%</td><td>24</td><td>Nevada</td><td>11,099</td><td>1.3%</td></tr>
<tr><td>14</td><td>Missouri</td><td>20,359</td><td>2.4%</td><td>25</td><td>Virginia</td><td>10,319</td><td>1.2%</td></tr>
<tr><td>43</td><td>Montana</td><td>2,008</td><td>0.2%</td><td>26</td><td>Arkansas</td><td>10,082</td><td>1.2%</td></tr>
<tr><td>39</td><td>Nebraska</td><td>3,466</td><td>0.4%</td><td>27</td><td>New Mexico</td><td>9,443</td><td>1.1%</td></tr>
<tr><td>24</td><td>Nevada</td><td>11,099</td><td>1.3%</td><td>28</td><td>Wisconsin</td><td>9,029</td><td>1.1%</td></tr>
<tr><td>45</td><td>New Hampshire</td><td>1,246</td><td>0.1%</td><td>29</td><td>Kansas</td><td>8,518</td><td>1.0%</td></tr>
<tr><td>18</td><td>New Jersey</td><td>14,152</td><td>1.7%</td><td>30</td><td>Minnesota</td><td>7,626</td><td>0.9%</td></tr>
<tr><td>27</td><td>New Mexico</td><td>9,443</td><td>1.1%</td><td>31</td><td>Kentucky</td><td>7,036</td><td>0.8%</td></tr>
<tr><td>4</td><td>New York</td><td>42,170</td><td>5.1%</td><td>32</td><td>Iowa</td><td>6,308</td><td>0.8%</td></tr>
<tr><td>10</td><td>North Carolina</td><td>25,877</td><td>3.1%</td><td>33</td><td>Oregon</td><td>5,868</td><td>0.7%</td></tr>
<tr><td>49</td><td>North Dakota</td><td>761</td><td>0.1%</td><td>34</td><td>Connecticut</td><td>5,723</td><td>0.7%</td></tr>
<tr><td>17</td><td>Ohio</td><td>16,316</td><td>2.0%</td><td>35</td><td>Mississippi</td><td>4,230</td><td>0.5%</td></tr>
<tr><td>19</td><td>Oklahoma</td><td>13,823</td><td>1.7%</td><td>36</td><td>Delaware</td><td>3,880</td><td>0.5%</td></tr>
<tr><td>33</td><td>Oregon</td><td>5,868</td><td>0.7%</td><td>37</td><td>Utah</td><td>3,717</td><td>0.4%</td></tr>
<tr><td>8</td><td>Pennsylvania</td><td>27,984</td><td>3.4%</td><td>38</td><td>West Virginia</td><td>3,657</td><td>0.4%</td></tr>
<tr><td>44</td><td>Rhode Island</td><td>1,436</td><td>0.2%</td><td>39</td><td>Nebraska</td><td>3,466</td><td>0.4%</td></tr>
<tr><td>11</td><td>South Carolina</td><td>24,149</td><td>2.9%</td><td>40</td><td>Alaska</td><td>3,360</td><td>0.4%</td></tr>
<tr><td>46</td><td>South Dakota</td><td>1,042</td><td>0.1%</td><td>41</td><td>Idaho</td><td>2,668</td><td>0.3%</td></tr>
<tr><td>7</td><td>Tennessee</td><td>31,627</td><td>3.8%</td><td>42</td><td>Hawaii</td><td>2,036</td><td>0.2%</td></tr>
<tr><td>3</td><td>Texas</td><td>76,423</td><td>9.2%</td><td>43</td><td>Montana</td><td>2,008</td><td>0.2%</td></tr>
<tr><td>37</td><td>Utah</td><td>3,717</td><td>0.4%</td><td>44</td><td>Rhode Island</td><td>1,436</td><td>0.2%</td></tr>
<tr><td>50</td><td>Vermont</td><td>611</td><td>0.1%</td><td>45</td><td>New Hampshire</td><td>1,246</td><td>0.1%</td></tr>
<tr><td>25</td><td>Virginia</td><td>10,319</td><td>1.2%</td><td>46</td><td>South Dakota</td><td>1,042</td><td>0.1%</td></tr>
<tr><td>20</td><td>Washington</td><td>12,524</td><td>1.5%</td><td>47</td><td>Wyoming</td><td>960</td><td>0.1%</td></tr>
<tr><td>38</td><td>West Virginia</td><td>3,657</td><td>0.4%</td><td>48</td><td>Maine</td><td>808</td><td>0.1%</td></tr>
<tr><td>28</td><td>Wisconsin</td><td>9,029</td><td>1.1%</td><td>49</td><td>North Dakota</td><td>761</td><td>0.1%</td></tr>
<tr><td>47</td><td>Wyoming</td><td>960</td><td>0.1%</td><td>50</td><td>Vermont</td><td>611</td><td>0.1%</td></tr>
<tr><td></td><td></td><td></td><td></td><td></td><td>District of Columbia</td><td>3,707</td><td>0.4%</td></tr>
</table>

Source: Reported data from the Federal Bureau of Investigation
   "Crime in the United States 2008" (Uniform Crime Reports, September 14, 2009, http://www.fbi.gov/ucr/ucr.htm)
*Aggravated assault is an attack for the purpose of inflicting severe bodily injury.

Aggravated Assault Rate in 2008

National Rate = 274.6 Aggravated Assaults per 100,000 Population*

ALPHA ORDER

RANK	STATE	RATE
22	Alabama	253.0
3	Alaska	489.6
21	Arizona	265.9
11	Arkansas	353.1
18	California	285.0
23	Colorado	229.3
35	Connecticut	163.5
7	Delaware	444.4
6	Florida	452.0
20	Georgia	270.5
38	Hawaii	158.1
33	Idaho	175.1
17	Illinois	300.9
31	Indiana	183.5
26	Iowa	210.1
16	Kansas	304.0
34	Kentucky	164.8
4	Louisiana	480.4
50	Maine	61.4
10	Maryland	365.1
15	Massachusetts	310.9
13	Michigan	321.5
40	Minnesota	146.1
41	Mississippi	143.9
12	Missouri	344.4
27	Montana	207.6
29	Nebraska	194.3
8	Nevada	426.9
49	New Hampshire	94.7
36	New Jersey	163.0
5	New Mexico	475.9
25	New York	216.4
19	North Carolina	280.6
47	North Dakota	118.6
42	Ohio	142.1
9	Oklahoma	379.5
39	Oregon	154.8
24	Pennsylvania	224.8
43	Rhode Island	136.7
1	South Carolina	539.1
46	South Dakota	129.6
2	Tennessee	508.9
14	Texas	314.1
44	Utah	135.8
48	Vermont	98.3
45	Virginia	132.8
30	Washington	191.2
28	West Virginia	201.5
37	Wisconsin	160.4
32	Wyoming	180.2

RANK ORDER

RANK	STATE	RATE
1	South Carolina	539.1
2	Tennessee	508.9
3	Alaska	489.6
4	Louisiana	480.4
5	New Mexico	475.9
6	Florida	452.0
7	Delaware	444.4
8	Nevada	426.9
9	Oklahoma	379.5
10	Maryland	365.1
11	Arkansas	353.1
12	Missouri	344.4
13	Michigan	321.5
14	Texas	314.1
15	Massachusetts	310.9
16	Kansas	304.0
17	Illinois	300.9
18	California	285.0
19	North Carolina	280.6
20	Georgia	270.5
21	Arizona	265.9
22	Alabama	253.0
23	Colorado	229.3
24	Pennsylvania	224.8
25	New York	216.4
26	Iowa	210.1
27	Montana	207.6
28	West Virginia	201.5
29	Nebraska	194.3
30	Washington	191.2
31	Indiana	183.5
32	Wyoming	180.2
33	Idaho	175.1
34	Kentucky	164.8
35	Connecticut	163.5
36	New Jersey	163.0
37	Wisconsin	160.4
38	Hawaii	158.1
39	Oregon	154.8
40	Minnesota	146.1
41	Mississippi	143.9
42	Ohio	142.1
43	Rhode Island	136.7
44	Utah	135.8
45	Virginia	132.8
46	South Dakota	129.6
47	North Dakota	118.6
48	Vermont	98.3
49	New Hampshire	94.7
50	Maine	61.4
	District of Columbia	626.4

Source: Reported data from the Federal Bureau of Investigation
"Crime in the United States 2008" (Uniform Crime Reports, September 14, 2009, http://www.fbi.gov/ucr/ucr.htm)
*Aggravated assault is an attack for the purpose of inflicting severe bodily injury.

Property Crimes in 2008

National Total = 9,767,915 Property Crimes*

ALPHA ORDER

RANK	STATE	CRIMES	% of USA
19	Alabama	190,343	1.9%
46	Alaska	20,124	0.2%
11	Arizona	278,920	2.9%
29	Arkansas	109,508	1.1%
1	California	1,080,747	11.1%
25	Colorado	140,725	1.4%
34	Connecticut	86,087	0.9%
42	Delaware	31,303	0.3%
3	Florida	758,934	7.8%
5	Georgia	388,935	4.0%
39	Hawaii	46,004	0.5%
41	Idaho	32,019	0.3%
7	Illinois	378,355	3.9%
15	Indiana	212,715	2.2%
36	Iowa	72,689	0.7%
30	Kansas	94,635	1.0%
28	Kentucky	110,314	1.1%
21	Louisiana	168,630	1.7%
40	Maine	32,285	0.3%
17	Maryland	198,165	2.0%
22	Massachusetts	155,959	1.6%
10	Michigan	293,585	3.0%
24	Minnesota	148,810	1.5%
33	Mississippi	86,408	0.9%
14	Missouri	216,585	2.2%
45	Montana	25,182	0.3%
37	Nebraska	51,338	0.5%
32	Nevada	89,640	0.9%
44	New Hampshire	27,526	0.3%
16	New Jersey	199,126	2.0%
35	New Mexico	77,572	0.8%
6	New York	388,533	4.0%
8	North Carolina	372,961	3.8%
50	North Dakota	12,152	0.1%
4	Ohio	391,862	4.0%
26	Oklahoma	125,384	1.3%
27	Oregon	124,397	1.3%
9	Pennsylvania	300,032	3.1%
43	Rhode Island	29,849	0.3%
20	South Carolina	189,683	1.9%
49	South Dakota	13,234	0.1%
12	Tennessee	251,245	2.6%
2	Texas	969,570	9.9%
31	Utah	91,873	0.9%
47	Vermont	15,771	0.2%
18	Virginia	195,634	2.0%
13	Washington	246,148	2.5%
38	West Virginia	46,607	0.5%
23	Wisconsin	155,127	1.6%
48	Wyoming	14,474	0.1%

RANK ORDER

RANK	STATE	CRIMES	% of USA
1	California	1,080,747	11.1%
2	Texas	969,570	9.9%
3	Florida	758,934	7.8%
4	Ohio	391,862	4.0%
5	Georgia	388,935	4.0%
6	New York	388,533	4.0%
7	Illinois	378,355	3.9%
8	North Carolina	372,961	3.8%
9	Pennsylvania	300,032	3.1%
10	Michigan	293,585	3.0%
11	Arizona	278,920	2.9%
12	Tennessee	251,245	2.6%
13	Washington	246,148	2.5%
14	Missouri	216,585	2.2%
15	Indiana	212,715	2.2%
16	New Jersey	199,126	2.0%
17	Maryland	198,165	2.0%
18	Virginia	195,634	2.0%
19	Alabama	190,343	1.9%
20	South Carolina	189,683	1.9%
21	Louisiana	168,630	1.7%
22	Massachusetts	155,959	1.6%
23	Wisconsin	155,127	1.6%
24	Minnesota	148,810	1.5%
25	Colorado	140,725	1.4%
26	Oklahoma	125,384	1.3%
27	Oregon	124,397	1.3%
28	Kentucky	110,314	1.1%
29	Arkansas	109,508	1.1%
30	Kansas	94,635	1.0%
31	Utah	91,873	0.9%
32	Nevada	89,640	0.9%
33	Mississippi	86,408	0.9%
34	Connecticut	86,087	0.9%
35	New Mexico	77,572	0.8%
36	Iowa	72,689	0.7%
37	Nebraska	51,338	0.5%
38	West Virginia	46,607	0.5%
39	Hawaii	46,004	0.5%
40	Maine	32,285	0.3%
41	Idaho	32,019	0.3%
42	Delaware	31,303	0.3%
43	Rhode Island	29,849	0.3%
44	New Hampshire	27,526	0.3%
45	Montana	25,182	0.3%
46	Alaska	20,124	0.2%
47	Vermont	15,771	0.2%
48	Wyoming	14,474	0.1%
49	South Dakota	13,234	0.1%
50	North Dakota	12,152	0.1%
	District of Columbia	30,211	0.3%

Source: Reported data from the Federal Bureau of Investigation
  "Crime in the United States 2008" (Uniform Crime Reports, September 14, 2009, http://www.fbi.gov/ucr/ucr.htm)
*Property crimes are offenses of burglary, larceny-theft, and motor vehicle theft.

Percent Change in Number of Property Crimes: 2007 to 2008

National Percent Change = 0.8% Decrease*

ALPHA ORDER

RANK	STATE	PERCENT CHANGE
7	Alabama	3.6
49	Alaska	(12.9)
25	Arizona	(0.3)
32	Arkansas	(2.3)
34	California	(2.5)
37	Colorado	(3.7)
12	Connecticut	2.4
4	Delaware	7.4
16	Florida	1.7
6	Georgia	4.5
50	Hawaii	(15.2)
38	Idaho	(4.9)
23	Illinois	0.3
28	Indiana	(1.3)
44	Iowa	(7.0)
45	Kansas	(7.3)
9	Kentucky	3.3
36	Louisiana	(3.6)
18	Maine	0.9
11	Maryland	2.8
17	Massachusetts	1.1
38	Michigan	(4.9)
42	Minnesota	(5.7)
46	Mississippi	(7.5)
29	Missouri	(1.4)
38	Montana	(4.9)
48	Nebraska	(8.5)
46	Nevada	(7.5)
1	New Hampshire	10.6
7	New Jersey	3.6
5	New Mexico	5.7
15	New York	1.8
19	North Carolina	0.7
22	North Dakota	0.5
27	Ohio	(1.1)
31	Oklahoma	(1.7)
43	Oregon	(5.9)
13	Pennsylvania	2.2
3	Rhode Island	7.6
19	South Carolina	0.7
21	South Dakota	0.6
24	Tennessee	(0.2)
30	Texas	(1.6)
26	Utah	(0.8)
2	Vermont	9.3
10	Virginia	2.9
41	Washington	(5.6)
14	West Virginia	1.9
33	Wisconsin	(2.4)
35	Wyoming	(3.4)

RANK ORDER

RANK	STATE	PERCENT CHANGE
1	New Hampshire	10.6
2	Vermont	9.3
3	Rhode Island	7.6
4	Delaware	7.4
5	New Mexico	5.7
6	Georgia	4.5
7	Alabama	3.6
7	New Jersey	3.6
9	Kentucky	3.3
10	Virginia	2.9
11	Maryland	2.8
12	Connecticut	2.4
13	Pennsylvania	2.2
14	West Virginia	1.9
15	New York	1.8
16	Florida	1.7
17	Massachusetts	1.1
18	Maine	0.9
19	North Carolina	0.7
19	South Carolina	0.7
21	South Dakota	0.6
22	North Dakota	0.5
23	Illinois	0.3
24	Tennessee	(0.2)
25	Arizona	(0.3)
26	Utah	(0.8)
27	Ohio	(1.1)
28	Indiana	(1.3)
29	Missouri	(1.4)
30	Texas	(1.6)
31	Oklahoma	(1.7)
32	Arkansas	(2.3)
33	Wisconsin	(2.4)
34	California	(2.5)
35	Wyoming	(3.4)
36	Louisiana	(3.6)
37	Colorado	(3.7)
38	Idaho	(4.9)
38	Michigan	(4.9)
38	Montana	(4.9)
41	Washington	(5.6)
42	Minnesota	(5.7)
43	Oregon	(5.9)
44	Iowa	(7.0)
45	Kansas	(7.3)
46	Mississippi	(7.5)
46	Nevada	(7.5)
48	Nebraska	(8.5)
49	Alaska	(12.9)
50	Hawaii	(15.2)
	District of Columbia	4.5

Source: Reported data from the Federal Bureau of Investigation
"Crime in the United States 2008" (Uniform Crime Reports, September 14, 2009, http://www.fbi.gov/ucr/ucr.htm)
*Property crimes are offenses of burglary, larceny-theft, and motor vehicle theft.

Property Crime Rate in 2008

National Rate = 3,212.5 Property Crimes per 100,000 Population*

ALPHA ORDER			RANK ORDER		
RANK	STATE	RATE	RANK	STATE	RATE
4	Alabama	4,082.9	1	Arizona	4,291.0
28	Alaska	2,932.3	2	South Carolina	4,234.2
1	Arizona	4,291.0	3	Florida	4,140.8
10	Arkansas	3,835.1	4	Alabama	4,082.9
25	California	2,940.3	5	North Carolina	4,044.1
31	Colorado	2,849.0	6	Tennessee	4,042.6
40	Connecticut	2,458.7	7	Georgia	4,015.5
14	Delaware	3,585.3	8	Texas	3,985.6
3	Florida	4,140.8	9	New Mexico	3,909.2
7	Georgia	4,015.5	10	Arkansas	3,835.1
15	Hawaii	3,571.2	11	Louisiana	3,823.1
46	Idaho	2,101.2	12	Washington	3,758.4
27	Illinois	2,932.6	13	Missouri	3,663.7
22	Indiana	3,335.8	14	Delaware	3,585.3
42	Iowa	2,420.9	15	Hawaii	3,571.2
20	Kansas	3,377.2	16	Maryland	3,517.6
36	Kentucky	2,583.9	17	Nevada	3,447.5
11	Louisiana	3,823.1	18	Oklahoma	3,442.4
41	Maine	2,452.4	19	Ohio	3,411.7
16	Maryland	3,517.6	20	Kansas	3,377.2
44	Massachusetts	2,400.1	21	Utah	3,357.4
26	Michigan	2,934.8	22	Indiana	3,335.8
30	Minnesota	2,850.6	23	Oregon	3,282.2
24	Mississippi	2,940.4	24	Mississippi	2,940.4
13	Missouri	3,663.7	25	California	2,940.3
35	Montana	2,603.0	26	Michigan	2,934.8
29	Nebraska	2,878.6	27	Illinois	2,932.6
17	Nevada	3,447.5	28	Alaska	2,932.3
47	New Hampshire	2,091.9	29	Nebraska	2,878.6
45	New Jersey	2,293.4	30	Minnesota	2,850.6
9	New Mexico	3,909.2	31	Colorado	2,849.0
48	New York	1,993.5	32	Rhode Island	2,840.6
5	North Carolina	4,044.1	33	Wisconsin	2,756.4
49	North Dakota	1,894.4	34	Wyoming	2,717.3
19	Ohio	3,411.7	35	Montana	2,603.0
18	Oklahoma	3,442.4	36	Kentucky	2,583.9
23	Oregon	3,282.2	37	West Virginia	2,568.6
43	Pennsylvania	2,410.2	38	Vermont	2,538.5
32	Rhode Island	2,840.6	39	Virginia	2,518.1
2	South Carolina	4,234.2	40	Connecticut	2,458.7
50	South Dakota	1,645.6	41	Maine	2,452.4
6	Tennessee	4,042.6	42	Iowa	2,420.9
8	Texas	3,985.6	43	Pennsylvania	2,410.2
21	Utah	3,357.4	44	Massachusetts	2,400.1
38	Vermont	2,538.5	45	New Jersey	2,293.4
39	Virginia	2,518.1	46	Idaho	2,101.2
12	Washington	3,758.4	47	New Hampshire	2,091.9
37	West Virginia	2,568.6	48	New York	1,993.5
33	Wisconsin	2,756.4	49	North Dakota	1,894.4
34	Wyoming	2,717.3	50	South Dakota	1,645.6

	District of Columbia	5,104.6

Source: Reported data from the Federal Bureau of Investigation
"Crime in the United States 2008" (Uniform Crime Reports, September 14, 2009, http://www.fbi.gov/ucr/ucr.htm)
*Property crimes are offenses of burglary, larceny-theft, and motor vehicle theft.

Percent Change in Property Crime Rate: 2007 to 2008

National Percent Change = 1.6% Decrease*

ALPHA ORDER

RANK	STATE	PERCENT CHANGE
8	Alabama	2.8
49	Alaska	(13.2)
29	Arizona	(2.8)
31	Arkansas	(3.0)
32	California	(3.1)
36	Colorado	(5.2)
10	Connecticut	2.5
4	Delaware	6.4
15	Florida	1.3
7	Georgia	2.9
50	Hawaii	(15.5)
41	Idaho	(6.5)
20	Illinois	(0.1)
26	Indiana	(1.8)
44	Iowa	(7.4)
46	Kansas	(8.2)
9	Kentucky	2.6
40	Louisiana	(6.2)
16	Maine	1.0
10	Maryland	2.5
18	Massachusetts	0.4
35	Michigan	(4.3)
39	Minnesota	(6.1)
45	Mississippi	(8.1)
27	Missouri	(2.0)
38	Montana	(5.9)
48	Nebraska	(8.9)
47	Nevada	(8.7)
1	New Hampshire	10.6
6	New Jersey	3.6
5	New Mexico	4.9
17	New York	0.8
23	North Carolina	(1.1)
19	North Dakota	0.3
25	Ohio	(1.3)
28	Oklahoma	(2.4)
43	Oregon	(6.9)
12	Pennsylvania	2.1
3	Rhode Island	8.3
22	South Carolina	(0.9)
21	South Dakota	(0.4)
23	Tennessee	(1.1)
33	Texas	(3.3)
34	Utah	(4.1)
2	Vermont	9.3
12	Virginia	2.1
42	Washington	(6.8)
14	West Virginia	1.7
30	Wisconsin	(2.9)
36	Wyoming	(5.2)

RANK ORDER

RANK	STATE	PERCENT CHANGE
1	New Hampshire	10.6
2	Vermont	9.3
3	Rhode Island	8.3
4	Delaware	6.4
5	New Mexico	4.9
6	New Jersey	3.6
7	Georgia	2.9
8	Alabama	2.8
9	Kentucky	2.6
10	Connecticut	2.5
10	Maryland	2.5
12	Pennsylvania	2.1
12	Virginia	2.1
14	West Virginia	1.7
15	Florida	1.3
16	Maine	1.0
17	New York	0.8
18	Massachusetts	0.4
19	North Dakota	0.3
20	Illinois	(0.1)
21	South Dakota	(0.4)
22	South Carolina	(0.9)
23	North Carolina	(1.1)
23	Tennessee	(1.1)
25	Ohio	(1.3)
26	Indiana	(1.8)
27	Missouri	(2.0)
28	Oklahoma	(2.4)
29	Arizona	(2.8)
30	Wisconsin	(2.9)
31	Arkansas	(3.0)
32	California	(3.1)
33	Texas	(3.3)
34	Utah	(4.1)
35	Michigan	(4.3)
36	Colorado	(5.2)
36	Wyoming	(5.2)
38	Montana	(5.9)
39	Minnesota	(6.1)
40	Louisiana	(6.2)
41	Idaho	(6.5)
42	Washington	(6.8)
43	Oregon	(6.9)
44	Iowa	(7.4)
45	Mississippi	(8.1)
46	Kansas	(8.2)
47	Nevada	(8.7)
48	Nebraska	(8.9)
49	Alaska	(13.2)
50	Hawaii	(15.5)

District of Columbia	3.9

Source: Reported data from the Federal Bureau of Investigation
"Crime in the United States 2008" (Uniform Crime Reports, September 14, 2009, http://www.fbi.gov/ucr/ucr.htm)
*Property crimes are offenses of burglary, larceny-theft, and motor vehicle theft.

Burglaries in 2008

National Total = 2,222,196 Burglaries*

ALPHA ORDER

RANK	STATE	BURGLARIES	% of USA
14	Alabama	50,408	2.3%
47	Alaska	3,240	0.1%
12	Arizona	56,481	2.5%
23	Arkansas	33,694	1.5%
1	California	237,835	10.7%
26	Colorado	28,256	1.3%
35	Connecticut	15,011	0.7%
40	Delaware	6,760	0.3%
3	Florida	188,467	8.5%
6	Georgia	100,629	4.5%
38	Hawaii	9,379	0.4%
41	Idaho	6,701	0.3%
7	Illinois	78,968	3.6%
15	Indiana	48,645	2.2%
34	Iowa	16,450	0.7%
33	Kansas	19,612	0.9%
25	Kentucky	28,839	1.3%
18	Louisiana	43,320	1.9%
42	Maine	6,522	0.3%
20	Maryland	38,849	1.7%
21	Massachusetts	36,094	1.6%
8	Michigan	74,176	3.3%
28	Minnesota	26,410	1.2%
29	Mississippi	26,024	1.2%
17	Missouri	45,788	2.1%
46	Montana	3,332	0.1%
39	Nebraska	8,775	0.4%
30	Nevada	24,156	1.1%
44	New Hampshire	4,286	0.2%
19	New Jersey	40,401	1.8%
31	New Mexico	21,713	1.0%
9	New York	65,735	3.0%
4	North Carolina	111,602	5.0%
50	North Dakota	2,106	0.1%
5	Ohio	102,544	4.6%
22	Oklahoma	35,081	1.6%
32	Oregon	20,879	0.9%
11	Pennsylvania	58,620	2.6%
43	Rhode Island	5,750	0.3%
16	South Carolina	45,967	2.1%
48	South Dakota	2,430	0.1%
10	Tennessee	65,006	2.9%
2	Texas	230,123	10.4%
36	Utah	14,682	0.7%
45	Vermont	3,462	0.2%
24	Virginia	31,993	1.4%
13	Washington	52,478	2.4%
37	West Virginia	11,066	0.5%
27	Wisconsin	27,479	1.2%
49	Wyoming	2,184	0.1%

RANK ORDER

RANK	STATE	BURGLARIES	% of USA
1	California	237,835	10.7%
2	Texas	230,123	10.4%
3	Florida	188,467	8.5%
4	North Carolina	111,602	5.0%
5	Ohio	102,544	4.6%
6	Georgia	100,629	4.5%
7	Illinois	78,968	3.6%
8	Michigan	74,176	3.3%
9	New York	65,735	3.0%
10	Tennessee	65,006	2.9%
11	Pennsylvania	58,620	2.6%
12	Arizona	56,481	2.5%
13	Washington	52,478	2.4%
14	Alabama	50,408	2.3%
15	Indiana	48,645	2.2%
16	South Carolina	45,967	2.1%
17	Missouri	45,788	2.1%
18	Louisiana	43,320	1.9%
19	New Jersey	40,401	1.8%
20	Maryland	38,849	1.7%
21	Massachusetts	36,094	1.6%
22	Oklahoma	35,081	1.6%
23	Arkansas	33,694	1.5%
24	Virginia	31,993	1.4%
25	Kentucky	28,839	1.3%
26	Colorado	28,256	1.3%
27	Wisconsin	27,479	1.2%
28	Minnesota	26,410	1.2%
29	Mississippi	26,024	1.2%
30	Nevada	24,156	1.1%
31	New Mexico	21,713	1.0%
32	Oregon	20,879	0.9%
33	Kansas	19,612	0.9%
34	Iowa	16,450	0.7%
35	Connecticut	15,011	0.7%
36	Utah	14,682	0.7%
37	West Virginia	11,066	0.5%
38	Hawaii	9,379	0.4%
39	Nebraska	8,775	0.4%
40	Delaware	6,760	0.3%
41	Idaho	6,701	0.3%
42	Maine	6,522	0.3%
43	Rhode Island	5,750	0.3%
44	New Hampshire	4,286	0.2%
45	Vermont	3,462	0.2%
46	Montana	3,332	0.1%
47	Alaska	3,240	0.1%
48	South Dakota	2,430	0.1%
49	Wyoming	2,184	0.1%
50	North Dakota	2,106	0.1%
	District of Columbia	3,788	0.2%

Source: Reported data from the Federal Bureau of Investigation
   "Crime in the United States 2008" (Uniform Crime Reports, September 14, 2009, http://www.fbi.gov/ucr/ucr.htm)
*Burglary is the unlawful entry of a structure to commit a felony or theft. Attempts are included.

Burglary Rate in 2008

National Rate = 730.8 Burglaries per 100,000 Population*

ALPHA ORDER

RANK	STATE	RATE
4	Alabama	1,081.3
39	Alaska	472.1
15	Arizona	868.9
2	Arkansas	1,180.0
25	California	647.1
28	Colorado	572.0
43	Connecticut	428.7
18	Delaware	774.3
7	Florida	1,028.3
6	Georgia	1,038.9
21	Hawaii	728.1
42	Idaho	439.8
26	Illinois	612.1
19	Indiana	762.8
32	Iowa	547.9
22	Kansas	699.9
24	Kentucky	675.5
9	Louisiana	982.1
36	Maine	495.4
23	Maryland	689.6
30	Massachusetts	555.5
20	Michigan	741.5
35	Minnesota	505.9
14	Mississippi	885.6
17	Missouri	774.5
46	Montana	344.4
37	Nebraska	492.0
12	Nevada	929.0
49	New Hampshire	325.7
41	New Jersey	465.3
3	New Mexico	1,094.2
47	New York	337.3
1	North Carolina	1,210.1
48	North Dakota	328.3
13	Ohio	892.8
10	Oklahoma	963.1
31	Oregon	550.9
40	Pennsylvania	470.9
33	Rhode Island	547.2
8	South Carolina	1,026.1
50	South Dakota	302.2
5	Tennessee	1,046.0
11	Texas	946.0
34	Utah	536.5
29	Vermont	557.2
44	Virginia	411.8
16	Washington	801.3
27	West Virginia	609.9
38	Wisconsin	488.3
45	Wyoming	410.0

RANK ORDER

RANK	STATE	RATE
1	North Carolina	1,210.1
2	Arkansas	1,180.0
3	New Mexico	1,094.2
4	Alabama	1,081.3
5	Tennessee	1,046.0
6	Georgia	1,038.9
7	Florida	1,028.3
8	South Carolina	1,026.1
9	Louisiana	982.1
10	Oklahoma	963.1
11	Texas	946.0
12	Nevada	929.0
13	Ohio	892.8
14	Mississippi	885.6
15	Arizona	868.9
16	Washington	801.3
17	Missouri	774.5
18	Delaware	774.3
19	Indiana	762.8
20	Michigan	741.5
21	Hawaii	728.1
22	Kansas	699.9
23	Maryland	689.6
24	Kentucky	675.5
25	California	647.1
26	Illinois	612.1
27	West Virginia	609.9
28	Colorado	572.0
29	Vermont	557.2
30	Massachusetts	555.5
31	Oregon	550.9
32	Iowa	547.9
33	Rhode Island	547.2
34	Utah	536.5
35	Minnesota	505.9
36	Maine	495.4
37	Nebraska	492.0
38	Wisconsin	488.3
39	Alaska	472.1
40	Pennsylvania	470.9
41	New Jersey	465.3
42	Idaho	439.8
43	Connecticut	428.7
44	Virginia	411.8
45	Wyoming	410.0
46	Montana	344.4
47	New York	337.3
48	North Dakota	328.3
49	New Hampshire	325.7
50	South Dakota	302.2
	District of Columbia	640.0

Source: Reported data from the Federal Bureau of Investigation
   "Crime in the United States 2008" (Uniform Crime Reports, September 14, 2009, http://www.fbi.gov/ucr/ucr.htm)
*Burglary is the unlawful entry of a structure to commit a felony or theft. Attempts are included.

Larceny-Thefts in 2008

National Total = 6,588,873 Larceny-Thefts*

ALPHA ORDER					RANK ORDER			
RANK	STATE	THEFTS	% of USA		RANK	STATE	THEFTS	% of USA
19	Alabama	126,477	1.9%		1	Texas	654,097	9.9%
46	Alaska	15,246	0.2%		2	California	650,385	9.9%
10	Arizona	185,221	2.8%		3	Florida	506,958	7.7%
30	Arkansas	69,303	1.1%		4	New York	297,684	4.5%
2	California	650,385	9.9%		5	Illinois	266,815	4.0%
25	Colorado	98,950	1.5%		6	Ohio	260,786	4.0%
32	Connecticut	62,113	0.9%		7	Georgia	248,678	3.8%
42	Delaware	22,002	0.3%		8	North Carolina	234,616	3.6%
3	Florida	506,958	7.7%		9	Pennsylvania	218,941	3.3%
7	Georgia	248,678	3.8%		10	Arizona	185,221	2.8%
39	Hawaii	31,492	0.5%		11	Michigan	183,168	2.8%
41	Idaho	23,650	0.4%		12	Tennessee	167,015	2.5%
5	Illinois	266,815	4.0%		13	Washington	165,339	2.5%
16	Indiana	146,615	2.2%		14	Virginia	150,382	2.3%
34	Iowa	51,907	0.8%		15	Missouri	150,032	2.3%
31	Kansas	67,628	1.0%		16	Indiana	146,615	2.2%
28	Kentucky	73,808	1.1%		17	New Jersey	138,545	2.1%
23	Louisiana	111,567	1.7%		18	Maryland	133,983	2.0%
40	Maine	24,587	0.4%		19	Alabama	126,477	1.9%
18	Maryland	133,983	2.0%		20	South Carolina	126,064	1.9%
24	Massachusetts	107,128	1.6%		21	Wisconsin	116,128	1.8%
11	Michigan	183,168	2.8%		22	Minnesota	112,322	1.7%
22	Minnesota	112,322	1.7%		23	Louisiana	111,567	1.7%
33	Mississippi	54,032	0.8%		24	Massachusetts	107,128	1.6%
15	Missouri	150,032	2.3%		25	Colorado	98,950	1.5%
45	Montana	20,277	0.3%		26	Oregon	92,187	1.4%
37	Nebraska	38,375	0.6%		27	Oklahoma	79,422	1.2%
35	Nevada	49,581	0.8%		28	Kentucky	73,808	1.1%
43	New Hampshire	21,853	0.3%		29	Utah	69,996	1.1%
17	New Jersey	138,545	2.1%		30	Arkansas	69,303	1.1%
36	New Mexico	47,855	0.7%		31	Kansas	67,628	1.0%
4	New York	297,684	4.5%		32	Connecticut	62,113	0.9%
8	North Carolina	234,616	3.6%		33	Mississippi	54,032	0.8%
50	North Dakota	9,164	0.1%		34	Iowa	51,907	0.8%
6	Ohio	260,786	4.0%		35	Nevada	49,581	0.8%
27	Oklahoma	79,422	1.2%		36	New Mexico	47,855	0.7%
26	Oregon	92,187	1.4%		37	Nebraska	38,375	0.6%
9	Pennsylvania	218,941	3.3%		38	West Virginia	32,337	0.5%
44	Rhode Island	20,899	0.3%		39	Hawaii	31,492	0.5%
20	South Carolina	126,064	1.9%		40	Maine	24,587	0.4%
49	South Dakota	10,004	0.2%		41	Idaho	23,650	0.4%
12	Tennessee	167,015	2.5%		42	Delaware	22,002	0.3%
1	Texas	654,097	9.9%		43	New Hampshire	21,853	0.3%
29	Utah	69,996	1.1%		44	Rhode Island	20,899	0.3%
47	Vermont	11,724	0.2%		45	Montana	20,277	0.3%
14	Virginia	150,382	2.3%		46	Alaska	15,246	0.2%
13	Washington	165,339	2.5%		47	Vermont	11,724	0.2%
38	West Virginia	32,337	0.5%		48	Wyoming	11,577	0.2%
21	Wisconsin	116,128	1.8%		49	South Dakota	10,004	0.2%
48	Wyoming	11,577	0.2%		50	North Dakota	9,164	0.1%
						District of Columbia	19,958	0.3%

Source: Reported data from the Federal Bureau of Investigation
   "Crime in the United States 2008" (Uniform Crime Reports, September 14, 2009, http://www.fbi.gov/ucr/ucr.htm)
*Larceny-theft is the unlawful taking of property without use of force, violence, or fraud. Attempts are included. Motor vehicle thefts are excluded.

Larceny-Theft Rate in 2008

National Rate = 2,167.0 Larceny-Thefts per 100,000 Population*

ALPHA ORDER

RANK	STATE	RATE
4	Alabama	2,713.0
22	Alaska	2,221.5
1	Arizona	2,849.5
16	Arkansas	2,427.1
40	California	1,769.4
30	Colorado	2,003.3
39	Connecticut	1,774.0
13	Delaware	2,520.0
3	Florida	2,766.0
7	Georgia	2,567.5
14	Hawaii	2,444.7
47	Idaho	1,552.0
28	Illinois	2,068.1
20	Indiana	2,299.2
42	Iowa	1,728.8
17	Kansas	2,413.4
42	Kentucky	1,728.8
11	Louisiana	2,529.4
35	Maine	1,867.7
19	Maryland	2,378.3
45	Massachusetts	1,648.6
37	Michigan	1,831.1
26	Minnesota	2,151.6
36	Mississippi	1,838.7
10	Missouri	2,537.9
27	Montana	2,095.9
25	Nebraska	2,151.8
33	Nevada	1,906.8
44	New Hampshire	1,660.8
46	New Jersey	1,595.7
18	New Mexico	2,411.6
48	New York	1,527.3
9	North Carolina	2,544.0
49	North Dakota	1,428.6
21	Ohio	2,270.5
23	Oklahoma	2,180.5
15	Oregon	2,432.3
41	Pennsylvania	1,758.8
31	Rhode Island	1,988.9
2	South Carolina	2,814.1
50	South Dakota	1,244.0
6	Tennessee	2,687.3
5	Texas	2,688.8
8	Utah	2,557.9
34	Vermont	1,887.1
32	Virginia	1,935.6
12	Washington	2,524.6
38	West Virginia	1,782.2
29	Wisconsin	2,063.4
24	Wyoming	2,173.4

RANK ORDER

RANK	STATE	RATE
1	Arizona	2,849.5
2	South Carolina	2,814.1
3	Florida	2,766.0
4	Alabama	2,713.0
5	Texas	2,688.8
6	Tennessee	2,687.3
7	Georgia	2,567.5
8	Utah	2,557.9
9	North Carolina	2,544.0
10	Missouri	2,537.9
11	Louisiana	2,529.4
12	Washington	2,524.6
13	Delaware	2,520.0
14	Hawaii	2,444.7
15	Oregon	2,432.3
16	Arkansas	2,427.1
17	Kansas	2,413.4
18	New Mexico	2,411.6
19	Maryland	2,378.3
20	Indiana	2,299.2
21	Ohio	2,270.5
22	Alaska	2,221.5
23	Oklahoma	2,180.5
24	Wyoming	2,173.4
25	Nebraska	2,151.8
26	Minnesota	2,151.6
27	Montana	2,095.9
28	Illinois	2,068.1
29	Wisconsin	2,063.4
30	Colorado	2,003.3
31	Rhode Island	1,988.9
32	Virginia	1,935.6
33	Nevada	1,906.8
34	Vermont	1,887.1
35	Maine	1,867.7
36	Mississippi	1,838.7
37	Michigan	1,831.1
38	West Virginia	1,782.2
39	Connecticut	1,774.0
40	California	1,769.4
41	Pennsylvania	1,758.8
42	Iowa	1,728.8
42	Kentucky	1,728.8
44	New Hampshire	1,660.8
45	Massachusetts	1,648.6
46	New Jersey	1,595.7
47	Idaho	1,552.0
48	New York	1,527.3
49	North Dakota	1,428.6
50	South Dakota	1,244.0

District of Columbia   3,372.2

Source: Reported data from the Federal Bureau of Investigation

"Crime in the United States 2008" (Uniform Crime Reports, September 14, 2009, http://www.fbi.gov/ucr/ucr.htm)
*Larceny-theft is the unlawful taking of property without use of force, violence, or fraud. Attempts are included. Motor vehicle thefts are excluded.

Motor Vehicle Thefts in 2008

National Total = 956,846 Motor Vehicle Thefts*

<table>
<tr><td colspan="4">ALPHA ORDER</td><td colspan="4">RANK ORDER</td></tr>
<tr><td>RANK</td><td>STATE</td><td>THEFTS</td><td>% of USA</td><td>RANK</td><td>STATE</td><td>THEFTS</td><td>% of USA</td></tr>
<tr><td>22</td><td>Alabama</td><td>13,458</td><td>1.4%</td><td>1</td><td>California</td><td>192,527</td><td>20.1%</td></tr>
<tr><td>43</td><td>Alaska</td><td>1,638</td><td>0.2%</td><td>2</td><td>Texas</td><td>85,350</td><td>8.9%</td></tr>
<tr><td>5</td><td>Arizona</td><td>37,218</td><td>3.9%</td><td>3</td><td>Florida</td><td>63,509</td><td>6.6%</td></tr>
<tr><td>34</td><td>Arkansas</td><td>6,511</td><td>0.7%</td><td>4</td><td>Georgia</td><td>39,628</td><td>4.1%</td></tr>
<tr><td>1</td><td>California</td><td>192,527</td><td>20.1%</td><td>5</td><td>Arizona</td><td>37,218</td><td>3.9%</td></tr>
<tr><td>21</td><td>Colorado</td><td>13,519</td><td>1.4%</td><td>6</td><td>Michigan</td><td>36,241</td><td>3.8%</td></tr>
<tr><td>29</td><td>Connecticut</td><td>8,963</td><td>0.9%</td><td>7</td><td>Illinois</td><td>32,572</td><td>3.4%</td></tr>
<tr><td>41</td><td>Delaware</td><td>2,541</td><td>0.3%</td><td>8</td><td>Ohio</td><td>28,532</td><td>3.0%</td></tr>
<tr><td>3</td><td>Florida</td><td>63,509</td><td>6.6%</td><td>9</td><td>Washington</td><td>28,331</td><td>3.0%</td></tr>
<tr><td>4</td><td>Georgia</td><td>39,628</td><td>4.1%</td><td>10</td><td>North Carolina</td><td>26,743</td><td>2.8%</td></tr>
<tr><td>36</td><td>Hawaii</td><td>5,133</td><td>0.5%</td><td>11</td><td>Maryland</td><td>25,333</td><td>2.6%</td></tr>
<tr><td>42</td><td>Idaho</td><td>1,668</td><td>0.2%</td><td>12</td><td>New York</td><td>25,114</td><td>2.6%</td></tr>
<tr><td>7</td><td>Illinois</td><td>32,572</td><td>3.4%</td><td>13</td><td>Pennsylvania</td><td>22,471</td><td>2.3%</td></tr>
<tr><td>18</td><td>Indiana</td><td>17,455</td><td>1.8%</td><td>14</td><td>Missouri</td><td>20,765</td><td>2.2%</td></tr>
<tr><td>37</td><td>Iowa</td><td>4,332</td><td>0.5%</td><td>15</td><td>New Jersey</td><td>20,180</td><td>2.1%</td></tr>
<tr><td>32</td><td>Kansas</td><td>7,395</td><td>0.8%</td><td>16</td><td>Tennessee</td><td>19,224</td><td>2.0%</td></tr>
<tr><td>31</td><td>Kentucky</td><td>7,667</td><td>0.8%</td><td>17</td><td>South Carolina</td><td>17,652</td><td>1.8%</td></tr>
<tr><td>20</td><td>Louisiana</td><td>13,743</td><td>1.4%</td><td>18</td><td>Indiana</td><td>17,455</td><td>1.8%</td></tr>
<tr><td>46</td><td>Maine</td><td>1,176</td><td>0.1%</td><td>19</td><td>Nevada</td><td>15,903</td><td>1.7%</td></tr>
<tr><td>11</td><td>Maryland</td><td>25,333</td><td>2.6%</td><td>20</td><td>Louisiana</td><td>13,743</td><td>1.4%</td></tr>
<tr><td>24</td><td>Massachusetts</td><td>12,737</td><td>1.3%</td><td>21</td><td>Colorado</td><td>13,519</td><td>1.4%</td></tr>
<tr><td>6</td><td>Michigan</td><td>36,241</td><td>3.8%</td><td>22</td><td>Alabama</td><td>13,458</td><td>1.4%</td></tr>
<tr><td>28</td><td>Minnesota</td><td>10,078</td><td>1.1%</td><td>23</td><td>Virginia</td><td>13,259</td><td>1.4%</td></tr>
<tr><td>35</td><td>Mississippi</td><td>6,352</td><td>0.7%</td><td>24</td><td>Massachusetts</td><td>12,737</td><td>1.3%</td></tr>
<tr><td>14</td><td>Missouri</td><td>20,765</td><td>2.2%</td><td>25</td><td>Wisconsin</td><td>11,520</td><td>1.2%</td></tr>
<tr><td>44</td><td>Montana</td><td>1,573</td><td>0.2%</td><td>26</td><td>Oregon</td><td>11,331</td><td>1.2%</td></tr>
<tr><td>38</td><td>Nebraska</td><td>4,188</td><td>0.4%</td><td>27</td><td>Oklahoma</td><td>10,881</td><td>1.1%</td></tr>
<tr><td>19</td><td>Nevada</td><td>15,903</td><td>1.7%</td><td>28</td><td>Minnesota</td><td>10,078</td><td>1.1%</td></tr>
<tr><td>45</td><td>New Hampshire</td><td>1,387</td><td>0.1%</td><td>29</td><td>Connecticut</td><td>8,963</td><td>0.9%</td></tr>
<tr><td>15</td><td>New Jersey</td><td>20,180</td><td>2.1%</td><td>30</td><td>New Mexico</td><td>8,004</td><td>0.8%</td></tr>
<tr><td>30</td><td>New Mexico</td><td>8,004</td><td>0.8%</td><td>31</td><td>Kentucky</td><td>7,667</td><td>0.8%</td></tr>
<tr><td>12</td><td>New York</td><td>25,114</td><td>2.6%</td><td>32</td><td>Kansas</td><td>7,395</td><td>0.8%</td></tr>
<tr><td>10</td><td>North Carolina</td><td>26,743</td><td>2.8%</td><td>33</td><td>Utah</td><td>7,195</td><td>0.8%</td></tr>
<tr><td>47</td><td>North Dakota</td><td>882</td><td>0.1%</td><td>34</td><td>Arkansas</td><td>6,511</td><td>0.7%</td></tr>
<tr><td>8</td><td>Ohio</td><td>28,532</td><td>3.0%</td><td>35</td><td>Mississippi</td><td>6,352</td><td>0.7%</td></tr>
<tr><td>27</td><td>Oklahoma</td><td>10,881</td><td>1.1%</td><td>36</td><td>Hawaii</td><td>5,133</td><td>0.5%</td></tr>
<tr><td>26</td><td>Oregon</td><td>11,331</td><td>1.2%</td><td>37</td><td>Iowa</td><td>4,332</td><td>0.5%</td></tr>
<tr><td>13</td><td>Pennsylvania</td><td>22,471</td><td>2.3%</td><td>38</td><td>Nebraska</td><td>4,188</td><td>0.4%</td></tr>
<tr><td>40</td><td>Rhode Island</td><td>3,200</td><td>0.3%</td><td>39</td><td>West Virginia</td><td>3,204</td><td>0.3%</td></tr>
<tr><td>17</td><td>South Carolina</td><td>17,652</td><td>1.8%</td><td>40</td><td>Rhode Island</td><td>3,200</td><td>0.3%</td></tr>
<tr><td>48</td><td>South Dakota</td><td>800</td><td>0.1%</td><td>41</td><td>Delaware</td><td>2,541</td><td>0.3%</td></tr>
<tr><td>16</td><td>Tennessee</td><td>19,224</td><td>2.0%</td><td>42</td><td>Idaho</td><td>1,668</td><td>0.2%</td></tr>
<tr><td>2</td><td>Texas</td><td>85,350</td><td>8.9%</td><td>43</td><td>Alaska</td><td>1,638</td><td>0.2%</td></tr>
<tr><td>33</td><td>Utah</td><td>7,195</td><td>0.8%</td><td>44</td><td>Montana</td><td>1,573</td><td>0.2%</td></tr>
<tr><td>50</td><td>Vermont</td><td>585</td><td>0.1%</td><td>45</td><td>New Hampshire</td><td>1,387</td><td>0.1%</td></tr>
<tr><td>23</td><td>Virginia</td><td>13,259</td><td>1.4%</td><td>46</td><td>Maine</td><td>1,176</td><td>0.1%</td></tr>
<tr><td>9</td><td>Washington</td><td>28,331</td><td>3.0%</td><td>47</td><td>North Dakota</td><td>882</td><td>0.1%</td></tr>
<tr><td>39</td><td>West Virginia</td><td>3,204</td><td>0.3%</td><td>48</td><td>South Dakota</td><td>800</td><td>0.1%</td></tr>
<tr><td>25</td><td>Wisconsin</td><td>11,520</td><td>1.2%</td><td>49</td><td>Wyoming</td><td>713</td><td>0.1%</td></tr>
<tr><td>49</td><td>Wyoming</td><td>713</td><td>0.1%</td><td>50</td><td>Vermont</td><td>585</td><td>0.1%</td></tr>
<tr><td></td><td></td><td></td><td></td><td></td><td>District of Columbia</td><td>6,465</td><td>0.7%</td></tr>
</table>

Source: Reported data from the Federal Bureau of Investigation
"Crime in the United States 2008" (Uniform Crime Reports, September 14, 2009, http://www.fbi.gov/ucr/ucr.htm)
*Includes the theft or attempted theft of a self-propelled vehicle. Excludes motorboats, construction equipment, airplanes, and farming equipment.

Motor Vehicle Theft Rate in 2008

National Rate = 314.7 Motor Vehicle Thefts per 100,000 Population*

ALPHA ORDER			RANK ORDER		
RANK	STATE	RATE	RANK	STATE	RATE
21	Alabama	288.7	1	Nevada	611.6
29	Alaska	238.7	2	Arizona	572.6
2	Arizona	572.6	3	California	523.8
32	Arkansas	228.0	4	Maryland	449.7
3	California	523.8	5	Washington	432.6
22	Colorado	273.7	6	Georgia	409.1
26	Connecticut	256.0	7	New Mexico	403.4
19	Delaware	291.0	8	Hawaii	398.5
13	Florida	346.5	9	South Carolina	394.0
6	Georgia	409.1	10	Michigan	362.3
8	Hawaii	398.5	11	Missouri	351.3
46	Idaho	109.5	12	Texas	350.8
27	Illinois	252.5	13	Florida	346.5
22	Indiana	273.7	14	Louisiana	311.6
42	Iowa	144.3	15	Tennessee	309.3
24	Kansas	263.9	16	Rhode Island	304.5
38	Kentucky	179.6	17	Oregon	299.0
14	Louisiana	311.6	18	Oklahoma	298.7
50	Maine	89.3	19	Delaware	291.0
4	Maryland	449.7	20	North Carolina	290.0
35	Massachusetts	196.0	21	Alabama	288.7
10	Michigan	362.3	22	Colorado	273.7
36	Minnesota	193.1	22	Indiana	273.7
33	Mississippi	216.2	24	Kansas	263.9
11	Missouri	351.3	25	Utah	262.9
41	Montana	162.6	26	Connecticut	256.0
30	Nebraska	234.8	27	Illinois	252.5
1	Nevada	611.6	28	Ohio	248.4
47	New Hampshire	105.4	29	Alaska	238.7
31	New Jersey	232.4	30	Nebraska	234.8
7	New Mexico	403.4	31	New Jersey	232.4
45	New York	128.9	32	Arkansas	228.0
20	North Carolina	290.0	33	Mississippi	216.2
43	North Dakota	137.5	34	Wisconsin	204.7
28	Ohio	248.4	35	Massachusetts	196.0
18	Oklahoma	298.7	36	Minnesota	193.1
17	Oregon	299.0	37	Pennsylvania	180.5
37	Pennsylvania	180.5	38	Kentucky	179.6
16	Rhode Island	304.5	39	West Virginia	176.6
9	South Carolina	394.0	40	Virginia	170.7
48	South Dakota	99.5	41	Montana	162.6
15	Tennessee	309.3	42	Iowa	144.3
12	Texas	350.8	43	North Dakota	137.5
25	Utah	262.9	44	Wyoming	133.9
49	Vermont	94.2	45	New York	128.9
40	Virginia	170.7	46	Idaho	109.5
5	Washington	432.6	47	New Hampshire	105.4
39	West Virginia	176.6	48	South Dakota	99.5
34	Wisconsin	204.7	49	Vermont	94.2
44	Wyoming	133.9	50	Maine	89.3
				District of Columbia	1,092.4

Source: Reported data from the Federal Bureau of Investigation
    "Crime in the United States 2008" (Uniform Crime Reports, September 14, 2009, http://www.fbi.gov/ucr/ucr.htm)
*Includes the theft or attempted theft of a self-propelled vehicle. Excludes motorboats, construction equipment, airplanes, and farming equipment.

Rate of Consumer Fraud Complaints in 2008

National Rate = 299.1 Complaints per 100,000 Population*

ALPHA ORDER

RANK	STATE	RATE
29	Alabama	244.9
6	Alaska	328.3
8	Arizona	317.1
46	Arkansas	192.3
12	California	290.1
1	Colorado	359.5
30	Connecticut	244.3
11	Delaware	301.2
9	Florida	313.6
16	Georgia	283.6
14	Hawaii	286.4
19	Idaho	260.5
36	Illinois	237.0
35	Indiana	237.7
45	Iowa	196.3
23	Kansas	253.4
47	Kentucky	191.4
44	Louisiana	203.5
34	Maine	238.4
2	Maryland	347.6
33	Massachusetts	238.8
41	Michigan	228.0
22	Minnesota	254.0
50	Mississippi	153.1
13	Missouri	288.5
26	Montana	249.1
31	Nebraska	244.1
3	Nevada	344.3
10	New Hampshire	302.9
15	New Jersey	286.0
32	New Mexico	242.2
39	New York	230.9
24	North Carolina	250.8
49	North Dakota	162.3
20	Ohio	256.9
42	Oklahoma	222.4
4	Oregon	332.0
28	Pennsylvania	246.7
40	Rhode Island	230.0
37	South Carolina	235.6
48	South Dakota	165.8
21	Tennessee	255.7
25	Texas	249.2
17	Utah	268.4
27	Vermont	247.1
7	Virginia	317.9
5	Washington	331.8
43	West Virginia	204.4
38	Wisconsin	233.5
18	Wyoming	262.3

RANK ORDER

RANK	STATE	RATE
1	Colorado	359.5
2	Maryland	347.6
3	Nevada	344.3
4	Oregon	332.0
5	Washington	331.8
6	Alaska	328.3
7	Virginia	317.9
8	Arizona	317.1
9	Florida	313.6
10	New Hampshire	302.9
11	Delaware	301.2
12	California	290.1
13	Missouri	288.5
14	Hawaii	286.4
15	New Jersey	286.0
16	Georgia	283.6
17	Utah	268.4
18	Wyoming	262.3
19	Idaho	260.5
20	Ohio	256.9
21	Tennessee	255.7
22	Minnesota	254.0
23	Kansas	253.4
24	North Carolina	250.8
25	Texas	249.2
26	Montana	249.1
27	Vermont	247.1
28	Pennsylvania	246.7
29	Alabama	244.9
30	Connecticut	244.3
31	Nebraska	244.1
32	New Mexico	242.2
33	Massachusetts	238.8
34	Maine	238.4
35	Indiana	237.7
36	Illinois	237.0
37	South Carolina	235.6
38	Wisconsin	233.5
39	New York	230.9
40	Rhode Island	230.0
41	Michigan	228.0
42	Oklahoma	222.4
43	West Virginia	204.4
44	Louisiana	203.5
45	Iowa	196.3
46	Arkansas	192.3
47	Kentucky	191.4
48	South Dakota	165.8
49	North Dakota	162.3
50	Mississippi	153.1
	District of Columbia	453.7

Source: Federal Trade Commission, Consumer Sentinel

"Consumer Fraud and Identify Theft Complaint Data, January - December 2008" (February 2009, http://www.ftc.gov/sentinel/)

*Total includes complaints not shown by state. Total does not include identity theft or "Do Not Call" registry complaints.

Rate of Identity Theft Complaints in 2008

National Rate = 103.3 Complaints per 100,000 Population*

ALPHA ORDER				RANK ORDER		
RANK	STATE	RATE		RANK	STATE	RATE
13	Alabama	93.1		1	Arizona	149.0
34	Alaska	71.4		2	California	139.1
1	Arizona	149.0		3	Florida	133.3
30	Arkansas	72.4		4	Texas	130.3
2	California	139.1		5	Nevada	126.0
10	Colorado	100.9		6	New York	116.2
16	Connecticut	86.6		7	Georgia	111.0
15	Delaware	86.9		8	Illinois	106.4
3	Florida	133.3		9	New Mexico	104.9
7	Georgia	111.0		10	Colorado	100.9
42	Hawaii	55.2		11	Maryland	96.1
39	Idaho	56.9		12	New Jersey	94.2
8	Illinois	106.4		13	Alabama	93.1
31	Indiana	72.0		14	Washington	89.4
48	Iowa	44.9		15	Delaware	86.9
33	Kansas	71.6		16	Connecticut	86.6
40	Kentucky	56.1		16	Louisiana	86.6
16	Louisiana	86.6		18	Pennsylvania	86.1
45	Maine	47.3		19	Michigan	83.6
11	Maryland	96.1		20	Massachusetts	83.2
20	Massachusetts	83.2		21	North Carolina	82.5
19	Michigan	83.6		22	Virginia	81.7
35	Minnesota	67.6		23	Mississippi	80.5
23	Mississippi	80.5		24	Tennessee	80.2
27	Missouri	75.0		25	Rhode Island	78.4
47	Montana	46.5		26	Oregon	77.5
37	Nebraska	59.2		27	Missouri	75.0
5	Nevada	126.0		28	Oklahoma	74.0
38	New Hampshire	57.7		29	South Carolina	73.5
12	New Jersey	94.2		30	Arkansas	72.4
9	New Mexico	104.9		31	Indiana	72.0
6	New York	116.2		32	Ohio	71.7
21	North Carolina	82.5		33	Kansas	71.6
49	North Dakota	35.7		34	Alaska	71.4
32	Ohio	71.7		35	Minnesota	67.6
28	Oklahoma	74.0		36	Utah	64.9
26	Oregon	77.5		37	Nebraska	59.2
18	Pennsylvania	86.1		38	New Hampshire	57.7
25	Rhode Island	78.4		39	Idaho	56.9
29	South Carolina	73.5		40	Kentucky	56.1
50	South Dakota	33.8		41	Wisconsin	56.0
24	Tennessee	80.2		42	Hawaii	55.2
4	Texas	130.3		43	West Virginia	47.7
36	Utah	64.9		44	Vermont	47.6
44	Vermont	47.6		45	Maine	47.3
22	Virginia	81.7		46	Wyoming	46.9
14	Washington	89.4		47	Montana	46.5
43	West Virginia	47.7		48	Iowa	44.9
41	Wisconsin	56.0		49	North Dakota	35.7
46	Wyoming	46.9		50	South Dakota	33.8
					District of Columbia	165.4

Source: Federal Trade Commission, Consumer Sentinel

"Consumer Fraud and Identify Theft Complaint Data, January - December 2008" (February 2009, http://www.ftc.gov/sentinel/)

*Total includes complaints not shown by state. Total does not include consumer fraud or "Do Not Call" registry complaints.

Reported Arrest Rate in 2008

National Rate = 4,759.1 Reported Arrests per 100,000 Population*

ALPHA ORDER

RANK	STATE	RATE
12	Alabama	5,624.0
10	Alaska	5,745.7
16	Arizona	5,210.5
9	Arkansas	5,756.5
33	California	4,234.2
17	Colorado	5,073.3
40	Connecticut	3,824.4
19	Delaware	4,883.9
5	Florida	6,285.1
27	Georgia	4,484.7
26	Hawaii	4,612.1
18	Idaho	5,006.7
NA	Illinois**	NA
24	Indiana	4,737.7
35	Iowa	4,216.3
32	Kansas	4,238.4
NA	Kentucky**	NA
11	Louisiana	5,684.5
31	Maine	4,341.8
15	Maryland	5,384.8
48	Massachusetts	2,570.2
46	Michigan	3,195.7
38	Minnesota	4,027.7
1	Mississippi	8,278.2
8	Missouri	5,992.0
43	Montana	3,471.7
13	Nebraska	5,464.6
4	Nevada	6,536.8
34	New Hampshire	4,226.0
25	New Jersey	4,625.0
14	New Mexico	5,429.0
45	New York	3,259.9
7	North Carolina	6,258.9
22	North Dakota	4,804.8
42	Ohio	3,628.1
28	Oklahoma	4,438.2
36	Oregon	4,045.6
39	Pennsylvania	4,024.1
44	Rhode Island	3,345.8
37	South Carolina	4,033.1
29	South Dakota	4,398.7
6	Tennessee	6,264.7
20	Texas	4,883.7
23	Utah	4,797.0
47	Vermont	2,654.7
30	Virginia	4,390.0
21	Washington	4,809.6
41	West Virginia	3,757.3
3	Wisconsin	7,435.5
2	Wyoming	7,761.0

RANK ORDER

RANK	STATE	RATE
1	Mississippi	8,278.2
2	Wyoming	7,761.0
3	Wisconsin	7,435.5
4	Nevada	6,536.8
5	Florida	6,285.1
6	Tennessee	6,264.7
7	North Carolina	6,258.9
8	Missouri	5,992.0
9	Arkansas	5,756.5
10	Alaska	5,745.7
11	Louisiana	5,684.5
12	Alabama	5,624.0
13	Nebraska	5,464.6
14	New Mexico	5,429.0
15	Maryland	5,384.8
16	Arizona	5,210.5
17	Colorado	5,073.3
18	Idaho	5,006.7
19	Delaware	4,883.9
20	Texas	4,883.7
21	Washington	4,809.6
22	North Dakota	4,804.8
23	Utah	4,797.0
24	Indiana	4,737.7
25	New Jersey	4,625.0
26	Hawaii	4,612.1
27	Georgia	4,484.7
28	Oklahoma	4,438.2
29	South Dakota	4,398.7
30	Virginia	4,390.0
31	Maine	4,341.8
32	Kansas	4,238.4
33	California	4,234.2
34	New Hampshire	4,226.0
35	Iowa	4,216.3
36	Oregon	4,045.6
37	South Carolina	4,033.1
38	Minnesota	4,027.7
39	Pennsylvania	4,024.1
40	Connecticut	3,824.4
41	West Virginia	3,757.3
42	Ohio	3,628.1
43	Montana	3,471.7
44	Rhode Island	3,345.8
45	New York	3,259.9
46	Michigan	3,195.7
47	Vermont	2,654.7
48	Massachusetts	2,570.2
NA	Illinois**	NA
NA	Kentucky**	NA
	District of Columbia**	NA

Source: CQ Press using reported data from the Federal Bureau of Investigation
    "Crime in the United States 2008" (Uniform Crime Reports, September 14, 2009, http://www.fbi.gov/ucr/ucr.htm)
*By law enforcement agencies submitting complete reports to the F.B.I. for 12 months in 2008. These rates based on population estimates for areas under the jurisdiction of those agencies reporting. Arrest rate based on the F.B.I. estimate of total arrests is 4,637.7 reported and unreported arrests per 100,000 population. See important note at beginning of this chapter.
**Not available.

Reported Juvenile Arrest Rate in 2008

National Rate = 6,470.5 Reported Arrests per 100,000 Juvenile Population*

ALPHA ORDER

RANK	STATE	RATE
45	Alabama	3,149.1
41	Alaska	5,066.8
17	Arizona	7,559.5
40	Arkansas	5,088.1
34	California	5,513.6
5	Colorado	9,571.7
33	Connecticut	5,532.3
13	Delaware	7,928.2
24	Florida	6,666.2
30	Georgia	5,728.3
4	Hawaii	11,056.7
6	Idaho	8,927.9
NA	Illinois**	NA
18	Indiana	7,479.3
20	Iowa	7,126.5
35	Kansas	5,411.8
NA	Kentucky**	NA
21	Louisiana	6,887.2
36	Maine	5,318.9
14	Maryland	7,836.1
46	Massachusetts	3,057.8
44	Michigan	3,712.4
10	Minnesota	8,464.2
22	Mississippi	6,878.6
16	Missouri	7,570.8
19	Montana	7,475.8
8	Nebraska	8,631.6
7	Nevada	8,805.6
26	New Hampshire	6,250.9
31	New Jersey	5,710.3
27	New Mexico	6,082.8
42	New York	4,184.6
29	North Carolina	5,881.7
3	North Dakota	11,572.7
38	Ohio	5,207.7
32	Oklahoma	5,573.7
15	Oregon	7,690.2
12	Pennsylvania	8,207.6
39	Rhode Island	5,202.5
43	South Carolina	3,963.0
9	South Dakota	8,511.2
23	Tennessee	6,769.8
25	Texas	6,325.8
11	Utah	8,338.5
47	Vermont	2,725.0
37	Virginia	5,269.1
28	Washington	6,076.8
48	West Virginia	2,153.2
1	Wisconsin	17,047.8
2	Wyoming	12,375.3

RANK ORDER

RANK	STATE	RATE
1	Wisconsin	17,047.8
2	Wyoming	12,375.3
3	North Dakota	11,572.7
4	Hawaii	11,056.7
5	Colorado	9,571.7
6	Idaho	8,927.9
7	Nevada	8,805.6
8	Nebraska	8,631.6
9	South Dakota	8,511.2
10	Minnesota	8,464.2
11	Utah	8,338.5
12	Pennsylvania	8,207.6
13	Delaware	7,928.2
14	Maryland	7,836.1
15	Oregon	7,690.2
16	Missouri	7,570.8
17	Arizona	7,559.5
18	Indiana	7,479.3
19	Montana	7,475.8
20	Iowa	7,126.5
21	Louisiana	6,887.2
22	Mississippi	6,878.6
23	Tennessee	6,769.8
24	Florida	6,666.2
25	Texas	6,325.8
26	New Hampshire	6,250.9
27	New Mexico	6,082.8
28	Washington	6,076.8
29	North Carolina	5,881.7
30	Georgia	5,728.3
31	New Jersey	5,710.3
32	Oklahoma	5,573.7
33	Connecticut	5,532.3
34	California	5,513.6
35	Kansas	5,411.8
36	Maine	5,318.9
37	Virginia	5,269.1
38	Ohio	5,207.7
39	Rhode Island	5,202.5
40	Arkansas	5,088.1
41	Alaska	5,066.8
42	New York	4,184.6
43	South Carolina	3,963.0
44	Michigan	3,712.4
45	Alabama	3,149.1
46	Massachusetts	3,057.8
47	Vermont	2,725.0
48	West Virginia	2,153.2
NA	Illinois**	NA
NA	Kentucky**	NA
	District of Columbia**	NA

Source: CQ Press using reported data from the Federal Bureau of Investigation
"Crime in the United States 2008" (Uniform Crime Reports, September 14, 2009, http://www.fbi.gov/ucr/ucr.htm)
*By law enforcement agencies submitting complete reports to the F.B.I. for 12 months in 2008. Arrests of youths 17 years and younger divided into population of 10 to 17 year olds. See important note at beginning of this chapter.
**Not available.

Prisoners in State Correctional Institutions: Year End 2008

National Total = 1,409,166 State Prisoners*

ALPHA ORDER

RANK	STATE	PRISONERS	% of USA
14	Alabama	30,508	2.2%
41	Alaska	5,014	0.4%
10	Arizona	39,589	2.8%
28	Arkansas	14,716	1.0%
1	California	173,670	12.3%
23	Colorado	23,274	1.7%
26	Connecticut	20,661	1.5%
36	Delaware	7,075	0.5%
3	Florida	102,388	7.3%
5	Georgia	52,719	3.7%
40	Hawaii	5,955	0.4%
35	Idaho	7,290	0.5%
9	Illinois	45,474	3.2%
16	Indiana	28,322	2.0%
33	Iowa	8,766	0.6%
34	Kansas	8,539	0.6%
25	Kentucky	21,706	1.5%
12	Louisiana	38,381	2.7%
47	Maine	2,195	0.2%
22	Maryland	23,324	1.7%
31	Massachusetts	11,408	0.8%
8	Michigan	48,738	3.5%
32	Minnesota	9,406	0.7%
24	Mississippi	22,754	1.6%
15	Missouri	30,186	2.1%
44	Montana	3,607	0.3%
42	Nebraska	4,520	0.3%
30	Nevada	12,743	0.9%
46	New Hampshire	2,904	0.2%
18	New Jersey	25,953	1.8%
38	New Mexico	6,402	0.5%
4	New York	60,347	4.3%
11	North Carolina	39,482	2.8%
50	North Dakota	1,452	0.1%
6	Ohio	51,686	3.7%
19	Oklahoma	25,864	1.8%
29	Oregon	14,167	1.0%
7	Pennsylvania	50,147	3.6%
43	Rhode Island	4,045	0.3%
20	South Carolina	24,326	1.7%
45	South Dakota	3,342	0.2%
17	Tennessee	27,228	1.9%
2	Texas	172,506	12.2%
37	Utah	6,546	0.5%
48	Vermont	2,116	0.2%
13	Virginia	38,276	2.7%
27	Washington	17,926	1.3%
39	West Virginia	6,059	0.4%
21	Wisconsin	23,380	1.7%
49	Wyoming	2,084	0.1%

RANK ORDER

RANK	STATE	PRISONERS	% of USA
1	California	173,670	12.3%
2	Texas	172,506	12.2%
3	Florida	102,388	7.3%
4	New York	60,347	4.3%
5	Georgia	52,719	3.7%
6	Ohio	51,686	3.7%
7	Pennsylvania	50,147	3.6%
8	Michigan	48,738	3.5%
9	Illinois	45,474	3.2%
10	Arizona	39,589	2.8%
11	North Carolina	39,482	2.8%
12	Louisiana	38,381	2.7%
13	Virginia	38,276	2.7%
14	Alabama	30,508	2.2%
15	Missouri	30,186	2.1%
16	Indiana	28,322	2.0%
17	Tennessee	27,228	1.9%
18	New Jersey	25,953	1.8%
19	Oklahoma	25,864	1.8%
20	South Carolina	24,326	1.7%
21	Wisconsin	23,380	1.7%
22	Maryland	23,324	1.7%
23	Colorado	23,274	1.7%
24	Mississippi	22,754	1.6%
25	Kentucky	21,706	1.5%
26	Connecticut	20,661	1.5%
27	Washington	17,926	1.3%
28	Arkansas	14,716	1.0%
29	Oregon	14,167	1.0%
30	Nevada	12,743	0.9%
31	Massachusetts	11,408	0.8%
32	Minnesota	9,406	0.7%
33	Iowa	8,766	0.6%
34	Kansas	8,539	0.6%
35	Idaho	7,290	0.5%
36	Delaware	7,075	0.5%
37	Utah	6,546	0.5%
38	New Mexico	6,402	0.5%
39	West Virginia	6,059	0.4%
40	Hawaii	5,955	0.4%
41	Alaska	5,014	0.4%
42	Nebraska	4,520	0.3%
43	Rhode Island	4,045	0.3%
44	Montana	3,607	0.3%
45	South Dakota	3,342	0.2%
46	New Hampshire	2,904	0.2%
47	Maine	2,195	0.2%
48	Vermont	2,116	0.2%
49	Wyoming	2,084	0.1%
50	North Dakota	1,452	0.1%
	District of Columbia**	NA	NA

Source: U.S. Department of Justice, Bureau of Justice Statistics
   "Prisoners in 2008" (December 2009, NCJ 228417, http://bjs.ojp.usdoj.gov/)
*Advance figures as of December 31, 2008. Totals reflect all prisoners, including those sentenced to a year or less and those unsentenced. National total does not include 201,280 prisoners under federal jurisdiction. State and federal prisoners combined total 1,610,446.
**Responsibility for sentenced felons in D.C. was transferred to the Federal Bureau of Prisons in 2001.

State Prisoner Imprisonment Rate in 2008

National Rate = 445 State Prisoners per 100,000 Population*

ALPHA ORDER

RANK	STATE	RATE
5	Alabama	634
23	Alaska	430
6	Arizona	567
10	Arkansas	511
17	California	467
17	Colorado	467
25	Connecticut	407
19	Delaware	463
7	Florida	557
8	Georgia	540
34	Hawaii	332
16	Idaho	474
33	Illinois	351
21	Indiana	442
40	Iowa	291
38	Kansas	303
12	Kentucky	492
1	Louisiana	853
50	Maine	151
26	Maryland	403
48	Massachusetts	218
14	Michigan	488
49	Minnesota	179
2	Mississippi	735
11	Missouri	509
31	Montana	368
43	Nebraska	247
15	Nevada	486
47	New Hampshire	220
39	New Jersey	298
36	New Mexico	316
37	New York	307
31	North Carolina	368
46	North Dakota	225
20	Ohio	449
3	Oklahoma	661
30	Oregon	371
27	Pennsylvania	393
44	Rhode Island	240
9	South Carolina	519
24	South Dakota	412
22	Tennessee	436
4	Texas	639
45	Utah	232
42	Vermont	260
13	Virginia	489
41	Washington	272
35	West Virginia	331
29	Wisconsin	374
28	Wyoming	387

RANK ORDER

RANK	STATE	RATE
1	Louisiana	853
2	Mississippi	735
3	Oklahoma	661
4	Texas	639
5	Alabama	634
6	Arizona	567
7	Florida	557
8	Georgia	540
9	South Carolina	519
10	Arkansas	511
11	Missouri	509
12	Kentucky	492
13	Virginia	489
14	Michigan	488
15	Nevada	486
16	Idaho	474
17	California	467
17	Colorado	467
19	Delaware	463
20	Ohio	449
21	Indiana	442
22	Tennessee	436
23	Alaska	430
24	South Dakota	412
25	Connecticut	407
26	Maryland	403
27	Pennsylvania	393
28	Wyoming	387
29	Wisconsin	374
30	Oregon	371
31	Montana	368
31	North Carolina	368
33	Illinois	351
34	Hawaii	332
35	West Virginia	331
36	New Mexico	316
37	New York	307
38	Kansas	303
39	New Jersey	298
40	Iowa	291
41	Washington	272
42	Vermont	260
43	Nebraska	247
44	Rhode Island	240
45	Utah	232
46	North Dakota	225
47	New Hampshire	220
48	Massachusetts	218
49	Minnesota	179
50	Maine	151
	District of Columbia**	NA

Source: U.S. Department of Justice, Bureau of Justice Statistics
"Prisoners in 2008" (December 2009, NCJ 228417, http://bjs.ojp.usdoj.gov/)
*As of December 31, 2008. Includes only inmates sentenced to more than one year. Does not include federal imprisonment rate
of 60 prisoners per 100,000 population. State and federal combined imprisonment rate is 504 prisoners per 100,000 population.
**Responsibility for sentenced felons in D.C. was transferred to the Federal Bureau of Prisons in 2001.

Percent Change in Number of State Prisoners: 2007 to 2008

National Percent Change = 0.8% Increase*

ALPHA ORDER				RANK ORDER		
RANK	STATE	PERCENT CHANGE		RANK	STATE	PERCENT CHANGE
7	Alabama	3.7		1	Pennsylvania	9.1
45	Alaska	(3.0)		2	Arizona	4.9
2	Arizona	4.9		3	Indiana	4.4
9	Arkansas	2.8		4	Florida	4.2
32	California	(0.4)		4	Montana	4.2
13	Colorado	1.9		6	North Carolina	4.0
38	Connecticut	(1.3)		7	Alabama	3.7
43	Delaware	(2.8)		7	Tennessee	3.7
4	Florida	4.2		9	Arkansas	2.8
43	Georgia	(2.8)		10	North Dakota	2.5
32	Hawaii	(0.4)		11	Louisiana	2.2
32	Idaho	(0.4)		11	Maine	2.2
21	Illinois	0.6		13	Colorado	1.9
3	Indiana	4.4		13	Ohio	1.9
24	Iowa	0.4		15	Oregon	1.6
42	Kansas	(1.8)		16	Mississippi	1.4
47	Kentucky	(3.3)		17	Missouri	1.1
11	Louisiana	2.2		18	South Dakota	0.9
11	Maine	2.2		18	Washington	0.9
35	Maryland	(0.5)		20	Rhode Island	0.7
31	Massachusetts	(0.2)		21	Illinois	0.6
45	Michigan	(3.0)		22	Utah	0.5
36	Minnesota	(0.7)		22	Virginia	0.5
16	Mississippi	1.4		24	Iowa	0.4
17	Missouri	1.1		24	South Carolina	0.4
4	Montana	4.2		24	Texas	0.4
27	Nebraska	0.3		27	Nebraska	0.3
NA	Nevada**	NA		28	Oklahoma	0.1
38	New Hampshire	(1.3)		29	West Virginia	0.0
47	New Jersey	(3.3)		29	Wyoming	0.0
37	New Mexico	(1.0)		31	Massachusetts	(0.2)
49	New York	(3.6)		32	California	(0.4)
6	North Carolina	4.0		32	Hawaii	(0.4)
10	North Dakota	2.5		32	Idaho	(0.4)
13	Ohio	1.9		35	Maryland	(0.5)
28	Oklahoma	0.1		36	Minnesota	(0.7)
15	Oregon	1.6		37	New Mexico	(1.0)
1	Pennsylvania	9.1		38	Connecticut	(1.3)
20	Rhode Island	0.7		38	New Hampshire	(1.3)
24	South Carolina	0.4		40	Vermont	(1.4)
18	South Dakota	0.9		41	Wisconsin	(1.5)
7	Tennessee	3.7		42	Kansas	(1.8)
24	Texas	0.4		43	Delaware	(2.8)
22	Utah	0.5		43	Georgia	(2.8)
40	Vermont	(1.4)		45	Alaska	(3.0)
22	Virginia	0.5		45	Michigan	(3.0)
18	Washington	0.9		47	Kentucky	(3.3)
29	West Virginia	0.0		47	New Jersey	(3.3)
41	Wisconsin	(1.5)		49	New York	(3.6)
29	Wyoming	0.0		NA	Nevada**	NA
					District of Columbia***	NA

Source: U.S. Department of Justice, Bureau of Justice Statistics
  "Prisoners in 2008" (December 2009, NCJ 228417, http://bjs.ojp.usdoj.gov/)
*From December 31, 2007 to December 31, 2008. Includes inmates sentenced to more than one year and those sentenced to a year or less or with no sentence. The percent change in number of prisoners under federal jurisdiction during the same period was an 0.8% increase. The combined state and federal increase was 0.8%. **Not available.
***Responsibility for sentenced felons in D.C. was transferred to the Federal Bureau of Prisons in 2001.

Prisoners Under Sentence of Death in 2008

National Total = 3,156 State Prisoners*

RANK	STATE	PRISONERS	% of USA
5	Alabama	205	6.5%
NA	Alaska**	NA	NA
8	Arizona	119	3.8%
17	Arkansas	41	1.3%
1	California	669	21.2%
32	Colorado	2	0.1%
25	Connecticut	10	0.3%
20	Delaware	20	0.6%
2	Florida	390	12.4%
9	Georgia	105	3.3%
NA	Hawaii**	NA	NA
21	Idaho	17	0.5%
22	Illinois	15	0.5%
24	Indiana	13	0.4%
NA	Iowa**	NA	NA
28	Kansas	8	0.3%
18	Kentucky	36	1.1%
12	Louisiana	84	2.7%
NA	Maine**	NA	NA
30	Maryland	5	0.2%
NA	Massachusetts**	NA	NA
NA	Michigan**	NA	NA
NA	Minnesota**	NA	NA
14	Mississippi	60	1.9%
16	Missouri	50	1.6%
32	Montana	2	0.1%
27	Nebraska	9	0.3%
13	Nevada	81	2.6%
35	New Hampshire	1	0.0%
NA	New Jersey**	NA	NA
32	New Mexico	2	0.1%
37	New York	0	0.0%
7	North Carolina	161	5.1%
NA	North Dakota**	NA	NA
6	Ohio	172	5.4%
11	Oklahoma	85	2.7%
19	Oregon	35	1.1%
4	Pennsylvania	223	7.1%
NA	Rhode Island**	NA	NA
15	South Carolina	58	1.8%
31	South Dakota	3	0.1%
10	Tennessee	87	2.8%
3	Texas	354	11.2%
25	Utah	10	0.3%
NA	Vermont**	NA	NA
22	Virginia	15	0.5%
28	Washington	8	0.3%
NA	West Virginia**	NA	NA
NA	Wisconsin**	NA	NA
35	Wyoming	1	0.0%

RANK	STATE	PRISONERS	% of USA
1	California	669	21.2%
2	Florida	390	12.4%
3	Texas	354	11.2%
4	Pennsylvania	223	7.1%
5	Alabama	205	6.5%
6	Ohio	172	5.4%
7	North Carolina	161	5.1%
8	Arizona	119	3.8%
9	Georgia	105	3.3%
10	Tennessee	87	2.8%
11	Oklahoma	85	2.7%
12	Louisiana	84	2.7%
13	Nevada	81	2.6%
14	Mississippi	60	1.9%
15	South Carolina	58	1.8%
16	Missouri	50	1.6%
17	Arkansas	41	1.3%
18	Kentucky	36	1.1%
19	Oregon	35	1.1%
20	Delaware	20	0.6%
21	Idaho	17	0.5%
22	Illinois	15	0.5%
22	Virginia	15	0.5%
24	Indiana	13	0.4%
25	Connecticut	10	0.3%
25	Utah	10	0.3%
27	Nebraska	9	0.3%
28	Kansas	8	0.3%
28	Washington	8	0.3%
30	Maryland	5	0.2%
31	South Dakota	3	0.1%
32	Colorado	2	0.1%
32	Montana	2	0.1%
32	New Mexico	2	0.1%
35	New Hampshire	1	0.0%
35	Wyoming	1	0.0%
37	New York	0	0.0%
NA	Alaska**	NA	NA
NA	Hawaii**	NA	NA
NA	Iowa**	NA	NA
NA	Maine**	NA	NA
NA	Massachusetts**	NA	NA
NA	Michigan**	NA	NA
NA	Minnesota**	NA	NA
NA	New Jersey**	NA	NA
NA	North Dakota**	NA	NA
NA	Rhode Island**	NA	NA
NA	Vermont**	NA	NA
NA	West Virginia**	NA	NA
NA	Wisconsin**	NA	NA
	District of Columbia**	NA	NA

Source: U.S. Department of Justice, Bureau of Justice Statistics
   "Capital Punishment 2008" (Bulletin, December 2009, NCJ 228662, http://bjs.ojp.usdoj.gov/)
*As of December 31, 2008. Does not include 51 federal prisoners under sentence of death. There were 37 executions in 2008.
**No death penalty as of December 31, 2008.

Rate of Full-Time Sworn Officers in Law Enforcement Agencies in 2004

National Rate = 249 Officers per 100,000 Population*

ALPHA ORDER

RANK	STATE	RATE
21	Alabama	241
33	Alaska	215
30	Arizona	220
26	Arkansas	230
36	California	211
21	Colorado	241
27	Connecticut	229
23	Delaware	239
11	Florida	262
10	Georgia	266
24	Hawaii	238
35	Idaho	213
5	Illinois	312
42	Indiana	194
46	Iowa	184
12	Kansas	261
45	Kentucky	185
1	Louisiana	399
41	Maine	195
9	Maryland	272
8	Massachusetts	283
40	Michigan	205
47	Minnesota	177
20	Mississippi	242
18	Missouri	245
38	Montana	206
31	Nebraska	217
15	Nevada	256
32	New Hampshire	216
2	New Jersey	366
14	New Mexico	257
3	New York	344
17	North Carolina	246
38	North Dakota	206
29	Ohio	226
28	Oklahoma	227
49	Oregon	176
33	Pennsylvania	215
7	Rhode Island	284
15	South Carolina	256
37	South Dakota	210
13	Tennessee	258
19	Texas	244
43	Utah	191
44	Vermont	186
6	Virginia	290
50	Washington	174
47	West Virginia	177
25	Wisconsin	237
4	Wyoming	328

RANK ORDER

RANK	STATE	RATE
1	Louisiana	399
2	New Jersey	366
3	New York	344
4	Wyoming	328
5	Illinois	312
6	Virginia	290
7	Rhode Island	284
8	Massachusetts	283
9	Maryland	272
10	Georgia	266
11	Florida	262
12	Kansas	261
13	Tennessee	258
14	New Mexico	257
15	Nevada	256
15	South Carolina	256
17	North Carolina	246
18	Missouri	245
19	Texas	244
20	Mississippi	242
21	Alabama	241
21	Colorado	241
23	Delaware	239
24	Hawaii	238
25	Wisconsin	237
26	Arkansas	230
27	Connecticut	229
28	Oklahoma	227
29	Ohio	226
30	Arizona	220
31	Nebraska	217
32	New Hampshire	216
33	Alaska	215
33	Pennsylvania	215
35	Idaho	213
36	California	211
37	South Dakota	210
38	Montana	206
38	North Dakota	206
40	Michigan	205
41	Maine	195
42	Indiana	194
43	Utah	191
44	Vermont	186
45	Kentucky	185
46	Iowa	184
47	Minnesota	177
47	West Virginia	177
49	Oregon	176
50	Washington	174
	District of Columbia	799

Source: CQ Press using data from U.S. Department of Justice, Bureau of Justice Statistics
"Census of State and Local Law Enforcement Agencies, 2004" (June 2007, NCJ 212749, www.ojp.usdoj.gov/bjs/sandlle.htm)
*Includes state and local police, sheriffs' departments, and special police agencies.

Per Capita State and Local Government Expenditures for Police Protection in 2007
National Per Capita = $279*

ALPHA ORDER

RANK	STATE	PER CAPITA
37	Alabama	$211
6	Alaska	347
9	Arizona	322
47	Arkansas	170
3	California	381
15	Colorado	278
19	Connecticut	261
4	Delaware	359
7	Florida	345
30	Georgia	224
24	Hawaii	239
40	Idaho	200
10	Illinois	317
45	Indiana	175
42	Iowa	197
23	Kansas	244
49	Kentucky	148
16	Louisiana	277
44	Maine	176
10	Maryland	317
14	Massachusetts	282
26	Michigan	233
17	Minnesota	272
43	Mississippi	196
25	Missouri	238
35	Montana	215
39	Nebraska	202
2	Nevada	385
28	New Hampshire	225
5	New Jersey	353
13	New Mexico	304
1	New York	393
28	North Carolina	225
48	North Dakota	166
21	Ohio	258
41	Oklahoma	199
20	Oregon	259
35	Pennsylvania	215
12	Rhode Island	311
38	South Carolina	205
46	South Dakota	172
31	Tennessee	221
32	Texas	220
33	Utah	219
27	Vermont	228
22	Virginia	248
33	Washington	219
49	West Virginia	148
18	Wisconsin	267
8	Wyoming	335

RANK ORDER

RANK	STATE	PER CAPITA
1	New York	$393
2	Nevada	385
3	California	381
4	Delaware	359
5	New Jersey	353
6	Alaska	347
7	Florida	345
8	Wyoming	335
9	Arizona	322
10	Illinois	317
10	Maryland	317
12	Rhode Island	311
13	New Mexico	304
14	Massachusetts	282
15	Colorado	278
16	Louisiana	277
17	Minnesota	272
18	Wisconsin	267
19	Connecticut	261
20	Oregon	259
21	Ohio	258
22	Virginia	248
23	Kansas	244
24	Hawaii	239
25	Missouri	238
26	Michigan	233
27	Vermont	228
28	New Hampshire	225
28	North Carolina	225
30	Georgia	224
31	Tennessee	221
32	Texas	220
33	Utah	219
33	Washington	219
35	Montana	215
35	Pennsylvania	215
37	Alabama	211
38	South Carolina	205
39	Nebraska	202
40	Idaho	200
41	Oklahoma	199
42	Iowa	197
43	Mississippi	196
44	Maine	176
45	Indiana	175
46	South Dakota	172
47	Arkansas	169
48	North Dakota	166
49	Kentucky	148
49	West Virginia	148

District of Columbia — 851

Source: CQ Press using data from U.S. Bureau of the Census, Governments Division
"State and Local Government Finances 2006-2007" (http://www.census.gov/govs/estimate/index.html)
*Direct general expenditures.

Per Capita State and Local Government Expenditures for Corrections in 2007

National Per Capita = $226*

ALPHA ORDER				RANK ORDER		
RANK	STATE	PER CAPITA		RANK	STATE	PER CAPITA
33	Alabama	$166		1	Alaska	$353
1	Alaska	353		2	California	347
14	Arizona	243		3	Wyoming	328
35	Arkansas	158		4	Delaware	309
2	California	347		5	Maryland	296
14	Colorado	243		6	New York	291
25	Connecticut	189		7	Oregon	265
4	Delaware	309		8	Nevada	259
19	Florida	232		9	Virginia	252
19	Georgia	232		10	Louisiana	245
37	Hawaii	154		10	Pennsylvania	245
30	Idaho	180		10	Washington	245
44	Illinois	146		13	Wisconsin	244
37	Indiana	154		14	Arizona	243
44	Iowa	146		14	Colorado	243
48	Kansas	138		16	New Mexico	239
36	Kentucky	155		17	Michigan	236
10	Louisiana	245		18	New Jersey	235
40	Maine	151		19	Florida	232
5	Maryland	296		19	Georgia	232
22	Massachusetts	199		21	Rhode Island	209
17	Michigan	236		22	Massachusetts	199
34	Minnesota	162		23	Texas	198
43	Mississippi	148		24	North Carolina	193
49	Missouri	136		25	Connecticut	189
25	Montana	189		25	Montana	189
28	Nebraska	184		27	Oklahoma	185
8	Nevada	259		28	Nebraska	184
50	New Hampshire	125		29	Vermont	183
18	New Jersey	235		30	Idaho	180
16	New Mexico	239		31	Utah	179
6	New York	291		32	South Dakota	176
24	North Carolina	193		33	Alabama	166
47	North Dakota	140		34	Minnesota	162
46	Ohio	142		35	Arkansas	158
27	Oklahoma	185		36	Kentucky	155
7	Oregon	265		37	Hawaii	154
10	Pennsylvania	245		37	Indiana	154
21	Rhode Island	209		37	Tennessee	154
42	South Carolina	150		40	Maine	151
32	South Dakota	176		40	West Virginia	151
37	Tennessee	154		42	South Carolina	150
23	Texas	198		43	Mississippi	148
31	Utah	179		44	Illinois	146
29	Vermont	183		44	Iowa	146
9	Virginia	252		46	Ohio	142
10	Washington	245		47	North Dakota	140
40	West Virginia	151		48	Kansas	138
13	Wisconsin	244		49	Missouri	136
3	Wyoming	328		50	New Hampshire	125
				District of Columbia		384

Source: CQ Press using data from U.S. Bureau of the Census, Governments Division
"State and Local Government Finances 2006-2007" (http://www.census.gov/govs/estimate/index.html)
*Direct general expenditures.

Per Capita State and Local Government Expenditures for Judicial and Legal Services in 2007
National Per Capita = $129*

ALPHA ORDER

RANK	STATE	PER CAPITA
40	Alabama	$87
1	Alaska	280
11	Arizona	143
46	Arkansas	73
2	California	236
31	Colorado	98
5	Connecticut	177
4	Delaware	181
19	Florida	119
35	Georgia	96
3	Hawaii	220
27	Idaho	102
24	Illinois	104
48	Indiana	71
28	Iowa	101
31	Kansas	98
31	Kentucky	98
16	Louisiana	128
43	Maine	79
15	Maryland	132
10	Massachusetts	153
24	Michigan	104
17	Minnesota	121
47	Mississippi	72
45	Missouri	78
14	Montana	134
41	Nebraska	85
8	Nevada	159
37	New Hampshire	93
8	New Jersey	159
11	New Mexico	143
6	New York	176
49	North Carolina	67
35	North Dakota	96
13	Ohio	139
42	Oklahoma	83
24	Oregon	104
19	Pennsylvania	119
18	Rhode Island	120
50	South Carolina	61
43	South Dakota	79
38	Tennessee	91
39	Texas	88
22	Utah	113
34	Vermont	97
28	Virginia	101
22	Washington	113
21	West Virginia	114
30	Wisconsin	100
7	Wyoming	174

RANK ORDER

RANK	STATE	PER CAPITA
1	Alaska	$280
2	California	236
3	Hawaii	220
4	Delaware	181
5	Connecticut	177
6	New York	176
7	Wyoming	174
8	Nevada	159
8	New Jersey	159
10	Massachusetts	153
11	Arizona	143
11	New Mexico	143
13	Ohio	139
14	Montana	134
15	Maryland	132
16	Louisiana	128
17	Minnesota	121
18	Rhode Island	120
19	Florida	119
19	Pennsylvania	119
21	West Virginia	114
22	Utah	113
22	Washington	113
24	Illinois	104
24	Michigan	104
24	Oregon	104
27	Idaho	102
28	Iowa	101
28	Virginia	101
30	Wisconsin	100
31	Colorado	98
31	Kansas	98
31	Kentucky	98
34	Vermont	97
35	Georgia	96
35	North Dakota	96
37	New Hampshire	93
38	Tennessee	91
39	Texas	88
40	Alabama	87
41	Nebraska	85
42	Oklahoma	83
43	Maine	79
43	South Dakota	79
45	Missouri	78
46	Arkansas	73
47	Mississippi	72
48	Indiana	71
49	North Carolina	67
50	South Carolina	61

| | District of Columbia | 139 |

Source: CQ Press using data from U.S. Bureau of the Census, Governments Division
"State and Local Government Finances 2006-2007" (http://www.census.gov/govs/estimate/index.html)
*Direct general expenditures. Includes courts, prosecution and legal services, and public defense.

III. Defense

Homeland Security Grants in 2010

National Total = $1,726,359,956*

ALPHA ORDER

RANK	STATE	GRANTS	% of USA
30	Alabama	$11,293,846	0.7%
36	Alaska	7,358,300	0.4%
14	Arizona	30,086,524	1.7%
39	Arkansas	7,093,544	0.4%
2	California	268,685,401	15.6%
22	Colorado	19,209,759	1.1%
25	Connecticut	14,954,871	0.9%
46	Delaware	6,727,997	0.4%
5	Florida	71,139,501	4.1%
11	Georgia	33,716,473	2.0%
29	Hawaii	11,810,295	0.7%
43	Idaho	6,743,796	0.4%
4	Illinois	87,934,150	5.1%
21	Indiana	19,314,399	1.1%
37	Iowa	7,097,117	0.4%
35	Kansas	7,409,670	0.4%
31	Kentucky	11,045,187	0.6%
17	Louisiana	23,694,494	1.4%
44	Maine	6,738,762	0.4%
16	Maryland	27,342,383	1.6%
9	Massachusetts	35,713,314	2.1%
10	Michigan	34,075,707	2.0%
19	Minnesota	19,907,805	1.2%
38	Mississippi	7,095,565	0.4%
15	Missouri	28,169,120	1.6%
45	Montana	6,730,288	0.4%
34	Nebraska	8,398,024	0.5%
23	Nevada	16,492,596	1.0%
41	New Hampshire	7,056,165	0.4%
6	New Jersey	62,035,995	3.6%
40	New Mexico	7,072,396	0.4%
1	New York	277,150,581	16.1%
18	North Carolina	21,273,139	1.2%
48	North Dakota	6,722,374	0.4%
8	Ohio	40,437,889	2.3%
27	Oklahoma	13,999,310	0.8%
24	Oregon	15,401,772	0.9%
7	Pennsylvania	57,855,730	3.4%
28	Rhode Island	11,814,031	0.7%
33	South Carolina	8,412,080	0.5%
47	South Dakota	6,726,325	0.4%
20	Tennessee	19,564,050	1.1%
3	Texas	143,036,730	8.3%
32	Utah	9,990,734	0.6%
49	Vermont	6,721,884	0.4%
12	Virginia	30,915,010	1.8%
13	Washington	30,615,761	1.8%
42	West Virginia	6,750,853	0.4%
26	Wisconsin	14,609,829	0.8%
50	Wyoming	6,719,732	0.4%

RANK ORDER

RANK	STATE	GRANTS	% of USA
1	New York	$277,150,581	16.1%
2	California	268,685,401	15.6%
3	Texas	143,036,730	8.3%
4	Illinois	87,934,150	5.1%
5	Florida	71,139,501	4.1%
6	New Jersey	62,035,995	3.6%
7	Pennsylvania	57,855,730	3.4%
8	Ohio	40,437,889	2.3%
9	Massachusetts	35,713,314	2.1%
10	Michigan	34,075,707	2.0%
11	Georgia	33,716,473	2.0%
12	Virginia	30,915,010	1.8%
13	Washington	30,615,761	1.8%
14	Arizona	30,086,524	1.7%
15	Missouri	28,169,120	1.6%
16	Maryland	27,342,383	1.6%
17	Louisiana	23,694,494	1.4%
18	North Carolina	21,273,139	1.2%
19	Minnesota	19,907,805	1.2%
20	Tennessee	19,564,050	1.1%
21	Indiana	19,314,399	1.1%
22	Colorado	19,209,759	1.1%
23	Nevada	16,492,596	1.0%
24	Oregon	15,401,772	0.9%
25	Connecticut	14,954,871	0.9%
26	Wisconsin	14,609,829	0.8%
27	Oklahoma	13,999,310	0.8%
28	Rhode Island	11,814,031	0.7%
29	Hawaii	11,810,295	0.7%
30	Alabama	11,293,846	0.7%
31	Kentucky	11,045,187	0.6%
32	Utah	9,990,734	0.6%
33	South Carolina	8,412,080	0.5%
34	Nebraska	8,398,024	0.5%
35	Kansas	7,409,670	0.4%
36	Alaska	7,358,300	0.4%
37	Iowa	7,097,117	0.4%
38	Mississippi	7,095,565	0.4%
39	Arkansas	7,093,544	0.4%
40	New Mexico	7,072,396	0.4%
41	New Hampshire	7,056,165	0.4%
42	West Virginia	6,750,853	0.4%
43	Idaho	6,743,796	0.4%
44	Maine	6,738,762	0.4%
45	Montana	6,730,288	0.4%
46	Delaware	6,727,997	0.4%
47	South Dakota	6,726,325	0.4%
48	North Dakota	6,722,374	0.4%
49	Vermont	6,721,884	0.4%
50	Wyoming	6,719,732	0.4%
	District of Columbia	69,574,433	4.0%

Source: CQ Press using data from U.S. Department of Homeland Security
  "FY 2010 Preparedness Grant Programs Overview" (http://www.dhs.gov/xgovt/grants/)
*For fiscal year ending September 30. National total includes $15,924,265 in grants to U.S. territories. The Homeland Security Grant Program includes several sub-grant programs such as State Homeland Security, Urban Area Security Initiative, Law Enforcement Terrorism Prevention Program, and Emergency Management Performance.

Per Capita Homeland Security Grants in 2010

National Per Capita = $5.57*

ALPHA ORDER				RANK ORDER		
RANK	STATE	PER CAPITA		RANK	STATE	PER CAPITA
46	Alabama	$2.40		1	New York	$14.18
5	Alaska	10.53		2	Wyoming	12.35
25	Arizona	4.56		3	Rhode Island	11.22
45	Arkansas	2.45		4	Vermont	10.81
10	California	7.27		5	Alaska	10.53
31	Colorado	3.82		6	North Dakota	10.39
27	Connecticut	4.25		7	Hawaii	9.12
9	Delaware	7.60		8	South Dakota	8.28
30	Florida	3.84		9	Delaware	7.60
38	Georgia	3.43		10	California	7.27
7	Hawaii	9.12		11	New Jersey	7.12
26	Idaho	4.36		12	Montana	6.90
13	Illinois	6.81		13	Illinois	6.81
41	Indiana	3.01		14	Nevada	6.24
48	Iowa	2.36		15	Texas	5.77
42	Kansas	2.63		16	Massachusetts	5.42
44	Kentucky	2.56		17	New Hampshire	5.33
18	Louisiana	5.27		18	Louisiana	5.27
19	Maine	5.11		19	Maine	5.11
20	Maryland	4.80		20	Maryland	4.80
16	Massachusetts	5.42		21	Missouri	4.70
39	Michigan	3.42		22	Nebraska	4.67
33	Minnesota	3.78		23	Pennsylvania	4.59
46	Mississippi	2.40		23	Washington	4.59
21	Missouri	4.70		25	Arizona	4.56
12	Montana	6.90		26	Idaho	4.36
22	Nebraska	4.67		27	Connecticut	4.25
14	Nevada	6.24		28	Oregon	4.03
17	New Hampshire	5.33		29	Virginia	3.92
11	New Jersey	7.12		30	Florida	3.84
36	New Mexico	3.52		31	Colorado	3.82
1	New York	14.18		32	Oklahoma	3.80
49	North Carolina	2.27		33	Minnesota	3.78
6	North Dakota	10.39		34	West Virginia	3.71
37	Ohio	3.50		35	Utah	3.59
32	Oklahoma	3.80		36	New Mexico	3.52
28	Oregon	4.03		37	Ohio	3.50
23	Pennsylvania	4.59		38	Georgia	3.43
3	Rhode Island	11.22		39	Michigan	3.42
50	South Carolina	1.84		40	Tennessee	3.11
8	South Dakota	8.28		41	Indiana	3.01
40	Tennessee	3.11		42	Kansas	2.63
15	Texas	5.77		43	Wisconsin	2.58
35	Utah	3.59		44	Kentucky	2.56
4	Vermont	10.81		45	Arkansas	2.45
29	Virginia	3.92		46	Alabama	2.40
23	Washington	4.59		46	Mississippi	2.40
34	West Virginia	3.71		48	Iowa	2.36
43	Wisconsin	2.58		49	North Carolina	2.27
2	Wyoming	12.35		50	South Carolina	1.84

District of Columbia   116.02

Source: CQ Press using data from U.S. Department of Homeland Security
   "FY 2010 Preparedness Grant Programs Overview" (http://www.dhs.gov/xgovt/grants/)
*For fiscal year ending September 30. National per capita does not include grants to U.S. territories. The Homeland Security Grant Program includes several sub-grant programs such as State Homeland Security, Urban Area Security Initiative, Law Enforcement Terrorism Prevention Program, and Emergency Management Performance.

U.S. Department of Defense Domestic Expenditures in 2008

National Total = $501,031,750,000*

RANK	STATE	EXPENDITURES	% of USA
13	Alabama	$12,388,829,000	2.5%
31	Alaska	3,813,958,000	0.8%
8	Arizona	14,950,285,000	3.0%
37	Arkansas	2,171,155,000	0.4%
3	California	50,845,643,000	10.1%
21	Colorado	8,532,494,000	1.7%
10	Connecticut	12,862,936,000	2.6%
48	Delaware	715,970,000	0.1%
4	Florida	20,960,184,000	4.2%
7	Georgia	15,312,859,000	3.1%
24	Hawaii	6,803,856,000	1.4%
45	Idaho	782,219,000	0.2%
14	Illinois	11,823,927,000	2.4%
18	Indiana	9,767,529,000	1.9%
41	Iowa	1,636,874,000	0.3%
28	Kansas	5,301,011,000	1.1%
20	Kentucky	8,873,951,000	1.8%
25	Louisiana	6,750,148,000	1.3%
40	Maine	1,741,698,000	0.3%
5	Maryland	18,862,525,000	3.8%
11	Massachusetts	12,656,077,000	2.5%
23	Michigan	7,756,312,000	1.5%
34	Minnesota	2,791,078,000	0.6%
26	Mississippi	6,141,143,000	1.2%
9	Missouri	14,787,493,000	3.0%
47	Montana	734,531,000	0.1%
39	Nebraska	1,782,951,000	0.4%
35	Nevada	2,386,818,000	0.5%
38	New Hampshire	1,972,353,000	0.4%
19	New Jersey	9,443,071,000	1.9%
33	New Mexico	2,966,845,000	0.6%
12	New York	12,584,527,000	2.5%
16	North Carolina	10,387,930,000	2.1%
46	North Dakota	751,877,000	0.2%
17	Ohio	10,294,759,000	2.1%
27	Oklahoma	5,364,454,000	1.1%
36	Oregon	2,218,851,000	0.4%
6	Pennsylvania	17,178,876,000	3.4%
42	Rhode Island	1,344,177,000	0.3%
22	South Carolina	7,843,732,000	1.6%
43	South Dakota	822,948,000	0.2%
29	Tennessee	5,273,556,000	1.1%
1	Texas	65,420,016,000	13.1%
32	Utah	3,746,666,000	0.7%
50	Vermont	541,963,000	0.1%
2	Virginia	54,526,362,000	10.9%
15	Washington	11,526,956,000	2.3%
44	West Virginia	819,821,000	0.2%
30	Wisconsin	4,097,011,000	0.8%
49	Wyoming	544,424,000	0.1%

RANK	STATE	EXPENDITURES	% of USA
1	Texas	$65,420,016,000	13.1%
2	Virginia	54,526,362,000	10.9%
3	California	50,845,643,000	10.1%
4	Florida	20,960,184,000	4.2%
5	Maryland	18,862,525,000	3.8%
6	Pennsylvania	17,178,876,000	3.4%
7	Georgia	15,312,859,000	3.1%
8	Arizona	14,950,285,000	3.0%
9	Missouri	14,787,493,000	3.0%
10	Connecticut	12,862,936,000	2.6%
11	Massachusetts	12,656,077,000	2.5%
12	New York	12,584,527,000	2.5%
13	Alabama	12,388,829,000	2.5%
14	Illinois	11,823,927,000	2.4%
15	Washington	11,526,956,000	2.3%
16	North Carolina	10,387,930,000	2.1%
17	Ohio	10,294,759,000	2.1%
18	Indiana	9,767,529,000	1.9%
19	New Jersey	9,443,071,000	1.9%
20	Kentucky	8,873,951,000	1.8%
21	Colorado	8,532,494,000	1.7%
22	South Carolina	7,843,732,000	1.6%
23	Michigan	7,756,312,000	1.5%
24	Hawaii	6,803,856,000	1.4%
25	Louisiana	6,750,148,000	1.3%
26	Mississippi	6,141,143,000	1.2%
27	Oklahoma	5,364,454,000	1.1%
28	Kansas	5,301,011,000	1.1%
29	Tennessee	5,273,556,000	1.1%
30	Wisconsin	4,097,011,000	0.8%
31	Alaska	3,813,958,000	0.8%
32	Utah	3,746,666,000	0.7%
33	New Mexico	2,966,845,000	0.6%
34	Minnesota	2,791,078,000	0.6%
35	Nevada	2,386,818,000	0.5%
36	Oregon	2,218,851,000	0.4%
37	Arkansas	2,171,155,000	0.4%
38	New Hampshire	1,972,353,000	0.4%
39	Nebraska	1,782,951,000	0.4%
40	Maine	1,741,698,000	0.3%
41	Iowa	1,636,874,000	0.3%
42	Rhode Island	1,344,177,000	0.3%
43	South Dakota	822,948,000	0.2%
44	West Virginia	819,821,000	0.2%
45	Idaho	782,219,000	0.2%
46	North Dakota	751,877,000	0.2%
47	Montana	734,531,000	0.1%
48	Delaware	715,970,000	0.1%
49	Wyoming	544,424,000	0.1%
50	Vermont	541,963,000	0.1%
	District of Columbia	7,426,121,000	1.5%

Source: U.S. Department of Defense

"Atlas/Data Abstract for the United States" (http://siadapp.dmdc.osd.mil/personnel/L03/fy08/08top.htm)

*Expenditures for payroll, grants, and prime contracts ($25,000 or more) for civil and military functions. Does not include payroll, contracts, or grants to U.S. territories and other countries.

Per Capita U.S. Department of Defense Domestic Expenditures in 2008

National Per Capita = $1,648*

ALPHA ORDER

RANK	STATE	PER CAPITA
7	Alabama	$2,657
2	Alaska	5,557
9	Arizona	2,300
42	Arkansas	760
23	California	1,383
16	Colorado	1,727
4	Connecticut	3,674
40	Delaware	820
29	Florida	1,144
17	Georgia	1,581
3	Hawaii	5,282
49	Idaho	513
36	Illinois	916
18	Indiana	1,532
47	Iowa	545
13	Kansas	1,892
11	Kentucky	2,079
19	Louisiana	1,530
26	Maine	1,323
5	Maryland	3,348
12	Massachusetts	1,948
41	Michigan	775
48	Minnesota	535
10	Mississippi	2,090
8	Missouri	2,501
43	Montana	759
34	Nebraska	1,000
35	Nevada	918
20	New Hampshire	1,499
31	New Jersey	1,088
21	New Mexico	1,495
45	New York	646
30	North Carolina	1,126
28	North Dakota	1,172
37	Ohio	896
22	Oklahoma	1,473
46	Oregon	585
24	Pennsylvania	1,380
27	Rhode Island	1,279
15	South Carolina	1,751
32	South Dakota	1,023
39	Tennessee	849
6	Texas	2,689
25	Utah	1,369
38	Vermont	872
1	Virginia	7,018
14	Washington	1,760
50	West Virginia	452
44	Wisconsin	728
33	Wyoming	1,022

RANK ORDER

RANK	STATE	PER CAPITA
1	Virginia	$7,018
2	Alaska	5,557
3	Hawaii	5,282
4	Connecticut	3,674
5	Maryland	3,348
6	Texas	2,689
7	Alabama	2,657
8	Missouri	2,501
9	Arizona	2,300
10	Mississippi	2,090
11	Kentucky	2,079
12	Massachusetts	1,948
13	Kansas	1,892
14	Washington	1,760
15	South Carolina	1,751
16	Colorado	1,727
17	Georgia	1,581
18	Indiana	1,532
19	Louisiana	1,530
20	New Hampshire	1,499
21	New Mexico	1,495
22	Oklahoma	1,473
23	California	1,383
24	Pennsylvania	1,380
25	Utah	1,369
26	Maine	1,323
27	Rhode Island	1,279
28	North Dakota	1,172
29	Florida	1,144
30	North Carolina	1,126
31	New Jersey	1,088
32	South Dakota	1,023
33	Wyoming	1,022
34	Nebraska	1,000
35	Nevada	918
36	Illinois	916
37	Ohio	896
38	Vermont	872
39	Tennessee	849
40	Delaware	820
41	Michigan	775
42	Arkansas	760
43	Montana	759
44	Wisconsin	728
45	New York	646
46	Oregon	585
47	Iowa	545
48	Minnesota	535
49	Idaho	513
50	West Virginia	452

District of Columbia   12,548

Source: CQ Press using data from U.S. Department of Defense
   "Atlas/Data Abstract for the United States" (http://siadapp.dmdc.osd.mil/personnel/L03/fy08/08top.htm)
*Expenditures for payroll, grants, and prime contracts ($25,000 or more) for civil and military functions. Does not include payroll, contracts, or grants to U.S. territories and other countries.

U.S. Department of Defense Total Contracts in 2008

National Total = $349,557,369,000*

ALPHA ORDER

RANK	STATE	CONTRACTS	% of USA
13	Alabama	$8,441,882,000	2.4%
31	Alaska	2,015,818,000	0.6%
7	Arizona	12,247,557,000	3.5%
40	Arkansas	828,306,000	0.2%
3	California	37,819,506,000	10.8%
22	Colorado	4,876,852,000	1.4%
9	Connecticut	12,208,015,000	3.5%
47	Delaware	225,151,000	0.1%
6	Florida	12,393,640,000	3.5%
15	Georgia	7,406,624,000	2.1%
29	Hawaii	2,258,591,000	0.6%
50	Idaho	164,483,000	0.0%
12	Illinois	9,180,322,000	2.6%
14	Indiana	7,996,420,000	2.3%
38	Iowa	1,071,040,000	0.3%
28	Kansas	3,000,420,000	0.9%
19	Kentucky	5,677,008,000	1.6%
23	Louisiana	4,840,348,000	1.4%
39	Maine	869,553,000	0.2%
5	Maryland	13,137,520,000	3.8%
10	Massachusetts	11,283,433,000	3.2%
18	Michigan	6,188,117,000	1.8%
32	Minnesota	1,913,486,000	0.5%
24	Mississippi	4,391,500,000	1.3%
8	Missouri	12,212,362,000	3.5%
46	Montana	246,660,000	0.1%
41	Nebraska	788,584,000	0.2%
37	Nevada	1,131,137,000	0.3%
34	New Hampshire	1,606,367,000	0.5%
16	New Jersey	7,194,152,000	2.1%
35	New Mexico	1,508,491,000	0.4%
11	New York	9,398,099,000	2.7%
25	North Carolina	3,646,609,000	1.0%
49	North Dakota	187,731,000	0.1%
17	Ohio	6,937,930,000	2.0%
30	Oklahoma	2,032,428,000	0.6%
36	Oregon	1,343,170,000	0.4%
4	Pennsylvania	13,587,534,000	3.9%
42	Rhode Island	682,367,000	0.2%
21	South Carolina	4,972,682,000	1.4%
43	South Dakota	404,485,000	0.1%
26	Tennessee	3,475,185,000	1.0%
1	Texas	51,905,267,000	14.8%
33	Utah	1,895,267,000	0.5%
45	Vermont	346,511,000	0.1%
2	Virginia	39,384,200,000	11.3%
20	Washington	5,598,464,000	1.6%
44	West Virginia	357,089,000	0.1%
27	Wisconsin	3,303,145,000	0.9%
48	Wyoming	205,552,000	0.1%

RANK ORDER

RANK	STATE	CONTRACTS	% of USA
1	Texas	$51,905,267,000	14.8%
2	Virginia	39,384,200,000	11.3%
3	California	37,819,506,000	10.8%
4	Pennsylvania	13,587,534,000	3.9%
5	Maryland	13,137,520,000	3.8%
6	Florida	12,393,640,000	3.5%
7	Arizona	12,247,557,000	3.5%
8	Missouri	12,212,362,000	3.5%
9	Connecticut	12,208,015,000	3.5%
10	Massachusetts	11,283,433,000	3.2%
11	New York	9,398,099,000	2.7%
12	Illinois	9,180,322,000	2.6%
13	Alabama	8,441,882,000	2.4%
14	Indiana	7,996,420,000	2.3%
15	Georgia	7,406,624,000	2.1%
16	New Jersey	7,194,152,000	2.1%
17	Ohio	6,937,930,000	2.0%
18	Michigan	6,188,117,000	1.8%
19	Kentucky	5,677,008,000	1.6%
20	Washington	5,598,464,000	1.6%
21	South Carolina	4,972,682,000	1.4%
22	Colorado	4,876,852,000	1.4%
23	Louisiana	4,840,348,000	1.4%
24	Mississippi	4,391,500,000	1.3%
25	North Carolina	3,646,609,000	1.0%
26	Tennessee	3,475,185,000	1.0%
27	Wisconsin	3,303,145,000	0.9%
28	Kansas	3,000,420,000	0.9%
29	Hawaii	2,258,591,000	0.6%
30	Oklahoma	2,032,428,000	0.6%
31	Alaska	2,015,818,000	0.6%
32	Minnesota	1,913,486,000	0.5%
33	Utah	1,895,267,000	0.5%
34	New Hampshire	1,606,367,000	0.5%
35	New Mexico	1,508,491,000	0.4%
36	Oregon	1,343,170,000	0.4%
37	Nevada	1,131,137,000	0.3%
38	Iowa	1,071,040,000	0.3%
39	Maine	869,553,000	0.2%
40	Arkansas	828,306,000	0.2%
41	Nebraska	788,584,000	0.2%
42	Rhode Island	682,367,000	0.2%
43	South Dakota	404,485,000	0.1%
44	West Virginia	357,089,000	0.1%
45	Vermont	346,511,000	0.1%
46	Montana	246,660,000	0.1%
47	Delaware	225,151,000	0.1%
48	Wyoming	205,552,000	0.1%
49	North Dakota	187,731,000	0.1%
50	Idaho	164,483,000	0.0%
	District of Columbia	4,770,309,000	1.4%

Source: U.S. Department of Defense
"Atlas/Data Abstract for the United States" (http://siadapp.dmdc.osd.mil/personnel/L03/fy08/08top.htm)
*Includes prime contracts ($25,000 or more) for civil and military functions. Does not include contracts to U.S. territories and other countries.

Per Capita U.S. Department of Defense Total Contracts in 2008

National Per Capita = $1,150*

ALPHA ORDER

RANK	STATE	PER CAPITA
8	Alabama	$1,811
3	Alaska	2,937
7	Arizona	1,884
46	Arkansas	290
19	California	1,029
20	Colorado	987
2	Connecticut	3,487
47	Delaware	258
27	Florida	676
23	Georgia	765
9	Hawaii	1,753
50	Idaho	108
25	Illinois	712
13	Indiana	1,254
43	Iowa	357
18	Kansas	1,071
12	Kentucky	1,330
16	Louisiana	1,097
28	Maine	661
4	Maryland	2,332
10	Massachusetts	1,736
30	Michigan	619
42	Minnesota	367
11	Mississippi	1,494
6	Missouri	2,066
48	Montana	255
38	Nebraska	442
39	Nevada	435
14	New Hampshire	1,221
22	New Jersey	829
24	New Mexico	760
37	New York	482
40	North Carolina	395
45	North Dakota	293
31	Ohio	604
34	Oklahoma	558
44	Oregon	354
17	Pennsylvania	1,092
29	Rhode Island	649
15	South Carolina	1,110
36	South Dakota	503
33	Tennessee	559
5	Texas	2,134
26	Utah	693
34	Vermont	558
1	Virginia	5,069
21	Washington	855
49	West Virginia	197
32	Wisconsin	587
41	Wyoming	386

RANK ORDER

RANK	STATE	PER CAPITA
1	Virginia	$5,069
2	Connecticut	3,487
3	Alaska	2,937
4	Maryland	2,332
5	Texas	2,134
6	Missouri	2,066
7	Arizona	1,884
8	Alabama	1,811
9	Hawaii	1,753
10	Massachusetts	1,736
11	Mississippi	1,494
12	Kentucky	1,330
13	Indiana	1,254
14	New Hampshire	1,221
15	South Carolina	1,110
16	Louisiana	1,097
17	Pennsylvania	1,092
18	Kansas	1,071
19	California	1,029
20	Colorado	987
21	Washington	855
22	New Jersey	829
23	Georgia	765
24	New Mexico	760
25	Illinois	712
26	Utah	693
27	Florida	676
28	Maine	661
29	Rhode Island	649
30	Michigan	619
31	Ohio	604
32	Wisconsin	587
33	Tennessee	559
34	Oklahoma	558
34	Vermont	558
36	South Dakota	503
37	New York	482
38	Nebraska	442
39	Nevada	435
40	North Carolina	395
41	Wyoming	386
42	Minnesota	367
43	Iowa	357
44	Oregon	354
45	North Dakota	293
46	Arkansas	290
47	Delaware	258
48	Montana	255
49	West Virginia	197
50	Idaho	108

District of Columbia   8,060

Source: CQ Press using data from U.S. Department of Defense
   "Atlas/Data Abstract for the United States" (http://siadapp.dmdc.osd.mil/personnel/L03/fy08/08top.htm)
*Includes prime contracts ($25,000 or more) for civil and military functions. Does not include contracts to U.S. territories and other countries.

U.S. Department of Defense Grants in 2008

National Total = $4,693,564,000*

ALPHA ORDER

RANK	STATE	GRANTS	% of USA
13	Alabama	$116,112,000	2.5%
34	Alaska	45,510,000	1.0%
31	Arizona	50,216,000	1.1%
30	Arkansas	51,099,000	1.1%
1	California	463,129,000	9.9%
24	Colorado	72,112,000	1.5%
22	Connecticut	74,978,000	1.6%
43	Delaware	30,308,000	0.6%
6	Florida	190,373,000	4.1%
16	Georgia	95,246,000	2.0%
27	Hawaii	57,010,000	1.2%
39	Idaho	34,092,000	0.7%
8	Illinois	153,527,000	3.3%
15	Indiana	101,864,000	2.2%
25	Iowa	69,301,000	1.5%
23	Kansas	73,932,000	1.6%
38	Kentucky	36,873,000	0.8%
28	Louisiana	56,735,000	1.2%
32	Maine	49,814,000	1.1%
3	Maryland	304,204,000	6.5%
5	Massachusetts	202,422,000	4.3%
11	Michigan	121,335,000	2.6%
20	Minnesota	81,199,000	1.7%
48	Mississippi	19,612,000	0.4%
19	Missouri	86,540,000	1.8%
29	Montana	53,107,000	1.1%
37	Nebraska	38,274,000	0.8%
45	Nevada	24,682,000	0.5%
40	New Hampshire	31,958,000	0.7%
17	New Jersey	88,731,000	1.9%
42	New Mexico	30,608,000	0.7%
7	New York	175,151,000	3.7%
18	North Carolina	88,532,000	1.9%
41	North Dakota	31,323,000	0.7%
14	Ohio	108,538,000	2.3%
10	Oklahoma	123,510,000	2.6%
21	Oregon	75,704,000	1.6%
4	Pennsylvania	226,037,000	4.8%
46	Rhode Island	24,626,000	0.5%
33	South Carolina	46,158,000	1.0%
47	South Dakota	20,495,000	0.4%
44	Tennessee	26,553,000	0.6%
2	Texas	342,295,000	7.3%
35	Utah	41,672,000	0.9%
50	Vermont	18,581,000	0.4%
12	Virginia	118,496,000	2.5%
9	Washington	129,461,000	2.8%
36	West Virginia	41,614,000	0.9%
26	Wisconsin	59,658,000	1.3%
49	Wyoming	18,645,000	0.4%

RANK ORDER

RANK	STATE	GRANTS	% of USA
1	California	$463,129,000	9.9%
2	Texas	342,295,000	7.3%
3	Maryland	304,204,000	6.5%
4	Pennsylvania	226,037,000	4.8%
5	Massachusetts	202,422,000	4.3%
6	Florida	190,373,000	4.1%
7	New York	175,151,000	3.7%
8	Illinois	153,527,000	3.3%
9	Washington	129,461,000	2.8%
10	Oklahoma	123,510,000	2.6%
11	Michigan	121,335,000	2.6%
12	Virginia	118,496,000	2.5%
13	Alabama	116,112,000	2.5%
14	Ohio	108,538,000	2.3%
15	Indiana	101,864,000	2.2%
16	Georgia	95,246,000	2.0%
17	New Jersey	88,731,000	1.9%
18	North Carolina	88,532,000	1.9%
19	Missouri	86,540,000	1.8%
20	Minnesota	81,199,000	1.7%
21	Oregon	75,704,000	1.6%
22	Connecticut	74,978,000	1.6%
23	Kansas	73,932,000	1.6%
24	Colorado	72,112,000	1.5%
25	Iowa	69,301,000	1.5%
26	Wisconsin	59,658,000	1.3%
27	Hawaii	57,010,000	1.2%
28	Louisiana	56,735,000	1.2%
29	Montana	53,107,000	1.1%
30	Arkansas	51,099,000	1.1%
31	Arizona	50,216,000	1.1%
32	Maine	49,814,000	1.1%
33	South Carolina	46,158,000	1.0%
34	Alaska	45,510,000	1.0%
35	Utah	41,672,000	0.9%
36	West Virginia	41,614,000	0.9%
37	Nebraska	38,274,000	0.8%
38	Kentucky	36,873,000	0.8%
39	Idaho	34,092,000	0.7%
40	New Hampshire	31,958,000	0.7%
41	North Dakota	31,323,000	0.7%
42	New Mexico	30,608,000	0.7%
43	Delaware	30,308,000	0.6%
44	Tennessee	26,553,000	0.6%
45	Nevada	24,682,000	0.5%
46	Rhode Island	24,626,000	0.5%
47	South Dakota	20,495,000	0.4%
48	Mississippi	19,612,000	0.4%
49	Wyoming	18,645,000	0.4%
50	Vermont	18,581,000	0.4%
	District of Columbia	71,612,000	1.5%

Source: U.S. Department of Defense
   "Atlas/Data Abstract for the United States" (http://siadapp.dmdc.osd.mil/personnel/L03/fy08/08top.htm)
*Includes grants for civil and military functions. Does not include contracts to U.S. territories and other countries.

Per Capita U.S. Department of Defense Grants in 2008

National Per Capita = $15.44*

ALPHA ORDER

RANK	STATE	PER CAPITA
14	Alabama	$24.91
1	Alaska	66.31
48	Arizona	7.73
25	Arkansas	17.90
35	California	12.60
32	Colorado	14.60
21	Connecticut	21.41
8	Delaware	34.71
39	Florida	10.39
42	Georgia	9.83
5	Hawaii	44.26
19	Idaho	22.37
37	Illinois	11.90
26	Indiana	15.97
17	Iowa	23.08
12	Kansas	26.38
47	Kentucky	8.64
34	Louisiana	12.86
6	Maine	37.84
3	Maryland	54.00
10	Massachusetts	31.15
36	Michigan	12.13
27	Minnesota	15.55
49	Mississippi	6.67
31	Missouri	14.64
2	Montana	54.89
20	Nebraska	21.46
44	Nevada	9.49
15	New Hampshire	24.29
41	New Jersey	10.22
28	New Mexico	15.42
46	New York	8.99
43	North Carolina	9.60
4	North Dakota	48.83
45	Ohio	9.45
9	Oklahoma	33.91
22	Oregon	19.97
24	Pennsylvania	18.16
16	Rhode Island	23.44
40	South Carolina	10.30
13	South Dakota	25.49
50	Tennessee	4.27
33	Texas	14.07
30	Utah	15.23
11	Vermont	29.91
29	Virginia	15.25
23	Washington	19.77
18	West Virginia	22.93
38	Wisconsin	10.60
7	Wyoming	35.00

RANK ORDER

RANK	STATE	PER CAPITA
1	Alaska	$66.31
2	Montana	54.89
3	Maryland	54.00
4	North Dakota	48.83
5	Hawaii	44.26
6	Maine	37.84
7	Wyoming	35.00
8	Delaware	34.71
9	Oklahoma	33.91
10	Massachusetts	31.15
11	Vermont	29.91
12	Kansas	26.38
13	South Dakota	25.49
14	Alabama	24.91
15	New Hampshire	24.29
16	Rhode Island	23.44
17	Iowa	23.08
18	West Virginia	22.93
19	Idaho	22.37
20	Nebraska	21.46
21	Connecticut	21.41
22	Oregon	19.97
23	Washington	19.77
24	Pennsylvania	18.16
25	Arkansas	17.90
26	Indiana	15.97
27	Minnesota	15.55
28	New Mexico	15.42
29	Virginia	15.25
30	Utah	15.23
31	Missouri	14.64
32	Colorado	14.60
33	Texas	14.07
34	Louisiana	12.86
35	California	12.60
36	Michigan	12.13
37	Illinois	11.90
38	Wisconsin	10.60
39	Florida	10.39
40	South Carolina	10.30
41	New Jersey	10.22
42	Georgia	9.83
43	North Carolina	9.60
44	Nevada	9.49
45	Ohio	9.45
46	New York	8.99
47	Kentucky	8.64
48	Arizona	7.73
49	Mississippi	6.67
50	Tennessee	4.27
	District of Columbia	121.00

Source: CQ Press using data from U.S. Department of Defense
   "Atlas/Data Abstract for the United States" (http://siadapp.dmdc.osd.mil/personnel/L03/fy08/08top.htm)
*Includes grants for civil and military functions. Does not include contracts to U.S. territories and other countries.

U.S. Department of Defense Domestic Personnel in 2008

National Total = 2,706,173 Personnel*

RANK	STATE	PERSONNEL	% of USA
16	Alabama	57,870	2.1%
29	Alaska	31,471	1.2%
20	Arizona	49,756	1.8%
32	Arkansas	24,504	0.9%
1	California	258,344	9.5%
17	Colorado	57,033	2.1%
43	Connecticut	11,715	0.4%
45	Delaware	10,607	0.4%
6	Florida	116,979	4.3%
5	Georgia	141,966	5.2%
11	Hawaii	67,916	2.5%
41	Idaho	13,271	0.5%
18	Illinois	56,990	2.1%
25	Indiana	34,873	1.3%
38	Iowa	16,252	0.6%
22	Kansas	41,634	1.5%
13	Kentucky	64,981	2.4%
21	Louisiana	44,175	1.6%
40	Maine	13,350	0.5%
8	Maryland	81,223	3.0%
30	Massachusetts	26,896	1.0%
28	Michigan	32,155	1.2%
31	Minnesota	26,375	1.0%
24	Mississippi	36,207	1.3%
19	Missouri	55,180	2.0%
44	Montana	10,733	0.4%
36	Nebraska	18,711	0.7%
35	Nevada	20,378	0.8%
49	New Hampshire	6,204	0.2%
23	New Jersey	40,963	1.5%
34	New Mexico	22,859	0.8%
9	New York	74,324	2.7%
4	North Carolina	149,641	5.5%
39	North Dakota	13,982	0.5%
14	Ohio	64,742	2.4%
15	Oklahoma	61,997	2.3%
37	Oregon	17,451	0.6%
10	Pennsylvania	68,932	2.5%
46	Rhode Island	10,420	0.4%
12	South Carolina	67,713	2.5%
47	South Dakota	10,246	0.4%
26	Tennessee	34,450	1.3%
2	Texas	245,978	9.1%
27	Utah	32,680	1.2%
50	Vermont	5,108	0.2%
3	Virginia	186,794	6.9%
7	Washington	93,181	3.4%
42	West Virginia	12,971	0.5%
33	Wisconsin	23,453	0.9%
48	Wyoming	8,107	0.3%

RANK	STATE	PERSONNEL	% of USA
1	California	258,344	9.5%
2	Texas	245,978	9.1%
3	Virginia	186,794	6.9%
4	North Carolina	149,641	5.5%
5	Georgia	141,966	5.2%
6	Florida	116,979	4.3%
7	Washington	93,181	3.4%
8	Maryland	81,223	3.0%
9	New York	74,324	2.7%
10	Pennsylvania	68,932	2.5%
11	Hawaii	67,916	2.5%
12	South Carolina	67,713	2.5%
13	Kentucky	64,981	2.4%
14	Ohio	64,742	2.4%
15	Oklahoma	61,997	2.3%
16	Alabama	57,870	2.1%
17	Colorado	57,033	2.1%
18	Illinois	56,990	2.1%
19	Missouri	55,180	2.0%
20	Arizona	49,756	1.8%
21	Louisiana	44,175	1.6%
22	Kansas	41,634	1.5%
23	New Jersey	40,963	1.5%
24	Mississippi	36,207	1.3%
25	Indiana	34,873	1.3%
26	Tennessee	34,450	1.3%
27	Utah	32,680	1.2%
28	Michigan	32,155	1.2%
29	Alaska	31,471	1.2%
30	Massachusetts	26,896	1.0%
31	Minnesota	26,375	1.0%
32	Arkansas	24,504	0.9%
33	Wisconsin	23,453	0.9%
34	New Mexico	22,859	0.8%
35	Nevada	20,378	0.8%
36	Nebraska	18,711	0.7%
37	Oregon	17,451	0.6%
38	Iowa	16,252	0.6%
39	North Dakota	13,982	0.5%
40	Maine	13,350	0.5%
41	Idaho	13,271	0.5%
42	West Virginia	12,971	0.5%
43	Connecticut	11,715	0.4%
44	Montana	10,733	0.4%
45	Delaware	10,607	0.4%
46	Rhode Island	10,420	0.4%
47	South Dakota	10,246	0.4%
48	Wyoming	8,107	0.3%
49	New Hampshire	6,204	0.2%
50	Vermont	5,108	0.2%
	District of Columbia	32,432	1.2%

Source: U.S. Department of Defense
"Atlas/Data Abstract for the United States" (http://siadapp.dmdc.osd.mil/personnel/L03/fy08/08top.htm)
*Includes Active Duty Military, Civilian, Reserve, and National Guard personnel. Does not include personnel in U.S. territories or in other countries.

U.S. Department of Defense Active Duty Military Personnel in 2008

National Total = 1,009,000 Personnel*

ALPHA ORDER

RANK	STATE	PERSONNEL	% of USA
21	Alabama	9,485	0.9%
17	Alaska	20,827	2.1%
15	Arizona	21,371	2.1%
29	Arkansas	5,321	0.5%
2	California	117,637	11.7%
11	Colorado	29,527	2.9%
40	Connecticut	1,386	0.1%
32	Delaware	3,511	0.3%
6	Florida	42,346	4.2%
4	Georgia	70,495	7.0%
9	Hawaii	39,770	3.9%
31	Idaho	4,386	0.4%
22	Illinois	9,480	0.9%
44	Indiana	970	0.1%
48	Iowa	482	0.0%
16	Kansas	21,033	2.1%
8	Kentucky	41,288	4.1%
19	Louisiana	16,160	1.6%
46	Maine	808	0.1%
12	Maryland	27,659	2.7%
38	Massachusetts	2,283	0.2%
39	Michigan	1,639	0.2%
45	Minnesota	936	0.1%
24	Mississippi	8,317	0.8%
18	Missouri	18,520	1.8%
33	Montana	3,422	0.3%
27	Nebraska	6,226	0.6%
20	Nevada	9,745	1.0%
49	New Hampshire	389	0.0%
28	New Jersey	6,011	0.6%
23	New Mexico	8,943	0.9%
13	New York	23,454	2.3%
3	North Carolina	100,031	9.9%
26	North Dakota	6,626	0.7%
25	Ohio	6,723	0.7%
14	Oklahoma	22,005	2.2%
43	Oregon	971	0.1%
36	Pennsylvania	3,022	0.3%
42	Rhode Island	1,236	0.1%
10	South Carolina	35,425	3.5%
34	South Dakota	3,389	0.3%
37	Tennessee	2,285	0.2%
1	Texas	124,598	12.3%
30	Utah	4,926	0.5%
50	Vermont	256	0.0%
5	Virginia	66,324	6.6%
7	Washington	41,608	4.1%
47	West Virginia	747	0.1%
41	Wisconsin	1,267	0.1%
35	Wyoming	3,142	0.3%

RANK ORDER

RANK	STATE	PERSONNEL	% of USA
1	Texas	124,598	12.3%
2	California	117,637	11.7%
3	North Carolina	100,031	9.9%
4	Georgia	70,495	7.0%
5	Virginia	66,324	6.6%
6	Florida	42,346	4.2%
7	Washington	41,608	4.1%
8	Kentucky	41,288	4.1%
9	Hawaii	39,770	3.9%
10	South Carolina	35,425	3.5%
11	Colorado	29,527	2.9%
12	Maryland	27,659	2.7%
13	New York	23,454	2.3%
14	Oklahoma	22,005	2.2%
15	Arizona	21,371	2.1%
16	Kansas	21,033	2.1%
17	Alaska	20,827	2.1%
18	Missouri	18,520	1.8%
19	Louisiana	16,160	1.6%
20	Nevada	9,745	1.0%
21	Alabama	9,485	0.9%
22	Illinois	9,480	0.9%
23	New Mexico	8,943	0.9%
24	Mississippi	8,317	0.8%
25	Ohio	6,723	0.7%
26	North Dakota	6,626	0.7%
27	Nebraska	6,226	0.6%
28	New Jersey	6,011	0.6%
29	Arkansas	5,321	0.5%
30	Utah	4,926	0.5%
31	Idaho	4,386	0.4%
32	Delaware	3,511	0.3%
33	Montana	3,422	0.3%
34	South Dakota	3,389	0.3%
35	Wyoming	3,142	0.3%
36	Pennsylvania	3,022	0.3%
37	Tennessee	2,285	0.2%
38	Massachusetts	2,283	0.2%
39	Michigan	1,639	0.2%
40	Connecticut	1,386	0.1%
41	Wisconsin	1,267	0.1%
42	Rhode Island	1,236	0.1%
43	Oregon	971	0.1%
44	Indiana	970	0.1%
45	Minnesota	936	0.1%
46	Maine	808	0.1%
47	West Virginia	747	0.1%
48	Iowa	482	0.0%
49	New Hampshire	389	0.0%
50	Vermont	256	0.0%
	District of Columbia	10,592	1.0%

Source: U.S. Department of Defense
"Atlas/Data Abstract for the United States" (http://siadapp.dmdc.osd.mil/personnel/L03/fy08/08top.htm)
*Does not include active duty personnel in U.S. territories, in other countries or others undistributed.

U.S. Department of Defense Domestic Civilian Personnel in 2008

National Total = 665,467 Personnel*

ALPHA ORDER

RANK	STATE	PERSONNEL	% of USA
9	Alabama	23,446	3.5%
32	Alaska	4,933	0.7%
22	Arizona	9,140	1.4%
34	Arkansas	4,066	0.6%
2	California	57,186	8.6%
18	Colorado	10,896	1.6%
39	Connecticut	2,428	0.4%
45	Delaware	1,582	0.2%
6	Florida	26,458	4.0%
4	Georgia	35,110	5.3%
13	Hawaii	17,340	2.6%
43	Idaho	1,642	0.2%
14	Illinois	14,653	2.2%
19	Indiana	9,998	1.5%
44	Iowa	1,637	0.2%
27	Kansas	6,945	1.0%
25	Kentucky	8,096	1.2%
31	Louisiana	6,397	1.0%
28	Maine	6,767	1.0%
5	Maryland	32,521	4.9%
30	Massachusetts	6,404	1.0%
24	Michigan	8,320	1.3%
37	Minnesota	2,656	0.4%
23	Mississippi	8,714	1.3%
21	Missouri	9,257	1.4%
46	Montana	1,474	0.2%
35	Nebraska	3,486	0.5%
40	Nevada	2,190	0.3%
49	New Hampshire	992	0.1%
15	New Jersey	14,426	2.2%
29	New Mexico	6,652	1.0%
17	New York	11,807	1.8%
12	North Carolina	19,164	2.9%
42	North Dakota	1,820	0.3%
10	Ohio	23,120	3.5%
11	Oklahoma	20,845	3.1%
36	Oregon	3,281	0.5%
7	Pennsylvania	26,041	3.9%
33	Rhode Island	4,213	0.6%
20	South Carolina	9,748	1.5%
47	South Dakota	1,287	0.2%
26	Tennessee	7,507	1.1%
3	Texas	45,056	6.8%
16	Utah	14,258	2.1%
50	Vermont	651	0.1%
1	Virginia	84,492	12.7%
8	Washington	25,969	3.9%
41	West Virginia	1,848	0.3%
38	Wisconsin	2,524	0.4%
48	Wyoming	1,078	0.2%

RANK ORDER

RANK	STATE	PERSONNEL	% of USA
1	Virginia	84,492	12.7%
2	California	57,186	8.6%
3	Texas	45,056	6.8%
4	Georgia	35,110	5.3%
5	Maryland	32,521	4.9%
6	Florida	26,458	4.0%
7	Pennsylvania	26,041	3.9%
8	Washington	25,969	3.9%
9	Alabama	23,446	3.5%
10	Ohio	23,120	3.5%
11	Oklahoma	20,845	3.1%
12	North Carolina	19,164	2.9%
13	Hawaii	17,340	2.6%
14	Illinois	14,653	2.2%
15	New Jersey	14,426	2.2%
16	Utah	14,258	2.1%
17	New York	11,807	1.8%
18	Colorado	10,896	1.6%
19	Indiana	9,998	1.5%
20	South Carolina	9,748	1.5%
21	Missouri	9,257	1.4%
22	Arizona	9,140	1.4%
23	Mississippi	8,714	1.3%
24	Michigan	8,320	1.3%
25	Kentucky	8,096	1.2%
26	Tennessee	7,507	1.1%
27	Kansas	6,945	1.0%
28	Maine	6,767	1.0%
29	New Mexico	6,652	1.0%
30	Massachusetts	6,404	1.0%
31	Louisiana	6,397	1.0%
32	Alaska	4,933	0.7%
33	Rhode Island	4,213	0.6%
34	Arkansas	4,066	0.6%
35	Nebraska	3,486	0.5%
36	Oregon	3,281	0.5%
37	Minnesota	2,656	0.4%
38	Wisconsin	2,524	0.4%
39	Connecticut	2,428	0.4%
40	Nevada	2,190	0.3%
41	West Virginia	1,848	0.3%
42	North Dakota	1,820	0.3%
43	Idaho	1,642	0.2%
44	Iowa	1,637	0.2%
45	Delaware	1,582	0.2%
46	Montana	1,474	0.2%
47	South Dakota	1,287	0.2%
48	Wyoming	1,078	0.2%
49	New Hampshire	992	0.1%
50	Vermont	651	0.1%
	District of Columbia	14,946	2.2%

Source: U.S. Department of Defense
    "Atlas/Data Abstract for the United States" (http://siadapp.dmdc.osd.mil/personnel/L03/fy08/08top.htm)
*Does not include civilian personnel in U.S. territories or civilian personnel in other countries. Includes military and civil functions.

U.S. Department of Defense Reserve and National Guard Personnel in 2008

National Total = 1,031,706 Personnel*

ALPHA ORDER

RANK	STATE	PERSONNEL	% of USA
13	Alabama	24,939	2.4%
43	Alaska	5,711	0.6%
23	Arizona	19,245	1.9%
29	Arkansas	15,117	1.5%
1	California	83,521	8.1%
27	Colorado	16,610	1.6%
38	Connecticut	7,901	0.8%
46	Delaware	5,514	0.5%
3	Florida	48,175	4.7%
6	Georgia	36,361	3.5%
34	Hawaii	10,806	1.0%
40	Idaho	7,243	0.7%
9	Illinois	32,857	3.2%
15	Indiana	23,905	2.3%
30	Iowa	14,133	1.4%
31	Kansas	13,656	1.3%
28	Kentucky	15,597	1.5%
19	Louisiana	21,618	2.1%
42	Maine	5,775	0.6%
20	Maryland	21,043	2.0%
26	Massachusetts	18,209	1.8%
18	Michigan	22,196	2.2%
16	Minnesota	22,783	2.2%
24	Mississippi	19,176	1.9%
11	Missouri	27,403	2.7%
41	Montana	5,837	0.6%
36	Nebraska	8,999	0.9%
37	Nevada	8,443	0.8%
48	New Hampshire	4,823	0.5%
21	New Jersey	20,526	2.0%
39	New Mexico	7,264	0.7%
5	New York	39,063	3.8%
10	North Carolina	30,446	3.0%
45	North Dakota	5,536	0.5%
8	Ohio	34,899	3.4%
25	Oklahoma	19,147	1.9%
33	Oregon	13,199	1.3%
4	Pennsylvania	39,869	3.9%
47	Rhode Island	4,971	0.5%
17	South Carolina	22,540	2.2%
44	South Dakota	5,570	0.5%
14	Tennessee	24,658	2.4%
2	Texas	76,324	7.4%
32	Utah	13,496	1.3%
49	Vermont	4,201	0.4%
7	Virginia	35,978	3.5%
12	Washington	25,604	2.5%
35	West Virginia	10,376	1.0%
22	Wisconsin	19,662	1.9%
50	Wyoming	3,887	0.4%

RANK ORDER

RANK	STATE	PERSONNEL	% of USA
1	California	83,521	8.1%
2	Texas	76,324	7.4%
3	Florida	48,175	4.7%
4	Pennsylvania	39,869	3.9%
5	New York	39,063	3.8%
6	Georgia	36,361	3.5%
7	Virginia	35,978	3.5%
8	Ohio	34,899	3.4%
9	Illinois	32,857	3.2%
10	North Carolina	30,446	3.0%
11	Missouri	27,403	2.7%
12	Washington	25,604	2.5%
13	Alabama	24,939	2.4%
14	Tennessee	24,658	2.4%
15	Indiana	23,905	2.3%
16	Minnesota	22,783	2.2%
17	South Carolina	22,540	2.2%
18	Michigan	22,196	2.2%
19	Louisiana	21,618	2.1%
20	Maryland	21,043	2.0%
21	New Jersey	20,526	2.0%
22	Wisconsin	19,662	1.9%
23	Arizona	19,245	1.9%
24	Mississippi	19,176	1.9%
25	Oklahoma	19,147	1.9%
26	Massachusetts	18,209	1.8%
27	Colorado	16,610	1.6%
28	Kentucky	15,597	1.5%
29	Arkansas	15,117	1.5%
30	Iowa	14,133	1.4%
31	Kansas	13,656	1.3%
32	Utah	13,496	1.3%
33	Oregon	13,199	1.3%
34	Hawaii	10,806	1.0%
35	West Virginia	10,376	1.0%
36	Nebraska	8,999	0.9%
37	Nevada	8,443	0.8%
38	Connecticut	7,901	0.8%
39	New Mexico	7,264	0.7%
40	Idaho	7,243	0.7%
41	Montana	5,837	0.6%
42	Maine	5,775	0.6%
43	Alaska	5,711	0.6%
44	South Dakota	5,570	0.5%
45	North Dakota	5,536	0.5%
46	Delaware	5,514	0.5%
47	Rhode Island	4,971	0.5%
48	New Hampshire	4,823	0.5%
49	Vermont	4,201	0.4%
50	Wyoming	3,887	0.4%
	District of Columbia	6,894	0.7%

Source: U.S. Department of Defense
 "Atlas/Data Abstract for the United States" (http://siadapp.dmdc.osd.mil/personnel/L03/fy08/08top.htm)
*Does not include reserve and national guard personnel in U.S. territories.

U.S. Department of Defense Total Compensation in 2008

National Total = $146,780,817,000*

ALPHA ORDER

RANK	STATE	COMPENSATION	% of USA
10	Alabama	$3,830,835,000	2.6%
26	Alaska	1,752,630,000	1.2%
18	Arizona	2,652,512,000	1.8%
31	Arkansas	1,291,750,000	0.9%
3	California	12,563,008,000	8.6%
11	Colorado	3,583,530,000	2.4%
41	Connecticut	579,943,000	0.4%
44	Delaware	460,511,000	0.3%
4	Florida	8,376,171,000	5.7%
5	Georgia	7,810,989,000	5.3%
9	Hawaii	4,488,255,000	3.1%
40	Idaho	583,644,000	0.4%
19	Illinois	2,490,078,000	1.7%
28	Indiana	1,669,245,000	1.1%
43	Iowa	496,533,000	0.3%
21	Kansas	2,226,659,000	1.5%
15	Kentucky	3,160,070,000	2.2%
23	Louisiana	1,853,065,000	1.3%
35	Maine	822,331,000	0.6%
8	Maryland	5,420,801,000	3.7%
33	Massachusetts	1,170,222,000	0.8%
29	Michigan	1,446,860,000	1.0%
37	Minnesota	796,393,000	0.5%
27	Mississippi	1,730,031,000	1.2%
20	Missouri	2,488,591,000	1.7%
45	Montana	434,764,000	0.3%
34	Nebraska	956,093,000	0.7%
32	Nevada	1,230,999,000	0.8%
48	New Hampshire	334,028,000	0.2%
22	New Jersey	2,160,188,000	1.5%
30	New Mexico	1,427,746,000	1.0%
16	New York	3,011,277,000	2.1%
6	North Carolina	6,652,789,000	4.5%
42	North Dakota	532,823,000	0.4%
13	Ohio	3,248,291,000	2.2%
14	Oklahoma	3,208,516,000	2.2%
36	Oregon	799,977,000	0.5%
12	Pennsylvania	3,365,305,000	2.3%
39	Rhode Island	637,184,000	0.4%
17	South Carolina	2,824,892,000	1.9%
47	South Dakota	397,968,000	0.3%
25	Tennessee	1,771,818,000	1.2%
2	Texas	13,172,454,000	9.0%
24	Utah	1,809,727,000	1.2%
50	Vermont	176,871,000	0.1%
1	Virginia	15,023,666,000	10.2%
7	Washington	5,799,031,000	4.0%
46	West Virginia	421,118,000	0.3%
38	Wisconsin	734,208,000	0.5%
49	Wyoming	320,227,000	0.2%

RANK ORDER

RANK	STATE	COMPENSATION	% of USA
1	Virginia	$15,023,666,000	10.2%
2	Texas	13,172,454,000	9.0%
3	California	12,563,008,000	8.6%
4	Florida	8,376,171,000	5.7%
5	Georgia	7,810,989,000	5.3%
6	North Carolina	6,652,789,000	4.5%
7	Washington	5,799,031,000	4.0%
8	Maryland	5,420,801,000	3.7%
9	Hawaii	4,488,255,000	3.1%
10	Alabama	3,830,835,000	2.6%
11	Colorado	3,583,530,000	2.4%
12	Pennsylvania	3,365,305,000	2.3%
13	Ohio	3,248,291,000	2.2%
14	Oklahoma	3,208,516,000	2.2%
15	Kentucky	3,160,070,000	2.2%
16	New York	3,011,277,000	2.1%
17	South Carolina	2,824,892,000	1.9%
18	Arizona	2,652,512,000	1.8%
19	Illinois	2,490,078,000	1.7%
20	Missouri	2,488,591,000	1.7%
21	Kansas	2,226,659,000	1.5%
22	New Jersey	2,160,188,000	1.5%
23	Louisiana	1,853,065,000	1.3%
24	Utah	1,809,727,000	1.2%
25	Tennessee	1,771,818,000	1.2%
26	Alaska	1,752,630,000	1.2%
27	Mississippi	1,730,031,000	1.2%
28	Indiana	1,669,245,000	1.1%
29	Michigan	1,446,860,000	1.0%
30	New Mexico	1,427,746,000	1.0%
31	Arkansas	1,291,750,000	0.9%
32	Nevada	1,230,999,000	0.8%
33	Massachusetts	1,170,222,000	0.8%
34	Nebraska	956,093,000	0.7%
35	Maine	822,331,000	0.6%
36	Oregon	799,977,000	0.5%
37	Minnesota	796,393,000	0.5%
38	Wisconsin	734,208,000	0.5%
39	Rhode Island	637,184,000	0.4%
40	Idaho	583,644,000	0.4%
41	Connecticut	579,943,000	0.4%
42	North Dakota	532,823,000	0.4%
43	Iowa	496,533,000	0.3%
44	Delaware	460,511,000	0.3%
45	Montana	434,764,000	0.3%
46	West Virginia	421,118,000	0.3%
47	South Dakota	397,968,000	0.3%
48	New Hampshire	334,028,000	0.2%
49	Wyoming	320,227,000	0.2%
50	Vermont	176,871,000	0.1%
	District of Columbia	2,584,200,000	1.8%

Source: U.S. Department of Defense
"Atlas/Data Abstract for the United States" (http://siadapp.dmdc.osd.mil/personnel/L03/fy08/08top.htm)
*Includes Civilian Pay, Military Active Duty Pay, Reserve, National Guard Pay, and Retired Military Pay. Based on location of recipient. Does not include recipients in U.S. territories and other countries.

U.S. Department of Defense Military Active Duty Pay in 2008

National Total = $52,159,197,000*

ALPHA ORDER

RANK	STATE	PAYROLL	% of USA
19	Alabama	$721,421,000	1.4%
14	Alaska	1,210,690,000	2.3%
17	Arizona	926,690,000	1.8%
28	Arkansas	335,575,000	0.6%
3	California	4,112,691,000	7.9%
10	Colorado	1,675,070,000	3.2%
39	Connecticut	155,900,000	0.3%
34	Delaware	189,109,000	0.4%
8	Florida	2,391,169,000	4.6%
5	Georgia	3,632,949,000	7.0%
6	Hawaii	2,715,315,000	5.2%
33	Idaho	217,359,000	0.4%
21	Illinois	574,505,000	1.1%
35	Indiana	187,851,000	0.4%
47	Iowa	75,122,000	0.1%
13	Kansas	1,273,008,000	2.4%
9	Kentucky	2,079,851,000	4.0%
18	Louisiana	832,561,000	1.6%
44	Maine	94,916,000	0.2%
11	Maryland	1,420,584,000	2.7%
32	Massachusetts	220,554,000	0.4%
41	Michigan	147,427,000	0.3%
43	Minnesota	113,434,000	0.2%
23	Mississippi	502,922,000	1.0%
20	Missouri	708,112,000	1.4%
37	Montana	163,792,000	0.3%
27	Nebraska	381,481,000	0.7%
22	Nevada	518,362,000	1.0%
49	New Hampshire	52,197,000	0.1%
26	New Jersey	404,392,000	0.8%
25	New Mexico	475,977,000	0.9%
12	New York	1,339,934,000	2.6%
4	North Carolina	3,667,592,000	7.0%
31	North Dakota	300,899,000	0.6%
24	Ohio	497,827,000	1.0%
15	Oklahoma	1,040,291,000	2.0%
45	Oregon	85,808,000	0.2%
29	Pennsylvania	317,632,000	0.6%
46	Rhode Island	85,325,000	0.2%
16	South Carolina	1,006,575,000	1.9%
38	South Dakota	159,437,000	0.3%
36	Tennessee	179,874,000	0.3%
1	Texas	6,151,030,000	11.8%
30	Utah	311,333,000	0.6%
50	Vermont	37,329,000	0.1%
2	Virginia	4,525,046,000	8.7%
7	Washington	2,511,799,000	4.8%
48	West Virginia	61,235,000	0.1%
42	Wisconsin	121,299,000	0.2%
40	Wyoming	150,244,000	0.3%

RANK ORDER

RANK	STATE	PAYROLL	% of USA
1	Texas	$6,151,030,000	11.8%
2	Virginia	4,525,046,000	8.7%
3	California	4,112,691,000	7.9%
4	North Carolina	3,667,592,000	7.0%
5	Georgia	3,632,949,000	7.0%
6	Hawaii	2,715,315,000	5.2%
7	Washington	2,511,799,000	4.8%
8	Florida	2,391,169,000	4.6%
9	Kentucky	2,079,851,000	4.0%
10	Colorado	1,675,070,000	3.2%
11	Maryland	1,420,584,000	2.7%
12	New York	1,339,934,000	2.6%
13	Kansas	1,273,008,000	2.4%
14	Alaska	1,210,690,000	2.3%
15	Oklahoma	1,040,291,000	2.0%
16	South Carolina	1,006,575,000	1.9%
17	Arizona	926,690,000	1.8%
18	Louisiana	832,561,000	1.6%
19	Alabama	721,421,000	1.4%
20	Missouri	708,112,000	1.4%
21	Illinois	574,505,000	1.1%
22	Nevada	518,362,000	1.0%
23	Mississippi	502,922,000	1.0%
24	Ohio	497,827,000	1.0%
25	New Mexico	475,977,000	0.9%
26	New Jersey	404,392,000	0.8%
27	Nebraska	381,481,000	0.7%
28	Arkansas	335,575,000	0.6%
29	Pennsylvania	317,632,000	0.6%
30	Utah	311,333,000	0.6%
31	North Dakota	300,899,000	0.6%
32	Massachusetts	220,554,000	0.4%
33	Idaho	217,359,000	0.4%
34	Delaware	189,109,000	0.4%
35	Indiana	187,851,000	0.4%
36	Tennessee	179,874,000	0.3%
37	Montana	163,792,000	0.3%
38	South Dakota	159,437,000	0.3%
39	Connecticut	155,900,000	0.3%
40	Wyoming	150,244,000	0.3%
41	Michigan	147,427,000	0.3%
42	Wisconsin	121,299,000	0.2%
43	Minnesota	113,434,000	0.2%
44	Maine	94,916,000	0.2%
45	Oregon	85,808,000	0.2%
46	Rhode Island	85,325,000	0.2%
47	Iowa	75,122,000	0.1%
48	West Virginia	61,235,000	0.1%
49	New Hampshire	52,197,000	0.1%
50	Vermont	37,329,000	0.1%
	District of Columbia	1,097,702,000	2.1%

Source: U.S. Department of Defense
"Atlas/Data Abstract for the United States" (http://siadapp.dmdc.osd.mil/personnel/L03/fy08/08top.htm)
*Based on location of recipient. Does not include recipients in U.S. territories and other countries.

U.S. Department of Defense Civilian Pay in 2008

National Total = $46,169,500,000*

ALPHA ORDER

RANK	STATE	PAYROLL	% of USA
8	Alabama	$1,768,760,000	3.8%
33	Alaska	329,137,000	0.7%
22	Arizona	564,296,000	1.2%
34	Arkansas	225,229,000	0.5%
2	California	4,345,009,000	9.4%
18	Colorado	706,492,000	1.5%
37	Connecticut	167,250,000	0.4%
43	Delaware	88,882,000	0.2%
7	Florida	1,774,968,000	3.8%
5	Georgia	2,174,930,000	4.7%
12	Hawaii	1,309,241,000	2.8%
44	Idaho	85,470,000	0.2%
16	Illinois	1,001,399,000	2.2%
19	Indiana	664,471,000	1.4%
45	Iowa	84,777,000	0.2%
31	Kansas	384,135,000	0.8%
28	Kentucky	439,846,000	1.0%
30	Louisiana	385,132,000	0.8%
25	Maine	479,539,000	1.0%
4	Maryland	2,694,968,000	5.8%
26	Massachusetts	475,443,000	1.0%
20	Michigan	658,104,000	1.4%
38	Minnesota	148,546,000	0.3%
23	Mississippi	539,937,000	1.2%
24	Missouri	527,351,000	1.1%
46	Montana	75,733,000	0.2%
35	Nebraska	217,367,000	0.5%
40	Nevada	125,582,000	0.3%
48	New Hampshire	63,882,000	0.1%
13	New Jersey	1,217,231,000	2.6%
27	New Mexico	460,503,000	1.0%
17	New York	726,054,000	1.6%
14	North Carolina	1,115,442,000	2.4%
42	North Dakota	94,615,000	0.2%
9	Ohio	1,703,191,000	3.7%
11	Oklahoma	1,321,156,000	2.9%
36	Oregon	212,315,000	0.5%
6	Pennsylvania	1,805,977,000	3.9%
32	Rhode Island	373,229,000	0.8%
21	South Carolina	574,785,000	1.2%
47	South Dakota	65,645,000	0.1%
29	Tennessee	431,870,000	0.9%
3	Texas	2,705,926,000	5.9%
15	Utah	1,007,352,000	2.2%
50	Vermont	31,038,000	0.1%
1	Virginia	6,479,499,000	14.0%
10	Washington	1,691,310,000	3.7%
41	West Virginia	105,793,000	0.2%
39	Wisconsin	133,631,000	0.3%
49	Wyoming	57,953,000	0.1%

RANK ORDER

RANK	STATE	PAYROLL	% of USA
1	Virginia	$6,479,499,000	14.0%
2	California	4,345,009,000	9.4%
3	Texas	2,705,926,000	5.9%
4	Maryland	2,694,968,000	5.8%
5	Georgia	2,174,930,000	4.7%
6	Pennsylvania	1,805,977,000	3.9%
7	Florida	1,774,968,000	3.8%
8	Alabama	1,768,760,000	3.8%
9	Ohio	1,703,191,000	3.7%
10	Washington	1,691,310,000	3.7%
11	Oklahoma	1,321,156,000	2.9%
12	Hawaii	1,309,241,000	2.8%
13	New Jersey	1,217,231,000	2.6%
14	North Carolina	1,115,442,000	2.4%
15	Utah	1,007,352,000	2.2%
16	Illinois	1,001,399,000	2.2%
17	New York	726,054,000	1.6%
18	Colorado	706,492,000	1.5%
19	Indiana	664,471,000	1.4%
20	Michigan	658,104,000	1.4%
21	South Carolina	574,785,000	1.2%
22	Arizona	564,296,000	1.2%
23	Mississippi	539,937,000	1.2%
24	Missouri	527,351,000	1.1%
25	Maine	479,539,000	1.0%
26	Massachusetts	475,443,000	1.0%
27	New Mexico	460,503,000	1.0%
28	Kentucky	439,846,000	1.0%
29	Tennessee	431,870,000	0.9%
30	Louisiana	385,132,000	0.8%
31	Kansas	384,135,000	0.8%
32	Rhode Island	373,229,000	0.8%
33	Alaska	329,137,000	0.7%
34	Arkansas	225,229,000	0.5%
35	Nebraska	217,367,000	0.5%
36	Oregon	212,315,000	0.5%
37	Connecticut	167,250,000	0.4%
38	Minnesota	148,546,000	0.3%
39	Wisconsin	133,631,000	0.3%
40	Nevada	125,582,000	0.3%
41	West Virginia	105,793,000	0.2%
42	North Dakota	94,615,000	0.2%
43	Delaware	88,882,000	0.2%
44	Idaho	85,470,000	0.2%
45	Iowa	84,777,000	0.2%
46	Montana	75,733,000	0.2%
47	South Dakota	65,645,000	0.1%
48	New Hampshire	63,882,000	0.1%
49	Wyoming	57,953,000	0.1%
50	Vermont	31,038,000	0.1%
	District of Columbia	1,349,109,000	2.9%

Source: U.S. Department of Defense
"Atlas/Data Abstract for the United States" (http://siadapp.dmdc.osd.mil/personnel/L03/fy08/08top.htm)
*Based on location of recipient. Does not include recipients in U.S. territories and other countries.

U.S. Department of Defense Reserve and National Guard Pay in 2008

National Total = $11,068,074,000*

RANK	STATE	PAYROLL	% of USA
10	Alabama	$329,973,000	3.0%
45	Alaska	49,537,000	0.4%
34	Arizona	107,508,000	1.0%
12	Arkansas	306,500,000	2.8%
1	California	694,806,000	6.3%
31	Colorado	141,239,000	1.3%
37	Connecticut	72,294,000	0.7%
48	Delaware	38,581,000	0.3%
6	Florida	416,397,000	3.8%
8	Georgia	379,449,000	3.4%
32	Hawaii	136,373,000	1.2%
42	Idaho	56,592,000	0.5%
14	Illinois	291,644,000	2.6%
4	Indiana	450,230,000	4.1%
29	Iowa	160,905,000	1.5%
28	Kansas	183,924,000	1.7%
25	Kentucky	209,722,000	1.9%
26	Louisiana	194,625,000	1.8%
47	Maine	44,920,000	0.4%
22	Maryland	230,854,000	2.1%
30	Massachusetts	160,068,000	1.4%
21	Michigan	231,184,000	2.1%
16	Minnesota	275,615,000	2.5%
18	Mississippi	248,349,000	2.2%
3	Missouri	645,998,000	5.8%
46	Montana	49,398,000	0.4%
35	Nebraska	95,580,000	0.9%
38	Nevada	71,713,000	0.6%
49	New Hampshire	36,797,000	0.3%
24	New Jersey	212,171,000	1.9%
39	New Mexico	70,636,000	0.6%
7	New York	409,835,000	3.7%
11	North Carolina	313,328,000	2.8%
41	North Dakota	63,552,000	0.6%
13	Ohio	306,361,000	2.8%
17	Oklahoma	274,587,000	2.5%
33	Oregon	127,471,000	1.2%
5	Pennsylvania	428,354,000	3.9%
40	Rhode Island	66,344,000	0.6%
20	South Carolina	241,639,000	2.2%
43	South Dakota	55,382,000	0.5%
15	Tennessee	281,697,000	2.5%
2	Texas	675,577,000	6.1%
23	Utah	220,423,000	2.0%
44	Vermont	50,438,000	0.5%
9	Virginia	330,950,000	3.0%
19	Washington	242,379,000	2.2%
36	West Virginia	90,594,000	0.8%
27	Wisconsin	190,929,000	1.7%
50	Wyoming	26,063,000	0.2%

RANK	STATE	PAYROLL	% of USA
1	California	$694,806,000	6.3%
2	Texas	675,577,000	6.1%
3	Missouri	645,998,000	5.8%
4	Indiana	450,230,000	4.1%
5	Pennsylvania	428,354,000	3.9%
6	Florida	416,397,000	3.8%
7	New York	409,835,000	3.7%
8	Georgia	379,449,000	3.4%
9	Virginia	330,950,000	3.0%
10	Alabama	329,973,000	3.0%
11	North Carolina	313,328,000	2.8%
12	Arkansas	306,500,000	2.8%
13	Ohio	306,361,000	2.8%
14	Illinois	291,644,000	2.6%
15	Tennessee	281,697,000	2.5%
16	Minnesota	275,615,000	2.5%
17	Oklahoma	274,587,000	2.5%
18	Mississippi	248,349,000	2.2%
19	Washington	242,379,000	2.2%
20	South Carolina	241,639,000	2.2%
21	Michigan	231,184,000	2.1%
22	Maryland	230,854,000	2.1%
23	Utah	220,423,000	2.0%
24	New Jersey	212,171,000	1.9%
25	Kentucky	209,722,000	1.9%
26	Louisiana	194,625,000	1.8%
27	Wisconsin	190,929,000	1.7%
28	Kansas	183,924,000	1.7%
29	Iowa	160,905,000	1.5%
30	Massachusetts	160,068,000	1.4%
31	Colorado	141,239,000	1.3%
32	Hawaii	136,373,000	1.2%
33	Oregon	127,471,000	1.2%
34	Arizona	107,508,000	1.0%
35	Nebraska	95,580,000	0.9%
36	West Virginia	90,594,000	0.8%
37	Connecticut	72,294,000	0.7%
38	Nevada	71,713,000	0.6%
39	New Mexico	70,636,000	0.6%
40	Rhode Island	66,344,000	0.6%
41	North Dakota	63,552,000	0.6%
42	Idaho	56,592,000	0.5%
43	South Dakota	55,382,000	0.5%
44	Vermont	50,438,000	0.5%
45	Alaska	49,537,000	0.4%
46	Montana	49,398,000	0.4%
47	Maine	44,920,000	0.4%
48	Delaware	38,581,000	0.3%
49	New Hampshire	36,797,000	0.3%
50	Wyoming	26,063,000	0.2%
	District of Columbia	78,589,000	0.7%

Source: U.S. Department of Defense
"Atlas/Data Abstract for the United States" (http://siadapp.dmdc.osd.mil/personnel/L03/fy08/08top.htm)
*Based on location of recipient. Does not include recipients in U.S. territories and other countries.

U.S. Department of Defense Retired Military Pay in 2008

National Total = $37,384,046,000*

RANK	STATE	PAYROLL	% of USA
11	Alabama	$1,010,681,000	2.7%
43	Alaska	163,266,000	0.4%
10	Arizona	1,054,018,000	2.8%
24	Arkansas	424,446,000	1.1%
4	California	3,410,502,000	9.1%
9	Colorado	1,060,729,000	2.8%
39	Connecticut	184,499,000	0.5%
45	Delaware	143,939,000	0.4%
1	Florida	3,793,637,000	10.1%
5	Georgia	1,623,661,000	4.3%
30	Hawaii	327,326,000	0.9%
37	Idaho	224,223,000	0.6%
16	Illinois	622,530,000	1.7%
29	Indiana	366,693,000	1.0%
41	Iowa	175,729,000	0.5%
27	Kansas	385,592,000	1.0%
23	Kentucky	430,651,000	1.2%
21	Louisiana	440,747,000	1.2%
38	Maine	202,956,000	0.5%
8	Maryland	1,074,395,000	2.9%
32	Massachusetts	314,157,000	0.8%
26	Michigan	410,145,000	1.1%
36	Minnesota	258,798,000	0.7%
22	Mississippi	438,823,000	1.2%
17	Missouri	607,130,000	1.6%
44	Montana	145,841,000	0.4%
35	Nebraska	261,665,000	0.7%
20	Nevada	515,342,000	1.4%
40	New Hampshire	181,152,000	0.5%
31	New Jersey	326,394,000	0.9%
25	New Mexico	420,630,000	1.1%
19	New York	535,454,000	1.4%
6	North Carolina	1,556,427,000	4.2%
49	North Dakota	73,757,000	0.2%
15	Ohio	740,912,000	2.0%
18	Oklahoma	572,482,000	1.5%
28	Oregon	374,383,000	1.0%
14	Pennsylvania	813,342,000	2.2%
47	Rhode Island	112,286,000	0.3%
12	South Carolina	1,001,893,000	2.7%
46	South Dakota	117,504,000	0.3%
13	Tennessee	878,377,000	2.3%
3	Texas	3,639,921,000	9.7%
34	Utah	270,619,000	0.7%
50	Vermont	58,066,000	0.2%
2	Virginia	3,688,171,000	9.9%
7	Washington	1,353,543,000	3.6%
42	West Virginia	163,496,000	0.4%
33	Wisconsin	288,349,000	0.8%
48	Wyoming	85,967,000	0.2%

RANK	STATE	PAYROLL	% of USA
1	Florida	$3,793,637,000	10.1%
2	Virginia	3,688,171,000	9.9%
3	Texas	3,639,921,000	9.7%
4	California	3,410,502,000	9.1%
5	Georgia	1,623,661,000	4.3%
6	North Carolina	1,556,427,000	4.2%
7	Washington	1,353,543,000	3.6%
8	Maryland	1,074,395,000	2.9%
9	Colorado	1,060,729,000	2.8%
10	Arizona	1,054,018,000	2.8%
11	Alabama	1,010,681,000	2.7%
12	South Carolina	1,001,893,000	2.7%
13	Tennessee	878,377,000	2.3%
14	Pennsylvania	813,342,000	2.2%
15	Ohio	740,912,000	2.0%
16	Illinois	622,530,000	1.7%
17	Missouri	607,130,000	1.6%
18	Oklahoma	572,482,000	1.5%
19	New York	535,454,000	1.4%
20	Nevada	515,342,000	1.4%
21	Louisiana	440,747,000	1.2%
22	Mississippi	438,823,000	1.2%
23	Kentucky	430,651,000	1.2%
24	Arkansas	424,446,000	1.1%
25	New Mexico	420,630,000	1.1%
26	Michigan	410,145,000	1.1%
27	Kansas	385,592,000	1.0%
28	Oregon	374,383,000	1.0%
29	Indiana	366,693,000	1.0%
30	Hawaii	327,326,000	0.9%
31	New Jersey	326,394,000	0.9%
32	Massachusetts	314,157,000	0.8%
33	Wisconsin	288,349,000	0.8%
34	Utah	270,619,000	0.7%
35	Nebraska	261,665,000	0.7%
36	Minnesota	258,798,000	0.7%
37	Idaho	224,223,000	0.6%
38	Maine	202,956,000	0.5%
39	Connecticut	184,499,000	0.5%
40	New Hampshire	181,152,000	0.5%
41	Iowa	175,729,000	0.5%
42	West Virginia	163,496,000	0.4%
43	Alaska	163,266,000	0.4%
44	Montana	145,841,000	0.4%
45	Delaware	143,939,000	0.4%
46	South Dakota	117,504,000	0.3%
47	Rhode Island	112,286,000	0.3%
48	Wyoming	85,967,000	0.2%
49	North Dakota	73,757,000	0.2%
50	Vermont	58,066,000	0.2%
	District of Columbia	58,800,000	0.2%

Source: U.S. Department of Defense
  "Atlas/Data Abstract for the United States" (http://siadapp.dmdc.osd.mil/personnel/L03/fy08/08top.htm)
*Based on location of recipient. Does not include recipients in U.S. territories and other countries.

Veterans in 2009

National Total = 23,066,965 Veterans*

ALPHA ORDER

RANK	STATE	VETERANS	% of USA
21	Alabama	409,997	1.8%
45	Alaska	76,468	0.3%
13	Arizona	561,387	2.4%
29	Arkansas	257,625	1.1%
1	California	2,025,934	8.8%
20	Colorado	424,228	1.8%
32	Connecticut	237,696	1.0%
44	Delaware	79,166	0.3%
3	Florida	1,683,899	7.3%
9	Georgia	772,832	3.4%
42	Hawaii	117,254	0.5%
40	Idaho	137,099	0.6%
8	Illinois	802,834	3.5%
16	Indiana	500,806	2.2%
31	Iowa	240,317	1.0%
33	Kansas	229,145	1.0%
26	Kentucky	339,942	1.5%
28	Louisiana	312,087	1.4%
39	Maine	140,552	0.6%
17	Maryland	476,202	2.1%
22	Massachusetts	409,184	1.8%
11	Michigan	723,368	3.1%
24	Minnesota	390,576	1.7%
34	Mississippi	209,242	0.9%
14	Missouri	514,724	2.2%
43	Montana	102,986	0.4%
38	Nebraska	147,928	0.6%
30	Nevada	245,064	1.1%
41	New Hampshire	129,629	0.6%
18	New Jersey	463,720	2.0%
35	New Mexico	176,566	0.8%
5	New York	988,217	4.3%
10	North Carolina	770,080	3.3%
48	North Dakota	57,074	0.2%
6	Ohio	913,296	4.0%
27	Oklahoma	329,601	1.4%
25	Oregon	340,020	1.5%
4	Pennsylvania	995,135	4.3%
46	Rhode Island	73,957	0.3%
23	South Carolina	408,747	1.8%
47	South Dakota	72,704	0.3%
15	Tennessee	501,907	2.2%
2	Texas	1,701,675	7.4%
37	Utah	155,052	0.7%
50	Vermont	53,222	0.2%
7	Virginia	819,490	3.6%
12	Washington	637,019	2.8%
36	West Virginia	170,783	0.7%
19	Wisconsin	427,527	1.9%
49	Wyoming	56,079	0.2%

RANK ORDER

RANK	STATE	VETERANS	% of USA
1	California	2,025,934	8.8%
2	Texas	1,701,675	7.4%
3	Florida	1,683,899	7.3%
4	Pennsylvania	995,135	4.3%
5	New York	988,217	4.3%
6	Ohio	913,296	4.0%
7	Virginia	819,490	3.6%
8	Illinois	802,834	3.5%
9	Georgia	772,832	3.4%
10	North Carolina	770,080	3.3%
11	Michigan	723,368	3.1%
12	Washington	637,019	2.8%
13	Arizona	561,387	2.4%
14	Missouri	514,724	2.2%
15	Tennessee	501,907	2.2%
16	Indiana	500,806	2.2%
17	Maryland	476,202	2.1%
18	New Jersey	463,720	2.0%
19	Wisconsin	427,527	1.9%
20	Colorado	424,228	1.8%
21	Alabama	409,997	1.8%
22	Massachusetts	409,184	1.8%
23	South Carolina	408,747	1.8%
24	Minnesota	390,576	1.7%
25	Oregon	340,020	1.5%
26	Kentucky	339,942	1.5%
27	Oklahoma	329,601	1.4%
28	Louisiana	312,087	1.4%
29	Arkansas	257,625	1.1%
30	Nevada	245,064	1.1%
31	Iowa	240,317	1.0%
32	Connecticut	237,696	1.0%
33	Kansas	229,145	1.0%
34	Mississippi	209,242	0.9%
35	New Mexico	176,566	0.8%
36	West Virginia	170,783	0.7%
37	Utah	155,052	0.7%
38	Nebraska	147,928	0.6%
39	Maine	140,552	0.6%
40	Idaho	137,099	0.6%
41	New Hampshire	129,629	0.6%
42	Hawaii	117,254	0.5%
43	Montana	102,986	0.4%
44	Delaware	79,166	0.3%
45	Alaska	76,468	0.3%
46	Rhode Island	73,957	0.3%
47	South Dakota	72,704	0.3%
48	North Dakota	57,074	0.2%
49	Wyoming	56,079	0.2%
50	Vermont	53,222	0.2%
	District of Columbia	37,948	0.2%

Source: U.S. Department of Veteran Affairs
   "Veteran Data and Information" (http://www1.va.gov/vetdata/page.cfm?pg=15)
*Estimates based on 2006 data. Includes 218,975 veterans in U.S. territories or other countries.

Percent of Adult Population Who Are Veterans: 2009

National Percent = 9.9%*

ALPHA ORDER				RANK ORDER		
RANK	**STATE**	**PERCENT**		**RANK**	**STATE**	**PERCENT**
20	Alabama	11.6		1	Alaska	15.1
1	Alaska	15.1		2	Wyoming	13.9
18	Arizona	11.7		3	Montana	13.8
10	Arkansas	12.0		3	Virginia	13.8
48	California	7.4		5	Maine	13.5
24	Colorado	11.4		6	Nevada	12.7
44	Connecticut	8.8		6	New Hampshire	12.7
15	Delaware	11.9		6	Washington	12.7
17	Florida	11.8		9	Idaho	12.3
29	Georgia	10.8		10	Arkansas	12.0
18	Hawaii	11.7		10	Oklahoma	12.0
9	Idaho	12.3		10	South Carolina	12.0
45	Illinois	8.3		10	South Dakota	12.0
32	Indiana	10.5		10	West Virginia	12.0
32	Iowa	10.5		15	Delaware	11.9
28	Kansas	10.9		15	New Mexico	11.9
34	Kentucky	10.4		17	Florida	11.8
42	Louisiana	9.4		18	Arizona	11.7
5	Maine	13.5		18	Hawaii	11.7
25	Maryland	11.1		20	Alabama	11.6
47	Massachusetts	8.1		20	Oregon	11.6
41	Michigan	9.5		22	Missouri	11.5
38	Minnesota	9.8		22	North Dakota	11.5
40	Mississippi	9.6		24	Colorado	11.4
22	Missouri	11.5		25	Maryland	11.1
3	Montana	13.8		25	Nebraska	11.1
25	Nebraska	11.1		27	North Carolina	11.0
6	Nevada	12.7		28	Kansas	10.9
6	New Hampshire	12.7		29	Georgia	10.8
49	New Jersey	7.0		29	Vermont	10.8
15	New Mexico	11.9		31	Tennessee	10.6
50	New York	6.6		32	Indiana	10.5
27	North Carolina	11.0		32	Iowa	10.5
22	North Dakota	11.5		34	Kentucky	10.4
34	Ohio	10.4		34	Ohio	10.4
10	Oklahoma	12.0		36	Pennsylvania	10.3
20	Oregon	11.6		37	Wisconsin	9.9
36	Pennsylvania	10.3		38	Minnesota	9.8
43	Rhode Island	9.0		39	Texas	9.7
10	South Carolina	12.0		40	Mississippi	9.6
10	South Dakota	12.0		41	Michigan	9.5
31	Tennessee	10.6		42	Louisiana	9.4
39	Texas	9.7		43	Rhode Island	9.0
46	Utah	8.2		44	Connecticut	8.8
29	Vermont	10.8		45	Illinois	8.3
3	Virginia	13.8		46	Utah	8.2
6	Washington	12.7		47	Massachusetts	8.1
10	West Virginia	12.0		48	California	7.4
37	Wisconsin	9.9		49	New Jersey	7.0
2	Wyoming	13.9		50	New York	6.6
					District of Columbia	7.9

Source: CQ Press using data from U.S. Department of Veteran Affairs
"Veteran Data and Information" (http://www1.va.gov/vetdata/page.cfm?pg=15)
*Estimates based on 2006 data. National figures does not include veterans in U.S. territories or other countries. Percent calculated with population 18 years old and older in 2008.

U.S. Military Fatalities in Iraq and Afghanistan as of January 30, 2010

National Total = 5,329 Fatalities*

ALPHA ORDER

RANK	STATE	FATALITIES	% of USA
24	Alabama	87	1.6%
46	Alaska	20	0.4%
12	Arizona	121	2.3%
29	Arkansas	67	1.3%
1	California	564	10.6%
27	Colorado	75	1.4%
39	Connecticut	34	0.6%
49	Delaware	16	0.3%
3	Florida	248	4.7%
9	Georgia	167	3.1%
43	Hawaii	27	0.5%
39	Idaho	34	0.6%
7	Illinois	207	3.9%
13	Indiana	119	2.2%
31	Iowa	55	1.0%
31	Kansas	55	1.0%
25	Kentucky	83	1.6%
19	Louisiana	99	1.9%
36	Maine	37	0.7%
20	Maryland	94	1.8%
17	Massachusetts	103	1.9%
8	Michigan	179	3.4%
26	Minnesota	76	1.4%
30	Mississippi	62	1.2%
15	Missouri	111	2.1%
38	Montana	35	0.7%
33	Nebraska	51	1.0%
34	Nevada	50	0.9%
42	New Hampshire	32	0.6%
22	New Jersey	90	1.7%
35	New Mexico	47	0.9%
4	New York	238	4.5%
11	North Carolina	135	2.5%
47	North Dakota	18	0.3%
6	Ohio	208	3.9%
21	Oklahoma	91	1.7%
22	Oregon	90	1.7%
5	Pennsylvania	237	4.4%
50	Rhode Island	11	0.2%
28	South Carolina	70	1.3%
45	South Dakota	22	0.4%
16	Tennessee	109	2.0%
2	Texas	476	8.9%
39	Utah	34	0.6%
44	Vermont	23	0.4%
10	Virginia	152	2.9%
14	Washington	115	2.2%
37	West Virginia	36	0.7%
17	Wisconsin	103	1.9%
48	Wyoming	17	0.3%

RANK ORDER

RANK	STATE	FATALITIES	% of USA
1	California	564	10.6%
2	Texas	476	8.9%
3	Florida	248	4.7%
4	New York	238	4.5%
5	Pennsylvania	237	4.4%
6	Ohio	208	3.9%
7	Illinois	207	3.9%
8	Michigan	179	3.4%
9	Georgia	167	3.1%
10	Virginia	152	2.9%
11	North Carolina	135	2.5%
12	Arizona	121	2.3%
13	Indiana	119	2.2%
14	Washington	115	2.2%
15	Missouri	111	2.1%
16	Tennessee	109	2.0%
17	Massachusetts	103	1.9%
17	Wisconsin	103	1.9%
19	Louisiana	99	1.9%
20	Maryland	94	1.8%
21	Oklahoma	91	1.7%
22	New Jersey	90	1.7%
22	Oregon	90	1.7%
24	Alabama	87	1.6%
25	Kentucky	83	1.6%
26	Minnesota	76	1.4%
27	Colorado	75	1.4%
28	South Carolina	70	1.3%
29	Arkansas	67	1.3%
30	Mississippi	62	1.2%
31	Iowa	55	1.0%
31	Kansas	55	1.0%
33	Nebraska	51	1.0%
34	Nevada	50	0.9%
35	New Mexico	47	0.9%
36	Maine	37	0.7%
37	West Virginia	36	0.7%
38	Montana	35	0.7%
39	Connecticut	34	0.6%
39	Idaho	34	0.6%
39	Utah	34	0.6%
42	New Hampshire	32	0.6%
43	Hawaii	27	0.5%
44	Vermont	23	0.4%
45	South Dakota	22	0.4%
46	Alaska	20	0.4%
47	North Dakota	18	0.3%
48	Wyoming	17	0.3%
49	Delaware	16	0.3%
50	Rhode Island	11	0.2%
	District of Columbia	8	0.2%

Source: U.S. Department of Defense, Statistical Information Analysis Department
"Military Casualty Information (http://siadapp.dmdc.osd.mil/personnel/CASUALTY/castop.htm)
*Total includes 91 deaths of soldiers from U.S. territories. Total does not include deaths of United Kingdom soldiers or other coalition nations. Includes 4,163 combat and 1,166 noncombat deaths. Includes 4,365 deaths in Iraq and 964 deaths in Afghanistan.

Rate of U.S. Military Fatalities in Iraq and Afghanistan as of January 30, 2010

National Rate = 1.7 Fatalities per 100,000 Population*

<table>
<tr><td colspan="3"><u>ALPHA ORDER</u></td><td colspan="3"><u>RANK ORDER</u></td></tr>
<tr><td>RANK</td><td>STATE</td><td>RATE</td><td>RANK</td><td>STATE</td><td>RATE</td></tr>
<tr><td>27</td><td>Alabama</td><td>1.8</td><td>1</td><td>Vermont</td><td>3.7</td></tr>
<tr><td>4</td><td>Alaska</td><td>2.9</td><td>2</td><td>Montana</td><td>3.6</td></tr>
<tr><td>27</td><td>Arizona</td><td>1.8</td><td>3</td><td>Wyoming</td><td>3.1</td></tr>
<tr><td>12</td><td>Arkansas</td><td>2.3</td><td>4</td><td>Alaska</td><td>2.9</td></tr>
<tr><td>40</td><td>California</td><td>1.5</td><td>5</td><td>Maine</td><td>2.8</td></tr>
<tr><td>40</td><td>Colorado</td><td>1.5</td><td>5</td><td>Nebraska</td><td>2.8</td></tr>
<tr><td>48</td><td>Connecticut</td><td>1.0</td><td>5</td><td>North Dakota</td><td>2.8</td></tr>
<tr><td>27</td><td>Delaware</td><td>1.8</td><td>8</td><td>South Dakota</td><td>2.7</td></tr>
<tr><td>45</td><td>Florida</td><td>1.3</td><td>9</td><td>Oklahoma</td><td>2.5</td></tr>
<tr><td>34</td><td>Georgia</td><td>1.7</td><td>10</td><td>New Hampshire</td><td>2.4</td></tr>
<tr><td>16</td><td>Hawaii</td><td>2.1</td><td>10</td><td>Oregon</td><td>2.4</td></tr>
<tr><td>14</td><td>Idaho</td><td>2.2</td><td>12</td><td>Arkansas</td><td>2.3</td></tr>
<tr><td>37</td><td>Illinois</td><td>1.6</td><td>12</td><td>New Mexico</td><td>2.3</td></tr>
<tr><td>20</td><td>Indiana</td><td>1.9</td><td>14</td><td>Idaho</td><td>2.2</td></tr>
<tr><td>27</td><td>Iowa</td><td>1.8</td><td>14</td><td>Louisiana</td><td>2.2</td></tr>
<tr><td>18</td><td>Kansas</td><td>2.0</td><td>16</td><td>Hawaii</td><td>2.1</td></tr>
<tr><td>20</td><td>Kentucky</td><td>1.9</td><td>16</td><td>Mississippi</td><td>2.1</td></tr>
<tr><td>14</td><td>Louisiana</td><td>2.2</td><td>18</td><td>Kansas</td><td>2.0</td></tr>
<tr><td>5</td><td>Maine</td><td>2.8</td><td>18</td><td>West Virginia</td><td>2.0</td></tr>
<tr><td>37</td><td>Maryland</td><td>1.6</td><td>20</td><td>Indiana</td><td>1.9</td></tr>
<tr><td>37</td><td>Massachusetts</td><td>1.6</td><td>20</td><td>Kentucky</td><td>1.9</td></tr>
<tr><td>27</td><td>Michigan</td><td>1.8</td><td>20</td><td>Missouri</td><td>1.9</td></tr>
<tr><td>43</td><td>Minnesota</td><td>1.4</td><td>20</td><td>Nevada</td><td>1.9</td></tr>
<tr><td>16</td><td>Mississippi</td><td>2.1</td><td>20</td><td>Pennsylvania</td><td>1.9</td></tr>
<tr><td>20</td><td>Missouri</td><td>1.9</td><td>20</td><td>Texas</td><td>1.9</td></tr>
<tr><td>2</td><td>Montana</td><td>3.6</td><td>20</td><td>Virginia</td><td>1.9</td></tr>
<tr><td>5</td><td>Nebraska</td><td>2.8</td><td>27</td><td>Alabama</td><td>1.8</td></tr>
<tr><td>20</td><td>Nevada</td><td>1.9</td><td>27</td><td>Arizona</td><td>1.8</td></tr>
<tr><td>10</td><td>New Hampshire</td><td>2.4</td><td>27</td><td>Delaware</td><td>1.8</td></tr>
<tr><td>48</td><td>New Jersey</td><td>1.0</td><td>27</td><td>Iowa</td><td>1.8</td></tr>
<tr><td>12</td><td>New Mexico</td><td>2.3</td><td>27</td><td>Michigan</td><td>1.8</td></tr>
<tr><td>46</td><td>New York</td><td>1.2</td><td>27</td><td>Ohio</td><td>1.8</td></tr>
<tr><td>43</td><td>North Carolina</td><td>1.4</td><td>27</td><td>Wisconsin</td><td>1.8</td></tr>
<tr><td>5</td><td>North Dakota</td><td>2.8</td><td>34</td><td>Georgia</td><td>1.7</td></tr>
<tr><td>27</td><td>Ohio</td><td>1.8</td><td>34</td><td>Tennessee</td><td>1.7</td></tr>
<tr><td>9</td><td>Oklahoma</td><td>2.5</td><td>34</td><td>Washington</td><td>1.7</td></tr>
<tr><td>10</td><td>Oregon</td><td>2.4</td><td>37</td><td>Illinois</td><td>1.6</td></tr>
<tr><td>20</td><td>Pennsylvania</td><td>1.9</td><td>37</td><td>Maryland</td><td>1.6</td></tr>
<tr><td>48</td><td>Rhode Island</td><td>1.0</td><td>37</td><td>Massachusetts</td><td>1.6</td></tr>
<tr><td>40</td><td>South Carolina</td><td>1.5</td><td>40</td><td>California</td><td>1.5</td></tr>
<tr><td>8</td><td>South Dakota</td><td>2.7</td><td>40</td><td>Colorado</td><td>1.5</td></tr>
<tr><td>34</td><td>Tennessee</td><td>1.7</td><td>40</td><td>South Carolina</td><td>1.5</td></tr>
<tr><td>20</td><td>Texas</td><td>1.9</td><td>43</td><td>Minnesota</td><td>1.4</td></tr>
<tr><td>48</td><td>Utah</td><td>1.2</td><td>43</td><td>North Carolina</td><td>1.4</td></tr>
<tr><td>1</td><td>Vermont</td><td>3.7</td><td>45</td><td>Florida</td><td>1.3</td></tr>
<tr><td>20</td><td>Virginia</td><td>1.9</td><td>46</td><td>New York</td><td>1.2</td></tr>
<tr><td>34</td><td>Washington</td><td>1.7</td><td>46</td><td>Utah</td><td>1.2</td></tr>
<tr><td>18</td><td>West Virginia</td><td>2.0</td><td>48</td><td>Connecticut</td><td>1.0</td></tr>
<tr><td>27</td><td>Wisconsin</td><td>1.8</td><td>48</td><td>New Jersey</td><td>1.0</td></tr>
<tr><td>3</td><td>Wyoming</td><td>3.1</td><td>48</td><td>Rhode Island</td><td>1.0</td></tr>
<tr><td></td><td></td><td></td><td></td><td>District of Columbia</td><td>1.3</td></tr>
</table>

Source: CQ Press using data from U.S. Department of Defense, Statistical Information Analysis Department
"Military Casualty Information (http://siadapp.dmdc.osd.mil/personnel/CASUALTY/castop.htm)
*National rate does not include deaths of soldiers from U.S. territories. Includes combat and noncombat deaths. Calculated with 2009 population estimates.

IV. Economy

Gross Domestic Product in 2008

National Total = $14,165,565,000,000*

ALPHA ORDER

RANK	STATE	G.D.P.	% of USA
25	Alabama	$170,014,000,000	1.2%
44	Alaska	47,912,000,000	0.3%
19	Arizona	248,888,000,000	1.8%
34	Arkansas	98,331,000,000	0.7%
1	California	1,846,757,000,000	13.0%
20	Colorado	248,603,000,000	1.8%
24	Connecticut	216,174,000,000	1.5%
39	Delaware	61,828,000,000	0.4%
4	Florida	744,120,000,000	5.3%
10	Georgia	397,756,000,000	2.8%
38	Hawaii	63,847,000,000	0.5%
42	Idaho	52,747,000,000	0.4%
5	Illinois	633,697,000,000	4.5%
17	Indiana	254,861,000,000	1.8%
30	Iowa	135,702,000,000	1.0%
32	Kansas	122,731,000,000	0.9%
27	Kentucky	156,436,000,000	1.1%
23	Louisiana	222,218,000,000	1.6%
43	Maine	49,709,000,000	0.4%
15	Maryland	273,333,000,000	1.9%
13	Massachusetts	364,988,000,000	2.6%
12	Michigan	382,544,000,000	2.7%
16	Minnesota	262,847,000,000	1.9%
35	Mississippi	91,782,000,000	0.6%
22	Missouri	237,797,000,000	1.7%
47	Montana	35,891,000,000	0.3%
36	Nebraska	83,273,000,000	0.6%
31	Nevada	131,233,000,000	0.9%
41	New Hampshire	60,005,000,000	0.4%
7	New Jersey	474,936,000,000	3.4%
37	New Mexico	79,901,000,000	0.6%
3	New York	1,144,481,000,000	8.1%
9	North Carolina	400,192,000,000	2.8%
49	North Dakota	31,208,000,000	0.2%
8	Ohio	471,508,000,000	3.3%
29	Oklahoma	146,448,000,000	1.0%
26	Oregon	161,573,000,000	1.1%
6	Pennsylvania	553,301,000,000	3.9%
45	Rhode Island	47,364,000,000	0.3%
28	South Carolina	156,384,000,000	1.1%
46	South Dakota	36,959,000,000	0.3%
18	Tennessee	252,127,000,000	1.8%
2	Texas	1,223,511,000,000	8.6%
33	Utah	109,777,000,000	0.8%
50	Vermont	25,442,000,000	0.2%
11	Virginia	397,025,000,000	2.8%
14	Washington	322,778,000,000	2.3%
40	West Virginia	61,652,000,000	0.4%
21	Wisconsin	240,429,000,000	1.7%
48	Wyoming	35,310,000,000	0.2%

RANK ORDER

RANK	STATE	G.D.P.	% of USA
1	California	$1,846,757,000,000	13.0%
2	Texas	1,223,511,000,000	8.6%
3	New York	1,144,481,000,000	8.1%
4	Florida	744,120,000,000	5.3%
5	Illinois	633,697,000,000	4.5%
6	Pennsylvania	553,301,000,000	3.9%
7	New Jersey	474,936,000,000	3.4%
8	Ohio	471,508,000,000	3.3%
9	North Carolina	400,192,000,000	2.8%
10	Georgia	397,756,000,000	2.8%
11	Virginia	397,025,000,000	2.8%
12	Michigan	382,544,000,000	2.7%
13	Massachusetts	364,988,000,000	2.6%
14	Washington	322,778,000,000	2.3%
15	Maryland	273,333,000,000	1.9%
16	Minnesota	262,847,000,000	1.9%
17	Indiana	254,861,000,000	1.8%
18	Tennessee	252,127,000,000	1.8%
19	Arizona	248,888,000,000	1.8%
20	Colorado	248,603,000,000	1.8%
21	Wisconsin	240,429,000,000	1.7%
22	Missouri	237,797,000,000	1.7%
23	Louisiana	222,218,000,000	1.6%
24	Connecticut	216,174,000,000	1.5%
25	Alabama	170,014,000,000	1.2%
26	Oregon	161,573,000,000	1.1%
27	Kentucky	156,436,000,000	1.1%
28	South Carolina	156,384,000,000	1.1%
29	Oklahoma	146,448,000,000	1.0%
30	Iowa	135,702,000,000	1.0%
31	Nevada	131,233,000,000	0.9%
32	Kansas	122,731,000,000	0.9%
33	Utah	109,777,000,000	0.8%
34	Arkansas	98,331,000,000	0.7%
35	Mississippi	91,782,000,000	0.6%
36	Nebraska	83,273,000,000	0.6%
37	New Mexico	79,901,000,000	0.6%
38	Hawaii	63,847,000,000	0.5%
39	Delaware	61,828,000,000	0.4%
40	West Virginia	61,652,000,000	0.4%
41	New Hampshire	60,005,000,000	0.4%
42	Idaho	52,747,000,000	0.4%
43	Maine	49,709,000,000	0.4%
44	Alaska	47,912,000,000	0.3%
45	Rhode Island	47,364,000,000	0.3%
46	South Dakota	36,959,000,000	0.3%
47	Montana	35,891,000,000	0.3%
48	Wyoming	35,310,000,000	0.2%
49	North Dakota	31,208,000,000	0.2%
50	Vermont	25,442,000,000	0.2%
	District of Columbia	97,235,000,000	0.7%

Source: U.S. Department of Commerce, Bureau of Economic Analysis
      "Gross Domestic Product Data" (http://www.bea.gov/regional/gsp/)
*G.D.P. is the market value of goods and services produced by the labor and property located in a state. It is the state
counterpart to the nation's Gross Domestic Product. This was formerly known as Gross State Product (G.S.P.).

Percent Change in Gross Domestic Product: 2004 to 2008
(Adjusted to Constant 2000 Dollars)
National Percent Change = 8.9% Increase*

ALPHA ORDER

RANK ORDER

RANK	STATE	PERCENT CHANGE	RANK	STATE	PERCENT CHANGE
26	Alabama	7.2	1	North Dakota	21.6
46	Alaska	3.5	2	Utah	20.2
4	Arizona	16.4	3	Oregon	16.8
29	Arkansas	6.8	4	Arizona	16.4
19	California	9.9	5	New York	16.2
13	Colorado	12.4	6	Washington	15.1
26	Connecticut	7.2	7	Idaho	15.0
39	Delaware	5.6	8	Nevada	14.8
18	Florida	10.0	8	Texas	14.8
32	Georgia	6.0	10	Wyoming	14.2
14	Hawaii	11.5	11	South Dakota	14.1
7	Idaho	15.0	12	Montana	13.5
34	Illinois	5.9	13	Colorado	12.4
48	Indiana	0.2	14	Hawaii	11.5
21	Iowa	9.4	15	North Carolina	11.4
16	Kansas	11.1	16	Kansas	11.1
34	Kentucky	5.9	17	Virginia	10.3
42	Louisiana	4.0	18	Florida	10.0
45	Maine	3.6	19	California	9.9
25	Maryland	7.5	19	Oklahoma	9.9
23	Massachusetts	9.1	21	Iowa	9.4
50	Michigan	(3.5)	22	Nebraska	9.2
37	Minnesota	5.8	23	Massachusetts	9.1
40	Mississippi	5.5	24	New Mexico	7.9
42	Missouri	4.0	25	Maryland	7.5
12	Montana	13.5	26	Alabama	7.2
22	Nebraska	9.2	26	Connecticut	7.2
8	Nevada	14.8	28	Vermont	7.0
34	New Hampshire	5.9	29	Arkansas	6.8
44	New Jersey	3.9	30	Pennsylvania	6.6
24	New Mexico	7.9	30	Tennessee	6.6
5	New York	16.2	32	Georgia	6.0
15	North Carolina	11.4	32	South Carolina	6.0
1	North Dakota	21.6	34	Illinois	5.9
49	Ohio	(0.5)	34	Kentucky	5.9
19	Oklahoma	9.9	34	New Hampshire	5.9
3	Oregon	16.8	37	Minnesota	5.8
30	Pennsylvania	6.6	38	West Virginia	5.7
47	Rhode Island	0.8	39	Delaware	5.6
32	South Carolina	6.0	40	Mississippi	5.5
11	South Dakota	14.1	40	Wisconsin	5.5
30	Tennessee	6.6	42	Louisiana	4.0
8	Texas	14.8	42	Missouri	4.0
2	Utah	20.2	44	New Jersey	3.9
28	Vermont	7.0	45	Maine	3.6
17	Virginia	10.3	46	Alaska	3.5
6	Washington	15.1	47	Rhode Island	0.8
38	West Virginia	5.7	48	Indiana	0.2
40	Wisconsin	5.5	49	Ohio	(0.5)
10	Wyoming	14.2	50	Michigan	(3.5)
				District of Columbia	10.8

Source: CQ Press using data from U.S. Department of Commerce, Bureau of Economic Analysis
"Gross Domestic Product Data" (http://www.bea.gov/regional/gsp/)

*G.D.P. is the market value of goods and services produced by the labor and property located in a state. It is the state counterpart to the nation's Gross Domestic Product. This was formerly known as Gross State Product (G.S.P.). Adjusted for inflation using chained 2000 dollars.

Average Annual Change in Gross Domestic Product: 2004 to 2008
(Adjusted to Constant 2000 Dollars)
National Annual Percent Change = 1.7% Increase*

ALPHA ORDER

RANK	STATE	ANNUAL CHANGE
25	Alabama	1.4
45	Alaska	0.7
4	Arizona	3.1
29	Arkansas	1.3
18	California	1.9
13	Colorado	2.4
25	Connecticut	1.4
34	Delaware	1.1
18	Florida	1.9
32	Georgia	1.2
14	Hawaii	2.2
6	Idaho	2.8
34	Illinois	1.1
48	Indiana	0.0
21	Iowa	1.8
16	Kansas	2.1
34	Kentucky	1.1
42	Louisiana	0.8
45	Maine	0.7
25	Maryland	1.4
23	Massachusetts	1.7
50	Michigan	(0.7)
34	Minnesota	1.1
34	Mississippi	1.1
42	Missouri	0.8
12	Montana	2.6
21	Nebraska	1.8
6	Nevada	2.8
34	New Hampshire	1.1
42	New Jersey	0.8
24	New Mexico	1.5
4	New York	3.1
14	North Carolina	2.2
1	North Dakota	4.0
49	Ohio	(0.1)
18	Oklahoma	1.9
3	Oregon	3.2
29	Pennsylvania	1.3
47	Rhode Island	0.2
32	South Carolina	1.2
10	South Dakota	2.7
29	Tennessee	1.3
6	Texas	2.8
2	Utah	3.7
25	Vermont	1.4
17	Virginia	2.0
6	Washington	2.8
34	West Virginia	1.1
34	Wisconsin	1.1
10	Wyoming	2.7

RANK ORDER

RANK	STATE	ANNUAL CHANGE
1	North Dakota	4.0
2	Utah	3.7
3	Oregon	3.2
4	Arizona	3.1
4	New York	3.1
6	Idaho	2.8
6	Nevada	2.8
6	Texas	2.8
6	Washington	2.8
10	South Dakota	2.7
10	Wyoming	2.7
12	Montana	2.6
13	Colorado	2.4
14	Hawaii	2.2
14	North Carolina	2.2
16	Kansas	2.1
17	Virginia	2.0
18	California	1.9
18	Florida	1.9
18	Oklahoma	1.9
21	Iowa	1.8
21	Nebraska	1.8
23	Massachusetts	1.7
24	New Mexico	1.5
25	Alabama	1.4
25	Connecticut	1.4
25	Maryland	1.4
25	Vermont	1.4
29	Arkansas	1.3
29	Pennsylvania	1.3
29	Tennessee	1.3
32	Georgia	1.2
32	South Carolina	1.2
34	Delaware	1.1
34	Illinois	1.1
34	Kentucky	1.1
34	Minnesota	1.1
34	Mississippi	1.1
34	New Hampshire	1.1
34	West Virginia	1.1
34	Wisconsin	1.1
42	Louisiana	0.8
42	Missouri	0.8
42	New Jersey	0.8
45	Alaska	0.7
45	Maine	0.7
47	Rhode Island	0.2
48	Indiana	0.0
49	Ohio	(0.1)
50	Michigan	(0.7)

| | District of Columbia | 2.1 |

Source: CQ Press using data from U.S. Department of Commerce, Bureau of Economic Analysis
"Gross Domestic Product Data" (http://www.bea.gov/regional/gsp/)
*G.D.P. is the market value of goods and services produced by the labor and property located in a state. It is the state counterpart to the nation's Gross Domestic Product. This was formerly known as Gross State Product (G.S.P.). Adjusted for inflation using chained 2000 dollars.

Per Capita Gross Domestic Product in 2008

National Per Capita = $46,588*

ALPHA ORDER

RANK	STATE	PER CAPITA
45	Alabama	$36,469
2	Alaska	69,813
40	Arizona	38,289
48	Arkansas	34,437
14	California	50,243
12	Colorado	50,330
4	Connecticut	61,742
1	Delaware	70,815
33	Florida	40,599
30	Georgia	41,066
15	Hawaii	49,563
47	Idaho	34,615
17	Illinois	49,118
39	Indiana	39,967
23	Iowa	45,196
26	Kansas	43,799
44	Kentucky	36,643
10	Louisiana	50,380
42	Maine	37,760
19	Maryland	48,518
6	Massachusetts	56,170
41	Michigan	38,241
11	Minnesota	50,350
50	Mississippi	31,233
36	Missouri	40,225
43	Montana	37,099
20	Nebraska	46,693
9	Nevada	50,471
22	New Hampshire	45,603
7	New Jersey	54,699
35	New Mexico	40,265
5	New York	58,721
27	North Carolina	43,393
18	North Dakota	48,650
31	Ohio	41,051
37	Oklahoma	40,207
29	Oregon	42,631
25	Pennsylvania	44,448
24	Rhode Island	45,075
46	South Carolina	34,909
21	South Dakota	45,958
34	Tennessee	40,568
13	Texas	50,294
38	Utah	40,117
32	Vermont	40,952
8	Virginia	51,103
16	Washington	49,285
49	West Virginia	33,978
28	Wisconsin	42,720
3	Wyoming	66,289

RANK ORDER

RANK	STATE	PER CAPITA
1	Delaware	$70,815
2	Alaska	69,813
3	Wyoming	66,289
4	Connecticut	61,742
5	New York	58,721
6	Massachusetts	56,170
7	New Jersey	54,699
8	Virginia	51,103
9	Nevada	50,471
10	Louisiana	50,380
11	Minnesota	50,350
12	Colorado	50,330
13	Texas	50,294
14	California	50,243
15	Hawaii	49,563
16	Washington	49,285
17	Illinois	49,118
18	North Dakota	48,650
19	Maryland	48,518
20	Nebraska	46,693
21	South Dakota	45,958
22	New Hampshire	45,603
23	Iowa	45,196
24	Rhode Island	45,075
25	Pennsylvania	44,448
26	Kansas	43,799
27	North Carolina	43,393
28	Wisconsin	42,720
29	Oregon	42,631
30	Georgia	41,066
31	Ohio	41,051
32	Vermont	40,952
33	Florida	40,599
34	Tennessee	40,568
35	New Mexico	40,265
36	Missouri	40,225
37	Oklahoma	40,207
38	Utah	40,117
39	Indiana	39,967
40	Arizona	38,289
41	Michigan	38,241
42	Maine	37,760
43	Montana	37,099
44	Kentucky	36,643
45	Alabama	36,469
46	South Carolina	34,909
47	Idaho	34,615
48	Arkansas	34,437
49	West Virginia	33,978
50	Mississippi	31,233

District of Columbia	164,295

Source: CQ Press using data from U.S. Department of Commerce, Bureau of Economic Analysis
"Gross Domestic Product Data" (http://www.bea.gov/regional/gsp/)
*G.D.P. is the market value of goods and services produced by the labor and property located in a state. It is the state
counterpart to the nation's Gross Domestic Product. This was formerly known as Gross State Product (G.S.P.).

Percent Change in Per Capita Gross Domestic Product: 2004 to 2008
(Adjusted to Constant 2000 Dollars)
National Percent Change = 4.9% Increase*

ALPHA ORDER

RANK	STATE	PERCENT CHANGE
29	Alabama	3.7
45	Alaska	(0.3)
33	Arizona	3.0
40	Arkansas	2.5
14	California	6.5
25	Colorado	4.7
16	Connecticut	6.4
44	Delaware	(0.2)
27	Florida	3.9
49	Georgia	(2.5)
7	Hawaii	8.4
24	Idaho	4.9
27	Illinois	3.9
48	Indiana	(2.4)
11	Iowa	7.3
8	Kansas	8.3
40	Kentucky	2.5
18	Louisiana	5.8
33	Maine	3.0
21	Maryland	5.6
9	Massachusetts	8.0
50	Michigan	(2.6)
33	Minnesota	3.0
30	Mississippi	3.6
43	Missouri	1.0
5	Montana	8.6
13	Nebraska	6.7
39	Nevada	2.6
26	New Hampshire	4.0
32	New Jersey	3.1
37	New Mexico	2.7
2	New York	15.1
33	North Carolina	3.0
1	North Dakota	20.6
47	Ohio	(0.8)
17	Oklahoma	5.9
3	Oregon	10.2
21	Pennsylvania	5.6
37	Rhode Island	2.7
46	South Carolina	(0.7)
4	South Dakota	9.8
42	Tennessee	1.3
18	Texas	5.8
12	Utah	7.2
14	Vermont	6.5
18	Virginia	5.8
5	Washington	8.6
23	West Virginia	5.1
31	Wisconsin	3.3
10	Wyoming	7.8

RANK ORDER

RANK	STATE	PERCENT CHANGE
1	North Dakota	20.6
2	New York	15.1
3	Oregon	10.2
4	South Dakota	9.8
5	Montana	8.6
5	Washington	8.6
7	Hawaii	8.4
8	Kansas	8.3
9	Massachusetts	8.0
10	Wyoming	7.8
11	Iowa	7.3
12	Utah	7.2
13	Nebraska	6.7
14	California	6.5
14	Vermont	6.5
16	Connecticut	6.4
17	Oklahoma	5.9
18	Louisiana	5.8
18	Texas	5.8
18	Virginia	5.8
21	Maryland	5.6
21	Pennsylvania	5.6
23	West Virginia	5.1
24	Idaho	4.9
25	Colorado	4.7
26	New Hampshire	4.0
27	Florida	3.9
27	Illinois	3.9
29	Alabama	3.7
30	Mississippi	3.6
31	Wisconsin	3.3
32	New Jersey	3.1
33	Arizona	3.0
33	Maine	3.0
33	Minnesota	3.0
33	North Carolina	3.0
37	New Mexico	2.7
37	Rhode Island	2.7
39	Nevada	2.6
40	Arkansas	2.5
40	Kentucky	2.5
42	Tennessee	1.3
43	Missouri	1.0
44	Delaware	(0.2)
45	Alaska	(0.3)
46	South Carolina	(0.7)
47	Ohio	(0.8)
48	Indiana	(2.4)
49	Georgia	(2.5)
50	Michigan	(2.6)

| District of Columbia | 8.5 |

Source: CQ Press using data from U.S. Department of Commerce, Bureau of Economic Analysis
"Gross Domestic Product Data" (http://www.bea.gov/regional/gsp/)
*G.D.P. is the market value of goods and services produced by the labor and property located in a state. It is the state counterpart to the nation's Gross Domestic Product. This was formerly known as Gross State Product (G.S.P.). Adjusted for inflation using chained 2000 dollars.

Personal Income in 2008

National Total = $12,225,589,000,000*

ALPHA ORDER					RANK ORDER				
RANK	STATE	INCOME	% of USA		RANK	STATE	INCOME	% of USA	
25	Alabama	$157,421,997,000	1.3%		1	California	$1,604,112,764,000	13.1%	
47	Alaska	30,223,608,000	0.2%		2	New York	950,209,504,000	7.8%	
17	Arizona	223,184,451,000	1.8%		3	Texas	918,921,246,000	7.5%	
33	Arkansas	92,505,191,000	0.8%		4	Florida	719,707,709,000	5.9%	
1	California	1,604,112,764,000	13.1%		5	Illinois	546,344,259,000	4.5%	
22	Colorado	212,320,185,000	1.7%		6	Pennsylvania	499,669,401,000	4.1%	
23	Connecticut	197,023,620,000	1.6%		7	New Jersey	445,928,224,000	3.6%	
44	Delaware	35,376,923,000	0.3%		8	Ohio	413,732,085,000	3.4%	
4	Florida	719,707,709,000	5.9%		9	Michigan	349,612,178,000	2.9%	
11	Georgia	337,960,830,000	2.8%		10	Virginia	343,580,294,000	2.8%	
40	Hawaii	54,175,210,000	0.4%		11	Georgia	337,960,830,000	2.8%	
41	Idaho	50,398,859,000	0.4%		12	Massachusetts	333,046,494,000	2.7%	
5	Illinois	546,344,259,000	4.5%		13	North Carolina	325,953,820,000	2.7%	
18	Indiana	220,670,002,000	1.8%		14	Washington	280,677,561,000	2.3%	
30	Iowa	112,302,300,000	0.9%		15	Maryland	272,542,169,000	2.2%	
31	Kansas	108,778,736,000	0.9%		16	Minnesota	224,670,738,000	1.8%	
28	Kentucky	136,939,777,000	1.1%		17	Arizona	223,184,451,000	1.8%	
24	Louisiana	160,658,930,000	1.3%		18	Indiana	220,670,002,000	1.8%	
42	Maine	47,994,130,000	0.4%		19	Tennessee	217,372,834,000	1.8%	
15	Maryland	272,542,169,000	2.2%		20	Missouri	216,546,820,000	1.8%	
12	Massachusetts	333,046,494,000	2.7%		21	Wisconsin	212,553,339,000	1.7%	
9	Michigan	349,612,178,000	2.9%		22	Colorado	212,320,185,000	1.7%	
16	Minnesota	224,670,738,000	1.8%		23	Connecticut	197,023,620,000	1.6%	
34	Mississippi	89,331,219,000	0.7%		24	Louisiana	160,658,930,000	1.3%	
20	Missouri	216,546,820,000	1.8%		25	Alabama	157,421,997,000	1.3%	
45	Montana	33,515,577,000	0.3%		26	South Carolina	146,334,933,000	1.2%	
36	Nebraska	69,820,901,000	0.6%		27	Oregon	137,569,686,000	1.1%	
32	Nevada	107,079,263,000	0.9%		28	Kentucky	136,939,777,000	1.1%	
39	New Hampshire	57,399,130,000	0.5%		29	Oklahoma	131,070,218,000	1.1%	
7	New Jersey	445,928,224,000	3.6%		30	Iowa	112,302,300,000	0.9%	
37	New Mexico	66,336,940,000	0.5%		31	Kansas	108,778,736,000	0.9%	
2	New York	950,209,504,000	7.8%		32	Nevada	107,079,263,000	0.9%	
13	North Carolina	325,953,820,000	2.7%		33	Arkansas	92,505,191,000	0.8%	
49	North Dakota	25,575,905,000	0.2%		34	Mississippi	89,331,219,000	0.7%	
8	Ohio	413,732,085,000	3.4%		35	Utah	87,411,357,000	0.7%	
29	Oklahoma	131,070,218,000	1.1%		36	Nebraska	69,820,901,000	0.6%	
27	Oregon	137,569,686,000	1.1%		37	New Mexico	66,336,940,000	0.5%	
6	Pennsylvania	499,669,401,000	4.1%		38	West Virginia	57,410,905,000	0.5%	
43	Rhode Island	43,468,678,000	0.4%		39	New Hampshire	57,399,130,000	0.5%	
26	South Carolina	146,334,933,000	1.2%		40	Hawaii	54,175,210,000	0.4%	
46	South Dakota	31,090,547,000	0.3%		41	Idaho	50,398,859,000	0.4%	
19	Tennessee	217,372,834,000	1.8%		42	Maine	47,994,130,000	0.4%	
3	Texas	918,921,246,000	7.5%		43	Rhode Island	43,468,678,000	0.4%	
35	Utah	87,411,357,000	0.7%		44	Delaware	35,376,923,000	0.3%	
50	Vermont	24,034,394,000	0.2%		45	Montana	33,515,577,000	0.3%	
10	Virginia	343,580,294,000	2.8%		46	South Dakota	31,090,547,000	0.3%	
14	Washington	280,677,561,000	2.3%		47	Alaska	30,223,608,000	0.2%	
38	West Virginia	57,410,905,000	0.5%		48	Wyoming	25,892,041,000	0.2%	
21	Wisconsin	212,553,339,000	1.7%		49	North Dakota	25,575,905,000	0.2%	
48	Wyoming	25,892,041,000	0.2%		50	Vermont	24,034,394,000	0.2%	
						District of Columbia	39,131,118,000	0.3%	

Source: U.S. Department of Commerce, Bureau of Economic Analysis
   "Annual State Personal Income" (http://www.bea.gov/regional/spi/)
*The national total shown here is the sum of the state estimates. It differs from the national income and product accounts
(NIPA) estimate of personal income because it omits the earnings of federal civilian and military personnel stationed abroad and
of U.S. residents employed abroad temporarily by private U.S. firms.

Change in Personal Income: 2007 to 2008

National Percent Change = 2.9% Increase*

ALPHA ORDER				RANK ORDER		
RANK	STATE	PERCENT CHANGE		RANK	STATE	PERCENT CHANGE
20	Alabama	3.5		1	North Dakota	9.3
2	Alaska	7.8		2	Alaska	7.8
43	Arizona	2.1		3	South Dakota	7.1
22	Arkansas	3.3		4	Wyoming	5.9
46	California	2.0		5	Oklahoma	5.8
22	Colorado	3.3		6	Iowa	5.4
49	Connecticut	1.5		7	West Virginia	5.2
40	Delaware	2.4		8	New Mexico	5.0
50	Florida	0.9		9	Kansas	4.8
40	Georgia	2.4		10	Texas	4.6
16	Hawaii	3.7		11	Missouri	4.3
40	Idaho	2.4		12	Nebraska	4.1
38	Illinois	2.5		13	Maine	4.0
24	Indiana	3.2		14	Louisiana	3.9
6	Iowa	5.4		15	Minnesota	3.8
9	Kansas	4.8		16	Hawaii	3.7
17	Kentucky	3.6		17	Kentucky	3.6
14	Louisiana	3.9		17	South Carolina	3.6
13	Maine	4.0		17	Washington	3.6
28	Maryland	3.1		20	Alabama	3.5
24	Massachusetts	3.2		20	Mississippi	3.5
48	Michigan	1.8		22	Arkansas	3.3
15	Minnesota	3.8		22	Colorado	3.3
20	Mississippi	3.5		24	Indiana	3.2
11	Missouri	4.3		24	Massachusetts	3.2
24	Montana	3.2		24	Montana	3.2
12	Nebraska	4.1		24	Utah	3.2
47	Nevada	1.9		28	Maryland	3.1
43	New Hampshire	2.1		28	North Carolina	3.1
38	New Jersey	2.5		28	Oregon	3.1
8	New Mexico	5.0		28	Tennessee	3.1
34	New York	2.7		28	Virginia	3.1
28	North Carolina	3.1		33	Pennsylvania	3.0
1	North Dakota	9.3		34	New York	2.7
43	Ohio	2.1		34	Vermont	2.7
5	Oklahoma	5.8		36	Rhode Island	2.6
28	Oregon	3.1		36	Wisconsin	2.6
33	Pennsylvania	3.0		38	Illinois	2.5
36	Rhode Island	2.6		38	New Jersey	2.5
17	South Carolina	3.6		40	Delaware	2.4
3	South Dakota	7.1		40	Georgia	2.4
28	Tennessee	3.1		40	Idaho	2.4
10	Texas	4.6		43	Arizona	2.1
24	Utah	3.2		43	New Hampshire	2.1
34	Vermont	2.7		43	Ohio	2.1
28	Virginia	3.1		46	California	2.0
17	Washington	3.6		47	Nevada	1.9
7	West Virginia	5.2		48	Michigan	1.8
36	Wisconsin	2.6		49	Connecticut	1.5
4	Wyoming	5.9		50	Florida	0.9
					District of Columbia	4.2

Source: CQ Press using data from U.S. Department of Commerce, Bureau of Economic Analysis
"Annual State Personal Income" (http://www.bea.gov/regional/spi/)
*Based on revised 2007 figures.

Per Capita Personal Income in 2008

National Per Capita = $40,208*

ALPHA ORDER

RANK	STATE	PER CAPITA
42	Alabama	$33,768
8	Alaska	44,039
41	Arizona	34,335
46	Arkansas	32,397
9	California	43,641
12	Colorado	42,985
1	Connecticut	56,272
18	Delaware	40,519
21	Florida	39,267
38	Georgia	34,893
15	Hawaii	42,055
44	Idaho	33,074
14	Illinois	42,347
40	Indiana	34,605
28	Iowa	37,402
23	Kansas	38,820
47	Kentucky	32,076
31	Louisiana	36,424
30	Maine	36,457
6	Maryland	48,378
3	Massachusetts	51,254
37	Michigan	34,949
11	Minnesota	43,037
50	Mississippi	30,399
29	Missouri	36,631
39	Montana	34,644
22	Nebraska	39,150
17	Nevada	41,182
10	New Hampshire	43,623
2	New Jersey	51,358
43	New Mexico	33,430
4	New York	48,753
35	North Carolina	35,344
20	North Dakota	39,870
33	Ohio	36,021
34	Oklahoma	35,985
32	Oregon	36,297
19	Pennsylvania	40,140
16	Rhode Island	41,368
45	South Carolina	32,666
25	South Dakota	38,661
36	Tennessee	34,976
26	Texas	37,774
48	Utah	31,944
24	Vermont	38,686
7	Virginia	44,224
13	Washington	42,857
49	West Virginia	31,641
27	Wisconsin	37,767
5	Wyoming	48,608

RANK ORDER

RANK	STATE	PER CAPITA
1	Connecticut	$56,272
2	New Jersey	51,358
3	Massachusetts	51,254
4	New York	48,753
5	Wyoming	48,608
6	Maryland	48,378
7	Virginia	44,224
8	Alaska	44,039
9	California	43,641
10	New Hampshire	43,623
11	Minnesota	43,037
12	Colorado	42,985
13	Washington	42,857
14	Illinois	42,347
15	Hawaii	42,055
16	Rhode Island	41,368
17	Nevada	41,182
18	Delaware	40,519
19	Pennsylvania	40,140
20	North Dakota	39,870
21	Florida	39,267
22	Nebraska	39,150
23	Kansas	38,820
24	Vermont	38,686
25	South Dakota	38,661
26	Texas	37,774
27	Wisconsin	37,767
28	Iowa	37,402
29	Missouri	36,631
30	Maine	36,457
31	Louisiana	36,424
32	Oregon	36,297
33	Ohio	36,021
34	Oklahoma	35,985
35	North Carolina	35,344
36	Tennessee	34,976
37	Michigan	34,949
38	Georgia	34,893
39	Montana	34,644
40	Indiana	34,605
41	Arizona	34,335
42	Alabama	33,768
43	New Mexico	33,430
44	Idaho	33,074
45	South Carolina	32,666
46	Arkansas	32,397
47	Kentucky	32,076
48	Utah	31,944
49	West Virginia	31,641
50	Mississippi	30,399
	District of Columbia	66,119

Source: U.S. Department of Commerce, Bureau of Economic Analysis
"Annual State Personal Income" (http://www.bea.gov/regional/spi/)
*The national figure is based on the sum of the state estimates. It differs from the national income and product accounts (NIPA) estimate of personal income because it omits the earnings of federal civilian and military personnel stationed abroad and of U.S. residents employed abroad temporarily by private U.S. firms.

Change in Per Capita Personal Income: 2007 to 2008

National Percent Change = 2.0% Increase*

ALPHA ORDER				RANK ORDER		
RANK	STATE	PERCENT CHANGE		RANK	STATE	PERCENT CHANGE
21	Alabama	2.7		1	North Dakota	8.7
2	Alaska	7.0		2	Alaska	7.0
50	Arizona	(0.2)		3	South Dakota	6.0
26	Arkansas	2.4		4	West Virginia	5.0
44	California	1.0		5	Iowa	4.8
40	Colorado	1.3		5	Oklahoma	4.8
41	Connecticut	1.2		7	Wyoming	4.0
42	Delaware	1.1		8	Maine	3.9
48	Florida	0.2		8	New Mexico	3.9
45	Georgia	0.7		10	Kansas	3.8
17	Hawaii	2.8		11	Missouri	3.7
47	Idaho	0.5		12	Nebraska	3.3
36	Illinois	1.9		13	Louisiana	3.0
25	Indiana	2.5		13	Minnesota	3.0
5	Iowa	4.8		15	Mississippi	2.9
10	Kansas	3.8		15	Rhode Island	2.9
17	Kentucky	2.8		17	Hawaii	2.8
13	Louisiana	3.0		17	Kentucky	2.8
8	Maine	3.9		17	Maryland	2.8
17	Maryland	2.8		17	Pennsylvania	2.8
21	Massachusetts	2.7		21	Alabama	2.7
28	Michigan	2.2		21	Massachusetts	2.7
13	Minnesota	3.0		23	Texas	2.6
15	Mississippi	2.9		23	Vermont	2.6
11	Missouri	3.7		25	Indiana	2.5
31	Montana	2.1		26	Arkansas	2.4
12	Nebraska	3.3		26	New York	2.4
49	Nevada	0.1		28	Michigan	2.2
38	New Hampshire	1.8		28	New Jersey	2.2
28	New Jersey	2.2		28	Virginia	2.2
8	New Mexico	3.9		31	Montana	2.1
26	New York	2.4		31	Wisconsin	2.1
42	North Carolina	1.1		33	Ohio	2.0
1	North Dakota	8.7		33	Tennessee	2.0
33	Ohio	2.0		33	Washington	2.0
5	Oklahoma	4.8		36	Illinois	1.9
39	Oregon	1.6		36	South Carolina	1.9
17	Pennsylvania	2.8		38	New Hampshire	1.8
15	Rhode Island	2.9		39	Oregon	1.6
36	South Carolina	1.9		40	Colorado	1.3
3	South Dakota	6.0		41	Connecticut	1.2
33	Tennessee	2.0		42	Delaware	1.1
23	Texas	2.6		42	North Carolina	1.1
46	Utah	0.6		44	California	1.0
23	Vermont	2.6		45	Georgia	0.7
28	Virginia	2.2		46	Utah	0.6
33	Washington	2.0		47	Idaho	0.5
4	West Virginia	5.0		48	Florida	0.2
31	Wisconsin	2.1		49	Nevada	0.1
7	Wyoming	4.0		50	Arizona	(0.2)

District of Columbia 3.5

Source: CQ Press using data from U.S. Department of Commerce, Bureau of Economic Analysis
"Annual State Personal Income" (http://www.bea.gov/regional/spi/)
*Based on revised 2007 figures.

Per Capita Disposable Personal Income in 2008

National Per Capita = $35,501*

ALPHA ORDER				RANK ORDER		
RANK	STATE	INCOME		RANK	STATE	INCOME
42	Alabama	$30,540		1	Connecticut	$46,615
7	Alaska	40,052		2	New Jersey	44,299
40	Arizona	30,960		3	Massachusetts	43,610
46	Arkansas	29,365		4	Wyoming	42,852
11	California	38,123		5	Maryland	41,828
12	Colorado	37,796		6	New York	40,862
1	Connecticut	46,615		7	Alaska	40,052
19	Delaware	35,707		8	New Hampshire	39,167
22	Florida	35,355		9	Virginia	38,727
38	Georgia	31,132		10	Washington	38,546
14	Hawaii	37,626		11	California	38,123
44	Idaho	29,742		12	Colorado	37,796
15	Illinois	37,255		13	Minnesota	37,672
41	Indiana	30,931		14	Hawaii	37,626
27	Iowa	33,656		15	Illinois	37,255
24	Kansas	34,496		16	Nevada	37,025
48	Kentucky	28,683		17	Rhode Island	36,754
29	Louisiana	33,197		18	North Dakota	36,268
30	Maine	32,745		19	Delaware	35,707
5	Maryland	41,828		20	South Dakota	35,542
3	Massachusetts	43,610		21	Pennsylvania	35,373
37	Michigan	31,340		22	Florida	35,355
13	Minnesota	37,672		23	Nebraska	35,130
50	Mississippi	28,009		24	Kansas	34,496
31	Missouri	32,733		25	Vermont	34,430
39	Montana	31,054		26	Texas	34,249
23	Nebraska	35,130		27	Iowa	33,656
16	Nevada	37,025		28	Wisconsin	33,430
8	New Hampshire	39,167		29	Louisiana	33,197
2	New Jersey	44,299		30	Maine	32,745
43	New Mexico	30,335		31	Missouri	32,733
6	New York	40,862		32	Oklahoma	32,263
36	North Carolina	31,342		33	Tennessee	32,108
18	North Dakota	36,268		34	Ohio	31,992
34	Ohio	31,992		35	Oregon	31,739
32	Oklahoma	32,263		36	North Carolina	31,342
35	Oregon	31,739		37	Michigan	31,340
21	Pennsylvania	35,373		38	Georgia	31,132
17	Rhode Island	36,754		39	Montana	31,054
45	South Carolina	29,465		40	Arizona	30,960
20	South Dakota	35,542		41	Indiana	30,931
33	Tennessee	32,108		42	Alabama	30,540
26	Texas	34,249		43	New Mexico	30,335
49	Utah	28,490		44	Idaho	29,742
25	Vermont	34,430		45	South Carolina	29,465
9	Virginia	38,727		46	Arkansas	29,365
10	Washington	38,546		47	West Virginia	28,709
47	West Virginia	28,709		48	Kentucky	28,683
28	Wisconsin	33,430		49	Utah	28,490
4	Wyoming	42,852		50	Mississippi	28,009
					District of Columbia	57,301

Source: U.S. Department of Commerce, Bureau of Economic Analysis
"Annual State Personal Income" (http://www.bea.gov/regional/spi/)
*Disposable personal income is personal income less personal tax and nontax payments. It is the income available to persons for spending or saving.

Median Household Income in 2008

National Median = $51,297*

ALPHA ORDER

RANK	STATE	INCOME
44	Alabama	$42,946
6	Alaska	63,217
32	Arizona	48,589
48	Arkansas	40,507
13	California	57,988
8	Colorado	61,304
4	Connecticut	65,976
16	Delaware	54,462
37	Florida	47,062
27	Georgia	49,810
5	Hawaii	64,193
29	Idaho	49,281
17	Illinois	53,251
34	Indiana	48,095
26	Iowa	50,774
31	Kansas	48,961
46	Kentucky	41,427
49	Louisiana	40,476
33	Maine	48,568
3	Maryland	66,618
9	Massachusetts	60,038
24	Michigan	51,001
12	Minnesota	58,414
50	Mississippi	37,416
36	Missouri	47,139
40	Montana	44,043
23	Nebraska	51,068
15	Nevada	55,570
1	New Hampshire	67,508
2	New Jersey	66,939
41	New Mexico	43,636
25	New York	50,927
42	North Carolina	43,538
35	North Dakota	47,494
30	Ohio	48,978
39	Oklahoma	44,154
21	Oregon	51,394
22	Pennsylvania	51,156
14	Rhode Island	55,639
43	South Carolina	43,458
28	South Dakota	49,437
45	Tennessee	41,978
38	Texas	46,853
10	Utah	58,820
19	Vermont	51,809
7	Virginia	61,472
11	Washington	58,460
47	West Virginia	40,910
18	Wisconsin	53,216
20	Wyoming	51,396

RANK ORDER

RANK	STATE	INCOME
1	New Hampshire	$67,508
2	New Jersey	66,939
3	Maryland	66,618
4	Connecticut	65,976
5	Hawaii	64,193
6	Alaska	63,217
7	Virginia	61,472
8	Colorado	61,304
9	Massachusetts	60,038
10	Utah	58,820
11	Washington	58,460
12	Minnesota	58,414
13	California	57,988
14	Rhode Island	55,639
15	Nevada	55,570
16	Delaware	54,462
17	Illinois	53,251
18	Wisconsin	53,216
19	Vermont	51,809
20	Wyoming	51,396
21	Oregon	51,394
22	Pennsylvania	51,156
23	Nebraska	51,068
24	Michigan	51,001
25	New York	50,927
26	Iowa	50,774
27	Georgia	49,810
28	South Dakota	49,437
29	Idaho	49,281
30	Ohio	48,978
31	Kansas	48,961
32	Arizona	48,589
33	Maine	48,568
34	Indiana	48,095
35	North Dakota	47,494
36	Missouri	47,139
37	Florida	47,062
38	Texas	46,853
39	Oklahoma	44,154
40	Montana	44,043
41	New Mexico	43,636
42	North Carolina	43,538
43	South Carolina	43,458
44	Alabama	42,946
45	Tennessee	41,978
46	Kentucky	41,427
47	West Virginia	40,910
48	Arkansas	40,507
49	Louisiana	40,476
50	Mississippi	37,416
	District of Columbia**	NA

Source: U.S. Bureau of the Census
  "Income 2008" (http://www.census.gov/hhes/www/income/income08.html)
*This is a 3-year-average of inflation-adjusted single-year medians for the years 2006 through 2008.
**Not available.

Bankruptcy Filings in 2009

National Total = 1,402,816 Bankruptcies*

ALPHA ORDER

RANK ORDER

RANK	STATE	BANKRUPTCIES	% of USA
13	Alabama	34,714	2.5%
50	Alaska	933	0.1%
15	Arizona	31,017	2.2%
28	Arkansas	16,223	1.2%
1	California	190,838	13.6%
20	Colorado	26,608	1.9%
35	Connecticut	9,710	0.7%
42	Delaware	4,592	0.3%
2	Florida	90,947	6.5%
3	Georgia	73,632	5.2%
44	Hawaii	2,941	0.2%
37	Idaho	7,203	0.5%
4	Illinois	69,695	5.0%
10	Indiana	46,888	3.3%
33	Iowa	9,892	0.7%
32	Kansas	10,588	0.8%
22	Kentucky	24,723	1.8%
26	Louisiana	18,268	1.3%
43	Maine	3,761	0.3%
23	Maryland	24,179	1.7%
25	Massachusetts	19,805	1.4%
6	Michigan	67,005	4.8%
24	Minnesota	20,490	1.5%
29	Mississippi	14,454	1.0%
16	Missouri	30,025	2.1%
45	Montana	2,593	0.2%
36	Nebraska	7,347	0.5%
18	Nevada	27,560	2.0%
41	New Hampshire	4,976	0.4%
14	New Jersey	34,070	2.4%
39	New Mexico	5,765	0.4%
7	New York	55,402	3.9%
19	North Carolina	26,917	1.9%
47	North Dakota	1,590	0.1%
5	Ohio	69,615	5.0%
31	Oklahoma	13,605	1.0%
27	Oregon	17,200	1.2%
11	Pennsylvania	36,765	2.6%
40	Rhode Island	5,096	0.4%
34	South Carolina	9,739	0.7%
46	South Dakota	1,790	0.1%
8	Tennessee	54,281	3.9%
9	Texas	52,889	3.8%
30	Utah	13,660	1.0%
48	Vermont	1,527	0.1%
12	Virginia	35,368	2.5%
17	Washington	29,520	2.1%
38	West Virginia	6,352	0.5%
21	Wisconsin	26,538	1.9%
49	Wyoming	1,249	0.1%

RANK	STATE	BANKRUPTCIES	% of USA
1	California	190,838	13.6%
2	Florida	90,947	6.5%
3	Georgia	73,632	5.2%
4	Illinois	69,695	5.0%
5	Ohio	69,615	5.0%
6	Michigan	67,005	4.8%
7	New York	55,402	3.9%
8	Tennessee	54,281	3.9%
9	Texas	52,889	3.8%
10	Indiana	46,888	3.3%
11	Pennsylvania	36,765	2.6%
12	Virginia	35,368	2.5%
13	Alabama	34,714	2.5%
14	New Jersey	34,070	2.4%
15	Arizona	31,017	2.2%
16	Missouri	30,025	2.1%
17	Washington	29,520	2.1%
18	Nevada	27,560	2.0%
19	North Carolina	26,917	1.9%
20	Colorado	26,608	1.9%
21	Wisconsin	26,538	1.9%
22	Kentucky	24,723	1.8%
23	Maryland	24,179	1.7%
24	Minnesota	20,490	1.5%
25	Massachusetts	19,805	1.4%
26	Louisiana	18,268	1.3%
27	Oregon	17,200	1.2%
28	Arkansas	16,223	1.2%
29	Mississippi	14,454	1.0%
30	Utah	13,660	1.0%
31	Oklahoma	13,605	1.0%
32	Kansas	10,588	0.8%
33	Iowa	9,892	0.7%
34	South Carolina	9,739	0.7%
35	Connecticut	9,710	0.7%
36	Nebraska	7,347	0.5%
37	Idaho	7,203	0.5%
38	West Virginia	6,352	0.5%
39	New Mexico	5,765	0.4%
40	Rhode Island	5,096	0.4%
41	New Hampshire	4,976	0.4%
42	Delaware	4,592	0.3%
43	Maine	3,761	0.3%
44	Hawaii	2,941	0.2%
45	Montana	2,593	0.2%
46	South Dakota	1,790	0.1%
47	North Dakota	1,590	0.1%
48	Vermont	1,527	0.1%
49	Wyoming	1,249	0.1%
50	Alaska	933	0.1%
	District of Columbia	1,095	0.1%

Source: CQ Press using data from Administrative Office of the U.S. Courts
"Table F-2, U.S. Bankruptcy Courts" (press release, November 25, 2009, http://www.uscourts.gov/news.cfm)
*For 12 months through September 2009. Includes business (58,721) and non-business (1,344,095) filings. Includes all chapters of bankruptcy. National total includes 10,771 bankruptcies in U.S. territories.

Personal Bankruptcy Rate in 2009

National Rate = 434 Personal Bankruptcies per 100,000 Population*

ALPHA ORDER

RANK	STATE	RATE
3	Alabama	722
50	Alaska	120
19	Arizona	447
9	Arkansas	539
12	California	493
11	Colorado	503
41	Connecticut	263
34	Delaware	309
17	Florida	465
4	Georgia	718
45	Hawaii	218
20	Idaho	446
10	Illinois	522
5	Indiana	716
33	Iowa	316
29	Kansas	363
8	Kentucky	559
26	Louisiana	388
39	Maine	267
24	Maryland	409
35	Massachusetts	290
6	Michigan	652
28	Minnesota	372
14	Mississippi	475
13	Missouri	488
42	Montana	253
25	Nebraska	392
1	Nevada	1,009
32	New Hampshire	336
27	New Jersey	374
37	New Mexico	273
40	New York	266
37	North Carolina	273
44	North Dakota	235
7	Ohio	585
30	Oklahoma	353
21	Oregon	434
36	Pennsylvania	280
16	Rhode Island	468
48	South Carolina	204
47	South Dakota	206
2	Tennessee	843
49	Texas	196
15	Utah	469
43	Vermont	236
21	Virginia	434
23	Washington	426
31	West Virginia	338
18	Wisconsin	455
46	Wyoming	214

RANK ORDER

RANK	STATE	RATE
1	Nevada	1,009
2	Tennessee	843
3	Alabama	722
4	Georgia	718
5	Indiana	716
6	Michigan	652
7	Ohio	585
8	Kentucky	559
9	Arkansas	539
10	Illinois	522
11	Colorado	503
12	California	493
13	Missouri	488
14	Mississippi	475
15	Utah	469
16	Rhode Island	468
17	Florida	465
18	Wisconsin	455
19	Arizona	447
20	Idaho	446
21	Oregon	434
21	Virginia	434
23	Washington	426
24	Maryland	409
25	Nebraska	392
26	Louisiana	388
27	New Jersey	374
28	Minnesota	372
29	Kansas	363
30	Oklahoma	353
31	West Virginia	338
32	New Hampshire	336
33	Iowa	316
34	Delaware	309
35	Massachusetts	290
36	Pennsylvania	280
37	New Mexico	273
37	North Carolina	273
39	Maine	267
40	New York	266
41	Connecticut	263
42	Montana	253
43	Vermont	236
44	North Dakota	235
45	Hawaii	218
46	Wyoming	214
47	South Dakota	206
48	South Carolina	204
49	Texas	196
50	Alaska	120

District of Columbia	169

Source: CQ Press using data from Administrative Office of the U.S. Courts
"Table F-2, U.S. Bankruptcy Courts" (press release, November 25, 2009, http://www.uscourts.gov/news.cfm)
*For 12 months through September 2009. National rate does not include bankruptcies or population in U.S. territories. Includes all nonbusiness bankruptcies.

Percent Change in Personal Bankruptcy Rate: 2008 to 2009

National Percent Change = 32.3% Increase*

ALPHA ORDER

RANK	STATE	PERCENT CHANGE
31	Alabama	24.3
50	Alaska	7.1
1	Arizona	81.0
40	Arkansas	20.3
2	California	62.7
19	Colorado	31.7
29	Connecticut	25.8
24	Delaware	28.8
8	Florida	48.1
33	Georgia	24.2
3	Hawaii	61.5
7	Idaho	49.2
20	Illinois	31.5
31	Indiana	24.3
26	Iowa	26.4
39	Kansas	21.0
41	Kentucky	19.4
47	Louisiana	15.5
14	Maine	33.5
11	Maryland	40.5
34	Massachusetts	23.4
28	Michigan	25.9
21	Minnesota	31.0
36	Mississippi	21.5
37	Missouri	21.4
13	Montana	35.3
48	Nebraska	13.0
4	Nevada	60.7
16	New Hampshire	32.8
12	New Jersey	36.5
15	New Mexico	33.2
42	New York	19.3
38	North Carolina	21.3
43	North Dakota	18.7
27	Ohio	26.3
25	Oklahoma	27.9
9	Oregon	45.6
49	Pennsylvania	12.0
22	Rhode Island	30.0
44	South Carolina	17.9
35	South Dakota	21.9
44	Tennessee	17.9
46	Texas	16.7
5	Utah	59.0
18	Vermont	31.8
17	Virginia	32.3
10	Washington	44.9
30	West Virginia	25.2
22	Wisconsin	30.0
6	Wyoming	57.4

RANK ORDER

RANK	STATE	PERCENT CHANGE
1	Arizona	81.0
2	California	62.7
3	Hawaii	61.5
4	Nevada	60.7
5	Utah	59.0
6	Wyoming	57.4
7	Idaho	49.2
8	Florida	48.1
9	Oregon	45.6
10	Washington	44.9
11	Maryland	40.5
12	New Jersey	36.5
13	Montana	35.3
14	Maine	33.5
15	New Mexico	33.2
16	New Hampshire	32.8
17	Virginia	32.3
18	Vermont	31.8
19	Colorado	31.7
20	Illinois	31.5
21	Minnesota	31.0
22	Rhode Island	30.0
22	Wisconsin	30.0
24	Delaware	28.8
25	Oklahoma	27.9
26	Iowa	26.4
27	Ohio	26.3
28	Michigan	25.9
29	Connecticut	25.8
30	West Virginia	25.2
31	Alabama	24.3
31	Indiana	24.3
33	Georgia	24.2
34	Massachusetts	23.4
35	South Dakota	21.9
36	Mississippi	21.5
37	Missouri	21.4
38	North Carolina	21.3
39	Kansas	21.0
40	Arkansas	20.3
41	Kentucky	19.4
42	New York	19.3
43	North Dakota	18.7
44	South Carolina	17.9
44	Tennessee	17.9
46	Texas	16.7
47	Louisiana	15.5
48	Nebraska	13.0
49	Pennsylvania	12.0
50	Alaska	7.1

District of Columbia — 22.5

Source: CQ Press using data from Administrative Office of the U.S. Courts
    "Table F-2, U.S. Bankruptcy Courts" (press release, November 25, 2009, http://www.uscourts.gov/news.cfm)
*Twelve months ending in September 2008 to 12 months ending in September 2009. National rate does not include bankruptcies or population in U.S. territories. Includes all nonbusiness bankruptcies.

Business Bankruptcy Rate in 2008

National Rate = 0.6% of Existing Firms*

ALPHA ORDER

RANK	STATE	RATE
16	Alabama	0.5
16	Alaska	0.5
10	Arizona	0.6
4	Arkansas	0.7
16	California	0.5
16	Colorado	0.5
28	Connecticut	0.4
1	Delaware	2.7
4	Florida	0.7
2	Georgia	0.9
45	Hawaii	0.2
28	Idaho	0.4
16	Illinois	0.5
10	Indiana	0.6
28	Iowa	0.4
40	Kansas	0.3
16	Kentucky	0.5
10	Louisiana	0.6
28	Maine	0.4
28	Maryland	0.4
45	Massachusetts	0.2
4	Michigan	0.7
10	Minnesota	0.6
10	Mississippi	0.6
16	Missouri	0.5
45	Montana	0.2
16	Nebraska	0.5
4	Nevada	0.7
3	New Hampshire	0.8
28	New Jersey	0.4
28	New Mexico	0.4
40	New York	0.3
28	North Carolina	0.4
40	North Dakota	0.3
10	Ohio	0.6
16	Oklahoma	0.5
40	Oregon	0.3
28	Pennsylvania	0.4
28	Rhode Island	0.4
45	South Carolina	0.2
28	South Dakota	0.4
4	Tennessee	0.7
4	Texas	0.7
16	Utah	0.5
45	Vermont	0.2
16	Virginia	0.5
40	Washington	0.3
16	West Virginia	0.5
28	Wisconsin	0.4
45	Wyoming	0.2

RANK ORDER

RANK	STATE	RATE
1	Delaware	2.7
2	Georgia	0.9
3	New Hampshire	0.8
4	Arkansas	0.7
4	Florida	0.7
4	Michigan	0.7
4	Nevada	0.7
4	Tennessee	0.7
4	Texas	0.7
10	Arizona	0.6
10	Indiana	0.6
10	Louisiana	0.6
10	Minnesota	0.6
10	Mississippi	0.6
10	Ohio	0.6
16	Alabama	0.5
16	Alaska	0.5
16	California	0.5
16	Colorado	0.5
16	Illinois	0.5
16	Kentucky	0.5
16	Missouri	0.5
16	Nebraska	0.5
16	Oklahoma	0.5
16	Utah	0.5
16	Virginia	0.5
16	West Virginia	0.5
28	Connecticut	0.4
28	Idaho	0.4
28	Iowa	0.4
28	Maine	0.4
28	Maryland	0.4
28	New Jersey	0.4
28	New Mexico	0.4
28	North Carolina	0.4
28	Pennsylvania	0.4
28	Rhode Island	0.4
28	South Dakota	0.4
28	Wisconsin	0.4
40	Kansas	0.3
40	New York	0.3
40	North Dakota	0.3
40	Oregon	0.3
40	Washington	0.3
45	Hawaii	0.2
45	Massachusetts	0.2
45	Montana	0.2
45	South Carolina	0.2
45	Vermont	0.2
45	Wyoming	0.2
	District of Columbia	0.2

Source: CQ Press using data from U.S. Small Business Administration and Administrative Office of the U.S. Courts
"The Small Business Economy 2009" and unpublished data (http://www.sba.gov/advo/research/) and
"Table F-2, U.S. Bankruptcy Courts" (press release, December 12, 2008, http://www.uscourts.gov/news.cfm)
*Firms can be in more than one state. Firms filing for bankruptcy in 2008 as a percent of employer firms existing in 2008.

State Business Tax Climate Index 2010

National Average Score = 5.00*

ALPHA ORDER

RANK ORDER

RANK	STATE	SCORE		RANK	STATE	SCORE
19	Alabama	5.19		1	South Dakota	7.42
2	Alaska	7.38		2	Alaska	7.38
28	Arizona	5.01		2	Wyoming	7.38
40	Arkansas	4.61		4	Nevada	7.05
48	California	3.89		5	Florida	6.62
13	Colorado	5.63		6	Montana	6.32
38	Connecticut	4.72		7	New Hampshire	6.25
8	Delaware	5.98		8	Delaware	5.98
5	Florida	6.62		9	Washington	5.81
28	Georgia	5.01		10	Utah	5.80
24	Hawaii	5.05		11	Texas	5.70
18	Idaho	5.21		12	Indiana	5.67
28	Illinois	5.01		13	Colorado	5.63
12	Indiana	5.67		14	Oregon	5.59
46	Iowa	4.23		15	Virginia	5.53
32	Kansas	4.93		16	Missouri	5.37
20	Kentucky	5.18		17	Michigan	5.35
35	Louisiana	4.74		18	Idaho	5.21
34	Maine	4.83		19	Alabama	5.19
45	Maryland	4.26		20	Kentucky	5.18
36	Massachusetts	4.73		21	Mississippi	5.16
17	Michigan	5.35		22	Tennessee	5.10
43	Minnesota	4.44		23	New Mexico	5.06
21	Mississippi	5.16		24	Hawaii	5.05
16	Missouri	5.37		25	North Dakota	5.04
6	Montana	6.32		26	Pennsylvania	5.03
33	Nebraska	4.88		26	South Carolina	5.03
4	Nevada	7.05		28	Arizona	5.01
7	New Hampshire	6.25		28	Georgia	5.01
50	New Jersey	3.60		28	Illinois	5.01
23	New Mexico	5.06		31	Oklahoma	4.97
49	New York	3.66		32	Kansas	4.93
39	North Carolina	4.66		33	Nebraska	4.88
25	North Dakota	5.04		34	Maine	4.83
47	Ohio	4.04		35	Louisiana	4.74
31	Oklahoma	4.97		36	Massachusetts	4.73
14	Oregon	5.59		36	West Virginia	4.73
26	Pennsylvania	5.03		38	Connecticut	4.72
44	Rhode Island	4.33		39	North Carolina	4.66
26	South Carolina	5.03		40	Arkansas	4.61
1	South Dakota	7.42		41	Vermont	4.56
22	Tennessee	5.10		42	Wisconsin	4.54
11	Texas	5.70		43	Minnesota	4.44
10	Utah	5.80		44	Rhode Island	4.33
41	Vermont	4.56		45	Maryland	4.26
15	Virginia	5.53		46	Iowa	4.23
9	Washington	5.81		47	Ohio	4.04
36	West Virginia	4.73		48	California	3.89
42	Wisconsin	4.54		49	New York	3.66
2	Wyoming	7.38		50	New Jersey	3.60
					District of Columbia	4.72

Source: The Tax Foundation
   "State Business Tax Climate Index" (September 2009, http://www.taxfoundation.org/publications/show/22658.html)
*This index looks at levels of taxation and complexity of compliance to compare the states on how "business friendly" each state is compared to the others. The scale for each factor considered is one to ten, with ten being the "best."

Fortune 500 Companies in 2008

National Total = 500 Companies*

ALPHA ORDER

RANK	STATE	COMPANIES	% of USA
35	Alabama	1	0.2%
40	Alaska	0	0.0%
23	Arizona	5	1.0%
25	Arkansas	4	0.8%
3	California	51	10.2%
15	Colorado	11	2.2%
15	Connecticut	11	2.2%
35	Delaware	1	0.2%
11	Florida	14	2.8%
12	Georgia	13	2.6%
40	Hawaii	0	0.0%
35	Idaho	1	0.2%
4	Illinois	33	6.6%
22	Indiana	6	1.2%
29	Iowa	2	0.4%
28	Kansas	3	0.6%
23	Kentucky	5	1.0%
29	Louisiana	2	0.4%
40	Maine	0	0.0%
21	Maryland	7	1.4%
14	Massachusetts	12	2.4%
7	Michigan	21	4.2%
9	Minnesota	19	3.8%
40	Mississippi	0	0.0%
18	Missouri	8	1.6%
40	Montana	0	0.0%
25	Nebraska	4	0.8%
29	Nevada	2	0.4%
40	New Hampshire	0	0.0%
7	New Jersey	21	4.2%
40	New Mexico	0	0.0%
2	New York	56	11.2%
12	North Carolina	13	2.6%
35	North Dakota	1	0.2%
5	Ohio	27	5.4%
25	Oklahoma	4	0.8%
29	Oregon	2	0.4%
6	Pennsylvania	24	4.8%
29	Rhode Island	2	0.4%
29	South Carolina	2	0.4%
40	South Dakota	0	0.0%
18	Tennessee	8	1.6%
1	Texas	64	12.8%
35	Utah	1	0.2%
40	Vermont	0	0.0%
10	Virginia	18	3.6%
18	Washington	8	1.6%
40	West Virginia	0	0.0%
17	Wisconsin	10	2.0%
40	Wyoming	0	0.0%

RANK ORDER

RANK	STATE	COMPANIES	% of USA
1	Texas	64	12.8%
2	New York	56	11.2%
3	California	51	10.2%
4	Illinois	33	6.6%
5	Ohio	27	5.4%
6	Pennsylvania	24	4.8%
7	Michigan	21	4.2%
7	New Jersey	21	4.2%
9	Minnesota	19	3.8%
10	Virginia	18	3.6%
11	Florida	14	2.8%
12	Georgia	13	2.6%
12	North Carolina	13	2.6%
14	Massachusetts	12	2.4%
15	Colorado	11	2.2%
15	Connecticut	11	2.2%
17	Wisconsin	10	2.0%
18	Missouri	8	1.6%
18	Tennessee	8	1.6%
18	Washington	8	1.6%
21	Maryland	7	1.4%
22	Indiana	6	1.2%
23	Arizona	5	1.0%
23	Kentucky	5	1.0%
25	Arkansas	4	0.8%
25	Nebraska	4	0.8%
25	Oklahoma	4	0.8%
28	Kansas	3	0.6%
29	Iowa	2	0.4%
29	Louisiana	2	0.4%
29	Nevada	2	0.4%
29	Oregon	2	0.4%
29	Rhode Island	2	0.4%
29	South Carolina	2	0.4%
35	Alabama	1	0.2%
35	Delaware	1	0.2%
35	Idaho	1	0.2%
35	North Dakota	1	0.2%
35	Utah	1	0.2%
40	Alaska	0	0.0%
40	Hawaii	0	0.0%
40	Maine	0	0.0%
40	Mississippi	0	0.0%
40	Montana	0	0.0%
40	New Hampshire	0	0.0%
40	New Mexico	0	0.0%
40	South Dakota	0	0.0%
40	Vermont	0	0.0%
40	West Virginia	0	0.0%
40	Wyoming	0	0.0%
	District of Columbia	3	0.6%

Source: Fortune Magazine
   "Fortune 500" (http://money.cnn.com/magazines/fortune/fortune500/2009/index.html)
*By state where each company's headquarters is located.

Employer Firms in 2008

National Total = 6,145,500 Firms*

<table>
<tr><td colspan="4">ALPHA ORDER</td><td colspan="4">RANK ORDER</td></tr>
<tr><th>RANK</th><th>STATE</th><th>FIRMS</th><th>% of USA</th><th>RANK</th><th>STATE</th><th>FIRMS</th><th>% of USA</th></tr>
<tr><td>27</td><td>Alabama</td><td>90,134</td><td>1.5%</td><td>1</td><td>California</td><td>1,204,455</td><td>19.6%</td></tr>
<tr><td>50</td><td>Alaska</td><td>17,445</td><td>0.3%</td><td>2</td><td>Florida</td><td>502,192</td><td>8.2%</td></tr>
<tr><td>19</td><td>Arizona</td><td>135,104</td><td>2.2%</td><td>3</td><td>New York</td><td>494,713</td><td>8.1%</td></tr>
<tr><td>33</td><td>Arkansas</td><td>68,425</td><td>1.1%</td><td>4</td><td>Texas</td><td>449,681</td><td>7.3%</td></tr>
<tr><td>1</td><td>California</td><td>1,204,455</td><td>19.6%</td><td>5</td><td>Illinois</td><td>303,224</td><td>4.9%</td></tr>
<tr><td>15</td><td>Colorado</td><td>158,538</td><td>2.6%</td><td>6</td><td>Pennsylvania</td><td>287,417</td><td>4.7%</td></tr>
<tr><td>26</td><td>Connecticut</td><td>99,084</td><td>1.6%</td><td>7</td><td>New Jersey</td><td>245,902</td><td>4.0%</td></tr>
<tr><td>45</td><td>Delaware</td><td>26,361</td><td>0.4%</td><td>8</td><td>Ohio</td><td>227,876</td><td>3.7%</td></tr>
<tr><td>2</td><td>Florida</td><td>502,192</td><td>8.2%</td><td>9</td><td>Georgia</td><td>217,801</td><td>3.5%</td></tr>
<tr><td>9</td><td>Georgia</td><td>217,801</td><td>3.5%</td><td>10</td><td>Michigan</td><td>213,493</td><td>3.5%</td></tr>
<tr><td>44</td><td>Hawaii</td><td>31,452</td><td>0.5%</td><td>11</td><td>Washington</td><td>203,835</td><td>3.3%</td></tr>
<tr><td>36</td><td>Idaho</td><td>51,053</td><td>0.8%</td><td>12</td><td>North Carolina</td><td>202,450</td><td>3.3%</td></tr>
<tr><td>5</td><td>Illinois</td><td>303,224</td><td>4.9%</td><td>13</td><td>Massachusetts</td><td>189,123</td><td>3.1%</td></tr>
<tr><td>21</td><td>Indiana</td><td>131,143</td><td>2.1%</td><td>14</td><td>Virginia</td><td>189,089</td><td>3.1%</td></tr>
<tr><td>30</td><td>Iowa</td><td>72,210</td><td>1.2%</td><td>15</td><td>Colorado</td><td>158,538</td><td>2.6%</td></tr>
<tr><td>31</td><td>Kansas</td><td>71,779</td><td>1.2%</td><td>16</td><td>Maryland</td><td>141,659</td><td>2.3%</td></tr>
<tr><td>28</td><td>Kentucky</td><td>86,011</td><td>1.4%</td><td>17</td><td>Missouri</td><td>138,942</td><td>2.3%</td></tr>
<tr><td>24</td><td>Louisiana</td><td>103,564</td><td>1.7%</td><td>18</td><td>Minnesota</td><td>136,144</td><td>2.2%</td></tr>
<tr><td>39</td><td>Maine</td><td>42,627</td><td>0.7%</td><td>19</td><td>Arizona</td><td>135,104</td><td>2.2%</td></tr>
<tr><td>16</td><td>Maryland</td><td>141,659</td><td>2.3%</td><td>20</td><td>Wisconsin</td><td>134,248</td><td>2.2%</td></tr>
<tr><td>13</td><td>Massachusetts</td><td>189,123</td><td>3.1%</td><td>21</td><td>Indiana</td><td>131,143</td><td>2.1%</td></tr>
<tr><td>10</td><td>Michigan</td><td>213,493</td><td>3.5%</td><td>22</td><td>Tennessee</td><td>115,887</td><td>1.9%</td></tr>
<tr><td>18</td><td>Minnesota</td><td>136,144</td><td>2.2%</td><td>23</td><td>Oregon</td><td>111,746</td><td>1.8%</td></tr>
<tr><td>35</td><td>Mississippi</td><td>56,214</td><td>0.9%</td><td>24</td><td>Louisiana</td><td>103,564</td><td>1.7%</td></tr>
<tr><td>17</td><td>Missouri</td><td>138,942</td><td>2.3%</td><td>25</td><td>South Carolina</td><td>100,724</td><td>1.6%</td></tr>
<tr><td>41</td><td>Montana</td><td>37,788</td><td>0.6%</td><td>26</td><td>Connecticut</td><td>99,084</td><td>1.6%</td></tr>
<tr><td>37</td><td>Nebraska</td><td>48,324</td><td>0.8%</td><td>27</td><td>Alabama</td><td>90,134</td><td>1.5%</td></tr>
<tr><td>34</td><td>Nevada</td><td>60,346</td><td>1.0%</td><td>28</td><td>Kentucky</td><td>86,011</td><td>1.4%</td></tr>
<tr><td>40</td><td>New Hampshire</td><td>41,483</td><td>0.7%</td><td>29</td><td>Oklahoma</td><td>82,752</td><td>1.3%</td></tr>
<tr><td>7</td><td>New Jersey</td><td>245,902</td><td>4.0%</td><td>30</td><td>Iowa</td><td>72,210</td><td>1.2%</td></tr>
<tr><td>38</td><td>New Mexico</td><td>45,896</td><td>0.7%</td><td>31</td><td>Kansas</td><td>71,779</td><td>1.2%</td></tr>
<tr><td>3</td><td>New York</td><td>494,713</td><td>8.1%</td><td>32</td><td>Utah</td><td>71,351</td><td>1.2%</td></tr>
<tr><td>12</td><td>North Carolina</td><td>202,450</td><td>3.3%</td><td>33</td><td>Arkansas</td><td>68,425</td><td>1.1%</td></tr>
<tr><td>49</td><td>North Dakota</td><td>20,480</td><td>0.3%</td><td>34</td><td>Nevada</td><td>60,346</td><td>1.0%</td></tr>
<tr><td>8</td><td>Ohio</td><td>227,876</td><td>3.7%</td><td>35</td><td>Mississippi</td><td>56,214</td><td>0.9%</td></tr>
<tr><td>29</td><td>Oklahoma</td><td>82,752</td><td>1.3%</td><td>36</td><td>Idaho</td><td>51,053</td><td>0.8%</td></tr>
<tr><td>23</td><td>Oregon</td><td>111,746</td><td>1.8%</td><td>37</td><td>Nebraska</td><td>48,324</td><td>0.8%</td></tr>
<tr><td>6</td><td>Pennsylvania</td><td>287,417</td><td>4.7%</td><td>38</td><td>New Mexico</td><td>45,896</td><td>0.7%</td></tr>
<tr><td>43</td><td>Rhode Island</td><td>33,773</td><td>0.5%</td><td>39</td><td>Maine</td><td>42,627</td><td>0.7%</td></tr>
<tr><td>25</td><td>South Carolina</td><td>100,724</td><td>1.6%</td><td>40</td><td>New Hampshire</td><td>41,483</td><td>0.7%</td></tr>
<tr><td>46</td><td>South Dakota</td><td>25,401</td><td>0.4%</td><td>41</td><td>Montana</td><td>37,788</td><td>0.6%</td></tr>
<tr><td>22</td><td>Tennessee</td><td>115,887</td><td>1.9%</td><td>42</td><td>West Virginia</td><td>36,233</td><td>0.6%</td></tr>
<tr><td>4</td><td>Texas</td><td>449,681</td><td>7.3%</td><td>43</td><td>Rhode Island</td><td>33,773</td><td>0.5%</td></tr>
<tr><td>32</td><td>Utah</td><td>71,351</td><td>1.2%</td><td>44</td><td>Hawaii</td><td>31,452</td><td>0.5%</td></tr>
<tr><td>47</td><td>Vermont</td><td>22,176</td><td>0.4%</td><td>45</td><td>Delaware</td><td>26,361</td><td>0.4%</td></tr>
<tr><td>14</td><td>Virginia</td><td>189,089</td><td>3.1%</td><td>46</td><td>South Dakota</td><td>25,401</td><td>0.4%</td></tr>
<tr><td>11</td><td>Washington</td><td>203,835</td><td>3.3%</td><td>47</td><td>Vermont</td><td>22,176</td><td>0.4%</td></tr>
<tr><td>42</td><td>West Virginia</td><td>36,233</td><td>0.6%</td><td>48</td><td>Wyoming</td><td>22,015</td><td>0.4%</td></tr>
<tr><td>20</td><td>Wisconsin</td><td>134,248</td><td>2.2%</td><td>49</td><td>North Dakota</td><td>20,480</td><td>0.3%</td></tr>
<tr><td>48</td><td>Wyoming</td><td>22,015</td><td>0.4%</td><td>50</td><td>Alaska</td><td>17,445</td><td>0.3%</td></tr>
<tr><td></td><td></td><td></td><td></td><td></td><td>District of Columbia</td><td>28,253</td><td>0.5%</td></tr>
</table>

Source: U.S. Small Business Administration
"The Small Business Economy 2009" (http://www.sba.gov/advo/research/)
*State totals do not add to the U.S. figure as firms can be in more than one state.

New Employer Firms in 2008

National Total = 874,816 New Firms*

RANK	STATE	FIRMS	% of USA
28	Alabama	9,194	1.1%
49	Alaska	1,922	0.2%
18	Arizona	15,847	1.8%
32	Arkansas	8,499	1.0%
1	California	103,572	11.8%
13	Colorado	21,921	2.5%
29	Connecticut	9,164	1.0%
45	Delaware	2,980	0.3%
2	Florida	72,203	8.3%
8	Georgia	28,980	3.3%
42	Hawaii	3,475	0.4%
34	Idaho	6,854	0.8%
7	Illinois	31,493	3.6%
20	Indiana	13,959	1.6%
36	Iowa	5,893	0.7%
33	Kansas	8,156	0.9%
31	Kentucky	8,821	1.0%
27	Louisiana	9,527	1.1%
40	Maine	4,202	0.5%
16	Maryland	18,392	2.1%
15	Massachusetts	18,581	2.1%
12	Michigan	22,090	2.5%
23	Minnesota	11,811	1.4%
37	Mississippi	5,776	0.7%
19	Missouri	15,061	1.7%
41	Montana	4,181	0.5%
38	Nebraska	4,602	0.5%
26	Nevada	10,202	1.2%
39	New Hampshire	4,587	0.5%
9	New Jersey	26,774	3.1%
35	New Mexico	5,971	0.7%
3	New York	65,624	7.5%
11	North Carolina	24,153	2.8%
50	North Dakota	1,842	0.2%
14	Ohio	20,361	2.3%
30	Oklahoma	8,943	1.0%
21	Oregon	13,952	1.6%
5	Pennsylvania	35,587	4.1%
44	Rhode Island	3,310	0.4%
24	South Carolina	11,634	1.3%
48	South Dakota	2,127	0.2%
17	Tennessee	17,167	2.0%
4	Texas	55,214	6.3%
25	Utah	11,238	1.3%
47	Vermont	2,146	0.2%
10	Virginia	25,517	2.9%
6	Washington	33,701	3.9%
43	West Virginia	3,363	0.4%
22	Wisconsin	12,905	1.5%
46	Wyoming	2,593	0.3%

RANK	STATE	FIRMS	% of USA
1	California	103,572	11.8%
2	Florida	72,203	8.3%
3	New York	65,624	7.5%
4	Texas	55,214	6.3%
5	Pennsylvania	35,587	4.1%
6	Washington	33,701	3.9%
7	Illinois	31,493	3.6%
8	Georgia	28,980	3.3%
9	New Jersey	26,774	3.1%
10	Virginia	25,517	2.9%
11	North Carolina	24,153	2.8%
12	Michigan	22,090	2.5%
13	Colorado	21,921	2.5%
14	Ohio	20,361	2.3%
15	Massachusetts	18,581	2.1%
16	Maryland	18,392	2.1%
17	Tennessee	17,167	2.0%
18	Arizona	15,847	1.8%
19	Missouri	15,061	1.7%
20	Indiana	13,959	1.6%
21	Oregon	13,952	1.6%
22	Wisconsin	12,905	1.5%
23	Minnesota	11,811	1.4%
24	South Carolina	11,634	1.3%
25	Utah	11,238	1.3%
26	Nevada	10,202	1.2%
27	Louisiana	9,527	1.1%
28	Alabama	9,194	1.1%
29	Connecticut	9,164	1.0%
30	Oklahoma	8,943	1.0%
31	Kentucky	8,821	1.0%
32	Arkansas	8,499	1.0%
33	Kansas	8,156	0.9%
34	Idaho	6,854	0.8%
35	New Mexico	5,971	0.7%
36	Iowa	5,893	0.7%
37	Mississippi	5,776	0.7%
38	Nebraska	4,602	0.5%
39	New Hampshire	4,587	0.5%
40	Maine	4,202	0.5%
41	Montana	4,181	0.5%
42	Hawaii	3,475	0.4%
43	West Virginia	3,363	0.4%
44	Rhode Island	3,310	0.4%
45	Delaware	2,980	0.3%
46	Wyoming	2,593	0.3%
47	Vermont	2,146	0.2%
48	South Dakota	2,127	0.2%
49	Alaska	1,922	0.2%
50	North Dakota	1,842	0.2%
	District of Columbia	3,939	0.5%

Source: U.S. Small Business Administration
   "The Small Business Economy 2009" (http://www.sba.gov/advo/research/)
*National total includes Puerto Rico and Virgin Islands.

Rate of New Employer Firms in 2008

National Rate = 14.3% of Existing Firms*

ALPHA ORDER

RANK	STATE	RATE
33	Alabama	10.2
22	Alaska	11.1
19	Arizona	11.8
13	Arkansas	12.6
47	California	8.8
6	Colorado	13.7
43	Connecticut	9.2
22	Delaware	11.1
5	Florida	14.3
8	Georgia	13.4
22	Hawaii	11.1
8	Idaho	13.4
31	Illinois	10.5
30	Indiana	10.7
50	Iowa	8.2
21	Kansas	11.5
33	Kentucky	10.2
42	Louisiana	9.3
36	Maine	9.9
12	Maryland	12.9
35	Massachusetts	10.0
36	Michigan	9.9
48	Minnesota	8.7
32	Mississippi	10.3
29	Missouri	10.8
22	Montana	11.1
41	Nebraska	9.6
1	Nevada	17.0
22	New Hampshire	11.1
27	New Jersey	11.0
10	New Mexico	13.1
10	New York	13.1
17	North Carolina	12.1
45	North Dakota	9.1
46	Ohio	9.0
27	Oklahoma	11.0
14	Oregon	12.4
16	Pennsylvania	12.3
39	Rhode Island	9.8
19	South Carolina	11.8
49	South Dakota	8.5
4	Tennessee	14.9
14	Texas	12.4
3	Utah	15.9
40	Vermont	9.7
7	Virginia	13.6
2	Washington	16.6
43	West Virginia	9.2
36	Wisconsin	9.9
17	Wyoming	12.1

RANK ORDER

RANK	STATE	RATE
1	Nevada	17.0
2	Washington	16.6
3	Utah	15.9
4	Tennessee	14.9
5	Florida	14.3
6	Colorado	13.7
7	Virginia	13.6
8	Georgia	13.4
8	Idaho	13.4
10	New Mexico	13.1
10	New York	13.1
12	Maryland	12.9
13	Arkansas	12.6
14	Oregon	12.4
14	Texas	12.4
16	Pennsylvania	12.3
17	North Carolina	12.1
17	Wyoming	12.1
19	Arizona	11.8
19	South Carolina	11.8
21	Kansas	11.5
22	Alaska	11.1
22	Delaware	11.1
22	Hawaii	11.1
22	Montana	11.1
22	New Hampshire	11.1
27	New Jersey	11.0
27	Oklahoma	11.0
29	Missouri	10.8
30	Indiana	10.7
31	Illinois	10.5
32	Mississippi	10.3
33	Alabama	10.2
33	Kentucky	10.2
35	Massachusetts	10.0
36	Maine	9.9
36	Michigan	9.9
36	Wisconsin	9.9
39	Rhode Island	9.8
40	Vermont	9.7
41	Nebraska	9.6
42	Louisiana	9.3
43	Connecticut	9.2
43	West Virginia	9.2
45	North Dakota	9.1
46	Ohio	9.0
47	California	8.8
48	Minnesota	8.7
49	South Dakota	8.5
50	Iowa	8.2
	District of Columbia	14.2

Source: CQ Press using data from U.S. Small Business Administration
"The Small Business Economy 2009" and unpublished data (http://www.sba.gov/advo/research/)
*Firms can be in more than one state. Rate figure represents the number of employer firms started in 2008 as a percent of existing firms at the beginning of 2008.

Employer Firm Terminations in 2008

National Total = 966,647 Terminations*

<u>ALPHA ORDER</u>

RANK	STATE	FIRMS	% of USA
26	Alabama	11,468	1.2%
46	Alaska	2,879	0.3%
16	Arizona	21,219	2.2%
34	Arkansas	7,511	0.8%
1	California	150,314	15.6%
11	Colorado	27,591	2.9%
25	Connecticut	11,488	1.2%
45	Delaware	3,698	0.4%
2	Florida	72,003	7.4%
10	Georgia	29,945	3.1%
44	Hawaii	3,973	0.4%
35	Idaho	7,273	0.8%
7	Illinois	35,689	3.7%
20	Indiana	14,380	1.5%
31	Iowa	7,679	0.8%
33	Kansas	7,648	0.8%
28	Kentucky	8,790	0.9%
32	Louisiana	7,656	0.8%
40	Maine	5,095	0.5%
15	Maryland	21,251	2.2%
18	Massachusetts	20,223	2.1%
8	Michigan	34,272	3.5%
23	Minnesota	12,597	1.3%
36	Mississippi	6,800	0.7%
14	Missouri	21,290	2.2%
41	Montana	4,771	0.5%
39	Nebraska	5,200	0.5%
27	Nevada	10,771	1.1%
38	New Hampshire	5,515	0.6%
9	New Jersey	31,167	3.2%
37	New Mexico	5,972	0.6%
3	New York	69,267	7.2%
13	North Carolina	23,734	2.5%
49	North Dakota	2,344	0.2%
17	Ohio	21,038	2.2%
30	Oklahoma	7,787	0.8%
21	Oregon	14,182	1.5%
4	Pennsylvania	42,318	4.4%
43	Rhode Island	4,459	0.5%
24	South Carolina	11,657	1.2%
50	South Dakota	2,311	0.2%
19	Tennessee	18,614	1.9%
6	Texas	36,108	3.7%
29	Utah	8,105	0.8%
48	Vermont	2,555	0.3%
12	Virginia	23,971	2.5%
5	Washington	37,955	3.9%
42	West Virginia	4,644	0.5%
22	Wisconsin	12,711	1.3%
47	Wyoming	2,703	0.3%

<u>RANK ORDER</u>

RANK	STATE	FIRMS	% of USA
1	California	150,314	15.6%
2	Florida	72,003	7.4%
3	New York	69,267	7.2%
4	Pennsylvania	42,318	4.4%
5	Washington	37,955	3.9%
6	Texas	36,108	3.7%
7	Illinois	35,689	3.7%
8	Michigan	34,272	3.5%
9	New Jersey	31,167	3.2%
10	Georgia	29,945	3.1%
11	Colorado	27,591	2.9%
12	Virginia	23,971	2.5%
13	North Carolina	23,734	2.5%
14	Missouri	21,290	2.2%
15	Maryland	21,251	2.2%
16	Arizona	21,219	2.2%
17	Ohio	21,038	2.2%
18	Massachusetts	20,223	2.1%
19	Tennessee	18,614	1.9%
20	Indiana	14,380	1.5%
21	Oregon	14,182	1.5%
22	Wisconsin	12,711	1.3%
23	Minnesota	12,597	1.3%
24	South Carolina	11,657	1.2%
25	Connecticut	11,488	1.2%
26	Alabama	11,468	1.2%
27	Nevada	10,771	1.1%
28	Kentucky	8,790	0.9%
29	Utah	8,105	0.8%
30	Oklahoma	7,787	0.8%
31	Iowa	7,679	0.8%
32	Louisiana	7,656	0.8%
33	Kansas	7,648	0.8%
34	Arkansas	7,511	0.8%
35	Idaho	7,273	0.8%
36	Mississippi	6,800	0.7%
37	New Mexico	5,972	0.6%
38	New Hampshire	5,515	0.6%
39	Nebraska	5,200	0.5%
40	Maine	5,095	0.5%
41	Montana	4,771	0.5%
42	West Virginia	4,644	0.5%
43	Rhode Island	4,459	0.5%
44	Hawaii	3,973	0.4%
45	Delaware	3,698	0.4%
46	Alaska	2,879	0.3%
47	Wyoming	2,703	0.3%
48	Vermont	2,555	0.3%
49	North Dakota	2,344	0.2%
50	South Dakota	2,311	0.2%
	District of Columbia	2,765	0.3%

Source: U.S. Small Business Administration
   "The Small Business Economy 2009" (http://www.sba.gov/advo/research/)
*National total includes Puerto Rico and Virgin Islands.

Rate of Employer Firm Terminations in 2008

National Rate = 15.8% of Existing Firms*

ALPHA ORDER

RANK	STATE	RATE
21	Alabama	12.7
4	Alaska	16.7
6	Arizona	15.9
37	Arkansas	11.1
21	California	12.7
3	Colorado	17.2
33	Connecticut	11.6
14	Delaware	13.8
11	Florida	14.3
14	Georgia	13.8
21	Hawaii	12.7
12	Idaho	14.2
29	Illinois	11.9
38	Indiana	11.0
41	Iowa	10.7
41	Kansas	10.7
43	Kentucky	10.2
50	Louisiana	7.5
29	Maine	11.9
9	Maryland	14.9
39	Massachusetts	10.9
7	Michigan	15.3
46	Minnesota	9.3
28	Mississippi	12.1
8	Missouri	15.2
21	Montana	12.7
40	Nebraska	10.8
2	Nevada	17.9
16	New Hampshire	13.4
19	New Jersey	12.8
18	New Mexico	13.1
13	New York	13.9
31	North Carolina	11.8
33	North Dakota	11.6
46	Ohio	9.3
45	Oklahoma	9.6
26	Oregon	12.6
10	Pennsylvania	14.6
17	Rhode Island	13.2
31	South Carolina	11.8
48	South Dakota	9.2
5	Tennessee	16.1
49	Texas	8.1
36	Utah	11.5
33	Vermont	11.6
19	Virginia	12.8
1	Washington	18.7
21	West Virginia	12.7
44	Wisconsin	9.7
26	Wyoming	12.6

RANK ORDER

RANK	STATE	RATE
1	Washington	18.7
2	Nevada	17.9
3	Colorado	17.2
4	Alaska	16.7
5	Tennessee	16.1
6	Arizona	15.9
7	Michigan	15.3
8	Missouri	15.2
9	Maryland	14.9
10	Pennsylvania	14.6
11	Florida	14.3
12	Idaho	14.2
13	New York	13.9
14	Delaware	13.8
14	Georgia	13.8
16	New Hampshire	13.4
17	Rhode Island	13.2
18	New Mexico	13.1
19	New Jersey	12.8
19	Virginia	12.8
21	Alabama	12.7
21	California	12.7
21	Hawaii	12.7
21	Montana	12.7
21	West Virginia	12.7
26	Oregon	12.6
26	Wyoming	12.6
28	Mississippi	12.1
29	Illinois	11.9
29	Maine	11.9
31	North Carolina	11.8
31	South Carolina	11.8
33	Connecticut	11.6
33	North Dakota	11.6
33	Vermont	11.6
36	Utah	11.5
37	Arkansas	11.1
38	Indiana	11.0
39	Massachusetts	10.9
40	Nebraska	10.8
41	Iowa	10.7
41	Kansas	10.7
43	Kentucky	10.2
44	Wisconsin	9.7
45	Oklahoma	9.6
46	Minnesota	9.3
46	Ohio	9.3
48	South Dakota	9.2
49	Texas	8.1
50	Louisiana	7.5
	District of Columbia	9.9

Source: CQ Press using data from U.S. Small Business Administration
"The Small Business Economy 2009" and unpublished data (http://www.sba.gov/advo/research/)
*Firms can be in more than one state. Firms with paid employees ceasing operations in 2008 as a percent of employer firms existing in 2008. Some state terminations result in successor firms which are not listed as new firms, thus making terminations higher than formations for most states.

V. Education

Estimated Percent of School-Age Population in Public Schools in 2008

National Percent = 94.1%*

ALPHA ORDER

ALPHA ORDER			RANK ORDER		
RANK	STATE	PERCENT	RANK	STATE	PERCENT
31	Alabama	92.4	1	Texas	103.7
2	Alaska	103.3	2	Alaska	103.3
3	Arizona	101.7	3	Arizona	101.7
9	Arkansas	96.9	4	Oklahoma	100.5
8	California	97.2	5	West Virginia	99.0
10	Colorado	95.7	6	Florida	98.2
21	Connecticut	93.4	7	Nevada	97.5
49	Delaware	85.1	8	California	97.2
6	Florida	98.2	9	Arkansas	96.9
16	Georgia	94.7	10	Colorado	95.7
26	Hawaii	92.9	11	Michigan	95.5
14	Idaho	94.9	11	Virginia	95.5
25	Illinois	93.0	13	Utah	95.4
33	Indiana	91.5	14	Idaho	94.9
17	Iowa	94.3	15	Kentucky	94.8
28	Kansas	92.6	16	Georgia	94.7
15	Kentucky	94.8	17	Iowa	94.3
50	Louisiana	75.5	18	North Carolina	94.0
35	Maine	91.4	19	New Jersey	93.5
45	Maryland	87.7	19	Vermont	93.5
36	Massachusetts	91.2	21	Connecticut	93.4
11	Michigan	95.5	22	New Mexico	93.2
29	Minnesota	92.5	23	Washington	93.1
39	Mississippi	90.7	23	Wyoming	93.1
41	Missouri	89.7	25	Illinois	93.0
43	Montana	89.2	26	Hawaii	92.9
33	Nebraska	91.5	26	North Dakota	92.9
7	Nevada	97.5	28	Kansas	92.6
38	New Hampshire	90.8	29	Minnesota	92.5
19	New Jersey	93.5	29	South Carolina	92.5
22	New Mexico	93.2	31	Alabama	92.4
48	New York	85.5	32	Tennessee	91.7
18	North Carolina	94.0	33	Indiana	91.5
26	North Dakota	92.9	33	Nebraska	91.5
36	Ohio	91.2	35	Maine	91.4
4	Oklahoma	100.5	36	Massachusetts	91.2
42	Oregon	89.4	36	Ohio	91.2
44	Pennsylvania	88.8	38	New Hampshire	90.8
46	Rhode Island	86.5	39	Mississippi	90.7
29	South Carolina	92.5	40	Wisconsin	90.3
47	South Dakota	85.9	41	Missouri	89.7
32	Tennessee	91.7	42	Oregon	89.4
1	Texas	103.7	43	Montana	89.2
13	Utah	95.4	44	Pennsylvania	88.8
19	Vermont	93.5	45	Maryland	87.7
11	Virginia	95.5	46	Rhode Island	86.5
23	Washington	93.1	47	South Dakota	85.9
5	West Virginia	99.0	48	New York	85.5
40	Wisconsin	90.3	49	Delaware	85.1
23	Wyoming	93.1	50	Louisiana	75.5
				District of Columbia	99.1

Source: CQ Press using data from U.S. Department of Education, National Center for Education Statistics
"Common Core of Data (CCD) Database" (http://nces.ed.gov/ccd/)
*Estimate based on 2008 Census population estimates for 5 to 17 year olds compared to estimated 2007-2008 school year public school student membership. Student membership figures include counts for pre-kindergarten programs. Figures higher than 100 percent reflect using different sources for population and for student membership.

Regular Public Elementary and Secondary School Districts in 2008

National Total = 13,924 Districts*

ALPHA ORDER

RANK	STATE	DISTRICTS	% of USA
34	Alabama	134	1.0%
43	Alaska	53	0.4%
23	Arizona	238	1.7%
22	Arkansas	245	1.8%
2	California	1,026	7.4%
27	Colorado	178	1.3%
30	Connecticut	169	1.2%
48	Delaware	19	0.1%
41	Florida	67	0.5%
26	Georgia	180	1.3%
50	Hawaii	1	0.0%
37	Idaho	115	0.8%
3	Illinois	870	6.2%
18	Indiana	294	2.1%
13	Iowa	364	2.6%
16	Kansas	319	2.3%
29	Kentucky	174	1.2%
40	Louisiana	69	0.5%
20	Maine	290	2.1%
47	Maryland	24	0.2%
14	Massachusetts	352	2.5%
7	Michigan	552	4.0%
15	Minnesota	340	2.4%
32	Mississippi	152	1.1%
9	Missouri	524	3.8%
12	Montana	421	3.0%
21	Nebraska	254	1.8%
49	Nevada	18	0.1%
28	New Hampshire	177	1.3%
5	New Jersey	616	4.4%
38	New Mexico	89	0.6%
4	New York	697	5.0%
36	North Carolina	116	0.8%
25	North Dakota	192	1.4%
6	Ohio	614	4.4%
8	Oklahoma	539	3.9%
24	Oregon	195	1.4%
10	Pennsylvania	501	3.6%
46	Rhode Island	32	0.2%
39	South Carolina	86	0.6%
31	South Dakota	168	1.2%
33	Tennessee	136	1.0%
1	Texas	1,033	7.4%
45	Utah	40	0.3%
19	Vermont	292	2.1%
34	Virginia	134	1.0%
17	Washington	295	2.1%
42	West Virginia	55	0.4%
11	Wisconsin	426	3.1%
44	Wyoming	48	0.3%

RANK ORDER

RANK	STATE	DISTRICTS	% of USA
1	Texas	1,033	7.4%
2	California	1,026	7.4%
3	Illinois	870	6.2%
4	New York	697	5.0%
5	New Jersey	616	4.4%
6	Ohio	614	4.4%
7	Michigan	552	4.0%
8	Oklahoma	539	3.9%
9	Missouri	524	3.8%
10	Pennsylvania	501	3.6%
11	Wisconsin	426	3.1%
12	Montana	421	3.0%
13	Iowa	364	2.6%
14	Massachusetts	352	2.5%
15	Minnesota	340	2.4%
16	Kansas	319	2.3%
17	Washington	295	2.1%
18	Indiana	294	2.1%
19	Vermont	292	2.1%
20	Maine	290	2.1%
21	Nebraska	254	1.8%
22	Arkansas	245	1.8%
23	Arizona	238	1.7%
24	Oregon	195	1.4%
25	North Dakota	192	1.4%
26	Georgia	180	1.3%
27	Colorado	178	1.3%
28	New Hampshire	177	1.3%
29	Kentucky	174	1.2%
30	Connecticut	169	1.2%
31	South Dakota	168	1.2%
32	Mississippi	152	1.1%
33	Tennessee	136	1.0%
34	Alabama	134	1.0%
34	Virginia	134	1.0%
36	North Carolina	116	0.8%
37	Idaho	115	0.8%
38	New Mexico	89	0.6%
39	South Carolina	86	0.6%
40	Louisiana	69	0.5%
41	Florida	67	0.5%
42	West Virginia	55	0.4%
43	Alaska	53	0.4%
44	Wyoming	48	0.3%
45	Utah	40	0.3%
46	Rhode Island	32	0.2%
47	Maryland	24	0.2%
48	Delaware	19	0.1%
49	Nevada	18	0.1%
50	Hawaii	1	0.0%
	District of Columbia	1	0.0%

Source: U.S. Department of Education, National Center for Education Statistics
"Numbers and Types of Public Elementary and Secondary Local Education Agencies"
(http://nces.ed.gov/pubs2010/2010306/index.asp)

*For school year 2007-2008. Regular school districts are agencies responsible for providing free public education for school-age children residing within their jurisdiction.

Public Elementary and Secondary Schools in 2008

National Total = 98,916 Schools*

ALPHA ORDER

RANK	STATE	SCHOOLS	% of USA
23	Alabama	1,605	1.6%
44	Alaska	501	0.5%
16	Arizona	2,135	2.2%
32	Arkansas	1,121	1.1%
1	California	9,983	10.1%
21	Colorado	1,757	1.8%
33	Connecticut	1,117	1.1%
50	Delaware	235	0.2%
6	Florida	3,935	4.0%
12	Georgia	2,452	2.5%
49	Hawaii	287	0.3%
40	Idaho	727	0.7%
4	Illinois	4,399	4.4%
18	Indiana	1,970	2.0%
25	Iowa	1,511	1.5%
28	Kansas	1,422	1.4%
24	Kentucky	1,528	1.5%
26	Louisiana	1,470	1.5%
41	Maine	670	0.7%
27	Maryland	1,453	1.5%
19	Massachusetts	1,878	1.9%
5	Michigan	4,096	4.1%
9	Minnesota	2,679	2.7%
34	Mississippi	1,068	1.1%
13	Missouri	2,417	2.4%
37	Montana	831	0.8%
31	Nebraska	1,143	1.2%
42	Nevada	610	0.6%
45	New Hampshire	488	0.5%
10	New Jersey	2,591	2.6%
36	New Mexico	851	0.9%
3	New York	4,631	4.7%
11	North Carolina	2,516	2.5%
43	North Dakota	528	0.5%
7	Ohio	3,924	4.0%
20	Oklahoma	1,798	1.8%
29	Oregon	1,295	1.3%
8	Pennsylvania	3,246	3.3%
48	Rhode Island	328	0.3%
30	South Carolina	1,195	1.2%
39	South Dakota	730	0.7%
22	Tennessee	1,718	1.7%
2	Texas	8,758	8.9%
35	Utah	1,010	1.0%
47	Vermont	329	0.3%
17	Virginia	2,027	2.0%
14	Washington	2,311	2.3%
38	West Virginia	762	0.8%
15	Wisconsin	2,268	2.3%
46	Wyoming	368	0.4%

RANK ORDER

RANK	STATE	SCHOOLS	% of USA
1	California	9,983	10.1%
2	Texas	8,758	8.9%
3	New York	4,631	4.7%
4	Illinois	4,399	4.4%
5	Michigan	4,096	4.1%
6	Florida	3,935	4.0%
7	Ohio	3,924	4.0%
8	Pennsylvania	3,246	3.3%
9	Minnesota	2,679	2.7%
10	New Jersey	2,591	2.6%
11	North Carolina	2,516	2.5%
12	Georgia	2,452	2.5%
13	Missouri	2,417	2.4%
14	Washington	2,311	2.3%
15	Wisconsin	2,268	2.3%
16	Arizona	2,135	2.2%
17	Virginia	2,027	2.0%
18	Indiana	1,970	2.0%
19	Massachusetts	1,878	1.9%
20	Oklahoma	1,798	1.8%
21	Colorado	1,757	1.8%
22	Tennessee	1,718	1.7%
23	Alabama	1,605	1.6%
24	Kentucky	1,528	1.5%
25	Iowa	1,511	1.5%
26	Louisiana	1,470	1.5%
27	Maryland	1,453	1.5%
28	Kansas	1,422	1.4%
29	Oregon	1,295	1.3%
30	South Carolina	1,195	1.2%
31	Nebraska	1,143	1.2%
32	Arkansas	1,121	1.1%
33	Connecticut	1,117	1.1%
34	Mississippi	1,068	1.1%
35	Utah	1,010	1.0%
36	New Mexico	851	0.9%
37	Montana	831	0.8%
38	West Virginia	762	0.8%
39	South Dakota	730	0.7%
40	Idaho	727	0.7%
41	Maine	670	0.7%
42	Nevada	610	0.6%
43	North Dakota	528	0.5%
44	Alaska	501	0.5%
45	New Hampshire	488	0.5%
46	Wyoming	368	0.4%
47	Vermont	329	0.3%
48	Rhode Island	328	0.3%
49	Hawaii	287	0.3%
50	Delaware	235	0.2%
	District of Columbia	244	0.2%

Source: U.S. Department of Education, National Center for Education Statistics
"Numbers and Types of Public Elementary and Secondary Schools" (http://nces.ed.gov/pubs2010/2010305/index.asp)
*For school year 2007-2008. Includes all operating schools.

Private Elementary and Secondary Schools in 2008

National Total = 33,740 Schools*

ALPHA ORDER

RANK	STATE	SCHOOLS	% of USA
22	Alabama	423	1.3%
48	Alaska	63	0.2%
28	Arizona	361	1.1%
30	Arkansas**	305	0.9%
1	California	4,013	11.9%
24	Colorado	415	1.2%
22	Connecticut	423	1.3%
37	Delaware**	214	0.6%
4	Florida	1,938	5.7%
11	Georgia	910	2.7%
46	Hawaii	136	0.4%
40	Idaho**	190	0.6%
5	Illinois	1,924	5.7%
15	Indiana	807	2.4%
33	Iowa	242	0.7%
32	Kansas	246	0.7%
26	Kentucky	404	1.2%
27	Louisiana	393	1.2%
39	Maine	200	0.6%
14	Maryland	823	2.4%
10	Massachusetts	947	2.8%
12	Michigan	908	2.7%
19	Minnesota	585	1.7%
36	Mississippi	219	0.6%
17	Missouri	690	2.0%
44	Montana**	141	0.4%
35	Nebraska	223	0.7%
41	Nevada	161	0.5%
29	New Hampshire	312	0.9%
7	New Jersey	1,441	4.3%
38	New Mexico	212	0.6%
3	New York	2,130	6.3%
18	North Carolina	656	1.9%
49	North Dakota	50	0.1%
8	Ohio	1,189	3.5%
31	Oklahoma**	300	0.9%
20	Oregon	564	1.7%
2	Pennsylvania	2,503	7.4%
34	Rhode Island	226	0.7%
25	South Carolina	409	1.2%
47	South Dakota	80	0.2%
21	Tennessee	557	1.7%
6	Texas	1,651	4.9%
43	Utah	146	0.4%
42	Vermont	150	0.4%
13	Virginia	872	2.6%
16	Washington	730	2.2%
45	West Virginia	139	0.4%
9	Wisconsin	990	2.9%
50	Wyoming	38	0.1%

RANK ORDER

RANK	STATE	SCHOOLS	% of USA
1	California	4,013	11.9%
2	Pennsylvania	2,503	7.4%
3	New York	2,130	6.3%
4	Florida	1,938	5.7%
5	Illinois	1,924	5.7%
6	Texas	1,651	4.9%
7	New Jersey	1,441	4.3%
8	Ohio	1,189	3.5%
9	Wisconsin	990	2.9%
10	Massachusetts	947	2.8%
11	Georgia	910	2.7%
12	Michigan	908	2.7%
13	Virginia	872	2.6%
14	Maryland	823	2.4%
15	Indiana	807	2.4%
16	Washington	730	2.2%
17	Missouri	690	2.0%
18	North Carolina	656	1.9%
19	Minnesota	585	1.7%
20	Oregon	564	1.7%
21	Tennessee	557	1.7%
22	Alabama	423	1.3%
22	Connecticut	423	1.3%
24	Colorado	415	1.2%
25	South Carolina	409	1.2%
26	Kentucky	404	1.2%
27	Louisiana	393	1.2%
28	Arizona	361	1.1%
29	New Hampshire	312	0.9%
30	Arkansas**	305	0.9%
31	Oklahoma**	300	0.9%
32	Kansas	246	0.7%
33	Iowa	242	0.7%
34	Rhode Island	226	0.7%
35	Nebraska	223	0.7%
36	Mississippi	219	0.6%
37	Delaware**	214	0.6%
38	New Mexico	212	0.6%
39	Maine	200	0.6%
40	Idaho**	190	0.6%
41	Nevada	161	0.5%
42	Vermont	150	0.4%
43	Utah	146	0.4%
44	Montana**	141	0.4%
45	West Virginia	139	0.4%
46	Hawaii	136	0.4%
47	South Dakota	80	0.2%
48	Alaska	63	0.2%
49	North Dakota	50	0.1%
50	Wyoming	38	0.1%
	District of Columbia	92	0.3%

Source: U.S. Department of Education, National Center for Education Statistics
   "Characteristics of Private Schools in the United States" (http://nces.ed.gov/pubs2009/2009313.pdf)
*For school year 2007-2008.
**Interpret data for these states with caution.

Private Elementary and Secondary School Enrollment in 2008

National Total = 5,072,451 Students*

ALPHA ORDER

RANK	STATE	STUDENTS	% of USA
23	Alabama	72,037	1.4%
49	Alaska	4,173	0.1%
27	Arizona	51,590	1.0%
33	Arkansas**	34,850	0.7%
1	California	607,141	12.0%
28	Colorado	48,945	1.0%
22	Connecticut	76,520	1.5%
36	Delaware	26,403	0.5%
3	Florida	329,646	6.5%
11	Georgia	136,987	2.7%
35	Hawaii	33,441	0.7%
41	Idaho**	20,878	0.4%
5	Illinois	264,012	5.2%
19	Indiana	104,062	2.1%
31	Iowa	41,796	0.8%
30	Kansas	43,413	0.9%
24	Kentucky	67,376	1.3%
13	Louisiana	123,476	2.4%
42	Maine	19,553	0.4%
9	Maryland	143,661	2.8%
12	Massachusetts	127,967	2.5%
10	Michigan	139,314	2.7%
20	Minnesota	90,973	1.8%
29	Mississippi	47,955	0.9%
16	Missouri	112,368	2.2%
44	Montana**	13,778	0.3%
32	Nebraska	35,872	0.7%
40	Nevada	22,310	0.4%
39	New Hampshire	23,200	0.5%
8	New Jersey	204,486	4.0%
38	New Mexico	23,582	0.5%
2	New York	458,231	9.0%
17	North Carolina	108,810	2.1%
48	North Dakota	6,345	0.1%
7	Ohio	215,592	4.3%
34	Oklahoma	34,354	0.7%
26	Oregon	53,243	1.0%
4	Pennsylvania	281,958	5.6%
37	Rhode Island	23,951	0.5%
25	South Carolina	56,492	1.1%
47	South Dakota	10,692	0.2%
18	Tennessee	106,097	2.1%
6	Texas	235,241	4.6%
43	Utah	17,551	0.3%
46	Vermont	11,713	0.2%
15	Virginia	116,934	2.3%
21	Washington	86,811	1.7%
45	West Virginia	13,400	0.3%
14	Wisconsin	123,174	2.4%
50	Wyoming	2,113	0.0%

RANK ORDER

RANK	STATE	STUDENTS	% of USA
1	California	607,141	12.0%
2	New York	458,231	9.0%
3	Florida	329,646	6.5%
4	Pennsylvania	281,958	5.6%
5	Illinois	264,012	5.2%
6	Texas	235,241	4.6%
7	Ohio	215,592	4.3%
8	New Jersey	204,486	4.0%
9	Maryland	143,661	2.8%
10	Michigan	139,314	2.7%
11	Georgia	136,987	2.7%
12	Massachusetts	127,967	2.5%
13	Louisiana	123,476	2.4%
14	Wisconsin	123,174	2.4%
15	Virginia	116,934	2.3%
16	Missouri	112,368	2.2%
17	North Carolina	108,810	2.1%
18	Tennessee	106,097	2.1%
19	Indiana	104,062	2.1%
20	Minnesota	90,973	1.8%
21	Washington	86,811	1.7%
22	Connecticut	76,520	1.5%
23	Alabama	72,037	1.4%
24	Kentucky	67,376	1.3%
25	South Carolina	56,492	1.1%
26	Oregon	53,243	1.0%
27	Arizona	51,590	1.0%
28	Colorado	48,945	1.0%
29	Mississippi	47,955	0.9%
30	Kansas	43,413	0.9%
31	Iowa	41,796	0.8%
32	Nebraska	35,872	0.7%
33	Arkansas**	34,850	0.7%
34	Oklahoma	34,354	0.7%
35	Hawaii	33,441	0.7%
36	Delaware	26,403	0.5%
37	Rhode Island	23,951	0.5%
38	New Mexico	23,582	0.5%
39	New Hampshire	23,200	0.5%
40	Nevada	22,310	0.4%
41	Idaho**	20,878	0.4%
42	Maine	19,553	0.4%
43	Utah	17,551	0.3%
44	Montana**	13,778	0.3%
45	West Virginia	13,400	0.3%
46	Vermont	11,713	0.2%
47	South Dakota	10,692	0.2%
48	North Dakota	6,345	0.1%
49	Alaska	4,173	0.1%
50	Wyoming	2,113	0.0%
	District of Columbia	17,985	0.4%

Source: U.S. Department of Education, National Center for Education Statistics
"Characteristics of Private Schools in the United States" (http://nces.ed.gov/pubs2009/2009313.pdf)
*For school year 2007-2008.
**Interpret data for these states with caution.

Enrollment in Public Elementary and Secondary Schools in 2008

National Total = 49,252,507 Students*

ALPHA ORDER					RANK ORDER			
RANK	STATE	ENROLLMENT	% of USA		RANK	STATE	ENROLLMENT	% of USA
23	Alabama	744,865	1.5%		1	California	6,343,471	12.9%
45	Alaska	131,029	0.3%		2	Texas	4,674,832	9.5%
13	Arizona	1,087,447	2.2%		3	New York	2,765,435	5.6%
33	Arkansas	479,016	1.0%		4	Florida	2,666,811	5.4%
1	California	6,343,471	12.9%		5	Illinois	2,112,805	4.3%
22	Colorado	801,867	1.6%		6	Ohio	1,827,184	3.7%
29	Connecticut	570,626	1.2%		7	Pennsylvania	1,801,971	3.7%
46	Delaware	122,574	0.2%		8	Michigan	1,692,739	3.4%
4	Florida	2,666,811	5.4%		9	Georgia	1,649,589	3.3%
9	Georgia	1,649,589	3.3%		10	North Carolina	1,489,492	3.0%
42	Hawaii	179,897	0.4%		11	New Jersey	1,382,348	2.8%
39	Idaho	272,119	0.6%		12	Virginia	1,230,857	2.5%
5	Illinois	2,112,805	4.3%		13	Arizona	1,087,447	2.2%
14	Indiana	1,046,766	2.1%		14	Indiana	1,046,766	2.1%
32	Iowa	485,115	1.0%		15	Washington	1,030,247	2.1%
34	Kansas	468,295	1.0%		16	Tennessee	964,259	2.0%
26	Kentucky	666,225	1.4%		17	Massachusetts	962,958	2.0%
25	Louisiana	681,038	1.4%		18	Missouri	917,188	1.9%
41	Maine	196,245	0.4%		19	Wisconsin	874,633	1.8%
20	Maryland	845,700	1.7%		20	Maryland	845,700	1.7%
17	Massachusetts	962,958	2.0%		21	Minnesota	837,578	1.7%
8	Michigan	1,692,739	3.4%		22	Colorado	801,867	1.6%
21	Minnesota	837,578	1.7%		23	Alabama	744,865	1.5%
31	Mississippi	494,122	1.0%		24	South Carolina	712,317	1.4%
18	Missouri	917,188	1.9%		25	Louisiana	681,038	1.4%
44	Montana	142,823	0.3%		26	Kentucky	666,225	1.4%
37	Nebraska	291,244	0.6%		27	Oklahoma	642,065	1.3%
35	Nevada	429,362	0.9%		28	Utah	576,244	1.2%
40	New Hampshire	200,772	0.4%		29	Connecticut	570,626	1.2%
11	New Jersey	1,382,348	2.8%		30	Oregon	565,586	1.1%
36	New Mexico	329,040	0.7%		31	Mississippi	494,122	1.0%
3	New York	2,765,435	5.6%		32	Iowa	485,115	1.0%
10	North Carolina	1,489,492	3.0%		33	Arkansas	479,016	1.0%
48	North Dakota	95,059	0.2%		34	Kansas	468,295	1.0%
6	Ohio	1,827,184	3.7%		35	Nevada	429,362	0.9%
27	Oklahoma	642,065	1.3%		36	New Mexico	329,040	0.7%
30	Oregon	565,586	1.1%		37	Nebraska	291,244	0.6%
7	Pennsylvania	1,801,971	3.7%		38	West Virginia	282,535	0.6%
43	Rhode Island	147,629	0.3%		39	Idaho	272,119	0.6%
24	South Carolina	712,317	1.4%		40	New Hampshire	200,772	0.4%
47	South Dakota	121,606	0.2%		41	Maine	196,245	0.4%
16	Tennessee	964,259	2.0%		42	Hawaii	179,897	0.4%
2	Texas	4,674,832	9.5%		43	Rhode Island	147,629	0.3%
28	Utah	576,244	1.2%		44	Montana	142,823	0.3%
49	Vermont	94,038	0.2%		45	Alaska	131,029	0.3%
12	Virginia	1,230,857	2.5%		46	Delaware	122,574	0.2%
15	Washington	1,030,247	2.1%		47	South Dakota	121,606	0.2%
38	West Virginia	282,535	0.6%		48	North Dakota	95,059	0.2%
19	Wisconsin	874,633	1.8%		49	Vermont	94,038	0.2%
50	Wyoming	86,422	0.2%		50	Wyoming	86,422	0.2%
						District of Columbia	78,422	0.2%

Source: U.S. Department of Education, National Center for Education Statistics
   "Public Elementary and Secondary School Student Enrollment and Staff Counts" (http://nces.ed.gov/pubs2010/2010309/)
*For school year 2007-2008.

Public Elementary and Secondary School Teachers in 2008

National Total = 3,178,142 Teachers*

ALPHA ORDER

RANK	STATE	TEACHERS	% of USA
22	Alabama	50,420	1.6%
49	Alaska	7,613	0.2%
19	Arizona	54,032	1.7%
31	Arkansas	33,882	1.1%
2	California	305,230	9.6%
24	Colorado	47,761	1.5%
28	Connecticut	39,304	1.2%
47	Delaware	8,198	0.3%
4	Florida	168,737	5.3%
7	Georgia	116,857	3.7%
42	Hawaii	11,397	0.4%
41	Idaho	15,013	0.5%
5	Illinois	136,571	4.3%
16	Indiana	62,334	2.0%
29	Iowa	36,089	1.1%
30	Kansas	35,359	1.1%
27	Kentucky	43,536	1.4%
23	Louisiana	48,610	1.5%
39	Maine	16,558	0.5%
17	Maryland	59,320	1.9%
13	Massachusetts	70,719	2.2%
11	Michigan	96,204	3.0%
21	Minnesota	52,975	1.7%
32	Mississippi	33,560	1.1%
14	Missouri	68,430	2.2%
44	Montana	10,519	0.3%
37	Nebraska	21,930	0.7%
35	Nevada	23,423	0.7%
40	New Hampshire	15,484	0.5%
8	New Jersey	111,500	3.5%
36	New Mexico	22,300	0.7%
3	New York	211,854	6.7%
10	North Carolina	106,562	3.4%
48	North Dakota	8,068	0.3%
9	Ohio	109,766	3.5%
26	Oklahoma	46,735	1.5%
33	Oregon	30,013	0.9%
6	Pennsylvania	135,234	4.3%
43	Rhode Island	11,271	0.4%
25	South Carolina	47,382	1.5%
45	South Dakota	9,416	0.3%
15	Tennessee	64,659	2.0%
1	Texas	321,929	10.1%
34	Utah	24,336	0.8%
46	Vermont	8,749	0.3%
12	Virginia	71,861	2.3%
20	Washington	53,960	1.7%
38	West Virginia	20,306	0.6%
18	Wisconsin	58,914	1.9%
50	Wyoming	6,915	0.2%

RANK ORDER

RANK	STATE	TEACHERS	% of USA
1	Texas	321,929	10.1%
2	California	305,230	9.6%
3	New York	211,854	6.7%
4	Florida	168,737	5.3%
5	Illinois	136,571	4.3%
6	Pennsylvania	135,234	4.3%
7	Georgia	116,857	3.7%
8	New Jersey	111,500	3.5%
9	Ohio	109,766	3.5%
10	North Carolina	106,562	3.4%
11	Michigan	96,204	3.0%
12	Virginia	71,861	2.3%
13	Massachusetts	70,719	2.2%
14	Missouri	68,430	2.2%
15	Tennessee	64,659	2.0%
16	Indiana	62,334	2.0%
17	Maryland	59,320	1.9%
18	Wisconsin	58,914	1.9%
19	Arizona	54,032	1.7%
20	Washington	53,960	1.7%
21	Minnesota	52,975	1.7%
22	Alabama	50,420	1.6%
23	Louisiana	48,610	1.5%
24	Colorado	47,761	1.5%
25	South Carolina	47,382	1.5%
26	Oklahoma	46,735	1.5%
27	Kentucky	43,536	1.4%
28	Connecticut	39,304	1.2%
29	Iowa	36,089	1.1%
30	Kansas	35,359	1.1%
31	Arkansas	33,882	1.1%
32	Mississippi	33,560	1.1%
33	Oregon	30,013	0.9%
34	Utah	24,336	0.8%
35	Nevada	23,423	0.7%
36	New Mexico	22,300	0.7%
37	Nebraska	21,930	0.7%
38	West Virginia	20,306	0.6%
39	Maine	16,558	0.5%
40	New Hampshire	15,484	0.5%
41	Idaho	15,013	0.5%
42	Hawaii	11,397	0.4%
43	Rhode Island	11,271	0.4%
44	Montana	10,519	0.3%
45	South Dakota	9,416	0.3%
46	Vermont	8,749	0.3%
47	Delaware	8,198	0.3%
48	North Dakota	8,068	0.3%
49	Alaska	7,613	0.2%
50	Wyoming	6,915	0.2%
	District of Columbia	6,347	0.2%

Source: U.S. Department of Education, National Center for Education Statistics
    "Public Elementary and Secondary School Student Enrollment and Staff Counts" (http://nces.ed.gov/pubs2010/2010309/)
*For school year 2007-2008.

Pupil-Teacher Ratio in
Public Elementary and Secondary Schools in 2008
National Ratio = 15.5 Pupils per Teacher*

ALPHA ORDER

RANK ORDER

RANK	STATE	RATIO	RANK	STATE	RATIO
22	Alabama	14.8	1	Utah	23.7
9	Alaska	17.2	2	California	20.8
3	Arizona	20.1	3	Arizona	20.1
29	Arkansas	14.1	4	Washington	19.1
2	California	20.8	5	Oregon	18.8
11	Colorado	16.8	6	Nevada	18.3
26	Connecticut	14.5	7	Idaho	18.1
19	Delaware	15.0	8	Michigan	17.6
14	Florida	15.8	9	Alaska	17.2
29	Georgia	14.1	10	Virginia	17.1
14	Hawaii	15.8	11	Colorado	16.8
7	Idaho	18.1	11	Indiana	16.8
17	Illinois	15.5	13	Ohio	16.6
11	Indiana	16.8	14	Florida	15.8
37	Iowa	13.4	14	Hawaii	15.8
41	Kansas	13.2	14	Minnesota	15.8
18	Kentucky	15.3	17	Illinois	15.5
31	Louisiana	14.0	18	Kentucky	15.3
48	Maine	11.9	19	Delaware	15.0
28	Maryland	14.3	19	South Carolina	15.0
35	Massachusetts	13.6	21	Tennessee	14.9
8	Michigan	17.6	22	Alabama	14.8
14	Minnesota	15.8	22	New Mexico	14.8
25	Mississippi	14.7	22	Wisconsin	14.8
37	Missouri	13.4	25	Mississippi	14.7
35	Montana	13.6	26	Connecticut	14.5
39	Nebraska	13.3	26	Texas	14.5
6	Nevada	18.3	28	Maryland	14.3
44	New Hampshire	13.0	29	Arkansas	14.1
47	New Jersey	12.4	29	Georgia	14.1
22	New Mexico	14.8	31	Louisiana	14.0
42	New York	13.1	31	North Carolina	14.0
31	North Carolina	14.0	33	West Virginia	13.9
49	North Dakota	11.8	34	Oklahoma	13.7
13	Ohio	16.6	35	Massachusetts	13.6
34	Oklahoma	13.7	35	Montana	13.6
5	Oregon	18.8	37	Iowa	13.4
39	Pennsylvania	13.3	37	Missouri	13.4
42	Rhode Island	13.1	39	Nebraska	13.3
19	South Carolina	15.0	39	Pennsylvania	13.3
45	South Dakota	12.9	41	Kansas	13.2
21	Tennessee	14.9	42	New York	13.1
26	Texas	14.5	42	Rhode Island	13.1
1	Utah	23.7	44	New Hampshire	13.0
50	Vermont	10.7	45	South Dakota	12.9
10	Virginia	17.1	46	Wyoming	12.5
4	Washington	19.1	47	New Jersey	12.4
33	West Virginia	13.9	48	Maine	11.9
22	Wisconsin	14.8	49	North Dakota	11.8
46	Wyoming	12.5	50	Vermont	10.7

	District of Columbia	12.4

Source: U.S. Department of Education, National Center for Education Statistics
   "Public Elementary and Secondary School Student Enrollment and Staff Counts" (http://nces.ed.gov/pubs2010/2010309/)
*For school year 2007-2008.

Estimated Average Salary of Public School Teachers in 2010
(National Education Association)
National Average = $55,350*

<u>ALPHA ORDER</u>

RANK	STATE	SALARY
34	Alabama	$47,156
8	Alaska	59,729
36	Arizona	46,952
29	Arkansas	49,051
2	California	70,458
27	Colorado	49,505
6	Connecticut	64,350
13	Delaware	57,080
37	Florida	46,912
17	Georgia	54,274
10	Hawaii	58,168
40	Idaho	46,283
7	Illinois	62,077
26	Indiana	49,986
23	Iowa	50,547
35	Kansas	46,957
32	Kentucky	48,354
24	Louisiana	50,349
41	Maine	46,106
4	Maryland	65,333
3	Massachusetts	68,000
12	Michigan	57,958
19	Minnesota	53,069
45	Mississippi	45,644
46	Missouri	45,317
44	Montana	45,759
42	Nebraska	46,080
21	Nevada	51,524
22	New Hampshire	51,365
5	New Jersey	64,809
38	New Mexico	46,401
1	New York	71,470
30	North Carolina	48,648
49	North Dakota	42,964
14	Ohio	55,931
47	Oklahoma	44,143
16	Oregon	55,224
11	Pennsylvania	58,124
9	Rhode Island	59,636
31	South Carolina	48,417
50	South Dakota	35,136
39	Tennessee	46,290
33	Texas	47,157
48	Utah	43,068
28	Vermont	49,053
25	Virginia	49,999
18	Washington	53,653
43	West Virginia	45,959
20	Wisconsin	52,644
15	Wyoming	55,694

<u>RANK ORDER</u>

RANK	STATE	SALARY
1	New York	$71,470
2	California	70,458
3	Massachusetts	68,000
4	Maryland	65,333
5	New Jersey	64,809
6	Connecticut	64,350
7	Illinois	62,077
8	Alaska	59,729
9	Rhode Island	59,636
10	Hawaii	58,168
11	Pennsylvania	58,124
12	Michigan	57,958
13	Delaware	57,080
14	Ohio	55,931
15	Wyoming	55,694
16	Oregon	55,224
17	Georgia	54,274
18	Washington	53,653
19	Minnesota	53,069
20	Wisconsin	52,644
21	Nevada	51,524
22	New Hampshire	51,365
23	Iowa	50,547
24	Louisiana	50,349
25	Virginia	49,999
26	Indiana	49,986
27	Colorado	49,505
28	Vermont	49,053
29	Arkansas	49,051
30	North Carolina	48,648
31	South Carolina	48,417
32	Kentucky	48,354
33	Texas	47,157
34	Alabama	47,156
35	Kansas	46,957
36	Arizona	46,952
37	Florida	46,912
38	New Mexico	46,401
39	Tennessee	46,290
40	Idaho	46,283
41	Maine	46,106
42	Nebraska	46,080
43	West Virginia	45,959
44	Montana	45,759
45	Mississippi	45,644
46	Missouri	45,317
47	Oklahoma	44,143
48	Utah	43,068
49	North Dakota	42,964
50	South Dakota	35,136
	District of Columbia	64,548

Source: National Education Association, Washington, D.C.
    "Rankings and Estimates" (Copyright © 2010, NEA, used with permission, http://www.nea.org/home/30896.htm)
*Estimates for school year 2009-2010 for classroom teachers.

Average Teacher's Salary as a Percent of Average Annual Pay in 2008

National Average = 117.6% of Average Annual Pay*

ALPHA ORDER

RANK	STATE	PERCENT
29	Alabama	120.7
18	Alaska	125.7
43	Arizona	108.3
3	Arkansas	133.5
8	California	130.0
46	Colorado	102.9
45	Connecticut	107.1
31	Delaware	118.4
35	Florida	115.7
24	Georgia	122.6
2	Hawaii	134.2
6	Idaho	131.7
20	Illinois	125.0
11	Indiana	128.5
16	Iowa	127.6
30	Kansas	119.4
17	Kentucky	127.0
31	Louisiana	118.4
26	Maine	121.3
21	Maryland	124.1
36	Massachusetts	115.0
13	Michigan	128.2
39	Minnesota	111.9
9	Mississippi	129.7
43	Missouri	108.3
7	Montana	131.1
25	Nebraska	122.2
37	Nevada	113.7
19	New Hampshire	125.4
49	New Jersey	97.9
21	New Mexico	124.1
40	New York	111.6
28	North Carolina	120.8
34	North Dakota	116.8
4	Ohio	132.5
33	Oklahoma	117.2
5	Oregon	131.8
15	Pennsylvania	127.7
1	Rhode Island	134.3
11	South Carolina	128.5
50	South Dakota	97.4
38	Tennessee	113.0
47	Texas	101.6
41	Utah	110.5
23	Vermont	123.2
48	Virginia	100.6
42	Washington	110.0
27	West Virginia	121.2
14	Wisconsin	128.0
10	Wyoming	129.6

RANK ORDER

RANK	STATE	PERCENT
1	Rhode Island	134.3
2	Hawaii	134.2
3	Arkansas	133.5
4	Ohio	132.5
5	Oregon	131.8
6	Idaho	131.7
7	Montana	131.1
8	California	130.0
9	Mississippi	129.7
10	Wyoming	129.6
11	Indiana	128.5
11	South Carolina	128.5
13	Michigan	128.2
14	Wisconsin	128.0
15	Pennsylvania	127.7
16	Iowa	127.6
17	Kentucky	127.0
18	Alaska	125.7
19	New Hampshire	125.4
20	Illinois	125.0
21	Maryland	124.1
21	New Mexico	124.1
23	Vermont	123.2
24	Georgia	122.6
25	Nebraska	122.2
26	Maine	121.3
27	West Virginia	121.2
28	North Carolina	120.8
29	Alabama	120.7
30	Kansas	119.4
31	Delaware	118.4
31	Louisiana	118.4
33	Oklahoma	117.2
34	North Dakota	116.8
35	Florida	115.7
36	Massachusetts	115.0
37	Nevada	113.7
38	Tennessee	113.0
39	Minnesota	111.9
40	New York	111.6
41	Utah	110.5
42	Washington	110.0
43	Arizona	108.3
43	Missouri	108.3
45	Connecticut	107.1
46	Colorado	102.9
47	Texas	101.6
48	Virginia	100.6
49	New Jersey	97.9
50	South Dakota	97.4

| | District of Columbia | 80.5 |

Source: CQ Press using data from National Education Association, Washington, D.C.
"Rankings and Estimates" (Copyright © 2010, NEA, used with permission, http://www.nea.org/home/30896.htm)
"Quarterly Census of Employment and Wages" (http://www.bls.gov/cew/home.htm)
*Average of public elementary and secondary teacher salary for school years 2007-2008 and 2008-2009 compared to each state's 2008 average annual pay for all workers covered by federal unemployment.

Percent of Public School Fourth Graders
Proficient or Better in Reading in 2007
National Percent = 32%*

ALPHA ORDER

RANK	STATE	PERCENT
34	Alabama	29
34	Alaska	29
45	Arizona	24
34	Arkansas	29
48	California	23
10	Colorado	36
3	Connecticut	41
23	Delaware	34
23	Florida	34
38	Georgia	28
43	Hawaii	26
20	Idaho	35
29	Illinois	32
27	Indiana	33
10	Iowa	36
10	Kansas	36
27	Kentucky	33
49	Louisiana	20
10	Maine	36
10	Maryland	36
1	Massachusetts	49
29	Michigan	32
9	Minnesota	37
50	Mississippi	19
29	Missouri	32
7	Montana	39
20	Nebraska	35
45	Nevada	24
3	New Hampshire	41
2	New Jersey	43
45	New Mexico	24
10	New York	36
34	North Carolina	29
20	North Dakota	35
10	Ohio	36
41	Oklahoma	27
38	Oregon	28
6	Pennsylvania	40
32	Rhode Island	31
43	South Carolina	26
23	South Dakota	34
41	Tennessee	27
33	Texas	30
23	Utah	34
3	Vermont	41
8	Virginia	38
10	Washington	36
38	West Virginia	28
10	Wisconsin	36
10	Wyoming	36

RANK ORDER

RANK	STATE	PERCENT
1	Massachusetts	49
2	New Jersey	43
3	Connecticut	41
3	New Hampshire	41
3	Vermont	41
6	Pennsylvania	40
7	Montana	39
8	Virginia	38
9	Minnesota	37
10	Colorado	36
10	Iowa	36
10	Kansas	36
10	Maine	36
10	Maryland	36
10	New York	36
10	Ohio	36
10	Washington	36
10	Wisconsin	36
10	Wyoming	36
20	Idaho	35
20	Nebraska	35
20	North Dakota	35
23	Delaware	34
23	Florida	34
23	South Dakota	34
23	Utah	34
27	Indiana	33
27	Kentucky	33
29	Illinois	32
29	Michigan	32
29	Missouri	32
32	Rhode Island	31
33	Texas	30
34	Alabama	29
34	Alaska	29
34	Arkansas	29
34	North Carolina	29
38	Georgia	28
38	Oregon	28
38	West Virginia	28
41	Oklahoma	27
41	Tennessee	27
43	Hawaii	26
43	South Carolina	26
45	Arizona	24
45	Nevada	24
45	New Mexico	24
48	California	23
49	Louisiana	20
50	Mississippi	19

| | District of Columbia | 14 |

Source: U.S. Department of Education, National Center for Education Statistics
    "NAEP 2007: Reading Report Card for the Nation and the States" (NCES 2007-496, http://nces.ed.gov/nationsreportcard/)
*There are four achievement levels: Below Basic, Basic, Proficient, and Advanced. Proficient represents solid academic mastery for 4th graders. Students reaching this level have demonstrated competency over challenging subject matter, including subject matter knowledge, application of such knowledge to real-world situations, and analytical skills appropriate to the subject matter.

Percent of Public School Eighth Graders
Proficient or Better in Reading in 2007
National Percent = 29%*

ALPHA ORDER

RANK	STATE	PERCENT
45	Alabama	21
35	Alaska	27
42	Arizona	24
40	Arkansas	25
45	California	21
13	Colorado	35
5	Connecticut	37
25	Delaware	31
30	Florida	28
37	Georgia	26
47	Hawaii	20
22	Idaho	32
28	Illinois	30
25	Indiana	31
10	Iowa	36
13	Kansas	35
30	Kentucky	28
48	Louisiana	19
5	Maine	37
19	Maryland	33
1	Massachusetts	43
30	Michigan	28
5	Minnesota	37
49	Mississippi	17
25	Missouri	31
3	Montana	39
13	Nebraska	35
44	Nevada	22
5	New Hampshire	37
3	New Jersey	39
49	New Mexico	17
22	New York	32
30	North Carolina	28
22	North Dakota	32
10	Ohio	36
37	Oklahoma	26
16	Oregon	34
10	Pennsylvania	36
35	Rhode Island	27
40	South Carolina	25
5	South Dakota	37
37	Tennessee	26
30	Texas	28
28	Utah	30
2	Vermont	42
16	Virginia	34
16	Washington	34
43	West Virginia	23
19	Wisconsin	33
19	Wyoming	33

RANK ORDER

RANK	STATE	PERCENT
1	Massachusetts	43
2	Vermont	42
3	Montana	39
3	New Jersey	39
5	Connecticut	37
5	Maine	37
5	Minnesota	37
5	New Hampshire	37
5	South Dakota	37
10	Iowa	36
10	Ohio	36
10	Pennsylvania	36
13	Colorado	35
13	Kansas	35
13	Nebraska	35
16	Oregon	34
16	Virginia	34
16	Washington	34
19	Maryland	33
19	Wisconsin	33
19	Wyoming	33
22	Idaho	32
22	New York	32
22	North Dakota	32
25	Delaware	31
25	Indiana	31
25	Missouri	31
28	Illinois	30
28	Utah	30
30	Florida	28
30	Kentucky	28
30	Michigan	28
30	North Carolina	28
30	Texas	28
35	Alaska	27
35	Rhode Island	27
37	Georgia	26
37	Oklahoma	26
37	Tennessee	26
40	Arkansas	25
40	South Carolina	25
42	Arizona	24
43	West Virginia	23
44	Nevada	22
45	Alabama	21
45	California	21
47	Hawaii	20
48	Louisiana	19
49	Mississippi	17
49	New Mexico	17
	District of Columbia	12

Source: U.S. Department of Education, National Center for Education Statistics

"NAEP 2007: Reading Report Card for the Nation and the States" (NCES 2007-496, http://nces.ed.gov/nationsreportcard/)

*There are four achievement levels: Below Basic, Basic, Proficient, and Advanced. Proficient represents solid academic mastery for 8th graders. Students reaching this level have demonstrated competency over challenging subject matter, including subject matter knowledge, application of such knowledge to real-world situations, and analytical skills appropriate to the subject matter.

Percent of Public School Fourth Graders Proficient or Better in Mathematics in 2009
National Percent = 38%*

ALPHA ORDER

RANK	STATE	PERCENT
48	Alabama	24
29	Alaska	38
44	Arizona	28
36	Arkansas	36
43	California	30
9	Colorado	45
6	Connecticut	46
36	Delaware	36
25	Florida	40
39	Georgia	34
33	Hawaii	37
21	Idaho	41
29	Illinois	38
19	Indiana	42
21	Iowa	41
6	Kansas	46
33	Kentucky	37
49	Louisiana	23
9	Maine	45
15	Maryland	44
1	Massachusetts	57
38	Michigan	35
3	Minnesota	54
50	Mississippi	22
21	Missouri	41
9	Montana	45
29	Nebraska	38
42	Nevada	32
2	New Hampshire	56
5	New Jersey	49
47	New Mexico	26
25	New York	40
16	North Carolina	43
9	North Dakota	45
9	Ohio	45
41	Oklahoma	33
33	Oregon	37
6	Pennsylvania	46
28	Rhode Island	39
39	South Carolina	34
19	South Dakota	42
44	Tennessee	28
29	Texas	38
21	Utah	41
4	Vermont	51
16	Virginia	43
16	Washington	43
44	West Virginia	28
9	Wisconsin	45
25	Wyoming	40

RANK ORDER

RANK	STATE	PERCENT
1	Massachusetts	57
2	New Hampshire	56
3	Minnesota	54
4	Vermont	51
5	New Jersey	49
6	Connecticut	46
6	Kansas	46
6	Pennsylvania	46
9	Colorado	45
9	Maine	45
9	Montana	45
9	North Dakota	45
9	Ohio	45
9	Wisconsin	45
15	Maryland	44
16	North Carolina	43
16	Virginia	43
16	Washington	43
19	Indiana	42
19	South Dakota	42
21	Idaho	41
21	Iowa	41
21	Missouri	41
21	Utah	41
25	Florida	40
25	New York	40
25	Wyoming	40
28	Rhode Island	39
29	Alaska	38
29	Illinois	38
29	Nebraska	38
29	Texas	38
33	Hawaii	37
33	Kentucky	37
33	Oregon	37
36	Arkansas	36
36	Delaware	36
38	Michigan	35
39	Georgia	34
39	South Carolina	34
41	Oklahoma	33
42	Nevada	32
43	California	30
44	Arizona	28
44	Tennessee	28
44	West Virginia	28
47	New Mexico	26
48	Alabama	24
49	Louisiana	23
50	Mississippi	22
	District of Columbia	17

Source: U.S. Department of Education, National Center for Education Statistics
    "NAEP 2009: The Nation's Report Card, Mathematics 2009" (NCES 2010-451, http://nces.ed.gov/nationsreportcard/)
*There are four achievement levels: Below Basic, Basic, Proficient, and Advanced. Proficient represents solid academic mastery for 4th graders. Students reaching this level have demonstrated competency over challenging subject matter, including subject matter knowledge, application of such knowledge to real-world situations, and analytical skills appropriate to the subject matter.

Percent of Public School Eighth Graders Proficient or Better in Mathematics in 2009
National Percent = 33%*

ALPHA ORDER

RANK	STATE	PERCENT
46	Alabama	20
30	Alaska	33
35	Arizona	29
38	Arkansas	27
45	California	23
9	Colorado	40
9	Connecticut	40
32	Delaware	32
35	Florida	29
38	Georgia	27
41	Hawaii	25
16	Idaho	38
30	Illinois	33
18	Indiana	36
28	Iowa	34
13	Kansas	39
38	Kentucky	27
46	Louisiana	20
23	Maine	35
9	Maryland	40
1	Massachusetts	52
33	Michigan	31
2	Minnesota	47
50	Mississippi	15
23	Missouri	35
3	Montana	44
23	Nebraska	35
41	Nevada	25
5	New Hampshire	43
3	New Jersey	44
46	New Mexico	20
28	New York	34
18	North Carolina	36
5	North Dakota	43
18	Ohio	36
44	Oklahoma	24
17	Oregon	37
9	Pennsylvania	40
37	Rhode Island	28
34	South Carolina	30
8	South Dakota	42
41	Tennessee	25
18	Texas	36
23	Utah	35
5	Vermont	43
18	Virginia	36
13	Washington	39
49	West Virginia	19
13	Wisconsin	39
23	Wyoming	35

RANK ORDER

RANK	STATE	PERCENT
1	Massachusetts	52
2	Minnesota	47
3	Montana	44
3	New Jersey	44
5	New Hampshire	43
5	North Dakota	43
5	Vermont	43
8	South Dakota	42
9	Colorado	40
9	Connecticut	40
9	Maryland	40
9	Pennsylvania	40
13	Kansas	39
13	Washington	39
13	Wisconsin	39
16	Idaho	38
17	Oregon	37
18	Indiana	36
18	North Carolina	36
18	Ohio	36
18	Texas	36
18	Virginia	36
23	Maine	35
23	Missouri	35
23	Nebraska	35
23	Utah	35
23	Wyoming	35
28	Iowa	34
28	New York	34
30	Alaska	33
30	Illinois	33
32	Delaware	32
33	Michigan	31
34	South Carolina	30
35	Arizona	29
35	Florida	29
37	Rhode Island	28
38	Arkansas	27
38	Georgia	27
38	Kentucky	27
41	Hawaii	25
41	Nevada	25
41	Tennessee	25
44	Oklahoma	24
45	California	23
46	Alabama	20
46	Louisiana	20
46	New Mexico	20
49	West Virginia	19
50	Mississippi	15
	District of Columbia	11

Source: U.S. Department of Education, National Center for Education Statistics

"NAEP 2009: The Nation's Report Card, Mathematics 2009" (NCES 2010-451, http://nces.ed.gov/nationsreportcard/)

*There are four achievement levels: Below Basic, Basic, Proficient, and Advanced. Proficient represents solid academic mastery for 8th graders. Students reaching this level have demonstrated competency over challenging subject matter, including subject matter knowledge, application of such knowledge to real-world situations, and analytical skills appropriate to the subject matter.

Percent of Population Graduated from High School in 2008

National Percent = 85.0%*

ALPHA ORDER

RANK	STATE	PERCENT
45	Alabama	81.9
2	Alaska	91.6
36	Arizona	83.8
44	Arkansas	82.0
48	California	80.2
17	Colorado	88.9
19	Connecticut	88.6
27	Delaware	87.2
33	Florida	85.2
35	Georgia	83.9
8	Hawaii	90.3
23	Idaho	87.9
30	Illinois	85.9
29	Indiana	86.2
8	Iowa	90.3
16	Kansas	89.5
46	Kentucky	81.3
47	Louisiana	81.2
12	Maine	89.7
22	Maryland	88.0
18	Massachusetts	88.7
21	Michigan	88.1
2	Minnesota	91.6
49	Mississippi	79.9
28	Missouri	86.5
4	Montana	90.9
11	Nebraska	90.1
39	Nevada	83.5
4	New Hampshire	90.9
26	New Jersey	87.4
42	New Mexico	82.4
34	New York	84.1
38	North Carolina	83.6
13	North Dakota	89.6
24	Ohio	87.6
32	Oklahoma	85.5
19	Oregon	88.6
25	Pennsylvania	87.5
37	Rhode Island	83.7
40	South Carolina	83.2
8	South Dakota	90.3
41	Tennessee	83.0
50	Texas	79.6
7	Utah	90.4
6	Vermont	90.6
30	Virginia	85.9
13	Washington	89.6
43	West Virginia	82.2
13	Wisconsin	89.6
1	Wyoming	91.7

RANK ORDER

RANK	STATE	PERCENT
1	Wyoming	91.7
2	Alaska	91.6
2	Minnesota	91.6
4	Montana	90.9
4	New Hampshire	90.9
6	Vermont	90.6
7	Utah	90.4
8	Hawaii	90.3
8	Iowa	90.3
8	South Dakota	90.3
11	Nebraska	90.1
12	Maine	89.7
13	North Dakota	89.6
13	Washington	89.6
13	Wisconsin	89.6
16	Kansas	89.5
17	Colorado	88.9
18	Massachusetts	88.7
19	Connecticut	88.6
19	Oregon	88.6
21	Michigan	88.1
22	Maryland	88.0
23	Idaho	87.9
24	Ohio	87.6
25	Pennsylvania	87.5
26	New Jersey	87.4
27	Delaware	87.2
28	Missouri	86.5
29	Indiana	86.2
30	Illinois	85.9
30	Virginia	85.9
32	Oklahoma	85.5
33	Florida	85.2
34	New York	84.1
35	Georgia	83.9
36	Arizona	83.8
37	Rhode Island	83.7
38	North Carolina	83.6
39	Nevada	83.5
40	South Carolina	83.2
41	Tennessee	83.0
42	New Mexico	82.4
43	West Virginia	82.2
44	Arkansas	82.0
45	Alabama	81.9
46	Kentucky	81.3
47	Louisiana	81.2
48	California	80.2
49	Mississippi	79.9
50	Texas	79.6

| | District of Columbia | 85.8 |

Source: U.S. Bureau of the Census, American Community Survey
   "Percent of People 25 Years and Over Who Have Completed High School" (http://www.census.gov/acs/www/index.html)
*Persons age 25 and older. Includes equivalency status.

Public High School Graduates in 2007

National Total = 2,892,351 Graduates*

ALPHA ORDER

RANK	STATE	GRADUATES	% of USA
24	Alabama	38,912	1.3%
46	Alaska	7,666	0.3%
20	Arizona	55,954	1.9%
33	Arkansas	27,166	0.9%
1	California	356,641	12.3%
22	Colorado	45,628	1.6%
25	Connecticut	37,541	1.3%
48	Delaware	7,205	0.2%
4	Florida	142,284	4.9%
10	Georgia	77,829	2.7%
42	Hawaii	11,063	0.4%
38	Idaho	16,242	0.6%
5	Illinois	130,220	4.5%
17	Indiana	59,887	2.1%
29	Iowa	34,127	1.2%
31	Kansas	30,139	1.0%
23	Kentucky	39,099	1.4%
28	Louisiana	34,274	1.2%
41	Maine	13,151	0.5%
19	Maryland	57,564	2.0%
14	Massachusetts	63,903	2.2%
8	Michigan	111,838	3.9%
18	Minnesota	59,497	2.1%
34	Mississippi	24,186	0.8%
16	Missouri	60,275	2.1%
44	Montana	10,122	0.3%
35	Nebraska	19,873	0.7%
37	Nevada	16,455	0.6%
40	New Hampshire	14,452	0.5%
9	New Jersey	93,013	3.2%
39	New Mexico	16,131	0.6%
3	New York	168,333	5.8%
11	North Carolina	76,031	2.6%
49	North Dakota	7,159	0.2%
7	Ohio	117,658	4.1%
26	Oklahoma	37,100	1.3%
30	Oregon	33,446	1.2%
6	Pennsylvania	128,603	4.4%
43	Rhode Island	10,384	0.4%
27	South Carolina	35,108	1.2%
45	South Dakota	8,346	0.3%
21	Tennessee	54,502	1.9%
2	Texas	241,193	8.3%
32	Utah	28,276	1.0%
47	Vermont	7,317	0.3%
12	Virginia	73,997	2.6%
15	Washington	62,801	2.2%
36	West Virginia	17,407	0.6%
13	Wisconsin	63,968	2.2%
50	Wyoming	5,441	0.2%

RANK ORDER

RANK	STATE	GRADUATES	% of USA
1	California	356,641	12.3%
2	Texas	241,193	8.3%
3	New York	168,333	5.8%
4	Florida	142,284	4.9%
5	Illinois	130,220	4.5%
6	Pennsylvania	128,603	4.4%
7	Ohio	117,658	4.1%
8	Michigan	111,838	3.9%
9	New Jersey	93,013	3.2%
10	Georgia	77,829	2.7%
11	North Carolina	76,031	2.6%
12	Virginia	73,997	2.6%
13	Wisconsin	63,968	2.2%
14	Massachusetts	63,903	2.2%
15	Washington	62,801	2.2%
16	Missouri	60,275	2.1%
17	Indiana	59,887	2.1%
18	Minnesota	59,497	2.1%
19	Maryland	57,564	2.0%
20	Arizona	55,954	1.9%
21	Tennessee	54,502	1.9%
22	Colorado	45,628	1.6%
23	Kentucky	39,099	1.4%
24	Alabama	38,912	1.3%
25	Connecticut	37,541	1.3%
26	Oklahoma	37,100	1.3%
27	South Carolina	35,108	1.2%
28	Louisiana	34,274	1.2%
29	Iowa	34,127	1.2%
30	Oregon	33,446	1.2%
31	Kansas	30,139	1.0%
32	Utah	28,276	1.0%
33	Arkansas	27,166	0.9%
34	Mississippi	24,186	0.8%
35	Nebraska	19,873	0.7%
36	West Virginia	17,407	0.6%
37	Nevada	16,455	0.6%
38	Idaho	16,242	0.6%
39	New Mexico	16,131	0.6%
40	New Hampshire	14,452	0.5%
41	Maine	13,151	0.5%
42	Hawaii	11,063	0.4%
43	Rhode Island	10,384	0.4%
44	Montana	10,122	0.3%
45	South Dakota	8,346	0.3%
46	Alaska	7,666	0.3%
47	Vermont	7,317	0.3%
48	Delaware	7,205	0.2%
49	North Dakota	7,159	0.2%
50	Wyoming	5,441	0.2%
	District of Columbia	2,944	0.1%

Source: U.S. Department of Education, National Center for Education Statistics
"Public Elementary and Secondary School Student Enrollment and Staff Counts" (http://nces.ed.gov/pubs2010/2010313.pdf)
*For school year 2006-2007.

Averaged Freshman Graduation Rate for Public High Schools in 2007

National Average = 73.9%*

ALPHA ORDER

RANK	STATE	RATE
43	Alabama	67.1
40	Alaska	69.1
39	Arizona	69.6
32	Arkansas	74.4
38	California	70.7
25	Colorado	76.6
11	Connecticut	81.8
36	Delaware	71.9
44	Florida	65.0
45	Georgia	64.1
30	Hawaii	75.4
15	Idaho	80.4
17	Illinois	79.5
33	Indiana	73.9
3	Iowa	86.5
18	Kansas	78.9
27	Kentucky	76.4
47	Louisiana	61.3
20	Maine	78.5
16	Maryland	80.0
14	Massachusetts	80.8
24	Michigan	77.0
3	Minnesota	86.5
46	Mississippi	63.6
10	Missouri	81.9
13	Montana	81.5
5	Nebraska	86.3
50	Nevada	52.0
12	New Hampshire	81.7
6	New Jersey	84.4
48	New Mexico	59.1
41	New York	68.8
42	North Carolina	68.6
7	North Dakota	83.1
19	Ohio	78.7
23	Oklahoma	77.8
34	Oregon	73.8
8	Pennsylvania	83.0
21	Rhode Island	78.4
49	South Carolina	58.9
9	South Dakota	82.5
35	Tennessee	72.6
36	Texas	71.9
25	Utah	76.6
1	Vermont	88.6
29	Virginia	75.5
31	Washington	74.8
22	West Virginia	78.2
2	Wisconsin	88.5
28	Wyoming	75.8

RANK ORDER

RANK	STATE	RATE
1	Vermont	88.6
2	Wisconsin	88.5
3	Iowa	86.5
3	Minnesota	86.5
5	Nebraska	86.3
6	New Jersey	84.4
7	North Dakota	83.1
8	Pennsylvania	83.0
9	South Dakota	82.5
10	Missouri	81.9
11	Connecticut	81.8
12	New Hampshire	81.7
13	Montana	81.5
14	Massachusetts	80.8
15	Idaho	80.4
16	Maryland	80.0
17	Illinois	79.5
18	Kansas	78.9
19	Ohio	78.7
20	Maine	78.5
21	Rhode Island	78.4
22	West Virginia	78.2
23	Oklahoma	77.8
24	Michigan	77.0
25	Colorado	76.6
25	Utah	76.6
27	Kentucky	76.4
28	Wyoming	75.8
29	Virginia	75.5
30	Hawaii	75.4
31	Washington	74.8
32	Arkansas	74.4
33	Indiana	73.9
34	Oregon	73.8
35	Tennessee	72.6
36	Delaware	71.9
36	Texas	71.9
38	California	70.7
39	Arizona	69.6
40	Alaska	69.1
41	New York	68.8
42	North Carolina	68.6
43	Alabama	67.1
44	Florida	65.0
45	Georgia	64.1
46	Mississippi	63.6
47	Louisiana	61.3
48	New Mexico	59.1
49	South Carolina	58.9
50	Nevada	52.0
	District of Columbia	54.9

Source: U.S. Department of Education, National Center for Education Statistics
   "Public Elementary and Secondary School Student Enrollment and Staff Counts" (http://nces.ed.gov/pubs2010/2010313.pdf)
*This rate is calculated by comparing the incoming freshman class enrollment of school year 2003-2004 with the number of graduates with regular diplomas four years later (2006-2007). The incoming class enrollment figure is an average of the eighth grade from five years earlier, the ninth grade four years earlier and the tenth grade from three years earlier.

Public High School Dropout Rate in 2007

National Rate = 4.4%*

ALPHA ORDER

RANK	STATE	RATE
43	Alabama	2.3
4	Alaska	7.3
1	Arizona	7.6
16	Arkansas	4.6
9	California	5.5
5	Colorado	6.9
47	Connecticut	2.1
9	Delaware	5.5
27	Florida	3.8
16	Georgia	4.6
11	Hawaii	5.4
41	Idaho	2.6
22	Illinois	4.0
39	Indiana	2.7
43	Iowa	2.3
39	Kansas	2.7
36	Kentucky	3.0
2	Louisiana	7.4
12	Maine	5.3
27	Maryland	3.8
27	Massachusetts	3.8
2	Michigan	7.4
36	Minnesota	3.0
21	Mississippi	4.3
30	Missouri	3.7
30	Montana	3.7
38	Nebraska	2.8
19	Nevada	4.5
33	New Hampshire	3.2
48	New Jersey	2.0
6	New Mexico	6.1
12	New York	5.3
8	North Carolina	5.7
43	North Dakota	2.3
19	Ohio	4.5
32	Oklahoma	3.5
16	Oregon	4.6
NA	Pennsylvania**	NA
7	Rhode Island	5.8
25	South Carolina	3.9
25	South Dakota	3.9
34	Tennessee	3.1
22	Texas	4.0
34	Utah	3.1
NA	Vermont**	NA
41	Virginia	2.6
14	Washington	5.1
22	West Virginia	4.0
46	Wisconsin	2.2
14	Wyoming	5.1

RANK ORDER

RANK	STATE	RATE
1	Arizona	7.6
2	Louisiana	7.4
2	Michigan	7.4
4	Alaska	7.3
5	Colorado	6.9
6	New Mexico	6.1
7	Rhode Island	5.8
8	North Carolina	5.7
9	California	5.5
9	Delaware	5.5
11	Hawaii	5.4
12	Maine	5.3
12	New York	5.3
14	Washington	5.1
14	Wyoming	5.1
16	Arkansas	4.6
16	Georgia	4.6
16	Oregon	4.6
19	Nevada	4.5
19	Ohio	4.5
21	Mississippi	4.3
22	Illinois	4.0
22	Texas	4.0
22	West Virginia	4.0
25	South Carolina	3.9
25	South Dakota	3.9
27	Florida	3.8
27	Maryland	3.8
27	Massachusetts	3.8
30	Missouri	3.7
30	Montana	3.7
32	Oklahoma	3.5
33	New Hampshire	3.2
34	Tennessee	3.1
34	Utah	3.1
36	Kentucky	3.0
36	Minnesota	3.0
38	Nebraska	2.8
39	Indiana	2.7
39	Kansas	2.7
41	Idaho	2.6
41	Virginia	2.6
43	Alabama	2.3
43	Iowa	2.3
43	North Dakota	2.3
46	Wisconsin	2.2
47	Connecticut	2.1
48	New Jersey	2.0
NA	Pennsylvania**	NA
NA	Vermont**	NA
	District of Columbia	7.1

Source: U.S. Department of Education, National Center for Education Statistics
 "Public Elementary and Secondary School Student Enrollment and Staff Counts" (http://nces.ed.gov/pubs2010/2010313.pdf)
*"Event" dropout rates showing the number of 9th-12th grade dropouts divided by the number of students enrolled at the beginning of the school year in those grades. National rate is for reporting states.
**Not available.

ACT Average Composite Score in 2009

National Average = 21.1*

ALPHA ORDER				RANK ORDER		
RANK	**STATE**	**AVERAGE SCORE**		**RANK**	**STATE**	**AVERAGE SCORE**
42	Alabama	20.3		1	Massachusetts	23.9
33	Alaska	21.0		2	Connecticut	23.5
21	Arizona	21.9		2	New Hampshire	23.5
39	Arkansas	20.6		4	Maine	23.1
14	California	22.2		4	New Jersey	23.1
34	Colorado	20.8		4	New York	23.1
2	Connecticut	23.5		4	Vermont	23.1
11	Delaware	22.6		8	Rhode Island	22.8
48	Florida	19.5		8	Washington	22.8
39	Georgia	20.6		10	Minnesota	22.7
29	Hawaii	21.5		11	Delaware	22.6
26	Idaho	21.6		12	Iowa	22.4
34	Illinois	20.8		13	Wisconsin	22.3
14	Indiana	22.2		14	California	22.2
12	Iowa	22.4		14	Indiana	22.2
21	Kansas	21.9		16	Maryland	22.1
49	Kentucky	19.4		16	Nebraska	22.1
43	Louisiana	20.1		16	Pennsylvania	22.1
4	Maine	23.1		19	Montana	22.0
16	Maryland	22.1		19	South Dakota	22.0
1	Massachusetts	23.9		21	Arizona	21.9
47	Michigan	19.6		21	Kansas	21.9
10	Minnesota	22.7		21	Virginia	21.9
50	Mississippi	18.9		24	Utah	21.8
26	Missouri	21.6		25	Ohio	21.7
19	Montana	22.0		26	Idaho	21.6
16	Nebraska	22.1		26	Missouri	21.6
29	Nevada	21.5		26	North Carolina	21.6
2	New Hampshire	23.5		29	Hawaii	21.5
4	New Jersey	23.1		29	Nevada	21.5
44	New Mexico	20.0		29	North Dakota	21.5
4	New York	23.1		32	Oregon	21.4
26	North Carolina	21.6		33	Alaska	21.0
29	North Dakota	21.5		34	Colorado	20.8
25	Ohio	21.7		34	Illinois	20.8
37	Oklahoma	20.7		34	Texas	20.8
32	Oregon	21.4		37	Oklahoma	20.7
16	Pennsylvania	22.1		37	West Virginia	20.7
8	Rhode Island	22.8		39	Arkansas	20.6
46	South Carolina	19.8		39	Georgia	20.6
19	South Dakota	22.0		39	Tennessee	20.6
39	Tennessee	20.6		42	Alabama	20.3
34	Texas	20.8		43	Louisiana	20.1
24	Utah	21.8		44	New Mexico	20.0
4	Vermont	23.1		44	Wyoming	20.0
21	Virginia	21.9		46	South Carolina	19.8
8	Washington	22.8		47	Michigan	19.6
37	West Virginia	20.7		48	Florida	19.5
13	Wisconsin	22.3		49	Kentucky	19.4
44	Wyoming	20.0		50	Mississippi	18.9
					District of Columbia	19.4

Source: The American College Testing Program (Copyright © 2009)
"Average ACT Scores by State" (http://www.act.org/news/data/09/states-text.html)

*The ACT score range is 1 to 36. Approximately 1.5 million 2009 U.S. high school students took the test. Caution should be used in using ACT scores to compare states. The percentage of high school students taking the test varies greatly from one state to another. For example, all 11th grade students in Colorado, Illinois, Kentucky, Michigan, and Wyoming are required to take the test but, in Maine, only 9 percent of 11th grade students took the test.

Education Expenditures by State and Local Governments in 2007

National Total = $776,625,800,000*

<table>
<tr><td colspan="4">ALPHA ORDER</td><td colspan="4">RANK ORDER</td></tr>
<tr><td>RANK</td><td>STATE</td><td>EXPENDITURES</td><td>% of USA</td><td>RANK</td><td>STATE</td><td>EXPENDITURES</td><td>% of USA</td></tr>
<tr><td>21</td><td>Alabama</td><td>$11,734,198,000</td><td>1.5%</td><td>1</td><td>California</td><td>$99,600,406,000</td><td>12.8%</td></tr>
<tr><td>45</td><td>Alaska</td><td>2,606,123,000</td><td>0.3%</td><td>2</td><td>New York</td><td>60,844,427,000</td><td>7.8%</td></tr>
<tr><td>19</td><td>Arizona</td><td>12,972,448,000</td><td>1.7%</td><td>3</td><td>Texas</td><td>59,001,610,000</td><td>7.6%</td></tr>
<tr><td>32</td><td>Arkansas</td><td>6,777,620,000</td><td>0.9%</td><td>4</td><td>Florida</td><td>39,515,603,000</td><td>5.1%</td></tr>
<tr><td>1</td><td>California</td><td>99,600,406,000</td><td>12.8%</td><td>5</td><td>Pennsylvania</td><td>32,976,299,000</td><td>4.2%</td></tr>
<tr><td>22</td><td>Colorado</td><td>11,544,256,000</td><td>1.5%</td><td>6</td><td>Illinois</td><td>30,630,820,000</td><td>3.9%</td></tr>
<tr><td>25</td><td>Connecticut</td><td>10,673,782,000</td><td>1.4%</td><td>7</td><td>Ohio</td><td>29,964,729,000</td><td>3.9%</td></tr>
<tr><td>44</td><td>Delaware</td><td>2,710,088,000</td><td>0.3%</td><td>8</td><td>New Jersey</td><td>29,610,513,000</td><td>3.8%</td></tr>
<tr><td>4</td><td>Florida</td><td>39,515,603,000</td><td>5.1%</td><td>9</td><td>Michigan</td><td>28,208,497,000</td><td>3.6%</td></tr>
<tr><td>10</td><td>Georgia</td><td>23,257,533,000</td><td>3.0%</td><td>10</td><td>Georgia</td><td>23,257,533,000</td><td>3.0%</td></tr>
<tr><td>40</td><td>Hawaii</td><td>3,239,601,000</td><td>0.4%</td><td>11</td><td>North Carolina</td><td>21,571,985,000</td><td>2.8%</td></tr>
<tr><td>42</td><td>Idaho</td><td>2,970,026,000</td><td>0.4%</td><td>12</td><td>Virginia</td><td>20,970,191,000</td><td>2.7%</td></tr>
<tr><td>6</td><td>Illinois</td><td>30,630,820,000</td><td>3.9%</td><td>13</td><td>Massachusetts</td><td>16,793,027,000</td><td>2.2%</td></tr>
<tr><td>16</td><td>Indiana</td><td>15,464,902,000</td><td>2.0%</td><td>14</td><td>Washington</td><td>16,536,672,000</td><td>2.1%</td></tr>
<tr><td>30</td><td>Iowa</td><td>8,099,088,000</td><td>1.0%</td><td>15</td><td>Maryland</td><td>15,654,825,000</td><td>2.0%</td></tr>
<tr><td>31</td><td>Kansas</td><td>7,069,075,000</td><td>0.9%</td><td>16</td><td>Indiana</td><td>15,464,902,000</td><td>2.0%</td></tr>
<tr><td>27</td><td>Kentucky</td><td>9,740,093,000</td><td>1.3%</td><td>17</td><td>Wisconsin</td><td>14,879,043,000</td><td>1.9%</td></tr>
<tr><td>26</td><td>Louisiana</td><td>10,039,985,000</td><td>1.3%</td><td>18</td><td>Minnesota</td><td>13,882,299,000</td><td>1.8%</td></tr>
<tr><td>41</td><td>Maine</td><td>3,091,252,000</td><td>0.4%</td><td>19</td><td>Arizona</td><td>12,972,448,000</td><td>1.7%</td></tr>
<tr><td>15</td><td>Maryland</td><td>15,654,825,000</td><td>2.0%</td><td>20</td><td>Missouri</td><td>12,794,545,000</td><td>1.6%</td></tr>
<tr><td>13</td><td>Massachusetts</td><td>16,793,027,000</td><td>2.2%</td><td>21</td><td>Alabama</td><td>11,734,198,000</td><td>1.5%</td></tr>
<tr><td>9</td><td>Michigan</td><td>28,208,497,000</td><td>3.6%</td><td>22</td><td>Colorado</td><td>11,544,256,000</td><td>1.5%</td></tr>
<tr><td>18</td><td>Minnesota</td><td>13,882,299,000</td><td>1.8%</td><td>23</td><td>Tennessee</td><td>11,430,205,000</td><td>1.5%</td></tr>
<tr><td>33</td><td>Mississippi</td><td>6,716,970,000</td><td>0.9%</td><td>24</td><td>South Carolina</td><td>11,395,667,000</td><td>1.5%</td></tr>
<tr><td>20</td><td>Missouri</td><td>12,794,545,000</td><td>1.6%</td><td>25</td><td>Connecticut</td><td>10,673,782,000</td><td>1.4%</td></tr>
<tr><td>46</td><td>Montana</td><td>2,333,494,000</td><td>0.3%</td><td>26</td><td>Louisiana</td><td>10,039,985,000</td><td>1.3%</td></tr>
<tr><td>37</td><td>Nebraska</td><td>4,717,228,000</td><td>0.6%</td><td>27</td><td>Kentucky</td><td>9,740,093,000</td><td>1.3%</td></tr>
<tr><td>35</td><td>Nevada</td><td>5,679,475,000</td><td>0.7%</td><td>28</td><td>Oklahoma</td><td>8,677,242,000</td><td>1.1%</td></tr>
<tr><td>39</td><td>New Hampshire</td><td>3,260,812,000</td><td>0.4%</td><td>29</td><td>Oregon</td><td>8,652,780,000</td><td>1.1%</td></tr>
<tr><td>8</td><td>New Jersey</td><td>29,610,513,000</td><td>3.8%</td><td>30</td><td>Iowa</td><td>8,099,088,000</td><td>1.0%</td></tr>
<tr><td>36</td><td>New Mexico</td><td>5,551,934,000</td><td>0.7%</td><td>31</td><td>Kansas</td><td>7,069,075,000</td><td>0.9%</td></tr>
<tr><td>2</td><td>New York</td><td>60,844,427,000</td><td>7.8%</td><td>32</td><td>Arkansas</td><td>6,777,620,000</td><td>0.9%</td></tr>
<tr><td>11</td><td>North Carolina</td><td>21,571,985,000</td><td>2.8%</td><td>33</td><td>Mississippi</td><td>6,716,970,000</td><td>0.9%</td></tr>
<tr><td>49</td><td>North Dakota</td><td>1,743,775,000</td><td>0.2%</td><td>34</td><td>Utah</td><td>6,373,999,000</td><td>0.8%</td></tr>
<tr><td>7</td><td>Ohio</td><td>29,964,729,000</td><td>3.9%</td><td>35</td><td>Nevada</td><td>5,679,475,000</td><td>0.7%</td></tr>
<tr><td>28</td><td>Oklahoma</td><td>8,677,242,000</td><td>1.1%</td><td>36</td><td>New Mexico</td><td>5,551,934,000</td><td>0.7%</td></tr>
<tr><td>29</td><td>Oregon</td><td>8,652,780,000</td><td>1.1%</td><td>37</td><td>Nebraska</td><td>4,717,228,000</td><td>0.6%</td></tr>
<tr><td>5</td><td>Pennsylvania</td><td>32,976,299,000</td><td>4.2%</td><td>38</td><td>West Virginia</td><td>4,543,396,000</td><td>0.6%</td></tr>
<tr><td>43</td><td>Rhode Island</td><td>2,797,137,000</td><td>0.4%</td><td>39</td><td>New Hampshire</td><td>3,260,812,000</td><td>0.4%</td></tr>
<tr><td>24</td><td>South Carolina</td><td>11,395,667,000</td><td>1.5%</td><td>40</td><td>Hawaii</td><td>3,239,601,000</td><td>0.4%</td></tr>
<tr><td>50</td><td>South Dakota</td><td>1,615,672,000</td><td>0.2%</td><td>41</td><td>Maine</td><td>3,091,252,000</td><td>0.4%</td></tr>
<tr><td>23</td><td>Tennessee</td><td>11,430,205,000</td><td>1.5%</td><td>42</td><td>Idaho</td><td>2,970,026,000</td><td>0.4%</td></tr>
<tr><td>3</td><td>Texas</td><td>59,001,610,000</td><td>7.6%</td><td>43</td><td>Rhode Island</td><td>2,797,137,000</td><td>0.4%</td></tr>
<tr><td>34</td><td>Utah</td><td>6,373,999,000</td><td>0.8%</td><td>44</td><td>Delaware</td><td>2,710,088,000</td><td>0.3%</td></tr>
<tr><td>47</td><td>Vermont</td><td>2,154,135,000</td><td>0.3%</td><td>45</td><td>Alaska</td><td>2,606,123,000</td><td>0.3%</td></tr>
<tr><td>12</td><td>Virginia</td><td>20,970,191,000</td><td>2.7%</td><td>46</td><td>Montana</td><td>2,333,494,000</td><td>0.3%</td></tr>
<tr><td>14</td><td>Washington</td><td>16,536,672,000</td><td>2.1%</td><td>47</td><td>Vermont</td><td>2,154,135,000</td><td>0.3%</td></tr>
<tr><td>38</td><td>West Virginia</td><td>4,543,396,000</td><td>0.6%</td><td>48</td><td>Wyoming</td><td>2,010,036,000</td><td>0.3%</td></tr>
<tr><td>17</td><td>Wisconsin</td><td>14,879,043,000</td><td>1.9%</td><td>49</td><td>North Dakota</td><td>1,743,775,000</td><td>0.2%</td></tr>
<tr><td>48</td><td>Wyoming</td><td>2,010,036,000</td><td>0.3%</td><td>50</td><td>South Dakota</td><td>1,615,672,000</td><td>0.2%</td></tr>
<tr><td></td><td></td><td></td><td></td><td></td><td>District of Columbia</td><td>1,546,282,000</td><td>0.2%</td></tr>
</table>

Source: U.S. Bureau of the Census, Governments Division
    "State and Local Government Finances 2006-2007" (http://www.census.gov/govs/estimate/index.html)
*Direct general expenditures for higher, secondary, elementary, and, "other" education. Includes capital outlays.

Per Capita State and Local Government Expenditures for Education in 2007

National Per Capita = $2,575*

ALPHA ORDER

ALPHA ORDER

RANK	STATE	PER CAPITA
26	Alabama	$2,530
2	Alaska	3,820
47	Arizona	2,039
36	Arkansas	2,385
11	California	2,749
37	Colorado	2,384
7	Connecticut	3,060
5	Delaware	3,133
46	Florida	2,162
30	Georgia	2,439
25	Hawaii	2,537
49	Idaho	1,981
34	Illinois	2,397
32	Indiana	2,437
13	Iowa	2,719
24	Kansas	2,547
43	Kentucky	2,288
42	Louisiana	2,294
39	Maine	2,347
10	Maryland	2,779
21	Massachusetts	2,584
9	Michigan	2,807
15	Minnesota	2,674
41	Mississippi	2,299
45	Missouri	2,165
31	Montana	2,438
16	Nebraska	2,665
44	Nevada	2,212
28	New Hampshire	2,475
4	New Jersey	3,429
8	New Mexico	2,820
5	New York	3,133
38	North Carolina	2,380
12	North Dakota	2,732
20	Ohio	2,601
33	Oklahoma	2,402
40	Oregon	2,318
19	Pennsylvania	2,633
18	Rhode Island	2,651
22	South Carolina	2,576
48	South Dakota	2,027
50	Tennessee	1,852
28	Texas	2,475
35	Utah	2,393
3	Vermont	3,472
14	Virginia	2,716
23	Washington	2,558
27	West Virginia	2,509
17	Wisconsin	2,656
1	Wyoming	3,840

RANK ORDER

RANK	STATE	PER CAPITA
1	Wyoming	$3,840
2	Alaska	3,820
3	Vermont	3,472
4	New Jersey	3,429
5	Delaware	3,133
5	New York	3,133
7	Connecticut	3,060
8	New Mexico	2,820
9	Michigan	2,807
10	Maryland	2,779
11	California	2,749
12	North Dakota	2,732
13	Iowa	2,719
14	Virginia	2,716
15	Minnesota	2,674
16	Nebraska	2,665
17	Wisconsin	2,656
18	Rhode Island	2,651
19	Pennsylvania	2,633
20	Ohio	2,601
21	Massachusetts	2,584
22	South Carolina	2,576
23	Washington	2,558
24	Kansas	2,547
25	Hawaii	2,537
26	Alabama	2,530
27	West Virginia	2,509
28	New Hampshire	2,475
28	Texas	2,475
30	Georgia	2,439
31	Montana	2,438
32	Indiana	2,437
33	Oklahoma	2,402
34	Illinois	2,397
35	Utah	2,393
36	Arkansas	2,385
37	Colorado	2,384
38	North Carolina	2,380
39	Maine	2,347
40	Oregon	2,318
41	Mississippi	2,299
42	Louisiana	2,294
43	Kentucky	2,288
44	Nevada	2,212
45	Missouri	2,165
46	Florida	2,162
47	Arizona	2,039
48	South Dakota	2,027
49	Idaho	1,981
50	Tennessee	1,852
	District of Columbia	2,637

Source: CQ Press using data from U.S. Bureau of the Census, Governments Division
"State and Local Government Finances 2006-2007" (http://www.census.gov/govs/estimate/index.html)
*Direct general expenditures for higher, secondary, elementary, and, "other" education. Includes capital outlays.

Expenditures for Education as a Percent of
All State and Local Government Expenditures in 2007
National Percent = 34.4%*

ALPHA ORDER

RANK	STATE	PERCENT
9	Alabama	38.2
50	Alaska	25.2
37	Arizona	32.9
4	Arkansas	39.7
42	California	31.5
29	Colorado	34.4
15	Connecticut	36.9
27	Delaware	35.0
45	Florida	30.3
21	Georgia	36.5
48	Hawaii	29.6
34	Idaho	33.1
32	Illinois	33.8
16	Indiana	36.8
14	Iowa	37.4
12	Kansas	37.7
23	Kentucky	35.9
49	Louisiana	29.0
44	Maine	30.8
16	Maryland	36.8
43	Massachusetts	31.1
2	Michigan	40.3
31	Minnesota	33.9
46	Mississippi	30.2
28	Missouri	34.9
26	Montana	35.1
12	Nebraska	37.7
36	Nevada	33.0
7	New Hampshire	38.5
5	New Jersey	39.5
30	New Mexico	34.2
47	New York	29.8
22	North Carolina	36.4
16	North Dakota	36.8
24	Ohio	35.3
9	Oklahoma	38.2
37	Oregon	32.9
24	Pennsylvania	35.3
39	Rhode Island	32.6
20	South Carolina	36.6
40	South Dakota	32.4
41	Tennessee	31.8
3	Texas	40.0
11	Utah	38.0
1	Vermont	40.8
6	Virginia	39.4
34	Washington	33.1
8	West Virginia	38.3
16	Wisconsin	36.8
33	Wyoming	33.3

RANK ORDER

RANK	STATE	PERCENT
1	Vermont	40.8
2	Michigan	40.3
3	Texas	40.0
4	Arkansas	39.7
5	New Jersey	39.5
6	Virginia	39.4
7	New Hampshire	38.5
8	West Virginia	38.3
9	Alabama	38.2
9	Oklahoma	38.2
11	Utah	38.0
12	Kansas	37.7
12	Nebraska	37.7
14	Iowa	37.4
15	Connecticut	36.9
16	Indiana	36.8
16	Maryland	36.8
16	North Dakota	36.8
16	Wisconsin	36.8
20	South Carolina	36.6
21	Georgia	36.5
22	North Carolina	36.4
23	Kentucky	35.9
24	Ohio	35.3
24	Pennsylvania	35.3
26	Montana	35.1
27	Delaware	35.0
28	Missouri	34.9
29	Colorado	34.4
30	New Mexico	34.2
31	Minnesota	33.9
32	Illinois	33.8
33	Wyoming	33.3
34	Idaho	33.1
34	Washington	33.1
36	Nevada	33.0
37	Arizona	32.9
37	Oregon	32.9
39	Rhode Island	32.6
40	South Dakota	32.4
41	Tennessee	31.8
42	California	31.5
43	Massachusetts	31.1
44	Maine	30.8
45	Florida	30.3
46	Mississippi	30.2
47	New York	29.8
48	Hawaii	29.6
49	Louisiana	29.0
50	Alaska	25.2

District of Columbia	18.2

Source: CQ Press using data from U.S. Bureau of the Census, Governments Division

"State and Local Government Finances 2006-2007" (http://www.census.gov/govs/estimate/index.html)

*Direct general expenditures for higher, secondary, elementary, and "other" education as a percent of all direct general expenditures. Includes capital outlays.

State and Local Government Expenditures for Elementary and Secondary Education in 2007
National Total = $534,919,416,000*

ALPHA ORDER

RANK	STATE	EXPENDITURES	% of USA
25	Alabama	$7,125,629,000	1.3%
44	Alaska	1,898,678,000	0.4%
20	Arizona	8,509,080,000	1.6%
32	Arkansas	4,382,977,000	0.8%
1	California	68,435,443,000	12.8%
23	Colorado	7,651,185,000	1.4%
21	Connecticut	7,957,113,000	1.5%
45	Delaware	1,669,343,000	0.3%
4	Florida	29,196,985,000	5.5%
10	Georgia	16,970,886,000	3.2%
41	Hawaii	2,159,608,000	0.4%
43	Idaho	1,908,989,000	0.4%
7	Illinois	21,499,679,000	4.0%
16	Indiana	10,004,993,000	1.9%
30	Iowa	4,906,485,000	0.9%
31	Kansas	4,479,603,000	0.8%
27	Kentucky	5,922,449,000	1.1%
26	Louisiana	6,556,970,000	1.2%
40	Maine	2,188,118,000	0.4%
14	Maryland	10,658,705,000	2.0%
13	Massachusetts	12,073,218,000	2.3%
9	Michigan	18,938,540,000	3.5%
18	Minnesota	9,260,415,000	1.7%
34	Mississippi	4,088,245,000	0.8%
19	Missouri	8,930,556,000	1.7%
46	Montana	1,429,433,000	0.3%
37	Nebraska	3,030,085,000	0.6%
33	Nevada	4,134,312,000	0.8%
39	New Hampshire	2,395,607,000	0.4%
5	New Jersey	23,659,539,000	4.4%
36	New Mexico	3,229,964,000	0.6%
2	New York	47,952,937,000	9.0%
12	North Carolina	12,591,860,000	2.4%
50	North Dakota	971,784,000	0.2%
8	Ohio	20,623,682,000	3.9%
28	Oklahoma	5,424,683,000	1.0%
29	Oregon	5,400,856,000	1.0%
6	Pennsylvania	22,915,387,000	4.3%
42	Rhode Island	2,072,949,000	0.4%
24	South Carolina	7,499,761,000	1.4%
49	South Dakota	1,063,926,000	0.2%
22	Tennessee	7,655,956,000	1.4%
3	Texas	41,071,449,000	7.7%
35	Utah	3,533,738,000	0.7%
48	Vermont	1,313,835,000	0.2%
11	Virginia	14,228,006,000	2.7%
15	Washington	10,267,382,000	1.9%
38	West Virginia	2,729,078,000	0.5%
17	Wisconsin	9,546,602,000	1.8%
47	Wyoming	1,379,469,000	0.3%

RANK ORDER

RANK	STATE	EXPENDITURES	% of USA
1	California	$68,435,443,000	12.8%
2	New York	47,952,937,000	9.0%
3	Texas	41,071,449,000	7.7%
4	Florida	29,196,985,000	5.5%
5	New Jersey	23,659,539,000	4.4%
6	Pennsylvania	22,915,387,000	4.3%
7	Illinois	21,499,679,000	4.0%
8	Ohio	20,623,682,000	3.9%
9	Michigan	18,938,540,000	3.5%
10	Georgia	16,970,886,000	3.2%
11	Virginia	14,228,006,000	2.7%
12	North Carolina	12,591,860,000	2.4%
13	Massachusetts	12,073,218,000	2.3%
14	Maryland	10,658,705,000	2.0%
15	Washington	10,267,382,000	1.9%
16	Indiana	10,004,993,000	1.9%
17	Wisconsin	9,546,602,000	1.8%
18	Minnesota	9,260,415,000	1.7%
19	Missouri	8,930,556,000	1.7%
20	Arizona	8,509,080,000	1.6%
21	Connecticut	7,957,113,000	1.5%
22	Tennessee	7,655,956,000	1.4%
23	Colorado	7,651,185,000	1.4%
24	South Carolina	7,499,761,000	1.4%
25	Alabama	7,125,629,000	1.3%
26	Louisiana	6,556,970,000	1.2%
27	Kentucky	5,922,449,000	1.1%
28	Oklahoma	5,424,683,000	1.0%
29	Oregon	5,400,856,000	1.0%
30	Iowa	4,906,485,000	0.9%
31	Kansas	4,479,603,000	0.8%
32	Arkansas	4,382,977,000	0.8%
33	Nevada	4,134,312,000	0.8%
34	Mississippi	4,088,245,000	0.8%
35	Utah	3,533,738,000	0.7%
36	New Mexico	3,229,964,000	0.6%
37	Nebraska	3,030,085,000	0.6%
38	West Virginia	2,729,078,000	0.5%
39	New Hampshire	2,395,607,000	0.4%
40	Maine	2,188,118,000	0.4%
41	Hawaii	2,159,608,000	0.4%
42	Rhode Island	2,072,949,000	0.4%
43	Idaho	1,908,989,000	0.4%
44	Alaska	1,898,678,000	0.4%
45	Delaware	1,669,343,000	0.3%
46	Montana	1,429,433,000	0.3%
47	Wyoming	1,379,469,000	0.3%
48	Vermont	1,313,835,000	0.2%
49	South Dakota	1,063,926,000	0.2%
50	North Dakota	971,784,000	0.2%
	District of Columbia	1,423,244,000	0.3%

Source: U.S. Bureau of the Census, Governments Division
   "State and Local Government Finances 2006-2007" (http://www.census.gov/govs/estimate/index.html)
*Direct general expenditures. Includes capital outlays.

Per Capita State and Local Government Expenditures for Elementary and Secondary Education in 2007
National Per Capita = $1,774*

ALPHA ORDER

RANK	STATE	PER CAPITA
35	Alabama	$1,536
1	Alaska	2,783
46	Arizona	1,337
34	Arkansas	1,542
10	California	1,889
32	Colorado	1,580
5	Connecticut	2,281
8	Delaware	1,930
30	Florida	1,597
18	Georgia	1,780
23	Hawaii	1,691
49	Idaho	1,273
24	Illinois	1,682
33	Indiana	1,577
26	Iowa	1,647
28	Kansas	1,614
44	Kentucky	1,391
40	Louisiana	1,498
25	Maine	1,661
9	Maryland	1,892
12	Massachusetts	1,858
11	Michigan	1,884
17	Minnesota	1,784
43	Mississippi	1,399
37	Missouri	1,511
41	Montana	1,493
20	Nebraska	1,712
29	Nevada	1,610
15	New Hampshire	1,819
2	New Jersey	2,740
27	New Mexico	1,641
4	New York	2,469
45	North Carolina	1,389
36	North Dakota	1,523
16	Ohio	1,790
39	Oklahoma	1,502
42	Oregon	1,447
14	Pennsylvania	1,830
7	Rhode Island	1,965
22	South Carolina	1,695
47	South Dakota	1,335
50	Tennessee	1,240
19	Texas	1,723
48	Utah	1,327
6	Vermont	2,118
13	Virginia	1,843
31	Washington	1,588
38	West Virginia	1,507
21	Wisconsin	1,704
3	Wyoming	2,636

RANK ORDER

RANK	STATE	PER CAPITA
1	Alaska	$2,783
2	New Jersey	2,740
3	Wyoming	2,636
4	New York	2,469
5	Connecticut	2,281
6	Vermont	2,118
7	Rhode Island	1,965
8	Delaware	1,930
9	Maryland	1,892
10	California	1,889
11	Michigan	1,884
12	Massachusetts	1,858
13	Virginia	1,843
14	Pennsylvania	1,830
15	New Hampshire	1,819
16	Ohio	1,790
17	Minnesota	1,784
18	Georgia	1,780
19	Texas	1,723
20	Nebraska	1,712
21	Wisconsin	1,704
22	South Carolina	1,695
23	Hawaii	1,691
24	Illinois	1,682
25	Maine	1,661
26	Iowa	1,647
27	New Mexico	1,641
28	Kansas	1,614
29	Nevada	1,610
30	Florida	1,597
31	Washington	1,588
32	Colorado	1,580
33	Indiana	1,577
34	Arkansas	1,542
35	Alabama	1,536
36	North Dakota	1,523
37	Missouri	1,511
38	West Virginia	1,507
39	Oklahoma	1,502
40	Louisiana	1,498
41	Montana	1,493
42	Oregon	1,447
43	Mississippi	1,399
44	Kentucky	1,391
45	North Carolina	1,389
46	Arizona	1,337
47	South Dakota	1,335
48	Utah	1,327
49	Idaho	1,273
50	Tennessee	1,240

District of Columbia   2,427

Source: CQ Press using data from U.S. Bureau of the Census, Governments Division
"State and Local Government Finances 2006-2007" (http://www.census.gov/govs/estimate/index.html)
*Direct general expenditures. Includes capital outlays.

State and Local Government Expenditures for Elementary and Secondary Education as a Percent of All Education Expenditures in 2007
National Percent = 23.7%*

ALPHA ORDER

RANK ORDER

RANK	STATE	PERCENT	RANK	STATE	PERCENT
24	Alabama	23.2	1	New Jersey	31.6
50	Alaska	18.3	2	New Hampshire	28.3
35	Arizona	21.6	3	Texas	27.9
8	Arkansas	25.7	4	Connecticut	27.5
34	California	21.7	5	Michigan	27.1
26	Colorado	22.8	6	Virginia	26.8
4	Connecticut	27.5	7	Georgia	26.6
36	Delaware	21.5	8	Arkansas	25.7
30	Florida	22.4	9	Maryland	25.0
7	Georgia	26.6	10	Vermont	24.9
47	Hawaii	19.8	11	Pennsylvania	24.5
38	Idaho	21.3	12	Missouri	24.4
21	Illinois	23.7	13	Ohio	24.3
20	Indiana	23.8	14	Nebraska	24.2
28	Iowa	22.7	15	Rhode Island	24.1
18	Kansas	23.9	15	South Carolina	24.1
32	Kentucky	21.8	17	Nevada	24.0
48	Louisiana	19.0	18	Kansas	23.9
32	Maine	21.8	18	Oklahoma	23.9
9	Maryland	25.0	20	Indiana	23.8
30	Massachusetts	22.4	21	Illinois	23.7
5	Michigan	27.1	22	Wisconsin	23.6
29	Minnesota	22.6	23	New York	23.5
49	Mississippi	18.4	24	Alabama	23.2
12	Missouri	24.4	25	West Virginia	23.0
36	Montana	21.5	26	Colorado	22.8
14	Nebraska	24.2	26	Wyoming	22.8
17	Nevada	24.0	28	Iowa	22.7
2	New Hampshire	28.3	29	Minnesota	22.6
1	New Jersey	31.6	30	Florida	22.4
46	New Mexico	19.9	30	Massachusetts	22.4
23	New York	23.5	32	Kentucky	21.8
41	North Carolina	21.2	32	Maine	21.8
44	North Dakota	20.5	34	California	21.7
13	Ohio	24.3	35	Arizona	21.6
18	Oklahoma	23.9	36	Delaware	21.5
44	Oregon	20.5	36	Montana	21.5
11	Pennsylvania	24.5	38	Idaho	21.3
15	Rhode Island	24.1	38	South Dakota	21.3
15	South Carolina	24.1	38	Tennessee	21.3
38	South Dakota	21.3	41	North Carolina	21.2
38	Tennessee	21.3	42	Utah	21.1
3	Texas	27.9	43	Washington	20.6
42	Utah	21.1	44	North Dakota	20.5
10	Vermont	24.9	44	Oregon	20.5
6	Virginia	26.8	46	New Mexico	19.9
43	Washington	20.6	47	Hawaii	19.8
25	West Virginia	23.0	48	Louisiana	19.0
22	Wisconsin	23.6	49	Mississippi	18.4
26	Wyoming	22.8	50	Alaska	18.3
				District of Columbia	16.8

Source: CQ Press using data from U.S. Bureau of the Census, Governments Division
"State and Local Government Finances 2006-2007" (http://www.census.gov/govs/estimate/index.html)
*Direct general expenditures as a percent of all direct general expenditures. Includes capital outlays.

Estimated Per Pupil Public Elementary and Secondary School Expenditures in 2010
National Per Pupil = $10,506*

ALPHA ORDER

RANK ORDER

RANK	STATE	PER PUPIL		RANK	STATE	PER PUPIL
35	Alabama	$9,418		1	Rhode Island	$18,729
20	Alaska	11,137		2	New Jersey	16,967
49	Arizona	6,170		3	New York	16,769
18	Arkansas	11,171		4	Vermont	15,466
44	California	8,520		5	Wyoming	15,459
29	Colorado	9,828		6	Connecticut	14,472
6	Connecticut	14,472		7	Maine	13,978
9	Delaware	13,496		8	Massachusetts	13,804
41	Florida	8,930		9	Delaware	13,496
24	Georgia	10,182		10	New Hampshire	13,112
13	Hawaii	11,968		11	Pennsylvania	12,541
47	Idaho	7,875		12	Maryland	12,281
19	Illinois	11,142		13	Hawaii	11,968
27	Indiana	10,037		14	Virginia	11,672
33	Iowa	9,472		15	Michigan	11,579
32	Kansas	9,662		16	Minnesota	11,447
37	Kentucky	9,325		17	Wisconsin	11,299
25	Louisiana	10,158		18	Arkansas	11,171
7	Maine	13,978		19	Illinois	11,142
12	Maryland	12,281		20	Alaska	11,137
8	Massachusetts	13,804		21	West Virginia	11,043
15	Michigan	11,579		22	New Mexico	10,551
16	Minnesota	11,447		23	Oregon	10,381
48	Mississippi	7,752		24	Georgia	10,182
39	Missouri	9,076		25	Louisiana	10,158
31	Montana	9,676		26	Washington	10,082
30	Nebraska	9,781		27	Indiana	10,037
46	Nevada	7,951		28	South Dakota	9,858
10	New Hampshire	13,112		29	Colorado	9,828
2	New Jersey	16,967		30	Nebraska	9,781
22	New Mexico	10,551		31	Montana	9,676
3	New York	16,769		32	Kansas	9,662
40	North Carolina	8,974		33	Iowa	9,472
42	North Dakota	8,687		34	Ohio	9,445
34	Ohio	9,445		35	Alabama	9,418
45	Oklahoma	8,348		36	South Carolina	9,375
23	Oregon	10,381		37	Kentucky	9,325
11	Pennsylvania	12,541		38	Texas	9,288
1	Rhode Island	18,729		39	Missouri	9,076
36	South Carolina	9,375		40	North Carolina	8,974
28	South Dakota	9,858		41	Florida	8,930
43	Tennessee	8,617		42	North Dakota	8,687
38	Texas	9,288		43	Tennessee	8,617
50	Utah	6,095		44	California	8,520
4	Vermont	15,466		45	Oklahoma	8,348
14	Virginia	11,672		46	Nevada	7,951
26	Washington	10,082		47	Idaho	7,875
21	West Virginia	11,043		48	Mississippi	7,752
17	Wisconsin	11,299		49	Arizona	6,170
5	Wyoming	15,459		50	Utah	6,095
					District of Columbia	18,273

Source: CQ Press using data from National Education Association, Washington, D.C.
   "Rankings and Estimates" (Copyright © 2010, NEA, used with permission, http://www.nea.org)
*Estimates for school year 2009-2010. Based on student membership.

Higher Education Expenditures by State and Local Governments in 2007

National Total = $204,372,261,000*

ALPHA ORDER

RANK	STATE	EXPENDITURES	% of USA
17	Alabama	$4,004,786,000	2.0%
47	Alaska	625,456,000	0.3%
18	Arizona	3,925,486,000	1.9%
34	Arkansas	2,064,323,000	1.0%
1	California	26,804,621,000	13.1%
21	Colorado	3,554,266,000	1.7%
33	Connecticut	2,109,882,000	1.0%
41	Delaware	861,741,000	0.4%
6	Florida	8,141,028,000	4.0%
13	Georgia	4,789,556,000	2.3%
39	Hawaii	1,030,768,000	0.5%
40	Idaho	926,194,000	0.5%
7	Illinois	7,668,080,000	3.8%
15	Indiana	4,599,222,000	2.3%
28	Iowa	2,828,439,000	1.4%
31	Kansas	2,395,650,000	1.2%
24	Kentucky	2,998,522,000	1.5%
29	Louisiana	2,691,405,000	1.3%
44	Maine	752,104,000	0.4%
16	Maryland	4,326,941,000	2.1%
19	Massachusetts	3,699,368,000	1.8%
4	Michigan	8,437,172,000	4.1%
20	Minnesota	3,666,828,000	1.8%
32	Mississippi	2,305,238,000	1.1%
22	Missouri	3,322,722,000	1.6%
43	Montana	754,045,000	0.4%
36	Nebraska	1,493,545,000	0.7%
37	Nevada	1,386,333,000	0.7%
42	New Hampshire	764,942,000	0.4%
14	New Jersey	4,761,884,000	2.3%
35	New Mexico	1,960,045,000	1.0%
3	New York	10,922,023,000	5.3%
5	North Carolina	8,344,318,000	4.1%
45	North Dakota	713,979,000	0.3%
8	Ohio	7,483,461,000	3.7%
27	Oklahoma	2,831,124,000	1.4%
25	Oregon	2,978,533,000	1.5%
9	Pennsylvania	6,835,293,000	3.3%
48	Rhode Island	564,386,000	0.3%
26	South Carolina	2,977,059,000	1.5%
50	South Dakota	465,806,000	0.2%
23	Tennessee	3,016,360,000	1.5%
2	Texas	16,343,270,000	8.0%
30	Utah	2,587,036,000	1.3%
46	Vermont	711,271,000	0.3%
10	Virginia	5,966,515,000	2.9%
11	Washington	5,123,128,000	2.5%
38	West Virginia	1,372,903,000	0.7%
12	Wisconsin	4,824,377,000	2.4%
49	Wyoming	537,789,000	0.3%

RANK ORDER

RANK	STATE	EXPENDITURES	% of USA
1	California	$26,804,621,000	13.1%
2	Texas	16,343,270,000	8.0%
3	New York	10,922,023,000	5.3%
4	Michigan	8,437,172,000	4.1%
5	North Carolina	8,344,318,000	4.1%
6	Florida	8,141,028,000	4.0%
7	Illinois	7,668,080,000	3.8%
8	Ohio	7,483,461,000	3.7%
9	Pennsylvania	6,835,293,000	3.3%
10	Virginia	5,966,515,000	2.9%
11	Washington	5,123,128,000	2.5%
12	Wisconsin	4,824,377,000	2.4%
13	Georgia	4,789,556,000	2.3%
14	New Jersey	4,761,884,000	2.3%
15	Indiana	4,599,222,000	2.3%
16	Maryland	4,326,941,000	2.1%
17	Alabama	4,004,786,000	2.0%
18	Arizona	3,925,486,000	1.9%
19	Massachusetts	3,699,368,000	1.8%
20	Minnesota	3,666,828,000	1.8%
21	Colorado	3,554,266,000	1.7%
22	Missouri	3,322,722,000	1.6%
23	Tennessee	3,016,360,000	1.5%
24	Kentucky	2,998,522,000	1.5%
25	Oregon	2,978,533,000	1.5%
26	South Carolina	2,977,059,000	1.5%
27	Oklahoma	2,831,124,000	1.4%
28	Iowa	2,828,439,000	1.4%
29	Louisiana	2,691,405,000	1.3%
30	Utah	2,587,036,000	1.3%
31	Kansas	2,395,650,000	1.2%
32	Mississippi	2,305,238,000	1.1%
33	Connecticut	2,109,882,000	1.0%
34	Arkansas	2,064,323,000	1.0%
35	New Mexico	1,960,045,000	1.0%
36	Nebraska	1,493,545,000	0.7%
37	Nevada	1,386,333,000	0.7%
38	West Virginia	1,372,903,000	0.7%
39	Hawaii	1,030,768,000	0.5%
40	Idaho	926,194,000	0.5%
41	Delaware	861,741,000	0.4%
42	New Hampshire	764,942,000	0.4%
43	Montana	754,045,000	0.4%
44	Maine	752,104,000	0.4%
45	North Dakota	713,979,000	0.3%
46	Vermont	711,271,000	0.3%
47	Alaska	625,456,000	0.3%
48	Rhode Island	564,386,000	0.3%
49	Wyoming	537,789,000	0.3%
50	South Dakota	465,806,000	0.2%
	District of Columbia	123,038,000	0.1%

Source: U.S. Bureau of the Census, Governments Division
   "State and Local Government Finances 2006-2007" (http://www.census.gov/govs/estimate/index.html)
*Direct general expenditures. Includes capital outlays.

Per Capita State and Local Government Expenditures for Higher Education in 2007
National Per Capita = $678*

<table>
<tr><td colspan="3">ALPHA ORDER</td><td colspan="3">RANK ORDER</td></tr>
<tr><th>RANK</th><th>STATE</th><th>PER CAPITA</th><th>RANK</th><th>STATE</th><th>PER CAPITA</th></tr>
<tr><td>10</td><td>Alabama</td><td>$863</td><td>1</td><td>Vermont</td><td>$1,146</td></tr>
<tr><td>9</td><td>Alaska</td><td>917</td><td>2</td><td>North Dakota</td><td>1,119</td></tr>
<tr><td>34</td><td>Arizona</td><td>617</td><td>3</td><td>Wyoming</td><td>1,027</td></tr>
<tr><td>26</td><td>Arkansas</td><td>726</td><td>4</td><td>Delaware</td><td>996</td></tr>
<tr><td>24</td><td>California</td><td>740</td><td>4</td><td>New Mexico</td><td>996</td></tr>
<tr><td>25</td><td>Colorado</td><td>734</td><td>6</td><td>Utah</td><td>971</td></tr>
<tr><td>36</td><td>Connecticut</td><td>605</td><td>7</td><td>Iowa</td><td>950</td></tr>
<tr><td>4</td><td>Delaware</td><td>996</td><td>8</td><td>North Carolina</td><td>921</td></tr>
<tr><td>50</td><td>Florida</td><td>445</td><td>9</td><td>Alaska</td><td>917</td></tr>
<tr><td>48</td><td>Georgia</td><td>502</td><td>10</td><td>Alabama</td><td>863</td></tr>
<tr><td>15</td><td>Hawaii</td><td>807</td><td>10</td><td>Kansas</td><td>863</td></tr>
<tr><td>33</td><td>Idaho</td><td>618</td><td>12</td><td>Wisconsin</td><td>861</td></tr>
<tr><td>37</td><td>Illinois</td><td>600</td><td>13</td><td>Nebraska</td><td>844</td></tr>
<tr><td>27</td><td>Indiana</td><td>725</td><td>14</td><td>Michigan</td><td>839</td></tr>
<tr><td>7</td><td>Iowa</td><td>950</td><td>15</td><td>Hawaii</td><td>807</td></tr>
<tr><td>10</td><td>Kansas</td><td>863</td><td>16</td><td>Oregon</td><td>798</td></tr>
<tr><td>29</td><td>Kentucky</td><td>704</td><td>17</td><td>Washington</td><td>792</td></tr>
<tr><td>35</td><td>Louisiana</td><td>615</td><td>18</td><td>Mississippi</td><td>789</td></tr>
<tr><td>40</td><td>Maine</td><td>571</td><td>19</td><td>Montana</td><td>788</td></tr>
<tr><td>22</td><td>Maryland</td><td>768</td><td>20</td><td>Oklahoma</td><td>784</td></tr>
<tr><td>41</td><td>Massachusetts</td><td>569</td><td>21</td><td>Virginia</td><td>773</td></tr>
<tr><td>14</td><td>Michigan</td><td>839</td><td>22</td><td>Maryland</td><td>768</td></tr>
<tr><td>28</td><td>Minnesota</td><td>706</td><td>23</td><td>West Virginia</td><td>758</td></tr>
<tr><td>18</td><td>Mississippi</td><td>789</td><td>24</td><td>California</td><td>740</td></tr>
<tr><td>42</td><td>Missouri</td><td>562</td><td>25</td><td>Colorado</td><td>734</td></tr>
<tr><td>19</td><td>Montana</td><td>788</td><td>26</td><td>Arkansas</td><td>726</td></tr>
<tr><td>13</td><td>Nebraska</td><td>844</td><td>27</td><td>Indiana</td><td>725</td></tr>
<tr><td>46</td><td>Nevada</td><td>540</td><td>28</td><td>Minnesota</td><td>706</td></tr>
<tr><td>39</td><td>New Hampshire</td><td>581</td><td>29</td><td>Kentucky</td><td>704</td></tr>
<tr><td>44</td><td>New Jersey</td><td>551</td><td>30</td><td>Texas</td><td>686</td></tr>
<tr><td>4</td><td>New Mexico</td><td>996</td><td>31</td><td>South Carolina</td><td>673</td></tr>
<tr><td>42</td><td>New York</td><td>562</td><td>32</td><td>Ohio</td><td>650</td></tr>
<tr><td>8</td><td>North Carolina</td><td>921</td><td>33</td><td>Idaho</td><td>618</td></tr>
<tr><td>2</td><td>North Dakota</td><td>1,119</td><td>34</td><td>Arizona</td><td>617</td></tr>
<tr><td>32</td><td>Ohio</td><td>650</td><td>35</td><td>Louisiana</td><td>615</td></tr>
<tr><td>20</td><td>Oklahoma</td><td>784</td><td>36</td><td>Connecticut</td><td>605</td></tr>
<tr><td>16</td><td>Oregon</td><td>798</td><td>37</td><td>Illinois</td><td>600</td></tr>
<tr><td>45</td><td>Pennsylvania</td><td>546</td><td>38</td><td>South Dakota</td><td>584</td></tr>
<tr><td>47</td><td>Rhode Island</td><td>535</td><td>39</td><td>New Hampshire</td><td>581</td></tr>
<tr><td>31</td><td>South Carolina</td><td>673</td><td>40</td><td>Maine</td><td>571</td></tr>
<tr><td>38</td><td>South Dakota</td><td>584</td><td>41</td><td>Massachusetts</td><td>569</td></tr>
<tr><td>49</td><td>Tennessee</td><td>489</td><td>42</td><td>Missouri</td><td>562</td></tr>
<tr><td>30</td><td>Texas</td><td>686</td><td>42</td><td>New York</td><td>562</td></tr>
<tr><td>6</td><td>Utah</td><td>971</td><td>44</td><td>New Jersey</td><td>551</td></tr>
<tr><td>1</td><td>Vermont</td><td>1,146</td><td>45</td><td>Pennsylvania</td><td>546</td></tr>
<tr><td>21</td><td>Virginia</td><td>773</td><td>46</td><td>Nevada</td><td>540</td></tr>
<tr><td>17</td><td>Washington</td><td>792</td><td>47</td><td>Rhode Island</td><td>535</td></tr>
<tr><td>23</td><td>West Virginia</td><td>758</td><td>48</td><td>Georgia</td><td>502</td></tr>
<tr><td>12</td><td>Wisconsin</td><td>861</td><td>49</td><td>Tennessee</td><td>489</td></tr>
<tr><td>3</td><td>Wyoming</td><td>1,027</td><td>50</td><td>Florida</td><td>445</td></tr>
<tr><td></td><td></td><td></td><td></td><td>District of Columbia</td><td>210</td></tr>
</table>

Source: CQ Press using data from U.S. Bureau of the Census, Governments Division
"State and Local Government Finances 2006-2007" (http://www.census.gov/govs/estimate/index.html)
*Direct general expenditures. Includes capital outlays.

Expenditures for Higher Education as a Percent
of All State and Local Government Expenditures in 2007
National Percent = 9.0%*

ALPHA ORDER

RANK	STATE	PERCENT
6	Alabama	13.0
49	Alaska	6.0
27	Arizona	10.0
9	Arkansas	12.1
36	California	8.5
22	Colorado	10.6
43	Connecticut	7.3
18	Delaware	11.1
48	Florida	6.2
41	Georgia	7.5
29	Hawaii	9.4
23	Idaho	10.3
36	Illinois	8.5
21	Indiana	10.9
5	Iowa	13.1
7	Kansas	12.8
18	Kentucky	11.1
40	Louisiana	7.8
41	Maine	7.5
26	Maryland	10.2
45	Massachusetts	6.9
9	Michigan	12.1
32	Minnesota	9.0
23	Mississippi	10.3
31	Missouri	9.1
15	Montana	11.3
12	Nebraska	11.9
39	Nevada	8.0
32	New Hampshire	9.0
47	New Jersey	6.4
9	New Mexico	12.1
50	New York	5.4
3	North Carolina	14.1
2	North Dakota	15.1
35	Ohio	8.8
8	Oklahoma	12.5
15	Oregon	11.3
43	Pennsylvania	7.3
46	Rhode Island	6.6
28	South Carolina	9.6
30	South Dakota	9.3
38	Tennessee	8.4
18	Texas	11.1
1	Utah	15.4
4	Vermont	13.5
17	Virginia	11.2
23	Washington	10.3
14	West Virginia	11.6
12	Wisconsin	11.9
34	Wyoming	8.9

RANK ORDER

RANK	STATE	PERCENT
1	Utah	15.4
2	North Dakota	15.1
3	North Carolina	14.1
4	Vermont	13.5
5	Iowa	13.1
6	Alabama	13.0
7	Kansas	12.8
8	Oklahoma	12.5
9	Arkansas	12.1
9	Michigan	12.1
9	New Mexico	12.1
12	Nebraska	11.9
12	Wisconsin	11.9
14	West Virginia	11.6
15	Montana	11.3
15	Oregon	11.3
17	Virginia	11.2
18	Delaware	11.1
18	Kentucky	11.1
18	Texas	11.1
21	Indiana	10.9
22	Colorado	10.6
23	Idaho	10.3
23	Mississippi	10.3
23	Washington	10.3
26	Maryland	10.2
27	Arizona	10.0
28	South Carolina	9.6
29	Hawaii	9.4
30	South Dakota	9.3
31	Missouri	9.1
32	Minnesota	9.0
32	New Hampshire	9.0
34	Wyoming	8.9
35	Ohio	8.8
36	California	8.5
36	Illinois	8.5
38	Tennessee	8.4
39	Nevada	8.0
40	Louisiana	7.8
41	Georgia	7.5
41	Maine	7.5
43	Connecticut	7.3
43	Pennsylvania	7.3
45	Massachusetts	6.9
46	Rhode Island	6.6
47	New Jersey	6.4
48	Florida	6.2
49	Alaska	6.0
50	New York	5.4

| | District of Columbia | 1.5 |

Source: CQ Press using data from U.S. Bureau of the Census, Governments Division
"State and Local Government Finances 2006-2007" (http://www.census.gov/govs/estimate/index.html)
*Direct general expenditures for higher education as a percent of all direct general expenditures. Includes capital outlays.

Average Faculty Salary at Institutions of Higher Education in 2007

National Average = $68,585*

ALPHA ORDER

RANK	STATE	AVERAGE SALARY
35	Alabama	$59,770
29	Alaska	61,861
11	Arizona	71,965
49	Arkansas	52,062
4	California	80,843
26	Colorado	63,281
2	Connecticut	83,336
5	Delaware	79,208
21	Florida	65,065
28	Georgia	62,839
17	Hawaii	66,635
44	Idaho	54,070
12	Illinois	70,404
22	Indiana	65,052
30	Iowa	61,109
38	Kansas	58,274
42	Kentucky	56,845
43	Louisiana	56,546
27	Maine	63,082
14	Maryland	69,179
1	Massachusetts	85,179
10	Michigan	72,106
18	Minnesota	65,826
48	Mississippi	52,277
31	Missouri	61,001
46	Montana	52,901
36	Nebraska	59,691
9	Nevada	72,581
13	New Hampshire	70,125
3	New Jersey	82,559
40	New Mexico	57,946
7	New York	76,918
32	North Carolina	60,919
50	North Dakota	50,399
20	Ohio	65,507
39	Oklahoma	58,120
33	Oregon	59,944
8	Pennsylvania	73,112
6	Rhode Island	77,582
41	South Carolina	57,941
47	South Dakota	52,532
34	Tennessee	59,855
25	Texas	63,709
19	Utah	65,763
23	Vermont	64,256
16	Virginia	66,950
15	Washington	67,453
45	West Virginia	53,951
24	Wisconsin	64,208
37	Wyoming	58,362

RANK ORDER

RANK	STATE	AVERAGE SALARY
1	Massachusetts	$85,179
2	Connecticut	83,336
3	New Jersey	82,559
4	California	80,843
5	Delaware	79,208
6	Rhode Island	77,582
7	New York	76,918
8	Pennsylvania	73,112
9	Nevada	72,581
10	Michigan	72,106
11	Arizona	71,965
12	Illinois	70,404
13	New Hampshire	70,125
14	Maryland	69,179
15	Washington	67,453
16	Virginia	66,950
17	Hawaii	66,635
18	Minnesota	65,826
19	Utah	65,763
20	Ohio	65,507
21	Florida	65,065
22	Indiana	65,052
23	Vermont	64,256
24	Wisconsin	64,208
25	Texas	63,709
26	Colorado	63,281
27	Maine	63,082
28	Georgia	62,839
29	Alaska	61,861
30	Iowa	61,109
31	Missouri	61,001
32	North Carolina	60,919
33	Oregon	59,944
34	Tennessee	59,855
35	Alabama	59,770
36	Nebraska	59,691
37	Wyoming	58,362
38	Kansas	58,274
39	Oklahoma	58,120
40	New Mexico	57,946
41	South Carolina	57,941
42	Kentucky	56,845
43	Louisiana	56,546
44	Idaho	54,070
45	West Virginia	53,951
46	Montana	52,901
47	South Dakota	52,532
48	Mississippi	52,277
49	Arkansas	52,062
50	North Dakota	50,399
	District of Columbia	81,791

Source: U.S. Department of Education, National Center for Education Statistics
   "Digest of Education Statistics 2007" (NCES 2008-022, March 2008, http://nces.ed.gov/programs/digest/d07/)
*For 2006-2007 school year. For full-time instructional faculty on 9-month contracts at four-year and two-year public and private degree-granting institutions.

Average Student Costs at Public Institutions of Higher Education in 2008

National Average = $13,424*

RANK	STATE	AVERAGE COSTS
38	Alabama	$11,035
32	Alaska	11,719
27	Arizona	12,289
45	Arkansas	10,598
14	California	14,893
23	Colorado	13,314
7	Connecticut	16,263
8	Delaware	16,165
42	Florida	10,709
39	Georgia	10,984
28	Hawaii	12,202
48	Idaho	9,871
5	Illinois	16,795
18	Indiana	14,096
24	Iowa	13,191
36	Kansas	11,338
25	Kentucky	12,641
50	Louisiana	9,479
15	Maine	14,791
12	Maryland	15,644
9	Massachusetts	16,159
10	Michigan	16,003
16	Minnesota	14,188
41	Mississippi	10,776
22	Missouri	13,385
33	Montana	11,609
30	Nebraska	11,852
29	Nevada	12,168
2	New Hampshire	18,293
1	New Jersey	19,548
43	New Mexico	10,610
17	New York	14,140
40	North Carolina	10,889
37	North Dakota	11,134
6	Ohio	16,354
44	Oklahoma	10,600
20	Oregon	13,868
4	Pennsylvania	17,187
11	Rhode Island	15,775
13	South Carolina	15,089
46	South Dakota	10,522
35	Tennessee	11,340
26	Texas	12,367
49	Utah	9,706
3	Vermont	18,245
19	Virginia	13,928
21	Washington	13,478
34	West Virginia	11,426
31	Wisconsin	11,747
47	Wyoming	10,068

RANK	STATE	AVERAGE COSTS
1	New Jersey	$19,548
2	New Hampshire	18,293
3	Vermont	18,245
4	Pennsylvania	17,187
5	Illinois	16,795
6	Ohio	16,354
7	Connecticut	16,263
8	Delaware	16,165
9	Massachusetts	16,159
10	Michigan	16,003
11	Rhode Island	15,775
12	Maryland	15,644
13	South Carolina	15,089
14	California	14,893
15	Maine	14,791
16	Minnesota	14,188
17	New York	14,140
18	Indiana	14,096
19	Virginia	13,928
20	Oregon	13,868
21	Washington	13,478
22	Missouri	13,385
23	Colorado	13,314
24	Iowa	13,191
25	Kentucky	12,641
26	Texas	12,367
27	Arizona	12,289
28	Hawaii	12,202
29	Nevada	12,168
30	Nebraska	11,852
31	Wisconsin	11,747
32	Alaska	11,719
33	Montana	11,609
34	West Virginia	11,426
35	Tennessee	11,340
36	Kansas	11,338
37	North Dakota	11,134
38	Alabama	11,035
39	Georgia	10,984
40	North Carolina	10,889
41	Mississippi	10,776
42	Florida	10,709
43	New Mexico	10,610
44	Oklahoma	10,600
45	Arkansas	10,598
46	South Dakota	10,522
47	Wyoming	10,068
48	Idaho	9,871
49	Utah	9,706
50	Louisiana	9,479
	District of Columbia**	NA

Source: U.S. Department of Education, National Center for Education Statistics
   "Digest of Education Statistics 2008" (NCES 2009-020, March 2009, http://nces.ed.gov/programs/digest/d08/)
*Data for 2007-2008 school year. Based on average in-state tuition, room and board, and fees for full-time students in public four-year institutions for an entire academic year.
**Not available.

Average Student Costs at Private Institutions of Higher Education in 2008

National Average = $30,393*

ALPHA ORDER

ALPHA ORDER

RANK	STATE	AVERAGE COSTS
42	Alabama	$21,014
25	Alaska	26,883
39	Arizona	21,809
45	Arkansas	20,096
8	California	35,006
15	Colorado	30,409
2	Connecticut	40,245
44	Delaware	20,170
23	Florida	27,534
21	Georgia	29,046
40	Hawaii	21,452
49	Idaho	10,788
14	Illinois	30,833
19	Indiana	29,953
29	Iowa	25,057
35	Kansas	22,653
36	Kentucky	22,303
16	Louisiana	30,363
11	Maine	32,753
5	Maryland	36,171
1	Massachusetts	41,458
38	Michigan	21,874
17	Minnesota	30,135
46	Mississippi	18,395
30	Missouri	25,008
41	Montana	21,072
33	Nebraska	23,022
28	Nevada	25,562
9	New Hampshire	34,643
7	New Jersey	35,182
32	New Mexico	24,023
4	New York	36,228
20	North Carolina	29,141
47	North Dakota	15,156
18	Ohio	30,093
34	Oklahoma	22,780
12	Oregon	31,810
6	Pennsylvania	36,019
3	Rhode Island	36,476
31	South Carolina	24,914
43	South Dakota	20,605
27	Tennessee	25,802
24	Texas	27,116
48	Utah	12,913
10	Vermont	33,879
26	Virginia	26,170
13	Washington	31,090
37	West Virginia	22,022
22	Wisconsin	28,422
NA	Wyoming**	NA

RANK ORDER

RANK	STATE	AVERAGE COSTS
1	Massachusetts	$41,458
2	Connecticut	40,245
3	Rhode Island	36,476
4	New York	36,228
5	Maryland	36,171
6	Pennsylvania	36,019
7	New Jersey	35,182
8	California	35,006
9	New Hampshire	34,643
10	Vermont	33,879
11	Maine	32,753
12	Oregon	31,810
13	Washington	31,090
14	Illinois	30,833
15	Colorado	30,409
16	Louisiana	30,363
17	Minnesota	30,135
18	Ohio	30,093
19	Indiana	29,953
20	North Carolina	29,141
21	Georgia	29,046
22	Wisconsin	28,422
23	Florida	27,534
24	Texas	27,116
25	Alaska	26,883
26	Virginia	26,170
27	Tennessee	25,802
28	Nevada	25,562
29	Iowa	25,057
30	Missouri	25,008
31	South Carolina	24,914
32	New Mexico	24,023
33	Nebraska	23,022
34	Oklahoma	22,780
35	Kansas	22,653
36	Kentucky	22,303
37	West Virginia	22,022
38	Michigan	21,874
39	Arizona	21,809
40	Hawaii	21,452
41	Montana	21,072
42	Alabama	21,014
43	South Dakota	20,605
44	Delaware	20,170
45	Arkansas	20,096
46	Mississippi	18,395
47	North Dakota	15,156
48	Utah	12,913
49	Idaho	10,788
NA	Wyoming**	NA
	District of Columbia	35,747

Source: U.S. Department of Education, National Center for Education Statistics
    "Digest of Education Statistics 2008" (NCES 2009-020, March 2009, http://nces.ed.gov/programs/digest/d08/)
*Data for 2007-2008 school year. Based on average in-state tuition, room and board, and fees for full-time students in private four-year institutions for an entire academic year.
**Not available or not applicable.

Institutions of Higher Education in 2008

National Total = 4,352 Institutions*

RANK	STATE	INSTITUTIONS	% of USA
23	Alabama	68	1.6%
50	Alaska	7	0.2%
19	Arizona	76	1.7%
31	Arkansas	49	1.1%
1	California	416	9.6%
18	Colorado	80	1.8%
32	Connecticut	46	1.1%
48	Delaware	10	0.2%
6	Florida	184	4.2%
8	Georgia	135	3.1%
44	Hawaii	22	0.5%
46	Idaho	14	0.3%
7	Illinois	177	4.1%
14	Indiana	106	2.4%
25	Iowa	65	1.5%
26	Kansas	60	1.4%
22	Kentucky	71	1.6%
17	Louisiana	84	1.9%
38	Maine	30	0.7%
30	Maryland	57	1.3%
11	Massachusetts	122	2.8%
15	Michigan	105	2.4%
12	Minnesota	112	2.6%
34	Mississippi	42	1.0%
10	Missouri	128	2.9%
42	Montana	23	0.5%
34	Nebraska	42	1.0%
42	Nevada	23	0.5%
39	New Hampshire	28	0.6%
26	New Jersey	60	1.4%
34	New Mexico	42	1.0%
2	New York	307	7.1%
9	North Carolina	130	3.0%
44	North Dakota	22	0.5%
5	Ohio	207	4.8%
29	Oklahoma	59	1.4%
26	Oregon	60	1.4%
3	Pennsylvania	263	6.0%
46	Rhode Island	14	0.3%
24	South Carolina	66	1.5%
41	South Dakota	24	0.6%
15	Tennessee	105	2.4%
4	Texas	214	4.9%
37	Utah	36	0.8%
40	Vermont	25	0.6%
12	Virginia	112	2.6%
19	Washington	76	1.7%
33	West Virginia	44	1.0%
21	Wisconsin	73	1.7%
48	Wyoming	10	0.2%

RANK ORDER

RANK	STATE	INSTITUTIONS	% of USA
1	California	416	9.6%
2	New York	307	7.1%
3	Pennsylvania	263	6.0%
4	Texas	214	4.9%
5	Ohio	207	4.8%
6	Florida	184	4.2%
7	Illinois	177	4.1%
8	Georgia	135	3.1%
9	North Carolina	130	3.0%
10	Missouri	128	2.9%
11	Massachusetts	122	2.8%
12	Minnesota	112	2.6%
12	Virginia	112	2.6%
14	Indiana	106	2.4%
15	Michigan	105	2.4%
15	Tennessee	105	2.4%
17	Louisiana	84	1.9%
18	Colorado	80	1.8%
19	Arizona	76	1.7%
19	Washington	76	1.7%
21	Wisconsin	73	1.7%
22	Kentucky	71	1.6%
23	Alabama	68	1.6%
24	South Carolina	66	1.5%
25	Iowa	65	1.5%
26	Kansas	60	1.4%
26	New Jersey	60	1.4%
26	Oregon	60	1.4%
29	Oklahoma	59	1.4%
30	Maryland	57	1.3%
31	Arkansas	49	1.1%
32	Connecticut	46	1.1%
33	West Virginia	44	1.0%
34	Mississippi	42	1.0%
34	Nebraska	42	1.0%
34	New Mexico	42	1.0%
37	Utah	36	0.8%
38	Maine	30	0.7%
39	New Hampshire	28	0.6%
40	Vermont	25	0.6%
41	South Dakota	24	0.6%
42	Montana	23	0.5%
42	Nevada	23	0.5%
44	Hawaii	22	0.5%
44	North Dakota	22	0.5%
46	Idaho	14	0.3%
46	Rhode Island	14	0.3%
48	Delaware	10	0.2%
48	Wyoming	10	0.2%
50	Alaska	7	0.2%
	District of Columbia	16	0.4%

Source: U.S. Department of Education, National Center for Education Statistics
   "Digest of Education Statistics 2008" (NCES 2009-020, March 2009, http://nces.ed.gov/programs/digest/index.asp)
*For 2007-2008 school year. Consists of 2,675 four-year and 1,677 two-year public and private degree-granting institutions.
Includes five U.S. Service Schools not shown by state.

Enrollment in Institutions of Higher Education in 2006

National Total = 17,758,870 Students*

ALPHA ORDER

RANK	STATE	ENROLLMENT	% of USA
23	Alabama	258,408	1.5%
50	Alaska	29,853	0.2%
9	Arizona	567,192	3.2%
34	Arkansas	147,391	0.8%
1	California	2,434,774	13.7%
21	Colorado	308,383	1.7%
32	Connecticut	176,716	1.0%
44	Delaware	51,238	0.3%
4	Florida	885,651	5.0%
13	Georgia	435,403	2.5%
42	Hawaii	66,893	0.4%
40	Idaho	77,872	0.4%
5	Illinois	830,676	4.7%
17	Indiana	368,013	2.1%
25	Iowa	238,634	1.3%
31	Kansas	193,146	1.1%
24	Kentucky	248,914	1.4%
26	Louisiana	224,147	1.3%
43	Maine	66,149	0.4%
20	Maryland	319,460	1.8%
12	Massachusetts	451,526	2.5%
7	Michigan	634,489	3.6%
16	Minnesota	375,899	2.1%
33	Mississippi	151,137	0.9%
15	Missouri	377,098	2.1%
47	Montana	47,501	0.3%
36	Nebraska	124,500	0.7%
37	Nevada	112,270	0.6%
41	New Hampshire	70,669	0.4%
14	New Jersey	385,656	2.2%
35	New Mexico	131,828	0.7%
3	New York	1,160,364	6.5%
10	North Carolina	495,633	2.8%
45	North Dakota	49,519	0.3%
8	Ohio	619,942	3.5%
28	Oklahoma	206,236	1.2%
30	Oregon	197,594	1.1%
6	Pennsylvania	707,132	4.0%
39	Rhode Island	81,734	0.5%
27	South Carolina	212,422	1.2%
46	South Dakota	48,931	0.3%
22	Tennessee	290,530	1.6%
2	Texas	1,252,709	7.1%
29	Utah	202,151	1.1%
48	Vermont	41,095	0.2%
11	Virginia	456,172	2.6%
18	Washington	348,154	2.0%
38	West Virginia	100,519	0.6%
19	Wisconsin	340,158	1.9%
49	Wyoming	34,693	0.2%

RANK ORDER

RANK	STATE	ENROLLMENT	% of USA
1	California	2,434,774	13.7%
2	Texas	1,252,709	7.1%
3	New York	1,160,364	6.5%
4	Florida	885,651	5.0%
5	Illinois	830,676	4.7%
6	Pennsylvania	707,132	4.0%
7	Michigan	634,489	3.6%
8	Ohio	619,942	3.5%
9	Arizona	567,192	3.2%
10	North Carolina	495,633	2.8%
11	Virginia	456,172	2.6%
12	Massachusetts	451,526	2.5%
13	Georgia	435,403	2.5%
14	New Jersey	385,656	2.2%
15	Missouri	377,098	2.1%
16	Minnesota	375,899	2.1%
17	Indiana	368,013	2.1%
18	Washington	348,154	2.0%
19	Wisconsin	340,158	1.9%
20	Maryland	319,460	1.8%
21	Colorado	308,383	1.7%
22	Tennessee	290,530	1.6%
23	Alabama	258,408	1.5%
24	Kentucky	248,914	1.4%
25	Iowa	238,634	1.3%
26	Louisiana	224,147	1.3%
27	South Carolina	212,422	1.2%
28	Oklahoma	206,236	1.2%
29	Utah	202,151	1.1%
30	Oregon	197,594	1.1%
31	Kansas	193,146	1.1%
32	Connecticut	176,716	1.0%
33	Mississippi	151,137	0.9%
34	Arkansas	147,391	0.8%
35	New Mexico	131,828	0.7%
36	Nebraska	124,500	0.7%
37	Nevada	112,270	0.6%
38	West Virginia	100,519	0.6%
39	Rhode Island	81,734	0.5%
40	Idaho	77,872	0.4%
41	New Hampshire	70,669	0.4%
42	Hawaii	66,893	0.4%
43	Maine	66,149	0.4%
44	Delaware	51,238	0.3%
45	North Dakota	49,519	0.3%
46	South Dakota	48,931	0.3%
47	Montana	47,501	0.3%
48	Vermont	41,095	0.2%
49	Wyoming	34,693	0.2%
50	Alaska	29,853	0.2%
	District of Columbia	109,505	0.6%

Source: U.S. Department of Education, National Center for Education Statistics
    "Digest of Education Statistics 2008" (NCES 2009-020, March 2009, http://nces.ed.gov/programs/digest/index.asp)
*Fall 2006 enrollment. Includes full-time and part-time students at Title IV eligible, degree-granting four-year and two-year institutions. National total includes 12,191 students at U.S. Service Schools not shown by state.

Enrollment Rate in Institutions of Higher Education in 2006

National Rate = 603 Students per 1,000 Population 18 to 24 Years Old*

ALPHA ORDER

RANK	STATE	RATE
31	Alabama	577
50	Alaska	416
1	Arizona	964
38	Arkansas	552
14	California	643
6	Colorado	671
37	Connecticut	553
18	Delaware	616
36	Florida	555
49	Georgia	476
39	Hawaii	535
42	Idaho	522
11	Illinois	648
24	Indiana	598
2	Iowa	765
9	Kansas	660
11	Kentucky	648
48	Louisiana	492
33	Maine	572
23	Maryland	599
4	Massachusetts	713
13	Michigan	646
3	Minnesota	723
47	Mississippi	498
7	Missouri	663
46	Montana	500
10	Nebraska	659
41	Nevada	526
28	New Hampshire	589
44	New Jersey	505
14	New Mexico	643
24	New York	598
26	North Carolina	594
21	North Dakota	606
34	Ohio	565
35	Oklahoma	559
30	Oregon	581
27	Pennsylvania	590
5	Rhode Island	704
45	South Carolina	502
28	South Dakota	589
40	Tennessee	529
43	Texas	512
17	Utah	634
8	Vermont	661
20	Virginia	611
32	Washington	573
19	West Virginia	615
21	Wisconsin	606
16	Wyoming	639

RANK ORDER

RANK	STATE	RATE
1	Arizona	964
2	Iowa	765
3	Minnesota	723
4	Massachusetts	713
5	Rhode Island	704
6	Colorado	671
7	Missouri	663
8	Vermont	661
9	Kansas	660
10	Nebraska	659
11	Illinois	648
11	Kentucky	648
13	Michigan	646
14	California	643
14	New Mexico	643
16	Wyoming	639
17	Utah	634
18	Delaware	616
19	West Virginia	615
20	Virginia	611
21	North Dakota	606
21	Wisconsin	606
23	Maryland	599
24	Indiana	598
24	New York	598
26	North Carolina	594
27	Pennsylvania	590
28	New Hampshire	589
28	South Dakota	589
30	Oregon	581
31	Alabama	577
32	Washington	573
33	Maine	572
34	Ohio	565
35	Oklahoma	559
36	Florida	555
37	Connecticut	553
38	Arkansas	552
39	Hawaii	535
40	Tennessee	529
41	Nevada	526
42	Idaho	522
43	Texas	512
44	New Jersey	505
45	South Carolina	502
46	Montana	500
47	Mississippi	498
48	Louisiana	492
49	Georgia	476
50	Alaska	416

District of Columbia 1,530

Source: CQ Press using data from U.S. Department of Education, National Center for Education Statistics
"Digest of Education Statistics 2008" (NCES 2009-020, March 2009, http://nces.ed.gov/programs/digest/index.asp)
*Based on fall 2006 enrollment and population. National rate includes U.S. Service Schools. Includes students at four-year and two-year public and private degree-granting institutions. Enrollment based on location of institution. Population based on residence.

Enrollment in Public Institutions of Higher Education in 2006

National Total = 13,180,133 Students*

ALPHA ORDER

RANK	STATE	ENROLLMENT	% of USA
20	Alabama	230,668	1.8%
49	Alaska	28,595	0.2%
12	Arizona	331,441	2.5%
33	Arkansas	131,407	1.0%
1	California	2,047,565	15.5%
19	Colorado	231,901	1.8%
35	Connecticut	112,476	0.9%
46	Delaware	38,118	0.3%
3	Florida	651,908	4.9%
11	Georgia	346,138	2.6%
40	Hawaii	49,990	0.4%
39	Idaho	59,211	0.4%
5	Illinois	552,777	4.2%
16	Indiana	271,704	2.1%
30	Iowa	151,052	1.1%
28	Kansas	170,531	1.3%
23	Kentucky	204,198	1.5%
24	Louisiana	192,554	1.5%
41	Maine	47,770	0.4%
17	Maryland	260,921	2.0%
25	Massachusetts	192,164	1.5%
6	Michigan	511,776	3.9%
18	Minnesota	244,106	1.9%
32	Mississippi	136,626	1.0%
21	Missouri	218,475	1.7%
42	Montana	42,995	0.3%
37	Nebraska	94,486	0.7%
36	Nevada	101,856	0.8%
44	New Hampshire	41,530	0.3%
13	New Jersey	308,374	2.3%
34	New Mexico	121,668	0.9%
4	New York	635,785	4.8%
8	North Carolina	406,068	3.1%
43	North Dakota	42,949	0.3%
7	Ohio	452,962	3.4%
26	Oklahoma	178,015	1.4%
29	Oregon	160,059	1.2%
9	Pennsylvania	388,251	2.9%
45	Rhode Island	40,374	0.3%
27	South Carolina	176,415	1.3%
47	South Dakota	38,028	0.3%
22	Tennessee	205,056	1.6%
2	Texas	1,094,139	8.3%
31	Utah	148,228	1.1%
50	Vermont	24,385	0.2%
10	Virginia	357,823	2.7%
14	Washington	297,048	2.3%
38	West Virginia	86,501	0.7%
15	Wisconsin	272,246	2.1%
48	Wyoming	32,860	0.2%

RANK ORDER

RANK	STATE	ENROLLMENT	% of USA
1	California	2,047,565	15.5%
2	Texas	1,094,139	8.3%
3	Florida	651,908	4.9%
4	New York	635,785	4.8%
5	Illinois	552,777	4.2%
6	Michigan	511,776	3.9%
7	Ohio	452,962	3.4%
8	North Carolina	406,068	3.1%
9	Pennsylvania	388,251	2.9%
10	Virginia	357,823	2.7%
11	Georgia	346,138	2.6%
12	Arizona	331,441	2.5%
13	New Jersey	308,374	2.3%
14	Washington	297,048	2.3%
15	Wisconsin	272,246	2.1%
16	Indiana	271,704	2.1%
17	Maryland	260,921	2.0%
18	Minnesota	244,106	1.9%
19	Colorado	231,901	1.8%
20	Alabama	230,668	1.8%
21	Missouri	218,475	1.7%
22	Tennessee	205,056	1.6%
23	Kentucky	204,198	1.5%
24	Louisiana	192,554	1.5%
25	Massachusetts	192,164	1.5%
26	Oklahoma	178,015	1.4%
27	South Carolina	176,415	1.3%
28	Kansas	170,531	1.3%
29	Oregon	160,059	1.2%
30	Iowa	151,052	1.1%
31	Utah	148,228	1.1%
32	Mississippi	136,626	1.0%
33	Arkansas	131,407	1.0%
34	New Mexico	121,668	0.9%
35	Connecticut	112,476	0.9%
36	Nevada	101,856	0.8%
37	Nebraska	94,486	0.7%
38	West Virginia	86,501	0.7%
39	Idaho	59,211	0.4%
40	Hawaii	49,990	0.4%
41	Maine	47,770	0.4%
42	Montana	42,995	0.3%
43	North Dakota	42,949	0.3%
44	New Hampshire	41,530	0.3%
45	Rhode Island	40,374	0.3%
46	Delaware	38,118	0.3%
47	South Dakota	38,028	0.3%
48	Wyoming	32,860	0.2%
49	Alaska	28,595	0.2%
50	Vermont	24,385	0.2%
	District of Columbia	5,769	0.0%

Source: U.S. Department of Education, National Center for Education Statistics
   "Digest of Education Statistics 2008" (NCES 2009-020, March 2009, http://nces.ed.gov/programs/digest/index.asp)
*Fall 2006 enrollment. Includes full-time and part-time students at Title IV eligible, degree-granting four-year and two-year institutions. National total includes 12,191 students at U.S. Service Schools not shown by state.

Enrollment in Private Institutions of Higher Education in 2006

National Total = 4,578,737 Students*

ALPHA ORDER

RANK	STATE	ENROLLMENT	% of USA
34	Alabama	27,740	0.6%
50	Alaska	1,258	0.0%
6	Arizona	235,751	5.1%
40	Arkansas	15,984	0.3%
2	California	387,209	8.5%
20	Colorado	76,482	1.7%
22	Connecticut	64,240	1.4%
43	Delaware	13,120	0.3%
7	Florida	233,743	5.1%
16	Georgia	89,265	1.9%
38	Hawaii	16,903	0.4%
36	Idaho	18,661	0.4%
4	Illinois	277,899	6.1%
14	Indiana	96,309	2.1%
17	Iowa	87,582	1.9%
35	Kansas	22,615	0.5%
26	Kentucky	44,716	1.0%
30	Louisiana	31,593	0.7%
37	Maine	18,379	0.4%
23	Maryland	58,539	1.3%
5	Massachusetts	259,362	5.7%
12	Michigan	122,713	2.7%
11	Minnesota	131,793	2.9%
41	Mississippi	14,511	0.3%
9	Missouri	158,623	3.5%
48	Montana	4,506	0.1%
31	Nebraska	30,014	0.7%
45	Nevada	10,414	0.2%
32	New Hampshire	29,139	0.6%
19	New Jersey	77,282	1.7%
46	New Mexico	10,160	0.2%
1	New York	524,579	11.5%
15	North Carolina	89,565	2.0%
47	North Dakota	6,570	0.1%
8	Ohio	166,980	3.6%
33	Oklahoma	28,221	0.6%
28	Oregon	37,535	0.8%
3	Pennsylvania	318,881	7.0%
27	Rhode Island	41,360	0.9%
29	South Carolina	36,007	0.8%
44	South Dakota	10,903	0.2%
18	Tennessee	85,474	1.9%
10	Texas	158,570	3.5%
24	Utah	53,923	1.2%
39	Vermont	16,710	0.4%
13	Virginia	98,349	2.1%
25	Washington	51,106	1.1%
42	West Virginia	14,018	0.3%
21	Wisconsin	67,912	1.5%
49	Wyoming	1,833	0.0%

RANK ORDER

RANK	STATE	ENROLLMENT	% of USA
1	New York	524,579	11.5%
2	California	387,209	8.5%
3	Pennsylvania	318,881	7.0%
4	Illinois	277,899	6.1%
5	Massachusetts	259,362	5.7%
6	Arizona	235,751	5.1%
7	Florida	233,743	5.1%
8	Ohio	166,980	3.6%
9	Missouri	158,623	3.5%
10	Texas	158,570	3.5%
11	Minnesota	131,793	2.9%
12	Michigan	122,713	2.7%
13	Virginia	98,349	2.1%
14	Indiana	96,309	2.1%
15	North Carolina	89,565	2.0%
16	Georgia	89,265	1.9%
17	Iowa	87,582	1.9%
18	Tennessee	85,474	1.9%
19	New Jersey	77,282	1.7%
20	Colorado	76,482	1.7%
21	Wisconsin	67,912	1.5%
22	Connecticut	64,240	1.4%
23	Maryland	58,539	1.3%
24	Utah	53,923	1.2%
25	Washington	51,106	1.1%
26	Kentucky	44,716	1.0%
27	Rhode Island	41,360	0.9%
28	Oregon	37,535	0.8%
29	South Carolina	36,007	0.8%
30	Louisiana	31,593	0.7%
31	Nebraska	30,014	0.7%
32	New Hampshire	29,139	0.6%
33	Oklahoma	28,221	0.6%
34	Alabama	27,740	0.6%
35	Kansas	22,615	0.5%
36	Idaho	18,661	0.4%
37	Maine	18,379	0.4%
38	Hawaii	16,903	0.4%
39	Vermont	16,710	0.4%
40	Arkansas	15,984	0.3%
41	Mississippi	14,511	0.3%
42	West Virginia	14,018	0.3%
43	Delaware	13,120	0.3%
44	South Dakota	10,903	0.2%
45	Nevada	10,414	0.2%
46	New Mexico	10,160	0.2%
47	North Dakota	6,570	0.1%
48	Montana	4,506	0.1%
49	Wyoming	1,833	0.0%
50	Alaska	1,258	0.0%
	District of Columbia	103,736	2.3%

Source: U.S. Department of Education, National Center for Education Statistics
  "Digest of Education Statistics 2008" (NCES 2009-020, March 2009, http://nces.ed.gov/programs/digest/index.asp)
*Fall 2006 enrollment. Includes full-time and part-time students at Title IV eligible, degree-granting four-year and two-year institutions.

Percent of Population With a Bachelor's Degree or More in 2008

National Percent = 27.7%*

<table>
<tr><td colspan="3">ALPHA ORDER</td><td colspan="3">RANK ORDER</td></tr>
<tr><th>RANK</th><th>STATE</th><th>PERCENT</th><th>RANK</th><th>STATE</th><th>PERCENT</th></tr>
<tr><td>44</td><td>Alabama</td><td>22.0</td><td>1</td><td>Massachusetts</td><td>38.1</td></tr>
<tr><td>21</td><td>Alaska</td><td>27.3</td><td>2</td><td>Colorado</td><td>35.6</td></tr>
<tr><td>31</td><td>Arizona</td><td>25.1</td><td>2</td><td>Connecticut</td><td>35.6</td></tr>
<tr><td>49</td><td>Arkansas</td><td>18.8</td><td>4</td><td>Maryland</td><td>35.2</td></tr>
<tr><td>14</td><td>California</td><td>29.6</td><td>5</td><td>New Jersey</td><td>34.4</td></tr>
<tr><td>2</td><td>Colorado</td><td>35.6</td><td>6</td><td>Virginia</td><td>33.7</td></tr>
<tr><td>2</td><td>Connecticut</td><td>35.6</td><td>7</td><td>New Hampshire</td><td>33.3</td></tr>
<tr><td>19</td><td>Delaware</td><td>27.5</td><td>8</td><td>Vermont</td><td>32.1</td></tr>
<tr><td>27</td><td>Florida</td><td>25.8</td><td>9</td><td>New York</td><td>31.9</td></tr>
<tr><td>19</td><td>Georgia</td><td>27.5</td><td>10</td><td>Minnesota</td><td>31.5</td></tr>
<tr><td>16</td><td>Hawaii</td><td>29.1</td><td>11</td><td>Washington</td><td>30.7</td></tr>
<tr><td>38</td><td>Idaho</td><td>24.0</td><td>12</td><td>Rhode Island</td><td>30.0</td></tr>
<tr><td>13</td><td>Illinois</td><td>29.9</td><td>13</td><td>Illinois</td><td>29.9</td></tr>
<tr><td>41</td><td>Indiana</td><td>22.9</td><td>14</td><td>California</td><td>29.6</td></tr>
<tr><td>36</td><td>Iowa</td><td>24.3</td><td>14</td><td>Kansas</td><td>29.6</td></tr>
<tr><td>14</td><td>Kansas</td><td>29.6</td><td>16</td><td>Hawaii</td><td>29.1</td></tr>
<tr><td>47</td><td>Kentucky</td><td>19.7</td><td>16</td><td>Utah</td><td>29.1</td></tr>
<tr><td>46</td><td>Louisiana</td><td>20.3</td><td>18</td><td>Oregon</td><td>28.1</td></tr>
<tr><td>29</td><td>Maine</td><td>25.4</td><td>19</td><td>Delaware</td><td>27.5</td></tr>
<tr><td>4</td><td>Maryland</td><td>35.2</td><td>19</td><td>Georgia</td><td>27.5</td></tr>
<tr><td>1</td><td>Massachusetts</td><td>38.1</td><td>21</td><td>Alaska</td><td>27.3</td></tr>
<tr><td>34</td><td>Michigan</td><td>24.7</td><td>22</td><td>Montana</td><td>27.1</td></tr>
<tr><td>10</td><td>Minnesota</td><td>31.5</td><td>22</td><td>Nebraska</td><td>27.1</td></tr>
<tr><td>48</td><td>Mississippi</td><td>19.4</td><td>24</td><td>North Dakota</td><td>26.9</td></tr>
<tr><td>33</td><td>Missouri</td><td>25.0</td><td>25</td><td>Pennsylvania</td><td>26.3</td></tr>
<tr><td>22</td><td>Montana</td><td>27.1</td><td>26</td><td>North Carolina</td><td>26.1</td></tr>
<tr><td>22</td><td>Nebraska</td><td>27.1</td><td>27</td><td>Florida</td><td>25.8</td></tr>
<tr><td>45</td><td>Nevada</td><td>21.9</td><td>28</td><td>Wisconsin</td><td>25.7</td></tr>
<tr><td>7</td><td>New Hampshire</td><td>33.3</td><td>29</td><td>Maine</td><td>25.4</td></tr>
<tr><td>5</td><td>New Jersey</td><td>34.4</td><td>30</td><td>Texas</td><td>25.3</td></tr>
<tr><td>34</td><td>New Mexico</td><td>24.7</td><td>31</td><td>Arizona</td><td>25.1</td></tr>
<tr><td>9</td><td>New York</td><td>31.9</td><td>31</td><td>South Dakota</td><td>25.1</td></tr>
<tr><td>26</td><td>North Carolina</td><td>26.1</td><td>33</td><td>Missouri</td><td>25.0</td></tr>
<tr><td>24</td><td>North Dakota</td><td>26.9</td><td>34</td><td>Michigan</td><td>24.7</td></tr>
<tr><td>37</td><td>Ohio</td><td>24.1</td><td>34</td><td>New Mexico</td><td>24.7</td></tr>
<tr><td>43</td><td>Oklahoma</td><td>22.2</td><td>36</td><td>Iowa</td><td>24.3</td></tr>
<tr><td>18</td><td>Oregon</td><td>28.1</td><td>37</td><td>Ohio</td><td>24.1</td></tr>
<tr><td>25</td><td>Pennsylvania</td><td>26.3</td><td>38</td><td>Idaho</td><td>24.0</td></tr>
<tr><td>12</td><td>Rhode Island</td><td>30.0</td><td>39</td><td>South Carolina</td><td>23.7</td></tr>
<tr><td>39</td><td>South Carolina</td><td>23.7</td><td>40</td><td>Wyoming</td><td>23.6</td></tr>
<tr><td>31</td><td>South Dakota</td><td>25.1</td><td>41</td><td>Indiana</td><td>22.9</td></tr>
<tr><td>41</td><td>Tennessee</td><td>22.9</td><td>41</td><td>Tennessee</td><td>22.9</td></tr>
<tr><td>30</td><td>Texas</td><td>25.3</td><td>43</td><td>Oklahoma</td><td>22.2</td></tr>
<tr><td>16</td><td>Utah</td><td>29.1</td><td>44</td><td>Alabama</td><td>22.0</td></tr>
<tr><td>8</td><td>Vermont</td><td>32.1</td><td>45</td><td>Nevada</td><td>21.9</td></tr>
<tr><td>6</td><td>Virginia</td><td>33.7</td><td>46</td><td>Louisiana</td><td>20.3</td></tr>
<tr><td>11</td><td>Washington</td><td>30.7</td><td>47</td><td>Kentucky</td><td>19.7</td></tr>
<tr><td>50</td><td>West Virginia</td><td>17.1</td><td>48</td><td>Mississippi</td><td>19.4</td></tr>
<tr><td>28</td><td>Wisconsin</td><td>25.7</td><td>49</td><td>Arkansas</td><td>18.8</td></tr>
<tr><td>40</td><td>Wyoming</td><td>23.6</td><td>50</td><td>West Virginia</td><td>17.1</td></tr>
<tr><td></td><td></td><td></td><td></td><td>District of Columbia</td><td>48.2</td></tr>
</table>

Source: U.S. Bureau of the Census, American Community Survey
   "Percent of People 25 Years and Over Who Have Completed a Bachelor's Degree" (http://www.census.gov/acs/www/)
*Persons age 25 and older.

Percent of Population Who Have Completed an Advanced Degree: 2008

National Percent = 10.2%*

ALPHA ORDER

RANK	STATE	PERCENT
40	Alabama	7.7
21	Alaska	9.7
25	Arizona	9.2
50	Arkansas	6.3
13	California	10.8
7	Colorado	12.7
3	Connecticut	15.2
13	Delaware	10.8
27	Florida	9.0
21	Georgia	9.7
20	Hawaii	9.9
41	Idaho	7.4
11	Illinois	11.2
36	Indiana	8.1
42	Iowa	7.3
16	Kansas	10.1
38	Kentucky	7.9
49	Louisiana	6.5
28	Maine	8.9
2	Maryland	15.4
1	Massachusetts	16.4
23	Michigan	9.4
18	Minnesota	10.0
46	Mississippi	6.8
26	Missouri	9.1
34	Montana	8.4
30	Nebraska	8.6
45	Nevada	7.0
9	New Hampshire	12.0
6	New Jersey	12.8
15	New Mexico	10.7
4	New York	13.8
30	North Carolina	8.6
48	North Dakota	6.6
29	Ohio	8.7
44	Oklahoma	7.2
16	Oregon	10.1
18	Pennsylvania	10.0
10	Rhode Island	11.3
33	South Carolina	8.5
42	South Dakota	7.3
37	Tennessee	8.0
35	Texas	8.3
23	Utah	9.4
8	Vermont	12.2
4	Virginia	13.8
12	Washington	10.9
47	West Virginia	6.7
30	Wisconsin	8.6
38	Wyoming	7.9

RANK ORDER

RANK	STATE	PERCENT
1	Massachusetts	16.4
2	Maryland	15.4
3	Connecticut	15.2
4	New York	13.8
4	Virginia	13.8
6	New Jersey	12.8
7	Colorado	12.7
8	Vermont	12.2
9	New Hampshire	12.0
10	Rhode Island	11.3
11	Illinois	11.2
12	Washington	10.9
13	California	10.8
13	Delaware	10.8
15	New Mexico	10.7
16	Kansas	10.1
16	Oregon	10.1
18	Minnesota	10.0
18	Pennsylvania	10.0
20	Hawaii	9.9
21	Alaska	9.7
21	Georgia	9.7
23	Michigan	9.4
23	Utah	9.4
25	Arizona	9.2
26	Missouri	9.1
27	Florida	9.0
28	Maine	8.9
29	Ohio	8.7
30	Nebraska	8.6
30	North Carolina	8.6
30	Wisconsin	8.6
33	South Carolina	8.5
34	Montana	8.4
35	Texas	8.3
36	Indiana	8.1
37	Tennessee	8.0
38	Kentucky	7.9
38	Wyoming	7.9
40	Alabama	7.7
41	Idaho	7.4
42	Iowa	7.3
42	South Dakota	7.3
44	Oklahoma	7.2
45	Nevada	7.0
46	Mississippi	6.8
47	West Virginia	6.7
48	North Dakota	6.6
49	Louisiana	6.5
50	Arkansas	6.3

	District of Columbia	26.7

Source: U.S. Bureau of the Census, American Community Survey
    "Percent of People 25 Years and Over Who Have Completed an Advanced Degree" (http://www.census.gov/acs/www/)
*Persons age 25 and older who have earned a master's degree or higher.

Public Libraries and Branches in 2007

National Total = 16,778 Libraries and Branches*

ALPHA ORDER

RANK	STATE	LIBRARIES	% of USA
24	Alabama	287	1.7%
44	Alaska	104	0.6%
33	Arizona	203	1.2%
30	Arkansas	218	1.3%
1	California	1,121	6.7%
26	Colorado	262	1.6%
27	Connecticut	245	1.5%
50	Delaware	35	0.2%
9	Florida	526	3.1%
15	Georgia	385	2.3%
49	Hawaii	51	0.3%
40	Idaho	141	0.8%
4	Illinois	781	4.7%
13	Indiana	433	2.6%
8	Iowa	559	3.3%
16	Kansas	375	2.2%
34	Kentucky	196	1.2%
21	Louisiana	327	1.9%
25	Maine	278	1.7%
35	Maryland	192	1.1%
10	Massachusetts	476	2.8%
6	Michigan	663	4.0%
18	Minnesota	369	2.2%
28	Mississippi	241	1.4%
17	Missouri	372	2.2%
43	Montana	109	0.6%
23	Nebraska	288	1.7%
46	Nevada	88	0.5%
29	New Hampshire	235	1.4%
12	New Jersey	454	2.7%
42	New Mexico	117	0.7%
2	New York	1,068	6.4%
14	North Carolina	399	2.4%
45	North Dakota	90	0.5%
5	Ohio	727	4.3%
32	Oklahoma	204	1.2%
30	Oregon	218	1.3%
7	Pennsylvania	634	3.8%
48	Rhode Island	73	0.4%
36	South Carolina	187	1.1%
39	South Dakota	145	0.9%
22	Tennessee	290	1.7%
3	Texas	864	5.1%
41	Utah	131	0.8%
37	Vermont	186	1.1%
19	Virginia	354	2.1%
20	Washington	341	2.0%
38	West Virginia	173	1.0%
11	Wisconsin	461	2.7%
47	Wyoming	75	0.4%

RANK ORDER

RANK	STATE	LIBRARIES	% of USA
1	California	1,121	6.7%
2	New York	1,068	6.4%
3	Texas	864	5.1%
4	Illinois	781	4.7%
5	Ohio	727	4.3%
6	Michigan	663	4.0%
7	Pennsylvania	634	3.8%
8	Iowa	559	3.3%
9	Florida	526	3.1%
10	Massachusetts	476	2.8%
11	Wisconsin	461	2.7%
12	New Jersey	454	2.7%
13	Indiana	433	2.6%
14	North Carolina	399	2.4%
15	Georgia	385	2.3%
16	Kansas	375	2.2%
17	Missouri	372	2.2%
18	Minnesota	369	2.2%
19	Virginia	354	2.1%
20	Washington	341	2.0%
21	Louisiana	327	1.9%
22	Tennessee	290	1.7%
23	Nebraska	288	1.7%
24	Alabama	287	1.7%
25	Maine	278	1.7%
26	Colorado	262	1.6%
27	Connecticut	245	1.5%
28	Mississippi	241	1.4%
29	New Hampshire	235	1.4%
30	Arkansas	218	1.3%
30	Oregon	218	1.3%
32	Oklahoma	204	1.2%
33	Arizona	203	1.2%
34	Kentucky	196	1.2%
35	Maryland	192	1.1%
36	South Carolina	187	1.1%
37	Vermont	186	1.1%
38	West Virginia	173	1.0%
39	South Dakota	145	0.9%
40	Idaho	141	0.8%
41	Utah	131	0.8%
42	New Mexico	117	0.7%
43	Montana	109	0.6%
44	Alaska	104	0.6%
45	North Dakota	90	0.5%
46	Nevada	88	0.5%
47	Wyoming	75	0.4%
48	Rhode Island	73	0.4%
49	Hawaii	51	0.3%
50	Delaware	35	0.2%
	District of Columbia	27	0.2%

Source: Institute of Museum and Library Services
   "Public Library Survey Fiscal Year 2007" (June 2009, http://harvester.census.gov/imls/index.asp)
*For fiscal year 2007. Total of central and branch outlets. Does not include bookmobiles. There are 9,214 public libraries.

Rate of Public Libraries and Branches in 2007

National Average = 17,975 Population per Library*

ALPHA ORDER

RANK	STATE	RATE
25	Alabama	16,160
44	Alaska	6,561
3	Arizona	31,341
35	Arkansas	13,038
2	California	32,316
19	Colorado	18,482
31	Connecticut	14,239
9	Delaware	24,711
1	Florida	34,749
8	Georgia	24,763
7	Hawaii	25,036
38	Idaho	10,633
24	Illinois	16,363
29	Indiana	14,656
48	Iowa	5,329
41	Kansas	7,402
13	Kentucky	21,716
34	Louisiana	13,383
49	Maine	4,739
4	Maryland	29,345
33	Massachusetts	13,654
28	Michigan	15,160
32	Minnesota	14,068
37	Mississippi	12,123
26	Missouri	15,887
40	Montana	8,782
45	Nebraska	6,146
5	Nevada	29,179
46	New Hampshire	5,606
17	New Jersey	19,022
23	New Mexico	16,827
20	New York	18,186
11	North Carolina	22,717
42	North Dakota	7,091
27	Ohio	15,847
21	Oklahoma	17,707
22	Oregon	17,124
16	Pennsylvania	19,752
30	Rhode Island	14,452
10	South Carolina	23,659
47	South Dakota	5,497
14	Tennessee	21,286
6	Texas	27,590
15	Utah	20,334
50	Vermont	3,336
12	Virginia	21,807
18	Washington	18,959
39	West Virginia	10,469
36	Wisconsin	12,151
43	Wyoming	6,979

RANK ORDER

RANK	STATE	RATE
1	Florida	34,749
2	California	32,316
3	Arizona	31,341
4	Maryland	29,345
5	Nevada	29,179
6	Texas	27,590
7	Hawaii	25,036
8	Georgia	24,763
9	Delaware	24,711
10	South Carolina	23,659
11	North Carolina	22,717
12	Virginia	21,807
13	Kentucky	21,716
14	Tennessee	21,286
15	Utah	20,334
16	Pennsylvania	19,752
17	New Jersey	19,022
18	Washington	18,959
19	Colorado	18,482
20	New York	18,186
21	Oklahoma	17,707
22	Oregon	17,124
23	New Mexico	16,827
24	Illinois	16,363
25	Alabama	16,160
26	Missouri	15,887
27	Ohio	15,847
28	Michigan	15,160
29	Indiana	14,656
30	Rhode Island	14,452
31	Connecticut	14,239
32	Minnesota	14,068
33	Massachusetts	13,654
34	Louisiana	13,383
35	Arkansas	13,038
36	Wisconsin	12,151
37	Mississippi	12,123
38	Idaho	10,633
39	West Virginia	10,469
40	Montana	8,782
41	Kansas	7,402
42	North Dakota	7,091
43	Wyoming	6,979
44	Alaska	6,561
45	Nebraska	6,146
46	New Hampshire	5,606
47	South Dakota	5,497
48	Iowa	5,329
49	Maine	4,739
50	Vermont	3,336
	District of Columbia	21,719

Source: CQ Press using data from Institute of Museum and Library Services
   "Public Library Survey Fiscal Year 2007" (June 2009, http://harvester.census.gov/imls/index.asp)
*For fiscal year 2007. Based on total of central and branch outlets. Does not include bookmobiles.

Books in Public Libraries Per Capita in 2007

National Per Capita = 2.8 Books*

ALPHA ORDER				RANK ORDER		
RANK	**STATE**	**PER CAPITA**		**RANK**	**STATE**	**PER CAPITA**
39	Alabama	2.2		1	Maine	5.5
18	Alaska	3.6		2	Nebraska	5.2
50	Arizona	1.5		3	Massachusetts	5.0
38	Arkansas	2.3		4	Vermont	4.8
42	California	2.0		5	Kansas	4.7
33	Colorado	2.5		5	New Hampshire	4.7
10	Connecticut	4.4		5	Wyoming	4.7
33	Delaware	2.5		8	South Dakota	4.6
47	Florida	1.7		9	Indiana	4.5
47	Georgia	1.7		10	Connecticut	4.4
30	Hawaii	2.6		11	Iowa	4.3
22	Idaho	3.1		11	North Dakota	4.3
16	Illinois	3.7		13	Ohio	4.1
9	Indiana	4.5		13	Rhode Island	4.1
11	Iowa	4.3		15	New York	3.9
5	Kansas	4.7		16	Illinois	3.7
40	Kentucky	2.1		16	New Jersey	3.7
28	Louisiana	2.7		18	Alaska	3.6
1	Maine	5.5		18	Missouri	3.6
30	Maryland	2.6		20	Michigan	3.5
3	Massachusetts	5.0		20	Wisconsin	3.5
20	Michigan	3.5		22	Idaho	3.1
24	Minnesota	3.0		22	Montana	3.1
42	Mississippi	2.0		24	Minnesota	3.0
18	Missouri	3.6		24	New Mexico	3.0
22	Montana	3.1		26	Oregon	2.8
2	Nebraska	5.2		26	West Virginia	2.8
47	Nevada	1.7		28	Louisiana	2.7
5	New Hampshire	4.7		28	Washington	2.7
16	New Jersey	3.7		30	Hawaii	2.6
24	New Mexico	3.0		30	Maryland	2.6
15	New York	3.9		30	Utah	2.6
44	North Carolina	1.9		33	Colorado	2.5
11	North Dakota	4.3		33	Delaware	2.5
13	Ohio	4.1		33	Pennsylvania	2.5
37	Oklahoma	2.4		33	Virginia	2.5
26	Oregon	2.8		37	Oklahoma	2.4
33	Pennsylvania	2.5		38	Arkansas	2.3
13	Rhode Island	4.1		39	Alabama	2.2
40	South Carolina	2.1		40	Kentucky	2.1
8	South Dakota	4.6		40	South Carolina	2.1
44	Tennessee	1.9		42	California	2.0
44	Texas	1.9		42	Mississippi	2.0
30	Utah	2.6		44	North Carolina	1.9
4	Vermont	4.8		44	Tennessee	1.9
33	Virginia	2.5		44	Texas	1.9
28	Washington	2.7		47	Florida	1.7
26	West Virginia	2.8		47	Georgia	1.7
20	Wisconsin	3.5		47	Nevada	1.7
5	Wyoming	4.7		50	Arizona	1.5
					District of Columbia	3.6

Source: Institute of Museum and Library Services
    "Public Library Survey Fiscal Year 2007" (June 2009, http://harvester.census.gov/imls/index.asp)
*For fiscal year 2007. Includes serial volumes but not serial subscriptions.

Internet Terminals in Public Libraries: 2007

National Total = 207,551 Terminals*

ALPHA ORDER

RANK	STATE	TERMINALS	% of USA
20	Alabama	4,100	2.0%
47	Alaska	510	0.2%
22	Arizona	3,614	1.7%
34	Arkansas	1,644	0.8%
1	California	15,856	7.6%
21	Colorado	3,748	1.8%
26	Connecticut	3,116	1.5%
50	Delaware	442	0.2%
4	Florida	12,349	5.9%
12	Georgia	5,953	2.9%
49	Hawaii	495	0.2%
39	Idaho	1,078	0.5%
7	Illinois	9,151	4.4%
9	Indiana	6,913	3.3%
25	Iowa	3,320	1.6%
29	Kansas	2,717	1.3%
27	Kentucky	2,956	1.4%
19	Louisiana	4,188	2.0%
36	Maine	1,369	0.7%
24	Maryland	3,554	1.7%
13	Massachusetts	4,847	2.3%
6	Michigan	9,572	4.6%
18	Minnesota	4,324	2.1%
32	Mississippi	1,964	0.9%
16	Missouri	4,644	2.2%
45	Montana	782	0.4%
33	Nebraska	1,833	0.9%
41	Nevada	1,046	0.5%
40	New Hampshire	1,054	0.5%
10	New Jersey	6,216	3.0%
37	New Mexico	1,324	0.6%
3	New York	13,497	6.5%
11	North Carolina	6,077	2.9%
48	North Dakota	509	0.2%
5	Ohio	10,993	5.3%
31	Oklahoma	2,141	1.0%
30	Oregon	2,213	1.1%
8	Pennsylvania	7,012	3.4%
42	Rhode Island	963	0.5%
28	South Carolina	2,898	1.4%
43	South Dakota	899	0.4%
23	Tennessee	3,558	1.7%
2	Texas	13,822	6.7%
35	Utah	1,485	0.7%
44	Vermont	859	0.4%
14	Virginia	4,816	2.3%
15	Washington	4,739	2.3%
38	West Virginia	1,115	0.5%
17	Wisconsin	4,378	2.1%
46	Wyoming	573	0.3%

RANK ORDER

RANK	STATE	TERMINALS	% of USA
1	California	15,856	7.6%
2	Texas	13,822	6.7%
3	New York	13,497	6.5%
4	Florida	12,349	5.9%
5	Ohio	10,993	5.3%
6	Michigan	9,572	4.6%
7	Illinois	9,151	4.4%
8	Pennsylvania	7,012	3.4%
9	Indiana	6,913	3.3%
10	New Jersey	6,216	3.0%
11	North Carolina	6,077	2.9%
12	Georgia	5,953	2.9%
13	Massachusetts	4,847	2.3%
14	Virginia	4,816	2.3%
15	Washington	4,739	2.3%
16	Missouri	4,644	2.2%
17	Wisconsin	4,378	2.1%
18	Minnesota	4,324	2.1%
19	Louisiana	4,188	2.0%
20	Alabama	4,100	2.0%
21	Colorado	3,748	1.8%
22	Arizona	3,614	1.7%
23	Tennessee	3,558	1.7%
24	Maryland	3,554	1.7%
25	Iowa	3,320	1.6%
26	Connecticut	3,116	1.5%
27	Kentucky	2,956	1.4%
28	South Carolina	2,898	1.4%
29	Kansas	2,717	1.3%
30	Oregon	2,213	1.1%
31	Oklahoma	2,141	1.0%
32	Mississippi	1,964	0.9%
33	Nebraska	1,833	0.9%
34	Arkansas	1,644	0.8%
35	Utah	1,485	0.7%
36	Maine	1,369	0.7%
37	New Mexico	1,324	0.6%
38	West Virginia	1,115	0.5%
39	Idaho	1,078	0.5%
40	New Hampshire	1,054	0.5%
41	Nevada	1,046	0.5%
42	Rhode Island	963	0.5%
43	South Dakota	899	0.4%
44	Vermont	859	0.4%
45	Montana	782	0.4%
46	Wyoming	573	0.3%
47	Alaska	510	0.2%
48	North Dakota	509	0.2%
49	Hawaii	495	0.2%
50	Delaware	442	0.2%
	District of Columbia	325	0.2%

Source: Institute of Museum and Library Services
"Public Library Survey Fiscal Year 2007" (June 2009, http://harvester.census.gov/imls/index.asp)
*For fiscal year 2007. Total of public-use Internet terminals in central and branch outlets.

Rate of Internet Terminals in Public Libraries: 2007

National Rate = 12.4 Terminals per Library*

ALPHA ORDER

RANK	STATE	RATE
12	Alabama	14.3
47	Alaska	4.9
3	Arizona	17.8
39	Arkansas	7.5
14	California	14.1
12	Colorado	14.3
20	Connecticut	12.7
21	Delaware	12.6
1	Florida	23.5
6	Georgia	15.5
34	Hawaii	9.7
37	Idaho	7.6
26	Illinois	11.7
4	Indiana	16.0
45	Iowa	5.9
40	Kansas	7.2
9	Kentucky	15.1
19	Louisiana	12.8
47	Maine	4.9
2	Maryland	18.5
32	Massachusetts	10.2
11	Michigan	14.4
26	Minnesota	11.7
36	Mississippi	8.1
23	Missouri	12.5
40	Montana	7.2
42	Nebraska	6.4
25	Nevada	11.9
50	New Hampshire	4.5
16	New Jersey	13.7
28	New Mexico	11.3
21	New York	12.6
8	North Carolina	15.2
46	North Dakota	5.7
9	Ohio	15.1
31	Oklahoma	10.5
32	Oregon	10.2
30	Pennsylvania	11.1
18	Rhode Island	13.2
6	South Carolina	15.5
44	South Dakota	6.2
24	Tennessee	12.3
4	Texas	16.0
28	Utah	11.3
49	Vermont	4.6
17	Virginia	13.6
15	Washington	13.9
42	West Virginia	6.4
35	Wisconsin	9.5
37	Wyoming	7.6

RANK ORDER

RANK	STATE	RATE
1	Florida	23.5
2	Maryland	18.5
3	Arizona	17.8
4	Indiana	16.0
4	Texas	16.0
6	Georgia	15.5
6	South Carolina	15.5
8	North Carolina	15.2
9	Kentucky	15.1
9	Ohio	15.1
11	Michigan	14.4
12	Alabama	14.3
12	Colorado	14.3
14	California	14.1
15	Washington	13.9
16	New Jersey	13.7
17	Virginia	13.6
18	Rhode Island	13.2
19	Louisiana	12.8
20	Connecticut	12.7
21	Delaware	12.6
21	New York	12.6
23	Missouri	12.5
24	Tennessee	12.3
25	Nevada	11.9
26	Illinois	11.7
26	Minnesota	11.7
28	New Mexico	11.3
28	Utah	11.3
30	Pennsylvania	11.1
31	Oklahoma	10.5
32	Massachusetts	10.2
32	Oregon	10.2
34	Hawaii	9.7
35	Wisconsin	9.5
36	Mississippi	8.1
37	Idaho	7.6
37	Wyoming	7.6
39	Arkansas	7.5
40	Kansas	7.2
40	Montana	7.2
42	Nebraska	6.4
42	West Virginia	6.4
44	South Dakota	6.2
45	Iowa	5.9
46	North Dakota	5.7
47	Alaska	4.9
47	Maine	4.9
49	Vermont	4.6
50	New Hampshire	4.5

	District of Columbia	12.0

Source: CQ Press using data from Institute of Museum and Library Services
"Public Library Survey Fiscal Year 2007" (June 2009, http://harvester.census.gov/imls/index.asp)
*For fiscal year 2007. Total of public-use Internet terminals in central and branch outlets divided by the number of outlets.

Per Capita State Art Agencies' Legislative Appropriations in 2010

National Per Capita = $0.97*

ALPHA ORDER		
RANK	STATE	PER CAPITA
18	Alabama	$0.98
18	Alaska	0.98
47	Arizona	0.14
27	Arkansas	0.73
50	California	0.12
46	Colorado	0.24
10	Connecticut	1.83
7	Delaware	1.97
49	Florida	0.13
45	Georgia	0.26
2	Hawaii	4.76
35	Idaho	0.51
29	Illinois	0.59
36	Indiana	0.47
42	Iowa	0.34
39	Kansas	0.45
26	Kentucky	0.76
15	Louisiana	1.24
33	Maine	0.55
4	Maryland	2.34
11	Massachusetts	1.47
47	Michigan	0.14
1	Minnesota	5.75
28	Mississippi	0.65
5	Missouri	2.27
36	Montana	0.47
23	Nebraska	0.83
41	Nevada	0.42
38	New Hampshire	0.46
8	New Jersey	1.96
20	New Mexico	0.97
3	New York	2.66
22	North Carolina	0.93
16	North Dakota	1.06
30	Ohio	0.57
13	Oklahoma	1.33
33	Oregon	0.55
21	Pennsylvania	0.95
9	Rhode Island	1.88
30	South Carolina	0.57
24	South Dakota	0.82
13	Tennessee	1.33
43	Texas	0.31
17	Utah	1.05
24	Vermont	0.82
32	Virginia	0.56
44	Washington	0.28
12	West Virginia	1.37
40	Wisconsin	0.43
6	Wyoming	2.10

RANK ORDER		
RANK	STATE	PER CAPITA
1	Minnesota	$5.75
2	Hawaii	4.76
3	New York	2.66
4	Maryland	2.34
5	Missouri	2.27
6	Wyoming	2.10
7	Delaware	1.97
8	New Jersey	1.96
9	Rhode Island	1.88
10	Connecticut	1.83
11	Massachusetts	1.47
12	West Virginia	1.37
13	Oklahoma	1.33
13	Tennessee	1.33
15	Louisiana	1.24
16	North Dakota	1.06
17	Utah	1.05
18	Alabama	0.98
18	Alaska	0.98
20	New Mexico	0.97
21	Pennsylvania	0.95
22	North Carolina	0.93
23	Nebraska	0.83
24	South Dakota	0.82
24	Vermont	0.82
26	Kentucky	0.76
27	Arkansas	0.73
28	Mississippi	0.65
29	Illinois	0.59
30	Ohio	0.57
30	South Carolina	0.57
32	Virginia	0.56
33	Maine	0.55
33	Oregon	0.55
35	Idaho	0.51
36	Indiana	0.47
36	Montana	0.47
38	New Hampshire	0.46
39	Kansas	0.45
40	Wisconsin	0.43
41	Nevada	0.42
42	Iowa	0.34
43	Texas	0.31
44	Washington	0.28
45	Georgia	0.26
46	Colorado	0.24
47	Arizona	0.14
47	Michigan	0.14
49	Florida	0.13
50	California	0.12
	District of Columbia	10.97

Source: CQ Press using data from National Assembly of State Arts Agencies
"State Arts Funding Grows in Fiscal Year 2010" (press release, January 11, 2010, http://www.nasaa-arts.org/nasaanews/)
*Preliminary figures for fiscal year 2010. Includes line item appropriations. Line items are legislative appropriations that are not controlled by the state art agencies but are passed through their budgets directly to another entity. Calculated using 2009 census population estimates. National per capita does not include appropriations or population in U.S. territories.

Federal Allocations for Head Start Program in 2007

National Total = $6,654,316,023*

ALPHA ORDER					RANK ORDER			
RANK	STATE	ALLOCATIONS	% of USA		RANK	STATE	ALLOCATIONS	% of USA
18	Alabama	$107,069,710	1.6%		1	California	$835,094,424	12.5%
49	Alaska	12,524,123	0.2%		2	Texas	480,685,049	7.2%
19	Arizona	103,928,297	1.6%		3	New York	434,979,286	6.5%
29	Arkansas	64,793,182	1.0%		4	Illinois	271,880,496	4.1%
1	California	835,094,424	12.5%		5	Florida	264,221,005	4.0%
28	Colorado	68,621,163	1.0%		6	Ohio	247,914,736	3.7%
32	Connecticut	52,112,641	0.8%		7	Michigan	235,517,531	3.5%
48	Delaware	13,290,490	0.2%		8	Pennsylvania	229,113,424	3.4%
5	Florida	264,221,005	4.0%		9	Georgia	169,203,527	2.5%
9	Georgia	169,203,527	2.5%		10	Mississippi	162,356,794	2.4%
40	Hawaii	22,980,561	0.3%		11	Louisiana	146,504,237	2.2%
41	Idaho	22,907,992	0.3%		12	North Carolina	141,857,656	2.1%
4	Illinois	271,880,496	4.1%		13	New Jersey	129,545,483	1.9%
22	Indiana	96,596,956	1.5%		14	Tennessee	119,832,346	1.8%
33	Iowa	51,762,241	0.8%		15	Missouri	119,482,617	1.8%
34	Kansas	51,136,866	0.8%		16	Massachusetts	108,797,056	1.6%
17	Kentucky	108,290,595	1.6%		17	Kentucky	108,290,595	1.6%
11	Louisiana	146,504,237	2.2%		18	Alabama	107,069,710	1.6%
38	Maine	27,724,725	0.4%		19	Arizona	103,928,297	1.6%
26	Maryland	78,356,161	1.2%		20	Washington	100,776,184	1.5%
16	Massachusetts	108,797,056	1.6%		21	Virginia	99,506,637	1.5%
7	Michigan	235,517,531	3.5%		22	Indiana	96,596,956	1.5%
27	Minnesota	72,300,453	1.1%		23	Wisconsin	91,252,718	1.4%
10	Mississippi	162,356,794	2.4%		24	South Carolina	82,842,414	1.2%
15	Missouri	119,482,617	1.8%		25	Oklahoma	81,384,010	1.2%
43	Montana	21,035,544	0.3%		26	Maryland	78,356,161	1.2%
37	Nebraska	36,207,292	0.5%		27	Minnesota	72,300,453	1.1%
39	Nevada	24,380,031	0.4%		28	Colorado	68,621,163	1.0%
47	New Hampshire	13,441,195	0.2%		29	Arkansas	64,793,182	1.0%
13	New Jersey	129,545,483	1.9%		30	Oregon	59,714,535	0.9%
31	New Mexico	52,515,381	0.8%		31	New Mexico	52,515,381	0.8%
3	New York	434,979,286	6.5%		32	Connecticut	52,112,641	0.8%
12	North Carolina	141,857,656	2.1%		33	Iowa	51,762,241	0.8%
45	North Dakota	17,245,660	0.3%		34	Kansas	51,136,866	0.8%
6	Ohio	247,914,736	3.7%		35	West Virginia	50,851,993	0.8%
25	Oklahoma	81,384,010	1.2%		36	Utah	37,920,068	0.6%
30	Oregon	59,714,535	0.9%		37	Nebraska	36,207,292	0.5%
8	Pennsylvania	229,113,424	3.4%		38	Maine	27,724,725	0.4%
42	Rhode Island	22,105,950	0.3%		39	Nevada	24,380,031	0.4%
24	South Carolina	82,842,414	1.2%		40	Hawaii	22,980,561	0.3%
44	South Dakota	18,902,974	0.3%		41	Idaho	22,907,992	0.3%
14	Tennessee	119,832,346	1.8%		42	Rhode Island	22,105,950	0.3%
2	Texas	480,685,049	7.2%		43	Montana	21,035,544	0.3%
36	Utah	37,920,068	0.6%		44	South Dakota	18,902,974	0.3%
46	Vermont	13,615,255	0.2%		45	North Dakota	17,245,660	0.3%
21	Virginia	99,506,637	1.5%		46	Vermont	13,615,255	0.2%
20	Washington	100,776,184	1.5%		47	New Hampshire	13,441,195	0.2%
35	West Virginia	50,851,993	0.8%		48	Delaware	13,290,490	0.2%
23	Wisconsin	91,252,718	1.4%		49	Alaska	12,524,123	0.2%
50	Wyoming	12,422,337	0.2%		50	Wyoming	12,422,337	0.2%
						District of Columbia	25,211,331	0.4%

Source: U.S. Department of Health and Human Services, Administration for Children and Families
"Head Start Fact Sheet" (http://www.acf.hhs.gov/programs/ohs/about/fy2008.html)
*For fiscal year 2007. National total includes $475,885,637 to Migrant and Native American programs and $265,717,054 to U.S. territories. Does not include $233,597,000 in "support activities" expenditures.

Head Start Program Enrollment in 2007

National Total = 908,412 Children*

ALPHA ORDER

RANK	STATE	CHILDREN	% of USA
15	Alabama	16,374	1.8%
49	Alaska	1,583	0.2%
22	Arizona	13,175	1.5%
26	Arkansas	10,778	1.2%
1	California	98,353	10.8%
29	Colorado	9,820	1.1%
35	Connecticut	7,076	0.8%
46	Delaware	2,071	0.2%
6	Florida	35,457	3.9%
10	Georgia	23,436	2.6%
40	Hawaii	3,049	0.3%
41	Idaho	2,943	0.3%
4	Illinois	39,640	4.4%
18	Indiana	14,213	1.6%
32	Iowa	7,710	0.8%
31	Kansas	8,178	0.9%
16	Kentucky	16,070	1.8%
11	Louisiana	21,592	2.4%
38	Maine	3,871	0.4%
27	Maryland	10,347	1.1%
23	Massachusetts	12,807	1.4%
8	Michigan	35,067	3.9%
28	Minnesota	10,332	1.1%
9	Mississippi	26,657	2.9%
13	Missouri	17,456	1.9%
42	Montana	2,919	0.3%
37	Nebraska	5,080	0.6%
44	Nevada	2,754	0.3%
48	New Hampshire	1,632	0.2%
17	New Jersey	14,854	1.6%
34	New Mexico	7,279	0.8%
3	New York	48,818	5.4%
12	North Carolina	18,963	2.1%
45	North Dakota	2,353	0.3%
5	Ohio	37,940	4.2%
21	Oklahoma	13,474	1.5%
30	Oregon	8,814	1.0%
7	Pennsylvania	35,362	3.9%
39	Rhode Island	3,104	0.3%
24	South Carolina	12,248	1.3%
43	South Dakota	2,827	0.3%
14	Tennessee	16,397	1.8%
2	Texas	67,630	7.4%
36	Utah	5,400	0.6%
50	Vermont	1,552	0.2%
20	Virginia	13,518	1.5%
25	Washington	11,278	1.2%
33	West Virginia	7,682	0.8%
19	Wisconsin	13,538	1.5%
47	Wyoming	1,840	0.2%

RANK ORDER

RANK	STATE	CHILDREN	% of USA
1	California	98,353	10.8%
2	Texas	67,630	7.4%
3	New York	48,818	5.4%
4	Illinois	39,640	4.4%
5	Ohio	37,940	4.2%
6	Florida	35,457	3.9%
7	Pennsylvania	35,362	3.9%
8	Michigan	35,067	3.9%
9	Mississippi	26,657	2.9%
10	Georgia	23,436	2.6%
11	Louisiana	21,592	2.4%
12	North Carolina	18,963	2.1%
13	Missouri	17,456	1.9%
14	Tennessee	16,397	1.8%
15	Alabama	16,374	1.8%
16	Kentucky	16,070	1.8%
17	New Jersey	14,854	1.6%
18	Indiana	14,213	1.6%
19	Wisconsin	13,538	1.5%
20	Virginia	13,518	1.5%
21	Oklahoma	13,474	1.5%
22	Arizona	13,175	1.5%
23	Massachusetts	12,807	1.4%
24	South Carolina	12,248	1.3%
25	Washington	11,278	1.2%
26	Arkansas	10,778	1.2%
27	Maryland	10,347	1.1%
28	Minnesota	10,332	1.1%
29	Colorado	9,820	1.1%
30	Oregon	8,814	1.0%
31	Kansas	8,178	0.9%
32	Iowa	7,710	0.8%
33	West Virginia	7,682	0.8%
34	New Mexico	7,279	0.8%
35	Connecticut	7,076	0.8%
36	Utah	5,400	0.6%
37	Nebraska	5,080	0.6%
38	Maine	3,871	0.4%
39	Rhode Island	3,104	0.3%
40	Hawaii	3,049	0.3%
41	Idaho	2,943	0.3%
42	Montana	2,919	0.3%
43	South Dakota	2,827	0.3%
44	Nevada	2,754	0.3%
45	North Dakota	2,353	0.3%
46	Delaware	2,071	0.2%
47	Wyoming	1,840	0.2%
48	New Hampshire	1,632	0.2%
49	Alaska	1,583	0.2%
50	Vermont	1,552	0.2%
	District of Columbia	3,403	0.4%

Source: U.S. Department of Health and Human Services, Administration for Children and Families
   "Head Start Fact Sheet" (http://www.acf.hhs.gov/programs/ohs/about/fy2008.html)
*For fiscal year 2007. National total includes 59,013 enrollees in Migrant and Native American programs and 40,685 enrollees in U.S. territories.

VI. Employment and Labor

Average Annual Pay in 2008

National Average = $45,563*

ALPHA ORDER

RANK	STATE	ANNUAL PAY
32	Alabama	$38,734
14	Alaska	45,805
21	Arizona	42,518
47	Arkansas	34,919
5	California	51,487
10	Colorado	46,614
2	Connecticut	58,395
8	Delaware	47,569
25	Florida	40,568
20	Georgia	42,585
24	Hawaii	40,675
48	Idaho	33,897
7	Illinois	48,719
33	Indiana	38,403
40	Iowa	36,964
35	Kansas	38,178
38	Kentucky	37,434
27	Louisiana	40,381
42	Maine	36,317
6	Maryland	49,535
3	Massachusetts	56,746
17	Michigan	44,245
13	Minnesota	45,826
49	Mississippi	33,508
28	Missouri	40,361
50	Montana	33,305
44	Nebraska	36,243
19	Nevada	42,984
16	New Hampshire	44,312
4	New Jersey	55,280
37	New Mexico	37,910
1	New York	60,288
30	North Carolina	39,740
46	North Dakota	35,075
23	Ohio	40,784
39	Oklahoma	37,284
26	Oregon	40,500
15	Pennsylvania	44,381
18	Rhode Island	43,029
43	South Carolina	36,252
41	South Dakota	36,822
29	Tennessee	39,996
12	Texas	45,939
36	Utah	37,980
34	Vermont	38,328
9	Virginia	47,241
11	Washington	46,569
45	West Virginia	35,987
31	Wisconsin	39,119
22	Wyoming	41,487

RANK ORDER

RANK	STATE	ANNUAL PAY
1	New York	$60,288
2	Connecticut	58,395
3	Massachusetts	56,746
4	New Jersey	55,280
5	California	51,487
6	Maryland	49,535
7	Illinois	48,719
8	Delaware	47,569
9	Virginia	47,241
10	Colorado	46,614
11	Washington	46,569
12	Texas	45,939
13	Minnesota	45,826
14	Alaska	45,805
15	Pennsylvania	44,381
16	New Hampshire	44,312
17	Michigan	44,245
18	Rhode Island	43,029
19	Nevada	42,984
20	Georgia	42,585
21	Arizona	42,518
22	Wyoming	41,487
23	Ohio	40,784
24	Hawaii	40,675
25	Florida	40,568
26	Oregon	40,500
27	Louisiana	40,381
28	Missouri	40,361
29	Tennessee	39,996
30	North Carolina	39,740
31	Wisconsin	39,119
32	Alabama	38,734
33	Indiana	38,403
34	Vermont	38,328
35	Kansas	38,178
36	Utah	37,980
37	New Mexico	37,910
38	Kentucky	37,434
39	Oklahoma	37,284
40	Iowa	36,964
41	South Dakota	36,822
42	Maine	36,317
43	South Carolina	36,252
44	Nebraska	36,243
45	West Virginia	35,987
46	North Dakota	35,075
47	Arkansas	34,919
48	Idaho	33,897
49	Mississippi	33,508
50	Montana	33,305
	District of Columbia	76,518

Source: U.S. Department of Labor, Bureau of Labor Statistics
    "Quarterly Census of Employment and Wages" (http://www.bls.gov/cew/home.htm)
*Computed by dividing total annual wages of employees covered by unemployment insurance programs by the average monthly number of these employees. Includes bonuses, cash value of meals and lodging, tips and, in many states, employer contributions to certain deferred compensation plans such as 401(k) plans.

Percent Change in Average Annual Pay: 2007 to 2008

National Percent Change = 2.5% Increase*

ALPHA ORDER

RANK	STATE	PERCENT CHANGE
16	Alabama	3.3
8	Alaska	4.2
34	Arizona	2.3
34	Arkansas	2.3
44	California	1.9
24	Colorado	2.7
49	Connecticut	0.6
49	Delaware	0.6
40	Florida	2.1
47	Georgia	1.0
19	Hawaii	3.1
46	Idaho	1.1
38	Illinois	2.2
34	Indiana	2.3
12	Iowa	3.4
19	Kansas	3.1
28	Kentucky	2.6
4	Louisiana	5.6
12	Maine	3.4
24	Maryland	2.7
24	Massachusetts	2.7
42	Michigan	2.0
16	Minnesota	3.3
10	Mississippi	3.8
7	Missouri	4.6
12	Montana	3.4
21	Nebraska	2.9
42	Nevada	2.0
47	New Hampshire	1.0
28	New Jersey	2.6
8	New Mexico	4.2
45	New York	1.4
40	North Carolina	2.1
2	North Dakota	6.0
38	Ohio	2.2
6	Oklahoma	5.1
32	Oregon	2.4
28	Pennsylvania	2.6
16	Rhode Island	3.3
32	South Carolina	2.4
1	South Dakota	16.3
34	Tennessee	2.3
22	Texas	2.8
31	Utah	2.5
11	Vermont	3.7
24	Virginia	2.7
12	Washington	3.4
5	West Virginia	5.5
22	Wisconsin	2.8
3	Wyoming	5.7

RANK ORDER

RANK	STATE	PERCENT CHANGE
1	South Dakota	16.3
2	North Dakota	6.0
3	Wyoming	5.7
4	Louisiana	5.6
5	West Virginia	5.5
6	Oklahoma	5.1
7	Missouri	4.6
8	Alaska	4.2
8	New Mexico	4.2
10	Mississippi	3.8
11	Vermont	3.7
12	Iowa	3.4
12	Maine	3.4
12	Montana	3.4
12	Washington	3.4
16	Alabama	3.3
16	Minnesota	3.3
16	Rhode Island	3.3
19	Hawaii	3.1
19	Kansas	3.1
21	Nebraska	2.9
22	Texas	2.8
22	Wisconsin	2.8
24	Colorado	2.7
24	Maryland	2.7
24	Massachusetts	2.7
24	Virginia	2.7
28	Kentucky	2.6
28	New Jersey	2.6
28	Pennsylvania	2.6
31	Utah	2.5
32	Oregon	2.4
32	South Carolina	2.4
34	Arizona	2.3
34	Arkansas	2.3
34	Indiana	2.3
34	Tennessee	2.3
38	Illinois	2.2
38	Ohio	2.2
40	Florida	2.1
40	North Carolina	2.1
42	Michigan	2.0
42	Nevada	2.0
44	California	1.9
45	New York	1.4
46	Idaho	1.1
47	Georgia	1.0
47	New Hampshire	1.0
49	Connecticut	0.6
49	Delaware	0.6
	District of Columbia	4.2

Source: CQ Press using data from U.S. Department of Labor, Bureau of Labor Statistics
 "Quarterly Census of Employment and Wages" (http://www.bls.gov/cew/home.htm)
*Includes bonuses, cash value of meals and lodging, tips and, in many states, employer contributions to certain deferred
compensation plans such as 401(k) plans.

Median Earnings of Male Full-Time Workers in 2008

National Median = $45,556

ALPHA ORDER

RANK	STATE	EARNINGS
35	Alabama	$41,411
6	Alaska	51,500
33	Arizona	41,524
50	Arkansas	36,839
15	California	47,758
16	Colorado	47,270
1	Connecticut	58,838
17	Delaware	46,898
43	Florida	40,672
28	Georgia	42,391
19	Hawaii	45,577
34	Idaho	41,461
9	Illinois	50,022
24	Indiana	44,906
31	Iowa	41,677
25	Kansas	43,346
38	Kentucky	40,977
26	Louisiana	43,326
40	Maine	40,908
4	Maryland	53,189
3	Massachusetts	55,555
12	Michigan	48,720
13	Minnesota	48,637
49	Mississippi	37,436
29	Missouri	42,106
47	Montana	38,440
42	Nebraska	40,860
22	Nevada	45,178
5	New Hampshire	51,655
2	New Jersey	55,980
45	New Mexico	40,359
11	New York	48,882
41	North Carolina	40,875
36	North Dakota	41,249
21	Ohio	45,214
46	Oklahoma	39,860
27	Oregon	43,226
18	Pennsylvania	46,455
10	Rhode Island	49,265
37	South Carolina	40,998
48	South Dakota	37,493
44	Tennessee	40,458
32	Texas	41,539
23	Utah	45,028
30	Vermont	41,778
8	Virginia	50,203
7	Washington	51,272
39	West Virginia	40,941
20	Wisconsin	45,266
14	Wyoming	48,555

RANK ORDER

RANK	STATE	EARNINGS
1	Connecticut	$58,838
2	New Jersey	55,980
3	Massachusetts	55,555
4	Maryland	53,189
5	New Hampshire	51,655
6	Alaska	51,500
7	Washington	51,272
8	Virginia	50,203
9	Illinois	50,022
10	Rhode Island	49,265
11	New York	48,882
12	Michigan	48,720
13	Minnesota	48,637
14	Wyoming	48,555
15	California	47,758
16	Colorado	47,270
17	Delaware	46,898
18	Pennsylvania	46,455
19	Hawaii	45,577
20	Wisconsin	45,266
21	Ohio	45,214
22	Nevada	45,178
23	Utah	45,028
24	Indiana	44,906
25	Kansas	43,346
26	Louisiana	43,326
27	Oregon	43,226
28	Georgia	42,391
29	Missouri	42,106
30	Vermont	41,778
31	Iowa	41,677
32	Texas	41,539
33	Arizona	41,524
34	Idaho	41,461
35	Alabama	41,411
36	North Dakota	41,249
37	South Carolina	40,998
38	Kentucky	40,977
39	West Virginia	40,941
40	Maine	40,908
41	North Carolina	40,875
42	Nebraska	40,860
43	Florida	40,672
44	Tennessee	40,458
45	New Mexico	40,359
46	Oklahoma	39,860
47	Montana	38,440
48	South Dakota	37,493
49	Mississippi	37,436
50	Arkansas	36,839

| | District of Columbia | 57,393 |

Source: U.S. Bureau of the Census
   "2008 American Community Survey" (http://www.census.gov/acs/www/index.html)

Median Earnings of Female Full-Time Workers in 2008

National Median = $35,471

RANK	STATE	EARNINGS
40	Alabama	$30,681
8	Alaska	37,861
20	Arizona	34,556
49	Arkansas	27,487
5	California	40,521
15	Colorado	36,618
1	Connecticut	44,625
11	Delaware	37,049
28	Florida	32,506
21	Georgia	34,513
14	Hawaii	36,709
43	Idaho	29,730
12	Illinois	36,968
31	Indiana	31,935
32	Iowa	31,903
30	Kansas	32,066
37	Kentucky	31,089
46	Louisiana	29,147
26	Maine	32,613
3	Maryland	44,188
4	Massachusetts	43,452
18	Michigan	35,260
10	Minnesota	37,281
48	Mississippi	27,697
33	Missouri	31,820
44	Montana	29,634
39	Nebraska	30,885
19	Nevada	34,724
13	New Hampshire	36,946
2	New Jersey	44,343
41	New Mexico	30,623
6	New York	40,490
29	North Carolina	32,397
45	North Dakota	29,589
25	Ohio	33,628
42	Oklahoma	30,123
23	Oregon	33,959
17	Pennsylvania	35,265
16	Rhode Island	36,536
38	South Carolina	31,063
47	South Dakota	28,431
36	Tennessee	31,091
27	Texas	32,530
35	Utah	31,183
22	Vermont	34,424
9	Virginia	37,859
7	Washington	37,932
50	West Virginia	27,472
24	Wisconsin	33,640
34	Wyoming	31,204

RANK	STATE	EARNINGS
1	Connecticut	$44,625
2	New Jersey	44,343
3	Maryland	44,188
4	Massachusetts	43,452
5	California	40,521
6	New York	40,490
7	Washington	37,932
8	Alaska	37,861
9	Virginia	37,859
10	Minnesota	37,281
11	Delaware	37,049
12	Illinois	36,968
13	New Hampshire	36,946
14	Hawaii	36,709
15	Colorado	36,618
16	Rhode Island	36,536
17	Pennsylvania	35,265
18	Michigan	35,260
19	Nevada	34,724
20	Arizona	34,556
21	Georgia	34,513
22	Vermont	34,424
23	Oregon	33,959
24	Wisconsin	33,640
25	Ohio	33,628
26	Maine	32,613
27	Texas	32,530
28	Florida	32,506
29	North Carolina	32,397
30	Kansas	32,066
31	Indiana	31,935
32	Iowa	31,903
33	Missouri	31,820
34	Wyoming	31,204
35	Utah	31,183
36	Tennessee	31,091
37	Kentucky	31,089
38	South Carolina	31,063
39	Nebraska	30,885
40	Alabama	30,681
41	New Mexico	30,623
42	Oklahoma	30,123
43	Idaho	29,730
44	Montana	29,634
45	North Dakota	29,589
46	Louisiana	29,147
47	South Dakota	28,431
48	Mississippi	27,697
49	Arkansas	27,487
50	West Virginia	27,472

District of Columbia   50,519

Source: U.S. Bureau of the Census
"2008 American Community Survey" (http://www.census.gov/acs/www/index.html)

State Minimum Wage Rates in 2010

National Rate = $7.25 per Hour*

ALPHA ORDER				RANK ORDER		
RANK	STATE	MINIMUM WAGE		RANK	STATE	MINIMUM WAGE
NA	Alabama**	NA		1	Washington	$8.55
8	Alaska	7.75		2	Oregon	8.40
15	Arizona	7.25		3	Connecticut	8.25
42	Arkansas	6.25		4	Vermont	8.06
5	California	8.00		5	California	8.00
41	Colorado	7.24		5	Illinois	8.00
3	Connecticut	8.25		5	Massachusetts	8.00
15	Delaware	7.25		8	Alaska	7.75
15	Florida	7.25		9	Nevada	7.55
44	Georgia	5.15		10	Maine	7.50
15	Hawaii	7.25		10	New Mexico	7.50
15	Idaho	7.25		12	Michigan	7.40
5	Illinois	8.00		12	Rhode Island	7.40
15	Indiana	7.25		14	Ohio	7.30
15	Iowa	7.25		15	Arizona	7.25
15	Kansas	7.25		15	Delaware	7.25
15	Kentucky	7.25		15	Florida	7.25
NA	Louisiana**	NA		15	Hawaii	7.25
10	Maine	7.50		15	Idaho	7.25
15	Maryland	7.25		15	Indiana	7.25
5	Massachusetts	8.00		15	Iowa	7.25
12	Michigan	7.40		15	Kansas	7.25
43	Minnesota	6.15		15	Kentucky	7.25
NA	Mississippi**	NA		15	Maryland	7.25
15	Missouri	7.25		15	Missouri	7.25
15	Montana	7.25		15	Montana	7.25
15	Nebraska	7.25		15	Nebraska	7.25
9	Nevada	7.55		15	New Hampshire	7.25
15	New Hampshire	7.25		15	New Jersey	7.25
15	New Jersey	7.25		15	New York	7.25
10	New Mexico	7.50		15	North Carolina	7.25
15	New York	7.25		15	North Dakota	7.25
15	North Carolina	7.25		15	Oklahoma	7.25
15	North Dakota	7.25		15	Pennsylvania	7.25
14	Ohio	7.30		15	South Dakota	7.25
15	Oklahoma	7.25		15	Texas	7.25
2	Oregon	8.40		15	Utah	7.25
15	Pennsylvania	7.25		15	Virginia	7.25
12	Rhode Island	7.40		15	West Virginia	7.25
NA	South Carolina**	NA		15	Wisconsin	7.25
15	South Dakota	7.25		41	Colorado	7.24
NA	Tennessee**	NA		42	Arkansas	6.25
15	Texas	7.25		43	Minnesota	6.15
15	Utah	7.25		44	Georgia	5.15
4	Vermont	8.06		44	Wyoming	5.15
15	Virginia	7.25		NA	Alabama**	NA
1	Washington	8.55		NA	Louisiana**	NA
15	West Virginia	7.25		NA	Mississippi**	NA
15	Wisconsin	7.25		NA	South Carolina**	NA
44	Wyoming	5.15		NA	Tennessee**	NA
				District of Columbia		8.25

Source: U.S. Department of Labor, Employment Standards Administration
   "Minimum Wage Laws in the States" (http://www.dol.gov/esa/minwage/america.htm)
*As of January 1, 2010. State minimum wage rates are for those employers and jobs not covered by the federal program.
**No separate state program.

Average Hourly Earnings of Production Workers
on Manufacturing Payrolls in 2009
National Average = $18.49*

ALPHA ORDER

RANK	STATE	HOURLY EARNINGS
42	Alabama	$15.51
3	Alaska	23.39
27	Arizona	17.64
50	Arkansas	14.18
22	California	18.43
5	Colorado	21.68
2	Connecticut	23.47
32	Delaware	16.55
9	Florida	20.29
37	Georgia	16.00
16	Hawaii	19.05
10	Idaho	20.10
30	Illinois	16.73
18	Indiana	18.78
31	Iowa	16.63
12	Kansas	19.58
20	Kentucky	18.65
7	Louisiana	20.58
11	Maine	20.07
14	Maryland	19.43
6	Massachusetts	20.75
4	Michigan	21.98
15	Minnesota	19.16
46	Mississippi	15.00
25	Missouri	18.34
33	Montana	16.54
40	Nebraska	15.66
44	Nevada	15.32
28	New Hampshire	17.59
26	New Jersey	18.17
41	New Mexico	15.56
24	New York	18.40
39	North Carolina	15.83
38	North Dakota	15.87
17	Ohio	18.83
48	Oklahoma	14.76
29	Oregon	17.39
35	Pennsylvania	16.51
49	Rhode Island	14.37
36	South Carolina	16.36
47	South Dakota	14.99
45	Tennessee	15.12
43	Texas	15.42
19	Utah	18.66
34	Vermont	16.52
13	Virginia	19.46
1	Washington	24.12
21	West Virginia	18.54
23	Wisconsin	18.42
8	Wyoming	20.52

RANK ORDER

RANK	STATE	HOURLY EARNINGS
1	Washington	$24.12
2	Connecticut	23.47
3	Alaska	23.39
4	Michigan	21.98
5	Colorado	21.68
6	Massachusetts	20.75
7	Louisiana	20.58
8	Wyoming	20.52
9	Florida	20.29
10	Idaho	20.10
11	Maine	20.07
12	Kansas	19.58
13	Virginia	19.46
14	Maryland	19.43
15	Minnesota	19.16
16	Hawaii	19.05
17	Ohio	18.83
18	Indiana	18.78
19	Utah	18.66
20	Kentucky	18.65
21	West Virginia	18.54
22	California	18.43
23	Wisconsin	18.42
24	New York	18.40
25	Missouri	18.34
26	New Jersey	18.17
27	Arizona	17.64
28	New Hampshire	17.59
29	Oregon	17.39
30	Illinois	16.73
31	Iowa	16.63
32	Delaware	16.55
33	Montana	16.54
34	Vermont	16.52
35	Pennsylvania	16.51
36	South Carolina	16.36
37	Georgia	16.00
38	North Dakota	15.87
39	North Carolina	15.83
40	Nebraska	15.66
41	New Mexico	15.56
42	Alabama	15.51
43	Texas	15.42
44	Nevada	15.32
45	Tennessee	15.12
46	Mississippi	15.00
47	South Dakota	14.99
48	Oklahoma	14.76
49	Rhode Island	14.37
50	Arkansas	14.18
	District of Columbia**	NA

Source: U.S. Department of Labor, Bureau of Labor Statistics
 "State and Metro Area Employment, Hours and Earnings" (http://www.bls.gov/sae/home.htm)
*Preliminary data for December 2009. Not seasonally adjusted.
**Not available.

Average Weekly Earnings of Production Workers
on Manufacturing Payrolls in 2009
National Average = $756.24*

ALPHA ORDER

RANK	STATE	WEEKLY EARNINGS
41	Alabama	$615.75
2	Alaska	1,043.19
28	Arizona	687.96
48	Arkansas	571.45
21	California	750.10
8	Colorado	836.85
4	Connecticut	969.31
29	Delaware	685.17
16	Florida	775.08
40	Georgia	622.40
34	Hawaii	653.42
11	Idaho	801.99
33	Illinois	667.53
13	Indiana	794.39
31	Iowa	668.53
12	Kansas	798.86
14	Kentucky	788.90
5	Louisiana	866.42
10	Maine	812.84
15	Maryland	781.09
9	Massachusetts	825.85
3	Michigan	969.32
19	Minnesota	756.82
44	Mississippi	604.50
23	Missouri	746.44
32	Montana	668.22
37	Nebraska	635.80
50	Nevada	465.73
26	New Hampshire	721.19
18	New Jersey	759.51
46	New Mexico	595.95
22	New York	748.88
38	North Carolina	634.78
47	North Dakota	590.36
20	Ohio	755.08
43	Oklahoma	605.16
30	Oregon	672.99
35	Pennsylvania	647.19
49	Rhode Island	548.93
27	South Carolina	710.02
45	South Dakota	598.10
42	Tennessee	607.82
36	Texas	644.56
17	Utah	766.93
39	Vermont	632.72
6	Virginia	842.62
1	Washington	1,370.14
25	West Virginia	726.77
24	Wisconsin	734.96
7	Wyoming	839.27

RANK ORDER

RANK	STATE	WEEKLY EARNINGS
1	Washington	$1,370.14
2	Alaska	1,043.19
3	Michigan	969.32
4	Connecticut	969.31
5	Louisiana	866.42
6	Virginia	842.62
7	Wyoming	839.27
8	Colorado	836.85
9	Massachusetts	825.85
10	Maine	812.84
11	Idaho	801.99
12	Kansas	798.86
13	Indiana	794.39
14	Kentucky	788.90
15	Maryland	781.09
16	Florida	775.08
17	Utah	766.93
18	New Jersey	759.51
19	Minnesota	756.82
20	Ohio	755.08
21	California	750.10
22	New York	748.88
23	Missouri	746.44
24	Wisconsin	734.96
25	West Virginia	726.77
26	New Hampshire	721.19
27	South Carolina	710.02
28	Arizona	687.96
29	Delaware	685.17
30	Oregon	672.99
31	Iowa	668.53
32	Montana	668.22
33	Illinois	667.53
34	Hawaii	653.42
35	Pennsylvania	647.19
36	Texas	644.56
37	Nebraska	635.80
38	North Carolina	634.78
39	Vermont	632.72
40	Georgia	622.40
41	Alabama	615.75
42	Tennessee	607.82
43	Oklahoma	605.16
44	Mississippi	604.50
45	South Dakota	598.10
46	New Mexico	595.95
47	North Dakota	590.36
48	Arkansas	571.45
49	Rhode Island	548.93
50	Nevada	465.73
	District of Columbia**	NA

Source: U.S. Department of Labor, Bureau of Labor Statistics
"State and Metro Area Employment, Hours and Earnings" (http://www.bls.gov/sae/home.htm)
*Preliminary data for December 2009. Not seasonally adjusted.
**Not available.

Average Work Week of Production Workers
on Manufacturing Payrolls in 2009
National Average = 40.9 Hours per Week*

ALPHA ORDER

RANK	STATE	WEEKLY HOURS
36	Alabama	39.7
1	Alaska	44.6
40	Arizona	39.0
25	Arkansas	40.3
19	California	40.7
44	Colorado	38.6
12	Connecticut	41.3
11	Delaware	41.4
46	Florida	38.2
41	Georgia	38.9
49	Hawaii	34.3
32	Idaho	39.9
32	Illinois	39.9
5	Indiana	42.3
27	Iowa	40.2
18	Kansas	40.8
5	Kentucky	42.3
7	Louisiana	42.1
23	Maine	40.5
27	Maryland	40.2
35	Massachusetts	39.8
2	Michigan	44.1
37	Minnesota	39.5
25	Mississippi	40.3
19	Missouri	40.7
24	Montana	40.4
22	Nebraska	40.6
50	Nevada	30.4
14	New Hampshire	41.0
9	New Jersey	41.8
45	New Mexico	38.3
19	New York	40.7
30	North Carolina	40.1
48	North Dakota	37.2
30	Ohio	40.1
14	Oklahoma	41.0
43	Oregon	38.7
38	Pennsylvania	39.2
16	Rhode Island	40.9
46	South Carolina	38.2
3	South Dakota	43.4
27	Tennessee	40.2
9	Texas	41.8
13	Utah	41.1
41	Vermont	38.9
4	Virginia	43.3
8	Washington	42.0
38	West Virginia	39.2
32	Wisconsin	39.9
16	Wyoming	40.9

RANK ORDER

RANK	STATE	WEEKLY HOURS
1	Alaska	44.6
2	Michigan	44.1
3	South Dakota	43.4
4	Virginia	43.3
5	Indiana	42.3
5	Kentucky	42.3
7	Louisiana	42.1
8	Washington	42.0
9	New Jersey	41.8
9	Texas	41.8
11	Delaware	41.4
12	Connecticut	41.3
13	Utah	41.1
14	New Hampshire	41.0
14	Oklahoma	41.0
16	Rhode Island	40.9
16	Wyoming	40.9
18	Kansas	40.8
19	California	40.7
19	Missouri	40.7
19	New York	40.7
22	Nebraska	40.6
23	Maine	40.5
24	Montana	40.4
25	Arkansas	40.3
25	Mississippi	40.3
27	Iowa	40.2
27	Maryland	40.2
27	Tennessee	40.2
30	North Carolina	40.1
30	Ohio	40.1
32	Idaho	39.9
32	Illinois	39.9
32	Wisconsin	39.9
35	Massachusetts	39.8
36	Alabama	39.7
37	Minnesota	39.5
38	Pennsylvania	39.2
38	West Virginia	39.2
40	Arizona	39.0
41	Georgia	38.9
41	Vermont	38.9
43	Oregon	38.7
44	Colorado	38.6
45	New Mexico	38.3
46	Florida	38.2
46	South Carolina	38.2
48	North Dakota	37.2
49	Hawaii	34.3
50	Nevada	30.4

District of Columbia**	NA

Source: U.S. Department of Labor, Bureau of Labor Statistics
  "State and Metro Area Employment, Hours and Earnings" (http://www.bls.gov/sae/home.htm)
*Preliminary data for December 2009. Not seasonally adjusted.
**Not available.

Average Weekly Unemployment Benefit in 2009

National Average = $309.94 a Week

RANK	STATE	BENEFIT
49	Alabama	$208.09
45	Alaska	235.03
48	Arizona	220.28
35	Arkansas	281.55
21	California	310.35
7	Colorado	360.79
11	Connecticut	342.07
39	Delaware	261.55
44	Florida	237.55
33	Georgia	282.99
1	Hawaii	422.96
36	Idaho	274.31
12	Illinois	332.04
26	Indiana	306.52
16	Iowa	319.77
8	Kansas	353.54
24	Kentucky	307.05
46	Louisiana	229.96
34	Maine	282.31
20	Maryland	310.87
2	Massachusetts	419.87
23	Michigan	308.38
6	Minnesota	367.92
50	Mississippi	195.58
40	Missouri	256.75
37	Montana	272.57
43	Nebraska	249.44
17	Nevada	317.54
32	New Hampshire	283.53
4	New Jersey	395.84
29	New Mexico	300.49
18	New York	314.40
25	North Carolina	306.70
22	North Dakota	309.94
14	Ohio	323.30
30	Oklahoma	295.14
19	Oregon	313.04
9	Pennsylvania	352.34
5	Rhode Island	383.50
42	South Carolina	249.68
41	South Dakota	253.48
47	Tennessee	226.30
13	Texas	324.59
15	Utah	320.65
27	Vermont	305.27
28	Virginia	303.43
3	Washington	402.57
38	West Virginia	271.50
31	Wisconsin	287.28
10	Wyoming	347.04

RANK	STATE	BENEFIT
1	Hawaii	$422.96
2	Massachusetts	419.87
3	Washington	402.57
4	New Jersey	395.84
5	Rhode Island	383.50
6	Minnesota	367.92
7	Colorado	360.79
8	Kansas	353.54
9	Pennsylvania	352.34
10	Wyoming	347.04
11	Connecticut	342.07
12	Illinois	332.04
13	Texas	324.59
14	Ohio	323.30
15	Utah	320.65
16	Iowa	319.77
17	Nevada	317.54
18	New York	314.40
19	Oregon	313.04
20	Maryland	310.87
21	California	310.35
22	North Dakota	309.94
23	Michigan	308.38
24	Kentucky	307.05
25	North Carolina	306.70
26	Indiana	306.52
27	Vermont	305.27
28	Virginia	303.43
29	New Mexico	300.49
30	Oklahoma	295.14
31	Wisconsin	287.28
32	New Hampshire	283.53
33	Georgia	282.99
34	Maine	282.31
35	Arkansas	281.55
36	Idaho	274.31
37	Montana	272.57
38	West Virginia	271.50
39	Delaware	261.55
40	Missouri	256.75
41	South Dakota	253.48
42	South Carolina	249.68
43	Nebraska	249.44
44	Florida	237.55
45	Alaska	235.03
46	Louisiana	229.96
47	Tennessee	226.30
48	Arizona	220.28
49	Alabama	208.09
50	Mississippi	195.58
	District of Columbia	302.82

Source: CQ Press using data from U.S. Department of Labor, Bureau of Labor Statistics
"Unemployment Insurance Data Summary" (http://workforcesecurity.doleta.gov/unemploy/content/data.asp)

Workers' Compensation Benefit Payments in 2007

National Total = $55,426,915,000*

ALPHA ORDER

RANK	STATE	PAYMENTS	% of USA
29	Alabama	$584,941,000	1.1%
45	Alaska	184,080,000	0.3%
26	Arizona	647,417,000	1.2%
40	Arkansas	242,743,000	0.4%
1	California	9,916,028,000	17.9%
19	Colorado	829,747,000	1.5%
22	Connecticut	725,915,000	1.3%
44	Delaware	195,339,000	0.4%
5	Florida	2,684,761,000	4.8%
12	Georgia	1,339,121,000	2.4%
39	Hawaii	247,294,000	0.4%
36	Idaho	276,108,000	0.5%
4	Illinois	2,722,402,000	4.9%
27	Indiana	643,783,000	1.2%
31	Iowa	509,546,000	0.9%
32	Kansas	393,722,000	0.7%
25	Kentucky	647,706,000	1.2%
30	Louisiana	579,810,000	1.0%
37	Maine	271,495,000	0.5%
18	Maryland	830,927,000	1.5%
16	Massachusetts	887,673,000	1.6%
9	Michigan	1,501,538,000	2.7%
15	Minnesota	936,085,000	1.7%
34	Mississippi	331,508,000	0.6%
17	Missouri	853,967,000	1.5%
41	Montana	240,997,000	0.4%
35	Nebraska	291,068,000	0.5%
33	Nevada	377,749,000	0.7%
43	New Hampshire	200,208,000	0.4%
8	New Jersey	1,967,609,000	3.5%
42	New Mexico	239,536,000	0.4%
2	New York	3,204,053,000	5.8%
11	North Carolina	1,340,245,000	2.4%
50	North Dakota	91,612,000	0.2%
6	Ohio	2,478,080,000	4.5%
24	Oklahoma	656,359,000	1.2%
28	Oregon	585,699,000	1.1%
3	Pennsylvania	2,747,847,000	5.0%
46	Rhode Island	154,931,000	0.3%
20	South Carolina	771,281,000	1.4%
48	South Dakota	119,351,000	0.2%
21	Tennessee	764,896,000	1.4%
10	Texas	1,423,150,000	2.6%
38	Utah	267,856,000	0.5%
49	Vermont	118,987,000	0.2%
14	Virginia	1,058,759,000	1.9%
7	Washington	1,994,598,000	3.6%
23	West Virginia	699,748,000	1.3%
13	Wisconsin	1,094,074,000	2.0%
47	Wyoming	126,983,000	0.2%

RANK ORDER

RANK	STATE	PAYMENTS	% of USA
1	California	$9,916,028,000	17.9%
2	New York	3,204,053,000	5.8%
3	Pennsylvania	2,747,847,000	5.0%
4	Illinois	2,722,402,000	4.9%
5	Florida	2,684,761,000	4.8%
6	Ohio	2,478,080,000	4.5%
7	Washington	1,994,598,000	3.6%
8	New Jersey	1,967,609,000	3.5%
9	Michigan	1,501,538,000	2.7%
10	Texas	1,423,150,000	2.6%
11	North Carolina	1,340,245,000	2.4%
12	Georgia	1,339,121,000	2.4%
13	Wisconsin	1,094,074,000	2.0%
14	Virginia	1,058,759,000	1.9%
15	Minnesota	936,085,000	1.7%
16	Massachusetts	887,673,000	1.6%
17	Missouri	853,967,000	1.5%
18	Maryland	830,927,000	1.5%
19	Colorado	829,747,000	1.5%
20	South Carolina	771,281,000	1.4%
21	Tennessee	764,896,000	1.4%
22	Connecticut	725,915,000	1.3%
23	West Virginia	699,748,000	1.3%
24	Oklahoma	656,359,000	1.2%
25	Kentucky	647,706,000	1.2%
26	Arizona	647,417,000	1.2%
27	Indiana	643,783,000	1.2%
28	Oregon	585,699,000	1.1%
29	Alabama	584,941,000	1.1%
30	Louisiana	579,810,000	1.0%
31	Iowa	509,546,000	0.9%
32	Kansas	393,722,000	0.7%
33	Nevada	377,749,000	0.7%
34	Mississippi	331,508,000	0.6%
35	Nebraska	291,068,000	0.5%
36	Idaho	276,108,000	0.5%
37	Maine	271,495,000	0.5%
38	Utah	267,856,000	0.5%
39	Hawaii	247,294,000	0.4%
40	Arkansas	242,743,000	0.4%
41	Montana	240,997,000	0.4%
42	New Mexico	239,536,000	0.4%
43	New Hampshire	200,208,000	0.4%
44	Delaware	195,339,000	0.4%
45	Alaska	184,080,000	0.3%
46	Rhode Island	154,931,000	0.3%
47	Wyoming	126,983,000	0.2%
48	South Dakota	119,351,000	0.2%
49	Vermont	118,987,000	0.2%
50	North Dakota	91,612,000	0.2%
	District of Columbia	87,695,000	0.2%

Source: National Academy of Social Insurance (Washington, DC)
  "Workers' Compensation: Benefits, Coverage, and Costs, 2007" (http://www.nasi.org)
*Estimated payments from private insurance, state and federal funds, and self insurance. National total includes payments for
federal civilian employee program, Black Lung Program, and other federal programs.

Workers' Compensation Benefit Payment per Covered Worker in 2007

National Average = $421*

ALPHA ORDER

RANK	STATE	AVERAGE
35	Alabama	$321
4	Alaska	626
46	Arizona	249
49	Arkansas	217
3	California	644
22	Colorado	370
14	Connecticut	436
11	Delaware	467
24	Florida	358
28	Georgia	344
17	Hawaii	416
16	Idaho	426
9	Illinois	471
48	Indiana	225
26	Iowa	347
42	Kansas	297
23	Kentucky	368
36	Louisiana	316
12	Maine	462
29	Maryland	343
44	Massachusetts	279
21	Michigan	372
25	Minnesota	353
37	Mississippi	314
31	Missouri	334
5	Montana	570
33	Nebraska	323
41	Nevada	299
34	New Hampshire	322
6	New Jersey	505
37	New Mexico	314
20	New York	380
29	North Carolina	343
45	North Dakota	278
8	Ohio	474
13	Oklahoma	441
27	Oregon	345
7	Pennsylvania	495
32	Rhode Island	330
15	South Carolina	430
39	South Dakota	313
43	Tennessee	294
50	Texas	186
47	Utah	226
19	Vermont	401
40	Virginia	308
2	Washington	698
1	West Virginia	1,023
18	Wisconsin	406
10	Wyoming	470

RANK ORDER

RANK	STATE	AVERAGE
1	West Virginia	$1,023
2	Washington	698
3	California	644
4	Alaska	626
5	Montana	570
6	New Jersey	505
7	Pennsylvania	495
8	Ohio	474
9	Illinois	471
10	Wyoming	470
11	Delaware	467
12	Maine	462
13	Oklahoma	441
14	Connecticut	436
15	South Carolina	430
16	Idaho	426
17	Hawaii	416
18	Wisconsin	406
19	Vermont	401
20	New York	380
21	Michigan	372
22	Colorado	370
23	Kentucky	368
24	Florida	358
25	Minnesota	353
26	Iowa	347
27	Oregon	345
28	Georgia	344
29	Maryland	343
29	North Carolina	343
31	Missouri	334
32	Rhode Island	330
33	Nebraska	323
34	New Hampshire	322
35	Alabama	321
36	Louisiana	316
37	Mississippi	314
37	New Mexico	314
39	South Dakota	313
40	Virginia	308
41	Nevada	299
42	Kansas	297
43	Tennessee	294
44	Massachusetts	279
45	North Dakota	278
46	Arizona	249
47	Utah	226
48	Indiana	225
49	Arkansas	217
50	Texas	186

District of Columbia   180

Source: CQ Press using data from National Academy of Social Insurance (Washington, DC)
    "Workers' Compensation: Benefits, Coverage, and Costs, 2007" (http://www.nasi.org)
*Estimated payments from private insurance, state and federal funds, and self insurance. National rate includes payments for
federal civilian employee program, Black Lung Program, and other federal programs. Total divided by number of workers covered
by workers' compensation.

Percent Change in Workers' Compensation Benefit Payments: 2006 to 2007

National Percent Change = 2.0% Increase*

ALPHA ORDER			RANK ORDER		
RANK	STATE	PERCENT CHANGE	RANK	STATE	PERCENT CHANGE
19	Alabama	4.0	1	Virginia	27.4
34	Alaska	1.1	2	Idaho	12.8
13	Arizona	6.4	3	North Dakota	12.7
9	Arkansas	8.7	4	Utah	10.7
40	California	(2.2)	5	Georgia	10.3
43	Colorado	(3.6)	6	South Dakota	9.9
26	Connecticut	2.5	7	Illinois	9.8
44	Delaware	(3.8)	8	Nebraska	9.5
24	Florida	2.8	9	Arkansas	8.7
5	Georgia	10.3	10	West Virginia	8.4
31	Hawaii	1.9	11	Wyoming	8.2
2	Idaho	12.8	12	New Jersey	7.1
7	Illinois	9.8	13	Arizona	6.4
14	Indiana	6.1	14	Indiana	6.1
23	Iowa	3.2	15	Missouri	5.6
26	Kansas	2.5	16	Wisconsin	4.9
38	Kentucky	(1.0)	17	Oklahoma	4.7
33	Louisiana	1.4	18	Oregon	4.1
47	Maine	(4.6)	19	Alabama	4.0
24	Maryland	2.8	19	Montana	4.0
48	Massachusetts	(5.4)	19	Ohio	4.0
26	Michigan	2.5	22	Washington	3.5
32	Minnesota	1.6	23	Iowa	3.2
39	Mississippi	(1.9)	24	Florida	2.8
15	Missouri	5.6	24	Maryland	2.8
19	Montana	4.0	26	Connecticut	2.5
8	Nebraska	9.5	26	Kansas	2.5
45	Nevada	(4.0)	26	Michigan	2.5
49	New Hampshire	(5.7)	29	Pennsylvania	2.4
12	New Jersey	7.1	30	Texas	2.2
35	New Mexico	0.8	31	Hawaii	1.9
41	New York	(3.0)	32	Minnesota	1.6
36	North Carolina	0.4	33	Louisiana	1.4
3	North Dakota	12.7	34	Alaska	1.1
19	Ohio	4.0	35	New Mexico	0.8
17	Oklahoma	4.7	36	North Carolina	0.4
18	Oregon	4.1	37	Rhode Island	0.1
29	Pennsylvania	2.4	38	Kentucky	(1.0)
37	Rhode Island	0.1	39	Mississippi	(1.9)
42	South Carolina	(3.1)	40	California	(2.2)
6	South Dakota	9.9	41	New York	(3.0)
50	Tennessee	(12.3)	42	South Carolina	(3.1)
30	Texas	2.2	43	Colorado	(3.6)
4	Utah	10.7	44	Delaware	(3.8)
46	Vermont	(4.4)	45	Nevada	(4.0)
1	Virginia	27.4	46	Vermont	(4.4)
22	Washington	3.5	47	Maine	(4.6)
10	West Virginia	8.4	48	Massachusetts	(5.4)
16	Wisconsin	4.9	49	New Hampshire	(5.7)
11	Wyoming	8.2	50	Tennessee	(12.3)
				District of Columbia	(4.2)

Source: National Academy of Social Insurance (Washington, DC)
   "Workers' Compensation: Benefits, Coverage, and Costs, 2007" (http://www.nasi.org)
*Estimated payments from private insurance, state and federal funds, and self insurance. National rate includes payments for federal civilian employee program, Black Lung Program, and other federal programs.

Civilian Labor Force in 2009

National Total = 153,059,000 Workers*

ALPHA ORDER

RANK	STATE	EMPLOYEES	% of USA
25	Alabama	2,059,700	1.3%
48	Alaska	357,900	0.2%
15	Arizona	3,141,200	2.1%
33	Arkansas	1,370,200	0.9%
1	California	18,232,300	11.9%
22	Colorado	2,656,800	1.7%
28	Connecticut	1,883,000	1.2%
46	Delaware	426,600	0.3%
4	Florida	9,179,700	6.0%
9	Georgia	4,702,200	3.1%
42	Hawaii	638,100	0.4%
39	Idaho	753,800	0.5%
5	Illinois	6,623,900	4.3%
16	Indiana	3,104,000	2.0%
30	Iowa	1,683,800	1.1%
31	Kansas	1,519,000	1.0%
24	Kentucky	2,061,800	1.3%
26	Louisiana	2,049,800	1.3%
41	Maine	703,100	0.5%
21	Maryland	2,936,700	1.9%
14	Massachusetts	3,431,800	2.2%
8	Michigan	4,812,700	3.1%
20	Minnesota	2,956,000	1.9%
35	Mississippi	1,292,700	0.8%
19	Missouri	2,979,800	1.9%
44	Montana	495,300	0.3%
36	Nebraska	983,200	0.6%
32	Nevada	1,375,100	0.9%
40	New Hampshire	737,700	0.5%
10	New Jersey	4,537,200	3.0%
37	New Mexico	962,200	0.6%
3	New York	9,669,200	6.3%
11	North Carolina	4,522,300	3.0%
47	North Dakota	363,100	0.2%
7	Ohio	5,900,500	3.9%
29	Oklahoma	1,773,300	1.2%
27	Oregon	1,949,300	1.3%
6	Pennsylvania	6,310,100	4.1%
43	Rhode Island	570,300	0.4%
23	South Carolina	2,166,700	1.4%
45	South Dakota	443,900	0.3%
18	Tennessee	2,986,300	2.0%
2	Texas	12,092,900	7.9%
34	Utah	1,356,100	0.9%
49	Vermont	357,800	0.2%
12	Virginia	4,131,100	2.7%
13	Washington	3,509,200	2.3%
38	West Virginia	786,500	0.5%
17	Wisconsin	3,028,000	2.0%
50	Wyoming	291,700	0.2%

RANK ORDER

RANK	STATE	EMPLOYEES	% of USA
1	California	18,232,300	11.9%
2	Texas	12,092,900	7.9%
3	New York	9,669,200	6.3%
4	Florida	9,179,700	6.0%
5	Illinois	6,623,900	4.3%
6	Pennsylvania	6,310,100	4.1%
7	Ohio	5,900,500	3.9%
8	Michigan	4,812,700	3.1%
9	Georgia	4,702,200	3.1%
10	New Jersey	4,537,200	3.0%
11	North Carolina	4,522,300	3.0%
12	Virginia	4,131,100	2.7%
13	Washington	3,509,200	2.3%
14	Massachusetts	3,431,800	2.2%
15	Arizona	3,141,200	2.1%
16	Indiana	3,104,000	2.0%
17	Wisconsin	3,028,000	2.0%
18	Tennessee	2,986,300	2.0%
19	Missouri	2,979,800	1.9%
20	Minnesota	2,956,000	1.9%
21	Maryland	2,936,700	1.9%
22	Colorado	2,656,800	1.7%
23	South Carolina	2,166,700	1.4%
24	Kentucky	2,061,800	1.3%
25	Alabama	2,059,700	1.3%
26	Louisiana	2,049,800	1.3%
27	Oregon	1,949,300	1.3%
28	Connecticut	1,883,000	1.2%
29	Oklahoma	1,773,300	1.2%
30	Iowa	1,683,800	1.1%
31	Kansas	1,519,000	1.0%
32	Nevada	1,375,100	0.9%
33	Arkansas	1,370,200	0.9%
34	Utah	1,356,100	0.9%
35	Mississippi	1,292,700	0.8%
36	Nebraska	983,200	0.6%
37	New Mexico	962,200	0.6%
38	West Virginia	786,500	0.5%
39	Idaho	753,800	0.5%
40	New Hampshire	737,700	0.5%
41	Maine	703,100	0.5%
42	Hawaii	638,100	0.4%
43	Rhode Island	570,300	0.4%
44	Montana	495,300	0.3%
45	South Dakota	443,900	0.3%
46	Delaware	426,600	0.3%
47	North Dakota	363,100	0.2%
48	Alaska	357,900	0.2%
49	Vermont	357,800	0.2%
50	Wyoming	291,700	0.2%
	District of Columbia	331,600	0.2%

Source: U.S. Department of Labor, Bureau of Labor Statistics
   "Regional and State Employment and Unemployment" (press release, January 22, 2010, www.bls.gov/bls/newsrels.htm)
*Seasonally adjusted preliminary data as of December 2009. National total calculated through a different formula.

Employed Civilian Labor Force in 2009

National Total = 137,792,000 Employed Workers*

ALPHA ORDER

RANK	STATE	EMPLOYED	% of USA
26	Alabama	1,834,100	1.3%
49	Alaska	326,300	0.2%
15	Arizona	2,855,500	2.1%
33	Arkansas	1,264,800	0.9%
1	California	15,977,900	11.6%
22	Colorado	2,458,400	1.8%
28	Connecticut	1,715,100	1.2%
46	Delaware	388,400	0.3%
4	Florida	8,092,600	5.9%
8	Georgia	4,217,100	3.1%
42	Hawaii	593,800	0.4%
40	Idaho	685,000	0.5%
5	Illinois	5,890,600	4.3%
16	Indiana	2,797,100	2.0%
30	Iowa	1,573,000	1.1%
31	Kansas	1,418,100	1.0%
25	Kentucky	1,840,700	1.3%
23	Louisiana	1,895,600	1.4%
41	Maine	644,800	0.5%
19	Maryland	2,716,800	2.0%
14	Massachusetts	3,108,600	2.3%
9	Michigan	4,111,700	3.0%
18	Minnesota	2,738,300	2.0%
35	Mississippi	1,155,200	0.8%
20	Missouri	2,695,100	2.0%
44	Montana	462,100	0.3%
36	Nebraska	936,900	0.7%
34	Nevada	1,196,600	0.9%
39	New Hampshire	686,100	0.5%
10	New Jersey	4,078,900	3.0%
37	New Mexico	882,400	0.6%
3	New York	8,800,600	6.4%
11	North Carolina	4,016,400	2.9%
47	North Dakota	347,100	0.3%
7	Ohio	5,259,800	3.8%
29	Oklahoma	1,655,500	1.2%
27	Oregon	1,734,600	1.3%
6	Pennsylvania	5,750,600	4.2%
43	Rhode Island	496,800	0.4%
24	South Carolina	1,893,500	1.4%
45	South Dakota	422,900	0.3%
21	Tennessee	2,660,600	1.9%
2	Texas	11,093,900	8.1%
32	Utah	1,264,900	0.9%
48	Vermont	333,100	0.2%
12	Virginia	3,846,800	2.8%
13	Washington	3,174,400	2.3%
38	West Virginia	714,900	0.5%
17	Wisconsin	2,764,700	2.0%
50	Wyoming	269,900	0.2%

RANK ORDER

RANK	STATE	EMPLOYED	% of USA
1	California	15,977,900	11.6%
2	Texas	11,093,900	8.1%
3	New York	8,800,600	6.4%
4	Florida	8,092,600	5.9%
5	Illinois	5,890,600	4.3%
6	Pennsylvania	5,750,600	4.2%
7	Ohio	5,259,800	3.8%
8	Georgia	4,217,100	3.1%
9	Michigan	4,111,700	3.0%
10	New Jersey	4,078,900	3.0%
11	North Carolina	4,016,400	2.9%
12	Virginia	3,846,800	2.8%
13	Washington	3,174,400	2.3%
14	Massachusetts	3,108,600	2.3%
15	Arizona	2,855,500	2.1%
16	Indiana	2,797,100	2.0%
17	Wisconsin	2,764,700	2.0%
18	Minnesota	2,738,300	2.0%
19	Maryland	2,716,800	2.0%
20	Missouri	2,695,100	2.0%
21	Tennessee	2,660,600	1.9%
22	Colorado	2,458,400	1.8%
23	Louisiana	1,895,600	1.4%
24	South Carolina	1,893,500	1.4%
25	Kentucky	1,840,700	1.3%
26	Alabama	1,834,100	1.3%
27	Oregon	1,734,600	1.3%
28	Connecticut	1,715,100	1.2%
29	Oklahoma	1,655,500	1.2%
30	Iowa	1,573,000	1.1%
31	Kansas	1,418,100	1.0%
32	Utah	1,264,900	0.9%
33	Arkansas	1,264,800	0.9%
34	Nevada	1,196,600	0.9%
35	Mississippi	1,155,200	0.8%
36	Nebraska	936,900	0.7%
37	New Mexico	882,400	0.6%
38	West Virginia	714,900	0.5%
39	New Hampshire	686,100	0.5%
40	Idaho	685,000	0.5%
41	Maine	644,800	0.5%
42	Hawaii	593,800	0.4%
43	Rhode Island	496,800	0.4%
44	Montana	462,100	0.3%
45	South Dakota	422,900	0.3%
46	Delaware	388,400	0.3%
47	North Dakota	347,100	0.3%
48	Vermont	333,100	0.2%
49	Alaska	326,300	0.2%
50	Wyoming	269,900	0.2%
	District of Columbia	291,600	0.2%

Source: CQ Press using data from U.S. Department of Labor, Bureau of Labor Statistics
"Regional and State Employment and Unemployment" (press release, January 22, 2010, www.bls.gov/bls/newsrels.htm)
*Seasonally adjusted preliminary data as of December 2009. National total calculated through a different formula.

Employment to Population Ratio in 2009

National Percent = 57.7% of Population 16 Years and Older Employed*

<table>
<tr><td colspan="3">ALPHA ORDER</td><td colspan="3">RANK ORDER</td></tr>
<tr><th>RANK</th><th>STATE</th><th>PERCENT</th><th>RANK</th><th>STATE</th><th>PERCENT</th></tr>
<tr><td>49</td><td>Alabama</td><td>50.0</td><td>1</td><td>Nebraska</td><td>67.5</td></tr>
<tr><td>13</td><td>Alaska</td><td>61.8</td><td>2</td><td>North Dakota</td><td>67.3</td></tr>
<tr><td>30</td><td>Arizona</td><td>57.4</td><td>3</td><td>South Dakota</td><td>67.2</td></tr>
<tr><td>36</td><td>Arkansas</td><td>56.6</td><td>4</td><td>Minnesota</td><td>66.6</td></tr>
<tr><td>40</td><td>California</td><td>56.1</td><td>5</td><td>Iowa</td><td>66.2</td></tr>
<tr><td>11</td><td>Colorado</td><td>63.6</td><td>6</td><td>Vermont</td><td>65.3</td></tr>
<tr><td>15</td><td>Connecticut</td><td>61.5</td><td>7</td><td>Kansas</td><td>65.0</td></tr>
<tr><td>38</td><td>Delaware</td><td>56.2</td><td>8</td><td>New Hampshire</td><td>64.7</td></tr>
<tr><td>43</td><td>Florida</td><td>54.7</td><td>9</td><td>Wyoming</td><td>64.4</td></tr>
<tr><td>35</td><td>Georgia</td><td>56.9</td><td>10</td><td>Utah</td><td>64.1</td></tr>
<tr><td>31</td><td>Hawaii</td><td>57.3</td><td>11</td><td>Colorado</td><td>63.6</td></tr>
<tr><td>24</td><td>Idaho</td><td>59.2</td><td>12</td><td>Virginia</td><td>62.5</td></tr>
<tr><td>25</td><td>Illinois</td><td>58.4</td><td>13</td><td>Alaska</td><td>61.8</td></tr>
<tr><td>38</td><td>Indiana</td><td>56.2</td><td>13</td><td>Wisconsin</td><td>61.8</td></tr>
<tr><td>5</td><td>Iowa</td><td>66.2</td><td>15</td><td>Connecticut</td><td>61.5</td></tr>
<tr><td>7</td><td>Kansas</td><td>65.0</td><td>16</td><td>Washington</td><td>61.1</td></tr>
<tr><td>44</td><td>Kentucky</td><td>54.5</td><td>17</td><td>Maryland</td><td>61.0</td></tr>
<tr><td>42</td><td>Louisiana</td><td>55.2</td><td>18</td><td>Texas</td><td>60.6</td></tr>
<tr><td>19</td><td>Maine</td><td>59.8</td><td>19</td><td>Maine</td><td>59.8</td></tr>
<tr><td>17</td><td>Maryland</td><td>61.0</td><td>20</td><td>Montana</td><td>59.7</td></tr>
<tr><td>22</td><td>Massachusetts</td><td>59.3</td><td>20</td><td>Nevada</td><td>59.7</td></tr>
<tr><td>47</td><td>Michigan</td><td>52.0</td><td>22</td><td>Massachusetts</td><td>59.3</td></tr>
<tr><td>4</td><td>Minnesota</td><td>66.6</td><td>22</td><td>New Jersey</td><td>59.3</td></tr>
<tr><td>48</td><td>Mississippi</td><td>51.1</td><td>24</td><td>Idaho</td><td>59.2</td></tr>
<tr><td>29</td><td>Missouri</td><td>57.8</td><td>25</td><td>Illinois</td><td>58.4</td></tr>
<tr><td>20</td><td>Montana</td><td>59.7</td><td>25</td><td>Rhode Island</td><td>58.4</td></tr>
<tr><td>1</td><td>Nebraska</td><td>67.5</td><td>27</td><td>Oklahoma</td><td>58.3</td></tr>
<tr><td>20</td><td>Nevada</td><td>59.7</td><td>28</td><td>Ohio</td><td>57.9</td></tr>
<tr><td>8</td><td>New Hampshire</td><td>64.7</td><td>29</td><td>Missouri</td><td>57.8</td></tr>
<tr><td>22</td><td>New Jersey</td><td>59.3</td><td>30</td><td>Arizona</td><td>57.4</td></tr>
<tr><td>31</td><td>New Mexico</td><td>57.3</td><td>31</td><td>Hawaii</td><td>57.3</td></tr>
<tr><td>37</td><td>New York</td><td>56.3</td><td>31</td><td>New Mexico</td><td>57.3</td></tr>
<tr><td>41</td><td>North Carolina</td><td>55.6</td><td>31</td><td>Oregon</td><td>57.3</td></tr>
<tr><td>2</td><td>North Dakota</td><td>67.3</td><td>31</td><td>Pennsylvania</td><td>57.3</td></tr>
<tr><td>28</td><td>Ohio</td><td>57.9</td><td>35</td><td>Georgia</td><td>56.9</td></tr>
<tr><td>27</td><td>Oklahoma</td><td>58.3</td><td>36</td><td>Arkansas</td><td>56.6</td></tr>
<tr><td>31</td><td>Oregon</td><td>57.3</td><td>37</td><td>New York</td><td>56.3</td></tr>
<tr><td>31</td><td>Pennsylvania</td><td>57.3</td><td>38</td><td>Delaware</td><td>56.2</td></tr>
<tr><td>25</td><td>Rhode Island</td><td>58.4</td><td>38</td><td>Indiana</td><td>56.2</td></tr>
<tr><td>46</td><td>South Carolina</td><td>53.5</td><td>40</td><td>California</td><td>56.1</td></tr>
<tr><td>3</td><td>South Dakota</td><td>67.2</td><td>41</td><td>North Carolina</td><td>55.6</td></tr>
<tr><td>45</td><td>Tennessee</td><td>54.2</td><td>42</td><td>Louisiana</td><td>55.2</td></tr>
<tr><td>18</td><td>Texas</td><td>60.6</td><td>43</td><td>Florida</td><td>54.7</td></tr>
<tr><td>10</td><td>Utah</td><td>64.1</td><td>44</td><td>Kentucky</td><td>54.5</td></tr>
<tr><td>6</td><td>Vermont</td><td>65.3</td><td>45</td><td>Tennessee</td><td>54.2</td></tr>
<tr><td>12</td><td>Virginia</td><td>62.5</td><td>46</td><td>South Carolina</td><td>53.5</td></tr>
<tr><td>16</td><td>Washington</td><td>61.1</td><td>47</td><td>Michigan</td><td>52.0</td></tr>
<tr><td>50</td><td>West Virginia</td><td>48.5</td><td>48</td><td>Mississippi</td><td>51.1</td></tr>
<tr><td>13</td><td>Wisconsin</td><td>61.8</td><td>49</td><td>Alabama</td><td>50.0</td></tr>
<tr><td>9</td><td>Wyoming</td><td>64.4</td><td>50</td><td>West Virginia</td><td>48.5</td></tr>
<tr><td></td><td></td><td></td><td></td><td>District of Columbia</td><td>59.2</td></tr>
</table>

Source: CQ Press using data from U.S. Department of Labor, Bureau of Labor Statistics
   "Regional and State Employment and Unemployment" (press release, January 22, 2010, www.bls.gov/bls/newsrels.htm)
*Seasonally adjusted preliminary data as of December 2009. Calculated with 2008 population data.

Unemployed Civilian Labor Force in 2009

National Total = 15,267,000 Unemployed Workers*

ALPHA ORDER

RANK	STATE	UNEMPLOYED	% of USA
21	Alabama	225,600	1.5%
46	Alaska	31,600	0.2%
16	Arizona	285,700	1.9%
33	Arkansas	105,400	0.7%
1	California	2,254,400	14.8%
26	Colorado	198,400	1.3%
28	Connecticut	167,900	1.1%
44	Delaware	38,200	0.3%
2	Florida	1,087,100	7.1%
10	Georgia	485,100	3.2%
43	Hawaii	44,300	0.3%
39	Idaho	68,800	0.5%
5	Illinois	733,300	4.8%
15	Indiana	306,900	2.0%
32	Iowa	110,800	0.7%
34	Kansas	100,900	0.7%
22	Kentucky	221,100	1.4%
29	Louisiana	154,200	1.0%
40	Maine	58,300	0.4%
23	Maryland	219,900	1.4%
14	Massachusetts	323,200	2.1%
6	Michigan	701,000	4.6%
24	Minnesota	217,700	1.4%
30	Mississippi	137,500	0.9%
17	Missouri	284,700	1.9%
45	Montana	33,200	0.2%
42	Nebraska	46,300	0.3%
27	Nevada	178,500	1.2%
41	New Hampshire	51,600	0.3%
11	New Jersey	458,300	3.0%
36	New Mexico	79,800	0.5%
4	New York	868,600	5.7%
9	North Carolina	505,900	3.3%
50	North Dakota	16,000	0.1%
7	Ohio	640,700	4.2%
31	Oklahoma	117,800	0.8%
25	Oregon	214,700	1.4%
8	Pennsylvania	559,500	3.7%
37	Rhode Island	73,500	0.5%
19	South Carolina	273,200	1.8%
49	South Dakota	21,000	0.1%
13	Tennessee	325,700	2.1%
3	Texas	999,000	6.5%
35	Utah	91,200	0.6%
47	Vermont	24,700	0.2%
18	Virginia	284,300	1.9%
12	Washington	334,800	2.2%
38	West Virginia	71,600	0.5%
20	Wisconsin	263,300	1.7%
48	Wyoming	21,800	0.1%

RANK ORDER

RANK	STATE	UNEMPLOYED	% of USA
1	California	2,254,400	14.8%
2	Florida	1,087,100	7.1%
3	Texas	999,000	6.5%
4	New York	868,600	5.7%
5	Illinois	733,300	4.8%
6	Michigan	701,000	4.6%
7	Ohio	640,700	4.2%
8	Pennsylvania	559,500	3.7%
9	North Carolina	505,900	3.3%
10	Georgia	485,100	3.2%
11	New Jersey	458,300	3.0%
12	Washington	334,800	2.2%
13	Tennessee	325,700	2.1%
14	Massachusetts	323,200	2.1%
15	Indiana	306,900	2.0%
16	Arizona	285,700	1.9%
17	Missouri	284,700	1.9%
18	Virginia	284,300	1.9%
19	South Carolina	273,200	1.8%
20	Wisconsin	263,300	1.7%
21	Alabama	225,600	1.5%
22	Kentucky	221,100	1.4%
23	Maryland	219,900	1.4%
24	Minnesota	217,700	1.4%
25	Oregon	214,700	1.4%
26	Colorado	198,400	1.3%
27	Nevada	178,500	1.2%
28	Connecticut	167,900	1.1%
29	Louisiana	154,200	1.0%
30	Mississippi	137,500	0.9%
31	Oklahoma	117,800	0.8%
32	Iowa	110,800	0.7%
33	Arkansas	105,400	0.7%
34	Kansas	100,900	0.7%
35	Utah	91,200	0.6%
36	New Mexico	79,800	0.5%
37	Rhode Island	73,500	0.5%
38	West Virginia	71,600	0.5%
39	Idaho	68,800	0.5%
40	Maine	58,300	0.4%
41	New Hampshire	51,600	0.3%
42	Nebraska	46,300	0.3%
43	Hawaii	44,300	0.3%
44	Delaware	38,200	0.3%
45	Montana	33,200	0.2%
46	Alaska	31,600	0.2%
47	Vermont	24,700	0.2%
48	Wyoming	21,800	0.1%
49	South Dakota	21,000	0.1%
50	North Dakota	16,000	0.1%
	District of Columbia	40,000	0.3%

Source: U.S. Department of Labor, Bureau of Labor Statistics
"Regional and State Employment and Unemployment" (press release, January 22, 2010, www.bls.gov/bls/newsrels.htm)
*Seasonally adjusted preliminary data as of December 2009. National total calculated through a different formula.

Unemployment Rate in 2009

National Rate = 10.0% of Labor Force Unemployed*

ALPHA ORDER

RANK	STATE	PERCENT
9	Alabama	11.0
28	Alaska	8.8
21	Arizona	9.1
33	Arkansas	7.7
5	California	12.4
34	Colorado	7.5
26	Connecticut	8.9
24	Delaware	9.0
6	Florida	11.8
15	Georgia	10.3
40	Hawaii	6.9
21	Idaho	9.1
8	Illinois	11.1
17	Indiana	9.9
45	Iowa	6.6
45	Kansas	6.6
13	Kentucky	10.7
34	Louisiana	7.5
30	Maine	8.3
34	Maryland	7.5
20	Massachusetts	9.4
1	Michigan	14.6
38	Minnesota	7.4
14	Mississippi	10.6
18	Missouri	9.6
43	Montana	6.7
48	Nebraska	4.7
2	Nevada	13.0
39	New Hampshire	7.0
16	New Jersey	10.1
30	New Mexico	8.3
24	New York	9.0
7	North Carolina	11.2
50	North Dakota	4.4
11	Ohio	10.9
45	Oklahoma	6.6
9	Oregon	11.0
26	Pennsylvania	8.9
3	Rhode Island	12.9
4	South Carolina	12.6
48	South Dakota	4.7
11	Tennessee	10.9
30	Texas	8.3
43	Utah	6.7
40	Vermont	6.9
40	Virginia	6.9
19	Washington	9.5
21	West Virginia	9.1
29	Wisconsin	8.7
34	Wyoming	7.5

RANK ORDER

RANK	STATE	PERCENT
1	Michigan	14.6
2	Nevada	13.0
3	Rhode Island	12.9
4	South Carolina	12.6
5	California	12.4
6	Florida	11.8
7	North Carolina	11.2
8	Illinois	11.1
9	Alabama	11.0
9	Oregon	11.0
11	Ohio	10.9
11	Tennessee	10.9
13	Kentucky	10.7
14	Mississippi	10.6
15	Georgia	10.3
16	New Jersey	10.1
17	Indiana	9.9
18	Missouri	9.6
19	Washington	9.5
20	Massachusetts	9.4
21	Arizona	9.1
21	Idaho	9.1
21	West Virginia	9.1
24	Delaware	9.0
24	New York	9.0
26	Connecticut	8.9
26	Pennsylvania	8.9
28	Alaska	8.8
29	Wisconsin	8.7
30	Maine	8.3
30	New Mexico	8.3
30	Texas	8.3
33	Arkansas	7.7
34	Colorado	7.5
34	Louisiana	7.5
34	Maryland	7.5
34	Wyoming	7.5
38	Minnesota	7.4
39	New Hampshire	7.0
40	Hawaii	6.9
40	Vermont	6.9
40	Virginia	6.9
43	Montana	6.7
43	Utah	6.7
45	Iowa	6.6
45	Kansas	6.6
45	Oklahoma	6.6
48	Nebraska	4.7
48	South Dakota	4.7
50	North Dakota	4.4

| | District of Columbia | 12.1 |

Source: U.S. Department of Labor, Bureau of Labor Statistics
   "Regional and State Employment and Unemployment" (press release, January 22, 2010, www.bls.gov/bls/newsrels.htm)
*Seasonally adjusted preliminary data as of December 2009. National rate calculated through a different formula.

Women in Civilian Labor Force in 2008

National Total = 72,019,000 Women*

ALPHA ORDER				RANK ORDER			
RANK	STATE	WOMEN	% of USA	RANK	STATE	WOMEN	% of USA
24	Alabama	1,013,000	1.4%	1	California	8,290,000	11.5%
49	Alaska	165,000	0.2%	2	Texas	5,295,000	7.4%
20	Arizona	1,418,000	2.0%	3	New York	4,622,000	6.4%
32	Arkansas	640,000	0.9%	4	Florida	4,291,000	6.0%
1	California	8,290,000	11.5%	5	Illinois	3,106,000	4.3%
22	Colorado	1,228,000	1.7%	6	Pennsylvania	3,005,000	4.2%
28	Connecticut	913,000	1.3%	7	Ohio	2,839,000	3.9%
46	Delaware	212,000	0.3%	8	Michigan	2,307,000	3.2%
4	Florida	4,291,000	6.0%	9	Georgia	2,223,000	3.1%
9	Georgia	2,223,000	3.1%	10	North Carolina	2,165,000	3.0%
42	Hawaii	300,000	0.4%	11	New Jersey	2,141,000	3.0%
40	Idaho	336,000	0.5%	12	Virginia	1,982,000	2.8%
5	Illinois	3,106,000	4.3%	13	Massachusetts	1,672,000	2.3%
15	Indiana	1,511,000	2.1%	14	Washington	1,650,000	2.3%
30	Iowa	814,000	1.1%	15	Indiana	1,511,000	2.1%
31	Kansas	720,000	1.0%	16	Wisconsin	1,496,000	2.1%
26	Kentucky	967,000	1.3%	17	Maryland	1,480,000	2.1%
25	Louisiana	974,000	1.4%	18	Missouri	1,471,000	2.0%
41	Maine	335,000	0.5%	19	Tennessee	1,425,000	2.0%
17	Maryland	1,480,000	2.1%	20	Arizona	1,418,000	2.0%
13	Massachusetts	1,672,000	2.3%	21	Minnesota	1,394,000	1.9%
8	Michigan	2,307,000	3.2%	22	Colorado	1,228,000	1.7%
21	Minnesota	1,394,000	1.9%	23	South Carolina	1,040,000	1.4%
33	Mississippi	610,000	0.8%	24	Alabama	1,013,000	1.4%
18	Missouri	1,471,000	2.0%	25	Louisiana	974,000	1.4%
44	Montana	236,000	0.3%	26	Kentucky	967,000	1.3%
36	Nebraska	471,000	0.7%	27	Oregon	923,000	1.3%
34	Nevada	600,000	0.8%	28	Connecticut	913,000	1.3%
39	New Hampshire	352,000	0.5%	29	Oklahoma	831,000	1.2%
11	New Jersey	2,141,000	3.0%	30	Iowa	814,000	1.1%
37	New Mexico	445,000	0.6%	31	Kansas	720,000	1.0%
3	New York	4,622,000	6.4%	32	Arkansas	640,000	0.9%
10	North Carolina	2,165,000	3.0%	33	Mississippi	610,000	0.8%
48	North Dakota	171,000	0.2%	34	Nevada	600,000	0.8%
7	Ohio	2,839,000	3.9%	34	Utah	600,000	0.8%
29	Oklahoma	831,000	1.2%	36	Nebraska	471,000	0.7%
27	Oregon	923,000	1.3%	37	New Mexico	445,000	0.6%
6	Pennsylvania	3,005,000	4.2%	38	West Virginia	369,000	0.5%
43	Rhode Island	273,000	0.4%	39	New Hampshire	352,000	0.5%
23	South Carolina	1,040,000	1.4%	40	Idaho	336,000	0.5%
45	South Dakota	215,000	0.3%	41	Maine	335,000	0.5%
19	Tennessee	1,425,000	2.0%	42	Hawaii	300,000	0.4%
2	Texas	5,295,000	7.4%	43	Rhode Island	273,000	0.4%
34	Utah	600,000	0.8%	44	Montana	236,000	0.3%
47	Vermont	178,000	0.2%	45	South Dakota	215,000	0.3%
12	Virginia	1,982,000	2.8%	46	Delaware	212,000	0.3%
14	Washington	1,650,000	2.3%	47	Vermont	178,000	0.2%
38	West Virginia	369,000	0.5%	48	North Dakota	171,000	0.2%
16	Wisconsin	1,496,000	2.1%	49	Alaska	165,000	0.2%
50	Wyoming	133,000	0.2%	50	Wyoming	133,000	0.2%
				District of Columbia		169,000	0.2%

Source: U.S. Department of Labor, Bureau of Labor Statistics
 "Geographic Profiles of Employment and Unemployment, 2008" (http://www.bls.gov/gps/)
*Annual averages.

Percent of Women in the Civilian Labor Force in 2008

National Percent = 59.2% of Women*

ALPHA ORDER

RANK	STATE	PERCENT
48	Alabama	53.1
9	Alaska	65.6
42	Arizona	56.2
45	Arkansas	55.9
36	California	57.7
14	Colorado	63.5
13	Connecticut	63.9
29	Delaware	59.0
40	Florida	56.8
32	Georgia	58.2
31	Hawaii	58.3
33	Idaho	57.9
23	Illinois	60.6
28	Indiana	59.8
4	Iowa	68.0
8	Kansas	65.9
46	Kentucky	55.8
47	Louisiana	54.8
23	Maine	60.6
12	Maryland	64.0
18	Massachusetts	61.9
37	Michigan	57.4
6	Minnesota	67.4
49	Mississippi	52.1
19	Missouri	61.7
21	Montana	60.9
1	Nebraska	72.1
25	Nevada	60.4
10	New Hampshire	65.5
22	New Jersey	60.8
42	New Mexico	56.2
38	New York	57.3
33	North Carolina	57.9
5	North Dakota	67.7
20	Ohio	61.1
35	Oklahoma	57.8
27	Oregon	59.9
30	Pennsylvania	58.6
17	Rhode Island	62.6
41	South Carolina	56.5
3	South Dakota	68.3
42	Tennessee	56.2
39	Texas	57.0
25	Utah	60.4
2	Vermont	68.8
15	Virginia	63.3
16	Washington	62.9
50	West Virginia	49.2
7	Wisconsin	66.5
11	Wyoming	64.2

RANK ORDER

RANK	STATE	PERCENT
1	Nebraska	72.1
2	Vermont	68.8
3	South Dakota	68.3
4	Iowa	68.0
5	North Dakota	67.7
6	Minnesota	67.4
7	Wisconsin	66.5
8	Kansas	65.9
9	Alaska	65.6
10	New Hampshire	65.5
11	Wyoming	64.2
12	Maryland	64.0
13	Connecticut	63.9
14	Colorado	63.5
15	Virginia	63.3
16	Washington	62.9
17	Rhode Island	62.6
18	Massachusetts	61.9
19	Missouri	61.7
20	Ohio	61.1
21	Montana	60.9
22	New Jersey	60.8
23	Illinois	60.6
23	Maine	60.6
25	Nevada	60.4
25	Utah	60.4
27	Oregon	59.9
28	Indiana	59.8
29	Delaware	59.0
30	Pennsylvania	58.6
31	Hawaii	58.3
32	Georgia	58.2
33	Idaho	57.9
33	North Carolina	57.9
35	Oklahoma	57.8
36	California	57.7
37	Michigan	57.4
38	New York	57.3
39	Texas	57.0
40	Florida	56.8
41	South Carolina	56.5
42	Arizona	56.2
42	New Mexico	56.2
42	Tennessee	56.2
45	Arkansas	55.9
46	Kentucky	55.8
47	Louisiana	54.8
48	Alabama	53.1
49	Mississippi	52.1
50	West Virginia	49.2
	District of Columbia	64.4

Source: U.S. Department of Labor, Bureau of Labor Statistics
  "Geographic Profiles of Employment and Unemployment, 2008" (http://www.bls.gov/gps/)
*Annual averages.

Percent of Civilian Labor Force Comprised of Women in 2008

National Percent = 46.7% of Civilian Labor Force*

<u>ALPHA ORDER</u>

RANK	STATE	PERCENT
27	Alabama	47.1
40	Alaska	46.2
45	Arizona	44.8
37	Arkansas	46.7
43	California	45.0
44	Colorado	44.9
7	Connecticut	48.3
4	Delaware	48.6
22	Florida	47.3
40	Georgia	46.2
31	Hawaii	46.9
46	Idaho	44.6
37	Illinois	46.7
25	Indiana	47.2
13	Iowa	48.0
31	Kansas	46.9
31	Kentucky	46.9
22	Louisiana	47.3
9	Maine	48.2
2	Maryland	49.0
6	Massachusetts	48.5
29	Michigan	47.0
18	Minnesota	47.5
13	Mississippi	48.0
7	Missouri	48.3
20	Montana	47.4
16	Nebraska	47.8
49	Nevada	44.2
17	New Hampshire	47.6
31	New Jersey	46.9
25	New Mexico	47.2
20	New York	47.4
22	North Carolina	47.3
29	North Dakota	47.0
9	Ohio	48.2
35	Oklahoma	46.8
35	Oregon	46.8
18	Pennsylvania	47.5
4	Rhode Island	48.6
3	South Carolina	48.8
13	South Dakota	48.0
27	Tennessee	47.1
48	Texas	44.3
50	Utah	43.1
1	Vermont	49.6
9	Virginia	48.2
37	Washington	46.7
42	West Virginia	45.1
9	Wisconsin	48.2
47	Wyoming	44.5

<u>RANK ORDER</u>

RANK	STATE	PERCENT
1	Vermont	49.6
2	Maryland	49.0
3	South Carolina	48.8
4	Delaware	48.6
4	Rhode Island	48.6
6	Massachusetts	48.5
7	Connecticut	48.3
7	Missouri	48.3
9	Maine	48.2
9	Ohio	48.2
9	Virginia	48.2
9	Wisconsin	48.2
13	Iowa	48.0
13	Mississippi	48.0
13	South Dakota	48.0
16	Nebraska	47.8
17	New Hampshire	47.6
18	Minnesota	47.5
18	Pennsylvania	47.5
20	Montana	47.4
20	New York	47.4
22	Florida	47.3
22	Louisiana	47.3
22	North Carolina	47.3
25	Indiana	47.2
25	New Mexico	47.2
27	Alabama	47.1
27	Tennessee	47.1
29	Michigan	47.0
29	North Dakota	47.0
31	Hawaii	46.9
31	Kansas	46.9
31	Kentucky	46.9
31	New Jersey	46.9
35	Oklahoma	46.8
35	Oregon	46.8
37	Arkansas	46.7
37	Illinois	46.7
37	Washington	46.7
40	Alaska	46.2
40	Georgia	46.2
42	West Virginia	45.1
43	California	45.0
44	Colorado	44.9
45	Arizona	44.8
46	Idaho	44.6
47	Wyoming	44.5
48	Texas	44.3
49	Nevada	44.2
50	Utah	43.1

District of Columbia   50.3

Source: CQ Press using data from U.S. Department of Labor, Bureau of Labor Statistics
"Geographic Profiles of Employment and Unemployment, 2008" (http://www.bls.gov/gps/)
*Annual averages.

Percent of Children Under 6 Years Old With All Parents Working: 2008

National Percent = 64.5%

<table>
<tr><td colspan="3">ALPHA ORDER</td><td colspan="3">RANK ORDER</td></tr>
<tr><td>RANK</td><td>STATE</td><td>PERCENT</td><td>RANK</td><td>STATE</td><td>PERCENT</td></tr>
<tr><td>32</td><td>Alabama</td><td>64.6</td><td>1</td><td>South Dakota</td><td>78.1</td></tr>
<tr><td>29</td><td>Alaska</td><td>64.9</td><td>2</td><td>Vermont</td><td>75.4</td></tr>
<tr><td>48</td><td>Arizona</td><td>59.7</td><td>3</td><td>Nebraska</td><td>75.1</td></tr>
<tr><td>35</td><td>Arkansas</td><td>63.5</td><td>4</td><td>North Dakota</td><td>74.8</td></tr>
<tr><td>45</td><td>California</td><td>60.2</td><td>5</td><td>Iowa</td><td>74.0</td></tr>
<tr><td>36</td><td>Colorado</td><td>63.4</td><td>6</td><td>Wisconsin</td><td>73.8</td></tr>
<tr><td>19</td><td>Connecticut</td><td>67.6</td><td>7</td><td>Minnesota</td><td>73.7</td></tr>
<tr><td>10</td><td>Delaware</td><td>70.9</td><td>8</td><td>Maryland</td><td>71.8</td></tr>
<tr><td>20</td><td>Florida</td><td>67.4</td><td>9</td><td>Rhode Island</td><td>71.1</td></tr>
<tr><td>38</td><td>Georgia</td><td>63.1</td><td>10</td><td>Delaware</td><td>70.9</td></tr>
<tr><td>24</td><td>Hawaii</td><td>66.3</td><td>11</td><td>New Hampshire</td><td>70.1</td></tr>
<tr><td>49</td><td>Idaho</td><td>58.2</td><td>12</td><td>Maine</td><td>69.1</td></tr>
<tr><td>31</td><td>Illinois</td><td>64.7</td><td>12</td><td>Missouri</td><td>69.1</td></tr>
<tr><td>17</td><td>Indiana</td><td>68.1</td><td>14</td><td>Kansas</td><td>68.7</td></tr>
<tr><td>5</td><td>Iowa</td><td>74.0</td><td>15</td><td>Mississippi</td><td>68.6</td></tr>
<tr><td>14</td><td>Kansas</td><td>68.7</td><td>15</td><td>Ohio</td><td>68.6</td></tr>
<tr><td>39</td><td>Kentucky</td><td>62.5</td><td>17</td><td>Indiana</td><td>68.1</td></tr>
<tr><td>25</td><td>Louisiana</td><td>65.9</td><td>18</td><td>Massachusetts</td><td>67.9</td></tr>
<tr><td>12</td><td>Maine</td><td>69.1</td><td>19</td><td>Connecticut</td><td>67.6</td></tr>
<tr><td>8</td><td>Maryland</td><td>71.8</td><td>20</td><td>Florida</td><td>67.4</td></tr>
<tr><td>18</td><td>Massachusetts</td><td>67.9</td><td>21</td><td>Virginia</td><td>66.6</td></tr>
<tr><td>23</td><td>Michigan</td><td>66.4</td><td>22</td><td>North Carolina</td><td>66.5</td></tr>
<tr><td>7</td><td>Minnesota</td><td>73.7</td><td>23</td><td>Michigan</td><td>66.4</td></tr>
<tr><td>15</td><td>Mississippi</td><td>68.6</td><td>24</td><td>Hawaii</td><td>66.3</td></tr>
<tr><td>12</td><td>Missouri</td><td>69.1</td><td>25</td><td>Louisiana</td><td>65.9</td></tr>
<tr><td>32</td><td>Montana</td><td>64.6</td><td>25</td><td>South Carolina</td><td>65.9</td></tr>
<tr><td>3</td><td>Nebraska</td><td>75.1</td><td>27</td><td>Pennsylvania</td><td>65.2</td></tr>
<tr><td>40</td><td>Nevada</td><td>62.4</td><td>28</td><td>New Jersey</td><td>65.0</td></tr>
<tr><td>11</td><td>New Hampshire</td><td>70.1</td><td>29</td><td>Alaska</td><td>64.9</td></tr>
<tr><td>28</td><td>New Jersey</td><td>65.0</td><td>29</td><td>Tennessee</td><td>64.9</td></tr>
<tr><td>41</td><td>New Mexico</td><td>61.8</td><td>31</td><td>Illinois</td><td>64.7</td></tr>
<tr><td>37</td><td>New York</td><td>63.2</td><td>32</td><td>Alabama</td><td>64.6</td></tr>
<tr><td>22</td><td>North Carolina</td><td>66.5</td><td>32</td><td>Montana</td><td>64.6</td></tr>
<tr><td>4</td><td>North Dakota</td><td>74.8</td><td>34</td><td>Wyoming</td><td>64.1</td></tr>
<tr><td>15</td><td>Ohio</td><td>68.6</td><td>35</td><td>Arkansas</td><td>63.5</td></tr>
<tr><td>42</td><td>Oklahoma</td><td>61.4</td><td>36</td><td>Colorado</td><td>63.4</td></tr>
<tr><td>43</td><td>Oregon</td><td>61.3</td><td>37</td><td>New York</td><td>63.2</td></tr>
<tr><td>27</td><td>Pennsylvania</td><td>65.2</td><td>38</td><td>Georgia</td><td>63.1</td></tr>
<tr><td>9</td><td>Rhode Island</td><td>71.1</td><td>39</td><td>Kentucky</td><td>62.5</td></tr>
<tr><td>25</td><td>South Carolina</td><td>65.9</td><td>40</td><td>Nevada</td><td>62.4</td></tr>
<tr><td>1</td><td>South Dakota</td><td>78.1</td><td>41</td><td>New Mexico</td><td>61.8</td></tr>
<tr><td>29</td><td>Tennessee</td><td>64.9</td><td>42</td><td>Oklahoma</td><td>61.4</td></tr>
<tr><td>46</td><td>Texas</td><td>60.0</td><td>43</td><td>Oregon</td><td>61.3</td></tr>
<tr><td>50</td><td>Utah</td><td>51.5</td><td>44</td><td>West Virginia</td><td>60.8</td></tr>
<tr><td>2</td><td>Vermont</td><td>75.4</td><td>45</td><td>California</td><td>60.2</td></tr>
<tr><td>21</td><td>Virginia</td><td>66.6</td><td>46</td><td>Texas</td><td>60.0</td></tr>
<tr><td>46</td><td>Washington</td><td>60.0</td><td>46</td><td>Washington</td><td>60.0</td></tr>
<tr><td>44</td><td>West Virginia</td><td>60.8</td><td>48</td><td>Arizona</td><td>59.7</td></tr>
<tr><td>6</td><td>Wisconsin</td><td>73.8</td><td>49</td><td>Idaho</td><td>58.2</td></tr>
<tr><td>34</td><td>Wyoming</td><td>64.1</td><td>50</td><td>Utah</td><td>51.5</td></tr>
<tr><td></td><td></td><td></td><td></td><td>District of Columbia</td><td>63.2</td></tr>
</table>

Source: U.S. Bureau of the Census
"2008 American Community Survey" (http://www.census.gov/acs/www/index.html)

Job Growth: 2008 to 2009

National Percent Change = 3.1% Decrease*

ALPHA ORDER				RANK ORDER		
RANK	STATE	PERCENT CHANGE		RANK	STATE	PERCENT CHANGE
39	Alabama	(4.4)		1	North Dakota	1.6
2	Alaska	0.2		2	Alaska	0.2
46	Arizona	(5.2)		3	Arkansas	(1.3)
3	Arkansas	(1.3)		3	New York	(1.3)
44	California	(5.1)		5	Oklahoma	(1.9)
36	Colorado	(4.2)		6	West Virginia	(2.2)
32	Connecticut	(3.7)		7	Pennsylvania	(2.3)
44	Delaware	(5.1)		7	Virginia	(2.3)
49	Florida	(5.7)		9	Louisiana	(2.4)
43	Georgia	(5.0)		9	Mississippi	(2.4)
37	Hawaii	(4.3)		9	Missouri	(2.4)
14	Idaho	(2.7)		12	Massachusetts	(2.5)
40	Illinois	(4.6)		13	Texas	(2.6)
23	Indiana	(3.0)		14	Idaho	(2.7)
20	Iowa	(2.9)		14	New Hampshire	(2.7)
35	Kansas	(4.0)		14	New Jersey	(2.7)
37	Kentucky	(4.3)		14	New Mexico	(2.7)
9	Louisiana	(2.4)		14	South Dakota	(2.7)
26	Maine	(3.2)		19	Montana	(2.8)
28	Maryland	(3.3)		20	Iowa	(2.9)
12	Massachusetts	(2.5)		20	Minnesota	(2.9)
47	Michigan	(5.5)		20	Washington	(2.9)
20	Minnesota	(2.9)		23	Indiana	(3.0)
9	Mississippi	(2.4)		23	South Carolina	(3.0)
9	Missouri	(2.4)		23	Utah	(3.0)
19	Montana	(2.8)		26	Maine	(3.2)
28	Nebraska	(3.3)		26	Rhode Island	(3.2)
50	Nevada	(8.4)		28	Maryland	(3.3)
14	New Hampshire	(2.7)		28	Nebraska	(3.3)
14	New Jersey	(2.7)		30	North Carolina	(3.5)
14	New Mexico	(2.7)		30	Vermont	(3.5)
3	New York	(1.3)		32	Connecticut	(3.7)
30	North Carolina	(3.5)		33	Wisconsin	(3.8)
1	North Dakota	1.6		34	Tennessee	(3.9)
40	Ohio	(4.6)		35	Kansas	(4.0)
5	Oklahoma	(1.9)		36	Colorado	(4.2)
40	Oregon	(4.6)		37	Hawaii	(4.3)
7	Pennsylvania	(2.3)		37	Kentucky	(4.3)
26	Rhode Island	(3.2)		39	Alabama	(4.4)
23	South Carolina	(3.0)		40	Illinois	(4.6)
14	South Dakota	(2.7)		40	Ohio	(4.6)
34	Tennessee	(3.9)		40	Oregon	(4.6)
13	Texas	(2.6)		43	Georgia	(5.0)
23	Utah	(3.0)		44	California	(5.1)
30	Vermont	(3.5)		44	Delaware	(5.1)
7	Virginia	(2.3)		46	Arizona	(5.2)
20	Washington	(2.9)		47	Michigan	(5.5)
6	West Virginia	(2.2)		48	Wyoming	(5.6)
33	Wisconsin	(3.8)		49	Florida	(5.7)
48	Wyoming	(5.6)		50	Nevada	(8.4)

District of Columbia   1.3

Source: CQ Press using data from U.S. Department of Labor, Bureau of Labor Statistics

"Regional and State Employment and Unemployment" (press release, January 22, 2010, www.bls.gov/bls/newsrels.htm)

*Nonfarm jobs. December 2008 to December 2009, seasonally adjusted. National figure based on nonfarm employment from a different survey.

Employees on Nonfarm Payrolls in 2009

National Total = 130,910,000 Employees*

ALPHA ORDER

RANK	STATE	EMPLOYEES	% of USA
24	Alabama	1,888,500	1.3%
48	Alaska	320,900	0.2%
21	Arizona	2,412,000	1.7%
33	Arkansas	1,172,100	0.8%
1	California	14,148,000	10.1%
22	Colorado	2,234,000	1.6%
28	Connecticut	1,614,900	1.2%
45	Delaware	409,800	0.3%
4	Florida	7,343,700	5.2%
10	Georgia	3,839,700	2.7%
42	Hawaii	586,100	0.4%
40	Idaho	612,000	0.4%
5	Illinois	5,612,200	4.0%
15	Indiana	2,796,300	2.0%
30	Iowa	1,468,800	1.0%
31	Kansas	1,329,900	1.0%
26	Kentucky	1,764,500	1.3%
23	Louisiana	1,901,700	1.4%
41	Maine	588,800	0.4%
20	Maryland	2,524,000	1.8%
13	Massachusetts	3,164,000	2.3%
11	Michigan	3,831,000	2.7%
18	Minnesota	2,642,400	1.9%
35	Mississippi	1,101,400	0.8%
17	Missouri	2,708,300	1.9%
44	Montana	431,000	0.3%
36	Nebraska	938,300	0.7%
34	Nevada	1,154,600	0.8%
39	New Hampshire	629,500	0.4%
9	New Jersey	3,910,400	2.8%
37	New Mexico	817,100	0.6%
3	New York	8,544,900	6.1%
8	North Carolina	3,924,000	2.8%
47	North Dakota	367,800	0.3%
7	Ohio	5,086,900	3.6%
29	Oklahoma	1,558,900	1.1%
27	Oregon	1,617,200	1.2%
6	Pennsylvania	5,598,900	4.0%
43	Rhode Island	453,800	0.3%
25	South Carolina	1,846,400	1.3%
46	South Dakota	400,500	0.3%
19	Tennessee	2,636,700	1.9%
2	Texas	10,355,300	7.4%
32	Utah	1,200,100	0.9%
49	Vermont	292,200	0.2%
12	Virginia	3,656,500	2.6%
14	Washington	2,834,900	2.0%
38	West Virginia	738,500	0.5%
16	Wisconsin	2,712,300	1.9%
50	Wyoming	282,400	0.2%

RANK ORDER

RANK	STATE	EMPLOYEES	% of USA
1	California	14,148,000	10.1%
2	Texas	10,355,300	7.4%
3	New York	8,544,900	6.1%
4	Florida	7,343,700	5.2%
5	Illinois	5,612,200	4.0%
6	Pennsylvania	5,598,900	4.0%
7	Ohio	5,086,900	3.6%
8	North Carolina	3,924,000	2.8%
9	New Jersey	3,910,400	2.8%
10	Georgia	3,839,700	2.7%
11	Michigan	3,831,000	2.7%
12	Virginia	3,656,500	2.6%
13	Massachusetts	3,164,000	2.3%
14	Washington	2,834,900	2.0%
15	Indiana	2,796,300	2.0%
16	Wisconsin	2,712,300	1.9%
17	Missouri	2,708,300	1.9%
18	Minnesota	2,642,400	1.9%
19	Tennessee	2,636,700	1.9%
20	Maryland	2,524,000	1.8%
21	Arizona	2,412,000	1.7%
22	Colorado	2,234,000	1.6%
23	Louisiana	1,901,700	1.4%
24	Alabama	1,888,500	1.3%
25	South Carolina	1,846,400	1.3%
26	Kentucky	1,764,500	1.3%
27	Oregon	1,617,200	1.2%
28	Connecticut	1,614,900	1.2%
29	Oklahoma	1,558,900	1.1%
30	Iowa	1,468,800	1.0%
31	Kansas	1,329,900	1.0%
32	Utah	1,200,100	0.9%
33	Arkansas	1,172,100	0.8%
34	Nevada	1,154,600	0.8%
35	Mississippi	1,101,400	0.8%
36	Nebraska	938,300	0.7%
37	New Mexico	817,100	0.6%
38	West Virginia	738,500	0.5%
39	New Hampshire	629,500	0.4%
40	Idaho	612,000	0.4%
41	Maine	588,800	0.4%
42	Hawaii	586,100	0.4%
43	Rhode Island	453,800	0.3%
44	Montana	431,000	0.3%
45	Delaware	409,800	0.3%
46	South Dakota	400,500	0.3%
47	North Dakota	367,800	0.3%
48	Alaska	320,900	0.2%
49	Vermont	292,200	0.2%
50	Wyoming	282,400	0.2%
	District of Columbia	710,900	0.5%

Source: U.S. Department of Labor, Bureau of Labor Statistics
"Regional and State Employment and Unemployment" (press release, January 22, 2010, www.bls.gov/bls/newsrels.htm)
*Seasonally adjusted preliminary data as of December 2009. National total calculated through a different formula.

Employees in Construction in 2009

National Total = 5,907,000 Employees*

ALPHA ORDER

RANK	STATE	EMPLOYEES	% of USA
25	Alabama	85,200	1.4%
49	Alaska	15,900	0.3%
15	Arizona	132,000	2.2%
35	Arkansas	51,200	0.9%
1	California	606,500	10.3%
16	Colorado	130,400	2.2%
34	Connecticut	51,300	0.9%
44	Delaware**	21,600	0.4%
3	Florida	405,100	6.9%
10	Georgia	160,800	2.7%
40	Hawaii**	31,600	0.5%
39	Idaho	35,900	0.6%
6	Illinois	209,800	3.6%
17	Indiana	120,900	2.0%
31	Iowa	62,800	1.1%
32	Kansas	56,800	1.0%
30	Kentucky	64,800	1.1%
14	Louisiana	133,500	2.3%
41	Maine	24,400	0.4%
12	Maryland**	139,400	2.4%
20	Massachusetts	107,000	1.8%
19	Michigan	119,000	2.0%
24	Minnesota	91,900	1.6%
33	Mississippi	52,700	0.9%
18	Missouri	119,900	2.0%
42	Montana	22,900	0.4%
37	Nebraska**	46,400	0.8%
26	Nevada	77,600	1.3%
45	New Hampshire	20,900	0.4%
13	New Jersey	134,800	2.3%
36	New Mexico	47,800	0.8%
4	New York	321,300	5.4%
8	North Carolina	187,100	3.2%
47	North Dakota	19,700	0.3%
9	Ohio	176,400	3.0%
28	Oklahoma	73,500	1.2%
27	Oregon	75,100	1.3%
5	Pennsylvania	227,100	3.8%
48	Rhode Island	17,600	0.3%
23	South Carolina	96,300	1.6%
46	South Dakota**	20,600	0.3%
21	Tennessee**	99,100	1.7%
2	Texas	555,800	9.4%
29	Utah	70,300	1.2%
50	Vermont	11,900	0.2%
7	Virginia	195,600	3.3%
11	Washington	155,500	2.6%
38	West Virginia	36,300	0.6%
21	Wisconsin	99,100	1.7%
43	Wyoming	21,800	0.4%

RANK ORDER

RANK	STATE	EMPLOYEES	% of USA
1	California	606,500	10.3%
2	Texas	555,800	9.4%
3	Florida	405,100	6.9%
4	New York	321,300	5.4%
5	Pennsylvania	227,100	3.8%
6	Illinois	209,800	3.6%
7	Virginia	195,600	3.3%
8	North Carolina	187,100	3.2%
9	Ohio	176,400	3.0%
10	Georgia	160,800	2.7%
11	Washington	155,500	2.6%
12	Maryland**	139,400	2.4%
13	New Jersey	134,800	2.3%
14	Louisiana	133,500	2.3%
15	Arizona	132,000	2.2%
16	Colorado	130,400	2.2%
17	Indiana	120,900	2.0%
18	Missouri	119,900	2.0%
19	Michigan	119,000	2.0%
20	Massachusetts	107,000	1.8%
21	Tennessee**	99,100	1.7%
21	Wisconsin	99,100	1.7%
23	South Carolina	96,300	1.6%
24	Minnesota	91,900	1.6%
25	Alabama	85,200	1.4%
26	Nevada	77,600	1.3%
27	Oregon	75,100	1.3%
28	Oklahoma	73,500	1.2%
29	Utah	70,300	1.2%
30	Kentucky	64,800	1.1%
31	Iowa	62,800	1.1%
32	Kansas	56,800	1.0%
33	Mississippi	52,700	0.9%
34	Connecticut	51,300	0.9%
35	Arkansas	51,200	0.9%
36	New Mexico	47,800	0.8%
37	Nebraska**	46,400	0.8%
38	West Virginia	36,300	0.6%
39	Idaho	35,900	0.6%
40	Hawaii**	31,600	0.5%
41	Maine	24,400	0.4%
42	Montana	22,900	0.4%
43	Wyoming	21,800	0.4%
44	Delaware**	21,600	0.4%
45	New Hampshire	20,900	0.4%
46	South Dakota**	20,600	0.3%
47	North Dakota	19,700	0.3%
48	Rhode Island	17,600	0.3%
49	Alaska	15,900	0.3%
50	Vermont	11,900	0.2%
	District of Columbia**	12,000	0.2%

Source: U.S. Department of Labor, Bureau of Labor Statistics
   "Regional and State Employment and Unemployment" (press release, January 22, 2010, www.bls.gov/bls/newsrels.htm)
*Seasonally adjusted preliminary data as of December 2009. National total calculated through a different formula.
**Figures for states include employees in natural resources and mining.

Percent of Nonfarm Employees in Construction in 2009

National Percent = 4.5% of Employees*

<table>
<tr><td colspan="3">ALPHA ORDER</td><td colspan="3">RANK ORDER</td></tr>
<tr><td>RANK</td><td>STATE</td><td>PERCENT</td><td>RANK</td><td>STATE</td><td>PERCENT</td></tr>
<tr><td>27</td><td>Alabama</td><td>4.5</td><td>1</td><td>Wyoming</td><td>7.7</td></tr>
<tr><td>20</td><td>Alaska</td><td>5.0</td><td>2</td><td>Louisiana</td><td>7.0</td></tr>
<tr><td>8</td><td>Arizona</td><td>5.5</td><td>3</td><td>Nevada</td><td>6.7</td></tr>
<tr><td>28</td><td>Arkansas</td><td>4.4</td><td>4</td><td>Idaho</td><td>5.9</td></tr>
<tr><td>30</td><td>California</td><td>4.3</td><td>4</td><td>Utah</td><td>5.9</td></tr>
<tr><td>6</td><td>Colorado</td><td>5.8</td><td>6</td><td>Colorado</td><td>5.8</td></tr>
<tr><td>49</td><td>Connecticut</td><td>3.2</td><td>6</td><td>New Mexico</td><td>5.8</td></tr>
<tr><td>15</td><td>Delaware**</td><td>5.3</td><td>8</td><td>Arizona</td><td>5.5</td></tr>
<tr><td>8</td><td>Florida</td><td>5.5</td><td>8</td><td>Florida</td><td>5.5</td></tr>
<tr><td>34</td><td>Georgia</td><td>4.2</td><td>8</td><td>Maryland**</td><td>5.5</td></tr>
<tr><td>12</td><td>Hawaii**</td><td>5.4</td><td>8</td><td>Washington</td><td>5.5</td></tr>
<tr><td>4</td><td>Idaho</td><td>5.9</td><td>12</td><td>Hawaii**</td><td>5.4</td></tr>
<tr><td>41</td><td>Illinois</td><td>3.7</td><td>12</td><td>North Dakota</td><td>5.4</td></tr>
<tr><td>30</td><td>Indiana</td><td>4.3</td><td>12</td><td>Texas</td><td>5.4</td></tr>
<tr><td>30</td><td>Iowa</td><td>4.3</td><td>15</td><td>Delaware**</td><td>5.3</td></tr>
<tr><td>30</td><td>Kansas</td><td>4.3</td><td>15</td><td>Montana</td><td>5.3</td></tr>
<tr><td>41</td><td>Kentucky</td><td>3.7</td><td>15</td><td>Virginia</td><td>5.3</td></tr>
<tr><td>2</td><td>Louisiana</td><td>7.0</td><td>18</td><td>South Carolina</td><td>5.2</td></tr>
<tr><td>35</td><td>Maine</td><td>4.1</td><td>19</td><td>South Dakota**</td><td>5.1</td></tr>
<tr><td>8</td><td>Maryland**</td><td>5.5</td><td>20</td><td>Alaska</td><td>5.0</td></tr>
<tr><td>46</td><td>Massachusetts</td><td>3.4</td><td>21</td><td>Nebraska**</td><td>4.9</td></tr>
<tr><td>50</td><td>Michigan</td><td>3.1</td><td>21</td><td>West Virginia</td><td>4.9</td></tr>
<tr><td>44</td><td>Minnesota</td><td>3.5</td><td>23</td><td>Mississippi</td><td>4.8</td></tr>
<tr><td>23</td><td>Mississippi</td><td>4.8</td><td>23</td><td>North Carolina</td><td>4.8</td></tr>
<tr><td>28</td><td>Missouri</td><td>4.4</td><td>25</td><td>Oklahoma</td><td>4.7</td></tr>
<tr><td>15</td><td>Montana</td><td>5.3</td><td>26</td><td>Oregon</td><td>4.6</td></tr>
<tr><td>21</td><td>Nebraska**</td><td>4.9</td><td>27</td><td>Alabama</td><td>4.5</td></tr>
<tr><td>3</td><td>Nevada</td><td>6.7</td><td>28</td><td>Arkansas</td><td>4.4</td></tr>
<tr><td>48</td><td>New Hampshire</td><td>3.3</td><td>28</td><td>Missouri</td><td>4.4</td></tr>
<tr><td>46</td><td>New Jersey</td><td>3.4</td><td>30</td><td>California</td><td>4.3</td></tr>
<tr><td>6</td><td>New Mexico</td><td>5.8</td><td>30</td><td>Indiana</td><td>4.3</td></tr>
<tr><td>39</td><td>New York</td><td>3.8</td><td>30</td><td>Iowa</td><td>4.3</td></tr>
<tr><td>23</td><td>North Carolina</td><td>4.8</td><td>30</td><td>Kansas</td><td>4.3</td></tr>
<tr><td>12</td><td>North Dakota</td><td>5.4</td><td>34</td><td>Georgia</td><td>4.2</td></tr>
<tr><td>44</td><td>Ohio</td><td>3.5</td><td>35</td><td>Maine</td><td>4.1</td></tr>
<tr><td>25</td><td>Oklahoma</td><td>4.7</td><td>35</td><td>Pennsylvania</td><td>4.1</td></tr>
<tr><td>26</td><td>Oregon</td><td>4.6</td><td>35</td><td>Vermont</td><td>4.1</td></tr>
<tr><td>35</td><td>Pennsylvania</td><td>4.1</td><td>38</td><td>Rhode Island</td><td>3.9</td></tr>
<tr><td>38</td><td>Rhode Island</td><td>3.9</td><td>39</td><td>New York</td><td>3.8</td></tr>
<tr><td>18</td><td>South Carolina</td><td>5.2</td><td>39</td><td>Tennessee**</td><td>3.8</td></tr>
<tr><td>19</td><td>South Dakota**</td><td>5.1</td><td>41</td><td>Illinois</td><td>3.7</td></tr>
<tr><td>39</td><td>Tennessee**</td><td>3.8</td><td>41</td><td>Kentucky</td><td>3.7</td></tr>
<tr><td>12</td><td>Texas</td><td>5.4</td><td>41</td><td>Wisconsin</td><td>3.7</td></tr>
<tr><td>4</td><td>Utah</td><td>5.9</td><td>44</td><td>Minnesota</td><td>3.5</td></tr>
<tr><td>35</td><td>Vermont</td><td>4.1</td><td>44</td><td>Ohio</td><td>3.5</td></tr>
<tr><td>15</td><td>Virginia</td><td>5.3</td><td>46</td><td>Massachusetts</td><td>3.4</td></tr>
<tr><td>8</td><td>Washington</td><td>5.5</td><td>46</td><td>New Jersey</td><td>3.4</td></tr>
<tr><td>21</td><td>West Virginia</td><td>4.9</td><td>48</td><td>New Hampshire</td><td>3.3</td></tr>
<tr><td>41</td><td>Wisconsin</td><td>3.7</td><td>49</td><td>Connecticut</td><td>3.2</td></tr>
<tr><td>1</td><td>Wyoming</td><td>7.7</td><td>50</td><td>Michigan</td><td>3.1</td></tr>
<tr><td></td><td></td><td></td><td></td><td>District of Columbia**</td><td>1.7</td></tr>
</table>

Source: CQ Press using data from U.S. Department of Labor, Bureau of Labor Statistics
"Regional and State Employment and Unemployment" (press release, January 22, 2010, www.bls.gov/bls/newsrels.htm)
*Seasonally adjusted preliminary data as of December 2009. National figure calculated through a different formula.
**Figures for states include employees in natural resources and mining.

Employees in Education and Health Services in 2009

National Total = 19,456,000 Employees*

ALPHA ORDER

RANK	STATE	EMPLOYEES	% of USA
27	Alabama	219,000	1.1%
49	Alaska	39,700	0.2%
21	Arizona	326,200	1.7%
32	Arkansas	170,000	0.9%
1	California	1,764,500	9.1%
24	Colorado	261,000	1.3%
22	Connecticut	300,500	1.5%
45	Delaware	62,500	0.3%
5	Florida	1,070,000	5.5%
12	Georgia	483,900	2.5%
43	Hawaii	75,500	0.4%
42	Idaho	79,600	0.4%
7	Illinois	801,200	4.1%
16	Indiana	414,900	2.1%
28	Iowa	211,700	1.1%
31	Kansas	179,200	0.9%
25	Kentucky	246,400	1.3%
23	Louisiana	262,900	1.4%
37	Maine	120,000	0.6%
18	Maryland	396,600	2.0%
8	Massachusetts	656,600	3.4%
9	Michigan	623,800	3.2%
13	Minnesota	456,100	2.3%
35	Mississippi	133,100	0.7%
17	Missouri	408,200	2.1%
46	Montana	62,200	0.3%
34	Nebraska	139,100	0.7%
40	Nevada	99,700	0.5%
39	New Hampshire	107,700	0.6%
10	New Jersey	597,700	3.1%
36	New Mexico	120,500	0.6%
2	New York	1,688,900	8.7%
11	North Carolina	548,000	2.8%
48	North Dakota	54,100	0.3%
6	Ohio	834,000	4.3%
30	Oklahoma	204,100	1.0%
26	Oregon	228,400	1.2%
4	Pennsylvania	1,132,800	5.8%
41	Rhode Island	99,600	0.5%
29	South Carolina	211,100	1.1%
44	South Dakota	63,600	0.3%
19	Tennessee	372,000	1.9%
3	Texas	1,377,800	7.1%
33	Utah	156,100	0.8%
47	Vermont	62,000	0.3%
14	Virginia	452,400	2.3%
20	Washington	370,900	1.9%
38	West Virginia	119,100	0.6%
15	Wisconsin	418,200	2.1%
NA	Wyoming**	NA	NA

RANK ORDER

RANK	STATE	EMPLOYEES	% of USA
1	California	1,764,500	9.1%
2	New York	1,688,900	8.7%
3	Texas	1,377,800	7.1%
4	Pennsylvania	1,132,800	5.8%
5	Florida	1,070,000	5.5%
6	Ohio	834,000	4.3%
7	Illinois	801,200	4.1%
8	Massachusetts	656,600	3.4%
9	Michigan	623,800	3.2%
10	New Jersey	597,700	3.1%
11	North Carolina	548,000	2.8%
12	Georgia	483,900	2.5%
13	Minnesota	456,100	2.3%
14	Virginia	452,400	2.3%
15	Wisconsin	418,200	2.1%
16	Indiana	414,900	2.1%
17	Missouri	408,200	2.1%
18	Maryland	396,600	2.0%
19	Tennessee	372,000	1.9%
20	Washington	370,900	1.9%
21	Arizona	326,200	1.7%
22	Connecticut	300,500	1.5%
23	Louisiana	262,900	1.4%
24	Colorado	261,000	1.3%
25	Kentucky	246,400	1.3%
26	Oregon	228,400	1.2%
27	Alabama	219,000	1.1%
28	Iowa	211,700	1.1%
29	South Carolina	211,100	1.1%
30	Oklahoma	204,100	1.0%
31	Kansas	179,200	0.9%
32	Arkansas	170,000	0.9%
33	Utah	156,100	0.8%
34	Nebraska	139,100	0.7%
35	Mississippi	133,100	0.7%
36	New Mexico	120,500	0.6%
37	Maine	120,000	0.6%
38	West Virginia	119,100	0.6%
39	New Hampshire	107,700	0.6%
40	Nevada	99,700	0.5%
41	Rhode Island	99,600	0.5%
42	Idaho	79,600	0.4%
43	Hawaii	75,500	0.4%
44	South Dakota	63,600	0.3%
45	Delaware	62,500	0.3%
46	Montana	62,200	0.3%
47	Vermont	62,000	0.3%
48	North Dakota	54,100	0.3%
49	Alaska	39,700	0.2%
NA	Wyoming**	NA	NA
	District of Columbia	106,100	0.5%

Source: U.S. Department of Labor, Bureau of Labor Statistics
    "Regional and State Employment and Unemployment" (press release, January 22, 2010, www.bls.gov/bls/newsrels.htm)
*Seasonally adjusted preliminary data as of December 2009. National total calculated through a different formula.
**The Bureau of Labor Statistics does not publish seasonally adjusted figures in this category for Wyoming.

Percent of Nonfarm Employees in Education and Health Services in 2009

National Percent = 14.9% of Employees*

ALPHA ORDER

RANK	STATE	PERCENT
47	Alabama	11.6
43	Alaska	12.4
33	Arizona	13.5
24	Arkansas	14.5
42	California	12.5
46	Colorado	11.7
7	Connecticut	18.6
16	Delaware	15.3
23	Florida	14.6
41	Georgia	12.6
40	Hawaii	12.9
38	Idaho	13.0
27	Illinois	14.3
19	Indiana	14.8
25	Iowa	14.4
33	Kansas	13.5
30	Kentucky	14.0
32	Louisiana	13.8
4	Maine	20.4
14	Maryland	15.7
3	Massachusetts	20.8
11	Michigan	16.3
8	Minnesota	17.3
45	Mississippi	12.1
18	Missouri	15.1
25	Montana	14.4
19	Nebraska	14.8
49	Nevada	8.6
9	New Hampshire	17.1
16	New Jersey	15.3
21	New Mexico	14.7
6	New York	19.8
30	North Carolina	14.0
21	North Dakota	14.7
10	Ohio	16.4
36	Oklahoma	13.1
28	Oregon	14.1
5	Pennsylvania	20.2
1	Rhode Island	21.9
48	South Carolina	11.4
13	South Dakota	15.9
28	Tennessee	14.1
35	Texas	13.3
38	Utah	13.0
2	Vermont	21.2
43	Virginia	12.4
36	Washington	13.1
12	West Virginia	16.1
15	Wisconsin	15.4
NA	Wyoming**	NA

RANK ORDER

RANK	STATE	PERCENT
1	Rhode Island	21.9
2	Vermont	21.2
3	Massachusetts	20.8
4	Maine	20.4
5	Pennsylvania	20.2
6	New York	19.8
7	Connecticut	18.6
8	Minnesota	17.3
9	New Hampshire	17.1
10	Ohio	16.4
11	Michigan	16.3
12	West Virginia	16.1
13	South Dakota	15.9
14	Maryland	15.7
15	Wisconsin	15.4
16	Delaware	15.3
16	New Jersey	15.3
18	Missouri	15.1
19	Indiana	14.8
19	Nebraska	14.8
21	New Mexico	14.7
21	North Dakota	14.7
23	Florida	14.6
24	Arkansas	14.5
25	Iowa	14.4
25	Montana	14.4
27	Illinois	14.3
28	Oregon	14.1
28	Tennessee	14.1
30	Kentucky	14.0
30	North Carolina	14.0
32	Louisiana	13.8
33	Arizona	13.5
33	Kansas	13.5
35	Texas	13.3
36	Oklahoma	13.1
36	Washington	13.1
38	Idaho	13.0
38	Utah	13.0
40	Hawaii	12.9
41	Georgia	12.6
42	California	12.5
43	Alaska	12.4
43	Virginia	12.4
45	Mississippi	12.1
46	Colorado	11.7
47	Alabama	11.6
48	South Carolina	11.4
49	Nevada	8.6
NA	Wyoming**	NA

District of Columbia   14.9

Source: CQ Press using data from U.S. Department of Labor, Bureau of Labor Statistics
"Regional and State Employment and Unemployment" (press release, January 22, 2010, www.bls.gov/bls/newsrels.htm)
*Seasonally adjusted preliminary data as of December 2009. National figure calculated through a different formula.
**The Bureau of Labor Statistics does not publish seasonally adjusted figures in this category for Wyoming.

Employees in Financial Activities in 2009

National Total = 7,695,000 Employees*

ALPHA ORDER

RANK	STATE	EMPLOYEES	% of USA
27	Alabama	94,000	1.2%
47	Alaska	14,600	0.2%
15	Arizona	165,800	2.2%
35	Arkansas	49,700	0.6%
1	California	798,700	10.4%
18	Colorado	145,400	1.9%
21	Connecticut	137,400	1.8%
36	Delaware	43,200	0.6%
4	Florida	496,300	6.4%
9	Georgia	205,900	2.7%
44	Hawaii	27,700	0.4%
41	Idaho	30,900	0.4%
5	Illinois	369,700	4.8%
23	Indiana	133,400	1.7%
24	Iowa	104,100	1.4%
31	Kansas	73,200	1.0%
29	Kentucky	87,400	1.1%
28	Louisiana	91,000	1.2%
40	Maine	31,400	0.4%
20	Maryland	137,600	1.8%
10	Massachusetts	205,200	2.7%
12	Michigan	187,800	2.4%
14	Minnesota	174,600	2.3%
NA	Mississippi**	NA	NA
16	Missouri	162,300	2.1%
45	Montana	22,100	0.3%
33	Nebraska	68,500	0.9%
34	Nevada	57,600	0.7%
37	New Hampshire	36,200	0.5%
8	New Jersey	249,700	3.2%
38	New Mexico	32,800	0.4%
2	New York	680,200	8.8%
11	North Carolina	200,300	2.6%
46	North Dakota	20,600	0.3%
7	Ohio	276,800	3.6%
30	Oklahoma	81,500	1.1%
26	Oregon	94,200	1.2%
6	Pennsylvania	311,800	4.1%
39	Rhode Island	32,600	0.4%
25	South Carolina	101,700	1.3%
42	South Dakota	30,100	0.4%
22	Tennessee	135,400	1.8%
3	Texas	649,900	8.4%
32	Utah	70,200	0.9%
48	Vermont	12,600	0.2%
13	Virginia	186,400	2.4%
19	Washington	143,800	1.9%
43	West Virginia	28,500	0.4%
17	Wisconsin	157,100	2.0%
49	Wyoming	11,100	0.1%

RANK ORDER

RANK	STATE	EMPLOYEES	% of USA
1	California	798,700	10.4%
2	New York	680,200	8.8%
3	Texas	649,900	8.4%
4	Florida	496,300	6.4%
5	Illinois	369,700	4.8%
6	Pennsylvania	311,800	4.1%
7	Ohio	276,800	3.6%
8	New Jersey	249,700	3.2%
9	Georgia	205,900	2.7%
10	Massachusetts	205,200	2.7%
11	North Carolina	200,300	2.6%
12	Michigan	187,800	2.4%
13	Virginia	186,400	2.4%
14	Minnesota	174,600	2.3%
15	Arizona	165,800	2.2%
16	Missouri	162,300	2.1%
17	Wisconsin	157,100	2.0%
18	Colorado	145,400	1.9%
19	Washington	143,800	1.9%
20	Maryland	137,600	1.8%
21	Connecticut	137,400	1.8%
22	Tennessee	135,400	1.8%
23	Indiana	133,400	1.7%
24	Iowa	104,100	1.4%
25	South Carolina	101,700	1.3%
26	Oregon	94,200	1.2%
27	Alabama	94,000	1.2%
28	Louisiana	91,000	1.2%
29	Kentucky	87,400	1.1%
30	Oklahoma	81,500	1.1%
31	Kansas	73,200	1.0%
32	Utah	70,200	0.9%
33	Nebraska	68,500	0.9%
34	Nevada	57,600	0.7%
35	Arkansas	49,700	0.6%
36	Delaware	43,200	0.6%
37	New Hampshire	36,200	0.5%
38	New Mexico	32,800	0.4%
39	Rhode Island	32,600	0.4%
40	Maine	31,400	0.4%
41	Idaho	30,900	0.4%
42	South Dakota	30,100	0.4%
43	West Virginia	28,500	0.4%
44	Hawaii	27,700	0.4%
45	Montana	22,100	0.3%
46	North Dakota	20,600	0.3%
47	Alaska	14,600	0.2%
48	Vermont	12,600	0.2%
49	Wyoming	11,100	0.1%
NA	Mississippi**	NA	NA
	District of Columbia	26,700	0.3%

Source: U.S. Department of Labor, Bureau of Labor Statistics

"Regional and State Employment and Unemployment" (press release, January 22, 2010, www.bls.gov/bls/newsrels.htm)

*Seasonally adjusted preliminary data as of December 2009. National total calculated through a different formula. Financial activities include insurance and real estate.

**The Bureau of Labor Statistics does not publish seasonally adjusted figures in this category for these states.

Percent of Nonfarm Employees in Financial Activities in 2009

National Percent = 5.9% of Employees*

ALPHA ORDER

RANK	STATE	PERCENT
36	Alabama	5.0
44	Alaska	4.5
8	Arizona	6.9
46	Arkansas	4.2
21	California	5.6
12	Colorado	6.5
2	Connecticut	8.5
1	Delaware	10.5
9	Florida	6.8
27	Georgia	5.4
43	Hawaii	4.7
36	Idaho	5.0
10	Illinois	6.6
41	Indiana	4.8
7	Iowa	7.1
24	Kansas	5.5
36	Kentucky	5.0
41	Louisiana	4.8
29	Maine	5.3
24	Maryland	5.5
12	Massachusetts	6.5
40	Michigan	4.9
10	Minnesota	6.6
NA	Mississippi**	NA
16	Missouri	6.0
31	Montana	5.1
5	Nebraska	7.3
36	Nevada	5.0
17	New Hampshire	5.8
14	New Jersey	6.4
47	New Mexico	4.0
3	New York	8.0
31	North Carolina	5.1
21	North Dakota	5.6
27	Ohio	5.4
30	Oklahoma	5.2
17	Oregon	5.8
21	Pennsylvania	5.6
6	Rhode Island	7.2
24	South Carolina	5.5
4	South Dakota	7.5
31	Tennessee	5.1
15	Texas	6.3
17	Utah	5.8
45	Vermont	4.3
31	Virginia	5.1
31	Washington	5.1
48	West Virginia	3.9
17	Wisconsin	5.8
48	Wyoming	3.9

RANK ORDER

RANK	STATE	PERCENT
1	Delaware	10.5
2	Connecticut	8.5
3	New York	8.0
4	South Dakota	7.5
5	Nebraska	7.3
6	Rhode Island	7.2
7	Iowa	7.1
8	Arizona	6.9
9	Florida	6.8
10	Illinois	6.6
10	Minnesota	6.6
12	Colorado	6.5
12	Massachusetts	6.5
14	New Jersey	6.4
15	Texas	6.3
16	Missouri	6.0
17	New Hampshire	5.8
17	Oregon	5.8
17	Utah	5.8
17	Wisconsin	5.8
21	California	5.6
21	North Dakota	5.6
21	Pennsylvania	5.6
24	Kansas	5.5
24	Maryland	5.5
24	South Carolina	5.5
27	Georgia	5.4
27	Ohio	5.4
29	Maine	5.3
30	Oklahoma	5.2
31	Montana	5.1
31	North Carolina	5.1
31	Tennessee	5.1
31	Virginia	5.1
31	Washington	5.1
36	Alabama	5.0
36	Idaho	5.0
36	Kentucky	5.0
36	Nevada	5.0
40	Michigan	4.9
41	Indiana	4.8
41	Louisiana	4.8
43	Hawaii	4.7
44	Alaska	4.5
45	Vermont	4.3
46	Arkansas	4.2
47	New Mexico	4.0
48	West Virginia	3.9
48	Wyoming	3.9
NA	Mississippi**	NA

District of Columbia 3.8

Source: CQ Press using data from U.S. Department of Labor, Bureau of Labor Statistics
"Regional and State Employment and Unemployment" (press release, January 22, 2010, www.bls.gov/bls/newsrels.htm)
*Seasonally adjusted preliminary data as of December 2009. National figure calculated through a different formula. Financial activities include insurance and real estate.
**The Bureau of Labor Statistics does not publish seasonally adjusted figures in this category for these states.

Employees in Government in 2009

National Total = 22,467,000 Employees*

ALPHA ORDER

RANK	STATE	EMPLOYEES	% of USA
23	Alabama	385,800	1.7%
44	Alaska	84,600	0.4%
21	Arizona	414,400	1.8%
33	Arkansas	221,100	1.0%
1	California	2,470,900	11.0%
22	Colorado	391,100	1.7%
32	Connecticut	246,400	1.1%
48	Delaware	62,500	0.3%
4	Florida	1,114,200	5.0%
10	Georgia	683,500	3.0%
39	Hawaii	123,800	0.6%
40	Idaho	117,900	0.5%
5	Illinois	854,600	3.8%
16	Indiana	439,100	2.0%
30	Iowa	252,600	1.1%
29	Kansas	262,000	1.2%
27	Kentucky	316,700	1.4%
24	Louisiana	366,400	1.6%
41	Maine	101,900	0.5%
14	Maryland	491,100	2.2%
17	Massachusetts	428,700	1.9%
12	Michigan	630,600	2.8%
20	Minnesota	415,000	1.8%
31	Mississippi	252,500	1.1%
15	Missouri	451,800	2.0%
43	Montana	89,000	0.4%
36	Nebraska	167,900	0.7%
37	Nevada	154,100	0.7%
42	New Hampshire	95,000	0.4%
11	New Jersey	650,400	2.9%
35	New Mexico	201,500	0.9%
3	New York	1,494,200	6.7%
8	North Carolina	734,800	3.3%
45	North Dakota	77,800	0.3%
6	Ohio	788,100	3.5%
26	Oklahoma	332,900	1.5%
28	Oregon	298,000	1.3%
7	Pennsylvania	753,600	3.4%
49	Rhode Island	61,000	0.3%
25	South Carolina	342,200	1.5%
46	South Dakota	76,600	0.3%
18	Tennessee	428,600	1.9%
2	Texas	1,867,900	8.3%
34	Utah	217,300	1.0%
50	Vermont	53,800	0.2%
9	Virginia	702,300	3.1%
13	Washington	548,800	2.4%
38	West Virginia	148,700	0.7%
19	Wisconsin	420,700	1.9%
47	Wyoming	71,600	0.3%

RANK ORDER

RANK	STATE	EMPLOYEES	% of USA
1	California	2,470,900	11.0%
2	Texas	1,867,900	8.3%
3	New York	1,494,200	6.7%
4	Florida	1,114,200	5.0%
5	Illinois	854,600	3.8%
6	Ohio	788,100	3.5%
7	Pennsylvania	753,600	3.4%
8	North Carolina	734,800	3.3%
9	Virginia	702,300	3.1%
10	Georgia	683,500	3.0%
11	New Jersey	650,400	2.9%
12	Michigan	630,600	2.8%
13	Washington	548,800	2.4%
14	Maryland	491,100	2.2%
15	Missouri	451,800	2.0%
16	Indiana	439,100	2.0%
17	Massachusetts	428,700	1.9%
18	Tennessee	428,600	1.9%
19	Wisconsin	420,700	1.9%
20	Minnesota	415,000	1.8%
21	Arizona	414,400	1.8%
22	Colorado	391,100	1.7%
23	Alabama	385,800	1.7%
24	Louisiana	366,400	1.6%
25	South Carolina	342,200	1.5%
26	Oklahoma	332,900	1.5%
27	Kentucky	316,700	1.4%
28	Oregon	298,000	1.3%
29	Kansas	262,000	1.2%
30	Iowa	252,600	1.1%
31	Mississippi	252,500	1.1%
32	Connecticut	246,400	1.1%
33	Arkansas	221,100	1.0%
34	Utah	217,300	1.0%
35	New Mexico	201,500	0.9%
36	Nebraska	167,900	0.7%
37	Nevada	154,100	0.7%
38	West Virginia	148,700	0.7%
39	Hawaii	123,800	0.6%
40	Idaho	117,900	0.5%
41	Maine	101,900	0.5%
42	New Hampshire	95,000	0.4%
43	Montana	89,000	0.4%
44	Alaska	84,600	0.4%
45	North Dakota	77,800	0.3%
46	South Dakota	76,600	0.3%
47	Wyoming	71,600	0.3%
48	Delaware	62,500	0.3%
49	Rhode Island	61,000	0.3%
50	Vermont	53,800	0.2%
	District of Columbia	243,100	1.1%

Source: U.S. Department of Labor, Bureau of Labor Statistics
   "Regional and State Employment and Unemployment" (press release, January 22, 2010, www.bls.gov/bls/newsrels.htm)
*Seasonally adjusted preliminary data as of December 2009. National total calculated through a different formula.

Percent of Nonfarm Employees in Government in 2009

National Percent = 17.2% of Employees*

ALPHA ORDER

RANK	STATE	PERCENT
9	Alabama	20.4
1	Alaska	26.4
32	Arizona	17.2
18	Arkansas	18.9
28	California	17.5
28	Colorado	17.5
42	Connecticut	15.3
42	Delaware	15.3
44	Florida	15.2
27	Georgia	17.8
7	Hawaii	21.1
14	Idaho	19.3
44	Illinois	15.2
38	Indiana	15.7
32	Iowa	17.2
11	Kansas	19.7
25	Kentucky	17.9
14	Louisiana	19.3
31	Maine	17.3
12	Maryland	19.5
47	Massachusetts	13.5
36	Michigan	16.5
38	Minnesota	15.7
4	Mississippi	22.9
34	Missouri	16.7
8	Montana	20.6
25	Nebraska	17.9
50	Nevada	13.3
46	New Hampshire	15.1
35	New Jersey	16.6
3	New Mexico	24.7
28	New York	17.5
19	North Carolina	18.7
6	North Dakota	21.2
40	Ohio	15.5
5	Oklahoma	21.4
21	Oregon	18.4
47	Pennsylvania	13.5
49	Rhode Island	13.4
20	South Carolina	18.5
17	South Dakota	19.1
37	Tennessee	16.3
24	Texas	18.0
23	Utah	18.1
21	Vermont	18.4
16	Virginia	19.2
13	Washington	19.4
10	West Virginia	20.1
40	Wisconsin	15.5
2	Wyoming	25.4

RANK ORDER

RANK	STATE	PERCENT
1	Alaska	26.4
2	Wyoming	25.4
3	New Mexico	24.7
4	Mississippi	22.9
5	Oklahoma	21.4
6	North Dakota	21.2
7	Hawaii	21.1
8	Montana	20.6
9	Alabama	20.4
10	West Virginia	20.1
11	Kansas	19.7
12	Maryland	19.5
13	Washington	19.4
14	Idaho	19.3
14	Louisiana	19.3
16	Virginia	19.2
17	South Dakota	19.1
18	Arkansas	18.9
19	North Carolina	18.7
20	South Carolina	18.5
21	Oregon	18.4
21	Vermont	18.4
23	Utah	18.1
24	Texas	18.0
25	Kentucky	17.9
25	Nebraska	17.9
27	Georgia	17.8
28	California	17.5
28	Colorado	17.5
28	New York	17.5
31	Maine	17.3
32	Arizona	17.2
32	Iowa	17.2
34	Missouri	16.7
35	New Jersey	16.6
36	Michigan	16.5
37	Tennessee	16.3
38	Indiana	15.7
38	Minnesota	15.7
40	Ohio	15.5
40	Wisconsin	15.5
42	Connecticut	15.3
42	Delaware	15.3
44	Florida	15.2
44	Illinois	15.2
46	New Hampshire	15.1
47	Massachusetts	13.5
47	Pennsylvania	13.5
49	Rhode Island	13.4
50	Nevada	13.3

District of Columbia	34.2

Source: CQ Press using data from U.S. Department of Labor, Bureau of Labor Statistics
   "Regional and State Employment and Unemployment" (press release, January 22, 2010, www.bls.gov/bls/newsrels.htm)
*Seasonally adjusted preliminary data as of December 2009. National figure calculated through a different formula.

Employees in Leisure and Hospitality in 2009

National Total = 13,096,000 Employees*

ALPHA ORDER

ALPHA ORDER

RANK	STATE	EMPLOYEES	% of USA
27	Alabama	167,400	1.3%
50	Alaska	30,100	0.2%
20	Arizona	256,400	2.0%
35	Arkansas	101,000	0.8%
1	California	1,501,400	11.5%
19	Colorado	261,700	2.0%
30	Connecticut	138,700	1.1%
46	Delaware	37,600	0.3%
3	Florida	910,000	6.9%
8	Georgia	386,300	2.9%
36	Hawaii	99,600	0.8%
40	Idaho	61,600	0.5%
5	Illinois	508,700	3.9%
16	Indiana	276,600	2.1%
31	Iowa	130,600	1.0%
33	Kansas	112,600	0.9%
26	Kentucky	169,000	1.3%
25	Louisiana	192,400	1.5%
43	Maine	57,500	0.4%
23	Maryland	228,500	1.7%
14	Massachusetts	297,600	2.3%
10	Michigan	378,600	2.9%
22	Minnesota	235,300	1.8%
32	Mississippi	119,100	0.9%
17	Missouri	270,400	2.1%
42	Montana	57,600	0.4%
38	Nebraska	80,200	0.6%
13	Nevada	301,200	2.3%
41	New Hampshire	61,000	0.5%
12	New Jersey	340,300	2.6%
37	New Mexico	86,700	0.7%
4	New York	702,500	5.4%
9	North Carolina	384,600	2.9%
47	North Dakota	34,100	0.3%
6	Ohio	494,100	3.8%
29	Oklahoma	140,700	1.1%
28	Oregon	161,400	1.2%
7	Pennsylvania	488,900	3.7%
44	Rhode Island	47,800	0.4%
24	South Carolina	199,200	1.5%
45	South Dakota	42,800	0.3%
18	Tennessee	270,300	2.1%
2	Texas	1,000,100	7.6%
34	Utah	104,900	0.8%
49	Vermont	31,400	0.2%
11	Virginia	342,800	2.6%
15	Washington	281,900	2.2%
39	West Virginia	70,700	0.5%
21	Wisconsin	241,000	1.8%
48	Wyoming	33,100	0.3%

RANK ORDER

RANK	STATE	EMPLOYEES	% of USA
1	California	1,501,400	11.5%
2	Texas	1,000,100	7.6%
3	Florida	910,000	6.9%
4	New York	702,500	5.4%
5	Illinois	508,700	3.9%
6	Ohio	494,100	3.8%
7	Pennsylvania	488,900	3.7%
8	Georgia	386,300	2.9%
9	North Carolina	384,600	2.9%
10	Michigan	378,600	2.9%
11	Virginia	342,800	2.6%
12	New Jersey	340,300	2.6%
13	Nevada	301,200	2.3%
14	Massachusetts	297,600	2.3%
15	Washington	281,900	2.2%
16	Indiana	276,600	2.1%
17	Missouri	270,400	2.1%
18	Tennessee	270,300	2.1%
19	Colorado	261,700	2.0%
20	Arizona	256,400	2.0%
21	Wisconsin	241,000	1.8%
22	Minnesota	235,300	1.8%
23	Maryland	228,500	1.7%
24	South Carolina	199,200	1.5%
25	Louisiana	192,400	1.5%
26	Kentucky	169,000	1.3%
27	Alabama	167,400	1.3%
28	Oregon	161,400	1.2%
29	Oklahoma	140,700	1.1%
30	Connecticut	138,700	1.1%
31	Iowa	130,600	1.0%
32	Mississippi	119,100	0.9%
33	Kansas	112,600	0.9%
34	Utah	104,900	0.8%
35	Arkansas	101,000	0.8%
36	Hawaii	99,600	0.8%
37	New Mexico	86,700	0.7%
38	Nebraska	80,200	0.6%
39	West Virginia	70,700	0.5%
40	Idaho	61,600	0.5%
41	New Hampshire	61,000	0.5%
42	Montana	57,600	0.4%
43	Maine	57,500	0.4%
44	Rhode Island	47,800	0.4%
45	South Dakota	42,800	0.3%
46	Delaware	37,600	0.3%
47	North Dakota	34,100	0.3%
48	Wyoming	33,100	0.3%
49	Vermont	31,400	0.2%
50	Alaska	30,100	0.2%
	District of Columbia	59,800	0.5%

Source: U.S. Department of Labor, Bureau of Labor Statistics

"Regional and State Employment and Unemployment" (press release, January 22, 2010, www.bls.gov/bls/newsrels.htm)
*Seasonally adjusted preliminary data as of December 2009. National total calculated through a different formula.

Percent of Nonfarm Employees in Leisure and Hospitality in 2009

National Percent = 10.0% of Employees*

ALPHA ORDER				RANK ORDER		
RANK	STATE	PERCENT		RANK	STATE	PERCENT
39	Alabama	8.9		1	Nevada	26.1
31	Alaska	9.4		2	Hawaii	17.0
11	Arizona	10.6		3	Montana	13.4
46	Arkansas	8.6		4	Florida	12.4
11	California	10.6		5	Colorado	11.7
5	Colorado	11.7		5	Wyoming	11.7
46	Connecticut	8.6		7	Mississippi	10.8
35	Delaware	9.2		7	South Carolina	10.8
4	Florida	12.4		9	South Dakota	10.7
16	Georgia	10.1		9	Vermont	10.7
2	Hawaii	17.0		11	Arizona	10.6
16	Idaho	10.1		11	California	10.6
36	Illinois	9.1		11	New Mexico	10.6
21	Indiana	9.9		14	Rhode Island	10.5
39	Iowa	8.9		15	Tennessee	10.3
48	Kansas	8.5		16	Georgia	10.1
29	Kentucky	9.6		16	Idaho	10.1
16	Louisiana	10.1		16	Louisiana	10.1
24	Maine	9.8		19	Missouri	10.0
36	Maryland	9.1		19	Oregon	10.0
31	Massachusetts	9.4		21	Indiana	9.9
21	Michigan	9.9		21	Michigan	9.9
39	Minnesota	8.9		21	Washington	9.9
7	Mississippi	10.8		24	Maine	9.8
19	Missouri	10.0		24	North Carolina	9.8
3	Montana	13.4		26	New Hampshire	9.7
48	Nebraska	8.5		26	Ohio	9.7
1	Nevada	26.1		26	Texas	9.7
26	New Hampshire	9.7		29	Kentucky	9.6
43	New Jersey	8.7		29	West Virginia	9.6
11	New Mexico	10.6		31	Alaska	9.4
50	New York	8.2		31	Massachusetts	9.4
24	North Carolina	9.8		31	Virginia	9.4
34	North Dakota	9.3		34	North Dakota	9.3
26	Ohio	9.7		35	Delaware	9.2
38	Oklahoma	9.0		36	Illinois	9.1
19	Oregon	10.0		36	Maryland	9.1
43	Pennsylvania	8.7		38	Oklahoma	9.0
14	Rhode Island	10.5		39	Alabama	8.9
7	South Carolina	10.8		39	Iowa	8.9
9	South Dakota	10.7		39	Minnesota	8.9
15	Tennessee	10.3		39	Wisconsin	8.9
26	Texas	9.7		43	New Jersey	8.7
43	Utah	8.7		43	Pennsylvania	8.7
9	Vermont	10.7		43	Utah	8.7
31	Virginia	9.4		46	Arkansas	8.6
21	Washington	9.9		46	Connecticut	8.6
29	West Virginia	9.6		48	Kansas	8.5
39	Wisconsin	8.9		48	Nebraska	8.5
5	Wyoming	11.7		50	New York	8.2
					District of Columbia	8.4

Source: CQ Press using data from U.S. Department of Labor, Bureau of Labor Statistics
"Regional and State Employment and Unemployment" (press release, January 22, 2010, www.bls.gov/bls/newsrels.htm)
*Seasonally adjusted preliminary data as of December 2009. National figure calculated through a different formula.

Employees in Manufacturing in 2009

National Total = 11,630,000 Employees*

ALPHA ORDER

RANK	STATE	EMPLOYEES	% of USA
NA	Alabama**	NA	NA
46	Alaska	12,800	0.1%
27	Arizona	159,300	1.4%
25	Arkansas	162,800	1.4%
1	California	1,278,200	11.0%
31	Colorado	127,800	1.1%
23	Connecticut	169,300	1.5%
NA	Delaware**	NA	NA
12	Florida	319,400	2.7%
11	Georgia	343,600	3.0%
NA	Hawaii**	NA	NA
36	Idaho	56,200	0.5%
4	Illinois	572,900	4.9%
8	Indiana	441,300	3.8%
22	Iowa	202,400	1.7%
26	Kansas	159,500	1.4%
21	Kentucky	208,800	1.8%
29	Louisiana	138,700	1.2%
37	Maine	52,200	0.4%
32	Maryland	123,400	1.1%
16	Massachusetts	266,900	2.3%
7	Michigan	452,900	3.9%
14	Minnesota	294,400	2.5%
28	Mississippi	145,500	1.3%
18	Missouri	260,100	2.2%
45	Montana	19,100	0.2%
34	Nebraska	91,500	0.8%
39	Nevada	43,300	0.4%
35	New Hampshire	65,700	0.6%
15	New Jersey	270,200	2.3%
42	New Mexico	30,400	0.3%
6	New York	482,500	4.1%
9	North Carolina	437,600	3.8%
44	North Dakota	23,700	0.2%
3	Ohio	614,500	5.3%
30	Oklahoma	133,500	1.1%
24	Oregon	164,800	1.4%
5	Pennsylvania	564,900	4.9%
40	Rhode Island	41,400	0.4%
20	South Carolina	212,700	1.8%
41	South Dakota	37,200	0.3%
13	Tennessee	316,500	2.7%
2	Texas	820,000	7.1%
33	Utah	111,300	1.0%
43	Vermont	29,200	0.3%
19	Virginia	235,700	2.0%
17	Washington	260,800	2.2%
38	West Virginia	49,700	0.4%
10	Wisconsin	436,800	3.8%
47	Wyoming	9,000	0.1%

RANK ORDER

RANK	STATE	EMPLOYEES	% of USA
1	California	1,278,200	11.0%
2	Texas	820,000	7.1%
3	Ohio	614,500	5.3%
4	Illinois	572,900	4.9%
5	Pennsylvania	564,900	4.9%
6	New York	482,500	4.1%
7	Michigan	452,900	3.9%
8	Indiana	441,300	3.8%
9	North Carolina	437,600	3.8%
10	Wisconsin	436,800	3.8%
11	Georgia	343,600	3.0%
12	Florida	319,400	2.7%
13	Tennessee	316,500	2.7%
14	Minnesota	294,400	2.5%
15	New Jersey	270,200	2.3%
16	Massachusetts	266,900	2.3%
17	Washington	260,800	2.2%
18	Missouri	260,100	2.2%
19	Virginia	235,700	2.0%
20	South Carolina	212,700	1.8%
21	Kentucky	208,800	1.8%
22	Iowa	202,400	1.7%
23	Connecticut	169,300	1.5%
24	Oregon	164,800	1.4%
25	Arkansas	162,800	1.4%
26	Kansas	159,500	1.4%
27	Arizona	159,300	1.4%
28	Mississippi	145,500	1.3%
29	Louisiana	138,700	1.2%
30	Oklahoma	133,500	1.1%
31	Colorado	127,800	1.1%
32	Maryland	123,400	1.1%
33	Utah	111,300	1.0%
34	Nebraska	91,500	0.8%
35	New Hampshire	65,700	0.6%
36	Idaho	56,200	0.5%
37	Maine	52,200	0.4%
38	West Virginia	49,700	0.4%
39	Nevada	43,300	0.4%
40	Rhode Island	41,400	0.4%
41	South Dakota	37,200	0.3%
42	New Mexico	30,400	0.3%
43	Vermont	29,200	0.3%
44	North Dakota	23,700	0.2%
45	Montana	19,100	0.2%
46	Alaska	12,800	0.1%
47	Wyoming	9,000	0.1%
NA	Alabama**	NA	NA
NA	Delaware**	NA	NA
NA	Hawaii**	NA	NA
	District of Columbia**	NA	NA

Source: U.S. Department of Labor, Bureau of Labor Statistics
  "Regional and State Employment and Unemployment" (press release, January 22, 2010, www.bls.gov/bls/newsrels.htm)
*Seasonally adjusted preliminary data as of December 2009. National total calculated through a different formula.
**The Bureau of Labor Statistics does not publish seasonally adjusted figures in this category for these states.

Percent of Nonfarm Employees in Manufacturing in 2009

National Percent = 8.9% of Employees*

ALPHA ORDER			RANK ORDER		
RANK	STATE	PERCENT	RANK	STATE	PERCENT
NA	Alabama**	NA	1	Wisconsin	16.1
44	Alaska	4.0	2	Indiana	15.8
36	Arizona	6.6	3	Arkansas	13.9
3	Arkansas	13.9	4	Iowa	13.8
27	California	9.0	5	Mississippi	13.2
39	Colorado	5.7	6	Ohio	12.1
14	Connecticut	10.5	7	Kansas	12.0
NA	Delaware**	NA	7	Tennessee	12.0
43	Florida	4.3	9	Kentucky	11.8
28	Georgia	8.9	9	Michigan	11.8
NA	Hawaii**	NA	11	South Carolina	11.5
24	Idaho	9.2	12	North Carolina	11.2
16	Illinois	10.2	13	Minnesota	11.1
2	Indiana	15.8	14	Connecticut	10.5
4	Iowa	13.8	15	New Hampshire	10.4
7	Kansas	12.0	16	Illinois	10.2
9	Kentucky	11.8	16	Oregon	10.2
33	Louisiana	7.3	18	Pennsylvania	10.1
28	Maine	8.9	19	Vermont	10.0
41	Maryland	4.9	20	Nebraska	9.8
31	Massachusetts	8.4	21	Missouri	9.6
9	Michigan	11.8	22	South Dakota	9.3
13	Minnesota	11.1	22	Utah	9.3
5	Mississippi	13.2	24	Idaho	9.2
21	Missouri	9.6	24	Washington	9.2
42	Montana	4.4	26	Rhode Island	9.1
20	Nebraska	9.8	27	California	9.0
45	Nevada	3.8	28	Georgia	8.9
15	New Hampshire	10.4	28	Maine	8.9
34	New Jersey	6.9	30	Oklahoma	8.6
46	New Mexico	3.7	31	Massachusetts	8.4
40	New York	5.6	32	Texas	7.9
12	North Carolina	11.2	33	Louisiana	7.3
37	North Dakota	6.4	34	New Jersey	6.9
6	Ohio	12.1	35	West Virginia	6.7
30	Oklahoma	8.6	36	Arizona	6.6
16	Oregon	10.2	37	North Dakota	6.4
18	Pennsylvania	10.1	37	Virginia	6.4
26	Rhode Island	9.1	39	Colorado	5.7
11	South Carolina	11.5	40	New York	5.6
22	South Dakota	9.3	41	Maryland	4.9
7	Tennessee	12.0	42	Montana	4.4
32	Texas	7.9	43	Florida	4.3
22	Utah	9.3	44	Alaska	4.0
19	Vermont	10.0	45	Nevada	3.8
37	Virginia	6.4	46	New Mexico	3.7
24	Washington	9.2	47	Wyoming	3.2
35	West Virginia	6.7	NA	Alabama**	NA
1	Wisconsin	16.1	NA	Delaware**	NA
47	Wyoming	3.2	NA	Hawaii**	NA
				District of Columbia**	NA

Source: CQ Press using data from U.S. Department of Labor, Bureau of Labor Statistics
   "Regional and State Employment and Unemployment" (press release, January 22, 2010, www.bls.gov/bls/newsrels.htm)
*Seasonally adjusted preliminary data as of December 2009. National figure calculated through a different formula.
**The Bureau of Labor Statistics does not publish seasonally adjusted figures in this category for these states.

Employees in Natural Resources and Mining in 2009

National Total = 705,000 Employees*

RANK	STATE	EMPLOYEES	% of USA
13	Alabama	12,500	1.8%
11	Alaska	15,100	2.1%
17	Arizona	11,100	1.6%
15	Arkansas	11,800	1.7%
5	California	26,800	3.8%
9	Colorado	23,200	3.3%
43	Connecticut	600	0.1%
NA	Delaware**	NA	NA
30	Florida	5,900	0.8%
21	Georgia	9,700	1.4%
NA	Hawaii**	NA	NA
35	Idaho	3,400	0.5%
20	Illinois	10,200	1.4%
26	Indiana	6,800	1.0%
38	Iowa	2,000	0.3%
19	Kansas	10,300	1.5%
6	Kentucky	26,000	3.7%
2	Louisiana	50,700	7.2%
37	Maine	2,400	0.3%
NA	Maryland**	NA	NA
40	Massachusetts	1,200	0.2%
25	Michigan	7,400	1.0%
33	Minnesota	4,800	0.7%
22	Mississippi	9,400	1.3%
32	Missouri	4,900	0.7%
23	Montana	8,300	1.2%
NA	Nebraska**	NA	NA
14	Nevada	11,900	1.7%
41	New Hampshire	900	0.1%
39	New Jersey	1,700	0.2%
10	New Mexico	18,600	2.6%
31	New York	5,700	0.8%
28	North Carolina	6,300	0.9%
24	North Dakota	8,000	1.1%
16	Ohio	11,400	1.6%
3	Oklahoma	44,000	6.2%
29	Oregon	6,200	0.9%
8	Pennsylvania	23,700	3.4%
44	Rhode Island	200	0.0%
34	South Carolina	4,200	0.6%
NA	South Dakota**	NA	NA
NA	Tennessee**	NA	NA
1	Texas	210,400	29.8%
12	Utah	13,300	1.9%
42	Vermont	800	0.1%
17	Virginia	11,100	1.6%
27	Washington	6,700	1.0%
4	West Virginia	27,000	3.8%
36	Wisconsin	2,800	0.4%
7	Wyoming	24,400	3.5%

RANK	STATE	EMPLOYEES	% of USA
1	Texas	210,400	29.8%
2	Louisiana	50,700	7.2%
3	Oklahoma	44,000	6.2%
4	West Virginia	27,000	3.8%
5	California	26,800	3.8%
6	Kentucky	26,000	3.7%
7	Wyoming	24,400	3.5%
8	Pennsylvania	23,700	3.4%
9	Colorado	23,200	3.3%
10	New Mexico	18,600	2.6%
11	Alaska	15,100	2.1%
12	Utah	13,300	1.9%
13	Alabama	12,500	1.8%
14	Nevada	11,900	1.7%
15	Arkansas	11,800	1.7%
16	Ohio	11,400	1.6%
17	Arizona	11,100	1.6%
17	Virginia	11,100	1.6%
19	Kansas	10,300	1.5%
20	Illinois	10,200	1.4%
21	Georgia	9,700	1.4%
22	Mississippi	9,400	1.3%
23	Montana	8,300	1.2%
24	North Dakota	8,000	1.1%
25	Michigan	7,400	1.0%
26	Indiana	6,800	1.0%
27	Washington	6,700	1.0%
28	North Carolina	6,300	0.9%
29	Oregon	6,200	0.9%
30	Florida	5,900	0.8%
31	New York	5,700	0.8%
32	Missouri	4,900	0.7%
33	Minnesota	4,800	0.7%
34	South Carolina	4,200	0.6%
35	Idaho	3,400	0.5%
36	Wisconsin	2,800	0.4%
37	Maine	2,400	0.3%
38	Iowa	2,000	0.3%
39	New Jersey	1,700	0.2%
40	Massachusetts	1,200	0.2%
41	New Hampshire	900	0.1%
42	Vermont	800	0.1%
43	Connecticut	600	0.1%
44	Rhode Island	200	0.0%
NA	Delaware**	NA	NA
NA	Hawaii**	NA	NA
NA	Maryland**	NA	NA
NA	Nebraska**	NA	NA
NA	South Dakota**	NA	NA
NA	Tennessee**	NA	NA
	District of Columbia**	NA	NA

Source: U.S. Department of Labor, Bureau of Labor Statistics

"Regional and State Employment and Unemployment" (press release, January 22, 2010, www.bls.gov/bls/newsrels.htm)

*Not seasonally adjusted preliminary data as of December 2009. National total calculated through a different formula.

**Natural resources and mining is combined with construction for these states.

Percent of Nonfarm Employees in Natural Resources and Mining in 2009

National Percent = 0.5% of Employees*

ALPHA ORDER

RANK	STATE	PERCENT
17	Alabama	0.7
2	Alaska	4.7
19	Arizona	0.5
12	Arkansas	1.0
26	California	0.2
12	Colorado	1.0
41	Connecticut	0.0
NA	Delaware**	NA
36	Florida	0.1
23	Georgia	0.3
NA	Hawaii**	NA
18	Idaho	0.6
26	Illinois	0.2
26	Indiana	0.2
36	Iowa	0.1
16	Kansas	0.8
10	Kentucky	1.5
5	Louisiana	2.7
20	Maine	0.4
NA	Maryland**	NA
41	Massachusetts	0.0
26	Michigan	0.2
26	Minnesota	0.2
15	Mississippi	0.9
26	Missouri	0.2
9	Montana	1.9
NA	Nebraska**	NA
12	Nevada	1.0
36	New Hampshire	0.1
41	New Jersey	0.0
6	New Mexico	2.3
36	New York	0.1
26	North Carolina	0.2
7	North Dakota	2.2
26	Ohio	0.2
4	Oklahoma	2.8
20	Oregon	0.4
20	Pennsylvania	0.4
41	Rhode Island	0.0
26	South Carolina	0.2
NA	South Dakota**	NA
NA	Tennessee**	NA
8	Texas	2.0
11	Utah	1.1
23	Vermont	0.3
23	Virginia	0.3
26	Washington	0.2
3	West Virginia	3.7
36	Wisconsin	0.1
1	Wyoming	8.6

RANK ORDER

RANK	STATE	PERCENT
1	Wyoming	8.6
2	Alaska	4.7
3	West Virginia	3.7
4	Oklahoma	2.8
5	Louisiana	2.7
6	New Mexico	2.3
7	North Dakota	2.2
8	Texas	2.0
9	Montana	1.9
10	Kentucky	1.5
11	Utah	1.1
12	Arkansas	1.0
12	Colorado	1.0
12	Nevada	1.0
15	Mississippi	0.9
16	Kansas	0.8
17	Alabama	0.7
18	Idaho	0.6
19	Arizona	0.5
20	Maine	0.4
20	Oregon	0.4
20	Pennsylvania	0.4
23	Georgia	0.3
23	Vermont	0.3
23	Virginia	0.3
26	California	0.2
26	Illinois	0.2
26	Indiana	0.2
26	Michigan	0.2
26	Minnesota	0.2
26	Missouri	0.2
26	North Carolina	0.2
26	Ohio	0.2
26	South Carolina	0.2
26	Washington	0.2
36	Florida	0.1
36	Iowa	0.1
36	New Hampshire	0.1
36	New York	0.1
36	Wisconsin	0.1
41	Connecticut	0.0
41	Massachusetts	0.0
41	New Jersey	0.0
41	Rhode Island	0.0
NA	Delaware**	NA
NA	Hawaii**	NA
NA	Maryland**	NA
NA	Nebraska**	NA
NA	South Dakota**	NA
NA	Tennessee**	NA
	District of Columbia**	NA

Source: CQ Press using data from U.S. Department of Labor, Bureau of Labor Statistics
  "Regional and State Employment and Unemployment" (press release, January 22, 2010, www.bls.gov/bls/newsrels.htm)
*Not seasonally adjusted preliminary data as of December 2009. National figure calculated through a different formula.
**Natural resources and mining is combined with construction for these states.

Employees in Professional and Business Services in 2009

National Total = 16,814,000 Employees*

ALPHA ORDER

RANK	STATE	EMPLOYEES	% of USA	RANK	STATE	EMPLOYEES	% of USA
24	Alabama	204,100	1.2%	1	California	2,122,400	12.6%
48	Alaska	25,500	0.2%	2	Texas	1,273,200	7.6%
15	Arizona	345,800	2.1%	3	New York	1,097,400	6.5%
33	Arkansas	115,200	0.7%	4	Florida	1,079,900	6.4%
1	California	2,122,400	12.6%	5	Illinois	790,900	4.7%
18	Colorado	324,400	1.9%	6	Pennsylvania	671,800	4.0%
26	Connecticut	185,500	1.1%	7	Virginia	638,400	3.8%
43	Delaware	54,400	0.3%	8	Ohio	625,100	3.7%
4	Florida	1,079,900	6.4%	9	New Jersey	579,900	3.4%
11	Georgia	510,700	3.0%	10	Michigan	514,600	3.1%
39	Hawaii	70,600	0.4%	11	Georgia	510,700	3.0%
38	Idaho	75,400	0.4%	12	North Carolina	469,800	2.8%
5	Illinois	790,900	4.7%	13	Massachusetts	464,800	2.8%
21	Indiana	271,700	1.6%	14	Maryland	406,000	2.4%
34	Iowa	114,700	0.7%	15	Arizona	345,800	2.1%
32	Kansas	132,000	0.8%	16	Washington	333,300	2.0%
27	Kentucky	185,400	1.1%	17	Missouri	330,300	2.0%
25	Louisiana	201,400	1.2%	18	Colorado	324,400	1.9%
42	Maine	54,700	0.3%	19	Tennessee	307,600	1.8%
14	Maryland	406,000	2.4%	20	Minnesota	307,300	1.8%
13	Massachusetts	464,800	2.8%	21	Indiana	271,700	1.6%
10	Michigan	514,600	3.1%	22	Wisconsin	252,100	1.5%
20	Minnesota	307,300	1.8%	23	South Carolina	223,700	1.3%
37	Mississippi	85,000	0.5%	24	Alabama	204,100	1.2%
17	Missouri	330,300	2.0%	25	Louisiana	201,400	1.2%
45	Montana	38,000	0.2%	26	Connecticut	185,500	1.1%
36	Nebraska	96,900	0.6%	27	Kentucky	185,400	1.1%
31	Nevada	138,900	0.8%	28	Oregon	181,500	1.1%
40	New Hampshire	69,100	0.4%	29	Oklahoma	174,800	1.0%
9	New Jersey	579,900	3.4%	30	Utah	154,400	0.9%
35	New Mexico	100,100	0.6%	31	Nevada	138,900	0.8%
3	New York	1,097,400	6.5%	32	Kansas	132,000	0.8%
12	North Carolina	469,800	2.8%	33	Arkansas	115,200	0.7%
46	North Dakota	29,600	0.2%	34	Iowa	114,700	0.7%
8	Ohio	625,100	3.7%	35	New Mexico	100,100	0.6%
29	Oklahoma	174,800	1.0%	36	Nebraska	96,900	0.6%
28	Oregon	181,500	1.1%	37	Mississippi	85,000	0.5%
6	Pennsylvania	671,800	4.0%	38	Idaho	75,400	0.4%
44	Rhode Island	50,600	0.3%	39	Hawaii	70,600	0.4%
23	South Carolina	223,700	1.3%	40	New Hampshire	69,100	0.4%
47	South Dakota	26,300	0.2%	41	West Virginia	60,300	0.4%
19	Tennessee	307,600	1.8%	42	Maine	54,700	0.3%
2	Texas	1,273,200	7.6%	43	Delaware	54,400	0.3%
30	Utah	154,400	0.9%	44	Rhode Island	50,600	0.3%
49	Vermont	20,400	0.1%	45	Montana	38,000	0.2%
7	Virginia	638,400	3.8%	46	North Dakota	29,600	0.2%
16	Washington	333,300	2.0%	47	South Dakota	26,300	0.2%
41	West Virginia	60,300	0.4%	48	Alaska	25,500	0.2%
22	Wisconsin	252,100	1.5%	49	Vermont	20,400	0.1%
50	Wyoming	17,000	0.1%	50	Wyoming	17,000	0.1%
					District of Columbia	152,600	0.9%

RANK ORDER

Source: U.S. Department of Labor, Bureau of Labor Statistics

"Regional and State Employment and Unemployment" (press release, January 22, 2010, www.bls.gov/bls/newsrels.htm)

*Seasonally adjusted preliminary data as of December 2009. National total calculated through a different formula.

Percent of Nonfarm Employees in Professional and Business Services in 2009

National Percent = 12.8% of Employees*

ALPHA ORDER

RANK	STATE	PERCENT
33	Alabama	10.8
45	Alaska	7.9
8	Arizona	14.3
38	Arkansas	9.8
3	California	15.0
7	Colorado	14.5
28	Connecticut	11.5
11	Delaware	13.3
5	Florida	14.7
11	Georgia	13.3
21	Hawaii	12.0
15	Idaho	12.3
9	Illinois	14.1
39	Indiana	9.7
46	Iowa	7.8
37	Kansas	9.9
35	Kentucky	10.5
34	Louisiana	10.6
40	Maine	9.3
2	Maryland	16.1
5	Massachusetts	14.7
10	Michigan	13.4
27	Minnesota	11.6
47	Mississippi	7.7
19	Missouri	12.2
42	Montana	8.8
36	Nebraska	10.3
21	Nevada	12.0
32	New Hampshire	11.0
4	New Jersey	14.8
15	New Mexico	12.3
14	New York	12.8
21	North Carolina	12.0
44	North Dakota	8.0
15	Ohio	12.3
29	Oklahoma	11.2
29	Oregon	11.2
21	Pennsylvania	12.0
29	Rhode Island	11.2
20	South Carolina	12.1
49	South Dakota	6.6
26	Tennessee	11.7
15	Texas	12.3
13	Utah	12.9
48	Vermont	7.0
1	Virginia	17.5
25	Washington	11.8
43	West Virginia	8.2
40	Wisconsin	9.3
50	Wyoming	6.0

RANK ORDER

RANK	STATE	PERCENT
1	Virginia	17.5
2	Maryland	16.1
3	California	15.0
4	New Jersey	14.8
5	Florida	14.7
5	Massachusetts	14.7
7	Colorado	14.5
8	Arizona	14.3
9	Illinois	14.1
10	Michigan	13.4
11	Delaware	13.3
11	Georgia	13.3
13	Utah	12.9
14	New York	12.8
15	Idaho	12.3
15	New Mexico	12.3
15	Ohio	12.3
15	Texas	12.3
19	Missouri	12.2
20	South Carolina	12.1
21	Hawaii	12.0
21	Nevada	12.0
21	North Carolina	12.0
21	Pennsylvania	12.0
25	Washington	11.8
26	Tennessee	11.7
27	Minnesota	11.6
28	Connecticut	11.5
29	Oklahoma	11.2
29	Oregon	11.2
29	Rhode Island	11.2
32	New Hampshire	11.0
33	Alabama	10.8
34	Louisiana	10.6
35	Kentucky	10.5
36	Nebraska	10.3
37	Kansas	9.9
38	Arkansas	9.8
39	Indiana	9.7
40	Maine	9.3
40	Wisconsin	9.3
42	Montana	8.8
43	West Virginia	8.2
44	North Dakota	8.0
45	Alaska	7.9
46	Iowa	7.8
47	Mississippi	7.7
48	Vermont	7.0
49	South Dakota	6.6
50	Wyoming	6.0

District of Columbia 21.5

Source: CQ Press using data from U.S. Department of Labor, Bureau of Labor Statistics
"Regional and State Employment and Unemployment" (press release, January 22, 2010, www.bls.gov/bls/newsrels.htm)
*Seasonally adjusted preliminary data as of December 2009. National figure calculated through a different formula.

Employees in Trade, Transportation and Public Utilities in 2009

National Total = 24,962,000 Employees*

ALPHA ORDER					RANK ORDER			
RANK	STATE	EMPLOYEES	% of USA		RANK	STATE	EMPLOYEES	% of USA
23	Alabama	371,000	1.5%		1	California	2,639,900	10.6%
48	Alaska	64,200	0.3%		2	Texas	2,035,000	8.2%
20	Arizona	471,000	1.9%		3	Florida	1,467,900	5.9%
33	Arkansas	228,800	0.9%		4	New York	1,460,000	5.8%
1	California	2,639,900	10.6%		5	Illinois	1,132,400	4.5%
22	Colorado	405,200	1.6%		6	Pennsylvania	1,077,100	4.3%
29	Connecticut	289,400	1.2%		7	Ohio	975,700	3.9%
46	Delaware	74,600	0.3%		8	New Jersey	830,100	3.3%
3	Florida	1,467,900	5.9%		9	Georgia	800,700	3.2%
9	Georgia	800,700	3.2%		10	North Carolina	720,300	2.9%
42	Hawaii	109,000	0.4%		11	Michigan	695,300	2.8%
40	Idaho	120,500	0.5%		12	Virginia	627,400	2.5%
5	Illinois	1,132,400	4.5%		13	Tennessee	560,900	2.2%
14	Indiana	547,900	2.2%		14	Indiana	547,900	2.2%
28	Iowa	300,100	1.2%		15	Massachusetts	533,800	2.1%
31	Kansas	252,600	1.0%		16	Washington	527,900	2.1%
25	Kentucky	357,900	1.4%		17	Missouri	523,100	2.1%
24	Louisiana	370,100	1.5%		18	Wisconsin	507,300	2.0%
41	Maine	115,200	0.5%		19	Minnesota	495,600	2.0%
21	Maryland	439,100	1.8%		20	Arizona	471,000	1.9%
15	Massachusetts	533,800	2.1%		21	Maryland	439,100	1.8%
11	Michigan	695,300	2.8%		22	Colorado	405,200	1.6%
19	Minnesota	495,600	2.0%		23	Alabama	371,000	1.5%
35	Mississippi	211,100	0.8%		24	Louisiana	370,100	1.5%
17	Missouri	523,100	2.1%		25	Kentucky	357,900	1.4%
43	Montana	88,300	0.4%		26	South Carolina	353,400	1.4%
36	Nebraska	196,200	0.8%		27	Oregon	314,500	1.3%
34	Nevada	220,100	0.9%		28	Iowa	300,100	1.2%
37	New Hampshire	138,600	0.6%		29	Connecticut	289,400	1.2%
8	New Jersey	830,100	3.3%		30	Oklahoma	283,600	1.1%
39	New Mexico	129,900	0.5%		31	Kansas	252,600	1.0%
4	New York	1,460,000	5.8%		32	Utah	237,400	1.0%
10	North Carolina	720,300	2.9%		33	Arkansas	228,800	0.9%
45	North Dakota	77,900	0.3%		34	Nevada	220,100	0.9%
7	Ohio	975,700	3.9%		35	Mississippi	211,100	0.8%
30	Oklahoma	283,600	1.1%		36	Nebraska	196,200	0.8%
27	Oregon	314,500	1.3%		37	New Hampshire	138,600	0.6%
6	Pennsylvania	1,077,100	4.3%		38	West Virginia	133,000	0.5%
47	Rhode Island	71,400	0.3%		39	New Mexico	129,900	0.5%
26	South Carolina	353,400	1.4%		40	Idaho	120,500	0.5%
44	South Dakota	81,000	0.3%		41	Maine	115,200	0.5%
13	Tennessee	560,900	2.2%		42	Hawaii	109,000	0.4%
2	Texas	2,035,000	8.2%		43	Montana	88,300	0.4%
32	Utah	237,400	1.0%		44	South Dakota	81,000	0.3%
49	Vermont	54,800	0.2%		45	North Dakota	77,900	0.3%
12	Virginia	627,400	2.5%		46	Delaware	74,600	0.3%
16	Washington	527,900	2.1%		47	Rhode Island	71,400	0.3%
38	West Virginia	133,000	0.5%		48	Alaska	64,200	0.3%
18	Wisconsin	507,300	2.0%		49	Vermont	54,800	0.2%
50	Wyoming	53,600	0.2%		50	Wyoming	53,600	0.2%
						District of Columbia	26,700	0.1%

Source: U.S. Department of Labor, Bureau of Labor Statistics

"Regional and State Employment and Unemployment" (press release, January 22, 2010, www.bls.gov/bls/newsrels.htm)
*Seasonally adjusted preliminary data as of December 2009. National total calculated through a different formula.

Percent of Nonfarm Employees in
Trade, Transportation and Public Utilities in 2009
National Percent = 19.1% of Employees*

ALPHA ORDER

RANK	STATE	PERCENT
17	Alabama	19.6
12	Alaska	20.0
20	Arizona	19.5
20	Arkansas	19.5
34	California	18.7
41	Colorado	18.1
44	Connecticut	17.9
39	Delaware	18.2
12	Florida	20.0
5	Georgia	20.9
36	Hawaii	18.6
15	Idaho	19.7
10	Illinois	20.2
17	Indiana	19.6
8	Iowa	20.4
30	Kansas	19.0
9	Kentucky	20.3
20	Louisiana	19.5
17	Maine	19.6
45	Maryland	17.4
48	Massachusetts	16.9
41	Michigan	18.1
32	Minnesota	18.8
25	Mississippi	19.2
24	Missouri	19.3
7	Montana	20.5
5	Nebraska	20.9
28	Nevada	19.1
1	New Hampshire	22.0
3	New Jersey	21.2
49	New Mexico	15.9
47	New York	17.1
38	North Carolina	18.4
3	North Dakota	21.2
25	Ohio	19.2
39	Oklahoma	18.2
23	Oregon	19.4
25	Pennsylvania	19.2
50	Rhode Island	15.7
28	South Carolina	19.1
10	South Dakota	20.2
2	Tennessee	21.3
15	Texas	19.7
14	Utah	19.8
32	Vermont	18.8
46	Virginia	17.2
36	Washington	18.6
43	West Virginia	18.0
34	Wisconsin	18.7
30	Wyoming	19.0

RANK ORDER

RANK	STATE	PERCENT
1	New Hampshire	22.0
2	Tennessee	21.3
3	New Jersey	21.2
3	North Dakota	21.2
5	Georgia	20.9
5	Nebraska	20.9
7	Montana	20.5
8	Iowa	20.4
9	Kentucky	20.3
10	Illinois	20.2
10	South Dakota	20.2
12	Alaska	20.0
12	Florida	20.0
14	Utah	19.8
15	Idaho	19.7
15	Texas	19.7
17	Alabama	19.6
17	Indiana	19.6
17	Maine	19.6
20	Arizona	19.5
20	Arkansas	19.5
20	Louisiana	19.5
23	Oregon	19.4
24	Missouri	19.3
25	Mississippi	19.2
25	Ohio	19.2
25	Pennsylvania	19.2
28	Nevada	19.1
28	South Carolina	19.1
30	Kansas	19.0
30	Wyoming	19.0
32	Minnesota	18.8
32	Vermont	18.8
34	California	18.7
34	Wisconsin	18.7
36	Hawaii	18.6
36	Washington	18.6
38	North Carolina	18.4
39	Delaware	18.2
39	Oklahoma	18.2
41	Colorado	18.1
41	Michigan	18.1
43	West Virginia	18.0
44	Connecticut	17.9
45	Maryland	17.4
46	Virginia	17.2
47	New York	17.1
48	Massachusetts	16.9
49	New Mexico	15.9
50	Rhode Island	15.7

District of Columbia 3.8

Source: CQ Press using data from U.S. Department of Labor, Bureau of Labor Statistics
"Regional and State Employment and Unemployment" (press release, January 22, 2010, www.bls.gov/bls/newsrels.htm)
*Seasonally adjusted preliminary data as of December 2009. National figure calculated through a different formula.

VII. Energy and Environment

Energy Consumption in 2007

National Total = 101,468,000,000,000,000 BTUs*

ALPHA ORDER

RANK	STATE	BTUs	% of USA
16	Alabama	2,132,000,000,000,000	2.1%
37	Alaska	723,600,000,000,000	0.7%
24	Arizona	1,577,800,000,000,000	1.6%
30	Arkansas	1,149,300,000,000,000	1.1%
2	California	8,491,500,000,000,000	8.4%
27	Colorado	1,479,300,000,000,000	1.5%
33	Connecticut	870,700,000,000,000	0.9%
47	Delaware	302,000,000,000,000	0.3%
3	Florida	4,601,900,000,000,000	4.5%
9	Georgia	3,133,000,000,000,000	3.1%
45	Hawaii	343,700,000,000,000	0.3%
40	Idaho	529,600,000,000,000	0.5%
6	Illinois	4,043,200,000,000,000	4.0%
11	Indiana	2,904,000,000,000,000	2.9%
29	Iowa	1,235,200,000,000,000	1.2%
31	Kansas	1,136,200,000,000,000	1.1%
18	Kentucky	2,023,000,000,000,000	2.0%
8	Louisiana	3,766,200,000,000,000	3.7%
43	Maine	455,600,000,000,000	0.4%
26	Maryland	1,488,700,000,000,000	1.5%
25	Massachusetts	1,514,600,000,000,000	1.5%
10	Michigan	3,026,900,000,000,000	3.0%
20	Minnesota	1,874,600,000,000,000	1.8%
28	Mississippi	1,239,500,000,000,000	1.2%
19	Missouri	1,964,100,000,000,000	1.9%
42	Montana	462,100,000,000,000	0.5%
39	Nebraska	692,900,000,000,000	0.7%
36	Nevada	777,400,000,000,000	0.8%
46	New Hampshire	314,200,000,000,000	0.3%
12	New Jersey	2,743,700,000,000,000	2.7%
38	New Mexico	710,700,000,000,000	0.7%
4	New York	4,064,300,000,000,000	4.0%
13	North Carolina	2,700,000,000,000,000	2.7%
44	North Dakota	428,100,000,000,000	0.4%
5	Ohio	4,048,900,000,000,000	4.0%
23	Oklahoma	1,608,500,000,000,000	1.6%
32	Oregon	1,108,200,000,000,000	1.1%
7	Pennsylvania	4,006,200,000,000,000	3.9%
49	Rhode Island	217,600,000,000,000	0.2%
22	South Carolina	1,692,300,000,000,000	1.7%
48	South Dakota	292,200,000,000,000	0.3%
15	Tennessee	2,330,500,000,000,000	2.3%
1	Texas	11,834,500,000,000,000	11.7%
35	Utah	805,500,000,000,000	0.8%
50	Vermont	162,100,000,000,000	0.2%
14	Virginia	2,610,900,000,000,000	2.6%
17	Washington	2,067,200,000,000,000	2.0%
34	West Virginia	850,500,000,000,000	0.8%
21	Wisconsin	1,846,300,000,000,000	1.8%
41	Wyoming	496,400,000,000,000	0.5%

RANK ORDER

RANK	STATE	BTUs	% of USA
1	Texas	11,834,500,000,000,000	11.7%
2	California	8,491,500,000,000,000	8.4%
3	Florida	4,601,900,000,000,000	4.5%
4	New York	4,064,300,000,000,000	4.0%
5	Ohio	4,048,900,000,000,000	4.0%
6	Illinois	4,043,200,000,000,000	4.0%
7	Pennsylvania	4,006,200,000,000,000	3.9%
8	Louisiana	3,766,200,000,000,000	3.7%
9	Georgia	3,133,000,000,000,000	3.1%
10	Michigan	3,026,900,000,000,000	3.0%
11	Indiana	2,904,000,000,000,000	2.9%
12	New Jersey	2,743,700,000,000,000	2.7%
13	North Carolina	2,700,000,000,000,000	2.7%
14	Virginia	2,610,900,000,000,000	2.6%
15	Tennessee	2,330,500,000,000,000	2.3%
16	Alabama	2,132,000,000,000,000	2.1%
17	Washington	2,067,200,000,000,000	2.0%
18	Kentucky	2,023,000,000,000,000	2.0%
19	Missouri	1,964,100,000,000,000	1.9%
20	Minnesota	1,874,600,000,000,000	1.8%
21	Wisconsin	1,846,300,000,000,000	1.8%
22	South Carolina	1,692,300,000,000,000	1.7%
23	Oklahoma	1,608,500,000,000,000	1.6%
24	Arizona	1,577,800,000,000,000	1.6%
25	Massachusetts	1,514,600,000,000,000	1.5%
26	Maryland	1,488,700,000,000,000	1.5%
27	Colorado	1,479,300,000,000,000	1.5%
28	Mississippi	1,239,500,000,000,000	1.2%
29	Iowa	1,235,200,000,000,000	1.2%
30	Arkansas	1,149,300,000,000,000	1.1%
31	Kansas	1,136,200,000,000,000	1.1%
32	Oregon	1,108,200,000,000,000	1.1%
33	Connecticut	870,700,000,000,000	0.9%
34	West Virginia	850,500,000,000,000	0.8%
35	Utah	805,500,000,000,000	0.8%
36	Nevada	777,400,000,000,000	0.8%
37	Alaska	723,600,000,000,000	0.7%
38	New Mexico	710,700,000,000,000	0.7%
39	Nebraska	692,900,000,000,000	0.7%
40	Idaho	529,600,000,000,000	0.5%
41	Wyoming	496,400,000,000,000	0.5%
42	Montana	462,100,000,000,000	0.5%
43	Maine	455,600,000,000,000	0.4%
44	North Dakota	428,100,000,000,000	0.4%
45	Hawaii	343,700,000,000,000	0.3%
46	New Hampshire	314,200,000,000,000	0.3%
47	Delaware	302,000,000,000,000	0.3%
48	South Dakota	292,200,000,000,000	0.3%
49	Rhode Island	217,600,000,000,000	0.2%
50	Vermont	162,100,000,000,000	0.2%
	District of Columbia	187,200,000,000,000	0.2%

Source: U.S. Department of Energy, Energy Information Administration
   "State Energy Data 2007: Consumption" (http://www.eia.doe.gov/emeu/states/_seds.html)
*British Thermal Units: The amount of heat required to raise the temperature of one pound of water one degree. National total
includes 25.2 trillion Btu of net imports of coal coke that are not allocated to the states.

Per Capita Energy Consumption in 2007

National Per Capita = 336,454,789 BTUs*

<table>
<tr><td colspan="3">ALPHA ORDER</td><td colspan="3">RANK ORDER</td></tr>
<tr><td>RANK</td><td>STATE</td><td>BTUs</td><td>RANK</td><td>STATE</td><td>BTUs</td></tr>
<tr><td>9</td><td>Alabama</td><td>459,690,412</td><td>1</td><td>Alaska</td><td>1,060,535,221</td></tr>
<tr><td>1</td><td>Alaska</td><td>1,060,535,221</td><td>2</td><td>Wyoming</td><td>948,388,847</td></tr>
<tr><td>45</td><td>Arizona</td><td>247,994,378</td><td>3</td><td>Louisiana</td><td>860,625,001</td></tr>
<tr><td>15</td><td>Arkansas</td><td>404,370,708</td><td>4</td><td>North Dakota</td><td>670,790,753</td></tr>
<tr><td>47</td><td>California</td><td>234,402,678</td><td>5</td><td>Texas</td><td>496,461,467</td></tr>
<tr><td>34</td><td>Colorado</td><td>305,497,909</td><td>6</td><td>Montana</td><td>482,749,615</td></tr>
<tr><td>44</td><td>Connecticut</td><td>249,582,000</td><td>7</td><td>Kentucky</td><td>475,297,901</td></tr>
<tr><td>24</td><td>Delaware</td><td>349,174,930</td><td>8</td><td>West Virginia</td><td>469,578,699</td></tr>
<tr><td>43</td><td>Florida</td><td>251,774,166</td><td>9</td><td>Alabama</td><td>459,690,412</td></tr>
<tr><td>29</td><td>Georgia</td><td>328,621,622</td><td>10</td><td>Indiana</td><td>457,602,945</td></tr>
<tr><td>40</td><td>Hawaii</td><td>269,181,850</td><td>11</td><td>Oklahoma</td><td>445,298,221</td></tr>
<tr><td>22</td><td>Idaho</td><td>353,244,466</td><td>12</td><td>Mississippi</td><td>424,235,973</td></tr>
<tr><td>33</td><td>Illinois</td><td>316,383,760</td><td>13</td><td>Iowa</td><td>414,674,899</td></tr>
<tr><td>10</td><td>Indiana</td><td>457,602,945</td><td>14</td><td>Kansas</td><td>409,354,997</td></tr>
<tr><td>13</td><td>Iowa</td><td>414,674,899</td><td>15</td><td>Arkansas</td><td>404,370,708</td></tr>
<tr><td>14</td><td>Kansas</td><td>409,354,997</td><td>16</td><td>Nebraska</td><td>391,488,390</td></tr>
<tr><td>7</td><td>Kentucky</td><td>475,297,901</td><td>17</td><td>South Carolina</td><td>382,507,066</td></tr>
<tr><td>3</td><td>Louisiana</td><td>860,625,001</td><td>18</td><td>Tennessee</td><td>377,539,624</td></tr>
<tr><td>25</td><td>Maine</td><td>345,856,854</td><td>19</td><td>South Dakota</td><td>366,608,744</td></tr>
<tr><td>41</td><td>Maryland</td><td>264,223,652</td><td>20</td><td>Minnesota</td><td>361,110,694</td></tr>
<tr><td>48</td><td>Massachusetts</td><td>233,041,378</td><td>21</td><td>New Mexico</td><td>360,993,960</td></tr>
<tr><td>37</td><td>Michigan</td><td>301,158,698</td><td>22</td><td>Idaho</td><td>353,244,466</td></tr>
<tr><td>20</td><td>Minnesota</td><td>361,110,694</td><td>23</td><td>Ohio</td><td>351,442,151</td></tr>
<tr><td>12</td><td>Mississippi</td><td>424,235,973</td><td>24</td><td>Delaware</td><td>349,174,930</td></tr>
<tr><td>27</td><td>Missouri</td><td>332,344,923</td><td>25</td><td>Maine</td><td>345,856,854</td></tr>
<tr><td>6</td><td>Montana</td><td>482,749,615</td><td>26</td><td>Virginia</td><td>338,210,478</td></tr>
<tr><td>16</td><td>Nebraska</td><td>391,488,390</td><td>27</td><td>Missouri</td><td>332,344,923</td></tr>
<tr><td>35</td><td>Nevada</td><td>302,755,095</td><td>28</td><td>Wisconsin</td><td>329,603,963</td></tr>
<tr><td>46</td><td>New Hampshire</td><td>238,510,396</td><td>29</td><td>Georgia</td><td>328,621,622</td></tr>
<tr><td>32</td><td>New Jersey</td><td>317,703,374</td><td>30</td><td>Pennsylvania</td><td>319,919,352</td></tr>
<tr><td>21</td><td>New Mexico</td><td>360,993,960</td><td>31</td><td>Washington</td><td>319,753,552</td></tr>
<tr><td>49</td><td>New York</td><td>209,254,320</td><td>32</td><td>New Jersey</td><td>317,703,374</td></tr>
<tr><td>38</td><td>North Carolina</td><td>297,879,298</td><td>33</td><td>Illinois</td><td>316,383,760</td></tr>
<tr><td>4</td><td>North Dakota</td><td>670,790,753</td><td>34</td><td>Colorado</td><td>305,497,909</td></tr>
<tr><td>23</td><td>Ohio</td><td>351,442,151</td><td>35</td><td>Nevada</td><td>302,755,095</td></tr>
<tr><td>11</td><td>Oklahoma</td><td>445,298,221</td><td>36</td><td>Utah</td><td>302,388,021</td></tr>
<tr><td>39</td><td>Oregon</td><td>296,869,211</td><td>37</td><td>Michigan</td><td>301,158,698</td></tr>
<tr><td>30</td><td>Pennsylvania</td><td>319,919,352</td><td>38</td><td>North Carolina</td><td>297,879,298</td></tr>
<tr><td>50</td><td>Rhode Island</td><td>206,254,165</td><td>39</td><td>Oregon</td><td>296,869,211</td></tr>
<tr><td>17</td><td>South Carolina</td><td>382,507,066</td><td>40</td><td>Hawaii</td><td>269,181,850</td></tr>
<tr><td>19</td><td>South Dakota</td><td>366,608,744</td><td>41</td><td>Maryland</td><td>264,223,652</td></tr>
<tr><td>18</td><td>Tennessee</td><td>377,539,624</td><td>42</td><td>Vermont</td><td>261,257,776</td></tr>
<tr><td>5</td><td>Texas</td><td>496,461,467</td><td>43</td><td>Florida</td><td>251,774,166</td></tr>
<tr><td>36</td><td>Utah</td><td>302,388,021</td><td>44</td><td>Connecticut</td><td>249,582,000</td></tr>
<tr><td>42</td><td>Vermont</td><td>261,257,776</td><td>45</td><td>Arizona</td><td>247,994,378</td></tr>
<tr><td>26</td><td>Virginia</td><td>338,210,478</td><td>46</td><td>New Hampshire</td><td>238,510,396</td></tr>
<tr><td>31</td><td>Washington</td><td>319,753,552</td><td>47</td><td>California</td><td>234,402,678</td></tr>
<tr><td>8</td><td>West Virginia</td><td>469,578,699</td><td>48</td><td>Massachusetts</td><td>233,041,378</td></tr>
<tr><td>28</td><td>Wisconsin</td><td>329,603,963</td><td>49</td><td>New York</td><td>209,254,320</td></tr>
<tr><td>2</td><td>Wyoming</td><td>948,388,847</td><td>50</td><td>Rhode Island</td><td>206,254,165</td></tr>
<tr><td></td><td></td><td></td><td></td><td>District of Columbia</td><td>319,231,117</td></tr>
</table>

Source: CQ Press using data from U.S. Department of Energy, Energy Information Administration
  "State Energy Data 2007: Consumption" (http://www.eia.doe.gov/emeu/states/_seds.html)
*British Thermal Units: The amount of heat required to raise the temperature of one pound of water one degree. National figure includes 25.2 trillion Btu of net imports of coal coke that are not allocated to the states.

Energy Prices in 2007

National Rate = $18.23 per Million BTUs*

ALPHA ORDER

RANK	STATE	RATE
43	Alabama	$16.01
20	Alaska	17.87
12	Arizona	20.72
40	Arkansas	16.66
13	California	20.12
36	Colorado	17.00
2	Connecticut	24.93
11	Delaware	20.82
9	Florida	21.47
34	Georgia	17.10
1	Hawaii	25.20
45	Idaho	15.92
29	Illinois	17.27
48	Indiana	14.41
42	Iowa	16.12
31	Kansas	17.23
44	Kentucky	15.99
49	Louisiana	14.19
15	Maine	19.17
8	Maryland	21.60
3	Massachusetts	23.89
28	Michigan	17.37
36	Minnesota	17.00
33	Mississippi	17.16
22	Missouri	17.73
30	Montana	17.26
39	Nebraska	16.72
10	Nevada	21.12
4	New Hampshire	23.25
14	New Jersey	19.55
17	New Mexico	19.05
7	New York	21.78
15	North Carolina	19.17
50	North Dakota	13.22
23	Ohio	17.71
38	Oklahoma	16.76
19	Oregon	18.23
18	Pennsylvania	18.30
6	Rhode Island	22.72
35	South Carolina	17.04
27	South Dakota	17.45
32	Tennessee	17.19
25	Texas	17.60
41	Utah	16.44
5	Vermont	22.90
26	Virginia	17.58
24	Washington	17.63
46	West Virginia	15.28
21	Wisconsin	17.84
47	Wyoming	14.81

RANK ORDER

RANK	STATE	RATE
1	Hawaii	$25.20
2	Connecticut	24.93
3	Massachusetts	23.89
4	New Hampshire	23.25
5	Vermont	22.90
6	Rhode Island	22.72
7	New York	21.78
8	Maryland	21.60
9	Florida	21.47
10	Nevada	21.12
11	Delaware	20.82
12	Arizona	20.72
13	California	20.12
14	New Jersey	19.55
15	Maine	19.17
15	North Carolina	19.17
17	New Mexico	19.05
18	Pennsylvania	18.30
19	Oregon	18.23
20	Alaska	17.87
21	Wisconsin	17.84
22	Missouri	17.73
23	Ohio	17.71
24	Washington	17.63
25	Texas	17.60
26	Virginia	17.58
27	South Dakota	17.45
28	Michigan	17.37
29	Illinois	17.27
30	Montana	17.26
31	Kansas	17.23
32	Tennessee	17.19
33	Mississippi	17.16
34	Georgia	17.10
35	South Carolina	17.04
36	Colorado	17.00
36	Minnesota	17.00
38	Oklahoma	16.76
39	Nebraska	16.72
40	Arkansas	16.66
41	Utah	16.44
42	Iowa	16.12
43	Alabama	16.01
44	Kentucky	15.99
45	Idaho	15.92
46	West Virginia	15.28
47	Wyoming	14.81
48	Indiana	14.41
49	Louisiana	14.19
50	North Dakota	13.22

District of Columbia   24.68

Source: U.S. Department of Energy, Energy Information Administration
   "State Energy Data 2007: Prices and Expenditures" (http://www.eia.doe.gov/emeu/states/_seds.html)
*British Thermal Units: The amount of heat required to raise the temperature of one pound of water one degree.

Energy Expenditures in 2007

National Total = $1,233,058,500,000*

RANK	STATE	EXPENDITURES	% of USA
21	Alabama	$21,606,400,000	1.8%
40	Alaska	6,260,200,000	0.5%
24	Arizona	20,198,400,000	1.6%
33	Arkansas	12,533,300,000	1.0%
2	California	121,829,300,000	9.9%
26	Colorado	17,032,900,000	1.4%
28	Connecticut	15,145,900,000	1.2%
47	Delaware	3,848,900,000	0.3%
4	Florida	60,746,600,000	4.9%
10	Georgia	35,677,700,000	2.9%
41	Hawaii	6,173,500,000	0.5%
42	Idaho	5,417,700,000	0.4%
6	Illinois	48,296,900,000	3.9%
14	Indiana	28,627,100,000	2.3%
29	Iowa	14,333,700,000	1.2%
32	Kansas	12,802,800,000	1.0%
23	Kentucky	20,316,300,000	1.6%
11	Louisiana	33,623,600,000	2.7%
39	Maine	6,695,700,000	0.5%
22	Maryland	21,489,700,000	1.7%
15	Massachusetts	25,861,900,000	2.1%
9	Michigan	36,882,200,000	3.0%
20	Minnesota	21,708,200,000	1.8%
30	Mississippi	13,391,600,000	1.1%
17	Missouri	23,341,800,000	1.9%
44	Montana	5,265,100,000	0.4%
38	Nebraska	7,876,600,000	0.6%
34	Nevada	10,570,700,000	0.9%
43	New Hampshire	5,334,600,000	0.4%
8	New Jersey	39,609,000,000	3.2%
37	New Mexico	7,876,900,000	0.6%
3	New York	63,642,000,000	5.2%
12	North Carolina	32,574,200,000	2.6%
46	North Dakota	4,109,700,000	0.3%
7	Ohio	48,190,300,000	3.9%
27	Oklahoma	17,027,100,000	1.4%
31	Oregon	13,175,300,000	1.1%
5	Pennsylvania	49,300,600,000	4.0%
49	Rhode Island	3,566,700,000	0.3%
25	South Carolina	18,130,400,000	1.5%
48	South Dakota	3,585,200,000	0.3%
16	Tennessee	25,462,400,000	2.1%
1	Texas	140,651,200,000	11.4%
35	Utah	8,739,000,000	0.7%
50	Vermont	2,687,100,000	0.2%
13	Virginia	30,509,300,000	2.5%
18	Washington	23,224,300,000	1.9%
36	West Virginia	8,369,100,000	0.7%
19	Wisconsin	22,454,500,000	1.8%
45	Wyoming	4,545,700,000	0.4%

RANK	STATE	EXPENDITURES	% of USA
1	Texas	$140,651,200,000	11.4%
2	California	121,829,300,000	9.9%
3	New York	63,642,000,000	5.2%
4	Florida	60,746,600,000	4.9%
5	Pennsylvania	49,300,600,000	4.0%
6	Illinois	48,296,900,000	3.9%
7	Ohio	48,190,300,000	3.9%
8	New Jersey	39,609,000,000	3.2%
9	Michigan	36,882,200,000	3.0%
10	Georgia	35,677,700,000	2.9%
11	Louisiana	33,623,600,000	2.7%
12	North Carolina	32,574,200,000	2.6%
13	Virginia	30,509,300,000	2.5%
14	Indiana	28,627,100,000	2.3%
15	Massachusetts	25,861,900,000	2.1%
16	Tennessee	25,462,400,000	2.1%
17	Missouri	23,341,800,000	1.9%
18	Washington	23,224,300,000	1.9%
19	Wisconsin	22,454,500,000	1.8%
20	Minnesota	21,708,200,000	1.8%
21	Alabama	21,606,400,000	1.8%
22	Maryland	21,489,700,000	1.7%
23	Kentucky	20,316,300,000	1.6%
24	Arizona	20,198,400,000	1.6%
25	South Carolina	18,130,400,000	1.5%
26	Colorado	17,032,900,000	1.4%
27	Oklahoma	17,027,100,000	1.4%
28	Connecticut	15,145,900,000	1.2%
29	Iowa	14,333,700,000	1.2%
30	Mississippi	13,391,600,000	1.1%
31	Oregon	13,175,300,000	1.1%
32	Kansas	12,802,800,000	1.0%
33	Arkansas	12,533,300,000	1.0%
34	Nevada	10,570,700,000	0.9%
35	Utah	8,739,000,000	0.7%
36	West Virginia	8,369,100,000	0.7%
37	New Mexico	7,876,900,000	0.6%
38	Nebraska	7,876,600,000	0.6%
39	Maine	6,695,700,000	0.5%
40	Alaska	6,260,200,000	0.5%
41	Hawaii	6,173,500,000	0.5%
42	Idaho	5,417,700,000	0.4%
43	New Hampshire	5,334,600,000	0.4%
44	Montana	5,265,100,000	0.4%
45	Wyoming	4,545,700,000	0.4%
46	North Dakota	4,109,700,000	0.3%
47	Delaware	3,848,900,000	0.3%
48	South Dakota	3,585,200,000	0.3%
49	Rhode Island	3,566,700,000	0.3%
50	Vermont	2,687,100,000	0.2%
	District of Columbia	2,391,900,000	0.2%

Source: U.S. Department of Energy, Energy Information Administration
   "State Energy Data 2007: Prices and Expenditures" (http://www.eia.doe.gov/emeu/states/_seds.html)
*The national total includes $347.3 million for coal coke net imports, which are not allocated to the states.

Per Capita Energy Expenditures in 2007

National Per Capita = $4,089

<table>
<tr><td colspan="3">ALPHA ORDER</td><td colspan="3">RANK ORDER</td></tr>
<tr><th>RANK</th><th>STATE</th><th>PER CAPITA</th><th>RANK</th><th>STATE</th><th>PER CAPITA</th></tr>
<tr><td>12</td><td>Alabama</td><td>$4,659</td><td>1</td><td>Alaska</td><td>$9,175</td></tr>
<tr><td>1</td><td>Alaska</td><td>9,175</td><td>2</td><td>Wyoming</td><td>8,685</td></tr>
<tr><td>50</td><td>Arizona</td><td>3,175</td><td>3</td><td>Louisiana</td><td>7,683</td></tr>
<tr><td>21</td><td>Arkansas</td><td>4,410</td><td>4</td><td>North Dakota</td><td>6,439</td></tr>
<tr><td>46</td><td>California</td><td>3,363</td><td>5</td><td>Texas</td><td>5,900</td></tr>
<tr><td>44</td><td>Colorado</td><td>3,518</td><td>6</td><td>Montana</td><td>5,500</td></tr>
<tr><td>22</td><td>Connecticut</td><td>4,341</td><td>7</td><td>Maine</td><td>5,083</td></tr>
<tr><td>19</td><td>Delaware</td><td>4,450</td><td>8</td><td>Hawaii</td><td>4,835</td></tr>
<tr><td>47</td><td>Florida</td><td>3,324</td><td>9</td><td>Iowa</td><td>4,812</td></tr>
<tr><td>38</td><td>Georgia</td><td>3,742</td><td>10</td><td>Kentucky</td><td>4,773</td></tr>
<tr><td>8</td><td>Hawaii</td><td>4,835</td><td>11</td><td>Oklahoma</td><td>4,714</td></tr>
<tr><td>40</td><td>Idaho</td><td>3,614</td><td>12</td><td>Alabama</td><td>4,659</td></tr>
<tr><td>37</td><td>Illinois</td><td>3,779</td><td>13</td><td>West Virginia</td><td>4,621</td></tr>
<tr><td>17</td><td>Indiana</td><td>4,511</td><td>14</td><td>Kansas</td><td>4,613</td></tr>
<tr><td>9</td><td>Iowa</td><td>4,812</td><td>15</td><td>New Jersey</td><td>4,586</td></tr>
<tr><td>14</td><td>Kansas</td><td>4,613</td><td>16</td><td>Mississippi</td><td>4,583</td></tr>
<tr><td>10</td><td>Kentucky</td><td>4,773</td><td>17</td><td>Indiana</td><td>4,511</td></tr>
<tr><td>3</td><td>Louisiana</td><td>7,683</td><td>18</td><td>South Dakota</td><td>4,498</td></tr>
<tr><td>7</td><td>Maine</td><td>5,083</td><td>19</td><td>Delaware</td><td>4,450</td></tr>
<tr><td>36</td><td>Maryland</td><td>3,814</td><td>19</td><td>Nebraska</td><td>4,450</td></tr>
<tr><td>32</td><td>Massachusetts</td><td>3,979</td><td>21</td><td>Arkansas</td><td>4,410</td></tr>
<tr><td>39</td><td>Michigan</td><td>3,670</td><td>22</td><td>Connecticut</td><td>4,341</td></tr>
<tr><td>25</td><td>Minnesota</td><td>4,182</td><td>23</td><td>Vermont</td><td>4,331</td></tr>
<tr><td>16</td><td>Mississippi</td><td>4,583</td><td>24</td><td>Ohio</td><td>4,183</td></tr>
<tr><td>34</td><td>Missouri</td><td>3,950</td><td>25</td><td>Minnesota</td><td>4,182</td></tr>
<tr><td>6</td><td>Montana</td><td>5,500</td><td>26</td><td>Tennessee</td><td>4,125</td></tr>
<tr><td>19</td><td>Nebraska</td><td>4,450</td><td>27</td><td>Nevada</td><td>4,117</td></tr>
<tr><td>27</td><td>Nevada</td><td>4,117</td><td>28</td><td>South Carolina</td><td>4,098</td></tr>
<tr><td>29</td><td>New Hampshire</td><td>4,050</td><td>29</td><td>New Hampshire</td><td>4,050</td></tr>
<tr><td>15</td><td>New Jersey</td><td>4,586</td><td>30</td><td>Wisconsin</td><td>4,009</td></tr>
<tr><td>31</td><td>New Mexico</td><td>4,001</td><td>31</td><td>New Mexico</td><td>4,001</td></tr>
<tr><td>49</td><td>New York</td><td>3,277</td><td>32</td><td>Massachusetts</td><td>3,979</td></tr>
<tr><td>41</td><td>North Carolina</td><td>3,594</td><td>33</td><td>Virginia</td><td>3,952</td></tr>
<tr><td>4</td><td>North Dakota</td><td>6,439</td><td>34</td><td>Missouri</td><td>3,950</td></tr>
<tr><td>24</td><td>Ohio</td><td>4,183</td><td>35</td><td>Pennsylvania</td><td>3,937</td></tr>
<tr><td>11</td><td>Oklahoma</td><td>4,714</td><td>36</td><td>Maryland</td><td>3,814</td></tr>
<tr><td>43</td><td>Oregon</td><td>3,529</td><td>37</td><td>Illinois</td><td>3,779</td></tr>
<tr><td>35</td><td>Pennsylvania</td><td>3,937</td><td>38</td><td>Georgia</td><td>3,742</td></tr>
<tr><td>45</td><td>Rhode Island</td><td>3,381</td><td>39</td><td>Michigan</td><td>3,670</td></tr>
<tr><td>28</td><td>South Carolina</td><td>4,098</td><td>40</td><td>Idaho</td><td>3,614</td></tr>
<tr><td>18</td><td>South Dakota</td><td>4,498</td><td>41</td><td>North Carolina</td><td>3,594</td></tr>
<tr><td>26</td><td>Tennessee</td><td>4,125</td><td>42</td><td>Washington</td><td>3,592</td></tr>
<tr><td>5</td><td>Texas</td><td>5,900</td><td>43</td><td>Oregon</td><td>3,529</td></tr>
<tr><td>48</td><td>Utah</td><td>3,281</td><td>44</td><td>Colorado</td><td>3,518</td></tr>
<tr><td>23</td><td>Vermont</td><td>4,331</td><td>45</td><td>Rhode Island</td><td>3,381</td></tr>
<tr><td>33</td><td>Virginia</td><td>3,952</td><td>46</td><td>California</td><td>3,363</td></tr>
<tr><td>42</td><td>Washington</td><td>3,592</td><td>47</td><td>Florida</td><td>3,324</td></tr>
<tr><td>13</td><td>West Virginia</td><td>4,621</td><td>48</td><td>Utah</td><td>3,281</td></tr>
<tr><td>30</td><td>Wisconsin</td><td>4,009</td><td>49</td><td>New York</td><td>3,277</td></tr>
<tr><td>2</td><td>Wyoming</td><td>8,685</td><td>50</td><td>Arizona</td><td>3,175</td></tr>
<tr><td></td><td></td><td></td><td></td><td>District of Columbia</td><td>4,079</td></tr>
</table>

Source: CQ Press using data from U.S. Department of Energy, Energy Information Administration
"State Energy Data 2007: Prices and Expenditures" (http://www.eia.doe.gov/emeu/states/_seds.html)

Average Monthly Electric Bill for Industrial Customers in 2008

National Average = $7,414 a Month

ALPHA ORDER

RANK	STATE	MONTHLY BILL
10	Alabama	$19,244
19	Alaska	11,761
25	Arizona	9,639
46	Arkansas	2,639
38	California	5,524
34	Colorado	5,817
23	Connecticut	10,396
3	Delaware	41,964
35	Florida	5,816
21	Georgia	11,340
1	Hawaii	122,701
49	Idaho	1,328
6	Illinois	28,634
17	Indiana	12,173
16	Iowa	12,457
47	Kansas	2,611
5	Kentucky	29,405
26	Louisiana	8,780
22	Maine	10,952
37	Maryland	5,592
27	Massachusetts	8,212
12	Michigan	14,283
15	Minnesota	12,813
18	Mississippi	11,962
29	Missouri	7,763
33	Montana	5,881
50	Nebraska	1,014
9	Nevada	25,467
31	New Hampshire	6,608
30	New Jersey	7,123
36	New Mexico	5,629
14	New York	14,131
20	North Carolina	11,680
28	North Dakota	8,034
13	Ohio	14,263
41	Oklahoma	4,293
48	Oregon	2,510
24	Pennsylvania	10,223
32	Rhode Island	6,215
8	South Carolina	27,885
44	South Dakota	3,450
2	Tennessee	82,116
39	Texas	4,812
43	Utah	3,687
4	Vermont	38,055
11	Virginia	16,912
45	Washington	3,074
40	West Virginia	4,298
7	Wisconsin	28,583
42	Wyoming	4,009

RANK ORDER

RANK	STATE	MONTHLY BILL
1	Hawaii	$122,701
2	Tennessee	82,116
3	Delaware	41,964
4	Vermont	38,055
5	Kentucky	29,405
6	Illinois	28,634
7	Wisconsin	28,583
8	South Carolina	27,885
9	Nevada	25,467
10	Alabama	19,244
11	Virginia	16,912
12	Michigan	14,283
13	Ohio	14,263
14	New York	14,131
15	Minnesota	12,813
16	Iowa	12,457
17	Indiana	12,173
18	Mississippi	11,962
19	Alaska	11,761
20	North Carolina	11,680
21	Georgia	11,340
22	Maine	10,952
23	Connecticut	10,396
24	Pennsylvania	10,223
25	Arizona	9,639
26	Louisiana	8,780
27	Massachusetts	8,212
28	North Dakota	8,034
29	Missouri	7,763
30	New Jersey	7,123
31	New Hampshire	6,608
32	Rhode Island	6,215
33	Montana	5,881
34	Colorado	5,817
35	Florida	5,816
36	New Mexico	5,629
37	Maryland	5,592
38	California	5,524
39	Texas	4,812
40	West Virginia	4,298
41	Oklahoma	4,293
42	Wyoming	4,009
43	Utah	3,687
44	South Dakota	3,450
45	Washington	3,074
46	Arkansas	2,639
47	Kansas	2,611
48	Oregon	2,510
49	Idaho	1,328
50	Nebraska	1,014

District of Columbia — 205,297

Source: U.S. Department of Energy, Energy Information Administration
"Electric Sales, Revenue and Average Price 2008" (http://www.eia.doe.gov/cneaf/electricity/esr/esr_sum.html)

Average Monthly Electric Bill for Commercial Customers in 2008

National Average = $657 a Month

ALPHA ORDER

RANK	STATE	MONTHLY BILL
26	Alabama	$499
16	Alaska	689
10	Arizona	752
41	Arkansas	421
12	California	723
43	Colorado	408
3	Connecticut	1,255
7	Delaware	891
15	Florida	697
17	Georgia	652
1	Hawaii	1,406
49	Idaho	291
8	Illinois	867
33	Indiana	469
46	Iowa	345
38	Kansas	433
44	Kentucky	403
11	Louisiana	730
24	Maine	511
2	Maryland	1,322
6	Massachusetts	921
19	Michigan	576
20	Minnesota	549
28	Mississippi	492
34	Missouri	462
48	Montana	342
47	Nebraska	344
24	Nevada	511
23	New Hampshire	524
5	New Jersey	1,043
31	New Mexico	477
4	New York	1,052
35	North Carolina	451
36	North Dakota	448
18	Ohio	594
32	Oklahoma	472
40	Oregon	423
21	Pennsylvania	547
9	Rhode Island	847
37	South Carolina	445
45	South Dakota	379
28	Tennessee	492
13	Texas	720
27	Utah	496
39	Vermont	428
14	Virginia	708
30	Washington	481
50	West Virginia	288
22	Wisconsin	544
42	Wyoming	416

RANK ORDER

RANK	STATE	MONTHLY BILL
1	Hawaii	$1,406
2	Maryland	1,322
3	Connecticut	1,255
4	New York	1,052
5	New Jersey	1,043
6	Massachusetts	921
7	Delaware	891
8	Illinois	867
9	Rhode Island	847
10	Arizona	752
11	Louisiana	730
12	California	723
13	Texas	720
14	Virginia	708
15	Florida	697
16	Alaska	689
17	Georgia	652
18	Ohio	594
19	Michigan	576
20	Minnesota	549
21	Pennsylvania	547
22	Wisconsin	544
23	New Hampshire	524
24	Maine	511
24	Nevada	511
26	Alabama	499
27	Utah	496
28	Mississippi	492
28	Tennessee	492
30	Washington	481
31	New Mexico	477
32	Oklahoma	472
33	Indiana	469
34	Missouri	462
35	North Carolina	451
36	North Dakota	448
37	South Carolina	445
38	Kansas	433
39	Vermont	428
40	Oregon	423
41	Arkansas	421
42	Wyoming	416
43	Colorado	408
44	Kentucky	403
45	South Dakota	379
46	Iowa	345
47	Nebraska	344
48	Montana	342
49	Idaho	291
50	West Virginia	288

District of Columbia   3,315

Source: U.S. Department of Energy, Energy Information Administration
"Electric Sales, Revenue and Average Price 2008" (http://www.eia.doe.gov/cneaf/electricity/esr/esr_sum.html)

Average Monthly Electric Bill for Residential Customers in 2008

National Average = $104 a Month

ALPHA ORDER

RANK	STATE	MONTHLY BILL
5	Alabama	$132
17	Alaska	109
15	Arizona	112
21	Arkansas	103
40	California	81
48	Colorado	69
4	Connecticut	143
6	Delaware	131
6	Florida	131
12	Georgia	114
1	Hawaii	204
45	Idaho	76
31	Illinois	85
27	Indiana	92
32	Iowa	84
37	Kansas	82
26	Kentucky	95
8	Louisiana	129
32	Maine	84
3	Maryland	144
17	Massachusetts	109
47	Michigan	72
41	Minnesota	80
9	Mississippi	128
29	Missouri	88
44	Montana	77
41	Nebraska	80
12	Nevada	114
25	New Hampshire	97
16	New Jersey	111
50	New Mexico	63
19	New York	108
20	North Carolina	107
32	North Dakota	84
27	Ohio	92
23	Oklahoma	101
30	Oregon	87
24	Pennsylvania	98
21	Rhode Island	103
10	South Carolina	118
32	South Dakota	84
11	Tennessee	116
2	Texas	147
49	Utah	65
32	Vermont	84
14	Virginia	113
37	Washington	82
41	West Virginia	80
37	Wisconsin	82
46	Wyoming	74

RANK ORDER

RANK	STATE	MONTHLY BILL
1	Hawaii	$204
2	Texas	147
3	Maryland	144
4	Connecticut	143
5	Alabama	132
6	Delaware	131
6	Florida	131
8	Louisiana	129
9	Mississippi	128
10	South Carolina	118
11	Tennessee	116
12	Georgia	114
12	Nevada	114
14	Virginia	113
15	Arizona	112
16	New Jersey	111
17	Alaska	109
17	Massachusetts	109
19	New York	108
20	North Carolina	107
21	Arkansas	103
21	Rhode Island	103
23	Oklahoma	101
24	Pennsylvania	98
25	New Hampshire	97
26	Kentucky	95
27	Indiana	92
27	Ohio	92
29	Missouri	88
30	Oregon	87
31	Illinois	85
32	Iowa	84
32	Maine	84
32	North Dakota	84
32	South Dakota	84
32	Vermont	84
37	Kansas	82
37	Washington	82
37	Wisconsin	82
40	California	81
41	Minnesota	80
41	Nebraska	80
41	West Virginia	80
44	Montana	77
45	Idaho	76
46	Wyoming	74
47	Michigan	72
48	Colorado	69
49	Utah	65
50	New Mexico	63

| | District of Columbia | 94 |

Source: U.S. Department of Energy, Energy Information Administration
"Electric Sales, Revenue and Average Price 2008" (http://www.eia.doe.gov/cneaf/electricity/esr/esr_sum.html)

Electricity Generated Through Renewable Sources in 2007

National Total = 352,747,486,000 Kilowatthours*

ALPHA ORDER

RANK	STATE	KWH	% of USA
9	Alabama	7,936,734,000	2.2%
38	Alaska	1,302,453,000	0.4%
10	Arizona	6,639,310,000	1.9%
14	Arkansas	4,860,497,000	1.4%
2	California	52,173,008,000	14.7%
26	Colorado	3,054,362,000	0.9%
42	Connecticut	1,093,100,000	0.3%
50	Delaware	48,116,000	0.0%
18	Florida	4,457,264,000	1.3%
12	Georgia	5,651,610,000	1.6%
44	Hawaii	845,691,000	0.2%
7	Idaho	9,674,539,000	2.7%
36	Illinois	1,438,480,000	0.4%
47	Indiana	681,183,000	0.2%
19	Iowa	3,870,121,000	1.1%
40	Kansas	1,163,039,000	0.3%
30	Kentucky	2,134,210,000	0.6%
21	Louisiana	3,806,525,000	1.1%
8	Maine	7,945,147,000	2.2%
29	Maryland	2,255,678,000	0.6%
31	Massachusetts	2,037,706,000	0.6%
22	Michigan	3,686,736,000	1.0%
17	Minnesota	4,586,460,000	1.3%
34	Mississippi	1,493,365,000	0.4%
39	Missouri	1,233,635,000	0.3%
6	Montana	9,971,057,000	2.8%
48	Nebraska	625,468,000	0.2%
24	Nevada	3,299,849,000	0.9%
28	New Hampshire	2,388,501,000	0.7%
43	New Jersey	864,487,000	0.2%
33	New Mexico	1,677,211,000	0.5%
4	New York	28,027,639,000	7.9%
16	North Carolina	4,656,377,000	1.3%
32	North Dakota	1,939,672,000	0.5%
45	Ohio	845,579,000	0.2%
13	Oklahoma	5,194,860,000	1.5%
3	Oregon	35,815,732,000	10.1%
15	Pennsylvania	4,782,178,000	1.4%
49	Rhode Island	159,121,000	0.0%
23	South Carolina	3,551,946,000	1.0%
25	South Dakota	3,067,301,000	0.9%
11	Tennessee	5,910,127,000	1.7%
5	Texas	11,932,049,000	3.4%
46	Utah	733,738,000	0.2%
41	Vermont	1,110,153,000	0.3%
20	Virginia	3,813,835,000	1.1%
1	Washington	82,559,749,000	23.3%
37	West Virginia	1,421,985,000	0.4%
27	Wisconsin	2,845,600,000	0.8%
35	Wyoming	1,484,305,000	0.4%

RANK ORDER

RANK	STATE	KWH	% of USA
1	Washington	82,559,749,000	23.3%
2	California	52,173,008,000	14.7%
3	Oregon	35,815,732,000	10.1%
4	New York	28,027,639,000	7.9%
5	Texas	11,932,049,000	3.4%
6	Montana	9,971,057,000	2.8%
7	Idaho	9,674,539,000	2.7%
8	Maine	7,945,147,000	2.2%
9	Alabama	7,936,734,000	2.2%
10	Arizona	6,639,310,000	1.9%
11	Tennessee	5,910,127,000	1.7%
12	Georgia	5,651,610,000	1.6%
13	Oklahoma	5,194,860,000	1.5%
14	Arkansas	4,860,497,000	1.4%
15	Pennsylvania	4,782,178,000	1.4%
16	North Carolina	4,656,377,000	1.3%
17	Minnesota	4,586,460,000	1.3%
18	Florida	4,457,264,000	1.3%
19	Iowa	3,870,121,000	1.1%
20	Virginia	3,813,835,000	1.1%
21	Louisiana	3,806,525,000	1.1%
22	Michigan	3,686,736,000	1.0%
23	South Carolina	3,551,946,000	1.0%
24	Nevada	3,299,849,000	0.9%
25	South Dakota	3,067,301,000	0.9%
26	Colorado	3,054,362,000	0.9%
27	Wisconsin	2,845,600,000	0.8%
28	New Hampshire	2,388,501,000	0.7%
29	Maryland	2,255,678,000	0.6%
30	Kentucky	2,134,210,000	0.6%
31	Massachusetts	2,037,706,000	0.6%
32	North Dakota	1,939,672,000	0.5%
33	New Mexico	1,677,211,000	0.5%
34	Mississippi	1,493,365,000	0.4%
35	Wyoming	1,484,305,000	0.4%
36	Illinois	1,438,480,000	0.4%
37	West Virginia	1,421,985,000	0.4%
38	Alaska	1,302,453,000	0.4%
39	Missouri	1,233,635,000	0.3%
40	Kansas	1,163,039,000	0.3%
41	Vermont	1,110,153,000	0.3%
42	Connecticut	1,093,100,000	0.3%
43	New Jersey	864,487,000	0.2%
44	Hawaii	845,691,000	0.2%
45	Ohio	845,579,000	0.2%
46	Utah	733,738,000	0.2%
47	Indiana	681,183,000	0.2%
48	Nebraska	625,468,000	0.2%
49	Rhode Island	159,121,000	0.0%
50	Delaware	48,116,000	0.0%
	District of Columbia	0	0.0%

Source: U.S. Department of Energy, Energy Information Administration
   "Renewable Energy Trends, 2007" (http://www.eia.doe.gov/cneaf/solar.renewables/page/trends/rentrends.html)
*Includes hydroelectric, geothermal, solar, wind, MSW/landfill gas, wood/wood waste and other biomass.

Percent of Electricity Generated Through Renewable Sources in 2007

National Percent = 8.5%*

ALPHA ORDER

RANK	STATE	PERCENT
22	Alabama	5.5
9	Alaska	19.1
20	Arizona	5.9
13	Arkansas	8.9
7	California	24.7
21	Colorado	5.7
32	Connecticut	3.3
48	Delaware	0.6
41	Florida	2.0
29	Georgia	3.9
16	Hawaii	7.3
1	Idaho	84.2
47	Illinois	0.7
49	Indiana	0.5
15	Iowa	7.8
37	Kansas	2.3
39	Kentucky	2.2
28	Louisiana	4.1
5	Maine	49.3
25	Maryland	4.5
27	Massachusetts	4.3
34	Michigan	3.1
14	Minnesota	8.4
35	Mississippi	3.0
45	Missouri	1.4
6	Montana	34.5
42	Nebraska	1.9
12	Nevada	10.1
11	New Hampshire	10.3
45	New Jersey	1.4
24	New Mexico	4.7
8	New York	19.2
30	North Carolina	3.6
18	North Dakota	6.2
49	Ohio	0.5
17	Oklahoma	7.1
3	Oregon	65.0
40	Pennsylvania	2.1
37	Rhode Island	2.3
31	South Carolina	3.4
4	South Dakota	50.0
18	Tennessee	6.2
36	Texas	2.9
43	Utah	1.6
9	Vermont	19.1
23	Virginia	4.9
2	Washington	77.2
44	West Virginia	1.5
25	Wisconsin	4.5
32	Wyoming	3.3

RANK ORDER

RANK	STATE	PERCENT
1	Idaho	84.2
2	Washington	77.2
3	Oregon	65.0
4	South Dakota	50.0
5	Maine	49.3
6	Montana	34.5
7	California	24.7
8	New York	19.2
9	Alaska	19.1
9	Vermont	19.1
11	New Hampshire	10.3
12	Nevada	10.1
13	Arkansas	8.9
14	Minnesota	8.4
15	Iowa	7.8
16	Hawaii	7.3
17	Oklahoma	7.1
18	North Dakota	6.2
18	Tennessee	6.2
20	Arizona	5.9
21	Colorado	5.7
22	Alabama	5.5
23	Virginia	4.9
24	New Mexico	4.7
25	Maryland	4.5
25	Wisconsin	4.5
27	Massachusetts	4.3
28	Louisiana	4.1
29	Georgia	3.9
30	North Carolina	3.6
31	South Carolina	3.4
32	Connecticut	3.3
32	Wyoming	3.3
34	Michigan	3.1
35	Mississippi	3.0
36	Texas	2.9
37	Kansas	2.3
37	Rhode Island	2.3
39	Kentucky	2.2
40	Pennsylvania	2.1
41	Florida	2.0
42	Nebraska	1.9
43	Utah	1.6
44	West Virginia	1.5
45	Missouri	1.4
45	New Jersey	1.4
47	Illinois	0.7
48	Delaware	0.6
49	Indiana	0.5
49	Ohio	0.5
	District of Columbia	0.0

Source: U.S. Department of Energy, Energy Information Administration
  "Renewable Energy Trends, 2007" (http://www.eia.doe.gov/cneaf/solar.renewables/page/trends/rentrends.html)
*Includes hydroelectric, geothermal, solar, wind, MSW/landfill gas, wood/wood waste and other biomass.

Average Price of Natural Gas Delivered to Industrial Customers in 2008

National Average = $9.58 per Thousand Cubic Feet

ALPHA ORDER

RANK ORDER

RANK	STATE	RATE		RANK	STATE	RATE
23	Alabama	$10.54		1	Hawaii	$26.74
43	Alaska	5.49		2	Massachusetts	15.52
25	Arizona	10.48		3	New Hampshire	14.50
18	Arkansas	10.80		4	Maryland	13.38
19	California	10.71		5	Pennsylvania	13.24
40	Colorado	8.28		6	Ohio	13.19
8	Connecticut	12.40		7	New York	12.97
NA	Delaware*	NA		8	Connecticut	12.40
NA	Florida*	NA		9	North Carolina	12.14
11	Georgia	11.63		10	Virginia	11.72
1	Hawaii	26.74		11	Georgia	11.63
32	Idaho	9.19		12	Missouri	11.26
NA	Illinois*	NA		13	South Carolina	11.23
28	Indiana	10.04		14	Montana	11.08
37	Iowa	8.96		15	West Virginia	10.97
30	Kansas	9.51		16	Nevada	10.93
26	Kentucky	10.46		17	Oklahoma	10.92
31	Louisiana	9.27		18	Arkansas	10.80
NA	Maine*	NA		19	California	10.71
4	Maryland	13.38		20	Wisconsin	10.70
2	Massachusetts	15.52		21	Washington	10.58
27	Michigan	10.21		22	Tennessee	10.57
33	Minnesota	9.09		23	Alabama	10.54
24	Mississippi	10.50		24	Mississippi	10.50
12	Missouri	11.26		25	Arizona	10.48
14	Montana	11.08		26	Kentucky	10.46
38	Nebraska	8.94		27	Michigan	10.21
16	Nevada	10.93		28	Indiana	10.04
3	New Hampshire	14.50		29	Vermont	9.60
NA	New Jersey*	NA		30	Kansas	9.51
NA	New Mexico*	NA		31	Louisiana	9.27
7	New York	12.97		32	Idaho	9.19
9	North Carolina	12.14		33	Minnesota	9.09
39	North Dakota	8.30		34	Oregon	9.07
6	Ohio	13.19		35	South Dakota	9.00
17	Oklahoma	10.92		36	Texas	8.98
34	Oregon	9.07		37	Iowa	8.96
5	Pennsylvania	13.24		38	Nebraska	8.94
NA	Rhode Island*	NA		39	North Dakota	8.30
13	South Carolina	11.23		40	Colorado	8.28
35	South Dakota	9.00		41	Wyoming	7.46
22	Tennessee	10.57		42	Utah	7.21
36	Texas	8.98		43	Alaska	5.49
42	Utah	7.21		NA	Delaware*	NA
29	Vermont	9.60		NA	Florida*	NA
10	Virginia	11.72		NA	Illinois*	NA
21	Washington	10.58		NA	Maine*	NA
15	West Virginia	10.97		NA	New Jersey*	NA
20	Wisconsin	10.70		NA	New Mexico*	NA
41	Wyoming	7.46		NA	Rhode Island*	NA
					District of Columbia*	NA

Source: U.S. Department of Energy, Energy Information Administration
"Natural Gas Monthly January 2010" (http://www.eia.doe.gov/oil_gas/natural_gas/info_glance/natural_gas.html)
*Not available.

Average Price of Natural Gas Delivered to Commercial Customers in 2008

National Average = $11.99 per Thousand Cubic Feet

ALPHA ORDER				RANK ORDER		
RANK	STATE	RATE		RANK	STATE	RATE
2	Alabama	$16.07		1	Hawaii	$39.01
45	Alaska	7.91		2	Alabama	16.07
18	Arizona	12.91		3	Maine	15.84
31	Arkansas	11.41		4	New Hampshire	15.53
25	California	11.72		5	Massachusetts	15.42
43	Colorado	9.03		6	Florida	14.63
12	Connecticut	13.81		7	Vermont	14.31
NA	Delaware*	NA		8	South Carolina	14.23
6	Florida	14.63		9	North Carolina	14.20
11	Georgia	14.04		10	Pennsylvania	14.12
1	Hawaii	39.01		11	Georgia	14.04
38	Idaho	10.43		12	Connecticut	13.81
25	Illinois	11.72		13	West Virginia	13.60
28	Indiana	11.52		14	Louisiana	13.49
40	Iowa	10.22		15	Tennessee	13.32
23	Kansas	12.34		16	Kentucky	13.14
16	Kentucky	13.14		17	Maryland	12.96
14	Louisiana	13.49		18	Arizona	12.91
3	Maine	15.84		18	New York	12.91
17	Maryland	12.96		20	Virginia	12.85
5	Massachusetts	15.42		21	Ohio	12.58
36	Michigan	10.55		22	Mississippi	12.50
37	Minnesota	10.52		23	Kansas	12.34
22	Mississippi	12.50		24	Missouri	12.19
24	Missouri	12.19		25	California	11.72
32	Montana	11.37		25	Illinois	11.72
NA	Nebraska*	NA		27	Oregon	11.62
35	Nevada	11.19		28	Indiana	11.52
4	New Hampshire	15.53		29	Oklahoma	11.50
NA	New Jersey*	NA		30	Washington	11.49
39	New Mexico	10.30		31	Arkansas	11.41
18	New York	12.91		32	Montana	11.37
9	North Carolina	14.20		33	Wisconsin	11.28
42	North Dakota	9.58		34	Texas	11.25
21	Ohio	12.58		35	Nevada	11.19
29	Oklahoma	11.50		36	Michigan	10.55
27	Oregon	11.62		37	Minnesota	10.52
10	Pennsylvania	14.12		38	Idaho	10.43
NA	Rhode Island*	NA		39	New Mexico	10.30
8	South Carolina	14.23		40	Iowa	10.22
41	South Dakota	9.76		41	South Dakota	9.76
15	Tennessee	13.32		42	North Dakota	9.58
34	Texas	11.25		43	Colorado	9.03
46	Utah	7.74		44	Wyoming	8.82
7	Vermont	14.31		45	Alaska	7.91
20	Virginia	12.85		46	Utah	7.74
30	Washington	11.49		NA	Delaware*	NA
13	West Virginia	13.60		NA	Nebraska*	NA
33	Wisconsin	11.28		NA	New Jersey*	NA
44	Wyoming	8.82		NA	Rhode Island*	NA
				District of Columbia		13.88

Source: U.S. Department of Energy, Energy Information Administration
 "Natural Gas Monthly January 2010" (http://www.eia.doe.gov/oil_gas/natural_gas/info_glance/natural_gas.html)
*Not available.

Average Price of Natural Gas Delivered to Residential Customers in 2008

National Average = $13.68 per Thousand Cubic Feet

ALPHA ORDER

RANK	STATE	RATE
3	Alabama	$18.55
48	Alaska	8.72
7	Arizona	17.54
23	Arkansas	14.18
33	California	12.74
46	Colorado	9.76
6	Connecticut	17.84
16	Delaware	16.17
2	Florida	21.29
4	Georgia	18.50
1	Hawaii	44.75
42	Idaho	11.25
36	Illinois	12.09
NA	Indiana*	NA
37	Iowa	11.93
31	Kansas	13.03
27	Kentucky	13.77
18	Louisiana	15.51
8	Maine	17.52
17	Maryland	16.05
10	Massachusetts	17.11
38	Michigan	11.82
41	Minnesota	11.30
24	Mississippi	13.93
28	Missouri	13.39
39	Montana	11.52
43	Nebraska	11.15
29	Nevada	13.33
12	New Hampshire	16.74
19	New Jersey	15.19
34	New Mexico	12.31
11	New York	16.75
13	North Carolina	16.71
44	North Dakota	10.34
21	Ohio	14.51
35	Oklahoma	12.29
25	Oregon	13.89
14	Pennsylvania	16.24
NA	Rhode Island*	NA
9	South Carolina	17.23
40	South Dakota	11.32
22	Tennessee	14.36
26	Texas	13.79
47	Utah	9.00
5	Vermont	18.31
15	Virginia	16.20
30	Washington	13.06
20	West Virginia	14.61
32	Wisconsin	12.80
45	Wyoming	10.24

RANK ORDER

RANK	STATE	RATE
1	Hawaii	$44.75
2	Florida	21.29
3	Alabama	18.55
4	Georgia	18.50
5	Vermont	18.31
6	Connecticut	17.84
7	Arizona	17.54
8	Maine	17.52
9	South Carolina	17.23
10	Massachusetts	17.11
11	New York	16.75
12	New Hampshire	16.74
13	North Carolina	16.71
14	Pennsylvania	16.24
15	Virginia	16.20
16	Delaware	16.17
17	Maryland	16.05
18	Louisiana	15.51
19	New Jersey	15.19
20	West Virginia	14.61
21	Ohio	14.51
22	Tennessee	14.36
23	Arkansas	14.18
24	Mississippi	13.93
25	Oregon	13.89
26	Texas	13.79
27	Kentucky	13.77
28	Missouri	13.39
29	Nevada	13.33
30	Washington	13.06
31	Kansas	13.03
32	Wisconsin	12.80
33	California	12.74
34	New Mexico	12.31
35	Oklahoma	12.29
36	Illinois	12.09
37	Iowa	11.93
38	Michigan	11.82
39	Montana	11.52
40	South Dakota	11.32
41	Minnesota	11.30
42	Idaho	11.25
43	Nebraska	11.15
44	North Dakota	10.34
45	Wyoming	10.24
46	Colorado	9.76
47	Utah	9.00
48	Alaska	8.72
NA	Indiana*	NA
NA	Rhode Island*	NA
	District of Columbia	16.49

Source: U.S. Department of Energy, Energy Information Administration
   "Natural Gas Monthly January 2010" (http://www.eia.doe.gov/oil_gas/natural_gas/info_glance/natural_gas.html)
*Not available.

Natural Gas Consumption in 2007

National Total = 23,047,229,000,000 Cubic Feet*

ALPHA ORDER

RANK	STATE	CUBIC FEET	% of USA
15	Alabama	418,545,000,000	1.8%
20	Alaska	369,967,000,000	1.6%
18	Arizona	393,039,000,000	1.7%
32	Arkansas	226,437,000,000	1.0%
2	California	2,394,930,000,000	10.4%
13	Colorado	504,786,000,000	2.2%
36	Connecticut	180,178,000,000	0.8%
47	Delaware	47,948,000,000	0.2%
6	Florida	917,245,000,000	4.0%
14	Georgia	441,099,000,000	1.9%
50	Hawaii	2,850,000,000	0.0%
42	Idaho	81,943,000,000	0.4%
5	Illinois	965,756,000,000	4.2%
12	Indiana	535,805,000,000	2.3%
26	Iowa	259,286,000,000	1.1%
23	Kansas	286,427,000,000	1.2%
31	Kentucky	229,801,000,000	1.0%
3	Louisiana	1,290,326,000,000	5.6%
48	Maine	44,552,000,000	0.2%
35	Maryland	201,078,000,000	0.9%
16	Massachusetts	408,758,000,000	1.8%
7	Michigan	828,779,000,000	3.6%
19	Minnesota	388,705,000,000	1.7%
21	Mississippi	364,005,000,000	1.6%
25	Missouri	272,405,000,000	1.2%
43	Montana	73,822,000,000	0.3%
38	Nebraska	143,827,000,000	0.6%
27	Nevada	254,464,000,000	1.1%
44	New Hampshire	62,133,000,000	0.3%
11	New Jersey	619,053,000,000	2.7%
30	New Mexico	233,951,000,000	1.0%
4	New York	1,190,341,000,000	5.2%
29	North Carolina	237,364,000,000	1.0%
45	North Dakota	60,211,000,000	0.3%
8	Ohio	806,466,000,000	3.5%
10	Oklahoma	658,350,000,000	2.9%
28	Oregon	251,949,000,000	1.1%
9	Pennsylvania	752,321,000,000	3.3%
41	Rhode Island	88,003,000,000	0.4%
37	South Carolina	173,848,000,000	0.8%
46	South Dakota	53,938,000,000	0.2%
33	Tennessee	221,089,000,000	1.0%
1	Texas	3,515,902,000,000	15.3%
34	Utah	219,687,000,000	1.0%
49	Vermont	8,867,000,000	0.0%
22	Virginia	319,935,000,000	1.4%
24	Washington	272,637,000,000	1.2%
39	West Virginia	114,280,000,000	0.5%
17	Wisconsin	398,369,000,000	1.7%
40	Wyoming	113,266,000,000	0.5%

RANK ORDER

RANK	STATE	CUBIC FEET	% of USA
1	Texas	3,515,902,000,000	15.3%
2	California	2,394,930,000,000	10.4%
3	Louisiana	1,290,326,000,000	5.6%
4	New York	1,190,341,000,000	5.2%
5	Illinois	965,756,000,000	4.2%
6	Florida	917,245,000,000	4.0%
7	Michigan	828,779,000,000	3.6%
8	Ohio	806,466,000,000	3.5%
9	Pennsylvania	752,321,000,000	3.3%
10	Oklahoma	658,350,000,000	2.9%
11	New Jersey	619,053,000,000	2.7%
12	Indiana	535,805,000,000	2.3%
13	Colorado	504,786,000,000	2.2%
14	Georgia	441,099,000,000	1.9%
15	Alabama	418,545,000,000	1.8%
16	Massachusetts	408,758,000,000	1.8%
17	Wisconsin	398,369,000,000	1.7%
18	Arizona	393,039,000,000	1.7%
19	Minnesota	388,705,000,000	1.7%
20	Alaska	369,967,000,000	1.6%
21	Mississippi	364,005,000,000	1.6%
22	Virginia	319,935,000,000	1.4%
23	Kansas	286,427,000,000	1.2%
24	Washington	272,637,000,000	1.2%
25	Missouri	272,405,000,000	1.2%
26	Iowa	259,286,000,000	1.1%
27	Nevada	254,464,000,000	1.1%
28	Oregon	251,949,000,000	1.1%
29	North Carolina	237,364,000,000	1.0%
30	New Mexico	233,951,000,000	1.0%
31	Kentucky	229,801,000,000	1.0%
32	Arkansas	226,437,000,000	1.0%
33	Tennessee	221,089,000,000	1.0%
34	Utah	219,687,000,000	1.0%
35	Maryland	201,078,000,000	0.9%
36	Connecticut	180,178,000,000	0.8%
37	South Carolina	173,848,000,000	0.8%
38	Nebraska	143,827,000,000	0.6%
39	West Virginia	114,280,000,000	0.5%
40	Wyoming	113,266,000,000	0.5%
41	Rhode Island	88,003,000,000	0.4%
42	Idaho	81,943,000,000	0.4%
43	Montana	73,822,000,000	0.3%
44	New Hampshire	62,133,000,000	0.3%
45	North Dakota	60,211,000,000	0.3%
46	South Dakota	53,938,000,000	0.2%
47	Delaware	47,948,000,000	0.2%
48	Maine	44,552,000,000	0.2%
49	Vermont	8,867,000,000	0.0%
50	Hawaii	2,850,000,000	0.0%
	District of Columbia	32,974,000,000	0.1%

Source: U.S. Department of Energy, Energy Information Administration
"Natural Gas Annual 2007" (http://www.eia.doe.gov/oil_gas/natural_gas/info_glance/natural_gas.html)
*National total includes 115,528,000,000 cubic feet of consumption in the Gulf of Mexico not shown by state.

Coal Mines in 2008

National Total = 1,458 Mines*

ALPHA ORDER

RANK	STATE	MINES	% of USA
5	Alabama	59	4.0%
23	Alaska	1	0.1%
23	Arizona	1	0.1%
19	Arkansas	2	0.1%
NA	California**	NA	NA
12	Colorado	12	0.8%
NA	Connecticut**	NA	NA
NA	Delaware**	NA	NA
NA	Florida**	NA	NA
NA	Georgia**	NA	NA
NA	Hawaii**	NA	NA
NA	Idaho**	NA	NA
11	Illinois	19	1.3%
7	Indiana	30	2.1%
NA	Iowa**	NA	NA
19	Kansas	2	0.1%
1	Kentucky	469	32.2%
19	Louisiana	2	0.1%
NA	Maine**	NA	NA
9	Maryland	21	1.4%
NA	Massachusetts**	NA	NA
NA	Michigan**	NA	NA
NA	Minnesota**	NA	NA
23	Mississippi	1	0.1%
19	Missouri	2	0.1%
16	Montana	6	0.4%
NA	Nebraska**	NA	NA
NA	Nevada**	NA	NA
NA	New Hampshire**	NA	NA
NA	New Jersey**	NA	NA
17	New Mexico	5	0.3%
NA	New York**	NA	NA
NA	North Carolina**	NA	NA
18	North Dakota	4	0.3%
6	Ohio	48	3.3%
15	Oklahoma	7	0.5%
NA	Oregon**	NA	NA
3	Pennsylvania	266	18.2%
NA	Rhode Island**	NA	NA
NA	South Carolina**	NA	NA
NA	South Dakota**	NA	NA
8	Tennessee	23	1.6%
13	Texas	11	0.8%
14	Utah	9	0.6%
NA	Vermont**	NA	NA
4	Virginia	114	7.8%
NA	Washington**	NA	NA
2	West Virginia	301	20.6%
NA	Wisconsin**	NA	NA
10	Wyoming	20	1.4%

RANK ORDER

RANK	STATE	MINES	% of USA
1	Kentucky	469	32.2%
2	West Virginia	301	20.6%
3	Pennsylvania	266	18.2%
4	Virginia	114	7.8%
5	Alabama	59	4.0%
6	Ohio	48	3.3%
7	Indiana	30	2.1%
8	Tennessee	23	1.6%
9	Maryland	21	1.4%
10	Wyoming	20	1.4%
11	Illinois	19	1.3%
12	Colorado	12	0.8%
13	Texas	11	0.8%
14	Utah	9	0.6%
15	Oklahoma	7	0.5%
16	Montana	6	0.4%
17	New Mexico	5	0.3%
18	North Dakota	4	0.3%
19	Arkansas	2	0.1%
19	Kansas	2	0.1%
19	Louisiana	2	0.1%
19	Missouri	2	0.1%
23	Alaska	1	0.1%
23	Arizona	1	0.1%
23	Mississippi	1	0.1%
NA	California**	NA	NA
NA	Connecticut**	NA	NA
NA	Delaware**	NA	NA
NA	Florida**	NA	NA
NA	Georgia**	NA	NA
NA	Hawaii**	NA	NA
NA	Idaho**	NA	NA
NA	Iowa**	NA	NA
NA	Maine**	NA	NA
NA	Massachusetts**	NA	NA
NA	Michigan**	NA	NA
NA	Minnesota**	NA	NA
NA	Nebraska**	NA	NA
NA	Nevada**	NA	NA
NA	New Hampshire**	NA	NA
NA	New Jersey**	NA	NA
NA	New York**	NA	NA
NA	North Carolina**	NA	NA
NA	Oregon**	NA	NA
NA	Rhode Island**	NA	NA
NA	South Carolina**	NA	NA
NA	South Dakota**	NA	NA
NA	Vermont**	NA	NA
NA	Washington**	NA	NA
NA	Wisconsin**	NA	NA
	District of Columbia**	NA	NA

Source: U.S. Department of Energy, Energy Information Administration
   "Annual Coal Report" (http://www.eia.doe.gov/cneaf/coal/page/acr/acr_sum.html)
*National total includes 23 coal mines in refuse recovery not shown by state.
**Not available or no mines.

Coal Production in 2008

National Total = 1,171,809,000 Short Tons*

ALPHA ORDER					RANK ORDER			
RANK	STATE	SHORT TONS	% of USA		RANK	STATE	SHORT TONS	% of USA
15	Alabama	20,611,000	1.8%		1	Wyoming	467,644,000	39.9%
21	Alaska	1,477,000	0.1%		2	West Virginia	157,778,000	13.5%
16	Arizona	8,025,000	0.7%		3	Kentucky	120,323,000	10.3%
25	Arkansas	69,000	0.0%		4	Pennsylvania	65,414,000	5.6%
NA	California**	NA	NA		5	Montana	44,786,000	3.8%
9	Colorado	32,028,000	2.7%		6	Texas	39,017,000	3.3%
NA	Connecticut**	NA	NA		7	Indiana	35,893,000	3.1%
NA	Delaware**	NA	NA		8	Illinois	32,918,000	2.8%
NA	Florida**	NA	NA		9	Colorado	32,028,000	2.7%
NA	Georgia**	NA	NA		10	North Dakota	29,627,000	2.5%
NA	Hawaii**	NA	NA		11	Ohio	26,251,000	2.2%
NA	Idaho**	NA	NA		12	New Mexico	25,645,000	2.2%
8	Illinois	32,918,000	2.8%		13	Virginia	24,712,000	2.1%
7	Indiana	35,893,000	3.1%		14	Utah	24,365,000	2.1%
NA	Iowa**	NA	NA		15	Alabama	20,611,000	1.8%
24	Kansas	229,000	0.0%		16	Arizona	8,025,000	0.7%
3	Kentucky	120,323,000	10.3%		17	Louisiana	3,843,000	0.3%
17	Louisiana	3,843,000	0.3%		18	Maryland	2,860,000	0.2%
NA	Maine**	NA	NA		19	Mississippi	2,842,000	0.2%
18	Maryland	2,860,000	0.2%		20	Tennessee	2,333,000	0.2%
NA	Massachusetts**	NA	NA		21	Alaska	1,477,000	0.1%
NA	Michigan**	NA	NA		22	Oklahoma	1,463,000	0.1%
NA	Minnesota**	NA	NA		23	Missouri	247,000	0.0%
19	Mississippi	2,842,000	0.2%		24	Kansas	229,000	0.0%
23	Missouri	247,000	0.0%		25	Arkansas	69,000	0.0%
5	Montana	44,786,000	3.8%		NA	California**	NA	NA
NA	Nebraska**	NA	NA		NA	Connecticut**	NA	NA
NA	Nevada**	NA	NA		NA	Delaware**	NA	NA
NA	New Hampshire**	NA	NA		NA	Florida**	NA	NA
NA	New Jersey**	NA	NA		NA	Georgia**	NA	NA
12	New Mexico	25,645,000	2.2%		NA	Hawaii**	NA	NA
NA	New York**	NA	NA		NA	Idaho**	NA	NA
NA	North Carolina**	NA	NA		NA	Iowa**	NA	NA
10	North Dakota	29,627,000	2.5%		NA	Maine**	NA	NA
11	Ohio	26,251,000	2.2%		NA	Massachusetts**	NA	NA
22	Oklahoma	1,463,000	0.1%		NA	Michigan**	NA	NA
NA	Oregon**	NA	NA		NA	Minnesota**	NA	NA
4	Pennsylvania	65,414,000	5.6%		NA	Nebraska**	NA	NA
NA	Rhode Island**	NA	NA		NA	Nevada**	NA	NA
NA	South Carolina**	NA	NA		NA	New Hampshire**	NA	NA
NA	South Dakota**	NA	NA		NA	New Jersey**	NA	NA
20	Tennessee	2,333,000	0.2%		NA	New York**	NA	NA
6	Texas	39,017,000	3.3%		NA	North Carolina**	NA	NA
14	Utah	24,365,000	2.1%		NA	Oregon**	NA	NA
NA	Vermont**	NA	NA		NA	Rhode Island**	NA	NA
13	Virginia	24,712,000	2.1%		NA	South Carolina**	NA	NA
NA	Washington**	NA	NA		NA	South Dakota**	NA	NA
2	West Virginia	157,778,000	13.5%		NA	Vermont**	NA	NA
NA	Wisconsin**	NA	NA		NA	Washington**	NA	NA
1	Wyoming	467,644,000	39.9%		NA	Wisconsin**	NA	NA
					NA	District of Columbia**	NA	NA

Source: U.S. Department of Energy, Energy Information Administration
"Annual Coal Report" (http://www.eia.doe.gov/cneaf/coal/page/acr/acr_sum.html)
*National total includes 1,408,000 short tons from refuse recovery not shown by state.
**Not available or no production.

Gasoline Used in 2008

National Total = 136,499,418,000 Gallons*

ALPHA ORDER

RANK	STATE	GALLONS	% of USA
21	Alabama	2,584,399,000	1.9%
50	Alaska	287,242,000	0.2%
18	Arizona	2,720,165,000	2.0%
32	Arkansas	1,427,420,000	1.0%
1	California	15,051,929,000	11.0%
26	Colorado	2,101,660,000	1.5%
31	Connecticut	1,494,164,000	1.1%
44	Delaware	445,599,000	0.3%
3	Florida	8,257,419,000	6.0%
8	Georgia	4,767,156,000	3.5%
43	Hawaii	446,175,000	0.3%
41	Idaho	658,903,000	0.5%
7	Illinois	4,893,624,000	3.6%
14	Indiana	3,094,010,000	2.3%
29	Iowa	1,624,009,000	1.2%
33	Kansas	1,309,777,000	1.0%
25	Kentucky	2,144,275,000	1.6%
24	Louisiana	2,160,747,000	1.6%
40	Maine	686,724,000	0.5%
17	Maryland	2,789,508,000	2.0%
16	Massachusetts	2,807,736,000	2.1%
10	Michigan	4,598,352,000	3.4%
20	Minnesota	2,624,459,000	1.9%
28	Mississippi	1,645,279,000	1.2%
13	Missouri	3,205,200,000	2.3%
42	Montana	484,217,000	0.4%
37	Nebraska	837,249,000	0.6%
34	Nevada	1,130,626,000	0.8%
39	New Hampshire	719,080,000	0.5%
11	New Jersey	4,280,963,000	3.1%
36	New Mexico	919,522,000	0.7%
4	New York	5,634,401,000	4.1%
9	North Carolina	4,760,470,000	3.5%
47	North Dakota	361,883,000	0.3%
5	Ohio	5,073,858,000	3.7%
27	Oklahoma	1,838,668,000	1.3%
30	Oregon	1,511,333,000	1.1%
6	Pennsylvania	5,005,820,000	3.7%
46	Rhode Island	406,633,000	0.3%
22	South Carolina	2,575,137,000	1.9%
45	South Dakota	421,545,000	0.3%
15	Tennessee	3,074,634,000	2.3%
2	Texas	11,904,811,000	8.7%
35	Utah	1,049,532,000	0.8%
49	Vermont	331,499,000	0.2%
12	Virginia	3,946,339,000	2.9%
19	Washington	2,665,967,000	2.0%
38	West Virginia	766,898,000	0.6%
23	Wisconsin	2,511,570,000	1.8%
48	Wyoming	354,456,000	0.3%

RANK ORDER

RANK	STATE	GALLONS	% of USA
1	California	15,051,929,000	11.0%
2	Texas	11,904,811,000	8.7%
3	Florida	8,257,419,000	6.0%
4	New York	5,634,401,000	4.1%
5	Ohio	5,073,858,000	3.7%
6	Pennsylvania	5,005,820,000	3.7%
7	Illinois	4,893,624,000	3.6%
8	Georgia	4,767,156,000	3.5%
9	North Carolina	4,760,470,000	3.5%
10	Michigan	4,598,352,000	3.4%
11	New Jersey	4,280,963,000	3.1%
12	Virginia	3,946,339,000	2.9%
13	Missouri	3,205,200,000	2.3%
14	Indiana	3,094,010,000	2.3%
15	Tennessee	3,074,634,000	2.3%
16	Massachusetts	2,807,736,000	2.1%
17	Maryland	2,789,508,000	2.0%
18	Arizona	2,720,165,000	2.0%
19	Washington	2,665,967,000	2.0%
20	Minnesota	2,624,459,000	1.9%
21	Alabama	2,584,399,000	1.9%
22	South Carolina	2,575,137,000	1.9%
23	Wisconsin	2,511,570,000	1.8%
24	Louisiana	2,160,747,000	1.6%
25	Kentucky	2,144,275,000	1.6%
26	Colorado	2,101,660,000	1.5%
27	Oklahoma	1,838,668,000	1.3%
28	Mississippi	1,645,279,000	1.2%
29	Iowa	1,624,009,000	1.2%
30	Oregon	1,511,333,000	1.1%
31	Connecticut	1,494,164,000	1.1%
32	Arkansas	1,427,420,000	1.0%
33	Kansas	1,309,777,000	1.0%
34	Nevada	1,130,626,000	0.8%
35	Utah	1,049,532,000	0.8%
36	New Mexico	919,522,000	0.7%
37	Nebraska	837,249,000	0.6%
38	West Virginia	766,898,000	0.6%
39	New Hampshire	719,080,000	0.5%
40	Maine	686,724,000	0.5%
41	Idaho	658,903,000	0.5%
42	Montana	484,217,000	0.4%
43	Hawaii	446,175,000	0.3%
44	Delaware	445,599,000	0.3%
45	South Dakota	421,545,000	0.3%
46	Rhode Island	406,633,000	0.3%
47	North Dakota	361,883,000	0.3%
48	Wyoming	354,456,000	0.3%
49	Vermont	331,499,000	0.2%
50	Alaska	287,242,000	0.2%
	District of Columbia	106,376,000	0.1%

Source: U.S. Department of Transportation, Federal Highway Administration
"Highway Statistics 2008" (Table MF-21) (http://www.fhwa.dot.gov/policyinformation/statistics/2008/)
*Includes gasoline for highway and nonhighway uses. "Gasoline" includes gasohol but excludes "special fuels" such as diesel.

Per Capita Gasoline Used in 2008

National Per Capita = 448 Gallons*

ALPHA ORDER				RANK ORDER		
RANK	STATE	GALLONS		RANK	STATE	GALLONS
5	Alabama	553		1	Wyoming	665
41	Alaska	417		2	South Carolina	572
40	Arizona	419		3	North Dakota	564
19	Arkansas	498		4	Mississippi	560
42	California	411		5	Alabama	553
38	Colorado	426		6	New Hampshire	544
37	Connecticut	427		7	Iowa	542
13	Delaware	509		8	Missouri	538
31	Florida	448		9	Vermont	534
23	Georgia	492		10	South Dakota	524
49	Hawaii	347		11	Maine	520
35	Idaho	431		12	North Carolina	515
48	Illinois	381		13	Delaware	509
26	Indiana	484		14	Virginia	506
7	Iowa	542		15	Oklahoma	505
28	Kansas	468		16	Minnesota	502
17	Kentucky	500		17	Kentucky	500
25	Louisiana	485		17	Montana	500
11	Maine	520		19	Arkansas	498
21	Maryland	493		20	New Jersey	494
36	Massachusetts	429		21	Maryland	493
30	Michigan	460		21	Tennessee	493
16	Minnesota	502		23	Georgia	492
4	Mississippi	560		24	Texas	490
8	Missouri	538		25	Louisiana	485
17	Montana	500		26	Indiana	484
27	Nebraska	470		27	Nebraska	470
34	Nevada	432		28	Kansas	468
6	New Hampshire	544		29	New Mexico	463
20	New Jersey	494		30	Michigan	460
29	New Mexico	463		31	Florida	448
50	New York	289		32	Wisconsin	446
12	North Carolina	515		33	Ohio	440
3	North Dakota	564		34	Nevada	432
33	Ohio	440		35	Idaho	431
15	Oklahoma	505		36	Massachusetts	429
44	Oregon	400		37	Connecticut	427
45	Pennsylvania	398		38	Colorado	426
46	Rhode Island	386		39	West Virginia	423
2	South Carolina	572		40	Arizona	419
10	South Dakota	524		41	Alaska	417
21	Tennessee	493		42	California	411
24	Texas	490		43	Washington	406
47	Utah	385		44	Oregon	400
9	Vermont	534		45	Pennsylvania	398
14	Virginia	506		46	Rhode Island	386
43	Washington	406		47	Utah	385
39	West Virginia	423		48	Illinois	381
32	Wisconsin	446		49	Hawaii	347
1	Wyoming	665		50	New York	289
					District of Columbia	180

Source: CQ Press using data from U.S. Department of Transportation, Federal Highway Administration
"Highway Statistics 2008" (Table MF-21) (http://www.fhwa.dot.gov/policyinformation/statistics/2008/)
*Includes gasoline for highway and nonhighway uses. "Gasoline" includes gasohol but excludes "special fuels" such as diesel.

Daily Production of Crude Oil in 2008

National Total = 4,950,320 Barrels a Day*

ALPHA ORDER				RANK ORDER			
RANK	**STATE**	**BARRELS**	**% of USA**	**RANK**	**STATE**	**BARRELS**	**% of USA**
15	Alabama	20,617	0.4%	1	Texas	1,087,470	22.0%
2	Alaska	682,716	13.8%	2	Alaska	682,716	13.8%
30	Arizona	142	0.0%	3	California	586,186	11.8%
17	Arkansas	16,609	0.3%	4	Louisiana	199,484	4.0%
3	California	586,186	11.8%	5	Oklahoma	175,041	3.5%
11	Colorado	65,721	1.3%	6	North Dakota	171,519	3.5%
NA	Connecticut**	NA	NA	7	New Mexico	162,303	3.3%
NA	Delaware**	NA	NA	8	Wyoming	144,653	2.9%
22	Florida	5,344	0.1%	9	Kansas	108,148	2.2%
NA	Georgia**	NA	NA	10	Montana	86,189	1.7%
NA	Hawaii**	NA	NA	11	Colorado	65,721	1.3%
NA	Idaho**	NA	NA	12	Mississippi	60,388	1.2%
14	Illinois	25,746	0.5%	13	Utah	60,104	1.2%
23	Indiana	5,077	0.1%	14	Illinois	25,746	0.5%
NA	Iowa**	NA	NA	15	Alabama	20,617	0.4%
9	Kansas	108,148	2.2%	16	Michigan	17,003	0.3%
20	Kentucky	7,227	0.1%	17	Arkansas	16,609	0.3%
4	Louisiana	199,484	4.0%	18	Ohio	15,615	0.3%
NA	Maine**	NA	NA	19	Pennsylvania	9,866	0.2%
NA	Maryland**	NA	NA	20	Kentucky	7,227	0.1%
NA	Massachusetts**	NA	NA	21	Nebraska	6,541	0.1%
16	Michigan	17,003	0.3%	22	Florida	5,344	0.1%
NA	Minnesota**	NA	NA	23	Indiana	5,077	0.1%
12	Mississippi	60,388	1.2%	24	South Dakota	4,637	0.1%
29	Missouri	270	0.0%	25	West Virginia	4,352	0.1%
10	Montana	86,189	1.7%	26	Nevada	1,191	0.0%
21	Nebraska	6,541	0.1%	27	New York	1,055	0.0%
26	Nevada	1,191	0.0%	28	Tennessee	940	0.0%
NA	New Hampshire**	NA	NA	29	Missouri	270	0.0%
NA	New Jersey**	NA	NA	30	Arizona	142	0.0%
7	New Mexico	162,303	3.3%	31	Virginia	19	0.0%
27	New York	1,055	0.0%	NA	Connecticut**	NA	NA
NA	North Carolina**	NA	NA	NA	Delaware**	NA	NA
6	North Dakota	171,519	3.5%	NA	Georgia**	NA	NA
18	Ohio	15,615	0.3%	NA	Hawaii**	NA	NA
5	Oklahoma	175,041	3.5%	NA	Idaho**	NA	NA
NA	Oregon**	NA	NA	NA	Iowa**	NA	NA
19	Pennsylvania	9,866	0.2%	NA	Maine**	NA	NA
NA	Rhode Island**	NA	NA	NA	Maryland**	NA	NA
NA	South Carolina**	NA	NA	NA	Massachusetts**	NA	NA
24	South Dakota	4,637	0.1%	NA	Minnesota**	NA	NA
28	Tennessee	940	0.0%	NA	New Hampshire**	NA	NA
1	Texas	1,087,470	22.0%	NA	New Jersey**	NA	NA
13	Utah	60,104	1.2%	NA	North Carolina**	NA	NA
NA	Vermont**	NA	NA	NA	Oregon**	NA	NA
31	Virginia	19	0.0%	NA	Rhode Island**	NA	NA
NA	Washington**	NA	NA	NA	South Carolina**	NA	NA
25	West Virginia	4,352	0.1%	NA	Vermont**	NA	NA
NA	Wisconsin**	NA	NA	NA	Washington**	NA	NA
8	Wyoming	144,653	2.9%	NA	Wisconsin**	NA	NA
					District of Columbia**	NA	NA

Source: CQ Press using data from U.S. Department of Energy, Energy Information Administration
"Petroleum Supply Annual 2008, Volume 1" (http://tonto.eia.doe.gov/dnav/pet/pet_crd_crpdn_adc_mbbl_m.htm)
*National total includes 1,218,153 barrels a day in federal offshore production. Figures for Alaska, California, Louisiana, and Texas include state offshore production.
**No reported production.

Fossil Fuel Emissions in 2007

National Total = 5,735,800,000 Metric Tons of Carbon Dioxide (CO2)*

ALPHA ORDER

RANK ORDER

RANK	STATE	TONS OF CO2	% of USA		RANK	STATE	TONS OF CO2	% of USA
14	Alabama	145,240,000	2.4%		1	Texas	676,750,000	11.3%
39	Alaska	43,150,000	0.7%		2	California	402,770,000	6.7%
22	Arizona	101,510,000	1.7%		3	Pennsylvania	274,300,000	4.6%
34	Arkansas	63,700,000	1.1%		4	Ohio	267,670,000	4.5%
2	California	402,770,000	6.7%		5	Florida	256,270,000	4.3%
24	Colorado	98,120,000	1.6%		6	Illinois	242,830,000	4.1%
41	Connecticut	40,240,000	0.7%		7	Indiana	230,830,000	3.9%
46	Delaware	17,380,000	0.3%		8	New York	201,250,000	3.4%
5	Florida	256,270,000	4.3%		9	Louisiana	194,930,000	3.3%
10	Georgia	184,040,000	3.1%		10	Georgia	184,040,000	3.1%
43	Hawaii	24,170,000	0.4%		11	Michigan	182,980,000	3.1%
47	Idaho	16,280,000	0.3%		12	Kentucky	156,800,000	2.6%
6	Illinois	242,830,000	4.1%		13	North Carolina	153,560,000	2.6%
7	Indiana	230,830,000	3.9%		14	Alabama	145,240,000	2.4%
26	Iowa	85,190,000	1.4%		15	Missouri	140,040,000	2.3%
29	Kansas	78,460,000	1.3%		16	New Jersey	134,290,000	2.2%
12	Kentucky	156,800,000	2.6%		17	Tennessee	128,390,000	2.1%
9	Louisiana	194,930,000	3.3%		18	Virginia	127,950,000	2.1%
44	Maine	19,930,000	0.3%		19	West Virginia	116,380,000	1.9%
30	Maryland	77,940,000	1.3%		20	Oklahoma	109,300,000	1.8%
28	Massachusetts	79,900,000	1.3%		21	Wisconsin	104,380,000	1.7%
11	Michigan	182,980,000	3.1%		22	Arizona	101,510,000	1.7%
23	Minnesota	99,860,000	1.7%		23	Minnesota	99,860,000	1.7%
32	Mississippi	67,810,000	1.1%		24	Colorado	98,120,000	1.6%
15	Missouri	140,040,000	2.3%		25	South Carolina	89,340,000	1.5%
42	Montana	37,700,000	0.6%		26	Iowa	85,190,000	1.4%
37	Nebraska	43,870,000	0.7%		27	Washington	82,560,000	1.4%
40	Nevada	41,600,000	0.7%		28	Massachusetts	79,900,000	1.3%
45	New Hampshire	19,020,000	0.3%		29	Kansas	78,460,000	1.3%
16	New Jersey	134,290,000	2.2%		30	Maryland	77,940,000	1.3%
35	New Mexico	58,550,000	1.0%		31	Utah	69,230,000	1.2%
8	New York	201,250,000	3.4%		32	Mississippi	67,810,000	1.1%
13	North Carolina	153,560,000	2.6%		33	Wyoming	64,570,000	1.1%
36	North Dakota	48,980,000	0.8%		34	Arkansas	63,700,000	1.1%
4	Ohio	267,670,000	4.5%		35	New Mexico	58,550,000	1.0%
20	Oklahoma	109,300,000	1.8%		36	North Dakota	48,980,000	0.8%
38	Oregon	43,520,000	0.7%		37	Nebraska	43,870,000	0.7%
3	Pennsylvania	274,300,000	4.6%		38	Oregon	43,520,000	0.7%
49	Rhode Island	11,100,000	0.2%		39	Alaska	43,150,000	0.7%
25	South Carolina	89,340,000	1.5%		40	Nevada	41,600,000	0.7%
48	South Dakota	13,780,000	0.2%		41	Connecticut	40,240,000	0.7%
17	Tennessee	128,390,000	2.1%		42	Montana	37,700,000	0.6%
1	Texas	676,750,000	11.3%		43	Hawaii	24,170,000	0.4%
31	Utah	69,230,000	1.2%		44	Maine	19,930,000	0.3%
50	Vermont	6,490,000	0.1%		45	New Hampshire	19,020,000	0.3%
18	Virginia	127,950,000	2.1%		46	Delaware	17,380,000	0.3%
27	Washington	82,560,000	1.4%		47	Idaho	16,280,000	0.3%
19	West Virginia	116,380,000	1.9%		48	South Dakota	13,780,000	0.2%
21	Wisconsin	104,380,000	1.7%		49	Rhode Island	11,100,000	0.2%
33	Wyoming	64,570,000	1.1%		50	Vermont	6,490,000	0.1%
						District of Columbia	3,380,000	0.1%

Source: U.S. Environmental Protection Agency
   "Energy CO2 Emissions by State" (http://www.epa.gov/climatechange/emissions/state_energyco2inv.html)
*National total determined using a different methodology. Carbon dioxide (CO2) emissions from fossil fuel combustion represented the largest source (94%) of total CO2 emissions from all emission sources. The EPA estimates that an additional 367,600,000 metric tons of CO2 were emitted from other sources.

Per Capita Fossil Fuel Emissions in 2007

National Per Capita = 19.8 Metric Tons of Carbon Dioxide (CO2)*

ALPHA ORDER

RANK ORDER

RANK	STATE	TONS OF CO2		RANK	STATE	TONS OF CO2
9	Alabama	31.3		1	Wyoming	123.4
4	Alaska	63.2		2	North Dakota	76.7
36	Arizona	16.0		3	West Virginia	64.3
20	Arkansas	22.4		4	Alaska	63.2
46	California	11.1		5	Louisiana	44.5
23	Colorado	20.3		6	Montana	39.4
45	Connecticut	11.5		7	Kentucky	36.8
25	Delaware	20.1		8	Indiana	36.4
40	Florida	14.0		9	Alabama	31.3
26	Georgia	19.3		10	Oklahoma	30.3
29	Hawaii	18.9		11	New Mexico	29.7
47	Idaho	10.9		12	Iowa	28.6
28	Illinois	19.0		13	Texas	28.4
8	Indiana	36.4		14	Kansas	28.3
12	Iowa	28.6		15	Utah	26.0
14	Kansas	28.3		16	Nebraska	24.8
7	Kentucky	36.8		17	Missouri	23.7
5	Louisiana	44.5		18	Mississippi	23.2
38	Maine	15.1		18	Ohio	23.2
41	Maryland	13.8		20	Arkansas	22.4
43	Massachusetts	12.3		21	Pennsylvania	21.9
31	Michigan	18.2		22	Tennessee	20.8
27	Minnesota	19.2		23	Colorado	20.3
18	Mississippi	23.2		24	South Carolina	20.2
17	Missouri	23.7		25	Delaware	20.1
6	Montana	39.4		26	Georgia	19.3
16	Nebraska	24.8		27	Minnesota	19.2
35	Nevada	16.2		28	Illinois	19.0
39	New Hampshire	14.4		29	Hawaii	18.9
37	New Jersey	15.5		30	Wisconsin	18.6
11	New Mexico	29.7		31	Michigan	18.2
50	New York	10.4		32	South Dakota	17.3
33	North Carolina	16.9		33	North Carolina	16.9
2	North Dakota	76.7		34	Virginia	16.6
18	Ohio	23.2		35	Nevada	16.2
10	Oklahoma	30.3		36	Arizona	16.0
44	Oregon	11.7		37	New Jersey	15.5
21	Pennsylvania	21.9		38	Maine	15.1
48	Rhode Island	10.5		39	New Hampshire	14.4
24	South Carolina	20.2		40	Florida	14.0
32	South Dakota	17.3		41	Maryland	13.8
22	Tennessee	20.8		42	Washington	12.8
13	Texas	28.4		43	Massachusetts	12.3
15	Utah	26.0		44	Oregon	11.7
48	Vermont	10.5		45	Connecticut	11.5
34	Virginia	16.6		46	California	11.1
42	Washington	12.8		47	Idaho	10.9
3	West Virginia	64.3		48	Rhode Island	10.5
30	Wisconsin	18.6		48	Vermont	10.5
1	Wyoming	123.4		50	New York	10.4

District of Columbia   5.8

Source: CQ Press using data from U.S. Environmental Protection Agency
"Energy CO2 Emissions by State" (http://www.epa.gov/climatechange/emissions/state_energyco2inv.html)
*National figure determined using a different methodology. Carbon dioxide (CO2) emissions from fossil fuel combustion represented the largest source (94%) of total CO2 emissions from all emission sources. The EPA estimates that an additional 367,600,000 metric tons of CO2 were emitted from other sources.

Percent Change in Fossil Fuel Emissions: 2003 to 2007

National Percent Change = 2.2% Increase*

ALPHA ORDER			RANK ORDER		
RANK	STATE	PERCENT CHANGE	RANK	STATE	PERCENT CHANGE
14	Alabama	6.4	1	Montana	16.3
33	Alaska	0.6	2	Arizona	14.2
2	Arizona	14.2	2	Idaho	14.2
27	Arkansas	2.2	4	Hawaii	12.9
23	California	2.9	5	Utah	12.1
7	Colorado	9.9	6	Oregon	10.1
46	Connecticut	(4.9)	7	Colorado	9.9
24	Delaware	2.8	8	Georgia	9.5
19	Florida	5.0	8	Washington	9.5
8	Georgia	9.5	10	South Carolina	9.1
4	Hawaii	12.9	11	Iowa	8.7
2	Idaho	14.2	12	Kentucky	8.0
16	Illinois	6.2	12	Mississippi	8.0
38	Indiana	(0.3)	14	Alabama	6.4
11	Iowa	8.7	14	New Jersey	6.4
36	Kansas	0.2	16	Illinois	6.2
12	Kentucky	8.0	16	Oklahoma	6.2
35	Louisiana	0.5	18	North Carolina	5.6
50	Maine	(15.1)	19	Florida	5.0
44	Maryland	(3.6)	20	Virginia	4.1
47	Massachusetts	(5.3)	21	Tennessee	3.8
41	Michigan	(0.7)	22	North Dakota	3.0
40	Minnesota	(0.6)	23	California	2.9
12	Mississippi	8.0	24	Delaware	2.8
30	Missouri	1.6	24	New Mexico	2.8
1	Montana	16.3	26	Nebraska	2.5
26	Nebraska	2.5	27	Arkansas	2.2
43	Nevada	(3.5)	28	West Virginia	1.8
49	New Hampshire	(7.4)	29	Wyoming	1.7
14	New Jersey	6.4	30	Missouri	1.6
24	New Mexico	2.8	30	South Dakota	1.6
48	New York	(5.4)	32	Pennsylvania	1.2
18	North Carolina	5.6	33	Alaska	0.6
22	North Dakota	3.0	33	Ohio	0.6
33	Ohio	0.6	35	Louisiana	0.5
16	Oklahoma	6.2	36	Kansas	0.2
6	Oregon	10.1	37	Wisconsin	0.0
32	Pennsylvania	1.2	38	Indiana	(0.3)
42	Rhode Island	(2.9)	38	Vermont	(0.3)
10	South Carolina	9.1	40	Minnesota	(0.6)
30	South Dakota	1.6	41	Michigan	(0.7)
21	Tennessee	3.8	42	Rhode Island	(2.9)
45	Texas	(4.4)	43	Nevada	(3.5)
5	Utah	12.1	44	Maryland	(3.6)
38	Vermont	(0.3)	45	Texas	(4.4)
20	Virginia	4.1	46	Connecticut	(4.9)
8	Washington	9.5	47	Massachusetts	(5.3)
28	West Virginia	1.8	48	New York	(5.4)
37	Wisconsin	0.0	49	New Hampshire	(7.4)
29	Wyoming	1.7	50	Maine	(15.1)

District of Columbia   (13.6)

Source: CQ Press using data from U.S. Environmental Protection Agency
   "Energy CO2 Emissions by State" (http://www.epa.gov/climatechange/emissions/state_energyco2inv.html)
*Based on metric tons of carbon dioxide (CO2).

Toxic Releases: Total Pollution Released in 2007

National Total = 4,080,007,958 Pounds of Toxins*

ALPHA ORDER

RANK	STATE	POUNDS	% of USA
14	Alabama	113,473,893	2.8%
1	Alaska	584,716,753	14.3%
18	Arizona	88,011,463	2.2%
28	Arkansas	43,809,072	1.1%
24	California	54,023,294	1.3%
36	Colorado	24,449,862	0.6%
46	Connecticut	4,136,192	0.1%
41	Delaware	17,394,539	0.4%
11	Florida	120,461,757	3.0%
12	Georgia	117,175,962	2.9%
48	Hawaii	3,015,062	0.1%
20	Idaho	68,400,130	1.7%
13	Illinois	114,294,948	2.8%
3	Indiana	228,963,262	5.6%
29	Iowa	43,405,128	1.1%
35	Kansas	26,194,077	0.6%
15	Kentucky	98,230,101	2.4%
8	Louisiana	130,440,759	3.2%
43	Maine	11,124,513	0.3%
25	Maryland	50,535,275	1.2%
45	Massachusetts	6,539,205	0.2%
17	Michigan	96,223,791	2.4%
34	Minnesota	28,051,229	0.7%
23	Mississippi	59,521,069	1.5%
16	Missouri	96,839,277	2.4%
26	Montana	48,349,738	1.2%
32	Nebraska	32,884,831	0.8%
5	Nevada	221,495,219	5.4%
47	New Hampshire	4,018,879	0.1%
39	New Jersey	20,561,802	0.5%
40	New Mexico	18,342,054	0.4%
30	New York	34,901,068	0.9%
9	North Carolina	122,105,656	3.0%
38	North Dakota	22,129,548	0.5%
2	Ohio	274,396,441	6.7%
31	Oklahoma	34,080,993	0.8%
37	Oregon	22,363,434	0.5%
7	Pennsylvania	163,119,212	4.0%
49	Rhode Island	519,459	0.0%
22	South Carolina	67,099,407	1.6%
44	South Dakota	7,790,733	0.2%
10	Tennessee	120,567,890	3.0%
4	Texas	222,562,560	5.5%
6	Utah	169,070,157	4.1%
50	Vermont	336,289	0.0%
21	Virginia	67,926,500	1.7%
33	Washington	28,388,092	0.7%
19	West Virginia	85,723,920	2.1%
27	Wisconsin	46,273,673	1.1%
42	Wyoming	15,531,604	0.4%

RANK ORDER

RANK	STATE	POUNDS	% of USA
1	Alaska	584,716,753	14.3%
2	Ohio	274,396,441	6.7%
3	Indiana	228,963,262	5.6%
4	Texas	222,562,560	5.5%
5	Nevada	221,495,219	5.4%
6	Utah	169,070,157	4.1%
7	Pennsylvania	163,119,212	4.0%
8	Louisiana	130,440,759	3.2%
9	North Carolina	122,105,656	3.0%
10	Tennessee	120,567,890	3.0%
11	Florida	120,461,757	3.0%
12	Georgia	117,175,962	2.9%
13	Illinois	114,294,948	2.8%
14	Alabama	113,473,893	2.8%
15	Kentucky	98,230,101	2.4%
16	Missouri	96,839,277	2.4%
17	Michigan	96,223,791	2.4%
18	Arizona	88,011,463	2.2%
19	West Virginia	85,723,920	2.1%
20	Idaho	68,400,130	1.7%
21	Virginia	67,926,500	1.7%
22	South Carolina	67,099,407	1.6%
23	Mississippi	59,521,069	1.5%
24	California	54,023,294	1.3%
25	Maryland	50,535,275	1.2%
26	Montana	48,349,738	1.2%
27	Wisconsin	46,273,673	1.1%
28	Arkansas	43,809,072	1.1%
29	Iowa	43,405,128	1.1%
30	New York	34,901,068	0.9%
31	Oklahoma	34,080,993	0.8%
32	Nebraska	32,884,831	0.8%
33	Washington	28,388,092	0.7%
34	Minnesota	28,051,229	0.7%
35	Kansas	26,194,077	0.6%
36	Colorado	24,449,862	0.6%
37	Oregon	22,363,434	0.5%
38	North Dakota	22,129,548	0.5%
39	New Jersey	20,561,802	0.5%
40	New Mexico	18,342,054	0.4%
41	Delaware	17,394,539	0.4%
42	Wyoming	15,531,604	0.4%
43	Maine	11,124,513	0.3%
44	South Dakota	7,790,733	0.2%
45	Massachusetts	6,539,205	0.2%
46	Connecticut	4,136,192	0.1%
47	New Hampshire	4,018,879	0.1%
48	Hawaii	3,015,062	0.1%
49	Rhode Island	519,459	0.0%
50	Vermont	336,289	0.0%
	District of Columbia	38,186	0.0%

Source: U.S. Environmental Protection Agency, Office of Pollution Prevention and Toxics Information Management
"2007 Toxics Release Inventory" (http://www.epa.gov/tri/tridata/tri07/)
*National total does not include 6,225,016 pounds of toxins in U.S. territories. Includes discharges to air, surface water, underground injection, and surface land. Includes both original (or manufacturing) industries and those added by EPA since it began tracking releases.

Toxic Releases: Total Air Emissions in 2007

National Total = 1,306,164,691 Pounds*

<u>ALPHA ORDER</u>

RANK	STATE	POUNDS	% of USA
13	Alabama	47,183,706	3.6%
47	Alaska	1,389,452	0.1%
38	Arizona	3,971,665	0.3%
22	Arkansas	16,243,004	1.2%
23	California	15,329,864	1.2%
41	Colorado	2,886,925	0.2%
42	Connecticut	2,558,357	0.2%
32	Delaware	6,894,090	0.5%
8	Florida	61,401,211	4.7%
2	Georgia	83,337,231	6.4%
43	Hawaii	2,267,707	0.2%
37	Idaho	4,180,921	0.3%
16	Illinois	40,703,384	3.1%
6	Indiana	63,231,489	4.8%
18	Iowa	24,050,708	1.8%
26	Kansas	11,631,024	0.9%
7	Kentucky	61,817,497	4.7%
11	Louisiana	51,879,261	4.0%
34	Maine	5,039,441	0.4%
15	Maryland	40,978,686	3.1%
36	Massachusetts	4,237,727	0.3%
12	Michigan	49,353,621	3.8%
27	Minnesota	11,303,887	0.9%
19	Mississippi	22,257,707	1.7%
21	Missouri	18,303,380	1.4%
39	Montana	3,902,100	0.3%
33	Nebraska	5,822,401	0.4%
46	Nevada	1,439,778	0.1%
40	New Hampshire	3,848,919	0.3%
30	New Jersey	8,991,984	0.7%
48	New Mexico	950,236	0.1%
25	New York	14,214,281	1.1%
3	North Carolina	82,310,718	6.3%
35	North Dakota	4,491,315	0.3%
1	Ohio	115,101,631	8.8%
24	Oklahoma	15,317,877	1.2%
28	Oregon	9,837,543	0.8%
4	Pennsylvania	79,387,526	6.1%
49	Rhode Island	242,335	0.0%
14	South Carolina	46,873,186	3.6%
45	South Dakota	1,925,537	0.1%
9	Tennessee	53,665,743	4.1%
5	Texas	71,514,182	5.5%
29	Utah	9,292,720	0.7%
50	Vermont	22,875	0.0%
17	Virginia	40,179,013	3.1%
31	Washington	8,920,877	0.7%
10	West Virginia	53,329,544	4.1%
20	Wisconsin	19,925,757	1.5%
44	Wyoming	2,223,394	0.2%

<u>RANK ORDER</u>

RANK	STATE	POUNDS	% of USA
1	Ohio	115,101,631	8.8%
2	Georgia	83,337,231	6.4%
3	North Carolina	82,310,718	6.3%
4	Pennsylvania	79,387,526	6.1%
5	Texas	71,514,182	5.5%
6	Indiana	63,231,489	4.8%
7	Kentucky	61,817,497	4.7%
8	Florida	61,401,211	4.7%
9	Tennessee	53,665,743	4.1%
10	West Virginia	53,329,544	4.1%
11	Louisiana	51,879,261	4.0%
12	Michigan	49,353,621	3.8%
13	Alabama	47,183,706	3.6%
14	South Carolina	46,873,186	3.6%
15	Maryland	40,978,686	3.1%
16	Illinois	40,703,384	3.1%
17	Virginia	40,179,013	3.1%
18	Iowa	24,050,708	1.8%
19	Mississippi	22,257,707	1.7%
20	Wisconsin	19,925,757	1.5%
21	Missouri	18,303,380	1.4%
22	Arkansas	16,243,004	1.2%
23	California	15,329,864	1.2%
24	Oklahoma	15,317,877	1.2%
25	New York	14,214,281	1.1%
26	Kansas	11,631,024	0.9%
27	Minnesota	11,303,887	0.9%
28	Oregon	9,837,543	0.8%
29	Utah	9,292,720	0.7%
30	New Jersey	8,991,984	0.7%
31	Washington	8,920,877	0.7%
32	Delaware	6,894,090	0.5%
33	Nebraska	5,822,401	0.4%
34	Maine	5,039,441	0.4%
35	North Dakota	4,491,315	0.3%
36	Massachusetts	4,237,727	0.3%
37	Idaho	4,180,921	0.3%
38	Arizona	3,971,665	0.3%
39	Montana	3,902,100	0.3%
40	New Hampshire	3,848,919	0.3%
41	Colorado	2,886,925	0.2%
42	Connecticut	2,558,357	0.2%
43	Hawaii	2,267,707	0.2%
44	Wyoming	2,223,394	0.2%
45	South Dakota	1,925,537	0.1%
46	Nevada	1,439,778	0.1%
47	Alaska	1,389,452	0.1%
48	New Mexico	950,236	0.1%
49	Rhode Island	242,335	0.0%
50	Vermont	22,875	0.0%
	District of Columbia	1,274	0.0%

Source: U.S. Environmental Protection Agency, Office of Pollution Prevention and Toxics Information Management
   "2007 Toxics Release Inventory" (http://www.epa.gov/tri/tridata/tri07/)
*National total does not include 5,484,366 pounds of emissions in U.S. territories. Includes both original (or manufacturing) industries and those added by EPA since it began tracking releases.

Toxic Releases: Total Surface Water Discharges in 2007

National Total = 231,680,711 Pounds*

ALPHA ORDER

RANK	STATE	POUNDS	% of USA
15	Alabama	5,876,097	2.5%
43	Alaska	63,962	0.0%
49	Arizona	4,364	0.0%
14	Arkansas	6,084,676	2.6%
18	California	3,900,865	1.7%
23	Colorado	3,357,389	1.4%
38	Connecticut	437,974	0.2%
25	Delaware	2,950,375	1.3%
34	Florida	1,166,540	0.5%
7	Georgia	10,601,709	4.6%
37	Hawaii	446,948	0.2%
24	Idaho	3,185,716	1.4%
11	Illinois	8,768,573	3.8%
1	Indiana	27,304,625	11.8%
21	Iowa	3,445,959	1.5%
35	Kansas	586,162	0.3%
16	Kentucky	5,305,784	2.3%
5	Louisiana	12,811,400	5.5%
22	Maine	3,374,134	1.5%
31	Maryland	2,052,280	0.9%
46	Massachusetts	12,727	0.0%
36	Michigan	575,930	0.2%
30	Minnesota	2,072,875	0.9%
10	Mississippi	9,058,061	3.9%
32	Missouri	1,690,965	0.7%
40	Montana	170,145	0.1%
3	Nebraska	17,409,779	7.5%
50	Nevada	144	0.0%
45	New Hampshire	42,824	0.0%
12	New Jersey	7,668,127	3.3%
44	New Mexico	56,100	0.0%
13	New York	6,400,905	2.8%
9	North Carolina	9,156,743	4.0%
42	North Dakota	82,123	0.0%
8	Ohio	9,312,046	4.0%
20	Oklahoma	3,508,076	1.5%
27	Oregon	2,847,886	1.2%
6	Pennsylvania	10,706,605	4.6%
48	Rhode Island	5,130	0.0%
19	South Carolina	3,780,395	1.6%
29	South Dakota	2,424,482	1.0%
28	Tennessee	2,706,182	1.2%
4	Texas	13,204,634	5.7%
41	Utah	94,394	0.0%
39	Vermont	179,592	0.1%
2	Virginia	18,382,941	7.9%
33	Washington	1,354,439	0.6%
26	West Virginia	2,923,737	1.3%
17	Wisconsin	4,100,243	1.8%
47	Wyoming	9,916	0.0%

RANK ORDER

RANK	STATE	POUNDS	% of USA
1	Indiana	27,304,625	11.8%
2	Virginia	18,382,941	7.9%
3	Nebraska	17,409,779	7.5%
4	Texas	13,204,634	5.7%
5	Louisiana	12,811,400	5.5%
6	Pennsylvania	10,706,605	4.6%
7	Georgia	10,601,709	4.6%
8	Ohio	9,312,046	4.0%
9	North Carolina	9,156,743	4.0%
10	Mississippi	9,058,061	3.9%
11	Illinois	8,768,573	3.8%
12	New Jersey	7,668,127	3.3%
13	New York	6,400,905	2.8%
14	Arkansas	6,084,676	2.6%
15	Alabama	5,876,097	2.5%
16	Kentucky	5,305,784	2.3%
17	Wisconsin	4,100,243	1.8%
18	California	3,900,865	1.7%
19	South Carolina	3,780,395	1.6%
20	Oklahoma	3,508,076	1.5%
21	Iowa	3,445,959	1.5%
22	Maine	3,374,134	1.5%
23	Colorado	3,357,389	1.4%
24	Idaho	3,185,716	1.4%
25	Delaware	2,950,375	1.3%
26	West Virginia	2,923,737	1.3%
27	Oregon	2,847,886	1.2%
28	Tennessee	2,706,182	1.2%
29	South Dakota	2,424,482	1.0%
30	Minnesota	2,072,875	0.9%
31	Maryland	2,052,280	0.9%
32	Missouri	1,690,965	0.7%
33	Washington	1,354,439	0.6%
34	Florida	1,166,540	0.5%
35	Kansas	586,162	0.3%
36	Michigan	575,930	0.2%
37	Hawaii	446,948	0.2%
38	Connecticut	437,974	0.2%
39	Vermont	179,592	0.1%
40	Montana	170,145	0.1%
41	Utah	94,394	0.0%
42	North Dakota	82,123	0.0%
43	Alaska	63,962	0.0%
44	New Mexico	56,100	0.0%
45	New Hampshire	42,824	0.0%
46	Massachusetts	12,727	0.0%
47	Wyoming	9,916	0.0%
48	Rhode Island	5,130	0.0%
49	Arizona	4,364	0.0%
50	Nevada	144	0.0%
	District of Columbia	17,033	0.0%

Source: U.S. Environmental Protection Agency, Office of Pollution Prevention and Toxics Information Management
"2007 Toxics Release Inventory" (http://www.epa.gov/tri/tridata/tri07/)
*National total does not include 352,489 pounds of discharges in U.S. territories. Includes both original (or manufacturing) industries and those added by EPA since it began tracking releases.

Hazardous Waste Sites on the National Priority List in 2010

National Total = 1,333 Sites*

ALPHA ORDER

RANK	STATE	SITES	% of USA
25	Alabama	15	1.1%
44	Alaska	6	0.5%
39	Arizona	9	0.7%
39	Arkansas	9	0.7%
3	California	96	7.2%
20	Colorado	20	1.5%
25	Connecticut	15	1.1%
27	Delaware	14	1.1%
6	Florida	54	4.1%
23	Georgia	16	1.2%
46	Hawaii	3	0.2%
39	Idaho	9	0.7%
7	Illinois	50	3.8%
13	Indiana	32	2.4%
33	Iowa	12	0.9%
33	Kansas	12	0.9%
27	Kentucky	14	1.1%
33	Louisiana	12	0.9%
33	Maine	12	0.9%
22	Maryland	18	1.4%
13	Massachusetts	32	2.4%
5	Michigan	68	5.1%
18	Minnesota	25	1.9%
44	Mississippi	6	0.5%
16	Missouri	30	2.3%
23	Montana	16	1.2%
31	Nebraska	13	1.0%
49	Nevada	1	0.1%
19	New Hampshire	21	1.6%
1	New Jersey	113	8.5%
27	New Mexico	14	1.1%
4	New York	88	6.6%
12	North Carolina	35	2.6%
50	North Dakota	0	0.0%
10	Ohio	41	3.1%
39	Oklahoma	9	0.7%
31	Oregon	13	1.0%
2	Pennsylvania	97	7.3%
33	Rhode Island	12	0.9%
17	South Carolina	26	2.0%
47	South Dakota	2	0.2%
27	Tennessee	14	1.1%
7	Texas	50	3.8%
21	Utah	19	1.4%
38	Vermont	11	0.8%
15	Virginia	31	2.3%
9	Washington	48	3.6%
39	West Virginia	9	0.7%
11	Wisconsin	39	2.9%
47	Wyoming	2	0.2%

RANK ORDER

RANK	STATE	SITES	% of USA
1	New Jersey	113	8.5%
2	Pennsylvania	97	7.3%
3	California	96	7.2%
4	New York	88	6.6%
5	Michigan	68	5.1%
6	Florida	54	4.1%
7	Illinois	50	3.8%
7	Texas	50	3.8%
9	Washington	48	3.6%
10	Ohio	41	3.1%
11	Wisconsin	39	2.9%
12	North Carolina	35	2.6%
13	Indiana	32	2.4%
13	Massachusetts	32	2.4%
15	Virginia	31	2.3%
16	Missouri	30	2.3%
17	South Carolina	26	2.0%
18	Minnesota	25	1.9%
19	New Hampshire	21	1.6%
20	Colorado	20	1.5%
21	Utah	19	1.4%
22	Maryland	18	1.4%
23	Georgia	16	1.2%
23	Montana	16	1.2%
25	Alabama	15	1.1%
25	Connecticut	15	1.1%
27	Delaware	14	1.1%
27	Kentucky	14	1.1%
27	New Mexico	14	1.1%
27	Tennessee	14	1.1%
31	Nebraska	13	1.0%
31	Oregon	13	1.0%
33	Iowa	12	0.9%
33	Kansas	12	0.9%
33	Louisiana	12	0.9%
33	Maine	12	0.9%
33	Rhode Island	12	0.9%
38	Vermont	11	0.8%
39	Arizona	9	0.7%
39	Arkansas	9	0.7%
39	Idaho	9	0.7%
39	Oklahoma	9	0.7%
39	West Virginia	9	0.7%
44	Alaska	6	0.5%
44	Mississippi	6	0.5%
46	Hawaii	3	0.2%
47	South Dakota	2	0.2%
47	Wyoming	2	0.2%
49	Nevada	1	0.1%
50	North Dakota	0	0.0%
	District of Columbia	1	0.1%

Source: U.S. Environmental Protection Agency
    "National Priorities List (NPL) Sites in the United States" (http://www.epa.gov/superfund/sites/npl/)
*As of January 12, 2010. Includes final and proposed General Superfund and Federal Facilities Sites. National total includes 14 sites in Puerto Rico, two in Guam, and five in the other U.S. territories.

Hazardous Waste Sites on the National Priority List
per 10,000 Square Miles in 2010
National Rate = 3.5 Sites per 10,000 Square Miles*

ALPHA ORDER

RANK ORDER

RANK	STATE	RATE		RANK	STATE	RATE
27	Alabama	2.9		1	New Jersey	129.5
48	Alaska	0.1		2	Rhode Island	77.7
45	Arizona	0.8		3	Delaware	56.3
36	Arkansas	1.7		4	Massachusetts	30.3
21	California	5.9		5	Connecticut	27.1
34	Colorado	1.9		6	New Hampshire	22.5
5	Connecticut	27.1		7	Pennsylvania	21.1
3	Delaware	56.3		8	New York	16.1
14	Florida	8.2		9	Maryland	14.5
29	Georgia	2.7		10	Vermont	11.4
29	Hawaii	2.7		11	Ohio	9.1
43	Idaho	1.1		12	Indiana	8.8
13	Illinois	8.6		13	Illinois	8.6
12	Indiana	8.8		14	Florida	8.2
33	Iowa	2.1		15	South Carolina	8.1
38	Kansas	1.5		16	Virginia	7.2
24	Kentucky	3.5		17	Michigan	7.0
31	Louisiana	2.3		18	Washington	6.7
25	Maine	3.4		19	North Carolina	6.5
9	Maryland	14.5		20	Wisconsin	6.0
4	Massachusetts	30.3		21	California	5.9
17	Michigan	7.0		22	Missouri	4.3
27	Minnesota	2.9		23	West Virginia	3.7
41	Mississippi	1.2		24	Kentucky	3.5
22	Missouri	4.3		25	Maine	3.4
43	Montana	1.1		26	Tennessee	3.3
36	Nebraska	1.7		27	Alabama	2.9
48	Nevada	0.1		27	Minnesota	2.9
6	New Hampshire	22.5		29	Georgia	2.7
1	New Jersey	129.5		29	Hawaii	2.7
41	New Mexico	1.2		31	Louisiana	2.3
8	New York	16.1		32	Utah	2.2
19	North Carolina	6.5		33	Iowa	2.1
50	North Dakota	0.0		34	Colorado	1.9
11	Ohio	9.1		34	Texas	1.9
39	Oklahoma	1.3		36	Arkansas	1.7
39	Oregon	1.3		36	Nebraska	1.7
7	Pennsylvania	21.1		38	Kansas	1.5
2	Rhode Island	77.7		39	Oklahoma	1.3
15	South Carolina	8.1		39	Oregon	1.3
46	South Dakota	0.3		41	Mississippi	1.2
26	Tennessee	3.3		41	New Mexico	1.2
34	Texas	1.9		43	Idaho	1.1
32	Utah	2.2		43	Montana	1.1
10	Vermont	11.4		45	Arizona	0.8
16	Virginia	7.2		46	South Dakota	0.3
18	Washington	6.7		47	Wyoming	0.2
23	West Virginia	3.7		48	Alaska	0.1
20	Wisconsin	6.0		48	Nevada	0.1
47	Wyoming	0.2		50	North Dakota	0.0

District of Columbia**   NA

Source: CQ Press using data from U.S. Environmental Protection Agency
     "National Priorities List (NPL) Sites in the United States" (http://www.epa.gov/superfund/sites/npl/)
*As of January 12, 2010. Includes final and proposed General Superfund and Federal Facilities Sites. National rate excludes
sites and square miles in Puerto Rico, Guam and the Virgin Islands. Based on land and water area of states.
**The District of Columbia has one site in its 68 square miles.

Hazardous Waste Sites Deleted from the National Priorities List as of 2010

National Total = 340 Sites*

ALPHA ORDER

RANK	STATE	SITES	% of USA
42	Alabama	1	0.3%
30	Alaska	3	0.9%
30	Arizona	3	0.9%
14	Arkansas	6	1.8%
8	California	12	3.5%
30	Colorado	3	0.9%
30	Connecticut	3	0.9%
14	Delaware	6	1.8%
4	Florida	23	6.8%
22	Georgia	4	1.2%
42	Hawaii	1	0.3%
30	Idaho	3	0.9%
36	Illinois	2	0.6%
12	Indiana	9	2.6%
10	Iowa	10	2.9%
19	Kansas	5	1.5%
14	Kentucky	6	1.8%
9	Louisiana	11	3.2%
36	Maine	2	0.6%
22	Maryland	4	1.2%
22	Massachusetts	4	1.2%
6	Michigan	17	5.0%
5	Minnesota	21	6.2%
30	Mississippi	3	0.9%
19	Missouri	5	1.5%
48	Montana	0	0.0%
42	Nebraska	1	0.3%
48	Nevada	0	0.0%
48	New Hampshire	0	0.0%
1	New Jersey	29	8.5%
22	New Mexico	4	1.2%
3	New York	24	7.1%
42	North Carolina	1	0.3%
36	North Dakota	2	0.6%
13	Ohio	7	2.1%
19	Oklahoma	5	1.5%
22	Oregon	4	1.2%
2	Pennsylvania	28	8.2%
42	Rhode Island	1	0.3%
22	South Carolina	4	1.2%
36	South Dakota	2	0.6%
14	Tennessee	6	1.8%
10	Texas	10	2.9%
22	Utah	4	1.2%
36	Vermont	2	0.6%
22	Virginia	4	1.2%
6	Washington	17	5.0%
36	West Virginia	2	0.6%
14	Wisconsin	6	1.8%
42	Wyoming	1	0.3%

RANK ORDER

RANK	STATE	SITES	% of USA
1	New Jersey	29	8.5%
2	Pennsylvania	28	8.2%
3	New York	24	7.1%
4	Florida	23	6.8%
5	Minnesota	21	6.2%
6	Michigan	17	5.0%
6	Washington	17	5.0%
8	California	12	3.5%
9	Louisiana	11	3.2%
10	Iowa	10	2.9%
10	Texas	10	2.9%
12	Indiana	9	2.6%
13	Ohio	7	2.1%
14	Arkansas	6	1.8%
14	Delaware	6	1.8%
14	Kentucky	6	1.8%
14	Tennessee	6	1.8%
14	Wisconsin	6	1.8%
19	Kansas	5	1.5%
19	Missouri	5	1.5%
19	Oklahoma	5	1.5%
22	Georgia	4	1.2%
22	Maryland	4	1.2%
22	Massachusetts	4	1.2%
22	New Mexico	4	1.2%
22	Oregon	4	1.2%
22	South Carolina	4	1.2%
22	Utah	4	1.2%
22	Virginia	4	1.2%
30	Alaska	3	0.9%
30	Arizona	3	0.9%
30	Colorado	3	0.9%
30	Connecticut	3	0.9%
30	Idaho	3	0.9%
30	Mississippi	3	0.9%
36	Illinois	2	0.6%
36	Maine	2	0.6%
36	North Dakota	2	0.6%
36	South Dakota	2	0.6%
36	Vermont	2	0.6%
36	West Virginia	2	0.6%
42	Alabama	1	0.3%
42	Hawaii	1	0.3%
42	Nebraska	1	0.3%
42	North Carolina	1	0.3%
42	Rhode Island	1	0.3%
42	Wyoming	1	0.3%
48	Montana	0	0.0%
48	Nevada	0	0.0%
48	New Hampshire	0	0.0%
	District of Columbia	0	0.0%

Source: U.S. Environmental Protection Agency
   "National Priorities List (NPL) Sites in the United States" (http://www.epa.gov/superfund/sites/npl/)
*Cumulative total as of January 12, 2010. National total includes five sites in Puerto Rico and three in other U.S. territories.

VIII. Geography

Total Area of States in Square Miles in 2008

National Total = 3,795,951 Square Miles*

ALPHA ORDER

RANK	STATE	MILES	% of USA
30	Alabama	52,420	1.4%
1	Alaska	664,988	17.5%
6	Arizona	113,990	3.0%
29	Arkansas	53,178	1.4%
3	California	163,694	4.3%
8	Colorado	104,094	2.7%
48	Connecticut	5,544	0.1%
49	Delaware	2,489	0.1%
22	Florida	65,758	1.7%
24	Georgia	59,425	1.6%
43	Hawaii	10,926	0.3%
14	Idaho	83,568	2.2%
25	Illinois	57,916	1.5%
38	Indiana	36,417	1.0%
26	Iowa	56,273	1.5%
15	Kansas	82,278	2.2%
37	Kentucky	40,411	1.1%
31	Louisiana	51,988	1.4%
39	Maine	35,384	0.9%
42	Maryland	12,406	0.3%
44	Massachusetts	10,554	0.3%
11	Michigan	96,713	2.5%
12	Minnesota	86,935	2.3%
32	Mississippi	48,432	1.3%
21	Missouri	69,702	1.8%
4	Montana	147,039	3.9%
16	Nebraska	77,349	2.0%
7	Nevada	110,572	2.9%
46	New Hampshire	9,348	0.2%
47	New Jersey	8,723	0.2%
5	New Mexico	121,590	3.2%
27	New York	54,555	1.4%
28	North Carolina	53,819	1.4%
19	North Dakota	70,698	1.9%
34	Ohio	44,825	1.2%
20	Oklahoma	69,899	1.8%
9	Oregon	98,379	2.6%
33	Pennsylvania	46,055	1.2%
50	Rhode Island	1,545	0.0%
40	South Carolina	32,021	0.8%
17	South Dakota	77,116	2.0%
36	Tennessee	42,144	1.1%
2	Texas	268,597	7.1%
13	Utah	84,897	2.2%
45	Vermont	9,616	0.3%
35	Virginia	42,775	1.1%
18	Washington	71,298	1.9%
41	West Virginia	24,230	0.6%
23	Wisconsin	65,496	1.7%
10	Wyoming	97,812	2.6%

RANK ORDER

RANK	STATE	MILES	% of USA
1	Alaska	664,988	17.5%
2	Texas	268,597	7.1%
3	California	163,694	4.3%
4	Montana	147,039	3.9%
5	New Mexico	121,590	3.2%
6	Arizona	113,990	3.0%
7	Nevada	110,572	2.9%
8	Colorado	104,094	2.7%
9	Oregon	98,379	2.6%
10	Wyoming	97,812	2.6%
11	Michigan	96,713	2.5%
12	Minnesota	86,935	2.3%
13	Utah	84,897	2.2%
14	Idaho	83,568	2.2%
15	Kansas	82,278	2.2%
16	Nebraska	77,349	2.0%
17	South Dakota	77,116	2.0%
18	Washington	71,298	1.9%
19	North Dakota	70,698	1.9%
20	Oklahoma	69,899	1.8%
21	Missouri	69,702	1.8%
22	Florida	65,758	1.7%
23	Wisconsin	65,496	1.7%
24	Georgia	59,425	1.6%
25	Illinois	57,916	1.5%
26	Iowa	56,273	1.5%
27	New York	54,555	1.4%
28	North Carolina	53,819	1.4%
29	Arkansas	53,178	1.4%
30	Alabama	52,420	1.4%
31	Louisiana	51,988	1.4%
32	Mississippi	48,432	1.3%
33	Pennsylvania	46,055	1.2%
34	Ohio	44,825	1.2%
35	Virginia	42,775	1.1%
36	Tennessee	42,144	1.1%
37	Kentucky	40,411	1.1%
38	Indiana	36,417	1.0%
39	Maine	35,384	0.9%
40	South Carolina	32,021	0.8%
41	West Virginia	24,230	0.6%
42	Maryland	12,406	0.3%
43	Hawaii	10,926	0.3%
44	Massachusetts	10,554	0.3%
45	Vermont	9,616	0.3%
46	New Hampshire	9,348	0.2%
47	New Jersey	8,723	0.2%
48	Connecticut	5,544	0.1%
49	Delaware	2,489	0.1%
50	Rhode Island	1,545	0.0%
	District of Columbia	68	0.0%

Source: U.S. Bureau of the Census
    "Statistical Abstract 2010" (http://www.census.gov/compendia/statab/)
*Total of land and water area. Revised figures.

Land Area of States in Square Miles in 2008

National Total = 3,531,822 Square Miles of Land Area*

ALPHA ORDER					RANK ORDER			
RANK	STATE	MILES	% of USA		RANK	STATE	MILES	% of USA
28	Alabama	50,644	1.4%		1	Alaska	570,665	16.2%
1	Alaska	570,665	16.2%		2	Texas	261,226	7.4%
6	Arizona	113,595	3.2%		3	California	155,766	4.4%
27	Arkansas	52,030	1.5%		4	Montana	145,541	4.1%
3	California	155,766	4.4%		5	New Mexico	121,297	3.4%
8	Colorado	103,641	2.9%		6	Arizona	113,595	3.2%
48	Connecticut	4,840	0.1%		7	Nevada	109,780	3.1%
49	Delaware	1,949	0.1%		8	Colorado	103,641	2.9%
26	Florida	53,603	1.5%		9	Wyoming	97,088	2.7%
21	Georgia	57,501	1.6%		10	Oregon	95,985	2.7%
47	Hawaii	6,428	0.2%		11	Idaho	82,643	2.3%
11	Idaho	82,643	2.3%		12	Utah	82,191	2.3%
24	Illinois	55,518	1.6%		13	Kansas	81,762	2.3%
38	Indiana	35,823	1.0%		14	Minnesota	79,607	2.3%
23	Iowa	55,858	1.6%		15	Nebraska	76,825	2.2%
13	Kansas	81,762	2.3%		16	South Dakota	75,811	2.1%
37	Kentucky	39,492	1.1%		17	North Dakota	69,001	2.0%
33	Louisiana	43,199	1.2%		18	Missouri	68,716	1.9%
39	Maine	30,841	0.9%		19	Oklahoma	68,603	1.9%
42	Maryland	9,705	0.3%		20	Washington	66,449	1.9%
45	Massachusetts	7,801	0.2%		21	Georgia	57,501	1.6%
22	Michigan	56,528	1.6%		22	Michigan	56,528	1.6%
14	Minnesota	79,607	2.3%		23	Iowa	55,858	1.6%
31	Mississippi	46,920	1.3%		24	Illinois	55,518	1.6%
18	Missouri	68,716	1.9%		25	Wisconsin	54,154	1.5%
4	Montana	145,541	4.1%		26	Florida	53,603	1.5%
15	Nebraska	76,825	2.2%		27	Arkansas	52,030	1.5%
7	Nevada	109,780	3.1%		28	Alabama	50,644	1.4%
44	New Hampshire	8,952	0.3%		29	North Carolina	48,619	1.4%
46	New Jersey	7,354	0.2%		30	New York	47,126	1.3%
5	New Mexico	121,297	3.4%		31	Mississippi	46,920	1.3%
30	New York	47,126	1.3%		32	Pennsylvania	44,739	1.3%
29	North Carolina	48,619	1.4%		33	Louisiana	43,199	1.2%
17	North Dakota	69,001	2.0%		34	Tennessee	41,235	1.2%
35	Ohio	40,858	1.2%		35	Ohio	40,858	1.2%
19	Oklahoma	68,603	1.9%		36	Virginia	39,493	1.1%
10	Oregon	95,985	2.7%		37	Kentucky	39,492	1.1%
32	Pennsylvania	44,739	1.3%		38	Indiana	35,823	1.0%
50	Rhode Island	1,034	0.0%		39	Maine	30,841	0.9%
40	South Carolina	30,070	0.9%		40	South Carolina	30,070	0.9%
16	South Dakota	75,811	2.1%		41	West Virginia	24,038	0.7%
34	Tennessee	41,235	1.2%		42	Maryland	9,705	0.3%
2	Texas	261,226	7.4%		43	Vermont	9,217	0.3%
12	Utah	82,191	2.3%		44	New Hampshire	8,952	0.3%
43	Vermont	9,217	0.3%		45	Massachusetts	7,801	0.2%
36	Virginia	39,493	1.1%		46	New Jersey	7,354	0.2%
20	Washington	66,449	1.9%		47	Hawaii	6,428	0.2%
41	West Virginia	24,038	0.7%		48	Connecticut	4,840	0.1%
25	Wisconsin	54,154	1.5%		49	Delaware	1,949	0.1%
9	Wyoming	97,088	2.7%		50	Rhode Island	1,034	0.0%
						District of Columbia	61	0.0%

Source: U.S. Bureau of the Census
   "Statistical Abstract 2010" (http://www.census.gov/compendia/statab/)
*Includes dry land temporarily or partially covered by water, such as marshland, swamps, etc.; streams and canals under one-eighth mile wide; and lakes, reservoirs, and ponds under 40 acres. Revised figures.

Water Area of States in Square Miles in 2008

National Total = 264,129 Square Miles of Water*

ALPHA ORDER

RANK	STATE	MILES	% of USA
23	Alabama	1,776	0.7%
1	Alaska	94,323	35.7%
47	Arizona	396	0.1%
31	Arkansas	1,149	0.4%
6	California	7,928	3.0%
44	Colorado	454	0.2%
38	Connecticut	703	0.3%
40	Delaware	539	0.2%
3	Florida	12,154	4.6%
22	Georgia	1,924	0.7%
13	Hawaii	4,499	1.7%
33	Idaho	926	0.4%
19	Illinois	2,398	0.9%
39	Indiana	594	0.2%
45	Iowa	415	0.2%
42	Kansas	516	0.2%
34	Kentucky	919	0.3%
5	Louisiana	8,789	3.3%
12	Maine	4,543	1.7%
18	Maryland	2,700	1.0%
16	Massachusetts	2,754	1.0%
2	Michigan	40,185	15.2%
9	Minnesota	7,328	2.8%
25	Mississippi	1,512	0.6%
32	Missouri	987	0.4%
26	Montana	1,498	0.6%
41	Nebraska	524	0.2%
36	Nevada	792	0.3%
47	New Hampshire	396	0.1%
27	New Jersey	1,369	0.5%
49	New Mexico	293	0.1%
7	New York	7,429	2.8%
10	North Carolina	5,200	2.0%
24	North Dakota	1,697	0.6%
14	Ohio	3,967	1.5%
30	Oklahoma	1,296	0.5%
20	Oregon	2,394	0.9%
28	Pennsylvania	1,316	0.5%
43	Rhode Island	511	0.2%
21	South Carolina	1,951	0.7%
29	South Dakota	1,305	0.5%
35	Tennessee	910	0.3%
8	Texas	7,371	2.8%
17	Utah	2,706	1.0%
46	Vermont	400	0.2%
15	Virginia	3,282	1.2%
11	Washington	4,849	1.8%
50	West Virginia	192	0.1%
4	Wisconsin	11,342	4.3%
37	Wyoming	724	0.3%

RANK ORDER

RANK	STATE	MILES	% of USA
1	Alaska	94,323	35.7%
2	Michigan	40,185	15.2%
3	Florida	12,154	4.6%
4	Wisconsin	11,342	4.3%
5	Louisiana	8,789	3.3%
6	California	7,928	3.0%
7	New York	7,429	2.8%
8	Texas	7,371	2.8%
9	Minnesota	7,328	2.8%
10	North Carolina	5,200	2.0%
11	Washington	4,849	1.8%
12	Maine	4,543	1.7%
13	Hawaii	4,499	1.7%
14	Ohio	3,967	1.5%
15	Virginia	3,282	1.2%
16	Massachusetts	2,754	1.0%
17	Utah	2,706	1.0%
18	Maryland	2,700	1.0%
19	Illinois	2,398	0.9%
20	Oregon	2,394	0.9%
21	South Carolina	1,951	0.7%
22	Georgia	1,924	0.7%
23	Alabama	1,776	0.7%
24	North Dakota	1,697	0.6%
25	Mississippi	1,512	0.6%
26	Montana	1,498	0.6%
27	New Jersey	1,369	0.5%
28	Pennsylvania	1,316	0.5%
29	South Dakota	1,305	0.5%
30	Oklahoma	1,296	0.5%
31	Arkansas	1,149	0.4%
32	Missouri	987	0.4%
33	Idaho	926	0.4%
34	Kentucky	919	0.3%
35	Tennessee	910	0.3%
36	Nevada	792	0.3%
37	Wyoming	724	0.3%
38	Connecticut	703	0.3%
39	Indiana	594	0.2%
40	Delaware	539	0.2%
41	Nebraska	524	0.2%
42	Kansas	516	0.2%
43	Rhode Island	511	0.2%
44	Colorado	454	0.2%
45	Iowa	415	0.2%
46	Vermont	400	0.2%
47	Arizona	396	0.1%
47	New Hampshire	396	0.1%
49	New Mexico	293	0.1%
50	West Virginia	192	0.1%
	District of Columbia	7	0.0%

Source: U.S. Bureau of the Census
 "Statistical Abstract 2010" (http://www.census.gov/compendia/statab/)
*Includes permanent inland water surface, such as lakes, reservoirs, and ponds having an area of 40 acres or more, canals one-eighth mile or more in width; coastal waters behind or sheltered by headlands or islands separated by less than 1 nautical mile of water, and islands under 40 acres in area. Excludes areas of oceans, bays, etc., lying within U.S. jurisdiction but not defined as inland water. Revised figures.

Highest Point of Elevation in Feet

National High Point = 20,320 Feet Above Sea Level (Mt. McKinley, Alaska)

ALPHA ORDER

RANK	STATE	HIGHEST POINT
35	Alabama	2,407
1	Alaska	20,320
12	Arizona	12,633
34	Arkansas	2,753
2	California	14,494
3	Colorado	14,433
36	Connecticut	2,380
49	Delaware	448
50	Florida	345
25	Georgia	4,784
6	Hawaii	13,796
11	Idaho	12,662
45	Illinois	1,235
44	Indiana	1,257
42	Iowa	1,670
28	Kansas	4,039
27	Kentucky	4,145
48	Louisiana	535
22	Maine	5,268
32	Maryland	3,360
31	Massachusetts	3,491
38	Michigan	1,979
37	Minnesota	2,301
47	Mississippi	806
41	Missouri	1,772
10	Montana	12,799
20	Nebraska	5,424
9	Nevada	13,140
18	New Hampshire	6,288
40	New Jersey	1,803
8	New Mexico	13,161
21	New York	5,344
16	North Carolina	6,684
30	North Dakota	3,506
43	Ohio	1,550
23	Oklahoma	4,973
13	Oregon	11,239
33	Pennsylvania	3,213
46	Rhode Island	812
29	South Carolina	3,560
15	South Dakota	7,242
17	Tennessee	6,643
14	Texas	8,749
7	Utah	13,528
26	Vermont	4,393
19	Virginia	5,729
4	Washington	14,411
24	West Virginia	4,863
39	Wisconsin	1,951
5	Wyoming	13,804

RANK ORDER

RANK	STATE	HIGHEST POINT
1	Alaska	20,320
2	California	14,494
3	Colorado	14,433
4	Washington	14,411
5	Wyoming	13,804
6	Hawaii	13,796
7	Utah	13,528
8	New Mexico	13,161
9	Nevada	13,140
10	Montana	12,799
11	Idaho	12,662
12	Arizona	12,633
13	Oregon	11,239
14	Texas	8,749
15	South Dakota	7,242
16	North Carolina	6,684
17	Tennessee	6,643
18	New Hampshire	6,288
19	Virginia	5,729
20	Nebraska	5,424
21	New York	5,344
22	Maine	5,268
23	Oklahoma	4,973
24	West Virginia	4,863
25	Georgia	4,784
26	Vermont	4,393
27	Kentucky	4,145
28	Kansas	4,039
29	South Carolina	3,560
30	North Dakota	3,506
31	Massachusetts	3,491
32	Maryland	3,360
33	Pennsylvania	3,213
34	Arkansas	2,753
35	Alabama	2,407
36	Connecticut	2,380
37	Minnesota	2,301
38	Michigan	1,979
39	Wisconsin	1,951
40	New Jersey	1,803
41	Missouri	1,772
42	Iowa	1,670
43	Ohio	1,550
44	Indiana	1,257
45	Illinois	1,235
46	Rhode Island	812
47	Mississippi	806
48	Louisiana	535
49	Delaware	448
50	Florida	345
	District of Columbia	410

Source: U.S. Department of Interior, U.S. Geological Survey
"Elevations and Distances in the United States" (http://erg.usgs.gov/isb/pubs/booklets/elvadist/elvadist.html)

Lowest Point of Elevation in Feet

National Low Point = 282 Feet Below Sea Level (Death Valley, California)*

ALPHA ORDER

RANK	STATE	LOWEST POINT
3	Alabama	0
3	Alaska	0
26	Arizona	70
25	Arkansas	55
1	California	(282)
50	Colorado	3,315
3	Connecticut	0
3	Delaware	0
3	Florida	0
3	Georgia	0
3	Hawaii	0
42	Idaho	710
32	Illinois	279
34	Indiana	320
37	Iowa	480
41	Kansas	679
31	Kentucky	257
2	Louisiana	(8)
3	Maine	0
3	Maryland	0
3	Massachusetts	0
38	Michigan	571
40	Minnesota	601
3	Mississippi	0
29	Missouri	230
46	Montana	1,800
44	Nebraska	840
36	Nevada	479
3	New Hampshire	0
3	New Jersey	0
48	New Mexico	2,842
3	New York	0
3	North Carolina	0
43	North Dakota	750
35	Ohio	455
33	Oklahoma	289
3	Oregon	0
3	Pennsylvania	0
3	Rhode Island	0
3	South Carolina	0
45	South Dakota	966
28	Tennessee	178
3	Texas	0
47	Utah	2,000
27	Vermont	95
3	Virginia	0
3	Washington	0
30	West Virginia	240
39	Wisconsin	579
49	Wyoming	3,099

RANK ORDER

RANK	STATE	LOWEST POINT
1	California	(282)
2	Louisiana	(8)
3	Alabama*	0
3	Alaska	0
3	Connecticut	0
3	Delaware	0
3	Florida	0
3	Georgia	0
3	Hawaii	0
3	Maine	0
3	Maryland	0
3	Massachusetts	0
3	Mississippi	0
3	New Hampshire	0
3	New Jersey	0
3	New York	0
3	North Carolina	0
3	Oregon	0
3	Pennsylvania	0
3	Rhode Island	0
3	South Carolina	0
3	Texas	0
3	Virginia	0
3	Washington	0
25	Arkansas	55
26	Arizona	70
27	Vermont	95
28	Tennessee	178
29	Missouri	230
30	West Virginia	240
31	Kentucky	257
32	Illinois	279
33	Oklahoma	289
34	Indiana	320
35	Ohio	455
36	Nevada	479
37	Iowa	480
38	Michigan	571
39	Wisconsin	579
40	Minnesota	601
41	Kansas	679
42	Idaho	710
43	North Dakota	750
44	Nebraska	840
45	South Dakota	966
46	Montana	1,800
47	Utah	2,000
48	New Mexico	2,842
49	Wyoming	3,099
50	Colorado	3,315

District of Columbia   1

Source: U.S. Department of Interior, U.S. Geological Survey
  "Elevations and Distances in the United States" (http://erg.usgs.gov/isb/pubs/booklets/elvadist/elvadist.html)
*States with "0" have sea level as lowest point.

Approximate Mean Elevation in Feet

Approximate National Mean Elevation = 2,500 Feet Above Sea Level

ALPHA ORDER				RANK ORDER		
RANK	STATE	MEAN ELEVATION		RANK	STATE	MEAN ELEVATION
40	Alabama	500		1	Colorado	6,800
15	Alaska	1,900		2	Wyoming	6,700
7	Arizona	4,100		3	Utah	6,100
36	Arkansas	650		4	New Mexico	5,700
11	California	2,900		5	Nevada	5,500
1	Colorado	6,800		6	Idaho	5,000
40	Connecticut	500		7	Arizona	4,100
50	Delaware	60		8	Montana	3,400
48	Florida	100		9	Oregon	3,300
37	Georgia	600		10	Hawaii	3,030
10	Hawaii	3,030		11	California	2,900
6	Idaho	5,000		12	Nebraska	2,600
37	Illinois	600		13	South Dakota	2,200
34	Indiana	700		14	Kansas	2,000
22	Iowa	1,100		15	Alaska	1,900
14	Kansas	2,000		15	North Dakota	1,900
33	Kentucky	750		17	Texas	1,700
48	Louisiana	100		17	Washington	1,700
37	Maine	600		19	West Virginia	1,500
43	Maryland	350		20	Oklahoma	1,300
40	Massachusetts	500		21	Minnesota	1,200
29	Michigan	900		22	Iowa	1,100
21	Minnesota	1,200		22	Pennsylvania	1,100
45	Mississippi	300		24	Wisconsin	1,050
32	Missouri	800		25	New Hampshire	1,000
8	Montana	3,400		25	New York	1,000
12	Nebraska	2,600		25	Vermont	1,000
5	Nevada	5,500		28	Virginia	950
25	New Hampshire	1,000		29	Michigan	900
46	New Jersey	250		29	Tennessee	900
4	New Mexico	5,700		31	Ohio	850
25	New York	1,000		32	Missouri	800
34	North Carolina	700		33	Kentucky	750
15	North Dakota	1,900		34	Indiana	700
31	Ohio	850		34	North Carolina	700
20	Oklahoma	1,300		36	Arkansas	650
9	Oregon	3,300		37	Georgia	600
22	Pennsylvania	1,100		37	Illinois	600
47	Rhode Island	200		37	Maine	600
43	South Carolina	350		40	Alabama	500
13	South Dakota	2,200		40	Connecticut	500
29	Tennessee	900		40	Massachusetts	500
17	Texas	1,700		43	Maryland	350
3	Utah	6,100		43	South Carolina	350
25	Vermont	1,000		45	Mississippi	300
28	Virginia	950		46	New Jersey	250
17	Washington	1,700		47	Rhode Island	200
19	West Virginia	1,500		48	Florida	100
24	Wisconsin	1,050		48	Louisiana	100
2	Wyoming	6,700		50	Delaware	60
					District of Columbia	150

Source: U.S. Department of Interior, U.S. Geological Survey
  "Elevations and Distances in the United States" (http://erg.usgs.gov/isb/pubs/booklets/elvadist/elvadist.html)

Normal Daily Mean Temperature*

ALPHA ORDER

RANK	STATE	MEAN TEMPERATURE
5	Alabama	66.8
50	Alaska	41.5
2	Arizona	72.9
10	Arkansas	62.1
11	California**	61.5
35	Colorado	50.1
34	Connecticut	50.2
22	Delaware	54.4
3	Florida**	72.4
9	Georgia	62.2
1	Hawaii	77.5
28	Idaho	52.0
37	Illinois**	50.0
26	Indiana	52.5
37	Iowa	50.0
18	Kansas	56.4
16	Kentucky	57.0
4	Louisiana	68.8
42	Maine	45.8
20	Maryland	54.6
30	Massachusetts	51.6
45	Michigan**	45.0
48	Minnesota**	42.3
7	Mississippi	64.1
19	Missouri**	55.3
47	Montana	43.8
33	Nebraska	50.7
31	Nevada	51.3
41	New Hampshire	45.9
23	New Jersey	53.5
17	New Mexico	56.8
35	New York**	50.1
13	North Carolina**	60.5
48	North Dakota	42.3
27	Ohio**	52.3
14	Oklahoma	60.1
23	Oregon	53.5
25	Pennsylvania**	53.2
32	Rhode Island	51.1
8	South Carolina	63.6
44	South Dakota	45.1
12	Tennessee**	60.7
6	Texas**	66.3
28	Utah	52.0
43	Vermont	45.2
15	Virginia**	58.6
39	Washington**	49.8
21	West Virginia	54.5
40	Wisconsin	47.5
45	Wyoming	45.0

RANK ORDER

RANK	STATE	MEAN TEMPERATURE
1	Hawaii	77.5
2	Arizona	72.9
3	Florida**	72.4
4	Louisiana	68.8
5	Alabama	66.8
6	Texas**	66.3
7	Mississippi	64.1
8	South Carolina	63.6
9	Georgia	62.2
10	Arkansas	62.1
11	California**	61.5
12	Tennessee**	60.7
13	North Carolina**	60.5
14	Oklahoma	60.1
15	Virginia**	58.6
16	Kentucky	57.0
17	New Mexico	56.8
18	Kansas	56.4
19	Missouri**	55.3
20	Maryland	54.6
21	West Virginia	54.5
22	Delaware	54.4
23	New Jersey	53.5
23	Oregon	53.5
25	Pennsylvania**	53.2
26	Indiana	52.5
27	Ohio**	52.3
28	Idaho	52.0
28	Utah	52.0
30	Massachusetts	51.6
31	Nevada	51.3
32	Rhode Island	51.1
33	Nebraska	50.7
34	Connecticut	50.2
35	Colorado	50.1
35	New York**	50.1
37	Illinois**	50.0
37	Iowa	50.0
39	Washington**	49.8
40	Wisconsin	47.5
41	New Hampshire	45.9
42	Maine	45.8
43	Vermont	45.2
44	South Dakota	45.1
45	Michigan**	45.0
45	Wyoming	45.0
47	Montana	43.8
48	Minnesota**	42.3
48	North Dakota	42.3
50	Alaska	41.5
	District of Columbia	57.5

Source: U.S. Department of Commerce, National Oceanic and Atmospheric Administration
   "Climatography of the United States" (No. 81) (www.ncdc.noaa.gov/oa/climate/online/ccd/nrmavg.txt)
*Based on standard 30 year period, 1971-2000.
**Temperatures from multiple reporting cities within one state were averaged to determine a state's mean temperature.

Percent of Days That Are Sunny*

ALPHA ORDER

RANK	STATE	PERCENT OF DAYS SUNNY
26	Alabama	58
50	Alaska	38
1	Arizona	85
8	Arkansas	66
4	California	72
4	Colorado	72
35	Connecticut**	56
37	Delaware**	55
7	Florida	67
16	Georgia	63
11	Hawaii	65
14	Idaho	64
31	Illinois	57
26	Indiana	58
22	Iowa	60
8	Kansas	66
31	Kentucky	57
14	Louisiana	64
31	Maine**	57
31	Maryland	57
37	Massachusetts	55
44	Michigan	49
37	Minnesota	55
16	Mississippi	63
26	Missouri	58
24	Montana	59
16	Nebraska	63
2	Nevada	76
48	New Hampshire	44
35	New Jersey**	56
3	New Mexico	75
42	New York	51
22	North Carolina	60
24	North Dakota	59
42	Ohio	51
11	Oklahoma	65
46	Oregon**	48
41	Pennsylvania	53
26	Rhode Island**	58
20	South Carolina	62
16	South Dakota	63
26	Tennessee	58
11	Texas	65
6	Utah	68
44	Vermont**	49
21	Virginia	61
47	Washington	45
49	West Virginia**	40
40	Wisconsin	54
8	Wyoming	66

RANK ORDER

RANK	STATE	PERCENT OF DAYS SUNNY
1	Arizona	85
2	Nevada	76
3	New Mexico	75
4	California	72
4	Colorado	72
6	Utah	68
7	Florida	67
8	Arkansas	66
8	Kansas	66
8	Wyoming	66
11	Hawaii	65
11	Oklahoma	65
11	Texas	65
14	Idaho	64
14	Louisiana	64
16	Georgia	63
16	Mississippi	63
16	Nebraska	63
16	South Dakota	63
20	South Carolina	62
21	Virginia	61
22	Iowa	60
22	North Carolina	60
24	Montana	59
24	North Dakota	59
26	Alabama	58
26	Indiana	58
26	Missouri	58
26	Rhode Island**	58
26	Tennessee	58
31	Illinois	57
31	Kentucky	57
31	Maine**	57
31	Maryland	57
35	Connecticut**	56
35	New Jersey**	56
37	Delaware**	55
37	Massachusetts	55
37	Minnesota	55
40	Wisconsin	54
41	Pennsylvania	53
42	New York	51
42	Ohio	51
44	Michigan	49
44	Vermont**	49
46	Oregon**	48
47	Washington	45
48	New Hampshire	44
49	West Virginia**	40
50	Alaska	38
	District of Columbia**	56

Source: CQ Press using data from U.S. Department of Commerce, National Oceanic and Atmospheric Administration
"Comparative Climatic Data" (annual) (http://www.ncdc.noaa.gov/oa/climate/online/ccd/pctpos.txt)
*Averages over various years.
**Percentages from these states are from a single location. All other states are from two or more reporting cities within each state, which were averaged to determine each state's average percentage of sunny days.

Average Wind Speed (M.P.H.)*

ALPHA ORDER

RANK	STATE	MILES PER HOUR
29	Alabama	8.8
39	Alaska	8.2
49	Arizona	6.2
43	Arkansas	7.8
39	California**	8.2
34	Colorado	8.6
36	Connecticut	8.4
24	Delaware	9.0
35	Florida**	8.5
22	Georgia	9.1
7	Hawaii	11.3
32	Idaho	8.7
14	Illinois**	10.1
19	Indiana	9.6
10	Iowa	10.7
4	Kansas	12.2
38	Kentucky	8.3
39	Louisiana	8.2
32	Maine	8.7
29	Maryland	8.8
3	Massachusetts	12.4
18	Michigan**	9.7
9	Minnesota**	10.8
45	Mississippi	6.9
14	Missouri**	10.1
2	Montana	12.5
11	Nebraska	10.5
48	Nevada	6.6
47	New Hampshire	6.7
17	New Jersey	9.8
27	New Mexico	8.9
16	New York**	10.0
44	North Carolina**	7.5
13	North Dakota	10.2
20	Ohio**	9.3
4	Oklahoma	12.2
42	Oregon	7.9
20	Pennsylvania**	9.3
12	Rhode Island	10.4
46	South Carolina	6.8
8	South Dakota	11.0
36	Tennessee**	8.4
24	Texas**	9.0
29	Utah	8.8
24	Vermont	9.0
22	Virginia**	9.1
27	Washington**	8.9
50	West Virginia	5.8
6	Wisconsin	11.5
1	Wyoming	12.9

RANK ORDER

RANK	STATE	MILES PER HOUR
1	Wyoming	12.9
2	Montana	12.5
3	Massachusetts	12.4
4	Kansas	12.2
4	Oklahoma	12.2
6	Wisconsin	11.5
7	Hawaii	11.3
8	South Dakota	11.0
9	Minnesota**	10.8
10	Iowa	10.7
11	Nebraska	10.5
12	Rhode Island	10.4
13	North Dakota	10.2
14	Illinois**	10.1
14	Missouri**	10.1
16	New York**	10.0
17	New Jersey	9.8
18	Michigan**	9.7
19	Indiana	9.6
20	Ohio**	9.3
20	Pennsylvania**	9.3
22	Georgia	9.1
22	Virginia**	9.1
24	Delaware	9.0
24	Texas**	9.0
24	Vermont	9.0
27	New Mexico	8.9
27	Washington**	8.9
29	Alabama	8.8
29	Maryland	8.8
29	Utah	8.8
32	Idaho	8.7
32	Maine	8.7
34	Colorado	8.6
35	Florida**	8.5
36	Connecticut	8.4
36	Tennessee**	8.4
38	Kentucky	8.3
39	Alaska	8.2
39	California**	8.2
39	Louisiana	8.2
42	Oregon	7.9
43	Arkansas	7.8
44	North Carolina**	7.5
45	Mississippi	6.9
46	South Carolina	6.8
47	New Hampshire	6.7
48	Nevada	6.6
49	Arizona	6.2
50	West Virginia	5.8
	District of Columbia	9.4

Source: U.S. Department of Commerce, National Oceanic and Atmospheric Administration
"Comparative Climatic Data" (annual) (http://www.ncdc.noaa.gov/oa/climate/online/ccd/wndspd.txt)
*Averages over various years.
**Wind speeds from multiple reporting cities within one state were averaged to determine a state's average wind speed.

Tornadoes in 2009

National Total = 1,305 Tornadoes*

ALPHA ORDER

RANK	STATE	TORNADOES	% of USA
2	Alabama	105	8.0%
45	Alaska	0	0.0%
32	Arizona	4	0.3%
15	Arkansas	35	2.7%
38	California	2	0.2%
7	Colorado	58	4.4%
35	Connecticut	3	0.2%
45	Delaware	0	0.0%
17	Florida	34	2.6%
5	Georgia	72	5.5%
45	Hawaii	0	0.0%
38	Idaho	2	0.2%
9	Illinois	52	4.0%
24	Indiana	13	1.0%
12	Iowa	42	3.2%
4	Kansas	87	6.7%
14	Kentucky	38	2.9%
3	Louisiana	102	7.8%
25	Maine	12	0.9%
29	Maryland	8	0.6%
43	Massachusetts	1	0.1%
35	Michigan	3	0.2%
20	Minnesota	31	2.4%
10	Mississippi	50	3.8%
6	Missouri	63	4.8%
30	Montana	7	0.5%
11	Nebraska	46	3.5%
38	Nevada	2	0.2%
45	New Hampshire	0	0.0%
43	New Jersey	1	0.1%
32	New Mexico	4	0.3%
27	New York	11	0.8%
13	North Carolina	40	3.1%
19	North Dakota	33	2.5%
23	Ohio	16	1.2%
17	Oklahoma	34	2.6%
32	Oregon	4	0.3%
30	Pennsylvania	7	0.5%
45	Rhode Island	0	0.0%
22	South Carolina	17	1.3%
15	South Dakota	35	2.7%
8	Tennessee	57	4.4%
1	Texas	125	9.6%
35	Utah	3	0.2%
38	Vermont	2	0.2%
27	Virginia	11	0.8%
38	Washington	2	0.2%
45	West Virginia	0	0.0%
21	Wisconsin	19	1.5%
25	Wyoming	12	0.9%

RANK ORDER

RANK	STATE	TORNADOES	% of USA
1	Texas	125	9.6%
2	Alabama	105	8.0%
3	Louisiana	102	7.8%
4	Kansas	87	6.7%
5	Georgia	72	5.5%
6	Missouri	63	4.8%
7	Colorado	58	4.4%
8	Tennessee	57	4.4%
9	Illinois	52	4.0%
10	Mississippi	50	3.8%
11	Nebraska	46	3.5%
12	Iowa	42	3.2%
13	North Carolina	40	3.1%
14	Kentucky	38	2.9%
15	Arkansas	35	2.7%
15	South Dakota	35	2.7%
17	Florida	34	2.6%
17	Oklahoma	34	2.6%
19	North Dakota	33	2.5%
20	Minnesota	31	2.4%
21	Wisconsin	19	1.5%
22	South Carolina	17	1.3%
23	Ohio	16	1.2%
24	Indiana	13	1.0%
25	Maine	12	0.9%
25	Wyoming	12	0.9%
27	New York	11	0.8%
27	Virginia	11	0.8%
29	Maryland	8	0.6%
30	Montana	7	0.5%
30	Pennsylvania	7	0.5%
32	Arizona	4	0.3%
32	New Mexico	4	0.3%
32	Oregon	4	0.3%
35	Connecticut	3	0.2%
35	Michigan	3	0.2%
35	Utah	3	0.2%
38	California	2	0.2%
38	Idaho	2	0.2%
38	Nevada	2	0.2%
38	Vermont	2	0.2%
38	Washington	2	0.2%
43	Massachusetts	1	0.1%
43	New Jersey	1	0.1%
45	Alaska	0	0.0%
45	Delaware	0	0.0%
45	Hawaii	0	0.0%
45	New Hampshire	0	0.0%
45	Rhode Island	0	0.0%
45	West Virginia	0	0.0%
	District of Columbia	0	0.0%

Source: National Weather Service, Storm Prediction Center
"Annual Severe Weather Report Summary - 2009" (www.spc.ncep.noaa.gov/climo/online/monthly/2009_annual_summary.html)
*Preliminary figures. Tornadoes striking more than one state are counted in each state.

Hazardous Weather Fatalities in 2008

National Total = 551 Fatalities*

<u>ALPHA ORDER</u>

RANK	STATE	FATALITIES	% of USA
11	Alabama	16	2.9%
37	Alaska	3	0.5%
21	Arizona	9	1.6%
3	Arkansas	35	6.4%
12	California	15	2.7%
17	Colorado	12	2.2%
41	Connecticut	2	0.4%
47	Delaware	0	0.0%
5	Florida	32	5.8%
19	Georgia	10	1.8%
37	Hawaii	3	0.5%
37	Idaho	3	0.5%
3	Illinois	35	6.4%
8	Indiana	27	4.9%
10	Iowa	18	3.3%
30	Kansas	5	0.9%
21	Kentucky	9	1.6%
15	Louisiana	13	2.4%
41	Maine	2	0.4%
37	Maryland	3	0.5%
41	Massachusetts	2	0.4%
23	Michigan	8	1.5%
27	Minnesota	6	1.1%
34	Mississippi	4	0.7%
6	Missouri	31	5.6%
30	Montana	5	0.9%
47	Nebraska	0	0.0%
9	Nevada	21	3.8%
41	New Hampshire	2	0.4%
13	New Jersey	14	2.5%
24	New Mexico	7	1.3%
19	New York	10	1.8%
17	North Carolina	12	2.2%
45	North Dakota	1	0.2%
15	Ohio	13	2.4%
13	Oklahoma	14	2.5%
34	Oregon	4	0.7%
6	Pennsylvania	31	5.6%
30	Rhode Island	5	0.9%
30	South Carolina	5	0.9%
45	South Dakota	1	0.2%
1	Tennessee	37	6.7%
2	Texas	36	6.5%
27	Utah	6	1.1%
47	Vermont	0	0.0%
34	Virginia	4	0.7%
24	Washington	7	1.3%
47	West Virginia	0	0.0%
27	Wisconsin	6	1.1%
24	Wyoming	7	1.3%

<u>RANK ORDER</u>

RANK	STATE	FATALITIES	% of USA
1	Tennessee	37	6.7%
2	Texas	36	6.5%
3	Arkansas	35	6.4%
3	Illinois	35	6.4%
5	Florida	32	5.8%
6	Missouri	31	5.6%
6	Pennsylvania	31	5.6%
8	Indiana	27	4.9%
9	Nevada	21	3.8%
10	Iowa	18	3.3%
11	Alabama	16	2.9%
12	California	15	2.7%
13	New Jersey	14	2.5%
13	Oklahoma	14	2.5%
15	Louisiana	13	2.4%
15	Ohio	13	2.4%
17	Colorado	12	2.2%
17	North Carolina	12	2.2%
19	Georgia	10	1.8%
19	New York	10	1.8%
21	Arizona	9	1.6%
21	Kentucky	9	1.6%
23	Michigan	8	1.5%
24	New Mexico	7	1.3%
24	Washington	7	1.3%
24	Wyoming	7	1.3%
27	Minnesota	6	1.1%
27	Utah	6	1.1%
27	Wisconsin	6	1.1%
30	Kansas	5	0.9%
30	Montana	5	0.9%
30	Rhode Island	5	0.9%
30	South Carolina	5	0.9%
34	Mississippi	4	0.7%
34	Oregon	4	0.7%
34	Virginia	4	0.7%
37	Alaska	3	0.5%
37	Hawaii	3	0.5%
37	Idaho	3	0.5%
37	Maryland	3	0.5%
41	Connecticut	2	0.4%
41	Maine	2	0.4%
41	Massachusetts	2	0.4%
41	New Hampshire	2	0.4%
45	North Dakota	1	0.2%
45	South Dakota	1	0.2%
47	Delaware	0	0.0%
47	Nebraska	0	0.0%
47	Vermont	0	0.0%
47	West Virginia	0	0.0%
	District of Columbia	0	0.0%

Source: National Weather Service, Water and Weather Services
    "2008 Summary of Hazardous Weather Fatalities" (http://www.nws.noaa.gov/om/hazstats/state08.pdf)
*Includes lightning, tornado, thunderstorm, extreme temperature, flood, coastal storm, rip current, hurricane, winter storm, fog, avalanche, and other weather events. National total does not include 16 fatalities in U.S. waters or territories.

Cost of Damage from Hazardous Weather in 2008

National Total = $29,695,830,000*

ALPHA ORDER					RANK ORDER			
RANK	STATE	DAMAGE	% of USA		RANK	STATE	DAMAGE	% of USA
31	Alabama	$41,890,000	0.1%		1	Texas	$16,081,830,000	54.2%
39	Alaska	12,170,000	0.0%		2	Louisiana	2,400,930,000	8.1%
29	Arizona	48,800,000	0.2%		3	Ohio	1,675,750,000	5.6%
7	Arkansas	770,470,000	2.6%		4	Iowa	1,642,430,000	5.5%
14	California	282,860,000	1.0%		5	Indiana	1,584,610,000	5.3%
17	Colorado	166,590,000	0.6%		6	Oklahoma	834,490,000	2.8%
45	Connecticut	1,680,000	0.0%		7	Arkansas	770,470,000	2.6%
46	Delaware	1,460,000	0.0%		8	Wisconsin	720,280,000	2.4%
11	Florida	334,440,000	1.1%		9	Mississippi	389,870,000	1.3%
13	Georgia	309,690,000	1.0%		10	Missouri	341,410,000	1.1%
50	Hawaii	0	0.0%		11	Florida	334,440,000	1.1%
38	Idaho	13,950,000	0.0%		12	Kentucky	313,320,000	1.1%
16	Illinois	268,180,000	0.9%		13	Georgia	309,690,000	1.0%
5	Indiana	1,584,610,000	5.3%		14	California	282,860,000	1.0%
4	Iowa	1,642,430,000	5.5%		15	Tennessee	279,380,000	0.9%
22	Kansas	79,090,000	0.3%		16	Illinois	268,180,000	0.9%
12	Kentucky	313,320,000	1.1%		17	Colorado	166,590,000	0.6%
2	Louisiana	2,400,930,000	8.1%		18	New York	150,190,000	0.5%
33	Maine	35,180,000	0.1%		19	Nebraska	136,880,000	0.5%
43	Maryland	6,770,000	0.0%		20	Washington	136,780,000	0.5%
24	Massachusetts	57,140,000	0.2%		21	Minnesota	84,310,000	0.3%
23	Michigan	73,380,000	0.2%		22	Kansas	79,090,000	0.3%
21	Minnesota	84,310,000	0.3%		23	Michigan	73,380,000	0.2%
9	Mississippi	389,870,000	1.3%		24	Massachusetts	57,140,000	0.2%
10	Missouri	341,410,000	1.1%		25	North Carolina	56,200,000	0.2%
44	Montana	3,700,000	0.0%		26	Pennsylvania	52,740,000	0.2%
19	Nebraska	136,880,000	0.5%		27	Virginia	51,920,000	0.2%
42	Nevada	8,650,000	0.0%		28	New Hampshire	48,890,000	0.2%
28	New Hampshire	48,890,000	0.2%		29	Arizona	48,800,000	0.2%
34	New Jersey	26,950,000	0.1%		30	New Mexico	44,610,000	0.2%
30	New Mexico	44,610,000	0.2%		31	Alabama	41,890,000	0.1%
18	New York	150,190,000	0.5%		32	Oregon	38,470,000	0.1%
25	North Carolina	56,200,000	0.2%		33	Maine	35,180,000	0.1%
35	North Dakota	25,650,000	0.1%		34	New Jersey	26,950,000	0.1%
3	Ohio	1,675,750,000	5.6%		35	North Dakota	25,650,000	0.1%
6	Oklahoma	834,490,000	2.8%		36	South Dakota	22,810,000	0.1%
32	Oregon	38,470,000	0.1%		37	South Carolina	17,240,000	0.1%
26	Pennsylvania	52,740,000	0.2%		38	Idaho	13,950,000	0.0%
49	Rhode Island	550,000	0.0%		39	Alaska	12,170,000	0.0%
37	South Carolina	17,240,000	0.1%		40	Vermont	9,850,000	0.0%
36	South Dakota	22,810,000	0.1%		41	West Virginia	9,650,000	0.0%
15	Tennessee	279,380,000	0.9%		42	Nevada	8,650,000	0.0%
1	Texas	16,081,830,000	54.2%		43	Maryland	6,770,000	0.0%
48	Utah	800,000	0.0%		44	Montana	3,700,000	0.0%
40	Vermont	9,850,000	0.0%		45	Connecticut	1,680,000	0.0%
27	Virginia	51,920,000	0.2%		46	Delaware	1,460,000	0.0%
20	Washington	136,780,000	0.5%		47	Wyoming	870,000	0.0%
41	West Virginia	9,650,000	0.0%		48	Utah	800,000	0.0%
8	Wisconsin	720,280,000	2.4%		49	Rhode Island	550,000	0.0%
47	Wyoming	870,000	0.0%		50	Hawaii	0	0.0%
						District of Columbia	80,000	0.0%

Source: National Weather Service, Water and Weather Services
"2008 Summary of Hazardous Weather Fatalities" (http://www.nws.noaa.gov/om/hazstats/state08.pdf)
*Includes lightning, tornado, thunderstorm, extreme temperature, flood, coastal storm, rip current, hurricane, winter storm, fog, avalanche, and other weather events. National total does not include damage costs in U.S. territories.

Acres Owned by the Federal Government in 2004

National Total = 653,299,090 Acres*

ALPHA ORDER

ALPHA ORDER

RANK	STATE	ACRES	% of USA
38	Alabama	513,913	0.1%
1	Alaska	252,495,811	38.6%
4	Arizona	34,933,236	5.3%
20	Arkansas	2,407,948	0.4%
3	California	45,393,238	6.9%
11	Colorado	24,354,713	3.7%
49	Connecticut	13,938	0.0%
48	Delaware	25,874	0.0%
18	Florida	2,858,782	0.4%
26	Georgia	1,409,406	0.2%
31	Hawaii	796,726	0.1%
9	Idaho	26,565,412	4.1%
35	Illinois	641,959	0.1%
39	Indiana	463,245	0.1%
42	Iowa	273,954	0.0%
36	Kansas	631,351	0.1%
27	Kentucky	1,378,677	0.2%
25	Louisiana	1,474,788	0.2%
44	Maine	208,422	0.0%
45	Maryland	178,527	0.0%
47	Massachusetts	93,950	0.0%
14	Michigan	3,637,873	0.6%
17	Minnesota	2,873,517	0.4%
22	Mississippi	2,196,940	0.3%
21	Missouri	2,224,788	0.3%
8	Montana	27,910,152	4.3%
34	Nebraska	665,481	0.1%
2	Nevada	59,362,643	9.1%
32	New Hampshire	775,665	0.1%
46	New Jersey	148,441	0.0%
6	New Mexico	32,483,877	5.0%
43	New York	233,533	0.0%
13	North Carolina	3,710,338	0.6%
28	North Dakota	1,185,777	0.2%
40	Ohio	448,381	0.1%
24	Oklahoma	1,586,148	0.2%
5	Oregon	32,715,514	5.0%
33	Pennsylvania	719,864	0.1%
50	Rhode Island	2,923	0.0%
37	South Carolina	560,956	0.1%
16	South Dakota	3,028,003	0.5%
30	Tennessee	865,837	0.1%
15	Texas	3,130,345	0.5%
7	Utah	30,271,905	4.6%
41	Vermont	443,249	0.1%
19	Virginia	2,534,178	0.4%
12	Washington	12,949,662	2.0%
29	West Virginia	1,146,211	0.2%
23	Wisconsin	1,971,902	0.3%
10	Wyoming	26,391,487	4.0%

RANK ORDER

RANK ORDER

RANK	STATE	ACRES	% of USA
1	Alaska	252,495,811	38.6%
2	Nevada	59,362,643	9.1%
3	California	45,393,238	6.9%
4	Arizona	34,933,236	5.3%
5	Oregon	32,715,514	5.0%
6	New Mexico	32,483,877	5.0%
7	Utah	30,271,905	4.6%
8	Montana	27,910,152	4.3%
9	Idaho	26,565,412	4.1%
10	Wyoming	26,391,487	4.0%
11	Colorado	24,354,713	3.7%
12	Washington	12,949,662	2.0%
13	North Carolina	3,710,338	0.6%
14	Michigan	3,637,873	0.6%
15	Texas	3,130,345	0.5%
16	South Dakota	3,028,003	0.5%
17	Minnesota	2,873,517	0.4%
18	Florida	2,858,782	0.4%
19	Virginia	2,534,178	0.4%
20	Arkansas	2,407,948	0.4%
21	Missouri	2,224,788	0.3%
22	Mississippi	2,196,940	0.3%
23	Wisconsin	1,971,902	0.3%
24	Oklahoma	1,586,148	0.2%
25	Louisiana	1,474,788	0.2%
26	Georgia	1,409,406	0.2%
27	Kentucky	1,378,677	0.2%
28	North Dakota	1,185,777	0.2%
29	West Virginia	1,146,211	0.2%
30	Tennessee	865,837	0.1%
31	Hawaii	796,726	0.1%
32	New Hampshire	775,665	0.1%
33	Pennsylvania	719,864	0.1%
34	Nebraska	665,481	0.1%
35	Illinois	641,959	0.1%
36	Kansas	631,351	0.1%
37	South Carolina	560,956	0.1%
38	Alabama	513,913	0.1%
39	Indiana	463,245	0.1%
40	Ohio	448,381	0.1%
41	Vermont	443,249	0.1%
42	Iowa	273,954	0.0%
43	New York	233,533	0.0%
44	Maine	208,422	0.0%
45	Maryland	178,527	0.0%
46	New Jersey	148,441	0.0%
47	Massachusetts	93,950	0.0%
48	Delaware	25,874	0.0%
49	Connecticut	13,938	0.0%
50	Rhode Island	2,923	0.0%
	District of Columbia	9,631	0.0%

Source: Government Services Administration, Office of Governmentwide Real Property Policy
"Federal Real Property Profile" (http://www.gsa.gov/realpropertyprofile)
*As of September 30, 2004. Does not include land owned by the federal government in U.S. territories or in foreign countries.

Percent of Land Owned by the Federal Government in 2004

National Percent = 28.8%*

RANK	STATE	PERCENT
43	Alabama	1.6
2	Alaska	69.1
6	Arizona	48.1
22	Arkansas	7.2
7	California	45.3
10	Colorado	36.6
49	Connecticut	0.4
37	Delaware	2.0
18	Florida	8.2
29	Georgia	3.8
13	Hawaii	19.4
5	Idaho	50.2
41	Illinois	1.8
37	Indiana	2.0
47	Iowa	0.8
45	Kansas	1.2
26	Kentucky	5.4
27	Louisiana	5.1
46	Maine	1.1
34	Maryland	2.8
39	Massachusetts	1.9
16	Michigan	10.0
24	Minnesota	5.6
21	Mississippi	7.3
28	Missouri	5.0
12	Montana	29.9
44	Nebraska	1.4
1	Nevada	84.5
14	New Hampshire	13.5
32	New Jersey	3.1
9	New Mexico	41.8
47	New York	0.8
15	North Carolina	11.8
35	North Dakota	2.7
42	Ohio	1.7
30	Oklahoma	3.6
4	Oregon	53.1
36	Pennsylvania	2.5
49	Rhode Island	0.4
33	South Carolina	2.9
23	South Dakota	6.2
31	Tennessee	3.2
39	Texas	1.9
3	Utah	57.5
19	Vermont	7.5
17	Virginia	9.9
11	Washington	30.3
20	West Virginia	7.4
24	Wisconsin	5.6
8	Wyoming	42.3

RANK	STATE	PERCENT
1	Nevada	84.5
2	Alaska	69.1
3	Utah	57.5
4	Oregon	53.1
5	Idaho	50.2
6	Arizona	48.1
7	California	45.3
8	Wyoming	42.3
9	New Mexico	41.8
10	Colorado	36.6
11	Washington	30.3
12	Montana	29.9
13	Hawaii	19.4
14	New Hampshire	13.5
15	North Carolina	11.8
16	Michigan	10.0
17	Virginia	9.9
18	Florida	8.2
19	Vermont	7.5
20	West Virginia	7.4
21	Mississippi	7.3
22	Arkansas	7.2
23	South Dakota	6.2
24	Minnesota	5.6
24	Wisconsin	5.6
26	Kentucky	5.4
27	Louisiana	5.1
28	Missouri	5.0
29	Georgia	3.8
30	Oklahoma	3.6
31	Tennessee	3.2
32	New Jersey	3.1
33	South Carolina	2.9
34	Maryland	2.8
35	North Dakota	2.7
36	Pennsylvania	2.5
37	Delaware	2.0
37	Indiana	2.0
39	Massachusetts	1.9
39	Texas	1.9
41	Illinois	1.8
42	Ohio	1.7
43	Alabama	1.6
44	Nebraska	1.4
45	Kansas	1.2
46	Maine	1.1
47	Iowa	0.8
47	New York	0.8
49	Connecticut	0.4
49	Rhode Island	0.4
	District of Columbia	24.7

Source: Government Services Administration, Office of Governmentwide Real Property Policy
"Federal Real Property Profile" (http://www.gsa.gov/realpropertyprofile)
*As of September 30, 2004. Does not include land owned by the federal government in U.S. territories or in foreign countries.

National Park Service Land in 2009

National Total = 84,378,873 Acres*

ALPHA ORDER

RANK	STATE	ACRES	% of USA
41	Alabama	22,737	0.0%
1	Alaska	54,654,052	64.8%
3	Arizona	2,962,853	3.5%
25	Arkansas	104,976	0.1%
2	California	8,109,854	9.6%
12	Colorado	673,589	0.8%
46	Connecticut	7,782	0.0%
50	Delaware	0	0.0%
4	Florida	2,638,354	3.1%
34	Georgia	62,888	0.1%
17	Hawaii	369,122	0.4%
13	Idaho	517,904	0.6%
48	Illinois	13	0.0%
43	Indiana	15,378	0.0%
47	Iowa	2,713	0.0%
44	Kansas	11,636	0.0%
27	Kentucky	95,415	0.1%
39	Louisiana	24,107	0.0%
29	Maine	90,282	0.1%
31	Maryland	73,325	0.1%
35	Massachusetts	57,954	0.1%
11	Michigan	718,188	0.9%
19	Minnesota	301,343	0.4%
24	Mississippi	118,736	0.1%
30	Missouri	83,475	0.1%
8	Montana	1,274,374	1.5%
36	Nebraska	45,735	0.1%
10	Nevada	778,512	0.9%
42	New Hampshire	21,894	0.0%
26	New Jersey	99,206	0.1%
15	New Mexico	391,029	0.5%
32	New York	72,674	0.1%
14	North Carolina	406,159	0.5%
33	North Dakota	72,579	0.1%
37	Ohio	34,149	0.0%
45	Oklahoma	10,241	0.0%
21	Oregon	199,095	0.2%
22	Pennsylvania	137,660	0.2%
49	Rhode Island	5	0.0%
38	South Carolina	32,618	0.0%
20	South Dakota	297,417	0.4%
16	Tennessee	384,752	0.5%
9	Texas	1,244,635	1.5%
6	Utah	2,117,043	2.5%
40	Vermont	23,174	0.0%
18	Virginia	363,640	0.4%
7	Washington	1,967,116	2.3%
28	West Virginia	92,670	0.1%
23	Wisconsin	133,754	0.2%
5	Wyoming	2,396,390	2.8%

RANK ORDER

RANK	STATE	ACRES	% of USA
1	Alaska	54,654,052	64.8%
2	California	8,109,854	9.6%
3	Arizona	2,962,853	3.5%
4	Florida	2,638,354	3.1%
5	Wyoming	2,396,390	2.8%
6	Utah	2,117,043	2.5%
7	Washington	1,967,116	2.3%
8	Montana	1,274,374	1.5%
9	Texas	1,244,635	1.5%
10	Nevada	778,512	0.9%
11	Michigan	718,188	0.9%
12	Colorado	673,589	0.8%
13	Idaho	517,904	0.6%
14	North Carolina	406,159	0.5%
15	New Mexico	391,029	0.5%
16	Tennessee	384,752	0.5%
17	Hawaii	369,122	0.4%
18	Virginia	363,640	0.4%
19	Minnesota	301,343	0.4%
20	South Dakota	297,417	0.4%
21	Oregon	199,095	0.2%
22	Pennsylvania	137,660	0.2%
23	Wisconsin	133,754	0.2%
24	Mississippi	118,736	0.1%
25	Arkansas	104,976	0.1%
26	New Jersey	99,206	0.1%
27	Kentucky	95,415	0.1%
28	West Virginia	92,670	0.1%
29	Maine	90,282	0.1%
30	Missouri	83,475	0.1%
31	Maryland	73,325	0.1%
32	New York	72,674	0.1%
33	North Dakota	72,579	0.1%
34	Georgia	62,888	0.1%
35	Massachusetts	57,954	0.1%
36	Nebraska	45,735	0.1%
37	Ohio	34,149	0.0%
38	South Carolina	32,618	0.0%
39	Louisiana	24,107	0.0%
40	Vermont	23,174	0.0%
41	Alabama	22,737	0.0%
42	New Hampshire	21,894	0.0%
43	Indiana	15,378	0.0%
44	Kansas	11,636	0.0%
45	Oklahoma	10,241	0.0%
46	Connecticut	7,782	0.0%
47	Iowa	2,713	0.0%
48	Illinois	13	0.0%
49	Rhode Island	5	0.0%
50	Delaware	0	0.0%
	District of Columbia	7,090	0.0%

Source: National Park Service
   "Listing of Acreage by State" (unpublished data)
*As of December 31, 2009. Includes federal and nonfederal land in national parks, monuments, historic sites, recreation areas, preserves, battlefields, grasslands, seashores, parkways, trails, and rivers. Does not include land in national forest or wildlife areas. Includes 55,585 acres in U.S. territories.

Recreation Visits to National Park Service Areas in 2008

National Total = 274,852,949 Visits*

ALPHA ORDER

RANK	STATE	VISITS	% of USA
36	Alabama	789,451	0.3%
26	Alaska	2,403,877	0.9%
5	Arizona	10,681,127	3.9%
25	Arkansas	2,873,026	1.0%
1	California	34,374,981	12.5%
18	Colorado	5,383,786	2.0%
49	Connecticut	18,522	0.0%
50	Delaware	0	0.0%
9	Florida	7,937,737	2.9%
12	Georgia	6,425,910	2.3%
19	Hawaii	4,536,505	1.7%
39	Idaho	543,485	0.2%
42	Illinois	335,473	0.1%
27	Indiana	2,094,407	0.8%
44	Iowa	211,352	0.1%
45	Kansas	86,264	0.0%
30	Kentucky	1,708,529	0.6%
40	Louisiana	431,134	0.2%
28	Maine	2,075,857	0.8%
21	Maryland	3,544,992	1.3%
6	Massachusetts	10,281,657	3.7%
33	Michigan	1,420,947	0.5%
37	Minnesota	640,843	0.2%
13	Mississippi	5,898,917	2.1%
23	Missouri	3,436,201	1.3%
20	Montana	3,822,075	1.4%
43	Nebraska	265,858	0.1%
16	Nevada	5,770,632	2.1%
48	New Hampshire	29,819	0.0%
14	New Jersey	5,811,657	2.1%
31	New Mexico	1,556,586	0.6%
4	New York	16,913,720	6.2%
3	North Carolina	17,984,028	6.5%
38	North Dakota	553,135	0.2%
24	Ohio	3,121,019	1.1%
34	Oklahoma	1,245,188	0.5%
35	Oregon	832,095	0.3%
7	Pennsylvania	9,189,257	3.3%
46	Rhode Island	46,154	0.0%
32	South Carolina	1,441,433	0.5%
22	South Dakota	3,501,677	1.3%
10	Tennessee	7,733,827	2.8%
15	Texas	5,804,179	2.1%
8	Utah	8,451,252	3.1%
47	Vermont	37,121	0.0%
2	Virginia	22,542,952	8.2%
11	Washington	7,140,553	2.6%
29	West Virginia	1,812,908	0.7%
41	Wisconsin	424,669	0.2%
17	Wyoming	5,572,123	2.0%

RANK ORDER

RANK	STATE	VISITS	% of USA
1	California	34,374,981	12.5%
2	Virginia	22,542,952	8.2%
3	North Carolina	17,984,028	6.5%
4	New York	16,913,720	6.2%
5	Arizona	10,681,127	3.9%
6	Massachusetts	10,281,657	3.7%
7	Pennsylvania	9,189,257	3.3%
8	Utah	8,451,252	3.1%
9	Florida	7,937,737	2.9%
10	Tennessee	7,733,827	2.8%
11	Washington	7,140,553	2.6%
12	Georgia	6,425,910	2.3%
13	Mississippi	5,898,917	2.1%
14	New Jersey	5,811,657	2.1%
15	Texas	5,804,179	2.1%
16	Nevada	5,770,632	2.1%
17	Wyoming	5,572,123	2.0%
18	Colorado	5,383,786	2.0%
19	Hawaii	4,536,505	1.7%
20	Montana	3,822,075	1.4%
21	Maryland	3,544,992	1.3%
22	South Dakota	3,501,677	1.3%
23	Missouri	3,436,201	1.3%
24	Ohio	3,121,019	1.1%
25	Arkansas	2,873,026	1.0%
26	Alaska	2,403,877	0.9%
27	Indiana	2,094,407	0.8%
28	Maine	2,075,857	0.8%
29	West Virginia	1,812,908	0.7%
30	Kentucky	1,708,529	0.6%
31	New Mexico	1,556,586	0.6%
32	South Carolina	1,441,433	0.5%
33	Michigan	1,420,947	0.5%
34	Oklahoma	1,245,188	0.5%
35	Oregon	832,095	0.3%
36	Alabama	789,451	0.3%
37	Minnesota	640,843	0.2%
38	North Dakota	553,135	0.2%
39	Idaho	543,485	0.2%
40	Louisiana	431,134	0.2%
41	Wisconsin	424,669	0.2%
42	Illinois	335,473	0.1%
43	Nebraska	265,858	0.1%
44	Iowa	211,352	0.1%
45	Kansas	86,264	0.0%
46	Rhode Island	46,154	0.0%
47	Vermont	37,121	0.0%
48	New Hampshire	29,819	0.0%
49	Connecticut	18,522	0.0%
50	Delaware	0	0.0%
	District of Columbia	33,165,410	12.1%

Source: National Park Service, Public Use Statistics Office
"National Park Service Statistical Abstract 2008" (http://www.nature.nps.gov/stats/abstracts/abst2008.pdf)
*National total includes 1,948,644 visits in U.S. territories.

Percent Change in National Park Service Recreation Visits: 2007-2008

National Percent Change = 0.3% Decrease*

ALPHA ORDER

RANK	STATE	PERCENT CHANGE
46	Alabama	(10.5)
42	Alaska	(8.8)
21	Arizona	0.1
9	Arkansas	4.8
22	California	(0.1)
29	Colorado	(3.2)
1	Connecticut	47.8
NA	Delaware**	NA
24	Florida	(1.0)
18	Georgia	1.7
48	Hawaii	(11.4)
26	Idaho	(1.5)
37	Illinois	(6.5)
35	Indiana	(5.5)
17	Iowa	2.3
45	Kansas	(10.0)
42	Kentucky	(8.8)
4	Louisiana	12.6
36	Maine	(5.7)
8	Maryland	5.5
10	Massachusetts	3.8
47	Michigan	(10.7)
14	Minnesota	3.1
28	Mississippi	(2.3)
49	Missouri	(22.1)
41	Montana	(8.3)
30	Nebraska	(3.3)
23	Nevada	(0.5)
16	New Hampshire	2.5
7	New Jersey	5.6
34	New Mexico	(4.0)
6	New York	6.9
39	North Carolina	(6.9)
5	North Dakota	12.5
3	Ohio	14.3
44	Oklahoma	(9.9)
40	Oregon	(8.1)
19	Pennsylvania	0.2
37	Rhode Island	(6.5)
19	South Carolina	0.2
30	South Dakota	(3.3)
27	Tennessee	(2.0)
10	Texas	3.8
13	Utah	3.5
2	Vermont	15.4
25	Virginia	(1.2)
12	Washington	3.6
15	West Virginia	2.8
33	Wisconsin	(3.9)
32	Wyoming	(3.7)

RANK ORDER

RANK	STATE	PERCENT CHANGE
1	Connecticut	47.8
2	Vermont	15.4
3	Ohio	14.3
4	Louisiana	12.6
5	North Dakota	12.5
6	New York	6.9
7	New Jersey	5.6
8	Maryland	5.5
9	Arkansas	4.8
10	Massachusetts	3.8
10	Texas	3.8
12	Washington	3.6
13	Utah	3.5
14	Minnesota	3.1
15	West Virginia	2.8
16	New Hampshire	2.5
17	Iowa	2.3
18	Georgia	1.7
19	Pennsylvania	0.2
19	South Carolina	0.2
21	Arizona	0.1
22	California	(0.1)
23	Nevada	(0.5)
24	Florida	(1.0)
25	Virginia	(1.2)
26	Idaho	(1.5)
27	Tennessee	(2.0)
28	Mississippi	(2.3)
29	Colorado	(3.2)
30	Nebraska	(3.3)
30	South Dakota	(3.3)
32	Wyoming	(3.7)
33	Wisconsin	(3.9)
34	New Mexico	(4.0)
35	Indiana	(5.5)
36	Maine	(5.7)
37	Illinois	(6.5)
37	Rhode Island	(6.5)
39	North Carolina	(6.9)
40	Oregon	(8.1)
41	Montana	(8.3)
42	Alaska	(8.8)
42	Kentucky	(8.8)
44	Oklahoma	(9.9)
45	Kansas	(10.0)
46	Alabama	(10.5)
47	Michigan	(10.7)
48	Hawaii	(11.4)
49	Missouri	(22.1)
NA	Delaware**	NA
	District of Columbia	4.5

Source: National Park Service, Public Use Statistics Office
   "National Park Service Statistical Abstract 2008" (http://www.nature.nps.gov/stats/abstracts/abst2008.pdf)
*National percent change includes visits in U.S. territories.
**Not applicable.

State Parks, Recreation Areas and Natural Areas in 2008

National Total = 6,547 Areas*

ALPHA ORDER

ALPHA ORDER

RANK	STATE	AREAS	% of USA
50	Alabama	22	0.3%
12	Alaska	139	2.1%
45	Arizona	32	0.5%
35	Arkansas	52	0.8%
5	California	279	4.3%
10	Colorado	164	2.5%
13	Connecticut	137	2.1%
43	Delaware	34	0.5%
11	Florida	161	2.5%
26	Georgia	73	1.1%
27	Hawaii	70	1.1%
43	Idaho	34	0.5%
4	Illinois	316	4.8%
40	Indiana	37	0.6%
9	Iowa	179	2.7%
47	Kansas	25	0.4%
33	Kentucky	53	0.8%
31	Louisiana	58	0.9%
14	Maine	136	2.1%
30	Maryland	65	1.0%
3	Massachusetts	339	5.2%
19	Michigan	97	1.5%
8	Minnesota	212	3.2%
47	Mississippi	25	0.4%
22	Missouri	85	1.3%
2	Montana	392	6.0%
22	Nebraska	85	1.3%
47	Nevada	25	0.4%
21	New Hampshire	90	1.4%
17	New Jersey	118	1.8%
41	New Mexico	36	0.5%
1	New York	1,417	21.6%
29	North Carolina	66	1.0%
46	North Dakota	30	0.5%
24	Ohio	74	1.1%
36	Oklahoma	51	0.8%
6	Oregon	253	3.9%
16	Pennsylvania	120	1.8%
24	Rhode Island	74	1.1%
32	South Carolina	56	0.9%
15	South Dakota	131	2.0%
33	Tennessee	53	0.8%
20	Texas	93	1.4%
37	Utah	50	0.8%
18	Vermont	103	1.6%
39	Virginia	41	0.6%
7	Washington	214	3.3%
38	West Virginia	47	0.7%
28	Wisconsin	68	1.0%
41	Wyoming	36	0.5%

RANK ORDER

RANK	STATE	AREAS	% of USA
1	New York	1,417	21.6%
2	Montana	392	6.0%
3	Massachusetts	339	5.2%
4	Illinois	316	4.8%
5	California	279	4.3%
6	Oregon	253	3.9%
7	Washington	214	3.3%
8	Minnesota	212	3.2%
9	Iowa	179	2.7%
10	Colorado	164	2.5%
11	Florida	161	2.5%
12	Alaska	139	2.1%
13	Connecticut	137	2.1%
14	Maine	136	2.1%
15	South Dakota	131	2.0%
16	Pennsylvania	120	1.8%
17	New Jersey	118	1.8%
18	Vermont	103	1.6%
19	Michigan	97	1.5%
20	Texas	93	1.4%
21	New Hampshire	90	1.4%
22	Missouri	85	1.3%
22	Nebraska	85	1.3%
24	Ohio	74	1.1%
24	Rhode Island	74	1.1%
26	Georgia	73	1.1%
27	Hawaii	70	1.1%
28	Wisconsin	68	1.0%
29	North Carolina	66	1.0%
30	Maryland	65	1.0%
31	Louisiana	58	0.9%
32	South Carolina	56	0.9%
33	Kentucky	53	0.8%
33	Tennessee	53	0.8%
35	Arkansas	52	0.8%
36	Oklahoma	51	0.8%
37	Utah	50	0.8%
38	West Virginia	47	0.7%
39	Virginia	41	0.6%
40	Indiana	37	0.6%
41	New Mexico	36	0.5%
41	Wyoming	36	0.5%
43	Delaware	34	0.5%
43	Idaho	34	0.5%
45	Arizona	32	0.5%
46	North Dakota	30	0.5%
47	Kansas	25	0.4%
47	Mississippi	25	0.4%
47	Nevada	25	0.4%
50	Alabama	22	0.3%
	District of Columbia**	NA	NA

Source: The National Association of State Parks Directors
    "Annual Information Exchange" (http://www.naspd.org/)
*For the period July 1, 2007 through June 30, 2008. Includes operating and nonoperating state parks, recreation areas, natural areas, and other areas.
**Not applicable.

Visitors to State Parks and Recreation Areas in 2008

National Total = 744,943,195 Visitors*

ALPHA ORDER

RANK	STATE	VISITORS	% of USA
36	Alabama	5,141,690	0.7%
38	Alaska	4,976,546	0.7%
44	Arizona	2,348,313	0.3%
24	Arkansas	8,399,016	1.1%
1	California	76,833,187	10.3%
19	Colorado	11,833,500	1.6%
26	Connecticut	7,504,358	1.0%
37	Delaware	5,021,946	0.7%
10	Florida	20,737,052	2.8%
21	Georgia	10,351,102	1.4%
23	Hawaii	10,181,733	1.4%
41	Idaho	4,031,348	0.5%
4	Illinois	45,158,558	6.1%
13	Indiana	18,043,306	2.4%
17	Iowa	13,381,541	1.8%
33	Kansas	6,875,114	0.9%
30	Kentucky	7,081,930	1.0%
46	Louisiana	1,679,173	0.2%
45	Maine	2,124,134	0.3%
20	Maryland	11,329,786	1.5%
9	Massachusetts	31,635,247	4.2%
11	Michigan	19,309,161	2.6%
25	Minnesota	8,379,570	1.1%
48	Mississippi	1,212,391	0.2%
14	Missouri	15,142,186	2.0%
35	Montana	5,332,502	0.7%
22	Nebraska	10,236,147	1.4%
42	Nevada	3,131,766	0.4%
47	New Hampshire	1,625,683	0.2%
12	New Jersey	18,543,109	2.5%
39	New Mexico	4,603,901	0.6%
2	New York	61,771,320	8.3%
18	North Carolina	12,868,493	1.7%
49	North Dakota	878,550	0.1%
3	Ohio	49,658,857	6.7%
16	Oklahoma	13,485,280	1.8%
5	Oregon	42,604,811	5.7%
7	Pennsylvania	33,209,574	4.5%
34	Rhode Island	6,216,588	0.8%
31	South Carolina	7,050,146	0.9%
27	South Dakota	7,374,723	1.0%
8	Tennessee	32,264,499	4.3%
29	Texas	7,142,382	1.0%
40	Utah	4,553,590	0.6%
50	Vermont	697,989	0.1%
32	Virginia	7,039,993	0.9%
6	Washington	41,590,112	5.6%
28	West Virginia	7,324,322	1.0%
15	Wisconsin	14,516,272	1.9%
43	Wyoming	2,510,698	0.3%

RANK ORDER

RANK	STATE	VISITORS	% of USA
1	California	76,833,187	10.3%
2	New York	61,771,320	8.3%
3	Ohio	49,658,857	6.7%
4	Illinois	45,158,558	6.1%
5	Oregon	42,604,811	5.7%
6	Washington	41,590,112	5.6%
7	Pennsylvania	33,209,574	4.5%
8	Tennessee	32,264,499	4.3%
9	Massachusetts	31,635,247	4.2%
10	Florida	20,737,052	2.8%
11	Michigan	19,309,161	2.6%
12	New Jersey	18,543,109	2.5%
13	Indiana	18,043,306	2.4%
14	Missouri	15,142,186	2.0%
15	Wisconsin	14,516,272	1.9%
16	Oklahoma	13,485,280	1.8%
17	Iowa	13,381,541	1.8%
18	North Carolina	12,868,493	1.7%
19	Colorado	11,833,500	1.6%
20	Maryland	11,329,786	1.5%
21	Georgia	10,351,102	1.4%
22	Nebraska	10,236,147	1.4%
23	Hawaii	10,181,733	1.4%
24	Arkansas	8,399,016	1.1%
25	Minnesota	8,379,570	1.1%
26	Connecticut	7,504,358	1.0%
27	South Dakota	7,374,723	1.0%
28	West Virginia	7,324,322	1.0%
29	Texas	7,142,382	1.0%
30	Kentucky	7,081,930	1.0%
31	South Carolina	7,050,146	0.9%
32	Virginia	7,039,993	0.9%
33	Kansas	6,875,114	0.9%
34	Rhode Island	6,216,588	0.8%
35	Montana	5,332,502	0.7%
36	Alabama	5,141,690	0.7%
37	Delaware	5,021,946	0.7%
38	Alaska	4,976,546	0.7%
39	New Mexico	4,603,901	0.6%
40	Utah	4,553,590	0.6%
41	Idaho	4,031,348	0.5%
42	Nevada	3,131,766	0.4%
43	Wyoming	2,510,698	0.3%
44	Arizona	2,348,313	0.3%
45	Maine	2,124,134	0.3%
46	Louisiana	1,679,173	0.2%
47	New Hampshire	1,625,683	0.2%
48	Mississippi	1,212,391	0.2%
49	North Dakota	878,550	0.1%
50	Vermont	697,989	0.1%

District of Columbia** NA NA

Source: The National Association of State Parks Directors
  "Annual Information Exchange" (http://www.naspd.org/)
*For the period July 1, 2007 through June 30, 2008. Includes operating and nonoperating state parks, recreation areas, natural areas, and other areas. Includes day and overnight visitors.
**Not applicable.

Percent of Land That Is Developed: 2003

National Percent = 5.6%*

ALPHA ORDER				RANK ORDER		
RANK	STATE	PERCENT		RANK	STATE	PERCENT
20	Alabama	8.1		1	New Jersey	36.9
NA	Alaska**	NA		2	Connecticut	29.5
38	Arizona	2.6		2	Massachusetts	29.5
33	Arkansas	4.7		4	Rhode Island	27.0
25	California	5.8		5	Delaware	17.3
37	Colorado	2.8		6	Maryland	17.1
2	Connecticut	29.5		7	Florida	15.6
5	Delaware	17.3		8	Pennsylvania	14.7
7	Florida	15.6		9	Ohio	14.6
12	Georgia	12.1		10	North Carolina	13.8
NA	Hawaii**	NA		11	South Carolina	12.4
44	Idaho	1.5		12	Georgia	12.1
19	Illinois	9.3		13	New York	11.1
16	Indiana	10.5		14	Virginia	10.8
31	Iowa	4.9		15	New Hampshire	10.7
36	Kansas	3.8		16	Indiana	10.5
21	Kentucky	7.7		16	Michigan	10.5
26	Louisiana	5.7		18	Tennessee	9.7
35	Maine	3.9		19	Illinois	9.3
6	Maryland	17.1		20	Alabama	8.1
2	Massachusetts	29.5		21	Kentucky	7.7
16	Michigan	10.5		22	Wisconsin	7.2
34	Minnesota	4.3		23	West Virginia	6.5
29	Mississippi	5.5		24	Missouri	6.1
24	Missouri	6.1		25	California	5.8
46	Montana	1.1		26	Louisiana	5.7
39	Nebraska	2.5		27	Texas	5.6
48	Nevada	0.7		27	Vermont	5.6
15	New Hampshire	10.7		29	Mississippi	5.5
1	New Jersey	36.9		30	Washington	5.2
43	New Mexico	1.8		31	Iowa	4.9
13	New York	11.1		32	Oklahoma	4.8
10	North Carolina	13.8		33	Arkansas	4.7
40	North Dakota	2.2		34	Minnesota	4.3
9	Ohio	14.6		35	Maine	3.9
32	Oklahoma	4.8		36	Kansas	3.8
41	Oregon	2.1		37	Colorado	2.8
8	Pennsylvania	14.7		38	Arizona	2.6
4	Rhode Island	27.0		39	Nebraska	2.5
11	South Carolina	12.4		40	North Dakota	2.2
42	South Dakota	2.0		41	Oregon	2.1
18	Tennessee	9.7		42	South Dakota	2.0
27	Texas	5.6		43	New Mexico	1.8
45	Utah	1.4		44	Idaho	1.5
27	Vermont	5.6		45	Utah	1.4
14	Virginia	10.8		46	Montana	1.1
30	Washington	5.2		47	Wyoming	1.0
23	West Virginia	6.5		48	Nevada	0.7
22	Wisconsin	7.2		NA	Alaska**	NA
47	Wyoming	1.0		NA	Hawaii**	NA
					District of Columbia**	NA

Source: CQ Press using data from U.S. Department of Agriculture, Natural Resources Conservation Service
"2003 Annual NRI (http://www.nrcs.usda.gov/Technical/nri/2003/nri03landuse-mrb.html)
*National percent does not include land in Alaska, Hawaii or the District of Columbia. "Developed" does not include cropland, water areas, or federal land.

IX. Government Finances: Federal

Internal Revenue Service Gross Collections in 2008

National Total = $2,742,190,129,000*

ALPHA ORDER

RANK	STATE	COLLECTIONS	% of USA
29	Alabama	$24,563,503,000	0.9%
47	Alaska	4,748,628,000	0.2%
23	Arizona	35,813,663,000	1.3%
26	Arkansas	28,165,013,000	1.0%
1	California	318,083,114,000	11.6%
20	Colorado	48,257,249,000	1.8%
16	Connecticut	54,421,151,000	2.0%
31	Delaware	21,589,039,000	0.8%
5	Florida	134,337,889,000	4.9%
12	Georgia	69,069,197,000	2.5%
42	Hawaii	8,489,937,000	0.3%
41	Idaho	8,600,349,000	0.3%
4	Illinois	134,871,112,000	4.9%
22	Indiana	43,231,402,000	1.6%
34	Iowa	19,683,455,000	0.7%
30	Kansas	22,177,597,000	0.8%
28	Kentucky	24,937,707,000	0.9%
24	Louisiana	35,234,657,000	1.3%
44	Maine	6,736,963,000	0.2%
17	Maryland	54,131,790,000	2.0%
9	Massachusetts	81,367,437,000	3.0%
15	Michigan	66,618,158,000	2.4%
10	Minnesota	81,025,159,000	3.0%
37	Mississippi	12,697,324,000	0.5%
19	Missouri	48,298,002,000	1.8%
48	Montana	4,713,181,000	0.2%
32	Nebraska	21,366,643,000	0.8%
35	Nevada	17,753,419,000	0.6%
39	New Hampshire	10,640,725,000	0.4%
6	New Jersey	122,535,119,000	4.5%
40	New Mexico	9,858,908,000	0.4%
3	New York	229,647,494,000	8.4%
11	North Carolina	73,917,681,000	2.7%
49	North Dakota	4,149,764,000	0.2%
8	Ohio	111,029,042,000	4.0%
25	Oklahoma	30,202,018,000	1.1%
27	Oregon	26,138,979,000	1.0%
7	Pennsylvania	116,554,665,000	4.3%
38	Rhode Island	11,628,434,000	0.4%
33	South Carolina	20,379,879,000	0.7%
46	South Dakota	4,860,642,000	0.2%
18	Tennessee	49,227,614,000	1.8%
2	Texas	235,676,058,000	8.6%
36	Utah	17,124,954,000	0.6%
50	Vermont	3,721,718,000	0.1%
14	Virginia	66,865,525,000	2.4%
13	Washington	66,887,298,000	2.4%
43	West Virginia	6,884,310,000	0.3%
21	Wisconsin	45,586,757,000	1.7%
45	Wyoming	5,129,559,000	0.2%

RANK ORDER

RANK	STATE	COLLECTIONS	% of USA
1	California	$318,083,114,000	11.6%
2	Texas	235,676,058,000	8.6%
3	New York	229,647,494,000	8.4%
4	Illinois	134,871,112,000	4.9%
5	Florida	134,337,889,000	4.9%
6	New Jersey	122,535,119,000	4.5%
7	Pennsylvania	116,554,665,000	4.3%
8	Ohio	111,029,042,000	4.0%
9	Massachusetts	81,367,437,000	3.0%
10	Minnesota	81,025,159,000	3.0%
11	North Carolina	73,917,681,000	2.7%
12	Georgia	69,069,197,000	2.5%
13	Washington	66,887,298,000	2.4%
14	Virginia	66,865,525,000	2.4%
15	Michigan	66,618,158,000	2.4%
16	Connecticut	54,421,151,000	2.0%
17	Maryland	54,131,790,000	2.0%
18	Tennessee	49,227,614,000	1.8%
19	Missouri	48,298,002,000	1.8%
20	Colorado	48,257,249,000	1.8%
21	Wisconsin	45,586,757,000	1.7%
22	Indiana	43,231,402,000	1.6%
23	Arizona	35,813,663,000	1.3%
24	Louisiana	35,234,657,000	1.3%
25	Oklahoma	30,202,018,000	1.1%
26	Arkansas	28,165,013,000	1.0%
27	Oregon	26,138,979,000	1.0%
28	Kentucky	24,937,707,000	0.9%
29	Alabama	24,563,503,000	0.9%
30	Kansas	22,177,597,000	0.8%
31	Delaware	21,589,039,000	0.8%
32	Nebraska	21,366,643,000	0.8%
33	South Carolina	20,379,879,000	0.7%
34	Iowa	19,683,455,000	0.7%
35	Nevada	17,753,419,000	0.6%
36	Utah	17,124,954,000	0.6%
37	Mississippi	12,697,324,000	0.5%
38	Rhode Island	11,628,434,000	0.4%
39	New Hampshire	10,640,725,000	0.4%
40	New Mexico	9,858,908,000	0.4%
41	Idaho	8,600,349,000	0.3%
42	Hawaii	8,489,937,000	0.3%
43	West Virginia	6,884,310,000	0.3%
44	Maine	6,736,963,000	0.2%
45	Wyoming	5,129,559,000	0.2%
46	South Dakota	4,860,642,000	0.2%
47	Alaska	4,748,628,000	0.2%
48	Montana	4,713,181,000	0.2%
49	North Dakota	4,149,764,000	0.2%
50	Vermont	3,721,718,000	0.1%
	District of Columbia	19,432,111,000	0.7%

Source: U.S. Department of the Treasury, Internal Revenue Service
"Fiscal Year 2008 IRS Data Book" (http://www.irs.gov/taxstats/index.html)
*Total includes $25,973,418,000 from U.S. citizens abroad and other miscellaneous returns not shown separately.

Per Capita Internal Revenue Service Gross Collections in 2008

National Per Capita = $8,933*

ALPHA ORDER

RANK	STATE	PER CAPITA
44	Alabama	$5,251
31	Alaska	6,901
43	Arizona	5,510
11	Arkansas	9,821
18	California	8,695
12	Colorado	9,778
2	Connecticut	15,536
1	Delaware	24,639
28	Florida	7,292
29	Georgia	7,122
35	Hawaii	6,594
42	Idaho	5,630
9	Illinois	10,502
33	Indiana	6,767
36	Iowa	6,574
25	Kansas	7,928
41	Kentucky	5,816
26	Louisiana	7,915
45	Maine	5,105
16	Maryland	9,566
5	Massachusetts	12,435
34	Michigan	6,660
3	Minnesota	15,491
49	Mississippi	4,319
21	Missouri	8,109
47	Montana	4,869
6	Nebraska	11,991
32	Nevada	6,787
23	New Hampshire	8,050
4	New Jersey	14,144
46	New Mexico	4,962
7	New York	11,796
24	North Carolina	7,994
37	North Dakota	6,470
14	Ohio	9,631
20	Oklahoma	8,288
30	Oregon	6,910
17	Pennsylvania	9,275
8	Rhode Island	11,038
48	South Carolina	4,526
39	South Dakota	6,042
27	Tennessee	7,888
13	Texas	9,697
38	Utah	6,279
40	Vermont	5,993
19	Virginia	8,578
10	Washington	10,187
50	West Virginia	3,793
22	Wisconsin	8,101
15	Wyoming	9,624

RANK ORDER

RANK	STATE	PER CAPITA
1	Delaware	$24,639
2	Connecticut	15,536
3	Minnesota	15,491
4	New Jersey	14,144
5	Massachusetts	12,435
6	Nebraska	11,991
7	New York	11,796
8	Rhode Island	11,038
9	Illinois	10,502
10	Washington	10,187
11	Arkansas	9,821
12	Colorado	9,778
13	Texas	9,697
14	Ohio	9,631
15	Wyoming	9,624
16	Maryland	9,566
17	Pennsylvania	9,275
18	California	8,695
19	Virginia	8,578
20	Oklahoma	8,288
21	Missouri	8,109
22	Wisconsin	8,101
23	New Hampshire	8,050
24	North Carolina	7,994
25	Kansas	7,928
26	Louisiana	7,915
27	Tennessee	7,888
28	Florida	7,292
29	Georgia	7,122
30	Oregon	6,910
31	Alaska	6,901
32	Nevada	6,787
33	Indiana	6,767
34	Michigan	6,660
35	Hawaii	6,594
36	Iowa	6,574
37	North Dakota	6,470
38	Utah	6,279
39	South Dakota	6,042
40	Vermont	5,993
41	Kentucky	5,816
42	Idaho	5,630
43	Arizona	5,510
44	Alabama	5,251
45	Maine	5,105
46	New Mexico	4,962
47	Montana	4,869
48	South Carolina	4,526
49	Mississippi	4,319
50	West Virginia	3,793
	District of Columbia	32,932

Source: CQ Press using data from U.S. Department of the Treasury, Internal Revenue Service
"Fiscal Year 2008 IRS Data Book" (http://www.irs.gov/taxstats/index.html)
*National per capita does not include collections from U.S. citizens abroad and other miscellaneous returns not shown separately.

Federal Individual Income Tax Collections in 2008

National Total = $2,306,595,808,000*

ALPHA ORDER

RANK	STATE	COLLECTIONS	% of USA
27	Alabama	$21,938,012,000	1.0%
47	Alaska	4,359,791,000	0.2%
24	Arizona	32,008,838,000	1.4%
28	Arkansas	20,985,443,000	0.9%
1	California	268,461,994,000	11.6%
19	Colorado	41,964,442,000	1.8%
17	Connecticut	46,709,549,000	2.0%
36	Delaware	12,761,439,000	0.6%
4	Florida	125,089,899,000	5.4%
13	Georgia	57,924,061,000	2.5%
42	Hawaii	7,500,971,000	0.3%
41	Idaho	8,083,539,000	0.4%
5	Illinois	110,521,255,000	4.8%
22	Indiana	38,213,422,000	1.7%
32	Iowa	17,166,708,000	0.7%
31	Kansas	18,629,451,000	0.8%
26	Kentucky	22,840,375,000	1.0%
23	Louisiana	32,375,089,000	1.4%
44	Maine	6,040,922,000	0.3%
16	Maryland	48,907,217,000	2.1%
9	Massachusetts	72,230,278,000	3.1%
11	Michigan	60,809,236,000	2.6%
10	Minnesota	63,161,450,000	2.7%
37	Mississippi	10,766,668,000	0.5%
20	Missouri	41,038,981,000	1.8%
46	Montana	4,403,646,000	0.2%
35	Nebraska	13,777,188,000	0.6%
33	Nevada	15,847,639,000	0.7%
38	New Hampshire	10,303,644,000	0.4%
6	New Jersey	101,060,594,000	4.4%
39	New Mexico	8,897,827,000	0.4%
2	New York	192,567,025,000	8.3%
12	North Carolina	60,045,400,000	2.6%
49	North Dakota	3,684,185,000	0.2%
8	Ohio	95,002,155,000	4.1%
29	Oklahoma	19,755,434,000	0.9%
25	Oregon	23,778,334,000	1.0%
7	Pennsylvania	100,087,870,000	4.3%
40	Rhode Island	8,475,354,000	0.4%
30	South Carolina	18,850,001,000	0.8%
45	South Dakota	4,612,927,000	0.2%
18	Tennessee	43,751,658,000	1.9%
3	Texas	178,761,539,000	7.8%
34	Utah	14,199,560,000	0.6%
50	Vermont	3,456,136,000	0.1%
14	Virginia	54,324,275,000	2.4%
15	Washington	53,831,470,000	2.3%
43	West Virginia	6,183,472,000	0.3%
21	Wisconsin	38,456,081,000	1.7%
48	Wyoming	3,939,671,000	0.2%

RANK ORDER

RANK	STATE	COLLECTIONS	% of USA
1	California	$268,461,994,000	11.6%
2	New York	192,567,025,000	8.3%
3	Texas	178,761,539,000	7.8%
4	Florida	125,089,899,000	5.4%
5	Illinois	110,521,255,000	4.8%
6	New Jersey	101,060,594,000	4.4%
7	Pennsylvania	100,087,870,000	4.3%
8	Ohio	95,002,155,000	4.1%
9	Massachusetts	72,230,278,000	3.1%
10	Minnesota	63,161,450,000	2.7%
11	Michigan	60,809,236,000	2.6%
12	North Carolina	60,045,400,000	2.6%
13	Georgia	57,924,061,000	2.5%
14	Virginia	54,324,275,000	2.4%
15	Washington	53,831,470,000	2.3%
16	Maryland	48,907,217,000	2.1%
17	Connecticut	46,709,549,000	2.0%
18	Tennessee	43,751,658,000	1.9%
19	Colorado	41,964,442,000	1.8%
20	Missouri	41,038,981,000	1.8%
21	Wisconsin	38,456,081,000	1.7%
22	Indiana	38,213,422,000	1.7%
23	Louisiana	32,375,089,000	1.4%
24	Arizona	32,008,838,000	1.4%
25	Oregon	23,778,334,000	1.0%
26	Kentucky	22,840,375,000	1.0%
27	Alabama	21,938,012,000	1.0%
28	Arkansas	20,985,443,000	0.9%
29	Oklahoma	19,755,434,000	0.9%
30	South Carolina	18,850,001,000	0.8%
31	Kansas	18,629,451,000	0.8%
32	Iowa	17,166,708,000	0.7%
33	Nevada	15,847,639,000	0.7%
34	Utah	14,199,560,000	0.6%
35	Nebraska	13,777,188,000	0.6%
36	Delaware	12,761,439,000	0.6%
37	Mississippi	10,766,668,000	0.5%
38	New Hampshire	10,303,644,000	0.4%
39	New Mexico	8,897,827,000	0.4%
40	Rhode Island	8,475,354,000	0.4%
41	Idaho	8,083,539,000	0.4%
42	Hawaii	7,500,971,000	0.3%
43	West Virginia	6,183,472,000	0.3%
44	Maine	6,040,922,000	0.3%
45	South Dakota	4,612,927,000	0.2%
46	Montana	4,403,646,000	0.2%
47	Alaska	4,359,791,000	0.2%
48	Wyoming	3,939,671,000	0.2%
49	North Dakota	3,684,185,000	0.2%
50	Vermont	3,456,136,000	0.1%
	District of Columbia	17,581,931,000	0.8%

Source: U.S. Department of the Treasury, Internal Revenue Service
  "Fiscal Year 2008 IRS Data Book" (http://www.irs.gov/taxstats/index.html)
*Total includes $23,063,767,000 from U.S. citizens abroad and other miscellaneous returns not shown separately.

Average Revenue Collection per Federal Individual Income Tax Return in 2008

National Average = $14,944 per Return*

ALPHA ORDER

RANK	STATE	PER RETURN
44	Alabama	$9,346
33	Alaska	11,781
39	Arizona	11,050
14	Arkansas	15,098
13	California	15,285
7	Colorado	17,101
2	Connecticut	25,121
1	Delaware	28,189
27	Florida	12,944
28	Georgia	12,732
40	Hawaii	10,875
37	Idaho	11,183
8	Illinois	16,912
32	Indiana	11,807
36	Iowa	11,205
24	Kansas	13,309
42	Kentucky	10,734
16	Louisiana	15,005
48	Maine	8,308
9	Maryland	16,686
5	Massachusetts	21,005
30	Michigan	12,156
3	Minnesota	23,150
49	Mississippi	7,443
22	Missouri	13,658
46	Montana	8,586
15	Nebraska	15,037
34	Nevada	11,752
19	New Hampshire	14,270
4	New Jersey	22,142
45	New Mexico	9,091
6	New York	19,540
25	North Carolina	13,092
41	North Dakota	10,760
12	Ohio	15,573
35	Oklahoma	11,208
29	Oregon	12,458
18	Pennsylvania	14,997
17	Rhode Island	14,999
47	South Carolina	8,376
38	South Dakota	11,085
20	Tennessee	13,873
11	Texas	15,793
31	Utah	11,950
43	Vermont	10,036
23	Virginia	13,577
10	Washington	16,003
50	West Virginia	6,709
26	Wisconsin	13,025
21	Wyoming	13,857

RANK ORDER

RANK	STATE	PER RETURN
1	Delaware	$28,189
2	Connecticut	25,121
3	Minnesota	23,150
4	New Jersey	22,142
5	Massachusetts	21,005
6	New York	19,540
7	Colorado	17,101
8	Illinois	16,912
9	Maryland	16,686
10	Washington	16,003
11	Texas	15,793
12	Ohio	15,573
13	California	15,285
14	Arkansas	15,098
15	Nebraska	15,037
16	Louisiana	15,005
17	Rhode Island	14,999
18	Pennsylvania	14,997
19	New Hampshire	14,270
20	Tennessee	13,873
21	Wyoming	13,857
22	Missouri	13,658
23	Virginia	13,577
24	Kansas	13,309
25	North Carolina	13,092
26	Wisconsin	13,025
27	Florida	12,944
28	Georgia	12,732
29	Oregon	12,458
30	Michigan	12,156
31	Utah	11,950
32	Indiana	11,807
33	Alaska	11,781
34	Nevada	11,752
35	Oklahoma	11,208
36	Iowa	11,205
37	Idaho	11,183
38	South Dakota	11,085
39	Arizona	11,050
40	Hawaii	10,875
41	North Dakota	10,760
42	Kentucky	10,734
43	Vermont	10,036
44	Alabama	9,346
45	New Mexico	9,091
46	Montana	8,586
47	South Carolina	8,376
48	Maine	8,308
49	Mississippi	7,443
50	West Virginia	6,709

	District of Columbia	56,059

Source: CQ Press using data from U.S. Department of the Treasury, Internal Revenue Service
"Fiscal Year 2008 IRS Data Book" (http://www.irs.gov/taxstats/index.html)
*National Rate includes collections and returns from U.S. citizens abroad and other miscellaneous returns not shown separately.

Adjusted Gross Income in 2007

National Total = $8,564,745,048,000*

ALPHA ORDER

RANK	STATE	A.G.I.	% of USA
24	Alabama	$102,787,248,000	1.2%
46	Alaska	19,988,327,000	0.2%
18	Arizona	154,964,429,000	1.8%
34	Arkansas	54,795,910,000	0.6%
1	California	1,109,534,361,000	13.0%
19	Colorado	151,056,679,000	1.8%
16	Connecticut	158,353,186,000	1.8%
44	Delaware	25,625,753,000	0.3%
4	Florida	530,465,450,000	6.2%
12	Georgia	230,079,128,000	2.7%
39	Hawaii	35,510,051,000	0.4%
41	Idaho	33,553,278,000	0.4%
5	Illinois	392,664,916,000	4.6%
20	Indiana	150,941,776,000	1.8%
32	Iowa	71,960,985,000	0.8%
31	Kansas	72,231,184,000	0.8%
28	Kentucky	88,680,887,000	1.0%
27	Louisiana	92,468,118,000	1.1%
42	Maine	31,232,495,000	0.4%
15	Maryland	194,552,399,000	2.3%
11	Massachusetts	243,829,482,000	2.8%
9	Michigan	246,804,525,000	2.9%
17	Minnesota	156,772,069,000	1.8%
35	Mississippi	52,429,398,000	0.6%
23	Missouri	141,954,921,000	1.7%
45	Montana	22,343,926,000	0.3%
36	Nebraska	44,820,008,000	0.5%
30	Nevada	80,656,994,000	0.9%
37	New Hampshire	42,846,123,000	0.5%
7	New Jersey	329,024,354,000	3.8%
38	New Mexico	42,803,279,000	0.5%
2	New York	676,036,186,000	7.9%
13	North Carolina	219,982,102,000	2.6%
50	North Dakota	15,748,754,000	0.2%
8	Ohio	282,438,548,000	3.3%
29	Oklahoma	82,316,851,000	1.0%
26	Oregon	96,393,038,000	1.1%
6	Pennsylvania	346,909,184,000	4.1%
43	Rhode Island	29,957,771,000	0.3%
25	South Carolina	98,961,892,000	1.2%
47	South Dakota	19,186,319,000	0.2%
22	Tennessee	143,315,079,000	1.7%
3	Texas	606,392,582,000	7.1%
33	Utah	63,718,881,000	0.7%
49	Vermont	16,858,991,000	0.2%
10	Virginia	246,080,302,000	2.9%
14	Washington	206,825,480,000	2.4%
40	West Virginia	34,353,216,000	0.4%
21	Wisconsin	149,072,266,000	1.7%
48	Wyoming	18,951,175,000	0.2%

RANK ORDER

RANK	STATE	A.G.I.	% of USA
1	California	$1,109,534,361,000	13.0%
2	New York	676,036,186,000	7.9%
3	Texas	606,392,582,000	7.1%
4	Florida	530,465,450,000	6.2%
5	Illinois	392,664,916,000	4.6%
6	Pennsylvania	346,909,184,000	4.1%
7	New Jersey	329,024,354,000	3.8%
8	Ohio	282,438,548,000	3.3%
9	Michigan	246,804,525,000	2.9%
10	Virginia	246,080,302,000	2.9%
11	Massachusetts	243,829,482,000	2.8%
12	Georgia	230,079,128,000	2.7%
13	North Carolina	219,982,102,000	2.6%
14	Washington	206,825,480,000	2.4%
15	Maryland	194,552,399,000	2.3%
16	Connecticut	158,353,186,000	1.8%
17	Minnesota	156,772,069,000	1.8%
18	Arizona	154,964,429,000	1.8%
19	Colorado	151,056,679,000	1.8%
20	Indiana	150,941,776,000	1.8%
21	Wisconsin	149,072,266,000	1.7%
22	Tennessee	143,315,079,000	1.7%
23	Missouri	141,954,921,000	1.7%
24	Alabama	102,787,248,000	1.2%
25	South Carolina	98,961,892,000	1.2%
26	Oregon	96,393,038,000	1.1%
27	Louisiana	92,468,118,000	1.1%
28	Kentucky	88,680,887,000	1.0%
29	Oklahoma	82,316,851,000	1.0%
30	Nevada	80,656,994,000	0.9%
31	Kansas	72,231,184,000	0.8%
32	Iowa	71,960,985,000	0.8%
33	Utah	63,718,881,000	0.7%
34	Arkansas	54,795,910,000	0.6%
35	Mississippi	52,429,398,000	0.6%
36	Nebraska	44,820,008,000	0.5%
37	New Hampshire	42,846,123,000	0.5%
38	New Mexico	42,803,279,000	0.5%
39	Hawaii	35,510,051,000	0.4%
40	West Virginia	34,353,216,000	0.4%
41	Idaho	33,553,278,000	0.4%
42	Maine	31,232,495,000	0.4%
43	Rhode Island	29,957,771,000	0.3%
44	Delaware	25,625,753,000	0.3%
45	Montana	22,343,926,000	0.3%
46	Alaska	19,988,327,000	0.2%
47	South Dakota	19,186,319,000	0.2%
48	Wyoming	18,951,175,000	0.2%
49	Vermont	16,858,991,000	0.2%
50	North Dakota	15,748,754,000	0.2%
	District of Columbia	23,739,724,000	0.3%

Source: U.S. Department of the Treasury, Internal Revenue Service
"Individual Tax Statistics, State Income" (http://www.irs.gov/)
*Total includes $81,775,066,000 from U.S. citizens abroad and other miscellaneous returns not shown separately.

Per Capita Adjusted Gross Income in 2007

National Per Capita = $28,128*

ALPHA ORDER

RANK	STATE	PER CAPITA
44	Alabama	$22,162
16	Alaska	29,296
30	Arizona	24,357
48	Arkansas	19,279
13	California	30,628
11	Colorado	31,195
1	Connecticut	45,391
15	Delaware	29,629
17	Florida	29,022
33	Georgia	24,133
19	Hawaii	27,811
42	Idaho	22,380
12	Illinois	30,726
37	Indiana	23,785
32	Iowa	24,158
23	Kansas	26,024
47	Kentucky	20,835
46	Louisiana	21,130
38	Maine	23,709
6	Maryland	34,530
3	Massachusetts	37,516
28	Michigan	24,556
14	Minnesota	30,200
50	Mississippi	17,945
35	Missouri	24,020
39	Montana	23,342
26	Nebraska	25,323
10	Nevada	31,412
7	New Hampshire	32,525
2	New Jersey	38,099
45	New Mexico	21,742
5	New York	34,806
31	North Carolina	24,270
27	North Dakota	24,677
29	Ohio	24,516
41	Oklahoma	22,789
24	Oregon	25,822
20	Pennsylvania	27,703
18	Rhode Island	28,396
43	South Carolina	22,368
34	South Dakota	24,072
40	Tennessee	23,217
25	Texas	25,438
36	Utah	23,920
21	Vermont	27,172
9	Virginia	31,877
8	Washington	31,992
49	West Virginia	18,967
22	Wisconsin	26,613
4	Wyoming	36,207

RANK ORDER

RANK	STATE	PER CAPITA
1	Connecticut	$45,391
2	New Jersey	38,099
3	Massachusetts	37,516
4	Wyoming	36,207
5	New York	34,806
6	Maryland	34,530
7	New Hampshire	32,525
8	Washington	31,992
9	Virginia	31,877
10	Nevada	31,412
11	Colorado	31,195
12	Illinois	30,726
13	California	30,628
14	Minnesota	30,200
15	Delaware	29,629
16	Alaska	29,296
17	Florida	29,022
18	Rhode Island	28,396
19	Hawaii	27,811
20	Pennsylvania	27,703
21	Vermont	27,172
22	Wisconsin	26,613
23	Kansas	26,024
24	Oregon	25,822
25	Texas	25,438
26	Nebraska	25,323
27	North Dakota	24,677
28	Michigan	24,556
29	Ohio	24,516
30	Arizona	24,357
31	North Carolina	24,270
32	Iowa	24,158
33	Georgia	24,133
34	South Dakota	24,072
35	Missouri	24,020
36	Utah	23,920
37	Indiana	23,785
38	Maine	23,709
39	Montana	23,342
40	Tennessee	23,217
41	Oklahoma	22,789
42	Idaho	22,380
43	South Carolina	22,368
44	Alabama	22,162
45	New Mexico	21,742
46	Louisiana	21,130
47	Kentucky	20,835
48	Arkansas	19,279
49	West Virginia	18,967
50	Mississippi	17,945
	District of Columbia	40,483

Source: CQ Press using data from U.S. Department of the Treasury, Internal Revenue Service
 "Individual Tax Statistics, State Income" (http://www.irs.gov/)
*National per capita does not include income from U.S. citizens abroad and other miscellaneous returns not shown separately.

Federal Corporate Income Tax Collections in 2008

National Total = $354,062,546,000*

ALPHA ORDER

RANK	STATE	COLLECTIONS	% of USA
30	Alabama	$2,229,203,000	0.6%
46	Alaska	316,380,000	0.1%
31	Arizona	2,200,364,000	0.6%
18	Arkansas	6,254,333,000	1.8%
1	California	40,440,402,000	11.4%
23	Colorado	4,633,621,000	1.3%
16	Connecticut	6,682,419,000	1.9%
13	Delaware	8,705,946,000	2.5%
20	Florida	5,977,696,000	1.7%
12	Georgia	8,715,040,000	2.5%
41	Hawaii	735,937,000	0.2%
45	Idaho	391,321,000	0.1%
5	Illinois	18,753,405,000	5.3%
24	Indiana	4,433,185,000	1.3%
29	Iowa	2,300,782,000	0.6%
32	Kansas	2,095,324,000	0.6%
35	Kentucky	1,670,372,000	0.5%
28	Louisiana	2,344,846,000	0.7%
44	Maine	431,929,000	0.1%
25	Maryland	4,344,480,000	1.2%
14	Massachusetts	7,708,521,000	2.2%
22	Michigan	4,895,778,000	1.4%
6	Minnesota	16,202,949,000	4.6%
36	Mississippi	1,610,632,000	0.5%
21	Missouri	5,665,429,000	1.6%
47	Montana	212,189,000	0.1%
15	Nebraska	7,417,558,000	2.1%
37	Nevada	1,608,398,000	0.5%
50	New Hampshire	146,722,000	0.0%
4	New Jersey	19,649,720,000	5.5%
40	New Mexico	817,494,000	0.2%
3	New York	32,710,990,000	9.2%
7	North Carolina	13,017,527,000	3.7%
43	North Dakota	432,439,000	0.1%
9	Ohio	12,535,213,000	3.5%
19	Oklahoma	6,159,229,000	1.7%
34	Oregon	1,922,975,000	0.5%
8	Pennsylvania	12,901,103,000	3.6%
27	Rhode Island	3,017,092,000	0.9%
38	South Carolina	1,118,940,000	0.3%
49	South Dakota	179,045,000	0.1%
26	Tennessee	4,266,824,000	1.2%
2	Texas	39,971,658,000	11.3%
33	Utah	1,997,580,000	0.6%
48	Vermont	202,432,000	0.1%
11	Virginia	11,631,016,000	3.3%
10	Washington	11,794,598,000	3.3%
42	West Virginia	505,988,000	0.1%
17	Wisconsin	6,466,352,000	1.8%
39	Wyoming	984,343,000	0.3%

RANK ORDER

RANK	STATE	COLLECTIONS	% of USA
1	California	$40,440,402,000	11.4%
2	Texas	39,971,658,000	11.3%
3	New York	32,710,990,000	9.2%
4	New Jersey	19,649,720,000	5.5%
5	Illinois	18,753,405,000	5.3%
6	Minnesota	16,202,949,000	4.6%
7	North Carolina	13,017,527,000	3.7%
8	Pennsylvania	12,901,103,000	3.6%
9	Ohio	12,535,213,000	3.5%
10	Washington	11,794,598,000	3.3%
11	Virginia	11,631,016,000	3.3%
12	Georgia	8,715,040,000	2.5%
13	Delaware	8,705,946,000	2.5%
14	Massachusetts	7,708,521,000	2.2%
15	Nebraska	7,417,558,000	2.1%
16	Connecticut	6,682,419,000	1.9%
17	Wisconsin	6,466,352,000	1.8%
18	Arkansas	6,254,333,000	1.8%
19	Oklahoma	6,159,229,000	1.7%
20	Florida	5,977,696,000	1.7%
21	Missouri	5,665,429,000	1.6%
22	Michigan	4,895,778,000	1.4%
23	Colorado	4,633,621,000	1.3%
24	Indiana	4,433,185,000	1.3%
25	Maryland	4,344,480,000	1.2%
26	Tennessee	4,266,824,000	1.2%
27	Rhode Island	3,017,092,000	0.9%
28	Louisiana	2,344,846,000	0.7%
29	Iowa	2,300,782,000	0.6%
30	Alabama	2,229,203,000	0.6%
31	Arizona	2,200,364,000	0.6%
32	Kansas	2,095,324,000	0.6%
33	Utah	1,997,580,000	0.6%
34	Oregon	1,922,975,000	0.5%
35	Kentucky	1,670,372,000	0.5%
36	Mississippi	1,610,632,000	0.5%
37	Nevada	1,608,398,000	0.5%
38	South Carolina	1,118,940,000	0.3%
39	Wyoming	984,343,000	0.3%
40	New Mexico	817,494,000	0.2%
41	Hawaii	735,937,000	0.2%
42	West Virginia	505,988,000	0.1%
43	North Dakota	432,439,000	0.1%
44	Maine	431,929,000	0.1%
45	Idaho	391,321,000	0.1%
46	Alaska	316,380,000	0.1%
47	Montana	212,189,000	0.1%
48	Vermont	202,432,000	0.1%
49	South Dakota	179,045,000	0.1%
50	New Hampshire	146,722,000	0.0%
	District of Columbia	1,505,984,000	0.4%

Source: U.S. Department of the Treasury, Internal Revenue Service
  "Fiscal Year 2008 IRS Data Book" (http://www.irs.gov/taxstats/index.html)
*Total includes collections and returns from international sources and others not distributed by state.

Average Revenue Collection per Federal Corporate Income Tax Return in 2008

National Average = $50,741 per Return*

ALPHA ORDER

RANK	STATE	PER RETURN
30	Alabama	$30,144
35	Alaska	25,475
42	Arizona	17,635
6	Arkansas	109,008
19	California	54,047
31	Colorado	29,469
4	Connecticut	118,560
1	Delaware	341,852
48	Florida	7,225
26	Georgia	36,604
36	Hawaii	25,319
46	Idaho	10,605
18	Illinois	55,741
25	Indiana	36,615
24	Iowa	36,804
23	Kansas	38,822
37	Kentucky	23,787
34	Louisiana	25,614
43	Maine	13,352
28	Maryland	32,990
22	Massachusetts	51,578
39	Michigan	23,281
3	Minnesota	120,060
27	Mississippi	35,832
21	Missouri	51,982
49	Montana	6,233
2	Nebraska	169,011
41	Nevada	19,307
50	New Hampshire	5,973
8	New Jersey	89,421
33	New Mexico	25,736
20	New York	53,971
12	North Carolina	66,822
29	North Dakota	30,654
14	Ohio	64,436
9	Oklahoma	84,209
40	Oregon	23,263
16	Pennsylvania	58,318
5	Rhode Island	113,788
44	South Carolina	12,568
47	South Dakota	9,705
15	Tennessee	59,108
7	Texas	95,926
32	Utah	27,416
45	Vermont	11,641
11	Virginia	69,594
10	Washington	83,609
38	West Virginia	23,302
13	Wisconsin	65,187
17	Wyoming	57,497

RANK ORDER

RANK	STATE	PER RETURN
1	Delaware	$341,852
2	Nebraska	169,011
3	Minnesota	120,060
4	Connecticut	118,560
5	Rhode Island	113,788
6	Arkansas	109,008
7	Texas	95,926
8	New Jersey	89,421
9	Oklahoma	84,209
10	Washington	83,609
11	Virginia	69,594
12	North Carolina	66,822
13	Wisconsin	65,187
14	Ohio	64,436
15	Tennessee	59,108
16	Pennsylvania	58,318
17	Wyoming	57,497
18	Illinois	55,741
19	California	54,047
20	New York	53,971
21	Missouri	51,982
22	Massachusetts	51,578
23	Kansas	38,822
24	Iowa	36,804
25	Indiana	36,615
26	Georgia	36,604
27	Mississippi	35,832
28	Maryland	32,990
29	North Dakota	30,654
30	Alabama	30,144
31	Colorado	29,469
32	Utah	27,416
33	New Mexico	25,736
34	Louisiana	25,614
35	Alaska	25,475
36	Hawaii	25,319
37	Kentucky	23,787
38	West Virginia	23,302
39	Michigan	23,281
40	Oregon	23,263
41	Nevada	19,307
42	Arizona	17,635
43	Maine	13,352
44	South Carolina	12,568
45	Vermont	11,641
46	Idaho	10,605
47	South Dakota	9,705
48	Florida	7,225
49	Montana	6,233
50	New Hampshire	5,973
	District of Columbia	92,505

Source: CQ Press using data from U.S. Department of the Treasury, Internal Revenue Service
"Fiscal Year 2008 IRS Data Book" (http://www.irs.gov/taxstats/index.html)
*National rate includes collections and returns from U.S. citizens abroad and other miscellaneous returns not shown separately.

Federal Tax Returns Filed in 2008

National Total = 250,378,521 Returns*

ALPHA ORDER

RANK	STATE	RETURNS	% of USA
23	Alabama	3,495,270	1.4%
49	Alaska	602,540	0.2%
19	Arizona	4,729,353	1.9%
33	Arkansas	2,163,060	0.9%
1	California	29,627,618	11.8%
22	Colorado	4,410,907	1.8%
27	Connecticut	3,189,786	1.3%
45	Delaware	787,867	0.3%
3	Florida	16,844,774	6.7%
11	Georgia	7,159,198	2.9%
42	Hawaii	1,160,161	0.5%
39	Idaho	1,243,122	0.5%
5	Illinois	10,686,433	4.3%
15	Indiana	4,989,461	2.0%
30	Iowa	2,538,208	1.0%
31	Kansas	2,335,588	0.9%
28	Kentucky	3,185,464	1.3%
25	Louisiana	3,386,737	1.4%
40	Maine	1,221,938	0.5%
17	Maryland	4,813,492	1.9%
13	Massachusetts	5,880,244	2.3%
8	Michigan	7,813,139	3.1%
21	Minnesota	4,569,416	1.8%
34	Mississippi	2,103,766	0.8%
16	Missouri	4,826,785	1.9%
43	Montana	966,281	0.4%
37	Nebraska	1,541,450	0.6%
32	Nevada	2,186,103	0.9%
41	New Hampshire	1,201,306	0.5%
9	New Jersey	7,175,962	2.9%
36	New Mexico	1,542,492	0.6%
4	New York	16,550,328	6.6%
10	North Carolina	7,170,653	2.9%
48	North Dakota	607,359	0.2%
7	Ohio	9,347,647	3.7%
29	Oklahoma	2,856,468	1.1%
26	Oregon	3,323,198	1.3%
6	Pennsylvania	9,614,798	3.8%
44	Rhode Island	942,093	0.4%
24	South Carolina	3,435,333	1.4%
46	South Dakota	740,090	0.3%
20	Tennessee	4,668,201	1.9%
2	Texas	17,915,834	7.2%
35	Utah	2,030,430	0.8%
47	Vermont	623,037	0.2%
12	Virginia	6,430,981	2.6%
14	Washington	5,739,121	2.3%
38	West Virginia	1,346,688	0.5%
18	Wisconsin	4,738,514	1.9%
50	Wyoming	534,288	0.2%

RANK ORDER

RANK	STATE	RETURNS	% of USA
1	California	29,627,618	11.8%
2	Texas	17,915,834	7.2%
3	Florida	16,844,774	6.7%
4	New York	16,550,328	6.6%
5	Illinois	10,686,433	4.3%
6	Pennsylvania	9,614,798	3.8%
7	Ohio	9,347,647	3.7%
8	Michigan	7,813,139	3.1%
9	New Jersey	7,175,962	2.9%
10	North Carolina	7,170,653	2.9%
11	Georgia	7,159,198	2.9%
12	Virginia	6,430,981	2.6%
13	Massachusetts	5,880,244	2.3%
14	Washington	5,739,121	2.3%
15	Indiana	4,989,461	2.0%
16	Missouri	4,826,785	1.9%
17	Maryland	4,813,492	1.9%
18	Wisconsin	4,738,514	1.9%
19	Arizona	4,729,353	1.9%
20	Tennessee	4,668,201	1.9%
21	Minnesota	4,569,416	1.8%
22	Colorado	4,410,907	1.8%
23	Alabama	3,495,270	1.4%
24	South Carolina	3,435,333	1.4%
25	Louisiana	3,386,737	1.4%
26	Oregon	3,323,198	1.3%
27	Connecticut	3,189,786	1.3%
28	Kentucky	3,185,464	1.3%
29	Oklahoma	2,856,468	1.1%
30	Iowa	2,538,208	1.0%
31	Kansas	2,335,588	0.9%
32	Nevada	2,186,103	0.9%
33	Arkansas	2,163,060	0.9%
34	Mississippi	2,103,766	0.8%
35	Utah	2,030,430	0.8%
36	New Mexico	1,542,492	0.6%
37	Nebraska	1,541,450	0.6%
38	West Virginia	1,346,688	0.5%
39	Idaho	1,243,122	0.5%
40	Maine	1,221,938	0.5%
41	New Hampshire	1,201,306	0.5%
42	Hawaii	1,160,161	0.5%
43	Montana	966,281	0.4%
44	Rhode Island	942,093	0.4%
45	Delaware	787,867	0.3%
46	South Dakota	740,090	0.3%
47	Vermont	623,037	0.2%
48	North Dakota	607,359	0.2%
49	Alaska	602,540	0.2%
50	Wyoming	534,288	0.2%
	District of Columbia	556,271	0.2%

Source: U.S. Department of the Treasury, Internal Revenue Service
"Fiscal Year 2008 IRS Data Book" (http://www.irs.gov/taxstats/index.html)
*Total includes returns from international sources and other miscellaneous returns not shown separately.

Federal Individual Income Tax Returns Filed in 2008

National Total = 154,345,853 Returns*

ALPHA ORDER

RANK	STATE	RETURNS	% of USA
23	Alabama	2,347,362	1.5%
47	Alaska	370,060	0.2%
20	Arizona	2,896,610	1.9%
33	Arkansas	1,389,962	0.9%
1	California	17,563,412	11.4%
22	Colorado	2,453,848	1.6%
28	Connecticut	1,859,368	1.2%
45	Delaware	452,717	0.3%
4	Florida	9,664,265	6.3%
11	Georgia	4,549,608	2.9%
42	Hawaii	689,759	0.4%
40	Idaho	722,832	0.5%
6	Illinois	6,535,199	4.2%
15	Indiana	3,236,586	2.1%
30	Iowa	1,532,064	1.0%
32	Kansas	1,399,792	0.9%
26	Kentucky	2,127,944	1.4%
25	Louisiana	2,157,640	1.4%
39	Maine	727,153	0.5%
19	Maryland	2,931,023	1.9%
13	Massachusetts	3,438,640	2.2%
8	Michigan	5,002,295	3.2%
21	Minnesota	2,728,350	1.8%
31	Mississippi	1,446,455	0.9%
17	Missouri	3,004,744	1.9%
44	Montana	512,911	0.3%
38	Nebraska	916,204	0.6%
34	Nevada	1,348,460	0.9%
41	New Hampshire	722,069	0.5%
10	New Jersey	4,564,278	3.0%
36	New Mexico	978,795	0.6%
3	New York	9,855,141	6.4%
9	North Carolina	4,586,300	3.0%
49	North Dakota	342,402	0.2%
7	Ohio	6,100,438	4.0%
29	Oklahoma	1,762,605	1.1%
27	Oregon	1,908,694	1.2%
5	Pennsylvania	6,673,972	4.3%
43	Rhode Island	565,076	0.4%
24	South Carolina	2,250,363	1.5%
46	South Dakota	416,152	0.3%
16	Tennessee	3,153,675	2.0%
2	Texas	11,319,150	7.3%
35	Utah	1,188,237	0.8%
48	Vermont	344,386	0.2%
12	Virginia	4,001,212	2.6%
14	Washington	3,363,742	2.2%
37	West Virginia	921,661	0.6%
18	Wisconsin	2,952,500	1.9%
50	Wyoming	284,305	0.2%

RANK ORDER

RANK	STATE	RETURNS	% of USA
1	California	17,563,412	11.4%
2	Texas	11,319,150	7.3%
3	New York	9,855,141	6.4%
4	Florida	9,664,265	6.3%
5	Pennsylvania	6,673,972	4.3%
6	Illinois	6,535,199	4.2%
7	Ohio	6,100,438	4.0%
8	Michigan	5,002,295	3.2%
9	North Carolina	4,586,300	3.0%
10	New Jersey	4,564,278	3.0%
11	Georgia	4,549,608	2.9%
12	Virginia	4,001,212	2.6%
13	Massachusetts	3,438,640	2.2%
14	Washington	3,363,742	2.2%
15	Indiana	3,236,586	2.1%
16	Tennessee	3,153,675	2.0%
17	Missouri	3,004,744	1.9%
18	Wisconsin	2,952,500	1.9%
19	Maryland	2,931,023	1.9%
20	Arizona	2,896,610	1.9%
21	Minnesota	2,728,350	1.8%
22	Colorado	2,453,848	1.6%
23	Alabama	2,347,362	1.5%
24	South Carolina	2,250,363	1.5%
25	Louisiana	2,157,640	1.4%
26	Kentucky	2,127,944	1.4%
27	Oregon	1,908,694	1.2%
28	Connecticut	1,859,368	1.2%
29	Oklahoma	1,762,605	1.1%
30	Iowa	1,532,064	1.0%
31	Mississippi	1,446,455	0.9%
32	Kansas	1,399,792	0.9%
33	Arkansas	1,389,962	0.9%
34	Nevada	1,348,460	0.9%
35	Utah	1,188,237	0.8%
36	New Mexico	978,795	0.6%
37	West Virginia	921,661	0.6%
38	Nebraska	916,204	0.6%
39	Maine	727,153	0.5%
40	Idaho	722,832	0.5%
41	New Hampshire	722,069	0.5%
42	Hawaii	689,759	0.4%
43	Rhode Island	565,076	0.4%
44	Montana	512,911	0.3%
45	Delaware	452,717	0.3%
46	South Dakota	416,152	0.3%
47	Alaska	370,060	0.2%
48	Vermont	344,386	0.2%
49	North Dakota	342,402	0.2%
50	Wyoming	284,305	0.2%
	District of Columbia	313,634	0.2%

Source: U.S. Department of the Treasury, Internal Revenue Service
 "Fiscal Year 2008 IRS Data Book" (http://www.irs.gov/taxstats/index.html)
*Total includes returns from international sources and other miscellaneous returns not shown separately.

Federal Corporate Income Tax Returns Filed in 2008

National Total = 6,977,826 Returns*

ALPHA ORDER

RANK	STATE	RETURNS	% of USA
26	Alabama	73,952	1.1%
50	Alaska	12,419	0.2%
18	Arizona	124,775	1.8%
32	Arkansas	57,375	0.8%
2	California	748,247	10.7%
13	Colorado	157,237	2.3%
33	Connecticut	56,363	0.8%
43	Delaware	25,467	0.4%
1	Florida	827,342	11.9%
6	Georgia	238,087	3.4%
41	Hawaii	29,067	0.4%
37	Idaho	36,899	0.5%
5	Illinois	336,440	4.8%
19	Indiana	121,074	1.7%
31	Iowa	62,515	0.9%
34	Kansas	53,973	0.8%
30	Kentucky	70,223	1.0%
22	Louisiana	91,545	1.3%
39	Maine	32,349	0.5%
17	Maryland	131,690	1.9%
14	Massachusetts	149,453	2.1%
9	Michigan	210,294	3.0%
16	Minnesota	134,957	1.9%
35	Mississippi	44,949	0.6%
20	Missouri	108,989	1.6%
38	Montana	34,043	0.5%
36	Nebraska	43,888	0.6%
24	Nevada	83,305	1.2%
44	New Hampshire	24,563	0.4%
8	New Jersey	219,744	3.1%
40	New Mexico	31,764	0.5%
3	New York	606,084	8.7%
10	North Carolina	194,810	2.8%
49	North Dakota	14,107	0.2%
11	Ohio	194,537	2.8%
27	Oklahoma	73,142	1.0%
25	Oregon	82,661	1.2%
7	Pennsylvania	221,220	3.2%
42	Rhode Island	26,515	0.4%
23	South Carolina	89,034	1.3%
46	South Dakota	18,449	0.3%
29	Tennessee	72,187	1.0%
4	Texas	416,692	6.0%
28	Utah	72,862	1.0%
47	Vermont	17,389	0.2%
12	Virginia	167,126	2.4%
15	Washington	141,069	2.0%
45	West Virginia	21,714	0.3%
21	Wisconsin	99,197	1.4%
48	Wyoming	17,120	0.2%

RANK ORDER

RANK	STATE	RETURNS	% of USA
1	Florida	827,342	11.9%
2	California	748,247	10.7%
3	New York	606,084	8.7%
4	Texas	416,692	6.0%
5	Illinois	336,440	4.8%
6	Georgia	238,087	3.4%
7	Pennsylvania	221,220	3.2%
8	New Jersey	219,744	3.1%
9	Michigan	210,294	3.0%
10	North Carolina	194,810	2.8%
11	Ohio	194,537	2.8%
12	Virginia	167,126	2.4%
13	Colorado	157,237	2.3%
14	Massachusetts	149,453	2.1%
15	Washington	141,069	2.0%
16	Minnesota	134,957	1.9%
17	Maryland	131,690	1.9%
18	Arizona	124,775	1.8%
19	Indiana	121,074	1.7%
20	Missouri	108,989	1.6%
21	Wisconsin	99,197	1.4%
22	Louisiana	91,545	1.3%
23	South Carolina	89,034	1.3%
24	Nevada	83,305	1.2%
25	Oregon	82,661	1.2%
26	Alabama	73,952	1.1%
27	Oklahoma	73,142	1.0%
28	Utah	72,862	1.0%
29	Tennessee	72,187	1.0%
30	Kentucky	70,223	1.0%
31	Iowa	62,515	0.9%
32	Arkansas	57,375	0.8%
33	Connecticut	56,363	0.8%
34	Kansas	53,973	0.8%
35	Mississippi	44,949	0.6%
36	Nebraska	43,888	0.6%
37	Idaho	36,899	0.5%
38	Montana	34,043	0.5%
39	Maine	32,349	0.5%
40	New Mexico	31,764	0.5%
41	Hawaii	29,067	0.4%
42	Rhode Island	26,515	0.4%
43	Delaware	25,467	0.4%
44	New Hampshire	24,563	0.4%
45	West Virginia	21,714	0.3%
46	South Dakota	18,449	0.3%
47	Vermont	17,389	0.2%
48	Wyoming	17,120	0.2%
49	North Dakota	14,107	0.2%
50	Alaska	12,419	0.2%
	District of Columbia	16,280	0.2%

Source: U.S. Department of the Treasury, Internal Revenue Service
"Fiscal Year 2008 IRS Data Book" (http://www.irs.gov/taxstats/index.html)
*Total includes returns from international sources and other miscellaneous returns not shown separately.

Federal Tax Refunds in 2008

National Total = 237,689,335 Refunds*

ALPHA ORDER

ALPHA ORDER

RANK	STATE	REFUNDS	% of USA
23	Alabama	3,671,822	1.5%
47	Alaska	538,758	0.2%
20	Arizona	4,452,333	1.9%
32	Arkansas	2,162,356	0.9%
1	California	26,069,119	11.0%
22	Colorado	3,673,310	1.5%
28	Connecticut	2,752,065	1.2%
45	Delaware	708,142	0.3%
3	Florida	15,135,693	6.4%
9	Georgia	7,092,550	3.0%
42	Hawaii	1,081,714	0.5%
39	Idaho	1,123,876	0.5%
6	Illinois	10,048,102	4.2%
14	Indiana	5,173,312	2.2%
30	Iowa	2,384,885	1.0%
33	Kansas	2,148,751	0.9%
26	Kentucky	3,355,000	1.4%
25	Louisiana	3,407,363	1.4%
40	Maine	1,119,558	0.5%
19	Maryland	4,454,613	1.9%
15	Massachusetts	5,145,949	2.2%
8	Michigan	7,817,818	3.3%
21	Minnesota	4,150,056	1.7%
31	Mississippi	2,260,049	1.0%
17	Missouri	4,683,883	2.0%
44	Montana	778,759	0.3%
38	Nebraska	1,415,589	0.6%
34	Nevada	2,102,942	0.9%
41	New Hampshire	1,115,443	0.5%
11	New Jersey	6,783,396	2.9%
36	New Mexico	1,525,222	0.6%
4	New York	14,999,781	6.3%
10	North Carolina	7,040,103	3.0%
49	North Dakota	526,396	0.2%
7	Ohio	9,588,554	4.0%
29	Oklahoma	2,710,777	1.1%
27	Oregon	2,856,320	1.2%
5	Pennsylvania	10,371,942	4.4%
43	Rhode Island	879,276	0.4%
24	South Carolina	3,479,965	1.5%
46	South Dakota	645,462	0.3%
16	Tennessee	4,965,999	2.1%
2	Texas	17,809,244	7.5%
35	Utah	1,848,764	0.8%
48	Vermont	533,571	0.2%
12	Virginia	6,132,797	2.6%
13	Washington	5,206,885	2.2%
37	West Virginia	1,466,317	0.6%
18	Wisconsin	4,593,578	1.9%
50	Wyoming	446,731	0.2%

RANK ORDER

RANK	STATE	REFUNDS	% of USA
1	California	26,069,119	11.0%
2	Texas	17,809,244	7.5%
3	Florida	15,135,693	6.4%
4	New York	14,999,781	6.3%
5	Pennsylvania	10,371,942	4.4%
6	Illinois	10,048,102	4.2%
7	Ohio	9,588,554	4.0%
8	Michigan	7,817,818	3.3%
9	Georgia	7,092,550	3.0%
10	North Carolina	7,040,103	3.0%
11	New Jersey	6,783,396	2.9%
12	Virginia	6,132,797	2.6%
13	Washington	5,206,885	2.2%
14	Indiana	5,173,312	2.2%
15	Massachusetts	5,145,949	2.2%
16	Tennessee	4,965,999	2.1%
17	Missouri	4,683,883	2.0%
18	Wisconsin	4,593,578	1.9%
19	Maryland	4,454,613	1.9%
20	Arizona	4,452,333	1.9%
21	Minnesota	4,150,056	1.7%
22	Colorado	3,673,310	1.5%
23	Alabama	3,671,822	1.5%
24	South Carolina	3,479,965	1.5%
25	Louisiana	3,407,363	1.4%
26	Kentucky	3,355,000	1.4%
27	Oregon	2,856,320	1.2%
28	Connecticut	2,752,065	1.2%
29	Oklahoma	2,710,777	1.1%
30	Iowa	2,384,885	1.0%
31	Mississippi	2,260,049	1.0%
32	Arkansas	2,162,356	0.9%
33	Kansas	2,148,751	0.9%
34	Nevada	2,102,942	0.9%
35	Utah	1,848,764	0.8%
36	New Mexico	1,525,222	0.6%
37	West Virginia	1,466,317	0.6%
38	Nebraska	1,415,589	0.6%
39	Idaho	1,123,876	0.5%
40	Maine	1,119,558	0.5%
41	New Hampshire	1,115,443	0.5%
42	Hawaii	1,081,714	0.5%
43	Rhode Island	879,276	0.4%
44	Montana	778,759	0.3%
45	Delaware	708,142	0.3%
46	South Dakota	645,462	0.3%
47	Alaska	538,758	0.2%
48	Vermont	533,571	0.2%
49	North Dakota	526,396	0.2%
50	Wyoming	446,731	0.2%
	District of Columbia	464,327	0.2%

Source: U.S. Department of the Treasury, Internal Revenue Service
  "Fiscal Year 2008 IRS Data Book" (http://www.irs.gov/taxstats/index.html)
*Total includes refunds to international sources and other miscellaneous refunds not shown separately.

Value of Federal Tax Refunds in 2008

National Total = $425,675,913,000*

ALPHA ORDER

RANK	STATE	REFUNDS	% of USA
23	Alabama	$6,399,377,000	1.5%
47	Alaska	805,512,000	0.2%
19	Arizona	7,500,487,000	1.8%
34	Arkansas	3,278,251,000	0.8%
1	California	48,717,749,000	11.4%
24	Colorado	6,351,414,000	1.5%
20	Connecticut	7,341,332,000	1.7%
41	Delaware	1,619,264,000	0.4%
4	Florida	26,830,118,000	6.3%
10	Georgia	13,601,650,000	3.2%
42	Hawaii	1,604,152,000	0.4%
40	Idaho	1,666,497,000	0.4%
5	Illinois	19,067,481,000	4.5%
15	Indiana	8,625,141,000	2.0%
31	Iowa	3,548,477,000	0.8%
33	Kansas	3,370,380,000	0.8%
27	Kentucky	5,035,252,000	1.2%
25	Louisiana	5,565,584,000	1.3%
43	Maine	1,498,631,000	0.4%
17	Maryland	7,886,164,000	1.9%
14	Massachusetts	9,024,282,000	2.1%
7	Michigan	15,415,997,000	3.6%
21	Minnesota	7,154,386,000	1.7%
32	Mississippi	3,495,315,000	0.8%
18	Missouri	7,836,216,000	1.8%
45	Montana	1,019,585,000	0.2%
37	Nebraska	2,146,859,000	0.5%
30	Nevada	4,049,460,000	1.0%
39	New Hampshire	1,721,514,000	0.4%
9	New Jersey	13,671,114,000	3.2%
36	New Mexico	2,254,005,000	0.5%
2	New York	33,709,429,000	7.9%
11	North Carolina	11,886,652,000	2.8%
50	North Dakota	693,665,000	0.2%
8	Ohio	15,085,421,000	3.5%
28	Oklahoma	4,167,848,000	1.0%
29	Oregon	4,111,075,000	1.0%
6	Pennsylvania	16,916,127,000	4.0%
44	Rhode Island	1,376,727,000	0.3%
26	South Carolina	5,066,465,000	1.2%
46	South Dakota	928,823,000	0.2%
16	Tennessee	8,365,644,000	2.0%
3	Texas	33,587,800,000	7.9%
35	Utah	3,171,954,000	0.7%
48	Vermont	756,978,000	0.2%
13	Virginia	10,573,078,000	2.5%
12	Washington	11,376,059,000	2.7%
38	West Virginia	2,050,783,000	0.5%
22	Wisconsin	7,022,775,000	1.6%
49	Wyoming	716,776,000	0.2%

RANK ORDER

RANK	STATE	REFUNDS	% of USA
1	California	$48,717,749,000	11.4%
2	New York	33,709,429,000	7.9%
3	Texas	33,587,800,000	7.9%
4	Florida	26,830,118,000	6.3%
5	Illinois	19,067,481,000	4.5%
6	Pennsylvania	16,916,127,000	4.0%
7	Michigan	15,415,997,000	3.6%
8	Ohio	15,085,421,000	3.5%
9	New Jersey	13,671,114,000	3.2%
10	Georgia	13,601,650,000	3.2%
11	North Carolina	11,886,652,000	2.8%
12	Washington	11,376,059,000	2.7%
13	Virginia	10,573,078,000	2.5%
14	Massachusetts	9,024,282,000	2.1%
15	Indiana	8,625,141,000	2.0%
16	Tennessee	8,365,644,000	2.0%
17	Maryland	7,886,164,000	1.9%
18	Missouri	7,836,216,000	1.8%
19	Arizona	7,500,487,000	1.8%
20	Connecticut	7,341,332,000	1.7%
21	Minnesota	7,154,386,000	1.7%
22	Wisconsin	7,022,775,000	1.6%
23	Alabama	6,399,377,000	1.5%
24	Colorado	6,351,414,000	1.5%
25	Louisiana	5,565,584,000	1.3%
26	South Carolina	5,066,465,000	1.2%
27	Kentucky	5,035,252,000	1.2%
28	Oklahoma	4,167,848,000	1.0%
29	Oregon	4,111,075,000	1.0%
30	Nevada	4,049,460,000	1.0%
31	Iowa	3,548,477,000	0.8%
32	Mississippi	3,495,315,000	0.8%
33	Kansas	3,370,380,000	0.8%
34	Arkansas	3,278,251,000	0.8%
35	Utah	3,171,954,000	0.7%
36	New Mexico	2,254,005,000	0.5%
37	Nebraska	2,146,859,000	0.5%
38	West Virginia	2,050,783,000	0.5%
39	New Hampshire	1,721,514,000	0.4%
40	Idaho	1,666,497,000	0.4%
41	Delaware	1,619,264,000	0.4%
42	Hawaii	1,604,152,000	0.4%
43	Maine	1,498,631,000	0.4%
44	Rhode Island	1,376,727,000	0.3%
45	Montana	1,019,585,000	0.2%
46	South Dakota	928,823,000	0.2%
47	Alaska	805,512,000	0.2%
48	Vermont	756,978,000	0.2%
49	Wyoming	716,776,000	0.2%
50	North Dakota	693,665,000	0.2%
	District of Columbia	1,408,452,000	0.3%

Source: U.S. Department of the Treasury, Internal Revenue Service
"Fiscal Year 2008 IRS Data Book" (http://www.irs.gov/taxstats/index.html)
*Total includes refunds to international sources and other miscellaneous refunds not shown separately.

Average Value of Federal Tax Refunds in 2008

National Average = $1,791*

ALPHA ORDER

RANK	STATE	AVERAGE REFUND
15	Alabama	$1,743
38	Alaska	1,495
21	Arizona	1,685
36	Arkansas	1,516
11	California	1,869
16	Colorado	1,729
1	Connecticut	2,668
2	Delaware	2,287
12	Florida	1,773
8	Georgia	1,918
40	Hawaii	1,483
40	Idaho	1,483
9	Illinois	1,898
24	Indiana	1,667
39	Iowa	1,488
29	Kansas	1,569
37	Kentucky	1,501
25	Louisiana	1,633
48	Maine	1,339
13	Maryland	1,770
14	Massachusetts	1,754
6	Michigan	1,972
17	Minnesota	1,724
31	Mississippi	1,547
23	Missouri	1,673
50	Montana	1,309
35	Nebraska	1,517
7	Nevada	1,926
32	New Hampshire	1,543
5	New Jersey	2,015
42	New Mexico	1,478
3	New York	2,247
20	North Carolina	1,688
49	North Dakota	1,318
28	Ohio	1,573
33	Oklahoma	1,538
44	Oregon	1,439
26	Pennsylvania	1,631
30	Rhode Island	1,566
43	South Carolina	1,456
44	South Dakota	1,439
21	Tennessee	1,685
10	Texas	1,886
19	Utah	1,716
46	Vermont	1,419
17	Virginia	1,724
4	Washington	2,185
47	West Virginia	1,399
34	Wisconsin	1,529
27	Wyoming	1,604

RANK ORDER

RANK	STATE	AVERAGE REFUND
1	Connecticut	$2,668
2	Delaware	2,287
3	New York	2,247
4	Washington	2,185
5	New Jersey	2,015
6	Michigan	1,972
7	Nevada	1,926
8	Georgia	1,918
9	Illinois	1,898
10	Texas	1,886
11	California	1,869
12	Florida	1,773
13	Maryland	1,770
14	Massachusetts	1,754
15	Alabama	1,743
16	Colorado	1,729
17	Minnesota	1,724
17	Virginia	1,724
19	Utah	1,716
20	North Carolina	1,688
21	Arizona	1,685
21	Tennessee	1,685
23	Missouri	1,673
24	Indiana	1,667
25	Louisiana	1,633
26	Pennsylvania	1,631
27	Wyoming	1,604
28	Ohio	1,573
29	Kansas	1,569
30	Rhode Island	1,566
31	Mississippi	1,547
32	New Hampshire	1,543
33	Oklahoma	1,538
34	Wisconsin	1,529
35	Nebraska	1,517
36	Arkansas	1,516
37	Kentucky	1,501
38	Alaska	1,495
39	Iowa	1,488
40	Hawaii	1,483
40	Idaho	1,483
42	New Mexico	1,478
43	South Carolina	1,456
44	Oregon	1,439
44	South Dakota	1,439
46	Vermont	1,419
47	West Virginia	1,399
48	Maine	1,339
49	North Dakota	1,318
50	Montana	1,309
	District of Columbia	3,033

Source: CQ Press using data from U.S. Department of the Treasury, Internal Revenue Service
"Fiscal Year 2008 IRS Data Book" (http://www.irs.gov/taxstats/index.html)
*National average includes refunds to international sources and other miscellaneous refunds not shown separately.

Value of Federal Individual Income Tax Refunds in 2008

National Total = $270,378,034,000*

ALPHA ORDER

RANK	STATE	REFUNDS	% of USA
22	Alabama	$4,069,259,000	1.5%
47	Alaska	562,570,000	0.2%
18	Arizona	5,084,734,000	1.9%
33	Arkansas	2,164,917,000	0.8%
1	California	33,291,510,000	12.3%
24	Colorado	3,976,410,000	1.5%
25	Connecticut	3,556,364,000	1.3%
44	Delaware	839,900,000	0.3%
4	Florida	18,322,879,000	6.8%
9	Georgia	8,469,970,000	3.1%
41	Hawaii	1,072,024,000	0.4%
40	Idaho	1,080,281,000	0.4%
5	Illinois	12,361,728,000	4.6%
16	Indiana	5,514,634,000	2.0%
32	Iowa	2,226,199,000	0.8%
34	Kansas	2,120,181,000	0.8%
27	Kentucky	3,317,209,000	1.2%
23	Louisiana	3,998,774,000	1.5%
42	Maine	965,215,000	0.4%
15	Maryland	5,571,552,000	2.1%
13	Massachusetts	6,109,839,000	2.3%
10	Michigan	8,318,592,000	3.1%
21	Minnesota	4,120,361,000	1.5%
31	Mississippi	2,515,446,000	0.9%
19	Missouri	4,707,425,000	1.7%
45	Montana	654,347,000	0.2%
38	Nebraska	1,313,659,000	0.5%
28	Nevada	2,798,498,000	1.0%
39	New Hampshire	1,190,218,000	0.4%
8	New Jersey	9,062,288,000	3.4%
36	New Mexico	1,524,423,000	0.6%
3	New York	18,406,617,000	6.8%
11	North Carolina	7,364,430,000	2.7%
50	North Dakota	431,826,000	0.2%
7	Ohio	9,464,566,000	3.5%
29	Oklahoma	2,738,434,000	1.0%
30	Oregon	2,638,910,000	1.0%
6	Pennsylvania	10,679,495,000	3.9%
43	Rhode Island	945,394,000	0.3%
26	South Carolina	3,520,419,000	1.3%
46	South Dakota	586,757,000	0.2%
17	Tennessee	5,296,940,000	2.0%
2	Texas	21,689,548,000	8.0%
35	Utah	2,036,665,000	0.8%
49	Vermont	471,284,000	0.2%
12	Virginia	7,193,266,000	2.7%
14	Washington	5,751,773,000	2.1%
37	West Virginia	1,347,808,000	0.5%
20	Wisconsin	4,314,849,000	1.6%
48	Wyoming	502,650,000	0.2%

RANK ORDER

RANK	STATE	REFUNDS	% of USA
1	California	$33,291,510,000	12.3%
2	Texas	21,689,548,000	8.0%
3	New York	18,406,617,000	6.8%
4	Florida	18,322,879,000	6.8%
5	Illinois	12,361,728,000	4.6%
6	Pennsylvania	10,679,495,000	3.9%
7	Ohio	9,464,566,000	3.5%
8	New Jersey	9,062,288,000	3.4%
9	Georgia	8,469,970,000	3.1%
10	Michigan	8,318,592,000	3.1%
11	North Carolina	7,364,430,000	2.7%
12	Virginia	7,193,266,000	2.7%
13	Massachusetts	6,109,839,000	2.3%
14	Washington	5,751,773,000	2.1%
15	Maryland	5,571,552,000	2.1%
16	Indiana	5,514,634,000	2.0%
17	Tennessee	5,296,940,000	2.0%
18	Arizona	5,084,734,000	1.9%
19	Missouri	4,707,425,000	1.7%
20	Wisconsin	4,314,849,000	1.6%
21	Minnesota	4,120,361,000	1.5%
22	Alabama	4,069,259,000	1.5%
23	Louisiana	3,998,774,000	1.5%
24	Colorado	3,976,410,000	1.5%
25	Connecticut	3,556,364,000	1.3%
26	South Carolina	3,520,419,000	1.3%
27	Kentucky	3,317,209,000	1.2%
28	Nevada	2,798,498,000	1.0%
29	Oklahoma	2,738,434,000	1.0%
30	Oregon	2,638,910,000	1.0%
31	Mississippi	2,515,446,000	0.9%
32	Iowa	2,226,199,000	0.8%
33	Arkansas	2,164,917,000	0.8%
34	Kansas	2,120,181,000	0.8%
35	Utah	2,036,665,000	0.8%
36	New Mexico	1,524,423,000	0.6%
37	West Virginia	1,347,808,000	0.5%
38	Nebraska	1,313,659,000	0.5%
39	New Hampshire	1,190,218,000	0.4%
40	Idaho	1,080,281,000	0.4%
41	Hawaii	1,072,024,000	0.4%
42	Maine	965,215,000	0.4%
43	Rhode Island	945,394,000	0.3%
44	Delaware	839,900,000	0.3%
45	Montana	654,347,000	0.2%
46	South Dakota	586,757,000	0.2%
47	Alaska	562,570,000	0.2%
48	Wyoming	502,650,000	0.2%
49	Vermont	471,284,000	0.2%
50	North Dakota	431,826,000	0.2%
	District of Columbia	624,386,000	0.2%

Source: U.S. Department of the Treasury, Internal Revenue Service
"Fiscal Year 2008 IRS Data Book" (http://www.irs.gov/taxstats/index.html)
*Total includes refunds to international sources and other miscellaneous refunds not shown separately.

Average Value of Federal Individual Income Tax Refunds in 2008

National Average = $2,282*

ALPHA ORDER

RANK	STATE	AVERAGE REFUND
17	Alabama	$2,300
34	Alaska	2,077
18	Arizona	2,285
27	Arkansas	2,148
4	California	2,485
22	Colorado	2,185
2	Connecticut	2,593
11	Delaware	2,392
8	Florida	2,453
14	Georgia	2,341
39	Hawaii	2,035
40	Idaho	2,020
7	Illinois	2,459
25	Indiana	2,164
41	Iowa	2,019
37	Kansas	2,051
32	Kentucky	2,100
10	Louisiana	2,404
48	Maine	1,858
6	Maryland	2,463
9	Massachusetts	2,411
23	Michigan	2,177
35	Minnesota	2,063
16	Mississippi	2,325
31	Missouri	2,111
49	Montana	1,817
44	Nebraska	1,969
3	Nevada	2,568
23	New Hampshire	2,177
1	New Jersey	2,631
36	New Mexico	2,052
5	New York	2,473
28	North Carolina	2,141
50	North Dakota	1,803
38	Ohio	2,042
30	Oklahoma	2,117
46	Oregon	1,934
29	Pennsylvania	2,139
21	Rhode Island	2,200
33	South Carolina	2,085
45	South Dakota	1,958
20	Tennessee	2,201
12	Texas	2,362
26	Utah	2,163
47	Vermont	1,891
13	Virginia	2,358
19	Washington	2,229
42	West Virginia	2,011
43	Wisconsin	1,973
15	Wyoming	2,335

RANK ORDER

RANK	STATE	AVERAGE REFUND
1	New Jersey	$2,631
2	Connecticut	2,593
3	Nevada	2,568
4	California	2,485
5	New York	2,473
6	Maryland	2,463
7	Illinois	2,459
8	Florida	2,453
9	Massachusetts	2,411
10	Louisiana	2,404
11	Delaware	2,392
12	Texas	2,362
13	Virginia	2,358
14	Georgia	2,341
15	Wyoming	2,335
16	Mississippi	2,325
17	Alabama	2,300
18	Arizona	2,285
19	Washington	2,229
20	Tennessee	2,201
21	Rhode Island	2,200
22	Colorado	2,185
23	Michigan	2,177
23	New Hampshire	2,177
25	Indiana	2,164
26	Utah	2,163
27	Arkansas	2,148
28	North Carolina	2,141
29	Pennsylvania	2,139
30	Oklahoma	2,117
31	Missouri	2,111
32	Kentucky	2,100
33	South Carolina	2,085
34	Alaska	2,077
35	Minnesota	2,063
36	New Mexico	2,052
37	Kansas	2,051
38	Ohio	2,042
39	Hawaii	2,035
40	Idaho	2,020
41	Iowa	2,019
42	West Virginia	2,011
43	Wisconsin	1,973
44	Nebraska	1,969
45	South Dakota	1,958
46	Oregon	1,934
47	Vermont	1,891
48	Maine	1,858
49	Montana	1,817
50	North Dakota	1,803

| | District of Columbia | 2,595 |

Source: CQ Press using data from U.S. Department of the Treasury, Internal Revenue Service
   "Fiscal Year 2008 IRS Data Book" (http://www.irs.gov/taxstats/index.html)
*National average includes refunds to international sources and other miscellaneous refunds not shown separately.

Value of Federal Corporate Income Tax Refunds in 2008

National Total = $54,340,019,000*

ALPHA ORDER

RANK	STATE	REFUNDS	% of USA
18	Alabama	$808,929,000	1.5%
50	Alaska	5,703,000	0.0%
23	Arizona	551,512,000	1.0%
35	Arkansas	156,823,000	0.3%
2	California	4,925,497,000	9.1%
20	Colorado	756,217,000	1.4%
6	Connecticut	2,609,326,000	4.8%
25	Delaware	470,666,000	0.9%
7	Florida	2,552,448,000	4.7%
9	Georgia	2,259,163,000	4.2%
39	Hawaii	71,738,000	0.1%
41	Idaho	68,827,000	0.1%
8	Illinois	2,482,338,000	4.6%
17	Indiana	854,920,000	1.6%
31	Iowa	211,435,000	0.4%
27	Kansas	256,223,000	0.5%
28	Kentucky	250,926,000	0.5%
34	Louisiana	172,091,000	0.3%
43	Maine	56,774,000	0.1%
24	Maryland	479,919,000	0.9%
21	Massachusetts	754,072,000	1.4%
4	Michigan	3,702,297,000	6.8%
14	Minnesota	1,108,509,000	2.0%
40	Mississippi	70,110,000	0.1%
15	Missouri	1,077,567,000	2.0%
47	Montana	28,291,000	0.1%
33	Nebraska	180,159,000	0.3%
26	Nevada	390,013,000	0.7%
46	New Hampshire	44,935,000	0.1%
11	New Jersey	1,783,842,000	3.3%
37	New Mexico	100,604,000	0.2%
1	New York	8,829,812,000	16.2%
12	North Carolina	1,588,637,000	2.9%
48	North Dakota	19,930,000	0.0%
13	Ohio	1,574,042,000	2.9%
32	Oklahoma	202,734,000	0.4%
29	Oregon	250,913,000	0.5%
10	Pennsylvania	1,812,222,000	3.3%
38	Rhode Island	72,440,000	0.1%
36	South Carolina	125,642,000	0.2%
45	South Dakota	47,476,000	0.1%
16	Tennessee	969,866,000	1.8%
3	Texas	4,561,131,000	8.4%
30	Utah	230,489,000	0.4%
44	Vermont	52,825,000	0.1%
19	Virginia	797,533,000	1.5%
5	Washington	3,385,467,000	6.2%
42	West Virginia	67,991,000	0.1%
22	Wisconsin	651,531,000	1.2%
49	Wyoming	12,163,000	0.0%

RANK ORDER

RANK	STATE	REFUNDS	% of USA
1	New York	$8,829,812,000	16.2%
2	California	4,925,497,000	9.1%
3	Texas	4,561,131,000	8.4%
4	Michigan	3,702,297,000	6.8%
5	Washington	3,385,467,000	6.2%
6	Connecticut	2,609,326,000	4.8%
7	Florida	2,552,448,000	4.7%
8	Illinois	2,482,338,000	4.6%
9	Georgia	2,259,163,000	4.2%
10	Pennsylvania	1,812,222,000	3.3%
11	New Jersey	1,783,842,000	3.3%
12	North Carolina	1,588,637,000	2.9%
13	Ohio	1,574,042,000	2.9%
14	Minnesota	1,108,509,000	2.0%
15	Missouri	1,077,567,000	2.0%
16	Tennessee	969,866,000	1.8%
17	Indiana	854,920,000	1.6%
18	Alabama	808,929,000	1.5%
19	Virginia	797,533,000	1.5%
20	Colorado	756,217,000	1.4%
21	Massachusetts	754,072,000	1.4%
22	Wisconsin	651,531,000	1.2%
23	Arizona	551,512,000	1.0%
24	Maryland	479,919,000	0.9%
25	Delaware	470,666,000	0.9%
26	Nevada	390,013,000	0.7%
27	Kansas	256,223,000	0.5%
28	Kentucky	250,926,000	0.5%
29	Oregon	250,913,000	0.5%
30	Utah	230,489,000	0.4%
31	Iowa	211,435,000	0.4%
32	Oklahoma	202,734,000	0.4%
33	Nebraska	180,159,000	0.3%
34	Louisiana	172,091,000	0.3%
35	Arkansas	156,823,000	0.3%
36	South Carolina	125,642,000	0.2%
37	New Mexico	100,604,000	0.2%
38	Rhode Island	72,440,000	0.1%
39	Hawaii	71,738,000	0.1%
40	Mississippi	70,110,000	0.1%
41	Idaho	68,827,000	0.1%
42	West Virginia	67,991,000	0.1%
43	Maine	56,774,000	0.1%
44	Vermont	52,825,000	0.1%
45	South Dakota	47,476,000	0.1%
46	New Hampshire	44,935,000	0.1%
47	Montana	28,291,000	0.1%
48	North Dakota	19,930,000	0.0%
49	Wyoming	12,163,000	0.0%
50	Alaska	5,703,000	0.0%
	District of Columbia	612,184,000	1.1%

Source: U.S. Department of the Treasury, Internal Revenue Service
   "Fiscal Year 2008 IRS Data Book" (http://www.irs.gov/taxstats/index.html)
*Total includes refunds to international sources and other miscellaneous refunds not shown separately.

Average Value of Federal Corporate Income Tax Refunds in 2008

National Average = $86,227*

ALPHA ORDER

RANK	STATE	AVERAGE REFUND
7	Alabama	$128,137
50	Alaska	4,768
22	Arizona	56,076
31	Arkansas	32,096
20	California	59,436
18	Colorado	66,405
1	Connecticut	371,223
4	Delaware	193,929
19	Florida	61,497
6	Georgia	136,119
39	Hawaii	20,728
41	Idaho	19,161
12	Illinois	92,267
15	Indiana	83,668
38	Iowa	22,422
29	Kansas	35,956
25	Kentucky	43,830
40	Louisiana	19,410
44	Maine	17,550
28	Maryland	40,561
21	Massachusetts	57,092
5	Michigan	167,798
16	Minnesota	82,571
45	Mississippi	13,774
14	Missouri	86,267
48	Montana	6,342
32	Nebraska	30,950
23	Nevada	54,900
46	New Hampshire	12,569
11	New Jersey	95,037
33	New Mexico	29,356
3	New York	218,565
10	North Carolina	98,112
47	North Dakota	8,893
17	Ohio	75,108
34	Oklahoma	28,647
37	Oregon	26,213
13	Pennsylvania	90,702
30	Rhode Island	33,260
42	South Carolina	18,531
43	South Dakota	18,079
8	Tennessee	110,614
9	Texas	102,615
26	Utah	43,703
36	Vermont	27,034
24	Virginia	52,876
2	Washington	230,382
35	West Virginia	28,365
27	Wisconsin	43,639
49	Wyoming	5,800

RANK ORDER

RANK	STATE	AVERAGE REFUND
1	Connecticut	$371,223
2	Washington	230,382
3	New York	218,565
4	Delaware	193,929
5	Michigan	167,798
6	Georgia	136,119
7	Alabama	128,137
8	Tennessee	110,614
9	Texas	102,615
10	North Carolina	98,112
11	New Jersey	95,037
12	Illinois	92,267
13	Pennsylvania	90,702
14	Missouri	86,267
15	Indiana	83,668
16	Minnesota	82,571
17	Ohio	75,108
18	Colorado	66,405
19	Florida	61,497
20	California	59,436
21	Massachusetts	57,092
22	Arizona	56,076
23	Nevada	54,900
24	Virginia	52,876
25	Kentucky	43,830
26	Utah	43,703
27	Wisconsin	43,639
28	Maryland	40,561
29	Kansas	35,956
30	Rhode Island	33,260
31	Arkansas	32,096
32	Nebraska	30,950
33	New Mexico	29,356
34	Oklahoma	28,647
35	West Virginia	28,365
36	Vermont	27,034
37	Oregon	26,213
38	Iowa	22,422
39	Hawaii	20,728
40	Louisiana	19,410
41	Idaho	19,161
42	South Carolina	18,531
43	South Dakota	18,079
44	Maine	17,550
45	Mississippi	13,774
46	New Hampshire	12,569
47	North Dakota	8,893
48	Montana	6,342
49	Wyoming	5,800
50	Alaska	4,768

District of Columbia	347,634

Source: CQ Press using data from U.S. Department of the Treasury, Internal Revenue Service
"Fiscal Year 2008 IRS Data Book" (http://www.irs.gov/taxstats/index.html)
*National average includes refunds to international sources and other miscellaneous refunds not shown separately.

Federal Tax Burden per Household in 2007

National Average = $23,524*

ALPHA ORDER

RANK	STATE	TAXES
43	Alabama	$17,201
11	Alaska	25,955
24	Arizona	20,193
48	Arkansas	15,422
5	California	29,729
18	Colorado	24,030
1	Connecticut	38,331
9	Delaware	26,049
19	Florida	23,956
25	Georgia	20,104
14	Hawaii	24,716
42	Idaho	17,366
13	Illinois	25,808
33	Indiana	18,841
37	Iowa	17,913
29	Kansas	19,501
47	Kentucky	16,205
44	Louisiana	17,094
40	Maine	17,391
6	Maryland	29,483
3	Massachusetts	32,157
23	Michigan	20,263
17	Minnesota	24,368
50	Mississippi	14,126
36	Missouri	18,489
38	Montana	17,523
30	Nebraska	19,356
7	Nevada	27,367
10	New Hampshire	26,030
2	New Jersey	34,400
45	New Mexico	16,997
4	New York	29,919
34	North Carolina	18,602
41	North Dakota	17,371
32	Ohio	18,913
39	Oklahoma	17,508
27	Oregon	19,757
21	Pennsylvania	22,214
15	Rhode Island	24,643
46	South Carolina	16,734
31	South Dakota	19,340
35	Tennessee	18,529
20	Texas	22,539
28	Utah	19,752
26	Vermont	19,855
8	Virginia	26,058
16	Washington	24,613
49	West Virginia	14,408
22	Wisconsin	20,276
12	Wyoming	25,851

RANK ORDER

RANK	STATE	TAXES
1	Connecticut	$38,331
2	New Jersey	34,400
3	Massachusetts	32,157
4	New York	29,919
5	California	29,729
6	Maryland	29,483
7	Nevada	27,367
8	Virginia	26,058
9	Delaware	26,049
10	New Hampshire	26,030
11	Alaska	25,955
12	Wyoming	25,851
13	Illinois	25,808
14	Hawaii	24,716
15	Rhode Island	24,643
16	Washington	24,613
17	Minnesota	24,368
18	Colorado	24,030
19	Florida	23,956
20	Texas	22,539
21	Pennsylvania	22,214
22	Wisconsin	20,276
23	Michigan	20,263
24	Arizona	20,193
25	Georgia	20,104
26	Vermont	19,855
27	Oregon	19,757
28	Utah	19,752
29	Kansas	19,501
30	Nebraska	19,356
31	South Dakota	19,340
32	Ohio	18,913
33	Indiana	18,841
34	North Carolina	18,602
35	Tennessee	18,529
36	Missouri	18,489
37	Iowa	17,913
38	Montana	17,523
39	Oklahoma	17,508
40	Maine	17,391
41	North Dakota	17,371
42	Idaho	17,366
43	Alabama	17,201
44	Louisiana	17,094
45	New Mexico	16,997
46	South Carolina	16,734
47	Kentucky	16,205
48	Arkansas	15,422
49	West Virginia	14,408
50	Mississippi	14,126
	District of Columbia	34,777

Source: The Tax Foundation
  "2008 Facts and Figures" (http://www.taxfoundation.org/files/2008 facts and figures.pdf)
*A household is a separate living quarters occupied by one or more people.

Per Capita Federal Economic Stimulus Funds in 2009

National Per Capita = $640*

<table>
<tr><td colspan="3">ALPHA ORDER</td><td colspan="3">RANK ORDER</td></tr>
<tr><td>RANK</td><td>STATE</td><td>PER CAPITA</td><td>RANK</td><td>STATE</td><td>PER CAPITA</td></tr>
<tr><td>25</td><td>Alabama</td><td>$631</td><td>1</td><td>Alaska</td><td>$2,298</td></tr>
<tr><td>1</td><td>Alaska</td><td>2,298</td><td>2</td><td>North Dakota</td><td>1,379</td></tr>
<tr><td>46</td><td>Arizona</td><td>513</td><td>3</td><td>South Carolina</td><td>1,256</td></tr>
<tr><td>41</td><td>Arkansas</td><td>547</td><td>4</td><td>Idaho</td><td>1,211</td></tr>
<tr><td>31</td><td>California</td><td>585</td><td>5</td><td>Montana</td><td>1,196</td></tr>
<tr><td>22</td><td>Colorado</td><td>669</td><td>6</td><td>Washington</td><td>1,183</td></tr>
<tr><td>45</td><td>Connecticut</td><td>519</td><td>7</td><td>South Dakota</td><td>1,166</td></tr>
<tr><td>15</td><td>Delaware</td><td>758</td><td>8</td><td>New Mexico</td><td>1,108</td></tr>
<tr><td>50</td><td>Florida</td><td>487</td><td>9</td><td>Wyoming</td><td>1,040</td></tr>
<tr><td>49</td><td>Georgia</td><td>491</td><td>10</td><td>Vermont</td><td>1,001</td></tr>
<tr><td>14</td><td>Hawaii</td><td>784</td><td>11</td><td>Tennessee</td><td>927</td></tr>
<tr><td>4</td><td>Idaho</td><td>1,211</td><td>12</td><td>Maryland</td><td>815</td></tr>
<tr><td>29</td><td>Illinois</td><td>605</td><td>13</td><td>West Virginia</td><td>815</td></tr>
<tr><td>23</td><td>Indiana</td><td>646</td><td>14</td><td>Hawaii</td><td>784</td></tr>
<tr><td>20</td><td>Iowa</td><td>679</td><td>15</td><td>Delaware</td><td>758</td></tr>
<tr><td>40</td><td>Kansas</td><td>554</td><td>16</td><td>Rhode Island</td><td>745</td></tr>
<tr><td>32</td><td>Kentucky</td><td>581</td><td>17</td><td>Michigan</td><td>730</td></tr>
<tr><td>38</td><td>Louisiana</td><td>557</td><td>18</td><td>Massachusetts</td><td>713</td></tr>
<tr><td>21</td><td>Maine</td><td>671</td><td>19</td><td>Mississippi</td><td>694</td></tr>
<tr><td>12</td><td>Maryland</td><td>815</td><td>20</td><td>Iowa</td><td>679</td></tr>
<tr><td>18</td><td>Massachusetts</td><td>713</td><td>21</td><td>Maine</td><td>671</td></tr>
<tr><td>17</td><td>Michigan</td><td>730</td><td>22</td><td>Colorado</td><td>669</td></tr>
<tr><td>36</td><td>Minnesota</td><td>562</td><td>23</td><td>Indiana</td><td>646</td></tr>
<tr><td>19</td><td>Mississippi</td><td>694</td><td>24</td><td>New York</td><td>643</td></tr>
<tr><td>35</td><td>Missouri</td><td>564</td><td>25</td><td>Alabama</td><td>631</td></tr>
<tr><td>5</td><td>Montana</td><td>1,196</td><td>26</td><td>Oklahoma</td><td>630</td></tr>
<tr><td>30</td><td>Nebraska</td><td>598</td><td>27</td><td>Utah</td><td>623</td></tr>
<tr><td>43</td><td>Nevada</td><td>528</td><td>28</td><td>New Hampshire</td><td>616</td></tr>
<tr><td>28</td><td>New Hampshire</td><td>616</td><td>29</td><td>Illinois</td><td>605</td></tr>
<tr><td>47</td><td>New Jersey</td><td>510</td><td>30</td><td>Nebraska</td><td>598</td></tr>
<tr><td>8</td><td>New Mexico</td><td>1,108</td><td>31</td><td>California</td><td>585</td></tr>
<tr><td>24</td><td>New York</td><td>643</td><td>32</td><td>Kentucky</td><td>581</td></tr>
<tr><td>34</td><td>North Carolina</td><td>576</td><td>33</td><td>Oregon</td><td>577</td></tr>
<tr><td>2</td><td>North Dakota</td><td>1,379</td><td>34</td><td>North Carolina</td><td>576</td></tr>
<tr><td>37</td><td>Ohio</td><td>560</td><td>35</td><td>Missouri</td><td>564</td></tr>
<tr><td>26</td><td>Oklahoma</td><td>630</td><td>36</td><td>Minnesota</td><td>562</td></tr>
<tr><td>33</td><td>Oregon</td><td>577</td><td>37</td><td>Ohio</td><td>560</td></tr>
<tr><td>42</td><td>Pennsylvania</td><td>539</td><td>38</td><td>Louisiana</td><td>557</td></tr>
<tr><td>16</td><td>Rhode Island</td><td>745</td><td>39</td><td>Virginia</td><td>556</td></tr>
<tr><td>3</td><td>South Carolina</td><td>1,256</td><td>40</td><td>Kansas</td><td>554</td></tr>
<tr><td>7</td><td>South Dakota</td><td>1,166</td><td>41</td><td>Arkansas</td><td>547</td></tr>
<tr><td>11</td><td>Tennessee</td><td>927</td><td>42</td><td>Pennsylvania</td><td>539</td></tr>
<tr><td>48</td><td>Texas</td><td>499</td><td>43</td><td>Nevada</td><td>528</td></tr>
<tr><td>27</td><td>Utah</td><td>623</td><td>44</td><td>Wisconsin</td><td>520</td></tr>
<tr><td>10</td><td>Vermont</td><td>1,001</td><td>45</td><td>Connecticut</td><td>519</td></tr>
<tr><td>39</td><td>Virginia</td><td>556</td><td>46</td><td>Arizona</td><td>513</td></tr>
<tr><td>6</td><td>Washington</td><td>1,183</td><td>47</td><td>New Jersey</td><td>510</td></tr>
<tr><td>13</td><td>West Virginia</td><td>815</td><td>48</td><td>Texas</td><td>499</td></tr>
<tr><td>44</td><td>Wisconsin</td><td>520</td><td>49</td><td>Georgia</td><td>491</td></tr>
<tr><td>9</td><td>Wyoming</td><td>1,040</td><td>50</td><td>Florida</td><td>487</td></tr>
<tr><td></td><td></td><td></td><td></td><td>District of Columbia</td><td>5,275</td></tr>
</table>

Source: CQ Press using data from Recovery Accountability and Transparency Board
   "State and Territory Totals by Agency" (http://www.recovery.gov/Pages/home.aspx)
*Funds awarded from February 17 to December 31, 2009. Calculated using 2009 Census population estimates.

Federal Government Expenditures in 2008

National Total = $2,792,611,000,000*

ALPHA ORDER				RANK ORDER			
RANK	STATE	EXPENDITURES	% of USA	RANK	STATE	EXPENDITURES	% of USA
21	Alabama	$47,966,000,000	1.7%	1	California	$299,923,000,000	10.7%
44	Alaska	9,423,000,000	0.3%	2	Texas	210,005,000,000	7.5%
18	Arizona	54,314,000,000	1.9%	3	New York	174,071,000,000	6.2%
33	Arkansas	23,857,000,000	0.9%	4	Florida	149,872,000,000	5.4%
1	California	299,923,000,000	10.7%	5	Pennsylvania	121,551,000,000	4.4%
27	Colorado	38,015,000,000	1.4%	6	Virginia	118,527,000,000	4.2%
24	Connecticut	38,879,000,000	1.4%	7	Illinois	100,672,000,000	3.6%
48	Delaware	6,623,000,000	0.2%	8	Ohio	90,592,000,000	3.2%
4	Florida	149,872,000,000	5.4%	9	Michigan	82,933,000,000	3.0%
11	Georgia	74,165,000,000	2.7%	10	Maryland	77,905,000,000	2.8%
39	Hawaii	15,009,000,000	0.5%	11	Georgia	74,165,000,000	2.7%
41	Idaho	11,227,000,000	0.4%	12	Massachusetts	72,115,000,000	2.6%
7	Illinois	100,672,000,000	3.6%	13	New Jersey	72,085,000,000	2.6%
19	Indiana	52,813,000,000	1.9%	14	North Carolina	70,203,000,000	2.5%
32	Iowa	23,927,000,000	0.9%	15	Missouri	60,829,000,000	2.2%
31	Kansas	25,129,000,000	0.9%	16	Tennessee	58,672,000,000	2.1%
20	Kentucky	52,264,000,000	1.9%	17	Washington	56,436,000,000	2.0%
22	Louisiana	44,496,000,000	1.6%	18	Arizona	54,314,000,000	1.9%
40	Maine	11,974,000,000	0.4%	19	Indiana	52,813,000,000	1.9%
10	Maryland	77,905,000,000	2.8%	20	Kentucky	52,264,000,000	1.9%
12	Massachusetts	72,115,000,000	2.6%	21	Alabama	47,966,000,000	1.7%
9	Michigan	82,933,000,000	3.0%	22	Louisiana	44,496,000,000	1.6%
26	Minnesota	38,246,000,000	1.4%	23	Wisconsin	40,137,000,000	1.4%
29	Mississippi	30,098,000,000	1.1%	24	Connecticut	38,879,000,000	1.4%
15	Missouri	60,829,000,000	2.2%	25	South Carolina	38,832,000,000	1.4%
45	Montana	8,843,000,000	0.3%	26	Minnesota	38,246,000,000	1.4%
38	Nebraska	15,739,000,000	0.6%	27	Colorado	38,015,000,000	1.4%
36	Nevada	17,260,000,000	0.6%	28	Oklahoma	31,758,000,000	1.1%
42	New Hampshire	10,311,000,000	0.4%	29	Mississippi	30,098,000,000	1.1%
13	New Jersey	72,085,000,000	2.6%	30	Oregon	27,530,000,000	1.0%
34	New Mexico	23,846,000,000	0.9%	31	Kansas	25,129,000,000	0.9%
3	New York	174,071,000,000	6.2%	32	Iowa	23,927,000,000	0.9%
14	North Carolina	70,203,000,000	2.5%	33	Arkansas	23,857,000,000	0.9%
47	North Dakota	7,323,000,000	0.3%	34	New Mexico	23,846,000,000	0.9%
8	Ohio	90,592,000,000	3.2%	35	West Virginia	18,002,000,000	0.6%
28	Oklahoma	31,758,000,000	1.1%	36	Nevada	17,260,000,000	0.6%
30	Oregon	27,530,000,000	1.0%	37	Utah	17,117,000,000	0.6%
5	Pennsylvania	121,551,000,000	4.4%	38	Nebraska	15,739,000,000	0.6%
43	Rhode Island	9,841,000,000	0.4%	39	Hawaii	15,009,000,000	0.5%
25	South Carolina	38,832,000,000	1.4%	40	Maine	11,974,000,000	0.4%
46	South Dakota	8,552,000,000	0.3%	41	Idaho	11,227,000,000	0.4%
16	Tennessee	58,672,000,000	2.1%	42	New Hampshire	10,311,000,000	0.4%
2	Texas	210,005,000,000	7.5%	43	Rhode Island	9,841,000,000	0.4%
37	Utah	17,117,000,000	0.6%	44	Alaska	9,423,000,000	0.3%
49	Vermont	6,080,000,000	0.2%	45	Montana	8,843,000,000	0.3%
6	Virginia	118,527,000,000	4.2%	46	South Dakota	8,552,000,000	0.3%
17	Washington	56,436,000,000	2.0%	47	North Dakota	7,323,000,000	0.3%
35	West Virginia	18,002,000,000	0.6%	48	Delaware	6,623,000,000	0.2%
23	Wisconsin	40,137,000,000	1.4%	49	Vermont	6,080,000,000	0.2%
50	Wyoming	5,969,000,000	0.2%	50	Wyoming	5,969,000,000	0.2%
					District of Columbia	47,203,000,000	1.7%

Source: U.S. Bureau of the Census
   "Consolidated Federal Funds Report: 2008" (CFFR/08, July 2009, http://www.census.gov/govs/cffr/)
*Total includes $20,830,000,000 in U.S. territories ($17,958,000,000 in Puerto Rico) and $22,625,000,000 in expenditures not distributed by state.

Per Capita Federal Government Expenditures in 2008

National Per Capita = $9,032*

<table>
<tr><td colspan="3">ALPHA ORDER</td><td colspan="3">RANK ORDER</td></tr>
<tr><td>RANK</td><td>STATE</td><td>PER CAPITA</td><td>RANK</td><td>STATE</td><td>PER CAPITA</td></tr>
<tr><td>12</td><td>Alabama</td><td>$10,255</td><td>1</td><td>Virginia</td><td>$15,205</td></tr>
<tr><td>3</td><td>Alaska</td><td>13,694</td><td>2</td><td>Maryland</td><td>13,767</td></tr>
<tr><td>30</td><td>Arizona</td><td>8,357</td><td>3</td><td>Alaska</td><td>13,694</td></tr>
<tr><td>32</td><td>Arkansas</td><td>8,319</td><td>4</td><td>Kentucky</td><td>12,189</td></tr>
<tr><td>35</td><td>California</td><td>8,199</td><td>5</td><td>New Mexico</td><td>12,002</td></tr>
<tr><td>41</td><td>Colorado</td><td>7,703</td><td>6</td><td>Hawaii</td><td>11,658</td></tr>
<tr><td>9</td><td>Connecticut</td><td>11,099</td><td>7</td><td>North Dakota</td><td>11,417</td></tr>
<tr><td>44</td><td>Delaware</td><td>7,559</td><td>8</td><td>Wyoming</td><td>11,199</td></tr>
<tr><td>36</td><td>Florida</td><td>8,135</td><td>9</td><td>Connecticut</td><td>11,099</td></tr>
<tr><td>42</td><td>Georgia</td><td>7,648</td><td>10</td><td>Massachusetts</td><td>11,021</td></tr>
<tr><td>6</td><td>Hawaii</td><td>11,658</td><td>11</td><td>South Dakota</td><td>10,630</td></tr>
<tr><td>45</td><td>Idaho</td><td>7,350</td><td>12</td><td>Alabama</td><td>10,255</td></tr>
<tr><td>39</td><td>Illinois</td><td>7,839</td><td>13</td><td>Mississippi</td><td>10,237</td></tr>
<tr><td>34</td><td>Indiana</td><td>8,267</td><td>14</td><td>Missouri</td><td>10,212</td></tr>
<tr><td>37</td><td>Iowa</td><td>7,992</td><td>15</td><td>Louisiana</td><td>9,996</td></tr>
<tr><td>23</td><td>Kansas</td><td>8,983</td><td>16</td><td>West Virginia</td><td>9,919</td></tr>
<tr><td>4</td><td>Kentucky</td><td>12,189</td><td>17</td><td>Vermont</td><td>9,790</td></tr>
<tr><td>15</td><td>Louisiana</td><td>9,996</td><td>18</td><td>Pennsylvania</td><td>9,673</td></tr>
<tr><td>22</td><td>Maine</td><td>9,073</td><td>19</td><td>Tennessee</td><td>9,402</td></tr>
<tr><td>2</td><td>Maryland</td><td>13,767</td><td>20</td><td>Rhode Island</td><td>9,341</td></tr>
<tr><td>10</td><td>Massachusetts</td><td>11,021</td><td>21</td><td>Montana</td><td>9,135</td></tr>
<tr><td>33</td><td>Michigan</td><td>8,291</td><td>22</td><td>Maine</td><td>9,073</td></tr>
<tr><td>46</td><td>Minnesota</td><td>7,312</td><td>23</td><td>Kansas</td><td>8,983</td></tr>
<tr><td>13</td><td>Mississippi</td><td>10,237</td><td>24</td><td>New York</td><td>8,941</td></tr>
<tr><td>14</td><td>Missouri</td><td>10,212</td><td>25</td><td>Nebraska</td><td>8,832</td></tr>
<tr><td>21</td><td>Montana</td><td>9,135</td><td>26</td><td>Oklahoma</td><td>8,715</td></tr>
<tr><td>25</td><td>Nebraska</td><td>8,832</td><td>27</td><td>Texas</td><td>8,641</td></tr>
<tr><td>49</td><td>Nevada</td><td>6,598</td><td>28</td><td>South Carolina</td><td>8,623</td></tr>
<tr><td>40</td><td>New Hampshire</td><td>7,800</td><td>29</td><td>Washington</td><td>8,595</td></tr>
<tr><td>31</td><td>New Jersey</td><td>8,321</td><td>30</td><td>Arizona</td><td>8,357</td></tr>
<tr><td>5</td><td>New Mexico</td><td>12,002</td><td>31</td><td>New Jersey</td><td>8,321</td></tr>
<tr><td>24</td><td>New York</td><td>8,941</td><td>32</td><td>Arkansas</td><td>8,319</td></tr>
<tr><td>43</td><td>North Carolina</td><td>7,592</td><td>33</td><td>Michigan</td><td>8,291</td></tr>
<tr><td>7</td><td>North Dakota</td><td>11,417</td><td>34</td><td>Indiana</td><td>8,267</td></tr>
<tr><td>38</td><td>Ohio</td><td>7,858</td><td>35</td><td>California</td><td>8,199</td></tr>
<tr><td>26</td><td>Oklahoma</td><td>8,715</td><td>36</td><td>Florida</td><td>8,135</td></tr>
<tr><td>47</td><td>Oregon</td><td>7,277</td><td>37</td><td>Iowa</td><td>7,992</td></tr>
<tr><td>18</td><td>Pennsylvania</td><td>9,673</td><td>38</td><td>Ohio</td><td>7,858</td></tr>
<tr><td>20</td><td>Rhode Island</td><td>9,341</td><td>39</td><td>Illinois</td><td>7,839</td></tr>
<tr><td>28</td><td>South Carolina</td><td>8,623</td><td>40</td><td>New Hampshire</td><td>7,800</td></tr>
<tr><td>11</td><td>South Dakota</td><td>10,630</td><td>41</td><td>Colorado</td><td>7,703</td></tr>
<tr><td>19</td><td>Tennessee</td><td>9,402</td><td>42</td><td>Georgia</td><td>7,648</td></tr>
<tr><td>27</td><td>Texas</td><td>8,641</td><td>43</td><td>North Carolina</td><td>7,592</td></tr>
<tr><td>50</td><td>Utah</td><td>6,276</td><td>44</td><td>Delaware</td><td>7,559</td></tr>
<tr><td>17</td><td>Vermont</td><td>9,790</td><td>45</td><td>Idaho</td><td>7,350</td></tr>
<tr><td>1</td><td>Virginia</td><td>15,205</td><td>46</td><td>Minnesota</td><td>7,312</td></tr>
<tr><td>29</td><td>Washington</td><td>8,595</td><td>47</td><td>Oregon</td><td>7,277</td></tr>
<tr><td>16</td><td>West Virginia</td><td>9,919</td><td>48</td><td>Wisconsin</td><td>7,132</td></tr>
<tr><td>48</td><td>Wisconsin</td><td>7,132</td><td>49</td><td>Nevada</td><td>6,598</td></tr>
<tr><td>8</td><td>Wyoming</td><td>11,199</td><td>50</td><td>Utah</td><td>6,276</td></tr>
<tr><td></td><td></td><td></td><td></td><td>District of Columbia</td><td>79,995</td></tr>
</table>

Source: CQ Press using data from U.S. Bureau of the Census
"Consolidated Federal Funds Report: 2008" (CFFR/08, July 2009, http://www.census.gov/govs/cffr/)
*National per capita excludes expenditures and population for territories and undistributed amounts.

Federal Government Grants in 2008

National Total = $574,659,000,000*

ALPHA ORDER

RANK	STATE	GRANTS	% of USA
25	Alabama	$7,242,000,000	1.3%
40	Alaska	2,702,000,000	0.5%
18	Arizona	10,325,000,000	1.8%
33	Arkansas	5,050,000,000	0.9%
1	California	82,219,000,000	14.3%
27	Colorado	6,524,000,000	1.1%
24	Connecticut	7,378,000,000	1.3%
50	Delaware	1,435,000,000	0.2%
7	Florida	20,226,000,000	3.5%
12	Georgia	14,569,000,000	2.5%
43	Hawaii	2,283,000,000	0.4%
45	Idaho	2,133,000,000	0.4%
4	Illinois	22,737,000,000	4.0%
20	Indiana	8,857,000,000	1.5%
32	Iowa	5,057,000,000	0.9%
34	Kansas	4,280,000,000	0.7%
23	Kentucky	8,312,000,000	1.4%
14	Louisiana	12,337,000,000	2.1%
39	Maine	2,930,000,000	0.5%
16	Maryland	10,528,000,000	1.8%
6	Massachusetts	20,427,000,000	3.6%
8	Michigan	19,205,000,000	3.3%
19	Minnesota	9,230,000,000	1.6%
26	Mississippi	6,790,000,000	1.2%
17	Missouri	10,372,000,000	1.8%
44	Montana	2,185,000,000	0.4%
35	Nebraska	3,733,000,000	0.6%
38	Nevada	3,107,000,000	0.5%
47	New Hampshire	1,877,000,000	0.3%
10	New Jersey	16,204,000,000	2.8%
31	New Mexico	5,531,000,000	1.0%
2	New York	54,421,000,000	9.5%
11	North Carolina	15,165,000,000	2.6%
49	North Dakota	1,660,000,000	0.3%
9	Ohio	17,769,000,000	3.1%
29	Oklahoma	6,216,000,000	1.1%
30	Oregon	6,132,000,000	1.1%
5	Pennsylvania	21,678,000,000	3.8%
41	Rhode Island	2,441,000,000	0.4%
28	South Carolina	6,422,000,000	1.1%
48	South Dakota	1,794,000,000	0.3%
13	Tennessee	14,188,000,000	2.5%
3	Texas	38,300,000,000	6.7%
37	Utah	3,536,000,000	0.6%
46	Vermont	2,103,000,000	0.4%
21	Virginia	8,776,000,000	1.5%
15	Washington	11,023,000,000	1.9%
36	West Virginia	3,711,000,000	0.6%
22	Wisconsin	8,431,000,000	1.5%
42	Wyoming	2,422,000,000	0.4%

RANK ORDER

RANK	STATE	GRANTS	% of USA
1	California	$82,219,000,000	14.3%
2	New York	54,421,000,000	9.5%
3	Texas	38,300,000,000	6.7%
4	Illinois	22,737,000,000	4.0%
5	Pennsylvania	21,678,000,000	3.8%
6	Massachusetts	20,427,000,000	3.6%
7	Florida	20,226,000,000	3.5%
8	Michigan	19,205,000,000	3.3%
9	Ohio	17,769,000,000	3.1%
10	New Jersey	16,204,000,000	2.8%
11	North Carolina	15,165,000,000	2.6%
12	Georgia	14,569,000,000	2.5%
13	Tennessee	14,188,000,000	2.5%
14	Louisiana	12,337,000,000	2.1%
15	Washington	11,023,000,000	1.9%
16	Maryland	10,528,000,000	1.8%
17	Missouri	10,372,000,000	1.8%
18	Arizona	10,325,000,000	1.8%
19	Minnesota	9,230,000,000	1.6%
20	Indiana	8,857,000,000	1.5%
21	Virginia	8,776,000,000	1.5%
22	Wisconsin	8,431,000,000	1.5%
23	Kentucky	8,312,000,000	1.4%
24	Connecticut	7,378,000,000	1.3%
25	Alabama	7,242,000,000	1.3%
26	Mississippi	6,790,000,000	1.2%
27	Colorado	6,524,000,000	1.1%
28	South Carolina	6,422,000,000	1.1%
29	Oklahoma	6,216,000,000	1.1%
30	Oregon	6,132,000,000	1.1%
31	New Mexico	5,531,000,000	1.0%
32	Iowa	5,057,000,000	0.9%
33	Arkansas	5,050,000,000	0.9%
34	Kansas	4,280,000,000	0.7%
35	Nebraska	3,733,000,000	0.6%
36	West Virginia	3,711,000,000	0.6%
37	Utah	3,536,000,000	0.6%
38	Nevada	3,107,000,000	0.5%
39	Maine	2,930,000,000	0.5%
40	Alaska	2,702,000,000	0.5%
41	Rhode Island	2,441,000,000	0.4%
42	Wyoming	2,422,000,000	0.4%
43	Hawaii	2,283,000,000	0.4%
44	Montana	2,185,000,000	0.4%
45	Idaho	2,133,000,000	0.4%
46	Vermont	2,103,000,000	0.4%
47	New Hampshire	1,877,000,000	0.3%
48	South Dakota	1,794,000,000	0.3%
49	North Dakota	1,660,000,000	0.3%
50	Delaware	1,435,000,000	0.2%
	District of Columbia	6,163,000,000	1.1%

Source: U.S. Bureau of the Census

"Consolidated Federal Funds Report: 2008" (CFFR/08, July 2009, http://www.census.gov/govs/cffr/)

*Total includes $6,344,000,000 in U.S. territories ($5,219,000,000 in Puerto Rico) and $182,000,000 in expenditures not distributed by state.

Per Capita Expenditures for Federal Government Grants in 2008

National Per Capita = $1,867*

ALPHA ORDER

RANK	STATE	PER CAPITA
37	Alabama	$1,548
2	Alaska	3,927
35	Arizona	1,589
26	Arkansas	1,761
13	California	2,248
46	Colorado	1,322
16	Connecticut	2,106
33	Delaware	1,638
50	Florida	1,098
40	Georgia	1,502
23	Hawaii	1,773
44	Idaho	1,396
24	Illinois	1,770
45	Indiana	1,386
30	Iowa	1,689
39	Kansas	1,530
19	Kentucky	1,938
7	Louisiana	2,771
15	Maine	2,220
22	Maryland	1,861
4	Massachusetts	3,122
20	Michigan	1,920
25	Minnesota	1,765
10	Mississippi	2,309
27	Missouri	1,741
12	Montana	2,257
17	Nebraska	2,095
48	Nevada	1,188
43	New Hampshire	1,420
21	New Jersey	1,870
6	New Mexico	2,784
5	New York	2,795
32	North Carolina	1,640
8	North Dakota	2,588
38	Ohio	1,541
29	Oklahoma	1,706
34	Oregon	1,621
28	Pennsylvania	1,725
9	Rhode Island	2,317
42	South Carolina	1,426
14	South Dakota	2,230
11	Tennessee	2,274
36	Texas	1,576
47	Utah	1,296
3	Vermont	3,386
49	Virginia	1,126
31	Washington	1,679
18	West Virginia	2,045
41	Wisconsin	1,498
1	Wyoming	4,544

RANK ORDER

RANK	STATE	PER CAPITA
1	Wyoming	$4,544
2	Alaska	3,927
3	Vermont	3,386
4	Massachusetts	3,122
5	New York	2,795
6	New Mexico	2,784
7	Louisiana	2,771
8	North Dakota	2,588
9	Rhode Island	2,317
10	Mississippi	2,309
11	Tennessee	2,274
12	Montana	2,257
13	California	2,248
14	South Dakota	2,230
15	Maine	2,220
16	Connecticut	2,106
17	Nebraska	2,095
18	West Virginia	2,045
19	Kentucky	1,938
20	Michigan	1,920
21	New Jersey	1,870
22	Maryland	1,861
23	Hawaii	1,773
24	Illinois	1,770
25	Minnesota	1,765
26	Arkansas	1,761
27	Missouri	1,741
28	Pennsylvania	1,725
29	Oklahoma	1,706
30	Iowa	1,689
31	Washington	1,679
32	North Carolina	1,640
33	Delaware	1,638
34	Oregon	1,621
35	Arizona	1,589
36	Texas	1,576
37	Alabama	1,548
38	Ohio	1,541
39	Kansas	1,530
40	Georgia	1,502
41	Wisconsin	1,498
42	South Carolina	1,426
43	New Hampshire	1,420
44	Idaho	1,396
45	Indiana	1,386
46	Colorado	1,322
47	Utah	1,296
48	Nevada	1,188
49	Virginia	1,126
50	Florida	1,098

District of Columbia   10,444

Source: CQ Press using data from U.S. Bureau of the Census
  "Consolidated Federal Funds Report: 2008" (CFFR/08, July 2009, http://www.census.gov/govs/cffr/)
*National per capita excludes expenditures and population for territories and undistributed amounts.

Federal Government Procurement Contract Awards in 2008

National Total = $514,117,000,000*

ALPHA ORDER

RANK	STATE	EXPENDITURES	% of USA
15	Alabama	$10,253,000,000	2.0%
34	Alaska	2,480,000,000	0.5%
8	Arizona	13,832,000,000	2.7%
40	Arkansas	1,331,000,000	0.3%
3	California	52,045,000,000	10.1%
22	Colorado	7,709,000,000	1.5%
12	Connecticut	12,856,000,000	2.5%
50	Delaware	366,000,000	0.1%
6	Florida	16,625,000,000	3.2%
13	Georgia	11,069,000,000	2.2%
35	Hawaii	2,456,000,000	0.5%
37	Idaho	2,003,000,000	0.4%
11	Illinois	13,197,000,000	2.6%
19	Indiana	8,922,000,000	1.7%
39	Iowa	1,870,000,000	0.4%
29	Kansas	4,102,000,000	0.8%
21	Kentucky	7,729,000,000	1.5%
25	Louisiana	6,240,000,000	1.2%
43	Maine	1,130,000,000	0.2%
4	Maryland	25,602,000,000	5.0%
10	Massachusetts	13,350,000,000	2.6%
20	Michigan	8,612,000,000	1.7%
30	Minnesota	3,363,000,000	0.7%
27	Mississippi	5,539,000,000	1.1%
7	Missouri	14,450,000,000	2.8%
46	Montana	572,000,000	0.1%
42	Nebraska	1,208,000,000	0.2%
33	Nevada	2,701,000,000	0.5%
38	New Hampshire	1,914,000,000	0.4%
18	New Jersey	8,961,000,000	1.7%
24	New Mexico	6,914,000,000	1.3%
9	New York	13,732,000,000	2.7%
26	North Carolina	5,794,000,000	1.1%
48	North Dakota	552,000,000	0.1%
17	Ohio	9,096,000,000	1.8%
32	Oklahoma	2,853,000,000	0.6%
36	Oregon	2,375,000,000	0.5%
5	Pennsylvania	18,294,000,000	3.6%
44	Rhode Island	865,000,000	0.2%
23	South Carolina	7,621,000,000	1.5%
45	South Dakota	653,000,000	0.1%
16	Tennessee	9,876,000,000	1.9%
1	Texas	60,703,000,000	11.8%
31	Utah	3,030,000,000	0.6%
47	Vermont	564,000,000	0.1%
2	Virginia	53,868,000,000	10.5%
14	Washington	10,386,000,000	2.0%
41	West Virginia	1,328,000,000	0.3%
28	Wisconsin	4,487,000,000	0.9%
49	Wyoming	529,000,000	0.1%

RANK ORDER

RANK	STATE	EXPENDITURES	% of USA
1	Texas	$60,703,000,000	11.8%
2	Virginia	53,868,000,000	10.5%
3	California	52,045,000,000	10.1%
4	Maryland	25,602,000,000	5.0%
5	Pennsylvania	18,294,000,000	3.6%
6	Florida	16,625,000,000	3.2%
7	Missouri	14,450,000,000	2.8%
8	Arizona	13,832,000,000	2.7%
9	New York	13,732,000,000	2.7%
10	Massachusetts	13,350,000,000	2.6%
11	Illinois	13,197,000,000	2.6%
12	Connecticut	12,856,000,000	2.5%
13	Georgia	11,069,000,000	2.2%
14	Washington	10,386,000,000	2.0%
15	Alabama	10,253,000,000	2.0%
16	Tennessee	9,876,000,000	1.9%
17	Ohio	9,096,000,000	1.8%
18	New Jersey	8,961,000,000	1.7%
19	Indiana	8,922,000,000	1.7%
20	Michigan	8,612,000,000	1.7%
21	Kentucky	7,729,000,000	1.5%
22	Colorado	7,709,000,000	1.5%
23	South Carolina	7,621,000,000	1.5%
24	New Mexico	6,914,000,000	1.3%
25	Louisiana	6,240,000,000	1.2%
26	North Carolina	5,794,000,000	1.1%
27	Mississippi	5,539,000,000	1.1%
28	Wisconsin	4,487,000,000	0.9%
29	Kansas	4,102,000,000	0.8%
30	Minnesota	3,363,000,000	0.7%
31	Utah	3,030,000,000	0.6%
32	Oklahoma	2,853,000,000	0.6%
33	Nevada	2,701,000,000	0.5%
34	Alaska	2,480,000,000	0.5%
35	Hawaii	2,456,000,000	0.5%
36	Oregon	2,375,000,000	0.5%
37	Idaho	2,003,000,000	0.4%
38	New Hampshire	1,914,000,000	0.4%
39	Iowa	1,870,000,000	0.4%
40	Arkansas	1,331,000,000	0.3%
41	West Virginia	1,328,000,000	0.3%
42	Nebraska	1,208,000,000	0.2%
43	Maine	1,130,000,000	0.2%
44	Rhode Island	865,000,000	0.2%
45	South Dakota	653,000,000	0.1%
46	Montana	572,000,000	0.1%
47	Vermont	564,000,000	0.1%
48	North Dakota	552,000,000	0.1%
49	Wyoming	529,000,000	0.1%
50	Delaware	366,000,000	0.1%
	District of Columbia	16,541,000,000	3.2%

Source: U.S. Bureau of the Census

"Consolidated Federal Funds Report: 2008" (CFFR/08, July 2009, http://www.census.gov/govs/cffr/)

*Total includes $1,559,000,000 in U.S. territories ($887,000,000 in Puerto Rico) and $20,013,000,000 in expenditures not distributed by state.

Per Capita Expenditures for Federal Government Procurement Contract Awards in 2008
National Per Capita = $1,618*

ALPHA ORDER

RANK	STATE	PER CAPITA
8	Alabama	$2,192
4	Alaska	3,604
9	Arizona	2,128
49	Arkansas	464
21	California	1,423
17	Colorado	1,562
3	Connecticut	3,670
50	Delaware	418
32	Florida	902
25	Georgia	1,141
11	Hawaii	1,908
24	Idaho	1,311
29	Illinois	1,028
23	Indiana	1,397
47	Iowa	625
18	Kansas	1,466
13	Kentucky	1,803
22	Louisiana	1,402
35	Maine	856
2	Maryland	4,524
10	Massachusetts	2,040
33	Michigan	861
44	Minnesota	643
12	Mississippi	1,884
7	Missouri	2,426
48	Montana	591
43	Nebraska	678
28	Nevada	1,033
20	New Hampshire	1,448
27	New Jersey	1,034
5	New Mexico	3,480
42	New York	705
46	North Carolina	627
33	North Dakota	861
39	Ohio	789
40	Oklahoma	783
45	Oregon	628
19	Pennsylvania	1,456
36	Rhode Island	821
14	South Carolina	1,692
37	South Dakota	812
15	Tennessee	1,583
6	Texas	2,498
26	Utah	1,111
31	Vermont	908
1	Virginia	6,910
16	Washington	1,582
41	West Virginia	732
38	Wisconsin	797
30	Wyoming	993

RANK ORDER

RANK	STATE	PER CAPITA
1	Virginia	$6,910
2	Maryland	4,524
3	Connecticut	3,670
4	Alaska	3,604
5	New Mexico	3,480
6	Texas	2,498
7	Missouri	2,426
8	Alabama	2,192
9	Arizona	2,128
10	Massachusetts	2,040
11	Hawaii	1,908
12	Mississippi	1,884
13	Kentucky	1,803
14	South Carolina	1,692
15	Tennessee	1,583
16	Washington	1,582
17	Colorado	1,562
18	Kansas	1,466
19	Pennsylvania	1,456
20	New Hampshire	1,448
21	California	1,423
22	Louisiana	1,402
23	Indiana	1,397
24	Idaho	1,311
25	Georgia	1,141
26	Utah	1,111
27	New Jersey	1,034
28	Nevada	1,033
29	Illinois	1,028
30	Wyoming	993
31	Vermont	908
32	Florida	902
33	Michigan	861
33	North Dakota	861
35	Maine	856
36	Rhode Island	821
37	South Dakota	812
38	Wisconsin	797
39	Ohio	789
40	Oklahoma	783
41	West Virginia	732
42	New York	705
43	Nebraska	678
44	Minnesota	643
45	Oregon	628
46	North Carolina	627
47	Iowa	625
48	Montana	591
49	Arkansas	464
50	Delaware	418

District of Columbia	28,032

Source: CQ Press using data from U.S. Bureau of the Census
   "Consolidated Federal Funds Report: 2008" (CFFR/08, July 2009, http://www.census.gov/govs/cffr/)
*National per capita excludes expenditures and population for territories and undistributed amounts.

Federal Government Direct Payments for
Retirement and Disability in 2008
National Total = $818,525,000,000*

ALPHA ORDER

RANK	STATE	PAYMENTS	% of USA
20	Alabama	$16,200,000,000	2.0%
50	Alaska	1,373,000,000	0.2%
19	Arizona	16,243,000,000	2.0%
29	Arkansas	9,316,000,000	1.1%
1	California	75,904,000,000	9.3%
27	Colorado	11,263,000,000	1.4%
30	Connecticut	9,262,000,000	1.1%
45	Delaware	2,710,000,000	0.3%
2	Florida	57,665,000,000	7.0%
11	Georgia	22,919,000,000	2.8%
41	Hawaii	3,873,000,000	0.5%
40	Idaho	3,943,000,000	0.5%
7	Illinois	30,934,000,000	3.8%
15	Indiana	17,479,000,000	2.1%
32	Iowa	8,453,000,000	1.0%
33	Kansas	7,565,000,000	0.9%
23	Kentucky	13,313,000,000	1.6%
25	Louisiana	11,801,000,000	1.4%
39	Maine	4,458,000,000	0.5%
16	Maryland	17,243,000,000	2.1%
18	Massachusetts	16,860,000,000	2.1%
8	Michigan	28,688,000,000	3.5%
24	Minnesota	12,658,000,000	1.5%
31	Mississippi	8,854,000,000	1.1%
17	Missouri	17,098,000,000	2.1%
44	Montana	2,979,000,000	0.4%
38	Nebraska	4,800,000,000	0.6%
35	Nevada	6,323,000,000	0.8%
42	New Hampshire	3,841,000,000	0.5%
12	New Jersey	22,659,000,000	2.8%
36	New Mexico	5,941,000,000	0.7%
4	New York	49,371,000,000	6.0%
9	North Carolina	26,129,000,000	3.2%
48	North Dakota	1,747,000,000	0.2%
6	Ohio	31,753,000,000	3.9%
26	Oklahoma	11,347,000,000	1.4%
28	Oregon	10,551,000,000	1.3%
5	Pennsylvania	39,892,000,000	4.9%
43	Rhode Island	3,071,000,000	0.4%
22	South Carolina	14,034,000,000	1.7%
46	South Dakota	2,256,000,000	0.3%
13	Tennessee	18,717,000,000	2.3%
3	Texas	53,203,000,000	6.5%
37	Utah	5,251,000,000	0.6%
47	Vermont	1,791,000,000	0.2%
10	Virginia	25,441,000,000	3.1%
14	Washington	17,933,000,000	2.2%
34	West Virginia	7,221,000,000	0.9%
21	Wisconsin	14,978,000,000	1.8%
49	Wyoming	1,455,000,000	0.2%

RANK ORDER

RANK	STATE	PAYMENTS	% of USA
1	California	$75,904,000,000	9.3%
2	Florida	57,665,000,000	7.0%
3	Texas	53,203,000,000	6.5%
4	New York	49,371,000,000	6.0%
5	Pennsylvania	39,892,000,000	4.9%
6	Ohio	31,753,000,000	3.9%
7	Illinois	30,934,000,000	3.8%
8	Michigan	28,688,000,000	3.5%
9	North Carolina	26,129,000,000	3.2%
10	Virginia	25,441,000,000	3.1%
11	Georgia	22,919,000,000	2.8%
12	New Jersey	22,659,000,000	2.8%
13	Tennessee	18,717,000,000	2.3%
14	Washington	17,933,000,000	2.2%
15	Indiana	17,479,000,000	2.1%
16	Maryland	17,243,000,000	2.1%
17	Missouri	17,098,000,000	2.1%
18	Massachusetts	16,860,000,000	2.1%
19	Arizona	16,243,000,000	2.0%
20	Alabama	16,200,000,000	2.0%
21	Wisconsin	14,978,000,000	1.8%
22	South Carolina	14,034,000,000	1.7%
23	Kentucky	13,313,000,000	1.6%
24	Minnesota	12,658,000,000	1.5%
25	Louisiana	11,801,000,000	1.4%
26	Oklahoma	11,347,000,000	1.4%
27	Colorado	11,263,000,000	1.4%
28	Oregon	10,551,000,000	1.3%
29	Arkansas	9,316,000,000	1.1%
30	Connecticut	9,262,000,000	1.1%
31	Mississippi	8,854,000,000	1.1%
32	Iowa	8,453,000,000	1.0%
33	Kansas	7,565,000,000	0.9%
34	West Virginia	7,221,000,000	0.9%
35	Nevada	6,323,000,000	0.8%
36	New Mexico	5,941,000,000	0.7%
37	Utah	5,251,000,000	0.6%
38	Nebraska	4,800,000,000	0.6%
39	Maine	4,458,000,000	0.5%
40	Idaho	3,943,000,000	0.5%
41	Hawaii	3,873,000,000	0.5%
42	New Hampshire	3,841,000,000	0.5%
43	Rhode Island	3,071,000,000	0.4%
44	Montana	2,979,000,000	0.4%
45	Delaware	2,710,000,000	0.3%
46	South Dakota	2,256,000,000	0.3%
47	Vermont	1,791,000,000	0.2%
48	North Dakota	1,747,000,000	0.2%
49	Wyoming	1,455,000,000	0.2%
50	Alaska	1,373,000,000	0.2%
	District of Columbia	2,269,000,000	0.3%

Source: U.S. Bureau of the Census
   "Consolidated Federal Funds Report: 2008" (CFFR/08, July 2009, http://www.census.gov/govs/cffr/)
*Total includes $7,477,000,000 in U.S. territories ($6,945,000,000 in Puerto Rico) and $19,000,000 in expenditures not distributed
by state. "Direct Payments for Retirement and Disability" include Social Security, federal retirement and disability payments,
and veterans benefits.

Per Capita Federal Government Direct Payments for Retirement and Disability in 2008
National Per Capita = $2,665*

ALPHA ORDER

RANK	STATE	PER CAPITA
2	Alabama	$3,463
49	Alaska	1,995
41	Arizona	2,499
5	Arkansas	3,249
48	California	2,075
46	Colorado	2,282
36	Connecticut	2,644
11	Delaware	3,093
7	Florida	3,130
45	Georgia	2,363
15	Hawaii	3,008
38	Idaho	2,581
44	Illinois	2,409
28	Indiana	2,736
24	Iowa	2,823
32	Kansas	2,704
10	Kentucky	3,105
35	Louisiana	2,651
3	Maine	3,378
13	Maryland	3,047
39	Massachusetts	2,577
22	Michigan	2,868
42	Minnesota	2,420
14	Mississippi	3,011
21	Missouri	2,871
12	Montana	3,077
33	Nebraska	2,694
43	Nevada	2,417
19	New Hampshire	2,906
37	New Jersey	2,615
17	New Mexico	2,990
40	New York	2,536
23	North Carolina	2,826
31	North Dakota	2,724
27	Ohio	2,754
9	Oklahoma	3,114
26	Oregon	2,789
6	Pennsylvania	3,175
18	Rhode Island	2,915
8	South Carolina	3,116
25	South Dakota	2,804
16	Tennessee	2,999
47	Texas	2,189
50	Utah	1,925
20	Vermont	2,884
4	Virginia	3,264
29	Washington	2,731
1	West Virginia	3,979
34	Wisconsin	2,662
30	Wyoming	2,730

RANK ORDER

RANK	STATE	PER CAPITA
1	West Virginia	$3,979
2	Alabama	3,463
3	Maine	3,378
4	Virginia	3,264
5	Arkansas	3,249
6	Pennsylvania	3,175
7	Florida	3,130
8	South Carolina	3,116
9	Oklahoma	3,114
10	Kentucky	3,105
11	Delaware	3,093
12	Montana	3,077
13	Maryland	3,047
14	Mississippi	3,011
15	Hawaii	3,008
16	Tennessee	2,999
17	New Mexico	2,990
18	Rhode Island	2,915
19	New Hampshire	2,906
20	Vermont	2,884
21	Missouri	2,871
22	Michigan	2,868
23	North Carolina	2,826
24	Iowa	2,823
25	South Dakota	2,804
26	Oregon	2,789
27	Ohio	2,754
28	Indiana	2,736
29	Washington	2,731
30	Wyoming	2,730
31	North Dakota	2,724
32	Kansas	2,704
33	Nebraska	2,694
34	Wisconsin	2,662
35	Louisiana	2,651
36	Connecticut	2,644
37	New Jersey	2,615
38	Idaho	2,581
39	Massachusetts	2,577
40	New York	2,536
41	Arizona	2,499
42	Minnesota	2,420
43	Nevada	2,417
44	Illinois	2,409
45	Georgia	2,363
46	Colorado	2,282
47	Texas	2,189
48	California	2,075
49	Alaska	1,995
50	Utah	1,925
	District of Columbia	3,845

Source: CQ Press using data from U.S. Bureau of the Census

"Consolidated Federal Funds Report: 2008" (CFFR/08, July 2009, http://www.census.gov/govs/cffr/)

*National per capita excludes expenditures and population for territories and undistributed amounts. "Direct Payments for Retirement and Disability" include Social Security, federal retirement and disability payments, and veterans benefits.

Federal Government "Other" Direct Payments in 2008

National Total = $631,349,000,000*

ALPHA ORDER

RANK	STATE	PAYMENTS	% of USA
20	Alabama	$10,423,000,000	1.7%
50	Alaska	663,000,000	0.1%
24	Arizona	9,749,000,000	1.5%
32	Arkansas	6,224,000,000	1.0%
1	California	67,722,000,000	10.7%
28	Colorado	7,120,000,000	1.1%
26	Connecticut	7,660,000,000	1.2%
47	Delaware	1,514,000,000	0.2%
3	Florida	43,870,000,000	6.9%
12	Georgia	15,543,000,000	2.5%
43	Hawaii	2,265,000,000	0.4%
45	Idaho	2,101,000,000	0.3%
6	Illinois	26,612,000,000	4.2%
15	Indiana	14,365,000,000	2.3%
29	Iowa	7,059,000,000	1.1%
33	Kansas	6,127,000,000	1.0%
10	Kentucky	18,610,000,000	2.9%
19	Louisiana	11,056,000,000	1.8%
42	Maine	2,433,000,000	0.4%
17	Maryland	12,793,000,000	2.0%
11	Massachusetts	17,353,000,000	2.7%
8	Michigan	22,107,000,000	3.5%
21	Minnesota	10,191,000,000	1.6%
30	Mississippi	6,691,000,000	1.1%
16	Missouri	13,899,000,000	2.2%
44	Montana	2,104,000,000	0.3%
34	Nebraska	4,539,000,000	0.7%
36	Nevada	3,478,000,000	0.6%
46	New Hampshire	1,938,000,000	0.3%
9	New Jersey	19,316,000,000	3.1%
37	New Mexico	3,174,000,000	0.5%
2	New York	45,462,000,000	7.2%
13	North Carolina	15,180,000,000	2.4%
41	North Dakota	2,490,000,000	0.4%
7	Ohio	25,577,000,000	4.1%
27	Oklahoma	7,515,000,000	1.2%
31	Oregon	6,285,000,000	1.0%
5	Pennsylvania	33,974,000,000	5.4%
40	Rhode Island	2,631,000,000	0.4%
25	South Carolina	7,730,000,000	1.2%
38	South Dakota	2,993,000,000	0.5%
18	Tennessee	12,604,000,000	2.0%
4	Texas	39,202,000,000	6.2%
39	Utah	2,756,000,000	0.4%
48	Vermont	1,120,000,000	0.2%
14	Virginia	14,742,000,000	2.3%
22	Washington	10,164,000,000	1.6%
35	West Virginia	4,022,000,000	0.6%
23	Wisconsin	9,881,000,000	1.6%
49	Wyoming	976,000,000	0.2%

RANK ORDER

RANK	STATE	PAYMENTS	% of USA
1	California	$67,722,000,000	10.7%
2	New York	45,462,000,000	7.2%
3	Florida	43,870,000,000	6.9%
4	Texas	39,202,000,000	6.2%
5	Pennsylvania	33,974,000,000	5.4%
6	Illinois	26,612,000,000	4.2%
7	Ohio	25,577,000,000	4.1%
8	Michigan	22,107,000,000	3.5%
9	New Jersey	19,316,000,000	3.1%
10	Kentucky	18,610,000,000	2.9%
11	Massachusetts	17,353,000,000	2.7%
12	Georgia	15,543,000,000	2.5%
13	North Carolina	15,180,000,000	2.4%
14	Virginia	14,742,000,000	2.3%
15	Indiana	14,365,000,000	2.3%
16	Missouri	13,899,000,000	2.2%
17	Maryland	12,793,000,000	2.0%
18	Tennessee	12,604,000,000	2.0%
19	Louisiana	11,056,000,000	1.8%
20	Alabama	10,423,000,000	1.7%
21	Minnesota	10,191,000,000	1.6%
22	Washington	10,164,000,000	1.6%
23	Wisconsin	9,881,000,000	1.6%
24	Arizona	9,749,000,000	1.5%
25	South Carolina	7,730,000,000	1.2%
26	Connecticut	7,660,000,000	1.2%
27	Oklahoma	7,515,000,000	1.2%
28	Colorado	7,120,000,000	1.1%
29	Iowa	7,059,000,000	1.1%
30	Mississippi	6,691,000,000	1.1%
31	Oregon	6,285,000,000	1.0%
32	Arkansas	6,224,000,000	1.0%
33	Kansas	6,127,000,000	1.0%
34	Nebraska	4,539,000,000	0.7%
35	West Virginia	4,022,000,000	0.6%
36	Nevada	3,478,000,000	0.6%
37	New Mexico	3,174,000,000	0.5%
38	South Dakota	2,993,000,000	0.5%
39	Utah	2,756,000,000	0.4%
40	Rhode Island	2,631,000,000	0.4%
41	North Dakota	2,490,000,000	0.4%
42	Maine	2,433,000,000	0.4%
43	Hawaii	2,265,000,000	0.4%
44	Montana	2,104,000,000	0.3%
45	Idaho	2,101,000,000	0.3%
46	New Hampshire	1,938,000,000	0.3%
47	Delaware	1,514,000,000	0.2%
48	Vermont	1,120,000,000	0.2%
49	Wyoming	976,000,000	0.2%
50	Alaska	663,000,000	0.1%
	District of Columbia	3,204,000,000	0.5%

Source: U.S. Bureau of the Census
    "Consolidated Federal Funds Report: 2008" (CFFR/08, July 2009, http://www.census.gov/govs/cffr/)
*Total includes $4,035,000,000 in U.S. territories ($3,797,000,000 in Puerto Rico) and $106,000,000 in expenditures not distributed by state. "Other Direct Payments" include direct payments for programs other than retirement and disability. These include Medicare, excess earned income tax credits, unemployment compensation, food stamps, housing assistance, and agricultural assistance.

Per Capita Expenditures for Federal Government "Other" Direct Payments in 2008
National Per Capita = $2,061*

ALPHA ORDER

RANK	STATE	PER CAPITA
17	Alabama	$2,228
50	Alaska	963
44	Arizona	1,500
24	Arkansas	2,170
30	California	1,851
46	Colorado	1,443
22	Connecticut	2,187
36	Delaware	1,728
9	Florida	2,381
41	Georgia	1,603
34	Hawaii	1,759
47	Idaho	1,375
25	Illinois	2,072
15	Indiana	2,249
10	Iowa	2,358
21	Kansas	2,190
1	Kentucky	4,340
8	Louisiana	2,484
31	Maine	1,844
14	Maryland	2,261
5	Massachusetts	2,652
20	Michigan	2,210
28	Minnesota	1,948
13	Mississippi	2,276
12	Missouri	2,333
23	Montana	2,173
6	Nebraska	2,547
48	Nevada	1,330
45	New Hampshire	1,466
16	New Jersey	2,230
42	New Mexico	1,598
11	New York	2,335
39	North Carolina	1,642
2	North Dakota	3,882
18	Ohio	2,219
26	Oklahoma	2,062
38	Oregon	1,661
4	Pennsylvania	2,704
7	Rhode Island	2,497
37	South Carolina	1,717
3	South Dakota	3,720
27	Tennessee	2,020
40	Texas	1,613
49	Utah	1,011
33	Vermont	1,803
29	Virginia	1,891
43	Washington	1,548
19	West Virginia	2,216
35	Wisconsin	1,756
32	Wyoming	1,831

RANK ORDER

RANK	STATE	PER CAPITA
1	Kentucky	$4,340
2	North Dakota	3,882
3	South Dakota	3,720
4	Pennsylvania	2,704
5	Massachusetts	2,652
6	Nebraska	2,547
7	Rhode Island	2,497
8	Louisiana	2,484
9	Florida	2,381
10	Iowa	2,358
11	New York	2,335
12	Missouri	2,333
13	Mississippi	2,276
14	Maryland	2,261
15	Indiana	2,249
16	New Jersey	2,230
17	Alabama	2,228
18	Ohio	2,219
19	West Virginia	2,216
20	Michigan	2,210
21	Kansas	2,190
22	Connecticut	2,187
23	Montana	2,173
24	Arkansas	2,170
25	Illinois	2,072
26	Oklahoma	2,062
27	Tennessee	2,020
28	Minnesota	1,948
29	Virginia	1,891
30	California	1,851
31	Maine	1,844
32	Wyoming	1,831
33	Vermont	1,803
34	Hawaii	1,759
35	Wisconsin	1,756
36	Delaware	1,728
37	South Carolina	1,717
38	Oregon	1,661
39	North Carolina	1,642
40	Texas	1,613
41	Georgia	1,603
42	New Mexico	1,598
43	Washington	1,548
44	Arizona	1,500
45	New Hampshire	1,466
46	Colorado	1,443
47	Idaho	1,375
48	Nevada	1,330
49	Utah	1,011
50	Alaska	963

District of Columbia   5,430

Source: CQ Press using data from U.S. Bureau of the Census
"Consolidated Federal Funds Report: 2008" (CFFR/08, July 2009, http://www.census.gov/govs/cffr/)
*National per capita excludes expenditures and population for territories and undistributed amounts. "Other Direct Payments" include direct payments for programs other than retirement and disability. These include Medicare, excess earned income tax credits, unemployment compensation, food stamps, housing assistance, and agricultural assistance.

Federal Government Expenditures for Salaries and Wages in 2008

National Total = $253,962,000,000*

ALPHA ORDER					RANK ORDER			
RANK	STATE	SALARIES	% of USA		RANK	STATE	SALARIES	% of USA
21	Alabama	$3,847,000,000	1.5%		1	California	$22,033,000,000	8.7%
33	Alaska	2,206,000,000	0.9%		2	Texas	18,597,000,000	7.3%
18	Arizona	4,166,000,000	1.6%		3	Virginia	15,699,000,000	6.2%
35	Arkansas	1,936,000,000	0.8%		4	Maryland	11,739,000,000	4.6%
1	California	22,033,000,000	8.7%		5	Florida	11,486,000,000	4.5%
13	Colorado	5,399,000,000	2.1%		6	New York	11,085,000,000	4.4%
36	Connecticut	1,723,000,000	0.7%		7	Georgia	10,065,000,000	4.0%
48	Delaware	598,000,000	0.2%		8	North Carolina	7,934,000,000	3.1%
5	Florida	11,486,000,000	4.5%		9	Pennsylvania	7,713,000,000	3.0%
7	Georgia	10,065,000,000	4.0%		10	Illinois	7,192,000,000	2.8%
19	Hawaii	4,133,000,000	1.6%		11	Washington	6,929,000,000	2.7%
41	Idaho	1,047,000,000	0.4%		12	Ohio	6,397,000,000	2.5%
10	Illinois	7,192,000,000	2.8%		13	Colorado	5,399,000,000	2.1%
24	Indiana	3,189,000,000	1.3%		14	Missouri	5,010,000,000	2.0%
39	Iowa	1,488,000,000	0.6%		15	New Jersey	4,946,000,000	1.9%
26	Kansas	3,054,000,000	1.2%		16	Michigan	4,322,000,000	1.7%
17	Kentucky	4,300,000,000	1.7%		17	Kentucky	4,300,000,000	1.7%
25	Louisiana	3,062,000,000	1.2%		18	Arizona	4,166,000,000	1.6%
42	Maine	1,023,000,000	0.4%		19	Hawaii	4,133,000,000	1.6%
4	Maryland	11,739,000,000	4.6%		20	Massachusetts	4,124,000,000	1.6%
20	Massachusetts	4,124,000,000	1.6%		21	Alabama	3,847,000,000	1.5%
16	Michigan	4,322,000,000	1.7%		22	Oklahoma	3,828,000,000	1.5%
28	Minnesota	2,804,000,000	1.1%		23	Tennessee	3,288,000,000	1.3%
32	Mississippi	2,224,000,000	0.9%		24	Indiana	3,189,000,000	1.3%
14	Missouri	5,010,000,000	2.0%		25	Louisiana	3,062,000,000	1.2%
43	Montana	1,004,000,000	0.4%		26	Kansas	3,054,000,000	1.2%
40	Nebraska	1,459,000,000	0.6%		27	South Carolina	3,025,000,000	1.2%
38	Nevada	1,651,000,000	0.7%		28	Minnesota	2,804,000,000	1.1%
47	New Hampshire	742,000,000	0.3%		29	Utah	2,544,000,000	1.0%
15	New Jersey	4,946,000,000	1.9%		30	Wisconsin	2,358,000,000	0.9%
31	New Mexico	2,287,000,000	0.9%		31	New Mexico	2,287,000,000	0.9%
6	New York	11,085,000,000	4.4%		32	Mississippi	2,224,000,000	0.9%
8	North Carolina	7,934,000,000	3.1%		33	Alaska	2,206,000,000	0.9%
44	North Dakota	872,000,000	0.3%		34	Oregon	2,187,000,000	0.9%
12	Ohio	6,397,000,000	2.5%		35	Arkansas	1,936,000,000	0.8%
22	Oklahoma	3,828,000,000	1.5%		36	Connecticut	1,723,000,000	0.7%
34	Oregon	2,187,000,000	0.9%		37	West Virginia	1,720,000,000	0.7%
9	Pennsylvania	7,713,000,000	3.0%		38	Nevada	1,651,000,000	0.7%
46	Rhode Island	833,000,000	0.3%		39	Iowa	1,488,000,000	0.6%
27	South Carolina	3,025,000,000	1.2%		40	Nebraska	1,459,000,000	0.6%
45	South Dakota	855,000,000	0.3%		41	Idaho	1,047,000,000	0.4%
23	Tennessee	3,288,000,000	1.3%		42	Maine	1,023,000,000	0.4%
2	Texas	18,597,000,000	7.3%		43	Montana	1,004,000,000	0.4%
29	Utah	2,544,000,000	1.0%		44	North Dakota	872,000,000	0.3%
50	Vermont	502,000,000	0.2%		45	South Dakota	855,000,000	0.3%
3	Virginia	15,699,000,000	6.2%		46	Rhode Island	833,000,000	0.3%
11	Washington	6,929,000,000	2.7%		47	New Hampshire	742,000,000	0.3%
37	West Virginia	1,720,000,000	0.7%		48	Delaware	598,000,000	0.2%
30	Wisconsin	2,358,000,000	0.9%		49	Wyoming	588,000,000	0.2%
49	Wyoming	588,000,000	0.2%		50	Vermont	502,000,000	0.2%
						District of Columbia	19,027,000,000	7.5%

Source: U.S. Bureau of the Census
    "Consolidated Federal Funds Report: 2008" (CFFR/08, July 2009, http://www.census.gov/govs/cffr/)
*Total includes $1,413,000,000 in U.S. territories ($1,110,000,000 in Puerto Rico) and $2,306,000,000 in expenditures not distributed by state.

Per Capita Expenditures for Federal Government Salaries and Wages in 2008

National Per Capita = $822*

ALPHA ORDER

RANK	STATE	PER CAPITA
20	Alabama	$822
2	Alaska	3,206
32	Arizona	641
30	Arkansas	675
37	California	602
8	Colorado	1,094
48	Connecticut	492
29	Delaware	682
35	Florida	623
13	Georgia	1,038
1	Hawaii	3,210
28	Idaho	685
42	Illinois	560
46	Indiana	499
47	Iowa	497
9	Kansas	1,092
15	Kentucky	1,003
27	Louisiana	688
24	Maine	775
3	Maryland	2,075
34	Massachusetts	630
49	Michigan	432
44	Minnesota	536
26	Mississippi	756
19	Missouri	841
14	Montana	1,037
21	Nebraska	819
33	Nevada	631
41	New Hampshire	561
39	New Jersey	571
6	New Mexico	1,151
40	New York	569
18	North Carolina	858
5	North Dakota	1,359
43	Ohio	555
12	Oklahoma	1,050
38	Oregon	578
36	Pennsylvania	614
23	Rhode Island	791
31	South Carolina	672
10	South Dakota	1,063
45	Tennessee	527
25	Texas	765
17	Utah	933
22	Vermont	808
4	Virginia	2,014
11	Washington	1,055
16	West Virginia	948
50	Wisconsin	419
7	Wyoming	1,103

RANK ORDER

RANK	STATE	PER CAPITA
1	Hawaii	$3,210
2	Alaska	3,206
3	Maryland	2,075
4	Virginia	2,014
5	North Dakota	1,359
6	New Mexico	1,151
7	Wyoming	1,103
8	Colorado	1,094
9	Kansas	1,092
10	South Dakota	1,063
11	Washington	1,055
12	Oklahoma	1,050
13	Georgia	1,038
14	Montana	1,037
15	Kentucky	1,003
16	West Virginia	948
17	Utah	933
18	North Carolina	858
19	Missouri	841
20	Alabama	822
21	Nebraska	819
22	Vermont	808
23	Rhode Island	791
24	Maine	775
25	Texas	765
26	Mississippi	756
27	Louisiana	688
28	Idaho	685
29	Delaware	682
30	Arkansas	675
31	South Carolina	672
32	Arizona	641
33	Nevada	631
34	Massachusetts	630
35	Florida	623
36	Pennsylvania	614
37	California	602
38	Oregon	578
39	New Jersey	571
40	New York	569
41	New Hampshire	561
42	Illinois	560
43	Ohio	555
44	Minnesota	536
45	Tennessee	527
46	Indiana	499
47	Iowa	497
48	Connecticut	492
49	Michigan	432
50	Wisconsin	419
	District of Columbia	32,245

Source: CQ Press using data from U.S. Bureau of the Census
   "Consolidated Federal Funds Report: 2008" (CFFR/08, July 2009, http://www.census.gov/govs/cffr/)
*National per capita excludes expenditures and population for territories and undistributed amounts.

Average Salary of Federal Civilian Employees in 2006

National Average = $65,516*

ALPHA ORDER				RANK ORDER		
RANK	STATE	SALARY		RANK	STATE	SALARY
14	Alabama	$64,078		1	Maryland	$79,319
39	Alaska	56,525		2	New Hampshire	75,990
44	Arizona	55,393		3	Rhode Island	73,502
47	Arkansas	54,176		4	Virginia	73,224
11	California	66,212		5	New Jersey	72,313
6	Colorado	67,679		6	Colorado	67,679
10	Connecticut	66,343		7	Ohio	67,638
35	Delaware	57,176		8	Illinois	67,385
19	Florida	60,807		9	Massachusetts	67,035
17	Georgia	61,376		10	Connecticut	66,343
43	Hawaii	55,470		11	California	66,212
26	Idaho	58,057		12	Michigan	65,576
8	Illinois	67,385		13	New York	65,010
20	Indiana	60,658		14	Alabama	64,078
42	Iowa	55,799		15	Minnesota	62,953
27	Kansas	57,528		16	Washington	62,571
50	Kentucky	52,242		17	Georgia	61,376
28	Louisiana	57,446		18	Oregon	60,818
32	Maine	57,336		19	Florida	60,807
1	Maryland	79,319		20	Indiana	60,658
9	Massachusetts	67,035		21	Nevada	59,831
12	Michigan	65,576		22	Texas	59,618
15	Minnesota	62,953		23	Pennsylvania	59,092
37	Mississippi	56,978		24	West Virginia	58,964
40	Missouri	56,159		25	New Mexico	58,693
41	Montana	55,997		26	Idaho	58,057
29	Nebraska	57,406		27	Kansas	57,528
21	Nevada	59,831		28	Louisiana	57,446
2	New Hampshire	75,990		29	Nebraska	57,406
5	New Jersey	72,313		30	Wisconsin	57,404
25	New Mexico	58,693		31	Tennessee	57,349
13	New York	65,010		32	Maine	57,336
33	North Carolina	57,319		33	North Carolina	57,319
48	North Dakota	54,141		34	Vermont	57,279
7	Ohio	67,638		35	Delaware	57,176
38	Oklahoma	56,603		36	South Carolina	57,057
18	Oregon	60,818		37	Mississippi	56,978
23	Pennsylvania	59,092		38	Oklahoma	56,603
3	Rhode Island	73,502		39	Alaska	56,525
36	South Carolina	57,057		40	Missouri	56,159
49	South Dakota	53,000		41	Montana	55,997
31	Tennessee	57,349		42	Iowa	55,799
22	Texas	59,618		43	Hawaii	55,470
46	Utah	54,379		44	Arizona	55,393
34	Vermont	57,279		45	Wyoming	54,952
4	Virginia	73,224		46	Utah	54,379
16	Washington	62,571		47	Arkansas	54,176
24	West Virginia	58,964		48	North Dakota	54,141
30	Wisconsin	57,404		49	South Dakota	53,000
45	Wyoming	54,952		50	Kentucky	52,242
					District of Columbia	87,195

Source: Office of Personnel Management
   "The Fact Book: 2007 Edition" (http://www.opm.gov/feddata/factbook/)
*Full-time employees. National average includes employees not shown by state.

Federal Civilian Employees in 2006

National Total = 1,674,026 Full-Time Employees*

ALPHA ORDER					RANK ORDER			
RANK	STATE	EMPLOYEES	% of USA		RANK	STATE	EMPLOYEES	% of USA
12	Alabama	33,997	2.0%		1	California	139,804	8.4%
35	Alaska	11,922	0.7%		2	Virginia	121,337	7.2%
13	Arizona	33,871	2.0%		3	Texas	113,364	6.8%
34	Arkansas	12,090	0.7%		4	Maryland	103,438	6.2%
1	California	139,804	8.4%		5	Florida	71,858	4.3%
15	Colorado	33,196	2.0%		6	Georgia	66,314	4.0%
44	Connecticut	6,854	0.4%		7	Pennsylvania	62,486	3.7%
50	Delaware	2,864	0.2%		8	New York	57,472	3.4%
5	Florida	71,858	4.3%		9	Washington	45,948	2.7%
6	Georgia	66,314	4.0%		10	Illinois	42,382	2.5%
24	Hawaii	20,759	1.2%		11	Ohio	41,445	2.5%
41	Idaho	7,788	0.5%		12	Alabama	33,997	2.0%
10	Illinois	42,382	2.5%		13	Arizona	33,871	2.0%
27	Indiana	18,577	1.1%		14	Oklahoma	33,652	2.0%
42	Iowa	7,468	0.4%		15	Colorado	33,196	2.0%
31	Kansas	15,796	0.9%		16	North Carolina	33,163	2.0%
25	Kentucky	20,737	1.2%		17	Missouri	32,947	2.0%
26	Louisiana	19,011	1.1%		18	Utah	27,438	1.6%
38	Maine	9,128	0.5%		19	New Jersey	26,682	1.6%
4	Maryland	103,438	6.2%		20	Massachusetts	24,532	1.5%
20	Massachusetts	24,532	1.5%		21	Tennessee	23,514	1.4%
22	Michigan	23,345	1.4%		22	Michigan	23,345	1.4%
32	Minnesota	14,298	0.9%		23	New Mexico	22,298	1.3%
30	Mississippi	16,576	1.0%		24	Hawaii	20,759	1.2%
17	Missouri	32,947	2.0%		25	Kentucky	20,737	1.2%
39	Montana	8,858	0.5%		26	Louisiana	19,011	1.1%
40	Nebraska	8,826	0.5%		27	Indiana	18,577	1.1%
37	Nevada	9,146	0.5%		28	Oregon	17,649	1.1%
49	New Hampshire	3,433	0.2%		29	South Carolina	17,158	1.0%
19	New Jersey	26,682	1.6%		30	Mississippi	16,576	1.0%
23	New Mexico	22,298	1.3%		31	Kansas	15,796	0.9%
8	New York	57,472	3.4%		32	Minnesota	14,298	0.9%
16	North Carolina	33,163	2.0%		33	West Virginia	13,292	0.8%
46	North Dakota	5,581	0.3%		34	Arkansas	12,090	0.7%
11	Ohio	41,445	2.5%		35	Alaska	11,922	0.7%
14	Oklahoma	33,652	2.0%		36	Wisconsin	11,494	0.7%
28	Oregon	17,649	1.1%		37	Nevada	9,146	0.5%
7	Pennsylvania	62,486	3.7%		38	Maine	9,128	0.5%
45	Rhode Island	5,882	0.4%		39	Montana	8,858	0.5%
29	South Carolina	17,158	1.0%		40	Nebraska	8,826	0.5%
43	South Dakota	7,166	0.4%		41	Idaho	7,788	0.5%
21	Tennessee	23,514	1.4%		42	Iowa	7,468	0.4%
3	Texas	113,364	6.8%		43	South Dakota	7,166	0.4%
18	Utah	27,438	1.6%		44	Connecticut	6,854	0.4%
48	Vermont	3,537	0.2%		45	Rhode Island	5,882	0.4%
2	Virginia	121,337	7.2%		46	North Dakota	5,581	0.3%
9	Washington	45,948	2.7%		47	Wyoming	4,759	0.3%
33	West Virginia	13,292	0.8%		48	Vermont	3,537	0.2%
36	Wisconsin	11,494	0.7%		49	New Hampshire	3,433	0.2%
47	Wyoming	4,759	0.3%		50	Delaware	2,864	0.2%
						District of Columbia	138,622	8.3%

Source: Office of Personnel Management
   "The Fact Book: 2007 Edition" (http://www.opm.gov/feddata/factbook/)
*Full-time employees. National total includes 20,272 employees not shown by state.

Rate of Federal Civilian Employees in 2006

National Rate = 56 Full-Time Employees per 10,000 Population*

ALPHA ORDER

RANK	STATE	RATE
12	Alabama	73
2	Alaska	175
23	Arizona	53
30	Arkansas	43
32	California	39
16	Colorado	69
50	Connecticut	20
40	Delaware	33
32	Florida	39
15	Georgia	70
3	Hawaii	163
24	Idaho	52
40	Illinois	33
44	Indiana	29
47	Iowa	25
18	Kansas	57
27	Kentucky	49
30	Louisiana	43
16	Maine	69
1	Maryland	184
35	Massachusetts	38
48	Michigan	23
45	Minnesota	28
18	Mississippi	57
21	Missouri	56
7	Montana	93
25	Nebraska	50
38	Nevada	36
46	New Hampshire	26
42	New Jersey	31
5	New Mexico	113
43	New York	30
37	North Carolina	37
11	North Dakota	87
38	Ohio	36
7	Oklahoma	93
29	Oregon	47
25	Pennsylvania	50
21	Rhode Island	56
32	South Carolina	39
10	South Dakota	90
35	Tennessee	38
28	Texas	48
6	Utah	103
18	Vermont	57
4	Virginia	157
14	Washington	71
12	West Virginia	73
49	Wisconsin	21
9	Wyoming	91

RANK ORDER

RANK	STATE	RATE
1	Maryland	184
2	Alaska	175
3	Hawaii	163
4	Virginia	157
5	New Mexico	113
6	Utah	103
7	Montana	93
7	Oklahoma	93
9	Wyoming	91
10	South Dakota	90
11	North Dakota	87
12	Alabama	73
12	West Virginia	73
14	Washington	71
15	Georgia	70
16	Colorado	69
16	Maine	69
18	Kansas	57
18	Mississippi	57
18	Vermont	57
21	Missouri	56
21	Rhode Island	56
23	Arizona	53
24	Idaho	52
25	Nebraska	50
25	Pennsylvania	50
27	Kentucky	49
28	Texas	48
29	Oregon	47
30	Arkansas	43
30	Louisiana	43
32	California	39
32	Florida	39
32	South Carolina	39
35	Massachusetts	38
35	Tennessee	38
37	North Carolina	37
38	Nevada	36
38	Ohio	36
40	Delaware	33
40	Illinois	33
42	New Jersey	31
43	New York	30
44	Indiana	29
45	Minnesota	28
46	New Hampshire	26
47	Iowa	25
48	Michigan	23
49	Wisconsin	21
50	Connecticut	20

District of Columbia — 2,364

Source: CQ Press using data from Office of Personnel Management
"The Fact Book: 2007 Edition" (http://www.opm.gov/feddata/factbook/)
*Full-time employees. National rate includes employees not shown by state.

X. Government Finances: State and Local

State and Local Government Total Revenue in 2007

National Total = $3,065,725,782,000*

ALPHA ORDER

RANK	STATE	REVENUE	% of USA
25	Alabama	$40,677,099,000	1.3%
38	Alaska	15,469,206,000	0.5%
19	Arizona	51,388,643,000	1.7%
35	Arkansas	22,544,697,000	0.7%
1	California	467,567,348,000	15.3%
23	Colorado	46,779,002,000	1.5%
27	Connecticut	37,089,469,000	1.2%
45	Delaware	9,227,498,000	0.3%
4	Florida	172,878,476,000	5.6%
10	Georgia	76,042,772,000	2.5%
40	Hawaii	13,550,965,000	0.4%
42	Idaho	12,345,051,000	0.4%
7	Illinois	119,470,878,000	3.9%
21	Indiana	49,064,964,000	1.6%
31	Iowa	27,670,763,000	0.9%
32	Kansas	23,662,363,000	0.8%
28	Kentucky	33,812,270,000	1.1%
22	Louisiana	46,816,594,000	1.5%
41	Maine	12,366,853,000	0.4%
17	Maryland	53,951,995,000	1.8%
14	Massachusetts	70,289,337,000	2.3%
9	Michigan	92,612,061,000	3.0%
16	Minnesota	54,346,982,000	1.8%
30	Mississippi	29,599,235,000	1.0%
20	Missouri	49,776,866,000	1.6%
46	Montana	9,184,816,000	0.3%
37	Nebraska	18,486,551,000	0.6%
33	Nevada	23,207,119,000	0.8%
44	New Hampshire	10,365,591,000	0.3%
8	New Jersey	95,280,994,000	3.1%
36	New Mexico	20,975,006,000	0.7%
2	New York	292,789,459,000	9.6%
11	North Carolina	75,896,621,000	2.5%
50	North Dakota	6,351,841,000	0.2%
5	Ohio	121,881,844,000	4.0%
29	Oklahoma	30,364,662,000	1.0%
24	Oregon	41,742,283,000	1.4%
6	Pennsylvania	121,330,532,000	4.0%
43	Rhode Island	11,244,517,000	0.4%
26	South Carolina	39,460,585,000	1.3%
48	South Dakota	7,069,053,000	0.2%
18	Tennessee	52,156,823,000	1.7%
3	Texas	195,973,291,000	6.4%
34	Utah	23,193,931,000	0.8%
49	Vermont	6,364,541,000	0.2%
13	Virginia	70,506,512,000	2.3%
12	Washington	72,319,569,000	2.4%
39	West Virginia	14,816,266,000	0.5%
15	Wisconsin	55,834,185,000	1.8%
47	Wyoming	8,538,960,000	0.3%

RANK ORDER

RANK	STATE	REVENUE	% of USA
1	California	$467,567,348,000	15.3%
2	New York	292,789,459,000	9.6%
3	Texas	195,973,291,000	6.4%
4	Florida	172,878,476,000	5.6%
5	Ohio	121,881,844,000	4.0%
6	Pennsylvania	121,330,532,000	4.0%
7	Illinois	119,470,878,000	3.9%
8	New Jersey	95,280,994,000	3.1%
9	Michigan	92,612,061,000	3.0%
10	Georgia	76,042,772,000	2.5%
11	North Carolina	75,896,621,000	2.5%
12	Washington	72,319,569,000	2.4%
13	Virginia	70,506,512,000	2.3%
14	Massachusetts	70,289,337,000	2.3%
15	Wisconsin	55,834,185,000	1.8%
16	Minnesota	54,346,982,000	1.8%
17	Maryland	53,951,995,000	1.8%
18	Tennessee	52,156,823,000	1.7%
19	Arizona	51,388,643,000	1.7%
20	Missouri	49,776,866,000	1.6%
21	Indiana	49,064,964,000	1.6%
22	Louisiana	46,816,594,000	1.5%
23	Colorado	46,779,002,000	1.5%
24	Oregon	41,742,283,000	1.4%
25	Alabama	40,677,099,000	1.3%
26	South Carolina	39,460,585,000	1.3%
27	Connecticut	37,089,469,000	1.2%
28	Kentucky	33,812,270,000	1.1%
29	Oklahoma	30,364,662,000	1.0%
30	Mississippi	29,599,235,000	1.0%
31	Iowa	27,670,763,000	0.9%
32	Kansas	23,662,363,000	0.8%
33	Nevada	23,207,119,000	0.8%
34	Utah	23,193,931,000	0.8%
35	Arkansas	22,544,697,000	0.7%
36	New Mexico	20,975,006,000	0.7%
37	Nebraska	18,486,551,000	0.6%
38	Alaska	15,469,206,000	0.5%
39	West Virginia	14,816,266,000	0.5%
40	Hawaii	13,550,965,000	0.4%
41	Maine	12,366,853,000	0.4%
42	Idaho	12,345,051,000	0.4%
43	Rhode Island	11,244,517,000	0.4%
44	New Hampshire	10,365,591,000	0.3%
45	Delaware	9,227,498,000	0.3%
46	Montana	9,184,816,000	0.3%
47	Wyoming	8,538,960,000	0.3%
48	South Dakota	7,069,053,000	0.2%
49	Vermont	6,364,541,000	0.2%
50	North Dakota	6,351,841,000	0.2%
	District of Columbia	11,388,843,000	0.4%

Source: U.S. Bureau of the Census, Governments Division
"State and Local Government Finances 2006-2007" (http://www.census.gov/govs/estimate/index.html)
*Total revenue includes all money received from external sources. This includes taxes, intergovernmental transfers and insurance trust revenue, and revenue from government owned utilities and other commercial or auxiliary enterprise.

Per Capita State and Local Government Revenue in 2007

National Per Capita = $10,166*

ALPHA ORDER

RANK	STATE	PER CAPITA
35	Alabama	$8,771
1	Alaska	22,672
45	Arizona	8,077
48	Arkansas	7,932
4	California	12,907
23	Colorado	9,661
13	Connecticut	10,632
10	Delaware	10,669
26	Florida	9,458
46	Georgia	7,976
14	Hawaii	10,613
42	Idaho	8,234
28	Illinois	9,349
50	Indiana	7,731
29	Iowa	9,289
37	Kansas	8,525
47	Kentucky	7,944
9	Louisiana	10,698
27	Maine	9,388
25	Maryland	9,576
8	Massachusetts	10,815
30	Michigan	9,214
16	Minnesota	10,469
19	Mississippi	10,131
39	Missouri	8,423
24	Montana	9,595
17	Nebraska	10,445
32	Nevada	9,038
49	New Hampshire	7,869
7	New Jersey	11,033
12	New Mexico	10,654
3	New York	15,075
41	North Carolina	8,373
21	North Dakota	9,953
15	Ohio	10,579
40	Oklahoma	8,406
6	Oregon	11,182
22	Pennsylvania	9,689
11	Rhode Island	10,658
33	South Carolina	8,919
34	South Dakota	8,869
38	Tennessee	8,449
43	Texas	8,221
36	Utah	8,707
18	Vermont	10,258
31	Virginia	9,133
5	Washington	11,186
44	West Virginia	8,180
20	Wisconsin	9,968
2	Wyoming	16,314

RANK ORDER

RANK	STATE	PER CAPITA
1	Alaska	$22,672
2	Wyoming	16,314
3	New York	15,075
4	California	12,907
5	Washington	11,186
6	Oregon	11,182
7	New Jersey	11,033
8	Massachusetts	10,815
9	Louisiana	10,698
10	Delaware	10,669
11	Rhode Island	10,658
12	New Mexico	10,654
13	Connecticut	10,632
14	Hawaii	10,613
15	Ohio	10,579
16	Minnesota	10,469
17	Nebraska	10,445
18	Vermont	10,258
19	Mississippi	10,131
20	Wisconsin	9,968
21	North Dakota	9,953
22	Pennsylvania	9,689
23	Colorado	9,661
24	Montana	9,595
25	Maryland	9,576
26	Florida	9,458
27	Maine	9,388
28	Illinois	9,349
29	Iowa	9,289
30	Michigan	9,214
31	Virginia	9,133
32	Nevada	9,038
33	South Carolina	8,919
34	South Dakota	8,869
35	Alabama	8,771
36	Utah	8,707
37	Kansas	8,525
38	Tennessee	8,449
39	Missouri	8,423
40	Oklahoma	8,406
41	North Carolina	8,373
42	Idaho	8,234
43	Texas	8,221
44	West Virginia	8,180
45	Arizona	8,077
46	Georgia	7,976
47	Kentucky	7,944
48	Arkansas	7,932
49	New Hampshire	7,869
50	Indiana	7,731

| | District of Columbia | 19,421 |

Source: CQ Press using data from U.S. Bureau of the Census, Governments Division
"State and Local Government Finances 2006-2007" (http://www.census.gov/govs/estimate/index.html)
*Total revenue includes all money received from external sources. This includes taxes, intergovernmental transfers and insurance trust revenue, and revenue from government owned utilities and other commercial or auxiliary enterprise.

State and Local Government Revenue From the Federal Government in 2007

National Total = $467,584,497,000

ALPHA ORDER

RANK	STATE	REVENUE	% of USA
21	Alabama	$7,823,806,000	1.7%
38	Alaska	2,547,532,000	0.5%
17	Arizona	8,713,139,000	1.9%
32	Arkansas	4,506,781,000	1.0%
1	California	55,362,109,000	11.8%
27	Colorado	5,718,285,000	1.2%
30	Connecticut	4,575,839,000	1.0%
50	Delaware	1,263,676,000	0.3%
4	Florida	22,976,024,000	4.9%
10	Georgia	13,796,792,000	3.0%
41	Hawaii	2,236,107,000	0.5%
44	Idaho	1,977,904,000	0.4%
7	Illinois	16,910,386,000	3.6%
19	Indiana	8,190,335,000	1.8%
31	Iowa	4,562,001,000	1.0%
36	Kansas	3,353,281,000	0.7%
26	Kentucky	6,724,237,000	1.4%
11	Louisiana	13,298,054,000	2.8%
39	Maine	2,523,099,000	0.5%
20	Maryland	8,088,938,000	1.7%
13	Massachusetts	10,653,185,000	2.3%
8	Michigan	14,389,826,000	3.1%
23	Minnesota	7,332,754,000	1.6%
14	Mississippi	9,785,801,000	2.1%
18	Missouri	8,653,094,000	1.9%
43	Montana	2,016,761,000	0.4%
37	Nebraska	2,710,426,000	0.6%
40	Nevada	2,470,907,000	0.5%
46	New Hampshire	1,684,396,000	0.4%
12	New Jersey	11,778,255,000	2.5%
33	New Mexico	4,480,304,000	1.0%
2	New York	45,165,426,000	9.7%
9	North Carolina	14,258,745,000	3.0%
49	North Dakota	1,332,321,000	0.3%
6	Ohio	18,202,070,000	3.9%
28	Oklahoma	5,685,102,000	1.2%
29	Oregon	5,604,164,000	1.2%
5	Pennsylvania	18,949,089,000	4.1%
42	Rhode Island	2,102,983,000	0.4%
25	South Carolina	7,058,208,000	1.5%
48	South Dakota	1,413,809,000	0.3%
15	Tennessee	8,916,275,000	1.9%
3	Texas	31,043,533,000	6.6%
34	Utah	3,457,512,000	0.7%
47	Vermont	1,435,670,000	0.3%
22	Virginia	7,483,420,000	1.6%
16	Washington	8,911,410,000	1.9%
35	West Virginia	3,417,817,000	0.7%
24	Wisconsin	7,166,153,000	1.5%
45	Wyoming	1,877,732,000	0.4%

RANK ORDER

RANK	STATE	REVENUE	% of USA
1	California	$55,362,109,000	11.8%
2	New York	45,165,426,000	9.7%
3	Texas	31,043,533,000	6.6%
4	Florida	22,976,024,000	4.9%
5	Pennsylvania	18,949,089,000	4.1%
6	Ohio	18,202,070,000	3.9%
7	Illinois	16,910,386,000	3.6%
8	Michigan	14,389,826,000	3.1%
9	North Carolina	14,258,745,000	3.0%
10	Georgia	13,796,792,000	3.0%
11	Louisiana	13,298,054,000	2.8%
12	New Jersey	11,778,255,000	2.5%
13	Massachusetts	10,653,185,000	2.3%
14	Mississippi	9,785,801,000	2.1%
15	Tennessee	8,916,275,000	1.9%
16	Washington	8,911,410,000	1.9%
17	Arizona	8,713,139,000	1.9%
18	Missouri	8,653,094,000	1.9%
19	Indiana	8,190,335,000	1.8%
20	Maryland	8,088,938,000	1.7%
21	Alabama	7,823,806,000	1.7%
22	Virginia	7,483,420,000	1.6%
23	Minnesota	7,332,754,000	1.6%
24	Wisconsin	7,166,153,000	1.5%
25	South Carolina	7,058,208,000	1.5%
26	Kentucky	6,724,237,000	1.4%
27	Colorado	5,718,285,000	1.2%
28	Oklahoma	5,685,102,000	1.2%
29	Oregon	5,604,164,000	1.2%
30	Connecticut	4,575,839,000	1.0%
31	Iowa	4,562,001,000	1.0%
32	Arkansas	4,506,781,000	1.0%
33	New Mexico	4,480,304,000	1.0%
34	Utah	3,457,512,000	0.7%
35	West Virginia	3,417,817,000	0.7%
36	Kansas	3,353,281,000	0.7%
37	Nebraska	2,710,426,000	0.6%
38	Alaska	2,547,532,000	0.5%
39	Maine	2,523,099,000	0.5%
40	Nevada	2,470,907,000	0.5%
41	Hawaii	2,236,107,000	0.5%
42	Rhode Island	2,102,983,000	0.4%
43	Montana	2,016,761,000	0.4%
44	Idaho	1,977,904,000	0.4%
45	Wyoming	1,877,732,000	0.4%
46	New Hampshire	1,684,396,000	0.4%
47	Vermont	1,435,670,000	0.3%
48	South Dakota	1,413,809,000	0.3%
49	North Dakota	1,332,321,000	0.3%
50	Delaware	1,263,676,000	0.3%
	District of Columbia	2,999,024,000	0.6%

Source: U.S. Bureau of the Census, Governments Division
"State and Local Government Finances 2006-2007" (http://www.census.gov/govs/estimate/index.html)

Per Capita State and Local Government Revenue
From the Federal Government in 2007
National Per Capita = $1,550

RANK	STATE	PER CAPITA
15	Alabama	$1,687
1	Alaska	3,734
36	Arizona	1,370
18	Arkansas	1,586
25	California	1,528
48	Colorado	1,181
40	Connecticut	1,312
29	Delaware	1,461
46	Florida	1,257
30	Georgia	1,447
14	Hawaii	1,751
39	Idaho	1,319
38	Illinois	1,323
43	Indiana	1,291
23	Iowa	1,532
47	Kansas	1,208
19	Kentucky	1,580
4	Louisiana	3,039
11	Maine	1,915
32	Maryland	1,436
16	Massachusetts	1,639
33	Michigan	1,432
34	Minnesota	1,413
3	Mississippi	3,349
28	Missouri	1,464
8	Montana	2,107
24	Nebraska	1,531
50	Nevada	962
44	New Hampshire	1,279
37	New Jersey	1,364
7	New Mexico	2,276
5	New York	2,325
22	North Carolina	1,573
9	North Dakota	2,088
19	Ohio	1,580
21	Oklahoma	1,574
27	Oregon	1,501
26	Pennsylvania	1,513
10	Rhode Island	1,993
17	South Carolina	1,595
13	South Dakota	1,774
31	Tennessee	1,444
41	Texas	1,302
42	Utah	1,298
6	Vermont	2,314
49	Virginia	969
35	Washington	1,378
12	West Virginia	1,887
44	Wisconsin	1,279
2	Wyoming	3,587

RANK	STATE	PER CAPITA
1	Alaska	$3,734
2	Wyoming	3,587
3	Mississippi	3,349
4	Louisiana	3,039
5	New York	2,325
6	Vermont	2,314
7	New Mexico	2,276
8	Montana	2,107
9	North Dakota	2,088
10	Rhode Island	1,993
11	Maine	1,915
12	West Virginia	1,887
13	South Dakota	1,774
14	Hawaii	1,751
15	Alabama	1,687
16	Massachusetts	1,639
17	South Carolina	1,595
18	Arkansas	1,586
19	Kentucky	1,580
19	Ohio	1,580
21	Oklahoma	1,574
22	North Carolina	1,573
23	Iowa	1,532
24	Nebraska	1,531
25	California	1,528
26	Pennsylvania	1,513
27	Oregon	1,501
28	Missouri	1,464
29	Delaware	1,461
30	Georgia	1,447
31	Tennessee	1,444
32	Maryland	1,436
33	Michigan	1,432
34	Minnesota	1,413
35	Washington	1,378
36	Arizona	1,370
37	New Jersey	1,364
38	Illinois	1,323
39	Idaho	1,319
40	Connecticut	1,312
41	Texas	1,302
42	Utah	1,298
43	Indiana	1,291
44	New Hampshire	1,279
44	Wisconsin	1,279
46	Florida	1,257
47	Kansas	1,208
48	Colorado	1,181
49	Virginia	969
50	Nevada	962
	District of Columbia	5,114

Source: CQ Press using data from U.S. Bureau of the Census, Governments Division
"State and Local Government Finances 2006-2007" (http://www.census.gov/govs/estimate/index.html)

Percent of State and Local Government Revenue
from the Federal Government in 2007
National Percent = 15.3%*

ALPHA ORDER				RANK ORDER		
RANK	STATE	PERCENT		RANK	STATE	PERCENT
13	Alabama	19.2		1	Mississippi	33.1
23	Alaska	16.5		2	Louisiana	28.4
21	Arizona	17.0		3	West Virginia	23.1
10	Arkansas	20.0		4	Vermont	22.6
48	California	11.8		5	Montana	22.0
47	Colorado	12.2		5	Wyoming	22.0
45	Connecticut	12.3		7	New Mexico	21.4
39	Delaware	13.7		8	North Dakota	21.0
42	Florida	13.3		9	Maine	20.4
17	Georgia	18.1		10	Arkansas	20.0
23	Hawaii	16.5		10	South Dakota	20.0
27	Idaho	16.0		12	Kentucky	19.9
37	Illinois	14.2		13	Alabama	19.2
22	Indiana	16.7		14	North Carolina	18.8
23	Iowa	16.5		15	Oklahoma	18.7
37	Kansas	14.2		15	Rhode Island	18.7
12	Kentucky	19.9		17	Georgia	18.1
2	Louisiana	28.4		18	South Carolina	17.9
9	Maine	20.4		19	Missouri	17.4
33	Maryland	15.0		20	Tennessee	17.1
32	Massachusetts	15.2		21	Arizona	17.0
30	Michigan	15.5		22	Indiana	16.7
40	Minnesota	13.5		23	Alaska	16.5
1	Mississippi	33.1		23	Hawaii	16.5
19	Missouri	17.4		23	Iowa	16.5
5	Montana	22.0		26	New Hampshire	16.2
36	Nebraska	14.7		27	Idaho	16.0
49	Nevada	10.6		28	Texas	15.8
26	New Hampshire	16.2		29	Pennsylvania	15.6
44	New Jersey	12.4		30	Michigan	15.5
7	New Mexico	21.4		31	New York	15.4
31	New York	15.4		32	Massachusetts	15.2
14	North Carolina	18.8		33	Maryland	15.0
8	North Dakota	21.0		34	Ohio	14.9
34	Ohio	14.9		34	Utah	14.9
15	Oklahoma	18.7		36	Nebraska	14.7
41	Oregon	13.4		37	Illinois	14.2
29	Pennsylvania	15.6		37	Kansas	14.2
15	Rhode Island	18.7		39	Delaware	13.7
18	South Carolina	17.9		40	Minnesota	13.5
10	South Dakota	20.0		41	Oregon	13.4
20	Tennessee	17.1		42	Florida	13.3
28	Texas	15.8		43	Wisconsin	12.8
34	Utah	14.9		44	New Jersey	12.4
4	Vermont	22.6		45	Connecticut	12.3
49	Virginia	10.6		45	Washington	12.3
45	Washington	12.3		47	Colorado	12.2
3	West Virginia	23.1		48	California	11.8
43	Wisconsin	12.8		49	Nevada	10.6
5	Wyoming	22.0		49	Virginia	10.6
					District of Columbia	26.3

Source: CQ Press using data from U.S. Bureau of the Census, Governments Division
"State and Local Government Finances 2006-2007" (http://www.census.gov/govs/estimate/index.html)
*As a percent of total revenue.

State and Local Government Own Source Revenue in 2007

National Total = $1,861,430,544,000*

ALPHA ORDER

RANK	STATE	REVENUE	% of USA
26	Alabama	$23,463,761,000	1.3%
38	Alaska	10,442,688,000	0.6%
19	Arizona	32,605,800,000	1.8%
35	Arkansas	13,185,948,000	0.7%
1	California	254,640,917,000	13.7%
20	Colorado	29,688,291,000	1.6%
24	Connecticut	25,860,310,000	1.4%
45	Delaware	6,370,098,000	0.3%
4	Florida	110,744,545,000	5.9%
10	Georgia	48,550,396,000	2.6%
40	Hawaii	9,001,057,000	0.5%
42	Idaho	7,461,708,000	0.4%
6	Illinois	74,248,106,000	4.0%
17	Indiana	33,572,657,000	1.8%
30	Iowa	17,306,191,000	0.9%
31	Kansas	16,010,366,000	0.9%
28	Kentucky	20,235,714,000	1.1%
23	Louisiana	26,117,090,000	1.4%
41	Maine	7,724,270,000	0.4%
15	Maryland	35,677,641,000	1.9%
13	Massachusetts	44,254,468,000	2.4%
9	Michigan	58,651,174,000	3.2%
16	Minnesota	34,124,042,000	1.8%
34	Mississippi	14,003,517,000	0.8%
22	Missouri	28,906,783,000	1.6%
47	Montana	5,122,442,000	0.3%
37	Nebraska	10,887,167,000	0.6%
32	Nevada	15,367,525,000	0.8%
43	New Hampshire	6,865,441,000	0.4%
8	New Jersey	66,838,577,000	3.6%
36	New Mexico	11,888,805,000	0.6%
2	New York	177,468,498,000	9.5%
11	North Carolina	48,021,316,000	2.6%
49	North Dakota	4,037,782,000	0.2%
7	Ohio	66,838,587,000	3.6%
29	Oklahoma	18,446,421,000	1.0%
27	Oregon	21,208,637,000	1.1%
5	Pennsylvania	74,333,794,000	4.0%
44	Rhode Island	6,690,849,000	0.4%
25	South Carolina	24,255,214,000	1.3%
50	South Dakota	3,718,279,000	0.2%
21	Tennessee	29,543,102,000	1.6%
3	Texas	124,922,977,000	6.7%
33	Utah	14,635,605,000	0.8%
48	Vermont	4,042,086,000	0.2%
12	Virginia	47,467,945,000	2.6%
14	Washington	41,276,596,000	2.2%
39	West Virginia	9,862,220,000	0.5%
18	Wisconsin	32,854,398,000	1.8%
46	Wyoming	5,241,170,000	0.3%

RANK ORDER

RANK	STATE	REVENUE	% of USA
1	California	$254,640,917,000	13.7%
2	New York	177,468,498,000	9.5%
3	Texas	124,922,977,000	6.7%
4	Florida	110,744,545,000	5.9%
5	Pennsylvania	74,333,794,000	4.0%
6	Illinois	74,248,106,000	4.0%
7	Ohio	66,838,587,000	3.6%
8	New Jersey	66,838,577,000	3.6%
9	Michigan	58,651,174,000	3.2%
10	Georgia	48,550,396,000	2.6%
11	North Carolina	48,021,316,000	2.6%
12	Virginia	47,467,945,000	2.6%
13	Massachusetts	44,254,468,000	2.4%
14	Washington	41,276,596,000	2.2%
15	Maryland	35,677,641,000	1.9%
16	Minnesota	34,124,042,000	1.8%
17	Indiana	33,572,657,000	1.8%
18	Wisconsin	32,854,398,000	1.8%
19	Arizona	32,605,800,000	1.8%
20	Colorado	29,688,291,000	1.6%
21	Tennessee	29,543,102,000	1.6%
22	Missouri	28,906,783,000	1.6%
23	Louisiana	26,117,090,000	1.4%
24	Connecticut	25,860,310,000	1.4%
25	South Carolina	24,255,214,000	1.3%
26	Alabama	23,463,761,000	1.3%
27	Oregon	21,208,637,000	1.1%
28	Kentucky	20,235,714,000	1.1%
29	Oklahoma	18,446,421,000	1.0%
30	Iowa	17,306,191,000	0.9%
31	Kansas	16,010,366,000	0.9%
32	Nevada	15,367,525,000	0.8%
33	Utah	14,635,605,000	0.8%
34	Mississippi	14,003,517,000	0.8%
35	Arkansas	13,185,948,000	0.7%
36	New Mexico	11,888,805,000	0.6%
37	Nebraska	10,887,167,000	0.6%
38	Alaska	10,442,688,000	0.6%
39	West Virginia	9,862,220,000	0.5%
40	Hawaii	9,001,057,000	0.5%
41	Maine	7,724,270,000	0.4%
42	Idaho	7,461,708,000	0.4%
43	New Hampshire	6,865,441,000	0.4%
44	Rhode Island	6,690,849,000	0.4%
45	Delaware	6,370,098,000	0.3%
46	Wyoming	5,241,170,000	0.3%
47	Montana	5,122,442,000	0.3%
48	Vermont	4,042,086,000	0.2%
49	North Dakota	4,037,782,000	0.2%
50	South Dakota	3,718,279,000	0.2%
	District of Columbia	6,747,573,000	0.4%

Source: U.S. Bureau of the Census, Governments Division
"State and Local Government Finances 2006-2007" (http://www.census.gov/govs/estimate/index.html)
*Own source revenue includes taxes, current charges, and miscellaneous general revenue. Excluded are intergovernmental transfers, insurance trust revenue, and revenue from government owned utilities and other commercial or auxiliary enterprise.

Per Capita State and Local Government Own Source Revenue in 2007

National Per Capita = $6,172*

ALPHA ORDER				RANK ORDER		
RANK	STATE	PER CAPITA		RANK	STATE	PER CAPITA
43	Alabama	$5,059		1	Alaska	$15,305
1	Alaska	15,305		2	Wyoming	10,013
40	Arizona	5,125		3	New York	9,137
50	Arkansas	4,639		4	New Jersey	7,739
8	California	7,029		5	Connecticut	7,413
18	Colorado	6,131		6	Delaware	7,365
5	Connecticut	7,413		7	Hawaii	7,050
6	Delaware	7,365		8	California	7,029
19	Florida	6,059		9	Massachusetts	6,809
42	Georgia	5,092		10	Minnesota	6,573
7	Hawaii	7,050		11	Vermont	6,515
44	Idaho	4,977		12	Washington	6,385
27	Illinois	5,810		13	Rhode Island	6,342
37	Indiana	5,290		14	Maryland	6,332
27	Iowa	5,810		15	North Dakota	6,327
30	Kansas	5,768		16	Nebraska	6,151
48	Kentucky	4,754		17	Virginia	6,149
22	Louisiana	5,968		18	Colorado	6,131
25	Maine	5,864		19	Florida	6,059
14	Maryland	6,332		20	New Mexico	6,039
9	Massachusetts	6,809		21	Nevada	5,985
26	Michigan	5,835		22	Louisiana	5,968
10	Minnesota	6,573		23	Pennsylvania	5,936
46	Mississippi	4,793		24	Wisconsin	5,865
45	Missouri	4,891		25	Maine	5,864
35	Montana	5,351		26	Michigan	5,835
16	Nebraska	6,151		27	Illinois	5,810
21	Nevada	5,985		27	Iowa	5,810
39	New Hampshire	5,212		29	Ohio	5,802
4	New Jersey	7,739		30	Kansas	5,768
20	New Mexico	6,039		31	Oregon	5,681
3	New York	9,137		32	Utah	5,494
36	North Carolina	5,298		33	South Carolina	5,482
15	North Dakota	6,327		34	West Virginia	5,445
29	Ohio	5,802		35	Montana	5,351
41	Oklahoma	5,107		36	North Carolina	5,298
31	Oregon	5,681		37	Indiana	5,290
23	Pennsylvania	5,936		38	Texas	5,241
13	Rhode Island	6,342		39	New Hampshire	5,212
33	South Carolina	5,482		40	Arizona	5,125
49	South Dakota	4,665		41	Oklahoma	5,107
47	Tennessee	4,786		42	Georgia	5,092
38	Texas	5,241		43	Alabama	5,059
32	Utah	5,494		44	Idaho	4,977
11	Vermont	6,515		45	Missouri	4,891
17	Virginia	6,149		46	Mississippi	4,793
12	Washington	6,385		47	Tennessee	4,786
34	West Virginia	5,445		48	Kentucky	4,754
24	Wisconsin	5,865		49	South Dakota	4,665
2	Wyoming	10,013		50	Arkansas	4,639
					District of Columbia	11,507

Source: CQ Press using data from U.S. Bureau of the Census, Governments Division
"State and Local Government Finances 2006-2007" (http://www.census.gov/govs/estimate/index.html)
*Own source revenue includes taxes, current charges, and miscellaneous general revenue. Excluded are intergovernmental transfers, insurance trust revenue, and revenue from government owned utilities and other commercial or auxiliary enterprise.

State and Local Government Tax Revenue in 2007

National Total = $1,275,501,894,000

ALPHA ORDER

RANK	STATE	REVENUE	% of USA
27	Alabama	$13,457,018,000	1.1%
41	Alaska	4,950,170,000	0.4%
18	Arizona	23,334,711,000	1.8%
33	Arkansas	9,179,610,000	0.7%
1	California	172,933,246,000	13.6%
22	Colorado	18,632,752,000	1.5%
20	Connecticut	21,095,231,000	1.7%
45	Delaware	3,658,685,000	0.3%
4	Florida	72,963,487,000	5.7%
10	Georgia	33,153,023,000	2.6%
38	Hawaii	6,564,657,000	0.5%
43	Idaho	4,763,128,000	0.4%
5	Illinois	55,075,065,000	4.3%
19	Indiana	21,111,365,000	1.7%
31	Iowa	10,933,498,000	0.9%
30	Kansas	11,354,429,000	0.9%
26	Kentucky	13,705,597,000	1.1%
24	Louisiana	17,593,803,000	1.4%
40	Maine	5,628,235,000	0.4%
15	Maryland	27,064,783,000	2.1%
13	Massachusetts	32,120,073,000	2.5%
9	Michigan	37,094,769,000	2.9%
16	Minnesota	23,664,988,000	1.9%
35	Mississippi	8,732,575,000	0.7%
21	Missouri	19,192,645,000	1.5%
46	Montana	3,271,530,000	0.3%
37	Nebraska	7,141,849,000	0.6%
32	Nevada	10,443,909,000	0.8%
44	New Hampshire	4,742,721,000	0.4%
7	New Jersey	51,431,954,000	4.0%
36	New Mexico	7,456,363,000	0.6%
2	New York	134,017,241,000	10.5%
11	North Carolina	32,422,471,000	2.5%
49	North Dakota	2,605,298,000	0.2%
8	Ohio	46,042,915,000	3.6%
29	Oklahoma	11,950,235,000	0.9%
28	Oregon	12,748,735,000	1.0%
6	Pennsylvania	52,257,355,000	4.1%
42	Rhode Island	4,786,803,000	0.4%
25	South Carolina	13,803,722,000	1.1%
50	South Dakota	2,391,888,000	0.2%
23	Tennessee	18,363,984,000	1.4%
3	Texas	82,037,189,000	6.4%
34	Utah	8,907,029,000	0.7%
48	Vermont	2,931,481,000	0.2%
12	Virginia	32,375,037,000	2.5%
14	Washington	27,533,277,000	2.2%
39	West Virginia	6,102,322,000	0.5%
17	Wisconsin	23,339,993,000	1.8%
47	Wyoming	3,246,860,000	0.3%

RANK ORDER

RANK	STATE	REVENUE	% of USA
1	California	$172,933,246,000	13.6%
2	New York	134,017,241,000	10.5%
3	Texas	82,037,189,000	6.4%
4	Florida	72,963,487,000	5.7%
5	Illinois	55,075,065,000	4.3%
6	Pennsylvania	52,257,355,000	4.1%
7	New Jersey	51,431,954,000	4.0%
8	Ohio	46,042,915,000	3.6%
9	Michigan	37,094,769,000	2.9%
10	Georgia	33,153,023,000	2.6%
11	North Carolina	32,422,471,000	2.5%
12	Virginia	32,375,037,000	2.5%
13	Massachusetts	32,120,073,000	2.5%
14	Washington	27,533,277,000	2.2%
15	Maryland	27,064,783,000	2.1%
16	Minnesota	23,664,988,000	1.9%
17	Wisconsin	23,339,993,000	1.8%
18	Arizona	23,334,711,000	1.8%
19	Indiana	21,111,365,000	1.7%
20	Connecticut	21,095,231,000	1.7%
21	Missouri	19,192,645,000	1.5%
22	Colorado	18,632,752,000	1.5%
23	Tennessee	18,363,984,000	1.4%
24	Louisiana	17,593,803,000	1.4%
25	South Carolina	13,803,722,000	1.1%
26	Kentucky	13,705,597,000	1.1%
27	Alabama	13,457,018,000	1.1%
28	Oregon	12,748,735,000	1.0%
29	Oklahoma	11,950,235,000	0.9%
30	Kansas	11,354,429,000	0.9%
31	Iowa	10,933,498,000	0.9%
32	Nevada	10,443,909,000	0.8%
33	Arkansas	9,179,610,000	0.7%
34	Utah	8,907,029,000	0.7%
35	Mississippi	8,732,575,000	0.7%
36	New Mexico	7,456,363,000	0.6%
37	Nebraska	7,141,849,000	0.6%
38	Hawaii	6,564,657,000	0.5%
39	West Virginia	6,102,322,000	0.5%
40	Maine	5,628,235,000	0.4%
41	Alaska	4,950,170,000	0.4%
42	Rhode Island	4,786,803,000	0.4%
43	Idaho	4,763,128,000	0.4%
44	New Hampshire	4,742,721,000	0.4%
45	Delaware	3,658,685,000	0.3%
46	Montana	3,271,530,000	0.3%
47	Wyoming	3,246,860,000	0.3%
48	Vermont	2,931,481,000	0.2%
49	North Dakota	2,605,298,000	0.2%
50	South Dakota	2,391,888,000	0.2%
	District of Columbia	5,192,190,000	0.4%

Source: U.S. Bureau of the Census, Governments Division
"State and Local Government Finances 2006-2007" (http://www.census.gov/govs/estimate/index.html)

Per Capita State and Local Government Tax Revenue in 2007

National Per Capita = $4,229

ALPHA ORDER

RANK	STATE	PER CAPITA
50	Alabama	$2,902
1	Alaska	7,255
31	Arizona	3,668
43	Arkansas	3,230
9	California	4,774
27	Colorado	3,848
4	Connecticut	6,047
16	Delaware	4,230
26	Florida	3,992
34	Georgia	3,477
6	Hawaii	5,141
45	Idaho	3,177
13	Illinois	4,310
40	Indiana	3,327
30	Iowa	3,671
20	Kansas	4,091
44	Kentucky	3,220
24	Louisiana	4,020
14	Maine	4,273
8	Maryland	4,804
7	Massachusetts	4,942
29	Michigan	3,691
11	Minnesota	4,559
48	Mississippi	2,989
42	Missouri	3,248
36	Montana	3,418
23	Nebraska	4,035
22	Nevada	4,067
32	New Hampshire	3,600
5	New Jersey	5,955
28	New Mexico	3,787
2	New York	6,900
33	North Carolina	3,577
21	North Dakota	4,082
25	Ohio	3,996
41	Oklahoma	3,308
37	Oregon	3,415
18	Pennsylvania	4,173
12	Rhode Island	4,537
46	South Carolina	3,120
47	South Dakota	3,001
49	Tennessee	2,975
35	Texas	3,441
39	Utah	3,344
10	Vermont	4,725
17	Virginia	4,194
15	Washington	4,259
38	West Virginia	3,369
19	Wisconsin	4,167
3	Wyoming	6,203

RANK ORDER

RANK	STATE	PER CAPITA
1	Alaska	$7,255
2	New York	6,900
3	Wyoming	6,203
4	Connecticut	6,047
5	New Jersey	5,955
6	Hawaii	5,141
7	Massachusetts	4,942
8	Maryland	4,804
9	California	4,774
10	Vermont	4,725
11	Minnesota	4,559
12	Rhode Island	4,537
13	Illinois	4,310
14	Maine	4,273
15	Washington	4,259
16	Delaware	4,230
17	Virginia	4,194
18	Pennsylvania	4,173
19	Wisconsin	4,167
20	Kansas	4,091
21	North Dakota	4,082
22	Nevada	4,067
23	Nebraska	4,035
24	Louisiana	4,020
25	Ohio	3,996
26	Florida	3,992
27	Colorado	3,848
28	New Mexico	3,787
29	Michigan	3,691
30	Iowa	3,671
31	Arizona	3,668
32	New Hampshire	3,600
33	North Carolina	3,577
34	Georgia	3,477
35	Texas	3,441
36	Montana	3,418
37	Oregon	3,415
38	West Virginia	3,369
39	Utah	3,344
40	Indiana	3,327
41	Oklahoma	3,308
42	Missouri	3,248
43	Arkansas	3,230
44	Kentucky	3,220
45	Idaho	3,177
46	South Carolina	3,120
47	South Dakota	3,001
48	Mississippi	2,989
49	Tennessee	2,975
50	Alabama	2,902

	District of Columbia	8,854

Source: CQ Press using data from U.S. Bureau of the Census, Governments Division
"State and Local Government Finances 2006-2007" (http://www.census.gov/govs/estimate/index.html)

Percent of State and Local Government Revenue from Taxes in 2007

National Percent = 41.6%

<table>
<tr><td colspan="3">ALPHA ORDER</td><td colspan="3">RANK ORDER</td></tr>
<tr><th>RANK</th><th>STATE</th><th>PERCENT</th><th>RANK</th><th>STATE</th><th>PERCENT</th></tr>
<tr><td>47</td><td>Alabama</td><td>33.1</td><td>1</td><td>Connecticut</td><td>56.9</td></tr>
<tr><td>48</td><td>Alaska</td><td>32.0</td><td>2</td><td>New Jersey</td><td>54.0</td></tr>
<tr><td>13</td><td>Arizona</td><td>45.4</td><td>3</td><td>Maryland</td><td>50.2</td></tr>
<tr><td>26</td><td>Arkansas</td><td>40.7</td><td>4</td><td>Hawaii</td><td>48.4</td></tr>
<tr><td>41</td><td>California</td><td>37.0</td><td>5</td><td>Kansas</td><td>48.0</td></tr>
<tr><td>29</td><td>Colorado</td><td>39.8</td><td>6</td><td>Illinois</td><td>46.1</td></tr>
<tr><td>1</td><td>Connecticut</td><td>56.9</td><td>6</td><td>Vermont</td><td>46.1</td></tr>
<tr><td>30</td><td>Delaware</td><td>39.6</td><td>8</td><td>Virginia</td><td>45.9</td></tr>
<tr><td>21</td><td>Florida</td><td>42.2</td><td>9</td><td>New Hampshire</td><td>45.8</td></tr>
<tr><td>15</td><td>Georgia</td><td>43.6</td><td>9</td><td>New York</td><td>45.8</td></tr>
<tr><td>4</td><td>Hawaii</td><td>48.4</td><td>11</td><td>Massachusetts</td><td>45.7</td></tr>
<tr><td>33</td><td>Idaho</td><td>38.6</td><td>12</td><td>Maine</td><td>45.5</td></tr>
<tr><td>6</td><td>Illinois</td><td>46.1</td><td>13</td><td>Arizona</td><td>45.4</td></tr>
<tr><td>18</td><td>Indiana</td><td>43.0</td><td>14</td><td>Nevada</td><td>45.0</td></tr>
<tr><td>31</td><td>Iowa</td><td>39.5</td><td>15</td><td>Georgia</td><td>43.6</td></tr>
<tr><td>5</td><td>Kansas</td><td>48.0</td><td>16</td><td>Minnesota</td><td>43.5</td></tr>
<tr><td>27</td><td>Kentucky</td><td>40.5</td><td>17</td><td>Pennsylvania</td><td>43.1</td></tr>
<tr><td>40</td><td>Louisiana</td><td>37.6</td><td>18</td><td>Indiana</td><td>43.0</td></tr>
<tr><td>12</td><td>Maine</td><td>45.5</td><td>19</td><td>North Carolina</td><td>42.7</td></tr>
<tr><td>3</td><td>Maryland</td><td>50.2</td><td>20</td><td>Rhode Island</td><td>42.6</td></tr>
<tr><td>11</td><td>Massachusetts</td><td>45.7</td><td>21</td><td>Florida</td><td>42.2</td></tr>
<tr><td>28</td><td>Michigan</td><td>40.1</td><td>22</td><td>Texas</td><td>41.9</td></tr>
<tr><td>16</td><td>Minnesota</td><td>43.5</td><td>23</td><td>Wisconsin</td><td>41.8</td></tr>
<tr><td>50</td><td>Mississippi</td><td>29.5</td><td>24</td><td>West Virginia</td><td>41.2</td></tr>
<tr><td>33</td><td>Missouri</td><td>38.6</td><td>25</td><td>North Dakota</td><td>41.0</td></tr>
<tr><td>42</td><td>Montana</td><td>35.6</td><td>26</td><td>Arkansas</td><td>40.7</td></tr>
<tr><td>33</td><td>Nebraska</td><td>38.6</td><td>27</td><td>Kentucky</td><td>40.5</td></tr>
<tr><td>14</td><td>Nevada</td><td>45.0</td><td>28</td><td>Michigan</td><td>40.1</td></tr>
<tr><td>9</td><td>New Hampshire</td><td>45.8</td><td>29</td><td>Colorado</td><td>39.8</td></tr>
<tr><td>2</td><td>New Jersey</td><td>54.0</td><td>30</td><td>Delaware</td><td>39.6</td></tr>
<tr><td>43</td><td>New Mexico</td><td>35.5</td><td>31</td><td>Iowa</td><td>39.5</td></tr>
<tr><td>9</td><td>New York</td><td>45.8</td><td>32</td><td>Oklahoma</td><td>39.4</td></tr>
<tr><td>19</td><td>North Carolina</td><td>42.7</td><td>33</td><td>Idaho</td><td>38.6</td></tr>
<tr><td>25</td><td>North Dakota</td><td>41.0</td><td>33</td><td>Missouri</td><td>38.6</td></tr>
<tr><td>39</td><td>Ohio</td><td>37.8</td><td>33</td><td>Nebraska</td><td>38.6</td></tr>
<tr><td>32</td><td>Oklahoma</td><td>39.4</td><td>36</td><td>Utah</td><td>38.4</td></tr>
<tr><td>49</td><td>Oregon</td><td>30.5</td><td>37</td><td>Washington</td><td>38.1</td></tr>
<tr><td>17</td><td>Pennsylvania</td><td>43.1</td><td>38</td><td>Wyoming</td><td>38.0</td></tr>
<tr><td>20</td><td>Rhode Island</td><td>42.6</td><td>39</td><td>Ohio</td><td>37.8</td></tr>
<tr><td>45</td><td>South Carolina</td><td>35.0</td><td>40</td><td>Louisiana</td><td>37.6</td></tr>
<tr><td>46</td><td>South Dakota</td><td>33.8</td><td>41</td><td>California</td><td>37.0</td></tr>
<tr><td>44</td><td>Tennessee</td><td>35.2</td><td>42</td><td>Montana</td><td>35.6</td></tr>
<tr><td>22</td><td>Texas</td><td>41.9</td><td>43</td><td>New Mexico</td><td>35.5</td></tr>
<tr><td>36</td><td>Utah</td><td>38.4</td><td>44</td><td>Tennessee</td><td>35.2</td></tr>
<tr><td>6</td><td>Vermont</td><td>46.1</td><td>45</td><td>South Carolina</td><td>35.0</td></tr>
<tr><td>8</td><td>Virginia</td><td>45.9</td><td>46</td><td>South Dakota</td><td>33.8</td></tr>
<tr><td>37</td><td>Washington</td><td>38.1</td><td>47</td><td>Alabama</td><td>33.1</td></tr>
<tr><td>24</td><td>West Virginia</td><td>41.2</td><td>48</td><td>Alaska</td><td>32.0</td></tr>
<tr><td>23</td><td>Wisconsin</td><td>41.8</td><td>49</td><td>Oregon</td><td>30.5</td></tr>
<tr><td>38</td><td>Wyoming</td><td>38.0</td><td>50</td><td>Mississippi</td><td>29.5</td></tr>
<tr><td></td><td></td><td></td><td></td><td>District of Columbia</td><td>45.6</td></tr>
</table>

Source: CQ Press using data from U.S. Bureau of the Census, Governments Division
"State and Local Government Finances 2006-2007" (http://www.census.gov/govs/estimate/index.html)

State and Local Government Tax Revenue
as a Percent of Personal Income in 2007
National Percent = 10.7% of Personal Income*

ALPHA ORDER

RANK	STATE	PERCENT
47	Alabama	8.8
1	Alaska	17.7
21	Arizona	10.7
29	Arkansas	10.2
15	California	11.0
46	Colorado	9.1
16	Connecticut	10.9
22	Delaware	10.6
29	Florida	10.2
35	Georgia	10.0
4	Hawaii	12.6
40	Idaho	9.7
26	Illinois	10.3
37	Indiana	9.9
26	Iowa	10.3
16	Kansas	10.9
25	Kentucky	10.4
9	Louisiana	11.4
6	Maine	12.2
29	Maryland	10.2
35	Massachusetts	10.0
19	Michigan	10.8
16	Minnesota	10.9
33	Mississippi	10.1
45	Missouri	9.2
33	Montana	10.1
22	Nebraska	10.6
37	Nevada	9.9
49	New Hampshire	8.4
7	New Jersey	11.8
7	New Mexico	11.8
2	New York	14.5
26	North Carolina	10.3
14	North Dakota	11.1
9	Ohio	11.4
42	Oklahoma	9.6
42	Oregon	9.6
19	Pennsylvania	10.8
11	Rhode Island	11.3
39	South Carolina	9.8
50	South Dakota	8.2
48	Tennessee	8.7
44	Texas	9.3
24	Utah	10.5
5	Vermont	12.5
40	Virginia	9.7
29	Washington	10.2
13	West Virginia	11.2
11	Wisconsin	11.3
3	Wyoming	13.3

RANK ORDER

RANK	STATE	PERCENT
1	Alaska	17.7
2	New York	14.5
3	Wyoming	13.3
4	Hawaii	12.6
5	Vermont	12.5
6	Maine	12.2
7	New Jersey	11.8
7	New Mexico	11.8
9	Louisiana	11.4
9	Ohio	11.4
11	Rhode Island	11.3
11	Wisconsin	11.3
13	West Virginia	11.2
14	North Dakota	11.1
15	California	11.0
16	Connecticut	10.9
16	Kansas	10.9
16	Minnesota	10.9
19	Michigan	10.8
19	Pennsylvania	10.8
21	Arizona	10.7
22	Delaware	10.6
22	Nebraska	10.6
24	Utah	10.5
25	Kentucky	10.4
26	Illinois	10.3
26	Iowa	10.3
26	North Carolina	10.3
29	Arkansas	10.2
29	Florida	10.2
29	Maryland	10.2
29	Washington	10.2
33	Mississippi	10.1
33	Montana	10.1
35	Georgia	10.0
35	Massachusetts	10.0
37	Indiana	9.9
37	Nevada	9.9
39	South Carolina	9.8
40	Idaho	9.7
40	Virginia	9.7
42	Oklahoma	9.6
42	Oregon	9.6
44	Texas	9.3
45	Missouri	9.2
46	Colorado	9.1
47	Alabama	8.8
48	Tennessee	8.7
49	New Hampshire	8.4
50	South Dakota	8.2

District of Columbia 13.8

Source: CQ Press using data from Bureau of Economic Analysis and U.S. Census Bureau
"Annual State Personal Income" (http://www.bea.gov/regional/spi/) and
"State and Local Government Finances 2006-2007" (http://www.census.gov/govs/estimate/index.html)
*The personal income total used for this table is the sum of state estimates. This total differs from the national income and product accounts (NIPA) estimate of personal income because it omits the earnings of federal civilian and military personnel stationed abroad and of U.S. residents employed abroad temporarily by private U.S. firms.

State and Local Government General Sales Tax Revenue in 2007

National Total = $299,232,314,000*

ALPHA ORDER

RANK	STATE	REVENUE	% of USA
23	Alabama	$4,024,592,000	1.3%
46	Alaska	179,427,000	0.1%
8	Arizona	9,365,648,000	3.1%
24	Arkansas	3,788,833,000	1.3%
1	California	41,900,336,000	14.0%
17	Colorado	5,067,255,000	1.7%
30	Connecticut	3,030,353,000	1.0%
47	Delaware	0	0.0%
3	Florida	24,195,392,000	8.1%
6	Georgia	9,886,053,000	3.3%
35	Hawaii	2,557,644,000	0.9%
38	Idaho	1,279,199,000	0.4%
9	Illinois	9,143,042,000	3.1%
16	Indiana	5,423,501,000	1.8%
36	Iowa	2,320,660,000	0.8%
31	Kansas	3,016,119,000	1.0%
32	Kentucky	2,817,636,000	0.9%
15	Louisiana	7,045,914,000	2.4%
40	Maine	1,054,812,000	0.4%
26	Maryland	3,447,828,000	1.2%
22	Massachusetts	4,075,549,000	1.4%
13	Michigan	7,983,098,000	2.7%
20	Minnesota	4,545,576,000	1.5%
29	Mississippi	3,156,462,000	1.1%
18	Missouri	5,020,230,000	1.7%
47	Montana	0	0.0%
37	Nebraska	1,735,754,000	0.6%
25	Nevada	3,532,908,000	1.2%
47	New Hampshire	0	0.0%
11	New Jersey	8,609,639,000	2.9%
33	New Mexico	2,689,355,000	0.9%
4	New York	21,990,539,000	7.3%
14	North Carolina	7,116,554,000	2.4%
44	North Dakota	570,551,000	0.2%
7	Ohio	9,404,320,000	3.1%
27	Oklahoma	3,405,211,000	1.1%
47	Oregon	0	0.0%
10	Pennsylvania	8,873,053,000	3.0%
43	Rhode Island	875,619,000	0.3%
28	South Carolina	3,353,364,000	1.1%
41	South Dakota	969,211,000	0.3%
12	Tennessee	8,453,679,000	2.8%
2	Texas	25,314,527,000	8.5%
34	Utah	2,560,427,000	0.9%
45	Vermont	339,903,000	0.1%
19	Virginia	4,695,496,000	1.6%
5	Washington	13,082,548,000	4.4%
39	West Virginia	1,131,459,000	0.4%
21	Wisconsin	4,445,533,000	1.5%
42	Wyoming	919,096,000	0.3%

RANK ORDER

RANK	STATE	REVENUE	% of USA
1	California	$41,900,336,000	14.0%
2	Texas	25,314,527,000	8.5%
3	Florida	24,195,392,000	8.1%
4	New York	21,990,539,000	7.3%
5	Washington	13,082,548,000	4.4%
6	Georgia	9,886,053,000	3.3%
7	Ohio	9,404,320,000	3.1%
8	Arizona	9,365,648,000	3.1%
9	Illinois	9,143,042,000	3.1%
10	Pennsylvania	8,873,053,000	3.0%
11	New Jersey	8,609,639,000	2.9%
12	Tennessee	8,453,679,000	2.8%
13	Michigan	7,983,098,000	2.7%
14	North Carolina	7,116,554,000	2.4%
15	Louisiana	7,045,914,000	2.4%
16	Indiana	5,423,501,000	1.8%
17	Colorado	5,067,255,000	1.7%
18	Missouri	5,020,230,000	1.7%
19	Virginia	4,695,496,000	1.6%
20	Minnesota	4,545,576,000	1.5%
21	Wisconsin	4,445,533,000	1.5%
22	Massachusetts	4,075,549,000	1.4%
23	Alabama	4,024,592,000	1.3%
24	Arkansas	3,788,833,000	1.3%
25	Nevada	3,532,908,000	1.2%
26	Maryland	3,447,828,000	1.2%
27	Oklahoma	3,405,211,000	1.1%
28	South Carolina	3,353,364,000	1.1%
29	Mississippi	3,156,462,000	1.1%
30	Connecticut	3,030,353,000	1.0%
31	Kansas	3,016,119,000	1.0%
32	Kentucky	2,817,636,000	0.9%
33	New Mexico	2,689,355,000	0.9%
34	Utah	2,560,427,000	0.9%
35	Hawaii	2,557,644,000	0.9%
36	Iowa	2,320,660,000	0.8%
37	Nebraska	1,735,754,000	0.6%
38	Idaho	1,279,199,000	0.4%
39	West Virginia	1,131,459,000	0.4%
40	Maine	1,054,812,000	0.4%
41	South Dakota	969,211,000	0.3%
42	Wyoming	919,096,000	0.3%
43	Rhode Island	875,619,000	0.3%
44	North Dakota	570,551,000	0.2%
45	Vermont	339,903,000	0.1%
46	Alaska	179,427,000	0.1%
47	Delaware	0	0.0%
47	Montana	0	0.0%
47	New Hampshire	0	0.0%
47	Oregon	0	0.0%
	District of Columbia	838,409,000	0.3%

Source: U.S. Bureau of the Census, Governments Division
"State and Local Government Finances 2006-2007" (http://www.census.gov/govs/estimate/index.html)
*Does not include special sales taxes such as those on sale of alcohol, gasoline, or tobacco.

Per Capita State and Local Government General Sales Tax Revenue in 2007

National Per Capita = $992*

ALPHA ORDER				RANK ORDER		
RANK	STATE	PER CAPITA		RANK	STATE	PER CAPITA
26	Alabama	$868		1	Washington	$2,024
46	Alaska	263		2	Hawaii	2,003
5	Arizona	1,472		3	Wyoming	1,756
9	Arkansas	1,333		4	Louisiana	1,610
12	California	1,157		5	Arizona	1,472
17	Colorado	1,046		6	Nevada	1,376
25	Connecticut	869		7	Tennessee	1,369
47	Delaware	0		8	New Mexico	1,366
10	Florida	1,324		9	Arkansas	1,333
18	Georgia	1,037		10	Florida	1,324
2	Hawaii	2,003		11	South Dakota	1,216
28	Idaho	853		12	California	1,157
38	Illinois	715		13	New York	1,132
27	Indiana	855		14	Kansas	1,087
36	Iowa	779		15	Mississippi	1,080
14	Kansas	1,087		16	Texas	1,062
40	Kentucky	662		17	Colorado	1,046
4	Louisiana	1,610		18	Georgia	1,037
32	Maine	801		19	New Jersey	997
43	Maryland	612		20	Nebraska	981
41	Massachusetts	627		21	Utah	961
33	Michigan	794		22	Oklahoma	943
24	Minnesota	876		23	North Dakota	894
15	Mississippi	1,080		24	Minnesota	876
29	Missouri	849		25	Connecticut	869
47	Montana	0		26	Alabama	868
20	Nebraska	981		27	Indiana	855
6	Nevada	1,376		28	Idaho	853
47	New Hampshire	0		29	Missouri	849
19	New Jersey	997		30	Rhode Island	830
8	New Mexico	1,366		31	Ohio	816
13	New York	1,132		32	Maine	801
35	North Carolina	785		33	Michigan	794
23	North Dakota	894		33	Wisconsin	794
31	Ohio	816		35	North Carolina	785
22	Oklahoma	943		36	Iowa	779
47	Oregon	0		37	South Carolina	758
39	Pennsylvania	709		38	Illinois	715
30	Rhode Island	830		39	Pennsylvania	709
37	South Carolina	758		40	Kentucky	662
11	South Dakota	1,216		41	Massachusetts	627
7	Tennessee	1,369		42	West Virginia	625
16	Texas	1,062		43	Maryland	612
21	Utah	961		44	Virginia	608
45	Vermont	548		45	Vermont	548
44	Virginia	608		46	Alaska	263
1	Washington	2,024		47	Delaware	0
42	West Virginia	625		47	Montana	0
33	Wisconsin	794		47	New Hampshire	0
3	Wyoming	1,756		47	Oregon	0
					District of Columbia	1,430

Source: CQ Press using data from U.S. Bureau of the Census, Governments Division
   "State and Local Government Finances 2006-2007" (http://www.census.gov/govs/estimate/index.html)
*Does not include special sales taxes such as those on sale of alcohol, gasoline, or tobacco.

State and Local Government Property Tax Revenue in 2007

National Total = $383,100,800,000

ALPHA ORDER

RANK	STATE	REVENUE	% of USA
34	Alabama	$2,095,509,000	0.5%
46	Alaska	1,036,824,000	0.3%
18	Arizona	6,221,217,000	1.6%
39	Arkansas	1,348,784,000	0.4%
1	California	41,720,253,000	10.9%
21	Colorado	5,660,332,000	1.5%
14	Connecticut	8,070,674,000	2.1%
50	Delaware	568,858,000	0.1%
4	Florida	26,833,764,000	7.0%
12	Georgia	9,519,656,000	2.5%
42	Hawaii	1,136,744,000	0.3%
44	Idaho	1,114,771,000	0.3%
6	Illinois	20,461,677,000	5.3%
19	Indiana	6,146,902,000	1.6%
26	Iowa	3,615,818,000	0.9%
27	Kansas	3,458,667,000	0.9%
31	Kentucky	2,580,082,000	0.7%
30	Louisiana	2,610,610,000	0.7%
35	Maine	2,058,663,000	0.5%
17	Maryland	6,547,182,000	1.7%
10	Massachusetts	11,041,925,000	2.9%
8	Michigan	14,537,374,000	3.8%
20	Minnesota	6,119,214,000	1.6%
33	Mississippi	2,206,445,000	0.6%
22	Missouri	5,258,109,000	1.4%
45	Montana	1,106,838,000	0.3%
32	Nebraska	2,388,497,000	0.6%
29	Nevada	2,874,957,000	0.8%
28	New Hampshire	2,911,703,000	0.8%
5	New Jersey	21,485,654,000	5.6%
47	New Mexico	1,009,890,000	0.3%
2	New York	38,077,006,000	9.9%
16	North Carolina	7,306,444,000	1.9%
49	North Dakota	698,403,000	0.2%
9	Ohio	13,349,114,000	3.5%
38	Oklahoma	1,931,218,000	0.5%
25	Oregon	3,957,923,000	1.0%
7	Pennsylvania	15,462,920,000	4.0%
37	Rhode Island	1,963,620,000	0.5%
24	South Carolina	4,294,654,000	1.1%
48	South Dakota	820,321,000	0.2%
23	Tennessee	4,375,223,000	1.1%
3	Texas	34,193,824,000	8.9%
36	Utah	2,038,390,000	0.5%
40	Vermont	1,236,699,000	0.3%
11	Virginia	10,018,135,000	2.6%
15	Washington	7,372,865,000	1.9%
43	West Virginia	1,136,217,000	0.3%
13	Wisconsin	8,407,167,000	2.2%
41	Wyoming	1,197,016,000	0.3%

RANK ORDER

RANK	STATE	REVENUE	% of USA
1	California	$41,720,253,000	10.9%
2	New York	38,077,006,000	9.9%
3	Texas	34,193,824,000	8.9%
4	Florida	26,833,764,000	7.0%
5	New Jersey	21,485,654,000	5.6%
6	Illinois	20,461,677,000	5.3%
7	Pennsylvania	15,462,920,000	4.0%
8	Michigan	14,537,374,000	3.8%
9	Ohio	13,349,114,000	3.5%
10	Massachusetts	11,041,925,000	2.9%
11	Virginia	10,018,135,000	2.6%
12	Georgia	9,519,656,000	2.5%
13	Wisconsin	8,407,167,000	2.2%
14	Connecticut	8,070,674,000	2.1%
15	Washington	7,372,865,000	1.9%
16	North Carolina	7,306,444,000	1.9%
17	Maryland	6,547,182,000	1.7%
18	Arizona	6,221,217,000	1.6%
19	Indiana	6,146,902,000	1.6%
20	Minnesota	6,119,214,000	1.6%
21	Colorado	5,660,332,000	1.5%
22	Missouri	5,258,109,000	1.4%
23	Tennessee	4,375,223,000	1.1%
24	South Carolina	4,294,654,000	1.1%
25	Oregon	3,957,923,000	1.0%
26	Iowa	3,615,818,000	0.9%
27	Kansas	3,458,667,000	0.9%
28	New Hampshire	2,911,703,000	0.8%
29	Nevada	2,874,957,000	0.8%
30	Louisiana	2,610,610,000	0.7%
31	Kentucky	2,580,082,000	0.7%
32	Nebraska	2,388,497,000	0.6%
33	Mississippi	2,206,445,000	0.6%
34	Alabama	2,095,509,000	0.5%
35	Maine	2,058,663,000	0.5%
36	Utah	2,038,390,000	0.5%
37	Rhode Island	1,963,620,000	0.5%
38	Oklahoma	1,931,218,000	0.5%
39	Arkansas	1,348,784,000	0.4%
40	Vermont	1,236,699,000	0.3%
41	Wyoming	1,197,016,000	0.3%
42	Hawaii	1,136,744,000	0.3%
43	West Virginia	1,136,217,000	0.3%
44	Idaho	1,114,771,000	0.3%
45	Montana	1,106,838,000	0.3%
46	Alaska	1,036,824,000	0.3%
47	New Mexico	1,009,890,000	0.3%
48	South Dakota	820,321,000	0.2%
49	North Dakota	698,403,000	0.2%
50	Delaware	568,858,000	0.1%
	District of Columbia	1,516,048,000	0.4%

Source: U.S. Bureau of the Census, Governments Division
"State and Local Government Finances 2006-2007" (http://www.census.gov/govs/estimate/index.html)

Per Capita State and Local Government Property Tax Revenue in 2007

National Per Capita = $1,270

<table>
<tr><td colspan="3">ALPHA ORDER</td><td colspan="3">RANK ORDER</td></tr>
<tr><td>RANK</td><td>STATE</td><td>PER CAPITA</td><td>RANK</td><td>STATE</td><td>PER CAPITA</td></tr>
<tr><td>50</td><td>Alabama</td><td>$452</td><td>1</td><td>New Jersey</td><td>$2,488</td></tr>
<tr><td>11</td><td>Alaska</td><td>1,520</td><td>2</td><td>Connecticut</td><td>2,313</td></tr>
<tr><td>33</td><td>Arizona</td><td>978</td><td>3</td><td>Wyoming</td><td>2,287</td></tr>
<tr><td>49</td><td>Arkansas</td><td>475</td><td>4</td><td>New Hampshire</td><td>2,210</td></tr>
<tr><td>26</td><td>California</td><td>1,152</td><td>5</td><td>Vermont</td><td>1,993</td></tr>
<tr><td>22</td><td>Colorado</td><td>1,169</td><td>6</td><td>New York</td><td>1,960</td></tr>
<tr><td>2</td><td>Connecticut</td><td>2,313</td><td>7</td><td>Rhode Island</td><td>1,861</td></tr>
<tr><td>43</td><td>Delaware</td><td>658</td><td>8</td><td>Massachusetts</td><td>1,699</td></tr>
<tr><td>13</td><td>Florida</td><td>1,468</td><td>9</td><td>Illinois</td><td>1,601</td></tr>
<tr><td>32</td><td>Georgia</td><td>999</td><td>10</td><td>Maine</td><td>1,563</td></tr>
<tr><td>36</td><td>Hawaii</td><td>890</td><td>11</td><td>Alaska</td><td>1,520</td></tr>
<tr><td>41</td><td>Idaho</td><td>744</td><td>12</td><td>Wisconsin</td><td>1,501</td></tr>
<tr><td>9</td><td>Illinois</td><td>1,601</td><td>13</td><td>Florida</td><td>1,468</td></tr>
<tr><td>35</td><td>Indiana</td><td>969</td><td>14</td><td>Michigan</td><td>1,446</td></tr>
<tr><td>20</td><td>Iowa</td><td>1,214</td><td>15</td><td>Texas</td><td>1,434</td></tr>
<tr><td>18</td><td>Kansas</td><td>1,246</td><td>16</td><td>Nebraska</td><td>1,350</td></tr>
<tr><td>45</td><td>Kentucky</td><td>606</td><td>17</td><td>Virginia</td><td>1,298</td></tr>
<tr><td>46</td><td>Louisiana</td><td>597</td><td>18</td><td>Kansas</td><td>1,246</td></tr>
<tr><td>10</td><td>Maine</td><td>1,563</td><td>19</td><td>Pennsylvania</td><td>1,235</td></tr>
<tr><td>23</td><td>Maryland</td><td>1,162</td><td>20</td><td>Iowa</td><td>1,214</td></tr>
<tr><td>8</td><td>Massachusetts</td><td>1,699</td><td>21</td><td>Minnesota</td><td>1,179</td></tr>
<tr><td>14</td><td>Michigan</td><td>1,446</td><td>22</td><td>Colorado</td><td>1,169</td></tr>
<tr><td>21</td><td>Minnesota</td><td>1,179</td><td>23</td><td>Maryland</td><td>1,162</td></tr>
<tr><td>40</td><td>Mississippi</td><td>755</td><td>24</td><td>Ohio</td><td>1,159</td></tr>
<tr><td>36</td><td>Missouri</td><td>890</td><td>25</td><td>Montana</td><td>1,156</td></tr>
<tr><td>25</td><td>Montana</td><td>1,156</td><td>26</td><td>California</td><td>1,152</td></tr>
<tr><td>16</td><td>Nebraska</td><td>1,350</td><td>27</td><td>Washington</td><td>1,140</td></tr>
<tr><td>28</td><td>Nevada</td><td>1,120</td><td>28</td><td>Nevada</td><td>1,120</td></tr>
<tr><td>4</td><td>New Hampshire</td><td>2,210</td><td>29</td><td>North Dakota</td><td>1,094</td></tr>
<tr><td>1</td><td>New Jersey</td><td>2,488</td><td>30</td><td>Oregon</td><td>1,060</td></tr>
<tr><td>48</td><td>New Mexico</td><td>513</td><td>31</td><td>South Dakota</td><td>1,029</td></tr>
<tr><td>6</td><td>New York</td><td>1,960</td><td>32</td><td>Georgia</td><td>999</td></tr>
<tr><td>38</td><td>North Carolina</td><td>806</td><td>33</td><td>Arizona</td><td>978</td></tr>
<tr><td>29</td><td>North Dakota</td><td>1,094</td><td>34</td><td>South Carolina</td><td>971</td></tr>
<tr><td>24</td><td>Ohio</td><td>1,159</td><td>35</td><td>Indiana</td><td>969</td></tr>
<tr><td>47</td><td>Oklahoma</td><td>535</td><td>36</td><td>Hawaii</td><td>890</td></tr>
<tr><td>30</td><td>Oregon</td><td>1,060</td><td>36</td><td>Missouri</td><td>890</td></tr>
<tr><td>19</td><td>Pennsylvania</td><td>1,235</td><td>38</td><td>North Carolina</td><td>806</td></tr>
<tr><td>7</td><td>Rhode Island</td><td>1,861</td><td>39</td><td>Utah</td><td>765</td></tr>
<tr><td>34</td><td>South Carolina</td><td>971</td><td>40</td><td>Mississippi</td><td>755</td></tr>
<tr><td>31</td><td>South Dakota</td><td>1,029</td><td>41</td><td>Idaho</td><td>744</td></tr>
<tr><td>42</td><td>Tennessee</td><td>709</td><td>42</td><td>Tennessee</td><td>709</td></tr>
<tr><td>15</td><td>Texas</td><td>1,434</td><td>43</td><td>Delaware</td><td>658</td></tr>
<tr><td>39</td><td>Utah</td><td>765</td><td>44</td><td>West Virginia</td><td>627</td></tr>
<tr><td>5</td><td>Vermont</td><td>1,993</td><td>45</td><td>Kentucky</td><td>606</td></tr>
<tr><td>17</td><td>Virginia</td><td>1,298</td><td>46</td><td>Louisiana</td><td>597</td></tr>
<tr><td>27</td><td>Washington</td><td>1,140</td><td>47</td><td>Oklahoma</td><td>535</td></tr>
<tr><td>44</td><td>West Virginia</td><td>627</td><td>48</td><td>New Mexico</td><td>513</td></tr>
<tr><td>12</td><td>Wisconsin</td><td>1,501</td><td>49</td><td>Arkansas</td><td>475</td></tr>
<tr><td>3</td><td>Wyoming</td><td>2,287</td><td>50</td><td>Alabama</td><td>452</td></tr>
<tr><td colspan="3"></td><td colspan="2">District of Columbia</td><td>2,585</td></tr>
</table>

Source: CQ Press using data from U.S. Bureau of the Census, Governments Division
"State and Local Government Finances 2006-2007" (http://www.census.gov/govs/estimate/index.html)

State and Local Government Property Tax as a Percent of State and Local Government Total Revenue in 2007
National Percent = 12.5%

ALPHA ORDER

RANK	STATE	PERCENT
49	Alabama	5.2
44	Alaska	6.7
23	Arizona	12.1
47	Arkansas	6.0
37	California	8.9
23	Colorado	12.1
3	Connecticut	21.8
46	Delaware	6.2
11	Florida	15.5
20	Georgia	12.5
39	Hawaii	8.4
36	Idaho	9.0
7	Illinois	17.1
20	Indiana	12.5
16	Iowa	13.1
13	Kansas	14.6
42	Kentucky	7.6
48	Louisiana	5.6
8	Maine	16.6
23	Maryland	12.1
9	Massachusetts	15.7
9	Michigan	15.7
28	Minnesota	11.3
43	Mississippi	7.5
32	Missouri	10.6
23	Montana	12.1
18	Nebraska	12.9
22	Nevada	12.4
1	New Hampshire	28.1
2	New Jersey	22.5
50	New Mexico	4.8
17	New York	13.0
34	North Carolina	9.6
29	North Dakota	11.0
29	Ohio	11.0
45	Oklahoma	6.4
35	Oregon	9.5
19	Pennsylvania	12.7
5	Rhode Island	17.5
31	South Carolina	10.9
27	South Dakota	11.6
39	Tennessee	8.4
6	Texas	17.4
38	Utah	8.8
4	Vermont	19.4
14	Virginia	14.2
33	Washington	10.2
41	West Virginia	7.7
12	Wisconsin	15.1
15	Wyoming	14.0

RANK ORDER

RANK	STATE	PERCENT
1	New Hampshire	28.1
2	New Jersey	22.5
3	Connecticut	21.8
4	Vermont	19.4
5	Rhode Island	17.5
6	Texas	17.4
7	Illinois	17.1
8	Maine	16.6
9	Massachusetts	15.7
9	Michigan	15.7
11	Florida	15.5
12	Wisconsin	15.1
13	Kansas	14.6
14	Virginia	14.2
15	Wyoming	14.0
16	Iowa	13.1
17	New York	13.0
18	Nebraska	12.9
19	Pennsylvania	12.7
20	Georgia	12.5
20	Indiana	12.5
22	Nevada	12.4
23	Arizona	12.1
23	Colorado	12.1
23	Maryland	12.1
23	Montana	12.1
27	South Dakota	11.6
28	Minnesota	11.3
29	North Dakota	11.0
29	Ohio	11.0
31	South Carolina	10.9
32	Missouri	10.6
33	Washington	10.2
34	North Carolina	9.6
35	Oregon	9.5
36	Idaho	9.0
37	California	8.9
38	Utah	8.8
39	Hawaii	8.4
39	Tennessee	8.4
41	West Virginia	7.7
42	Kentucky	7.6
43	Mississippi	7.5
44	Alaska	6.7
45	Oklahoma	6.4
46	Delaware	6.2
47	Arkansas	6.0
48	Louisiana	5.6
49	Alabama	5.2
50	New Mexico	4.8

District of Columbia	13.3

Source: CQ Press using data from U.S. Bureau of the Census, Governments Division
"State and Local Government Finances 2006-2007" (http://www.census.gov/govs/estimate/index.html)

State and Local Government Property Tax Revenue as a Percent of State and Local Government Own Source Revenue in 2007
National Percent = 20.6%*

ALPHA ORDER

RANK	STATE	PERCENT
48	Alabama	8.9
47	Alaska	9.9
24	Arizona	19.1
45	Arkansas	10.2
35	California	16.4
24	Colorado	19.1
3	Connecticut	31.2
48	Delaware	8.9
12	Florida	24.2
23	Georgia	19.6
42	Hawaii	12.6
38	Idaho	14.9
6	Illinois	27.6
29	Indiana	18.3
20	Iowa	20.9
16	Kansas	21.6
41	Kentucky	12.8
46	Louisiana	10.0
8	Maine	26.7
28	Maryland	18.4
10	Massachusetts	25.0
11	Michigan	24.8
31	Minnesota	17.9
36	Mississippi	15.8
30	Missouri	18.2
16	Montana	21.6
15	Nebraska	21.9
26	Nevada	18.7
1	New Hampshire	42.4
2	New Jersey	32.1
50	New Mexico	8.5
18	New York	21.5
37	North Carolina	15.2
34	North Dakota	17.3
22	Ohio	20.0
44	Oklahoma	10.5
26	Oregon	18.7
21	Pennsylvania	20.8
5	Rhode Island	29.3
33	South Carolina	17.7
14	South Dakota	22.1
39	Tennessee	14.8
7	Texas	27.4
40	Utah	13.9
4	Vermont	30.6
19	Virginia	21.1
31	Washington	17.9
43	West Virginia	11.5
9	Wisconsin	25.6
13	Wyoming	22.8

RANK ORDER

RANK	STATE	PERCENT
1	New Hampshire	42.4
2	New Jersey	32.1
3	Connecticut	31.2
4	Vermont	30.6
5	Rhode Island	29.3
6	Illinois	27.6
7	Texas	27.4
8	Maine	26.7
9	Wisconsin	25.6
10	Massachusetts	25.0
11	Michigan	24.8
12	Florida	24.2
13	Wyoming	22.8
14	South Dakota	22.1
15	Nebraska	21.9
16	Kansas	21.6
16	Montana	21.6
18	New York	21.5
19	Virginia	21.1
20	Iowa	20.9
21	Pennsylvania	20.8
22	Ohio	20.0
23	Georgia	19.6
24	Arizona	19.1
24	Colorado	19.1
26	Nevada	18.7
26	Oregon	18.7
28	Maryland	18.4
29	Indiana	18.3
30	Missouri	18.2
31	Minnesota	17.9
31	Washington	17.9
33	South Carolina	17.7
34	North Dakota	17.3
35	California	16.4
36	Mississippi	15.8
37	North Carolina	15.2
38	Idaho	14.9
39	Tennessee	14.8
40	Utah	13.9
41	Kentucky	12.8
42	Hawaii	12.6
43	West Virginia	11.5
44	Oklahoma	10.5
45	Arkansas	10.2
46	Louisiana	10.0
47	Alaska	9.9
48	Alabama	8.9
48	Delaware	8.9
50	New Mexico	8.5

District of Columbia   22.5

Source: CQ Press using data from U.S. Bureau of the Census, Governments Division
   "State and Local Government Finances 2006-2007" (http://www.census.gov/govs/estimate/index.html)
*Own source revenue includes taxes, current charges, and miscellaneous general revenue. Excluded are intergovernmental transfers, insurance trust revenue, and revenue from government owned utilities and other commercial or auxiliary enterprise.

State and Local Tax Burden as a Percentage of Income in 2008

National Percent = 9.7% of Income*

ALPHA ORDER

RANK	STATE	PERCENT
38	Alabama	8.6
50	Alaska	6.4
41	Arizona	8.5
14	Arkansas	10.0
6	California	10.5
34	Colorado	9.0
3	Connecticut	11.1
23	Delaware	9.5
47	Florida	7.4
16	Georgia	9.9
5	Hawaii	10.6
13	Idaho	10.1
29	Illinois	9.3
25	Indiana	9.4
29	Iowa	9.3
21	Kansas	9.6
25	Kentucky	9.4
42	Louisiana	8.4
14	Maine	10.0
4	Maryland	10.8
23	Massachusetts	9.5
25	Michigan	9.4
9	Minnesota	10.2
35	Mississippi	8.9
32	Missouri	9.2
38	Montana	8.6
17	Nebraska	9.8
49	Nevada	6.6
46	New Hampshire	7.6
1	New Jersey	11.8
38	New Mexico	8.6
2	New York	11.7
17	North Carolina	9.8
32	North Dakota	9.2
7	Ohio	10.4
17	Oklahoma	9.8
25	Oregon	9.4
9	Pennsylvania	10.2
9	Rhode Island	10.2
37	South Carolina	8.8
45	South Dakota	7.9
44	Tennessee	8.3
42	Texas	8.4
21	Utah	9.6
8	Vermont	10.3
17	Virginia	9.8
35	Washington	8.9
29	West Virginia	9.3
9	Wisconsin	10.2
48	Wyoming	7.0

RANK ORDER

RANK	STATE	PERCENT
1	New Jersey	11.8
2	New York	11.7
3	Connecticut	11.1
4	Maryland	10.8
5	Hawaii	10.6
6	California	10.5
7	Ohio	10.4
8	Vermont	10.3
9	Minnesota	10.2
9	Pennsylvania	10.2
9	Rhode Island	10.2
9	Wisconsin	10.2
13	Idaho	10.1
14	Arkansas	10.0
14	Maine	10.0
16	Georgia	9.9
17	Nebraska	9.8
17	North Carolina	9.8
17	Oklahoma	9.8
17	Virginia	9.8
21	Kansas	9.6
21	Utah	9.6
23	Delaware	9.5
23	Massachusetts	9.5
25	Indiana	9.4
25	Kentucky	9.4
25	Michigan	9.4
25	Oregon	9.4
29	Illinois	9.3
29	Iowa	9.3
29	West Virginia	9.3
32	Missouri	9.2
32	North Dakota	9.2
34	Colorado	9.0
35	Mississippi	8.9
35	Washington	8.9
37	South Carolina	8.8
38	Alabama	8.6
38	Montana	8.6
38	New Mexico	8.6
41	Arizona	8.5
42	Louisiana	8.4
42	Texas	8.4
44	Tennessee	8.3
45	South Dakota	7.9
46	New Hampshire	7.6
47	Florida	7.4
48	Wyoming	7.0
49	Nevada	6.6
50	Alaska	6.4

District of Columbia   10.3

Source: The Tax Foundation
"State and Local Tax Burdens: All States, One Year, 1977-2008" (www.taxfoundation.org/research/show/336.html)
*All state and local taxes.

State and Local Government Total Expenditures in 2007

National Total = $2,667,921,122,000*

RANK	STATE	EXPENDITURES	% of USA
25	Alabama	$35,911,308,000	1.3%
40	Alaska	11,672,052,000	0.4%
17	Arizona	47,294,034,000	1.8%
35	Arkansas	19,128,997,000	0.7%
1	California	391,609,617,000	14.7%
22	Colorado	40,490,421,000	1.5%
26	Connecticut	33,197,713,000	1.2%
45	Delaware	8,702,076,000	0.3%
4	Florida	148,374,788,000	5.6%
10	Georgia	73,585,072,000	2.8%
39	Hawaii	12,166,556,000	0.5%
43	Idaho	9,936,932,000	0.4%
6	Illinois	108,476,220,000	4.1%
19	Indiana	46,691,217,000	1.8%
31	Iowa	24,248,183,000	0.9%
32	Kansas	21,157,383,000	0.8%
28	Kentucky	31,743,821,000	1.2%
23	Louisiana	39,234,653,000	1.5%
41	Maine	10,862,116,000	0.4%
16	Maryland	47,679,537,000	1.8%
12	Massachusetts	64,312,050,000	2.4%
9	Michigan	81,083,862,000	3.0%
18	Minnesota	47,221,920,000	1.8%
30	Mississippi	24,883,994,000	0.9%
21	Missouri	42,040,362,000	1.6%
46	Montana	7,448,776,000	0.3%
37	Nebraska	16,853,162,000	0.6%
33	Nevada	20,016,775,000	0.8%
44	New Hampshire	9,415,523,000	0.4%
8	New Jersey	87,091,981,000	3.3%
36	New Mexico	18,127,904,000	0.7%
2	New York	249,751,983,000	9.4%
11	North Carolina	68,138,085,000	2.6%
50	North Dakota	5,235,396,000	0.2%
7	Ohio	100,292,295,000	3.8%
29	Oklahoma	26,075,994,000	1.0%
27	Oregon	32,234,625,000	1.2%
5	Pennsylvania	108,925,964,000	4.1%
42	Rhode Island	10,073,478,000	0.4%
24	South Carolina	36,676,411,000	1.4%
49	South Dakota	5,585,661,000	0.2%
15	Tennessee	49,063,208,000	1.8%
3	Texas	171,226,241,000	6.4%
34	Utah	19,986,810,000	0.7%
48	Vermont	5,808,494,000	0.2%
14	Virginia	59,069,014,000	2.2%
13	Washington	62,544,533,000	2.3%
38	West Virginia	12,658,441,000	0.5%
20	Wisconsin	46,612,424,000	1.7%
47	Wyoming	6,718,313,000	0.3%

RANK	STATE	EXPENDITURES	% of USA
1	California	$391,609,617,000	14.7%
2	New York	249,751,983,000	9.4%
3	Texas	171,226,241,000	6.4%
4	Florida	148,374,788,000	5.6%
5	Pennsylvania	108,925,964,000	4.1%
6	Illinois	108,476,220,000	4.1%
7	Ohio	100,292,295,000	3.8%
8	New Jersey	87,091,981,000	3.3%
9	Michigan	81,083,862,000	3.0%
10	Georgia	73,585,072,000	2.8%
11	North Carolina	68,138,085,000	2.6%
12	Massachusetts	64,312,050,000	2.4%
13	Washington	62,544,533,000	2.3%
14	Virginia	59,069,014,000	2.2%
15	Tennessee	49,063,208,000	1.8%
16	Maryland	47,679,537,000	1.8%
17	Arizona	47,294,034,000	1.8%
18	Minnesota	47,221,920,000	1.8%
19	Indiana	46,691,217,000	1.8%
20	Wisconsin	46,612,424,000	1.7%
21	Missouri	42,040,362,000	1.6%
22	Colorado	40,490,421,000	1.5%
23	Louisiana	39,234,653,000	1.5%
24	South Carolina	36,676,411,000	1.4%
25	Alabama	35,911,308,000	1.3%
26	Connecticut	33,197,713,000	1.2%
27	Oregon	32,234,625,000	1.2%
28	Kentucky	31,743,821,000	1.2%
29	Oklahoma	26,075,994,000	1.0%
30	Mississippi	24,883,994,000	0.9%
31	Iowa	24,248,183,000	0.9%
32	Kansas	21,157,383,000	0.8%
33	Nevada	20,016,775,000	0.8%
34	Utah	19,986,810,000	0.7%
35	Arkansas	19,128,997,000	0.7%
36	New Mexico	18,127,904,000	0.7%
37	Nebraska	16,853,162,000	0.6%
38	West Virginia	12,658,441,000	0.5%
39	Hawaii	12,166,556,000	0.5%
40	Alaska	11,672,052,000	0.4%
41	Maine	10,862,116,000	0.4%
42	Rhode Island	10,073,478,000	0.4%
43	Idaho	9,936,932,000	0.4%
44	New Hampshire	9,415,523,000	0.4%
45	Delaware	8,702,076,000	0.3%
46	Montana	7,448,776,000	0.3%
47	Wyoming	6,718,313,000	0.3%
48	Vermont	5,808,494,000	0.2%
49	South Dakota	5,585,661,000	0.2%
50	North Dakota	5,235,396,000	0.2%
	District of Columbia	10,584,747,000	0.4%

Source: U.S. Bureau of the Census, Governments Division
   "State and Local Government Finances 2006-2007" (http://www.census.gov/govs/estimate/index.html)
*Total expenditures includes all money paid other than for retirement of debt and extension of loans. Includes payments from all sources of funds including current revenues and proceeds from borrowing and prior year fund balances. Includes intergovernmental transfers and expenditures for government owned utilities and other commercial or auxiliary enterprise, and insurance trust expenditures.

Per Capita State and Local Government Total Expenditures in 2007

National Per Capita = $8,846*

ALPHA ORDER

RANK	STATE	PER CAPITA		RANK	STATE	PER CAPITA
34	Alabama	$7,743		1	Alaska	$17,107
1	Alaska	17,107		2	New York	12,859
41	Arizona	7,434		3	Wyoming	12,836
49	Arkansas	6,730		4	California	10,810
4	California	10,810		5	New Jersey	10,085
23	Colorado	8,362		6	Delaware	10,061
12	Connecticut	9,516		7	Massachusetts	9,895
6	Delaware	10,061		8	Washington	9,674
29	Florida	8,118		9	Rhode Island	9,548
35	Georgia	7,718		10	Hawaii	9,529
10	Hawaii	9,529		11	Nebraska	9,522
50	Idaho	6,628		12	Connecticut	9,516
21	Illinois	8,488		13	Vermont	9,362
42	Indiana	7,357		14	New Mexico	9,208
28	Iowa	8,140		15	Minnesota	9,097
37	Kansas	7,623		16	Louisiana	8,966
40	Kentucky	7,458		17	Ohio	8,705
16	Louisiana	8,966		18	Pennsylvania	8,698
26	Maine	8,246		19	Oregon	8,635
22	Maryland	8,462		20	Mississippi	8,517
7	Massachusetts	9,895		21	Illinois	8,488
30	Michigan	8,067		22	Maryland	8,462
15	Minnesota	9,097		23	Colorado	8,362
20	Mississippi	8,517		24	Wisconsin	8,321
46	Missouri	7,114		25	South Carolina	8,290
33	Montana	7,782		26	Maine	8,246
11	Nebraska	9,522		27	North Dakota	8,203
32	Nevada	7,795		28	Iowa	8,140
45	New Hampshire	7,147		29	Florida	8,118
5	New Jersey	10,085		30	Michigan	8,067
14	New Mexico	9,208		31	Tennessee	7,948
2	New York	12,859		32	Nevada	7,795
38	North Carolina	7,517		33	Montana	7,782
27	North Dakota	8,203		34	Alabama	7,743
17	Ohio	8,705		35	Georgia	7,718
43	Oklahoma	7,219		36	Virginia	7,652
19	Oregon	8,635		37	Kansas	7,623
18	Pennsylvania	8,698		38	North Carolina	7,517
9	Rhode Island	9,548		39	Utah	7,503
25	South Carolina	8,290		40	Kentucky	7,458
47	South Dakota	7,008		41	Arizona	7,434
31	Tennessee	7,948		42	Indiana	7,357
44	Texas	7,183		43	Oklahoma	7,219
39	Utah	7,503		44	Texas	7,183
13	Vermont	9,362		45	New Hampshire	7,147
36	Virginia	7,652		46	Missouri	7,114
8	Washington	9,674		47	South Dakota	7,008
48	West Virginia	6,989		48	West Virginia	6,989
24	Wisconsin	8,321		49	Arkansas	6,730
3	Wyoming	12,836		50	Idaho	6,628

District of Columbia   18,050

Source: CQ Press using data from U.S. Bureau of the Census, Governments Division
"State and Local Government Finances 2006-2007" (http://www.census.gov/govs/estimate/index.html)
*Total expenditures includes all money paid other than for retirement of debt and extension of loans. Includes payments from all sources of funds including current revenues and proceeds from borrowing and prior year fund balances. Includes intergovernmental transfers and expenditures for government owned utilities and other commercial or auxiliary enterprise, and insurance trust expenditures.

State and Local Government Direct General Expenditures in 2007

National Total = $2,260,613,271,000*

ALPHA ORDER				RANK ORDER			
RANK	STATE	EXPENDITURES	% of USA	RANK	STATE	EXPENDITURES	% of USA
25	Alabama	$30,699,725,000	1.4%	1	California	$315,948,145,000	14.0%
40	Alaska	10,347,821,000	0.5%	2	New York	203,958,779,000	9.0%
19	Arizona	39,416,869,000	1.7%	3	Texas	147,466,764,000	6.5%
34	Arkansas	17,057,914,000	0.8%	4	Florida	130,530,382,000	5.8%
1	California	315,948,145,000	14.0%	5	Pennsylvania	93,496,829,000	4.1%
23	Colorado	33,599,540,000	1.5%	6	Illinois	90,689,586,000	4.0%
26	Connecticut	28,915,018,000	1.3%	7	Ohio	84,791,397,000	3.8%
45	Delaware	7,749,843,000	0.3%	8	New Jersey	74,976,042,000	3.3%
4	Florida	130,530,382,000	5.8%	9	Michigan	69,993,377,000	3.1%
10	Georgia	63,684,986,000	2.8%	10	Georgia	63,684,986,000	2.8%
39	Hawaii	10,932,793,000	0.5%	11	North Carolina	59,321,085,000	2.6%
42	Idaho	8,959,433,000	0.4%	12	Massachusetts	53,991,474,000	2.4%
6	Illinois	90,689,586,000	4.0%	13	Virginia	53,163,098,000	2.4%
16	Indiana	42,027,853,000	1.9%	14	Washington	49,920,286,000	2.2%
31	Iowa	21,634,423,000	1.0%	15	Maryland	42,571,976,000	1.9%
32	Kansas	18,735,663,000	0.8%	16	Indiana	42,027,853,000	1.9%
27	Kentucky	27,133,080,000	1.2%	17	Minnesota	40,939,634,000	1.8%
22	Louisiana	34,580,991,000	1.5%	18	Wisconsin	40,406,999,000	1.8%
41	Maine	10,045,219,000	0.4%	19	Arizona	39,416,869,000	1.7%
15	Maryland	42,571,976,000	1.9%	20	Missouri	36,647,428,000	1.6%
12	Massachusetts	53,991,474,000	2.4%	21	Tennessee	35,996,374,000	1.6%
9	Michigan	69,993,377,000	3.1%	22	Louisiana	34,580,991,000	1.5%
17	Minnesota	40,939,634,000	1.8%	23	Colorado	33,599,540,000	1.5%
30	Mississippi	22,278,457,000	1.0%	24	South Carolina	31,166,609,000	1.4%
20	Missouri	36,647,428,000	1.6%	25	Alabama	30,699,725,000	1.4%
46	Montana	6,650,592,000	0.3%	26	Connecticut	28,915,018,000	1.3%
37	Nebraska	12,521,904,000	0.6%	27	Kentucky	27,133,080,000	1.2%
33	Nevada	17,224,876,000	0.8%	28	Oregon	26,308,454,000	1.2%
44	New Hampshire	8,469,581,000	0.4%	29	Oklahoma	22,712,417,000	1.0%
8	New Jersey	74,976,042,000	3.3%	30	Mississippi	22,278,457,000	1.0%
36	New Mexico	16,219,771,000	0.7%	31	Iowa	21,634,423,000	1.0%
2	New York	203,958,779,000	9.0%	32	Kansas	18,735,663,000	0.8%
11	North Carolina	59,321,085,000	2.6%	33	Nevada	17,224,876,000	0.8%
50	North Dakota	4,738,673,000	0.2%	34	Arkansas	17,057,914,000	0.8%
7	Ohio	84,791,397,000	3.8%	35	Utah	16,759,751,000	0.7%
29	Oklahoma	22,712,417,000	1.0%	36	New Mexico	16,219,771,000	0.7%
28	Oregon	26,308,454,000	1.2%	37	Nebraska	12,521,904,000	0.6%
5	Pennsylvania	93,496,829,000	4.1%	38	West Virginia	11,852,681,000	0.5%
43	Rhode Island	8,589,924,000	0.4%	39	Hawaii	10,932,793,000	0.5%
24	South Carolina	31,166,609,000	1.4%	40	Alaska	10,347,821,000	0.5%
49	South Dakota	4,991,520,000	0.2%	41	Maine	10,045,219,000	0.4%
21	Tennessee	35,996,374,000	1.6%	42	Idaho	8,959,433,000	0.4%
3	Texas	147,466,764,000	6.5%	43	Rhode Island	8,589,924,000	0.4%
35	Utah	16,759,751,000	0.7%	44	New Hampshire	8,469,581,000	0.4%
48	Vermont	5,275,200,000	0.2%	45	Delaware	7,749,843,000	0.3%
13	Virginia	53,163,098,000	2.4%	46	Montana	6,650,592,000	0.3%
14	Washington	49,920,286,000	2.2%	47	Wyoming	6,041,600,000	0.3%
38	West Virginia	11,852,681,000	0.5%	48	Vermont	5,275,200,000	0.2%
18	Wisconsin	40,406,999,000	1.8%	49	South Dakota	4,991,520,000	0.2%
47	Wyoming	6,041,600,000	0.3%	50	North Dakota	4,738,673,000	0.2%
					District of Columbia	8,480,435,000	0.4%

Source: U.S. Bureau of the Census, Governments Division
  "State and Local Government Finances 2006-2007" (http://www.census.gov/govs/estimate/index.html)
*Direct general expenditures include expenditures for current operations, assistance and subsidies, interest on debt, and capital outlay. Excludes intergovernmental transfers, expenditures for government owned utilities and other commercial or auxiliary enterprise, and insurance trust expenditures.

Per Capita State and Local Government Direct General Expenditures in 2007

National Per Capita = $7,496*

ALPHA ORDER

RANK	STATE	PER CAPITA
37	Alabama	$6,619
1	Alaska	15,166
46	Arizona	6,195
48	Arkansas	6,002
5	California	8,722
31	Colorado	6,939
10	Connecticut	8,288
4	Delaware	8,960
24	Florida	7,141
35	Georgia	6,680
7	Hawaii	8,562
49	Idaho	5,976
25	Illinois	7,097
36	Indiana	6,623
22	Iowa	7,263
33	Kansas	6,750
41	Kentucky	6,375
13	Louisiana	7,902
16	Maine	7,626
18	Maryland	7,556
9	Massachusetts	8,307
29	Michigan	6,964
14	Minnesota	7,886
17	Mississippi	7,625
45	Missouri	6,201
30	Montana	6,948
26	Nebraska	7,075
34	Nevada	6,708
40	New Hampshire	6,429
6	New Jersey	8,682
11	New Mexico	8,239
3	New York	10,501
38	North Carolina	6,545
20	North Dakota	7,425
21	Ohio	7,360
43	Oklahoma	6,288
27	Oregon	7,048
19	Pennsylvania	7,466
12	Rhode Island	8,142
28	South Carolina	7,045
44	South Dakota	6,263
50	Tennessee	5,831
47	Texas	6,186
42	Utah	6,292
8	Vermont	8,502
32	Virginia	6,887
15	Washington	7,722
39	West Virginia	6,544
23	Wisconsin	7,214
2	Wyoming	11,543

RANK ORDER

RANK	STATE	PER CAPITA
1	Alaska	$15,166
2	Wyoming	11,543
3	New York	10,501
4	Delaware	8,960
5	California	8,722
6	New Jersey	8,682
7	Hawaii	8,562
8	Vermont	8,502
9	Massachusetts	8,307
10	Connecticut	8,288
11	New Mexico	8,239
12	Rhode Island	8,142
13	Louisiana	7,902
14	Minnesota	7,886
15	Washington	7,722
16	Maine	7,626
17	Mississippi	7,625
18	Maryland	7,556
19	Pennsylvania	7,466
20	North Dakota	7,425
21	Ohio	7,360
22	Iowa	7,263
23	Wisconsin	7,214
24	Florida	7,141
25	Illinois	7,097
26	Nebraska	7,075
27	Oregon	7,048
28	South Carolina	7,045
29	Michigan	6,964
30	Montana	6,948
31	Colorado	6,939
32	Virginia	6,887
33	Kansas	6,750
34	Nevada	6,708
35	Georgia	6,680
36	Indiana	6,623
37	Alabama	6,619
38	North Carolina	6,545
39	West Virginia	6,544
40	New Hampshire	6,429
41	Kentucky	6,375
42	Utah	6,292
43	Oklahoma	6,288
44	South Dakota	6,263
45	Missouri	6,201
46	Arizona	6,195
47	Texas	6,186
48	Arkansas	6,002
49	Idaho	5,976
50	Tennessee	5,831

District of Columbia	14,462

Source: CQ Press using data from U.S. Bureau of the Census, Governments Division
"State and Local Government Finances 2006-2007" (http://www.census.gov/govs/estimate/index.html)
*Direct general expenditures include expenditures for current operations, assistance and subsidies, interest on debt, and capital outlay. Excludes intergovernmental transfers, expenditures for government owned utilities and other commercial or auxiliary enterprise, and insurance trust expenditures.

State and Local Government Debt Outstanding in 2007

National Total = $2,409,735,658,000*

ALPHA ORDER

RANK	STATE	DEBT	% of USA
28	Alabama	$24,588,876,000	1.0%
41	Alaska	9,997,365,000	0.4%
18	Arizona	39,330,127,000	1.6%
35	Arkansas	12,209,979,000	0.5%
1	California	330,150,197,000	13.7%
15	Colorado	46,185,886,000	1.9%
25	Connecticut	32,726,987,000	1.4%
44	Delaware	7,372,297,000	0.3%
4	Florida	133,954,511,000	5.6%
14	Georgia	48,462,885,000	2.0%
39	Hawaii	10,335,062,000	0.4%
46	Idaho	5,228,718,000	0.2%
5	Illinois	116,536,798,000	4.8%
17	Indiana	41,527,827,000	1.7%
33	Iowa	14,771,928,000	0.6%
30	Kansas	19,702,116,000	0.8%
21	Kentucky	36,771,491,000	1.5%
27	Louisiana	28,115,924,000	1.2%
43	Maine	7,985,668,000	0.3%
23	Maryland	34,453,591,000	1.4%
7	Massachusetts	89,641,103,000	3.7%
9	Michigan	73,082,101,000	3.0%
20	Minnesota	38,710,749,000	1.6%
34	Mississippi	12,556,063,000	0.5%
19	Missouri	38,816,919,000	1.6%
45	Montana	6,161,569,000	0.3%
37	Nebraska	11,516,101,000	0.5%
29	Nevada	22,083,059,000	0.9%
40	New Hampshire	10,253,124,000	0.4%
8	New Jersey	85,696,936,000	3.6%
36	New Mexico	12,194,625,000	0.5%
2	New York	259,517,419,000	10.8%
13	North Carolina	50,154,710,000	2.1%
49	North Dakota	3,631,762,000	0.2%
10	Ohio	68,172,350,000	2.8%
31	Oklahoma	16,565,656,000	0.7%
26	Oregon	28,946,400,000	1.2%
6	Pennsylvania	111,912,187,000	4.6%
38	Rhode Island	10,498,135,000	0.4%
22	South Carolina	35,870,206,000	1.5%
47	South Dakota	4,853,849,000	0.2%
24	Tennessee	33,980,198,000	1.4%
3	Texas	189,396,988,000	7.9%
32	Utah	15,924,509,000	0.7%
48	Vermont	4,048,370,000	0.2%
12	Virginia	50,976,455,000	2.1%
11	Washington	62,109,246,000	2.6%
42	West Virginia	9,082,567,000	0.4%
16	Wisconsin	41,818,829,000	1.7%
50	Wyoming	2,239,393,000	0.1%

RANK ORDER

RANK	STATE	DEBT	% of USA
1	California	$330,150,197,000	13.7%
2	New York	259,517,419,000	10.8%
3	Texas	189,396,988,000	7.9%
4	Florida	133,954,511,000	5.6%
5	Illinois	116,536,798,000	4.8%
6	Pennsylvania	111,912,187,000	4.6%
7	Massachusetts	89,641,103,000	3.7%
8	New Jersey	85,696,936,000	3.6%
9	Michigan	73,082,101,000	3.0%
10	Ohio	68,172,350,000	2.8%
11	Washington	62,109,246,000	2.6%
12	Virginia	50,976,455,000	2.1%
13	North Carolina	50,154,710,000	2.1%
14	Georgia	48,462,885,000	2.0%
15	Colorado	46,185,886,000	1.9%
16	Wisconsin	41,818,829,000	1.7%
17	Indiana	41,527,827,000	1.7%
18	Arizona	39,330,127,000	1.6%
19	Missouri	38,816,919,000	1.6%
20	Minnesota	38,710,749,000	1.6%
21	Kentucky	36,771,491,000	1.5%
22	South Carolina	35,870,206,000	1.5%
23	Maryland	34,453,591,000	1.4%
24	Tennessee	33,980,198,000	1.4%
25	Connecticut	32,726,987,000	1.4%
26	Oregon	28,946,400,000	1.2%
27	Louisiana	28,115,924,000	1.2%
28	Alabama	24,588,876,000	1.0%
29	Nevada	22,083,059,000	0.9%
30	Kansas	19,702,116,000	0.8%
31	Oklahoma	16,565,656,000	0.7%
32	Utah	15,924,509,000	0.7%
33	Iowa	14,771,928,000	0.6%
34	Mississippi	12,556,063,000	0.5%
35	Arkansas	12,209,979,000	0.5%
36	New Mexico	12,194,625,000	0.5%
37	Nebraska	11,516,101,000	0.5%
38	Rhode Island	10,498,135,000	0.4%
39	Hawaii	10,335,062,000	0.4%
40	New Hampshire	10,253,124,000	0.4%
41	Alaska	9,997,365,000	0.4%
42	West Virginia	9,082,567,000	0.4%
43	Maine	7,985,668,000	0.3%
44	Delaware	7,372,297,000	0.3%
45	Montana	6,161,569,000	0.3%
46	Idaho	5,228,718,000	0.2%
47	South Dakota	4,853,849,000	0.2%
48	Vermont	4,048,370,000	0.2%
49	North Dakota	3,631,762,000	0.2%
50	Wyoming	2,239,393,000	0.1%

| | District of Columbia | 8,915,847,000 | 0.4% |

Source: U.S. Bureau of the Census, Governments Division
   "State and Local Government Finances 2006-2007" (http://www.census.gov/govs/estimate/index.html)
*Includes short-term, long-term, full faith and credit, nonguaranteed, and public debt for private purposes.

Per Capita State and Local Government Debt Outstanding in 2007

National Per Capita = $7,990*

ALPHA ORDER				RANK ORDER		
RANK	STATE	PER CAPITA		RANK	STATE	PER CAPITA
42	Alabama	$5,302		1	Alaska	$14,653
1	Alaska	14,653		2	Massachusetts	13,792
33	Arizona	6,182		3	New York	13,361
48	Arkansas	4,296		4	Rhode Island	9,951
10	California	9,114		5	New Jersey	9,923
7	Colorado	9,538		6	Washington	9,607
8	Connecticut	9,381		7	Colorado	9,538
14	Delaware	8,524		8	Connecticut	9,381
22	Florida	7,329		9	Illinois	9,119
43	Georgia	5,083		10	California	9,114
16	Hawaii	8,094		11	Pennsylvania	8,937
50	Idaho	3,488		12	Kentucky	8,639
9	Illinois	9,119		13	Nevada	8,600
27	Indiana	6,544		14	Delaware	8,524
45	Iowa	4,959		15	South Carolina	8,108
24	Kansas	7,098		16	Hawaii	8,094
12	Kentucky	8,639		17	Texas	7,945
31	Louisiana	6,425		18	New Hampshire	7,783
36	Maine	6,062		19	Oregon	7,754
34	Maryland	6,115		20	Wisconsin	7,466
2	Massachusetts	13,792		21	Minnesota	7,457
23	Michigan	7,271		22	Florida	7,329
21	Minnesota	7,457		23	Michigan	7,271
47	Mississippi	4,297		24	Kansas	7,098
26	Missouri	6,568		25	Virginia	6,603
30	Montana	6,437		26	Missouri	6,568
29	Nebraska	6,507		27	Indiana	6,544
13	Nevada	8,600		28	Vermont	6,525
18	New Hampshire	7,783		29	Nebraska	6,507
5	New Jersey	9,923		30	Montana	6,437
32	New Mexico	6,194		31	Louisiana	6,425
3	New York	13,361		32	New Mexico	6,194
40	North Carolina	5,533		33	Arizona	6,182
39	North Dakota	5,691		34	Maryland	6,115
38	Ohio	5,917		35	South Dakota	6,090
46	Oklahoma	4,586		36	Maine	6,062
19	Oregon	7,754		37	Utah	5,978
11	Pennsylvania	8,937		38	Ohio	5,917
4	Rhode Island	9,951		39	North Dakota	5,691
15	South Carolina	8,108		40	North Carolina	5,533
35	South Dakota	6,090		41	Tennessee	5,505
41	Tennessee	5,505		42	Alabama	5,302
17	Texas	7,945		43	Georgia	5,083
37	Utah	5,978		44	West Virginia	5,015
28	Vermont	6,525		45	Iowa	4,959
25	Virginia	6,603		46	Oklahoma	4,586
6	Washington	9,607		47	Mississippi	4,297
44	West Virginia	5,015		48	Arkansas	4,296
20	Wisconsin	7,466		49	Wyoming	4,278
49	Wyoming	4,278		50	Idaho	3,488

District of Columbia   15,204

Source: CQ Press using data from U.S. Bureau of the Census, Governments Division
"State and Local Government Finances 2006-2007" (http://www.census.gov/govs/estimate/index.html)
*Includes short-term, long-term, full faith and credit, nonguaranteed, and public debt for private purposes.

State and Local Government Full-Time Equivalent Employees in 2008

National Total = 16,668,184 FTE Employees*

ALPHA ORDER

RANK	STATE	EMPLOYEES	% of USA
20	Alabama	288,830	1.7%
44	Alaska	53,513	0.3%
18	Arizona	324,168	1.9%
33	Arkansas	166,044	1.0%
1	California	1,845,608	11.1%
24	Colorado	264,696	1.6%
30	Connecticut	191,593	1.1%
46	Delaware	50,682	0.3%
4	Florida	909,649	5.5%
9	Georgia	539,073	3.2%
41	Hawaii	74,727	0.4%
39	Idaho	81,301	0.5%
5	Illinois	647,750	3.9%
13	Indiana	354,182	2.1%
32	Iowa	182,333	1.1%
28	Kansas	195,117	1.2%
26	Kentucky	246,292	1.5%
22	Louisiana	282,279	1.7%
40	Maine	78,134	0.5%
19	Maryland	300,139	1.8%
15	Massachusetts	342,979	2.1%
11	Michigan	475,014	2.8%
23	Minnesota	280,399	1.7%
29	Mississippi	191,687	1.2%
17	Missouri	328,324	2.0%
43	Montana	55,191	0.3%
36	Nebraska	117,027	0.7%
37	Nevada	114,287	0.7%
42	New Hampshire	72,187	0.4%
10	New Jersey	506,476	3.0%
35	New Mexico	129,362	0.8%
3	New York	1,235,728	7.4%
8	North Carolina	566,792	3.4%
49	North Dakota	41,252	0.2%
6	Ohio	620,383	3.7%
27	Oklahoma	216,152	1.3%
31	Oregon	190,867	1.1%
7	Pennsylvania	595,202	3.6%
45	Rhode Island	52,004	0.3%
25	South Carolina	261,048	1.6%
48	South Dakota	43,439	0.3%
16	Tennessee	328,347	2.0%
2	Texas	1,370,719	8.2%
34	Utah	134,939	0.8%
50	Vermont	39,871	0.2%
12	Virginia	450,997	2.7%
14	Washington	349,729	2.1%
38	West Virginia	101,681	0.6%
21	Wisconsin	283,351	1.7%
47	Wyoming	49,400	0.3%

RANK ORDER

RANK	STATE	EMPLOYEES	% of USA
1	California	1,845,608	11.1%
2	Texas	1,370,719	8.2%
3	New York	1,235,728	7.4%
4	Florida	909,649	5.5%
5	Illinois	647,750	3.9%
6	Ohio	620,383	3.7%
7	Pennsylvania	595,202	3.6%
8	North Carolina	566,792	3.4%
9	Georgia	539,073	3.2%
10	New Jersey	506,476	3.0%
11	Michigan	475,014	2.8%
12	Virginia	450,997	2.7%
13	Indiana	354,182	2.1%
14	Washington	349,729	2.1%
15	Massachusetts	342,979	2.1%
16	Tennessee	328,347	2.0%
17	Missouri	328,324	2.0%
18	Arizona	324,168	1.9%
19	Maryland	300,139	1.8%
20	Alabama	288,830	1.7%
21	Wisconsin	283,351	1.7%
22	Louisiana	282,279	1.7%
23	Minnesota	280,399	1.7%
24	Colorado	264,696	1.6%
25	South Carolina	261,048	1.6%
26	Kentucky	246,292	1.5%
27	Oklahoma	216,152	1.3%
28	Kansas	195,117	1.2%
29	Mississippi	191,687	1.2%
30	Connecticut	191,593	1.1%
31	Oregon	190,867	1.1%
32	Iowa	182,333	1.1%
33	Arkansas	166,044	1.0%
34	Utah	134,939	0.8%
35	New Mexico	129,362	0.8%
36	Nebraska	117,027	0.7%
37	Nevada	114,287	0.7%
38	West Virginia	101,681	0.6%
39	Idaho	81,301	0.5%
40	Maine	78,134	0.5%
41	Hawaii	74,727	0.4%
42	New Hampshire	72,187	0.4%
43	Montana	55,191	0.3%
44	Alaska	53,513	0.3%
45	Rhode Island	52,004	0.3%
46	Delaware	50,682	0.3%
47	Wyoming	49,400	0.3%
48	South Dakota	43,439	0.3%
49	North Dakota	41,252	0.2%
50	Vermont	39,871	0.2%
	District of Columbia	47,240	0.3%

Source: U.S. Bureau of the Census, Governments Division
"Government Employment and Payroll" (http://www.census.gov/govs/apes/index.html)
*As of March 2008.

Rate of State and Local Government Full-Time Equivalent Employees in 2008

National Rate = 548 State/Local Government Employees per 10,000 Population*

ALPHA ORDER				RANK ORDER		
RANK	**STATE**	**RATE**		**RANK**	**STATE**	**RATE**
11	Alabama	617		1	Wyoming	927
2	Alaska	778		2	Alaska	778
44	Arizona	499		3	Kansas	698
19	Arkansas	579		4	Nebraska	657
40	California	505		5	Mississippi	652
33	Colorado	536		6	New Mexico	651
29	Connecticut	547		7	North Dakota	643
21	Delaware	578		8	Vermont	642
46	Florida	494		9	New York	635
26	Georgia	556		10	Louisiana	634
17	Hawaii	580		11	Alabama	617
36	Idaho	532		12	North Carolina	613
42	Illinois	504		13	Iowa	609
27	Indiana	554		14	Oklahoma	593
13	Iowa	609		15	Maine	592
3	Kansas	698		16	New Jersey	585
22	Kentucky	574		17	Hawaii	580
10	Louisiana	634		17	South Carolina	580
15	Maine	592		19	Arkansas	579
37	Maryland	530		19	Virginia	579
39	Massachusetts	524		21	Delaware	578
48	Michigan	475		22	Kentucky	574
33	Minnesota	536		23	Montana	570
5	Mississippi	652		24	Texas	564
28	Missouri	551		25	West Virginia	560
23	Montana	570		26	Georgia	556
4	Nebraska	657		27	Indiana	554
50	Nevada	437		28	Missouri	551
30	New Hampshire	546		29	Connecticut	547
16	New Jersey	585		30	New Hampshire	546
6	New Mexico	651		31	South Dakota	540
9	New York	635		32	Ohio	538
12	North Carolina	613		33	Colorado	536
7	North Dakota	643		33	Minnesota	536
32	Ohio	538		35	Washington	533
14	Oklahoma	593		36	Idaho	532
40	Oregon	505		37	Maryland	530
49	Pennsylvania	474		38	Tennessee	526
46	Rhode Island	494		39	Massachusetts	524
17	South Carolina	580		40	California	505
31	South Dakota	540		40	Oregon	505
38	Tennessee	526		42	Illinois	504
24	Texas	564		42	Wisconsin	504
45	Utah	495		44	Arizona	499
8	Vermont	642		45	Utah	495
19	Virginia	579		46	Florida	494
35	Washington	533		46	Rhode Island	494
25	West Virginia	560		48	Michigan	475
42	Wisconsin	504		49	Pennsylvania	474
1	Wyoming	927		50	Nevada	437
					District of Columbia	801

Source: CQ Press using data from U.S. Bureau of the Census, Governments Division
   "Government Employment and Payroll" (http://www.census.gov/govs/apes/index.html)
*As of March 2008.

Average Annual Earnings of Full-Time State and Local Government Employees in 2008
National Average = $50,479*

ALPHA ORDER

RANK	STATE	SALARY
40	Alabama	$40,846
9	Alaska	55,865
18	Arizona	50,185
49	Arkansas	36,961
1	California	68,488
16	Colorado	51,167
3	Connecticut	60,681
14	Delaware	51,897
24	Florida	47,624
36	Georgia	41,611
17	Hawaii	50,619
35	Idaho	41,788
13	Illinois	52,749
32	Indiana	43,040
22	Iowa	47,678
42	Kansas	40,735
45	Kentucky	39,332
43	Louisiana	40,719
34	Maine	41,827
7	Maryland	57,400
10	Massachusetts	55,246
11	Michigan	54,147
12	Minnesota	53,885
50	Mississippi	36,121
44	Missouri	39,629
37	Montana	41,566
29	Nebraska	44,112
5	Nevada	58,726
25	New Hampshire	47,201
2	New Jersey	63,458
41	New Mexico	40,789
4	New York	58,786
31	North Carolina	43,272
30	North Dakota	43,829
21	Ohio	48,724
47	Oklahoma	38,051
15	Oregon	51,516
20	Pennsylvania	48,787
8	Rhode Island	56,594
38	South Carolina	41,043
46	South Dakota	38,381
39	Tennessee	40,897
33	Texas	43,018
23	Utah	47,632
27	Vermont	46,134
26	Virginia	47,025
6	Washington	58,592
48	West Virginia	37,129
19	Wisconsin	49,761
28	Wyoming	45,857

RANK ORDER

RANK	STATE	SALARY
1	California	$68,488
2	New Jersey	63,458
3	Connecticut	60,681
4	New York	58,786
5	Nevada	58,726
6	Washington	58,592
7	Maryland	57,400
8	Rhode Island	56,594
9	Alaska	55,865
10	Massachusetts	55,246
11	Michigan	54,147
12	Minnesota	53,885
13	Illinois	52,749
14	Delaware	51,897
15	Oregon	51,516
16	Colorado	51,167
17	Hawaii	50,619
18	Arizona	50,185
19	Wisconsin	49,761
20	Pennsylvania	48,787
21	Ohio	48,724
22	Iowa	47,678
23	Utah	47,632
24	Florida	47,624
25	New Hampshire	47,201
26	Virginia	47,025
27	Vermont	46,134
28	Wyoming	45,857
29	Nebraska	44,112
30	North Dakota	43,829
31	North Carolina	43,272
32	Indiana	43,040
33	Texas	43,018
34	Maine	41,827
35	Idaho	41,788
36	Georgia	41,611
37	Montana	41,566
38	South Carolina	41,043
39	Tennessee	40,897
40	Alabama	40,846
41	New Mexico	40,789
42	Kansas	40,735
43	Louisiana	40,719
44	Missouri	39,629
45	Kentucky	39,332
46	South Dakota	38,381
47	Oklahoma	38,051
48	West Virginia	37,129
49	Arkansas	36,961
50	Mississippi	36,121
	District of Columbia	64,841

Source: CQ Press using data from U.S. Bureau of the Census, Governments Division
"Government Employment and Payroll" (http://www.census.gov/govs/apes/index.html)
*March 2008 full-time payroll (multiplied by 12) divided by full-time employees.

State Government Total Revenue in 2007

National Total = $2,000,211,558,000*

ALPHA ORDER					RANK ORDER			
RANK	STATE	REVENUE	% of USA		RANK	STATE	REVENUE	% of USA
24	Alabama	$27,536,360,000	1.4%		1	California	$299,948,562,000	15.0%
37	Alaska	12,723,515,000	0.6%		2	New York	178,908,359,000	8.9%
21	Arizona	31,885,916,000	1.6%		3	Texas	114,728,001,000	5.7%
32	Arkansas	18,175,873,000	0.9%		4	Florida	98,133,857,000	4.9%
1	California	299,948,562,000	15.0%		5	Ohio	87,604,512,000	4.4%
26	Colorado	26,892,432,000	1.3%		6	Pennsylvania	83,384,773,000	4.2%
27	Connecticut	25,492,170,000	1.3%		7	Illinois	70,742,539,000	3.5%
44	Delaware	7,432,741,000	0.4%		8	New Jersey	65,876,296,000	3.3%
4	Florida	98,133,857,000	4.9%		9	Michigan	63,056,739,000	3.2%
14	Georgia	45,212,826,000	2.3%		10	North Carolina	51,841,493,000	2.6%
39	Hawaii	11,172,950,000	0.6%		11	Massachusetts	49,455,210,000	2.5%
42	Idaho	9,095,154,000	0.5%		12	Virginia	47,251,108,000	2.4%
7	Illinois	70,742,539,000	3.5%		13	Washington	47,030,140,000	2.4%
20	Indiana	32,429,387,000	1.6%		14	Georgia	45,212,826,000	2.3%
31	Iowa	19,053,312,000	1.0%		15	Wisconsin	40,164,298,000	2.0%
35	Kansas	14,998,530,000	0.7%		16	Minnesota	38,733,292,000	1.9%
28	Kentucky	25,425,381,000	1.3%		17	Maryland	34,848,081,000	1.7%
18	Louisiana	33,395,630,000	1.7%		18	Louisiana	33,395,630,000	1.7%
41	Maine	9,434,179,000	0.5%		19	Missouri	32,729,141,000	1.6%
17	Maryland	34,848,081,000	1.7%		20	Indiana	32,429,387,000	1.6%
11	Massachusetts	49,455,210,000	2.5%		21	Arizona	31,885,916,000	1.6%
9	Michigan	63,056,739,000	3.2%		22	Oregon	30,556,715,000	1.5%
16	Minnesota	38,733,292,000	1.9%		23	Tennessee	29,488,884,000	1.5%
29	Mississippi	22,466,811,000	1.1%		24	Alabama	27,536,360,000	1.4%
19	Missouri	32,729,141,000	1.6%		25	South Carolina	27,530,567,000	1.4%
46	Montana	7,129,303,000	0.4%		26	Colorado	26,892,432,000	1.3%
40	Nebraska	9,991,123,000	0.5%		27	Connecticut	25,492,170,000	1.3%
36	Nevada	14,183,611,000	0.7%		28	Kentucky	25,425,381,000	1.3%
45	New Hampshire	7,171,927,000	0.4%		29	Mississippi	22,466,811,000	1.1%
8	New Jersey	65,876,296,000	3.3%		30	Oklahoma	22,329,933,000	1.1%
33	New Mexico	17,103,483,000	0.9%		31	Iowa	19,053,312,000	1.0%
2	New York	178,908,359,000	8.9%		32	Arkansas	18,175,873,000	0.9%
10	North Carolina	51,841,493,000	2.6%		33	New Mexico	17,103,483,000	0.9%
50	North Dakota	4,786,348,000	0.2%		34	Utah	15,868,687,000	0.8%
5	Ohio	87,604,512,000	4.4%		35	Kansas	14,998,530,000	0.7%
30	Oklahoma	22,329,933,000	1.1%		36	Nevada	14,183,611,000	0.7%
22	Oregon	30,556,715,000	1.5%		37	Alaska	12,723,515,000	0.6%
6	Pennsylvania	83,384,773,000	4.2%		38	West Virginia	11,931,058,000	0.6%
43	Rhode Island	8,417,797,000	0.4%		39	Hawaii	11,172,950,000	0.6%
25	South Carolina	27,530,567,000	1.4%		40	Nebraska	9,991,123,000	0.5%
49	South Dakota	4,929,034,000	0.2%		41	Maine	9,434,179,000	0.5%
23	Tennessee	29,488,884,000	1.5%		42	Idaho	9,095,154,000	0.5%
3	Texas	114,728,001,000	5.7%		43	Rhode Island	8,417,797,000	0.4%
34	Utah	15,868,687,000	0.8%		44	Delaware	7,432,741,000	0.4%
48	Vermont	5,442,194,000	0.3%		45	New Hampshire	7,171,927,000	0.4%
12	Virginia	47,251,108,000	2.4%		46	Montana	7,129,303,000	0.4%
13	Washington	47,030,140,000	2.4%		47	Wyoming	6,091,326,000	0.3%
38	West Virginia	11,931,058,000	0.6%		48	Vermont	5,442,194,000	0.3%
15	Wisconsin	40,164,298,000	2.0%		49	South Dakota	4,929,034,000	0.2%
47	Wyoming	6,091,326,000	0.3%		50	North Dakota	4,786,348,000	0.2%
					District of Columbia**		NA	NA

Source: U.S. Bureau of the Census, Governments Division
"State and Local Government Finances 2006-2007" (http://www.census.gov/govs/estimate/index.html)
*Total revenue includes all money received from external sources. This includes taxes, intergovernmental transfers and insurance trust revenue, and revenue from government owned utilities and other commercial or auxiliary enterprise.
**Not applicable.

Per Capita State Government Total Revenue in 2007

National Per Capita = $6,645*

ALPHA ORDER

RANK	STATE	PER CAPITA
36	Alabama	$5,937
1	Alaska	18,648
47	Arizona	5,012
26	Arkansas	6,395
8	California	8,280
39	Colorado	5,554
19	Connecticut	7,307
7	Delaware	8,594
45	Florida	5,369
50	Georgia	4,742
5	Hawaii	8,751
33	Idaho	6,066
41	Illinois	5,536
46	Indiana	5,110
25	Iowa	6,396
44	Kansas	5,404
34	Kentucky	5,974
12	Louisiana	7,631
22	Maine	7,162
29	Maryland	6,185
14	Massachusetts	7,609
27	Michigan	6,274
17	Minnesota	7,461
11	Mississippi	7,690
40	Missouri	5,538
18	Montana	7,448
38	Nebraska	5,645
42	Nevada	5,524
43	New Hampshire	5,444
13	New Jersey	7,628
6	New Mexico	8,688
3	New York	9,211
37	North Carolina	5,719
16	North Dakota	7,500
15	Ohio	7,604
31	Oklahoma	6,182
9	Oregon	8,186
23	Pennsylvania	6,659
10	Rhode Island	7,979
28	South Carolina	6,223
30	South Dakota	6,184
49	Tennessee	4,777
48	Texas	4,813
35	Utah	5,957
4	Vermont	8,771
32	Virginia	6,121
20	Washington	7,275
24	West Virginia	6,587
21	Wisconsin	7,170
2	Wyoming	11,638

RANK ORDER

RANK	STATE	PER CAPITA
1	Alaska	$18,648
2	Wyoming	11,638
3	New York	9,211
4	Vermont	8,771
5	Hawaii	8,751
6	New Mexico	8,688
7	Delaware	8,594
8	California	8,280
9	Oregon	8,186
10	Rhode Island	7,979
11	Mississippi	7,690
12	Louisiana	7,631
13	New Jersey	7,628
14	Massachusetts	7,609
15	Ohio	7,604
16	North Dakota	7,500
17	Minnesota	7,461
18	Montana	7,448
19	Connecticut	7,307
20	Washington	7,275
21	Wisconsin	7,170
22	Maine	7,162
23	Pennsylvania	6,659
24	West Virginia	6,587
25	Iowa	6,396
26	Arkansas	6,395
27	Michigan	6,274
28	South Carolina	6,223
29	Maryland	6,185
30	South Dakota	6,184
31	Oklahoma	6,182
32	Virginia	6,121
33	Idaho	6,066
34	Kentucky	5,974
35	Utah	5,957
36	Alabama	5,937
37	North Carolina	5,719
38	Nebraska	5,645
39	Colorado	5,554
40	Missouri	5,538
41	Illinois	5,536
42	Nevada	5,524
43	New Hampshire	5,444
44	Kansas	5,404
45	Florida	5,369
46	Indiana	5,110
47	Arizona	5,012
48	Texas	4,813
49	Tennessee	4,777
50	Georgia	4,742
	District of Columbia**	NA

Source: CQ Press using data from U.S. Bureau of the Census, Governments Division
"State and Local Government Finances 2006-2007" (http://www.census.gov/govs/estimate/index.html)
*Total revenue includes all money received from external sources. This includes taxes, intergovernmental transfers and insurance trust revenue, and revenue from government owned utilities and other commercial or auxiliary enterprise.
**Not applicable.

State Government Intergovernmental Revenue in 2007

National Total = $430,242,378,000*

ALPHA ORDER					RANK ORDER			
RANK	STATE	REVENUE	% of USA		RANK	STATE	REVENUE	% of USA
20	Alabama	$7,732,269,000	1.8%		1	California	$49,889,749,000	11.6%
39	Alaska	2,288,253,000	0.5%		2	New York	47,324,109,000	11.0%
16	Arizona	8,123,983,000	1.9%		3	Texas	28,277,613,000	6.6%
31	Arkansas	4,286,094,000	1.0%		4	Florida	19,239,807,000	4.5%
1	California	49,889,749,000	11.6%		5	Ohio	16,691,614,000	3.9%
28	Colorado	4,732,975,000	1.1%		6	Pennsylvania	16,323,614,000	3.8%
33	Connecticut	4,167,175,000	1.0%		7	Illinois	14,234,320,000	3.3%
49	Delaware	1,241,741,000	0.3%		8	North Carolina	13,231,264,000	3.1%
4	Florida	19,239,807,000	4.5%		9	Michigan	13,083,153,000	3.0%
10	Georgia	13,005,370,000	3.0%		10	Georgia	13,005,370,000	3.0%
42	Hawaii	2,063,945,000	0.5%		11	Louisiana	12,417,474,000	2.9%
44	Idaho	1,842,758,000	0.4%		12	New Jersey	11,462,648,000	2.7%
7	Illinois	14,234,320,000	3.3%		13	Massachusetts	9,617,501,000	2.2%
18	Indiana	7,941,998,000	1.8%		14	Mississippi	9,167,368,000	2.1%
30	Iowa	4,378,744,000	1.0%		15	Tennessee	8,341,938,000	1.9%
35	Kansas	3,156,389,000	0.7%		16	Arizona	8,123,983,000	1.9%
26	Kentucky	6,338,156,000	1.5%		17	Missouri	8,005,044,000	1.9%
11	Louisiana	12,417,474,000	2.9%		18	Indiana	7,941,998,000	1.8%
38	Maine	2,393,954,000	0.6%		19	Washington	7,892,810,000	1.8%
21	Maryland	7,199,413,000	1.7%		20	Alabama	7,732,269,000	1.8%
13	Massachusetts	9,617,501,000	2.2%		21	Maryland	7,199,413,000	1.7%
9	Michigan	13,083,153,000	3.0%		22	South Carolina	7,097,636,000	1.6%
25	Minnesota	6,680,661,000	1.6%		23	Virginia	6,883,654,000	1.6%
14	Mississippi	9,167,368,000	2.1%		24	Wisconsin	6,769,288,000	1.6%
17	Missouri	8,005,044,000	1.9%		25	Minnesota	6,680,661,000	1.6%
45	Montana	1,813,956,000	0.4%		26	Kentucky	6,338,156,000	1.5%
37	Nebraska	2,532,557,000	0.6%		27	Oklahoma	5,406,356,000	1.3%
40	Nevada	2,091,256,000	0.5%		28	Colorado	4,732,975,000	1.1%
46	New Hampshire	1,775,088,000	0.4%		29	Oregon	4,623,287,000	1.1%
12	New Jersey	11,462,648,000	2.7%		30	Iowa	4,378,744,000	1.0%
32	New Mexico	4,219,834,000	1.0%		31	Arkansas	4,286,094,000	1.0%
2	New York	47,324,109,000	11.0%		32	New Mexico	4,219,834,000	1.0%
8	North Carolina	13,231,264,000	3.1%		33	Connecticut	4,167,175,000	1.0%
50	North Dakota	1,227,870,000	0.3%		34	West Virginia	3,256,627,000	0.8%
5	Ohio	16,691,614,000	3.9%		35	Kansas	3,156,389,000	0.7%
27	Oklahoma	5,406,356,000	1.3%		36	Utah	3,081,010,000	0.7%
29	Oregon	4,623,287,000	1.1%		37	Nebraska	2,532,557,000	0.6%
6	Pennsylvania	16,323,614,000	3.8%		38	Maine	2,393,954,000	0.6%
41	Rhode Island	2,086,752,000	0.5%		39	Alaska	2,288,253,000	0.5%
22	South Carolina	7,097,636,000	1.6%		40	Nevada	2,091,256,000	0.5%
48	South Dakota	1,276,075,000	0.3%		41	Rhode Island	2,086,752,000	0.5%
15	Tennessee	8,341,938,000	1.9%		42	Hawaii	2,063,945,000	0.5%
3	Texas	28,277,613,000	6.6%		43	Wyoming	1,947,258,000	0.5%
36	Utah	3,081,010,000	0.7%		44	Idaho	1,842,758,000	0.4%
47	Vermont	1,379,970,000	0.3%		45	Montana	1,813,956,000	0.4%
23	Virginia	6,883,654,000	1.6%		46	New Hampshire	1,775,088,000	0.4%
19	Washington	7,892,810,000	1.8%		47	Vermont	1,379,970,000	0.3%
34	West Virginia	3,256,627,000	0.8%		48	South Dakota	1,276,075,000	0.3%
24	Wisconsin	6,769,288,000	1.6%		49	Delaware	1,241,741,000	0.3%
43	Wyoming	1,947,258,000	0.5%		50	North Dakota	1,227,870,000	0.3%
					District of Columbia**		NA	NA

Source: U.S. Bureau of the Census, Governments Division
"State and Local Government Finances 2006-2007" (http://www.census.gov/govs/estimate/index.html)
*Includes revenue from federal and local government sources.
**Not applicable.

Per Capita State Government Intergovernmental Revenue in 2007

National Per Capita = $1,429*

ALPHA ORDER

RANK ORDER

RANK	STATE	PER CAPITA		RANK	STATE	PER CAPITA
13	Alabama	$1,667		1	Wyoming	$3,720
2	Alaska	3,354		2	Alaska	3,354
36	Arizona	1,277		3	Mississippi	3,138
17	Arkansas	1,508		4	Louisiana	2,838
26	California	1,377		5	New York	2,437
48	Colorado	977		6	Vermont	2,224
42	Connecticut	1,195		7	New Mexico	2,143
24	Delaware	1,436		8	Rhode Island	1,978
47	Florida	1,053		9	North Dakota	1,924
27	Georgia	1,364		10	Montana	1,895
14	Hawaii	1,616		11	Maine	1,817
39	Idaho	1,229		12	West Virginia	1,798
46	Illinois	1,114		13	Alabama	1,667
37	Indiana	1,251		14	Hawaii	1,616
21	Iowa	1,470		15	South Carolina	1,604
45	Kansas	1,137		16	South Dakota	1,601
19	Kentucky	1,489		17	Arkansas	1,508
4	Louisiana	2,838		18	Oklahoma	1,497
11	Maine	1,817		19	Kentucky	1,489
35	Maryland	1,278		20	Massachusetts	1,480
20	Massachusetts	1,480		21	Iowa	1,470
33	Michigan	1,302		22	North Carolina	1,460
34	Minnesota	1,287		23	Ohio	1,449
3	Mississippi	3,138		24	Delaware	1,436
28	Missouri	1,355		25	Nebraska	1,431
10	Montana	1,895		26	California	1,377
25	Nebraska	1,431		27	Georgia	1,364
50	Nevada	814		28	Missouri	1,355
30	New Hampshire	1,347		29	Tennessee	1,351
31	New Jersey	1,327		30	New Hampshire	1,347
7	New Mexico	2,143		31	New Jersey	1,327
5	New York	2,437		32	Pennsylvania	1,304
22	North Carolina	1,460		33	Michigan	1,302
9	North Dakota	1,924		34	Minnesota	1,287
23	Ohio	1,449		35	Maryland	1,278
18	Oklahoma	1,497		36	Arizona	1,277
38	Oregon	1,239		37	Indiana	1,251
32	Pennsylvania	1,304		38	Oregon	1,239
8	Rhode Island	1,978		39	Idaho	1,229
15	South Carolina	1,604		40	Washington	1,221
16	South Dakota	1,601		41	Wisconsin	1,208
29	Tennessee	1,351		42	Connecticut	1,195
43	Texas	1,186		43	Texas	1,186
44	Utah	1,157		44	Utah	1,157
6	Vermont	2,224		45	Kansas	1,137
49	Virginia	892		46	Illinois	1,114
40	Washington	1,221		47	Florida	1,053
12	West Virginia	1,798		48	Colorado	977
41	Wisconsin	1,208		49	Virginia	892
1	Wyoming	3,720		50	Nevada	814

District of Columbia**   NA

Source: CQ Press using data from U.S. Bureau of the Census, Governments Division
"State and Local Government Finances 2006-2007" (http://www.census.gov/govs/estimate/index.html)
*Includes revenue from federal and local government sources.
**Not applicable.

State Government Own Source Revenue in 2007

National Total = $1,027,531,249,000*

ALPHA ORDER

RANK	STATE	REVENUE	% of USA
27	Alabama	$13,554,959,000	1.3%
36	Alaska	8,293,595,000	0.8%
19	Arizona	18,068,106,000	1.8%
30	Arkansas	9,874,912,000	1.0%
1	California	139,654,167,000	13.6%
25	Colorado	13,759,276,000	1.3%
21	Connecticut	16,215,095,000	1.6%
41	Delaware	5,071,311,000	0.5%
4	Florida	49,854,642,000	4.9%
13	Georgia	23,454,056,000	2.3%
39	Hawaii	7,006,031,000	0.7%
43	Idaho	4,566,257,000	0.4%
7	Illinois	37,630,542,000	3.7%
18	Indiana	19,395,516,000	1.9%
31	Iowa	9,741,029,000	0.9%
33	Kansas	8,847,455,000	0.9%
26	Kentucky	13,719,940,000	1.3%
22	Louisiana	15,103,422,000	1.5%
42	Maine	5,034,392,000	0.5%
16	Maryland	20,174,720,000	2.0%
10	Massachusetts	29,120,584,000	2.8%
9	Michigan	35,687,533,000	3.5%
15	Minnesota	21,783,712,000	2.1%
35	Mississippi	8,298,192,000	0.8%
23	Missouri	15,094,326,000	1.5%
47	Montana	3,377,684,000	0.3%
40	Nebraska	5,852,564,000	0.6%
37	Nevada	7,642,443,000	0.7%
45	New Hampshire	3,696,634,000	0.4%
6	New Jersey	38,665,020,000	3.8%
34	New Mexico	8,774,073,000	0.9%
2	New York	83,074,907,000	8.1%
11	North Carolina	29,109,208,000	2.8%
49	North Dakota	2,714,466,000	0.3%
8	Ohio	36,631,049,000	3.6%
29	Oklahoma	11,828,061,000	1.2%
28	Oregon	12,356,811,000	1.2%
5	Pennsylvania	43,062,777,000	4.2%
44	Rhode Island	4,192,416,000	0.4%
24	South Carolina	13,844,749,000	1.3%
50	South Dakota	2,026,059,000	0.2%
20	Tennessee	16,489,139,000	1.6%
3	Texas	60,585,843,000	5.9%
32	Utah	9,387,096,000	0.9%
46	Vermont	3,410,261,000	0.3%
12	Virginia	28,357,173,000	2.8%
14	Washington	23,319,718,000	2.3%
38	West Virginia	7,377,282,000	0.7%
17	Wisconsin	19,878,844,000	1.9%
48	Wyoming	2,873,202,000	0.3%

RANK ORDER

RANK	STATE	REVENUE	% of USA
1	California	$139,654,167,000	13.6%
2	New York	83,074,907,000	8.1%
3	Texas	60,585,843,000	5.9%
4	Florida	49,854,642,000	4.9%
5	Pennsylvania	43,062,777,000	4.2%
6	New Jersey	38,665,020,000	3.8%
7	Illinois	37,630,542,000	3.7%
8	Ohio	36,631,049,000	3.6%
9	Michigan	35,687,533,000	3.5%
10	Massachusetts	29,120,584,000	2.8%
11	North Carolina	29,109,208,000	2.8%
12	Virginia	28,357,173,000	2.8%
13	Georgia	23,454,056,000	2.3%
14	Washington	23,319,718,000	2.3%
15	Minnesota	21,783,712,000	2.1%
16	Maryland	20,174,720,000	2.0%
17	Wisconsin	19,878,844,000	1.9%
18	Indiana	19,395,516,000	1.9%
19	Arizona	18,068,106,000	1.8%
20	Tennessee	16,489,139,000	1.6%
21	Connecticut	16,215,095,000	1.6%
22	Louisiana	15,103,422,000	1.5%
23	Missouri	15,094,326,000	1.5%
24	South Carolina	13,844,749,000	1.3%
25	Colorado	13,759,276,000	1.3%
26	Kentucky	13,719,940,000	1.3%
27	Alabama	13,554,959,000	1.3%
28	Oregon	12,356,811,000	1.2%
29	Oklahoma	11,828,061,000	1.2%
30	Arkansas	9,874,912,000	1.0%
31	Iowa	9,741,029,000	0.9%
32	Utah	9,387,096,000	0.9%
33	Kansas	8,847,455,000	0.9%
34	New Mexico	8,774,073,000	0.9%
35	Mississippi	8,298,192,000	0.8%
36	Alaska	8,293,595,000	0.8%
37	Nevada	7,642,443,000	0.7%
38	West Virginia	7,377,282,000	0.7%
39	Hawaii	7,006,031,000	0.7%
40	Nebraska	5,852,564,000	0.6%
41	Delaware	5,071,311,000	0.5%
42	Maine	5,034,392,000	0.5%
43	Idaho	4,566,257,000	0.4%
44	Rhode Island	4,192,416,000	0.4%
45	New Hampshire	3,696,634,000	0.4%
46	Vermont	3,410,261,000	0.3%
47	Montana	3,377,684,000	0.3%
48	Wyoming	2,873,202,000	0.3%
49	North Dakota	2,714,466,000	0.3%
50	South Dakota	2,026,059,000	0.2%

District of Columbia** — NA — NA

Source: U.S. Bureau of the Census, Governments Division
   "State and Local Government Finances 2006-2007" (http://www.census.gov/govs/estimate/index.html)
*Own source revenue includes taxes, current charges, and miscellaneous general revenue. Excluded are intergovernmental transfers, insurance trust revenue, and revenue from government owned utilities and other commercial or auxiliary enterprise.
**Not applicable.

Per Capita State Government Own Source Revenue in 2007

National Per Capita = $3,414*

ALPHA ORDER

RANK	STATE	PER CAPITA
40	Alabama	$2,923
1	Alaska	12,155
42	Arizona	2,840
24	Arkansas	3,474
15	California	3,855
41	Colorado	2,841
6	Connecticut	4,648
2	Delaware	5,863
45	Florida	2,728
50	Georgia	2,460
5	Hawaii	5,487
37	Idaho	3,046
39	Illinois	2,945
36	Indiana	3,056
30	Iowa	3,270
33	Kansas	3,188
31	Kentucky	3,223
25	Louisiana	3,451
16	Maine	3,822
19	Maryland	3,581
7	Massachusetts	4,481
20	Michigan	3,551
12	Minnesota	4,196
42	Mississippi	2,840
47	Missouri	2,554
22	Montana	3,529
28	Nebraska	3,307
38	Nevada	2,976
44	New Hampshire	2,806
8	New Jersey	4,477
9	New Mexico	4,457
10	New York	4,277
32	North Carolina	3,211
11	North Dakota	4,253
34	Ohio	3,180
29	Oklahoma	3,274
27	Oregon	3,310
26	Pennsylvania	3,439
14	Rhode Island	3,974
35	South Carolina	3,129
48	South Dakota	2,542
46	Tennessee	2,671
48	Texas	2,542
23	Utah	3,524
3	Vermont	5,496
17	Virginia	3,673
18	Washington	3,607
13	West Virginia	4,073
21	Wisconsin	3,549
4	Wyoming	5,489

RANK ORDER

RANK	STATE	PER CAPITA
1	Alaska	$12,155
2	Delaware	5,863
3	Vermont	5,496
4	Wyoming	5,489
5	Hawaii	5,487
6	Connecticut	4,648
7	Massachusetts	4,481
8	New Jersey	4,477
9	New Mexico	4,457
10	New York	4,277
11	North Dakota	4,253
12	Minnesota	4,196
13	West Virginia	4,073
14	Rhode Island	3,974
15	California	3,855
16	Maine	3,822
17	Virginia	3,673
18	Washington	3,607
19	Maryland	3,581
20	Michigan	3,551
21	Wisconsin	3,549
22	Montana	3,529
23	Utah	3,524
24	Arkansas	3,474
25	Louisiana	3,451
26	Pennsylvania	3,439
27	Oregon	3,310
28	Nebraska	3,307
29	Oklahoma	3,274
30	Iowa	3,270
31	Kentucky	3,223
32	North Carolina	3,211
33	Kansas	3,188
34	Ohio	3,180
35	South Carolina	3,129
36	Indiana	3,056
37	Idaho	3,046
38	Nevada	2,976
39	Illinois	2,945
40	Alabama	2,923
41	Colorado	2,841
42	Arizona	2,840
42	Mississippi	2,840
44	New Hampshire	2,806
45	Florida	2,728
46	Tennessee	2,671
47	Missouri	2,554
48	South Dakota	2,542
48	Texas	2,542
50	Georgia	2,460

District of Columbia**   NA

Source: CQ Press using data from U.S. Bureau of the Census, Governments Division
"State and Local Government Finances 2006-2007" (http://www.census.gov/govs/estimate/index.html)
*Own source revenue includes taxes, current charges, and miscellaneous general revenue. Excluded are intergovernmental transfers, insurance trust revenue, and revenue from government owned utilities and other commercial or auxiliary enterprise.
**Not applicable.

Profits of State Lotteries in 2008

National Total = $17,763,300,000*

ALPHA ORDER

RANK	STATE	PROFITS	% of USA
NA	Alabama**	NA	NA
NA	Alaska**	NA	NA
25	Arizona	144,600,000	0.8%
NA	Arkansas**	NA	NA
3	California	1,069,400,000	6.0%
30	Colorado	122,300,000	0.7%
18	Connecticut	285,100,000	1.6%
22	Delaware	252,500,000	1.4%
2	Florida	1,280,000,000	7.2%
8	Georgia	867,700,000	4.9%
NA	Hawaii**	NA	NA
38	Idaho	36,200,000	0.2%
12	Illinois	657,000,000	3.7%
23	Indiana	217,100,000	1.2%
35	Iowa	57,000,000	0.3%
34	Kansas	71,000,000	0.4%
24	Kentucky	192,100,000	1.1%
27	Louisiana	131,800,000	0.7%
36	Maine	49,490,000	0.3%
14	Maryland	529,400,000	3.0%
6	Massachusetts	913,000,000	5.1%
9	Michigan	740,700,000	4.2%
31	Minnesota	116,270,000	0.7%
NA	Mississippi**	NA	NA
20	Missouri	266,600,000	1.5%
41	Montana	11,000,000	0.1%
39	Nebraska	31,030,000	0.2%
NA	Nevada**	NA	NA
32	New Hampshire	75,650,000	0.4%
7	New Jersey	882,100,000	5.0%
37	New Mexico	40,800,000	0.2%
1	New York	2,556,100,000	14.4%
17	North Carolina	350,010,000	2.0%
42	North Dakota	6,070,000	0.0%
11	Ohio	672,200,000	3.8%
33	Oklahoma	71,610,000	0.4%
10	Oregon	678,700,000	3.8%
5	Pennsylvania	928,050,000	5.2%
16	Rhode Island	355,570,000	2.0%
21	South Carolina	263,900,000	1.5%
29	South Dakota	122,560,000	0.7%
19	Tennessee	283,100,000	1.6%
4	Texas	1,038,000,000	5.8%
NA	Utah**	NA	NA
40	Vermont	22,600,000	0.1%
15	Virginia	455,260,000	2.6%
28	Washington	130,300,000	0.7%
13	West Virginia	579,000,000	3.3%
26	Wisconsin	140,000,000	0.8%
NA	Wyoming**	NA	NA

RANK ORDER

RANK	STATE	PROFITS	% of USA
1	New York	$2,556,100,000	14.4%
2	Florida	1,280,000,000	7.2%
3	California	1,069,400,000	6.0%
4	Texas	1,038,000,000	5.8%
5	Pennsylvania	928,050,000	5.2%
6	Massachusetts	913,000,000	5.1%
7	New Jersey	882,100,000	5.0%
8	Georgia	867,700,000	4.9%
9	Michigan	740,700,000	4.2%
10	Oregon	678,700,000	3.8%
11	Ohio	672,200,000	3.8%
12	Illinois	657,000,000	3.7%
13	West Virginia	579,000,000	3.3%
14	Maryland	529,400,000	3.0%
15	Virginia	455,260,000	2.6%
16	Rhode Island	355,570,000	2.0%
17	North Carolina	350,010,000	2.0%
18	Connecticut	285,100,000	1.6%
19	Tennessee	283,100,000	1.6%
20	Missouri	266,600,000	1.5%
21	South Carolina	263,900,000	1.5%
22	Delaware	252,500,000	1.4%
23	Indiana	217,100,000	1.2%
24	Kentucky	192,100,000	1.1%
25	Arizona	144,600,000	0.8%
26	Wisconsin	140,000,000	0.8%
27	Louisiana	131,800,000	0.7%
28	Washington	130,300,000	0.7%
29	South Dakota	122,560,000	0.7%
30	Colorado	122,300,000	0.7%
31	Minnesota	116,270,000	0.7%
32	New Hampshire	75,650,000	0.4%
33	Oklahoma	71,610,000	0.4%
34	Kansas	71,000,000	0.4%
35	Iowa	57,000,000	0.3%
36	Maine	49,490,000	0.3%
37	New Mexico	40,800,000	0.2%
38	Idaho	36,200,000	0.2%
39	Nebraska	31,030,000	0.2%
40	Vermont	22,600,000	0.1%
41	Montana	11,000,000	0.1%
42	North Dakota	6,070,000	0.0%
NA	Alabama**	NA	NA
NA	Alaska**	NA	NA
NA	Arkansas**	NA	NA
NA	Hawaii**	NA	NA
NA	Mississippi**	NA	NA
NA	Nevada**	NA	NA
NA	Utah**	NA	NA
NA	Wyoming**	NA	NA
	District of Columbia	70,430,000	0.4%

Source: North American Association of State and Provincial Lotteries, Willoughby Hills, OH

"Sales and Profits" (http://www.naspl.org/index.cfm?fuseaction=content&PageID=3&PageCategory=3)

*Reported profits for fiscal year 2007 on sales of $60,261,990,000. National total does not include $126,500,000 in profits for Puerto Rico.

**No lottery as of fiscal year 2008.

Per Capita Profits of State Lotteries in 2008

National Per Capita = $62.72*

ALPHA ORDER				RANK ORDER		
RANK	**STATE**	**PER CAPITA**		**RANK**	**STATE**	**PER CAPITA**
NA	Alabama**	NA		1	Rhode Island	$337.63
NA	Alaska**	NA		2	West Virginia	319.92
34	Arizona	22.76		3	Delaware	292.94
NA	Arkansas**	NA		4	Oregon	181.69
29	California	29.40		5	South Dakota	154.03
31	Colorado	25.25		6	Massachusetts	141.16
11	Connecticut	81.69		7	New York	131.56
3	Delaware	292.94		8	New Jersey	101.94
14	Florida	70.33		9	Maryland	94.22
10	Georgia	91.11		10	Georgia	91.11
NA	Hawaii**	NA		11	Connecticut	81.69
33	Idaho	24.20		12	Pennsylvania	74.72
19	Illinois	51.22		13	Michigan	73.70
27	Indiana	34.27		14	Florida	70.33
39	Iowa	19.11		15	South Carolina	59.91
30	Kansas	25.56		16	Virginia	59.13
21	Kentucky	45.35		17	Ohio	58.57
28	Louisiana	30.14		18	New Hampshire	57.65
25	Maine	37.62		19	Illinois	51.22
9	Maryland	94.22		20	Tennessee	46.04
6	Massachusetts	141.16		21	Kentucky	45.35
13	Michigan	73.70		21	Missouri	45.35
35	Minnesota	22.44		23	Texas	43.53
NA	Mississippi**	NA		24	North Carolina	38.71
21	Missouri	45.35		25	Maine	37.62
41	Montana	11.50		26	Vermont	36.41
40	Nebraska	17.54		27	Indiana	34.27
NA	Nevada**	NA		28	Louisiana	30.14
18	New Hampshire	57.65		29	California	29.40
8	New Jersey	101.94		30	Kansas	25.56
36	New Mexico	20.77		31	Colorado	25.25
7	New York	131.56		32	Wisconsin	25.00
24	North Carolina	38.71		33	Idaho	24.20
42	North Dakota	9.52		34	Arizona	22.76
17	Ohio	58.57		35	Minnesota	22.44
38	Oklahoma	19.85		36	New Mexico	20.77
4	Oregon	181.69		37	Washington	20.20
12	Pennsylvania	74.72		38	Oklahoma	19.85
1	Rhode Island	337.63		39	Iowa	19.11
15	South Carolina	59.91		40	Nebraska	17.54
5	South Dakota	154.03		41	Montana	11.50
20	Tennessee	46.04		42	North Dakota	9.52
23	Texas	43.53		NA	Alabama**	NA
NA	Utah**	NA		NA	Alaska**	NA
26	Vermont	36.41		NA	Arkansas**	NA
16	Virginia	59.13		NA	Hawaii**	NA
37	Washington	20.20		NA	Mississippi**	NA
2	West Virginia	319.92		NA	Nevada**	NA
32	Wisconsin	25.00		NA	Utah**	NA
NA	Wyoming**	NA		NA	Wyoming**	NA
					District of Columbia	119.81

Source: CQ Press using data from North American Association of State and Provincial Lotteries, Willoughby Hills, OH
"Sales and Profits" (http://www.naspl.org/index.cfm?fuseaction=content&PageID=3&PageCategory=3)
*For fiscal year 2007. National rate is based on population of states with a lottery.
**No lottery as of fiscal year 2008.

Projected vs. Actual State Tax Collections in 2009

National Percent = 91.3% of Projected Taxes*

ALPHA ORDER

RANK	STATE	PERCENT
42	Alabama	83.6
39	Alaska	84.6
46	Arizona	76.0
10	Arkansas	97.2
NA	California**	NA
4	Colorado	100.9
40	Connecticut	84.5
18	Delaware	92.7
36	Florida	86.2
17	Georgia	93.6
22	Hawaii	90.7
13	Idaho	96.2
27	Illinois	90.0
28	Indiana	89.7
NA	Iowa**	NA
7	Kansas	97.5
19	Kentucky	92.5
9	Louisiana	97.3
6	Maine	97.8
25	Maryland	90.3
38	Massachusetts	85.3
32	Michigan	88.4
22	Minnesota	90.7
21	Mississippi	91.7
28	Missouri	89.7
12	Montana	97.1
16	Nebraska	94.0
NA	Nevada**	NA
45	New Hampshire	78.1
NA	New Jersey**	NA
30	New Mexico	89.4
14	New York	94.7
33	North Carolina	87.9
1	North Dakota	127.1
35	Ohio	86.4
15	Oklahoma	94.5
44	Oregon	78.8
26	Pennsylvania	90.1
10	Rhode Island	97.2
43	South Carolina	80.8
7	South Dakota	97.5
31	Tennessee	88.6
3	Texas	102.5
41	Utah	84.3
19	Vermont	92.5
22	Virginia	90.7
36	Washington	86.2
5	West Virginia	99.2
33	Wisconsin	87.9
2	Wyoming	107.6

RANK ORDER

RANK	STATE	PERCENT
1	North Dakota	127.1
2	Wyoming	107.6
3	Texas	102.5
4	Colorado	100.9
5	West Virginia	99.2
6	Maine	97.8
7	Kansas	97.5
7	South Dakota	97.5
9	Louisiana	97.3
10	Arkansas	97.2
10	Rhode Island	97.2
12	Montana	97.1
13	Idaho	96.2
14	New York	94.7
15	Oklahoma	94.5
16	Nebraska	94.0
17	Georgia	93.6
18	Delaware	92.7
19	Kentucky	92.5
19	Vermont	92.5
21	Mississippi	91.7
22	Hawaii	90.7
22	Minnesota	90.7
22	Virginia	90.7
25	Maryland	90.3
26	Pennsylvania	90.1
27	Illinois	90.0
28	Indiana	89.7
28	Missouri	89.7
30	New Mexico	89.4
31	Tennessee	88.6
32	Michigan	88.4
33	North Carolina	87.9
33	Wisconsin	87.9
35	Ohio	86.4
36	Florida	86.2
36	Washington	86.2
38	Massachusetts	85.3
39	Alaska	84.6
40	Connecticut	84.5
41	Utah	84.3
42	Alabama	83.6
43	South Carolina	80.8
44	Oregon	78.8
45	New Hampshire	78.1
46	Arizona	76.0
NA	California**	NA
NA	Iowa**	NA
NA	Nevada**	NA
NA	New Jersey**	NA
	District of Columbia**	NA

Source: CQ Press using data from National Association of State Budget Officers

"The Fiscal Survey of States" (December 2009, http://www.nasbo.org/Publications/FiscalSurvey/tabid/65/Default.aspx)

*For fiscal year 2009. This table compares sales, personal, and corporate income tax collections projected in adopting budgets with the amount collected.

**Not available.

State Government Tax Revenue in 2008

National Total = $780,675,722,000

RANK	STATE	REVENUE	% of USA
26	Alabama	$9,070,530,000	1.2%
29	Alaska	8,424,714,000	1.1%
19	Arizona	13,705,901,000	1.8%
30	Arkansas	7,530,504,000	1.0%
1	California	117,361,976,000	15.0%
25	Colorado	9,624,636,000	1.2%
20	Connecticut	13,367,631,000	1.7%
43	Delaware	2,930,955,000	0.4%
4	Florida	35,849,998,000	4.6%
14	Georgia	18,183,117,000	2.3%
38	Hawaii	5,147,569,000	0.7%
42	Idaho	3,651,917,000	0.5%
6	Illinois	31,890,597,000	4.1%
18	Indiana	14,916,295,000	1.9%
33	Iowa	6,892,026,000	0.9%
32	Kansas	7,159,748,000	0.9%
24	Kentucky	10,056,293,000	1.3%
22	Louisiana	11,003,870,000	1.4%
41	Maine	3,681,614,000	0.5%
16	Maryland	15,713,987,000	2.0%
11	Massachusetts	21,904,897,000	2.8%
9	Michigan	24,781,626,000	3.2%
13	Minnesota	18,320,891,000	2.3%
34	Mississippi	6,761,759,000	0.9%
23	Missouri	10,965,171,000	1.4%
46	Montana	2,457,929,000	0.3%
40	Nebraska	4,228,800,000	0.5%
35	Nevada	6,115,584,000	0.8%
48	New Hampshire	2,257,977,000	0.3%
7	New Jersey	30,616,510,000	3.9%
37	New Mexico	5,645,649,000	0.7%
2	New York	65,370,654,000	8.4%
10	North Carolina	22,781,202,000	2.9%
47	North Dakota	2,312,056,000	0.3%
8	Ohio	26,373,813,000	3.4%
27	Oklahoma	8,484,227,000	1.1%
31	Oregon	7,278,717,000	0.9%
5	Pennsylvania	32,123,740,000	4.1%
44	Rhode Island	2,761,356,000	0.4%
28	South Carolina	8,455,463,000	1.1%
50	South Dakota	1,321,368,000	0.2%
21	Tennessee	11,538,430,000	1.5%
3	Texas	44,675,953,000	5.7%
36	Utah	5,944,879,000	0.8%
45	Vermont	2,544,163,000	0.3%
12	Virginia	18,408,276,000	2.4%
15	Washington	17,944,925,000	2.3%
39	West Virginia	4,879,151,000	0.6%
17	Wisconsin	15,088,662,000	1.9%
49	Wyoming	2,168,016,000	0.3%

RANK	STATE	REVENUE	% of USA
1	California	$117,361,976,000	15.0%
2	New York	65,370,654,000	8.4%
3	Texas	44,675,953,000	5.7%
4	Florida	35,849,998,000	4.6%
5	Pennsylvania	32,123,740,000	4.1%
6	Illinois	31,890,597,000	4.1%
7	New Jersey	30,616,510,000	3.9%
8	Ohio	26,373,813,000	3.4%
9	Michigan	24,781,626,000	3.2%
10	North Carolina	22,781,202,000	2.9%
11	Massachusetts	21,904,897,000	2.8%
12	Virginia	18,408,276,000	2.4%
13	Minnesota	18,320,891,000	2.3%
14	Georgia	18,183,117,000	2.3%
15	Washington	17,944,925,000	2.3%
16	Maryland	15,713,987,000	2.0%
17	Wisconsin	15,088,662,000	1.9%
18	Indiana	14,916,295,000	1.9%
19	Arizona	13,705,901,000	1.8%
20	Connecticut	13,367,631,000	1.7%
21	Tennessee	11,538,430,000	1.5%
22	Louisiana	11,003,870,000	1.4%
23	Missouri	10,965,171,000	1.4%
24	Kentucky	10,056,293,000	1.3%
25	Colorado	9,624,636,000	1.2%
26	Alabama	9,070,530,000	1.2%
27	Oklahoma	8,484,227,000	1.1%
28	South Carolina	8,455,463,000	1.1%
29	Alaska	8,424,714,000	1.1%
30	Arkansas	7,530,504,000	1.0%
31	Oregon	7,278,717,000	0.9%
32	Kansas	7,159,748,000	0.9%
33	Iowa	6,892,026,000	0.9%
34	Mississippi	6,761,759,000	0.9%
35	Nevada	6,115,584,000	0.8%
36	Utah	5,944,879,000	0.8%
37	New Mexico	5,645,649,000	0.7%
38	Hawaii	5,147,569,000	0.7%
39	West Virginia	4,879,151,000	0.6%
40	Nebraska	4,228,800,000	0.5%
41	Maine	3,681,614,000	0.5%
42	Idaho	3,651,917,000	0.5%
43	Delaware	2,930,955,000	0.4%
44	Rhode Island	2,761,356,000	0.4%
45	Vermont	2,544,163,000	0.3%
46	Montana	2,457,929,000	0.3%
47	North Dakota	2,312,056,000	0.3%
48	New Hampshire	2,257,977,000	0.3%
49	Wyoming	2,168,016,000	0.3%
50	South Dakota	1,321,368,000	0.2%
	District of Columbia*	NA	NA

Source: U.S. Bureau of the Census, Governments Division
"2008 State Government Tax Collections" (http://www.census.gov/govs/statetax/)
*Not applicable.

Per Capita State Government Tax Revenue in 2008

National Per Capita = $2,575

	ALPHA ORDER				RANK ORDER	
RANK	STATE	PER CAPITA		RANK	STATE	PER CAPITA
42	Alabama	$1,939		1	Alaska	$12,243
1	Alaska	12,243		2	Vermont	4,097
39	Arizona	2,109		3	Wyoming	4,068
19	Arkansas	2,626		4	Hawaii	3,998
12	California	3,208		5	Connecticut	3,816
40	Colorado	1,950		6	North Dakota	3,605
5	Connecticut	3,816		7	New Jersey	3,534
11	Delaware	3,345		8	Minnesota	3,503
41	Florida	1,946		9	New York	3,358
45	Georgia	1,875		10	Massachusetts	3,348
4	Hawaii	3,998		11	Delaware	3,345
28	Idaho	2,391		12	California	3,208
24	Illinois	2,483		13	New Mexico	2,842
33	Indiana	2,335		14	Maine	2,790
35	Iowa	2,302		15	Maryland	2,777
21	Kansas	2,559		16	Washington	2,733
31	Kentucky	2,345		17	West Virginia	2,688
26	Louisiana	2,472		18	Wisconsin	2,681
14	Maine	2,790		19	Arkansas	2,626
15	Maryland	2,777		20	Rhode Island	2,621
10	Massachusetts	3,348		21	Kansas	2,559
25	Michigan	2,478		22	Pennsylvania	2,556
8	Minnesota	3,503		23	Montana	2,539
36	Mississippi	2,300		24	Illinois	2,483
47	Missouri	1,841		25	Michigan	2,478
23	Montana	2,539		26	Louisiana	2,472
29	Nebraska	2,373		27	North Carolina	2,464
32	Nevada	2,338		28	Idaho	2,391
49	New Hampshire	1,708		29	Nebraska	2,373
7	New Jersey	3,534		30	Virginia	2,361
13	New Mexico	2,842		31	Kentucky	2,345
9	New York	3,358		32	Nevada	2,338
27	North Carolina	2,464		33	Indiana	2,335
6	North Dakota	3,605		34	Oklahoma	2,328
37	Ohio	2,288		35	Iowa	2,302
34	Oklahoma	2,328		36	Mississippi	2,300
43	Oregon	1,924		37	Ohio	2,288
22	Pennsylvania	2,556		38	Utah	2,180
20	Rhode Island	2,621		39	Arizona	2,109
44	South Carolina	1,878		40	Colorado	1,950
50	South Dakota	1,642		41	Florida	1,946
46	Tennessee	1,849		42	Alabama	1,939
48	Texas	1,838		43	Oregon	1,924
38	Utah	2,180		44	South Carolina	1,878
2	Vermont	4,097		45	Georgia	1,875
30	Virginia	2,361		46	Tennessee	1,849
16	Washington	2,733		47	Missouri	1,841
17	West Virginia	2,688		48	Texas	1,838
18	Wisconsin	2,681		49	New Hampshire	1,708
3	Wyoming	4,068		50	South Dakota	1,642
					District of Columbia*	NA

Source: CQ Press using data from U.S. Bureau of the Census, Governments Division
"2008 State Government Tax Collections" (http://www.census.gov/govs/statetax/)
*Not applicable.

State Government Tax Revenue as a Percent of Personal Income in 2008

National Percent = 6.4% of Personal Income*

ALPHA ORDER

RANK	STATE	PERCENT
36	Alabama	5.8
1	Alaska	27.9
33	Arizona	6.1
10	Arkansas	8.1
13	California	7.3
48	Colorado	4.5
22	Connecticut	6.8
8	Delaware	8.3
46	Florida	5.0
41	Georgia	5.4
3	Hawaii	9.5
16	Idaho	7.2
36	Illinois	5.8
22	Indiana	6.8
33	Iowa	6.1
26	Kansas	6.6
13	Kentucky	7.3
22	Louisiana	6.8
11	Maine	7.7
36	Maryland	5.8
26	Massachusetts	6.6
17	Michigan	7.1
9	Minnesota	8.2
12	Mississippi	7.6
45	Missouri	5.1
13	Montana	7.3
33	Nebraska	6.1
40	Nevada	5.7
50	New Hampshire	3.9
20	New Jersey	6.9
5	New Mexico	8.5
20	New York	6.9
19	North Carolina	7.0
4	North Dakota	9.0
29	Ohio	6.4
28	Oklahoma	6.5
43	Oregon	5.3
29	Pennsylvania	6.4
29	Rhode Island	6.4
36	South Carolina	5.8
49	South Dakota	4.3
43	Tennessee	5.3
47	Texas	4.9
22	Utah	6.8
2	Vermont	10.6
41	Virginia	5.4
29	Washington	6.4
5	West Virginia	8.5
17	Wisconsin	7.1
7	Wyoming	8.4

RANK ORDER

RANK	STATE	PERCENT
1	Alaska	27.9
2	Vermont	10.6
3	Hawaii	9.5
4	North Dakota	9.0
5	New Mexico	8.5
5	West Virginia	8.5
7	Wyoming	8.4
8	Delaware	8.3
9	Minnesota	8.2
10	Arkansas	8.1
11	Maine	7.7
12	Mississippi	7.6
13	California	7.3
13	Kentucky	7.3
13	Montana	7.3
16	Idaho	7.2
17	Michigan	7.1
17	Wisconsin	7.1
19	North Carolina	7.0
20	New Jersey	6.9
20	New York	6.9
22	Connecticut	6.8
22	Indiana	6.8
22	Louisiana	6.8
22	Utah	6.8
26	Kansas	6.6
26	Massachusetts	6.6
28	Oklahoma	6.5
29	Ohio	6.4
29	Pennsylvania	6.4
29	Rhode Island	6.4
29	Washington	6.4
33	Arizona	6.1
33	Iowa	6.1
33	Nebraska	6.1
36	Alabama	5.8
36	Illinois	5.8
36	Maryland	5.8
36	South Carolina	5.8
40	Nevada	5.7
41	Georgia	5.4
41	Virginia	5.4
43	Oregon	5.3
43	Tennessee	5.3
45	Missouri	5.1
46	Florida	5.0
47	Texas	4.9
48	Colorado	4.5
49	South Dakota	4.3
50	New Hampshire	3.9

District of Columbia**		NA

Source: CQ Press using data from U.S. Bureau of the Census, Governments Division
   "2008 State Government Tax Collections" (http://www.census.gov/govs/statetax/)
   U.S. Department of Commerce, Bureau of Economic Analysis
   "Annual State Personal Income" (http://www.bea.doc.gov/bea/regional/spi/)
*National figure does not include personal income or taxes from the District of Columbia.
**Not applicable.

State Government Individual Income Tax Revenue in 2008

National Total = $278,230,889,000

ALPHA ORDER

RANK	STATE	REVENUE	% of USA
24	Alabama	$3,077,553,000	1.1%
44	Alaska	0	0.0%
21	Arizona	3,408,576,000	1.2%
29	Arkansas	2,344,876,000	0.8%
1	California	55,745,970,000	20.0%
17	Colorado	5,067,981,000	1.8%
13	Connecticut	7,000,225,000	2.5%
38	Delaware	1,006,859,000	0.4%
44	Florida	0	0.0%
10	Georgia	8,845,476,000	3.2%
32	Hawaii	1,544,835,000	0.6%
35	Idaho	1,438,518,000	0.5%
7	Illinois	10,320,239,000	3.7%
19	Indiana	4,837,524,000	1.7%
26	Iowa	2,848,393,000	1.0%
25	Kansas	2,944,851,000	1.1%
20	Kentucky	3,483,138,000	1.3%
23	Louisiana	3,169,686,000	1.1%
34	Maine	1,448,273,000	0.5%
14	Maryland	6,940,134,000	2.5%
4	Massachusetts	12,496,142,000	4.5%
12	Michigan	7,181,055,000	2.6%
11	Minnesota	7,777,259,000	2.8%
31	Mississippi	1,551,079,000	0.6%
16	Missouri	5,118,849,000	1.8%
39	Montana	870,064,000	0.3%
30	Nebraska	1,726,145,000	0.6%
44	Nevada	0	0.0%
43	New Hampshire	117,936,000	0.0%
3	New Jersey	12,605,545,000	4.5%
36	New Mexico	1,213,522,000	0.4%
2	New York	36,563,948,000	13.1%
5	North Carolina	10,993,927,000	4.0%
41	North Dakota	317,249,000	0.1%
9	Ohio	9,847,506,000	3.5%
27	Oklahoma	2,787,445,000	1.0%
18	Oregon	4,968,791,000	1.8%
6	Pennsylvania	10,408,439,000	3.7%
37	Rhode Island	1,091,705,000	0.4%
22	South Carolina	3,339,935,000	1.2%
44	South Dakota	0	0.0%
42	Tennessee	290,986,000	0.1%
44	Texas	0	0.0%
28	Utah	2,593,129,000	0.9%
40	Vermont	623,019,000	0.2%
8	Virginia	10,114,833,000	3.6%
44	Washington	0	0.0%
33	West Virginia	1,518,746,000	0.5%
15	Wisconsin	6,640,528,000	2.4%
44	Wyoming	0	0.0%

RANK ORDER

RANK	STATE	REVENUE	% of USA
1	California	$55,745,970,000	20.0%
2	New York	36,563,948,000	13.1%
3	New Jersey	12,605,545,000	4.5%
4	Massachusetts	12,496,142,000	4.5%
5	North Carolina	10,993,927,000	4.0%
6	Pennsylvania	10,408,439,000	3.7%
7	Illinois	10,320,239,000	3.7%
8	Virginia	10,114,833,000	3.6%
9	Ohio	9,847,506,000	3.5%
10	Georgia	8,845,476,000	3.2%
11	Minnesota	7,777,259,000	2.8%
12	Michigan	7,181,055,000	2.6%
13	Connecticut	7,000,225,000	2.5%
14	Maryland	6,940,134,000	2.5%
15	Wisconsin	6,640,528,000	2.4%
16	Missouri	5,118,849,000	1.8%
17	Colorado	5,067,981,000	1.8%
18	Oregon	4,968,791,000	1.8%
19	Indiana	4,837,524,000	1.7%
20	Kentucky	3,483,138,000	1.3%
21	Arizona	3,408,576,000	1.2%
22	South Carolina	3,339,935,000	1.2%
23	Louisiana	3,169,686,000	1.1%
24	Alabama	3,077,553,000	1.1%
25	Kansas	2,944,851,000	1.1%
26	Iowa	2,848,393,000	1.0%
27	Oklahoma	2,787,445,000	1.0%
28	Utah	2,593,129,000	0.9%
29	Arkansas	2,344,876,000	0.8%
30	Nebraska	1,726,145,000	0.6%
31	Mississippi	1,551,079,000	0.6%
32	Hawaii	1,544,835,000	0.6%
33	West Virginia	1,518,746,000	0.5%
34	Maine	1,448,273,000	0.5%
35	Idaho	1,438,518,000	0.5%
36	New Mexico	1,213,522,000	0.4%
37	Rhode Island	1,091,705,000	0.4%
38	Delaware	1,006,859,000	0.4%
39	Montana	870,064,000	0.3%
40	Vermont	623,019,000	0.2%
41	North Dakota	317,249,000	0.1%
42	Tennessee	290,986,000	0.1%
43	New Hampshire	117,936,000	0.0%
44	Alaska	0	0.0%
44	Florida	0	0.0%
44	Nevada	0	0.0%
44	South Dakota	0	0.0%
44	Texas	0	0.0%
44	Washington	0	0.0%
44	Wyoming	0	0.0%
	District of Columbia*	NA	NA

Source: U.S. Bureau of the Census, Governments Division
"2008 State Government Tax Collections" (http://www.census.gov/govs/statetax/)
*Not applicable.

Per Capita State Government Individual Income Tax Revenue in 2008

National Per Capita = $918

ALPHA ORDER

RANK	STATE	PER CAPITA
37	Alabama	$658
44	Alaska	0
40	Arizona	524
29	Arkansas	818
4	California	1,524
17	Colorado	1,027
1	Connecticut	1,998
13	Delaware	1,149
44	Florida	0
23	Georgia	912
10	Hawaii	1,200
22	Idaho	942
31	Illinois	804
33	Indiana	757
20	Iowa	951
15	Kansas	1,053
30	Kentucky	812
36	Louisiana	712
14	Maine	1,097
9	Maryland	1,226
2	Massachusetts	1,910
35	Michigan	718
5	Minnesota	1,487
39	Mississippi	528
25	Missouri	859
24	Montana	899
19	Nebraska	969
44	Nevada	0
42	New Hampshire	89
6	New Jersey	1,455
38	New Mexico	611
3	New York	1,878
11	North Carolina	1,189
41	North Dakota	495
26	Ohio	854
32	Oklahoma	765
7	Oregon	1,313
28	Pennsylvania	828
16	Rhode Island	1,036
34	South Carolina	742
44	South Dakota	0
43	Tennessee	47
44	Texas	0
20	Utah	951
18	Vermont	1,003
8	Virginia	1,298
44	Washington	0
27	West Virginia	837
12	Wisconsin	1,180
44	Wyoming	0

RANK ORDER

RANK	STATE	PER CAPITA
1	Connecticut	$1,998
2	Massachusetts	1,910
3	New York	1,878
4	California	1,524
5	Minnesota	1,487
6	New Jersey	1,455
7	Oregon	1,313
8	Virginia	1,298
9	Maryland	1,226
10	Hawaii	1,200
11	North Carolina	1,189
12	Wisconsin	1,180
13	Delaware	1,149
14	Maine	1,097
15	Kansas	1,053
16	Rhode Island	1,036
17	Colorado	1,027
18	Vermont	1,003
19	Nebraska	969
20	Iowa	951
20	Utah	951
22	Idaho	942
23	Georgia	912
24	Montana	899
25	Missouri	859
26	Ohio	854
27	West Virginia	837
28	Pennsylvania	828
29	Arkansas	818
30	Kentucky	812
31	Illinois	804
32	Oklahoma	765
33	Indiana	757
34	South Carolina	742
35	Michigan	718
36	Louisiana	712
37	Alabama	658
38	New Mexico	611
39	Mississippi	528
40	Arizona	524
41	North Dakota	495
42	New Hampshire	89
43	Tennessee	47
44	Alaska	0
44	Florida	0
44	Nevada	0
44	South Dakota	0
44	Texas	0
44	Washington	0
44	Wyoming	0

District of Columbia*   NA

Source: CQ Press using data from U.S. Bureau of the Census, Governments Division
   "2008 State Government Tax Collections" (http://www.census.gov/govs/statetax/)
*Not applicable.

State Government Corporation Net Income Tax Revenue in 2008

National Total = $50,688,869,000

ALPHA ORDER

RANK	STATE	REVENUE	% of USA
26	Alabama	$524,808,000	1.0%
12	Alaska	981,673,000	1.9%
17	Arizona	784,511,000	1.5%
35	Arkansas	342,529,000	0.7%
1	California	11,849,097,000	23.4%
27	Colorado	507,986,000	1.0%
23	Connecticut	534,201,000	1.1%
37	Delaware	308,676,000	0.6%
5	Florida	2,208,600,000	4.4%
13	Georgia	943,042,000	1.9%
44	Hawaii	105,294,000	0.2%
39	Idaho	190,194,000	0.4%
3	Illinois	3,115,604,000	6.1%
14	Indiana	909,494,000	1.8%
34	Iowa	347,248,000	0.7%
25	Kansas	528,011,000	1.0%
24	Kentucky	533,630,000	1.1%
20	Louisiana	703,196,000	1.4%
40	Maine	184,515,000	0.4%
19	Maryland	735,324,000	1.5%
7	Massachusetts	2,179,956,000	4.3%
8	Michigan	1,778,317,000	3.5%
10	Minnesota	1,040,479,000	2.1%
30	Mississippi	384,643,000	0.8%
31	Missouri	384,010,000	0.8%
42	Montana	161,713,000	0.3%
38	Nebraska	232,852,000	0.5%
47	Nevada	0	0.0%
21	New Hampshire	614,794,000	1.2%
4	New Jersey	2,819,906,000	5.6%
33	New Mexico	354,588,000	0.7%
2	New York	5,037,830,000	9.9%
9	North Carolina	1,206,412,000	2.4%
41	North Dakota	161,925,000	0.3%
18	Ohio	754,633,000	1.5%
32	Oklahoma	360,065,000	0.7%
28	Oregon	477,113,000	0.9%
6	Pennsylvania	2,191,420,000	4.3%
43	Rhode Island	145,866,000	0.3%
36	South Carolina	320,378,000	0.6%
46	South Dakota	69,879,000	0.1%
11	Tennessee	1,005,880,000	2.0%
47	Texas	0	0.0%
29	Utah	394,638,000	0.8%
45	Vermont	84,783,000	0.2%
16	Virginia	787,229,000	1.6%
47	Washington	0	0.0%
22	West Virginia	538,839,000	1.1%
15	Wisconsin	863,088,000	1.7%
47	Wyoming	0	0.0%

RANK ORDER

RANK	STATE	REVENUE	% of USA
1	California	$11,849,097,000	23.4%
2	New York	5,037,830,000	9.9%
3	Illinois	3,115,604,000	6.1%
4	New Jersey	2,819,906,000	5.6%
5	Florida	2,208,600,000	4.4%
6	Pennsylvania	2,191,420,000	4.3%
7	Massachusetts	2,179,956,000	4.3%
8	Michigan	1,778,317,000	3.5%
9	North Carolina	1,206,412,000	2.4%
10	Minnesota	1,040,479,000	2.1%
11	Tennessee	1,005,880,000	2.0%
12	Alaska	981,673,000	1.9%
13	Georgia	943,042,000	1.9%
14	Indiana	909,494,000	1.8%
15	Wisconsin	863,088,000	1.7%
16	Virginia	787,229,000	1.6%
17	Arizona	784,511,000	1.5%
18	Ohio	754,633,000	1.5%
19	Maryland	735,324,000	1.5%
20	Louisiana	703,196,000	1.4%
21	New Hampshire	614,794,000	1.2%
22	West Virginia	538,839,000	1.1%
23	Connecticut	534,201,000	1.1%
24	Kentucky	533,630,000	1.1%
25	Kansas	528,011,000	1.0%
26	Alabama	524,808,000	1.0%
27	Colorado	507,986,000	1.0%
28	Oregon	477,113,000	0.9%
29	Utah	394,638,000	0.8%
30	Mississippi	384,643,000	0.8%
31	Missouri	384,010,000	0.8%
32	Oklahoma	360,065,000	0.7%
33	New Mexico	354,588,000	0.7%
34	Iowa	347,248,000	0.7%
35	Arkansas	342,529,000	0.7%
36	South Carolina	320,378,000	0.6%
37	Delaware	308,676,000	0.6%
38	Nebraska	232,852,000	0.5%
39	Idaho	190,194,000	0.4%
40	Maine	184,515,000	0.4%
41	North Dakota	161,925,000	0.3%
42	Montana	161,713,000	0.3%
43	Rhode Island	145,866,000	0.3%
44	Hawaii	105,294,000	0.2%
45	Vermont	84,783,000	0.2%
46	South Dakota	69,879,000	0.1%
47	Nevada	0	0.0%
47	Texas	0	0.0%
47	Washington	0	0.0%
47	Wyoming	0	0.0%
	District of Columbia*	NA	NA

Source: U.S. Bureau of the Census, Governments Division
"2008 State Government Tax Collections" (http://www.census.gov/govs/statetax/)
*Not applicable.

Per Capita State Government Corporation Net Income Tax Revenue in 2008

National Per Capita = $167

<table>
<tr><td colspan="3">ALPHA ORDER</td><td colspan="3">RANK ORDER</td></tr>
<tr><td>RANK</td><td>STATE</td><td>PER CAPITA</td><td>RANK</td><td>STATE</td><td>PER CAPITA</td></tr>
<tr><td>37</td><td>Alabama</td><td>$112</td><td>1</td><td>Alaska</td><td>$1,427</td></tr>
<tr><td>1</td><td>Alaska</td><td>1,427</td><td>2</td><td>New Hampshire</td><td>465</td></tr>
<tr><td>33</td><td>Arizona</td><td>121</td><td>3</td><td>Delaware</td><td>352</td></tr>
<tr><td>35</td><td>Arkansas</td><td>119</td><td>4</td><td>Massachusetts</td><td>333</td></tr>
<tr><td>6</td><td>California</td><td>324</td><td>5</td><td>New Jersey</td><td>325</td></tr>
<tr><td>38</td><td>Colorado</td><td>103</td><td>6</td><td>California</td><td>324</td></tr>
<tr><td>19</td><td>Connecticut</td><td>153</td><td>7</td><td>West Virginia</td><td>297</td></tr>
<tr><td>3</td><td>Delaware</td><td>352</td><td>8</td><td>New York</td><td>259</td></tr>
<tr><td>34</td><td>Florida</td><td>120</td><td>9</td><td>North Dakota</td><td>252</td></tr>
<tr><td>41</td><td>Georgia</td><td>97</td><td>10</td><td>Illinois</td><td>243</td></tr>
<tr><td>43</td><td>Hawaii</td><td>82</td><td>11</td><td>Minnesota</td><td>199</td></tr>
<tr><td>31</td><td>Idaho</td><td>125</td><td>12</td><td>Kansas</td><td>189</td></tr>
<tr><td>10</td><td>Illinois</td><td>243</td><td>13</td><td>Michigan</td><td>178</td></tr>
<tr><td>22</td><td>Indiana</td><td>142</td><td>13</td><td>New Mexico</td><td>178</td></tr>
<tr><td>36</td><td>Iowa</td><td>116</td><td>15</td><td>Pennsylvania</td><td>174</td></tr>
<tr><td>12</td><td>Kansas</td><td>189</td><td>16</td><td>Montana</td><td>167</td></tr>
<tr><td>32</td><td>Kentucky</td><td>124</td><td>17</td><td>Tennessee</td><td>161</td></tr>
<tr><td>18</td><td>Louisiana</td><td>158</td><td>18</td><td>Louisiana</td><td>158</td></tr>
<tr><td>23</td><td>Maine</td><td>140</td><td>19</td><td>Connecticut</td><td>153</td></tr>
<tr><td>28</td><td>Maryland</td><td>130</td><td>19</td><td>Wisconsin</td><td>153</td></tr>
<tr><td>4</td><td>Massachusetts</td><td>333</td><td>21</td><td>Utah</td><td>145</td></tr>
<tr><td>13</td><td>Michigan</td><td>178</td><td>22</td><td>Indiana</td><td>142</td></tr>
<tr><td>11</td><td>Minnesota</td><td>199</td><td>23</td><td>Maine</td><td>140</td></tr>
<tr><td>26</td><td>Mississippi</td><td>131</td><td>24</td><td>Rhode Island</td><td>138</td></tr>
<tr><td>46</td><td>Missouri</td><td>64</td><td>25</td><td>Vermont</td><td>137</td></tr>
<tr><td>16</td><td>Montana</td><td>167</td><td>26</td><td>Mississippi</td><td>131</td></tr>
<tr><td>26</td><td>Nebraska</td><td>131</td><td>26</td><td>Nebraska</td><td>131</td></tr>
<tr><td>47</td><td>Nevada</td><td>0</td><td>28</td><td>Maryland</td><td>130</td></tr>
<tr><td>2</td><td>New Hampshire</td><td>465</td><td>28</td><td>North Carolina</td><td>130</td></tr>
<tr><td>5</td><td>New Jersey</td><td>325</td><td>30</td><td>Oregon</td><td>126</td></tr>
<tr><td>13</td><td>New Mexico</td><td>178</td><td>31</td><td>Idaho</td><td>125</td></tr>
<tr><td>8</td><td>New York</td><td>259</td><td>32</td><td>Kentucky</td><td>124</td></tr>
<tr><td>28</td><td>North Carolina</td><td>130</td><td>33</td><td>Arizona</td><td>121</td></tr>
<tr><td>9</td><td>North Dakota</td><td>252</td><td>34</td><td>Florida</td><td>120</td></tr>
<tr><td>45</td><td>Ohio</td><td>65</td><td>35</td><td>Arkansas</td><td>119</td></tr>
<tr><td>40</td><td>Oklahoma</td><td>99</td><td>36</td><td>Iowa</td><td>116</td></tr>
<tr><td>30</td><td>Oregon</td><td>126</td><td>37</td><td>Alabama</td><td>112</td></tr>
<tr><td>15</td><td>Pennsylvania</td><td>174</td><td>38</td><td>Colorado</td><td>103</td></tr>
<tr><td>24</td><td>Rhode Island</td><td>138</td><td>39</td><td>Virginia</td><td>101</td></tr>
<tr><td>44</td><td>South Carolina</td><td>71</td><td>40</td><td>Oklahoma</td><td>99</td></tr>
<tr><td>42</td><td>South Dakota</td><td>87</td><td>41</td><td>Georgia</td><td>97</td></tr>
<tr><td>17</td><td>Tennessee</td><td>161</td><td>42</td><td>South Dakota</td><td>87</td></tr>
<tr><td>47</td><td>Texas</td><td>0</td><td>43</td><td>Hawaii</td><td>82</td></tr>
<tr><td>21</td><td>Utah</td><td>145</td><td>44</td><td>South Carolina</td><td>71</td></tr>
<tr><td>25</td><td>Vermont</td><td>137</td><td>45</td><td>Ohio</td><td>65</td></tr>
<tr><td>39</td><td>Virginia</td><td>101</td><td>46</td><td>Missouri</td><td>64</td></tr>
<tr><td>47</td><td>Washington</td><td>0</td><td>47</td><td>Nevada</td><td>0</td></tr>
<tr><td>7</td><td>West Virginia</td><td>297</td><td>47</td><td>Texas</td><td>0</td></tr>
<tr><td>19</td><td>Wisconsin</td><td>153</td><td>47</td><td>Washington</td><td>0</td></tr>
<tr><td>47</td><td>Wyoming</td><td>0</td><td>47</td><td>Wyoming</td><td>0</td></tr>
<tr><td></td><td></td><td></td><td></td><td>District of Columbia*</td><td>NA</td></tr>
</table>

Source: CQ Press using data from U.S. Bureau of the Census, Governments Division
   "2008 State Government Tax Collections" (http://www.census.gov/govs/statetax/)
*Not applicable.

State Government General Sales Tax Revenue in 2008

National Total = $240,415,097,000*

ALPHA ORDER

ALPHA ORDER

RANK	STATE	REVENUE	% of USA
31	Alabama	$2,287,288,000	1.0%
46	Alaska	0	0.0%
12	Arizona	6,433,468,000	2.7%
28	Arkansas	2,807,943,000	1.2%
1	California	31,972,874,000	13.3%
30	Colorado	2,312,731,000	1.0%
23	Connecticut	3,178,903,000	1.3%
46	Delaware	0	0.0%
3	Florida	21,518,100,000	9.0%
13	Georgia	5,796,653,000	2.4%
29	Hawaii	2,619,595,000	1.1%
38	Idaho	1,347,327,000	0.6%
9	Illinois	7,935,417,000	3.3%
14	Indiana	5,738,829,000	2.4%
36	Iowa	1,840,862,000	0.8%
32	Kansas	2,264,747,000	0.9%
27	Kentucky	2,875,836,000	1.2%
21	Louisiana	3,459,383,000	1.4%
40	Maine	1,071,653,000	0.4%
19	Maryland	3,748,933,000	1.6%
18	Massachusetts	4,098,089,000	1.7%
8	Michigan	8,225,599,000	3.4%
16	Minnesota	4,550,838,000	1.9%
24	Mississippi	3,135,390,000	1.3%
22	Missouri	3,228,274,000	1.3%
46	Montana	0	0.0%
37	Nebraska	1,534,134,000	0.6%
25	Nevada	3,077,433,000	1.3%
46	New Hampshire	0	0.0%
6	New Jersey	8,915,515,000	3.7%
35	New Mexico	1,949,768,000	0.8%
5	New York	11,294,737,000	4.7%
15	North Carolina	5,269,929,000	2.2%
44	North Dakota	530,078,000	0.2%
10	Ohio	7,865,674,000	3.3%
33	Oklahoma	2,096,220,000	0.9%
46	Oregon	0	0.0%
7	Pennsylvania	8,873,309,000	3.7%
41	Rhode Island	846,870,000	0.4%
26	South Carolina	3,051,608,000	1.3%
43	South Dakota	732,438,000	0.3%
11	Tennessee	6,832,948,000	2.8%
2	Texas	21,668,972,000	9.0%
34	Utah	1,964,119,000	0.8%
45	Vermont	338,941,000	0.1%
20	Virginia	3,656,789,000	1.5%
4	Washington	11,344,622,000	4.7%
39	West Virginia	1,109,822,000	0.5%
17	Wisconsin	4,268,068,000	1.8%
42	Wyoming	744,371,000	0.3%

RANK ORDER

RANK	STATE	REVENUE	% of USA
1	California	$31,972,874,000	13.3%
2	Texas	21,668,972,000	9.0%
3	Florida	21,518,100,000	9.0%
4	Washington	11,344,622,000	4.7%
5	New York	11,294,737,000	4.7%
6	New Jersey	8,915,515,000	3.7%
7	Pennsylvania	8,873,309,000	3.7%
8	Michigan	8,225,599,000	3.4%
9	Illinois	7,935,417,000	3.3%
10	Ohio	7,865,674,000	3.3%
11	Tennessee	6,832,948,000	2.8%
12	Arizona	6,433,468,000	2.7%
13	Georgia	5,796,653,000	2.4%
14	Indiana	5,738,829,000	2.4%
15	North Carolina	5,269,929,000	2.2%
16	Minnesota	4,550,838,000	1.9%
17	Wisconsin	4,268,068,000	1.8%
18	Massachusetts	4,098,089,000	1.7%
19	Maryland	3,748,933,000	1.6%
20	Virginia	3,656,789,000	1.5%
21	Louisiana	3,459,383,000	1.4%
22	Missouri	3,228,274,000	1.3%
23	Connecticut	3,178,903,000	1.3%
24	Mississippi	3,135,390,000	1.3%
25	Nevada	3,077,433,000	1.3%
26	South Carolina	3,051,608,000	1.3%
27	Kentucky	2,875,836,000	1.2%
28	Arkansas	2,807,943,000	1.2%
29	Hawaii	2,619,595,000	1.1%
30	Colorado	2,312,731,000	1.0%
31	Alabama	2,287,288,000	1.0%
32	Kansas	2,264,747,000	0.9%
33	Oklahoma	2,096,220,000	0.9%
34	Utah	1,964,119,000	0.8%
35	New Mexico	1,949,768,000	0.8%
36	Iowa	1,840,862,000	0.8%
37	Nebraska	1,534,134,000	0.6%
38	Idaho	1,347,327,000	0.6%
39	West Virginia	1,109,822,000	0.5%
40	Maine	1,071,653,000	0.4%
41	Rhode Island	846,870,000	0.4%
42	Wyoming	744,371,000	0.3%
43	South Dakota	732,438,000	0.3%
44	North Dakota	530,078,000	0.2%
45	Vermont	338,941,000	0.1%
46	Alaska	0	0.0%
46	Delaware	0	0.0%
46	Montana	0	0.0%
46	New Hampshire	0	0.0%
46	Oregon	0	0.0%
	District of Columbia**	NA	NA

Source: U.S. Bureau of the Census, Governments Division
"2008 State Government Tax Collections" (http://www.census.gov/govs/statetax/)
*Does not include special sales taxes such as those on sale of alcohol, gasoline, or tobacco.
**Not applicable.

Per Capita State Government General Sales Tax Revenue in 2008

National Per Capita = $793*

<table>
<tr><td colspan="3">ALPHA ORDER</td><td colspan="3">RANK ORDER</td></tr>
<tr><td>RANK</td><td>STATE</td><td>PER CAPITA</td><td>RANK</td><td>STATE</td><td>PER CAPITA</td></tr>
<tr><td>43</td><td>Alabama</td><td>$489</td><td>1</td><td>Hawaii</td><td>$2,035</td></tr>
<tr><td>46</td><td>Alaska</td><td>0</td><td>2</td><td>Washington</td><td>1,728</td></tr>
<tr><td>9</td><td>Arizona</td><td>990</td><td>3</td><td>Wyoming</td><td>1,397</td></tr>
<tr><td>11</td><td>Arkansas</td><td>979</td><td>4</td><td>Nevada</td><td>1,176</td></tr>
<tr><td>17</td><td>California</td><td>874</td><td>5</td><td>Florida</td><td>1,168</td></tr>
<tr><td>44</td><td>Colorado</td><td>469</td><td>6</td><td>Tennessee</td><td>1,095</td></tr>
<tr><td>13</td><td>Connecticut</td><td>907</td><td>7</td><td>Mississippi</td><td>1,066</td></tr>
<tr><td>46</td><td>Delaware</td><td>0</td><td>8</td><td>New Jersey</td><td>1,029</td></tr>
<tr><td>5</td><td>Florida</td><td>1,168</td><td>9</td><td>Arizona</td><td>990</td></tr>
<tr><td>37</td><td>Georgia</td><td>598</td><td>10</td><td>New Mexico</td><td>981</td></tr>
<tr><td>1</td><td>Hawaii</td><td>2,035</td><td>11</td><td>Arkansas</td><td>979</td></tr>
<tr><td>16</td><td>Idaho</td><td>882</td><td>12</td><td>South Dakota</td><td>910</td></tr>
<tr><td>34</td><td>Illinois</td><td>618</td><td>13</td><td>Connecticut</td><td>907</td></tr>
<tr><td>14</td><td>Indiana</td><td>898</td><td>14</td><td>Indiana</td><td>898</td></tr>
<tr><td>35</td><td>Iowa</td><td>615</td><td>15</td><td>Texas</td><td>892</td></tr>
<tr><td>23</td><td>Kansas</td><td>810</td><td>16</td><td>Idaho</td><td>882</td></tr>
<tr><td>31</td><td>Kentucky</td><td>671</td><td>17</td><td>California</td><td>874</td></tr>
<tr><td>25</td><td>Louisiana</td><td>777</td><td>18</td><td>Minnesota</td><td>870</td></tr>
<tr><td>22</td><td>Maine</td><td>812</td><td>19</td><td>Nebraska</td><td>861</td></tr>
<tr><td>32</td><td>Maryland</td><td>663</td><td>20</td><td>North Dakota</td><td>826</td></tr>
<tr><td>33</td><td>Massachusetts</td><td>626</td><td>21</td><td>Michigan</td><td>822</td></tr>
<tr><td>21</td><td>Michigan</td><td>822</td><td>22</td><td>Maine</td><td>812</td></tr>
<tr><td>18</td><td>Minnesota</td><td>870</td><td>23</td><td>Kansas</td><td>810</td></tr>
<tr><td>7</td><td>Mississippi</td><td>1,066</td><td>24</td><td>Rhode Island</td><td>804</td></tr>
<tr><td>42</td><td>Missouri</td><td>542</td><td>25</td><td>Louisiana</td><td>777</td></tr>
<tr><td>46</td><td>Montana</td><td>0</td><td>26</td><td>Wisconsin</td><td>758</td></tr>
<tr><td>19</td><td>Nebraska</td><td>861</td><td>27</td><td>Utah</td><td>720</td></tr>
<tr><td>4</td><td>Nevada</td><td>1,176</td><td>28</td><td>Pennsylvania</td><td>706</td></tr>
<tr><td>46</td><td>New Hampshire</td><td>0</td><td>29</td><td>Ohio</td><td>682</td></tr>
<tr><td>8</td><td>New Jersey</td><td>1,029</td><td>30</td><td>South Carolina</td><td>678</td></tr>
<tr><td>10</td><td>New Mexico</td><td>981</td><td>31</td><td>Kentucky</td><td>671</td></tr>
<tr><td>38</td><td>New York</td><td>580</td><td>32</td><td>Maryland</td><td>663</td></tr>
<tr><td>40</td><td>North Carolina</td><td>570</td><td>33</td><td>Massachusetts</td><td>626</td></tr>
<tr><td>20</td><td>North Dakota</td><td>826</td><td>34</td><td>Illinois</td><td>618</td></tr>
<tr><td>29</td><td>Ohio</td><td>682</td><td>35</td><td>Iowa</td><td>615</td></tr>
<tr><td>39</td><td>Oklahoma</td><td>575</td><td>36</td><td>West Virginia</td><td>612</td></tr>
<tr><td>46</td><td>Oregon</td><td>0</td><td>37</td><td>Georgia</td><td>598</td></tr>
<tr><td>28</td><td>Pennsylvania</td><td>706</td><td>38</td><td>New York</td><td>580</td></tr>
<tr><td>24</td><td>Rhode Island</td><td>804</td><td>39</td><td>Oklahoma</td><td>575</td></tr>
<tr><td>30</td><td>South Carolina</td><td>678</td><td>40</td><td>North Carolina</td><td>570</td></tr>
<tr><td>12</td><td>South Dakota</td><td>910</td><td>41</td><td>Vermont</td><td>546</td></tr>
<tr><td>6</td><td>Tennessee</td><td>1,095</td><td>42</td><td>Missouri</td><td>542</td></tr>
<tr><td>15</td><td>Texas</td><td>892</td><td>43</td><td>Alabama</td><td>489</td></tr>
<tr><td>27</td><td>Utah</td><td>720</td><td>44</td><td>Colorado</td><td>469</td></tr>
<tr><td>41</td><td>Vermont</td><td>546</td><td>44</td><td>Virginia</td><td>469</td></tr>
<tr><td>44</td><td>Virginia</td><td>469</td><td>46</td><td>Alaska</td><td>0</td></tr>
<tr><td>2</td><td>Washington</td><td>1,728</td><td>46</td><td>Delaware</td><td>0</td></tr>
<tr><td>36</td><td>West Virginia</td><td>612</td><td>46</td><td>Montana</td><td>0</td></tr>
<tr><td>26</td><td>Wisconsin</td><td>758</td><td>46</td><td>New Hampshire</td><td>0</td></tr>
<tr><td>3</td><td>Wyoming</td><td>1,397</td><td>46</td><td>Oregon</td><td>0</td></tr>
<tr><td></td><td></td><td></td><td></td><td>District of Columbia**</td><td>NA</td></tr>
</table>

Source: CQ Press using data from U.S. Bureau of the Census, Governments Division
"2008 State Government Tax Collections" (http://www.census.gov/govs/statetax/)
*Does not include special sales taxes such as those on sale of alcohol, gasoline, or tobacco.
**Not applicable.

State Government Motor Fuels Sales Tax Revenue in 2008

National Total = $36,437,108,000

ALPHA ORDER

RANK	STATE	REVENUE	% of USA
24	Alabama	$545,726,000	1.5%
50	Alaska	41,985,000	0.1%
17	Arizona	731,345,000	2.0%
27	Arkansas	471,214,000	1.3%
1	California	3,421,457,000	9.4%
20	Colorado	637,193,000	1.7%
28	Connecticut	450,095,000	1.2%
46	Delaware	117,746,000	0.3%
3	Florida	2,289,166,000	6.3%
9	Georgia	1,011,202,000	2.8%
47	Hawaii	94,080,000	0.3%
39	Idaho	239,881,000	0.7%
7	Illinois	1,334,664,000	3.7%
14	Indiana	856,301,000	2.4%
29	Iowa	442,183,000	1.2%
31	Kansas	431,755,000	1.2%
21	Kentucky	617,826,000	1.7%
22	Louisiana	604,377,000	1.7%
40	Maine	229,849,000	0.6%
15	Maryland	808,964,000	2.2%
18	Massachusetts	672,654,000	1.8%
11	Michigan	994,937,000	2.7%
19	Minnesota	648,565,000	1.8%
30	Mississippi	442,119,000	1.2%
16	Missouri	736,303,000	2.0%
41	Montana	205,819,000	0.6%
37	Nebraska	294,149,000	0.8%
36	Nevada	311,953,000	0.9%
43	New Hampshire	137,206,000	0.4%
23	New Jersey	563,266,000	1.5%
38	New Mexico	250,418,000	0.7%
26	New York	527,840,000	1.4%
6	North Carolina	1,582,400,000	4.3%
42	North Dakota	143,389,000	0.4%
5	Ohio	1,842,595,000	5.1%
34	Oklahoma	384,814,000	1.1%
32	Oregon	413,521,000	1.1%
4	Pennsylvania	2,102,168,000	5.8%
45	Rhode Island	126,718,000	0.3%
25	South Carolina	534,252,000	1.5%
44	South Dakota	129,619,000	0.4%
13	Tennessee	872,892,000	2.4%
2	Texas	3,103,170,000	8.5%
35	Utah	377,261,000	1.0%
48	Vermont	91,535,000	0.3%
12	Virginia	920,063,000	2.5%
8	Washington	1,169,900,000	3.2%
33	West Virginia	404,221,000	1.1%
10	Wisconsin	1,001,339,000	2.7%
49	Wyoming	75,013,000	0.2%

RANK ORDER

RANK	STATE	REVENUE	% of USA
1	California	$3,421,457,000	9.4%
2	Texas	3,103,170,000	8.5%
3	Florida	2,289,166,000	6.3%
4	Pennsylvania	2,102,168,000	5.8%
5	Ohio	1,842,595,000	5.1%
6	North Carolina	1,582,400,000	4.3%
7	Illinois	1,334,664,000	3.7%
8	Washington	1,169,900,000	3.2%
9	Georgia	1,011,202,000	2.8%
10	Wisconsin	1,001,339,000	2.7%
11	Michigan	994,937,000	2.7%
12	Virginia	920,063,000	2.5%
13	Tennessee	872,892,000	2.4%
14	Indiana	856,301,000	2.4%
15	Maryland	808,964,000	2.2%
16	Missouri	736,303,000	2.0%
17	Arizona	731,345,000	2.0%
18	Massachusetts	672,654,000	1.8%
19	Minnesota	648,565,000	1.8%
20	Colorado	637,193,000	1.7%
21	Kentucky	617,826,000	1.7%
22	Louisiana	604,377,000	1.7%
23	New Jersey	563,266,000	1.5%
24	Alabama	545,726,000	1.5%
25	South Carolina	534,252,000	1.5%
26	New York	527,840,000	1.4%
27	Arkansas	471,214,000	1.3%
28	Connecticut	450,095,000	1.2%
29	Iowa	442,183,000	1.2%
30	Mississippi	442,119,000	1.2%
31	Kansas	431,755,000	1.2%
32	Oregon	413,521,000	1.1%
33	West Virginia	404,221,000	1.1%
34	Oklahoma	384,814,000	1.1%
35	Utah	377,261,000	1.0%
36	Nevada	311,953,000	0.9%
37	Nebraska	294,149,000	0.8%
38	New Mexico	250,418,000	0.7%
39	Idaho	239,881,000	0.7%
40	Maine	229,849,000	0.6%
41	Montana	205,819,000	0.6%
42	North Dakota	143,389,000	0.4%
43	New Hampshire	137,206,000	0.4%
44	South Dakota	129,619,000	0.4%
45	Rhode Island	126,718,000	0.3%
46	Delaware	117,746,000	0.3%
47	Hawaii	94,080,000	0.3%
48	Vermont	91,535,000	0.3%
49	Wyoming	75,013,000	0.2%
50	Alaska	41,985,000	0.1%

District of Columbia*   NA   NA

Source: U.S. Bureau of the Census, Governments Division
  "2008 State Government Tax Collections" (http://www.census.gov/govs/statetax/)
*Not applicable.

Per Capita State Government Motor Fuel Sales Tax Revenue in 2008

National Per Capita = $120

ALPHA ORDER

RANK	STATE	PER CAPITA
37	Alabama	$117
49	Alaska	61
38	Arizona	113
10	Arkansas	164
46	California	94
26	Colorado	129
27	Connecticut	128
24	Delaware	134
30	Florida	124
41	Georgia	104
47	Hawaii	73
13	Idaho	157
41	Illinois	104
24	Indiana	134
16	Iowa	148
14	Kansas	154
18	Kentucky	144
23	Louisiana	136
6	Maine	174
19	Maryland	143
44	Massachusetts	103
45	Michigan	99
30	Minnesota	124
15	Mississippi	150
30	Missouri	124
3	Montana	213
9	Nebraska	165
34	Nevada	119
41	New Hampshire	104
48	New Jersey	65
29	New Mexico	126
50	New York	27
7	North Carolina	171
1	North Dakota	224
12	Ohio	160
40	Oklahoma	106
39	Oregon	109
8	Pennsylvania	167
33	Rhode Island	120
34	South Carolina	119
11	South Dakota	161
21	Tennessee	140
27	Texas	128
22	Utah	138
17	Vermont	147
36	Virginia	118
4	Washington	178
2	West Virginia	223
4	Wisconsin	178
20	Wyoming	141

RANK ORDER

RANK	STATE	PER CAPITA
1	North Dakota	$224
2	West Virginia	223
3	Montana	213
4	Washington	178
4	Wisconsin	178
6	Maine	174
7	North Carolina	171
8	Pennsylvania	167
9	Nebraska	165
10	Arkansas	164
11	South Dakota	161
12	Ohio	160
13	Idaho	157
14	Kansas	154
15	Mississippi	150
16	Iowa	148
17	Vermont	147
18	Kentucky	144
19	Maryland	143
20	Wyoming	141
21	Tennessee	140
22	Utah	138
23	Louisiana	136
24	Delaware	134
24	Indiana	134
26	Colorado	129
27	Connecticut	128
27	Texas	128
29	New Mexico	126
30	Florida	124
30	Minnesota	124
30	Missouri	124
33	Rhode Island	120
34	Nevada	119
34	South Carolina	119
36	Virginia	118
37	Alabama	117
38	Arizona	113
39	Oregon	109
40	Oklahoma	106
41	Georgia	104
41	Illinois	104
41	New Hampshire	104
44	Massachusetts	103
45	Michigan	99
46	California	94
47	Hawaii	73
48	New Jersey	65
49	Alaska	61
50	New York	27

District of Columbia*	NA

Source: CQ Press using data from U.S. Bureau of the Census, Governments Division
   "2008 State Government Tax Collections" (http://www.census.gov/govs/statetax/)
*Not applicable.

State Tax Rates on Gasoline in 2008

National Median = 21.00 Cents per Gallon*

<table>
<tr><td colspan="3">ALPHA ORDER</td><td colspan="3">RANK ORDER</td></tr>
<tr><th>RANK</th><th>STATE</th><th>CENTS PER GALLON</th><th>RANK</th><th>STATE</th><th>CENTS PER GALLON</th></tr>
<tr><td>38</td><td>Alabama</td><td>18.00</td><td>1</td><td>Washington</td><td>36.00</td></tr>
<tr><td>50</td><td>Alaska</td><td>8.00</td><td>2</td><td>Wisconsin</td><td>32.90</td></tr>
<tr><td>38</td><td>Arizona</td><td>18.00</td><td>3</td><td>West Virginia</td><td>32.20</td></tr>
<tr><td>23</td><td>Arkansas</td><td>21.50</td><td>4</td><td>Pennsylvania</td><td>31.20</td></tr>
<tr><td>38</td><td>California</td><td>18.00</td><td>5</td><td>Rhode Island</td><td>31.00</td></tr>
<tr><td>21</td><td>Colorado</td><td>22.00</td><td>6</td><td>North Carolina</td><td>30.15</td></tr>
<tr><td>11</td><td>Connecticut</td><td>25.00</td><td>7</td><td>Ohio</td><td>28.00</td></tr>
<tr><td>19</td><td>Delaware</td><td>23.00</td><td>8</td><td>Maine</td><td>27.60</td></tr>
<tr><td>47</td><td>Florida</td><td>15.60</td><td>9</td><td>Montana</td><td>27.00</td></tr>
<tr><td>36</td><td>Georgia</td><td>18.50</td><td>10</td><td>Idaho</td><td>26.00</td></tr>
<tr><td>44</td><td>Hawaii</td><td>17.00</td><td>11</td><td>Connecticut</td><td>25.00</td></tr>
<tr><td>10</td><td>Idaho</td><td>26.00</td><td>12</td><td>Utah</td><td>24.50</td></tr>
<tr><td>28</td><td>Illinois</td><td>20.10</td><td>13</td><td>New York</td><td>24.40</td></tr>
<tr><td>38</td><td>Indiana</td><td>18.00</td><td>14</td><td>Nevada</td><td>24.06</td></tr>
<tr><td>27</td><td>Iowa</td><td>20.70</td><td>15</td><td>Kansas</td><td>24.00</td></tr>
<tr><td>15</td><td>Kansas</td><td>24.00</td><td>15</td><td>Oregon</td><td>24.00</td></tr>
<tr><td>25</td><td>Kentucky</td><td>21.00</td><td>17</td><td>Nebraska</td><td>23.90</td></tr>
<tr><td>29</td><td>Louisiana</td><td>20.00</td><td>18</td><td>Maryland</td><td>23.50</td></tr>
<tr><td>8</td><td>Maine</td><td>27.60</td><td>19</td><td>Delaware</td><td>23.00</td></tr>
<tr><td>18</td><td>Maryland</td><td>23.50</td><td>19</td><td>North Dakota</td><td>23.00</td></tr>
<tr><td>25</td><td>Massachusetts</td><td>21.00</td><td>21</td><td>Colorado</td><td>22.00</td></tr>
<tr><td>34</td><td>Michigan</td><td>19.00</td><td>21</td><td>South Dakota</td><td>22.00</td></tr>
<tr><td>29</td><td>Minnesota</td><td>20.00</td><td>23</td><td>Arkansas</td><td>21.50</td></tr>
<tr><td>37</td><td>Mississippi</td><td>18.40</td><td>24</td><td>Tennessee</td><td>21.40</td></tr>
<tr><td>42</td><td>Missouri</td><td>17.55</td><td>25</td><td>Kentucky</td><td>21.00</td></tr>
<tr><td>9</td><td>Montana</td><td>27.00</td><td>25</td><td>Massachusetts</td><td>21.00</td></tr>
<tr><td>17</td><td>Nebraska</td><td>23.90</td><td>27</td><td>Iowa</td><td>20.70</td></tr>
<tr><td>14</td><td>Nevada</td><td>24.06</td><td>28</td><td>Illinois</td><td>20.10</td></tr>
<tr><td>33</td><td>New Hampshire</td><td>19.63</td><td>29</td><td>Louisiana</td><td>20.00</td></tr>
<tr><td>48</td><td>New Jersey</td><td>14.50</td><td>29</td><td>Minnesota</td><td>20.00</td></tr>
<tr><td>35</td><td>New Mexico</td><td>18.88</td><td>29</td><td>Texas</td><td>20.00</td></tr>
<tr><td>13</td><td>New York</td><td>24.40</td><td>29</td><td>Vermont</td><td>20.00</td></tr>
<tr><td>6</td><td>North Carolina</td><td>30.15</td><td>33</td><td>New Hampshire</td><td>19.63</td></tr>
<tr><td>19</td><td>North Dakota</td><td>23.00</td><td>34</td><td>Michigan</td><td>19.00</td></tr>
<tr><td>7</td><td>Ohio</td><td>28.00</td><td>35</td><td>New Mexico</td><td>18.88</td></tr>
<tr><td>44</td><td>Oklahoma</td><td>17.00</td><td>36</td><td>Georgia</td><td>18.50</td></tr>
<tr><td>15</td><td>Oregon</td><td>24.00</td><td>37</td><td>Mississippi</td><td>18.40</td></tr>
<tr><td>4</td><td>Pennsylvania</td><td>31.20</td><td>38</td><td>Alabama</td><td>18.00</td></tr>
<tr><td>5</td><td>Rhode Island</td><td>31.00</td><td>38</td><td>Arizona</td><td>18.00</td></tr>
<tr><td>46</td><td>South Carolina</td><td>16.00</td><td>38</td><td>California</td><td>18.00</td></tr>
<tr><td>21</td><td>South Dakota</td><td>22.00</td><td>38</td><td>Indiana</td><td>18.00</td></tr>
<tr><td>24</td><td>Tennessee</td><td>21.40</td><td>42</td><td>Missouri</td><td>17.55</td></tr>
<tr><td>29</td><td>Texas</td><td>20.00</td><td>43</td><td>Virginia</td><td>17.50</td></tr>
<tr><td>12</td><td>Utah</td><td>24.50</td><td>44</td><td>Hawaii</td><td>17.00</td></tr>
<tr><td>29</td><td>Vermont</td><td>20.00</td><td>44</td><td>Oklahoma</td><td>17.00</td></tr>
<tr><td>43</td><td>Virginia</td><td>17.50</td><td>46</td><td>South Carolina</td><td>16.00</td></tr>
<tr><td>1</td><td>Washington</td><td>36.00</td><td>47</td><td>Florida</td><td>15.60</td></tr>
<tr><td>3</td><td>West Virginia</td><td>32.20</td><td>48</td><td>New Jersey</td><td>14.50</td></tr>
<tr><td>2</td><td>Wisconsin</td><td>32.90</td><td>49</td><td>Wyoming</td><td>14.00</td></tr>
<tr><td>49</td><td>Wyoming</td><td>14.00</td><td>50</td><td>Alaska</td><td>8.00</td></tr>
<tr><td></td><td></td><td></td><td></td><td>District of Columbia</td><td>20.00</td></tr>
</table>

Source: Federation of Tax Administrators
  "Motor Fuel Excise Tax Rates" (http://www.taxadmin.org/fta/rate/motor_fl.html)
*As of January 1, 2008. Federal gasoline tax rate is an additional 18.4 cents per gallon. Many states also allow additional local option taxes on gasoline.

State Government Motor Vehicle and Operators' License Tax Revenue in 2008

National Total = $21,716,028,000

ALPHA ORDER

RANK	STATE	REVENUE	% of USA
28	Alabama	$230,449,000	1.1%
47	Alaska	53,453,000	0.2%
24	Arizona	245,845,000	1.1%
34	Arkansas	154,928,000	0.7%
1	California	2,939,817,000	13.5%
26	Colorado	233,177,000	1.1%
25	Connecticut	240,566,000	1.1%
50	Delaware	49,227,000	0.2%
4	Florida	1,314,729,000	6.1%
21	Georgia	361,544,000	1.7%
38	Hawaii	111,666,000	0.5%
36	Idaho	131,662,000	0.6%
3	Illinois	1,435,073,000	6.6%
18	Indiana	416,261,000	1.9%
17	Iowa	419,006,000	1.9%
29	Kansas	189,381,000	0.9%
27	Kentucky	231,982,000	1.1%
41	Louisiana	98,644,000	0.5%
42	Maine	97,586,000	0.4%
14	Maryland	471,391,000	2.2%
20	Massachusetts	380,619,000	1.8%
6	Michigan	944,745,000	4.4%
11	Minnesota	561,681,000	2.6%
33	Mississippi	157,588,000	0.7%
23	Missouri	285,001,000	1.3%
35	Montana	151,888,000	0.7%
40	Nebraska	99,580,000	0.5%
31	Nevada	186,029,000	0.9%
39	New Hampshire	106,905,000	0.5%
15	New Jersey	469,743,000	2.2%
32	New Mexico	184,147,000	0.8%
5	New York	1,005,603,000	4.6%
9	North Carolina	743,354,000	3.4%
43	North Dakota	92,540,000	0.4%
7	Ohio	890,789,000	4.1%
10	Oklahoma	646,321,000	3.0%
13	Oregon	516,197,000	2.4%
8	Pennsylvania	876,367,000	4.0%
48	Rhode Island	52,908,000	0.2%
30	South Carolina	186,837,000	0.9%
49	South Dakota	49,798,000	0.2%
22	Tennessee	314,003,000	1.4%
2	Texas	1,634,123,000	7.5%
37	Utah	129,415,000	0.6%
45	Vermont	84,117,000	0.4%
19	Virginia	401,108,000	1.8%
12	Washington	549,400,000	2.5%
44	West Virginia	87,701,000	0.4%
16	Wisconsin	443,197,000	2.0%
46	Wyoming	57,937,000	0.3%

RANK ORDER

RANK	STATE	REVENUE	% of USA
1	California	$2,939,817,000	13.5%
2	Texas	1,634,123,000	7.5%
3	Illinois	1,435,073,000	6.6%
4	Florida	1,314,729,000	6.1%
5	New York	1,005,603,000	4.6%
6	Michigan	944,745,000	4.4%
7	Ohio	890,789,000	4.1%
8	Pennsylvania	876,367,000	4.0%
9	North Carolina	743,354,000	3.4%
10	Oklahoma	646,321,000	3.0%
11	Minnesota	561,681,000	2.6%
12	Washington	549,400,000	2.5%
13	Oregon	516,197,000	2.4%
14	Maryland	471,391,000	2.2%
15	New Jersey	469,743,000	2.2%
16	Wisconsin	443,197,000	2.0%
17	Iowa	419,006,000	1.9%
18	Indiana	416,261,000	1.9%
19	Virginia	401,108,000	1.8%
20	Massachusetts	380,619,000	1.8%
21	Georgia	361,544,000	1.7%
22	Tennessee	314,003,000	1.4%
23	Missouri	285,001,000	1.3%
24	Arizona	245,845,000	1.1%
25	Connecticut	240,566,000	1.1%
26	Colorado	233,177,000	1.1%
27	Kentucky	231,982,000	1.1%
28	Alabama	230,449,000	1.1%
29	Kansas	189,381,000	0.9%
30	South Carolina	186,837,000	0.9%
31	Nevada	186,029,000	0.9%
32	New Mexico	184,147,000	0.8%
33	Mississippi	157,588,000	0.7%
34	Arkansas	154,928,000	0.7%
35	Montana	151,888,000	0.7%
36	Idaho	131,662,000	0.6%
37	Utah	129,415,000	0.6%
38	Hawaii	111,666,000	0.5%
39	New Hampshire	106,905,000	0.5%
40	Nebraska	99,580,000	0.5%
41	Louisiana	98,644,000	0.5%
42	Maine	97,586,000	0.4%
43	North Dakota	92,540,000	0.4%
44	West Virginia	87,701,000	0.4%
45	Vermont	84,117,000	0.4%
46	Wyoming	57,937,000	0.3%
47	Alaska	53,453,000	0.2%
48	Rhode Island	52,908,000	0.2%
49	South Dakota	49,798,000	0.2%
50	Delaware	49,227,000	0.2%
	District of Columbia*	NA	NA

Source: U.S. Bureau of the Census, Governments Division
   "2008 State Government Tax Collections" (http://www.census.gov/govs/statetax/)
*Not applicable.

Per Capita State Government Motor Vehicle and Operators' License Tax Revenue in 2008
National Per Capita = $71.62

ALPHA ORDER

ALPHA ORDER

RANK	STATE	PER CAPITA		RANK	STATE	PER CAPITA
42	Alabama	$49.27		1	Oklahoma	$177.36
20	Alaska	77.68		2	Montana	156.90
48	Arizona	37.83		3	North Dakota	144.27
36	Arkansas	54.02		4	Iowa	139.95
18	California	80.37		5	Oregon	136.45
46	Colorado	47.25		6	Vermont	135.44
26	Connecticut	68.68		7	Illinois	111.74
32	Delaware	56.18		8	Wyoming	108.70
23	Florida	71.36		9	Minnesota	107.38
49	Georgia	37.28		10	Michigan	94.45
12	Hawaii	86.73		11	New Mexico	92.69
13	Idaho	86.19		12	Hawaii	86.73
7	Illinois	111.74		13	Idaho	86.19
29	Indiana	65.16		14	Washington	83.67
4	Iowa	139.95		15	Maryland	83.30
27	Kansas	67.70		16	New Hampshire	80.87
35	Kentucky	54.10		17	North Carolina	80.39
50	Louisiana	22.16		18	California	80.37
22	Maine	73.95		19	Wisconsin	78.75
15	Maryland	83.30		20	Alaska	77.68
31	Massachusetts	58.17		21	Ohio	77.27
10	Michigan	94.45		22	Maine	73.95
9	Minnesota	107.38		23	Florida	71.36
37	Mississippi	53.60		24	Nevada	71.12
44	Missouri	47.85		25	Pennsylvania	69.74
2	Montana	156.90		26	Connecticut	68.68
33	Nebraska	55.88		27	Kansas	67.70
24	Nevada	71.12		28	Texas	67.24
16	New Hampshire	80.87		29	Indiana	65.16
34	New Jersey	54.22		30	South Dakota	61.90
11	New Mexico	92.69		31	Massachusetts	58.17
38	New York	51.65		32	Delaware	56.18
17	North Carolina	80.39		33	Nebraska	55.88
3	North Dakota	144.27		34	New Jersey	54.22
21	Ohio	77.27		35	Kentucky	54.10
1	Oklahoma	177.36		36	Arkansas	54.02
5	Oregon	136.45		37	Mississippi	53.60
25	Pennsylvania	69.74		38	New York	51.65
41	Rhode Island	50.22		39	Virginia	51.45
47	South Carolina	41.49		40	Tennessee	50.32
30	South Dakota	61.90		41	Rhode Island	50.22
40	Tennessee	50.32		42	Alabama	49.27
28	Texas	67.24		43	West Virginia	48.32
45	Utah	47.45		44	Missouri	47.85
6	Vermont	135.44		45	Utah	47.45
39	Virginia	51.45		46	Colorado	47.25
14	Washington	83.67		47	South Carolina	41.49
43	West Virginia	48.32		48	Arizona	37.83
19	Wisconsin	78.75		49	Georgia	37.28
8	Wyoming	108.70		50	Louisiana	22.16

District of Columbia*   NA

Source: CQ Press using data from U.S. Bureau of the Census, Governments Division
   "2008 State Government Tax Collections" (http://www.census.gov/govs/statetax/)
*Not applicable.

State Government Tobacco Product Sales Tax Revenue in 2008

National Total = $16,050,425,000

ALPHA ORDER

RANK	STATE	REVENUE	% of USA
31	Alabama	$145,020,000	0.9%
41	Alaska	73,451,000	0.5%
15	Arizona	407,420,000	2.5%
29	Arkansas	147,482,000	0.9%
3	California	1,037,457,000	6.5%
24	Colorado	220,699,000	1.4%
17	Connecticut	317,257,000	2.0%
33	Delaware	125,337,000	0.8%
11	Florida	443,732,000	2.8%
23	Georgia	233,158,000	1.5%
39	Hawaii	89,265,000	0.6%
46	Idaho	54,781,000	0.3%
8	Illinois	613,651,000	3.8%
9	Indiana	519,871,000	3.2%
20	Iowa	252,857,000	1.6%
34	Kansas	118,253,000	0.7%
25	Kentucky	178,558,000	1.1%
30	Louisiana	145,578,000	0.9%
28	Maine	150,499,000	0.9%
16	Maryland	376,112,000	2.3%
12	Massachusetts	436,942,000	2.7%
2	Michigan	1,076,087,000	6.7%
13	Minnesota	419,127,000	2.6%
45	Mississippi	58,327,000	0.4%
37	Missouri	109,365,000	0.7%
38	Montana	94,020,000	0.6%
40	Nebraska	75,479,000	0.5%
32	Nevada	134,617,000	0.8%
26	New Hampshire	169,789,000	1.1%
7	New Jersey	789,351,000	4.9%
47	New Mexico	48,115,000	0.3%
5	New York	973,489,000	6.1%
22	North Carolina	248,159,000	1.5%
50	North Dakota	24,127,000	0.2%
6	Ohio	950,940,000	5.9%
21	Oklahoma	252,374,000	1.6%
19	Oregon	254,955,000	1.6%
4	Pennsylvania	1,025,822,000	6.4%
36	Rhode Island	113,998,000	0.7%
48	South Carolina	31,073,000	0.2%
42	South Dakota	63,903,000	0.4%
18	Tennessee	272,433,000	1.7%
1	Texas	1,446,895,000	9.0%
43	Utah	62,246,000	0.4%
44	Vermont	59,247,000	0.4%
27	Virginia	168,118,000	1.0%
14	Washington	413,488,000	2.6%
35	West Virginia	114,669,000	0.7%
10	Wisconsin	485,470,000	3.0%
49	Wyoming	27,362,000	0.2%

RANK ORDER

RANK	STATE	REVENUE	% of USA
1	Texas	$1,446,895,000	9.0%
2	Michigan	1,076,087,000	6.7%
3	California	1,037,457,000	6.5%
4	Pennsylvania	1,025,822,000	6.4%
5	New York	973,489,000	6.1%
6	Ohio	950,940,000	5.9%
7	New Jersey	789,351,000	4.9%
8	Illinois	613,651,000	3.8%
9	Indiana	519,871,000	3.2%
10	Wisconsin	485,470,000	3.0%
11	Florida	443,732,000	2.8%
12	Massachusetts	436,942,000	2.7%
13	Minnesota	419,127,000	2.6%
14	Washington	413,488,000	2.6%
15	Arizona	407,420,000	2.5%
16	Maryland	376,112,000	2.3%
17	Connecticut	317,257,000	2.0%
18	Tennessee	272,433,000	1.7%
19	Oregon	254,955,000	1.6%
20	Iowa	252,857,000	1.6%
21	Oklahoma	252,374,000	1.6%
22	North Carolina	248,159,000	1.5%
23	Georgia	233,158,000	1.5%
24	Colorado	220,699,000	1.4%
25	Kentucky	178,558,000	1.1%
26	New Hampshire	169,789,000	1.1%
27	Virginia	168,118,000	1.0%
28	Maine	150,499,000	0.9%
29	Arkansas	147,482,000	0.9%
30	Louisiana	145,578,000	0.9%
31	Alabama	145,020,000	0.9%
32	Nevada	134,617,000	0.8%
33	Delaware	125,337,000	0.8%
34	Kansas	118,253,000	0.7%
35	West Virginia	114,669,000	0.7%
36	Rhode Island	113,998,000	0.7%
37	Missouri	109,365,000	0.7%
38	Montana	94,020,000	0.6%
39	Hawaii	89,265,000	0.6%
40	Nebraska	75,479,000	0.5%
41	Alaska	73,451,000	0.5%
42	South Dakota	63,903,000	0.4%
43	Utah	62,246,000	0.4%
44	Vermont	59,247,000	0.4%
45	Mississippi	58,327,000	0.4%
46	Idaho	54,781,000	0.3%
47	New Mexico	48,115,000	0.3%
48	South Carolina	31,073,000	0.2%
49	Wyoming	27,362,000	0.2%
50	North Dakota	24,127,000	0.2%
	District of Columbia*	NA	NA

Source: U.S. Bureau of the Census, Governments Division
"2008 State Government Tax Collections" (http://www.census.gov/govs/statetax/)
*Not applicable.

Per Capita State Government Tobacco Sales Tax Revenue in 2008

National Per Capita = $52.94

ALPHA ORDER

RANK	STATE	PER CAPITA
40	Alabama	$31.00
6	Alaska	106.74
25	Arizona	62.69
28	Arkansas	51.43
41	California	28.36
32	Colorado	44.72
10	Connecticut	90.57
1	Delaware	143.04
44	Florida	24.08
45	Georgia	24.04
18	Hawaii	69.33
38	Idaho	35.86
31	Illinois	47.78
15	Indiana	81.38
12	Iowa	84.45
35	Kansas	42.27
36	Kentucky	41.64
39	Louisiana	32.70
3	Maine	114.04
22	Maryland	66.47
21	Massachusetts	66.77
5	Michigan	107.58
16	Minnesota	80.13
48	Mississippi	19.84
49	Missouri	18.36
7	Montana	97.12
34	Nebraska	42.36
27	Nevada	51.46
2	New Hampshire	128.45
9	New Jersey	91.11
43	New Mexico	24.22
30	New York	50.01
42	North Carolina	26.84
37	North Dakota	37.61
13	Ohio	82.49
19	Oklahoma	69.26
20	Oregon	67.40
14	Pennsylvania	81.63
4	Rhode Island	108.21
50	South Carolina	6.90
17	South Dakota	79.43
33	Tennessee	43.66
26	Texas	59.53
46	Utah	22.82
8	Vermont	95.40
47	Virginia	21.57
24	Washington	62.97
23	West Virginia	63.18
11	Wisconsin	86.27
29	Wyoming	51.34

RANK ORDER

RANK	STATE	PER CAPITA
1	Delaware	$143.04
2	New Hampshire	128.45
3	Maine	114.04
4	Rhode Island	108.21
5	Michigan	107.58
6	Alaska	106.74
7	Montana	97.12
8	Vermont	95.40
9	New Jersey	91.11
10	Connecticut	90.57
11	Wisconsin	86.27
12	Iowa	84.45
13	Ohio	82.49
14	Pennsylvania	81.63
15	Indiana	81.38
16	Minnesota	80.13
17	South Dakota	79.43
18	Hawaii	69.33
19	Oklahoma	69.26
20	Oregon	67.40
21	Massachusetts	66.77
22	Maryland	66.47
23	West Virginia	63.18
24	Washington	62.97
25	Arizona	62.69
26	Texas	59.53
27	Nevada	51.46
28	Arkansas	51.43
29	Wyoming	51.34
30	New York	50.01
31	Illinois	47.78
32	Colorado	44.72
33	Tennessee	43.66
34	Nebraska	42.36
35	Kansas	42.27
36	Kentucky	41.64
37	North Dakota	37.61
38	Idaho	35.86
39	Louisiana	32.70
40	Alabama	31.00
41	California	28.36
42	North Carolina	26.84
43	New Mexico	24.22
44	Florida	24.08
45	Georgia	24.04
46	Utah	22.82
47	Virginia	21.57
48	Mississippi	19.84
49	Missouri	18.36
50	South Carolina	6.90
	District of Columbia*	NA

Source: CQ Press using data from U.S. Bureau of the Census, Governments Division
"2008 State Government Tax Collections" (http://www.census.gov/govs/statetax/)
*Not applicable.

State Tax on a Pack of Cigarettes in 2009

National Median = $1.18 per Pack*

ALPHA ORDER				RANK ORDER		
RANK	STATE	TAX PER PACK		RANK	STATE	TAX PER PACK
45	Alabama	$0.43		1	Rhode Island	$3.46
10	Alaska	2.00		2	Connecticut	3.00
10	Arizona	2.00		3	New York	2.75
26	Arkansas	1.15		4	New Jersey	2.70
31	California	0.87		5	Hawaii	2.60
32	Colorado	0.84		6	Wisconsin	2.52
2	Connecticut	3.00		7	Massachusetts	2.51
17	Delaware	1.60		8	Vermont	2.24
23	Florida	1.34		9	Washington	2.03
46	Georgia	0.37		10	Alaska	2.00
5	Hawaii	2.60		10	Arizona	2.00
41	Idaho	0.57		10	Maine	2.00
29	Illinois	0.98		10	Maryland	2.00
28	Indiana	1.00		10	Michigan	2.00
22	Iowa	1.36		15	New Hampshire	1.78
34	Kansas	0.79		16	Montana	1.70
39	Kentucky	0.60		17	Delaware	1.60
47	Louisiana	0.36		17	Pennsylvania	1.60
10	Maine	2.00		19	Minnesota	1.56
10	Maryland	2.00		20	South Dakota	1.53
7	Massachusetts	2.51		21	Texas	1.41
10	Michigan	2.00		22	Iowa	1.36
19	Minnesota	1.56		23	Florida	1.34
36	Mississippi	0.68		24	Ohio	1.25
49	Missouri	0.17		25	Oregon	1.18
16	Montana	1.70		26	Arkansas	1.15
37	Nebraska	0.64		27	Oklahoma	1.03
33	Nevada	0.80		28	Indiana	1.00
15	New Hampshire	1.78		29	Illinois	0.98
4	New Jersey	2.70		30	New Mexico	0.91
30	New Mexico	0.91		31	California	0.87
3	New York	2.75		32	Colorado	0.84
43	North Carolina	0.45		33	Nevada	0.80
44	North Dakota	0.44		34	Kansas	0.79
24	Ohio	1.25		35	Utah	0.70
27	Oklahoma	1.03		36	Mississippi	0.68
25	Oregon	1.18		37	Nebraska	0.64
17	Pennsylvania	1.60		38	Tennessee	0.62
1	Rhode Island	3.46		39	Kentucky	0.60
50	South Carolina	0.07		39	Wyoming	0.60
20	South Dakota	1.53		41	Idaho	0.57
38	Tennessee	0.62		42	West Virginia	0.55
21	Texas	1.41		43	North Carolina	0.45
35	Utah	0.70		44	North Dakota	0.44
8	Vermont	2.24		45	Alabama	0.43
48	Virginia	0.30		46	Georgia	0.37
9	Washington	2.03		47	Louisiana	0.36
42	West Virginia	0.55		48	Virginia	0.30
6	Wisconsin	2.52		49	Missouri	0.17
39	Wyoming	0.60		50	South Carolina	0.07
					District of Columbia	2.50

Source: Campaign for Tobacco-Free Kids
   "State Cigarette Excise Tax Rates" (http://www.tobaccofreekids.org/research/factsheets/pdf/0097.pdf)
*As of November 1, 2009. Many states also allow additional local option taxes on cigarettes.

State Government Alcoholic Beverage Sales Tax Revenue in 2008

National Total = $5,291,245,000

ALPHA ORDER				RANK ORDER			
RANK	STATE	REVENUE	% of USA	RANK	STATE	REVENUE	% of USA
10	Alabama	$164,827,000	3.1%	1	Texas	$784,069,000	14.8%
33	Alaska	39,103,000	0.7%	2	Florida	609,185,000	11.5%
22	Arizona	64,556,000	1.2%	3	California	327,260,000	6.2%
27	Arkansas	42,843,000	0.8%	4	Pennsylvania	277,427,000	5.2%
3	California	327,260,000	6.2%	5	Washington	266,939,000	5.0%
34	Colorado	35,472,000	0.7%	6	North Carolina	260,382,000	4.9%
28	Connecticut	42,311,000	0.8%	7	New York	205,253,000	3.9%
42	Delaware	14,735,000	0.3%	8	Virginia	175,654,000	3.3%
2	Florida	609,185,000	11.5%	9	Georgia	165,640,000	3.1%
9	Georgia	165,640,000	3.1%	10	Alabama	164,827,000	3.1%
25	Hawaii	45,620,000	0.9%	11	Illinois	158,067,000	3.0%
48	Idaho	7,562,000	0.1%	12	South Carolina	150,065,000	2.8%
11	Illinois	158,067,000	3.0%	13	Michigan	138,779,000	2.6%
26	Indiana	44,707,000	0.8%	14	Tennessee	116,189,000	2.2%
43	Iowa	14,449,000	0.3%	15	Kentucky	107,507,000	2.0%
16	Kansas	106,299,000	2.0%	16	Kansas	106,299,000	2.0%
15	Kentucky	107,507,000	2.0%	17	New Jersey	104,104,000	2.0%
23	Louisiana	54,993,000	1.0%	18	Ohio	92,696,000	1.8%
39	Maine	20,673,000	0.4%	19	Oklahoma	86,433,000	1.6%
36	Maryland	28,966,000	0.5%	20	Minnesota	72,563,000	1.4%
21	Massachusetts	71,935,000	1.4%	21	Massachusetts	71,935,000	1.4%
13	Michigan	138,779,000	2.6%	22	Arizona	64,556,000	1.2%
20	Minnesota	72,563,000	1.4%	23	Louisiana	54,993,000	1.0%
29	Mississippi	42,092,000	0.8%	24	Wisconsin	54,789,000	1.0%
35	Missouri	31,173,000	0.6%	25	Hawaii	45,620,000	0.9%
37	Montana	27,166,000	0.5%	26	Indiana	44,707,000	0.8%
38	Nebraska	26,254,000	0.5%	27	Arkansas	42,843,000	0.8%
31	Nevada	40,401,000	0.8%	28	Connecticut	42,311,000	0.8%
45	New Hampshire	12,508,000	0.2%	29	Mississippi	42,092,000	0.8%
17	New Jersey	104,104,000	2.0%	30	New Mexico	41,230,000	0.8%
30	New Mexico	41,230,000	0.8%	31	Nevada	40,401,000	0.8%
7	New York	205,253,000	3.9%	32	Utah	39,697,000	0.8%
6	North Carolina	260,382,000	4.9%	33	Alaska	39,103,000	0.7%
49	North Dakota	6,916,000	0.1%	34	Colorado	35,472,000	0.7%
18	Ohio	92,696,000	1.8%	35	Missouri	31,173,000	0.6%
19	Oklahoma	86,433,000	1.6%	36	Maryland	28,966,000	0.5%
41	Oregon	15,543,000	0.3%	37	Montana	27,166,000	0.5%
4	Pennsylvania	277,427,000	5.2%	38	Nebraska	26,254,000	0.5%
46	Rhode Island	11,495,000	0.2%	39	Maine	20,673,000	0.4%
12	South Carolina	150,065,000	2.8%	40	Vermont	19,812,000	0.4%
44	South Dakota	13,808,000	0.3%	41	Oregon	15,543,000	0.3%
14	Tennessee	116,189,000	2.2%	42	Delaware	14,735,000	0.3%
1	Texas	784,069,000	14.8%	43	Iowa	14,449,000	0.3%
32	Utah	39,697,000	0.8%	44	South Dakota	13,808,000	0.3%
40	Vermont	19,812,000	0.4%	45	New Hampshire	12,508,000	0.2%
8	Virginia	175,654,000	3.3%	46	Rhode Island	11,495,000	0.2%
5	Washington	266,939,000	5.0%	47	West Virginia	9,465,000	0.2%
47	West Virginia	9,465,000	0.2%	48	Idaho	7,562,000	0.1%
24	Wisconsin	54,789,000	1.0%	49	North Dakota	6,916,000	0.1%
50	Wyoming	1,633,000	0.0%	50	Wyoming	1,633,000	0.0%
					District of Columbia*	NA	NA

Source: U.S. Bureau of the Census, Governments Division
   "2008 State Government Tax Collections" (http://www.census.gov/govs/statetax/)
*Not applicable.

Per Capita State Government Alcoholic Beverage Sales Tax Revenue in 2008

National Per Capita = $17.45

ALPHA ORDER

ALPHA ORDER

RANK	STATE	PER CAPITA
5	Alabama	$35.24
1	Alaska	56.83
37	Arizona	9.93
23	Arkansas	14.94
40	California	8.95
42	Colorado	7.19
31	Connecticut	12.08
20	Delaware	16.82
7	Florida	33.06
19	Georgia	17.08
4	Hawaii	35.43
47	Idaho	4.95
30	Illinois	12.31
43	Indiana	7.00
48	Iowa	4.83
3	Kansas	38.00
12	Kentucky	25.07
29	Louisiana	12.35
21	Maine	15.67
46	Maryland	5.12
33	Massachusetts	10.99
27	Michigan	13.87
27	Minnesota	13.87
26	Mississippi	14.32
44	Missouri	5.23
11	Montana	28.06
24	Nebraska	14.73
22	Nevada	15.45
39	New Hampshire	9.46
32	New Jersey	12.02
16	New Mexico	20.75
36	New York	10.54
10	North Carolina	28.16
35	North Dakota	10.78
41	Ohio	8.04
13	Oklahoma	23.72
49	Oregon	4.11
15	Pennsylvania	22.08
34	Rhode Island	10.91
6	South Carolina	33.32
18	South Dakota	17.16
17	Tennessee	18.62
8	Texas	32.26
25	Utah	14.56
9	Vermont	31.90
14	Virginia	22.53
2	Washington	40.65
45	West Virginia	5.22
38	Wisconsin	9.74
50	Wyoming	3.06

RANK ORDER

RANK	STATE	PER CAPITA
1	Alaska	$56.83
2	Washington	40.65
3	Kansas	38.00
4	Hawaii	35.43
5	Alabama	35.24
6	South Carolina	33.32
7	Florida	33.06
8	Texas	32.26
9	Vermont	31.90
10	North Carolina	28.16
11	Montana	28.06
12	Kentucky	25.07
13	Oklahoma	23.72
14	Virginia	22.53
15	Pennsylvania	22.08
16	New Mexico	20.75
17	Tennessee	18.62
18	South Dakota	17.16
19	Georgia	17.08
20	Delaware	16.82
21	Maine	15.67
22	Nevada	15.45
23	Arkansas	14.94
24	Nebraska	14.73
25	Utah	14.56
26	Mississippi	14.32
27	Michigan	13.87
27	Minnesota	13.87
29	Louisiana	12.35
30	Illinois	12.31
31	Connecticut	12.08
32	New Jersey	12.02
33	Massachusetts	10.99
34	Rhode Island	10.91
35	North Dakota	10.78
36	New York	10.54
37	Arizona	9.93
38	Wisconsin	9.74
39	New Hampshire	9.46
40	California	8.95
41	Ohio	8.04
42	Colorado	7.19
43	Indiana	7.00
44	Missouri	5.23
45	West Virginia	5.22
46	Maryland	5.12
47	Idaho	4.95
48	Iowa	4.83
49	Oregon	4.11
50	Wyoming	3.06
	District of Columbia*	NA

Source: CQ Press using data from U.S. Bureau of the Census, Governments Division
"2008 State Government Tax Collections" (http://www.census.gov/govs/statetax/)
*Not applicable.

State Government Total Expenditures in 2007

National Total = $1,635,729,450,000*

ALPHA ORDER			
RANK	STATE	EXPENDITURES	% of USA
25	Alabama	$23,192,507,000	1.4%
39	Alaska	9,191,744,000	0.6%
18	Arizona	28,828,472,000	1.8%
32	Arkansas	14,948,566,000	0.9%
1	California	233,578,021,000	14.3%
27	Colorado	21,243,982,000	1.3%
26	Connecticut	22,115,190,000	1.4%
44	Delaware	6,735,984,000	0.4%
4	Florida	72,785,123,000	4.4%
12	Georgia	41,843,352,000	2.6%
37	Hawaii	9,848,210,000	0.6%
43	Idaho	6,895,319,000	0.4%
7	Illinois	59,302,221,000	3.6%
19	Indiana	28,809,586,000	1.8%
31	Iowa	15,461,766,000	0.9%
34	Kansas	13,182,916,000	0.8%
24	Kentucky	23,680,419,000	1.4%
20	Louisiana	27,855,931,000	1.7%
40	Maine	7,935,673,000	0.5%
16	Maryland	31,610,548,000	1.9%
10	Massachusetts	44,049,996,000	2.7%
9	Michigan	54,765,658,000	3.3%
15	Minnesota	31,880,478,000	1.9%
29	Mississippi	18,744,353,000	1.1%
21	Missouri	25,318,686,000	1.5%
46	Montana	5,554,244,000	0.3%
41	Nebraska	7,834,295,000	0.5%
36	Nevada	10,755,326,000	0.7%
45	New Hampshire	6,226,121,000	0.4%
8	New Jersey	56,076,165,000	3.4%
33	New Mexico	14,907,222,000	0.9%
2	New York	151,338,991,000	9.3%
11	North Carolina	44,009,293,000	2.7%
49	North Dakota	3,777,523,000	0.2%
6	Ohio	66,494,460,000	4.1%
30	Oklahoma	18,104,268,000	1.1%
28	Oregon	20,605,597,000	1.3%
5	Pennsylvania	68,292,746,000	4.2%
42	Rhode Island	7,071,396,000	0.4%
23	South Carolina	24,824,628,000	1.5%
50	South Dakota	3,571,741,000	0.2%
22	Tennessee	24,992,628,000	1.5%
3	Texas	90,623,748,000	5.5%
35	Utah	12,774,196,000	0.8%
47	Vermont	4,993,860,000	0.3%
14	Virginia	36,774,042,000	2.2%
13	Washington	37,116,177,000	2.3%
38	West Virginia	9,766,972,000	0.6%
17	Wisconsin	30,902,737,000	1.9%
48	Wyoming	4,536,373,000	0.3%

RANK ORDER			
RANK	STATE	EXPENDITURES	% of USA
1	California	$233,578,021,000	14.3%
2	New York	151,338,991,000	9.3%
3	Texas	90,623,748,000	5.5%
4	Florida	72,785,123,000	4.4%
5	Pennsylvania	68,292,746,000	4.2%
6	Ohio	66,494,460,000	4.1%
7	Illinois	59,302,221,000	3.6%
8	New Jersey	56,076,165,000	3.4%
9	Michigan	54,765,658,000	3.3%
10	Massachusetts	44,049,996,000	2.7%
11	North Carolina	44,009,293,000	2.7%
12	Georgia	41,843,352,000	2.6%
13	Washington	37,116,177,000	2.3%
14	Virginia	36,774,042,000	2.2%
15	Minnesota	31,880,478,000	1.9%
16	Maryland	31,610,548,000	1.9%
17	Wisconsin	30,902,737,000	1.9%
18	Arizona	28,828,472,000	1.8%
19	Indiana	28,809,586,000	1.8%
20	Louisiana	27,855,931,000	1.7%
21	Missouri	25,318,686,000	1.5%
22	Tennessee	24,992,628,000	1.5%
23	South Carolina	24,824,628,000	1.5%
24	Kentucky	23,680,419,000	1.4%
25	Alabama	23,192,507,000	1.4%
26	Connecticut	22,115,190,000	1.4%
27	Colorado	21,243,982,000	1.3%
28	Oregon	20,605,597,000	1.3%
29	Mississippi	18,744,353,000	1.1%
30	Oklahoma	18,104,268,000	1.1%
31	Iowa	15,461,766,000	0.9%
32	Arkansas	14,948,566,000	0.9%
33	New Mexico	14,907,222,000	0.9%
34	Kansas	13,182,916,000	0.8%
35	Utah	12,774,196,000	0.8%
36	Nevada	10,755,326,000	0.7%
37	Hawaii	9,848,210,000	0.6%
38	West Virginia	9,766,972,000	0.6%
39	Alaska	9,191,744,000	0.6%
40	Maine	7,935,673,000	0.5%
41	Nebraska	7,834,295,000	0.5%
42	Rhode Island	7,071,396,000	0.4%
43	Idaho	6,895,319,000	0.4%
44	Delaware	6,735,984,000	0.4%
45	New Hampshire	6,226,121,000	0.4%
46	Montana	5,554,244,000	0.3%
47	Vermont	4,993,860,000	0.3%
48	Wyoming	4,536,373,000	0.3%
49	North Dakota	3,777,523,000	0.2%
50	South Dakota	3,571,741,000	0.2%
	District of Columbia**	NA	NA

Source: U.S. Bureau of the Census, Governments Division
    "State and Local Government Finances 2006-2007" (http://www.census.gov/govs/estimate/index.html)
*Total expenditures includes all money paid other than for retirement of debt and extension of loans. Includes payments from all sources of funds including current revenues and proceeds from borrowing and prior year fund balances. Includes intergovernmental transfers and expenditures for government owned utilities and other commercial or auxiliary enterprise, and insurance trust expenditures. **Not applicable.

Per Capita State Government Total Expenditures in 2007

National Per Capita = $5,434*

RANK	STATE	PER CAPITA
32	Alabama	$5,001
1	Alaska	13,472
41	Arizona	4,531
29	Arkansas	5,260
11	California	6,448
45	Colorado	4,387
14	Connecticut	6,339
5	Delaware	7,788
49	Florida	3,982
44	Georgia	4,389
6	Hawaii	7,713
39	Idaho	4,599
38	Illinois	4,640
40	Indiana	4,540
30	Iowa	5,191
36	Kansas	4,750
23	Kentucky	5,564
13	Louisiana	6,365
16	Maine	6,024
22	Maryland	5,610
8	Massachusetts	6,778
27	Michigan	5,449
15	Minnesota	6,141
12	Mississippi	6,416
46	Missouri	4,284
18	Montana	5,802
43	Nebraska	4,426
47	Nevada	4,189
37	New Hampshire	4,726
10	New Jersey	6,493
7	New Mexico	7,572
4	New York	7,792
33	North Carolina	4,855
17	North Dakota	5,919
19	Ohio	5,772
31	Oklahoma	5,012
24	Oregon	5,520
26	Pennsylvania	5,454
9	Rhode Island	6,703
21	South Carolina	5,611
42	South Dakota	4,481
48	Tennessee	4,049
50	Texas	3,802
34	Utah	4,795
3	Vermont	8,049
35	Virginia	4,764
20	Washington	5,741
28	West Virginia	5,393
25	Wisconsin	5,517
2	Wyoming	8,667

RANK	STATE	PER CAPITA
1	Alaska	$13,472
2	Wyoming	8,667
3	Vermont	8,049
4	New York	7,792
5	Delaware	7,788
6	Hawaii	7,713
7	New Mexico	7,572
8	Massachusetts	6,778
9	Rhode Island	6,703
10	New Jersey	6,493
11	California	6,448
12	Mississippi	6,416
13	Louisiana	6,365
14	Connecticut	6,339
15	Minnesota	6,141
16	Maine	6,024
17	North Dakota	5,919
18	Montana	5,802
19	Ohio	5,772
20	Washington	5,741
21	South Carolina	5,611
22	Maryland	5,610
23	Kentucky	5,564
24	Oregon	5,520
25	Wisconsin	5,517
26	Pennsylvania	5,454
27	Michigan	5,449
28	West Virginia	5,393
29	Arkansas	5,260
30	Iowa	5,191
31	Oklahoma	5,012
32	Alabama	5,001
33	North Carolina	4,855
34	Utah	4,795
35	Virginia	4,764
36	Kansas	4,750
37	New Hampshire	4,726
38	Illinois	4,640
39	Idaho	4,599
40	Indiana	4,540
41	Arizona	4,531
42	South Dakota	4,481
43	Nebraska	4,426
44	Georgia	4,389
45	Colorado	4,387
46	Missouri	4,284
47	Nevada	4,189
48	Tennessee	4,049
49	Florida	3,982
50	Texas	3,802

District of Columbia**   NA

Source: CQ Press using data from U.S. Bureau of the Census, Governments Division
  "State and Local Government Finances 2006-2007" (http://www.census.gov/govs/estimate/index.html)
*Total expenditures includes all money paid other than for retirement of debt and extension of loans. Includes payments from all sources of funds including current revenues and proceeds from borrowing and prior year fund balances. Includes intergovernmental transfers and expenditures for government owned utilities total other commercial or auxiliary enterprise, and insurance trust expenditures. **Not applicable.

State Government Direct General Expenditures in 2007

National Total = $966,157,329,000*

RANK	STATE	EXPENDITURES	% of USA
26	Alabama	$14,585,279,000	1.5%
38	Alaska	6,924,835,000	0.7%
24	Arizona	15,627,690,000	1.6%
33	Arkansas	9,461,914,000	1.0%
1	California	106,125,618,000	11.0%
27	Colorado	11,980,347,000	1.2%
25	Connecticut	15,177,542,000	1.6%
42	Delaware	5,056,225,000	0.5%
4	Florida	46,069,270,000	4.8%
11	Georgia	27,232,882,000	2.8%
35	Hawaii	8,831,690,000	0.9%
44	Idaho	4,213,785,000	0.4%
6	Illinois	36,777,216,000	3.8%
17	Indiana	18,343,822,000	1.9%
31	Iowa	9,950,442,000	1.0%
36	Kansas	8,110,997,000	0.8%
22	Kentucky	16,394,104,000	1.7%
16	Louisiana	18,754,141,000	1.9%
39	Maine	5,986,893,000	0.6%
15	Maryland	20,697,960,000	2.1%
9	Massachusetts	30,068,676,000	3.1%
10	Michigan	28,665,153,000	3.0%
18	Minnesota	17,476,979,000	1.8%
28	Mississippi	11,928,637,000	1.2%
21	Missouri	16,815,361,000	1.7%
46	Montana	3,720,570,000	0.4%
40	Nebraska	5,641,761,000	0.6%
41	Nevada	5,631,977,000	0.6%
45	New Hampshire	3,973,499,000	0.4%
8	New Jersey	34,253,102,000	3.5%
32	New Mexico	9,495,898,000	1.0%
2	New York	74,308,658,000	7.7%
12	North Carolina	27,089,674,000	2.8%
48	North Dakota	2,699,640,000	0.3%
7	Ohio	36,197,810,000	3.7%
29	Oklahoma	11,778,981,000	1.2%
30	Oregon	11,655,988,000	1.2%
5	Pennsylvania	43,307,310,000	4.5%
43	Rhode Island	4,900,043,000	0.5%
23	South Carolina	16,016,460,000	1.7%
49	South Dakota	2,611,292,000	0.3%
19	Tennessee	17,168,261,000	1.8%
3	Texas	58,851,832,000	6.1%
34	Utah	9,009,514,000	0.9%
47	Vermont	3,270,912,000	0.3%
14	Virginia	23,213,637,000	2.4%
13	Washington	23,335,662,000	2.4%
37	West Virginia	7,215,415,000	0.7%
20	Wisconsin	17,060,476,000	1.8%
50	Wyoming	2,491,499,000	0.3%

RANK	STATE	EXPENDITURES	% of USA
1	California	$106,125,618,000	11.0%
2	New York	74,308,658,000	7.7%
3	Texas	58,851,832,000	6.1%
4	Florida	46,069,270,000	4.8%
5	Pennsylvania	43,307,310,000	4.5%
6	Illinois	36,777,216,000	3.8%
7	Ohio	36,197,810,000	3.7%
8	New Jersey	34,253,102,000	3.5%
9	Massachusetts	30,068,676,000	3.1%
10	Michigan	28,665,153,000	3.0%
11	Georgia	27,232,882,000	2.8%
12	North Carolina	27,089,674,000	2.8%
13	Washington	23,335,662,000	2.4%
14	Virginia	23,213,637,000	2.4%
15	Maryland	20,697,960,000	2.1%
16	Louisiana	18,754,141,000	1.9%
17	Indiana	18,343,822,000	1.9%
18	Minnesota	17,476,979,000	1.8%
19	Tennessee	17,168,261,000	1.8%
20	Wisconsin	17,060,476,000	1.8%
21	Missouri	16,815,361,000	1.7%
22	Kentucky	16,394,104,000	1.7%
23	South Carolina	16,016,460,000	1.7%
24	Arizona	15,627,690,000	1.6%
25	Connecticut	15,177,542,000	1.6%
26	Alabama	14,585,279,000	1.5%
27	Colorado	11,980,347,000	1.2%
28	Mississippi	11,928,637,000	1.2%
29	Oklahoma	11,778,981,000	1.2%
30	Oregon	11,655,988,000	1.2%
31	Iowa	9,950,442,000	1.0%
32	New Mexico	9,495,898,000	1.0%
33	Arkansas	9,461,914,000	1.0%
34	Utah	9,009,514,000	0.9%
35	Hawaii	8,831,690,000	0.9%
36	Kansas	8,110,997,000	0.8%
37	West Virginia	7,215,415,000	0.7%
38	Alaska	6,924,835,000	0.7%
39	Maine	5,986,893,000	0.6%
40	Nebraska	5,641,761,000	0.6%
41	Nevada	5,631,977,000	0.6%
42	Delaware	5,056,225,000	0.5%
43	Rhode Island	4,900,043,000	0.5%
44	Idaho	4,213,785,000	0.4%
45	New Hampshire	3,973,499,000	0.4%
46	Montana	3,720,570,000	0.4%
47	Vermont	3,270,912,000	0.3%
48	North Dakota	2,699,640,000	0.3%
49	South Dakota	2,611,292,000	0.3%
50	Wyoming	2,491,499,000	0.3%
	District of Columbia**	NA	NA

Source: U.S. Bureau of the Census, Governments Division
"State and Local Government Finances 2006-2007" (http://www.census.gov/govs/estimate/index.html)
*Direct general expenditures include expenditures for current operations, assistance and subsidies, interest on debt, and capital outlay. Excludes intergovernmental transfers, expenditures for government owned utilities and other commercial or auxiliary enterprise, and insurance trust expenditures.
**Not applicable.

Per Capita State Government Direct General Expenditures in 2007

National Per Capita = $3,210*

ALPHA ORDER

RANK	STATE	PER CAPITA
30	Alabama	$3,145
1	Alaska	10,149
49	Arizona	2,456
26	Arkansas	3,329
37	California	2,930
47	Colorado	2,474
10	Connecticut	4,351
3	Delaware	5,846
46	Florida	2,520
41	Georgia	2,856
2	Hawaii	6,917
44	Idaho	2,811
40	Illinois	2,878
39	Indiana	2,891
25	Iowa	3,341
38	Kansas	2,922
17	Kentucky	3,852
11	Louisiana	4,286
9	Maine	4,545
19	Maryland	3,674
8	Massachusetts	4,626
42	Michigan	2,852
24	Minnesota	3,367
13	Mississippi	4,083
43	Missouri	2,845
16	Montana	3,887
29	Nebraska	3,188
50	Nevada	2,193
34	New Hampshire	3,016
15	New Jersey	3,966
5	New Mexico	4,823
18	New York	3,826
36	North Carolina	2,989
12	North Dakota	4,230
31	Ohio	3,142
28	Oklahoma	3,261
32	Oregon	3,122
22	Pennsylvania	3,458
7	Rhode Island	4,645
20	South Carolina	3,620
27	South Dakota	3,276
45	Tennessee	2,781
48	Texas	2,469
23	Utah	3,382
4	Vermont	5,272
35	Virginia	3,007
21	Washington	3,610
14	West Virginia	3,984
33	Wisconsin	3,046
6	Wyoming	4,760

RANK ORDER

RANK	STATE	PER CAPITA
1	Alaska	$10,149
2	Hawaii	6,917
3	Delaware	5,846
4	Vermont	5,272
5	New Mexico	4,823
6	Wyoming	4,760
7	Rhode Island	4,645
8	Massachusetts	4,626
9	Maine	4,545
10	Connecticut	4,351
11	Louisiana	4,286
12	North Dakota	4,230
13	Mississippi	4,083
14	West Virginia	3,984
15	New Jersey	3,966
16	Montana	3,887
17	Kentucky	3,852
18	New York	3,826
19	Maryland	3,674
20	South Carolina	3,620
21	Washington	3,610
22	Pennsylvania	3,458
23	Utah	3,382
24	Minnesota	3,367
25	Iowa	3,341
26	Arkansas	3,329
27	South Dakota	3,276
28	Oklahoma	3,261
29	Nebraska	3,188
30	Alabama	3,145
31	Ohio	3,142
32	Oregon	3,122
33	Wisconsin	3,046
34	New Hampshire	3,016
35	Virginia	3,007
36	North Carolina	2,989
37	California	2,930
38	Kansas	2,922
39	Indiana	2,891
40	Illinois	2,878
41	Georgia	2,856
42	Michigan	2,852
43	Missouri	2,845
44	Idaho	2,811
45	Tennessee	2,781
46	Florida	2,520
47	Colorado	2,474
48	Texas	2,469
49	Arizona	2,456
50	Nevada	2,193

| | District of Columbia** | NA |

Source: CQ Press using data from U.S. Bureau of the Census, Governments Division
   "State and Local Government Finances 2006-2007" (http://www.census.gov/govs/estimate/index.html)
*Direct general expenditures include expenditures for current operations, assistance and subsidies, interest on debt, and capital outlay. Excludes intergovernmental transfers, expenditures for government owned utilities and other commercial or auxiliary enterprise, and insurance trust expenditures.
**Not applicable.

State Government Debt Outstanding in 2007

National Total = $933,801,534,000*

ALPHA ORDER

RANK	STATE	DEBT	% of USA
31	Alabama	$7,059,343,000	0.7%
33	Alaska	6,553,080,000	0.7%
25	Arizona	9,546,428,000	1.0%
42	Arkansas	4,508,511,000	0.5%
1	California	114,701,797,000	11.9%
20	Colorado	14,905,758,000	1.5%
11	Connecticut	23,836,187,000	2.5%
39	Delaware	5,390,504,000	0.6%
7	Florida	36,483,336,000	3.8%
22	Georgia	11,370,040,000	1.2%
34	Hawaii	5,959,064,000	0.6%
47	Idaho	2,812,655,000	0.3%
4	Illinois	54,535,159,000	5.6%
16	Indiana	19,180,194,000	2.0%
32	Iowa	6,727,065,000	0.7%
37	Kansas	5,638,261,000	0.6%
24	Kentucky	10,857,128,000	1.1%
21	Louisiana	14,251,968,000	1.5%
40	Maine	5,326,692,000	0.6%
17	Maryland	19,017,465,000	2.0%
3	Massachusetts	68,675,081,000	7.1%
8	Michigan	28,521,830,000	3.0%
26	Minnesota	8,866,611,000	0.9%
36	Mississippi	5,858,340,000	0.6%
18	Missouri	18,715,821,000	1.9%
41	Montana	4,649,819,000	0.5%
48	Nebraska	2,331,711,000	0.2%
44	Nevada	4,140,910,000	0.4%
29	New Hampshire	7,690,409,000	0.8%
5	New Jersey	51,384,806,000	5.3%
30	New Mexico	7,323,101,000	0.8%
2	New York	110,084,829,000	11.4%
15	North Carolina	19,245,613,000	2.0%
49	North Dakota	1,792,485,000	0.2%
9	Ohio	26,065,238,000	2.7%
27	Oklahoma	8,667,100,000	0.9%
23	Oregon	11,303,477,000	1.2%
6	Pennsylvania	37,125,118,000	3.8%
28	Rhode Island	8,418,744,000	0.9%
19	South Carolina	14,981,290,000	1.6%
45	South Dakota	3,232,457,000	0.3%
43	Tennessee	4,141,541,000	0.4%
10	Texas	23,909,021,000	2.5%
35	Utah	5,926,589,000	0.6%
46	Vermont	3,052,469,000	0.3%
14	Virginia	19,683,529,000	2.0%
13	Washington	21,058,558,000	2.2%
38	West Virginia	5,628,065,000	0.6%
12	Wisconsin	21,461,270,000	2.2%
50	Wyoming	1,205,067,000	0.1%

RANK ORDER

RANK	STATE	DEBT	% of USA
1	California	$114,701,797,000	11.9%
2	New York	110,084,829,000	11.4%
3	Massachusetts	68,675,081,000	7.1%
4	Illinois	54,535,159,000	5.6%
5	New Jersey	51,384,806,000	5.3%
6	Pennsylvania	37,125,118,000	3.8%
7	Florida	36,483,336,000	3.8%
8	Michigan	28,521,830,000	3.0%
9	Ohio	26,065,238,000	2.7%
10	Texas	23,909,021,000	2.5%
11	Connecticut	23,836,187,000	2.5%
12	Wisconsin	21,461,270,000	2.2%
13	Washington	21,058,558,000	2.2%
14	Virginia	19,683,529,000	2.0%
15	North Carolina	19,245,613,000	2.0%
16	Indiana	19,180,194,000	2.0%
17	Maryland	19,017,465,000	2.0%
18	Missouri	18,715,821,000	1.9%
19	South Carolina	14,981,290,000	1.6%
20	Colorado	14,905,758,000	1.5%
21	Louisiana	14,251,968,000	1.5%
22	Georgia	11,370,040,000	1.2%
23	Oregon	11,303,477,000	1.2%
24	Kentucky	10,857,128,000	1.1%
25	Arizona	9,546,428,000	1.0%
26	Minnesota	8,866,611,000	0.9%
27	Oklahoma	8,667,100,000	0.9%
28	Rhode Island	8,418,744,000	0.9%
29	New Hampshire	7,690,409,000	0.8%
30	New Mexico	7,323,101,000	0.8%
31	Alabama	7,059,343,000	0.7%
32	Iowa	6,727,065,000	0.7%
33	Alaska	6,553,080,000	0.7%
34	Hawaii	5,959,064,000	0.6%
35	Utah	5,926,589,000	0.6%
36	Mississippi	5,858,340,000	0.6%
37	Kansas	5,638,261,000	0.6%
38	West Virginia	5,628,065,000	0.6%
39	Delaware	5,390,504,000	0.6%
40	Maine	5,326,692,000	0.6%
41	Montana	4,649,819,000	0.5%
42	Arkansas	4,508,511,000	0.5%
43	Tennessee	4,141,541,000	0.4%
44	Nevada	4,140,910,000	0.4%
45	South Dakota	3,232,457,000	0.3%
46	Vermont	3,052,469,000	0.3%
47	Idaho	2,812,655,000	0.3%
48	Nebraska	2,331,711,000	0.2%
49	North Dakota	1,792,485,000	0.2%
50	Wyoming	1,205,067,000	0.1%
	District of Columbia**	NA	NA

Source: U.S. Bureau of the Census, Governments Division
   "State and Local Government Finances 2006-2007" (http://www.census.gov/govs/estimate/index.html)
*Includes short-term, long-term, full faith and credit, nonguaranteed, and public debt for private purposes.
**Not applicable.

Per Capita State Government Debt Outstanding in 2007

National Per Capita = $3,102*

ALPHA ORDER

RANK	STATE	PER CAPITA
45	Alabama	$1,522
2	Alaska	9,604
46	Arizona	1,500
44	Arkansas	1,586
22	California	3,166
24	Colorado	3,078
4	Connecticut	6,833
5	Delaware	6,233
40	Florida	1,996
48	Georgia	1,193
11	Hawaii	4,667
41	Idaho	1,876
12	Illinois	4,267
26	Indiana	3,022
35	Iowa	2,258
38	Kansas	2,031
30	Kentucky	2,551
19	Louisiana	3,257
14	Maine	4,044
18	Maryland	3,375
1	Massachusetts	10,567
28	Michigan	2,838
42	Minnesota	1,708
39	Mississippi	2,005
21	Missouri	3,167
10	Montana	4,858
47	Nebraska	1,317
43	Nevada	1,613
7	New Hampshire	5,838
6	New Jersey	5,950
16	New Mexico	3,720
8	New York	5,668
37	North Carolina	2,123
29	North Dakota	2,809
34	Ohio	2,262
32	Oklahoma	2,399
25	Oregon	3,028
27	Pennsylvania	2,965
3	Rhode Island	7,980
17	South Carolina	3,386
13	South Dakota	4,056
50	Tennessee	671
49	Texas	1,003
36	Utah	2,225
9	Vermont	4,920
31	Virginia	2,550
19	Washington	3,257
23	West Virginia	3,107
15	Wisconsin	3,831
33	Wyoming	2,302

RANK ORDER

RANK	STATE	PER CAPITA
1	Massachusetts	$10,567
2	Alaska	9,604
3	Rhode Island	7,980
4	Connecticut	6,833
5	Delaware	6,233
6	New Jersey	5,950
7	New Hampshire	5,838
8	New York	5,668
9	Vermont	4,920
10	Montana	4,858
11	Hawaii	4,667
12	Illinois	4,267
13	South Dakota	4,056
14	Maine	4,044
15	Wisconsin	3,831
16	New Mexico	3,720
17	South Carolina	3,386
18	Maryland	3,375
19	Louisiana	3,257
19	Washington	3,257
21	Missouri	3,167
22	California	3,166
23	West Virginia	3,107
24	Colorado	3,078
25	Oregon	3,028
26	Indiana	3,022
27	Pennsylvania	2,965
28	Michigan	2,838
29	North Dakota	2,809
30	Kentucky	2,551
31	Virginia	2,550
32	Oklahoma	2,399
33	Wyoming	2,302
34	Ohio	2,262
35	Iowa	2,258
36	Utah	2,225
37	North Carolina	2,123
38	Kansas	2,031
39	Mississippi	2,005
40	Florida	1,996
41	Idaho	1,876
42	Minnesota	1,708
43	Nevada	1,613
44	Arkansas	1,586
45	Alabama	1,522
46	Arizona	1,500
47	Nebraska	1,317
48	Georgia	1,193
49	Texas	1,003
50	Tennessee	671
	District of Columbia**	NA

Source: CQ Press using data from U.S. Bureau of the Census, Governments Division
"State and Local Government Finances 2006-2007" (http://www.census.gov/govs/estimate/index.html)
*Includes short-term, long-term, full faith and credit, nonguaranteed, and public debt for private purposes.
**Not applicable.

State Government Full-Time Equivalent Employees in 2008

National Total = 4,362,688 FTE Employees*

ALPHA ORDER

RANK	STATE	EMPLOYEES	% of USA
17	Alabama	89,456	2.1%
41	Alaska	25,885	0.6%
24	Arizona	73,004	1.7%
29	Arkansas	61,103	1.4%
1	California	393,989	9.0%
26	Colorado	69,400	1.6%
28	Connecticut	66,183	1.5%
40	Delaware	26,756	0.6%
4	Florida	189,226	4.3%
10	Georgia	129,749	3.0%
31	Hawaii	59,868	1.4%
43	Idaho	22,721	0.5%
11	Illinois	128,605	2.9%
16	Indiana	91,166	2.1%
33	Iowa	54,547	1.3%
36	Kansas	45,989	1.1%
21	Kentucky	81,190	1.9%
15	Louisiana	91,854	2.1%
42	Maine	23,075	0.5%
19	Maryland	89,153	2.0%
14	Massachusetts	97,601	2.2%
9	Michigan	140,585	3.2%
22	Minnesota	79,128	1.8%
32	Mississippi	57,337	1.3%
18	Missouri	89,349	2.0%
45	Montana	19,881	0.5%
38	Nebraska	32,251	0.7%
39	Nevada	28,437	0.7%
46	New Hampshire	19,753	0.5%
6	New Jersey	156,373	3.6%
35	New Mexico	48,532	1.1%
3	New York	254,883	5.8%
7	North Carolina	145,881	3.3%
47	North Dakota	17,983	0.4%
8	Ohio	142,727	3.3%
25	Oklahoma	71,971	1.6%
30	Oregon	60,387	1.4%
5	Pennsylvania	161,528	3.7%
44	Rhode Island	20,426	0.5%
23	South Carolina	77,957	1.8%
49	South Dakota	13,410	0.3%
20	Tennessee	86,099	2.0%
2	Texas	290,022	6.6%
34	Utah	50,879	1.2%
48	Vermont	15,103	0.3%
12	Virginia	127,645	2.9%
13	Washington	122,541	2.8%
37	West Virginia	39,065	0.9%
27	Wisconsin	69,019	1.6%
50	Wyoming	13,016	0.3%

RANK ORDER

RANK	STATE	EMPLOYEES	% of USA
1	California	393,989	9.0%
2	Texas	290,022	6.6%
3	New York	254,883	5.8%
4	Florida	189,226	4.3%
5	Pennsylvania	161,528	3.7%
6	New Jersey	156,373	3.6%
7	North Carolina	145,881	3.3%
8	Ohio	142,727	3.3%
9	Michigan	140,585	3.2%
10	Georgia	129,749	3.0%
11	Illinois	128,605	2.9%
12	Virginia	127,645	2.9%
13	Washington	122,541	2.8%
14	Massachusetts	97,601	2.2%
15	Louisiana	91,854	2.1%
16	Indiana	91,166	2.1%
17	Alabama	89,456	2.1%
18	Missouri	89,349	2.0%
19	Maryland	89,153	2.0%
20	Tennessee	86,099	2.0%
21	Kentucky	81,190	1.9%
22	Minnesota	79,128	1.8%
23	South Carolina	77,957	1.8%
24	Arizona	73,004	1.7%
25	Oklahoma	71,971	1.6%
26	Colorado	69,400	1.6%
27	Wisconsin	69,019	1.6%
28	Connecticut	66,183	1.5%
29	Arkansas	61,103	1.4%
30	Oregon	60,387	1.4%
31	Hawaii	59,868	1.4%
32	Mississippi	57,337	1.3%
33	Iowa	54,547	1.3%
34	Utah	50,879	1.2%
35	New Mexico	48,532	1.1%
36	Kansas	45,989	1.1%
37	West Virginia	39,065	0.9%
38	Nebraska	32,251	0.7%
39	Nevada	28,437	0.7%
40	Delaware	26,756	0.6%
41	Alaska	25,885	0.6%
42	Maine	23,075	0.5%
43	Idaho	22,721	0.5%
44	Rhode Island	20,426	0.5%
45	Montana	19,881	0.5%
46	New Hampshire	19,753	0.5%
47	North Dakota	17,983	0.4%
48	Vermont	15,103	0.3%
49	South Dakota	13,410	0.3%
50	Wyoming	13,016	0.3%
	District of Columbia**	NA	NA

Source: U.S. Bureau of the Census, Governments Division
 "Government Employment and Payroll" (http://www.census.gov/govs/apes/index.html)
*As of March 2008.
**Not applicable.

Rate of State Government Full-Time Equivalent Employees in 2008

National Rate = 144 State Government Employees per 10,000 Population*

ALPHA ORDER

RANK	STATE	RATE
15	Alabama	191
2	Alaska	376
46	Arizona	112
9	Arkansas	213
48	California	108
37	Colorado	141
16	Connecticut	189
3	Delaware	305
49	Florida	103
40	Georgia	134
1	Hawaii	465
33	Idaho	149
50	Illinois	100
36	Indiana	143
20	Iowa	182
26	Kansas	164
16	Kentucky	189
10	Louisiana	206
23	Maine	175
29	Maryland	158
33	Massachusetts	149
37	Michigan	141
31	Minnesota	151
13	Mississippi	195
32	Missouri	150
11	Montana	205
21	Nebraska	181
47	Nevada	109
33	New Hampshire	149
22	New Jersey	180
5	New Mexico	244
41	New York	131
29	North Carolina	158
4	North Dakota	280
43	Ohio	124
12	Oklahoma	198
28	Oregon	160
42	Pennsylvania	129
14	Rhode Island	194
24	South Carolina	173
25	South Dakota	167
39	Tennessee	138
45	Texas	119
18	Utah	187
7	Vermont	243
26	Virginia	164
18	Washington	187
8	West Virginia	215
44	Wisconsin	123
5	Wyoming	244

RANK ORDER

RANK	STATE	RATE
1	Hawaii	465
2	Alaska	376
3	Delaware	305
4	North Dakota	280
5	New Mexico	244
5	Wyoming	244
7	Vermont	243
8	West Virginia	215
9	Arkansas	213
10	Louisiana	206
11	Montana	205
12	Oklahoma	198
13	Mississippi	195
14	Rhode Island	194
15	Alabama	191
16	Connecticut	189
16	Kentucky	189
18	Utah	187
18	Washington	187
20	Iowa	182
21	Nebraska	181
22	New Jersey	180
23	Maine	175
24	South Carolina	173
25	South Dakota	167
26	Kansas	164
26	Virginia	164
28	Oregon	160
29	Maryland	158
29	North Carolina	158
31	Minnesota	151
32	Missouri	150
33	Idaho	149
33	Massachusetts	149
33	New Hampshire	149
36	Indiana	143
37	Colorado	141
37	Michigan	141
39	Tennessee	138
40	Georgia	134
41	New York	131
42	Pennsylvania	129
43	Ohio	124
44	Wisconsin	123
45	Texas	119
46	Arizona	112
47	Nevada	109
48	California	108
49	Florida	103
50	Illinois	100
	District of Columbia**	NA

Source: CQ Press using data from U.S. Bureau of the Census, Governments Division
   "Government Employment and Payroll" (http://www.census.gov/govs/apes/index.html)
*Full-time equivalent as of March 2008.
**Not applicable.

Average Annual Earnings of Full-Time State Government Employees in 2008

National Average = $53,344*

ALPHA ORDER

RANK	STATE	SALARY
31	Alabama	$47,882
14	Alaska	55,913
21	Arizona	51,088
47	Arkansas	41,510
1	California	70,950
8	Colorado	58,813
3	Connecticut	65,763
23	Delaware	50,124
37	Florida	45,700
41	Georgia	44,691
28	Hawaii	48,774
26	Idaho	49,277
7	Illinois	58,968
27	Indiana	48,871
4	Iowa	61,980
34	Kansas	46,736
35	Kentucky	46,537
30	Louisiana	48,087
32	Maine	47,602
17	Maryland	53,907
10	Massachusetts	57,871
13	Michigan	56,955
5	Minnesota	60,843
48	Mississippi	40,376
50	Missouri	39,494
36	Montana	45,861
43	Nebraska	44,345
12	Nevada	57,029
19	New Hampshire	52,409
2	New Jersey	66,962
39	New Mexico	45,208
6	New York	60,619
33	North Carolina	47,173
44	North Dakota	43,674
15	Ohio	55,617
42	Oklahoma	44,387
18	Oregon	53,551
22	Pennsylvania	50,252
9	Rhode Island	58,232
46	South Carolina	42,358
45	South Dakota	43,090
38	Tennessee	45,528
29	Texas	48,678
25	Utah	49,823
20	Vermont	51,996
24	Virginia	49,952
16	Washington	54,978
49	West Virginia	40,163
11	Wisconsin	57,364
40	Wyoming	44,721

RANK ORDER

RANK	STATE	SALARY
1	California	$70,950
2	New Jersey	66,962
3	Connecticut	65,763
4	Iowa	61,980
5	Minnesota	60,843
6	New York	60,619
7	Illinois	58,968
8	Colorado	58,813
9	Rhode Island	58,232
10	Massachusetts	57,871
11	Wisconsin	57,364
12	Nevada	57,029
13	Michigan	56,955
14	Alaska	55,913
15	Ohio	55,617
16	Washington	54,978
17	Maryland	53,907
18	Oregon	53,551
19	New Hampshire	52,409
20	Vermont	51,996
21	Arizona	51,088
22	Pennsylvania	50,252
23	Delaware	50,124
24	Virginia	49,952
25	Utah	49,823
26	Idaho	49,277
27	Indiana	48,871
28	Hawaii	48,774
29	Texas	48,678
30	Louisiana	48,087
31	Alabama	47,882
32	Maine	47,602
33	North Carolina	47,173
34	Kansas	46,736
35	Kentucky	46,537
36	Montana	45,861
37	Florida	45,700
38	Tennessee	45,528
39	New Mexico	45,208
40	Wyoming	44,721
41	Georgia	44,691
42	Oklahoma	44,387
43	Nebraska	44,345
44	North Dakota	43,674
45	South Dakota	43,090
46	South Carolina	42,358
47	Arkansas	41,510
48	Mississippi	40,376
49	West Virginia	40,163
50	Missouri	39,494

District of Columbia**   NA

Source: CQ Press using data from U.S. Bureau of the Census, Governments Division
"Government Employment and Payroll" (http://www.census.gov/govs/apes/index.html)
*March 2008 full-time payroll (multiplied by 12) divided by full-time employees.
**Not applicable.

Local Government Total Revenue in 2007

National Total = $1,536,299,851,000*

ALPHA ORDER

RANK	STATE	REVENUE	% of USA
23	Alabama	$19,588,287,000	1.3%
44	Alaska	3,969,049,000	0.3%
15	Arizona	29,111,990,000	1.9%
36	Arkansas	8,400,937,000	0.5%
1	California	263,561,329,000	17.2%
20	Colorado	24,906,882,000	1.6%
27	Connecticut	15,733,269,000	1.0%
46	Delaware	3,073,643,000	0.2%
4	Florida	96,594,924,000	6.3%
9	Georgia	41,684,410,000	2.7%
48	Hawaii	2,575,974,000	0.2%
38	Idaho	5,214,367,000	0.3%
5	Illinois	64,700,190,000	4.2%
21	Indiana	24,611,734,000	1.6%
29	Iowa	12,662,433,000	0.8%
31	Kansas	12,360,063,000	0.8%
30	Kentucky	12,587,191,000	0.8%
24	Louisiana	18,840,074,000	1.2%
41	Maine	4,268,660,000	0.3%
19	Maryland	25,479,844,000	1.7%
14	Massachusetts	31,017,152,000	2.0%
8	Michigan	47,748,028,000	3.1%
17	Minnesota	25,832,679,000	1.7%
33	Mississippi	11,549,074,000	0.8%
22	Missouri	22,483,264,000	1.5%
45	Montana	3,140,994,000	0.2%
34	Nebraska	10,307,246,000	0.7%
28	Nevada	13,641,386,000	0.9%
40	New Hampshire	4,744,694,000	0.3%
10	New Jersey	41,215,393,000	2.7%
37	New Mexico	7,661,117,000	0.5%
2	New York	166,261,944,000	10.8%
11	North Carolina	36,703,780,000	2.4%
50	North Dakota	2,265,663,000	0.1%
7	Ohio	53,075,177,000	3.5%
32	Oklahoma	12,062,222,000	0.8%
26	Oregon	16,306,689,000	1.1%
6	Pennsylvania	57,232,955,000	3.7%
42	Rhode Island	4,085,701,000	0.3%
25	South Carolina	16,597,404,000	1.1%
47	South Dakota	2,767,171,000	0.2%
16	Tennessee	28,208,852,000	1.8%
3	Texas	105,000,767,000	6.8%
35	Utah	9,984,636,000	0.6%
49	Vermont	2,300,709,000	0.1%
13	Virginia	33,708,633,000	2.2%
12	Washington	34,649,059,000	2.3%
39	West Virginia	4,893,745,000	0.3%
18	Wisconsin	25,491,397,000	1.7%
43	Wyoming	4,048,227,000	0.3%

RANK ORDER

RANK	STATE	REVENUE	% of USA
1	California	$263,561,329,000	17.2%
2	New York	166,261,944,000	10.8%
3	Texas	105,000,767,000	6.8%
4	Florida	96,594,924,000	6.3%
5	Illinois	64,700,190,000	4.2%
6	Pennsylvania	57,232,955,000	3.7%
7	Ohio	53,075,177,000	3.5%
8	Michigan	47,748,028,000	3.1%
9	Georgia	41,684,410,000	2.7%
10	New Jersey	41,215,393,000	2.7%
11	North Carolina	36,703,780,000	2.4%
12	Washington	34,649,059,000	2.3%
13	Virginia	33,708,633,000	2.2%
14	Massachusetts	31,017,152,000	2.0%
15	Arizona	29,111,990,000	1.9%
16	Tennessee	28,208,852,000	1.8%
17	Minnesota	25,832,679,000	1.7%
18	Wisconsin	25,491,397,000	1.7%
19	Maryland	25,479,844,000	1.7%
20	Colorado	24,906,882,000	1.6%
21	Indiana	24,611,734,000	1.6%
22	Missouri	22,483,264,000	1.5%
23	Alabama	19,588,287,000	1.3%
24	Louisiana	18,840,074,000	1.2%
25	South Carolina	16,597,404,000	1.1%
26	Oregon	16,306,689,000	1.1%
27	Connecticut	15,733,269,000	1.0%
28	Nevada	13,641,386,000	0.9%
29	Iowa	12,662,433,000	0.8%
30	Kentucky	12,587,191,000	0.8%
31	Kansas	12,360,063,000	0.8%
32	Oklahoma	12,062,222,000	0.8%
33	Mississippi	11,549,074,000	0.8%
34	Nebraska	10,307,246,000	0.7%
35	Utah	9,984,636,000	0.6%
36	Arkansas	8,400,937,000	0.5%
37	New Mexico	7,661,117,000	0.5%
38	Idaho	5,214,367,000	0.3%
39	West Virginia	4,893,745,000	0.3%
40	New Hampshire	4,744,694,000	0.3%
41	Maine	4,268,660,000	0.3%
42	Rhode Island	4,085,701,000	0.3%
43	Wyoming	4,048,227,000	0.3%
44	Alaska	3,969,049,000	0.3%
45	Montana	3,140,994,000	0.2%
46	Delaware	3,073,643,000	0.2%
47	South Dakota	2,767,171,000	0.2%
48	Hawaii	2,575,974,000	0.2%
49	Vermont	2,300,709,000	0.1%
50	North Dakota	2,265,663,000	0.1%
	District of Columbia	11,388,843,000	0.7%

Source: U.S. Bureau of the Census, Governments Division
   "State and Local Government Finances 2006-2007" (http://www.census.gov/govs/estimate/index.html)
*Total revenue includes all money received from external sources. This includes taxes, intergovernmental transfers and
insurance trust revenue, and revenue from government owned utilities and other commercial or auxiliary enterprise.

Per Capita Local Government Total Revenue in 2007

National Per Capita = $5,094*

<table>
<tr><td colspan="3">ALPHA ORDER</td><td colspan="3">RANK ORDER</td></tr>
<tr><td>RANK</td><td>STATE</td><td>PER CAPITA</td><td>RANK</td><td>STATE</td><td>PER CAPITA</td></tr>
<tr><td>29</td><td>Alabama</td><td>$4,224</td><td>1</td><td>New York</td><td>$8,560</td></tr>
<tr><td>5</td><td>Alaska</td><td>5,817</td><td>2</td><td>Wyoming</td><td>7,734</td></tr>
<tr><td>16</td><td>Arizona</td><td>4,576</td><td>3</td><td>California</td><td>7,275</td></tr>
<tr><td>48</td><td>Arkansas</td><td>2,956</td><td>4</td><td>Nebraska</td><td>5,824</td></tr>
<tr><td>3</td><td>California</td><td>7,275</td><td>5</td><td>Alaska</td><td>5,817</td></tr>
<tr><td>9</td><td>Colorado</td><td>5,144</td><td>6</td><td>Washington</td><td>5,360</td></tr>
<tr><td>21</td><td>Connecticut</td><td>4,510</td><td>7</td><td>Nevada</td><td>5,313</td></tr>
<tr><td>40</td><td>Delaware</td><td>3,554</td><td>8</td><td>Florida</td><td>5,285</td></tr>
<tr><td>8</td><td>Florida</td><td>5,285</td><td>9</td><td>Colorado</td><td>5,144</td></tr>
<tr><td>24</td><td>Georgia</td><td>4,372</td><td>10</td><td>Illinois</td><td>5,063</td></tr>
<tr><td>50</td><td>Hawaii</td><td>2,017</td><td>11</td><td>Minnesota</td><td>4,976</td></tr>
<tr><td>42</td><td>Idaho</td><td>3,478</td><td>12</td><td>Massachusetts</td><td>4,772</td></tr>
<tr><td>10</td><td>Illinois</td><td>5,063</td><td>12</td><td>New Jersey</td><td>4,772</td></tr>
<tr><td>33</td><td>Indiana</td><td>3,878</td><td>14</td><td>Michigan</td><td>4,751</td></tr>
<tr><td>28</td><td>Iowa</td><td>4,251</td><td>15</td><td>Ohio</td><td>4,607</td></tr>
<tr><td>22</td><td>Kansas</td><td>4,453</td><td>16</td><td>Arizona</td><td>4,576</td></tr>
<tr><td>47</td><td>Kentucky</td><td>2,957</td><td>17</td><td>Pennsylvania</td><td>4,570</td></tr>
<tr><td>27</td><td>Louisiana</td><td>4,305</td><td>17</td><td>Tennessee</td><td>4,570</td></tr>
<tr><td>46</td><td>Maine</td><td>3,240</td><td>19</td><td>Wisconsin</td><td>4,551</td></tr>
<tr><td>20</td><td>Maryland</td><td>4,522</td><td>20</td><td>Maryland</td><td>4,522</td></tr>
<tr><td>12</td><td>Massachusetts</td><td>4,772</td><td>21</td><td>Connecticut</td><td>4,510</td></tr>
<tr><td>14</td><td>Michigan</td><td>4,751</td><td>22</td><td>Kansas</td><td>4,453</td></tr>
<tr><td>11</td><td>Minnesota</td><td>4,976</td><td>23</td><td>Texas</td><td>4,405</td></tr>
<tr><td>31</td><td>Mississippi</td><td>3,953</td><td>24</td><td>Georgia</td><td>4,372</td></tr>
<tr><td>35</td><td>Missouri</td><td>3,804</td><td>25</td><td>Oregon</td><td>4,368</td></tr>
<tr><td>45</td><td>Montana</td><td>3,281</td><td>26</td><td>Virginia</td><td>4,367</td></tr>
<tr><td>4</td><td>Nebraska</td><td>5,824</td><td>27</td><td>Louisiana</td><td>4,305</td></tr>
<tr><td>7</td><td>Nevada</td><td>5,313</td><td>28</td><td>Iowa</td><td>4,251</td></tr>
<tr><td>39</td><td>New Hampshire</td><td>3,602</td><td>29</td><td>Alabama</td><td>4,224</td></tr>
<tr><td>12</td><td>New Jersey</td><td>4,772</td><td>30</td><td>North Carolina</td><td>4,049</td></tr>
<tr><td>32</td><td>New Mexico</td><td>3,891</td><td>31</td><td>Mississippi</td><td>3,953</td></tr>
<tr><td>1</td><td>New York</td><td>8,560</td><td>32</td><td>New Mexico</td><td>3,891</td></tr>
<tr><td>30</td><td>North Carolina</td><td>4,049</td><td>33</td><td>Indiana</td><td>3,878</td></tr>
<tr><td>41</td><td>North Dakota</td><td>3,550</td><td>34</td><td>Rhode Island</td><td>3,873</td></tr>
<tr><td>15</td><td>Ohio</td><td>4,607</td><td>35</td><td>Missouri</td><td>3,804</td></tr>
<tr><td>44</td><td>Oklahoma</td><td>3,339</td><td>36</td><td>South Carolina</td><td>3,751</td></tr>
<tr><td>25</td><td>Oregon</td><td>4,368</td><td>37</td><td>Utah</td><td>3,748</td></tr>
<tr><td>17</td><td>Pennsylvania</td><td>4,570</td><td>38</td><td>Vermont</td><td>3,708</td></tr>
<tr><td>34</td><td>Rhode Island</td><td>3,873</td><td>39</td><td>New Hampshire</td><td>3,602</td></tr>
<tr><td>36</td><td>South Carolina</td><td>3,751</td><td>40</td><td>Delaware</td><td>3,554</td></tr>
<tr><td>43</td><td>South Dakota</td><td>3,472</td><td>41</td><td>North Dakota</td><td>3,550</td></tr>
<tr><td>17</td><td>Tennessee</td><td>4,570</td><td>42</td><td>Idaho</td><td>3,478</td></tr>
<tr><td>23</td><td>Texas</td><td>4,405</td><td>43</td><td>South Dakota</td><td>3,472</td></tr>
<tr><td>37</td><td>Utah</td><td>3,748</td><td>44</td><td>Oklahoma</td><td>3,339</td></tr>
<tr><td>38</td><td>Vermont</td><td>3,708</td><td>45</td><td>Montana</td><td>3,281</td></tr>
<tr><td>26</td><td>Virginia</td><td>4,367</td><td>46</td><td>Maine</td><td>3,240</td></tr>
<tr><td>6</td><td>Washington</td><td>5,360</td><td>47</td><td>Kentucky</td><td>2,957</td></tr>
<tr><td>49</td><td>West Virginia</td><td>2,702</td><td>48</td><td>Arkansas</td><td>2,956</td></tr>
<tr><td>19</td><td>Wisconsin</td><td>4,551</td><td>49</td><td>West Virginia</td><td>2,702</td></tr>
<tr><td>2</td><td>Wyoming</td><td>7,734</td><td>50</td><td>Hawaii</td><td>2,017</td></tr>
<tr><td></td><td></td><td></td><td></td><td>District of Columbia</td><td>19,421</td></tr>
</table>

Source: CQ Press using data from U.S. Bureau of the Census, Governments Division
   "State and Local Government Finances 2006-2007" (http://www.census.gov/govs/estimate/index.html)
*Total revenue includes all money received from external sources. This includes taxes, intergovernmental transfers and insurance trust revenue, and revenue from government owned utilities and other commercial or auxiliary enterprise.

Local Government Revenue From the Federal Government in 2007

National Total = $57,766,657,000

<table>
<tr><td colspan="4">ALPHA ORDER</td><td colspan="4">RANK ORDER</td></tr>
<tr><td>RANK</td><td>STATE</td><td>REVENUE</td><td>% of USA</td><td>RANK</td><td>STATE</td><td>REVENUE</td><td>% of USA</td></tr>
<tr><td>20</td><td>Alabama</td><td>$871,353,000</td><td>1.5%</td><td>1</td><td>California</td><td>$8,111,529,000</td><td>14.0%</td></tr>
<tr><td>35</td><td>Alaska</td><td>264,141,000</td><td>0.5%</td><td>2</td><td>New York</td><td>5,570,887,000</td><td>9.6%</td></tr>
<tr><td>18</td><td>Arizona</td><td>943,079,000</td><td>1.6%</td><td>3</td><td>Florida</td><td>4,033,146,000</td><td>7.0%</td></tr>
<tr><td>36</td><td>Arkansas</td><td>240,454,000</td><td>0.4%</td><td>4</td><td>Texas</td><td>3,669,289,000</td><td>6.4%</td></tr>
<tr><td>1</td><td>California</td><td>8,111,529,000</td><td>14.0%</td><td>5</td><td>Illinois</td><td>3,184,098,000</td><td>5.5%</td></tr>
<tr><td>14</td><td>Colorado</td><td>1,063,736,000</td><td>1.8%</td><td>6</td><td>Pennsylvania</td><td>3,098,180,000</td><td>5.4%</td></tr>
<tr><td>28</td><td>Connecticut</td><td>421,800,000</td><td>0.7%</td><td>7</td><td>Ohio</td><td>2,012,588,000</td><td>3.5%</td></tr>
<tr><td>49</td><td>Delaware</td><td>67,605,000</td><td>0.1%</td><td>8</td><td>North Carolina</td><td>1,799,347,000</td><td>3.1%</td></tr>
<tr><td>3</td><td>Florida</td><td>4,033,146,000</td><td>7.0%</td><td>9</td><td>Michigan</td><td>1,583,198,000</td><td>2.7%</td></tr>
<tr><td>15</td><td>Georgia</td><td>1,030,337,000</td><td>1.8%</td><td>10</td><td>Massachusetts</td><td>1,424,923,000</td><td>2.5%</td></tr>
<tr><td>41</td><td>Hawaii</td><td>176,015,000</td><td>0.3%</td><td>11</td><td>Washington</td><td>1,329,778,000</td><td>2.3%</td></tr>
<tr><td>43</td><td>Idaho</td><td>149,748,000</td><td>0.3%</td><td>12</td><td>Maryland</td><td>1,162,917,000</td><td>2.0%</td></tr>
<tr><td>5</td><td>Illinois</td><td>3,184,098,000</td><td>5.5%</td><td>13</td><td>Virginia</td><td>1,075,314,000</td><td>1.9%</td></tr>
<tr><td>27</td><td>Indiana</td><td>423,728,000</td><td>0.7%</td><td>14</td><td>Colorado</td><td>1,063,736,000</td><td>1.8%</td></tr>
<tr><td>30</td><td>Iowa</td><td>409,967,000</td><td>0.7%</td><td>15</td><td>Georgia</td><td>1,030,337,000</td><td>1.8%</td></tr>
<tr><td>38</td><td>Kansas</td><td>236,567,000</td><td>0.4%</td><td>16</td><td>Oregon</td><td>994,784,000</td><td>1.7%</td></tr>
<tr><td>29</td><td>Kentucky</td><td>418,298,000</td><td>0.7%</td><td>17</td><td>Louisiana</td><td>970,340,000</td><td>1.7%</td></tr>
<tr><td>17</td><td>Louisiana</td><td>970,340,000</td><td>1.7%</td><td>18</td><td>Arizona</td><td>943,079,000</td><td>1.6%</td></tr>
<tr><td>45</td><td>Maine</td><td>139,739,000</td><td>0.2%</td><td>19</td><td>New Jersey</td><td>880,778,000</td><td>1.5%</td></tr>
<tr><td>12</td><td>Maryland</td><td>1,162,917,000</td><td>2.0%</td><td>20</td><td>Alabama</td><td>871,353,000</td><td>1.5%</td></tr>
<tr><td>10</td><td>Massachusetts</td><td>1,424,923,000</td><td>2.5%</td><td>21</td><td>Missouri</td><td>806,661,000</td><td>1.4%</td></tr>
<tr><td>9</td><td>Michigan</td><td>1,583,198,000</td><td>2.7%</td><td>22</td><td>Minnesota</td><td>762,164,000</td><td>1.3%</td></tr>
<tr><td>22</td><td>Minnesota</td><td>762,164,000</td><td>1.3%</td><td>23</td><td>Mississippi</td><td>761,043,000</td><td>1.3%</td></tr>
<tr><td>23</td><td>Mississippi</td><td>761,043,000</td><td>1.3%</td><td>24</td><td>Tennessee</td><td>670,340,000</td><td>1.2%</td></tr>
<tr><td>21</td><td>Missouri</td><td>806,661,000</td><td>1.4%</td><td>25</td><td>Wisconsin</td><td>558,394,000</td><td>1.0%</td></tr>
<tr><td>40</td><td>Montana</td><td>211,078,000</td><td>0.4%</td><td>26</td><td>Nevada</td><td>522,585,000</td><td>0.9%</td></tr>
<tr><td>37</td><td>Nebraska</td><td>239,324,000</td><td>0.4%</td><td>27</td><td>Indiana</td><td>423,728,000</td><td>0.7%</td></tr>
<tr><td>26</td><td>Nevada</td><td>522,585,000</td><td>0.9%</td><td>28</td><td>Connecticut</td><td>421,800,000</td><td>0.7%</td></tr>
<tr><td>47</td><td>New Hampshire</td><td>128,450,000</td><td>0.2%</td><td>29</td><td>Kentucky</td><td>418,298,000</td><td>0.7%</td></tr>
<tr><td>19</td><td>New Jersey</td><td>880,778,000</td><td>1.5%</td><td>30</td><td>Iowa</td><td>409,967,000</td><td>0.7%</td></tr>
<tr><td>34</td><td>New Mexico</td><td>363,419,000</td><td>0.6%</td><td>31</td><td>Oklahoma</td><td>406,081,000</td><td>0.7%</td></tr>
<tr><td>2</td><td>New York</td><td>5,570,887,000</td><td>9.6%</td><td>32</td><td>Utah</td><td>384,900,000</td><td>0.7%</td></tr>
<tr><td>8</td><td>North Carolina</td><td>1,799,347,000</td><td>3.1%</td><td>33</td><td>South Carolina</td><td>367,004,000</td><td>0.6%</td></tr>
<tr><td>46</td><td>North Dakota</td><td>136,338,000</td><td>0.2%</td><td>34</td><td>New Mexico</td><td>363,419,000</td><td>0.6%</td></tr>
<tr><td>7</td><td>Ohio</td><td>2,012,588,000</td><td>3.5%</td><td>35</td><td>Alaska</td><td>264,141,000</td><td>0.5%</td></tr>
<tr><td>31</td><td>Oklahoma</td><td>406,081,000</td><td>0.7%</td><td>36</td><td>Arkansas</td><td>240,454,000</td><td>0.4%</td></tr>
<tr><td>16</td><td>Oregon</td><td>994,784,000</td><td>1.7%</td><td>37</td><td>Nebraska</td><td>239,324,000</td><td>0.4%</td></tr>
<tr><td>6</td><td>Pennsylvania</td><td>3,098,180,000</td><td>5.4%</td><td>38</td><td>Kansas</td><td>236,567,000</td><td>0.4%</td></tr>
<tr><td>44</td><td>Rhode Island</td><td>140,130,000</td><td>0.2%</td><td>39</td><td>West Virginia</td><td>231,534,000</td><td>0.4%</td></tr>
<tr><td>33</td><td>South Carolina</td><td>367,004,000</td><td>0.6%</td><td>40</td><td>Montana</td><td>211,078,000</td><td>0.4%</td></tr>
<tr><td>42</td><td>South Dakota</td><td>158,290,000</td><td>0.3%</td><td>41</td><td>Hawaii</td><td>176,015,000</td><td>0.3%</td></tr>
<tr><td>24</td><td>Tennessee</td><td>670,340,000</td><td>1.2%</td><td>42</td><td>South Dakota</td><td>158,290,000</td><td>0.3%</td></tr>
<tr><td>4</td><td>Texas</td><td>3,669,289,000</td><td>6.4%</td><td>43</td><td>Idaho</td><td>149,748,000</td><td>0.3%</td></tr>
<tr><td>32</td><td>Utah</td><td>384,900,000</td><td>0.7%</td><td>44</td><td>Rhode Island</td><td>140,130,000</td><td>0.2%</td></tr>
<tr><td>50</td><td>Vermont</td><td>60,506,000</td><td>0.1%</td><td>45</td><td>Maine</td><td>139,739,000</td><td>0.2%</td></tr>
<tr><td>13</td><td>Virginia</td><td>1,075,314,000</td><td>1.9%</td><td>46</td><td>North Dakota</td><td>136,338,000</td><td>0.2%</td></tr>
<tr><td>11</td><td>Washington</td><td>1,329,778,000</td><td>2.3%</td><td>47</td><td>New Hampshire</td><td>128,450,000</td><td>0.2%</td></tr>
<tr><td>39</td><td>West Virginia</td><td>231,534,000</td><td>0.4%</td><td>48</td><td>Wyoming</td><td>101,729,000</td><td>0.2%</td></tr>
<tr><td>25</td><td>Wisconsin</td><td>558,394,000</td><td>1.0%</td><td>49</td><td>Delaware</td><td>67,605,000</td><td>0.1%</td></tr>
<tr><td>48</td><td>Wyoming</td><td>101,729,000</td><td>0.2%</td><td>50</td><td>Vermont</td><td>60,506,000</td><td>0.1%</td></tr>
<tr><td></td><td></td><td></td><td></td><td></td><td>District of Columbia</td><td>2,999,024,000</td><td>5.2%</td></tr>
</table>

Source: U.S. Bureau of the Census, Governments Division
"State and Local Government Finances 2006-2007" (http://www.census.gov/govs/estimate/index.html)

Per Capita Local Government Revenue From the Federal Government in 2007

National Per Capita = $192

<table>
<tr><td colspan="3">ALPHA ORDER</td><td colspan="3">RANK ORDER</td></tr>
<tr><td>RANK</td><td>STATE</td><td>PER CAPITA</td><td>RANK</td><td>STATE</td><td>PER CAPITA</td></tr>
<tr><td>20</td><td>Alabama</td><td>$188</td><td>1</td><td>Alaska</td><td>$387</td></tr>
<tr><td>1</td><td>Alaska</td><td>387</td><td>2</td><td>New York</td><td>287</td></tr>
<tr><td>25</td><td>Arizona</td><td>148</td><td>3</td><td>Oregon</td><td>266</td></tr>
<tr><td>46</td><td>Arkansas</td><td>85</td><td>4</td><td>Mississippi</td><td>260</td></tr>
<tr><td>7</td><td>California</td><td>224</td><td>5</td><td>Illinois</td><td>249</td></tr>
<tr><td>11</td><td>Colorado</td><td>220</td><td>6</td><td>Pennsylvania</td><td>247</td></tr>
<tr><td>35</td><td>Connecticut</td><td>121</td><td>7</td><td>California</td><td>224</td></tr>
<tr><td>49</td><td>Delaware</td><td>78</td><td>8</td><td>Louisiana</td><td>222</td></tr>
<tr><td>9</td><td>Florida</td><td>221</td><td>9</td><td>Florida</td><td>221</td></tr>
<tr><td>38</td><td>Georgia</td><td>108</td><td>9</td><td>Montana</td><td>221</td></tr>
<tr><td>29</td><td>Hawaii</td><td>138</td><td>11</td><td>Colorado</td><td>220</td></tr>
<tr><td>41</td><td>Idaho</td><td>100</td><td>12</td><td>Massachusetts</td><td>219</td></tr>
<tr><td>5</td><td>Illinois</td><td>249</td><td>13</td><td>North Dakota</td><td>214</td></tr>
<tr><td>50</td><td>Indiana</td><td>67</td><td>14</td><td>Maryland</td><td>206</td></tr>
<tr><td>29</td><td>Iowa</td><td>138</td><td>14</td><td>Washington</td><td>206</td></tr>
<tr><td>46</td><td>Kansas</td><td>85</td><td>16</td><td>Nevada</td><td>204</td></tr>
<tr><td>43</td><td>Kentucky</td><td>98</td><td>17</td><td>North Carolina</td><td>199</td></tr>
<tr><td>8</td><td>Louisiana</td><td>222</td><td>17</td><td>South Dakota</td><td>199</td></tr>
<tr><td>39</td><td>Maine</td><td>106</td><td>19</td><td>Wyoming</td><td>194</td></tr>
<tr><td>14</td><td>Maryland</td><td>206</td><td>20</td><td>Alabama</td><td>188</td></tr>
<tr><td>12</td><td>Massachusetts</td><td>219</td><td>21</td><td>New Mexico</td><td>185</td></tr>
<tr><td>23</td><td>Michigan</td><td>158</td><td>22</td><td>Ohio</td><td>175</td></tr>
<tr><td>26</td><td>Minnesota</td><td>147</td><td>23</td><td>Michigan</td><td>158</td></tr>
<tr><td>4</td><td>Mississippi</td><td>260</td><td>24</td><td>Texas</td><td>154</td></tr>
<tr><td>31</td><td>Missouri</td><td>136</td><td>25</td><td>Arizona</td><td>148</td></tr>
<tr><td>9</td><td>Montana</td><td>221</td><td>26</td><td>Minnesota</td><td>147</td></tr>
<tr><td>32</td><td>Nebraska</td><td>135</td><td>27</td><td>Utah</td><td>144</td></tr>
<tr><td>16</td><td>Nevada</td><td>204</td><td>28</td><td>Virginia</td><td>139</td></tr>
<tr><td>43</td><td>New Hampshire</td><td>98</td><td>29</td><td>Hawaii</td><td>138</td></tr>
<tr><td>40</td><td>New Jersey</td><td>102</td><td>29</td><td>Iowa</td><td>138</td></tr>
<tr><td>21</td><td>New Mexico</td><td>185</td><td>31</td><td>Missouri</td><td>136</td></tr>
<tr><td>2</td><td>New York</td><td>287</td><td>32</td><td>Nebraska</td><td>135</td></tr>
<tr><td>17</td><td>North Carolina</td><td>199</td><td>33</td><td>Rhode Island</td><td>133</td></tr>
<tr><td>13</td><td>North Dakota</td><td>214</td><td>34</td><td>West Virginia</td><td>128</td></tr>
<tr><td>22</td><td>Ohio</td><td>175</td><td>35</td><td>Connecticut</td><td>121</td></tr>
<tr><td>36</td><td>Oklahoma</td><td>112</td><td>36</td><td>Oklahoma</td><td>112</td></tr>
<tr><td>3</td><td>Oregon</td><td>266</td><td>37</td><td>Tennessee</td><td>109</td></tr>
<tr><td>6</td><td>Pennsylvania</td><td>247</td><td>38</td><td>Georgia</td><td>108</td></tr>
<tr><td>33</td><td>Rhode Island</td><td>133</td><td>39</td><td>Maine</td><td>106</td></tr>
<tr><td>48</td><td>South Carolina</td><td>83</td><td>40</td><td>New Jersey</td><td>102</td></tr>
<tr><td>17</td><td>South Dakota</td><td>199</td><td>41</td><td>Idaho</td><td>100</td></tr>
<tr><td>37</td><td>Tennessee</td><td>109</td><td>41</td><td>Wisconsin</td><td>100</td></tr>
<tr><td>24</td><td>Texas</td><td>154</td><td>43</td><td>Kentucky</td><td>98</td></tr>
<tr><td>27</td><td>Utah</td><td>144</td><td>43</td><td>New Hampshire</td><td>98</td></tr>
<tr><td>43</td><td>Vermont</td><td>98</td><td>43</td><td>Vermont</td><td>98</td></tr>
<tr><td>28</td><td>Virginia</td><td>139</td><td>46</td><td>Arkansas</td><td>85</td></tr>
<tr><td>14</td><td>Washington</td><td>206</td><td>46</td><td>Kansas</td><td>85</td></tr>
<tr><td>34</td><td>West Virginia</td><td>128</td><td>48</td><td>South Carolina</td><td>83</td></tr>
<tr><td>41</td><td>Wisconsin</td><td>100</td><td>49</td><td>Delaware</td><td>78</td></tr>
<tr><td>19</td><td>Wyoming</td><td>194</td><td>50</td><td>Indiana</td><td>67</td></tr>
</table>

District of Columbia   5,114

Source: CQ Press using data from U.S. Bureau of the Census, Governments Division
"State and Local Government Finances 2006-2007" (http://www.census.gov/govs/estimate/index.html)

Local Government Own Source Revenue in 2007

National Total = $833,899,295,000*

ALPHA ORDER

RANK	STATE	REVENUE	% of USA
25	Alabama	$9,908,802,000	1.2%
44	Alaska	2,149,093,000	0.3%
17	Arizona	14,537,694,000	1.7%
36	Arkansas	3,311,036,000	0.4%
1	California	114,986,750,000	13.8%
14	Colorado	15,929,015,000	1.9%
26	Connecticut	9,645,215,000	1.2%
49	Delaware	1,298,787,000	0.2%
4	Florida	60,889,903,000	7.3%
9	Georgia	25,096,340,000	3.0%
45	Hawaii	1,995,026,000	0.2%
39	Idaho	2,895,451,000	0.3%
5	Illinois	36,617,564,000	4.4%
18	Indiana	14,177,141,000	1.7%
29	Iowa	7,565,162,000	0.9%
30	Kansas	7,162,911,000	0.9%
32	Kentucky	6,515,774,000	0.8%
23	Louisiana	11,013,668,000	1.3%
40	Maine	2,689,878,000	0.3%
15	Maryland	15,502,921,000	1.9%
16	Massachusetts	15,133,884,000	1.8%
10	Michigan	22,963,641,000	2.8%
22	Minnesota	12,340,330,000	1.5%
33	Mississippi	5,705,325,000	0.7%
19	Missouri	13,812,457,000	1.7%
46	Montana	1,744,758,000	0.2%
35	Nebraska	5,034,603,000	0.6%
28	Nevada	7,725,082,000	0.9%
37	New Hampshire	3,168,807,000	0.4%
8	New Jersey	28,173,557,000	3.4%
38	New Mexico	3,114,732,000	0.4%
2	New York	94,393,591,000	11.3%
12	North Carolina	18,912,108,000	2.3%
48	North Dakota	1,323,316,000	0.2%
7	Ohio	30,207,538,000	3.6%
31	Oklahoma	6,618,360,000	0.8%
27	Oregon	8,851,826,000	1.1%
6	Pennsylvania	31,271,017,000	3.7%
41	Rhode Island	2,498,433,000	0.3%
24	South Carolina	10,410,465,000	1.2%
47	South Dakota	1,692,220,000	0.2%
20	Tennessee	13,053,963,000	1.6%
3	Texas	64,337,134,000	7.7%
34	Utah	5,248,509,000	0.6%
50	Vermont	631,825,000	0.1%
11	Virginia	19,110,772,000	2.3%
13	Washington	17,956,878,000	2.2%
42	West Virginia	2,484,938,000	0.3%
21	Wisconsin	12,975,554,000	1.6%
43	Wyoming	2,367,968,000	0.3%

RANK ORDER

RANK	STATE	REVENUE	% of USA
1	California	$114,986,750,000	13.8%
2	New York	94,393,591,000	11.3%
3	Texas	64,337,134,000	7.7%
4	Florida	60,889,903,000	7.3%
5	Illinois	36,617,564,000	4.4%
6	Pennsylvania	31,271,017,000	3.7%
7	Ohio	30,207,538,000	3.6%
8	New Jersey	28,173,557,000	3.4%
9	Georgia	25,096,340,000	3.0%
10	Michigan	22,963,641,000	2.8%
11	Virginia	19,110,772,000	2.3%
12	North Carolina	18,912,108,000	2.3%
13	Washington	17,956,878,000	2.2%
14	Colorado	15,929,015,000	1.9%
15	Maryland	15,502,921,000	1.9%
16	Massachusetts	15,133,884,000	1.8%
17	Arizona	14,537,694,000	1.7%
18	Indiana	14,177,141,000	1.7%
19	Missouri	13,812,457,000	1.7%
20	Tennessee	13,053,963,000	1.6%
21	Wisconsin	12,975,554,000	1.6%
22	Minnesota	12,340,330,000	1.5%
23	Louisiana	11,013,668,000	1.3%
24	South Carolina	10,410,465,000	1.2%
25	Alabama	9,908,802,000	1.2%
26	Connecticut	9,645,215,000	1.2%
27	Oregon	8,851,826,000	1.1%
28	Nevada	7,725,082,000	0.9%
29	Iowa	7,565,162,000	0.9%
30	Kansas	7,162,911,000	0.9%
31	Oklahoma	6,618,360,000	0.8%
32	Kentucky	6,515,774,000	0.8%
33	Mississippi	5,705,325,000	0.7%
34	Utah	5,248,509,000	0.6%
35	Nebraska	5,034,603,000	0.6%
36	Arkansas	3,311,036,000	0.4%
37	New Hampshire	3,168,807,000	0.4%
38	New Mexico	3,114,732,000	0.4%
39	Idaho	2,895,451,000	0.3%
40	Maine	2,689,878,000	0.3%
41	Rhode Island	2,498,433,000	0.3%
42	West Virginia	2,484,938,000	0.3%
43	Wyoming	2,367,968,000	0.3%
44	Alaska	2,149,093,000	0.3%
45	Hawaii	1,995,026,000	0.2%
46	Montana	1,744,758,000	0.2%
47	South Dakota	1,692,220,000	0.2%
48	North Dakota	1,323,316,000	0.2%
49	Delaware	1,298,787,000	0.2%
50	Vermont	631,825,000	0.1%
	District of Columbia	6,747,573,000	0.8%

Source: U.S. Bureau of the Census, Governments Division
"State and Local Government Finances 2006-2007" (http://www.census.gov/govs/estimate/index.html)
*Own source revenue includes taxes, current charges, and miscellaneous general revenue. Excluded are intergovernmental transfers, insurance trust revenue, and revenue from government owned utilities and other commercial or auxiliary enterprise.

Per Capita Local Government Own Source Revenue in 2007

National Per Capita = $2,765*

ALPHA ORDER			RANK ORDER		
RANK	STATE	PER CAPITA	RANK	STATE	PER CAPITA
33	Alabama	$2,136	1	New York	$4,860
7	Alaska	3,150	2	Wyoming	4,524
30	Arizona	2,285	3	Florida	3,331
49	Arkansas	1,165	4	Colorado	3,290
6	California	3,174	5	New Jersey	3,262
4	Colorado	3,290	6	California	3,174
12	Connecticut	2,765	7	Alaska	3,150
47	Delaware	1,502	8	Nevada	3,009
3	Florida	3,331	9	Illinois	2,865
15	Georgia	2,632	10	Nebraska	2,845
45	Hawaii	1,562	11	Washington	2,778
41	Idaho	1,931	12	Connecticut	2,765
9	Illinois	2,865	13	Maryland	2,752
32	Indiana	2,234	14	Texas	2,699
18	Iowa	2,540	15	Georgia	2,632
17	Kansas	2,581	16	Ohio	2,622
46	Kentucky	1,531	17	Kansas	2,581
19	Louisiana	2,517	18	Iowa	2,540
38	Maine	2,042	19	Louisiana	2,517
13	Maryland	2,752	20	Pennsylvania	2,497
28	Massachusetts	2,329	21	Virginia	2,476
30	Michigan	2,285	22	New Hampshire	2,405
23	Minnesota	2,377	23	Minnesota	2,377
40	Mississippi	1,953	24	Oregon	2,371
27	Missouri	2,337	25	Rhode Island	2,368
43	Montana	1,823	26	South Carolina	2,353
10	Nebraska	2,845	27	Missouri	2,337
8	Nevada	3,009	28	Massachusetts	2,329
22	New Hampshire	2,405	29	Wisconsin	2,316
5	New Jersey	3,262	30	Arizona	2,285
44	New Mexico	1,582	30	Michigan	2,285
1	New York	4,860	32	Indiana	2,234
36	North Carolina	2,086	33	Alabama	2,136
37	North Dakota	2,074	34	South Dakota	2,123
16	Ohio	2,622	35	Tennessee	2,115
42	Oklahoma	1,832	36	North Carolina	2,086
24	Oregon	2,371	37	North Dakota	2,074
20	Pennsylvania	2,497	38	Maine	2,042
25	Rhode Island	2,368	39	Utah	1,970
26	South Carolina	2,353	40	Mississippi	1,953
34	South Dakota	2,123	41	Idaho	1,931
35	Tennessee	2,115	42	Oklahoma	1,832
14	Texas	2,699	43	Montana	1,823
39	Utah	1,970	44	New Mexico	1,582
50	Vermont	1,018	45	Hawaii	1,562
21	Virginia	2,476	46	Kentucky	1,531
11	Washington	2,778	47	Delaware	1,502
48	West Virginia	1,372	48	West Virginia	1,372
29	Wisconsin	2,316	49	Arkansas	1,165
2	Wyoming	4,524	50	Vermont	1,018
				District of Columbia	11,507

Source: CQ Press using data from U.S. Bureau of the Census, Governments Division
  "State and Local Government Finances 2006-2007" (http://www.census.gov/govs/estimate/index.html)
*Own source revenue includes taxes, current charges, and miscellaneous general revenue. Excluded are intergovernmental
transfers, insurance trust revenue, and revenue from government owned utilities and other commercial or auxiliary enterprise.

Local Government Tax Revenue in 2007

National Total = $518,622,988,000

ALPHA ORDER

RANK	STATE	REVENUE	% of USA
27	Alabama	$4,588,704,000	0.9%
43	Alaska	1,261,723,000	0.2%
17	Arizona	8,929,735,000	1.7%
40	Arkansas	1,787,832,000	0.3%
2	California	58,196,265,000	11.2%
16	Colorado	9,415,769,000	1.8%
20	Connecticut	8,247,677,000	1.6%
49	Delaware	752,780,000	0.1%
4	Florida	34,144,780,000	6.6%
9	Georgia	14,836,315,000	2.9%
41	Hawaii	1,474,158,000	0.3%
44	Idaho	1,226,554,000	0.2%
5	Illinois	25,009,548,000	4.8%
21	Indiana	7,103,332,000	1.4%
28	Iowa	4,463,746,000	0.9%
29	Kansas	4,461,070,000	0.9%
31	Kentucky	3,810,390,000	0.7%
23	Louisiana	6,620,688,000	1.3%
37	Maine	2,046,555,000	0.4%
12	Maryland	11,970,600,000	2.3%
13	Massachusetts	11,425,397,000	2.2%
11	Michigan	13,246,016,000	2.6%
24	Minnesota	5,896,554,000	1.1%
36	Mississippi	2,338,061,000	0.5%
19	Missouri	8,486,958,000	1.6%
47	Montana	951,538,000	0.2%
33	Nebraska	3,070,817,000	0.6%
30	Nevada	4,139,156,000	0.8%
35	New Hampshire	2,567,664,000	0.5%
6	New Jersey	21,944,092,000	4.2%
39	New Mexico	1,929,146,000	0.4%
1	New York	70,855,659,000	13.7%
15	North Carolina	9,809,673,000	1.9%
48	North Dakota	822,308,000	0.2%
8	Ohio	20,057,465,000	3.9%
32	Oklahoma	3,682,629,000	0.7%
26	Oregon	5,005,873,000	1.0%
7	Pennsylvania	21,419,698,000	4.1%
38	Rhode Island	2,020,757,000	0.4%
25	South Carolina	5,114,787,000	1.0%
46	South Dakota	1,125,963,000	0.2%
22	Tennessee	6,973,947,000	1.3%
3	Texas	41,722,475,000	8.0%
34	Utah	3,017,606,000	0.6%
50	Vermont	367,975,000	0.1%
10	Virginia	13,708,350,000	2.6%
14	Washington	9,840,510,000	1.9%
42	West Virginia	1,462,364,000	0.3%
18	Wisconsin	8,857,369,000	1.7%
45	Wyoming	1,221,770,000	0.2%

RANK ORDER

RANK	STATE	REVENUE	% of USA
1	New York	$70,855,659,000	13.7%
2	California	58,196,265,000	11.2%
3	Texas	41,722,475,000	8.0%
4	Florida	34,144,780,000	6.6%
5	Illinois	25,009,548,000	4.8%
6	New Jersey	21,944,092,000	4.2%
7	Pennsylvania	21,419,698,000	4.1%
8	Ohio	20,057,465,000	3.9%
9	Georgia	14,836,315,000	2.9%
10	Virginia	13,708,350,000	2.6%
11	Michigan	13,246,016,000	2.6%
12	Maryland	11,970,600,000	2.3%
13	Massachusetts	11,425,397,000	2.2%
14	Washington	9,840,510,000	1.9%
15	North Carolina	9,809,673,000	1.9%
16	Colorado	9,415,769,000	1.8%
17	Arizona	8,929,735,000	1.7%
18	Wisconsin	8,857,369,000	1.7%
19	Missouri	8,486,958,000	1.6%
20	Connecticut	8,247,677,000	1.6%
21	Indiana	7,103,332,000	1.4%
22	Tennessee	6,973,947,000	1.3%
23	Louisiana	6,620,688,000	1.3%
24	Minnesota	5,896,554,000	1.1%
25	South Carolina	5,114,787,000	1.0%
26	Oregon	5,005,873,000	1.0%
27	Alabama	4,588,704,000	0.9%
28	Iowa	4,463,746,000	0.9%
29	Kansas	4,461,070,000	0.9%
30	Nevada	4,139,156,000	0.8%
31	Kentucky	3,810,390,000	0.7%
32	Oklahoma	3,682,629,000	0.7%
33	Nebraska	3,070,817,000	0.6%
34	Utah	3,017,606,000	0.6%
35	New Hampshire	2,567,664,000	0.5%
36	Mississippi	2,338,061,000	0.5%
37	Maine	2,046,555,000	0.4%
38	Rhode Island	2,020,757,000	0.4%
39	New Mexico	1,929,146,000	0.4%
40	Arkansas	1,787,832,000	0.3%
41	Hawaii	1,474,158,000	0.3%
42	West Virginia	1,462,364,000	0.3%
43	Alaska	1,261,723,000	0.2%
44	Idaho	1,226,554,000	0.2%
45	Wyoming	1,221,770,000	0.2%
46	South Dakota	1,125,963,000	0.2%
47	Montana	951,538,000	0.2%
48	North Dakota	822,308,000	0.2%
49	Delaware	752,780,000	0.1%
50	Vermont	367,975,000	0.1%
	District of Columbia	5,192,190,000	1.0%

Source: U.S. Bureau of the Census, Governments Division
"State and Local Government Finances 2006-2007" (http://www.census.gov/govs/estimate/index.html)

Per Capita Local Government Tax Revenue in 2007

National Per Capita = $1,720

RANK	STATE	PER CAPITA
42	Alabama	$989
11	Alaska	1,849
29	Arizona	1,404
49	Arkansas	629
20	California	1,606
8	Colorado	1,944
3	Connecticut	2,364
45	Delaware	870
10	Florida	1,868
22	Georgia	1,556
34	Hawaii	1,155
46	Idaho	818
6	Illinois	1,957
38	Indiana	1,119
26	Iowa	1,499
19	Kansas	1,607
44	Kentucky	895
25	Louisiana	1,513
23	Maine	1,554
5	Maryland	2,125
13	Massachusetts	1,758
31	Michigan	1,318
35	Minnesota	1,136
48	Mississippi	800
27	Missouri	1,436
41	Montana	994
16	Nebraska	1,735
18	Nevada	1,612
7	New Hampshire	1,949
2	New Jersey	2,541
43	New Mexico	980
1	New York	3,648
39	North Carolina	1,082
32	North Dakota	1,288
15	Ohio	1,741
40	Oklahoma	1,020
30	Oregon	1,341
17	Pennsylvania	1,710
9	Rhode Island	1,915
33	South Carolina	1,156
28	South Dakota	1,413
37	Tennessee	1,130
14	Texas	1,750
36	Utah	1,133
50	Vermont	593
12	Virginia	1,776
24	Washington	1,522
47	West Virginia	807
21	Wisconsin	1,581
4	Wyoming	2,334

RANK	STATE	PER CAPITA
1	New York	$3,648
2	New Jersey	2,541
3	Connecticut	2,364
4	Wyoming	2,334
5	Maryland	2,125
6	Illinois	1,957
7	New Hampshire	1,949
8	Colorado	1,944
9	Rhode Island	1,915
10	Florida	1,868
11	Alaska	1,849
12	Virginia	1,776
13	Massachusetts	1,758
14	Texas	1,750
15	Ohio	1,741
16	Nebraska	1,735
17	Pennsylvania	1,710
18	Nevada	1,612
19	Kansas	1,607
20	California	1,606
21	Wisconsin	1,581
22	Georgia	1,556
23	Maine	1,554
24	Washington	1,522
25	Louisiana	1,513
26	Iowa	1,499
27	Missouri	1,436
28	South Dakota	1,413
29	Arizona	1,404
30	Oregon	1,341
31	Michigan	1,318
32	North Dakota	1,288
33	South Carolina	1,156
34	Hawaii	1,155
35	Minnesota	1,136
36	Utah	1,133
37	Tennessee	1,130
38	Indiana	1,119
39	North Carolina	1,082
40	Oklahoma	1,020
41	Montana	994
42	Alabama	989
43	New Mexico	980
44	Kentucky	895
45	Delaware	870
46	Idaho	818
47	West Virginia	807
48	Mississippi	800
49	Arkansas	629
50	Vermont	593

| | District of Columbia | 8,854 |

Source: CQ Press using data from U.S. Bureau of the Census, Governments Division
"State and Local Government Finances 2006-2007" (http://www.census.gov/govs/estimate/index.html)

Local Government Total Expenditures in 2007

National Total = $1,499,477,792,000*

ALPHA ORDER

RANK	STATE	EXPENDITURES	% of USA
23	Alabama	$18,822,328,000	1.2%
43	Alaska	3,846,110,000	0.2%
16	Arizona	29,058,159,000	1.8%
36	Arkansas	8,488,973,000	0.5%
1	California	247,207,963,000	15.5%
20	Colorado	25,298,865,000	1.6%
27	Connecticut	14,924,856,000	0.9%
45	Delaware	3,123,320,000	0.2%
4	Florida	95,535,952,000	6.0%
9	Georgia	42,296,728,000	2.6%
48	Hawaii	2,456,095,000	0.2%
38	Idaho	4,975,454,000	0.3%
5	Illinois	63,446,540,000	4.0%
17	Indiana	26,169,419,000	1.6%
29	Iowa	12,770,976,000	0.8%
32	Kansas	11,869,937,000	0.7%
30	Kentucky	12,534,229,000	0.8%
24	Louisiana	17,653,629,000	1.1%
41	Maine	4,190,515,000	0.3%
21	Maryland	23,963,666,000	1.5%
15	Massachusetts	30,198,624,000	1.9%
8	Michigan	45,953,104,000	2.9%
18	Minnesota	26,156,416,000	1.6%
33	Mississippi	11,227,295,000	0.7%
22	Missouri	22,348,583,000	1.4%
46	Montana	3,071,745,000	0.2%
34	Nebraska	10,785,830,000	0.7%
28	Nevada	13,089,810,000	0.8%
40	New Hampshire	4,669,674,000	0.3%
10	New Jersey	42,062,254,000	2.6%
37	New Mexico	7,395,166,000	0.5%
2	New York	156,259,283,000	9.8%
11	North Carolina	37,523,164,000	2.3%
50	North Dakota	2,207,768,000	0.1%
7	Ohio	52,188,728,000	3.3%
31	Oklahoma	11,995,146,000	0.7%
26	Oregon	16,689,506,000	1.0%
6	Pennsylvania	55,670,923,000	3.5%
42	Rhode Island	3,983,889,000	0.2%
25	South Carolina	16,751,830,000	1.0%
47	South Dakota	2,666,713,000	0.2%
14	Tennessee	30,237,735,000	1.9%
3	Texas	103,972,127,000	6.5%
35	Utah	9,828,083,000	0.6%
49	Vermont	2,231,129,000	0.1%
13	Virginia	32,762,640,000	2.0%
12	Washington	34,119,801,000	2.1%
39	West Virginia	4,969,646,000	0.3%
19	Wisconsin	25,489,495,000	1.6%
44	Wyoming	3,753,224,000	0.2%

RANK ORDER

RANK	STATE	EXPENDITURES	% of USA
1	California	$247,207,963,000	15.5%
2	New York	156,259,283,000	9.8%
3	Texas	103,972,127,000	6.5%
4	Florida	95,535,952,000	6.0%
5	Illinois	63,446,540,000	4.0%
6	Pennsylvania	55,670,923,000	3.5%
7	Ohio	52,188,728,000	3.3%
8	Michigan	45,953,104,000	2.9%
9	Georgia	42,296,728,000	2.6%
10	New Jersey	42,062,254,000	2.6%
11	North Carolina	37,523,164,000	2.3%
12	Washington	34,119,801,000	2.1%
13	Virginia	32,762,640,000	2.0%
14	Tennessee	30,237,735,000	1.9%
15	Massachusetts	30,198,624,000	1.9%
16	Arizona	29,058,159,000	1.8%
17	Indiana	26,169,419,000	1.6%
18	Minnesota	26,156,416,000	1.6%
19	Wisconsin	25,489,495,000	1.6%
20	Colorado	25,298,865,000	1.6%
21	Maryland	23,963,666,000	1.5%
22	Missouri	22,348,583,000	1.4%
23	Alabama	18,822,328,000	1.2%
24	Louisiana	17,653,629,000	1.1%
25	South Carolina	16,751,830,000	1.0%
26	Oregon	16,689,506,000	1.0%
27	Connecticut	14,924,856,000	0.9%
28	Nevada	13,089,810,000	0.8%
29	Iowa	12,770,976,000	0.8%
30	Kentucky	12,534,229,000	0.8%
31	Oklahoma	11,995,146,000	0.7%
32	Kansas	11,869,937,000	0.7%
33	Mississippi	11,227,295,000	0.7%
34	Nebraska	10,785,830,000	0.7%
35	Utah	9,828,083,000	0.6%
36	Arkansas	8,488,973,000	0.5%
37	New Mexico	7,395,166,000	0.5%
38	Idaho	4,975,454,000	0.3%
39	West Virginia	4,969,646,000	0.3%
40	New Hampshire	4,669,674,000	0.3%
41	Maine	4,190,515,000	0.3%
42	Rhode Island	3,983,889,000	0.2%
43	Alaska	3,846,110,000	0.2%
44	Wyoming	3,753,224,000	0.2%
45	Delaware	3,123,320,000	0.2%
46	Montana	3,071,745,000	0.2%
47	South Dakota	2,666,713,000	0.2%
48	Hawaii	2,456,095,000	0.2%
49	Vermont	2,231,129,000	0.1%
50	North Dakota	2,207,768,000	0.1%
	District of Columbia	10,584,747,000	0.7%

Source: U.S. Bureau of the Census, Governments Division
"State and Local Government Finances 2006-2007" (http://www.census.gov/govs/estimate/index.html)
*Total expenditures includes all money paid other than for retirement of debt and extension of loans. Includes payments from all sources of funds including current revenues and proceeds from borrowing and prior year fund balances. Includes intergovernmental transfers and expenditures for government owned utilities and other commercial or auxiliary enterprise and insurance trust expenditures.

Per Capita Local Government Total Expenditures in 2007

National Per Capita = $4,972*

ALPHA ORDER

RANK	STATE	PER CAPITA
30	Alabama	$4,058
5	Alaska	5,637
16	Arizona	4,567
47	Arkansas	2,987
3	California	6,824
8	Colorado	5,225
24	Connecticut	4,278
38	Delaware	3,611
7	Florida	5,227
21	Georgia	4,437
50	Hawaii	1,924
44	Idaho	3,319
11	Illinois	4,965
29	Indiana	4,124
23	Iowa	4,287
25	Kansas	4,277
48	Kentucky	2,945
31	Louisiana	4,034
46	Maine	3,181
26	Maryland	4,253
14	Massachusetts	4,646
15	Michigan	4,572
10	Minnesota	5,039
32	Mississippi	3,843
34	Missouri	3,782
45	Montana	3,209
4	Nebraska	6,094
9	Nevada	5,098
40	New Hampshire	3,545
13	New Jersey	4,871
36	New Mexico	3,756
1	New York	8,045
28	North Carolina	4,140
41	North Dakota	3,459
18	Ohio	4,530
43	Oklahoma	3,321
19	Oregon	4,471
20	Pennsylvania	4,446
35	Rhode Island	3,776
33	South Carolina	3,786
42	South Dakota	3,346
12	Tennessee	4,898
22	Texas	4,362
37	Utah	3,690
39	Vermont	3,596
27	Virginia	4,244
6	Washington	5,278
49	West Virginia	2,744
17	Wisconsin	4,550
2	Wyoming	7,171

RANK ORDER

RANK	STATE	PER CAPITA
1	New York	$8,045
2	Wyoming	7,171
3	California	6,824
4	Nebraska	6,094
5	Alaska	5,637
6	Washington	5,278
7	Florida	5,227
8	Colorado	5,225
9	Nevada	5,098
10	Minnesota	5,039
11	Illinois	4,965
12	Tennessee	4,898
13	New Jersey	4,871
14	Massachusetts	4,646
15	Michigan	4,572
16	Arizona	4,567
17	Wisconsin	4,550
18	Ohio	4,530
19	Oregon	4,471
20	Pennsylvania	4,446
21	Georgia	4,437
22	Texas	4,362
23	Iowa	4,287
24	Connecticut	4,278
25	Kansas	4,277
26	Maryland	4,253
27	Virginia	4,244
28	North Carolina	4,140
29	Indiana	4,124
30	Alabama	4,058
31	Louisiana	4,034
32	Mississippi	3,843
33	South Carolina	3,786
34	Missouri	3,782
35	Rhode Island	3,776
36	New Mexico	3,756
37	Utah	3,690
38	Delaware	3,611
39	Vermont	3,596
40	New Hampshire	3,545
41	North Dakota	3,459
42	South Dakota	3,346
43	Oklahoma	3,321
44	Idaho	3,319
45	Montana	3,209
46	Maine	3,181
47	Arkansas	2,987
48	Kentucky	2,945
49	West Virginia	2,744
50	Hawaii	1,924

District of Columbia   18,050

Source: CQ Press using data from U.S. Bureau of the Census, Governments Division
"State and Local Government Finances 2006-2007" (http://www.census.gov/govs/estimate/index.html)
*Total expenditures includes all money paid other than for retirement of debt and extension of loans. Includes payments from all sources of funds including current revenues and proceeds from borrowing and prior year fund balances. Includes intergovernmental transfers and expenditures for government owned utilities and other commercial or auxiliary enterprise and insurance trust expenditures.

Local Government Direct General Expenditures in 2007

National Total = $1,294,455,942,000*

ALPHA ORDER

RANK	STATE	EXPENDITURES	% of USA
23	Alabama	$16,114,446,000	1.2%
44	Alaska	3,422,986,000	0.3%
15	Arizona	23,789,179,000	1.8%
35	Arkansas	7,596,000,000	0.6%
1	California	209,822,527,000	16.2%
20	Colorado	21,619,193,000	1.7%
27	Connecticut	13,737,476,000	1.1%
46	Delaware	2,693,618,000	0.2%
4	Florida	84,461,112,000	6.5%
10	Georgia	36,452,104,000	2.8%
48	Hawaii	2,101,103,000	0.2%
38	Idaho	4,745,648,000	0.4%
5	Illinois	53,912,370,000	4.2%
16	Indiana	23,684,031,000	1.8%
28	Iowa	11,683,981,000	0.9%
32	Kansas	10,624,666,000	0.8%
31	Kentucky	10,738,976,000	0.8%
24	Louisiana	15,826,850,000	1.2%
41	Maine	4,058,326,000	0.3%
19	Maryland	21,874,016,000	1.7%
14	Massachusetts	23,922,798,000	1.8%
8	Michigan	41,328,224,000	3.2%
17	Minnesota	23,462,655,000	1.8%
33	Mississippi	10,349,820,000	0.8%
21	Missouri	19,832,067,000	1.5%
45	Montana	2,930,022,000	0.2%
36	Nebraska	6,880,143,000	0.5%
29	Nevada	11,592,899,000	0.9%
40	New Hampshire	4,496,082,000	0.3%
9	New Jersey	40,722,940,000	3.1%
37	New Mexico	6,723,873,000	0.5%
2	New York	129,650,121,000	10.0%
11	North Carolina	32,231,411,000	2.5%
49	North Dakota	2,039,033,000	0.2%
7	Ohio	48,593,587,000	3.8%
30	Oklahoma	10,933,436,000	0.8%
26	Oregon	14,652,466,000	1.1%
6	Pennsylvania	50,189,519,000	3.9%
42	Rhode Island	3,689,881,000	0.3%
25	South Carolina	15,150,149,000	1.2%
47	South Dakota	2,380,228,000	0.2%
22	Tennessee	18,828,113,000	1.5%
3	Texas	88,614,932,000	6.8%
34	Utah	7,750,237,000	0.6%
50	Vermont	2,004,288,000	0.2%
12	Virginia	29,949,461,000	2.3%
13	Washington	26,584,624,000	2.1%
39	West Virginia	4,637,266,000	0.4%
18	Wisconsin	23,346,523,000	1.8%
43	Wyoming	3,550,101,000	0.3%

RANK ORDER

RANK	STATE	EXPENDITURES	% of USA
1	California	$209,822,527,000	16.2%
2	New York	129,650,121,000	10.0%
3	Texas	88,614,932,000	6.8%
4	Florida	84,461,112,000	6.5%
5	Illinois	53,912,370,000	4.2%
6	Pennsylvania	50,189,519,000	3.9%
7	Ohio	48,593,587,000	3.8%
8	Michigan	41,328,224,000	3.2%
9	New Jersey	40,722,940,000	3.1%
10	Georgia	36,452,104,000	2.8%
11	North Carolina	32,231,411,000	2.5%
12	Virginia	29,949,461,000	2.3%
13	Washington	26,584,624,000	2.1%
14	Massachusetts	23,922,798,000	1.8%
15	Arizona	23,789,179,000	1.8%
16	Indiana	23,684,031,000	1.8%
17	Minnesota	23,462,655,000	1.8%
18	Wisconsin	23,346,523,000	1.8%
19	Maryland	21,874,016,000	1.7%
20	Colorado	21,619,193,000	1.7%
21	Missouri	19,832,067,000	1.5%
22	Tennessee	18,828,113,000	1.5%
23	Alabama	16,114,446,000	1.2%
24	Louisiana	15,826,850,000	1.2%
25	South Carolina	15,150,149,000	1.2%
26	Oregon	14,652,466,000	1.1%
27	Connecticut	13,737,476,000	1.1%
28	Iowa	11,683,981,000	0.9%
29	Nevada	11,592,899,000	0.9%
30	Oklahoma	10,933,436,000	0.8%
31	Kentucky	10,738,976,000	0.8%
32	Kansas	10,624,666,000	0.8%
33	Mississippi	10,349,820,000	0.8%
34	Utah	7,750,237,000	0.6%
35	Arkansas	7,596,000,000	0.6%
36	Nebraska	6,880,143,000	0.5%
37	New Mexico	6,723,873,000	0.5%
38	Idaho	4,745,648,000	0.4%
39	West Virginia	4,637,266,000	0.4%
40	New Hampshire	4,496,082,000	0.3%
41	Maine	4,058,326,000	0.3%
42	Rhode Island	3,689,881,000	0.3%
43	Wyoming	3,550,101,000	0.3%
44	Alaska	3,422,986,000	0.3%
45	Montana	2,930,022,000	0.2%
46	Delaware	2,693,618,000	0.2%
47	South Dakota	2,380,228,000	0.2%
48	Hawaii	2,101,103,000	0.2%
49	North Dakota	2,039,033,000	0.2%
50	Vermont	2,004,288,000	0.2%
	District of Columbia	8,480,435,000	0.7%

Source: U.S. Bureau of the Census, Governments Division
"State and Local Government Finances 2006-2007" (http://www.census.gov/govs/estimate/index.html)
*Direct general expenditures include expenditures for current operations, assistance and subsidies, interest on debt, and capital outlay. Excludes intergovernmental transfers, expenditures for government owned utilities and other commercial or auxiliary enterprise, and insurance trust expenditures.

Per Capita Local Government Direct General Expenditures in 2007

National Per Capita = $4,292*

<table>
<tr><td colspan="3">ALPHA ORDER</td><td colspan="3">RANK ORDER</td></tr>
<tr><td>RANK</td><td>STATE</td><td>PER CAPITA</td><td>RANK</td><td>STATE</td><td>PER CAPITA</td></tr>
<tr><td>32</td><td>Alabama</td><td>$3,475</td><td>1</td><td>Wyoming</td><td>$6,783</td></tr>
<tr><td>4</td><td>Alaska</td><td>5,017</td><td>2</td><td>New York</td><td>6,675</td></tr>
<tr><td>24</td><td>Arizona</td><td>3,739</td><td>3</td><td>California</td><td>5,792</td></tr>
<tr><td>47</td><td>Arkansas</td><td>2,673</td><td>4</td><td>Alaska</td><td>5,017</td></tr>
<tr><td>3</td><td>California</td><td>5,792</td><td>5</td><td>New Jersey</td><td>4,715</td></tr>
<tr><td>9</td><td>Colorado</td><td>4,465</td><td>6</td><td>Florida</td><td>4,621</td></tr>
<tr><td>16</td><td>Connecticut</td><td>3,938</td><td>7</td><td>Minnesota</td><td>4,520</td></tr>
<tr><td>40</td><td>Delaware</td><td>3,114</td><td>8</td><td>Nevada</td><td>4,515</td></tr>
<tr><td>6</td><td>Florida</td><td>4,621</td><td>9</td><td>Colorado</td><td>4,465</td></tr>
<tr><td>23</td><td>Georgia</td><td>3,823</td><td>10</td><td>Illinois</td><td>4,219</td></tr>
<tr><td>50</td><td>Hawaii</td><td>1,646</td><td>11</td><td>Ohio</td><td>4,218</td></tr>
<tr><td>39</td><td>Idaho</td><td>3,165</td><td>12</td><td>Wisconsin</td><td>4,168</td></tr>
<tr><td>10</td><td>Illinois</td><td>4,219</td><td>13</td><td>Michigan</td><td>4,112</td></tr>
<tr><td>25</td><td>Indiana</td><td>3,732</td><td>13</td><td>Washington</td><td>4,112</td></tr>
<tr><td>18</td><td>Iowa</td><td>3,922</td><td>15</td><td>Pennsylvania</td><td>4,008</td></tr>
<tr><td>22</td><td>Kansas</td><td>3,828</td><td>16</td><td>Connecticut</td><td>3,938</td></tr>
<tr><td>49</td><td>Kentucky</td><td>2,523</td><td>17</td><td>Oregon</td><td>3,925</td></tr>
<tr><td>28</td><td>Louisiana</td><td>3,617</td><td>18</td><td>Iowa</td><td>3,922</td></tr>
<tr><td>41</td><td>Maine</td><td>3,081</td><td>19</td><td>Nebraska</td><td>3,887</td></tr>
<tr><td>20</td><td>Maryland</td><td>3,882</td><td>20</td><td>Maryland</td><td>3,882</td></tr>
<tr><td>27</td><td>Massachusetts</td><td>3,681</td><td>21</td><td>Virginia</td><td>3,880</td></tr>
<tr><td>13</td><td>Michigan</td><td>4,112</td><td>22</td><td>Kansas</td><td>3,828</td></tr>
<tr><td>7</td><td>Minnesota</td><td>4,520</td><td>23</td><td>Georgia</td><td>3,823</td></tr>
<tr><td>30</td><td>Mississippi</td><td>3,542</td><td>24</td><td>Arizona</td><td>3,739</td></tr>
<tr><td>36</td><td>Missouri</td><td>3,356</td><td>25</td><td>Indiana</td><td>3,732</td></tr>
<tr><td>42</td><td>Montana</td><td>3,061</td><td>26</td><td>Texas</td><td>3,717</td></tr>
<tr><td>19</td><td>Nebraska</td><td>3,887</td><td>27</td><td>Massachusetts</td><td>3,681</td></tr>
<tr><td>8</td><td>Nevada</td><td>4,515</td><td>28</td><td>Louisiana</td><td>3,617</td></tr>
<tr><td>35</td><td>New Hampshire</td><td>3,413</td><td>29</td><td>North Carolina</td><td>3,556</td></tr>
<tr><td>5</td><td>New Jersey</td><td>4,715</td><td>30</td><td>Mississippi</td><td>3,542</td></tr>
<tr><td>34</td><td>New Mexico</td><td>3,415</td><td>31</td><td>Rhode Island</td><td>3,497</td></tr>
<tr><td>2</td><td>New York</td><td>6,675</td><td>32</td><td>Alabama</td><td>3,475</td></tr>
<tr><td>29</td><td>North Carolina</td><td>3,556</td><td>33</td><td>South Carolina</td><td>3,424</td></tr>
<tr><td>38</td><td>North Dakota</td><td>3,195</td><td>34</td><td>New Mexico</td><td>3,415</td></tr>
<tr><td>11</td><td>Ohio</td><td>4,218</td><td>35</td><td>New Hampshire</td><td>3,413</td></tr>
<tr><td>44</td><td>Oklahoma</td><td>3,027</td><td>36</td><td>Missouri</td><td>3,356</td></tr>
<tr><td>17</td><td>Oregon</td><td>3,925</td><td>37</td><td>Vermont</td><td>3,230</td></tr>
<tr><td>15</td><td>Pennsylvania</td><td>4,008</td><td>38</td><td>North Dakota</td><td>3,195</td></tr>
<tr><td>31</td><td>Rhode Island</td><td>3,497</td><td>39</td><td>Idaho</td><td>3,165</td></tr>
<tr><td>33</td><td>South Carolina</td><td>3,424</td><td>40</td><td>Delaware</td><td>3,114</td></tr>
<tr><td>45</td><td>South Dakota</td><td>2,986</td><td>41</td><td>Maine</td><td>3,081</td></tr>
<tr><td>43</td><td>Tennessee</td><td>3,050</td><td>42</td><td>Montana</td><td>3,061</td></tr>
<tr><td>26</td><td>Texas</td><td>3,717</td><td>43</td><td>Tennessee</td><td>3,050</td></tr>
<tr><td>46</td><td>Utah</td><td>2,909</td><td>44</td><td>Oklahoma</td><td>3,027</td></tr>
<tr><td>37</td><td>Vermont</td><td>3,230</td><td>45</td><td>South Dakota</td><td>2,986</td></tr>
<tr><td>21</td><td>Virginia</td><td>3,880</td><td>46</td><td>Utah</td><td>2,909</td></tr>
<tr><td>13</td><td>Washington</td><td>4,112</td><td>47</td><td>Arkansas</td><td>2,673</td></tr>
<tr><td>48</td><td>West Virginia</td><td>2,560</td><td>48</td><td>West Virginia</td><td>2,560</td></tr>
<tr><td>12</td><td>Wisconsin</td><td>4,168</td><td>49</td><td>Kentucky</td><td>2,523</td></tr>
<tr><td>1</td><td>Wyoming</td><td>6,783</td><td>50</td><td>Hawaii</td><td>1,646</td></tr>
<tr><td></td><td></td><td></td><td></td><td>District of Columbia</td><td>14,462</td></tr>
</table>

Source: CQ Press using data from U.S. Bureau of the Census, Governments Division
  "State and Local Government Finances 2006-2007" (http://www.census.gov/govs/estimate/index.html)
*Direct general expenditures include expenditures for current operations, assistance and subsidies, interest on debt, and capital outlay. Excludes intergovernmental transfers, expenditures for government owned utilities and other commercial or auxiliary enterprise, and insurance trust expenditures.

Local Government Debt Outstanding in 2007

National Total = $1,475,934,124,000*

ALPHA ORDER

RANK	STATE	DEBT	% of USA
26	Alabama	$17,529,533,000	1.2%
40	Alaska	3,444,285,000	0.2%
17	Arizona	29,783,699,000	2.0%
35	Arkansas	7,701,468,000	0.5%
1	California	215,448,400,000	14.6%
13	Colorado	31,280,128,000	2.1%
32	Connecticut	8,890,800,000	0.6%
45	Delaware	1,981,793,000	0.1%
4	Florida	97,471,175,000	6.6%
10	Georgia	37,092,845,000	2.5%
38	Hawaii	4,375,998,000	0.3%
43	Idaho	2,416,063,000	0.2%
6	Illinois	62,001,639,000	4.2%
19	Indiana	22,347,633,000	1.5%
33	Iowa	8,044,863,000	0.5%
28	Kansas	14,063,855,000	1.0%
18	Kentucky	25,914,363,000	1.8%
29	Louisiana	13,863,956,000	0.9%
41	Maine	2,658,976,000	0.2%
27	Maryland	15,436,126,000	1.0%
20	Massachusetts	20,966,022,000	1.4%
7	Michigan	44,560,271,000	3.0%
15	Minnesota	29,844,138,000	2.0%
36	Mississippi	6,697,723,000	0.5%
23	Missouri	20,101,098,000	1.4%
48	Montana	1,511,750,000	0.1%
31	Nebraska	9,184,390,000	0.6%
24	Nevada	17,942,149,000	1.2%
42	New Hampshire	2,562,715,000	0.2%
11	New Jersey	34,312,130,000	2.3%
37	New Mexico	4,871,524,000	0.3%
3	New York	149,432,590,000	10.1%
14	North Carolina	30,909,097,000	2.1%
46	North Dakota	1,839,277,000	0.1%
8	Ohio	42,107,112,000	2.9%
34	Oklahoma	7,898,556,000	0.5%
25	Oregon	17,642,923,000	1.2%
5	Pennsylvania	74,787,069,000	5.1%
44	Rhode Island	2,079,391,000	0.1%
21	South Carolina	20,888,916,000	1.4%
47	South Dakota	1,621,392,000	0.1%
16	Tennessee	29,838,657,000	2.0%
2	Texas	165,487,967,000	11.2%
30	Utah	9,997,920,000	0.7%
50	Vermont	995,901,000	0.1%
12	Virginia	31,292,926,000	2.1%
9	Washington	41,050,688,000	2.8%
39	West Virginia	3,454,502,000	0.2%
22	Wisconsin	20,357,559,000	1.4%
49	Wyoming	1,034,326,000	0.1%

RANK ORDER

RANK	STATE	DEBT	% of USA
1	California	$215,448,400,000	14.6%
2	Texas	165,487,967,000	11.2%
3	New York	149,432,590,000	10.1%
4	Florida	97,471,175,000	6.6%
5	Pennsylvania	74,787,069,000	5.1%
6	Illinois	62,001,639,000	4.2%
7	Michigan	44,560,271,000	3.0%
8	Ohio	42,107,112,000	2.9%
9	Washington	41,050,688,000	2.8%
10	Georgia	37,092,845,000	2.5%
11	New Jersey	34,312,130,000	2.3%
12	Virginia	31,292,926,000	2.1%
13	Colorado	31,280,128,000	2.1%
14	North Carolina	30,909,097,000	2.1%
15	Minnesota	29,844,138,000	2.0%
16	Tennessee	29,838,657,000	2.0%
17	Arizona	29,783,699,000	2.0%
18	Kentucky	25,914,363,000	1.8%
19	Indiana	22,347,633,000	1.5%
20	Massachusetts	20,966,022,000	1.4%
21	South Carolina	20,888,916,000	1.4%
22	Wisconsin	20,357,559,000	1.4%
23	Missouri	20,101,098,000	1.4%
24	Nevada	17,942,149,000	1.2%
25	Oregon	17,642,923,000	1.2%
26	Alabama	17,529,533,000	1.2%
27	Maryland	15,436,126,000	1.0%
28	Kansas	14,063,855,000	1.0%
29	Louisiana	13,863,956,000	0.9%
30	Utah	9,997,920,000	0.7%
31	Nebraska	9,184,390,000	0.6%
32	Connecticut	8,890,800,000	0.6%
33	Iowa	8,044,863,000	0.5%
34	Oklahoma	7,898,556,000	0.5%
35	Arkansas	7,701,468,000	0.5%
36	Mississippi	6,697,723,000	0.5%
37	New Mexico	4,871,524,000	0.3%
38	Hawaii	4,375,998,000	0.3%
39	West Virginia	3,454,502,000	0.2%
40	Alaska	3,444,285,000	0.2%
41	Maine	2,658,976,000	0.2%
42	New Hampshire	2,562,715,000	0.2%
43	Idaho	2,416,063,000	0.2%
44	Rhode Island	2,079,391,000	0.1%
45	Delaware	1,981,793,000	0.1%
46	North Dakota	1,839,277,000	0.1%
47	South Dakota	1,621,392,000	0.1%
48	Montana	1,511,750,000	0.1%
49	Wyoming	1,034,326,000	0.1%
50	Vermont	995,901,000	0.1%
	District of Columbia	8,915,847,000	0.6%

Source: U.S. Bureau of the Census, Governments Division
"State and Local Government Finances 2006-2007" (http://www.census.gov/govs/estimate/index.html)
*Includes short-term, long-term, full faith and credit, nonguaranteed, and public debt for private purposes.

Per Capita Local Government Debt Outstanding in 2007

National Per Capita = $4,894*

ALPHA ORDER

RANK	STATE	PER CAPITA
23	Alabama	$3,780
13	Alaska	5,048
18	Arizona	4,681
35	Arkansas	2,710
8	California	5,947
4	Colorado	6,460
37	Connecticut	2,549
40	Delaware	2,291
10	Florida	5,333
22	Georgia	3,891
28	Hawaii	3,427
48	Idaho	1,612
14	Illinois	4,852
27	Indiana	3,521
36	Iowa	2,701
12	Kansas	5,067
6	Kentucky	6,089
32	Louisiana	3,168
43	Maine	2,018
34	Maryland	2,740
31	Massachusetts	3,226
19	Michigan	4,433
9	Minnesota	5,749
39	Mississippi	2,292
30	Missouri	3,401
50	Montana	1,579
11	Nebraska	5,189
2	Nevada	6,987
46	New Hampshire	1,945
21	New Jersey	3,973
38	New Mexico	2,474
1	New York	7,694
29	North Carolina	3,410
33	North Dakota	2,882
25	Ohio	3,655
41	Oklahoma	2,187
16	Oregon	4,726
7	Pennsylvania	5,972
45	Rhode Island	1,971
17	South Carolina	4,721
42	South Dakota	2,034
15	Tennessee	4,834
3	Texas	6,942
24	Utah	3,753
49	Vermont	1,605
20	Virginia	4,054
5	Washington	6,350
47	West Virginia	1,907
26	Wisconsin	3,634
44	Wyoming	1,976

RANK ORDER

RANK	STATE	PER CAPITA
1	New York	$7,694
2	Nevada	6,987
3	Texas	6,942
4	Colorado	6,460
5	Washington	6,350
6	Kentucky	6,089
7	Pennsylvania	5,972
8	California	5,947
9	Minnesota	5,749
10	Florida	5,333
11	Nebraska	5,189
12	Kansas	5,067
13	Alaska	5,048
14	Illinois	4,852
15	Tennessee	4,834
16	Oregon	4,726
17	South Carolina	4,721
18	Arizona	4,681
19	Michigan	4,433
20	Virginia	4,054
21	New Jersey	3,973
22	Georgia	3,891
23	Alabama	3,780
24	Utah	3,753
25	Ohio	3,655
26	Wisconsin	3,634
27	Indiana	3,521
28	Hawaii	3,427
29	North Carolina	3,410
30	Missouri	3,401
31	Massachusetts	3,226
32	Louisiana	3,168
33	North Dakota	2,882
34	Maryland	2,740
35	Arkansas	2,710
36	Iowa	2,701
37	Connecticut	2,549
38	New Mexico	2,474
39	Mississippi	2,292
40	Delaware	2,291
41	Oklahoma	2,187
42	South Dakota	2,034
43	Maine	2,018
44	Wyoming	1,976
45	Rhode Island	1,971
46	New Hampshire	1,945
47	West Virginia	1,907
48	Idaho	1,612
49	Vermont	1,605
50	Montana	1,579
	District of Columbia	15,204

Source: CQ Press using data from U.S. Bureau of the Census, Governments Division
"State and Local Government Finances 2006-2007" (http://www.census.gov/govs/estimate/index.html)
*Includes short-term, long-term, full faith and credit, nonguaranteed, and public debt for private purposes.

Local Government Full-Time Equivalent Employees in 2008

National Total = 12,305,496 FTE Employees*

ALPHA ORDER

RANK ORDER

RANK	STATE	EMPLOYEES	% of USA	RANK	STATE	EMPLOYEES	% of USA
22	Alabama	199,374	1.6%	1	California	1,451,619	11.8%
46	Alaska	27,628	0.2%	2	Texas	1,080,697	8.8%
14	Arizona	251,164	2.0%	3	New York	980,845	8.0%
33	Arkansas	104,941	0.9%	4	Florida	720,423	5.9%
1	California	1,451,619	11.8%	5	Illinois	519,145	4.2%
23	Colorado	195,296	1.6%	6	Ohio	477,656	3.9%
32	Connecticut	125,410	1.0%	7	Pennsylvania	433,674	3.5%
48	Delaware	23,926	0.2%	8	North Carolina	420,911	3.4%
4	Florida	720,423	5.9%	9	Georgia	409,324	3.3%
9	Georgia	409,324	3.3%	10	New Jersey	350,103	2.8%
50	Hawaii	14,859	0.1%	11	Michigan	334,429	2.7%
39	Idaho	58,580	0.5%	12	Virginia	323,352	2.6%
5	Illinois	519,145	4.2%	13	Indiana	263,016	2.1%
13	Indiana	263,016	2.1%	14	Arizona	251,164	2.0%
31	Iowa	127,786	1.0%	15	Massachusetts	245,378	2.0%
27	Kansas	149,128	1.2%	16	Tennessee	242,248	2.0%
26	Kentucky	165,102	1.3%	17	Missouri	238,975	1.9%
24	Louisiana	190,425	1.5%	18	Washington	227,188	1.8%
40	Maine	55,059	0.4%	19	Wisconsin	214,332	1.7%
20	Maryland	210,986	1.7%	20	Maryland	210,986	1.7%
15	Massachusetts	245,378	2.0%	21	Minnesota	201,271	1.6%
11	Michigan	334,429	2.7%	22	Alabama	199,374	1.6%
21	Minnesota	201,271	1.6%	23	Colorado	195,296	1.6%
29	Mississippi	134,350	1.1%	24	Louisiana	190,425	1.5%
17	Missouri	238,975	1.9%	25	South Carolina	183,091	1.5%
43	Montana	35,310	0.3%	26	Kentucky	165,102	1.3%
35	Nebraska	84,776	0.7%	27	Kansas	149,128	1.2%
34	Nevada	85,850	0.7%	28	Oklahoma	144,181	1.2%
41	New Hampshire	52,434	0.4%	29	Mississippi	134,350	1.1%
10	New Jersey	350,103	2.8%	30	Oregon	130,480	1.1%
37	New Mexico	80,830	0.7%	31	Iowa	127,786	1.0%
3	New York	980,845	8.0%	32	Connecticut	125,410	1.0%
8	North Carolina	420,911	3.4%	33	Arkansas	104,941	0.9%
49	North Dakota	23,269	0.2%	34	Nevada	85,850	0.7%
6	Ohio	477,656	3.9%	35	Nebraska	84,776	0.7%
28	Oklahoma	144,181	1.2%	36	Utah	84,060	0.7%
30	Oregon	130,480	1.1%	37	New Mexico	80,830	0.7%
7	Pennsylvania	433,674	3.5%	38	West Virginia	62,616	0.5%
44	Rhode Island	31,578	0.3%	39	Idaho	58,580	0.5%
25	South Carolina	183,091	1.5%	40	Maine	55,059	0.4%
45	South Dakota	30,029	0.2%	41	New Hampshire	52,434	0.4%
16	Tennessee	242,248	2.0%	42	Wyoming	36,384	0.3%
2	Texas	1,080,697	8.8%	43	Montana	35,310	0.3%
36	Utah	84,060	0.7%	44	Rhode Island	31,578	0.3%
47	Vermont	24,768	0.2%	45	South Dakota	30,029	0.2%
12	Virginia	323,352	2.6%	46	Alaska	27,628	0.2%
18	Washington	227,188	1.8%	47	Vermont	24,768	0.2%
38	West Virginia	62,616	0.5%	48	Delaware	23,926	0.2%
19	Wisconsin	214,332	1.7%	49	North Dakota	23,269	0.2%
42	Wyoming	36,384	0.3%	50	Hawaii	14,859	0.1%
					District of Columbia	47,240	0.4%

Source: U.S. Bureau of the Census, Governments Division

"Government Employment and Payroll" (http://www.census.gov/govs/apes/index.html)

*As of March 2008.

Rate of Local Government Full-Time Equivalent Employees in 2008

National Rate = 404 Local Government Employees per 10,000 Population*

ALPHA ORDER

RANK	STATE	RATE
10	Alabama	426
20	Alaska	401
29	Arizona	386
37	Arkansas	366
23	California	397
25	Colorado	396
40	Connecticut	358
49	Delaware	273
27	Florida	391
11	Georgia	422
50	Hawaii	115
32	Idaho	384
18	Illinois	404
15	Indiana	412
9	Iowa	427
2	Kansas	533
30	Kentucky	385
8	Louisiana	428
12	Maine	417
35	Maryland	373
34	Massachusetts	375
45	Michigan	334
30	Minnesota	385
5	Mississippi	457
20	Missouri	401
38	Montana	365
4	Nebraska	476
46	Nevada	328
23	New Hampshire	397
18	New Jersey	404
16	New Mexico	407
3	New York	504
6	North Carolina	455
39	North Dakota	363
14	Ohio	414
25	Oklahoma	396
42	Oregon	345
42	Pennsylvania	345
48	Rhode Island	300
16	South Carolina	407
35	South Dakota	373
28	Tennessee	388
7	Texas	445
47	Utah	308
22	Vermont	399
13	Virginia	415
41	Washington	346
42	West Virginia	345
33	Wisconsin	381
1	Wyoming	683

RANK ORDER

RANK	STATE	RATE
1	Wyoming	683
2	Kansas	533
3	New York	504
4	Nebraska	476
5	Mississippi	457
6	North Carolina	455
7	Texas	445
8	Louisiana	428
9	Iowa	427
10	Alabama	426
11	Georgia	422
12	Maine	417
13	Virginia	415
14	Ohio	414
15	Indiana	412
16	New Mexico	407
16	South Carolina	407
18	Illinois	404
18	New Jersey	404
20	Alaska	401
20	Missouri	401
22	Vermont	399
23	California	397
23	New Hampshire	397
25	Colorado	396
25	Oklahoma	396
27	Florida	391
28	Tennessee	388
29	Arizona	386
30	Kentucky	385
30	Minnesota	385
32	Idaho	384
33	Wisconsin	381
34	Massachusetts	375
35	Maryland	373
35	South Dakota	373
37	Arkansas	366
38	Montana	365
39	North Dakota	363
40	Connecticut	358
41	Washington	346
42	Oregon	345
42	Pennsylvania	345
42	West Virginia	345
45	Michigan	334
46	Nevada	328
47	Utah	308
48	Rhode Island	300
49	Delaware	273
50	Hawaii	115
	District of Columbia	801

Source: CQ Press using data from U.S. Bureau of the Census, Governments Division
  "Government Employment and Payroll" (http://www.census.gov/govs/apes/index.html)
*Full-time equivalent as of March 2008.

Average Annual Earnings of Full-Time Local Government Employees in 2008

National Average = $49,487*

ALPHA ORDER				RANK ORDER		
RANK	STATE	SALARY		RANK	STATE	SALARY
43	Alabama	$37,855		1	California	$67,818
9	Alaska	55,819		2	New Jersey	61,901
17	Arizona	49,934		3	Washington	60,604
49	Arkansas	34,388		4	Nevada	59,304
1	California	67,818		5	Maryland	58,924
18	Colorado	48,803		6	New York	58,298
7	Connecticut	58,112		7	Connecticut	58,112
12	Delaware	53,924		8	Hawaii	57,487
20	Florida	48,124		9	Alaska	55,819
34	Georgia	40,691		10	Rhode Island	55,567
8	Hawaii	57,487		11	Massachusetts	54,219
40	Idaho	39,092		12	Delaware	53,924
14	Illinois	51,267		13	Michigan	53,002
33	Indiana	41,078		14	Illinois	51,267
30	Iowa	42,134		15	Minnesota	51,180
41	Kansas	38,909		16	Oregon	50,520
46	Kentucky	35,952		17	Arizona	49,934
44	Louisiana	37,252		18	Colorado	48,803
37	Maine	39,355		19	Pennsylvania	48,250
5	Maryland	58,924		20	Florida	48,124
11	Massachusetts	54,219		21	Wisconsin	47,499
13	Michigan	53,002		22	Ohio	46,761
15	Minnesota	51,180		23	Wyoming	46,301
50	Mississippi	34,376		24	Utah	46,284
36	Missouri	39,679		25	Virginia	45,948
39	Montana	39,134		26	New Hampshire	45,317
27	Nebraska	44,029		27	Nebraska	44,029
4	Nevada	59,304		28	North Dakota	43,947
26	New Hampshire	45,317		29	Vermont	42,305
2	New Jersey	61,901		30	Iowa	42,134
42	New Mexico	38,290		31	North Carolina	41,956
6	New York	58,298		32	Texas	41,579
31	North Carolina	41,956		33	Indiana	41,078
28	North Dakota	43,947		34	Georgia	40,691
22	Ohio	46,761		35	South Carolina	40,489
48	Oklahoma	35,092		36	Missouri	39,679
16	Oregon	50,520		37	Maine	39,355
19	Pennsylvania	48,250		38	Tennessee	39,313
10	Rhode Island	55,567		39	Montana	39,134
35	South Carolina	40,489		40	Idaho	39,092
45	South Dakota	36,334		41	Kansas	38,909
38	Tennessee	39,313		42	New Mexico	38,290
32	Texas	41,579		43	Alabama	37,855
24	Utah	46,284		44	Louisiana	37,252
29	Vermont	42,305		45	South Dakota	36,334
25	Virginia	45,948		46	Kentucky	35,952
3	Washington	60,604		47	West Virginia	35,300
47	West Virginia	35,300		48	Oklahoma	35,092
21	Wisconsin	47,499		49	Arkansas	34,388
23	Wyoming	46,301		50	Mississippi	34,376
					District of Columbia	64,841

Source: CQ Press using data from U.S. Bureau of the Census, Governments Division
   "Government Employment and Payroll" (http://www.census.gov/govs/apes/index.html)
*March 2008 full-time payroll (multiplied by 12) divided by full-time employees.

XI. Health

Average Medical Malpractice Payment in 2006

National Average = $311,965*

ALPHA ORDER			RANK ORDER		
RANK	STATE	AVERAGE PAYMENT	RANK	STATE	AVERAGE PAYMENT
7	Alabama	$453,665	1	Illinois	$619,205
39	Alaska	240,511	2	Wisconsin**	524,041
30	Arizona	286,898	3	Delaware	521,177
37	Arkansas	246,959	4	Connecticut	500,289
41	California	223,039	5	Minnesota	480,822
24	Colorado	312,138	6	Massachusetts	465,236
4	Connecticut	500,289	7	Alabama	453,665
3	Delaware	521,177	8	South Dakota	422,033
40	Florida**	240,363	9	Wyoming	413,553
29	Georgia	292,902	10	New York	405,558
14	Hawaii	342,316	11	New Jersey	401,144
31	Idaho	281,751	12	North Carolina	366,966
1	Illinois	619,205	13	Maryland	347,477
20	Indiana**	322,822	14	Hawaii	342,316
34	Iowa	274,281	15	Nevada	340,211
48	Kansas**	155,285	16	New Hampshire	336,032
32	Kentucky	280,599	17	Pennsylvania**	332,376
43	Louisiana**	207,878	18	Missouri	330,115
21	Maine	322,325	19	Rhode Island	326,542
13	Maryland	347,477	20	Indiana**	322,822
6	Massachusetts	465,236	21	Maine	322,325
49	Michigan	138,433	22	Montana	320,849
5	Minnesota	480,822	23	Tennessee	317,305
35	Mississippi	258,806	24	Colorado	312,138
18	Missouri	330,115	25	Ohio	310,573
22	Montana	320,849	26	Oregon	305,725
42	Nebraska**	213,081	27	North Dakota	301,422
15	Nevada	340,211	28	Virginia	295,840
16	New Hampshire	336,032	29	Georgia	292,902
11	New Jersey	401,144	30	Arizona	286,898
45	New Mexico**	199,917	31	Idaho	281,751
10	New York	405,558	32	Kentucky	280,599
12	North Carolina	366,966	33	Washington	277,493
27	North Dakota	301,422	34	Iowa	274,281
25	Ohio	310,573	35	Mississippi	258,806
38	Oklahoma	245,127	36	Utah	247,349
26	Oregon	305,725	37	Arkansas	246,959
17	Pennsylvania**	332,376	38	Oklahoma	245,127
19	Rhode Island	326,542	39	Alaska	240,511
47	South Carolina**	174,454	40	Florida**	240,363
8	South Dakota	422,033	41	California	223,039
23	Tennessee	317,305	42	Nebraska**	213,081
46	Texas	175,644	43	Louisiana**	207,878
36	Utah	247,349	44	West Virginia	204,794
50	Vermont	125,795	45	New Mexico**	199,917
28	Virginia	295,840	46	Texas	175,644
33	Washington	277,493	47	South Carolina**	174,454
44	West Virginia	204,794	48	Kansas**	155,285
2	Wisconsin**	524,041	49	Michigan	138,433
9	Wyoming	413,553	50	Vermont	125,795
				District of Columbia	331,628

Source: U.S. Department of Health and Human Services, Bureau of Health Professions
"National Practitioner Data Bank, 2006 Annual Report" (http://www.npdb-hipdb.com/annualrpt.html)
*National figure includes U.S. territories and U.S. Armed Forces locations overseas.
**The figures for these states have not been adjusted for payments by state compensation funds and other similar funds.
Average payments for these states understate the actual average amounts received by claimants.

Average Annual Single Coverage Health Insurance Premium per Enrolled Employee in 2008
National Average = $4,386*

ALPHA ORDER

RANK	STATE	PREMIUM
38	Alabama	$4,139
1	Alaska	5,293
31	Arizona	4,214
48	Arkansas	3,923
28	California	4,280
27	Colorado	4,303
10	Connecticut	4,740
11	Delaware	4,733
15	Florida	4,517
36	Georgia	4,160
49	Hawaii	3,831
41	Idaho	4,104
12	Illinois	4,643
17	Indiana	4,495
37	Iowa	4,146
34	Kansas	4,197
46	Kentucky	4,009
45	Louisiana	4,055
4	Maine	4,910
25	Maryland	4,360
7	Massachusetts	4,836
23	Michigan	4,388
20	Minnesota	4,432
39	Mississippi	4,124
39	Missouri	4,124
26	Montana	4,355
22	Nebraska	4,392
47	Nevada	3,927
2	New Hampshire	5,247
8	New Jersey	4,798
43	New Mexico	4,074
13	New York	4,638
19	North Carolina	4,460
50	North Dakota	3,830
42	Ohio	4,089
44	Oklahoma	4,072
24	Oregon	4,384
16	Pennsylvania	4,499
3	Rhode Island	4,930
18	South Carolina	4,477
30	South Dakota	4,233
29	Tennessee	4,276
32	Texas	4,205
34	Utah	4,197
5	Vermont	4,900
33	Virginia	4,202
21	Washington	4,404
6	West Virginia	4,892
9	Wisconsin	4,777
14	Wyoming	4,622

RANK ORDER

RANK	STATE	PREMIUM
1	Alaska	$5,293
2	New Hampshire	5,247
3	Rhode Island	4,930
4	Maine	4,910
5	Vermont	4,900
6	West Virginia	4,892
7	Massachusetts	4,836
8	New Jersey	4,798
9	Wisconsin	4,777
10	Connecticut	4,740
11	Delaware	4,733
12	Illinois	4,643
13	New York	4,638
14	Wyoming	4,622
15	Florida	4,517
16	Pennsylvania	4,499
17	Indiana	4,495
18	South Carolina	4,477
19	North Carolina	4,460
20	Minnesota	4,432
21	Washington	4,404
22	Nebraska	4,392
23	Michigan	4,388
24	Oregon	4,384
25	Maryland	4,360
26	Montana	4,355
27	Colorado	4,303
28	California	4,280
29	Tennessee	4,276
30	South Dakota	4,233
31	Arizona	4,214
32	Texas	4,205
33	Virginia	4,202
34	Kansas	4,197
34	Utah	4,197
36	Georgia	4,160
37	Iowa	4,146
38	Alabama	4,139
39	Mississippi	4,124
39	Missouri	4,124
41	Idaho	4,104
42	Ohio	4,089
43	New Mexico	4,074
44	Oklahoma	4,072
45	Louisiana	4,055
46	Kentucky	4,009
47	Nevada	3,927
48	Arkansas	3,923
49	Hawaii	3,831
50	North Dakota	3,830
	District of Columbia	4,890

Source: U.S. Department of Health and Human Services, Agency for Healthcare Research and Quality
"Private-Sector Data by Firm Size and State" (Table II Series, Medical Expenditures Panel Survey)
(http://www.meps.ahrq.gov/mepsweb/survey_comp/Insurance.jsp)
*Enrolled employees at private-sector establishments that offer health insurance coverage.

Average Annual Family Coverage Health Insurance Premium per Enrolled Employee in 2008
National Average = $12,298*

ALPHA ORDER

RANK	STATE	PREMIUM
46	Alabama	$11,119
7	Alaska	13,383
24	Arizona	12,292
43	Arkansas	11,220
25	California	12,254
29	Colorado	11,952
5	Connecticut	13,436
6	Delaware	13,386
17	Florida	12,697
33	Georgia	11,659
48	Hawaii	11,044
50	Idaho	10,837
18	Illinois	12,603
4	Indiana	13,504
49	Iowa	10,947
32	Kansas	11,662
36	Kentucky	11,506
44	Louisiana	11,207
9	Maine	13,102
20	Maryland	12,541
1	Massachusetts	13,788
42	Michigan	11,321
2	Minnesota	13,639
41	Mississippi	11,363
35	Missouri	11,557
38	Montana	11,438
34	Nebraska	11,648
37	Nevada	11,487
3	New Hampshire	13,592
15	New Jersey	12,789
26	New Mexico	12,071
14	New York	12,824
22	North Carolina	12,308
45	North Dakota	11,178
39	Ohio	11,425
47	Oklahoma	11,053
19	Oregon	12,585
21	Pennsylvania	12,339
8	Rhode Island	13,363
27	South Carolina	12,068
40	South Dakota	11,382
23	Tennessee	12,302
28	Texas	11,967
31	Utah	11,783
10	Vermont	13,091
30	Virginia	11,935
11	Washington	13,036
13	West Virginia	12,887
12	Wisconsin	12,956
16	Wyoming	12,734

RANK ORDER

RANK	STATE	PREMIUM
1	Massachusetts	$13,788
2	Minnesota	13,639
3	New Hampshire	13,592
4	Indiana	13,504
5	Connecticut	13,436
6	Delaware	13,386
7	Alaska	13,383
8	Rhode Island	13,363
9	Maine	13,102
10	Vermont	13,091
11	Washington	13,036
12	Wisconsin	12,956
13	West Virginia	12,887
14	New York	12,824
15	New Jersey	12,789
16	Wyoming	12,734
17	Florida	12,697
18	Illinois	12,603
19	Oregon	12,585
20	Maryland	12,541
21	Pennsylvania	12,339
22	North Carolina	12,308
23	Tennessee	12,302
24	Arizona	12,292
25	California	12,254
26	New Mexico	12,071
27	South Carolina	12,068
28	Texas	11,967
29	Colorado	11,952
30	Virginia	11,935
31	Utah	11,783
32	Kansas	11,662
33	Georgia	11,659
34	Nebraska	11,648
35	Missouri	11,557
36	Kentucky	11,506
37	Nevada	11,487
38	Montana	11,438
39	Ohio	11,425
40	South Dakota	11,382
41	Mississippi	11,363
42	Michigan	11,321
43	Arkansas	11,220
44	Louisiana	11,207
45	North Dakota	11,178
46	Alabama	11,119
47	Oklahoma	11,053
48	Hawaii	11,044
49	Iowa	10,947
50	Idaho	10,837

| | District of Columbia | 13,427 |

Source: U.S. Department of Health and Human Services, Agency for Healthcare Research and Quality
"Private-Sector Data by Firm Size and State" (Table II Series, Medical Expenditures Panel Survey)
(http://www.meps.ahrq.gov/mepsweb/survey_comp/Insurance.jsp)
*Enrolled employees at private-sector establishments that offer health insurance coverage.

Percent of Private-Sector Establishments That Offer Health Insurance: 2008

National Percent = 56.4%

ALPHA ORDER

RANK	STATE	PERCENT
7	Alabama	62.9
45	Alaska	46.0
32	Arizona	53.4
45	Arkansas	46.0
16	California	57.6
38	Colorado	52.1
5	Connecticut	63.6
10	Delaware	61.4
26	Florida	55.1
32	Georgia	53.4
1	Hawaii	88.5
49	Idaho	43.9
23	Illinois	55.6
29	Indiana	53.8
25	Iowa	55.2
24	Kansas	55.3
20	Kentucky	56.6
34	Louisiana	52.8
17	Maine	57.1
15	Maryland	58.2
2	Massachusetts	68.7
18	Michigan	56.9
31	Minnesota	53.5
43	Mississippi	47.7
18	Missouri	56.9
50	Montana	40.2
48	Nebraska	44.8
8	Nevada	62.8
4	New Hampshire	64.8
3	New Jersey	67.5
39	New Mexico	51.1
13	New York	58.7
28	North Carolina	54.4
36	North Dakota	52.2
9	Ohio	61.6
41	Oklahoma	50.8
35	Oregon	52.6
11	Pennsylvania	61.3
6	Rhode Island	63.0
27	South Carolina	54.8
44	South Dakota	47.3
21	Tennessee	56.3
42	Texas	48.8
39	Utah	51.1
22	Vermont	56.0
12	Virginia	59.1
14	Washington	58.6
30	West Virginia	53.7
36	Wisconsin	52.2
45	Wyoming	46.0

RANK ORDER

RANK	STATE	PERCENT
1	Hawaii	88.5
2	Massachusetts	68.7
3	New Jersey	67.5
4	New Hampshire	64.8
5	Connecticut	63.6
6	Rhode Island	63.0
7	Alabama	62.9
8	Nevada	62.8
9	Ohio	61.6
10	Delaware	61.4
11	Pennsylvania	61.3
12	Virginia	59.1
13	New York	58.7
14	Washington	58.6
15	Maryland	58.2
16	California	57.6
17	Maine	57.1
18	Michigan	56.9
18	Missouri	56.9
20	Kentucky	56.6
21	Tennessee	56.3
22	Vermont	56.0
23	Illinois	55.6
24	Kansas	55.3
25	Iowa	55.2
26	Florida	55.1
27	South Carolina	54.8
28	North Carolina	54.4
29	Indiana	53.8
30	West Virginia	53.7
31	Minnesota	53.5
32	Arizona	53.4
32	Georgia	53.4
34	Louisiana	52.8
35	Oregon	52.6
36	North Dakota	52.2
36	Wisconsin	52.2
38	Colorado	52.1
39	New Mexico	51.1
39	Utah	51.1
41	Oklahoma	50.8
42	Texas	48.8
43	Mississippi	47.7
44	South Dakota	47.3
45	Alaska	46.0
45	Arkansas	46.0
45	Wyoming	46.0
48	Nebraska	44.8
49	Idaho	43.9
50	Montana	40.2
	District of Columbia	72.5

Source: U.S. Department of Health and Human Services, Agency for Healthcare Research and Quality
   "Private-Sector Data by Firm Size and State" (Table II Series, Medical Expenditures Panel Survey)
   (http://www.meps.ahrq.gov/mepsweb/survey_comp/Insurance.jsp)

Persons Not Covered by Health Insurance in 2008

National Total = 46,340,000 Uninsured

ALPHA ORDER

RANK	STATE	UNINSURED	% of USA
24	Alabama	561,000	1.2%
42	Alaska	133,000	0.3%
9	Arizona	1,273,000	2.7%
27	Arkansas	505,000	1.1%
1	California	6,822,000	14.7%
17	Colorado	780,000	1.7%
34	Connecticut	343,000	0.7%
47	Delaware	94,000	0.2%
3	Florida	3,619,000	7.8%
5	Georgia	1,703,000	3.7%
46	Hawaii	98,000	0.2%
38	Idaho	236,000	0.5%
6	Illinois	1,638,000	3.5%
18	Indiana	772,000	1.7%
36	Iowa	283,000	0.6%
35	Kansas	330,000	0.7%
21	Kentucky	682,000	1.5%
15	Louisiana	869,000	1.9%
41	Maine	137,000	0.3%
22	Maryland	669,000	1.4%
33	Massachusetts	352,000	0.8%
12	Michigan	1,151,000	2.5%
31	Minnesota	444,000	1.0%
26	Mississippi	519,000	1.1%
19	Missouri	739,000	1.6%
40	Montana	158,000	0.3%
39	Nebraska	211,000	0.5%
29	Nevada	487,000	1.1%
42	New Hampshire	133,000	0.3%
11	New Jersey	1,201,000	2.6%
30	New Mexico	468,000	1.0%
4	New York	2,720,000	5.9%
7	North Carolina	1,421,000	3.1%
48	North Dakota	74,000	0.2%
8	Ohio	1,309,000	2.8%
28	Oklahoma	498,000	1.1%
23	Oregon	621,000	1.3%
10	Pennsylvania	1,211,000	2.6%
44	Rhode Island	123,000	0.3%
20	South Carolina	707,000	1.5%
45	South Dakota	100,000	0.2%
14	Tennessee	931,000	2.0%
2	Texas	6,084,000	13.1%
32	Utah	364,000	0.8%
50	Vermont	57,000	0.1%
13	Virginia	962,000	2.1%
16	Washington	808,000	1.7%
37	West Virginia	271,000	0.6%
25	Wisconsin	535,000	1.2%
49	Wyoming	72,000	0.2%

RANK ORDER

RANK	STATE	UNINSURED	% of USA
1	California	6,822,000	14.7%
2	Texas	6,084,000	13.1%
3	Florida	3,619,000	7.8%
4	New York	2,720,000	5.9%
5	Georgia	1,703,000	3.7%
6	Illinois	1,638,000	3.5%
7	North Carolina	1,421,000	3.1%
8	Ohio	1,309,000	2.8%
9	Arizona	1,273,000	2.7%
10	Pennsylvania	1,211,000	2.6%
11	New Jersey	1,201,000	2.6%
12	Michigan	1,151,000	2.5%
13	Virginia	962,000	2.1%
14	Tennessee	931,000	2.0%
15	Louisiana	869,000	1.9%
16	Washington	808,000	1.7%
17	Colorado	780,000	1.7%
18	Indiana	772,000	1.7%
19	Missouri	739,000	1.6%
20	South Carolina	707,000	1.5%
21	Kentucky	682,000	1.5%
22	Maryland	669,000	1.4%
23	Oregon	621,000	1.3%
24	Alabama	561,000	1.2%
25	Wisconsin	535,000	1.2%
26	Mississippi	519,000	1.1%
27	Arkansas	505,000	1.1%
28	Oklahoma	498,000	1.1%
29	Nevada	487,000	1.1%
30	New Mexico	468,000	1.0%
31	Minnesota	444,000	1.0%
32	Utah	364,000	0.8%
33	Massachusetts	352,000	0.8%
34	Connecticut	343,000	0.7%
35	Kansas	330,000	0.7%
36	Iowa	283,000	0.6%
37	West Virginia	271,000	0.6%
38	Idaho	236,000	0.5%
39	Nebraska	211,000	0.5%
40	Montana	158,000	0.3%
41	Maine	137,000	0.3%
42	Alaska	133,000	0.3%
42	New Hampshire	133,000	0.3%
44	Rhode Island	123,000	0.3%
45	South Dakota	100,000	0.2%
46	Hawaii	98,000	0.2%
47	Delaware	94,000	0.2%
48	North Dakota	74,000	0.2%
49	Wyoming	72,000	0.2%
50	Vermont	57,000	0.1%
	District of Columbia	59,000	0.1%

Source: U.S. Bureau of the Census
"Health Insurance Coverage Status by State for All People: 2008" (http://www.census.gov/hhes/www/hlthins/hlthin08.html)

Percent of Population Not Covered by Health Insurance in 2008

National Percent = 15.5% of Population*

ALPHA ORDER				RANK ORDER		
RANK	STATE	PERCENT		RANK	STATE	PERCENT
29	Alabama	13.0		1	Texas	24.9
9	Alaska	18.2		2	New Mexico	23.0
5	Arizona	19.6		3	Florida	20.5
11	Arkansas	17.6		4	Louisiana	20.1
7	California	18.5		5	Arizona	19.6
15	Colorado	16.5		6	Mississippi	19.1
45	Connecticut	9.6		7	California	18.5
36	Delaware	11.4		7	Nevada	18.5
3	Florida	20.5		9	Alaska	18.2
10	Georgia	17.7		10	Georgia	17.7
49	Hawaii	8.1		11	Arkansas	17.6
19	Idaho	15.0		12	Oregon	17.0
27	Illinois	13.4		13	Oklahoma	16.9
33	Indiana	11.8		14	North Carolina	16.6
43	Iowa	9.8		15	Colorado	16.5
32	Kansas	12.4		16	Montana	16.3
19	Kentucky	15.0		17	South Carolina	16.1
4	Louisiana	20.1		18	New Jersey	15.1
46	Maine	9.5		19	Idaho	15.0
28	Maryland	13.2		19	Kentucky	15.0
50	Massachusetts	7.1		21	Utah	14.5
38	Michigan	11.3		22	Tennessee	14.4
48	Minnesota	8.7		23	West Virginia	14.2
6	Mississippi	19.1		24	Wyoming	13.9
30	Missouri	12.8		25	New York	13.8
16	Montana	16.3		26	Virginia	13.5
31	Nebraska	12.5		27	Illinois	13.4
7	Nevada	18.5		28	Maryland	13.2
40	New Hampshire	10.7		29	Alabama	13.0
18	New Jersey	15.1		30	Missouri	12.8
2	New Mexico	23.0		31	Nebraska	12.5
25	New York	13.8		32	Kansas	12.4
14	North Carolina	16.6		33	Indiana	11.8
36	North Dakota	11.4		33	Washington	11.8
39	Ohio	11.1		35	South Dakota	11.5
13	Oklahoma	16.9		36	Delaware	11.4
12	Oregon	17.0		36	North Dakota	11.4
43	Pennsylvania	9.8		38	Michigan	11.3
41	Rhode Island	10.4		39	Ohio	11.1
17	South Carolina	16.1		40	New Hampshire	10.7
35	South Dakota	11.5		41	Rhode Island	10.4
22	Tennessee	14.4		42	Vermont	10.2
1	Texas	24.9		43	Iowa	9.8
21	Utah	14.5		43	Pennsylvania	9.8
42	Vermont	10.2		45	Connecticut	9.6
26	Virginia	13.5		46	Maine	9.5
33	Washington	11.8		47	Wisconsin	8.9
23	West Virginia	14.2		48	Minnesota	8.7
47	Wisconsin	8.9		49	Hawaii	8.1
24	Wyoming	13.9		50	Massachusetts	7.1
					District of Columbia	10.4

Source: U.S. Bureau of the Census
"Health Insurance Coverage Status by State for All People: 2008" (http://www.census.gov/hhes/www/hlthins/hlthin08.html)
*Three-year average for 2006 through 2008.

Percent of Population Lacking Access to Primary Care in 2010

National Percent = 11.5% of Population*

ALPHA ORDER

RANK	STATE	PERCENT		RANK	STATE	PERCENT
9	Alabama	18.4		1	Louisiana	33.3
16	Alaska	14.0		2	New Mexico	31.5
12	Arizona	16.4		3	Mississippi	31.3
31	Arkansas	9.9		4	South Dakota	26.5
29	California	10.0		5	Montana	23.7
22	Colorado	11.7		6	North Dakota	22.3
33	Connecticut	9.0		7	Missouri	21.2
17	Delaware	13.6		8	Wyoming	19.0
13	Florida	14.9		9	Alabama	18.4
15	Georgia	14.3		10	Illinois	17.5
48	Hawaii	2.8		11	Idaho	16.7
11	Idaho	16.7		12	Arizona	16.4
10	Illinois	17.5		13	Florida	14.9
37	Indiana	7.1		14	Oklahoma	14.5
25	Iowa	10.8		15	Georgia	14.3
20	Kansas	12.5		16	Alaska	14.0
23	Kentucky	11.4		17	Delaware	13.6
1	Louisiana	33.3		18	South Carolina	13.0
42	Maine	5.8		19	Nevada	12.6
43	Maryland	5.7		20	Kansas	12.5
38	Massachusetts	6.9		21	Texas	12.4
25	Michigan	10.8		22	Colorado	11.7
45	Minnesota	5.4		23	Kentucky	11.4
3	Mississippi	31.3		24	New York	11.3
7	Missouri	21.2		25	Iowa	10.8
5	Montana	23.7		25	Michigan	10.8
46	Nebraska	4.7		27	Wisconsin	10.6
19	Nevada	12.6		28	Tennessee	10.4
47	New Hampshire	4.1		29	California	10.0
50	New Jersey	1.7		29	Utah	10.0
2	New Mexico	31.5		31	Arkansas	9.9
24	New York	11.3		32	Washington	9.4
43	North Carolina	5.7		33	Connecticut	9.0
6	North Dakota	22.3		34	West Virginia	8.8
40	Ohio	6.0		35	Virginia	8.2
14	Oklahoma	14.5		36	Oregon	7.8
36	Oregon	7.8		37	Indiana	7.1
41	Pennsylvania	5.9		38	Massachusetts	6.9
39	Rhode Island	6.3		39	Rhode Island	6.3
18	South Carolina	13.0		40	Ohio	6.0
4	South Dakota	26.5		41	Pennsylvania	5.9
28	Tennessee	10.4		42	Maine	5.8
21	Texas	12.4		43	Maryland	5.7
29	Utah	10.0		43	North Carolina	5.7
49	Vermont	2.7		45	Minnesota	5.4
35	Virginia	8.2		46	Nebraska	4.7
32	Washington	9.4		47	New Hampshire	4.1
34	West Virginia	8.8		48	Hawaii	2.8
27	Wisconsin	10.6		49	Vermont	2.7
8	Wyoming	19.0		50	New Jersey	1.7

RANK ORDER

	District of Columbia	25.2

Source: CQ Press using data from U.S. Department of Health and Human Services, Division of Shortage Designation
"Selected Statistics on Health Professional Shortage Areas" (as of January 15, 2010)
(http://datawarehouse.hrsa.gov/HPSADownload.aspx)

*Percent of population considered under-served by primary medical practitioners (Family and General Practice doctors, Internists, Ob/Gyns, and Pediatricians). An under-served population does not have primary medical care within reasonable economic and geographic bounds.

Physicians in 2008

National Total = 940,171 Physicians*

ALPHA ORDER

RANK	STATE	PHYSICIANS	% of USA
27	Alabama	11,371	1.2%
49	Alaska	1,730	0.2%
19	Arizona	16,133	1.7%
31	Arkansas	6,631	0.7%
1	California	114,490	12.2%
23	Colorado	14,870	1.6%
22	Connecticut	14,931	1.6%
46	Delaware	2,477	0.3%
4	Florida	56,027	6.0%
14	Georgia	23,714	2.5%
39	Hawaii	4,723	0.5%
43	Idaho	3,063	0.3%
6	Illinois	40,255	4.3%
21	Indiana	15,642	1.7%
32	Iowa	6,564	0.7%
29	Kansas	7,325	0.8%
28	Kentucky	11,099	1.2%
24	Louisiana	13,009	1.4%
42	Maine	4,304	0.5%
12	Maryland	26,602	2.8%
8	Massachusetts	33,815	3.6%
10	Michigan	28,567	3.0%
17	Minnesota	17,462	1.9%
34	Mississippi	6,023	0.6%
20	Missouri	16,110	1.7%
45	Montana	2,604	0.3%
37	Nebraska	5,042	0.5%
35	Nevada	5,697	0.6%
41	New Hampshire	4,377	0.5%
9	New Jersey	30,700	3.3%
36	New Mexico	5,612	0.6%
2	New York	85,142	9.1%
11	North Carolina	26,744	2.8%
48	North Dakota	1,787	0.2%
7	Ohio	34,743	3.7%
30	Oklahoma	7,317	0.8%
25	Oregon	12,466	1.3%
5	Pennsylvania	43,726	4.7%
40	Rhode Island	4,452	0.5%
26	South Carolina	11,747	1.2%
47	South Dakota	2,046	0.2%
16	Tennessee	18,416	2.0%
3	Texas	57,939	6.2%
33	Utah	6,467	0.7%
44	Vermont	2,762	0.3%
13	Virginia	24,634	2.6%
15	Washington	20,842	2.2%
38	West Virginia	4,798	0.5%
18	Wisconsin	16,718	1.8%
50	Wyoming	1,212	0.1%

RANK ORDER

RANK	STATE	PHYSICIANS	% of USA
1	California	114,490	12.2%
2	New York	85,142	9.1%
3	Texas	57,939	6.2%
4	Florida	56,027	6.0%
5	Pennsylvania	43,726	4.7%
6	Illinois	40,255	4.3%
7	Ohio	34,743	3.7%
8	Massachusetts	33,815	3.6%
9	New Jersey	30,700	3.3%
10	Michigan	28,567	3.0%
11	North Carolina	26,744	2.8%
12	Maryland	26,602	2.8%
13	Virginia	24,634	2.6%
14	Georgia	23,714	2.5%
15	Washington	20,842	2.2%
16	Tennessee	18,416	2.0%
17	Minnesota	17,462	1.9%
18	Wisconsin	16,718	1.8%
19	Arizona	16,133	1.7%
20	Missouri	16,110	1.7%
21	Indiana	15,642	1.7%
22	Connecticut	14,931	1.6%
23	Colorado	14,870	1.6%
24	Louisiana	13,009	1.4%
25	Oregon	12,466	1.3%
26	South Carolina	11,747	1.2%
27	Alabama	11,371	1.2%
28	Kentucky	11,099	1.2%
29	Kansas	7,325	0.8%
30	Oklahoma	7,317	0.8%
31	Arkansas	6,631	0.7%
32	Iowa	6,564	0.7%
33	Utah	6,467	0.7%
34	Mississippi	6,023	0.6%
35	Nevada	5,697	0.6%
36	New Mexico	5,612	0.6%
37	Nebraska	5,042	0.5%
38	West Virginia	4,798	0.5%
39	Hawaii	4,723	0.5%
40	Rhode Island	4,452	0.5%
41	New Hampshire	4,377	0.5%
42	Maine	4,304	0.5%
43	Idaho	3,063	0.3%
44	Vermont	2,762	0.3%
45	Montana	2,604	0.3%
46	Delaware	2,477	0.3%
47	South Dakota	2,046	0.2%
48	North Dakota	1,787	0.2%
49	Alaska	1,730	0.2%
50	Wyoming	1,212	0.1%
	District of Columbia	5,244	0.6%

Source: American Medical Association (Chicago, Illinois)
     "Physician Characteristics and Distribution in the U.S." (2010 Edition)
*As of December 31, 2008. Total does not include 14,053 physicians in the U.S. territories and possessions, at APOs and FPOs, or whose addresses are unknown.

Rate of Physicians in 2008

National Rate = 309 Physicians per 100,000 Population*

ALPHA ORDER

RANK	STATE	RATE
41	Alabama	243
37	Alaska	251
38	Arizona	248
44	Arkansas	231
16	California	313
19	Colorado	301
5	Connecticut	426
26	Delaware	283
18	Florida	304
39	Georgia	245
7	Hawaii	367
49	Idaho	201
16	Illinois	313
39	Indiana	245
46	Iowa	219
33	Kansas	262
35	Kentucky	259
23	Louisiana	292
13	Maine	326
2	Maryland	470
1	Massachusetts	517
25	Michigan	286
10	Minnesota	334
48	Mississippi	205
30	Missouri	270
31	Montana	269
26	Nebraska	283
47	Nevada	218
11	New Hampshire	331
8	New Jersey	354
28	New Mexico	282
4	New York	437
24	North Carolina	289
29	North Dakota	279
19	Ohio	301
49	Oklahoma	201
12	Oregon	330
9	Pennsylvania	348
6	Rhode Island	423
34	South Carolina	261
36	South Dakota	254
22	Tennessee	295
42	Texas	238
43	Utah	237
3	Vermont	445
15	Virginia	316
14	Washington	317
32	West Virginia	264
21	Wisconsin	297
45	Wyoming	227

RANK ORDER

RANK	STATE	RATE
1	Massachusetts	517
2	Maryland	470
3	Vermont	445
4	New York	437
5	Connecticut	426
6	Rhode Island	423
7	Hawaii	367
8	New Jersey	354
9	Pennsylvania	348
10	Minnesota	334
11	New Hampshire	331
12	Oregon	330
13	Maine	326
14	Washington	317
15	Virginia	316
16	California	313
16	Illinois	313
18	Florida	304
19	Colorado	301
19	Ohio	301
21	Wisconsin	297
22	Tennessee	295
23	Louisiana	292
24	North Carolina	289
25	Michigan	286
26	Delaware	283
26	Nebraska	283
28	New Mexico	282
29	North Dakota	279
30	Missouri	270
31	Montana	269
32	West Virginia	264
33	Kansas	262
34	South Carolina	261
35	Kentucky	259
36	South Dakota	254
37	Alaska	251
38	Arizona	248
39	Georgia	245
39	Indiana	245
41	Alabama	243
42	Texas	238
43	Utah	237
44	Arkansas	231
45	Wyoming	227
46	Iowa	219
47	Nevada	218
48	Mississippi	205
49	Idaho	201
49	Oklahoma	201

District of Columbia — 889

Source: CQ Press using data from American Medical Association (Chicago, Illinois)
"Physician Characteristics and Distribution in the U.S." (2010 Edition)
*As of December 31, 2008. National rate does not include physicians in the U.S. territories and possessions, at APOs and FPOs, or whose addresses are unknown.

Rate of Registered Nurses in 2008

National Rate = 835 Nurses per 100,000 Population*

ALPHA ORDER

RANK	STATE	RATE
25	Alabama	889
38	Alaska	777
50	Arizona	581
33	Arkansas	802
46	California	657
34	Colorado	799
9	Connecticut	1,010
7	Delaware	1,034
35	Florida	793
45	Georgia	669
43	Hawaii	680
42	Idaho	710
30	Illinois	847
26	Indiana	884
11	Iowa	1,008
23	Kansas	894
16	Kentucky	958
24	Louisiana	890
4	Maine	1,065
22	Maryland	897
2	Massachusetts	1,218
29	Michigan	866
4	Minnesota	1,065
19	Mississippi	930
10	Missouri	1,009
39	Montana	773
6	Nebraska	1,062
48	Nevada	610
13	New Hampshire	992
27	New Jersey	873
49	New Mexico	599
28	New York	867
21	North Carolina	911
14	North Dakota	988
12	Ohio	997
41	Oklahoma	734
36	Oregon	792
8	Pennsylvania	1,027
3	Rhode Island	1,078
31	South Carolina	819
1	South Dakota	1,244
15	Tennessee	987
44	Texas	676
47	Utah	632
17	Vermont	950
40	Virginia	770
36	Washington	792
18	West Virginia	932
20	Wisconsin	919
32	Wyoming	807

RANK ORDER

RANK	STATE	RATE
1	South Dakota	1,244
2	Massachusetts	1,218
3	Rhode Island	1,078
4	Maine	1,065
4	Minnesota	1,065
6	Nebraska	1,062
7	Delaware	1,034
8	Pennsylvania	1,027
9	Connecticut	1,010
10	Missouri	1,009
11	Iowa	1,008
12	Ohio	997
13	New Hampshire	992
14	North Dakota	988
15	Tennessee	987
16	Kentucky	958
17	Vermont	950
18	West Virginia	932
19	Mississippi	930
20	Wisconsin	919
21	North Carolina	911
22	Maryland	897
23	Kansas	894
24	Louisiana	890
25	Alabama	889
26	Indiana	884
27	New Jersey	873
28	New York	867
29	Michigan	866
30	Illinois	847
31	South Carolina	819
32	Wyoming	807
33	Arkansas	802
34	Colorado	799
35	Florida	793
36	Oregon	792
36	Washington	792
38	Alaska	777
39	Montana	773
40	Virginia	770
41	Oklahoma	734
42	Idaho	710
43	Hawaii	680
44	Texas	676
45	Georgia	669
46	California	657
47	Utah	632
48	Nevada	610
49	New Mexico	599
50	Arizona	581

| | District of Columbia | 1,566 |

Source: CQ Press using data from U.S. Department of Labor, Bureau of Labor Statistics
   "Occupational Employment and Wages, 2008" (http://www.bls.gov/oes/)
*Does not include self-employed.

Rate of Dentists in 2007

National Rate = 60 Dentists per 100,000 Population*

ALPHA ORDER

RANK	STATE	RATE
48	Alabama	44
6	Alaska	76
30	Arizona	51
49	Arkansas	41
6	California	76
11	Colorado	66
4	Connecticut	78
41	Delaware	47
27	Florida	53
46	Georgia	45
1	Hawaii	82
20	Idaho	58
12	Illinois	65
38	Indiana	48
25	Iowa	54
29	Kansas	52
24	Kentucky	55
38	Louisiana	48
33	Maine	50
8	Maryland	75
1	Massachusetts	82
18	Michigan	61
16	Minnesota	62
49	Mississippi	41
38	Missouri	48
22	Montana	57
14	Nebraska	63
33	Nevada	50
14	New Hampshire	63
1	New Jersey	82
43	New Mexico	46
4	New York	78
46	North Carolina	45
30	North Dakota	51
27	Ohio	53
33	Oklahoma	50
10	Oregon	68
16	Pennsylvania	62
25	Rhode Island	54
43	South Carolina	46
33	South Dakota	50
33	Tennessee	50
43	Texas	46
13	Utah	64
20	Vermont	58
19	Virginia	59
9	Washington	70
41	West Virginia	47
22	Wisconsin	57
30	Wyoming	51

RANK ORDER

RANK	STATE	RATE
1	Hawaii	82
1	Massachusetts	82
1	New Jersey	82
4	Connecticut	78
4	New York	78
6	Alaska	76
6	California	76
8	Maryland	75
9	Washington	70
10	Oregon	68
11	Colorado	66
12	Illinois	65
13	Utah	64
14	Nebraska	63
14	New Hampshire	63
16	Minnesota	62
16	Pennsylvania	62
18	Michigan	61
19	Virginia	59
20	Idaho	58
20	Vermont	58
22	Montana	57
22	Wisconsin	57
24	Kentucky	55
25	Iowa	54
25	Rhode Island	54
27	Florida	53
27	Ohio	53
29	Kansas	52
30	Arizona	51
30	North Dakota	51
30	Wyoming	51
33	Maine	50
33	Nevada	50
33	Oklahoma	50
33	South Dakota	50
33	Tennessee	50
38	Indiana	48
38	Louisiana	48
38	Missouri	48
41	Delaware	47
41	West Virginia	47
43	New Mexico	46
43	South Carolina	46
43	Texas	46
46	Georgia	45
46	North Carolina	45
48	Alabama	44
49	Arkansas	41
49	Mississippi	41

District of Columbia	105

Source: CQ Press using data from American Dental Association
 "Distribution of Dentists, by Region and State, 2007"
*Professionally active dentists. Total includes 24 dentists for whom state is not known.

Community Hospitals in 2008

National Total = 5,010 Hospitals*

ALPHA ORDER

RANK	STATE	HOSPITALS	% of USA
20	Alabama	109	2.2%
47	Alaska	22	0.4%
30	Arizona	71	1.4%
24	Arkansas	86	1.7%
2	California	352	7.0%
27	Colorado	78	1.6%
42	Connecticut	35	0.7%
50	Delaware	7	0.1%
3	Florida	211	4.2%
8	Georgia	153	3.1%
45	Hawaii	25	0.5%
39	Idaho	39	0.8%
6	Illinois	191	3.8%
15	Indiana	123	2.5%
17	Iowa	118	2.4%
11	Kansas	132	2.6%
21	Kentucky	105	2.1%
12	Louisiana	130	2.6%
40	Maine	37	0.7%
35	Maryland	50	1.0%
28	Massachusetts	75	1.5%
8	Michigan	153	3.1%
12	Minnesota	130	2.6%
22	Mississippi	98	2.0%
15	Missouri	123	2.5%
36	Montana	48	1.0%
24	Nebraska	86	1.7%
42	Nevada	35	0.7%
44	New Hampshire	28	0.6%
29	New Jersey	73	1.5%
41	New Mexico	36	0.7%
5	New York	194	3.9%
18	North Carolina	116	2.3%
38	North Dakota	41	0.8%
7	Ohio	181	3.6%
19	Oklahoma	115	2.3%
32	Oregon	58	1.2%
4	Pennsylvania	201	4.0%
49	Rhode Island	11	0.2%
31	South Carolina	69	1.4%
34	South Dakota	53	1.1%
10	Tennessee	137	2.7%
1	Texas	426	8.5%
37	Utah	43	0.9%
48	Vermont	14	0.3%
23	Virginia	90	1.8%
24	Washington	86	1.7%
33	West Virginia	56	1.1%
14	Wisconsin	126	2.5%
46	Wyoming	24	0.5%

RANK ORDER

RANK	STATE	HOSPITALS	% of USA
1	Texas	426	8.5%
2	California	352	7.0%
3	Florida	211	4.2%
4	Pennsylvania	201	4.0%
5	New York	194	3.9%
6	Illinois	191	3.8%
7	Ohio	181	3.6%
8	Georgia	153	3.1%
8	Michigan	153	3.1%
10	Tennessee	137	2.7%
11	Kansas	132	2.6%
12	Louisiana	130	2.6%
12	Minnesota	130	2.6%
14	Wisconsin	126	2.5%
15	Indiana	123	2.5%
15	Missouri	123	2.5%
17	Iowa	118	2.4%
18	North Carolina	116	2.3%
19	Oklahoma	115	2.3%
20	Alabama	109	2.2%
21	Kentucky	105	2.1%
22	Mississippi	98	2.0%
23	Virginia	90	1.8%
24	Arkansas	86	1.7%
24	Nebraska	86	1.7%
24	Washington	86	1.7%
27	Colorado	78	1.6%
28	Massachusetts	75	1.5%
29	New Jersey	73	1.5%
30	Arizona	71	1.4%
31	South Carolina	69	1.4%
32	Oregon	58	1.2%
33	West Virginia	56	1.1%
34	South Dakota	53	1.1%
35	Maryland	50	1.0%
36	Montana	48	1.0%
37	Utah	43	0.9%
38	North Dakota	41	0.8%
39	Idaho	39	0.8%
40	Maine	37	0.7%
41	New Mexico	36	0.7%
42	Connecticut	35	0.7%
42	Nevada	35	0.7%
44	New Hampshire	28	0.6%
45	Hawaii	25	0.5%
46	Wyoming	24	0.5%
47	Alaska	22	0.4%
48	Vermont	14	0.3%
49	Rhode Island	11	0.2%
50	Delaware	7	0.1%
	District of Columbia	10	0.2%

Source: American Hospital Association (Chicago, IL)
"Hospital Statistics" (2010 edition)

*Community hospitals are all nonfederal, short-term general, and special hospitals whose facilities and services are available to the public.

Rate of Community Hospitals in 2008

National Rate = 1.6 Community Hospitals per 100,000 Population*

ALPHA ORDER

RANK	STATE	RATE
18	Alabama	2.3
9	Alaska	3.2
41	Arizona	1.1
12	Arkansas	3.0
44	California	1.0
28	Colorado	1.6
44	Connecticut	1.0
49	Delaware	0.8
41	Florida	1.1
28	Georgia	1.6
24	Hawaii	1.9
15	Idaho	2.6
33	Illinois	1.5
24	Indiana	1.9
7	Iowa	3.9
5	Kansas	4.7
17	Kentucky	2.4
13	Louisiana	2.9
14	Maine	2.8
48	Maryland	0.9
41	Massachusetts	1.1
33	Michigan	1.5
16	Minnesota	2.5
8	Mississippi	3.3
22	Missouri	2.1
3	Montana	5.0
4	Nebraska	4.8
37	Nevada	1.3
22	New Hampshire	2.1
49	New Jersey	0.8
26	New Mexico	1.8
44	New York	1.0
37	North Carolina	1.3
2	North Dakota	6.4
28	Ohio	1.6
9	Oklahoma	3.2
33	Oregon	1.5
28	Pennsylvania	1.6
44	Rhode Island	1.0
33	South Carolina	1.5
1	South Dakota	6.6
20	Tennessee	2.2
26	Texas	1.8
28	Utah	1.6
18	Vermont	2.3
40	Virginia	1.2
37	Washington	1.3
11	West Virginia	3.1
20	Wisconsin	2.2
6	Wyoming	4.5

RANK ORDER

RANK	STATE	RATE
1	South Dakota	6.6
2	North Dakota	6.4
3	Montana	5.0
4	Nebraska	4.8
5	Kansas	4.7
6	Wyoming	4.5
7	Iowa	3.9
8	Mississippi	3.3
9	Alaska	3.2
9	Oklahoma	3.2
11	West Virginia	3.1
12	Arkansas	3.0
13	Louisiana	2.9
14	Maine	2.8
15	Idaho	2.6
16	Minnesota	2.5
17	Kentucky	2.4
18	Alabama	2.3
18	Vermont	2.3
20	Tennessee	2.2
20	Wisconsin	2.2
22	Missouri	2.1
22	New Hampshire	2.1
24	Hawaii	1.9
24	Indiana	1.9
26	New Mexico	1.8
26	Texas	1.8
28	Colorado	1.6
28	Georgia	1.6
28	Ohio	1.6
28	Pennsylvania	1.6
28	Utah	1.6
33	Illinois	1.5
33	Michigan	1.5
33	Oregon	1.5
33	South Carolina	1.5
37	Nevada	1.3
37	North Carolina	1.3
37	Washington	1.3
40	Virginia	1.2
41	Arizona	1.1
41	Florida	1.1
41	Massachusetts	1.1
44	California	1.0
44	Connecticut	1.0
44	New York	1.0
44	Rhode Island	1.0
48	Maryland	0.9
49	Delaware	0.8
49	New Jersey	0.8
	District of Columbia	1.7

Source: CQ Press using data from American Hospital Association (Chicago, IL)
"Hospital Statistics" (2010 edition)

*Community hospitals are all nonfederal, short-term general, and special hospitals whose facilities and services are available to the public.

Births in 2007

National Total = 4,317,119 Live Births*

ALPHA ORDER

RANK	STATE	BIRTHS	% of USA
24	Alabama	64,749	1.5%
47	Alaska	11,101	0.3%
13	Arizona	102,992	2.4%
33	Arkansas	41,377	1.0%
1	California	566,352	13.1%
22	Colorado	70,805	1.6%
32	Connecticut	41,663	1.0%
46	Delaware	12,171	0.3%
4	Florida	239,143	5.5%
6	Georgia	152,021	3.5%
40	Hawaii	19,137	0.4%
38	Idaho	25,019	0.6%
5	Illinois	180,856	4.2%
14	Indiana	89,847	2.1%
35	Iowa	40,885	0.9%
31	Kansas	42,004	1.0%
26	Kentucky	59,370	1.4%
23	Louisiana	66,260	1.5%
42	Maine	14,120	0.3%
18	Maryland	78,096	1.8%
19	Massachusetts	77,962	1.8%
10	Michigan	125,394	2.9%
20	Minnesota	73,745	1.7%
30	Mississippi	46,501	1.1%
17	Missouri	81,928	1.9%
43	Montana	12,444	0.3%
37	Nebraska	26,923	0.6%
34	Nevada	41,202	1.0%
41	New Hampshire	14,169	0.3%
11	New Jersey	116,060	2.7%
36	New Mexico	30,555	0.7%
3	New York	253,458	5.9%
9	North Carolina	131,016	3.0%
48	North Dakota	8,840	0.2%
7	Ohio	150,882	3.5%
28	Oklahoma	55,078	1.3%
29	Oregon	49,372	1.1%
8	Pennsylvania	150,731	3.5%
44	Rhode Island	12,375	0.3%
25	South Carolina	62,891	1.5%
45	South Dakota	12,259	0.3%
16	Tennessee	86,707	2.0%
2	Texas	407,640	9.4%
27	Utah	55,131	1.3%
50	Vermont	6,513	0.2%
12	Virginia	108,874	2.5%
15	Washington	88,958	2.1%
39	West Virginia	21,992	0.5%
21	Wisconsin	72,796	1.7%
49	Wyoming	7,893	0.2%

RANK ORDER

RANK	STATE	BIRTHS	% of USA
1	California	566,352	13.1%
2	Texas	407,640	9.4%
3	New York	253,458	5.9%
4	Florida	239,143	5.5%
5	Illinois	180,856	4.2%
6	Georgia	152,021	3.5%
7	Ohio	150,882	3.5%
8	Pennsylvania	150,731	3.5%
9	North Carolina	131,016	3.0%
10	Michigan	125,394	2.9%
11	New Jersey	116,060	2.7%
12	Virginia	108,874	2.5%
13	Arizona	102,992	2.4%
14	Indiana	89,847	2.1%
15	Washington	88,958	2.1%
16	Tennessee	86,707	2.0%
17	Missouri	81,928	1.9%
18	Maryland	78,096	1.8%
19	Massachusetts	77,962	1.8%
20	Minnesota	73,745	1.7%
21	Wisconsin	72,796	1.7%
22	Colorado	70,805	1.6%
23	Louisiana	66,260	1.5%
24	Alabama	64,749	1.5%
25	South Carolina	62,891	1.5%
26	Kentucky	59,370	1.4%
27	Utah	55,131	1.3%
28	Oklahoma	55,078	1.3%
29	Oregon	49,372	1.1%
30	Mississippi	46,501	1.1%
31	Kansas	42,004	1.0%
32	Connecticut	41,663	1.0%
33	Arkansas	41,377	1.0%
34	Nevada	41,202	1.0%
35	Iowa	40,885	0.9%
36	New Mexico	30,555	0.7%
37	Nebraska	26,923	0.6%
38	Idaho	25,019	0.6%
39	West Virginia	21,992	0.5%
40	Hawaii	19,137	0.4%
41	New Hampshire	14,169	0.3%
42	Maine	14,120	0.3%
43	Montana	12,444	0.3%
44	Rhode Island	12,375	0.3%
45	South Dakota	12,259	0.3%
46	Delaware	12,171	0.3%
47	Alaska	11,101	0.3%
48	North Dakota	8,840	0.2%
49	Wyoming	7,893	0.2%
50	Vermont	6,513	0.2%
	District of Columbia	8,862	0.2%

Source: U.S. Department of Health and Human Services, National Center for Health Statistics
"National Vital Statistics Reports" (Vol. 57, No. 12, March 18, 2009, http://www.cdc.gov/nchs/births.htm)
*Revised preliminary data by state of residence.

Birth Rate in 2007

National Rate = 14.3 Live Births per 1,000 Population*

ALPHA ORDER

RANK	STATE	RATE
28	Alabama	14.0
4	Alaska	16.2
4	Arizona	16.2
18	Arkansas	14.6
9	California	15.5
18	Colorado	14.6
46	Connecticut	11.9
24	Delaware	14.1
38	Florida	13.1
7	Georgia	15.9
17	Hawaii	14.9
3	Idaho	16.7
24	Illinois	14.1
22	Indiana	14.2
34	Iowa	13.7
15	Kansas	15.1
28	Kentucky	14.0
11	Louisiana	15.4
49	Maine	10.7
30	Maryland	13.9
43	Massachusetts	12.1
42	Michigan	12.4
22	Minnesota	14.2
7	Mississippi	15.9
30	Missouri	13.9
40	Montana	13.0
13	Nebraska	15.2
6	Nevada	16.1
48	New Hampshire	10.8
35	New Jersey	13.4
9	New Mexico	15.5
38	New York	13.1
20	North Carolina	14.5
32	North Dakota	13.8
36	Ohio	13.2
13	Oklahoma	15.2
36	Oregon	13.2
43	Pennsylvania	12.1
47	Rhode Island	11.7
21	South Carolina	14.3
11	South Dakota	15.4
24	Tennessee	14.1
2	Texas	17.1
1	Utah	20.8
50	Vermont	10.5
24	Virginia	14.1
32	Washington	13.8
43	West Virginia	12.1
40	Wisconsin	13.0
15	Wyoming	15.1

RANK ORDER

RANK	STATE	RATE
1	Utah	20.8
2	Texas	17.1
3	Idaho	16.7
4	Alaska	16.2
4	Arizona	16.2
6	Nevada	16.1
7	Georgia	15.9
7	Mississippi	15.9
9	California	15.5
9	New Mexico	15.5
11	Louisiana	15.4
11	South Dakota	15.4
13	Nebraska	15.2
13	Oklahoma	15.2
15	Kansas	15.1
15	Wyoming	15.1
17	Hawaii	14.9
18	Arkansas	14.6
18	Colorado	14.6
20	North Carolina	14.5
21	South Carolina	14.3
22	Indiana	14.2
22	Minnesota	14.2
24	Delaware	14.1
24	Illinois	14.1
24	Tennessee	14.1
24	Virginia	14.1
28	Alabama	14.0
28	Kentucky	14.0
30	Maryland	13.9
30	Missouri	13.9
32	North Dakota	13.8
32	Washington	13.8
34	Iowa	13.7
35	New Jersey	13.4
36	Ohio	13.2
36	Oregon	13.2
38	Florida	13.1
38	New York	13.1
40	Montana	13.0
40	Wisconsin	13.0
42	Michigan	12.4
43	Massachusetts	12.1
43	Pennsylvania	12.1
43	West Virginia	12.1
46	Connecticut	11.9
47	Rhode Island	11.7
48	New Hampshire	10.8
49	Maine	10.7
50	Vermont	10.5
	District of Columbia	15.1

Source: U.S. Department of Health and Human Services, National Center for Health Statistics
"National Vital Statistics Reports" (Vol. 57, No. 12, March 18, 2009, http://www.cdc.gov/nchs/births.htm)
*Revised preliminary data by state of residence.

Births of Low Birthweight as a Percent of All Births in 2007

National Percent = 8.2% of Live Births*

ALPHA ORDER

RANK	STATE	PERCENT
3	Alabama	10.4
50	Alaska	5.7
34	Arizona	7.1
10	Arkansas	9.1
38	California	6.9
14	Colorado	9.0
28	Connecticut	8.1
7	Delaware	9.3
16	Florida	8.7
10	Georgia	9.1
29	Hawaii	8.0
42	Idaho	6.5
19	Illinois	8.5
19	Indiana	8.5
39	Iowa	6.8
49	Kansas	6.0
7	Kentucky	9.3
2	Louisiana	11.0
43	Maine	6.3
10	Maryland	9.1
31	Massachusetts	7.9
24	Michigan	8.2
40	Minnesota	6.7
1	Mississippi	12.3
32	Missouri	7.8
33	Montana	7.2
35	Nebraska	7.0
24	Nevada	8.2
43	New Hampshire	6.3
19	New Jersey	8.5
15	New Mexico	8.8
24	New York	8.2
9	North Carolina	9.2
43	North Dakota	6.3
16	Ohio	8.7
24	Oklahoma	8.2
48	Oregon	6.1
22	Pennsylvania	8.4
29	Rhode Island	8.0
4	South Carolina	10.1
35	South Dakota	7.0
6	Tennessee	9.4
22	Texas	8.4
40	Utah	6.7
47	Vermont	6.2
18	Virginia	8.6
43	Washington	6.3
5	West Virginia	9.5
35	Wisconsin	7.0
10	Wyoming	9.1

RANK ORDER

RANK	STATE	PERCENT
1	Mississippi	12.3
2	Louisiana	11.0
3	Alabama	10.4
4	South Carolina	10.1
5	West Virginia	9.5
6	Tennessee	9.4
7	Delaware	9.3
7	Kentucky	9.3
9	North Carolina	9.2
10	Arkansas	9.1
10	Georgia	9.1
10	Maryland	9.1
10	Wyoming	9.1
14	Colorado	9.0
15	New Mexico	8.8
16	Florida	8.7
16	Ohio	8.7
18	Virginia	8.6
19	Illinois	8.5
19	Indiana	8.5
19	New Jersey	8.5
22	Pennsylvania	8.4
22	Texas	8.4
24	Michigan	8.2
24	Nevada	8.2
24	New York	8.2
24	Oklahoma	8.2
28	Connecticut	8.1
29	Hawaii	8.0
29	Rhode Island	8.0
31	Massachusetts	7.9
32	Missouri	7.8
33	Montana	7.2
34	Arizona	7.1
35	Nebraska	7.0
35	South Dakota	7.0
35	Wisconsin	7.0
38	California	6.9
39	Iowa	6.8
40	Minnesota	6.7
40	Utah	6.7
42	Idaho	6.5
43	Maine	6.3
43	New Hampshire	6.3
43	North Dakota	6.3
43	Washington	6.3
47	Vermont	6.2
48	Oregon	6.1
49	Kansas	6.0
50	Alaska	5.7

| District of Columbia | | 11.1 |

Source: U.S. Department of Health and Human Services, National Center for Health Statistics
    "National Vital Statistics Reports" (Vol. 57, No. 12, March 18, 2009, http://www.cdc.gov/nchs/births.htm)
*Preliminary data by state of residence. Births of less than 2,500 grams (5 pounds 8 ounces).

Births to Teenage Mothers as a Percent of All Births in 2007

National Percent = 10.5% of Live Births*

ALPHA ORDER

RANK	STATE	PERCENT
6	Alabama	13.6
23	Alaska	10.1
11	Arizona	12.7
3	Arkansas	14.6
30	California	9.5
27	Colorado	9.7
46	Connecticut	6.9
21	Delaware	10.4
19	Florida	10.9
13	Georgia	12.2
39	Hawaii	8.5
32	Idaho	9.1
23	Illinois	10.1
17	Indiana	11.2
35	Iowa	8.7
22	Kansas	10.3
10	Kentucky	12.9
5	Louisiana	13.7
40	Maine	8.4
33	Maryland	8.9
49	Massachusetts	6.4
23	Michigan	10.1
44	Minnesota	7.1
1	Mississippi	17.1
16	Missouri	11.4
27	Montana	9.7
37	Nebraska	8.6
20	Nevada	10.8
48	New Hampshire	6.6
49	New Jersey	6.4
2	New Mexico	15.7
45	New York	7.0
15	North Carolina	11.7
42	North Dakota	8.0
18	Ohio	11.0
4	Oklahoma	13.9
33	Oregon	8.9
31	Pennsylvania	9.3
27	Rhode Island	9.7
8	South Carolina	13.4
26	South Dakota	9.8
9	Tennessee	13.2
7	Texas	13.5
46	Utah	6.9
43	Vermont	7.6
37	Virginia	8.6
40	Washington	8.4
12	West Virginia	12.5
35	Wisconsin	8.7
14	Wyoming	11.8

RANK ORDER

RANK	STATE	PERCENT
1	Mississippi	17.1
2	New Mexico	15.7
3	Arkansas	14.6
4	Oklahoma	13.9
5	Louisiana	13.7
6	Alabama	13.6
7	Texas	13.5
8	South Carolina	13.4
9	Tennessee	13.2
10	Kentucky	12.9
11	Arizona	12.7
12	West Virginia	12.5
13	Georgia	12.2
14	Wyoming	11.8
15	North Carolina	11.7
16	Missouri	11.4
17	Indiana	11.2
18	Ohio	11.0
19	Florida	10.9
20	Nevada	10.8
21	Delaware	10.4
22	Kansas	10.3
23	Alaska	10.1
23	Illinois	10.1
23	Michigan	10.1
26	South Dakota	9.8
27	Colorado	9.7
27	Montana	9.7
27	Rhode Island	9.7
30	California	9.5
31	Pennsylvania	9.3
32	Idaho	9.1
33	Maryland	8.9
33	Oregon	8.9
35	Iowa	8.7
35	Wisconsin	8.7
37	Nebraska	8.6
37	Virginia	8.6
39	Hawaii	8.5
40	Maine	8.4
40	Washington	8.4
42	North Dakota	8.0
43	Vermont	7.6
44	Minnesota	7.1
45	New York	7.0
46	Connecticut	6.9
46	Utah	6.9
48	New Hampshire	6.6
49	Massachusetts	6.4
49	New Jersey	6.4
	District of Columbia	12.1

Source: U.S. Department of Health and Human Services, National Center for Health Statistics
"National Vital Statistics Reports" (Vol. 57, No. 12, March 18, 2009, http://www.cdc.gov/nchs/births.htm)
*Preliminary data by state of residence.

Births to Unmarried Women as a Percent of All Births in 2007

National Percent = 39.7% of Live Births*

ALPHA ORDER

RANK	STATE	PERCENT		RANK	STATE	PERCENT
28	Alabama	38.4		1	Mississippi	53.7
30	Alaska	37.2		2	New Mexico	51.8
7	Arizona	45.2		3	Louisiana	50.9
9	Arkansas	43.4		4	Delaware	46.9
27	California	38.9		5	South Carolina	46.6
49	Colorado	25.4		6	Florida	46.1
37	Connecticut	35.1		7	Arizona	45.2
4	Delaware	46.9		8	Rhode Island	44.0
6	Florida	46.1		9	Arkansas	43.4
10	Georgia	43.3		10	Georgia	43.3
31	Hawaii	36.9		11	Tennessee	42.8
48	Idaho	25.5		12	Indiana	42.4
22	Illinois	40.1		13	Ohio	42.2
12	Indiana	42.4		14	Nevada	42.0
41	Iowa	34.3		15	Oklahoma	41.3
33	Kansas	36.5		16	North Carolina	41.2
25	Kentucky	39.3		17	Maryland	40.9
3	Louisiana	50.9		18	New York	40.7
26	Maine	39.1		18	Texas	40.7
17	Maryland	40.9		20	Missouri	40.5
42	Massachusetts	33.4		21	West Virginia	40.3
24	Michigan	39.4		22	Illinois	40.1
45	Minnesota	32.7		23	Pennsylvania	39.7
1	Mississippi	53.7		24	Michigan	39.4
20	Missouri	40.5		25	Kentucky	39.3
34	Montana	35.9		26	Maine	39.1
42	Nebraska	33.4		27	California	38.9
14	Nevada	42.0		28	Alabama	38.4
47	New Hampshire	31.4		28	South Dakota	38.4
40	New Jersey	34.4		30	Alaska	37.2
2	New Mexico	51.8		31	Hawaii	36.9
18	New York	40.7		32	Vermont	36.6
16	North Carolina	41.2		33	Kansas	36.5
46	North Dakota	32.6		34	Montana	35.9
13	Ohio	42.2		35	Wisconsin	35.4
15	Oklahoma	41.3		36	Virginia	35.2
37	Oregon	35.1		37	Connecticut	35.1
23	Pennsylvania	39.7		37	Oregon	35.1
8	Rhode Island	44.0		39	Wyoming	34.7
5	South Carolina	46.6		40	New Jersey	34.4
28	South Dakota	38.4		41	Iowa	34.3
11	Tennessee	42.8		42	Massachusetts	33.4
18	Texas	40.7		42	Nebraska	33.4
50	Utah	19.6		44	Washington	33.2
32	Vermont	36.6		45	Minnesota	32.7
36	Virginia	35.2		46	North Dakota	32.6
44	Washington	33.2		47	New Hampshire	31.4
21	West Virginia	40.3		48	Idaho	25.5
35	Wisconsin	35.4		49	Colorado	25.4
39	Wyoming	34.7		50	Utah	19.6
					District of Columbia	58.5

Source: U.S. Department of Health and Human Services, National Center for Health Statistics
    "National Vital Statistics Reports" (Vol. 57, No. 12, March 18, 2009, http://www.cdc.gov/nchs/births.htm)
*Preliminary data by state of residence.

Percent of Women Receiving Late or No Prenatal Care in 2006

National Percent = 3.6% of Women*

ALPHA ORDER				RANK ORDER		
RANK	STATE	PERCENT		RANK	STATE	PERCENT
9	Alabama	4.5		1	Nevada	8.8
6	Alaska	4.9		2	New Mexico	6.7
3	Arizona	6.1		3	Arizona	6.1
8	Arkansas	4.7		3	Oklahoma	6.1
24	California	2.8		5	New Jersey	5.0
9	Colorado	4.5		6	Alaska	4.9
32	Connecticut	1.8		6	New York*	4.9
NA	Delaware**	NA		8	Arkansas	4.7
NA	Florida**	NA		9	Alabama	4.5
14	Georgia	4.1		9	Colorado	4.5
17	Hawaii	3.6		9	Indiana	4.5
NA	Idaho**	NA		12	Maryland	4.3
27	Illinois	2.4		12	Oregon	4.3
9	Indiana	4.5		14	Georgia	4.1
26	Iowa	2.5		14	Virginia	4.1
NA	Kansas**	NA		16	Utah	3.9
NA	Kentucky**	NA		17	Hawaii	3.6
25	Louisiana	2.6		18	Mississippi	3.2
32	Maine	1.8		18	West Virginia	3.2
12	Maryland	4.3		20	Michigan	3.1
28	Massachusetts	2.3		20	Montana	3.1
20	Michigan	3.1		20	North Carolina	3.1
30	Minnesota	2.1		20	Wisconsin	3.1
18	Mississippi	3.2		24	California	2.8
28	Missouri	2.3		25	Louisiana	2.6
20	Montana	3.1		26	Iowa	2.5
NA	Nebraska**	NA		27	Illinois	2.4
1	Nevada	8.8		28	Massachusetts	2.3
NA	New Hampshire**	NA		28	Missouri	2.3
5	New Jersey	5.0		30	Minnesota	2.1
2	New Mexico	6.7		31	Rhode Island	1.9
6	New York*	4.9		32	Connecticut	1.8
20	North Carolina	3.1		32	Maine	1.8
NA	North Dakota**	NA		NA	Delaware**	NA
NA	Ohio**	NA		NA	Florida**	NA
3	Oklahoma	6.1		NA	Idaho**	NA
12	Oregon	4.3		NA	Kansas**	NA
NA	Pennsylvania**	NA		NA	Kentucky**	NA
31	Rhode Island	1.9		NA	Nebraska**	NA
NA	South Carolina**	NA		NA	New Hampshire**	NA
NA	South Dakota**	NA		NA	North Dakota**	NA
NA	Tennessee**	NA		NA	Ohio**	NA
NA	Texas**	NA		NA	Pennsylvania**	NA
16	Utah	3.9		NA	South Carolina**	NA
NA	Vermont**	NA		NA	South Dakota**	NA
14	Virginia	4.1		NA	Tennessee**	NA
NA	Washington**	NA		NA	Texas**	NA
18	West Virginia	3.2		NA	Vermont**	NA
20	Wisconsin	3.1		NA	Washington**	NA
NA	Wyoming**	NA		NA	Wyoming**	NA
					District of Columbia	5.5

Source: U.S. Department of Health and Human Services, National Center for Health Statistics
   "National Vital Statistics Reports" (Vol. 57, No. 7, January 7, 2009, http://www.cdc.gov/nchs/births.htm)
*Final data by state of residence. "Late" means care begun in third trimester. New York's figure is for New York City only.
**Not available. These states have implemented the 2003 Revision of the U.S. Certificate of Live Birth and their prenatal care data are not comparable with those based on the 1989 revision.

Reported Legal Abortions in 2006

Reporting States' Total = 846,181 Abortions*

RANK	STATE	ABORTIONS	% of USA
18	Alabama	11,654	1.4%
42	Alaska	1,923	0.2%
22	Arizona	10,836	1.3%
31	Arkansas	4,988	0.6%
NA	California**	NA	NA
21	Colorado	11,048	1.3%
15	Connecticut	14,112	1.7%
33	Delaware	4,804	0.6%
2	Florida	95,586	11.3%
9	Georgia	30,550	3.6%
34	Hawaii	3,990	0.5%
45	Idaho	1,249	0.1%
4	Illinois	46,467	5.5%
23	Indiana	10,614	1.3%
29	Iowa	6,722	0.8%
20	Kansas	11,173	1.3%
35	Kentucky	3,912	0.5%
NA	Louisiana**	NA	NA
39	Maine	2,670	0.3%
25	Maryland	9,530	1.1%
13	Massachusetts	24,246	2.9%
11	Michigan	25,636	3.0%
16	Minnesota	14,065	1.7%
37	Mississippi	2,949	0.3%
26	Missouri	7,556	0.9%
40	Montana	2,119	0.3%
38	Nebraska	2,927	0.3%
19	Nevada	11,471	1.4%
NA	New Hampshire**	NA	NA
8	New Jersey	30,986	3.7%
30	New Mexico	6,087	0.7%
1	New York	127,437	15.1%
6	North Carolina	35,088	4.1%
44	North Dakota	1,298	0.2%
7	Ohio	32,936	3.9%
27	Oklahoma	7,088	0.8%
17	Oregon	11,732	1.4%
5	Pennsylvania	36,731	4.3%
32	Rhode Island	4,828	0.6%
28	South Carolina	7,005	0.8%
46	South Dakota	748	0.1%
14	Tennessee	17,883	2.1%
3	Texas	81,883	9.7%
36	Utah	3,753	0.4%
43	Vermont	1,610	0.2%
10	Virginia	27,349	3.2%
12	Washington	24,627	2.9%
41	West Virginia	2,036	0.2%
24	Wisconsin	9,580	1.1%
47	Wyoming	7	0.0%

RANK ORDER

RANK	STATE	ABORTIONS	% of USA
1	New York	127,437	15.1%
2	Florida	95,586	11.3%
3	Texas	81,883	9.7%
4	Illinois	46,467	5.5%
5	Pennsylvania	36,731	4.3%
6	North Carolina	35,088	4.1%
7	Ohio	32,936	3.9%
8	New Jersey	30,986	3.7%
9	Georgia	30,550	3.6%
10	Virginia	27,349	3.2%
11	Michigan	25,636	3.0%
12	Washington	24,627	2.9%
13	Massachusetts	24,246	2.9%
14	Tennessee	17,883	2.1%
15	Connecticut	14,112	1.7%
16	Minnesota	14,065	1.7%
17	Oregon	11,732	1.4%
18	Alabama	11,654	1.4%
19	Nevada	11,471	1.4%
20	Kansas	11,173	1.3%
21	Colorado	11,048	1.3%
22	Arizona	10,836	1.3%
23	Indiana	10,614	1.3%
24	Wisconsin	9,580	1.1%
25	Maryland	9,530	1.1%
26	Missouri	7,556	0.9%
27	Oklahoma	7,088	0.8%
28	South Carolina	7,005	0.8%
29	Iowa	6,722	0.8%
30	New Mexico	6,087	0.7%
31	Arkansas	4,988	0.6%
32	Rhode Island	4,828	0.6%
33	Delaware	4,804	0.6%
34	Hawaii	3,990	0.5%
35	Kentucky	3,912	0.5%
36	Utah	3,753	0.4%
37	Mississippi	2,949	0.3%
38	Nebraska	2,927	0.3%
39	Maine	2,670	0.3%
40	Montana	2,119	0.3%
41	West Virginia	2,036	0.2%
42	Alaska	1,923	0.2%
43	Vermont	1,610	0.2%
44	North Dakota	1,298	0.2%
45	Idaho	1,249	0.1%
46	South Dakota	748	0.1%
47	Wyoming	7	0.0%
NA	California**	NA	NA
NA	Louisiana**	NA	NA
NA	New Hampshire**	NA	NA
	District of Columbia	2,692	0.3%

Source: U.S. Department of Health and Human Services, Centers for Disease Control and Prevention
"Abortion Surveillance-United States, 2006" (MMWR, Vol. 58, No. SS-8, 11/27/09, http://www.cdc.gov/mmwr/mmwr_ss.html)
*By state of occurrence. Total is for reporting states only.
**Not reported.

Reported Legal Abortions per 1,000 Live Births in 2006

Reporting States' Ratio = 233 Abortions per 1,000 Live Births*

ALPHA ORDER

RANK	STATE	RATIO
26	Alabama	184
27	Alaska	175
39	Arizona	106
35	Arkansas	122
NA	California**	NA
30	Colorado	156
5	Connecticut	337
3	Delaware	401
2	Florida	404
20	Georgia	206
19	Hawaii	210
46	Idaho	52
12	Illinois	257
36	Indiana	120
29	Iowa	166
10	Kansas	273
43	Kentucky	67
NA	Louisiana**	NA
25	Maine	189
34	Maryland	123
6	Massachusetts	312
23	Michigan	201
24	Minnesota	191
44	Mississippi	64
41	Missouri	93
28	Montana	169
38	Nebraska	110
7	Nevada	287
NA	New Hampshire**	NA
11	New Jersey	269
22	New Mexico	203
1	New York	510
9	North Carolina	274
31	North Dakota	151
17	Ohio	219
33	Oklahoma	131
16	Oregon	241
15	Pennsylvania	246
4	Rhode Island	390
37	South Carolina	113
45	South Dakota	63
18	Tennessee	212
21	Texas	205
42	Utah	70
14	Vermont	247
13	Virginia	254
8	Washington	283
40	West Virginia	97
32	Wisconsin	132
47	Wyoming	1

RANK ORDER

RANK	STATE	RATIO
1	New York	510
2	Florida	404
3	Delaware	401
4	Rhode Island	390
5	Connecticut	337
6	Massachusetts	312
7	Nevada	287
8	Washington	283
9	North Carolina	274
10	Kansas	273
11	New Jersey	269
12	Illinois	257
13	Virginia	254
14	Vermont	247
15	Pennsylvania	246
16	Oregon	241
17	Ohio	219
18	Tennessee	212
19	Hawaii	210
20	Georgia	206
21	Texas	205
22	New Mexico	203
23	Michigan	201
24	Minnesota	191
25	Maine	189
26	Alabama	184
27	Alaska	175
28	Montana	169
29	Iowa	166
30	Colorado	156
31	North Dakota	151
32	Wisconsin	132
33	Oklahoma	131
34	Maryland	123
35	Arkansas	122
36	Indiana	120
37	South Carolina	113
38	Nebraska	110
39	Arizona	106
40	West Virginia	97
41	Missouri	93
42	Utah	70
43	Kentucky	67
44	Mississippi	64
45	South Dakota	63
46	Idaho	52
47	Wyoming	1
NA	California**	NA
NA	Louisiana**	NA
NA	New Hampshire**	NA

District of Columbia   316

Source: U.S. Department of Health and Human Services, Centers for Disease Control and Prevention
"Abortion Surveillance-United States, 2006" (MMWR, Vol. 58, No. SS-8, 11/27/09, http://www.cdc.gov/mmwr/mmwr_ss.html)
*By state of occurrence. National figure is for reporting states only.
**Not reported.

Infant Deaths in 2006

National Total = 28,527 Infant Deaths*

ALPHA ORDER

RANK	STATE	DEATHS	% of USA
19	Alabama	571	2.0%
45	Alaska	76	0.3%
14	Arizona	651	2.3%
29	Arkansas	350	1.2%
1	California	2,835	9.9%
26	Colorado	404	1.4%
33	Connecticut	260	0.9%
41	Delaware	99	0.3%
3	Florida	1,717	6.0%
6	Georgia	1,206	4.2%
40	Hawaii	107	0.4%
37	Idaho	165	0.6%
5	Illinois	1,309	4.6%
13	Indiana	708	2.5%
35	Iowa	208	0.7%
30	Kansas	292	1.0%
23	Kentucky	438	1.5%
16	Louisiana	629	2.2%
42	Maine	89	0.3%
17	Maryland	616	2.2%
28	Massachusetts	370	1.3%
10	Michigan	940	3.3%
27	Minnesota	381	1.3%
21	Mississippi	488	1.7%
18	Missouri	603	2.1%
47	Montana	73	0.3%
39	Nebraska	149	0.5%
34	Nevada	257	0.9%
43	New Hampshire	87	0.3%
15	New Jersey	632	2.2%
36	New Mexico	173	0.6%
4	New York	1,407	4.9%
9	North Carolina	1,033	3.6%
49	North Dakota	50	0.2%
7	Ohio	1,170	4.1%
24	Oklahoma	432	1.5%
32	Oregon	267	0.9%
8	Pennsylvania	1,138	4.0%
45	Rhode Island	76	0.3%
20	South Carolina	522	1.8%
44	South Dakota	82	0.3%
12	Tennessee	733	2.6%
2	Texas	2,486	8.7%
31	Utah	273	1.0%
50	Vermont	36	0.1%
11	Virginia	765	2.7%
25	Washington	407	1.4%
38	West Virginia	155	0.5%
22	Wisconsin	462	1.6%
48	Wyoming	54	0.2%

RANK ORDER

RANK	STATE	DEATHS	% of USA
1	California	2,835	9.9%
2	Texas	2,486	8.7%
3	Florida	1,717	6.0%
4	New York	1,407	4.9%
5	Illinois	1,309	4.6%
6	Georgia	1,206	4.2%
7	Ohio	1,170	4.1%
8	Pennsylvania	1,138	4.0%
9	North Carolina	1,033	3.6%
10	Michigan	940	3.3%
11	Virginia	765	2.7%
12	Tennessee	733	2.6%
13	Indiana	708	2.5%
14	Arizona	651	2.3%
15	New Jersey	632	2.2%
16	Louisiana	629	2.2%
17	Maryland	616	2.2%
18	Missouri	603	2.1%
19	Alabama	571	2.0%
20	South Carolina	522	1.8%
21	Mississippi	488	1.7%
22	Wisconsin	462	1.6%
23	Kentucky	438	1.5%
24	Oklahoma	432	1.5%
25	Washington	407	1.4%
26	Colorado	404	1.4%
27	Minnesota	381	1.3%
28	Massachusetts	370	1.3%
29	Arkansas	350	1.2%
30	Kansas	292	1.0%
31	Utah	273	1.0%
32	Oregon	267	0.9%
33	Connecticut	260	0.9%
34	Nevada	257	0.9%
35	Iowa	208	0.7%
36	New Mexico	173	0.6%
37	Idaho	165	0.6%
38	West Virginia	155	0.5%
39	Nebraska	149	0.5%
40	Hawaii	107	0.4%
41	Delaware	99	0.3%
42	Maine	89	0.3%
43	New Hampshire	87	0.3%
44	South Dakota	82	0.3%
45	Alaska	76	0.3%
45	Rhode Island	76	0.3%
47	Montana	73	0.3%
48	Wyoming	54	0.2%
49	North Dakota	50	0.2%
50	Vermont	36	0.1%
	District of Columbia	96	0.3%

Source: U.S. Department of Health and Human Services, National Center for Health Statistics
"National Vital Statistics Reports" (Vol. 57, No. 14, April 17, 2009, http://www.cdc.gov/nchs/deaths.htm)
*Final data. Deaths of infants under 1 year old by state of residence.

Infant Mortality Rate in 2006

National Rate = 6.7 Infant Deaths per 1,000 Live Births*

ALPHA ORDER

RANK	STATE	RATE
3	Alabama	9.0
24	Alaska	6.9
27	Arizona	6.4
5	Arkansas	8.5
48	California	5.0
38	Colorado	5.7
31	Connecticut	6.2
7	Delaware	8.3
19	Florida	7.3
8	Georgia	8.1
39	Hawaii	5.6
26	Idaho	6.8
19	Illinois	7.3
10	Indiana	8.0
46	Iowa	5.1
21	Kansas	7.1
15	Kentucky	7.5
2	Louisiana	9.9
30	Maine	6.3
10	Maryland	8.0
49	Massachusetts	4.8
16	Michigan	7.4
45	Minnesota	5.2
1	Mississippi	10.6
16	Missouri	7.4
35	Montana	5.8
39	Nebraska	5.6
27	Nevada	6.4
33	New Hampshire	6.1
42	New Jersey	5.5
35	New Mexico	5.8
39	New York	5.6
8	North Carolina	8.1
35	North Dakota	5.8
13	Ohio	7.8
10	Oklahoma	8.0
42	Oregon	5.5
14	Pennsylvania	7.6
33	Rhode Island	6.1
6	South Carolina	8.4
24	South Dakota	6.9
4	Tennessee	8.7
31	Texas	6.2
46	Utah	5.1
42	Vermont	5.5
21	Virginia	7.1
50	Washington	4.7
16	West Virginia	7.4
27	Wisconsin	6.4
23	Wyoming	7.0

RANK ORDER

RANK	STATE	RATE
1	Mississippi	10.6
2	Louisiana	9.9
3	Alabama	9.0
4	Tennessee	8.7
5	Arkansas	8.5
6	South Carolina	8.4
7	Delaware	8.3
8	Georgia	8.1
8	North Carolina	8.1
10	Indiana	8.0
10	Maryland	8.0
10	Oklahoma	8.0
13	Ohio	7.8
14	Pennsylvania	7.6
15	Kentucky	7.5
16	Michigan	7.4
16	Missouri	7.4
16	West Virginia	7.4
19	Florida	7.3
19	Illinois	7.3
21	Kansas	7.1
21	Virginia	7.1
23	Wyoming	7.0
24	Alaska	6.9
24	South Dakota	6.9
26	Idaho	6.8
27	Arizona	6.4
27	Nevada	6.4
27	Wisconsin	6.4
30	Maine	6.3
31	Connecticut	6.2
31	Texas	6.2
33	New Hampshire	6.1
33	Rhode Island	6.1
35	Montana	5.8
35	New Mexico	5.8
35	North Dakota	5.8
38	Colorado	5.7
39	Hawaii	5.6
39	Nebraska	5.6
39	New York	5.6
42	New Jersey	5.5
42	Oregon	5.5
42	Vermont	5.5
45	Minnesota	5.2
46	Iowa	5.1
46	Utah	5.1
48	California	5.0
49	Massachusetts	4.8
50	Washington	4.7

	District of Columbia	11.3

Source: U.S. Department of Health and Human Services, National Center for Health Statistics
   "National Vital Statistics Reports" (Vol. 57, No. 14, April 17, 2009, http://www.cdc.gov/nchs/deaths.htm)
*Final data. Deaths of infants under 1 year old by state of residence.

Deaths in 2007

National Total = 2,423,995 Deaths*

ALPHA ORDER

RANK	STATE	DEATHS	% of USA
15	Alabama	46,671	1.9%
47	Alaska	3,470	0.1%
17	Arizona	45,595	1.9%
28	Arkansas	28,164	1.2%
NA	California**	NA	NA
25	Colorado	29,993	1.2%
26	Connecticut	28,654	1.2%
42	Delaware	7,330	0.3%
1	Florida	168,043	6.9%
NA	Georgia**	NA	NA
40	Hawaii	9,499	0.4%
37	Idaho	10,829	0.4%
5	Illinois	100,318	4.1%
12	Indiana	54,172	2.2%
29	Iowa	27,247	1.1%
30	Kansas	24,477	1.0%
19	Kentucky	40,120	1.7%
20	Louisiana	39,765	1.6%
36	Maine	12,491	0.5%
18	Maryland	43,772	1.8%
13	Massachusetts	52,936	2.2%
6	Michigan	86,727	3.6%
22	Minnesota	37,176	1.5%
27	Mississippi	28,271	1.2%
11	Missouri	54,174	2.2%
41	Montana	8,629	0.4%
34	Nebraska	15,261	0.6%
32	Nevada	18,642	0.8%
38	New Hampshire	10,305	0.4%
8	New Jersey	69,648	2.9%
33	New Mexico	15,388	0.6%
2	New York	147,727	6.1%
7	North Carolina	76,033	3.1%
44	North Dakota	5,571	0.2%
4	Ohio	106,534	4.4%
23	Oklahoma	36,014	1.5%
24	Oregon	31,418	1.3%
3	Pennsylvania	125,200	5.2%
39	Rhode Island	9,721	0.4%
21	South Carolina	39,497	1.6%
43	South Dakota	6,824	0.3%
10	Tennessee	57,078	2.4%
NA	Texas**	NA	NA
35	Utah	14,143	0.6%
45	Vermont	5,186	0.2%
9	Virginia	58,220	2.4%
14	Washington	47,363	2.0%
31	West Virginia	21,087	0.9%
16	Wisconsin	46,271	1.9%
46	Wyoming	4,264	0.2%

RANK ORDER

RANK	STATE	DEATHS	% of USA
1	Florida	168,043	6.9%
2	New York	147,727	6.1%
3	Pennsylvania	125,200	5.2%
4	Ohio	106,534	4.4%
5	Illinois	100,318	4.1%
6	Michigan	86,727	3.6%
7	North Carolina	76,033	3.1%
8	New Jersey	69,648	2.9%
9	Virginia	58,220	2.4%
10	Tennessee	57,078	2.4%
11	Missouri	54,174	2.2%
12	Indiana	54,172	2.2%
13	Massachusetts	52,936	2.2%
14	Washington	47,363	2.0%
15	Alabama	46,671	1.9%
16	Wisconsin	46,271	1.9%
17	Arizona	45,595	1.9%
18	Maryland	43,772	1.8%
19	Kentucky	40,120	1.7%
20	Louisiana	39,765	1.6%
21	South Carolina	39,497	1.6%
22	Minnesota	37,176	1.5%
23	Oklahoma	36,014	1.5%
24	Oregon	31,418	1.3%
25	Colorado	29,993	1.2%
26	Connecticut	28,654	1.2%
27	Mississippi	28,271	1.2%
28	Arkansas	28,164	1.2%
29	Iowa	27,247	1.1%
30	Kansas	24,477	1.0%
31	West Virginia	21,087	0.9%
32	Nevada	18,642	0.8%
33	New Mexico	15,388	0.6%
34	Nebraska	15,261	0.6%
35	Utah	14,143	0.6%
36	Maine	12,491	0.5%
37	Idaho	10,829	0.4%
38	New Hampshire	10,305	0.4%
39	Rhode Island	9,721	0.4%
40	Hawaii	9,499	0.4%
41	Montana	8,629	0.4%
42	Delaware	7,330	0.3%
43	South Dakota	6,824	0.3%
44	North Dakota	5,571	0.2%
45	Vermont	5,186	0.2%
46	Wyoming	4,264	0.2%
47	Alaska	3,470	0.1%
NA	California**	NA	NA
NA	Georgia**	NA	NA
NA	Texas**	NA	NA
	District of Columbia	5,190	0.2%

Source: U.S. Department of Health and Human Services, National Center for Health Statistics
   "National Vital Statistics Reports" (Vol. 58, No. 1, August 19, 2009, http://www.cdc.gov/nchs/deaths.htm)
*Preliminary data by state of residence.
**Not available. Data for these three states are not shown separately but are included in the U.S. total because their data did not meet the required criterion of completeness.

Age-Adjusted Death Rate in 2007

National Rate = 760.3 Deaths per 100,000 Population*

ALPHA ORDER

RANK	STATE	RATE
3	Alabama	930.3
25	Alaska	756.5
44	Arizona	682.5
8	Arkansas	881.8
NA	California**	NA
38	Colorado	700.8
40	Connecticut	694.1
20	Delaware	774.1
43	Florida	685.7
NA	Georgia**	NA
47	Hawaii	607.7
30	Idaho	734.9
24	Illinois	758.5
13	Indiana	812.5
36	Iowa	719.3
19	Kansas	782.5
6	Kentucky	897.6
4	Louisiana	921.8
21	Maine	773.5
18	Maryland	782.9
37	Massachusetts	707.7
14	Michigan	806.1
46	Minnesota	662.2
2	Mississippi	943.5
12	Missouri	826.8
22	Montana	772.9
29	Nebraska	743.5
15	Nevada	801.6
33	New Hampshire	727.2
34	New Jersey	724.0
27	New Mexico	751.0
42	New York	686.5
10	North Carolina	834.3
45	North Dakota	681.0
11	Ohio	830.8
5	Oklahoma	919.9
26	Oregon	753.9
17	Pennsylvania	790.7
28	Rhode Island	749.8
9	South Carolina	851.4
41	South Dakota	693.4
7	Tennessee	885.0
NA	Texas**	NA
39	Utah	694.2
32	Vermont	730.3
23	Virginia	770.6
35	Washington	722.8
1	West Virginia	951.7
31	Wisconsin	732.8
15	Wyoming	801.6

RANK ORDER

RANK	STATE	RATE
1	West Virginia	951.7
2	Mississippi	943.5
3	Alabama	930.3
4	Louisiana	921.8
5	Oklahoma	919.9
6	Kentucky	897.6
7	Tennessee	885.0
8	Arkansas	881.8
9	South Carolina	851.4
10	North Carolina	834.3
11	Ohio	830.8
12	Missouri	826.8
13	Indiana	812.5
14	Michigan	806.1
15	Nevada	801.6
15	Wyoming	801.6
17	Pennsylvania	790.7
18	Maryland	782.9
19	Kansas	782.5
20	Delaware	774.1
21	Maine	773.5
22	Montana	772.9
23	Virginia	770.6
24	Illinois	758.5
25	Alaska	756.5
26	Oregon	753.9
27	New Mexico	751.0
28	Rhode Island	749.8
29	Nebraska	743.5
30	Idaho	734.9
31	Wisconsin	732.8
32	Vermont	730.3
33	New Hampshire	727.2
34	New Jersey	724.0
35	Washington	722.8
36	Iowa	719.3
37	Massachusetts	707.7
38	Colorado	700.8
39	Utah	694.2
40	Connecticut	694.1
41	South Dakota	693.4
42	New York	686.5
43	Florida	685.7
44	Arizona	682.5
45	North Dakota	681.0
46	Minnesota	662.2
47	Hawaii	607.7
NA	California**	NA
NA	Georgia**	NA
NA	Texas**	NA

District of Columbia   866.9

Source: U.S. Department of Health and Human Services, National Center for Health Statistics
"National Vital Statistics Reports" (Vol. 58, No. 1, August 19, 2009, http://www.cdc.gov/nchs/deaths.htm)
*Preliminary data by state of residence. Age-adjusted rates eliminate the distorting effects of the aging of the population. Rates based on the year 2000 standard population.
**Not available.

Estimated Deaths by Cancer in 2009

National Estimated Total = 562,340 Deaths

ALPHA ORDER

RANK	STATE	DEATHS	% of USA
21	Alabama	9,900	1.8%
50	Alaska	830	0.1%
20	Arizona	10,260	1.8%
31	Arkansas	6,230	1.1%
1	California	54,600	9.7%
29	Colorado	6,740	1.2%
28	Connecticut	6,990	1.2%
45	Delaware	1,860	0.3%
2	Florida	41,270	7.3%
11	Georgia	14,970	2.7%
42	Hawaii	2,270	0.4%
41	Idaho	2,450	0.4%
7	Illinois	23,220	4.1%
15	Indiana	12,820	2.3%
30	Iowa	6,360	1.1%
33	Kansas	5,290	0.9%
22	Kentucky	9,410	1.7%
25	Louisiana	8,810	1.6%
38	Maine	3,190	0.6%
19	Maryland	10,320	1.8%
14	Massachusetts	13,140	2.3%
8	Michigan	20,450	3.6%
24	Minnesota	9,020	1.6%
32	Mississippi	6,090	1.1%
16	Missouri	12,620	2.2%
44	Montana	1,980	0.4%
36	Nebraska	3,360	0.6%
34	Nevada	4,600	0.8%
40	New Hampshire	2,620	0.5%
10	New Jersey	16,480	2.9%
37	New Mexico	3,300	0.6%
4	New York	34,190	6.1%
9	North Carolina	18,550	3.3%
47	North Dakota	1,300	0.2%
6	Ohio	24,350	4.3%
26	Oklahoma	7,420	1.3%
27	Oregon	7,380	1.3%
5	Pennsylvania	28,690	5.1%
43	Rhode Island	2,220	0.4%
23	South Carolina	9,100	1.6%
46	South Dakota	1,640	0.3%
13	Tennessee	13,340	2.4%
3	Texas	36,030	6.4%
39	Utah	2,760	0.5%
48	Vermont	1,150	0.2%
12	Virginia	13,920	2.5%
17	Washington	11,210	2.0%
35	West Virginia	4,530	0.8%
18	Wisconsin	11,170	2.0%
49	Wyoming	990	0.2%

RANK ORDER

RANK	STATE	DEATHS	% of USA
1	California	54,600	9.7%
2	Florida	41,270	7.3%
3	Texas	36,030	6.4%
4	New York	34,190	6.1%
5	Pennsylvania	28,690	5.1%
6	Ohio	24,350	4.3%
7	Illinois	23,220	4.1%
8	Michigan	20,450	3.6%
9	North Carolina	18,550	3.3%
10	New Jersey	16,480	2.9%
11	Georgia	14,970	2.7%
12	Virginia	13,920	2.5%
13	Tennessee	13,340	2.4%
14	Massachusetts	13,140	2.3%
15	Indiana	12,820	2.3%
16	Missouri	12,620	2.2%
17	Washington	11,210	2.0%
18	Wisconsin	11,170	2.0%
19	Maryland	10,320	1.8%
20	Arizona	10,260	1.8%
21	Alabama	9,900	1.8%
22	Kentucky	9,410	1.7%
23	South Carolina	9,100	1.6%
24	Minnesota	9,020	1.6%
25	Louisiana	8,810	1.6%
26	Oklahoma	7,420	1.3%
27	Oregon	7,380	1.3%
28	Connecticut	6,990	1.2%
29	Colorado	6,740	1.2%
30	Iowa	6,360	1.1%
31	Arkansas	6,230	1.1%
32	Mississippi	6,090	1.1%
33	Kansas	5,290	0.9%
34	Nevada	4,600	0.8%
35	West Virginia	4,530	0.8%
36	Nebraska	3,360	0.6%
37	New Mexico	3,300	0.6%
38	Maine	3,190	0.6%
39	Utah	2,760	0.5%
40	New Hampshire	2,620	0.5%
41	Idaho	2,450	0.4%
42	Hawaii	2,270	0.4%
43	Rhode Island	2,220	0.4%
44	Montana	1,980	0.4%
45	Delaware	1,860	0.3%
46	South Dakota	1,640	0.3%
47	North Dakota	1,300	0.2%
48	Vermont	1,150	0.2%
49	Wyoming	990	0.2%
50	Alaska	830	0.1%
	District of Columbia	970	0.2%

Source: American Cancer Society
"Cancer Facts & Figures 2009" (Copyright 2009, American Cancer Society, http://www.cancer.org/docroot/stt/stt_0.asp)

Estimated Death Rate by Cancer in 2009

National Estimated Rate = 183.2 Deaths per 100,000 Population*

ALPHA ORDER

RANK	STATE	RATE
12	Alabama	210.2
49	Alaska	118.8
44	Arizona	155.6
6	Arkansas	215.6
46	California	147.7
48	Colorado	134.1
23	Connecticut	198.7
13	Delaware	210.1
4	Florida	222.6
45	Georgia	152.3
37	Hawaii	175.3
43	Idaho	158.5
35	Illinois	179.9
20	Indiana	199.6
8	Iowa	211.4
30	Kansas	187.7
5	Kentucky	218.1
27	Louisiana	196.1
2	Maine	242.0
34	Maryland	181.1
22	Massachusetts	199.3
15	Michigan	205.1
40	Minnesota	171.3
14	Mississippi	206.3
10	Missouri	210.8
16	Montana	203.1
31	Nebraska	187.0
39	Nevada	174.0
24	New Hampshire	197.8
29	New Jersey	189.3
42	New Mexico	164.2
38	New York	175.0
25	North Carolina	197.7
19	North Dakota	201.0
9	Ohio	211.0
18	Oklahoma	201.2
28	Oregon	192.9
3	Pennsylvania	227.6
10	Rhode Island	210.8
21	South Carolina	199.5
17	South Dakota	201.9
7	Tennessee	211.9
47	Texas	145.4
50	Utah	99.1
32	Vermont	185.0
36	Virginia	176.6
41	Washington	168.2
1	West Virginia	248.9
26	Wisconsin	197.5
33	Wyoming	181.9

RANK ORDER

RANK	STATE	RATE
1	West Virginia	248.9
2	Maine	242.0
3	Pennsylvania	227.6
4	Florida	222.6
5	Kentucky	218.1
6	Arkansas	215.6
7	Tennessee	211.9
8	Iowa	211.4
9	Ohio	211.0
10	Missouri	210.8
10	Rhode Island	210.8
12	Alabama	210.2
13	Delaware	210.1
14	Mississippi	206.3
15	Michigan	205.1
16	Montana	203.1
17	South Dakota	201.9
18	Oklahoma	201.2
19	North Dakota	201.0
20	Indiana	199.6
21	South Carolina	199.5
22	Massachusetts	199.3
23	Connecticut	198.7
24	New Hampshire	197.8
25	North Carolina	197.7
26	Wisconsin	197.5
27	Louisiana	196.1
28	Oregon	192.9
29	New Jersey	189.3
30	Kansas	187.7
31	Nebraska	187.0
32	Vermont	185.0
33	Wyoming	181.9
34	Maryland	181.1
35	Illinois	179.9
36	Virginia	176.6
37	Hawaii	175.3
38	New York	175.0
39	Nevada	174.0
40	Minnesota	171.3
41	Washington	168.2
42	New Mexico	164.2
43	Idaho	158.5
44	Arizona	155.6
45	Georgia	152.3
46	California	147.7
47	Texas	145.4
48	Colorado	134.1
49	Alaska	118.8
50	Utah	99.1
	District of Columbia	161.8

Source: CQ Press using data from American Cancer Society
"Cancer Facts & Figures 2009" (Copyright 2009, American Cancer Society, http://www.cancer.org/docroot/stt/stt_0.asp)
*Rates calculated using 2009 Census resident population estimates. Not age-adjusted.

Estimated New Cancer Cases in 2009

National Estimated Total = 1,479,350 New Cases*

ALPHA ORDER

RANK	STATE	CASES	% of USA
21	Alabama	24,090	1.6%
49	Alaska	2,530	0.2%
18	Arizona	27,600	1.9%
31	Arkansas	14,800	1.0%
1	California	152,170	10.3%
27	Colorado	20,340	1.4%
26	Connecticut	20,650	1.4%
45	Delaware	4,690	0.3%
2	Florida	102,210	6.9%
11	Georgia	39,080	2.6%
42	Hawaii	6,400	0.4%
41	Idaho	6,800	0.5%
7	Illinois	60,960	4.1%
16	Indiana	31,320	2.1%
30	Iowa	16,740	1.1%
33	Kansas	13,080	0.9%
22	Kentucky	24,060	1.6%
24	Louisiana	22,170	1.5%
36	Maine	9,000	0.6%
20	Maryland	26,650	1.8%
12	Massachusetts	36,080	2.4%
8	Michigan	53,550	3.6%
23	Minnesota	23,670	1.6%
32	Mississippi	14,150	1.0%
17	Missouri	30,090	2.0%
44	Montana	5,340	0.4%
39	Nebraska	8,810	0.6%
34	Nevada	12,020	0.8%
40	New Hampshire	7,630	0.5%
9	New Jersey	47,920	3.2%
38	New Mexico	8,830	0.6%
3	New York	101,550	6.9%
10	North Carolina	42,270	2.9%
48	North Dakota	3,200	0.2%
6	Ohio	62,420	4.2%
29	Oklahoma	18,110	1.2%
28	Oregon	19,210	1.3%
5	Pennsylvania	74,170	5.0%
43	Rhode Island	6,250	0.4%
25	South Carolina	22,100	1.5%
46	South Dakota	4,120	0.3%
14	Tennessee	32,570	2.2%
4	Texas	98,200	6.6%
37	Utah	8,880	0.6%
47	Vermont	3,550	0.2%
13	Virginia	34,150	2.3%
15	Washington	32,290	2.2%
35	West Virginia	10,230	0.7%
19	Wisconsin	27,560	1.9%
50	Wyoming	2,500	0.2%

RANK ORDER

RANK	STATE	CASES	% of USA
1	California	152,170	10.3%
2	Florida	102,210	6.9%
3	New York	101,550	6.9%
4	Texas	98,200	6.6%
5	Pennsylvania	74,170	5.0%
6	Ohio	62,420	4.2%
7	Illinois	60,960	4.1%
8	Michigan	53,550	3.6%
9	New Jersey	47,920	3.2%
10	North Carolina	42,270	2.9%
11	Georgia	39,080	2.6%
12	Massachusetts	36,080	2.4%
13	Virginia	34,150	2.3%
14	Tennessee	32,570	2.2%
15	Washington	32,290	2.2%
16	Indiana	31,320	2.1%
17	Missouri	30,090	2.0%
18	Arizona	27,600	1.9%
19	Wisconsin	27,560	1.9%
20	Maryland	26,650	1.8%
21	Alabama	24,090	1.6%
22	Kentucky	24,060	1.6%
23	Minnesota	23,670	1.6%
24	Louisiana	22,170	1.5%
25	South Carolina	22,100	1.5%
26	Connecticut	20,650	1.4%
27	Colorado	20,340	1.4%
28	Oregon	19,210	1.3%
29	Oklahoma	18,110	1.2%
30	Iowa	16,740	1.1%
31	Arkansas	14,800	1.0%
32	Mississippi	14,150	1.0%
33	Kansas	13,080	0.9%
34	Nevada	12,020	0.8%
35	West Virginia	10,230	0.7%
36	Maine	9,000	0.6%
37	Utah	8,880	0.6%
38	New Mexico	8,830	0.6%
39	Nebraska	8,810	0.6%
40	New Hampshire	7,630	0.5%
41	Idaho	6,800	0.5%
42	Hawaii	6,400	0.4%
43	Rhode Island	6,250	0.4%
44	Montana	5,340	0.4%
45	Delaware	4,690	0.3%
46	South Dakota	4,120	0.3%
47	Vermont	3,550	0.2%
48	North Dakota	3,200	0.2%
49	Alaska	2,530	0.2%
50	Wyoming	2,500	0.2%
	District of Columbia	2,600	0.2%

Source: American Cancer Society
"Cancer Facts & Figures 2009" (Copyright 2009, American Cancer Society, http://www.cancer.org/docroot/stt/stt_0.asp)
*These estimates are offered as a rough guide and should not be regarded as definitive. They are calculated according to the distribution of estimated 2008 cancer deaths by state. Totals do not include basal and squamous cell skin cancers or in situ carcinomas except urinary bladder.

Estimated Rate of New Cancer Cases in 2009

National Estimated Rate = 481.9 New Cases per 100,000 Population*

ALPHA ORDER

RANK	STATE	RATE
20	Alabama	511.6
49	Alaska	362.2
44	Arizona	418.4
19	Arkansas	512.2
45	California	411.7
46	Colorado	404.8
4	Connecticut	586.9
16	Delaware	529.9
10	Florida	551.4
47	Georgia	397.6
25	Hawaii	494.1
41	Idaho	439.9
34	Illinois	472.2
29	Indiana	487.6
9	Iowa	556.5
36	Kansas	464.0
8	Kentucky	557.7
26	Louisiana	493.5
1	Maine	682.7
35	Maryland	467.6
13	Massachusetts	547.2
15	Michigan	537.1
40	Minnesota	449.5
33	Mississippi	479.3
22	Missouri	502.5
12	Montana	547.7
28	Nebraska	490.4
38	Nevada	454.8
5	New Hampshire	576.0
11	New Jersey	550.3
42	New Mexico	439.4
17	New York	519.7
39	North Carolina	450.6
24	North Dakota	494.7
14	Ohio	540.8
27	Oklahoma	491.2
23	Oregon	502.1
3	Pennsylvania	588.4
2	Rhode Island	593.4
31	South Carolina	484.5
21	South Dakota	507.1
18	Tennessee	517.3
48	Texas	396.3
50	Utah	318.9
6	Vermont	571.0
43	Virginia	433.2
31	Washington	484.5
7	West Virginia	562.2
30	Wisconsin	487.4
37	Wyoming	459.3

RANK ORDER

RANK	STATE	RATE
1	Maine	682.7
2	Rhode Island	593.4
3	Pennsylvania	588.4
4	Connecticut	586.9
5	New Hampshire	576.0
6	Vermont	571.0
7	West Virginia	562.2
8	Kentucky	557.7
9	Iowa	556.5
10	Florida	551.4
11	New Jersey	550.3
12	Montana	547.7
13	Massachusetts	547.2
14	Ohio	540.8
15	Michigan	537.1
16	Delaware	529.9
17	New York	519.7
18	Tennessee	517.3
19	Arkansas	512.2
20	Alabama	511.6
21	South Dakota	507.1
22	Missouri	502.5
23	Oregon	502.1
24	North Dakota	494.7
25	Hawaii	494.1
26	Louisiana	493.5
27	Oklahoma	491.2
28	Nebraska	490.4
29	Indiana	487.6
30	Wisconsin	487.4
31	South Carolina	484.5
31	Washington	484.5
33	Mississippi	479.3
34	Illinois	472.2
35	Maryland	467.6
36	Kansas	464.0
37	Wyoming	459.3
38	Nevada	454.8
39	North Carolina	450.6
40	Minnesota	449.5
41	Idaho	439.9
42	New Mexico	439.4
43	Virginia	433.2
44	Arizona	418.4
45	California	411.7
46	Colorado	404.8
47	Georgia	397.6
48	Texas	396.3
49	Alaska	362.2
50	Utah	318.9

District of Columbia 433.6

Source: CQ Press using data from American Cancer Society
"Cancer Facts & Figures 2009" (Copyright 2009, American Cancer Society, http://www.cancer.org/docroot/stt/stt_0.asp)
*These estimates are offered as a rough guide and should not be regarded as definitive. They are calculated according to the distribution of estimated 2009 cancer deaths by state. Totals do not include basal and squamous cell skin cancers or in situ carcinomas except urinary bladder. Rates calculated using 2009 Census resident population estimates.

Deaths by Accidents in 2006

National Total = 121,599 Deaths*

ALPHA ORDER

RANK	STATE	DEATHS	% of USA
18	Alabama	2,506	2.1%
47	Alaska	316	0.3%
11	Arizona	3,352	2.8%
30	Arkansas	1,415	1.2%
1	California	11,375	9.4%
26	Colorado	1,917	1.6%
31	Connecticut	1,302	1.1%
46	Delaware	329	0.3%
3	Florida	8,917	7.3%
9	Georgia	3,879	3.2%
44	Hawaii	441	0.4%
39	Idaho	682	0.6%
7	Illinois	4,451	3.7%
19	Indiana	2,480	2.0%
34	Iowa	1,188	1.0%
33	Kansas	1,198	1.0%
20	Kentucky	2,446	2.0%
21	Louisiana	2,422	2.0%
40	Maine	572	0.5%
29	Maryland	1,456	1.2%
23	Massachusetts	2,214	1.8%
10	Michigan	3,590	3.0%
25	Minnesota	1,919	1.6%
27	Mississippi	1,856	1.5%
13	Missouri	3,009	2.5%
41	Montana	558	0.5%
38	Nebraska	683	0.6%
36	Nevada	1,091	0.9%
42	New Hampshire	460	0.4%
16	New Jersey	2,590	2.1%
32	New Mexico	1,297	1.1%
5	New York	5,235	4.3%
8	North Carolina	4,156	3.4%
50	North Dakota	275	0.2%
6	Ohio	4,821	4.0%
24	Oklahoma	2,039	1.7%
28	Oregon	1,586	1.3%
4	Pennsylvania	5,299	4.4%
45	Rhode Island	434	0.4%
22	South Carolina	2,315	1.9%
43	South Dakota	452	0.4%
12	Tennessee	3,307	2.7%
2	Texas	9,140	7.5%
37	Utah	715	0.6%
49	Vermont	301	0.2%
14	Virginia	2,703	2.2%
15	Washington	2,679	2.2%
35	West Virginia	1,177	1.0%
17	Wisconsin	2,524	2.1%
48	Wyoming	306	0.3%

RANK ORDER

RANK	STATE	DEATHS	% of USA
1	California	11,375	9.4%
2	Texas	9,140	7.5%
3	Florida	8,917	7.3%
4	Pennsylvania	5,299	4.4%
5	New York	5,235	4.3%
6	Ohio	4,821	4.0%
7	Illinois	4,451	3.7%
8	North Carolina	4,156	3.4%
9	Georgia	3,879	3.2%
10	Michigan	3,590	3.0%
11	Arizona	3,352	2.8%
12	Tennessee	3,307	2.7%
13	Missouri	3,009	2.5%
14	Virginia	2,703	2.2%
15	Washington	2,679	2.2%
16	New Jersey	2,590	2.1%
17	Wisconsin	2,524	2.1%
18	Alabama	2,506	2.1%
19	Indiana	2,480	2.0%
20	Kentucky	2,446	2.0%
21	Louisiana	2,422	2.0%
22	South Carolina	2,315	1.9%
23	Massachusetts	2,214	1.8%
24	Oklahoma	2,039	1.7%
25	Minnesota	1,919	1.6%
26	Colorado	1,917	1.6%
27	Mississippi	1,856	1.5%
28	Oregon	1,586	1.3%
29	Maryland	1,456	1.2%
30	Arkansas	1,415	1.2%
31	Connecticut	1,302	1.1%
32	New Mexico	1,297	1.1%
33	Kansas	1,198	1.0%
34	Iowa	1,188	1.0%
35	West Virginia	1,177	1.0%
36	Nevada	1,091	0.9%
37	Utah	715	0.6%
38	Nebraska	683	0.6%
39	Idaho	682	0.6%
40	Maine	572	0.5%
41	Montana	558	0.5%
42	New Hampshire	460	0.4%
43	South Dakota	452	0.4%
44	Hawaii	441	0.4%
45	Rhode Island	434	0.4%
46	Delaware	329	0.3%
47	Alaska	316	0.3%
48	Wyoming	306	0.3%
49	Vermont	301	0.2%
50	North Dakota	275	0.2%
	District of Columbia	224	0.2%

Source: U.S. Department of Health and Human Services, National Center for Health Statistics
   "National Vital Statistics Reports" (Vol. 57, No. 14, April 17, 2009, http://www.cdc.gov/nchs/deaths.htm)
*Final data by state of residence. Includes motor vehicle deaths, poisoning, falls, drowning, and other accidents.

Age-Adjusted Death Rate by Accidents in 2006

National Rate = 39.8 Deaths per 100,000 Population*

ALPHA ORDER				RANK ORDER		
RANK	**STATE**	**RATE**		**RANK**	**STATE**	**RATE**
10	Alabama	53.8		1	New Mexico	67.1
14	Alaska	51.9		2	Mississippi	63.8
10	Arizona	53.8		3	West Virginia	62.2
16	Arkansas	49.1		4	Wyoming	58.9
46	California	31.6		5	Kentucky	57.5
24	Colorado	42.1		6	Louisiana	56.6
41	Connecticut	34.6		7	Oklahoma	56.3
34	Delaware	37.9		8	Montana	55.8
19	Florida	46.0		9	Tennessee	54.2
22	Georgia	43.8		10	Alabama	53.8
45	Hawaii	31.7		10	Arizona	53.8
17	Idaho	47.0		12	South Carolina	53.2
42	Illinois	34.3		13	South Dakota	53.0
33	Indiana	38.7		14	Alaska	51.9
38	Iowa	35.4		15	Missouri	49.7
25	Kansas	41.5		16	Arkansas	49.1
5	Kentucky	57.5		17	Idaho	47.0
6	Louisiana	56.6		17	North Carolina	47.0
28	Maine	40.6		19	Florida	46.0
49	Maryland	26.1		20	Vermont	45.2
44	Massachusetts	32.0		21	Nevada	44.5
40	Michigan	34.9		22	Georgia	43.8
39	Minnesota	35.2		23	Wisconsin	42.7
2	Mississippi	63.8		24	Colorado	42.1
15	Missouri	49.7		25	Kansas	41.5
8	Montana	55.8		26	Washington	41.1
36	Nebraska	35.9		27	Texas	41.0
21	Nevada	44.5		28	Maine	40.6
43	New Hampshire	33.7		29	Oregon	40.5
48	New Jersey	28.7		30	Ohio	40.2
1	New Mexico	67.1		31	North Dakota	39.5
50	New York	25.9		32	Pennsylvania	39.4
17	North Carolina	47.0		33	Indiana	38.7
31	North Dakota	39.5		34	Delaware	37.9
30	Ohio	40.2		35	Rhode Island	36.4
7	Oklahoma	56.3		36	Nebraska	35.9
29	Oregon	40.5		37	Virginia	35.7
32	Pennsylvania	39.4		38	Iowa	35.4
35	Rhode Island	36.4		39	Minnesota	35.2
12	South Carolina	53.2		40	Michigan	34.9
13	South Dakota	53.0		41	Connecticut	34.6
9	Tennessee	54.2		42	Illinois	34.3
27	Texas	41.0		43	New Hampshire	33.7
47	Utah	30.9		44	Massachusetts	32.0
20	Vermont	45.2		45	Hawaii	31.7
37	Virginia	35.7		46	California	31.6
26	Washington	41.1		47	Utah	30.9
3	West Virginia	62.2		48	New Jersey	28.7
23	Wisconsin	42.7		49	Maryland	26.1
4	Wyoming	58.9		50	New York	25.9
					District of Columbia	38.1

Source: U.S. Department of Health and Human Services, National Center for Health Statistics
    "National Vital Statistics Reports" (Vol. 57, No. 14, April 17, 2009, http://www.cdc.gov/nchs/deaths.htm)
*Final data by state of residence. Includes motor vehicle deaths, poisoning, falls, drowning, and other accidents. Age-adjusted rates based on the year 2000 standard population.

Deaths by Cerebrovascular Diseases in 2006

National Total = 137,119 Deaths*

ALPHA ORDER

ALPHA ORDER

RANK	STATE	DEATHS	% of USA
18	Alabama	2,740	2.0%
50	Alaska	177	0.1%
22	Arizona	2,226	1.6%
28	Arkansas	1,884	1.4%
1	California	15,039	11.0%
32	Colorado	1,532	1.1%
31	Connecticut	1,547	1.1%
47	Delaware	384	0.3%
3	Florida	8,925	6.5%
10	Georgia	3,889	2.8%
41	Hawaii	665	0.5%
38	Idaho	725	0.5%
6	Illinois	5,989	4.4%
15	Indiana	3,238	2.4%
29	Iowa	1,718	1.3%
33	Kansas	1,489	1.1%
24	Kentucky	2,197	1.6%
25	Louisiana	2,195	1.6%
40	Maine	670	0.5%
20	Maryland	2,365	1.7%
16	Massachusetts	2,880	2.1%
8	Michigan	4,752	3.5%
23	Minnesota	2,219	1.6%
30	Mississippi	1,585	1.2%
14	Missouri	3,247	2.4%
43	Montana	461	0.3%
35	Nebraska	922	0.7%
36	Nevada	847	0.6%
42	New Hampshire	494	0.4%
12	New Jersey	3,468	2.5%
37	New Mexico	739	0.5%
5	New York	6,398	4.7%
9	North Carolina	4,572	3.3%
45	North Dakota	428	0.3%
7	Ohio	5,828	4.3%
26	Oklahoma	2,085	1.5%
27	Oregon	1,978	1.4%
4	Pennsylvania	7,151	5.2%
46	Rhode Island	421	0.3%
21	South Carolina	2,291	1.7%
44	South Dakota	442	0.3%
13	Tennessee	3,407	2.5%
2	Texas	9,366	6.8%
39	Utah	674	0.5%
48	Vermont	264	0.2%
11	Virginia	3,523	2.6%
19	Washington	2,725	2.0%
34	West Virginia	1,072	0.8%
17	Wisconsin	2,829	2.1%
49	Wyoming	236	0.2%

RANK ORDER

RANK	STATE	DEATHS	% of USA
1	California	15,039	11.0%
2	Texas	9,366	6.8%
3	Florida	8,925	6.5%
4	Pennsylvania	7,151	5.2%
5	New York	6,398	4.7%
6	Illinois	5,989	4.4%
7	Ohio	5,828	4.3%
8	Michigan	4,752	3.5%
9	North Carolina	4,572	3.3%
10	Georgia	3,889	2.8%
11	Virginia	3,523	2.6%
12	New Jersey	3,468	2.5%
13	Tennessee	3,407	2.5%
14	Missouri	3,247	2.4%
15	Indiana	3,238	2.4%
16	Massachusetts	2,880	2.1%
17	Wisconsin	2,829	2.1%
18	Alabama	2,740	2.0%
19	Washington	2,725	2.0%
20	Maryland	2,365	1.7%
21	South Carolina	2,291	1.7%
22	Arizona	2,226	1.6%
23	Minnesota	2,219	1.6%
24	Kentucky	2,197	1.6%
25	Louisiana	2,195	1.6%
26	Oklahoma	2,085	1.5%
27	Oregon	1,978	1.4%
28	Arkansas	1,884	1.4%
29	Iowa	1,718	1.3%
30	Mississippi	1,585	1.2%
31	Connecticut	1,547	1.1%
32	Colorado	1,532	1.1%
33	Kansas	1,489	1.1%
34	West Virginia	1,072	0.8%
35	Nebraska	922	0.7%
36	Nevada	847	0.6%
37	New Mexico	739	0.5%
38	Idaho	725	0.5%
39	Utah	674	0.5%
40	Maine	670	0.5%
41	Hawaii	665	0.5%
42	New Hampshire	494	0.4%
43	Montana	461	0.3%
44	South Dakota	442	0.3%
45	North Dakota	428	0.3%
46	Rhode Island	421	0.3%
47	Delaware	384	0.3%
48	Vermont	264	0.2%
49	Wyoming	236	0.2%
50	Alaska	177	0.1%
	District of Columbia	221	0.2%

Source: U.S. Department of Health and Human Services, National Center for Health Statistics
   "National Vital Statistics Reports" (Vol. 57, No. 14, April 17, 2009, http://www.cdc.gov/nchs/deaths.htm)
*Final data by state of residence. Cerebrovascular diseases include stroke and other disorders of the blood vessels of the brain.

Age-Adjusted Death Rate by Cerebrovascular Diseases in 2006

National Rate = 43.6 Deaths per 100,000 Population*

ALPHA ORDER

RANK	STATE	RATE
2	Alabama	55.3
19	Alaska	47.2
48	Arizona	34.5
1	Arkansas	58.8
24	California	44.9
39	Colorado	38.9
44	Connecticut	36.3
34	Delaware	41.7
47	Florida	35.3
10	Georgia	51.3
30	Hawaii	43.2
7	Idaho	51.8
21	Illinois	45.3
14	Indiana	49.0
31	Iowa	42.9
20	Kansas	46.5
11	Kentucky	50.3
9	Louisiana	51.5
35	Maine	41.3
28	Maryland	43.6
41	Massachusetts	37.6
25	Michigan	44.7
38	Minnesota	39.4
4	Mississippi	53.4
12	Missouri	49.5
35	Montana	41.3
27	Nebraska	43.8
37	Nevada	39.6
46	New Hampshire	35.5
45	New Jersey	35.8
41	New Mexico	37.6
50	New York	29.8
6	North Carolina	52.4
13	North Dakota	49.3
23	Ohio	45.1
4	Oklahoma	53.4
17	Oregon	47.9
29	Pennsylvania	43.4
49	Rhode Island	31.2
8	South Carolina	51.6
31	South Dakota	42.9
3	Tennessee	54.9
16	Texas	48.3
43	Utah	36.4
40	Vermont	37.8
15	Virginia	48.8
31	Washington	42.9
18	West Virginia	47.6
26	Wisconsin	44.6
21	Wyoming	45.3

RANK ORDER

RANK	STATE	RATE
1	Arkansas	58.8
2	Alabama	55.3
3	Tennessee	54.9
4	Mississippi	53.4
4	Oklahoma	53.4
6	North Carolina	52.4
7	Idaho	51.8
8	South Carolina	51.6
9	Louisiana	51.5
10	Georgia	51.3
11	Kentucky	50.3
12	Missouri	49.5
13	North Dakota	49.3
14	Indiana	49.0
15	Virginia	48.8
16	Texas	48.3
17	Oregon	47.9
18	West Virginia	47.6
19	Alaska	47.2
20	Kansas	46.5
21	Illinois	45.3
21	Wyoming	45.3
23	Ohio	45.1
24	California	44.9
25	Michigan	44.7
26	Wisconsin	44.6
27	Nebraska	43.8
28	Maryland	43.6
29	Pennsylvania	43.4
30	Hawaii	43.2
31	Iowa	42.9
31	South Dakota	42.9
31	Washington	42.9
34	Delaware	41.7
35	Maine	41.3
35	Montana	41.3
37	Nevada	39.6
38	Minnesota	39.4
39	Colorado	38.9
40	Vermont	37.8
41	Massachusetts	37.6
41	New Mexico	37.6
43	Utah	36.4
44	Connecticut	36.3
45	New Jersey	35.8
46	New Hampshire	35.5
47	Florida	35.3
48	Arizona	34.5
49	Rhode Island	31.2
50	New York	29.8
	District of Columbia	36.9

Source: U.S. Department of Health and Human Services, National Center for Health Statistics
"National Vital Statistics Reports" (Vol. 57, No. 14, April 17, 2009, http://www.cdc.gov/nchs/deaths.htm)
*Final data by state of residence. Cerebrovascular diseases include stroke and other disorders of the blood vessels of the brain.
Age-adjusted rates based on the year 2000 standard population.

Deaths by Diseases of the Heart in 2006

National Total = 631,636 Deaths*

<u>ALPHA ORDER</u>

RANK	STATE	DEATHS	% of USA
17	Alabama	12,583	2.0%
50	Alaska	645	0.1%
20	Arizona	10,607	1.7%
29	Arkansas	7,431	1.2%
1	California	64,871	10.3%
32	Colorado	6,124	1.0%
28	Connecticut	7,490	1.2%
45	Delaware	1,866	0.3%
3	Florida	44,305	7.0%
11	Georgia	16,478	2.6%
43	Hawaii	2,244	0.4%
42	Idaho	2,399	0.4%
7	Illinois	27,007	4.3%
14	Indiana	14,375	2.3%
30	Iowa	7,172	1.1%
33	Kansas	5,849	0.9%
22	Kentucky	10,353	1.6%
23	Louisiana	10,026	1.6%
39	Maine	2,815	0.4%
19	Maryland	11,268	1.8%
16	Massachusetts	12,947	2.0%
8	Michigan	24,255	3.8%
27	Minnesota	7,525	1.2%
26	Mississippi	8,097	1.3%
12	Missouri	14,749	2.3%
44	Montana	1,869	0.3%
36	Nebraska	3,445	0.5%
35	Nevada	5,013	0.8%
41	New Hampshire	2,501	0.4%
9	New Jersey	19,548	3.1%
37	New Mexico	3,411	0.5%
2	New York	50,470	8.0%
10	North Carolina	17,271	2.7%
47	North Dakota	1,527	0.2%
6	Ohio	27,886	4.4%
24	Oklahoma	9,798	1.6%
31	Oregon	6,620	1.0%
5	Pennsylvania	33,744	5.3%
40	Rhode Island	2,718	0.4%
25	South Carolina	9,030	1.4%
46	South Dakota	1,757	0.3%
13	Tennessee	14,642	2.3%
4	Texas	38,782	6.1%
38	Utah	2,932	0.5%
48	Vermont	1,244	0.2%
15	Virginia	14,021	2.2%
21	Washington	10,604	1.7%
34	West Virginia	5,311	0.8%
18	Wisconsin	11,451	1.8%
49	Wyoming	994	0.2%

<u>RANK ORDER</u>

RANK	STATE	DEATHS	% of USA
1	California	64,871	10.3%
2	New York	50,470	8.0%
3	Florida	44,305	7.0%
4	Texas	38,782	6.1%
5	Pennsylvania	33,744	5.3%
6	Ohio	27,886	4.4%
7	Illinois	27,007	4.3%
8	Michigan	24,255	3.8%
9	New Jersey	19,548	3.1%
10	North Carolina	17,271	2.7%
11	Georgia	16,478	2.6%
12	Missouri	14,749	2.3%
13	Tennessee	14,642	2.3%
14	Indiana	14,375	2.3%
15	Virginia	14,021	2.2%
16	Massachusetts	12,947	2.0%
17	Alabama	12,583	2.0%
18	Wisconsin	11,451	1.8%
19	Maryland	11,268	1.8%
20	Arizona	10,607	1.7%
21	Washington	10,604	1.7%
22	Kentucky	10,353	1.6%
23	Louisiana	10,026	1.6%
24	Oklahoma	9,798	1.6%
25	South Carolina	9,030	1.4%
26	Mississippi	8,097	1.3%
27	Minnesota	7,525	1.2%
28	Connecticut	7,490	1.2%
29	Arkansas	7,431	1.2%
30	Iowa	7,172	1.1%
31	Oregon	6,620	1.0%
32	Colorado	6,124	1.0%
33	Kansas	5,849	0.9%
34	West Virginia	5,311	0.8%
35	Nevada	5,013	0.8%
36	Nebraska	3,445	0.5%
37	New Mexico	3,411	0.5%
38	Utah	2,932	0.5%
39	Maine	2,815	0.4%
40	Rhode Island	2,718	0.4%
41	New Hampshire	2,501	0.4%
42	Idaho	2,399	0.4%
43	Hawaii	2,244	0.4%
44	Montana	1,869	0.3%
45	Delaware	1,866	0.3%
46	South Dakota	1,757	0.3%
47	North Dakota	1,527	0.2%
48	Vermont	1,244	0.2%
49	Wyoming	994	0.2%
50	Alaska	645	0.1%
	District of Columbia	1,566	0.2%

Source: U.S. Department of Health and Human Services, National Center for Health Statistics
"National Vital Statistics Reports" (Vol. 57, No. 14, April 17, 2009, http://www.cdc.gov/nchs/deaths.htm)
*Final data by state of residence.

Age-Adjusted Death Rate by Diseases of the Heart in 2006

National Rate = 200.2 Deaths per 100,000 Population*

ALPHA ORDER				RANK ORDER		
RANK	STATE	RATE		RANK	STATE	RATE
2	Alabama	253.3		1	Mississippi	270.9
42	Alaska	167.2		2	Alabama	253.3
45	Arizona	164.2		3	Oklahoma	251.1
8	Arkansas	233.0		4	West Virginia	236.9
25	California	192.5		5	Kentucky	235.5
48	Colorado	151.6		6	Tennessee	233.3
33	Connecticut	177.3		7	New York	233.1
19	Delaware	201.2		8	Arkansas	233.0
36	Florida	175.1		9	Louisiana	232.3
15	Georgia	213.2		10	Michigan	227.0
49	Hawaii	147.2		11	Nevada	226.7
40	Idaho	168.5		12	Missouri	224.4
18	Illinois	204.4		13	Indiana	217.2
13	Indiana	217.2		14	Ohio	216.1
28	Iowa	184.7		15	Georgia	213.2
29	Kansas	183.6		16	Pennsylvania	207.1
5	Kentucky	235.5		17	Maryland	205.6
9	Louisiana	232.3		18	Illinois	204.4
37	Maine	174.0		19	Delaware	201.2
17	Maryland	205.6		20	New Jersey	200.9
39	Massachusetts	169.5		21	Rhode Island	200.8
10	Michigan	227.0		22	South Carolina	200.2
50	Minnesota	133.9		23	Texas	197.4
1	Mississippi	270.9		24	North Carolina	195.3
12	Missouri	224.4		25	California	192.5
41	Montana	168.4		26	Virginia	190.8
44	Nebraska	165.0		27	Wyoming	189.4
11	Nevada	226.7		28	Iowa	184.7
32	New Hampshire	178.3		29	Kansas	183.6
20	New Jersey	200.9		30	North Dakota	181.5
38	New Mexico	172.6		31	Wisconsin	181.1
7	New York	233.1		32	New Hampshire	178.3
24	North Carolina	195.3		33	Connecticut	177.3
30	North Dakota	181.5		34	South Dakota	177.0
14	Ohio	216.1		35	Vermont	175.5
3	Oklahoma	251.1		36	Florida	175.1
46	Oregon	160.0		37	Maine	174.0
16	Pennsylvania	207.1		38	New Mexico	172.6
21	Rhode Island	200.8		39	Massachusetts	169.5
22	South Carolina	200.2		40	Idaho	168.5
34	South Dakota	177.0		41	Montana	168.4
6	Tennessee	233.3		42	Alaska	167.2
23	Texas	197.4		43	Washington	165.8
47	Utah	156.3		44	Nebraska	165.0
35	Vermont	175.5		45	Arizona	164.2
26	Virginia	190.8		46	Oregon	160.0
43	Washington	165.8		47	Utah	156.3
4	West Virginia	236.9		48	Colorado	151.6
31	Wisconsin	181.1		49	Hawaii	147.2
27	Wyoming	189.4		50	Minnesota	133.9
					District of Columbia	260.0

Source: U.S. Department of Health and Human Services, National Center for Health Statistics
   "National Vital Statistics Reports" (Vol. 57, No. 14, April 17, 2009, http://www.cdc.gov/nchs/deaths.htm)
*Final data by state of residence. Age-adjusted rates based on the year 2000 standard population.

Deaths by Suicide in 2006

National Total = 33,300 Suicides*

ALPHA ORDER

RANK	STATE	DEATHS	% of USA
21	Alabama	580	1.7%
43	Alaska	135	0.4%
10	Arizona	979	2.9%
31	Arkansas	376	1.1%
1	California	3,334	10.0%
17	Colorado	730	2.2%
36	Connecticut	292	0.9%
47	Delaware	91	0.3%
2	Florida	2,440	7.3%
11	Georgia	923	2.8%
45	Hawaii	120	0.4%
38	Idaho	222	0.7%
9	Illinois	1,010	3.0%
14	Indiana	824	2.5%
34	Iowa	334	1.0%
30	Kansas	379	1.1%
19	Kentucky	622	1.9%
27	Louisiana	492	1.5%
41	Maine	158	0.5%
26	Maryland	495	1.5%
29	Massachusetts	450	1.4%
7	Michigan	1,139	3.4%
23	Minnesota	554	1.7%
35	Mississippi	325	1.0%
16	Missouri	799	2.4%
40	Montana	189	0.6%
39	Nebraska	202	0.6%
28	Nevada	486	1.5%
42	New Hampshire	151	0.5%
20	New Jersey	585	1.8%
33	New Mexico	352	1.1%
5	New York	1,326	4.0%
8	North Carolina	1,106	3.3%
48	North Dakota	90	0.3%
6	Ohio	1,325	4.0%
24	Oklahoma	537	1.6%
22	Oregon	579	1.7%
4	Pennsylvania	1,396	4.2%
48	Rhode Island	90	0.3%
25	South Carolina	524	1.6%
44	South Dakota	125	0.4%
13	Tennessee	874	2.6%
3	Texas	2,347	7.0%
32	Utah	362	1.1%
50	Vermont	81	0.2%
12	Virginia	876	2.6%
15	Washington	809	2.4%
37	West Virginia	269	0.8%
18	Wisconsin	670	2.0%
46	Wyoming	116	0.3%

RANK ORDER

RANK	STATE	DEATHS	% of USA
1	California	3,334	10.0%
2	Florida	2,440	7.3%
3	Texas	2,347	7.0%
4	Pennsylvania	1,396	4.2%
5	New York	1,326	4.0%
6	Ohio	1,325	4.0%
7	Michigan	1,139	3.4%
8	North Carolina	1,106	3.3%
9	Illinois	1,010	3.0%
10	Arizona	979	2.9%
11	Georgia	923	2.8%
12	Virginia	876	2.6%
13	Tennessee	874	2.6%
14	Indiana	824	2.5%
15	Washington	809	2.4%
16	Missouri	799	2.4%
17	Colorado	730	2.2%
18	Wisconsin	670	2.0%
19	Kentucky	622	1.9%
20	New Jersey	585	1.8%
21	Alabama	580	1.7%
22	Oregon	579	1.7%
23	Minnesota	554	1.7%
24	Oklahoma	537	1.6%
25	South Carolina	524	1.6%
26	Maryland	495	1.5%
27	Louisiana	492	1.5%
28	Nevada	486	1.5%
29	Massachusetts	450	1.4%
30	Kansas	379	1.1%
31	Arkansas	376	1.1%
32	Utah	362	1.1%
33	New Mexico	352	1.1%
34	Iowa	334	1.0%
35	Mississippi	325	1.0%
36	Connecticut	292	0.9%
37	West Virginia	269	0.8%
38	Idaho	222	0.7%
39	Nebraska	202	0.6%
40	Montana	189	0.6%
41	Maine	158	0.5%
42	New Hampshire	151	0.5%
43	Alaska	135	0.4%
44	South Dakota	125	0.4%
45	Hawaii	120	0.4%
46	Wyoming	116	0.3%
47	Delaware	91	0.3%
48	North Dakota	90	0.3%
48	Rhode Island	90	0.3%
50	Vermont	81	0.2%
	District of Columbia	30	0.1%

Source: U.S. Department of Health and Human Services, National Center for Health Statistics
"National Vital Statistics Reports" (Vol. 57, No. 14, April 17, 2009, http://www.cdc.gov/nchs/deaths.htm)
*Final data by state of residence.

Age-Adjusted Death Rate by Suicide in 2006

National Rate = 10.9 Deaths per 100,000 Population*

ALPHA ORDER				RANK ORDER		
RANK	STATE	RATE		RANK	STATE	RATE
22	Alabama	12.4		1	Wyoming	21.7
2	Alaska	20.0		2	Alaska	20.0
6	Arizona	16.0		3	Montana	19.7
19	Arkansas	13.3		4	Nevada	19.5
42	California	9.2		5	New Mexico	18.0
10	Colorado	15.2		6	Arizona	16.0
46	Connecticut	8.0		6	South Dakota	16.0
39	Delaware	10.4		8	Utah	15.8
21	Florida	12.6		9	Idaho	15.6
41	Georgia	10.0		10	Colorado	15.2
42	Hawaii	9.2		10	Oregon	15.2
9	Idaho	15.6		12	Oklahoma	15.0
47	Illinois	7.8		13	Kentucky	14.6
20	Indiana	13.0		14	Tennessee	14.2
32	Iowa	11.1		15	West Virginia	14.1
16	Kansas	13.8		16	Kansas	13.8
13	Kentucky	14.6		17	North Dakota	13.6
28	Louisiana	11.6		18	Missouri	13.5
35	Maine	11.0		19	Arkansas	13.3
44	Maryland	8.6		20	Indiana	13.0
48	Massachusetts	6.7		21	Florida	12.6
32	Michigan	11.1		22	Alabama	12.4
38	Minnesota	10.6		23	Washington	12.3
29	Mississippi	11.4		24	North Carolina	12.2
18	Missouri	13.5		25	Vermont	12.0
3	Montana	19.7		26	South Carolina	11.9
30	Nebraska	11.2		26	Wisconsin	11.9
4	Nevada	19.5		28	Louisiana	11.6
35	New Hampshire	11.0		29	Mississippi	11.4
50	New Jersey	6.5		30	Nebraska	11.2
5	New Mexico	18.0		30	Ohio	11.2
49	New York	6.6		32	Iowa	11.1
24	North Carolina	12.2		32	Michigan	11.1
17	North Dakota	13.6		32	Virginia	11.1
30	Ohio	11.2		35	Maine	11.0
12	Oklahoma	15.0		35	New Hampshire	11.0
10	Oregon	15.2		37	Pennsylvania	10.8
37	Pennsylvania	10.8		38	Minnesota	10.6
45	Rhode Island	8.1		39	Delaware	10.4
26	South Carolina	11.9		40	Texas	10.3
6	South Dakota	16.0		41	Georgia	10.0
14	Tennessee	14.2		42	California	9.2
40	Texas	10.3		42	Hawaii	9.2
8	Utah	15.8		44	Maryland	8.6
25	Vermont	12.0		45	Rhode Island	8.1
32	Virginia	11.1		46	Connecticut	8.0
23	Washington	12.3		47	Illinois	7.8
15	West Virginia	14.1		48	Massachusetts	6.7
26	Wisconsin	11.9		49	New York	6.6
1	Wyoming	21.7		50	New Jersey	6.5
					District of Columbia	5.1

Source: U.S. Department of Health and Human Services, National Center for Health Statistics

"National Vital Statistics Reports" (Vol. 57, No. 14, April 17, 2009, http://www.cdc.gov/nchs/deaths.htm)

*Final data by state of residence. Age-adjusted rates based on the year 2000 standard population.

Deaths by AIDS in 2006

National Total = 12,113 Deaths*

ALPHA ORDER

ALPHA ORDER

RANK	STATE	DEATHS	% of USA
16	Alabama	189	1.6%
44	Alaska	10	0.1%
21	Arizona	138	1.1%
28	Arkansas	74	0.6%
3	California	1,176	9.7%
26	Colorado	83	0.7%
22	Connecticut	127	1.0%
30	Delaware	54	0.4%
1	Florida	1,753	14.5%
5	Georgia	684	5.6%
40	Hawaii	18	0.1%
45	Idaho	8	0.1%
9	Illinois	382	3.2%
20	Indiana	141	1.2%
41	Iowa	16	0.1%
35	Kansas	28	0.2%
27	Kentucky	81	0.7%
11	Louisiana	338	2.8%
42	Maine	12	0.1%
7	Maryland	483	4.0%
19	Massachusetts	182	1.5%
18	Michigan	184	1.5%
31	Minnesota	53	0.4%
17	Mississippi	187	1.5%
23	Missouri	120	1.0%
47	Montana	6	0.0%
38	Nebraska	24	0.2%
28	Nevada	74	0.6%
42	New Hampshire	12	0.1%
6	New Jersey	539	4.4%
34	New Mexico	39	0.3%
2	New York	1,471	12.1%
8	North Carolina	427	3.5%
50	North Dakota	2	0.0%
15	Ohio	232	1.9%
25	Oklahoma	89	0.7%
33	Oregon	50	0.4%
10	Pennsylvania	367	3.0%
37	Rhode Island	27	0.2%
12	South Carolina	256	2.1%
45	South Dakota	8	0.1%
12	Tennessee	256	2.1%
4	Texas	1,034	8.5%
35	Utah	28	0.2%
47	Vermont	6	0.0%
14	Virginia	251	2.1%
24	Washington	100	0.8%
39	West Virginia	22	0.2%
32	Wisconsin	52	0.4%
49	Wyoming	3	0.0%

RANK ORDER

RANK	STATE	DEATHS	% of USA
1	Florida	1,753	14.5%
2	New York	1,471	12.1%
3	California	1,176	9.7%
4	Texas	1,034	8.5%
5	Georgia	684	5.6%
6	New Jersey	539	4.4%
7	Maryland	483	4.0%
8	North Carolina	427	3.5%
9	Illinois	382	3.2%
10	Pennsylvania	367	3.0%
11	Louisiana	338	2.8%
12	South Carolina	256	2.1%
12	Tennessee	256	2.1%
14	Virginia	251	2.1%
15	Ohio	232	1.9%
16	Alabama	189	1.6%
17	Mississippi	187	1.5%
18	Michigan	184	1.5%
19	Massachusetts	182	1.5%
20	Indiana	141	1.2%
21	Arizona	138	1.1%
22	Connecticut	127	1.0%
23	Missouri	120	1.0%
24	Washington	100	0.8%
25	Oklahoma	89	0.7%
26	Colorado	83	0.7%
27	Kentucky	81	0.7%
28	Arkansas	74	0.6%
28	Nevada	74	0.6%
30	Delaware	54	0.4%
31	Minnesota	53	0.4%
32	Wisconsin	52	0.4%
33	Oregon	50	0.4%
34	New Mexico	39	0.3%
35	Kansas	28	0.2%
35	Utah	28	0.2%
37	Rhode Island	27	0.2%
38	Nebraska	24	0.2%
39	West Virginia	22	0.2%
40	Hawaii	18	0.1%
41	Iowa	16	0.1%
42	Maine	12	0.1%
42	New Hampshire	12	0.1%
44	Alaska	10	0.1%
45	Idaho	8	0.1%
45	South Dakota	8	0.1%
47	Montana	6	0.0%
47	Vermont	6	0.0%
49	Wyoming	3	0.0%
50	North Dakota	2	0.0%
	District of Columbia	217	1.8%

Source: U.S. Department of Health and Human Services, National Center for Health Statistics
"National Vital Statistics Reports" (Vol. 57, No. 14, April 17, 2009, http://www.cdc.gov/nchs/deaths.htm)
*Final data by state of residence. AIDS is Acquired Immunodeficiency Syndrome. It is a specific group of diseases or
conditions which are indicative of severe immunosuppression related to infection with the Human Immunodeficiency Virus (HIV).

Age-Adjusted Death Rate by AIDS in 2006

National Rate = 4.0 Deaths per 100,000 Population*

ALPHA ORDER

RANK	STATE	RATE
12	Alabama	4.2
NA	Alaska**	NA
23	Arizona	2.4
20	Arkansas	2.8
15	California	3.3
31	Colorado	1.7
14	Connecticut	3.4
7	Delaware	6.1
1	Florida	9.7
5	Georgia	7.2
NA	Hawaii**	NA
NA	Idaho**	NA
17	Illinois	3.0
25	Indiana	2.2
NA	Iowa**	NA
37	Kansas	1.1
29	Kentucky	1.9
2	Louisiana	8.1
NA	Maine**	NA
2	Maryland	8.1
21	Massachusetts	2.7
30	Michigan	1.8
38	Minnesota	1.0
6	Mississippi	6.7
27	Missouri	2.1
NA	Montana**	NA
32	Nebraska	1.4
18	Nevada	2.9
NA	New Hampshire**	NA
9	New Jersey	5.8
25	New Mexico	2.2
4	New York	7.3
10	North Carolina	4.7
NA	North Dakota**	NA
28	Ohio	2.0
22	Oklahoma	2.6
32	Oregon	1.4
18	Pennsylvania	2.9
23	Rhode Island	2.4
8	South Carolina	5.9
NA	South Dakota**	NA
12	Tennessee	4.2
11	Texas	4.5
35	Utah	1.3
NA	Vermont**	NA
16	Virginia	3.1
32	Washington	1.4
36	West Virginia	1.2
39	Wisconsin	0.9
NA	Wyoming**	NA

RANK ORDER

RANK	STATE	RATE
1	Florida	9.7
2	Louisiana	8.1
2	Maryland	8.1
4	New York	7.3
5	Georgia	7.2
6	Mississippi	6.7
7	Delaware	6.1
8	South Carolina	5.9
9	New Jersey	5.8
10	North Carolina	4.7
11	Texas	4.5
12	Alabama	4.2
12	Tennessee	4.2
14	Connecticut	3.4
15	California	3.3
16	Virginia	3.1
17	Illinois	3.0
18	Nevada	2.9
18	Pennsylvania	2.9
20	Arkansas	2.8
21	Massachusetts	2.7
22	Oklahoma	2.6
23	Arizona	2.4
23	Rhode Island	2.4
25	Indiana	2.2
25	New Mexico	2.2
27	Missouri	2.1
28	Ohio	2.0
29	Kentucky	1.9
30	Michigan	1.8
31	Colorado	1.7
32	Nebraska	1.4
32	Oregon	1.4
32	Washington	1.4
35	Utah	1.3
36	West Virginia	1.2
37	Kansas	1.1
38	Minnesota	1.0
39	Wisconsin	0.9
NA	Alaska**	NA
NA	Hawaii**	NA
NA	Idaho**	NA
NA	Iowa**	NA
NA	Maine**	NA
NA	Montana**	NA
NA	New Hampshire**	NA
NA	North Dakota**	NA
NA	South Dakota**	NA
NA	Vermont**	NA
NA	Wyoming**	NA
	District of Columbia	37.3

Source: U.S. Department of Health and Human Services, National Center for Health Statistics
"National Vital Statistics Reports" (Vol. 57, No. 14, April 17, 2009, http://www.cdc.gov/nchs/deaths.htm)
*Final data by state of residence. AIDS is Acquired Immunodeficiency Syndrome. It is a specific group of diseases or
conditions which are indicative of severe immunosuppression related to infection with the Human Immunodeficiency Virus (HIV).
Age-adjusted rates based on the year 2000 standard population.
**Insufficient data to determine a reliable rate.

Adult Per Capita Alcohol Consumption in 2007

National Per Capita = 2.6 Gallons Consumed per Adult 21 Years and Older*

RANK	STATE	PER CAPITA		RANK	STATE	PER CAPITA
40	Alabama	2.3		1	New Hampshire	4.8
5	Alaska	3.3		2	Nevada	4.1
18	Arizona	2.8		3	Delaware	3.7
46	Arkansas	2.1		4	Wisconsin	3.4
24	California	2.7		5	Alaska	3.3
9	Colorado	3.1		5	North Dakota	3.3
24	Connecticut	2.7		7	Montana	3.2
3	Delaware	3.7		7	Wyoming	3.2
10	Florida	3.0		9	Colorado	3.1
37	Georgia	2.4		10	Florida	3.0
15	Hawaii	2.9		10	Idaho	3.0
10	Idaho	3.0		10	Louisiana	3.0
24	Illinois	2.7		10	South Dakota	3.0
37	Indiana	2.4		10	Vermont	3.0
30	Iowa	2.6		15	Hawaii	2.9
44	Kansas	2.2		15	Oregon	2.9
46	Kentucky	2.1		15	Rhode Island	2.9
10	Louisiana	3.0		18	Arizona	2.8
18	Maine	2.8		18	Maine	2.8
34	Maryland	2.5		18	Massachusetts	2.8
18	Massachusetts	2.8		18	Minnesota	2.8
34	Michigan	2.5		18	New Mexico	2.8
18	Minnesota	2.8		18	South Carolina	2.8
30	Mississippi	2.6		24	California	2.7
24	Missouri	2.7		24	Connecticut	2.7
7	Montana	3.2		24	Illinois	2.7
24	Nebraska	2.7		24	Missouri	2.7
2	Nevada	4.1		24	Nebraska	2.7
1	New Hampshire	4.8		24	Washington	2.7
30	New Jersey	2.6		30	Iowa	2.6
18	New Mexico	2.8		30	Mississippi	2.6
40	New York	2.3		30	New Jersey	2.6
40	North Carolina	2.3		30	Texas	2.6
5	North Dakota	3.3		34	Maryland	2.5
40	Ohio	2.3		34	Michigan	2.5
44	Oklahoma	2.2		34	Pennsylvania	2.5
15	Oregon	2.9		37	Georgia	2.4
34	Pennsylvania	2.5		37	Indiana	2.4
15	Rhode Island	2.9		37	Virginia	2.4
18	South Carolina	2.8		40	Alabama	2.3
10	South Dakota	3.0		40	New York	2.3
46	Tennessee	2.1		40	North Carolina	2.3
30	Texas	2.6		40	Ohio	2.3
50	Utah	1.6		44	Kansas	2.2
10	Vermont	3.0		44	Oklahoma	2.2
37	Virginia	2.4		46	Arkansas	2.1
24	Washington	2.7		46	Kentucky	2.1
49	West Virginia	2.0		46	Tennessee	2.1
4	Wisconsin	3.4		49	West Virginia	2.0
7	Wyoming	3.2		50	Utah	1.6

District of Columbia 4.5

Source: CQ Press using data from U.S. Dept of Health and Human Services, National Institute on Alcohol Abuse and Alcoholism
"Volume Beverage and Ethanol Consumption for States" (http://www.niaaa.nih.gov/Resources/)
*This is apparent consumption of actual alcohol, not entire volume of an alcoholic beverage (for example, wine is roughly 11%
absolute alcohol content). Apparent consumption is based on several sources which together approximate sales but do not
actually measure consumption. Accordingly, figures for some states may be skewed by purchases by nonresidents.

Percent of Adults Who Smoke: 2008

National Median = 18.4% of Adults*

ALPHA ORDER

RANK	STATE	PERCENT
10	Alabama	22.1
11	Alaska	21.5
43	Arizona	15.9
8	Arkansas	22.3
49	California	14.0
31	Colorado	17.6
43	Connecticut	15.9
30	Delaware	17.8
33	Florida	17.5
20	Georgia	19.5
46	Hawaii	15.4
37	Idaho	16.9
12	Illinois	21.3
2	Indiana	26.0
23	Iowa	18.8
29	Kansas	17.9
3	Kentucky	25.2
15	Louisiana	20.5
27	Maine	18.2
47	Maryland	14.9
42	Massachusetts	16.1
15	Michigan	20.5
31	Minnesota	17.6
7	Mississippi	22.7
4	Missouri	25.0
24	Montana	18.5
26	Nebraska	18.4
9	Nevada	22.2
36	New Hampshire	17.1
48	New Jersey	14.8
21	New Mexico	19.4
38	New York	16.8
14	North Carolina	20.9
28	North Dakota	18.1
17	Ohio	20.1
5	Oklahoma	24.7
41	Oregon	16.3
12	Pennsylvania	21.3
35	Rhode Island	17.4
18	South Carolina	20.0
33	South Dakota	17.5
6	Tennessee	23.1
24	Texas	18.5
50	Utah	9.3
38	Vermont	16.8
40	Virginia	16.4
45	Washington	15.7
1	West Virginia	26.5
19	Wisconsin	19.9
21	Wyoming	19.4

RANK ORDER

RANK	STATE	PERCENT
1	West Virginia	26.5
2	Indiana	26.0
3	Kentucky	25.2
4	Missouri	25.0
5	Oklahoma	24.7
6	Tennessee	23.1
7	Mississippi	22.7
8	Arkansas	22.3
9	Nevada	22.2
10	Alabama	22.1
11	Alaska	21.5
12	Illinois	21.3
12	Pennsylvania	21.3
14	North Carolina	20.9
15	Louisiana	20.5
15	Michigan	20.5
17	Ohio	20.1
18	South Carolina	20.0
19	Wisconsin	19.9
20	Georgia	19.5
21	New Mexico	19.4
21	Wyoming	19.4
23	Iowa	18.8
24	Montana	18.5
24	Texas	18.5
26	Nebraska	18.4
27	Maine	18.2
28	North Dakota	18.1
29	Kansas	17.9
30	Delaware	17.8
31	Colorado	17.6
31	Minnesota	17.6
33	Florida	17.5
33	South Dakota	17.5
35	Rhode Island	17.4
36	New Hampshire	17.1
37	Idaho	16.9
38	New York	16.8
38	Vermont	16.8
40	Virginia	16.4
41	Oregon	16.3
42	Massachusetts	16.1
43	Arizona	15.9
43	Connecticut	15.9
45	Washington	15.7
46	Hawaii	15.4
47	Maryland	14.9
48	New Jersey	14.8
49	California	14.0
50	Utah	9.3

| | District of Columbia | 16.2 |

Source: U.S. Department of Health and Human Services, Centers for Disease Control and Prevention
"2008 Behavioral Risk Factor Surveillance Summary Prevalence Data" (http://apps.nccd.cdc.gov/brfss/)
*Persons 18 and older who have smoked more than 100 cigarettes during their lifetime and who currently smoke every day or some days.

Percent of Adults Overweight or Obese: 2008

National Median = 63.2% of Adults*

ALPHA ORDER

RANK	STATE	PERCENT
3	Alabama	67.9
13	Alaska	65.5
40	Arizona	61.3
10	Arkansas	65.7
39	California	61.4
50	Colorado	55.3
45	Connecticut	59.7
21	Delaware	63.8
42	Florida	60.2
16	Georgia	64.7
49	Hawaii	57.3
31	Idaho	62.2
27	Illinois	63.3
23	Indiana	63.6
19	Iowa	64.3
10	Kansas	65.7
6	Kentucky	66.8
21	Louisiana	63.8
34	Maine	61.9
25	Maryland	63.4
48	Massachusetts	58.1
16	Michigan	64.7
29	Minnesota	62.8
4	Mississippi	67.5
13	Missouri	65.5
36	Montana	61.7
20	Nebraska	64.1
30	Nevada	62.6
28	New Hampshire	63.1
32	New Jersey	62.1
44	New Mexico	59.9
41	New York	60.3
10	North Carolina	65.7
5	North Dakota	67.4
25	Ohio	63.4
7	Oklahoma	66.6
36	Oregon	61.7
18	Pennsylvania	64.4
43	Rhode Island	60.0
9	South Carolina	65.9
15	South Dakota	64.9
2	Tennessee	68.0
8	Texas	66.2
47	Utah	58.2
46	Vermont	58.5
38	Virginia	61.6
35	Washington	61.8
1	West Virginia	68.8
23	Wisconsin	63.6
32	Wyoming	62.1

RANK ORDER

RANK	STATE	PERCENT
1	West Virginia	68.8
2	Tennessee	68.0
3	Alabama	67.9
4	Mississippi	67.5
5	North Dakota	67.4
6	Kentucky	66.8
7	Oklahoma	66.6
8	Texas	66.2
9	South Carolina	65.9
10	Arkansas	65.7
10	Kansas	65.7
10	North Carolina	65.7
13	Alaska	65.5
13	Missouri	65.5
15	South Dakota	64.9
16	Georgia	64.7
16	Michigan	64.7
18	Pennsylvania	64.4
19	Iowa	64.3
20	Nebraska	64.1
21	Delaware	63.8
21	Louisiana	63.8
23	Indiana	63.6
23	Wisconsin	63.6
25	Maryland	63.4
25	Ohio	63.4
27	Illinois	63.3
28	New Hampshire	63.1
29	Minnesota	62.8
30	Nevada	62.6
31	Idaho	62.2
32	New Jersey	62.1
32	Wyoming	62.1
34	Maine	61.9
35	Washington	61.8
36	Montana	61.7
36	Oregon	61.7
38	Virginia	61.6
39	California	61.4
40	Arizona	61.3
41	New York	60.3
42	Florida	60.2
43	Rhode Island	60.0
44	New Mexico	59.9
45	Connecticut	59.7
46	Vermont	58.5
47	Utah	58.2
48	Massachusetts	58.1
49	Hawaii	57.3
50	Colorado	55.3

District of Columbia 55.1

Source: CQ Press using data from U.S. Department of Health and Human Services, Centers for Disease Control and Prevention "2008 Behavioral Risk Factor Surveillance Summary Prevalence Data" (http://apps.nccd.cdc.gov/brfss/)

*Persons 18 and older. Overweight is defined as a Body Mass Index (BMI) of 25.0 to 29.9 regardless of sex. Obese is a BMI of 30.0 or greater. BMI is a ratio of height to weight. As an example, a person 5' 8" and weighing 165 pounds has a BMI of 25. The same height at 197 pounds has a BMI of 30. See http://www.cdc.gov/healthyweight/assessing/bmi/index.html.

Percent of Children Aged 19 to 35 Months Fully Immunized in 2008

National Percent = 76.1%*

ALPHA ORDER

RANK	STATE	PERCENT
25	Alabama	75.1
44	Alaska	69.2
21	Arizona	76.4
23	Arkansas	75.5
10	California	78.7
9	Colorado	79.4
42	Connecticut	69.8
37	Delaware	71.8
7	Florida	79.9
36	Georgia	71.9
15	Hawaii	77.4
49	Idaho	60.4
26	Illinois	74.8
23	Indiana	75.5
27	Iowa	74.7
18	Kansas	76.7
30	Kentucky	74.1
2	Louisiana	81.9
31	Maine	73.6
6	Maryland	80.2
1	Massachusetts	82.3
29	Michigan	74.5
28	Minnesota	74.6
22	Mississippi	75.8
34	Missouri	72.9
50	Montana	59.2
39	Nebraska	71.5
46	Nevada	67.8
5	New Hampshire	81.0
45	New Jersey	68.5
17	New Mexico	77.0
33	New York	73.3
41	North Carolina	70.8
42	North Dakota	69.8
3	Ohio	81.8
38	Oklahoma	71.7
40	Oregon	71.0
13	Pennsylvania	77.7
14	Rhode Island	77.5
11	South Carolina	78.4
15	South Dakota	77.4
4	Tennessee	81.2
12	Texas	77.8
19	Utah	76.6
48	Vermont	64.5
34	Virginia	72.9
32	Washington	73.5
20	West Virginia	76.5
8	Wisconsin	79.6
47	Wyoming	64.6

RANK ORDER

RANK	STATE	PERCENT
1	Massachusetts	82.3
2	Louisiana	81.9
3	Ohio	81.8
4	Tennessee	81.2
5	New Hampshire	81.0
6	Maryland	80.2
7	Florida	79.9
8	Wisconsin	79.6
9	Colorado	79.4
10	California	78.7
11	South Carolina	78.4
12	Texas	77.8
13	Pennsylvania	77.7
14	Rhode Island	77.5
15	Hawaii	77.4
15	South Dakota	77.4
17	New Mexico	77.0
18	Kansas	76.7
19	Utah	76.6
20	West Virginia	76.5
21	Arizona	76.4
22	Mississippi	75.8
23	Arkansas	75.5
23	Indiana	75.5
25	Alabama	75.1
26	Illinois	74.8
27	Iowa	74.7
28	Minnesota	74.6
29	Michigan	74.5
30	Kentucky	74.1
31	Maine	73.6
32	Washington	73.5
33	New York	73.3
34	Missouri	72.9
34	Virginia	72.9
36	Georgia	71.9
37	Delaware	71.8
38	Oklahoma	71.7
39	Nebraska	71.5
40	Oregon	71.0
41	North Carolina	70.8
42	Connecticut	69.8
42	North Dakota	69.8
44	Alaska	69.2
45	New Jersey	68.5
46	Nevada	67.8
47	Wyoming	64.6
48	Vermont	64.5
49	Idaho	60.4
50	Montana	59.2

	District of Columbia	77.6

Source: U.S. Department of Health and Human Services, Centers for Disease Control and Prevention

  "State Vaccination Coverage Levels" (MMWR, Vol. 58, No. 33, August 28, 2009, http://www.cdc.gov/mmwr/)

*Fully immunized (4:3:1:3:3:1 series) children received four doses of DTP/DT/DTaP (Diphtheria, Tetanus, Pertussis [Whooping Cough], Acellular Pertussis), three doses of OPV (Oral Poliovirus Vaccine), one dose of MCV (Measles-Containing Vaccine), three doses of Hib (Haemophilus influenzae type b), three doses of Hepatitis B vaccine, and one dose of Varicella (chickenpox) vaccine. This differs from previous "fully" immunized tables.

XII. Households and Housing

Households in 2008

National Total = 113,101,329 Households*

ALPHA ORDER

RANK	STATE	HOUSEHOLDS	% of USA
23	Alabama	1,815,865	1.6%
49	Alaska	237,607	0.2%
18	Arizona	2,273,842	2.0%
31	Arkansas	1,114,041	1.0%
1	California	12,176,760	10.8%
22	Colorado	1,897,835	1.7%
29	Connecticut	1,329,305	1.2%
45	Delaware	328,654	0.3%
4	Florida	7,057,285	6.2%
10	Georgia	3,469,845	3.1%
42	Hawaii	437,105	0.4%
39	Idaho	566,004	0.5%
6	Illinois	4,766,252	4.2%
14	Indiana	2,480,570	2.2%
30	Iowa	1,215,351	1.1%
32	Kansas	1,110,829	1.0%
25	Kentucky	1,686,277	1.5%
26	Louisiana	1,625,153	1.4%
40	Maine	542,363	0.5%
20	Maryland	2,092,692	1.9%
15	Massachusetts	2,467,323	2.2%
8	Michigan	3,810,801	3.4%
21	Minnesota	2,089,449	1.8%
33	Mississippi	1,094,208	1.0%
17	Missouri	2,330,040	2.1%
44	Montana	375,598	0.3%
38	Nebraska	704,143	0.6%
34	Nevada	952,856	0.8%
41	New Hampshire	505,286	0.4%
11	New Jersey	3,154,012	2.8%
37	New Mexico	741,399	0.7%
3	New York	7,137,482	6.3%
9	North Carolina	3,595,175	3.2%
47	North Dakota	274,743	0.2%
7	Ohio	4,508,871	4.0%
28	Oklahoma	1,407,933	1.2%
27	Oregon	1,474,755	1.3%
5	Pennsylvania	4,904,554	4.3%
43	Rhode Island	399,107	0.4%
24	South Carolina	1,702,300	1.5%
46	South Dakota	319,926	0.3%
16	Tennessee	2,434,683	2.2%
2	Texas	8,422,249	7.4%
35	Utah	854,244	0.8%
48	Vermont	249,986	0.2%
12	Virginia	2,961,083	2.6%
13	Washington	2,547,663	2.3%
36	West Virginia	749,586	0.7%
19	Wisconsin	2,249,630	2.0%
50	Wyoming	208,613	0.2%

RANK ORDER

RANK	STATE	HOUSEHOLDS	% of USA
1	California	12,176,760	10.8%
2	Texas	8,422,249	7.4%
3	New York	7,137,482	6.3%
4	Florida	7,057,285	6.2%
5	Pennsylvania	4,904,554	4.3%
6	Illinois	4,766,252	4.2%
7	Ohio	4,508,871	4.0%
8	Michigan	3,810,801	3.4%
9	North Carolina	3,595,175	3.2%
10	Georgia	3,469,845	3.1%
11	New Jersey	3,154,012	2.8%
12	Virginia	2,961,083	2.6%
13	Washington	2,547,663	2.3%
14	Indiana	2,480,570	2.2%
15	Massachusetts	2,467,323	2.2%
16	Tennessee	2,434,683	2.2%
17	Missouri	2,330,040	2.1%
18	Arizona	2,273,842	2.0%
19	Wisconsin	2,249,630	2.0%
20	Maryland	2,092,692	1.9%
21	Minnesota	2,089,449	1.8%
22	Colorado	1,897,835	1.7%
23	Alabama	1,815,865	1.6%
24	South Carolina	1,702,300	1.5%
25	Kentucky	1,686,277	1.5%
26	Louisiana	1,625,153	1.4%
27	Oregon	1,474,755	1.3%
28	Oklahoma	1,407,933	1.2%
29	Connecticut	1,329,305	1.2%
30	Iowa	1,215,351	1.1%
31	Arkansas	1,114,041	1.0%
32	Kansas	1,110,829	1.0%
33	Mississippi	1,094,208	1.0%
34	Nevada	952,856	0.8%
35	Utah	854,244	0.8%
36	West Virginia	749,586	0.7%
37	New Mexico	741,399	0.7%
38	Nebraska	704,143	0.6%
39	Idaho	566,004	0.5%
40	Maine	542,363	0.5%
41	New Hampshire	505,286	0.4%
42	Hawaii	437,105	0.4%
43	Rhode Island	399,107	0.4%
44	Montana	375,598	0.3%
45	Delaware	328,654	0.3%
46	South Dakota	319,926	0.3%
47	North Dakota	274,743	0.2%
48	Vermont	249,986	0.2%
49	Alaska	237,607	0.2%
50	Wyoming	208,613	0.2%
	District of Columbia	249,996	0.2%

Source: U.S. Bureau of the Census
   "2008 American Community Survey" (http://www.census.gov/acs/www/index.html)
*A household includes all persons who occupy a housing unit. A household consists of a single family, one person living alone, two or more families living together, or any other group of related or unrelated persons who share living arrangements.

Persons per Household in 2008

National Rate = 2.62 Persons per Household*

ALPHA ORDER

RANK	STATE	PERSONS
30	Alabama	2.50
6	Alaska	2.80
5	Arizona	2.81
32	Arkansas	2.49
2	California	2.95
19	Colorado	2.55
19	Connecticut	2.55
17	Delaware	2.58
22	Florida	2.54
7	Georgia	2.71
3	Hawaii	2.87
12	Idaho	2.63
12	Illinois	2.63
32	Indiana	2.49
47	Iowa	2.38
41	Kansas	2.45
38	Kentucky	2.46
11	Louisiana	2.64
48	Maine	2.36
14	Maryland	2.62
25	Massachusetts	2.53
18	Michigan	2.56
43	Minnesota	2.43
16	Mississippi	2.59
38	Missouri	2.46
30	Montana	2.50
38	Nebraska	2.46
8	Nevada	2.69
25	New Hampshire	2.53
8	New Jersey	2.69
14	New Mexico	2.62
10	New York	2.65
32	North Carolina	2.49
50	North Dakota	2.24
36	Ohio	2.48
27	Oklahoma	2.51
27	Oregon	2.51
42	Pennsylvania	2.44
22	Rhode Island	2.54
19	South Carolina	2.55
45	South Dakota	2.42
32	Tennessee	2.49
4	Texas	2.82
1	Utah	3.15
46	Vermont	2.40
22	Virginia	2.54
27	Washington	2.51
48	West Virginia	2.36
43	Wisconsin	2.43
36	Wyoming	2.48

RANK ORDER

RANK	STATE	PERSONS
1	Utah	3.15
2	California	2.95
3	Hawaii	2.87
4	Texas	2.82
5	Arizona	2.81
6	Alaska	2.80
7	Georgia	2.71
8	Nevada	2.69
8	New Jersey	2.69
10	New York	2.65
11	Louisiana	2.64
12	Idaho	2.63
12	Illinois	2.63
14	Maryland	2.62
14	New Mexico	2.62
16	Mississippi	2.59
17	Delaware	2.58
18	Michigan	2.56
19	Colorado	2.55
19	Connecticut	2.55
19	South Carolina	2.55
22	Florida	2.54
22	Rhode Island	2.54
22	Virginia	2.54
25	Massachusetts	2.53
25	New Hampshire	2.53
27	Oklahoma	2.51
27	Oregon	2.51
27	Washington	2.51
30	Alabama	2.50
30	Montana	2.50
32	Arkansas	2.49
32	Indiana	2.49
32	North Carolina	2.49
32	Tennessee	2.49
36	Ohio	2.48
36	Wyoming	2.48
38	Kentucky	2.46
38	Missouri	2.46
38	Nebraska	2.46
41	Kansas	2.45
42	Pennsylvania	2.44
43	Minnesota	2.43
43	Wisconsin	2.43
45	South Dakota	2.42
46	Vermont	2.40
47	Iowa	2.38
48	Maine	2.36
48	West Virginia	2.36
50	North Dakota	2.24
	District of Columbia	2.23

Source: U.S. Bureau of the Census
   "2008 American Community Survey" (http://www.census.gov/acs/www/index.html)
*A household includes all persons who occupy a housing unit. A household consists of a single family, one person living alone,
two or more families living together, or any other group of related or unrelated persons who share living arrangements.

Percent of Households With One Person in 2008

National Percent = 27.8% of Households*

ALPHA ORDER

RANK ORDER

RANK	STATE	PERCENT	RANK	STATE	PERCENT
13	Alabama	29.0	1	Rhode Island	31.3
45	Alaska	25.3	2	North Dakota	31.2
33	Arizona	27.7	3	South Dakota	30.2
30	Arkansas	27.9	4	Montana	29.8
46	California	25.1	4	West Virginia	29.8
13	Colorado	29.0	6	New York	29.7
35	Connecticut	27.4	7	Ohio	29.6
41	Delaware	26.7	8	Massachusetts	29.4
15	Florida	28.8	9	Nebraska	29.3
42	Georgia	26.6	10	Pennsylvania	29.2
47	Hawaii	24.1	11	Minnesota	29.1
48	Idaho	23.8	11	New Mexico	29.1
16	Illinois	28.7	13	Alabama	29.0
30	Indiana	27.9	13	Colorado	29.0
19	Iowa	28.6	15	Florida	28.8
26	Kansas	28.3	16	Illinois	28.7
19	Kentucky	28.6	16	Missouri	28.7
28	Louisiana	28.1	16	Wyoming	28.7
21	Maine	28.5	19	Iowa	28.6
35	Maryland	27.4	19	Kentucky	28.6
8	Massachusetts	29.4	21	Maine	28.5
23	Michigan	28.4	21	Tennessee	28.5
11	Minnesota	29.1	23	Michigan	28.4
37	Mississippi	27.0	23	Oklahoma	28.4
16	Missouri	28.7	23	Wisconsin	28.4
4	Montana	29.8	26	Kansas	28.3
9	Nebraska	29.3	26	Oregon	28.3
37	Nevada	27.0	28	Louisiana	28.1
48	New Hampshire	23.8	28	Washington	28.1
43	New Jersey	26.5	30	Arkansas	27.9
11	New Mexico	29.1	30	Indiana	27.9
6	New York	29.7	30	South Carolina	27.9
33	North Carolina	27.7	33	Arizona	27.7
2	North Dakota	31.2	33	North Carolina	27.7
7	Ohio	29.6	35	Connecticut	27.4
23	Oklahoma	28.4	35	Maryland	27.4
26	Oregon	28.3	37	Mississippi	27.0
10	Pennsylvania	29.2	37	Nevada	27.0
1	Rhode Island	31.3	37	Vermont	27.0
30	South Carolina	27.9	40	Virginia	26.8
3	South Dakota	30.2	41	Delaware	26.7
21	Tennessee	28.5	42	Georgia	26.6
44	Texas	25.5	43	New Jersey	26.5
50	Utah	20.4	44	Texas	25.5
37	Vermont	27.0	45	Alaska	25.3
40	Virginia	26.8	46	California	25.1
28	Washington	28.1	47	Hawaii	24.1
4	West Virginia	29.8	48	Idaho	23.8
23	Wisconsin	28.4	48	New Hampshire	23.8
16	Wyoming	28.7	50	Utah	20.4
				District of Columbia	47.1

Source: CQ Press using data from U.S. Bureau of the Census
   "2008 American Community Survey" (http://www.census.gov/acs/www/index.html)
*A household includes all persons who occupy a housing unit. A household consists of a single family, one person living alone, two or more families living together, or any other group of related or unrelated persons who share living arrangements.

Percent of Households Headed by Married Couples in 2008

National Percent = 49.2% of Households*

ALPHA ORDER

RANK	STATE	PERCENT
36	Alabama	48.8
34	Alaska	48.9
38	Arizona	48.7
28	Arkansas	49.6
33	California	49.1
24	Colorado	49.9
20	Connecticut	50.3
31	Delaware	49.5
43	Florida	47.8
39	Georgia	48.6
11	Hawaii	51.3
2	Idaho	56.3
36	Illinois	48.8
18	Indiana	50.4
5	Iowa	52.2
6	Kansas	52.0
20	Kentucky	50.3
46	Louisiana	46.7
23	Maine	50.0
42	Maryland	48.1
44	Massachusetts	47.3
28	Michigan	49.6
9	Minnesota	51.4
47	Mississippi	46.6
26	Missouri	49.8
13	Montana	51.2
7	Nebraska	51.8
45	Nevada	47.2
3	New Hampshire	54.6
8	New Jersey	51.5
48	New Mexico	45.9
50	New York	45.0
32	North Carolina	49.4
13	North Dakota	51.2
40	Ohio	48.3
20	Oklahoma	50.3
28	Oregon	49.6
34	Pennsylvania	48.9
49	Rhode Island	45.3
40	South Carolina	48.3
9	South Dakota	51.4
27	Tennessee	49.7
16	Texas	51.0
1	Utah	60.5
17	Vermont	50.6
11	Virginia	51.3
24	Washington	49.9
18	West Virginia	50.4
15	Wisconsin	51.1
4	Wyoming	52.4

RANK ORDER

RANK	STATE	PERCENT
1	Utah	60.5
2	Idaho	56.3
3	New Hampshire	54.6
4	Wyoming	52.4
5	Iowa	52.2
6	Kansas	52.0
7	Nebraska	51.8
8	New Jersey	51.5
9	Minnesota	51.4
9	South Dakota	51.4
11	Hawaii	51.3
11	Virginia	51.3
13	Montana	51.2
13	North Dakota	51.2
15	Wisconsin	51.1
16	Texas	51.0
17	Vermont	50.6
18	Indiana	50.4
18	West Virginia	50.4
20	Connecticut	50.3
20	Kentucky	50.3
20	Oklahoma	50.3
23	Maine	50.0
24	Colorado	49.9
24	Washington	49.9
26	Missouri	49.8
27	Tennessee	49.7
28	Arkansas	49.6
28	Michigan	49.6
28	Oregon	49.6
31	Delaware	49.5
32	North Carolina	49.4
33	California	49.1
34	Alaska	48.9
34	Pennsylvania	48.9
36	Alabama	48.8
36	Illinois	48.8
38	Arizona	48.7
39	Georgia	48.6
40	Ohio	48.3
40	South Carolina	48.3
42	Maryland	48.1
43	Florida	47.8
44	Massachusetts	47.3
45	Nevada	47.2
46	Louisiana	46.7
47	Mississippi	46.6
48	New Mexico	45.9
49	Rhode Island	45.3
50	New York	45.0
	District of Columbia	21.8

Source: CQ Press using data from U.S. Bureau of the Census
 "2008 American Community Survey" (http://www.census.gov/acs/www/index.html)
*A household includes all persons who occupy a housing unit. A household consists of a single family, one person living alone,
two or more families living together, or any other group of related or unrelated persons who share living arrangements.

Percent of Households Headed by Single Mothers in 2008

National Percent = 7.4% of Households*

ALPHA ORDER				RANK ORDER		
RANK	STATE	PERCENT		RANK	STATE	PERCENT
8	Alabama	8.0		1	Mississippi	10.4
17	Alaska	7.4		2	Louisiana	9.2
22	Arizona	7.1		3	Georgia	8.9
6	Arkansas	8.3		4	South Carolina	8.4
18	California	7.3		4	Texas	8.4
40	Colorado	6.0		6	Arkansas	8.3
20	Connecticut	7.2		6	New Mexico	8.3
18	Delaware	7.3		8	Alabama	8.0
28	Florida	7.0		9	New York	7.9
3	Georgia	8.9		9	North Carolina	7.9
49	Hawaii	5.4		11	Maryland	7.8
34	Idaho	6.5		12	Indiana	7.6
20	Illinois	7.2		12	Michigan	7.6
12	Indiana	7.6		12	Ohio	7.6
40	Iowa	6.0		15	Rhode Island	7.5
28	Kansas	7.0		15	Tennessee	7.5
28	Kentucky	7.0		17	Alaska	7.4
2	Louisiana	9.2		18	California	7.3
38	Maine	6.2		18	Delaware	7.3
11	Maryland	7.8		20	Connecticut	7.2
22	Massachusetts	7.1		20	Illinois	7.2
12	Michigan	7.6		22	Arizona	7.1
43	Minnesota	5.9		22	Massachusetts	7.1
1	Mississippi	10.4		22	Missouri	7.1
22	Missouri	7.1		22	Nevada	7.1
47	Montana	5.6		22	Oklahoma	7.1
45	Nebraska	5.7		22	Virginia	7.1
22	Nevada	7.1		28	Florida	7.0
45	New Hampshire	5.7		28	Kansas	7.0
32	New Jersey	6.8		28	Kentucky	7.0
6	New Mexico	8.3		31	Pennsylvania	6.9
9	New York	7.9		32	New Jersey	6.8
9	North Carolina	7.9		33	Vermont	6.7
49	North Dakota	5.4		34	Idaho	6.5
12	Ohio	7.6		34	Wisconsin	6.5
22	Oklahoma	7.1		36	South Dakota	6.4
39	Oregon	6.1		36	Washington	6.4
31	Pennsylvania	6.9		38	Maine	6.2
15	Rhode Island	7.5		39	Oregon	6.1
4	South Carolina	8.4		40	Colorado	6.0
36	South Dakota	6.4		40	Iowa	6.0
15	Tennessee	7.5		40	West Virginia	6.0
4	Texas	8.4		43	Minnesota	5.9
48	Utah	5.5		44	Wyoming	5.8
33	Vermont	6.7		45	Nebraska	5.7
22	Virginia	7.1		45	New Hampshire	5.7
36	Washington	6.4		47	Montana	5.6
40	West Virginia	6.0		48	Utah	5.5
34	Wisconsin	6.5		49	Hawaii	5.4
44	Wyoming	5.8		49	North Dakota	5.4
					District of Columbia	8.9

Source: CQ Press using data from U.S. Bureau of the Census
    "2008 American Community Survey" (http://www.census.gov/acs/www/index.html)
*No spouse present in household with children under 18 years old. A household includes all persons who occupy a housing unit.
A household consists of a single family, one person living alone, two or more families living together, or any other group of
related or unrelated persons who share living arrangements.

Percent of Households Headed by Single Fathers in 2008

National Percent = 2.3% of Households*

ALPHA ORDER

RANK	STATE	PERCENT
49	Alabama	1.7
1	Alaska	4.1
4	Arizona	2.7
41	Arkansas	2.0
4	California	2.7
14	Colorado	2.3
46	Connecticut	1.8
14	Delaware	2.3
27	Florida	2.2
38	Georgia	2.1
27	Hawaii	2.2
9	Idaho	2.4
27	Illinois	2.2
9	Indiana	2.4
14	Iowa	2.3
27	Kansas	2.2
9	Kentucky	2.4
14	Louisiana	2.3
14	Maine	2.3
38	Maryland	2.1
46	Massachusetts	1.8
41	Michigan	2.0
14	Minnesota	2.3
14	Mississippi	2.3
14	Missouri	2.3
27	Montana	2.2
14	Nebraska	2.3
2	Nevada	3.1
14	New Hampshire	2.3
46	New Jersey	1.8
3	New Mexico	2.9
41	New York	2.0
27	North Carolina	2.2
50	North Dakota	1.6
14	Ohio	2.3
9	Oklahoma	2.4
14	Oregon	2.3
27	Pennsylvania	2.2
27	Rhode Island	2.2
44	South Carolina	1.9
27	South Dakota	2.2
27	Tennessee	2.2
9	Texas	2.4
38	Utah	2.1
7	Vermont	2.5
44	Virginia	1.9
7	Washington	2.5
27	West Virginia	2.2
14	Wisconsin	2.3
6	Wyoming	2.6

RANK ORDER

RANK	STATE	PERCENT
1	Alaska	4.1
2	Nevada	3.1
3	New Mexico	2.9
4	Arizona	2.7
4	California	2.7
6	Wyoming	2.6
7	Vermont	2.5
7	Washington	2.5
9	Idaho	2.4
9	Indiana	2.4
9	Kentucky	2.4
9	Oklahoma	2.4
9	Texas	2.4
14	Colorado	2.3
14	Delaware	2.3
14	Iowa	2.3
14	Louisiana	2.3
14	Maine	2.3
14	Minnesota	2.3
14	Mississippi	2.3
14	Missouri	2.3
14	Nebraska	2.3
14	New Hampshire	2.3
14	Ohio	2.3
14	Oregon	2.3
14	Wisconsin	2.3
27	Florida	2.2
27	Hawaii	2.2
27	Illinois	2.2
27	Kansas	2.2
27	Montana	2.2
27	North Carolina	2.2
27	Pennsylvania	2.2
27	Rhode Island	2.2
27	South Dakota	2.2
27	Tennessee	2.2
27	West Virginia	2.2
38	Georgia	2.1
38	Maryland	2.1
38	Utah	2.1
41	Arkansas	2.0
41	Michigan	2.0
41	New York	2.0
44	South Carolina	1.9
44	Virginia	1.9
46	Connecticut	1.8
46	Massachusetts	1.8
46	New Jersey	1.8
49	Alabama	1.7
50	North Dakota	1.6

| | District of Columbia | 1.7 |

Source: CQ Press using data from U.S. Bureau of the Census
"2008 American Community Survey" (http://www.census.gov/acs/www/index.html)
*No spouse present in household with children under 18 years old. A household includes all persons who occupy a housing unit.
A household consists of a single family, one person living alone, two or more families living together, or any other group of
related or unrelated persons who share living arrangements.

Housing Units in 2008

National Total = 129,065,264 Housing Units*

ALPHA ORDER

RANK	STATE	HOUSING UNITS	% of USA
22	Alabama	2,158,576	1.7%
49	Alaska	283,357	0.2%
17	Arizona	2,722,725	2.1%
31	Arkansas	1,298,137	1.0%
1	California	13,393,878	10.4%
23	Colorado	2,152,040	1.7%
29	Connecticut	1,443,115	1.1%
45	Delaware	392,965	0.3%
3	Florida	8,800,294	6.8%
10	Georgia	4,026,082	3.1%
42	Hawaii	512,881	0.4%
40	Idaho	641,479	0.5%
6	Illinois	5,276,979	4.1%
13	Indiana	2,795,024	2.2%
30	Iowa	1,329,352	1.0%
33	Kansas	1,226,859	1.0%
25	Kentucky	1,920,581	1.5%
26	Louisiana	1,883,167	1.5%
39	Maine	700,480	0.5%
20	Maryland	2,333,064	1.8%
16	Massachusetts	2,735,443	2.1%
8	Michigan	4,535,323	3.5%
21	Minnesota	2,331,619	1.8%
32	Mississippi	1,267,231	1.0%
18	Missouri	2,663,977	2.1%
44	Montana	438,282	0.3%
38	Nebraska	786,334	0.6%
34	Nevada	1,127,061	0.9%
41	New Hampshire	597,129	0.5%
11	New Jersey	3,517,293	2.7%
37	New Mexico	871,700	0.7%
4	New York	7,977,286	6.2%
9	North Carolina	4,201,378	3.3%
47	North Dakota	313,332	0.2%
7	Ohio	5,079,873	3.9%
27	Oklahoma	1,637,138	1.3%
28	Oregon	1,628,826	1.3%
5	Pennsylvania	5,496,336	4.3%
43	Rhode Island	451,753	0.4%
24	South Carolina	2,056,127	1.6%
46	South Dakota	361,482	0.3%
15	Tennessee	2,758,171	2.1%
2	Texas	9,598,579	7.4%
35	Utah	944,347	0.7%
48	Vermont	312,617	0.2%
12	Virginia	3,306,389	2.6%
14	Washington	2,791,597	2.2%
36	West Virginia	886,430	0.7%
19	Wisconsin	2,569,430	2.0%
50	Wyoming	246,393	0.2%

RANK ORDER

RANK	STATE	HOUSING UNITS	% of USA
1	California	13,393,878	10.4%
2	Texas	9,598,579	7.4%
3	Florida	8,800,294	6.8%
4	New York	7,977,286	6.2%
5	Pennsylvania	5,496,336	4.3%
6	Illinois	5,276,979	4.1%
7	Ohio	5,079,873	3.9%
8	Michigan	4,535,323	3.5%
9	North Carolina	4,201,378	3.3%
10	Georgia	4,026,082	3.1%
11	New Jersey	3,517,293	2.7%
12	Virginia	3,306,389	2.6%
13	Indiana	2,795,024	2.2%
14	Washington	2,791,597	2.2%
15	Tennessee	2,758,171	2.1%
16	Massachusetts	2,735,443	2.1%
17	Arizona	2,722,725	2.1%
18	Missouri	2,663,977	2.1%
19	Wisconsin	2,569,430	2.0%
20	Maryland	2,333,064	1.8%
21	Minnesota	2,331,619	1.8%
22	Alabama	2,158,576	1.7%
23	Colorado	2,152,040	1.7%
24	South Carolina	2,056,127	1.6%
25	Kentucky	1,920,581	1.5%
26	Louisiana	1,883,167	1.5%
27	Oklahoma	1,637,138	1.3%
28	Oregon	1,628,826	1.3%
29	Connecticut	1,443,115	1.1%
30	Iowa	1,329,352	1.0%
31	Arkansas	1,298,137	1.0%
32	Mississippi	1,267,231	1.0%
33	Kansas	1,226,859	1.0%
34	Nevada	1,127,061	0.9%
35	Utah	944,347	0.7%
36	West Virginia	886,430	0.7%
37	New Mexico	871,700	0.7%
38	Nebraska	786,334	0.6%
39	Maine	700,480	0.5%
40	Idaho	641,479	0.5%
41	New Hampshire	597,129	0.5%
42	Hawaii	512,881	0.4%
43	Rhode Island	451,753	0.4%
44	Montana	438,282	0.3%
45	Delaware	392,965	0.3%
46	South Dakota	361,482	0.3%
47	North Dakota	313,332	0.2%
48	Vermont	312,617	0.2%
49	Alaska	283,357	0.2%
50	Wyoming	246,393	0.2%
	District of Columbia	285,353	0.2%

Source: U.S. Bureau of the Census
  "Housing Unit Estimates" (http://www.census.gov/popest/housing/HU-EST2008.html)
*A housing unit is a house, an apartment, a mobile home, a group of rooms, or a single room that is occupied (or if vacant, is intended for occupancy) as separate living quarters. Separate living quarters are those in which the occupants live and eat separately from any other persons in the building and which have direct access from the outside of the building or through a common hall.

Housing Units per Square Mile in 2008

National Average = 36.5 Housing Units*

ALPHA ORDER

RANK	STATE	HOUSING UNITS
25	Alabama	42.5
50	Alaska	0.5
34	Arizona	24.0
33	Arkansas	24.9
13	California	85.9
38	Colorado	20.7
4	Connecticut	297.9
6	Delaware	201.1
8	Florida	163.2
18	Georgia	69.5
15	Hawaii	79.9
44	Idaho	7.8
11	Illinois	94.9
17	Indiana	77.9
35	Iowa	23.8
40	Kansas	15.0
22	Kentucky	48.3
24	Louisiana	43.2
37	Maine	22.7
5	Maryland	238.7
3	Massachusetts	348.9
16	Michigan	79.8
31	Minnesota	29.3
32	Mississippi	27.0
27	Missouri	38.7
48	Montana	3.0
43	Nebraska	10.2
42	Nevada	10.3
21	New Hampshire	66.6
1	New Jersey	474.2
45	New Mexico	7.2
7	New York	169.0
12	North Carolina	86.3
47	North Dakota	4.5
9	Ohio	124.1
35	Oklahoma	23.8
39	Oregon	17.0
10	Pennsylvania	122.6
2	Rhode Island	432.3
19	South Carolina	68.3
46	South Dakota	4.8
20	Tennessee	66.9
29	Texas	36.7
41	Utah	11.5
30	Vermont	33.8
14	Virginia	83.5
26	Washington	42.0
28	West Virginia	36.8
23	Wisconsin	47.3
49	Wyoming	2.5

RANK ORDER

RANK	STATE	HOUSING UNITS
1	New Jersey	474.2
2	Rhode Island	432.3
3	Massachusetts	348.9
4	Connecticut	297.9
5	Maryland	238.7
6	Delaware	201.1
7	New York	169.0
8	Florida	163.2
9	Ohio	124.1
10	Pennsylvania	122.6
11	Illinois	94.9
12	North Carolina	86.3
13	California	85.9
14	Virginia	83.5
15	Hawaii	79.9
16	Michigan	79.8
17	Indiana	77.9
18	Georgia	69.5
19	South Carolina	68.3
20	Tennessee	66.9
21	New Hampshire	66.6
22	Kentucky	48.3
23	Wisconsin	47.3
24	Louisiana	43.2
25	Alabama	42.5
26	Washington	42.0
27	Missouri	38.7
28	West Virginia	36.8
29	Texas	36.7
30	Vermont	33.8
31	Minnesota	29.3
32	Mississippi	27.0
33	Arkansas	24.9
34	Arizona	24.0
35	Iowa	23.8
35	Oklahoma	23.8
37	Maine	22.7
38	Colorado	20.7
39	Oregon	17.0
40	Kansas	15.0
41	Utah	11.5
42	Nevada	10.3
43	Nebraska	10.2
44	Idaho	7.8
45	New Mexico	7.2
46	South Dakota	4.8
47	North Dakota	4.5
48	Montana	3.0
49	Wyoming	2.5
50	Alaska	0.5

District of Columbia — 4,677.9

Source: CQ Press using data from U.S. Bureau of the Census
"Housing Unit Estimates" (http://www.census.gov/popest/housing/HU-EST2008.html)
*Based on land area. A housing unit is a house, an apartment, a mobile home, a group of rooms, or a single room that is occupied (or if vacant, is intended for occupancy) as separate living quarters. Separate living quarters are those in which the occupants live and eat separately from any other persons in the building and which have direct access from the outside of the building or through a common hall.

Percent of Housing Units That Are Owner-Occupied: 2008

National Percent = 66.6% of Housing Units*

ALPHA ORDER

RANK	STATE	PERCENT
11	Alabama	71.0
42	Alaska	65.0
34	Arizona	68.1
36	Arkansas	67.4
49	California	57.0
35	Colorado	67.5
28	Connecticut	69.0
4	Delaware	73.5
20	Florida	69.7
36	Georgia	67.4
48	Hawaii	59.1
12	Idaho	70.9
24	Illinois	69.3
9	Indiana	71.8
5	Iowa	72.9
23	Kansas	69.4
21	Kentucky	69.5
31	Louisiana	68.5
8	Maine	72.1
21	Maryland	69.5
44	Massachusetts	64.5
2	Michigan	74.0
1	Minnesota	74.7
15	Mississippi	70.1
15	Missouri	70.1
31	Montana	68.5
24	Nebraska	69.3
47	Nevada	59.7
6	New Hampshire	72.3
39	New Jersey	67.0
26	New Mexico	69.2
50	New York	55.3
33	North Carolina	68.2
40	North Dakota	66.6
28	Ohio	69.0
38	Oklahoma	67.2
45	Oregon	64.3
13	Pennsylvania	70.8
46	Rhode Island	62.4
14	South Carolina	70.6
26	South Dakota	69.2
19	Tennessee	69.8
43	Texas	64.9
10	Utah	71.7
7	Vermont	72.2
30	Virginia	68.7
41	Washington	65.3
3	West Virginia	73.7
15	Wisconsin	70.1
15	Wyoming	70.1

RANK ORDER

RANK	STATE	PERCENT
1	Minnesota	74.7
2	Michigan	74.0
3	West Virginia	73.7
4	Delaware	73.5
5	Iowa	72.9
6	New Hampshire	72.3
7	Vermont	72.2
8	Maine	72.1
9	Indiana	71.8
10	Utah	71.7
11	Alabama	71.0
12	Idaho	70.9
13	Pennsylvania	70.8
14	South Carolina	70.6
15	Mississippi	70.1
15	Missouri	70.1
15	Wisconsin	70.1
15	Wyoming	70.1
19	Tennessee	69.8
20	Florida	69.7
21	Kentucky	69.5
21	Maryland	69.5
23	Kansas	69.4
24	Illinois	69.3
24	Nebraska	69.3
26	New Mexico	69.2
26	South Dakota	69.2
28	Connecticut	69.0
28	Ohio	69.0
30	Virginia	68.7
31	Louisiana	68.5
31	Montana	68.5
33	North Carolina	68.2
34	Arizona	68.1
35	Colorado	67.5
36	Arkansas	67.4
36	Georgia	67.4
38	Oklahoma	67.2
39	New Jersey	67.0
40	North Dakota	66.6
41	Washington	65.3
42	Alaska	65.0
43	Texas	64.9
44	Massachusetts	64.5
45	Oregon	64.3
46	Rhode Island	62.4
47	Nevada	59.7
48	Hawaii	59.1
49	California	57.0
50	New York	55.3
	District of Columbia	43.4

Source: U.S. Bureau of the Census
   "2008 American Community Survey" (http://www.census.gov/acs/www/index.html)
*For occupied housing units.

New Housing Units Authorized in 2009

National Total = 572,232 Units*

<table>
<tr><td colspan="4">ALPHA ORDER</td><td colspan="4">RANK ORDER</td></tr>
<tr><th>RANK</th><th>STATE</th><th>UNITS</th><th>% of USA</th><th>RANK</th><th>STATE</th><th>UNITS</th><th>% of USA</th></tr>
<tr><td>17</td><td>Alabama</td><td>12,171</td><td>2.1%</td><td>1</td><td>Texas</td><td>82,938</td><td>14.5%</td></tr>
<tr><td>50</td><td>Alaska</td><td>912</td><td>0.2%</td><td>2</td><td>Florida</td><td>35,858</td><td>6.3%</td></tr>
<tr><td>12</td><td>Arizona</td><td>14,134</td><td>2.5%</td><td>3</td><td>California</td><td>33,811</td><td>5.9%</td></tr>
<tr><td>34</td><td>Arkansas</td><td>6,637</td><td>1.2%</td><td>4</td><td>North Carolina</td><td>33,785</td><td>5.9%</td></tr>
<tr><td>3</td><td>California</td><td>33,811</td><td>5.9%</td><td>5</td><td>Virginia</td><td>21,078</td><td>3.7%</td></tr>
<tr><td>22</td><td>Colorado</td><td>9,393</td><td>1.6%</td><td>6</td><td>Pennsylvania</td><td>18,712</td><td>3.3%</td></tr>
<tr><td>39</td><td>Connecticut</td><td>3,343</td><td>0.6%</td><td>7</td><td>New York</td><td>17,356</td><td>3.0%</td></tr>
<tr><td>40</td><td>Delaware</td><td>3,140</td><td>0.5%</td><td>8</td><td>Georgia</td><td>17,202</td><td>3.0%</td></tr>
<tr><td>2</td><td>Florida</td><td>35,858</td><td>6.3%</td><td>9</td><td>Washington</td><td>16,754</td><td>2.9%</td></tr>
<tr><td>8</td><td>Georgia</td><td>17,202</td><td>3.0%</td><td>10</td><td>South Carolina</td><td>15,829</td><td>2.8%</td></tr>
<tr><td>43</td><td>Hawaii</td><td>2,617</td><td>0.5%</td><td>11</td><td>Tennessee</td><td>14,574</td><td>2.5%</td></tr>
<tr><td>35</td><td>Idaho</td><td>5,292</td><td>0.9%</td><td>12</td><td>Arizona</td><td>14,134</td><td>2.5%</td></tr>
<tr><td>19</td><td>Illinois</td><td>10,912</td><td>1.9%</td><td>13</td><td>Ohio</td><td>13,135</td><td>2.3%</td></tr>
<tr><td>15</td><td>Indiana</td><td>12,433</td><td>2.2%</td><td>14</td><td>Louisiana</td><td>12,562</td><td>2.2%</td></tr>
<tr><td>27</td><td>Iowa</td><td>7,130</td><td>1.2%</td><td>15</td><td>Indiana</td><td>12,433</td><td>2.2%</td></tr>
<tr><td>31</td><td>Kansas</td><td>6,837</td><td>1.2%</td><td>16</td><td>New Jersey</td><td>12,235</td><td>2.1%</td></tr>
<tr><td>30</td><td>Kentucky</td><td>6,878</td><td>1.2%</td><td>17</td><td>Alabama</td><td>12,171</td><td>2.1%</td></tr>
<tr><td>14</td><td>Louisiana</td><td>12,562</td><td>2.2%</td><td>18</td><td>Maryland</td><td>11,085</td><td>1.9%</td></tr>
<tr><td>42</td><td>Maine</td><td>2,766</td><td>0.5%</td><td>19</td><td>Illinois</td><td>10,912</td><td>1.9%</td></tr>
<tr><td>18</td><td>Maryland</td><td>11,085</td><td>1.9%</td><td>20</td><td>Wisconsin</td><td>10,818</td><td>1.9%</td></tr>
<tr><td>28</td><td>Massachusetts</td><td>7,097</td><td>1.2%</td><td>21</td><td>Utah</td><td>10,627</td><td>1.9%</td></tr>
<tr><td>29</td><td>Michigan</td><td>6,984</td><td>1.2%</td><td>22</td><td>Colorado</td><td>9,393</td><td>1.6%</td></tr>
<tr><td>23</td><td>Minnesota</td><td>9,255</td><td>1.6%</td><td>23</td><td>Minnesota</td><td>9,255</td><td>1.6%</td></tr>
<tr><td>33</td><td>Mississippi</td><td>6,665</td><td>1.2%</td><td>24</td><td>Oklahoma</td><td>8,845</td><td>1.5%</td></tr>
<tr><td>25</td><td>Missouri</td><td>8,346</td><td>1.5%</td><td>25</td><td>Missouri</td><td>8,346</td><td>1.5%</td></tr>
<tr><td>47</td><td>Montana</td><td>1,745</td><td>0.3%</td><td>26</td><td>Oregon</td><td>7,686</td><td>1.3%</td></tr>
<tr><td>36</td><td>Nebraska</td><td>5,180</td><td>0.9%</td><td>27</td><td>Iowa</td><td>7,130</td><td>1.2%</td></tr>
<tr><td>32</td><td>Nevada</td><td>6,752</td><td>1.2%</td><td>28</td><td>Massachusetts</td><td>7,097</td><td>1.2%</td></tr>
<tr><td>44</td><td>New Hampshire</td><td>2,224</td><td>0.4%</td><td>29</td><td>Michigan</td><td>6,984</td><td>1.2%</td></tr>
<tr><td>16</td><td>New Jersey</td><td>12,235</td><td>2.1%</td><td>30</td><td>Kentucky</td><td>6,878</td><td>1.2%</td></tr>
<tr><td>37</td><td>New Mexico</td><td>4,649</td><td>0.8%</td><td>31</td><td>Kansas</td><td>6,837</td><td>1.2%</td></tr>
<tr><td>7</td><td>New York</td><td>17,356</td><td>3.0%</td><td>32</td><td>Nevada</td><td>6,752</td><td>1.2%</td></tr>
<tr><td>4</td><td>North Carolina</td><td>33,785</td><td>5.9%</td><td>33</td><td>Mississippi</td><td>6,665</td><td>1.2%</td></tr>
<tr><td>41</td><td>North Dakota</td><td>3,065</td><td>0.5%</td><td>34</td><td>Arkansas</td><td>6,637</td><td>1.2%</td></tr>
<tr><td>13</td><td>Ohio</td><td>13,135</td><td>2.3%</td><td>35</td><td>Idaho</td><td>5,292</td><td>0.9%</td></tr>
<tr><td>24</td><td>Oklahoma</td><td>8,845</td><td>1.5%</td><td>36</td><td>Nebraska</td><td>5,180</td><td>0.9%</td></tr>
<tr><td>26</td><td>Oregon</td><td>7,686</td><td>1.3%</td><td>37</td><td>New Mexico</td><td>4,649</td><td>0.8%</td></tr>
<tr><td>6</td><td>Pennsylvania</td><td>18,712</td><td>3.3%</td><td>38</td><td>South Dakota</td><td>3,529</td><td>0.6%</td></tr>
<tr><td>49</td><td>Rhode Island</td><td>958</td><td>0.2%</td><td>39</td><td>Connecticut</td><td>3,343</td><td>0.6%</td></tr>
<tr><td>10</td><td>South Carolina</td><td>15,829</td><td>2.8%</td><td>40</td><td>Delaware</td><td>3,140</td><td>0.5%</td></tr>
<tr><td>38</td><td>South Dakota</td><td>3,529</td><td>0.6%</td><td>41</td><td>North Dakota</td><td>3,065</td><td>0.5%</td></tr>
<tr><td>11</td><td>Tennessee</td><td>14,574</td><td>2.5%</td><td>42</td><td>Maine</td><td>2,766</td><td>0.5%</td></tr>
<tr><td>1</td><td>Texas</td><td>82,938</td><td>14.5%</td><td>43</td><td>Hawaii</td><td>2,617</td><td>0.5%</td></tr>
<tr><td>21</td><td>Utah</td><td>10,627</td><td>1.9%</td><td>44</td><td>New Hampshire</td><td>2,224</td><td>0.4%</td></tr>
<tr><td>48</td><td>Vermont</td><td>1,209</td><td>0.2%</td><td>45</td><td>Wyoming</td><td>1,975</td><td>0.3%</td></tr>
<tr><td>5</td><td>Virginia</td><td>21,078</td><td>3.7%</td><td>46</td><td>West Virginia</td><td>1,966</td><td>0.3%</td></tr>
<tr><td>9</td><td>Washington</td><td>16,754</td><td>2.9%</td><td>47</td><td>Montana</td><td>1,745</td><td>0.3%</td></tr>
<tr><td>46</td><td>West Virginia</td><td>1,966</td><td>0.3%</td><td>48</td><td>Vermont</td><td>1,209</td><td>0.2%</td></tr>
<tr><td>20</td><td>Wisconsin</td><td>10,818</td><td>1.9%</td><td>49</td><td>Rhode Island</td><td>958</td><td>0.2%</td></tr>
<tr><td>45</td><td>Wyoming</td><td>1,975</td><td>0.3%</td><td>50</td><td>Alaska</td><td>912</td><td>0.2%</td></tr>
<tr><td></td><td></td><td></td><td></td><td></td><td>District of Columbia</td><td>1,148</td><td>0.2%</td></tr>
</table>

Source: U.S. Bureau of the Census
"New Privately Owned Housing Units Authorized" (http://www.census.gov/const/www/C40/table2.html)
*Preliminary and unadjusted year to date as of December 2009. Includes single and multifamily privately owned units. Based on approximately 19,000 places in the U.S. having building permit systems.

Value of New Housing Units Authorized in 2009

National Total = $94,516,031,000*

ALPHA ORDER

RANK	STATE	VALUE	% of USA
23	Alabama	$1,624,324,000	1.7%
48	Alaska	194,935,000	0.2%
9	Arizona	2,697,188,000	2.9%
36	Arkansas	778,594,000	0.8%
2	California	7,529,058,000	8.0%
12	Colorado	2,178,822,000	2.3%
39	Connecticut	637,743,000	0.7%
45	Delaware	359,528,000	0.4%
3	Florida	6,903,480,000	7.3%
11	Georgia	2,537,052,000	2.7%
35	Hawaii	779,010,000	0.8%
32	Idaho	848,081,000	0.9%
13	Illinois	2,174,791,000	2.3%
18	Indiana	1,963,669,000	2.1%
29	Iowa	1,123,915,000	1.2%
30	Kansas	884,954,000	0.9%
31	Kentucky	863,208,000	0.9%
19	Louisiana	1,863,527,000	2.0%
41	Maine	441,673,000	0.5%
16	Maryland	2,043,723,000	2.2%
25	Massachusetts	1,416,051,000	1.5%
28	Michigan	1,190,022,000	1.3%
22	Minnesota	1,656,107,000	1.8%
34	Mississippi	807,204,000	0.9%
27	Missouri	1,228,348,000	1.3%
47	Montana	258,312,000	0.3%
37	Nebraska	775,275,000	0.8%
33	Nevada	813,327,000	0.9%
42	New Hampshire	410,873,000	0.4%
15	New Jersey	2,068,397,000	2.2%
38	New Mexico	771,557,000	0.8%
8	New York	2,945,485,000	3.1%
4	North Carolina	4,935,616,000	5.2%
43	North Dakota	395,391,000	0.4%
14	Ohio	2,166,946,000	2.3%
26	Oklahoma	1,286,055,000	1.4%
24	Oregon	1,440,438,000	1.5%
7	Pennsylvania	3,006,142,000	3.2%
50	Rhode Island	161,443,000	0.2%
10	South Carolina	2,603,483,000	2.8%
40	South Dakota	451,296,000	0.5%
17	Tennessee	2,004,798,000	2.1%
1	Texas	12,408,061,000	13.1%
20	Utah	1,731,653,000	1.8%
49	Vermont	179,623,000	0.2%
6	Virginia	3,212,879,000	3.4%
5	Washington	3,263,934,000	3.5%
46	West Virginia	276,591,000	0.3%
21	Wisconsin	1,726,533,000	1.8%
44	Wyoming	362,516,000	0.4%

RANK ORDER

RANK	STATE	VALUE	% of USA
1	Texas	$12,408,061,000	13.1%
2	California	7,529,058,000	8.0%
3	Florida	6,903,480,000	7.3%
4	North Carolina	4,935,616,000	5.2%
5	Washington	3,263,934,000	3.5%
6	Virginia	3,212,879,000	3.4%
7	Pennsylvania	3,006,142,000	3.2%
8	New York	2,945,485,000	3.1%
9	Arizona	2,697,188,000	2.9%
10	South Carolina	2,603,483,000	2.8%
11	Georgia	2,537,052,000	2.7%
12	Colorado	2,178,822,000	2.3%
13	Illinois	2,174,791,000	2.3%
14	Ohio	2,166,946,000	2.3%
15	New Jersey	2,068,397,000	2.2%
16	Maryland	2,043,723,000	2.2%
17	Tennessee	2,004,798,000	2.1%
18	Indiana	1,963,669,000	2.1%
19	Louisiana	1,863,527,000	2.0%
20	Utah	1,731,653,000	1.8%
21	Wisconsin	1,726,533,000	1.8%
22	Minnesota	1,656,107,000	1.8%
23	Alabama	1,624,324,000	1.7%
24	Oregon	1,440,438,000	1.5%
25	Massachusetts	1,416,051,000	1.5%
26	Oklahoma	1,286,055,000	1.4%
27	Missouri	1,228,348,000	1.3%
28	Michigan	1,190,022,000	1.3%
29	Iowa	1,123,915,000	1.2%
30	Kansas	884,954,000	0.9%
31	Kentucky	863,208,000	0.9%
32	Idaho	848,081,000	0.9%
33	Nevada	813,327,000	0.9%
34	Mississippi	807,204,000	0.9%
35	Hawaii	779,010,000	0.8%
36	Arkansas	778,594,000	0.8%
37	Nebraska	775,275,000	0.8%
38	New Mexico	771,557,000	0.8%
39	Connecticut	637,743,000	0.7%
40	South Dakota	451,296,000	0.5%
41	Maine	441,673,000	0.5%
42	New Hampshire	410,873,000	0.4%
43	North Dakota	395,391,000	0.4%
44	Wyoming	362,516,000	0.4%
45	Delaware	359,528,000	0.4%
46	West Virginia	276,591,000	0.3%
47	Montana	258,312,000	0.3%
48	Alaska	194,935,000	0.2%
49	Vermont	179,623,000	0.2%
50	Rhode Island	161,443,000	0.2%
	District of Columbia	134,401,000	0.1%

Source: U.S. Bureau of the Census
"New Privately Owned Housing Units Authorized" (http://www.census.gov/const/www/C40/table2.html)
*Preliminary and unadjusted year to date as of December 2009. Includes single and multifamily privately owned units. Based on approximately 19,000 places in the U.S. having building permit systems.

Average Value of New Housing Units in 2009

National Average = $165,171 per Unit*

ALPHA ORDER				RANK ORDER		
RANK	STATE	VALUE		RANK	STATE	VALUE
42	Alabama	$133,459		1	Hawaii	$297,673
4	Alaska	213,745		2	Colorado	231,962
9	Arizona	190,830		3	California	222,681
49	Arkansas	117,311		4	Alaska	213,745
3	California	222,681		5	Massachusetts	199,528
2	Colorado	231,962		6	Illinois	199,303
10	Connecticut	190,770		7	Washington	194,815
50	Delaware	114,499		8	Florida	192,523
8	Florida	192,523		9	Arizona	190,830
36	Georgia	147,486		10	Connecticut	190,770
1	Hawaii	297,673		11	Oregon	187,411
25	Idaho	160,257		12	New Hampshire	184,745
6	Illinois	199,303		13	Maryland	184,368
28	Indiana	157,940		14	Wyoming	183,552
29	Iowa	157,632		15	Minnesota	178,942
43	Kansas	129,436		16	Michigan	170,393
46	Kentucky	125,503		17	New York	169,710
34	Louisiana	148,346		18	New Jersey	169,056
26	Maine	159,679		19	Rhode Island	168,521
13	Maryland	184,368		20	New Mexico	165,962
5	Massachusetts	199,528		21	Ohio	164,975
16	Michigan	170,393		22	South Carolina	164,476
15	Minnesota	178,942		23	Utah	162,948
47	Mississippi	121,111		24	Pennsylvania	160,653
37	Missouri	147,178		25	Idaho	160,257
35	Montana	148,030		26	Maine	159,679
31	Nebraska	149,667		27	Wisconsin	159,598
48	Nevada	120,457		28	Indiana	157,940
12	New Hampshire	184,745		29	Iowa	157,632
18	New Jersey	169,056		30	Virginia	152,428
20	New Mexico	165,962		31	Nebraska	149,667
17	New York	169,710		32	Texas	149,606
38	North Carolina	146,089		33	Vermont	148,572
44	North Dakota	129,002		34	Louisiana	148,346
21	Ohio	164,975		35	Montana	148,030
39	Oklahoma	145,399		36	Georgia	147,486
11	Oregon	187,411		37	Missouri	147,178
24	Pennsylvania	160,653		38	North Carolina	146,089
19	Rhode Island	168,521		39	Oklahoma	145,399
22	South Carolina	164,476		40	West Virginia	140,687
45	South Dakota	127,882		41	Tennessee	137,560
41	Tennessee	137,560		42	Alabama	133,459
32	Texas	149,606		43	Kansas	129,436
23	Utah	162,948		44	North Dakota	129,002
33	Vermont	148,572		45	South Dakota	127,882
30	Virginia	152,428		46	Kentucky	125,503
7	Washington	194,815		47	Mississippi	121,111
40	West Virginia	140,687		48	Nevada	120,457
27	Wisconsin	159,598		49	Arkansas	117,311
14	Wyoming	183,552		50	Delaware	114,499
					District of Columbia	117,074

Source: CQ Press using data from U.S. Bureau of the Census
   "New Privately Owned Housing Units Authorized" (http://www.census.gov/const/www/C40/table2.html)
*Preliminary and unadjusted year to date as of December 2009. Includes single and multifamily privately owned units. Based on approximately 19,000 places in the U.S. having building permit systems.

Median Value of Owner-Occupied Housing in 2008

National Median = $197,600*

ALPHA ORDER				RANK ORDER		
RANK	STATE	MEDIAN		RANK	STATE	MEDIAN
43	Alabama	$121,500		1	Hawaii	$560,200
16	Alaska	237,800		2	California	467,000
18	Arizona	229,200		3	New Jersey	364,100
47	Arkansas	105,700		4	Massachusetts	353,600
2	California	467,000		5	Maryland	341,200
15	Colorado	242,200		6	New York	318,900
8	Connecticut	306,000		7	Washington	308,100
14	Delaware	250,900		8	Connecticut	306,000
19	Florida	218,700		9	Rhode Island	286,000
28	Georgia	169,100		10	Oregon	273,300
1	Hawaii	560,200		11	Nevada	271,500
24	Idaho	183,700		12	Virginia	269,600
20	Illinois	214,900		13	New Hampshire	264,700
42	Indiana	125,200		14	Delaware	250,900
44	Iowa	120,700		15	Colorado	242,200
41	Kansas	125,700		16	Alaska	237,800
45	Kentucky	118,400		17	Utah	236,000
37	Louisiana	132,400		18	Arizona	229,200
26	Maine	180,200		19	Florida	218,700
5	Maryland	341,200		20	Illinois	214,900
4	Massachusetts	353,600		21	Vermont	214,700
32	Michigan	151,300		22	Minnesota	213,800
22	Minnesota	213,800		23	Wyoming	188,200
49	Mississippi	99,700		24	Idaho	183,700
33	Missouri	141,500		25	Montana	180,300
25	Montana	180,300		26	Maine	180,200
39	Nebraska	126,500		27	Wisconsin	173,300
11	Nevada	271,500		28	Georgia	169,100
13	New Hampshire	264,700		29	New Mexico	165,100
3	New Jersey	364,100		30	Pennsylvania	164,700
29	New Mexico	165,100		31	North Carolina	154,500
6	New York	318,900		32	Michigan	151,300
31	North Carolina	154,500		33	Missouri	141,500
46	North Dakota	112,500		34	Ohio	140,200
34	Ohio	140,200		35	South Carolina	138,700
48	Oklahoma	105,500		36	Tennessee	138,600
10	Oregon	273,300		37	Louisiana	132,400
30	Pennsylvania	164,700		38	Texas	126,800
9	Rhode Island	286,000		39	Nebraska	126,500
35	South Carolina	138,700		40	South Dakota	126,200
40	South Dakota	126,200		41	Kansas	125,700
36	Tennessee	138,600		42	Indiana	125,200
38	Texas	126,800		43	Alabama	121,500
17	Utah	236,000		44	Iowa	120,700
21	Vermont	214,700		45	Kentucky	118,400
12	Virginia	269,600		46	North Dakota	112,500
7	Washington	308,100		47	Arkansas	105,700
50	West Virginia	95,900		48	Oklahoma	105,500
27	Wisconsin	173,300		49	Mississippi	99,700
23	Wyoming	188,200		50	West Virginia	95,900
					District of Columbia	474,100

Source: U.S. Bureau of the Census
  "2008 American Community Survey" (http://www.census.gov/acs/www/index.html)
*Housing units with a mortgage.

Percent Change in House Prices: 2008 to 2009

National Percent Change = 3.8% Decrease*

ALPHA ORDER				RANK ORDER		
RANK	STATE	PERCENT CHANGE		RANK	STATE	PERCENT CHANGE
23	Alabama	(2.4)		1	Nebraska	2.6
27	Alaska	(2.9)		2	Vermont	2.2
49	Arizona	(17.1)		3	Kansas	1.6
24	Arkansas	(2.5)		4	Iowa	1.3
43	California	(7.7)		4	Oklahoma	1.3
8	Colorado	0.0		6	Mississippi	0.3
36	Connecticut	(4.6)		7	North Dakota	0.1
37	Delaware	(4.7)		8	Colorado	0.0
48	Florida	(13.4)		8	Texas	0.0
30	Georgia	(3.3)		10	South Dakota	(0.5)
42	Hawaii	(7.6)		11	South Carolina	(0.7)
44	Idaho	(8.7)		11	West Virginia	(0.7)
33	Illinois	(4.1)		13	Louisiana	(0.9)
19	Indiana	(2.2)		14	Kentucky	(1.0)
4	Iowa	1.3		15	North Carolina	(1.4)
3	Kansas	1.6		16	Massachusetts	(1.5)
14	Kentucky	(1.0)		17	Ohio	(2.0)
13	Louisiana	(0.9)		18	Missouri	(2.1)
25	Maine	(2.7)		19	Indiana	(2.2)
40	Maryland	(5.4)		19	Tennessee	(2.2)
16	Massachusetts	(1.5)		21	Pennsylvania	(2.3)
34	Michigan	(4.2)		21	Wisconsin	(2.3)
34	Minnesota	(4.2)		23	Alabama	(2.4)
6	Mississippi	0.3		24	Arkansas	(2.5)
18	Missouri	(2.1)		25	Maine	(2.7)
31	Montana	(3.6)		26	New York	(2.8)
1	Nebraska	2.6		27	Alaska	(2.9)
50	Nevada	(24.5)		28	Rhode Island	(3.0)
29	New Hampshire	(3.1)		29	New Hampshire	(3.1)
39	New Jersey	(4.9)		30	Georgia	(3.3)
40	New Mexico	(5.4)		31	Montana	(3.6)
26	New York	(2.8)		32	Virginia	(3.7)
15	North Carolina	(1.4)		33	Illinois	(4.1)
7	North Dakota	0.1		34	Michigan	(4.2)
17	Ohio	(2.0)		34	Minnesota	(4.2)
4	Oklahoma	1.3		36	Connecticut	(4.6)
46	Oregon	(8.8)		37	Delaware	(4.7)
21	Pennsylvania	(2.3)		37	Wyoming	(4.7)
28	Rhode Island	(3.0)		39	New Jersey	(4.9)
11	South Carolina	(0.7)		40	Maryland	(5.4)
10	South Dakota	(0.5)		40	New Mexico	(5.4)
19	Tennessee	(2.2)		42	Hawaii	(7.6)
8	Texas	0.0		43	California	(7.7)
47	Utah	(10.5)		44	Idaho	(8.7)
2	Vermont	2.2		44	Washington	(8.7)
32	Virginia	(3.7)		46	Oregon	(8.8)
44	Washington	(8.7)		47	Utah	(10.5)
11	West Virginia	(0.7)		48	Florida	(13.4)
21	Wisconsin	(2.3)		49	Arizona	(17.1)
37	Wyoming	(4.7)		50	Nevada	(24.5)
				District of Columbia		(1.0)

Source: Federal Housing Finance Agency
"House Price Index" (http://www.fhfa.gov/Default.aspx?Page=14)
*Single-family house prices. As of September 30, 2009.

Percent Change in House Prices: 2005 to 2009

National Percent Change = 4.6% Increase*

ALPHA ORDER				RANK ORDER		
RANK	STATE	PERCENT CHANGE		RANK	STATE	PERCENT CHANGE
19	Alabama	16.1		1	Wyoming	30.7
12	Alaska	19.4		2	Montana	27.5
43	Arizona	(5.6)		3	New Mexico	23.9
30	Arkansas	8.7		3	Utah	23.9
49	California	(25.1)		5	North Dakota	23.8
31	Colorado	6.9		6	Louisiana	21.9
38	Connecticut	2.4		7	Washington	21.7
25	Delaware	10.7		8	Idaho	21.3
47	Florida	(13.7)		9	Vermont	20.7
39	Georgia	2.3		10	Oklahoma	20.5
15	Hawaii	16.6		11	Oregon	20.3
8	Idaho	21.3		12	Alaska	19.4
37	Illinois	3.3		13	Texas	19.1
40	Indiana	1.5		14	North Carolina	18.8
28	Iowa	9.7		15	Hawaii	16.6
23	Kansas	12.1		15	South Carolina	16.6
29	Kentucky	9.2		17	South Dakota	16.3
6	Louisiana	21.9		18	Pennsylvania	16.2
32	Maine	6.7		19	Alabama	16.1
27	Maryland	9.9		19	Mississippi	16.1
45	Massachusetts	(7.1)		21	West Virginia	14.1
48	Michigan	(21.8)		22	Tennessee	13.7
44	Minnesota	(6.5)		23	Kansas	12.1
19	Mississippi	16.1		24	Virginia	11.3
34	Missouri	5.6		25	Delaware	10.7
2	Montana	27.5		26	New York	10.5
35	Nebraska	4.9		27	Maryland	9.9
50	Nevada	(36.4)		28	Iowa	9.7
42	New Hampshire	(4.9)		29	Kentucky	9.2
33	New Jersey	5.9		30	Arkansas	8.7
3	New Mexico	23.9		31	Colorado	6.9
26	New York	10.5		32	Maine	6.7
14	North Carolina	18.8		33	New Jersey	5.9
5	North Dakota	23.8		34	Missouri	5.6
41	Ohio	(4.5)		35	Nebraska	4.9
10	Oklahoma	20.5		36	Wisconsin	4.1
11	Oregon	20.3		37	Illinois	3.3
18	Pennsylvania	16.2		38	Connecticut	2.4
46	Rhode Island	(9.4)		39	Georgia	2.3
15	South Carolina	16.6		40	Indiana	1.5
17	South Dakota	16.3		41	Ohio	(4.5)
22	Tennessee	13.7		42	New Hampshire	(4.9)
13	Texas	19.1		43	Arizona	(5.6)
3	Utah	23.9		44	Minnesota	(6.5)
9	Vermont	20.7		45	Massachusetts	(7.1)
24	Virginia	11.3		46	Rhode Island	(9.4)
7	Washington	21.7		47	Florida	(13.7)
21	West Virginia	14.1		48	Michigan	(21.8)
36	Wisconsin	4.1		49	California	(25.1)
1	Wyoming	30.7		50	Nevada	(36.4)
				District of Columbia		26.0

Source: Federal Housing Finance Agency
   "House Price Index" (http://www.fhfa.gov/Default.aspx?Page=14)
*Single-family house prices. As of September 30, 2009.

Existing Home Sales in 2009

National Total = 5,300,000 Homes*

ALPHA ORDER

RANK	STATE	HOMES	% of USA
24	Alabama	75,200	1.4%
43	Alaska	18,800	0.4%
10	Arizona	153,200	2.9%
29	Arkansas	60,800	1.1%
1	California	517,200	9.8%
19	Colorado	92,800	1.8%
33	Connecticut	46,800	0.9%
48	Delaware	13,200	0.2%
3	Florida	353,600	6.7%
8	Georgia	174,000	3.3%
42	Hawaii	19,200	0.4%
39	Idaho	26,400	0.5%
6	Illinois	187,600	3.5%
17	Indiana	104,000	2.0%
28	Iowa	61,600	1.2%
30	Kansas	59,200	1.1%
26	Kentucky	74,400	1.4%
31	Louisiana	58,400	1.1%
40	Maine	22,800	0.4%
24	Maryland	75,200	1.4%
15	Massachusetts	108,800	2.1%
9	Michigan	169,200	3.2%
21	Minnesota	90,000	1.7%
34	Mississippi	44,800	0.8%
14	Missouri	110,800	2.1%
40	Montana	22,800	0.4%
35	Nebraska	35,600	0.7%
18	Nevada	98,400	1.9%
43	New Hampshire	18,800	0.4%
12	New Jersey	122,800	2.3%
36	New Mexico	33,200	0.6%
4	New York	268,400	5.1%
11	North Carolina	146,800	2.8%
47	North Dakota	14,800	0.3%
5	Ohio	251,600	4.7%
22	Oklahoma	87,200	1.6%
32	Oregon	56,400	1.1%
7	Pennsylvania	184,400	3.5%
46	Rhode Island	17,200	0.3%
27	South Carolina	74,000	1.4%
45	South Dakota	18,400	0.3%
16	Tennessee	107,600	2.0%
2	Texas	455,200	8.6%
37	Utah	30,800	0.6%
49	Vermont	11,200	0.2%
13	Virginia	120,000	2.3%
23	Washington	85,200	1.6%
38	West Virginia	29,200	0.6%
20	Wisconsin	90,600	1.7%
50	Wyoming	8,800	0.2%

RANK ORDER

RANK	STATE	HOMES	% of USA
1	California	517,200	9.8%
2	Texas	455,200	8.6%
3	Florida	353,600	6.7%
4	New York	268,400	5.1%
5	Ohio	251,600	4.7%
6	Illinois	187,600	3.5%
7	Pennsylvania	184,400	3.5%
8	Georgia	174,000	3.3%
9	Michigan	169,200	3.2%
10	Arizona	153,200	2.9%
11	North Carolina	146,800	2.8%
12	New Jersey	122,800	2.3%
13	Virginia	120,000	2.3%
14	Missouri	110,800	2.1%
15	Massachusetts	108,800	2.1%
16	Tennessee	107,600	2.0%
17	Indiana	104,000	2.0%
18	Nevada	98,400	1.9%
19	Colorado	92,800	1.8%
20	Wisconsin	90,600	1.7%
21	Minnesota	90,000	1.7%
22	Oklahoma	87,200	1.6%
23	Washington	85,200	1.6%
24	Alabama	75,200	1.4%
24	Maryland	75,200	1.4%
26	Kentucky	74,400	1.4%
27	South Carolina	74,000	1.4%
28	Iowa	61,600	1.2%
29	Arkansas	60,800	1.1%
30	Kansas	59,200	1.1%
31	Louisiana	58,400	1.1%
32	Oregon	56,400	1.1%
33	Connecticut	46,800	0.9%
34	Mississippi	44,800	0.8%
35	Nebraska	35,600	0.7%
36	New Mexico	33,200	0.6%
37	Utah	30,800	0.6%
38	West Virginia	29,200	0.6%
39	Idaho	26,400	0.5%
40	Maine	22,800	0.4%
40	Montana	22,800	0.4%
42	Hawaii	19,200	0.4%
43	Alaska	18,800	0.4%
43	New Hampshire	18,800	0.4%
45	South Dakota	18,400	0.3%
46	Rhode Island	17,200	0.3%
47	North Dakota	14,800	0.3%
48	Delaware	13,200	0.2%
49	Vermont	11,200	0.2%
50	Wyoming	8,800	0.2%
	District of Columbia	9,200	0.2%

Source: National Association of Realtors®, Economics and Research Division
    "Existing Home Sales" (http://www.realtor.org/research/research/metroprice)
*Seasonally adjusted preliminary data as of September 2009. Includes existing houses, apartment condos, and co-ops. Excludes new construction.

Percent Change in Existing Home Sales: 2008 to 2009

National Percent Change = 5.9% Increase*

ALPHA ORDER				RANK ORDER		
RANK	STATE	PERCENT CHANGE		RANK	STATE	PERCENT CHANGE
48	Alabama	(9.6)		1	Florida	36.8
46	Alaska	(7.8)		2	Nevada	36.7
16	Arizona	10.4		3	Idaho	31.3
33	Arkansas	0.0		4	Rhode Island	22.9
26	California	3.9		5	Nebraska	20.3
50	Colorado	(14.1)		6	North Dakota	19.4
24	Connecticut	4.5		7	Delaware	17.9
7	Delaware	17.9		8	Maryland	15.3
1	Florida	36.8		9	West Virginia	14.1
32	Georgia	1.2		10	Montana	14.0
44	Hawaii	(5.9)		11	South Dakota	12.2
3	Idaho	31.3		12	Vermont	12.0
31	Illinois	1.7		13	Maine	11.8
49	Indiana	(10.7)		14	Ohio	11.7
18	Iowa	7.7		15	Michigan	11.0
39	Kansas	(3.3)		16	Arizona	10.4
20	Kentucky	6.3		17	New Jersey	8.5
28	Louisiana	3.5		18	Iowa	7.7
13	Maine	11.8		19	Oregon	6.8
8	Maryland	15.3		20	Kentucky	6.3
34	Massachusetts	(1.1)		21	Wisconsin	5.8
15	Michigan	11.0		22	Pennsylvania	5.7
42	Minnesota	(4.7)		23	New York	4.7
47	Mississippi	(8.2)		24	Connecticut	4.5
30	Missouri	1.8		25	New Hampshire	4.4
10	Montana	14.0		26	California	3.9
5	Nebraska	20.3		27	New Mexico	3.8
2	Nevada	36.7		28	Louisiana	3.5
25	New Hampshire	4.4		29	Washington	1.9
17	New Jersey	8.5		30	Missouri	1.8
27	New Mexico	3.8		31	Illinois	1.7
23	New York	4.7		32	Georgia	1.2
41	North Carolina	(4.4)		33	Arkansas	0.0
6	North Dakota	19.4		34	Massachusetts	(1.1)
14	Ohio	11.7		35	Utah	(1.3)
36	Oklahoma	(1.8)		36	Oklahoma	(1.8)
19	Oregon	6.8		37	Texas	(1.9)
22	Pennsylvania	5.7		38	Virginia	(2.3)
4	Rhode Island	22.9		39	Kansas	(3.3)
45	South Carolina	(7.5)		40	Wyoming	(4.3)
11	South Dakota	12.2		41	North Carolina	(4.4)
43	Tennessee	(5.3)		42	Minnesota	(4.7)
37	Texas	(1.9)		43	Tennessee	(5.3)
35	Utah	(1.3)		44	Hawaii	(5.9)
12	Vermont	12.0		45	South Carolina	(7.5)
38	Virginia	(2.3)		46	Alaska	(7.8)
29	Washington	1.9		47	Mississippi	(8.2)
9	West Virginia	14.1		48	Alabama	(9.6)
21	Wisconsin	5.8		49	Indiana	(10.7)
40	Wyoming	(4.3)		50	Colorado	(14.1)

District of Columbia   27.8

Source: National Association of Realtors®, Economics and Research Division
   "Existing Home Sales" (http://www.realtor.org/research/research/metroprice)
*Seasonally adjusted preliminary data as of September 2009. Includes existing houses, apartment condos, and co-ops. Excludes new construction.

Median Monthly Mortgage Payment in 2008

National Median = $1,514*

<table>
<tr><td colspan="3"><u>ALPHA ORDER</u></td><td colspan="3"><u>RANK ORDER</u></td></tr>
<tr><th>RANK</th><th>STATE</th><th>MORTGAGE</th><th>RANK</th><th>STATE</th><th>MORTGAGE</th></tr>
<tr><td>45</td><td>Alabama</td><td>$1,089</td><td>1</td><td>California</td><td>$2,384</td></tr>
<tr><td>12</td><td>Alaska</td><td>1,732</td><td>2</td><td>New Jersey</td><td>2,360</td></tr>
<tr><td>20</td><td>Arizona</td><td>1,527</td><td>3</td><td>Hawaii</td><td>2,265</td></tr>
<tr><td>49</td><td>Arkansas</td><td>964</td><td>4</td><td>Connecticut</td><td>2,108</td></tr>
<tr><td>1</td><td>California</td><td>2,384</td><td>5</td><td>Massachusetts</td><td>2,105</td></tr>
<tr><td>15</td><td>Colorado</td><td>1,620</td><td>6</td><td>Maryland</td><td>1,983</td></tr>
<tr><td>4</td><td>Connecticut</td><td>2,108</td><td>7</td><td>New York</td><td>1,936</td></tr>
<tr><td>18</td><td>Delaware</td><td>1,580</td><td>8</td><td>New Hampshire</td><td>1,900</td></tr>
<tr><td>16</td><td>Florida</td><td>1,603</td><td>9</td><td>Rhode Island</td><td>1,888</td></tr>
<tr><td>25</td><td>Georgia</td><td>1,387</td><td>10</td><td>Nevada</td><td>1,818</td></tr>
<tr><td>3</td><td>Hawaii</td><td>2,265</td><td>11</td><td>Washington</td><td>1,763</td></tr>
<tr><td>35</td><td>Idaho</td><td>1,198</td><td>12</td><td>Alaska</td><td>1,732</td></tr>
<tr><td>14</td><td>Illinois</td><td>1,684</td><td>13</td><td>Virginia</td><td>1,715</td></tr>
<tr><td>40</td><td>Indiana</td><td>1,144</td><td>14</td><td>Illinois</td><td>1,684</td></tr>
<tr><td>43</td><td>Iowa</td><td>1,131</td><td>15</td><td>Colorado</td><td>1,620</td></tr>
<tr><td>34</td><td>Kansas</td><td>1,212</td><td>16</td><td>Florida</td><td>1,603</td></tr>
<tr><td>47</td><td>Kentucky</td><td>1,055</td><td>17</td><td>Oregon</td><td>1,585</td></tr>
<tr><td>44</td><td>Louisiana</td><td>1,111</td><td>18</td><td>Delaware</td><td>1,580</td></tr>
<tr><td>28</td><td>Maine</td><td>1,326</td><td>19</td><td>Minnesota</td><td>1,545</td></tr>
<tr><td>6</td><td>Maryland</td><td>1,983</td><td>20</td><td>Arizona</td><td>1,527</td></tr>
<tr><td>5</td><td>Massachusetts</td><td>2,105</td><td>21</td><td>Vermont</td><td>1,471</td></tr>
<tr><td>27</td><td>Michigan</td><td>1,351</td><td>22</td><td>Utah</td><td>1,445</td></tr>
<tr><td>19</td><td>Minnesota</td><td>1,545</td><td>23</td><td>Wisconsin</td><td>1,424</td></tr>
<tr><td>48</td><td>Mississippi</td><td>1,014</td><td>24</td><td>Pennsylvania</td><td>1,389</td></tr>
<tr><td>36</td><td>Missouri</td><td>1,180</td><td>25</td><td>Georgia</td><td>1,387</td></tr>
<tr><td>31</td><td>Montana</td><td>1,239</td><td>26</td><td>Texas</td><td>1,380</td></tr>
<tr><td>32</td><td>Nebraska</td><td>1,235</td><td>27</td><td>Michigan</td><td>1,351</td></tr>
<tr><td>10</td><td>Nevada</td><td>1,818</td><td>28</td><td>Maine</td><td>1,326</td></tr>
<tr><td>8</td><td>New Hampshire</td><td>1,900</td><td>29</td><td>Ohio</td><td>1,275</td></tr>
<tr><td>2</td><td>New Jersey</td><td>2,360</td><td>30</td><td>Wyoming</td><td>1,272</td></tr>
<tr><td>38</td><td>New Mexico</td><td>1,173</td><td>31</td><td>Montana</td><td>1,239</td></tr>
<tr><td>7</td><td>New York</td><td>1,936</td><td>32</td><td>Nebraska</td><td>1,235</td></tr>
<tr><td>33</td><td>North Carolina</td><td>1,218</td><td>33</td><td>North Carolina</td><td>1,218</td></tr>
<tr><td>42</td><td>North Dakota</td><td>1,140</td><td>34</td><td>Kansas</td><td>1,212</td></tr>
<tr><td>29</td><td>Ohio</td><td>1,275</td><td>35</td><td>Idaho</td><td>1,198</td></tr>
<tr><td>46</td><td>Oklahoma</td><td>1,064</td><td>36</td><td>Missouri</td><td>1,180</td></tr>
<tr><td>17</td><td>Oregon</td><td>1,585</td><td>37</td><td>South Dakota</td><td>1,174</td></tr>
<tr><td>24</td><td>Pennsylvania</td><td>1,389</td><td>38</td><td>New Mexico</td><td>1,173</td></tr>
<tr><td>9</td><td>Rhode Island</td><td>1,888</td><td>39</td><td>Tennessee</td><td>1,149</td></tr>
<tr><td>41</td><td>South Carolina</td><td>1,142</td><td>40</td><td>Indiana</td><td>1,144</td></tr>
<tr><td>37</td><td>South Dakota</td><td>1,174</td><td>41</td><td>South Carolina</td><td>1,142</td></tr>
<tr><td>39</td><td>Tennessee</td><td>1,149</td><td>42</td><td>North Dakota</td><td>1,140</td></tr>
<tr><td>26</td><td>Texas</td><td>1,380</td><td>43</td><td>Iowa</td><td>1,131</td></tr>
<tr><td>22</td><td>Utah</td><td>1,445</td><td>44</td><td>Louisiana</td><td>1,111</td></tr>
<tr><td>21</td><td>Vermont</td><td>1,471</td><td>45</td><td>Alabama</td><td>1,089</td></tr>
<tr><td>13</td><td>Virginia</td><td>1,715</td><td>46</td><td>Oklahoma</td><td>1,064</td></tr>
<tr><td>11</td><td>Washington</td><td>1,763</td><td>47</td><td>Kentucky</td><td>1,055</td></tr>
<tr><td>50</td><td>West Virginia</td><td>878</td><td>48</td><td>Mississippi</td><td>1,014</td></tr>
<tr><td>23</td><td>Wisconsin</td><td>1,424</td><td>49</td><td>Arkansas</td><td>964</td></tr>
<tr><td>30</td><td>Wyoming</td><td>1,272</td><td>50</td><td>West Virginia</td><td>878</td></tr>
<tr><td></td><td></td><td></td><td></td><td>District of Columbia</td><td>2,218</td></tr>
</table>

Source: U.S. Bureau of the Census
   "2008 American Community Survey" (http://www.census.gov/acs/www/index.html)
*For owner-occupied housing.

Percent of Home Owners Spending 30% or More of Household Income on Housing Costs: 2008
National Percent = 37.6% of Home Owners*

ALPHA ORDER

RANK	STATE	PERCENT
37	Alabama	28.8
30	Alaska	32.5
10	Arizona	41.3
43	Arkansas	27.5
1	California	53.3
18	Colorado	36.9
13	Connecticut	40.9
19	Delaware	36.5
3	Florida	49.1
26	Georgia	34.0
2	Hawaii	49.3
27	Idaho	33.8
16	Illinois	38.6
40	Indiana	28.1
49	Iowa	24.3
48	Kansas	25.1
42	Kentucky	27.7
38	Louisiana	28.6
17	Maine	37.1
14	Maryland	39.2
7	Massachusetts	41.9
20	Michigan	35.8
23	Minnesota	34.4
35	Mississippi	30.8
39	Missouri	28.4
28	Montana	33.5
45	Nebraska	26.6
4	Nevada	48.9
11	New Hampshire	41.1
5	New Jersey	46.3
23	New Mexico	34.4
11	New York	41.1
31	North Carolina	31.6
50	North Dakota	23.1
36	Ohio	30.7
46	Oklahoma	26.5
8	Oregon	41.4
29	Pennsylvania	33.1
6	Rhode Island	42.2
34	South Carolina	30.9
41	South Dakota	27.8
33	Tennessee	31.1
32	Texas	31.3
22	Utah	35.1
15	Vermont	38.8
21	Virginia	35.5
8	Washington	41.4
47	West Virginia	25.4
25	Wisconsin	34.1
44	Wyoming	27.0

RANK ORDER

RANK	STATE	PERCENT
1	California	53.3
2	Hawaii	49.3
3	Florida	49.1
4	Nevada	48.9
5	New Jersey	46.3
6	Rhode Island	42.2
7	Massachusetts	41.9
8	Oregon	41.4
8	Washington	41.4
10	Arizona	41.3
11	New Hampshire	41.1
11	New York	41.1
13	Connecticut	40.9
14	Maryland	39.2
15	Vermont	38.8
16	Illinois	38.6
17	Maine	37.1
18	Colorado	36.9
19	Delaware	36.5
20	Michigan	35.8
21	Virginia	35.5
22	Utah	35.1
23	Minnesota	34.4
23	New Mexico	34.4
25	Wisconsin	34.1
26	Georgia	34.0
27	Idaho	33.8
28	Montana	33.5
29	Pennsylvania	33.1
30	Alaska	32.5
31	North Carolina	31.6
32	Texas	31.3
33	Tennessee	31.1
34	South Carolina	30.9
35	Mississippi	30.8
36	Ohio	30.7
37	Alabama	28.8
38	Louisiana	28.6
39	Missouri	28.4
40	Indiana	28.1
41	South Dakota	27.8
42	Kentucky	27.7
43	Arkansas	27.5
44	Wyoming	27.0
45	Nebraska	26.6
46	Oklahoma	26.5
47	West Virginia	25.4
48	Kansas	25.1
49	Iowa	24.3
50	North Dakota	23.1
	District of Columbia	37.5

Source: U.S. Bureau of the Census
"2008 American Community Survey" (http://www.census.gov/acs/www/index.html)
*For owner-occupied housing units with a mortgage.

Homeownership Rate in 2008

National Rate = 67.8%*

ALPHA ORDER			RANK ORDER		
RANK	STATE	RATE	RANK	STATE	RATE
15	Alabama	73.0	1	West Virginia	77.8
41	Alaska	66.4	2	Delaware	76.2
33	Arizona	69.1	2	Utah	76.2
35	Arkansas	68.9	4	Michigan	75.9
49	California	57.5	5	Mississippi	75.4
34	Colorado	69.0	6	Idaho	75.0
23	Connecticut	70.7	6	New Hampshire	75.0
2	Delaware	76.2	8	Indiana	74.4
21	Florida	71.1	9	Iowa	74.0
38	Georgia	68.2	10	Maine	73.9
48	Hawaii	59.1	10	South Carolina	73.9
6	Idaho	75.0	12	Louisiana	73.5
35	Illinois	68.9	13	Wyoming	73.3
8	Indiana	74.4	14	Minnesota	73.1
9	Iowa	74.0	15	Alabama	73.0
37	Kansas	68.8	16	Kentucky	72.8
16	Kentucky	72.8	16	Vermont	72.8
12	Louisiana	73.5	18	Pennsylvania	72.6
10	Maine	73.9	19	Tennessee	71.7
24	Maryland	70.6	20	Missouri	71.4
44	Massachusetts	65.7	21	Florida	71.1
4	Michigan	75.9	22	Ohio	70.8
14	Minnesota	73.1	23	Connecticut	70.7
5	Mississippi	75.4	24	Maryland	70.6
20	Missouri	71.4	24	Virginia	70.6
30	Montana	70.3	26	New Mexico	70.4
31	Nebraska	69.6	26	Oklahoma	70.4
47	Nevada	63.6	26	South Dakota	70.4
6	New Hampshire	75.0	26	Wisconsin	70.4
39	New Jersey	67.3	30	Montana	70.3
26	New Mexico	70.4	31	Nebraska	69.6
50	New York	55.0	32	North Carolina	69.4
32	North Carolina	69.4	33	Arizona	69.1
40	North Dakota	66.6	34	Colorado	69.0
22	Ohio	70.8	35	Arkansas	68.9
26	Oklahoma	70.4	35	Illinois	68.9
42	Oregon	66.2	37	Kansas	68.8
18	Pennsylvania	72.6	38	Georgia	68.2
46	Rhode Island	64.5	39	New Jersey	67.3
10	South Carolina	73.9	40	North Dakota	66.6
26	South Dakota	70.4	41	Alaska	66.4
19	Tennessee	71.7	42	Oregon	66.2
45	Texas	65.5	42	Washington	66.2
2	Utah	76.2	44	Massachusetts	65.7
16	Vermont	72.8	45	Texas	65.5
24	Virginia	70.6	46	Rhode Island	64.5
42	Washington	66.2	47	Nevada	63.6
1	West Virginia	77.8	48	Hawaii	59.1
26	Wisconsin	70.4	49	California	57.5
13	Wyoming	73.3	50	New York	55.0
				District of Columbia	44.1

Source: U.S. Bureau of the Census
  "Housing Vacancies and Homeownership, Annual Statistics: 2008"
  (http://www.census.gov/hhes/www/housing/hvs/annual08/ann08ind.html)
*Percent of households occupied by the owner.

Properties With Foreclosure Filings in 2010

National Total = 2,824,674 Properties*

ALPHA ORDER

RANK	STATE	PROPERTIES	% of USA
27	Alabama	19,896	0.7%
43	Alaska	2,442	0.1%
3	Arizona	163,210	5.8%
30	Arkansas	16,547	0.6%
1	California	632,573	22.4%
12	Colorado	50,514	1.8%
28	Connecticut	19,679	0.7%
42	Delaware	3,034	0.1%
2	Florida	516,711	18.3%
7	Georgia	106,110	3.8%
35	Hawaii	9,002	0.3%
29	Idaho	17,161	0.6%
4	Illinois	131,132	4.6%
16	Indiana	41,405	1.5%
38	Iowa	5,681	0.2%
34	Kansas	9,056	0.3%
33	Kentucky	9,682	0.3%
32	Louisiana	11,750	0.4%
41	Maine	3,178	0.1%
15	Maryland	43,248	1.5%
18	Massachusetts	36,119	1.3%
5	Michigan	118,302	4.2%
22	Minnesota	31,697	1.1%
39	Mississippi	5,402	0.2%
23	Missouri	28,519	1.0%
46	Montana	1,373	0.0%
44	Nebraska	1,845	0.1%
6	Nevada	112,097	4.0%
37	New Hampshire	7,210	0.3%
10	New Jersey	63,208	2.2%
36	New Mexico	7,212	0.3%
13	New York	50,369	1.8%
24	North Carolina	28,384	1.0%
49	North Dakota	390	0.0%
8	Ohio	101,614	3.6%
31	Oklahoma	12,937	0.5%
21	Oregon	34,121	1.2%
14	Pennsylvania	44,732	1.6%
40	Rhode Island	5,065	0.2%
26	South Carolina	25,163	0.9%
47	South Dakota	765	0.0%
17	Tennessee	40,733	1.4%
9	Texas	100,045	3.5%
25	Utah	27,140	1.0%
50	Vermont	143	0.0%
11	Virginia	52,127	1.8%
19	Washington	35,268	1.2%
45	West Virginia	1,479	0.1%
20	Wisconsin	35,252	1.2%
48	Wyoming	717	0.0%

RANK ORDER

RANK	STATE	PROPERTIES	% of USA
1	California	632,573	22.4%
2	Florida	516,711	18.3%
3	Arizona	163,210	5.8%
4	Illinois	131,132	4.6%
5	Michigan	118,302	4.2%
6	Nevada	112,097	4.0%
7	Georgia	106,110	3.8%
8	Ohio	101,614	3.6%
9	Texas	100,045	3.5%
10	New Jersey	63,208	2.2%
11	Virginia	52,127	1.8%
12	Colorado	50,514	1.8%
13	New York	50,369	1.8%
14	Pennsylvania	44,732	1.6%
15	Maryland	43,248	1.5%
16	Indiana	41,405	1.5%
17	Tennessee	40,733	1.4%
18	Massachusetts	36,119	1.3%
19	Washington	35,268	1.2%
20	Wisconsin	35,252	1.2%
21	Oregon	34,121	1.2%
22	Minnesota	31,697	1.1%
23	Missouri	28,519	1.0%
24	North Carolina	28,384	1.0%
25	Utah	27,140	1.0%
26	South Carolina	25,163	0.9%
27	Alabama	19,896	0.7%
28	Connecticut	19,679	0.7%
29	Idaho	17,161	0.6%
30	Arkansas	16,547	0.6%
31	Oklahoma	12,937	0.5%
32	Louisiana	11,750	0.4%
33	Kentucky	9,682	0.3%
34	Kansas	9,056	0.3%
35	Hawaii	9,002	0.3%
36	New Mexico	7,212	0.3%
37	New Hampshire	7,210	0.3%
38	Iowa	5,681	0.2%
39	Mississippi	5,402	0.2%
40	Rhode Island	5,065	0.2%
41	Maine	3,178	0.1%
42	Delaware	3,034	0.1%
43	Alaska	2,442	0.1%
44	Nebraska	1,845	0.1%
45	West Virginia	1,479	0.1%
46	Montana	1,373	0.0%
47	South Dakota	765	0.0%
48	Wyoming	717	0.0%
49	North Dakota	390	0.0%
50	Vermont	143	0.0%
	District of Columbia	3,235	0.1%

Source: RealtyTrac

"Record 2.8 Million U.S. Properties with Foreclosure Filings in 2009" (Press Release, January 14, 2010, www.realtytrac.com)
*Foreclosure filings include foreclosure-related documents filed in all phases of foreclosure.

Percent of Housing Units Receiving Foreclosure Filings in 2009

National Rate = 2.2% of Housing Units*

ALPHA ORDER

RANK	STATE	PERCENT
30	Alabama	0.9
30	Alaska	0.9
2	Arizona	6.1
22	Arkansas	1.3
4	California	4.8
10	Colorado	2.4
19	Connecticut	1.4
32	Delaware	0.8
3	Florida	5.9
6	Georgia	2.7
14	Hawaii	1.8
6	Idaho	2.7
9	Illinois	2.5
17	Indiana	1.5
42	Iowa	0.4
36	Kansas	0.7
40	Kentucky	0.5
38	Louisiana	0.6
40	Maine	0.5
13	Maryland	1.9
22	Massachusetts	1.3
8	Michigan	2.6
19	Minnesota	1.4
42	Mississippi	0.4
27	Missouri	1.1
44	Montana	0.3
46	Nebraska	0.2
1	Nevada	10.2
25	New Hampshire	1.2
14	New Jersey	1.8
32	New Mexico	0.8
38	New York	0.6
36	North Carolina	0.7
49	North Dakota	0.1
12	Ohio	2.0
32	Oklahoma	0.8
11	Oregon	2.1
32	Pennsylvania	0.8
27	Rhode Island	1.1
25	South Carolina	1.2
46	South Dakota	0.2
17	Tennessee	1.5
27	Texas	1.1
5	Utah	2.9
49	Vermont	0.1
16	Virginia	1.6
22	Washington	1.3
46	West Virginia	0.2
19	Wisconsin	1.4
44	Wyoming	0.3

RANK ORDER

RANK	STATE	PERCENT
1	Nevada	10.2
2	Arizona	6.1
3	Florida	5.9
4	California	4.8
5	Utah	2.9
6	Georgia	2.7
6	Idaho	2.7
8	Michigan	2.6
9	Illinois	2.5
10	Colorado	2.4
11	Oregon	2.1
12	Ohio	2.0
13	Maryland	1.9
14	Hawaii	1.8
14	New Jersey	1.8
16	Virginia	1.6
17	Indiana	1.5
17	Tennessee	1.5
19	Connecticut	1.4
19	Minnesota	1.4
19	Wisconsin	1.4
22	Arkansas	1.3
22	Massachusetts	1.3
22	Washington	1.3
25	New Hampshire	1.2
25	South Carolina	1.2
27	Missouri	1.1
27	Rhode Island	1.1
27	Texas	1.1
30	Alabama	0.9
30	Alaska	0.9
32	Delaware	0.8
32	New Mexico	0.8
32	Oklahoma	0.8
32	Pennsylvania	0.8
36	Kansas	0.7
36	North Carolina	0.7
38	Louisiana	0.6
38	New York	0.6
40	Kentucky	0.5
40	Maine	0.5
42	Iowa	0.4
42	Mississippi	0.4
44	Montana	0.3
44	Wyoming	0.3
46	Nebraska	0.2
46	South Dakota	0.2
46	West Virginia	0.2
49	North Dakota	0.1
49	Vermont	0.1

| | District of Columbia | 1.1 |

Source: RealtyTrac

"Record 2.8 Million U.S. Properties with Foreclosure Filings in 2009" (Press Release, January 14, 2010, www.realtytrac.com)

*Foreclosure filings include foreclosure-related documents filed in all phases of foreclosure.

Percent Change in Properties Receiving Foreclosure Filings: 2008 to 2009

National Percent Change = 21.2% Increase*

ALPHA ORDER			RANK ORDER		
RANK	STATE	PERCENT CHANGE	RANK	STATE	PERCENT CHANGE
2	Alabama**	156.3	1	Hawaii	182.6
22	Alaska	25.5	2	Alabama**	156.3
16	Arizona	39.6	3	Mississippi**	135.6
27	Arkansas	15.9	4	West Virginia**	115.9
24	California	20.8	5	Idaho**	101.6
41	Colorado	0.2	6	New Mexico**	93.5
45	Connecticut	(10.2)	7	South Dakota**	90.3
25	Delaware	20.6	8	Oregon	89.6
18	Florida	34.1	9	Utah	82.9
23	Georgia	24.5	10	Wisconsin**	79.0
1	Hawaii	182.6	11	South Carolina**	67.8
5	Idaho**	101.6	12	Louisiana**	64.8
21	Illinois	31.8	13	Minnesota	56.3
44	Indiana	(9.9)	14	Kansas	45.6
34	Iowa	5.5	15	Nevada	44.3
14	Kansas	45.6	16	Arizona	39.6
19	Kentucky**	33.7	17	Washington	35.3
12	Louisiana**	64.8	18	Florida	34.1
28	Maine	11.5	19	Kentucky**	33.7
19	Maryland	33.7	19	Maryland	33.7
48	Massachusetts	(18.5)	21	Illinois	31.8
28	Michigan	11.5	22	Alaska	25.5
13	Minnesota	56.3	23	Georgia	24.5
3	Mississippi**	135.6	24	California	20.8
43	Missouri	(8.8)	25	Delaware	20.6
30	Montana	10.2	26	Pennsylvania	20.2
50	Nebraska	(42.2)	27	Arkansas	15.9
15	Nevada	44.3	28	Maine	11.5
31	New Hampshire	8.7	28	Michigan	11.5
39	New Jersey	1.1	30	Montana	10.2
6	New Mexico**	93.5	31	New Hampshire	8.7
40	New York	0.7	32	Virginia	6.4
47	North Carolina	(16.1)	33	Wyoming	5.9
35	North Dakota	5.1	34	Iowa	5.5
46	Ohio	(10.5)	35	North Dakota	5.1
38	Oklahoma	3.8	36	Vermont	4.4
8	Oregon	89.6	37	Texas	4.0
26	Pennsylvania	20.2	38	Oklahoma	3.8
49	Rhode Island	(23.1)	39	New Jersey	1.1
11	South Carolina**	67.8	40	New York	0.7
7	South Dakota**	90.3	41	Colorado	0.2
42	Tennessee	(7.8)	42	Tennessee	(7.8)
37	Texas	4.0	43	Missouri	(8.8)
9	Utah	82.9	44	Indiana	(9.9)
36	Vermont	4.4	45	Connecticut	(10.2)
32	Virginia	6.4	46	Ohio	(10.5)
17	Washington	35.3	47	North Carolina	(16.1)
4	West Virginia**	115.9	48	Massachusetts	(18.5)
10	Wisconsin**	79.0	49	Rhode Island	(23.1)
33	Wyoming	5.9	50	Nebraska	(42.2)
			District of Columbia		(22.6)

Source: RealtyTrac

"Record 2.8 Million U.S. Properties with Foreclosure Filings in 2009" (Press Release, January 14, 2010, www.realtytrac.com)

*Foreclosure filings include foreclosure-related documents filed in all phases of foreclosure.

**Actual increase may not be as high due to data collection changes or improvements.

Median Monthly Rental Payment in 2008

National Median = $824*

ALPHA ORDER				RANK ORDER		
RANK	STATE	RENT		RANK	STATE	RENT
41	Alabama	$631		1	Hawaii	$1,298
9	Alaska	949		2	California	1,135
15	Arizona	866		3	Maryland	1,074
46	Arkansas	606		4	New Jersey	1,068
2	California	1,135		5	Nevada	1,011
17	Colorado	848		6	Massachusetts	991
7	Connecticut	970		7	Connecticut	970
12	Delaware	917		8	New York	953
10	Florida	947		9	Alaska	949
20	Georgia	787		10	Florida	947
1	Hawaii	1,298		11	Virginia	934
31	Idaho	690		12	Delaware	917
18	Illinois	811		13	New Hampshire	914
33	Indiana	670		14	Washington	874
45	Iowa	607		15	Arizona	866
38	Kansas	654		16	Rhode Island	850
47	Kentucky	578		17	Colorado	848
29	Louisiana	698		18	Illinois	811
28	Maine	702		19	Vermont	797
3	Maryland	1,074		20	Georgia	787
6	Massachusetts	991		21	Utah	784
26	Michigan	706		22	Oregon	780
24	Minnesota	734		23	Texas	768
39	Mississippi	638		24	Minnesota	734
37	Missouri	657		25	Pennsylvania	726
41	Montana	631		26	Michigan	706
43	Nebraska	626		27	Wisconsin	704
5	Nevada	1,011		28	Maine	702
13	New Hampshire	914		29	Louisiana	698
4	New Jersey	1,068		30	North Carolina	694
34	New Mexico	668		31	Idaho	690
8	New York	953		32	South Carolina	675
30	North Carolina	694		33	Indiana	670
49	North Dakota	534		34	New Mexico	668
35	Ohio	667		35	Ohio	667
44	Oklahoma	614		36	Tennessee	660
22	Oregon	780		37	Missouri	657
25	Pennsylvania	726		38	Kansas	654
16	Rhode Island	850		39	Mississippi	638
32	South Carolina	675		40	Wyoming	636
48	South Dakota	569		41	Alabama	631
36	Tennessee	660		41	Montana	631
23	Texas	768		43	Nebraska	626
21	Utah	784		44	Oklahoma	614
19	Vermont	797		45	Iowa	607
11	Virginia	934		46	Arkansas	606
14	Washington	874		47	Kentucky	578
50	West Virginia	528		48	South Dakota	569
27	Wisconsin	704		49	North Dakota	534
40	Wyoming	636		50	West Virginia	528
					District of Columbia	1,011

Source: U.S. Bureau of the Census
   "2008 American Community Survey" (http://www.census.gov/acs/www/index.html)
*For renter-occupied housing.

Percent of Renters Spending 30% or More of Household Income on Rent and Utilities: 2008
National Percent = 46.1% of Renters

ALPHA ORDER

ALPHA ORDER

RANK	STATE	PERCENT
35	Alabama	41.3
46	Alaska	38.0
17	Arizona	46.4
33	Arkansas	42.3
2	California	52.1
11	Colorado	47.3
5	Connecticut	48.2
7	Delaware	47.5
1	Florida	53.7
21	Georgia	45.3
3	Hawaii	50.4
35	Idaho	41.3
20	Illinois	45.6
27	Indiana	43.5
44	Iowa	39.7
41	Kansas	40.3
39	Kentucky	40.7
27	Louisiana	43.5
11	Maine	47.3
14	Maryland	46.9
15	Massachusetts	46.5
4	Michigan	48.8
17	Minnesota	46.4
29	Mississippi	43.0
37	Missouri	41.1
40	Montana	40.4
47	Nebraska	37.7
11	Nevada	47.3
22	New Hampshire	44.9
7	New Jersey	47.5
31	New Mexico	42.7
6	New York	47.9
34	North Carolina	41.8
49	North Dakota	34.4
23	Ohio	44.1
43	Oklahoma	40.0
10	Oregon	47.4
26	Pennsylvania	43.6
15	Rhode Island	46.5
38	South Carolina	40.8
48	South Dakota	34.9
29	Tennessee	43.0
24	Texas	43.9
42	Utah	40.2
7	Vermont	47.5
25	Virginia	43.7
19	Washington	45.7
45	West Virginia	38.2
32	Wisconsin	42.5
50	Wyoming	32.5

RANK ORDER

RANK	STATE	PERCENT
1	Florida	53.7
2	California	52.1
3	Hawaii	50.4
4	Michigan	48.8
5	Connecticut	48.2
6	New York	47.9
7	Delaware	47.5
7	New Jersey	47.5
7	Vermont	47.5
10	Oregon	47.4
11	Colorado	47.3
11	Maine	47.3
11	Nevada	47.3
14	Maryland	46.9
15	Massachusetts	46.5
15	Rhode Island	46.5
17	Arizona	46.4
17	Minnesota	46.4
19	Washington	45.7
20	Illinois	45.6
21	Georgia	45.3
22	New Hampshire	44.9
23	Ohio	44.1
24	Texas	43.9
25	Virginia	43.7
26	Pennsylvania	43.6
27	Indiana	43.5
27	Louisiana	43.5
29	Mississippi	43.0
29	Tennessee	43.0
31	New Mexico	42.7
32	Wisconsin	42.5
33	Arkansas	42.3
34	North Carolina	41.8
35	Alabama	41.3
35	Idaho	41.3
37	Missouri	41.1
38	South Carolina	40.8
39	Kentucky	40.7
40	Montana	40.4
41	Kansas	40.3
42	Utah	40.2
43	Oklahoma	40.0
44	Iowa	39.7
45	West Virginia	38.2
46	Alaska	38.0
47	Nebraska	37.7
48	South Dakota	34.9
49	North Dakota	34.4
50	Wyoming	32.5
	District of Columbia	45.5

Source: U.S. Bureau of the Census
"2008 American Community Survey" (http://www.census.gov/acs/www/index.html)

State and Local Government Expenditures
for Housing and Community Development in 2007
National Total = $45,964,452,000*

ALPHA ORDER

RANK	STATE	EXPENDITURES	% of USA
25	Alabama	$451,654,000	1.0%
30	Alaska	270,835,000	0.6%
24	Arizona	472,286,000	1.0%
40	Arkansas	170,866,000	0.4%
1	California	8,685,831,000	18.9%
18	Colorado	697,394,000	1.5%
19	Connecticut	682,283,000	1.5%
45	Delaware	117,982,000	0.3%
4	Florida	2,137,167,000	4.6%
12	Georgia	1,061,653,000	2.3%
35	Hawaii	216,089,000	0.5%
49	Idaho	46,715,000	0.1%
6	Illinois	1,903,804,000	4.1%
21	Indiana	644,321,000	1.4%
41	Iowa	166,890,000	0.4%
36	Kansas	201,767,000	0.4%
29	Kentucky	284,651,000	0.6%
3	Louisiana	3,296,331,000	7.2%
32	Maine	250,988,000	0.5%
13	Maryland	1,037,724,000	2.3%
9	Massachusetts	1,708,004,000	3.7%
15	Michigan	971,917,000	2.1%
17	Minnesota	844,863,000	1.8%
34	Mississippi	217,494,000	0.5%
22	Missouri	615,820,000	1.3%
47	Montana	102,370,000	0.2%
37	Nebraska	198,281,000	0.4%
33	Nevada	226,456,000	0.5%
39	New Hampshire	174,856,000	0.4%
10	New Jersey	1,073,987,000	2.3%
42	New Mexico	145,850,000	0.3%
2	New York	4,839,725,000	10.5%
16	North Carolina	882,502,000	1.9%
48	North Dakota	60,392,000	0.1%
5	Ohio	1,959,176,000	4.3%
31	Oklahoma	264,186,000	0.6%
23	Oregon	513,527,000	1.1%
8	Pennsylvania	1,770,395,000	3.9%
38	Rhode Island	179,244,000	0.4%
26	South Carolina	364,154,000	0.8%
46	South Dakota	102,517,000	0.2%
20	Tennessee	665,866,000	1.4%
7	Texas	1,858,364,000	4.0%
28	Utah	300,966,000	0.7%
44	Vermont	121,955,000	0.3%
14	Virginia	984,139,000	2.1%
11	Washington	1,068,529,000	2.3%
43	West Virginia	134,255,000	0.3%
27	Wisconsin	343,434,000	0.7%
50	Wyoming	25,207,000	0.1%

RANK ORDER

RANK	STATE	EXPENDITURES	% of USA
1	California	$8,685,831,000	18.9%
2	New York	4,839,725,000	10.5%
3	Louisiana	3,296,331,000	7.2%
4	Florida	2,137,167,000	4.6%
5	Ohio	1,959,176,000	4.3%
6	Illinois	1,903,804,000	4.1%
7	Texas	1,858,364,000	4.0%
8	Pennsylvania	1,770,395,000	3.9%
9	Massachusetts	1,708,004,000	3.7%
10	New Jersey	1,073,987,000	2.3%
11	Washington	1,068,529,000	2.3%
12	Georgia	1,061,653,000	2.3%
13	Maryland	1,037,724,000	2.3%
14	Virginia	984,139,000	2.1%
15	Michigan	971,917,000	2.1%
16	North Carolina	882,502,000	1.9%
17	Minnesota	844,863,000	1.8%
18	Colorado	697,394,000	1.5%
19	Connecticut	682,283,000	1.5%
20	Tennessee	665,866,000	1.4%
21	Indiana	644,321,000	1.4%
22	Missouri	615,820,000	1.3%
23	Oregon	513,527,000	1.1%
24	Arizona	472,286,000	1.0%
25	Alabama	451,654,000	1.0%
26	South Carolina	364,154,000	0.8%
27	Wisconsin	343,434,000	0.7%
28	Utah	300,966,000	0.7%
29	Kentucky	284,651,000	0.6%
30	Alaska	270,835,000	0.6%
31	Oklahoma	264,186,000	0.6%
32	Maine	250,988,000	0.5%
33	Nevada	226,456,000	0.5%
34	Mississippi	217,494,000	0.5%
35	Hawaii	216,089,000	0.5%
36	Kansas	201,767,000	0.4%
37	Nebraska	198,281,000	0.4%
38	Rhode Island	179,244,000	0.4%
39	New Hampshire	174,856,000	0.4%
40	Arkansas	170,866,000	0.4%
41	Iowa	166,890,000	0.4%
42	New Mexico	145,850,000	0.3%
43	West Virginia	134,255,000	0.3%
44	Vermont	121,955,000	0.3%
45	Delaware	117,982,000	0.3%
46	South Dakota	102,517,000	0.2%
47	Montana	102,370,000	0.2%
48	North Dakota	60,392,000	0.1%
49	Idaho	46,715,000	0.1%
50	Wyoming	25,207,000	0.1%
	District of Columbia	448,790,000	1.0%

Source: U.S. Bureau of the Census, Governments Division
"State and Local Government Finances 2006-2007" (http://www.census.gov/govs/estimate/index.html)
*Direct general expenditures.

Per Capita State and Local Government Expenditures
for Housing and Community Development in 2007
National Per Capita = $152*

ALPHA ORDER

ALPHA ORDER

RANK	STATE	PER CAPITA
32	Alabama	$97
2	Alaska	397
39	Arizona	74
47	Arkansas	60
5	California	240
16	Colorado	144
7	Connecticut	196
19	Delaware	136
24	Florida	117
27	Georgia	111
12	Hawaii	169
50	Idaho	31
15	Illinois	149
31	Indiana	102
48	Iowa	56
43	Kansas	73
45	Kentucky	67
1	Louisiana	753
8	Maine	191
9	Maryland	184
3	Massachusetts	263
32	Michigan	97
14	Minnesota	163
39	Mississippi	74
30	Missouri	104
29	Montana	107
26	Nebraska	112
36	Nevada	88
20	New Hampshire	133
23	New Jersey	124
39	New Mexico	74
4	New York	249
32	North Carolina	97
35	North Dakota	95
10	Ohio	170
43	Oklahoma	73
18	Oregon	138
17	Pennsylvania	141
10	Rhode Island	170
37	South Carolina	82
21	South Dakota	129
28	Tennessee	108
38	Texas	78
25	Utah	113
6	Vermont	197
22	Virginia	127
13	Washington	165
39	West Virginia	74
46	Wisconsin	61
49	Wyoming	48

RANK ORDER

RANK	STATE	PER CAPITA
1	Louisiana	$753
2	Alaska	397
3	Massachusetts	263
4	New York	249
5	California	240
6	Vermont	197
7	Connecticut	196
8	Maine	191
9	Maryland	184
10	Ohio	170
10	Rhode Island	170
12	Hawaii	169
13	Washington	165
14	Minnesota	163
15	Illinois	149
16	Colorado	144
17	Pennsylvania	141
18	Oregon	138
19	Delaware	136
20	New Hampshire	133
21	South Dakota	129
22	Virginia	127
23	New Jersey	124
24	Florida	117
25	Utah	113
26	Nebraska	112
27	Georgia	111
28	Tennessee	108
29	Montana	107
30	Missouri	104
31	Indiana	102
32	Alabama	97
32	Michigan	97
32	North Carolina	97
35	North Dakota	95
36	Nevada	88
37	South Carolina	82
38	Texas	78
39	Arizona	74
39	Mississippi	74
39	New Mexico	74
39	West Virginia	74
43	Kansas	73
43	Oklahoma	73
45	Kentucky	67
46	Wisconsin	61
47	Arkansas	60
48	Iowa	56
49	Wyoming	48
50	Idaho	31

District of Columbia	765

Source: CQ Press using data from U.S. Bureau of the Census, Governments Division
   "State and Local Government Finances 2006-2007" (http://www.census.gov/govs/estimate/index.html)
*Direct general expenditures.

XIII. Population

Population in 2009

National Total = 307,006,550*

ALPHA ORDER

ALPHA ORDER

RANK	STATE	POPULATION	% of USA
23	Alabama	4,708,708	1.5%
47	Alaska	698,473	0.2%
14	Arizona	6,595,778	2.1%
32	Arkansas	2,889,450	0.9%
1	California	36,961,664	12.0%
22	Colorado	5,024,748	1.6%
29	Connecticut	3,518,288	1.1%
45	Delaware	885,122	0.3%
4	Florida	18,537,969	6.0%
9	Georgia	9,829,211	3.2%
42	Hawaii	1,295,178	0.4%
39	Idaho	1,545,801	0.5%
5	Illinois	12,910,409	4.2%
16	Indiana	6,423,113	2.1%
30	Iowa	3,007,856	1.0%
33	Kansas	2,818,747	0.9%
26	Kentucky	4,314,113	1.4%
25	Louisiana	4,492,076	1.5%
41	Maine	1,318,301	0.4%
19	Maryland	5,699,478	1.9%
15	Massachusetts	6,593,587	2.1%
8	Michigan	9,969,727	3.2%
21	Minnesota	5,266,214	1.7%
31	Mississippi	2,951,996	1.0%
18	Missouri	5,987,580	2.0%
44	Montana	974,989	0.3%
38	Nebraska	1,796,619	0.6%
35	Nevada	2,643,085	0.9%
40	New Hampshire	1,324,575	0.4%
11	New Jersey	8,707,739	2.8%
36	New Mexico	2,009,671	0.7%
3	New York	19,541,453	6.4%
10	North Carolina	9,380,884	3.1%
48	North Dakota	646,844	0.2%
7	Ohio	11,542,645	3.8%
28	Oklahoma	3,687,050	1.2%
27	Oregon	3,825,657	1.2%
6	Pennsylvania	12,604,767	4.1%
43	Rhode Island	1,053,209	0.3%
24	South Carolina	4,561,242	1.5%
46	South Dakota	812,383	0.3%
17	Tennessee	6,296,254	2.1%
2	Texas	24,782,302	8.1%
34	Utah	2,784,572	0.9%
49	Vermont	621,760	0.2%
12	Virginia	7,882,590	2.6%
13	Washington	6,664,195	2.2%
37	West Virginia	1,819,777	0.6%
20	Wisconsin	5,654,774	1.8%
50	Wyoming	544,270	0.2%

RANK ORDER

RANK	STATE	POPULATION	% of USA
1	California	36,961,664	12.0%
2	Texas	24,782,302	8.1%
3	New York	19,541,453	6.4%
4	Florida	18,537,969	6.0%
5	Illinois	12,910,409	4.2%
6	Pennsylvania	12,604,767	4.1%
7	Ohio	11,542,645	3.8%
8	Michigan	9,969,727	3.2%
9	Georgia	9,829,211	3.2%
10	North Carolina	9,380,884	3.1%
11	New Jersey	8,707,739	2.8%
12	Virginia	7,882,590	2.6%
13	Washington	6,664,195	2.2%
14	Arizona	6,595,778	2.1%
15	Massachusetts	6,593,587	2.1%
16	Indiana	6,423,113	2.1%
17	Tennessee	6,296,254	2.1%
18	Missouri	5,987,580	2.0%
19	Maryland	5,699,478	1.9%
20	Wisconsin	5,654,774	1.8%
21	Minnesota	5,266,214	1.7%
22	Colorado	5,024,748	1.6%
23	Alabama	4,708,708	1.5%
24	South Carolina	4,561,242	1.5%
25	Louisiana	4,492,076	1.5%
26	Kentucky	4,314,113	1.4%
27	Oregon	3,825,657	1.2%
28	Oklahoma	3,687,050	1.2%
29	Connecticut	3,518,288	1.1%
30	Iowa	3,007,856	1.0%
31	Mississippi	2,951,996	1.0%
32	Arkansas	2,889,450	0.9%
33	Kansas	2,818,747	0.9%
34	Utah	2,784,572	0.9%
35	Nevada	2,643,085	0.9%
36	New Mexico	2,009,671	0.7%
37	West Virginia	1,819,777	0.6%
38	Nebraska	1,796,619	0.6%
39	Idaho	1,545,801	0.5%
40	New Hampshire	1,324,575	0.4%
41	Maine	1,318,301	0.4%
42	Hawaii	1,295,178	0.4%
43	Rhode Island	1,053,209	0.3%
44	Montana	974,989	0.3%
45	Delaware	885,122	0.3%
46	South Dakota	812,383	0.3%
47	Alaska	698,473	0.2%
48	North Dakota	646,844	0.2%
49	Vermont	621,760	0.2%
50	Wyoming	544,270	0.2%
	District of Columbia	599,657	0.2%

Source: U.S. Bureau of the Census
   "Population Estimates" (December 23, 2009, http://www.census.gov/popest/estimates.php)
*Resident population.

Population in 2008

National Total = 304,374,846*

RANK	STATE	POPULATION	% of USA
23	Alabama	4,677,464	1.5%
47	Alaska	688,125	0.2%
15	Arizona	6,499,377	2.1%
32	Arkansas	2,867,764	0.9%
1	California	36,580,371	12.0%
22	Colorado	4,935,213	1.6%
29	Connecticut	3,502,932	1.2%
45	Delaware	876,211	0.3%
4	Florida	18,423,878	6.1%
9	Georgia	9,697,838	3.2%
42	Hawaii	1,287,481	0.4%
39	Idaho	1,527,506	0.5%
5	Illinois	12,842,954	4.2%
16	Indiana	6,388,309	2.1%
30	Iowa	2,993,987	1.0%
33	Kansas	2,797,375	0.9%
26	Kentucky	4,287,931	1.4%
25	Louisiana	4,451,513	1.5%
41	Maine	1,319,691	0.4%
19	Maryland	5,658,655	1.9%
14	Massachusetts	6,543,595	2.1%
8	Michigan	10,002,486	3.3%
21	Minnesota	5,230,567	1.7%
31	Mississippi	2,940,212	1.0%
18	Missouri	5,956,335	2.0%
44	Montana	968,035	0.3%
38	Nebraska	1,781,949	0.6%
35	Nevada	2,615,772	0.9%
40	New Hampshire	1,321,872	0.4%
11	New Jersey	8,663,398	2.8%
36	New Mexico	1,986,763	0.7%
3	New York	19,467,789	6.4%
10	North Carolina	9,247,134	3.0%
48	North Dakota	641,421	0.2%
7	Ohio	11,528,072	3.8%
28	Oklahoma	3,644,025	1.2%
27	Oregon	3,782,991	1.2%
6	Pennsylvania	12,566,368	4.1%
43	Rhode Island	1,053,502	0.3%
24	South Carolina	4,503,280	1.5%
46	South Dakota	804,532	0.3%
17	Tennessee	6,240,456	2.1%
2	Texas	24,304,290	8.0%
34	Utah	2,727,343	0.9%
49	Vermont	621,049	0.2%
12	Virginia	7,795,424	2.6%
13	Washington	6,566,073	2.2%
37	West Virginia	1,814,873	0.6%
20	Wisconsin	5,627,610	1.8%
50	Wyoming	532,981	0.2%

RANK	STATE	POPULATION	% of USA
1	California	36,580,371	12.0%
2	Texas	24,304,290	8.0%
3	New York	19,467,789	6.4%
4	Florida	18,423,878	6.1%
5	Illinois	12,842,954	4.2%
6	Pennsylvania	12,566,368	4.1%
7	Ohio	11,528,072	3.8%
8	Michigan	10,002,486	3.3%
9	Georgia	9,697,838	3.2%
10	North Carolina	9,247,134	3.0%
11	New Jersey	8,663,398	2.8%
12	Virginia	7,795,424	2.6%
13	Washington	6,566,073	2.2%
14	Massachusetts	6,543,595	2.1%
15	Arizona	6,499,377	2.1%
16	Indiana	6,388,309	2.1%
17	Tennessee	6,240,456	2.1%
18	Missouri	5,956,335	2.0%
19	Maryland	5,658,655	1.9%
20	Wisconsin	5,627,610	1.8%
21	Minnesota	5,230,567	1.7%
22	Colorado	4,935,213	1.6%
23	Alabama	4,677,464	1.5%
24	South Carolina	4,503,280	1.5%
25	Louisiana	4,451,513	1.5%
26	Kentucky	4,287,931	1.4%
27	Oregon	3,782,991	1.2%
28	Oklahoma	3,644,025	1.2%
29	Connecticut	3,502,932	1.2%
30	Iowa	2,993,987	1.0%
31	Mississippi	2,940,212	1.0%
32	Arkansas	2,867,764	0.9%
33	Kansas	2,797,375	0.9%
34	Utah	2,727,343	0.9%
35	Nevada	2,615,772	0.9%
36	New Mexico	1,986,763	0.7%
37	West Virginia	1,814,873	0.6%
38	Nebraska	1,781,949	0.6%
39	Idaho	1,527,506	0.5%
40	New Hampshire	1,321,872	0.4%
41	Maine	1,319,691	0.4%
42	Hawaii	1,287,481	0.4%
43	Rhode Island	1,053,502	0.3%
44	Montana	968,035	0.3%
45	Delaware	876,211	0.3%
46	South Dakota	804,532	0.3%
47	Alaska	688,125	0.2%
48	North Dakota	641,421	0.2%
49	Vermont	621,049	0.2%
50	Wyoming	532,981	0.2%
	District of Columbia	590,074	0.2%

Source: U.S. Bureau of the Census
"Population Estimates" (December 23, 2009, http://www.census.gov/popest/estimates.php)
*Resident population. Revised estimates.

Numerical Population Change: 2008 to 2009

National Total = 2,631,704 Increase*

ALPHA ORDER

RANK	STATE	GAIN/LOSS	% of USA
25	Alabama	31,244	1.2%
39	Alaska	10,348	0.4%
7	Arizona	96,401	3.7%
30	Arkansas	21,686	0.8%
2	California	381,293	14.5%
8	Colorado	89,535	3.4%
33	Connecticut	15,356	0.6%
40	Delaware	8,911	0.3%
5	Florida	114,091	4.3%
4	Georgia	131,373	5.0%
42	Hawaii	7,697	0.3%
32	Idaho	18,295	0.7%
11	Illinois	67,455	2.6%
23	Indiana	34,804	1.3%
36	Iowa	13,869	0.5%
31	Kansas	21,372	0.8%
28	Kentucky	26,182	1.0%
20	Louisiana	40,563	1.5%
49	Maine	(1,390)	
19	Maryland	40,823	1.6%
15	Massachusetts	49,992	1.9%
50	Michigan	(32,759)	
22	Minnesota	35,647	1.4%
37	Mississippi	11,784	0.4%
24	Missouri	31,245	1.2%
43	Montana	6,954	0.3%
34	Nebraska	14,670	0.6%
26	Nevada	27,313	1.0%
46	New Hampshire	2,703	0.1%
16	New Jersey	44,341	1.7%
29	New Mexico	22,908	0.9%
10	New York	73,664	2.8%
3	North Carolina	133,750	5.1%
44	North Dakota	5,423	0.2%
35	Ohio	14,573	0.6%
17	Oklahoma	43,025	1.6%
18	Oregon	42,666	1.6%
21	Pennsylvania	38,399	1.5%
48	Rhode Island	(293)	0.0%
12	South Carolina	57,962	2.2%
41	South Dakota	7,851	0.3%
14	Tennessee	55,798	2.1%
1	Texas	478,012	18.2%
13	Utah	57,229	2.2%
47	Vermont	711	0.0%
9	Virginia	87,166	3.3%
6	Washington	98,122	3.7%
45	West Virginia	4,904	0.2%
27	Wisconsin	27,164	1.0%
38	Wyoming	11,289	0.4%

RANK ORDER

RANK	STATE	GAIN/LOSS	% of USA
1	Texas	478,012	18.2%
2	California	381,293	14.5%
3	North Carolina	133,750	5.1%
4	Georgia	131,373	5.0%
5	Florida	114,091	4.3%
6	Washington	98,122	3.7%
7	Arizona	96,401	3.7%
8	Colorado	89,535	3.4%
9	Virginia	87,166	3.3%
10	New York	73,664	2.8%
11	Illinois	67,455	2.6%
12	South Carolina	57,962	2.2%
13	Utah	57,229	2.2%
14	Tennessee	55,798	2.1%
15	Massachusetts	49,992	1.9%
16	New Jersey	44,341	1.7%
17	Oklahoma	43,025	1.6%
18	Oregon	42,666	1.6%
19	Maryland	40,823	1.6%
20	Louisiana	40,563	1.5%
21	Pennsylvania	38,399	1.5%
22	Minnesota	35,647	1.4%
23	Indiana	34,804	1.3%
24	Missouri	31,245	1.2%
25	Alabama	31,244	1.2%
26	Nevada	27,313	1.0%
27	Wisconsin	27,164	1.0%
28	Kentucky	26,182	1.0%
29	New Mexico	22,908	0.9%
30	Arkansas	21,686	0.8%
31	Kansas	21,372	0.8%
32	Idaho	18,295	0.7%
33	Connecticut	15,356	0.6%
34	Nebraska	14,670	0.6%
35	Ohio	14,573	0.6%
36	Iowa	13,869	0.5%
37	Mississippi	11,784	0.4%
38	Wyoming	11,289	0.4%
39	Alaska	10,348	0.4%
40	Delaware	8,911	0.3%
41	South Dakota	7,851	0.3%
42	Hawaii	7,697	0.3%
43	Montana	6,954	0.3%
44	North Dakota	5,423	0.2%
45	West Virginia	4,904	0.2%
46	New Hampshire	2,703	0.1%
47	Vermont	711	0.0%
48	Rhode Island	(293)	0.0%
49	Maine	(1,390)	
50	Michigan	(32,759)	
	District of Columbia	9,583	0.4%

Source: U.S. Bureau of the Census
"Population Estimates" (December 23, 2009, http://www.census.gov/popest/estimates.php)
*Resident population from July 1, 2008 to July 1, 2009.

Percent Change in Population: 2008 to 2009

National Percent Change = 0.9% Increase*

<u>ALPHA ORDER</u>

RANK	STATE	PERCENT CHANGE
27	Alabama	0.7
5	Alaska	1.5
5	Arizona	1.5
22	Arkansas	0.8
16	California	1.0
4	Colorado	1.8
40	Connecticut	0.4
16	Delaware	1.0
31	Florida	0.6
8	Georgia	1.4
31	Hawaii	0.6
11	Idaho	1.2
34	Illinois	0.5
34	Indiana	0.5
34	Iowa	0.5
22	Kansas	0.8
31	Kentucky	0.6
20	Louisiana	0.9
49	Maine	(0.1)
27	Maryland	0.7
22	Massachusetts	0.8
50	Michigan	(0.3)
27	Minnesota	0.7
40	Mississippi	0.4
34	Missouri	0.5
27	Montana	0.7
22	Nebraska	0.8
16	Nevada	1.0
45	New Hampshire	0.2
34	New Jersey	0.5
11	New Mexico	1.2
40	New York	0.4
8	North Carolina	1.4
22	North Dakota	0.8
46	Ohio	0.1
11	Oklahoma	1.2
14	Oregon	1.1
43	Pennsylvania	0.3
48	Rhode Island	0.0
10	South Carolina	1.3
16	South Dakota	1.0
20	Tennessee	0.9
3	Texas	2.0
1	Utah	2.1
46	Vermont	0.1
14	Virginia	1.1
5	Washington	1.5
43	West Virginia	0.3
34	Wisconsin	0.5
1	Wyoming	2.1

<u>RANK ORDER</u>

RANK	STATE	PERCENT CHANGE
1	Utah	2.1
1	Wyoming	2.1
3	Texas	2.0
4	Colorado	1.8
5	Alaska	1.5
5	Arizona	1.5
5	Washington	1.5
8	Georgia	1.4
8	North Carolina	1.4
10	South Carolina	1.3
11	Idaho	1.2
11	New Mexico	1.2
11	Oklahoma	1.2
14	Oregon	1.1
14	Virginia	1.1
16	California	1.0
16	Delaware	1.0
16	Nevada	1.0
16	South Dakota	1.0
20	Louisiana	0.9
20	Tennessee	0.9
22	Arkansas	0.8
22	Kansas	0.8
22	Massachusetts	0.8
22	Nebraska	0.8
22	North Dakota	0.8
27	Alabama	0.7
27	Maryland	0.7
27	Minnesota	0.7
27	Montana	0.7
31	Florida	0.6
31	Hawaii	0.6
31	Kentucky	0.6
34	Illinois	0.5
34	Indiana	0.5
34	Iowa	0.5
34	Missouri	0.5
34	New Jersey	0.5
34	Wisconsin	0.5
40	Connecticut	0.4
40	Mississippi	0.4
40	New York	0.4
43	Pennsylvania	0.3
43	West Virginia	0.3
45	New Hampshire	0.2
46	Ohio	0.1
46	Vermont	0.1
48	Rhode Island	0.0
49	Maine	(0.1)
50	Michigan	(0.3)

| | District of Columbia | 1.6 |

Source: U.S. Bureau of the Census

   "Population Estimates" (December 23, 2009, http://www.census.gov/popest/estimates.php)

*Resident population from July 1, 2008 to July 1, 2009.

Population in 2000 Census

National Total = 281,421,906*

<u>ALPHA ORDER</u>

RANK	STATE	POPULATION	% of USA
23	Alabama	4,447,100	1.6%
48	Alaska	626,932	0.2%
20	Arizona	5,130,632	1.8%
33	Arkansas	2,673,400	0.9%
1	California	33,871,648	12.0%
24	Colorado	4,301,261	1.5%
29	Connecticut	3,405,565	1.2%
45	Delaware	783,600	0.3%
4	Florida	15,982,378	5.7%
10	Georgia	8,186,453	2.9%
42	Hawaii	1,211,537	0.4%
39	Idaho	1,293,953	0.5%
5	Illinois	12,419,293	4.4%
14	Indiana	6,080,485	2.2%
30	Iowa	2,926,324	1.0%
32	Kansas	2,688,418	1.0%
25	Kentucky	4,041,769	1.4%
22	Louisiana	4,468,976	1.6%
40	Maine	1,274,923	0.5%
19	Maryland	5,296,486	1.9%
13	Massachusetts	6,349,097	2.3%
8	Michigan	9,938,444	3.5%
21	Minnesota	4,919,479	1.7%
31	Mississippi	2,844,658	1.0%
17	Missouri	5,595,211	2.0%
44	Montana	902,195	0.3%
38	Nebraska	1,711,263	0.6%
35	Nevada	1,998,257	0.7%
41	New Hampshire	1,235,786	0.4%
9	New Jersey	8,414,350	3.0%
36	New Mexico	1,819,046	0.6%
3	New York	18,976,457	6.7%
11	North Carolina	8,049,313	2.9%
47	North Dakota	642,200	0.2%
7	Ohio	11,353,140	4.0%
27	Oklahoma	3,450,654	1.2%
28	Oregon	3,421,399	1.2%
6	Pennsylvania	12,281,054	4.4%
43	Rhode Island	1,048,319	0.4%
26	South Carolina	4,012,012	1.4%
46	South Dakota	754,844	0.3%
16	Tennessee	5,689,283	2.0%
2	Texas	20,851,820	7.4%
34	Utah	2,233,169	0.8%
49	Vermont	608,827	0.2%
12	Virginia	7,078,515	2.5%
15	Washington	5,894,121	2.1%
37	West Virginia	1,808,344	0.6%
18	Wisconsin	5,363,675	1.9%
50	Wyoming	493,782	0.2%

<u>RANK ORDER</u>

RANK	STATE	POPULATION	% of USA
1	California	33,871,648	12.0%
2	Texas	20,851,820	7.4%
3	New York	18,976,457	6.7%
4	Florida	15,982,378	5.7%
5	Illinois	12,419,293	4.4%
6	Pennsylvania	12,281,054	4.4%
7	Ohio	11,353,140	4.0%
8	Michigan	9,938,444	3.5%
9	New Jersey	8,414,350	3.0%
10	Georgia	8,186,453	2.9%
11	North Carolina	8,049,313	2.9%
12	Virginia	7,078,515	2.5%
13	Massachusetts	6,349,097	2.3%
14	Indiana	6,080,485	2.2%
15	Washington	5,894,121	2.1%
16	Tennessee	5,689,283	2.0%
17	Missouri	5,595,211	2.0%
18	Wisconsin	5,363,675	1.9%
19	Maryland	5,296,486	1.9%
20	Arizona	5,130,632	1.8%
21	Minnesota	4,919,479	1.7%
22	Louisiana	4,468,976	1.6%
23	Alabama	4,447,100	1.6%
24	Colorado	4,301,261	1.5%
25	Kentucky	4,041,769	1.4%
26	South Carolina	4,012,012	1.4%
27	Oklahoma	3,450,654	1.2%
28	Oregon	3,421,399	1.2%
29	Connecticut	3,405,565	1.2%
30	Iowa	2,926,324	1.0%
31	Mississippi	2,844,658	1.0%
32	Kansas	2,688,418	1.0%
33	Arkansas	2,673,400	0.9%
34	Utah	2,233,169	0.8%
35	Nevada	1,998,257	0.7%
36	New Mexico	1,819,046	0.6%
37	West Virginia	1,808,344	0.6%
38	Nebraska	1,711,263	0.6%
39	Idaho	1,293,953	0.5%
40	Maine	1,274,923	0.5%
41	New Hampshire	1,235,786	0.4%
42	Hawaii	1,211,537	0.4%
43	Rhode Island	1,048,319	0.4%
44	Montana	902,195	0.3%
45	Delaware	783,600	0.3%
46	South Dakota	754,844	0.3%
47	North Dakota	642,200	0.2%
48	Alaska	626,932	0.2%
49	Vermont	608,827	0.2%
50	Wyoming	493,782	0.2%
	District of Columbia	572,059	0.2%

Source: U.S. Bureau of the Census
"First Census 2000 Results" (December 28, 2000, http://www.census.gov/main/www/cen2000.html)
*Resident population as of April 2000 Census.

Projected State Population in 2030

National Total = 363,584,435

ALPHA ORDER					RANK ORDER			
RANK	STATE	POPULATION	% of USA		RANK	STATE	POPULATION	% of USA
24	Alabama	4,874,243	1.3%		1	California	46,444,861	12.8%
46	Alaska	867,674	0.2%		2	Texas	33,317,744	9.2%
10	Arizona	10,712,397	2.9%		3	Florida	28,685,769	7.9%
32	Arkansas	3,240,208	0.9%		4	New York	19,477,429	5.4%
1	California	46,444,861	12.8%		5	Illinois	13,432,892	3.7%
22	Colorado	5,792,357	1.6%		6	Pennsylvania	12,768,184	3.5%
30	Connecticut	3,688,630	1.0%		7	North Carolina	12,227,739	3.4%
45	Delaware	1,012,658	0.3%		8	Georgia	12,017,838	3.3%
3	Florida	28,685,769	7.9%		9	Ohio	11,550,528	3.2%
8	Georgia	12,017,838	3.3%		10	Arizona	10,712,397	2.9%
41	Hawaii	1,466,046	0.4%		11	Michigan	10,694,172	2.9%
37	Idaho	1,969,624	0.5%		12	Virginia	9,825,019	2.7%
5	Illinois	13,432,892	3.7%		13	New Jersey	9,802,440	2.7%
18	Indiana	6,810,108	1.9%		14	Washington	8,624,801	2.4%
34	Iowa	2,955,172	0.8%		15	Tennessee	7,380,634	2.0%
35	Kansas	2,940,084	0.8%		16	Maryland	7,022,251	1.9%
27	Kentucky	4,554,998	1.3%		17	Massachusetts	7,012,009	1.9%
26	Louisiana	4,802,633	1.3%		18	Indiana	6,810,108	1.9%
42	Maine	1,411,097	0.4%		19	Missouri	6,430,173	1.8%
16	Maryland	7,022,251	1.9%		20	Minnesota	6,306,130	1.7%
17	Massachusetts	7,012,009	1.9%		21	Wisconsin	6,150,764	1.7%
11	Michigan	10,694,172	2.9%		22	Colorado	5,792,357	1.6%
20	Minnesota	6,306,130	1.7%		23	South Carolina	5,148,569	1.4%
33	Mississippi	3,092,410	0.9%		24	Alabama	4,874,243	1.3%
19	Missouri	6,430,173	1.8%		25	Oregon	4,833,918	1.3%
44	Montana	1,044,898	0.3%		26	Louisiana	4,802,633	1.3%
38	Nebraska	1,820,247	0.5%		27	Kentucky	4,554,998	1.3%
28	Nevada	4,282,102	1.2%		28	Nevada	4,282,102	1.2%
40	New Hampshire	1,646,471	0.5%		29	Oklahoma	3,913,251	1.1%
13	New Jersey	9,802,440	2.7%		30	Connecticut	3,688,630	1.0%
36	New Mexico	2,099,708	0.6%		31	Utah	3,485,367	1.0%
4	New York	19,477,429	5.4%		32	Arkansas	3,240,208	0.9%
7	North Carolina	12,227,739	3.4%		33	Mississippi	3,092,410	0.9%
49	North Dakota	606,566	0.2%		34	Iowa	2,955,172	0.8%
9	Ohio	11,550,528	3.2%		35	Kansas	2,940,084	0.8%
29	Oklahoma	3,913,251	1.1%		36	New Mexico	2,099,708	0.6%
25	Oregon	4,833,918	1.3%		37	Idaho	1,969,624	0.5%
6	Pennsylvania	12,768,184	3.5%		38	Nebraska	1,820,247	0.5%
43	Rhode Island	1,152,941	0.3%		39	West Virginia	1,719,959	0.5%
23	South Carolina	5,148,569	1.4%		40	New Hampshire	1,646,471	0.5%
47	South Dakota	800,462	0.2%		41	Hawaii	1,466,046	0.4%
15	Tennessee	7,380,634	2.0%		42	Maine	1,411,097	0.4%
2	Texas	33,317,744	9.2%		43	Rhode Island	1,152,941	0.3%
31	Utah	3,485,367	1.0%		44	Montana	1,044,898	0.3%
48	Vermont	711,867	0.2%		45	Delaware	1,012,658	0.3%
12	Virginia	9,825,019	2.7%		46	Alaska	867,674	0.2%
14	Washington	8,624,801	2.4%		47	South Dakota	800,462	0.2%
39	West Virginia	1,719,959	0.5%		48	Vermont	711,867	0.2%
21	Wisconsin	6,150,764	1.7%		49	North Dakota	606,566	0.2%
50	Wyoming	522,979	0.1%		50	Wyoming	522,979	0.1%
						District of Columbia	433,414	0.1%

Source: U.S. Bureau of the Census
"State Interim Population Projections: 2004-2030 "
(http://www.census.gov/population/www/projections/projectionsagesex.html)

Population per Square Mile in 2009

National Rate = 86.8 Persons per Square Mile*

ALPHA ORDER			RANK ORDER		
RANK	STATE	RATE	RANK	STATE	RATE
27	Alabama	92.8	1	New Jersey	1,174.0
50	Alaska	1.2	2	Rhode Island	1,007.9
33	Arizona	58.0	3	Massachusetts	841.0
34	Arkansas	55.5	4	Connecticut	726.2
11	California	237.0	5	Maryland	583.1
37	Colorado	48.4	6	Delaware	453.0
4	Connecticut	726.2	7	New York	413.9
6	Delaware	453.0	8	Florida	343.8
8	Florida	343.8	9	Ohio	281.9
18	Georgia	169.7	10	Pennsylvania	281.2
13	Hawaii	201.6	11	California	237.0
44	Idaho	18.7	12	Illinois	232.3
12	Illinois	232.3	13	Hawaii	201.6
16	Indiana	179.1	14	Virginia	199.1
35	Iowa	53.8	15	North Carolina	192.6
40	Kansas	34.5	16	Indiana	179.1
22	Kentucky	108.6	17	Michigan	175.5
24	Louisiana	103.1	18	Georgia	169.7
38	Maine	42.7	19	Tennessee	152.8
5	Maryland	583.1	20	South Carolina	151.5
3	Massachusetts	841.0	21	New Hampshire	147.7
17	Michigan	175.5	22	Kentucky	108.6
31	Minnesota	66.2	23	Wisconsin	104.1
32	Mississippi	62.9	24	Louisiana	103.1
28	Missouri	86.9	25	Washington	100.1
48	Montana	6.7	26	Texas	94.7
43	Nebraska	23.4	27	Alabama	92.8
42	Nevada	24.1	28	Missouri	86.9
21	New Hampshire	147.7	29	West Virginia	75.6
1	New Jersey	1,174.0	30	Vermont	67.2
45	New Mexico	16.6	31	Minnesota	66.2
7	New York	413.9	32	Mississippi	62.9
15	North Carolina	192.6	33	Arizona	58.0
47	North Dakota	9.4	34	Arkansas	55.5
9	Ohio	281.9	35	Iowa	53.8
36	Oklahoma	53.7	36	Oklahoma	53.7
39	Oregon	39.9	37	Colorado	48.4
10	Pennsylvania	281.2	38	Maine	42.7
2	Rhode Island	1,007.9	39	Oregon	39.9
20	South Carolina	151.5	40	Kansas	34.5
46	South Dakota	10.7	41	Utah	33.9
19	Tennessee	152.8	42	Nevada	24.1
26	Texas	94.7	43	Nebraska	23.4
41	Utah	33.9	44	Idaho	18.7
30	Vermont	67.2	45	New Mexico	16.6
14	Virginia	199.1	46	South Dakota	10.7
25	Washington	100.1	47	North Dakota	9.4
29	West Virginia	75.6	48	Montana	6.7
23	Wisconsin	104.1	49	Wyoming	5.6
49	Wyoming	5.6	50	Alaska	1.2

District of Columbia	9,830.4

Source: CQ Press using data from U.S. Bureau of the Census
"Population Estimates" (December 23, 2009, http://www.census.gov/popest/estimates.php)
*Resident population. Based on land area of states.

Male Population in 2008

National Total = 149,924,604 Males

RANK	STATE	MALES	% of USA
23	Alabama	2,258,087	1.5%
47	Alaska	357,607	0.2%
14	Arizona	3,256,691	2.2%
32	Arkansas	1,398,635	0.9%
1	California	18,388,022	12.3%
22	Colorado	2,491,041	1.7%
29	Connecticut	1,707,410	1.1%
45	Delaware	423,336	0.3%
4	Florida	9,005,282	6.0%
9	Georgia	4,764,975	3.2%
40	Hawaii	649,519	0.4%
39	Idaho	766,580	0.5%
5	Illinois	6,359,906	4.2%
16	Indiana	3,142,510	2.1%
30	Iowa	1,482,872	1.0%
33	Kansas	1,391,821	0.9%
26	Kentucky	2,088,142	1.4%
25	Louisiana	2,140,798	1.4%
42	Maine	642,369	0.4%
20	Maryland	2,727,323	1.8%
15	Massachusetts	3,153,176	2.1%
8	Michigan	4,923,929	3.3%
21	Minnesota	2,599,899	1.7%
31	Mississippi	1,423,841	0.9%
18	Missouri	2,887,907	1.9%
44	Montana	484,485	0.3%
38	Nebraska	884,280	0.6%
35	Nevada	1,324,590	0.9%
41	New Hampshire	649,087	0.4%
11	New Jersey	4,251,782	2.8%
36	New Mexico	978,326	0.7%
3	New York	9,462,063	6.3%
10	North Carolina	4,516,987	3.0%
48	North Dakota	321,933	0.2%
7	Ohio	5,603,768	3.7%
28	Oklahoma	1,798,841	1.2%
27	Oregon	1,882,731	1.3%
6	Pennsylvania	6,060,170	4.0%
43	Rhode Island	508,705	0.3%
24	South Carolina	2,181,278	1.5%
46	South Dakota	400,861	0.3%
17	Tennessee	3,029,115	2.0%
2	Texas	12,143,558	8.1%
34	Utah	1,381,261	0.9%
49	Vermont	305,723	0.2%
12	Virginia	3,817,042	2.5%
13	Washington	3,269,925	2.2%
37	West Virginia	888,696	0.6%
19	Wisconsin	2,797,649	1.9%
50	Wyoming	270,190	0.2%

RANK	STATE	MALES	% of USA
1	California	18,388,022	12.3%
2	Texas	12,143,558	8.1%
3	New York	9,462,063	6.3%
4	Florida	9,005,282	6.0%
5	Illinois	6,359,906	4.2%
6	Pennsylvania	6,060,170	4.0%
7	Ohio	5,603,768	3.7%
8	Michigan	4,923,929	3.3%
9	Georgia	4,764,975	3.2%
10	North Carolina	4,516,987	3.0%
11	New Jersey	4,251,782	2.8%
12	Virginia	3,817,042	2.5%
13	Washington	3,269,925	2.2%
14	Arizona	3,256,691	2.2%
15	Massachusetts	3,153,176	2.1%
16	Indiana	3,142,510	2.1%
17	Tennessee	3,029,115	2.0%
18	Missouri	2,887,907	1.9%
19	Wisconsin	2,797,649	1.9%
20	Maryland	2,727,323	1.8%
21	Minnesota	2,599,899	1.7%
22	Colorado	2,491,041	1.7%
23	Alabama	2,258,087	1.5%
24	South Carolina	2,181,278	1.5%
25	Louisiana	2,140,798	1.4%
26	Kentucky	2,088,142	1.4%
27	Oregon	1,882,731	1.3%
28	Oklahoma	1,798,841	1.2%
29	Connecticut	1,707,410	1.1%
30	Iowa	1,482,872	1.0%
31	Mississippi	1,423,841	0.9%
32	Arkansas	1,398,635	0.9%
33	Kansas	1,391,821	0.9%
34	Utah	1,381,261	0.9%
35	Nevada	1,324,590	0.9%
36	New Mexico	978,326	0.7%
37	West Virginia	888,696	0.6%
38	Nebraska	884,280	0.6%
39	Idaho	766,580	0.5%
40	Hawaii	649,519	0.4%
41	New Hampshire	649,087	0.4%
42	Maine	642,369	0.4%
43	Rhode Island	508,705	0.3%
44	Montana	484,485	0.3%
45	Delaware	423,336	0.3%
46	South Dakota	400,861	0.3%
47	Alaska	357,607	0.2%
48	North Dakota	321,933	0.2%
49	Vermont	305,723	0.2%
50	Wyoming	270,190	0.2%
	District of Columbia	279,880	0.2%

Source: CQ Press using data from U.S. Bureau of the Census
"SC-EST2008-AGESEX_RES - State Characteristic Estimates" (http://www.census.gov/popest/datasets.html)

Female Population in 2008

National Total = 154,135,120 Females

RANK	STATE	FEMALES	% of USA
23	Alabama	2,403,813	1.6%
47	Alaska	328,686	0.2%
15	Arizona	3,243,489	2.1%
32	Arkansas	1,456,755	0.9%
1	California	18,368,644	11.9%
22	Colorado	2,448,415	1.6%
29	Connecticut	1,793,842	1.2%
45	Delaware	449,756	0.3%
4	Florida	9,323,058	6.0%
9	Georgia	4,920,769	3.2%
42	Hawaii	638,679	0.4%
39	Idaho	757,236	0.5%
5	Illinois	6,541,657	4.2%
16	Indiana	3,234,282	2.1%
30	Iowa	1,519,683	1.0%
33	Kansas	1,410,313	0.9%
26	Kentucky	2,181,103	1.4%
25	Louisiana	2,269,998	1.5%
40	Maine	674,087	0.4%
19	Maryland	2,906,274	1.9%
13	Massachusetts	3,344,791	2.2%
8	Michigan	5,079,493	3.3%
21	Minnesota	2,620,494	1.7%
31	Mississippi	1,514,777	1.0%
18	Missouri	3,023,698	2.0%
44	Montana	482,955	0.3%
38	Nebraska	899,152	0.6%
35	Nevada	1,275,577	0.8%
41	New Hampshire	666,722	0.4%
11	New Jersey	4,430,879	2.9%
36	New Mexico	1,006,030	0.7%
3	New York	10,028,234	6.5%
10	North Carolina	4,705,427	3.1%
48	North Dakota	319,548	0.2%
7	Ohio	5,882,142	3.8%
28	Oklahoma	1,843,520	1.2%
27	Oregon	1,907,329	1.2%
6	Pennsylvania	6,388,109	4.1%
43	Rhode Island	542,083	0.4%
24	South Carolina	2,298,522	1.5%
46	South Dakota	403,333	0.3%
17	Tennessee	3,185,773	2.1%
2	Texas	12,183,416	7.9%
34	Utah	1,355,163	0.9%
49	Vermont	315,547	0.2%
12	Virginia	3,952,047	2.6%
14	Washington	3,279,299	2.1%
37	West Virginia	925,772	0.6%
20	Wisconsin	2,830,318	1.8%
50	Wyoming	262,478	0.2%

RANK	STATE	FEMALES	% of USA
1	California	18,368,644	11.9%
2	Texas	12,183,416	7.9%
3	New York	10,028,234	6.5%
4	Florida	9,323,058	6.0%
5	Illinois	6,541,657	4.2%
6	Pennsylvania	6,388,109	4.1%
7	Ohio	5,882,142	3.8%
8	Michigan	5,079,493	3.3%
9	Georgia	4,920,769	3.2%
10	North Carolina	4,705,427	3.1%
11	New Jersey	4,430,879	2.9%
12	Virginia	3,952,047	2.6%
13	Massachusetts	3,344,791	2.2%
14	Washington	3,279,299	2.1%
15	Arizona	3,243,489	2.1%
16	Indiana	3,234,282	2.1%
17	Tennessee	3,185,773	2.1%
18	Missouri	3,023,698	2.0%
19	Maryland	2,906,274	1.9%
20	Wisconsin	2,830,318	1.8%
21	Minnesota	2,620,494	1.7%
22	Colorado	2,448,415	1.6%
23	Alabama	2,403,813	1.6%
24	South Carolina	2,298,522	1.5%
25	Louisiana	2,269,998	1.5%
26	Kentucky	2,181,103	1.4%
27	Oregon	1,907,329	1.2%
28	Oklahoma	1,843,520	1.2%
29	Connecticut	1,793,842	1.2%
30	Iowa	1,519,683	1.0%
31	Mississippi	1,514,777	1.0%
32	Arkansas	1,456,755	0.9%
33	Kansas	1,410,313	0.9%
34	Utah	1,355,163	0.9%
35	Nevada	1,275,577	0.8%
36	New Mexico	1,006,030	0.7%
37	West Virginia	925,772	0.6%
38	Nebraska	899,152	0.6%
39	Idaho	757,236	0.5%
40	Maine	674,087	0.4%
41	New Hampshire	666,722	0.4%
42	Hawaii	638,679	0.4%
43	Rhode Island	542,083	0.4%
44	Montana	482,955	0.3%
45	Delaware	449,756	0.3%
46	South Dakota	403,333	0.3%
47	Alaska	328,686	0.2%
48	North Dakota	319,548	0.2%
49	Vermont	315,547	0.2%
50	Wyoming	262,478	0.2%
	District of Columbia	311,953	0.2%

Source: CQ Press using data from U.S. Bureau of the Census
"SC-EST2008-AGESEX_RES - State Characteristic Estimates" (http://www.census.gov/popest/datasets.html)

Male to Female Ratio in 2008

National Ratio = 97.3 Males per 100 Females

ALPHA ORDER

RANK	STATE	RATIO
48	Alabama	93.9
1	Alaska	108.8
9	Arizona	100.4
31	Arkansas	96.0
11	California	100.1
5	Colorado	101.7
39	Connecticut	95.2
46	Delaware	94.1
29	Florida	96.6
28	Georgia	96.8
5	Hawaii	101.7
7	Idaho	101.2
23	Illinois	97.2
23	Indiana	97.2
20	Iowa	97.6
17	Kansas	98.7
35	Kentucky	95.7
44	Louisiana	94.3
37	Maine	95.3
49	Maryland	93.8
44	Massachusetts	94.3
26	Michigan	96.9
15	Minnesota	99.2
47	Mississippi	94.0
36	Missouri	95.5
10	Montana	100.3
19	Nebraska	98.3
2	Nevada	103.8
22	New Hampshire	97.4
31	New Jersey	96.0
23	New Mexico	97.2
43	New York	94.4
31	North Carolina	96.0
8	North Dakota	100.7
37	Ohio	95.3
20	Oklahoma	97.6
17	Oregon	98.7
41	Pennsylvania	94.9
49	Rhode Island	93.8
41	South Carolina	94.9
14	South Dakota	99.4
40	Tennessee	95.1
12	Texas	99.7
4	Utah	101.9
26	Vermont	96.9
29	Virginia	96.6
12	Washington	99.7
31	West Virginia	96.0
16	Wisconsin	98.8
3	Wyoming	102.9

RANK ORDER

RANK	STATE	RATIO
1	Alaska	108.8
2	Nevada	103.8
3	Wyoming	102.9
4	Utah	101.9
5	Colorado	101.7
5	Hawaii	101.7
7	Idaho	101.2
8	North Dakota	100.7
9	Arizona	100.4
10	Montana	100.3
11	California	100.1
12	Texas	99.7
12	Washington	99.7
14	South Dakota	99.4
15	Minnesota	99.2
16	Wisconsin	98.8
17	Kansas	98.7
17	Oregon	98.7
19	Nebraska	98.3
20	Iowa	97.6
20	Oklahoma	97.6
22	New Hampshire	97.4
23	Illinois	97.2
23	Indiana	97.2
23	New Mexico	97.2
26	Michigan	96.9
26	Vermont	96.9
28	Georgia	96.8
29	Florida	96.6
29	Virginia	96.6
31	Arkansas	96.0
31	New Jersey	96.0
31	North Carolina	96.0
31	West Virginia	96.0
35	Kentucky	95.7
36	Missouri	95.5
37	Maine	95.3
37	Ohio	95.3
39	Connecticut	95.2
40	Tennessee	95.1
41	Pennsylvania	94.9
41	South Carolina	94.9
43	New York	94.4
44	Louisiana	94.3
44	Massachusetts	94.3
46	Delaware	94.1
47	Mississippi	94.0
48	Alabama	93.9
49	Maryland	93.8
49	Rhode Island	93.8
	District of Columbia	89.7

Source: CQ Press using data from U.S. Bureau of the Census
"SC-EST2008-AGESEX_RES - State Characteristic Estimates" (http://www.census.gov/popest/datasets.html)

White Population in 2008

National Total = 242,639,242 White Persons*

ALPHA ORDER

RANK	STATE	WHITES	% of USA
25	Alabama	3,311,216	1.4%
49	Alaska	484,682	0.2%
13	Arizona	5,623,026	2.3%
33	Arkansas	2,306,697	1.0%
1	California	28,170,328	11.6%
21	Colorado	4,432,376	1.8%
27	Connecticut	2,950,808	1.2%
45	Delaware	648,411	0.3%
3	Florida	14,628,044	6.0%
11	Georgia	6,333,287	2.6%
50	Hawaii	382,174	0.2%
39	Idaho	1,441,540	0.6%
6	Illinois	10,209,408	4.2%
14	Indiana	5,611,577	2.3%
30	Iowa	2,827,520	1.2%
32	Kansas	2,485,597	1.0%
22	Kentucky	3,838,236	1.6%
28	Louisiana	2,859,940	1.2%
40	Maine	1,268,930	0.5%
23	Maryland	3,571,589	1.5%
15	Massachusetts	5,601,486	2.3%
8	Michigan	8,121,119	3.3%
20	Minnesota	4,648,528	1.9%
35	Mississippi	1,780,749	0.7%
18	Missouri	5,026,572	2.1%
43	Montana	875,221	0.4%
38	Nebraska	1,629,566	0.7%
34	Nevada	2,103,307	0.9%
41	New Hampshire	1,256,429	0.5%
10	New Jersey	6,601,611	2.7%
37	New Mexico	1,666,790	0.7%
4	New York	14,310,269	5.9%
9	North Carolina	6,818,808	2.8%
47	North Dakota	586,272	0.2%
7	Ohio	9,735,944	4.0%
29	Oklahoma	2,846,186	1.2%
24	Oregon	3,416,377	1.4%
5	Pennsylvania	10,633,888	4.4%
42	Rhode Island	929,778	0.4%
26	South Carolina	3,079,779	1.3%
44	South Dakota	709,217	0.3%
19	Tennessee	4,995,028	2.1%
2	Texas	20,046,078	8.3%
31	Utah	2,542,561	1.0%
46	Vermont	598,959	0.2%
12	Virginia	5,673,913	2.3%
16	Washington	5,520,400	2.3%
36	West Virginia	1,715,122	0.7%
17	Wisconsin	5,046,806	2.1%
48	Wyoming	500,001	0.2%

RANK ORDER

RANK	STATE	WHITES	% of USA
1	California	28,170,328	11.6%
2	Texas	20,046,078	8.3%
3	Florida	14,628,044	6.0%
4	New York	14,310,269	5.9%
5	Pennsylvania	10,633,888	4.4%
6	Illinois	10,209,408	4.2%
7	Ohio	9,735,944	4.0%
8	Michigan	8,121,119	3.3%
9	North Carolina	6,818,808	2.8%
10	New Jersey	6,601,611	2.7%
11	Georgia	6,333,287	2.6%
12	Virginia	5,673,913	2.3%
13	Arizona	5,623,026	2.3%
14	Indiana	5,611,577	2.3%
15	Massachusetts	5,601,486	2.3%
16	Washington	5,520,400	2.3%
17	Wisconsin	5,046,806	2.1%
18	Missouri	5,026,572	2.1%
19	Tennessee	4,995,028	2.1%
20	Minnesota	4,648,528	1.9%
21	Colorado	4,432,376	1.8%
22	Kentucky	3,838,236	1.6%
23	Maryland	3,571,589	1.5%
24	Oregon	3,416,377	1.4%
25	Alabama	3,311,216	1.4%
26	South Carolina	3,079,779	1.3%
27	Connecticut	2,950,808	1.2%
28	Louisiana	2,859,940	1.2%
29	Oklahoma	2,846,186	1.2%
30	Iowa	2,827,520	1.2%
31	Utah	2,542,561	1.0%
32	Kansas	2,485,597	1.0%
33	Arkansas	2,306,697	1.0%
34	Nevada	2,103,307	0.9%
35	Mississippi	1,780,749	0.7%
36	West Virginia	1,715,122	0.7%
37	New Mexico	1,666,790	0.7%
38	Nebraska	1,629,566	0.7%
39	Idaho	1,441,540	0.6%
40	Maine	1,268,930	0.5%
41	New Hampshire	1,256,429	0.5%
42	Rhode Island	929,778	0.4%
43	Montana	875,221	0.4%
44	South Dakota	709,217	0.3%
45	Delaware	648,411	0.3%
46	Vermont	598,959	0.2%
47	North Dakota	586,272	0.2%
48	Wyoming	500,001	0.2%
49	Alaska	484,682	0.2%
50	Hawaii	382,174	0.2%
	District of Columbia	237,092	0.1%

Source: U.S. Bureau of the Census

"State Population Estimates - Characteristics" (http://www.census.gov/popest/states/asrh/)

*"White" is defined by Census as a person having origins in any of the original peoples of Europe, North Africa, or the Middle East. There are 199,491,458 non-Hispanic whites. Census states "Race is a self-identification data item in which respondents choose the race or races with which they most closely identify."

Percent of Population White in 2008

National Percent = 79.8% White*

ALPHA ORDER				RANK ORDER		
RANK	STATE	PERCENT		RANK	STATE	PERCENT
43	Alabama	71.0		1	Maine	96.4
44	Alaska	70.6		1	Vermont	96.4
21	Arizona	86.5		3	New Hampshire	95.5
32	Arkansas	80.8		4	Idaho	94.6
37	California	76.6		5	West Virginia	94.5
14	Colorado	89.7		6	Iowa	94.2
26	Connecticut	84.3		7	Wyoming	93.9
39	Delaware	74.3		8	Utah	92.9
34	Florida	79.8		9	Nebraska	91.4
46	Georgia	65.4		9	North Dakota	91.4
50	Hawaii	29.7		11	Montana	90.5
4	Idaho	94.6		12	Oregon	90.1
35	Illinois	79.1		13	Kentucky	89.9
20	Indiana	88.0		14	Colorado	89.7
6	Iowa	94.2		14	Wisconsin	89.7
17	Kansas	88.7		16	Minnesota	89.0
13	Kentucky	89.9		17	Kansas	88.7
47	Louisiana	64.8		18	Rhode Island	88.5
1	Maine	96.4		19	South Dakota	88.2
48	Maryland	63.4		20	Indiana	88.0
22	Massachusetts	86.2		21	Arizona	86.5
30	Michigan	81.2		22	Massachusetts	86.2
16	Minnesota	89.0		23	Pennsylvania	85.4
49	Mississippi	60.6		24	Missouri	85.0
24	Missouri	85.0		25	Ohio	84.8
11	Montana	90.5		26	Connecticut	84.3
9	Nebraska	91.4		26	Washington	84.3
31	Nevada	80.9		28	New Mexico	84.0
3	New Hampshire	95.5		29	Texas	82.4
38	New Jersey	76.0		30	Michigan	81.2
28	New Mexico	84.0		31	Nevada	80.9
41	New York	73.4		32	Arkansas	80.8
40	North Carolina	73.9		33	Tennessee	80.4
9	North Dakota	91.4		34	Florida	79.8
25	Ohio	84.8		35	Illinois	79.1
36	Oklahoma	78.1		36	Oklahoma	78.1
12	Oregon	90.1		37	California	76.6
23	Pennsylvania	85.4		38	New Jersey	76.0
18	Rhode Island	88.5		39	Delaware	74.3
45	South Carolina	68.7		40	North Carolina	73.9
19	South Dakota	88.2		41	New York	73.4
33	Tennessee	80.4		42	Virginia	73.0
29	Texas	82.4		43	Alabama	71.0
8	Utah	92.9		44	Alaska	70.6
1	Vermont	96.4		45	South Carolina	68.7
42	Virginia	73.0		46	Georgia	65.4
26	Washington	84.3		47	Louisiana	64.8
5	West Virginia	94.5		48	Maryland	63.4
14	Wisconsin	89.7		49	Mississippi	60.6
7	Wyoming	93.9		50	Hawaii	29.7

District of Columbia   40.1

Source: CQ Press using data from U.S. Bureau of the Census
   "State Population Estimates - Characteristics" (http://www.census.gov/popest/states/asrh/)
*"White" is defined by Census as a person having origins in any of the original peoples of Europe, North Africa, or the Middle East. Non-Hispanic whites comprise 65.6% of the total population. Census states "Race is a self-identification data item in which respondents choose the race or races with which they most closely identify."

Black Population in 2008

National Total = 39,058,834 Black Persons*

ALPHA ORDER				RANK ORDER			
RANK	STATE	BLACKS	% of USA	RANK	STATE	BLACKS	% of USA
16	Alabama	1,229,787	3.1%	1	New York	3,362,736	8.6%
42	Alaska	29,274	0.1%	2	Florida	2,916,174	7.5%
27	Arizona	270,159	0.7%	3	Georgia	2,907,944	7.4%
22	Arkansas	450,037	1.2%	4	Texas	2,898,143	7.4%
5	California	2,451,453	6.3%	5	California	2,451,453	6.3%
30	Colorado	211,249	0.5%	6	North Carolina	1,991,654	5.1%
23	Connecticut	361,879	0.9%	7	Illinois	1,919,701	4.9%
32	Delaware	182,890	0.5%	8	Maryland	1,658,422	4.2%
2	Florida	2,916,174	7.5%	9	Virginia	1,546,444	4.0%
3	Georgia	2,907,944	7.4%	10	Michigan	1,424,595	3.6%
40	Hawaii	39,620	0.1%	11	Louisiana	1,410,457	3.6%
44	Idaho	14,470	0.0%	12	Ohio	1,382,358	3.5%
7	Illinois	1,919,701	4.9%	13	Pennsylvania	1,342,571	3.4%
20	Indiana	578,088	1.5%	14	South Carolina	1,275,815	3.3%
34	Iowa	80,516	0.2%	15	New Jersey	1,255,868	3.2%
33	Kansas	172,342	0.4%	16	Alabama	1,229,787	3.1%
25	Kentucky	329,225	0.8%	17	Mississippi	1,092,588	2.8%
11	Louisiana	1,410,457	3.6%	18	Tennessee	1,042,811	2.7%
45	Maine	13,588	0.0%	19	Missouri	679,223	1.7%
8	Maryland	1,658,422	4.2%	20	Indiana	578,088	1.5%
21	Massachusetts	455,880	1.2%	21	Massachusetts	455,880	1.2%
10	Michigan	1,424,595	3.6%	22	Arkansas	450,037	1.2%
29	Minnesota	238,531	0.6%	23	Connecticut	361,879	0.9%
17	Mississippi	1,092,588	2.8%	24	Wisconsin	341,723	0.9%
19	Missouri	679,223	1.7%	25	Kentucky	329,225	0.8%
49	Montana	6,504	0.0%	26	Oklahoma	289,993	0.7%
35	Nebraska	80,174	0.2%	27	Arizona	270,159	0.7%
31	Nevada	210,677	0.5%	28	Washington	245,000	0.6%
43	New Hampshire	16,015	0.0%	29	Minnesota	238,531	0.6%
15	New Jersey	1,255,868	3.2%	30	Colorado	211,249	0.5%
39	New Mexico	59,009	0.2%	31	Nevada	210,677	0.5%
1	New York	3,362,736	8.6%	32	Delaware	182,890	0.5%
6	North Carolina	1,991,654	5.1%	33	Kansas	172,342	0.4%
47	North Dakota	6,956	0.0%	34	Iowa	80,516	0.2%
12	Ohio	1,382,358	3.5%	35	Nebraska	80,174	0.2%
26	Oklahoma	289,993	0.7%	36	Oregon	76,109	0.2%
36	Oregon	76,109	0.2%	37	Rhode Island	66,847	0.2%
13	Pennsylvania	1,342,571	3.4%	38	West Virginia	64,987	0.2%
37	Rhode Island	66,847	0.2%	39	New Mexico	59,009	0.2%
14	South Carolina	1,275,815	3.3%	40	Hawaii	39,620	0.1%
46	South Dakota	9,185	0.0%	41	Utah	34,880	0.1%
18	Tennessee	1,042,811	2.7%	42	Alaska	29,274	0.1%
4	Texas	2,898,143	7.4%	43	New Hampshire	16,015	0.0%
41	Utah	34,880	0.1%	44	Idaho	14,470	0.0%
50	Vermont	5,378	0.0%	45	Maine	13,588	0.0%
9	Virginia	1,546,444	4.0%	46	South Dakota	9,185	0.0%
28	Washington	245,000	0.6%	47	North Dakota	6,956	0.0%
38	West Virginia	64,987	0.2%	48	Wyoming	6,884	0.0%
24	Wisconsin	341,723	0.9%	49	Montana	6,504	0.0%
48	Wyoming	6,884	0.0%	50	Vermont	5,378	0.0%
					District of Columbia	322,021	0.8%

Source: U.S. Bureau of the Census

"State Population Estimates - Characteristics" (http://www.census.gov/popest/states/asrh/)

*"Black" is defined by Census as a person having origins in any of the Black racial groups of Africa. Census states "Race is a self-identification data item in which respondents choose the race or races with which they most closely identify."

Percent of Population Black in 2008

National Percent = 12.8% Black*

ALPHA ORDER

RANK	STATE	PERCENT
6	Alabama	26.4
33	Alaska	4.3
35	Arizona	4.2
13	Arkansas	15.8
27	California	6.7
33	Colorado	4.3
21	Connecticut	10.3
8	Delaware	20.9
12	Florida	15.9
3	Georgia	30.0
38	Hawaii	3.1
48	Idaho	0.9
14	Illinois	14.9
22	Indiana	9.1
40	Iowa	2.7
29	Kansas	6.2
25	Kentucky	7.7
2	Louisiana	32.0
47	Maine	1.0
4	Maryland	29.4
26	Massachusetts	7.0
16	Michigan	14.2
31	Minnesota	4.6
1	Mississippi	37.2
19	Missouri	11.5
50	Montana	0.7
32	Nebraska	4.5
23	Nevada	8.1
44	New Hampshire	1.2
15	New Jersey	14.5
39	New Mexico	3.0
10	New York	17.3
7	North Carolina	21.6
45	North Dakota	1.1
17	Ohio	12.0
24	Oklahoma	8.0
41	Oregon	2.0
20	Pennsylvania	10.8
28	Rhode Island	6.4
5	South Carolina	28.5
45	South Dakota	1.1
11	Tennessee	16.8
18	Texas	11.9
42	Utah	1.3
48	Vermont	0.9
9	Virginia	19.9
36	Washington	3.7
37	West Virginia	3.6
30	Wisconsin	6.1
42	Wyoming	1.3

RANK ORDER

RANK	STATE	PERCENT
1	Mississippi	37.2
2	Louisiana	32.0
3	Georgia	30.0
4	Maryland	29.4
5	South Carolina	28.5
6	Alabama	26.4
7	North Carolina	21.6
8	Delaware	20.9
9	Virginia	19.9
10	New York	17.3
11	Tennessee	16.8
12	Florida	15.9
13	Arkansas	15.8
14	Illinois	14.9
15	New Jersey	14.5
16	Michigan	14.2
17	Ohio	12.0
18	Texas	11.9
19	Missouri	11.5
20	Pennsylvania	10.8
21	Connecticut	10.3
22	Indiana	9.1
23	Nevada	8.1
24	Oklahoma	8.0
25	Kentucky	7.7
26	Massachusetts	7.0
27	California	6.7
28	Rhode Island	6.4
29	Kansas	6.2
30	Wisconsin	6.1
31	Minnesota	4.6
32	Nebraska	4.5
33	Alaska	4.3
33	Colorado	4.3
35	Arizona	4.2
36	Washington	3.7
37	West Virginia	3.6
38	Hawaii	3.1
39	New Mexico	3.0
40	Iowa	2.7
41	Oregon	2.0
42	Utah	1.3
42	Wyoming	1.3
44	New Hampshire	1.2
45	North Dakota	1.1
45	South Dakota	1.1
47	Maine	1.0
48	Idaho	0.9
48	Vermont	0.9
50	Montana	0.7

District of Columbia	54.4

Source: CQ Press using data from U.S. Bureau of the Census
"State Population Estimates - Characteristics" (http://www.census.gov/popest/states/asrh/)
*"Black" is defined by Census as a person having origins in any of the Black racial groups of Africa. Census states "Race is a self-identification data item in which respondents choose the race or races with which they most closely identify."

Hispanic Population in 2008

National Total = 46,943,613 Hispanics*

ALPHA ORDER

RANK	STATE	HISPANICS	% of USA
35	Alabama	134,810	0.3%
42	Alaska	41,853	0.1%
6	Arizona	1,955,630	4.2%
31	Arkansas	159,525	0.3%
1	California	13,457,397	28.7%
8	Colorado	997,062	2.1%
17	Connecticut	419,391	0.9%
41	Delaware	59,093	0.1%
3	Florida	3,845,069	8.2%
10	Georgia	777,244	1.7%
38	Hawaii	112,320	0.2%
32	Idaho	155,827	0.3%
5	Illinois	1,967,121	4.2%
21	Indiana	332,225	0.7%
36	Iowa	126,453	0.3%
26	Kansas	255,409	0.5%
39	Kentucky	101,981	0.2%
33	Louisiana	148,463	0.3%
48	Maine	16,814	0.0%
20	Maryland	375,830	0.8%
15	Massachusetts	556,897	1.2%
19	Michigan	413,827	0.9%
28	Minnesota	216,574	0.5%
40	Mississippi	65,798	0.1%
29	Missouri	189,700	0.4%
45	Montana	28,804	0.1%
34	Nebraska	140,498	0.3%
12	Nevada	668,527	1.4%
44	New Hampshire	34,676	0.1%
7	New Jersey	1,418,545	3.0%
9	New Mexico	891,013	1.9%
4	New York	3,250,038	6.9%
11	North Carolina	684,770	1.5%
49	North Dakota	13,227	0.0%
23	Ohio	302,101	0.6%
25	Oklahoma	278,620	0.6%
18	Oregon	416,044	0.9%
14	Pennsylvania	593,986	1.3%
37	Rhode Island	122,206	0.3%
30	South Carolina	183,981	0.4%
46	South Dakota	21,016	0.0%
27	Tennessee	231,272	0.5%
2	Texas	8,870,475	18.9%
22	Utah	329,069	0.7%
50	Vermont	8,588	0.0%
16	Virginia	531,396	1.1%
13	Washington	643,687	1.4%
47	West Virginia	20,648	0.0%
24	Wisconsin	285,827	0.6%
43	Wyoming	41,162	0.1%

RANK ORDER

RANK	STATE	HISPANICS	% of USA
1	California	13,457,397	28.7%
2	Texas	8,870,475	18.9%
3	Florida	3,845,069	8.2%
4	New York	3,250,038	6.9%
5	Illinois	1,967,121	4.2%
6	Arizona	1,955,630	4.2%
7	New Jersey	1,418,545	3.0%
8	Colorado	997,062	2.1%
9	New Mexico	891,013	1.9%
10	Georgia	777,244	1.7%
11	North Carolina	684,770	1.5%
12	Nevada	668,527	1.4%
13	Washington	643,687	1.4%
14	Pennsylvania	593,986	1.3%
15	Massachusetts	556,897	1.2%
16	Virginia	531,396	1.1%
17	Connecticut	419,391	0.9%
18	Oregon	416,044	0.9%
19	Michigan	413,827	0.9%
20	Maryland	375,830	0.8%
21	Indiana	332,225	0.7%
22	Utah	329,069	0.7%
23	Ohio	302,101	0.6%
24	Wisconsin	285,827	0.6%
25	Oklahoma	278,620	0.6%
26	Kansas	255,409	0.5%
27	Tennessee	231,272	0.5%
28	Minnesota	216,574	0.5%
29	Missouri	189,700	0.4%
30	South Carolina	183,981	0.4%
31	Arkansas	159,525	0.3%
32	Idaho	155,827	0.3%
33	Louisiana	148,463	0.3%
34	Nebraska	140,498	0.3%
35	Alabama	134,810	0.3%
36	Iowa	126,453	0.3%
37	Rhode Island	122,206	0.3%
38	Hawaii	112,320	0.2%
39	Kentucky	101,981	0.2%
40	Mississippi	65,798	0.1%
41	Delaware	59,093	0.1%
42	Alaska	41,853	0.1%
43	Wyoming	41,162	0.1%
44	New Hampshire	34,676	0.1%
45	Montana	28,804	0.1%
46	South Dakota	21,016	0.0%
47	West Virginia	20,648	0.0%
48	Maine	16,814	0.0%
49	North Dakota	13,227	0.0%
50	Vermont	8,588	0.0%
	District of Columbia	51,124	0.1%

Source: U.S. Bureau of the Census
  "State Population Estimates - Characteristics" (http://www.census.gov/popest/states/asrh/)
*Persons of Hispanic origin may be of any race. Census states "Race is a self-identification data item in which respondents choose the race or races with which they most closely identify."

Percent of Population Hispanic in 2008

National Percent = 15.4% Hispanic*

ALPHA ORDER

ALPHA ORDER

RANK	STATE	PERCENT
41	Alabama	2.9
28	Alaska	6.1
4	Arizona	30.1
29	Arkansas	5.6
2	California	36.6
7	Colorado	20.2
11	Connecticut	12.0
25	Delaware	6.8
6	Florida	21.0
20	Georgia	8.0
18	Hawaii	8.7
15	Idaho	10.2
10	Illinois	15.2
30	Indiana	5.2
33	Iowa	4.2
17	Kansas	9.1
45	Kentucky	2.4
38	Louisiana	3.4
49	Maine	1.3
27	Maryland	6.7
19	Massachusetts	8.6
34	Michigan	4.1
34	Minnesota	4.1
46	Mississippi	2.2
39	Missouri	3.2
40	Montana	3.0
21	Nebraska	7.9
5	Nevada	25.7
42	New Hampshire	2.6
9	New Jersey	16.3
1	New Mexico	44.9
8	New York	16.7
24	North Carolina	7.4
47	North Dakota	2.1
42	Ohio	2.6
23	Oklahoma	7.6
14	Oregon	11.0
32	Pennsylvania	4.8
13	Rhode Island	11.6
34	South Carolina	4.1
42	South Dakota	2.6
37	Tennessee	3.7
3	Texas	36.5
11	Utah	12.0
48	Vermont	1.4
25	Virginia	6.8
16	Washington	9.8
50	West Virginia	1.1
31	Wisconsin	5.1
22	Wyoming	7.7

RANK ORDER

RANK	STATE	PERCENT
1	New Mexico	44.9
2	California	36.6
3	Texas	36.5
4	Arizona	30.1
5	Nevada	25.7
6	Florida	21.0
7	Colorado	20.2
8	New York	16.7
9	New Jersey	16.3
10	Illinois	15.2
11	Connecticut	12.0
11	Utah	12.0
13	Rhode Island	11.6
14	Oregon	11.0
15	Idaho	10.2
16	Washington	9.8
17	Kansas	9.1
18	Hawaii	8.7
19	Massachusetts	8.6
20	Georgia	8.0
21	Nebraska	7.9
22	Wyoming	7.7
23	Oklahoma	7.6
24	North Carolina	7.4
25	Delaware	6.8
25	Virginia	6.8
27	Maryland	6.7
28	Alaska	6.1
29	Arkansas	5.6
30	Indiana	5.2
31	Wisconsin	5.1
32	Pennsylvania	4.8
33	Iowa	4.2
34	Michigan	4.1
34	Minnesota	4.1
34	South Carolina	4.1
37	Tennessee	3.7
38	Louisiana	3.4
39	Missouri	3.2
40	Montana	3.0
41	Alabama	2.9
42	New Hampshire	2.6
42	Ohio	2.6
42	South Dakota	2.6
45	Kentucky	2.4
46	Mississippi	2.2
47	North Dakota	2.1
48	Vermont	1.4
49	Maine	1.3
50	West Virginia	1.1

District of Columbia   8.6

Source: CQ Press using data from U.S. Bureau of the Census
"State Population Estimates - Characteristics" (http://www.census.gov/popest/states/asrh/)
*Persons of Hispanic origin may be of any race. Census states "Race is a self-identification data item in which respondents choose the race or races with which they most closely identify."

Asian Population in 2008

National Total = 13,549,064 Asians*

ALPHA ORDER

RANK	STATE	ASIANS	% of USA
33	Alabama	44,541	0.3%
35	Alaska	31,043	0.2%
18	Arizona	162,014	1.2%
36	Arkansas	30,654	0.2%
1	California	4,581,890	33.8%
21	Colorado	131,084	1.0%
22	Connecticut	121,248	0.9%
41	Delaware	25,129	0.2%
8	Florida	416,318	3.1%
13	Georgia	276,615	2.0%
6	Hawaii	506,159	3.7%
43	Idaho	17,394	0.1%
5	Illinois	558,933	4.1%
24	Indiana	86,768	0.6%
32	Iowa	47,486	0.4%
29	Kansas	62,468	0.5%
34	Kentucky	42,335	0.3%
27	Louisiana	63,818	0.5%
45	Maine	11,693	0.1%
12	Maryland	286,333	2.1%
10	Massachusetts	321,130	2.4%
14	Michigan	236,559	1.7%
15	Minnesota	185,089	1.4%
42	Mississippi	23,699	0.2%
25	Missouri	85,898	0.6%
47	Montana	6,130	0.0%
37	Nebraska	30,409	0.2%
19	Nevada	161,366	1.2%
40	New Hampshire	25,147	0.2%
4	New Jersey	664,251	4.9%
39	New Mexico	27,884	0.2%
2	New York	1,368,585	10.1%
17	North Carolina	177,177	1.3%
49	North Dakota	4,759	0.0%
16	Ohio	181,362	1.3%
28	Oklahoma	62,770	0.5%
20	Oregon	137,893	1.0%
11	Pennsylvania	304,309	2.2%
38	Rhode Island	29,099	0.2%
30	South Carolina	54,622	0.4%
48	South Dakota	5,960	0.0%
26	Tennessee	82,539	0.6%
3	Texas	841,016	6.2%
31	Utah	53,996	0.4%
46	Vermont	7,055	0.1%
9	Virginia	378,226	2.8%
7	Washington	437,783	3.2%
44	West Virginia	11,977	0.1%
23	Wisconsin	114,503	0.8%
50	Wyoming	3,828	0.0%

RANK ORDER

RANK	STATE	ASIANS	% of USA
1	California	4,581,890	33.8%
2	New York	1,368,585	10.1%
3	Texas	841,016	6.2%
4	New Jersey	664,251	4.9%
5	Illinois	558,933	4.1%
6	Hawaii	506,159	3.7%
7	Washington	437,783	3.2%
8	Florida	416,318	3.1%
9	Virginia	378,226	2.8%
10	Massachusetts	321,130	2.4%
11	Pennsylvania	304,309	2.2%
12	Maryland	286,333	2.1%
13	Georgia	276,615	2.0%
14	Michigan	236,559	1.7%
15	Minnesota	185,089	1.4%
16	Ohio	181,362	1.3%
17	North Carolina	177,177	1.3%
18	Arizona	162,014	1.2%
19	Nevada	161,366	1.2%
20	Oregon	137,893	1.0%
21	Colorado	131,084	1.0%
22	Connecticut	121,248	0.9%
23	Wisconsin	114,503	0.8%
24	Indiana	86,768	0.6%
25	Missouri	85,898	0.6%
26	Tennessee	82,539	0.6%
27	Louisiana	63,818	0.5%
28	Oklahoma	62,770	0.5%
29	Kansas	62,468	0.5%
30	South Carolina	54,622	0.4%
31	Utah	53,996	0.4%
32	Iowa	47,486	0.4%
33	Alabama	44,541	0.3%
34	Kentucky	42,335	0.3%
35	Alaska	31,043	0.2%
36	Arkansas	30,654	0.2%
37	Nebraska	30,409	0.2%
38	Rhode Island	29,099	0.2%
39	New Mexico	27,884	0.2%
40	New Hampshire	25,147	0.2%
41	Delaware	25,129	0.2%
42	Mississippi	23,699	0.2%
43	Idaho	17,394	0.1%
44	West Virginia	11,977	0.1%
45	Maine	11,693	0.1%
46	Vermont	7,055	0.1%
47	Montana	6,130	0.0%
48	South Dakota	5,960	0.0%
49	North Dakota	4,759	0.0%
50	Wyoming	3,828	0.0%
	District of Columbia	20,120	0.1%

Source: U.S. Bureau of the Census

"State Population Estimates - Characteristics" (http://www.census.gov/popest/states/asrh/)

*Census states "Race is a self-identification data item in which respondents choose the race or races with which they most closely identify."

Percent of Population Asian in 2008

National Percent = 4.5% Asian*

<table>
<tr><th colspan="3">ALPHA ORDER</th><th colspan="3">RANK ORDER</th></tr>
<tr><th>RANK</th><th>STATE</th><th>PERCENT</th><th>RANK</th><th>STATE</th><th>PERCENT</th></tr>
<tr><td>42</td><td>Alabama</td><td>1.0</td><td>1</td><td>Hawaii</td><td>39.3</td></tr>
<tr><td>10</td><td>Alaska</td><td>4.5</td><td>2</td><td>California</td><td>12.5</td></tr>
<tr><td>20</td><td>Arizona</td><td>2.5</td><td>3</td><td>New Jersey</td><td>7.7</td></tr>
<tr><td>39</td><td>Arkansas</td><td>1.1</td><td>4</td><td>New York</td><td>7.0</td></tr>
<tr><td>2</td><td>California</td><td>12.5</td><td>5</td><td>Washington</td><td>6.7</td></tr>
<tr><td>19</td><td>Colorado</td><td>2.7</td><td>6</td><td>Nevada</td><td>6.2</td></tr>
<tr><td>13</td><td>Connecticut</td><td>3.5</td><td>7</td><td>Maryland</td><td>5.1</td></tr>
<tr><td>16</td><td>Delaware</td><td>2.9</td><td>8</td><td>Massachusetts</td><td>4.9</td></tr>
<tr><td>23</td><td>Florida</td><td>2.3</td><td>8</td><td>Virginia</td><td>4.9</td></tr>
<tr><td>16</td><td>Georgia</td><td>2.9</td><td>10</td><td>Alaska</td><td>4.5</td></tr>
<tr><td>1</td><td>Hawaii</td><td>39.3</td><td>11</td><td>Illinois</td><td>4.3</td></tr>
<tr><td>39</td><td>Idaho</td><td>1.1</td><td>12</td><td>Oregon</td><td>3.6</td></tr>
<tr><td>11</td><td>Illinois</td><td>4.3</td><td>13</td><td>Connecticut</td><td>3.5</td></tr>
<tr><td>34</td><td>Indiana</td><td>1.4</td><td>13</td><td>Minnesota</td><td>3.5</td></tr>
<tr><td>31</td><td>Iowa</td><td>1.6</td><td>13</td><td>Texas</td><td>3.5</td></tr>
<tr><td>24</td><td>Kansas</td><td>2.2</td><td>16</td><td>Delaware</td><td>2.9</td></tr>
<tr><td>42</td><td>Kentucky</td><td>1.0</td><td>16</td><td>Georgia</td><td>2.9</td></tr>
<tr><td>34</td><td>Louisiana</td><td>1.4</td><td>18</td><td>Rhode Island</td><td>2.8</td></tr>
<tr><td>44</td><td>Maine</td><td>0.9</td><td>19</td><td>Colorado</td><td>2.7</td></tr>
<tr><td>7</td><td>Maryland</td><td>5.1</td><td>20</td><td>Arizona</td><td>2.5</td></tr>
<tr><td>8</td><td>Massachusetts</td><td>4.9</td><td>21</td><td>Michigan</td><td>2.4</td></tr>
<tr><td>21</td><td>Michigan</td><td>2.4</td><td>21</td><td>Pennsylvania</td><td>2.4</td></tr>
<tr><td>13</td><td>Minnesota</td><td>3.5</td><td>23</td><td>Florida</td><td>2.3</td></tr>
<tr><td>45</td><td>Mississippi</td><td>0.8</td><td>24</td><td>Kansas</td><td>2.2</td></tr>
<tr><td>33</td><td>Missouri</td><td>1.5</td><td>25</td><td>Utah</td><td>2.0</td></tr>
<tr><td>50</td><td>Montana</td><td>0.6</td><td>25</td><td>Wisconsin</td><td>2.0</td></tr>
<tr><td>29</td><td>Nebraska</td><td>1.7</td><td>27</td><td>New Hampshire</td><td>1.9</td></tr>
<tr><td>6</td><td>Nevada</td><td>6.2</td><td>27</td><td>North Carolina</td><td>1.9</td></tr>
<tr><td>27</td><td>New Hampshire</td><td>1.9</td><td>29</td><td>Nebraska</td><td>1.7</td></tr>
<tr><td>3</td><td>New Jersey</td><td>7.7</td><td>29</td><td>Oklahoma</td><td>1.7</td></tr>
<tr><td>34</td><td>New Mexico</td><td>1.4</td><td>31</td><td>Iowa</td><td>1.6</td></tr>
<tr><td>4</td><td>New York</td><td>7.0</td><td>31</td><td>Ohio</td><td>1.6</td></tr>
<tr><td>27</td><td>North Carolina</td><td>1.9</td><td>33</td><td>Missouri</td><td>1.5</td></tr>
<tr><td>46</td><td>North Dakota</td><td>0.7</td><td>34</td><td>Indiana</td><td>1.4</td></tr>
<tr><td>31</td><td>Ohio</td><td>1.6</td><td>34</td><td>Louisiana</td><td>1.4</td></tr>
<tr><td>29</td><td>Oklahoma</td><td>1.7</td><td>34</td><td>New Mexico</td><td>1.4</td></tr>
<tr><td>12</td><td>Oregon</td><td>3.6</td><td>37</td><td>Tennessee</td><td>1.3</td></tr>
<tr><td>21</td><td>Pennsylvania</td><td>2.4</td><td>38</td><td>South Carolina</td><td>1.2</td></tr>
<tr><td>18</td><td>Rhode Island</td><td>2.8</td><td>39</td><td>Arkansas</td><td>1.1</td></tr>
<tr><td>38</td><td>South Carolina</td><td>1.2</td><td>39</td><td>Idaho</td><td>1.1</td></tr>
<tr><td>46</td><td>South Dakota</td><td>0.7</td><td>39</td><td>Vermont</td><td>1.1</td></tr>
<tr><td>37</td><td>Tennessee</td><td>1.3</td><td>42</td><td>Alabama</td><td>1.0</td></tr>
<tr><td>13</td><td>Texas</td><td>3.5</td><td>42</td><td>Kentucky</td><td>1.0</td></tr>
<tr><td>25</td><td>Utah</td><td>2.0</td><td>44</td><td>Maine</td><td>0.9</td></tr>
<tr><td>39</td><td>Vermont</td><td>1.1</td><td>45</td><td>Mississippi</td><td>0.8</td></tr>
<tr><td>8</td><td>Virginia</td><td>4.9</td><td>46</td><td>North Dakota</td><td>0.7</td></tr>
<tr><td>5</td><td>Washington</td><td>6.7</td><td>46</td><td>South Dakota</td><td>0.7</td></tr>
<tr><td>46</td><td>West Virginia</td><td>0.7</td><td>46</td><td>West Virginia</td><td>0.7</td></tr>
<tr><td>25</td><td>Wisconsin</td><td>2.0</td><td>46</td><td>Wyoming</td><td>0.7</td></tr>
<tr><td>46</td><td>Wyoming</td><td>0.7</td><td>50</td><td>Montana</td><td>0.6</td></tr>
<tr><td></td><td></td><td></td><td></td><td>District of Columbia</td><td>3.4</td></tr>
</table>

Source: CQ Press using data from U.S. Bureau of the Census
"State Population Estimates - Characteristics" (http://www.census.gov/popest/states/asrh/)
*Census states "Race is a self-identification data item in which respondents choose the race or races with which they most closely identify."

American Indian Population in 2008

National Total = 3,083,434 American Indians*

ALPHA ORDER

RANK	STATE	INDIANS	% of USA
30	Alabama	24,825	0.8%
9	Alaska	104,990	3.4%
2	Arizona	315,727	10.2%
31	Arkansas	24,302	0.8%
1	California	443,719	14.4%
15	Colorado	60,375	2.0%
41	Connecticut	13,387	0.4%
48	Delaware	3,691	0.1%
10	Florida	91,412	3.0%
22	Georgia	35,528	1.2%
45	Hawaii	7,569	0.2%
32	Idaho	23,209	0.8%
18	Illinois	45,128	1.5%
34	Indiana	20,390	0.7%
42	Iowa	12,644	0.4%
26	Kansas	28,895	0.9%
43	Kentucky	11,006	0.4%
28	Louisiana	28,230	0.9%
44	Maine	7,889	0.3%
36	Maryland	20,321	0.7%
35	Massachusetts	20,361	0.7%
14	Michigan	62,094	2.0%
12	Minnesota	64,503	2.1%
39	Mississippi	14,740	0.5%
24	Missouri	30,034	1.0%
13	Montana	62,303	2.0%
38	Nebraska	18,949	0.6%
19	Nevada	39,039	1.3%
49	New Hampshire	3,642	0.1%
23	New Jersey	30,132	1.0%
4	New Mexico	192,235	6.2%
8	New York	111,337	3.6%
6	North Carolina	115,635	3.8%
21	North Dakota	35,666	1.2%
25	Ohio	29,443	1.0%
3	Oklahoma	291,390	9.5%
17	Oregon	54,405	1.8%
29	Pennsylvania	27,181	0.9%
46	Rhode Island	6,591	0.2%
37	South Carolina	19,091	0.6%
11	South Dakota	68,000	2.2%
33	Tennessee	20,709	0.7%
5	Texas	184,649	6.0%
20	Utah	38,102	1.2%
50	Vermont	2,437	0.1%
27	Virginia	28,595	0.9%
7	Washington	112,965	3.7%
47	West Virginia	4,203	0.1%
16	Wisconsin	55,844	1.8%
40	Wyoming	13,555	0.4%

RANK ORDER

RANK	STATE	INDIANS	% of USA
1	California	443,719	14.4%
2	Arizona	315,727	10.2%
3	Oklahoma	291,390	9.5%
4	New Mexico	192,235	6.2%
5	Texas	184,649	6.0%
6	North Carolina	115,635	3.8%
7	Washington	112,965	3.7%
8	New York	111,337	3.6%
9	Alaska	104,990	3.4%
10	Florida	91,412	3.0%
11	South Dakota	68,000	2.2%
12	Minnesota	64,503	2.1%
13	Montana	62,303	2.0%
14	Michigan	62,094	2.0%
15	Colorado	60,375	2.0%
16	Wisconsin	55,844	1.8%
17	Oregon	54,405	1.8%
18	Illinois	45,128	1.5%
19	Nevada	39,039	1.3%
20	Utah	38,102	1.2%
21	North Dakota	35,666	1.2%
22	Georgia	35,528	1.2%
23	New Jersey	30,132	1.0%
24	Missouri	30,034	1.0%
25	Ohio	29,443	1.0%
26	Kansas	28,895	0.9%
27	Virginia	28,595	0.9%
28	Louisiana	28,230	0.9%
29	Pennsylvania	27,181	0.9%
30	Alabama	24,825	0.8%
31	Arkansas	24,302	0.8%
32	Idaho	23,209	0.8%
33	Tennessee	20,709	0.7%
34	Indiana	20,390	0.7%
35	Massachusetts	20,361	0.7%
36	Maryland	20,321	0.7%
37	South Carolina	19,091	0.6%
38	Nebraska	18,949	0.6%
39	Mississippi	14,740	0.5%
40	Wyoming	13,555	0.4%
41	Connecticut	13,387	0.4%
42	Iowa	12,644	0.4%
43	Kentucky	11,006	0.4%
44	Maine	7,889	0.3%
45	Hawaii	7,569	0.2%
46	Rhode Island	6,591	0.2%
47	West Virginia	4,203	0.1%
48	Delaware	3,691	0.1%
49	New Hampshire	3,642	0.1%
50	Vermont	2,437	0.1%
	District of Columbia	2,367	0.1%

Source: U.S. Bureau of the Census
"State Population Estimates - Characteristics" (http://www.census.gov/popest/states/asrh/)
*Includes Alaska Native populations. Census states "Race is a self-identification data item in which respondents choose the race or races with which they most closely identify."

Percent of Population American Indian in 2008

National Percent = 1.0% American Indian*

<table>
<tr><td colspan="3">ALPHA ORDER</td><td colspan="3">RANK ORDER</td></tr>
<tr><th>RANK</th><th>STATE</th><th>PERCENT</th><th>RANK</th><th>STATE</th><th>PERCENT</th></tr>
<tr><td>29</td><td>Alabama</td><td>0.5</td><td>1</td><td>Alaska</td><td>15.3</td></tr>
<tr><td>1</td><td>Alaska</td><td>15.3</td><td>2</td><td>New Mexico</td><td>9.7</td></tr>
<tr><td>7</td><td>Arizona</td><td>4.9</td><td>3</td><td>South Dakota</td><td>8.5</td></tr>
<tr><td>21</td><td>Arkansas</td><td>0.9</td><td>4</td><td>Oklahoma</td><td>8.0</td></tr>
<tr><td>15</td><td>California</td><td>1.2</td><td>5</td><td>Montana</td><td>6.4</td></tr>
<tr><td>15</td><td>Colorado</td><td>1.2</td><td>6</td><td>North Dakota</td><td>5.6</td></tr>
<tr><td>33</td><td>Connecticut</td><td>0.4</td><td>7</td><td>Arizona</td><td>4.9</td></tr>
<tr><td>33</td><td>Delaware</td><td>0.4</td><td>8</td><td>Wyoming</td><td>2.5</td></tr>
<tr><td>29</td><td>Florida</td><td>0.5</td><td>9</td><td>Washington</td><td>1.7</td></tr>
<tr><td>33</td><td>Georgia</td><td>0.4</td><td>10</td><td>Idaho</td><td>1.5</td></tr>
<tr><td>23</td><td>Hawaii</td><td>0.6</td><td>10</td><td>Nevada</td><td>1.5</td></tr>
<tr><td>10</td><td>Idaho</td><td>1.5</td><td>12</td><td>Oregon</td><td>1.4</td></tr>
<tr><td>41</td><td>Illinois</td><td>0.3</td><td>12</td><td>Utah</td><td>1.4</td></tr>
<tr><td>41</td><td>Indiana</td><td>0.3</td><td>14</td><td>North Carolina</td><td>1.3</td></tr>
<tr><td>33</td><td>Iowa</td><td>0.4</td><td>15</td><td>California</td><td>1.2</td></tr>
<tr><td>19</td><td>Kansas</td><td>1.0</td><td>15</td><td>Colorado</td><td>1.2</td></tr>
<tr><td>41</td><td>Kentucky</td><td>0.3</td><td>15</td><td>Minnesota</td><td>1.2</td></tr>
<tr><td>23</td><td>Louisiana</td><td>0.6</td><td>18</td><td>Nebraska</td><td>1.1</td></tr>
<tr><td>23</td><td>Maine</td><td>0.6</td><td>19</td><td>Kansas</td><td>1.0</td></tr>
<tr><td>33</td><td>Maryland</td><td>0.4</td><td>19</td><td>Wisconsin</td><td>1.0</td></tr>
<tr><td>41</td><td>Massachusetts</td><td>0.3</td><td>21</td><td>Arkansas</td><td>0.9</td></tr>
<tr><td>23</td><td>Michigan</td><td>0.6</td><td>22</td><td>Texas</td><td>0.8</td></tr>
<tr><td>15</td><td>Minnesota</td><td>1.2</td><td>23</td><td>Hawaii</td><td>0.6</td></tr>
<tr><td>29</td><td>Mississippi</td><td>0.5</td><td>23</td><td>Louisiana</td><td>0.6</td></tr>
<tr><td>29</td><td>Missouri</td><td>0.5</td><td>23</td><td>Maine</td><td>0.6</td></tr>
<tr><td>5</td><td>Montana</td><td>6.4</td><td>23</td><td>Michigan</td><td>0.6</td></tr>
<tr><td>18</td><td>Nebraska</td><td>1.1</td><td>23</td><td>New York</td><td>0.6</td></tr>
<tr><td>10</td><td>Nevada</td><td>1.5</td><td>23</td><td>Rhode Island</td><td>0.6</td></tr>
<tr><td>41</td><td>New Hampshire</td><td>0.3</td><td>29</td><td>Alabama</td><td>0.5</td></tr>
<tr><td>41</td><td>New Jersey</td><td>0.3</td><td>29</td><td>Florida</td><td>0.5</td></tr>
<tr><td>2</td><td>New Mexico</td><td>9.7</td><td>29</td><td>Mississippi</td><td>0.5</td></tr>
<tr><td>23</td><td>New York</td><td>0.6</td><td>29</td><td>Missouri</td><td>0.5</td></tr>
<tr><td>14</td><td>North Carolina</td><td>1.3</td><td>33</td><td>Connecticut</td><td>0.4</td></tr>
<tr><td>6</td><td>North Dakota</td><td>5.6</td><td>33</td><td>Delaware</td><td>0.4</td></tr>
<tr><td>41</td><td>Ohio</td><td>0.3</td><td>33</td><td>Georgia</td><td>0.4</td></tr>
<tr><td>4</td><td>Oklahoma</td><td>8.0</td><td>33</td><td>Iowa</td><td>0.4</td></tr>
<tr><td>12</td><td>Oregon</td><td>1.4</td><td>33</td><td>Maryland</td><td>0.4</td></tr>
<tr><td>49</td><td>Pennsylvania</td><td>0.2</td><td>33</td><td>South Carolina</td><td>0.4</td></tr>
<tr><td>23</td><td>Rhode Island</td><td>0.6</td><td>33</td><td>Vermont</td><td>0.4</td></tr>
<tr><td>33</td><td>South Carolina</td><td>0.4</td><td>33</td><td>Virginia</td><td>0.4</td></tr>
<tr><td>3</td><td>South Dakota</td><td>8.5</td><td>41</td><td>Illinois</td><td>0.3</td></tr>
<tr><td>41</td><td>Tennessee</td><td>0.3</td><td>41</td><td>Indiana</td><td>0.3</td></tr>
<tr><td>22</td><td>Texas</td><td>0.8</td><td>41</td><td>Kentucky</td><td>0.3</td></tr>
<tr><td>12</td><td>Utah</td><td>1.4</td><td>41</td><td>Massachusetts</td><td>0.3</td></tr>
<tr><td>33</td><td>Vermont</td><td>0.4</td><td>41</td><td>New Hampshire</td><td>0.3</td></tr>
<tr><td>33</td><td>Virginia</td><td>0.4</td><td>41</td><td>New Jersey</td><td>0.3</td></tr>
<tr><td>9</td><td>Washington</td><td>1.7</td><td>41</td><td>Ohio</td><td>0.3</td></tr>
<tr><td>49</td><td>West Virginia</td><td>0.2</td><td>41</td><td>Tennessee</td><td>0.3</td></tr>
<tr><td>19</td><td>Wisconsin</td><td>1.0</td><td>49</td><td>Pennsylvania</td><td>0.2</td></tr>
<tr><td>8</td><td>Wyoming</td><td>2.5</td><td>49</td><td>West Virginia</td><td>0.2</td></tr>
<tr><td></td><td></td><td></td><td></td><td>District of Columbia</td><td>0.4</td></tr>
</table>

Source: CQ Press using data from U.S. Bureau of the Census
"State Population Estimates - Characteristics" (http://www.census.gov/popest/states/asrh/)
*Includes Alaska Native populations. Census states "Race is a self-identification data item in which respondents choose the race or races with which they most closely identify."

Mixed Race Population in 2008

National Total = 5,167,029 Mixed Race*

ALPHA ORDER

RANK ORDER

RANK	STATE	MIXED RACE	% of USA	RANK	STATE	MIXED RACE	% of USA
29	Alabama	49,586	1.0%	1	California	952,164	18.4%
37	Alaska	31,805	0.6%	2	Texas	326,030	6.3%
15	Arizona	115,995	2.2%	3	New York	316,822	6.1%
34	Arkansas	40,817	0.8%	4	Florida	258,734	5.0%
1	California	952,164	18.4%	5	Hawaii	235,672	4.6%
17	Colorado	96,903	1.9%	6	Washington	201,254	3.9%
27	Connecticut	51,069	1.0%	7	Illinois	159,040	3.1%
46	Delaware	12,378	0.2%	8	Michigan	154,921	3.0%
4	Florida	258,734	5.0%	9	Ohio	152,708	3.0%
13	Georgia	124,055	2.4%	10	Oklahoma	148,159	2.9%
5	Hawaii	235,672	4.6%	11	Virginia	135,088	2.6%
39	Idaho	25,159	0.5%	12	Pennsylvania	134,234	2.6%
7	Illinois	159,040	3.1%	13	Georgia	124,055	2.4%
23	Indiana	76,833	1.5%	14	New Jersey	123,145	2.4%
36	Iowa	32,866	0.6%	15	Arizona	115,995	2.2%
28	Kansas	50,701	1.0%	16	North Carolina	112,364	2.2%
32	Kentucky	46,441	0.9%	17	Colorado	96,903	1.9%
31	Louisiana	46,505	0.9%	18	Oregon	94,242	1.8%
45	Maine	13,872	0.3%	19	Massachusetts	93,603	1.8%
20	Maryland	92,698	1.8%	20	Maryland	92,698	1.8%
19	Massachusetts	93,603	1.8%	21	Missouri	85,292	1.7%
8	Michigan	154,921	3.0%	22	Minnesota	80,491	1.6%
22	Minnesota	80,491	1.6%	23	Indiana	76,833	1.5%
38	Mississippi	25,747	0.5%	24	Nevada	71,508	1.4%
21	Missouri	85,292	1.7%	25	Tennessee	70,323	1.4%
43	Montana	16,592	0.3%	26	Wisconsin	66,613	1.3%
40	Nebraska	22,957	0.4%	27	Connecticut	51,069	1.0%
24	Nevada	71,508	1.4%	28	Kansas	50,701	1.0%
44	New Hampshire	14,027	0.3%	29	Alabama	49,586	1.0%
14	New Jersey	123,145	2.4%	30	South Carolina	47,749	0.9%
35	New Mexico	35,584	0.7%	31	Louisiana	46,505	0.9%
3	New York	316,822	6.1%	32	Kentucky	46,441	0.9%
16	North Carolina	112,364	2.2%	33	Utah	45,791	0.9%
49	North Dakota	7,492	0.1%	34	Arkansas	40,817	0.8%
9	Ohio	152,708	3.0%	35	New Mexico	35,584	0.7%
10	Oklahoma	148,159	2.9%	36	Iowa	32,866	0.6%
18	Oregon	94,242	1.8%	37	Alaska	31,805	0.6%
12	Pennsylvania	134,234	2.6%	38	Mississippi	25,747	0.5%
42	Rhode Island	17,179	0.3%	39	Idaho	25,159	0.5%
30	South Carolina	47,749	0.9%	40	Nebraska	22,957	0.4%
47	South Dakota	11,417	0.2%	41	West Virginia	17,643	0.3%
25	Tennessee	70,323	1.4%	42	Rhode Island	17,179	0.3%
2	Texas	326,030	6.3%	43	Montana	16,592	0.3%
33	Utah	45,791	0.9%	44	New Hampshire	14,027	0.3%
50	Vermont	7,238	0.1%	45	Maine	13,872	0.3%
11	Virginia	135,088	2.6%	46	Delaware	12,378	0.2%
6	Washington	201,254	3.9%	47	South Dakota	11,417	0.2%
41	West Virginia	17,643	0.3%	48	Wyoming	7,888	0.2%
26	Wisconsin	66,613	1.3%	49	North Dakota	7,492	0.1%
48	Wyoming	7,888	0.2%	50	Vermont	7,238	0.1%
					District of Columbia	9,635	0.2%

Source: U.S. Bureau of the Census

"State Population Estimates - Characteristics" (http://www.census.gov/popest/states/asrh/)

*Census states "Race is a self-identification data item in which respondents choose the race or races with which they most closely identify." The 2000 Census was the first to allow respondents to identify themselves as one or more races.

Percent of Population of Mixed Race in 2008

National Percent = 1.7% Mixed Race*

ALPHA ORDER			RANK ORDER		
RANK	STATE	PERCENT	RANK	STATE	PERCENT
40	Alabama	1.1	1	Hawaii	18.3
2	Alaska	4.6	2	Alaska	4.6
9	Arizona	1.8	3	Oklahoma	4.1
23	Arkansas	1.4	4	Washington	3.1
6	California	2.6	5	Nevada	2.8
8	Colorado	2.0	6	California	2.6
19	Connecticut	1.5	7	Oregon	2.5
23	Delaware	1.4	8	Colorado	2.0
23	Florida	1.4	9	Arizona	1.8
30	Georgia	1.3	9	Kansas	1.8
1	Hawaii	18.3	9	New Mexico	1.8
12	Idaho	1.7	12	Idaho	1.7
34	Illinois	1.2	12	Montana	1.7
34	Indiana	1.2	12	Utah	1.7
40	Iowa	1.1	12	Virginia	1.7
9	Kansas	1.8	16	Maryland	1.6
40	Kentucky	1.1	16	New York	1.6
40	Louisiana	1.1	16	Rhode Island	1.6
40	Maine	1.1	19	Connecticut	1.5
16	Maryland	1.6	19	Michigan	1.5
23	Massachusetts	1.4	19	Minnesota	1.5
19	Michigan	1.5	19	Wyoming	1.5
19	Minnesota	1.5	23	Arkansas	1.4
50	Mississippi	0.9	23	Delaware	1.4
23	Missouri	1.4	23	Florida	1.4
12	Montana	1.7	23	Massachusetts	1.4
30	Nebraska	1.3	23	Missouri	1.4
5	Nevada	2.8	23	New Jersey	1.4
40	New Hampshire	1.1	23	South Dakota	1.4
23	New Jersey	1.4	30	Georgia	1.3
9	New Mexico	1.8	30	Nebraska	1.3
16	New York	1.6	30	Ohio	1.3
34	North Carolina	1.2	30	Texas	1.3
34	North Dakota	1.2	34	Illinois	1.2
30	Ohio	1.3	34	Indiana	1.2
3	Oklahoma	4.1	34	North Carolina	1.2
7	Oregon	2.5	34	North Dakota	1.2
40	Pennsylvania	1.1	34	Vermont	1.2
16	Rhode Island	1.6	34	Wisconsin	1.2
40	South Carolina	1.1	40	Alabama	1.1
23	South Dakota	1.4	40	Iowa	1.1
40	Tennessee	1.1	40	Kentucky	1.1
30	Texas	1.3	40	Louisiana	1.1
12	Utah	1.7	40	Maine	1.1
34	Vermont	1.2	40	New Hampshire	1.1
12	Virginia	1.7	40	Pennsylvania	1.1
4	Washington	3.1	40	South Carolina	1.1
49	West Virginia	1.0	40	Tennessee	1.1
34	Wisconsin	1.2	49	West Virginia	1.0
19	Wyoming	1.5	50	Mississippi	0.9
				District of Columbia	1.6

Source: CQ Press using data from U.S. Bureau of the Census
 "State Population Estimates - Characteristics" (http://www.census.gov/popest/states/asrh/)
*Census states "Race is a self-identification data item in which respondents choose the race or races with which they most closely identify." The 2000 Census was the first to allow respondents to identify themselves as one or more races.

Median Age in 2008

National Median = 36.8 Years Old

RANK	STATE	MEDIAN AGE
25	Alabama	37.5
48	Alaska	33.3
44	Arizona	35.1
29	Arkansas	37.2
46	California	34.8
41	Colorado	35.7
7	Connecticut	39.4
12	Delaware	38.2
4	Florida	40.2
45	Georgia	34.9
19	Hawaii	38.0
47	Idaho	34.4
38	Illinois	36.0
34	Indiana	36.7
15	Iowa	38.1
36	Kansas	36.2
20	Kentucky	37.7
42	Louisiana	35.6
1	Maine	42.0
22	Maryland	37.7
11	Massachusetts	38.6
17	Michigan	38.0
26	Minnesota	37.3
43	Mississippi	35.3
24	Missouri	37.5
8	Montana	39.3
35	Nebraska	36.2
39	Nevada	35.9
5	New Hampshire	40.2
10	New Jersey	38.7
40	New Mexico	35.8
18	New York	38.0
32	North Carolina	36.9
31	North Dakota	37.1
14	Ohio	38.1
37	Oklahoma	36.1
16	Oregon	38.0
6	Pennsylvania	39.9
9	Rhode Island	38.8
23	South Carolina	37.6
27	South Dakota	37.3
21	Tennessee	37.7
49	Texas	33.2
50	Utah	28.7
2	Vermont	41.2
30	Virginia	37.1
28	Washington	37.2
3	West Virginia	40.6
13	Wisconsin	38.2
33	Wyoming	36.8

RANK	STATE	MEDIAN AGE
1	Maine	42.0
2	Vermont	41.2
3	West Virginia	40.6
4	Florida	40.2
5	New Hampshire	40.2
6	Pennsylvania	39.9
7	Connecticut	39.4
8	Montana	39.3
9	Rhode Island	38.8
10	New Jersey	38.7
11	Massachusetts	38.6
12	Delaware	38.2
13	Wisconsin	38.2
14	Ohio	38.1
15	Iowa	38.1
16	Oregon	38.0
17	Michigan	38.0
18	New York	38.0
19	Hawaii	38.0
20	Kentucky	37.7
21	Tennessee	37.7
22	Maryland	37.7
23	South Carolina	37.6
24	Missouri	37.5
25	Alabama	37.5
26	Minnesota	37.3
27	South Dakota	37.3
28	Washington	37.2
29	Arkansas	37.2
30	Virginia	37.1
31	North Dakota	37.1
32	North Carolina	36.9
33	Wyoming	36.8
34	Indiana	36.7
35	Nebraska	36.2
36	Kansas	36.2
37	Oklahoma	36.1
38	Illinois	36.0
39	Nevada	35.9
40	New Mexico	35.8
41	Colorado	35.7
42	Louisiana	35.6
43	Mississippi	35.3
44	Arizona	35.1
45	Georgia	34.9
46	California	34.8
47	Idaho	34.4
48	Alaska	33.3
49	Texas	33.2
50	Utah	28.7
	District of Columbia	34.9

Source: U.S. Bureau of the Census
 "State Population Estimates - Characteristics" (http://www.census.gov/popest/states/asrh/)

Population Under 5 Years Old in 2008

National Total = 21,005,852

RANK	STATE	POPULATION	% of USA
24	Alabama	310,504	1.5%
47	Alaska	52,083	0.2%
13	Arizona	515,910	2.5%
33	Arkansas	202,070	1.0%
1	California	2,704,659	12.9%
22	Colorado	358,280	1.7%
31	Connecticut	211,637	1.0%
45	Delaware	59,319	0.3%
4	Florida	1,140,516	5.4%
7	Georgia	740,521	3.5%
40	Hawaii	87,207	0.4%
38	Idaho	121,746	0.6%
5	Illinois	894,368	4.3%
14	Indiana	443,089	2.1%
34	Iowa	201,321	1.0%
32	Kansas	202,529	1.0%
26	Kentucky	284,601	1.4%
23	Louisiana	310,716	1.5%
42	Maine	71,459	0.3%
19	Maryland	371,787	1.8%
18	Massachusetts	383,568	1.8%
10	Michigan	625,526	3.0%
21	Minnesota	358,471	1.7%
30	Mississippi	220,813	1.1%
17	Missouri	399,450	1.9%
43	Montana	61,114	0.3%
37	Nebraska	132,092	0.6%
35	Nevada	199,175	0.9%
41	New Hampshire	75,297	0.4%
11	New Jersey	557,421	2.7%
36	New Mexico	148,323	0.7%
3	New York	1,208,495	5.8%
9	North Carolina	652,823	3.1%
48	North Dakota	41,896	0.2%
6	Ohio	743,750	3.5%
28	Oklahoma	266,547	1.3%
29	Oregon	243,483	1.2%
8	Pennsylvania	737,462	3.5%
44	Rhode Island	60,934	0.3%
25	South Carolina	303,024	1.4%
46	South Dakota	58,566	0.3%
16	Tennessee	416,334	2.0%
2	Texas	2,027,307	9.7%
27	Utah	268,916	1.3%
50	Vermont	32,635	0.2%
12	Virginia	522,672	2.5%
15	Washington	433,119	2.1%
39	West Virginia	105,435	0.5%
20	Wisconsin	362,277	1.7%
49	Wyoming	38,253	0.2%

RANK	STATE	POPULATION	% of USA
1	California	2,704,659	12.9%
2	Texas	2,027,307	9.7%
3	New York	1,208,495	5.8%
4	Florida	1,140,516	5.4%
5	Illinois	894,368	4.3%
6	Ohio	743,750	3.5%
7	Georgia	740,521	3.5%
8	Pennsylvania	737,462	3.5%
9	North Carolina	652,823	3.1%
10	Michigan	625,526	3.0%
11	New Jersey	557,421	2.7%
12	Virginia	522,672	2.5%
13	Arizona	515,910	2.5%
14	Indiana	443,089	2.1%
15	Washington	433,119	2.1%
16	Tennessee	416,334	2.0%
17	Missouri	399,450	1.9%
18	Massachusetts	383,568	1.8%
19	Maryland	371,787	1.8%
20	Wisconsin	362,277	1.7%
21	Minnesota	358,471	1.7%
22	Colorado	358,280	1.7%
23	Louisiana	310,716	1.5%
24	Alabama	310,504	1.5%
25	South Carolina	303,024	1.4%
26	Kentucky	284,601	1.4%
27	Utah	268,916	1.3%
28	Oklahoma	266,547	1.3%
29	Oregon	243,483	1.2%
30	Mississippi	220,813	1.1%
31	Connecticut	211,637	1.0%
32	Kansas	202,529	1.0%
33	Arkansas	202,070	1.0%
34	Iowa	201,321	1.0%
35	Nevada	199,175	0.9%
36	New Mexico	148,323	0.7%
37	Nebraska	132,092	0.6%
38	Idaho	121,746	0.6%
39	West Virginia	105,435	0.5%
40	Hawaii	87,207	0.4%
41	New Hampshire	75,297	0.4%
42	Maine	71,459	0.3%
43	Montana	61,114	0.3%
44	Rhode Island	60,934	0.3%
45	Delaware	59,319	0.3%
46	South Dakota	58,566	0.3%
47	Alaska	52,083	0.2%
48	North Dakota	41,896	0.2%
49	Wyoming	38,253	0.2%
50	Vermont	32,635	0.2%
	District of Columbia	36,352	0.2%

Source: U.S. Bureau of the Census
"State Population Estimates - Characteristics" (http://www.census.gov/popest/states/asrh/)

Percent of Population Under 5 Years Old in 2008

National Percent = 6.9% of Population

RANK	STATE	PERCENT
27	Alabama	6.7
6	Alaska	7.6
4	Arizona	7.9
17	Arkansas	7.1
10	California	7.4
12	Colorado	7.3
43	Connecticut	6.0
23	Delaware	6.8
41	Florida	6.2
6	Georgia	7.6
23	Hawaii	6.8
3	Idaho	8.0
20	Illinois	6.9
20	Indiana	6.9
27	Iowa	6.7
15	Kansas	7.2
27	Kentucky	6.7
19	Louisiana	7.0
49	Maine	5.4
32	Maryland	6.6
44	Massachusetts	5.9
39	Michigan	6.3
20	Minnesota	6.9
8	Mississippi	7.5
23	Missouri	6.8
39	Montana	6.3
10	Nebraska	7.4
5	Nevada	7.7
48	New Hampshire	5.7
36	New Jersey	6.4
8	New Mexico	7.5
41	New York	6.2
17	North Carolina	7.1
34	North Dakota	6.5
34	Ohio	6.5
12	Oklahoma	7.3
36	Oregon	6.4
44	Pennsylvania	5.9
46	Rhode Island	5.8
23	South Carolina	6.8
12	South Dakota	7.3
27	Tennessee	6.7
2	Texas	8.3
1	Utah	9.8
50	Vermont	5.3
27	Virginia	6.7
32	Washington	6.6
46	West Virginia	5.8
36	Wisconsin	6.4
15	Wyoming	7.2

RANK	STATE	PERCENT
1	Utah	9.8
2	Texas	8.3
3	Idaho	8.0
4	Arizona	7.9
5	Nevada	7.7
6	Alaska	7.6
6	Georgia	7.6
8	Mississippi	7.5
8	New Mexico	7.5
10	California	7.4
10	Nebraska	7.4
12	Colorado	7.3
12	Oklahoma	7.3
12	South Dakota	7.3
15	Kansas	7.2
15	Wyoming	7.2
17	Arkansas	7.1
17	North Carolina	7.1
19	Louisiana	7.0
20	Illinois	6.9
20	Indiana	6.9
20	Minnesota	6.9
23	Delaware	6.8
23	Hawaii	6.8
23	Missouri	6.8
23	South Carolina	6.8
27	Alabama	6.7
27	Iowa	6.7
27	Kentucky	6.7
27	Tennessee	6.7
27	Virginia	6.7
32	Maryland	6.6
32	Washington	6.6
34	North Dakota	6.5
34	Ohio	6.5
36	New Jersey	6.4
36	Oregon	6.4
36	Wisconsin	6.4
39	Michigan	6.3
39	Montana	6.3
41	Florida	6.2
41	New York	6.2
43	Connecticut	6.0
44	Massachusetts	5.9
44	Pennsylvania	5.9
46	Rhode Island	5.8
46	West Virginia	5.8
48	New Hampshire	5.7
49	Maine	5.4
50	Vermont	5.3
	District of Columbia	6.1

Source: CQ Press using data from U.S. Bureau of the Census
"State Population Estimates - Characteristics" (http://www.census.gov/popest/states/asrh/)

Population 5 to 17 Years Old in 2008

National Total = 52,935,996

ALPHA ORDER

RANK	STATE	POPULATION	% of USA
23	Alabama	811,373	1.5%
47	Alaska	127,793	0.2%
13	Arizona	1,191,311	2.3%
33	Arkansas	500,411	0.9%
1	California	6,659,871	12.6%
22	Colorado	848,855	1.6%
29	Connecticut	600,576	1.1%
45	Delaware	146,910	0.3%
4	Florida	2,863,755	5.4%
8	Georgia	1,808,320	3.4%
42	Hawaii	198,036	0.4%
38	Idaho	290,894	0.5%
5	Illinois	2,284,892	4.3%
14	Indiana	1,141,592	2.2%
32	Iowa	511,292	1.0%
34	Kansas	497,956	0.9%
26	Kentucky	723,463	1.4%
24	Louisiana	797,257	1.5%
41	Maine	203,408	0.4%
19	Maryland	968,796	1.8%
17	Massachusetts	1,043,465	2.0%
9	Michigan	1,764,672	3.3%
21	Minnesota	896,173	1.7%
31	Mississippi	545,907	1.0%
18	Missouri	1,022,019	1.9%
44	Montana	159,244	0.3%
37	Nebraska	314,903	0.6%
35	Nevada	468,626	0.9%
40	New Hampshire	218,061	0.4%
11	New Jersey	1,490,161	2.8%
36	New Mexico	354,127	0.7%
3	New York	3,199,521	6.0%
10	North Carolina	1,590,854	3.0%
48	North Dakota	101,152	0.2%
7	Ohio	1,986,627	3.8%
27	Oklahoma	639,488	1.2%
28	Oregon	624,092	1.2%
6	Pennsylvania	2,024,542	3.8%
43	Rhode Island	167,606	0.3%
25	South Carolina	763,203	1.4%
46	South Dakota	139,743	0.3%
16	Tennessee	1,062,260	2.0%
2	Texas	4,698,464	8.9%
30	Utah	580,719	1.1%
49	Vermont	96,295	0.2%
12	Virginia	1,300,529	2.5%
15	Washington	1,108,056	2.1%
39	West Virginia	280,723	0.5%
20	Wisconsin	952,135	1.8%
50	Wyoming	90,204	0.2%

RANK ORDER

RANK	STATE	POPULATION	% of USA
1	California	6,659,871	12.6%
2	Texas	4,698,464	8.9%
3	New York	3,199,521	6.0%
4	Florida	2,863,755	5.4%
5	Illinois	2,284,892	4.3%
6	Pennsylvania	2,024,542	3.8%
7	Ohio	1,986,627	3.8%
8	Georgia	1,808,320	3.4%
9	Michigan	1,764,672	3.3%
10	North Carolina	1,590,854	3.0%
11	New Jersey	1,490,161	2.8%
12	Virginia	1,300,529	2.5%
13	Arizona	1,191,311	2.3%
14	Indiana	1,141,592	2.2%
15	Washington	1,108,056	2.1%
16	Tennessee	1,062,260	2.0%
17	Massachusetts	1,043,465	2.0%
18	Missouri	1,022,019	1.9%
19	Maryland	968,796	1.8%
20	Wisconsin	952,135	1.8%
21	Minnesota	896,173	1.7%
22	Colorado	848,855	1.6%
23	Alabama	811,373	1.5%
24	Louisiana	797,257	1.5%
25	South Carolina	763,203	1.4%
26	Kentucky	723,463	1.4%
27	Oklahoma	639,488	1.2%
28	Oregon	624,092	1.2%
29	Connecticut	600,576	1.1%
30	Utah	580,719	1.1%
31	Mississippi	545,907	1.0%
32	Iowa	511,292	1.0%
33	Arkansas	500,411	0.9%
34	Kansas	497,956	0.9%
35	Nevada	468,626	0.9%
36	New Mexico	354,127	0.7%
37	Nebraska	314,903	0.6%
38	Idaho	290,894	0.5%
39	West Virginia	280,723	0.5%
40	New Hampshire	218,061	0.4%
41	Maine	203,408	0.4%
42	Hawaii	198,036	0.4%
43	Rhode Island	167,606	0.3%
44	Montana	159,244	0.3%
45	Delaware	146,910	0.3%
46	South Dakota	139,743	0.3%
47	Alaska	127,793	0.2%
48	North Dakota	101,152	0.2%
49	Vermont	96,295	0.2%
50	Wyoming	90,204	0.2%
	District of Columbia	75,664	0.1%

Source: U.S. Bureau of the Census
"State Population Estimates - Characteristics" (http://www.census.gov/popest/states/asrh/)

Percent of Population 5 to 17 Years Old in 2008

National Percent = 17.4% of Population

ALPHA ORDER

RANK	STATE	PERCENT
19	Alabama	17.4
5	Alaska	18.6
7	Arizona	18.3
18	Arkansas	17.5
8	California	18.1
23	Colorado	17.2
23	Connecticut	17.2
36	Delaware	16.8
46	Florida	15.6
4	Georgia	18.7
50	Hawaii	15.4
3	Idaho	19.1
14	Illinois	17.7
11	Indiana	17.9
30	Iowa	17.0
12	Kansas	17.8
32	Kentucky	16.9
8	Louisiana	18.1
47	Maine	15.5
23	Maryland	17.2
43	Massachusetts	16.1
16	Michigan	17.6
23	Minnesota	17.2
5	Mississippi	18.6
21	Missouri	17.3
39	Montana	16.5
14	Nebraska	17.7
10	Nevada	18.0
38	New Hampshire	16.6
23	New Jersey	17.2
12	New Mexico	17.8
41	New York	16.4
23	North Carolina	17.2
45	North Dakota	15.8
21	Ohio	17.3
16	Oklahoma	17.6
39	Oregon	16.5
42	Pennsylvania	16.3
44	Rhode Island	16.0
30	South Carolina	17.0
19	South Dakota	17.4
29	Tennessee	17.1
2	Texas	19.3
1	Utah	21.2
47	Vermont	15.5
37	Virginia	16.7
32	Washington	16.9
47	West Virginia	15.5
32	Wisconsin	16.9
32	Wyoming	16.9

RANK ORDER

RANK	STATE	PERCENT
1	Utah	21.2
2	Texas	19.3
3	Idaho	19.1
4	Georgia	18.7
5	Alaska	18.6
5	Mississippi	18.6
7	Arizona	18.3
8	California	18.1
8	Louisiana	18.1
10	Nevada	18.0
11	Indiana	17.9
12	Kansas	17.8
12	New Mexico	17.8
14	Illinois	17.7
14	Nebraska	17.7
16	Michigan	17.6
16	Oklahoma	17.6
18	Arkansas	17.5
19	Alabama	17.4
19	South Dakota	17.4
21	Missouri	17.3
21	Ohio	17.3
23	Colorado	17.2
23	Connecticut	17.2
23	Maryland	17.2
23	Minnesota	17.2
23	New Jersey	17.2
23	North Carolina	17.2
29	Tennessee	17.1
30	Iowa	17.0
30	South Carolina	17.0
32	Kentucky	16.9
32	Washington	16.9
32	Wisconsin	16.9
32	Wyoming	16.9
36	Delaware	16.8
37	Virginia	16.7
38	New Hampshire	16.6
39	Montana	16.5
39	Oregon	16.5
41	New York	16.4
42	Pennsylvania	16.3
43	Massachusetts	16.1
44	Rhode Island	16.0
45	North Dakota	15.8
46	Florida	15.6
47	Maine	15.5
47	Vermont	15.5
47	West Virginia	15.5
50	Hawaii	15.4
	District of Columbia	12.8

Source: CQ Press using data from U.S. Bureau of the Census
"State Population Estimates - Characteristics" (http://www.census.gov/popest/states/asrh/)

Population 18 Years Old and Older in 2008

National Total = 230,117,876

ALPHA ORDER

RANK	STATE	POPULATION	% of USA
23	Alabama	3,540,023	1.5%
47	Alaska	506,417	0.2%
15	Arizona	4,792,959	2.1%
32	Arkansas	2,152,909	0.9%
1	California	27,392,136	11.9%
22	Colorado	3,732,321	1.6%
29	Connecticut	2,689,039	1.2%
45	Delaware	666,863	0.3%
4	Florida	14,324,069	6.2%
9	Georgia	7,136,903	3.1%
42	Hawaii	1,002,955	0.4%
39	Idaho	1,111,176	0.5%
5	Illinois	9,722,303	4.2%
16	Indiana	4,792,111	2.1%
30	Iowa	2,289,942	1.0%
33	Kansas	2,101,649	0.9%
26	Kentucky	3,261,181	1.4%
25	Louisiana	3,302,823	1.4%
40	Maine	1,041,589	0.5%
20	Maryland	4,293,014	1.9%
13	Massachusetts	5,070,934	2.2%
8	Michigan	7,613,224	3.3%
21	Minnesota	3,965,749	1.7%
31	Mississippi	2,171,898	0.9%
18	Missouri	4,490,136	2.0%
44	Montana	747,082	0.3%
38	Nebraska	1,336,437	0.6%
34	Nevada	1,932,366	0.8%
41	New Hampshire	1,022,451	0.4%
11	New Jersey	6,635,079	2.9%
36	New Mexico	1,481,906	0.6%
3	New York	15,082,281	6.6%
10	North Carolina	6,978,737	3.0%
48	North Dakota	498,433	0.2%
7	Ohio	8,755,533	3.8%
28	Oklahoma	2,736,326	1.2%
27	Oregon	2,922,485	1.3%
6	Pennsylvania	9,686,275	4.2%
43	Rhode Island	822,248	0.4%
24	South Carolina	3,413,573	1.5%
46	South Dakota	605,885	0.3%
17	Tennessee	4,736,294	2.1%
2	Texas	17,601,203	7.6%
35	Utah	1,886,789	0.8%
49	Vermont	492,340	0.2%
12	Virginia	5,945,888	2.6%
14	Washington	5,008,049	2.2%
37	West Virginia	1,428,310	0.6%
19	Wisconsin	4,313,555	1.9%
50	Wyoming	404,211	0.2%

RANK ORDER

RANK	STATE	POPULATION	% of USA
1	California	27,392,136	11.9%
2	Texas	17,601,203	7.6%
3	New York	15,082,281	6.6%
4	Florida	14,324,069	6.2%
5	Illinois	9,722,303	4.2%
6	Pennsylvania	9,686,275	4.2%
7	Ohio	8,755,533	3.8%
8	Michigan	7,613,224	3.3%
9	Georgia	7,136,903	3.1%
10	North Carolina	6,978,737	3.0%
11	New Jersey	6,635,079	2.9%
12	Virginia	5,945,888	2.6%
13	Massachusetts	5,070,934	2.2%
14	Washington	5,008,049	2.2%
15	Arizona	4,792,959	2.1%
16	Indiana	4,792,111	2.1%
17	Tennessee	4,736,294	2.1%
18	Missouri	4,490,136	2.0%
19	Wisconsin	4,313,555	1.9%
20	Maryland	4,293,014	1.9%
21	Minnesota	3,965,749	1.7%
22	Colorado	3,732,321	1.6%
23	Alabama	3,540,023	1.5%
24	South Carolina	3,413,573	1.5%
25	Louisiana	3,302,823	1.4%
26	Kentucky	3,261,181	1.4%
27	Oregon	2,922,485	1.3%
28	Oklahoma	2,736,326	1.2%
29	Connecticut	2,689,039	1.2%
30	Iowa	2,289,942	1.0%
31	Mississippi	2,171,898	0.9%
32	Arkansas	2,152,909	0.9%
33	Kansas	2,101,649	0.9%
34	Nevada	1,932,366	0.8%
35	Utah	1,886,789	0.8%
36	New Mexico	1,481,906	0.6%
37	West Virginia	1,428,310	0.6%
38	Nebraska	1,336,437	0.6%
39	Idaho	1,111,176	0.5%
40	Maine	1,041,589	0.5%
41	New Hampshire	1,022,451	0.4%
42	Hawaii	1,002,955	0.4%
43	Rhode Island	822,248	0.4%
44	Montana	747,082	0.3%
45	Delaware	666,863	0.3%
46	South Dakota	605,885	0.3%
47	Alaska	506,417	0.2%
48	North Dakota	498,433	0.2%
49	Vermont	492,340	0.2%
50	Wyoming	404,211	0.2%
	District of Columbia	479,817	0.2%

Source: U.S. Bureau of the Census
   "State Population Estimates - Characteristics" (http://www.census.gov/popest/states/asrh/)

Percent of Population 18 Years Old and Older in 2008

National Percent = 75.7% of Population

ALPHA ORDER

RANK	STATE	PERCENT
29	Alabama	75.9
45	Alaska	73.8
46	Arizona	73.7
33	Arkansas	75.4
42	California	74.5
32	Colorado	75.6
14	Connecticut	76.8
18	Delaware	76.4
5	Florida	78.2
46	Georgia	73.7
7	Hawaii	77.9
48	Idaho	72.9
33	Illinois	75.4
36	Indiana	75.1
21	Iowa	76.3
38	Kansas	75.0
18	Kentucky	76.4
39	Louisiana	74.9
2	Maine	79.1
22	Maryland	76.2
6	Massachusetts	78.0
26	Michigan	76.1
27	Minnesota	76.0
44	Mississippi	73.9
27	Missouri	76.0
12	Montana	77.2
39	Nebraska	74.9
43	Nevada	74.3
9	New Hampshire	77.7
18	New Jersey	76.4
41	New Mexico	74.7
11	New York	77.4
31	North Carolina	75.7
9	North Dakota	77.7
22	Ohio	76.2
36	Oklahoma	75.1
13	Oregon	77.1
8	Pennsylvania	77.8
4	Rhode Island	78.3
22	South Carolina	76.2
35	South Dakota	75.3
22	Tennessee	76.2
49	Texas	72.4
50	Utah	69.0
1	Vermont	79.2
16	Virginia	76.5
16	Washington	76.5
3	West Virginia	78.7
15	Wisconsin	76.6
29	Wyoming	75.9

RANK ORDER

RANK	STATE	PERCENT
1	Vermont	79.2
2	Maine	79.1
3	West Virginia	78.7
4	Rhode Island	78.3
5	Florida	78.2
6	Massachusetts	78.0
7	Hawaii	77.9
8	Pennsylvania	77.8
9	New Hampshire	77.7
9	North Dakota	77.7
11	New York	77.4
12	Montana	77.2
13	Oregon	77.1
14	Connecticut	76.8
15	Wisconsin	76.6
16	Virginia	76.5
16	Washington	76.5
18	Delaware	76.4
18	Kentucky	76.4
18	New Jersey	76.4
21	Iowa	76.3
22	Maryland	76.2
22	Ohio	76.2
22	South Carolina	76.2
22	Tennessee	76.2
26	Michigan	76.1
27	Minnesota	76.0
27	Missouri	76.0
29	Alabama	75.9
29	Wyoming	75.9
31	North Carolina	75.7
32	Colorado	75.6
33	Arkansas	75.4
33	Illinois	75.4
35	South Dakota	75.3
36	Indiana	75.1
36	Oklahoma	75.1
38	Kansas	75.0
39	Louisiana	74.9
39	Nebraska	74.9
41	New Mexico	74.7
42	California	74.5
43	Nevada	74.3
44	Mississippi	73.9
45	Alaska	73.8
46	Arizona	73.7
46	Georgia	73.7
48	Idaho	72.9
49	Texas	72.4
50	Utah	69.0
	District of Columbia	81.1

Source: CQ Press using data from U.S. Bureau of the Census
  "State Population Estimates - Characteristics" (http://www.census.gov/popest/states/asrh/)

Population 18 to 24 Years Old in 2008

National Total = 29,757,219

ALPHA ORDER

RANK	STATE	POPULATION	% of USA
24	Alabama	450,818	1.5%
48	Alaska	74,257	0.2%
16	Arizona	601,943	2.0%
34	Arkansas	264,160	0.9%
1	California	3,853,788	13.0%
23	Colorado	466,194	1.6%
30	Connecticut	325,110	1.1%
45	Delaware	84,464	0.3%
4	Florida	1,607,297	5.4%
9	Georgia	919,876	3.1%
40	Hawaii	124,834	0.4%
39	Idaho	147,606	0.5%
5	Illinois	1,311,479	4.4%
15	Indiana	605,863	2.0%
31	Iowa	306,398	1.0%
33	Kansas	293,114	1.0%
26	Kentucky	381,394	1.3%
22	Louisiana	471,275	1.6%
43	Maine	112,682	0.4%
20	Maryland	543,470	1.8%
13	Massachusetts	665,879	2.2%
8	Michigan	974,480	3.3%
21	Minnesota	507,289	1.7%
32	Mississippi	305,964	1.0%
17	Missouri	560,463	1.9%
44	Montana	95,232	0.3%
37	Nebraska	186,657	0.6%
35	Nevada	212,379	0.7%
41	New Hampshire	119,114	0.4%
11	New Jersey	769,321	2.6%
36	New Mexico	203,097	0.7%
3	New York	1,999,120	6.7%
10	North Carolina	883,397	3.0%
47	North Dakota	82,629	0.3%
7	Ohio	1,081,734	3.6%
27	Oklahoma	369,916	1.2%
28	Oregon	338,162	1.1%
6	Pennsylvania	1,203,944	4.0%
42	Rhode Island	114,502	0.4%
25	South Carolina	438,147	1.5%
46	South Dakota	82,869	0.3%
19	Tennessee	550,612	1.9%
2	Texas	2,454,721	8.2%
29	Utah	329,585	1.1%
49	Vermont	61,679	0.2%
12	Virginia	768,475	2.6%
14	Washington	610,378	2.1%
38	West Virginia	157,989	0.5%
18	Wisconsin	553,914	1.9%
50	Wyoming	53,980	0.2%

RANK ORDER

RANK	STATE	POPULATION	% of USA
1	California	3,853,788	13.0%
2	Texas	2,454,721	8.2%
3	New York	1,999,120	6.7%
4	Florida	1,607,297	5.4%
5	Illinois	1,311,479	4.4%
6	Pennsylvania	1,203,944	4.0%
7	Ohio	1,081,734	3.6%
8	Michigan	974,480	3.3%
9	Georgia	919,876	3.1%
10	North Carolina	883,397	3.0%
11	New Jersey	769,321	2.6%
12	Virginia	768,475	2.6%
13	Massachusetts	665,879	2.2%
14	Washington	610,378	2.1%
15	Indiana	605,863	2.0%
16	Arizona	601,943	2.0%
17	Missouri	560,463	1.9%
18	Wisconsin	553,914	1.9%
19	Tennessee	550,612	1.9%
20	Maryland	543,470	1.8%
21	Minnesota	507,289	1.7%
22	Louisiana	471,275	1.6%
23	Colorado	466,194	1.6%
24	Alabama	450,818	1.5%
25	South Carolina	438,147	1.5%
26	Kentucky	381,394	1.3%
27	Oklahoma	369,916	1.2%
28	Oregon	338,162	1.1%
29	Utah	329,585	1.1%
30	Connecticut	325,110	1.1%
31	Iowa	306,398	1.0%
32	Mississippi	305,964	1.0%
33	Kansas	293,114	1.0%
34	Arkansas	264,160	0.9%
35	Nevada	212,379	0.7%
36	New Mexico	203,097	0.7%
37	Nebraska	186,657	0.6%
38	West Virginia	157,989	0.5%
39	Idaho	147,606	0.5%
40	Hawaii	124,834	0.4%
41	New Hampshire	119,114	0.4%
42	Rhode Island	114,502	0.4%
43	Maine	112,682	0.4%
44	Montana	95,232	0.3%
45	Delaware	84,464	0.3%
46	South Dakota	82,869	0.3%
47	North Dakota	82,629	0.3%
48	Alaska	74,257	0.2%
49	Vermont	61,679	0.2%
50	Wyoming	53,980	0.2%
	District of Columbia	75,569	0.3%

Source: U.S. Bureau of the Census
   "State Population Estimates - Characteristics" (http://www.census.gov/popest/states/asrh/)

Percent of Population 18 to 24 Years Old in 2008

National Percent = 9.8% of Population

RANK	STATE	PERCENT
24	Alabama	9.7
4	Alaska	10.8
38	Arizona	9.3
38	Arkansas	9.3
6	California	10.5
36	Colorado	9.4
38	Connecticut	9.3
24	Delaware	9.7
47	Florida	8.8
33	Georgia	9.5
24	Hawaii	9.7
24	Idaho	9.7
12	Illinois	10.2
33	Indiana	9.5
12	Iowa	10.2
6	Kansas	10.5
43	Kentucky	8.9
5	Louisiana	10.7
49	Maine	8.6
31	Maryland	9.6
12	Massachusetts	10.2
24	Michigan	9.7
24	Minnesota	9.7
9	Mississippi	10.4
33	Missouri	9.5
21	Montana	9.8
6	Nebraska	10.5
50	Nevada	8.2
42	New Hampshire	9.1
43	New Jersey	8.9
12	New Mexico	10.2
10	New York	10.3
31	North Carolina	9.6
1	North Dakota	12.9
36	Ohio	9.4
12	Oklahoma	10.2
43	Oregon	8.9
24	Pennsylvania	9.7
3	Rhode Island	10.9
21	South Carolina	9.8
10	South Dakota	10.3
43	Tennessee	8.9
17	Texas	10.1
2	Utah	12.0
19	Vermont	9.9
19	Virginia	9.9
38	Washington	9.3
48	West Virginia	8.7
21	Wisconsin	9.8
17	Wyoming	10.1

RANK	STATE	PERCENT
1	North Dakota	12.9
2	Utah	12.0
3	Rhode Island	10.9
4	Alaska	10.8
5	Louisiana	10.7
6	California	10.5
6	Kansas	10.5
6	Nebraska	10.5
9	Mississippi	10.4
10	New York	10.3
10	South Dakota	10.3
12	Illinois	10.2
12	Iowa	10.2
12	Massachusetts	10.2
12	New Mexico	10.2
12	Oklahoma	10.2
17	Texas	10.1
17	Wyoming	10.1
19	Vermont	9.9
19	Virginia	9.9
21	Montana	9.8
21	South Carolina	9.8
21	Wisconsin	9.8
24	Alabama	9.7
24	Delaware	9.7
24	Hawaii	9.7
24	Idaho	9.7
24	Michigan	9.7
24	Minnesota	9.7
24	Pennsylvania	9.7
31	Maryland	9.6
31	North Carolina	9.6
33	Georgia	9.5
33	Indiana	9.5
33	Missouri	9.5
36	Colorado	9.4
36	Ohio	9.4
38	Arizona	9.3
38	Arkansas	9.3
38	Connecticut	9.3
38	Washington	9.3
42	New Hampshire	9.1
43	Kentucky	8.9
43	New Jersey	8.9
43	Oregon	8.9
43	Tennessee	8.9
47	Florida	8.8
48	West Virginia	8.7
49	Maine	8.6
50	Nevada	8.2
	District of Columbia	12.8

Source: CQ Press using data from U.S. Bureau of the Census
"State Population Estimates - Characteristics" (http://www.census.gov/popest/states/asrh/)

Population 25 to 44 Years Old in 2008

National Total = 83,432,695

ALPHA ORDER

RANK	STATE	POPULATION	% of USA
23	Alabama	1,231,572	1.5%
46	Alaska	198,724	0.2%
14	Arizona	1,804,762	2.2%
33	Arkansas	754,420	0.9%
1	California	10,604,510	12.7%
21	Colorado	1,464,939	1.8%
29	Connecticut	916,955	1.1%
45	Delaware	230,183	0.3%
4	Florida	4,782,119	5.7%
8	Georgia	2,846,985	3.4%
40	Hawaii	356,237	0.4%
39	Idaho	406,247	0.5%
5	Illinois	3,596,343	4.3%
16	Indiana	1,724,528	2.1%
34	Iowa	750,505	0.9%
35	Kansas	728,166	0.9%
25	Kentucky	1,179,637	1.4%
26	Louisiana	1,162,463	1.4%
42	Maine	331,809	0.4%
19	Maryland	1,556,225	1.9%
15	Massachusetts	1,782,449	2.1%
9	Michigan	2,628,322	3.2%
22	Minnesota	1,416,063	1.7%
32	Mississippi	764,203	0.9%
18	Missouri	1,569,626	1.9%
44	Montana	236,297	0.3%
38	Nebraska	457,177	0.5%
31	Nevada	769,913	0.9%
41	New Hampshire	345,109	0.4%
11	New Jersey	2,379,649	2.9%
36	New Mexico	517,154	0.6%
3	New York	5,355,235	6.4%
10	North Carolina	2,575,603	3.1%
49	North Dakota	154,913	0.2%
7	Ohio	3,019,147	3.6%
28	Oklahoma	957,085	1.1%
27	Oregon	1,044,056	1.3%
6	Pennsylvania	3,157,759	3.8%
43	Rhode Island	277,779	0.3%
24	South Carolina	1,193,112	1.4%
47	South Dakota	196,738	0.2%
17	Tennessee	1,719,433	2.1%
2	Texas	7,017,731	8.4%
30	Utah	772,024	0.9%
48	Vermont	155,419	0.2%
12	Virginia	2,203,286	2.6%
13	Washington	1,850,983	2.2%
37	West Virginia	470,749	0.6%
20	Wisconsin	1,487,457	1.8%
50	Wyoming	137,338	0.2%

RANK ORDER

RANK	STATE	POPULATION	% of USA
1	California	10,604,510	12.7%
2	Texas	7,017,731	8.4%
3	New York	5,355,235	6.4%
4	Florida	4,782,119	5.7%
5	Illinois	3,596,343	4.3%
6	Pennsylvania	3,157,759	3.8%
7	Ohio	3,019,147	3.6%
8	Georgia	2,846,985	3.4%
9	Michigan	2,628,322	3.2%
10	North Carolina	2,575,603	3.1%
11	New Jersey	2,379,649	2.9%
12	Virginia	2,203,286	2.6%
13	Washington	1,850,983	2.2%
14	Arizona	1,804,762	2.2%
15	Massachusetts	1,782,449	2.1%
16	Indiana	1,724,528	2.1%
17	Tennessee	1,719,433	2.1%
18	Missouri	1,569,626	1.9%
19	Maryland	1,556,225	1.9%
20	Wisconsin	1,487,457	1.8%
21	Colorado	1,464,939	1.8%
22	Minnesota	1,416,063	1.7%
23	Alabama	1,231,572	1.5%
24	South Carolina	1,193,112	1.4%
25	Kentucky	1,179,637	1.4%
26	Louisiana	1,162,463	1.4%
27	Oregon	1,044,056	1.3%
28	Oklahoma	957,085	1.1%
29	Connecticut	916,955	1.1%
30	Utah	772,024	0.9%
31	Nevada	769,913	0.9%
32	Mississippi	764,203	0.9%
33	Arkansas	754,420	0.9%
34	Iowa	750,505	0.9%
35	Kansas	728,166	0.9%
36	New Mexico	517,154	0.6%
37	West Virginia	470,749	0.6%
38	Nebraska	457,177	0.5%
39	Idaho	406,247	0.5%
40	Hawaii	356,237	0.4%
41	New Hampshire	345,109	0.4%
42	Maine	331,809	0.4%
43	Rhode Island	277,779	0.3%
44	Montana	236,297	0.3%
45	Delaware	230,183	0.3%
46	Alaska	198,724	0.2%
47	South Dakota	196,738	0.2%
48	Vermont	155,419	0.2%
49	North Dakota	154,913	0.2%
50	Wyoming	137,338	0.2%
	District of Columbia	193,557	0.2%

Source: CQ Press using data from U.S. Bureau of the Census
"SC-EST2008-AGESEX_RES - State Characteristic Estimates" (http://www.census.gov/popest/datasets.html)

Percent of Population 25 to 44 Years Old in 2008

National Percent = 27.4% of Population

ALPHA ORDER

RANK	STATE	PERCENT
26	Alabama	26.4
4	Alaska	29.0
12	Arizona	27.8
26	Arkansas	26.4
5	California	28.9
1	Colorado	29.7
35	Connecticut	26.2
26	Delaware	26.4
37	Florida	26.1
3	Georgia	29.4
13	Hawaii	27.7
23	Idaho	26.7
10	Illinois	27.9
22	Indiana	27.0
46	Iowa	25.0
39	Kansas	26.0
15	Kentucky	27.6
26	Louisiana	26.4
45	Maine	25.2
15	Maryland	27.6
19	Massachusetts	27.4
32	Michigan	26.3
21	Minnesota	27.1
39	Mississippi	26.0
24	Missouri	26.6
49	Montana	24.4
43	Nebraska	25.6
2	Nevada	29.6
35	New Hampshire	26.2
19	New Jersey	27.4
37	New Mexico	26.1
17	New York	27.5
10	North Carolina	27.9
50	North Dakota	24.1
32	Ohio	26.3
32	Oklahoma	26.3
17	Oregon	27.5
44	Pennsylvania	25.4
26	Rhode Island	26.4
24	South Carolina	26.6
48	South Dakota	24.5
13	Tennessee	27.7
6	Texas	28.8
9	Utah	28.2
46	Vermont	25.0
7	Virginia	28.4
8	Washington	28.3
41	West Virginia	25.9
26	Wisconsin	26.4
42	Wyoming	25.8

RANK ORDER

RANK	STATE	PERCENT
1	Colorado	29.7
2	Nevada	29.6
3	Georgia	29.4
4	Alaska	29.0
5	California	28.9
6	Texas	28.8
7	Virginia	28.4
8	Washington	28.3
9	Utah	28.2
10	Illinois	27.9
10	North Carolina	27.9
12	Arizona	27.8
13	Hawaii	27.7
13	Tennessee	27.7
15	Kentucky	27.6
15	Maryland	27.6
17	New York	27.5
17	Oregon	27.5
19	Massachusetts	27.4
19	New Jersey	27.4
21	Minnesota	27.1
22	Indiana	27.0
23	Idaho	26.7
24	Missouri	26.6
24	South Carolina	26.6
26	Alabama	26.4
26	Arkansas	26.4
26	Delaware	26.4
26	Louisiana	26.4
26	Rhode Island	26.4
26	Wisconsin	26.4
32	Michigan	26.3
32	Ohio	26.3
32	Oklahoma	26.3
35	Connecticut	26.2
35	New Hampshire	26.2
37	Florida	26.1
37	New Mexico	26.1
39	Kansas	26.0
39	Mississippi	26.0
41	West Virginia	25.9
42	Wyoming	25.8
43	Nebraska	25.6
44	Pennsylvania	25.4
45	Maine	25.2
46	Iowa	25.0
46	Vermont	25.0
48	South Dakota	24.5
49	Montana	24.4
50	North Dakota	24.1
	District of Columbia	32.7

Source: CQ Press using data from U.S. Bureau of the Census
"SC-EST2008-AGESEX_RES - State Characteristic Estimates" (http://www.census.gov/popest/datasets.html)

Population 45 to 64 Years Old in 2008

National Total = 78,058,246

ALPHA ORDER

RANK	STATE	POPULATION	% of USA
23	Alabama	1,215,966	1.6%
48	Alaska	183,159	0.2%
18	Arizona	1,523,681	2.0%
32	Arkansas	727,124	0.9%
1	California	8,819,342	11.3%
22	Colorado	1,290,094	1.7%
28	Connecticut	968,967	1.2%
45	Delaware	230,528	0.3%
4	Florida	4,746,856	6.1%
9	Georgia	2,389,018	3.1%
42	Hawaii	331,817	0.4%
41	Idaho	375,173	0.5%
6	Illinois	3,239,173	4.1%
15	Indiana	1,647,881	2.1%
30	Iowa	788,485	1.0%
33	Kansas	713,663	0.9%
25	Kentucky	1,134,283	1.5%
26	Louisiana	1,128,771	1.4%
39	Maine	397,911	0.5%
20	Maryland	1,513,754	1.9%
14	Massachusetts	1,751,508	2.2%
8	Michigan	2,706,100	3.5%
21	Minnesota	1,391,878	1.8%
31	Mississippi	730,133	0.9%
17	Missouri	1,554,812	2.0%
44	Montana	278,241	0.4%
38	Nebraska	451,756	0.6%
34	Nevada	653,357	0.8%
40	New Hampshire	388,250	0.5%
11	New Jersey	2,335,168	3.0%
37	New Mexico	501,604	0.6%
3	New York	5,120,254	6.6%
10	North Carolina	2,380,685	3.0%
49	North Dakota	166,615	0.2%
7	Ohio	3,083,815	4.0%
29	Oklahoma	918,688	1.2%
27	Oregon	1,036,269	1.3%
5	Pennsylvania	3,414,001	4.4%
43	Rhode Island	282,321	0.4%
24	South Carolina	1,186,019	1.5%
46	South Dakota	210,178	0.3%
16	Tennessee	1,646,623	2.1%
2	Texas	5,656,528	7.2%
35	Utah	538,978	0.7%
47	Vermont	188,593	0.2%
12	Virginia	2,033,550	2.6%
13	Washington	1,762,811	2.3%
36	West Virginia	514,505	0.7%
19	Wisconsin	1,522,038	1.9%
50	Wyoming	147,279	0.2%

RANK ORDER

RANK	STATE	POPULATION	% of USA
1	California	8,819,342	11.3%
2	Texas	5,656,528	7.2%
3	New York	5,120,254	6.6%
4	Florida	4,746,856	6.1%
5	Pennsylvania	3,414,001	4.4%
6	Illinois	3,239,173	4.1%
7	Ohio	3,083,815	4.0%
8	Michigan	2,706,100	3.5%
9	Georgia	2,389,018	3.1%
10	North Carolina	2,380,685	3.0%
11	New Jersey	2,335,168	3.0%
12	Virginia	2,033,550	2.6%
13	Washington	1,762,811	2.3%
14	Massachusetts	1,751,508	2.2%
15	Indiana	1,647,881	2.1%
16	Tennessee	1,646,623	2.1%
17	Missouri	1,554,812	2.0%
18	Arizona	1,523,681	2.0%
19	Wisconsin	1,522,038	1.9%
20	Maryland	1,513,754	1.9%
21	Minnesota	1,391,878	1.8%
22	Colorado	1,290,094	1.7%
23	Alabama	1,215,966	1.6%
24	South Carolina	1,186,019	1.5%
25	Kentucky	1,134,283	1.5%
26	Louisiana	1,128,771	1.4%
27	Oregon	1,036,269	1.3%
28	Connecticut	968,967	1.2%
29	Oklahoma	918,688	1.2%
30	Iowa	788,485	1.0%
31	Mississippi	730,133	0.9%
32	Arkansas	727,124	0.9%
33	Kansas	713,663	0.9%
34	Nevada	653,357	0.8%
35	Utah	538,978	0.7%
36	West Virginia	514,505	0.7%
37	New Mexico	501,604	0.6%
38	Nebraska	451,756	0.6%
39	Maine	397,911	0.5%
40	New Hampshire	388,250	0.5%
41	Idaho	375,173	0.5%
42	Hawaii	331,817	0.4%
43	Rhode Island	282,321	0.4%
44	Montana	278,241	0.4%
45	Delaware	230,528	0.3%
46	South Dakota	210,178	0.3%
47	Vermont	188,593	0.2%
48	Alaska	183,159	0.2%
49	North Dakota	166,615	0.2%
50	Wyoming	147,279	0.2%
	District of Columbia	140,043	0.2%

Source: U.S. Bureau of the Census
"State Population Estimates - Characteristics" (http://www.census.gov/popest/states/asrh/)

Percent of Population 45 to 64 Years Old in 2008

National Percent = 25.7% of Population

ALPHA ORDER

RANK	STATE	PERCENT
28	Alabama	26.1
18	Alaska	26.7
48	Arizona	23.4
37	Arkansas	25.5
47	California	24.0
28	Colorado	26.1
6	Connecticut	27.7
23	Delaware	26.4
32	Florida	25.9
45	Georgia	24.7
33	Hawaii	25.8
46	Idaho	24.6
42	Illinois	25.1
33	Indiana	25.8
24	Iowa	26.3
37	Kansas	25.5
20	Kentucky	26.6
36	Louisiana	25.6
2	Maine	30.2
13	Maryland	26.9
11	Massachusetts	27.0
10	Michigan	27.1
18	Minnesota	26.7
44	Mississippi	24.8
24	Missouri	26.3
4	Montana	28.8
39	Nebraska	25.3
42	Nevada	25.1
3	New Hampshire	29.5
13	New Jersey	26.9
39	New Mexico	25.3
24	New York	26.3
33	North Carolina	25.8
31	North Dakota	26.0
17	Ohio	26.8
41	Oklahoma	25.2
9	Oregon	27.3
8	Pennsylvania	27.4
13	Rhode Island	26.9
21	South Carolina	26.5
28	South Dakota	26.1
21	Tennessee	26.5
49	Texas	23.3
50	Utah	19.7
1	Vermont	30.4
27	Virginia	26.2
13	Washington	26.9
5	West Virginia	28.4
11	Wisconsin	27.0
7	Wyoming	27.6

RANK ORDER

RANK	STATE	PERCENT
1	Vermont	30.4
2	Maine	30.2
3	New Hampshire	29.5
4	Montana	28.8
5	West Virginia	28.4
6	Connecticut	27.7
7	Wyoming	27.6
8	Pennsylvania	27.4
9	Oregon	27.3
10	Michigan	27.1
11	Massachusetts	27.0
11	Wisconsin	27.0
13	Maryland	26.9
13	New Jersey	26.9
13	Rhode Island	26.9
13	Washington	26.9
17	Ohio	26.8
18	Alaska	26.7
18	Minnesota	26.7
20	Kentucky	26.6
21	South Carolina	26.5
21	Tennessee	26.5
23	Delaware	26.4
24	Iowa	26.3
24	Missouri	26.3
24	New York	26.3
27	Virginia	26.2
28	Alabama	26.1
28	Colorado	26.1
28	South Dakota	26.1
31	North Dakota	26.0
32	Florida	25.9
33	Hawaii	25.8
33	Indiana	25.8
33	North Carolina	25.8
36	Louisiana	25.6
37	Arkansas	25.5
37	Kansas	25.5
39	Nebraska	25.3
39	New Mexico	25.3
41	Oklahoma	25.2
42	Illinois	25.1
42	Nevada	25.1
44	Mississippi	24.8
45	Georgia	24.7
46	Idaho	24.6
47	California	24.0
48	Arizona	23.4
49	Texas	23.3
50	Utah	19.7
	District of Columbia	23.7

Source: CQ Press using data from U.S. Bureau of the Census
"State Population Estimates - Characteristics" (http://www.census.gov/popest/states/asrh/)

Population 65 Years Old and Older in 2008

National Total = 38,869,716

ALPHA ORDER

ALPHA ORDER

RANK	STATE	POPULATION	% of USA
22	Alabama	641,667	1.7%
50	Alaska	50,277	0.1%
14	Arizona	862,573	2.2%
31	Arkansas	407,205	1.0%
1	California	4,114,496	10.6%
26	Colorado	511,094	1.3%
29	Connecticut	478,007	1.2%
45	Delaware	121,688	0.3%
2	Florida	3,187,797	8.2%
11	Georgia	981,024	2.5%
40	Hawaii	190,067	0.5%
41	Idaho	182,150	0.5%
6	Illinois	1,575,308	4.1%
16	Indiana	813,839	2.1%
30	Iowa	444,554	1.1%
33	Kansas	366,706	0.9%
24	Kentucky	565,867	1.5%
25	Louisiana	540,314	1.4%
39	Maine	199,187	0.5%
20	Maryland	679,565	1.7%
13	Massachusetts	871,098	2.2%
8	Michigan	1,304,322	3.4%
21	Minnesota	650,519	1.7%
32	Mississippi	371,598	1.0%
17	Missouri	805,235	2.1%
44	Montana	137,312	0.4%
38	Nebraska	240,847	0.6%
34	Nevada	296,717	0.8%
42	New Hampshire	169,978	0.4%
9	New Jersey	1,150,941	3.0%
36	New Mexico	260,051	0.7%
3	New York	2,607,672	6.7%
10	North Carolina	1,139,052	2.9%
47	North Dakota	94,276	0.2%
7	Ohio	1,570,837	4.0%
28	Oklahoma	490,637	1.3%
27	Oregon	503,998	1.3%
5	Pennsylvania	1,910,571	4.9%
43	Rhode Island	147,646	0.4%
23	South Carolina	596,295	1.5%
46	South Dakota	116,100	0.3%
15	Tennessee	819,626	2.1%
4	Texas	2,472,223	6.4%
37	Utah	246,202	0.6%
48	Vermont	86,649	0.2%
12	Virginia	940,577	2.4%
18	Washington	783,877	2.0%
35	West Virginia	285,067	0.7%
19	Wisconsin	750,146	1.9%
49	Wyoming	65,614	0.2%

RANK ORDER

RANK	STATE	POPULATION	% of USA
1	California	4,114,496	10.6%
2	Florida	3,187,797	8.2%
3	New York	2,607,672	6.7%
4	Texas	2,472,223	6.4%
5	Pennsylvania	1,910,571	4.9%
6	Illinois	1,575,308	4.1%
7	Ohio	1,570,837	4.0%
8	Michigan	1,304,322	3.4%
9	New Jersey	1,150,941	3.0%
10	North Carolina	1,139,052	2.9%
11	Georgia	981,024	2.5%
12	Virginia	940,577	2.4%
13	Massachusetts	871,098	2.2%
14	Arizona	862,573	2.2%
15	Tennessee	819,626	2.1%
16	Indiana	813,839	2.1%
17	Missouri	805,235	2.1%
18	Washington	783,877	2.0%
19	Wisconsin	750,146	1.9%
20	Maryland	679,565	1.7%
21	Minnesota	650,519	1.7%
22	Alabama	641,667	1.7%
23	South Carolina	596,295	1.5%
24	Kentucky	565,867	1.5%
25	Louisiana	540,314	1.4%
26	Colorado	511,094	1.3%
27	Oregon	503,998	1.3%
28	Oklahoma	490,637	1.3%
29	Connecticut	478,007	1.2%
30	Iowa	444,554	1.1%
31	Arkansas	407,205	1.0%
32	Mississippi	371,598	1.0%
33	Kansas	366,706	0.9%
34	Nevada	296,717	0.8%
35	West Virginia	285,067	0.7%
36	New Mexico	260,051	0.7%
37	Utah	246,202	0.6%
38	Nebraska	240,847	0.6%
39	Maine	199,187	0.5%
40	Hawaii	190,067	0.5%
41	Idaho	182,150	0.5%
42	New Hampshire	169,978	0.4%
43	Rhode Island	147,646	0.4%
44	Montana	137,312	0.4%
45	Delaware	121,688	0.3%
46	South Dakota	116,100	0.3%
47	North Dakota	94,276	0.2%
48	Vermont	86,649	0.2%
49	Wyoming	65,614	0.2%
50	Alaska	50,277	0.1%
	District of Columbia	70,648	0.2%

Source: U.S. Bureau of the Census
   "State Population Estimates - Characteristics" (http://www.census.gov/popest/states/asrh/)

Percent of Population 65 Years Old and Older in 2008

National Percent = 12.8% of Population

ALPHA ORDER				RANK ORDER		
RANK	STATE	PERCENT		RANK	STATE	PERCENT
14	Alabama	13.8		1	Florida	17.4
50	Alaska	7.3		2	West Virginia	15.7
22	Arizona	13.3		3	Pennsylvania	15.3
9	Arkansas	14.3		4	Maine	15.1
45	California	11.2		5	Hawaii	14.8
46	Colorado	10.3		5	Iowa	14.8
15	Connecticut	13.7		7	North Dakota	14.7
12	Delaware	13.9		8	South Dakota	14.4
1	Florida	17.4		9	Arkansas	14.3
48	Georgia	10.1		10	Montana	14.2
5	Hawaii	14.8		11	Rhode Island	14.1
42	Idaho	12.0		12	Delaware	13.9
38	Illinois	12.2		12	Vermont	13.9
33	Indiana	12.8		14	Alabama	13.8
5	Iowa	14.8		15	Connecticut	13.7
29	Kansas	13.1		15	Ohio	13.7
22	Kentucky	13.3		17	Missouri	13.6
38	Louisiana	12.2		18	Nebraska	13.5
4	Maine	15.1		18	Oklahoma	13.5
40	Maryland	12.1		20	Massachusetts	13.4
20	Massachusetts	13.4		20	New York	13.4
31	Michigan	13.0		22	Arizona	13.3
35	Minnesota	12.5		22	Kentucky	13.3
34	Mississippi	12.6		22	New Jersey	13.3
17	Missouri	13.6		22	Oregon	13.3
10	Montana	14.2		22	South Carolina	13.3
18	Nebraska	13.5		22	Wisconsin	13.3
44	Nevada	11.4		28	Tennessee	13.2
32	New Hampshire	12.9		29	Kansas	13.1
22	New Jersey	13.3		29	New Mexico	13.1
29	New Mexico	13.1		31	Michigan	13.0
20	New York	13.4		32	New Hampshire	12.9
36	North Carolina	12.4		33	Indiana	12.8
7	North Dakota	14.7		34	Mississippi	12.6
15	Ohio	13.7		35	Minnesota	12.5
18	Oklahoma	13.5		36	North Carolina	12.4
22	Oregon	13.3		37	Wyoming	12.3
3	Pennsylvania	15.3		38	Illinois	12.2
11	Rhode Island	14.1		38	Louisiana	12.2
22	South Carolina	13.3		40	Maryland	12.1
8	South Dakota	14.4		40	Virginia	12.1
28	Tennessee	13.2		42	Idaho	12.0
47	Texas	10.2		42	Washington	12.0
49	Utah	9.0		44	Nevada	11.4
12	Vermont	13.9		45	California	11.2
40	Virginia	12.1		46	Colorado	10.3
42	Washington	12.0		47	Texas	10.2
2	West Virginia	15.7		48	Georgia	10.1
22	Wisconsin	13.3		49	Utah	9.0
37	Wyoming	12.3		50	Alaska	7.3
				District of Columbia		11.9

Source: CQ Press using data from U.S. Bureau of the Census
"State Population Estimates - Characteristics" (http://www.census.gov/popest/states/asrh/)

Population 85 Years Old and Older in 2008

National Total = 5,721,768

RANK	STATE	POPULATION	% of USA
22	Alabama	85,079	1.5%
50	Alaska	4,844	0.1%
12	Arizona	122,985	2.1%
32	Arkansas	58,675	1.0%
1	California	612,463	10.7%
30	Colorado	67,286	1.2%
23	Connecticut	79,111	1.4%
47	Delaware	16,118	0.3%
2	Florida	521,366	9.1%
13	Georgia	122,419	2.1%
39	Hawaii	31,681	0.6%
42	Idaho	25,501	0.4%
6	Illinois	238,921	4.2%
16	Indiana	118,650	2.1%
24	Iowa	78,699	1.4%
31	Kansas	62,319	1.1%
27	Kentucky	74,759	1.3%
28	Louisiana	72,250	1.3%
40	Maine	28,719	0.5%
21	Maryland	91,884	1.6%
11	Massachusetts	143,097	2.5%
8	Michigan	186,744	3.3%
19	Minnesota	106,854	1.9%
33	Mississippi	52,235	0.9%
15	Missouri	121,678	2.1%
45	Montana	20,246	0.4%
34	Nebraska	41,008	0.7%
38	Nevada	31,930	0.6%
43	New Hampshire	24,480	0.4%
9	New Jersey	175,310	3.1%
36	New Mexico	35,849	0.6%
3	New York	397,954	7.0%
10	North Carolina	148,054	2.6%
46	North Dakota	17,772	0.3%
7	Ohio	228,649	4.0%
29	Oklahoma	69,824	1.2%
26	Oregon	76,229	1.3%
5	Pennsylvania	310,242	5.4%
41	Rhode Island	26,001	0.5%
25	South Carolina	76,604	1.3%
44	South Dakota	20,645	0.4%
20	Tennessee	106,162	1.9%
4	Texas	332,872	5.8%
37	Utah	32,898	0.6%
48	Vermont	12,364	0.2%
14	Virginia	121,693	2.1%
18	Washington	114,860	2.0%
35	West Virginia	38,502	0.7%
17	Wisconsin	117,154	2.0%
49	Wyoming	8,985	0.2%

RANK	STATE	POPULATION	% of USA
1	California	612,463	10.7%
2	Florida	521,366	9.1%
3	New York	397,954	7.0%
4	Texas	332,872	5.8%
5	Pennsylvania	310,242	5.4%
6	Illinois	238,921	4.2%
7	Ohio	228,649	4.0%
8	Michigan	186,744	3.3%
9	New Jersey	175,310	3.1%
10	North Carolina	148,054	2.6%
11	Massachusetts	143,097	2.5%
12	Arizona	122,985	2.1%
13	Georgia	122,419	2.1%
14	Virginia	121,693	2.1%
15	Missouri	121,678	2.1%
16	Indiana	118,650	2.1%
17	Wisconsin	117,154	2.0%
18	Washington	114,860	2.0%
19	Minnesota	106,854	1.9%
20	Tennessee	106,162	1.9%
21	Maryland	91,884	1.6%
22	Alabama	85,079	1.5%
23	Connecticut	79,111	1.4%
24	Iowa	78,699	1.4%
25	South Carolina	76,604	1.3%
26	Oregon	76,229	1.3%
27	Kentucky	74,759	1.3%
28	Louisiana	72,250	1.3%
29	Oklahoma	69,824	1.2%
30	Colorado	67,286	1.2%
31	Kansas	62,319	1.1%
32	Arkansas	58,675	1.0%
33	Mississippi	52,235	0.9%
34	Nebraska	41,008	0.7%
35	West Virginia	38,502	0.7%
36	New Mexico	35,849	0.6%
37	Utah	32,898	0.6%
38	Nevada	31,930	0.6%
39	Hawaii	31,681	0.6%
40	Maine	28,719	0.5%
41	Rhode Island	26,001	0.5%
42	Idaho	25,501	0.4%
43	New Hampshire	24,480	0.4%
44	South Dakota	20,645	0.4%
45	Montana	20,246	0.4%
46	North Dakota	17,772	0.3%
47	Delaware	16,118	0.3%
48	Vermont	12,364	0.2%
49	Wyoming	8,985	0.2%
50	Alaska	4,844	0.1%
	District of Columbia	11,144	0.2%

Source: U.S. Bureau of the Census
"State Population Estimates - Characteristics" (http://www.census.gov/popest/states/asrh/)

Percent of Population 85 Years Old and Older in 2008

National Percent = 1.9% of Population

ALPHA ORDER				RANK ORDER		
RANK	STATE	PERCENT		RANK	STATE	PERCENT
30	Alabama	1.8		1	Florida	2.8
50	Alaska	0.7		1	North Dakota	2.8
24	Arizona	1.9		3	Iowa	2.6
13	Arkansas	2.1		3	South Dakota	2.6
36	California	1.7		5	Hawaii	2.5
45	Colorado	1.4		5	Pennsylvania	2.5
8	Connecticut	2.3		5	Rhode Island	2.5
30	Delaware	1.8		8	Connecticut	2.3
1	Florida	2.8		8	Nebraska	2.3
47	Georgia	1.3		10	Kansas	2.2
5	Hawaii	2.5		10	Maine	2.2
36	Idaho	1.7		10	Massachusetts	2.2
24	Illinois	1.9		13	Arkansas	2.1
24	Indiana	1.9		13	Missouri	2.1
3	Iowa	2.6		13	Montana	2.1
10	Kansas	2.2		13	West Virginia	2.1
30	Kentucky	1.8		13	Wisconsin	2.1
41	Louisiana	1.6		18	Minnesota	2.0
10	Maine	2.2		18	New Jersey	2.0
41	Maryland	1.6		18	New York	2.0
10	Massachusetts	2.2		18	Ohio	2.0
24	Michigan	1.9		18	Oregon	2.0
18	Minnesota	2.0		18	Vermont	2.0
30	Mississippi	1.8		24	Arizona	1.9
13	Missouri	2.1		24	Illinois	1.9
13	Montana	2.1		24	Indiana	1.9
8	Nebraska	2.3		24	Michigan	1.9
48	Nevada	1.2		24	New Hampshire	1.9
24	New Hampshire	1.9		24	Oklahoma	1.9
18	New Jersey	2.0		30	Alabama	1.8
30	New Mexico	1.8		30	Delaware	1.8
18	New York	2.0		30	Kentucky	1.8
41	North Carolina	1.6		30	Mississippi	1.8
1	North Dakota	2.8		30	New Mexico	1.8
18	Ohio	2.0		30	Washington	1.8
24	Oklahoma	1.9		36	California	1.7
18	Oregon	2.0		36	Idaho	1.7
5	Pennsylvania	2.5		36	South Carolina	1.7
5	Rhode Island	2.5		36	Tennessee	1.7
36	South Carolina	1.7		36	Wyoming	1.7
3	South Dakota	2.6		41	Louisiana	1.6
36	Tennessee	1.7		41	Maryland	1.6
45	Texas	1.4		41	North Carolina	1.6
48	Utah	1.2		41	Virginia	1.6
18	Vermont	2.0		45	Colorado	1.4
41	Virginia	1.6		45	Texas	1.4
30	Washington	1.8		47	Georgia	1.3
13	West Virginia	2.1		48	Nevada	1.2
13	Wisconsin	2.1		48	Utah	1.2
36	Wyoming	1.7		50	Alaska	0.7
					District of Columbia	1.9

Source: CQ Press using data from U.S. Bureau of the Census
   "State Population Estimates - Characteristics" (http://www.census.gov/popest/states/asrh/)

Percent of Native Population Born in Their State of Residence: 2008

National Percent = 67.3%

ALPHA ORDER				RANK ORDER		
RANK	STATE	PERCENT		RANK	STATE	PERCENT
11	Alabama	73.4		1	Louisiana	82.1
49	Alaska	40.9		2	New York	82.0
47	Arizona	42.7		3	Michigan	81.0
29	Arkansas	63.9		4	Pennsylvania	79.0
14	California	72.9		5	Ohio	77.9
44	Colorado	46.9		6	Illinois	77.4
30	Connecticut	63.8		7	Iowa	75.8
42	Delaware	50.5		8	Wisconsin	75.1
48	Florida	42.2		9	Massachusetts	74.2
34	Georgia	61.3		10	Minnesota	74.1
28	Hawaii	64.3		11	Alabama	73.4
43	Idaho	49.8		12	Kentucky	73.2
6	Illinois	77.4		12	Mississippi	73.2
17	Indiana	71.3		14	California	72.9
7	Iowa	75.8		15	Texas	72.2
31	Kansas	63.1		16	West Virginia	71.4
12	Kentucky	73.2		17	Indiana	71.3
1	Louisiana	82.1		18	North Dakota	71.2
24	Maine	66.0		19	Nebraska	69.5
38	Maryland	55.3		20	Missouri	68.8
9	Massachusetts	74.2		21	South Dakota	68.6
3	Michigan	81.0		22	Utah	67.1
10	Minnesota	74.1		23	Rhode Island	67.0
12	Mississippi	73.2		24	Maine	66.0
20	Missouri	68.8		25	New Jersey	65.5
37	Montana	55.4		26	Tennessee	64.8
19	Nebraska	69.5		27	Oklahoma	64.6
50	Nevada	29.1		28	Hawaii	64.3
46	New Hampshire	43.3		29	Arkansas	63.9
25	New Jersey	65.5		30	Connecticut	63.8
35	New Mexico	57.0		31	Kansas	63.1
2	New York	82.0		32	North Carolina	62.9
32	North Carolina	62.9		33	South Carolina	62.8
18	North Dakota	71.2		34	Georgia	61.3
5	Ohio	77.9		35	New Mexico	57.0
27	Oklahoma	64.6		36	Virginia	56.0
41	Oregon	50.9		37	Montana	55.4
4	Pennsylvania	79.0		38	Maryland	55.3
23	Rhode Island	67.0		39	Vermont	53.7
33	South Carolina	62.8		39	Washington	53.7
21	South Dakota	68.6		41	Oregon	50.9
26	Tennessee	64.8		42	Delaware	50.5
15	Texas	72.2		43	Idaho	49.8
22	Utah	67.1		44	Colorado	46.9
39	Vermont	53.7		45	Wyoming	43.6
36	Virginia	56.0		46	New Hampshire	43.3
39	Washington	53.7		47	Arizona	42.7
16	West Virginia	71.4		48	Florida	42.2
8	Wisconsin	75.1		49	Alaska	40.9
45	Wyoming	43.6		50	Nevada	29.1

District of Columbia   46.4

Source: U.S. Bureau of the Census
"2008 American Community Survey" (http://www.census.gov/acs/www/index.html)

Domestic Migration of Population: 2008 to 2009

National Net Migration = 0 People*

ALPHA ORDER

RANK	STATE	NET MIGRATION
13	Alabama	11,044
27	Alaska	979
11	Arizona	15,111
17	Arkansas	5,298
50	California	(98,798)
4	Colorado	35,591
41	Connecticut	(7,824)
21	Delaware	2,580
44	Florida	(31,179)
6	Georgia	26,604
36	Hawaii	(5,298)
24	Idaho	1,555
47	Illinois	(48,249)
40	Indiana	(6,805)
32	Iowa	(2,135)
31	Kansas	(1,242)
16	Kentucky	6,268
12	Louisiana	14,647
34	Maine	(2,937)
43	Maryland	(11,163)
19	Massachusetts	3,614
48	Michigan	(87,339)
42	Minnesota	(8,813)
37	Mississippi	(5,529)
28	Missouri	(124)
22	Montana	2,410
29	Nebraska	(956)
35	Nevada	(3,801)
33	New Hampshire	(2,602)
45	New Jersey	(31,690)
20	New Mexico	3,366
49	New York	(98,178)
2	North Carolina	59,108
25	North Dakota	1,375
46	Ohio	(36,278)
8	Oklahoma	18,345
10	Oregon	16,173
26	Pennsylvania	1,346
39	Rhode Island	(6,172)
5	South Carolina	31,480
23	South Dakota	1,619
7	Tennessee	20,605
1	Texas	143,423
14	Utah	8,623
30	Vermont	(975)
9	Virginia	18,238
3	Washington	38,201
18	West Virginia	4,510
38	Wisconsin	(5,672)
15	Wyoming	7,192

RANK ORDER

RANK	STATE	NET MIGRATION
1	Texas	143,423
2	North Carolina	59,108
3	Washington	38,201
4	Colorado	35,591
5	South Carolina	31,480
6	Georgia	26,604
7	Tennessee	20,605
8	Oklahoma	18,345
9	Virginia	18,238
10	Oregon	16,173
11	Arizona	15,111
12	Louisiana	14,647
13	Alabama	11,044
14	Utah	8,623
15	Wyoming	7,192
16	Kentucky	6,268
17	Arkansas	5,298
18	West Virginia	4,510
19	Massachusetts	3,614
20	New Mexico	3,366
21	Delaware	2,580
22	Montana	2,410
23	South Dakota	1,619
24	Idaho	1,555
25	North Dakota	1,375
26	Pennsylvania	1,346
27	Alaska	979
28	Missouri	(124)
29	Nebraska	(956)
30	Vermont	(975)
31	Kansas	(1,242)
32	Iowa	(2,135)
33	New Hampshire	(2,602)
34	Maine	(2,937)
35	Nevada	(3,801)
36	Hawaii	(5,298)
37	Mississippi	(5,529)
38	Wisconsin	(5,672)
39	Rhode Island	(6,172)
40	Indiana	(6,805)
41	Connecticut	(7,824)
42	Minnesota	(8,813)
43	Maryland	(11,163)
44	Florida	(31,179)
45	New Jersey	(31,690)
46	Ohio	(36,278)
47	Illinois	(48,249)
48	Michigan	(87,339)
49	New York	(98,178)
50	California	(98,798)
	District of Columbia	4,454

Source: U.S. Bureau of the Census
   "Components of Population Change" (http://www.census.gov/popest/datasets.html)
*From July 1, 2008 to July 1, 2009. Includes armed forces residing in each state. Net Domestic Migration is the difference between domestic inmigration to an area and domestic outmigration from it during the period. Domestic inmigration and outmigration consist of moves where both the origins and destinations are within the United States (excluding Puerto Rico).

Net International Migration: 2008 to 2009

National Net = 854,905 Immigrants*

ALPHA ORDER

RANK	STATE	IMMIGRANTS	% of USA
29	Alabama	5,319	0.6%
43	Alaska	1,022	0.1%
8	Arizona	26,997	3.2%
34	Arkansas	3,662	0.4%
1	California	165,600	19.4%
16	Colorado	13,078	1.5%
18	Connecticut	11,322	1.3%
40	Delaware	2,016	0.2%
3	Florida	87,381	10.2%
7	Georgia	27,346	3.2%
33	Hawaii	4,033	0.5%
39	Idaho	2,179	0.3%
6	Illinois	35,839	4.2%
22	Indiana	9,194	1.1%
36	Iowa	3,189	0.4%
30	Kansas	5,003	0.6%
32	Kentucky	4,598	0.5%
35	Louisiana	3,476	0.4%
44	Maine	828	0.1%
13	Maryland	19,565	2.3%
9	Massachusetts	24,518	2.9%
15	Michigan	15,446	1.8%
20	Minnesota	10,066	1.2%
41	Mississippi	1,939	0.2%
26	Missouri	6,133	0.7%
50	Montana	344	0.0%
38	Nebraska	3,069	0.4%
19	Nevada	10,969	1.3%
42	New Hampshire	1,787	0.2%
5	New Jersey	37,360	4.4%
31	New Mexico	4,828	0.6%
4	New York	75,099	8.8%
10	North Carolina	21,211	2.5%
47	North Dakota	521	0.1%
17	Ohio	11,835	1.4%
28	Oklahoma	5,340	0.6%
23	Oregon	8,599	1.0%
14	Pennsylvania	18,480	2.2%
37	Rhode Island	3,096	0.4%
24	South Carolina	7,265	0.8%
45	South Dakota	688	0.1%
21	Tennessee	9,474	1.1%
2	Texas	88,116	10.3%
27	Utah	5,957	0.7%
48	Vermont	421	0.0%
11	Virginia	20,928	2.4%
12	Washington	19,956	2.3%
46	West Virginia	558	0.1%
25	Wisconsin	6,798	0.8%
49	Wyoming	361	0.0%

RANK ORDER

RANK	STATE	IMMIGRANTS	% of USA
1	California	165,600	19.4%
2	Texas	88,116	10.3%
3	Florida	87,381	10.2%
4	New York	75,099	8.8%
5	New Jersey	37,360	4.4%
6	Illinois	35,839	4.2%
7	Georgia	27,346	3.2%
8	Arizona	26,997	3.2%
9	Massachusetts	24,518	2.9%
10	North Carolina	21,211	2.5%
11	Virginia	20,928	2.4%
12	Washington	19,956	2.3%
13	Maryland	19,565	2.3%
14	Pennsylvania	18,480	2.2%
15	Michigan	15,446	1.8%
16	Colorado	13,078	1.5%
17	Ohio	11,835	1.4%
18	Connecticut	11,322	1.3%
19	Nevada	10,969	1.3%
20	Minnesota	10,066	1.2%
21	Tennessee	9,474	1.1%
22	Indiana	9,194	1.1%
23	Oregon	8,599	1.0%
24	South Carolina	7,265	0.8%
25	Wisconsin	6,798	0.8%
26	Missouri	6,133	0.7%
27	Utah	5,957	0.7%
28	Oklahoma	5,340	0.6%
29	Alabama	5,319	0.6%
30	Kansas	5,003	0.6%
31	New Mexico	4,828	0.6%
32	Kentucky	4,598	0.5%
33	Hawaii	4,033	0.5%
34	Arkansas	3,662	0.4%
35	Louisiana	3,476	0.4%
36	Iowa	3,189	0.4%
37	Rhode Island	3,096	0.4%
38	Nebraska	3,069	0.4%
39	Idaho	2,179	0.3%
40	Delaware	2,016	0.2%
41	Mississippi	1,939	0.2%
42	New Hampshire	1,787	0.2%
43	Alaska	1,022	0.1%
44	Maine	828	0.1%
45	South Dakota	688	0.1%
46	West Virginia	558	0.1%
47	North Dakota	521	0.1%
48	Vermont	421	0.0%
49	Wyoming	361	0.0%
50	Montana	344	0.0%
	District of Columbia	2,096	0.2%

Source: U.S. Bureau of the Census
    "Components of Population Change" (http://www.census.gov/popest/datasets.html)
*From July 1, 2008 to July 1, 2009. Net International Migration is the difference between migration to an area from outside the United States (immigration) and migration from the area to outside the United States (emigration) during the period. Includes legal immigration and estimates of undocumented immigration.

Percent of Population Foreign Born: 2008

National Percent = 12.5% of Population*

ALPHA ORDER

RANK	STATE	PERCENT
43	Alabama	2.8
23	Alaska	6.5
9	Arizona	14.3
37	Arkansas	3.8
1	California	26.8
16	Colorado	10.1
11	Connecticut	13.0
21	Delaware	7.7
5	Florida	18.5
19	Georgia	9.4
6	Hawaii	17.8
25	Idaho	5.9
10	Illinois	13.8
34	Indiana	4.0
38	Iowa	3.7
25	Kansas	5.9
43	Kentucky	2.8
41	Louisiana	3.1
42	Maine	3.0
12	Maryland	12.4
8	Massachusetts	14.4
27	Michigan	5.8
23	Minnesota	6.5
48	Mississippi	2.1
40	Missouri	3.6
47	Montana	2.2
28	Nebraska	5.5
4	Nevada	18.9
30	New Hampshire	5.0
3	New Jersey	19.8
18	New Mexico	9.6
2	New York	21.7
22	North Carolina	7.0
45	North Dakota	2.3
38	Ohio	3.7
30	Oklahoma	5.0
17	Oregon	9.7
29	Pennsylvania	5.3
14	Rhode Island	12.2
32	South Carolina	4.4
49	South Dakota	1.9
34	Tennessee	4.0
7	Texas	16.0
20	Utah	8.3
36	Vermont	3.9
15	Virginia	10.2
13	Washington	12.3
50	West Virginia	1.3
32	Wisconsin	4.4
45	Wyoming	2.3

RANK ORDER

RANK	STATE	PERCENT
1	California	26.8
2	New York	21.7
3	New Jersey	19.8
4	Nevada	18.9
5	Florida	18.5
6	Hawaii	17.8
7	Texas	16.0
8	Massachusetts	14.4
9	Arizona	14.3
10	Illinois	13.8
11	Connecticut	13.0
12	Maryland	12.4
13	Washington	12.3
14	Rhode Island	12.2
15	Virginia	10.2
16	Colorado	10.1
17	Oregon	9.7
18	New Mexico	9.6
19	Georgia	9.4
20	Utah	8.3
21	Delaware	7.7
22	North Carolina	7.0
23	Alaska	6.5
23	Minnesota	6.5
25	Idaho	5.9
25	Kansas	5.9
27	Michigan	5.8
28	Nebraska	5.5
29	Pennsylvania	5.3
30	New Hampshire	5.0
30	Oklahoma	5.0
32	South Carolina	4.4
32	Wisconsin	4.4
34	Indiana	4.0
34	Tennessee	4.0
36	Vermont	3.9
37	Arkansas	3.8
38	Iowa	3.7
38	Ohio	3.7
40	Missouri	3.6
41	Louisiana	3.1
42	Maine	3.0
43	Alabama	2.8
43	Kentucky	2.8
45	North Dakota	2.3
45	Wyoming	2.3
47	Montana	2.2
48	Mississippi	2.1
49	South Dakota	1.9
50	West Virginia	1.3

| | District of Columbia | 13.2 |

Source: U.S. Bureau of the Census
"2008 American Community Survey" (http://www.census.gov/acs/www/index.html)
*"Foreign born" are persons not born in the United States, Puerto Rico, a U.S. Island Area, or abroad of American parent or parents.

Percent of Population Speaking a Language
Other Than English at Home in 2008
National Percent = 19.7%*

ALPHA ORDER

RANK	STATE	PERCENT
48	Alabama	4.1
17	Alaska	14.8
7	Arizona	27.5
37	Arkansas	6.1
1	California	42.3
14	Colorado	17.0
13	Connecticut	19.8
22	Delaware	10.6
8	Florida	25.9
21	Georgia	12.5
9	Hawaii	25.4
23	Idaho	10.1
10	Illinois	21.9
34	Indiana	7.2
36	Iowa	6.4
24	Kansas	9.9
47	Kentucky	4.2
31	Louisiana	8.1
35	Maine	7.1
16	Maryland	15.1
11	Massachusetts	21.0
29	Michigan	8.8
26	Minnesota	9.7
49	Mississippi	3.6
43	Missouri	5.6
46	Montana	4.7
28	Nebraska	9.1
5	Nevada	27.9
33	New Hampshire	7.9
5	New Jersey	27.9
2	New Mexico	35.4
4	New York	29.0
25	North Carolina	9.8
44	North Dakota	5.5
39	Ohio	6.0
30	Oklahoma	8.4
18	Oregon	14.0
27	Pennsylvania	9.4
12	Rhode Island	20.0
37	South Carolina	6.1
39	South Dakota	6.0
42	Tennessee	5.7
3	Texas	33.8
18	Utah	14.0
45	Vermont	5.3
20	Virginia	13.3
15	Washington	16.7
50	West Virginia	2.1
31	Wisconsin	8.1
41	Wyoming	5.9

RANK ORDER

RANK	STATE	PERCENT
1	California	42.3
2	New Mexico	35.4
3	Texas	33.8
4	New York	29.0
5	Nevada	27.9
5	New Jersey	27.9
7	Arizona	27.5
8	Florida	25.9
9	Hawaii	25.4
10	Illinois	21.9
11	Massachusetts	21.0
12	Rhode Island	20.0
13	Connecticut	19.8
14	Colorado	17.0
15	Washington	16.7
16	Maryland	15.1
17	Alaska	14.8
18	Oregon	14.0
18	Utah	14.0
20	Virginia	13.3
21	Georgia	12.5
22	Delaware	10.6
23	Idaho	10.1
24	Kansas	9.9
25	North Carolina	9.8
26	Minnesota	9.7
27	Pennsylvania	9.4
28	Nebraska	9.1
29	Michigan	8.8
30	Oklahoma	8.4
31	Louisiana	8.1
31	Wisconsin	8.1
33	New Hampshire	7.9
34	Indiana	7.2
35	Maine	7.1
36	Iowa	6.4
37	Arkansas	6.1
37	South Carolina	6.1
39	Ohio	6.0
39	South Dakota	6.0
41	Wyoming	5.9
42	Tennessee	5.7
43	Missouri	5.6
44	North Dakota	5.5
45	Vermont	5.3
46	Montana	4.7
47	Kentucky	4.2
48	Alabama	4.1
49	Mississippi	3.6
50	West Virginia	2.1
	District of Columbia	14.4

Source: U.S. Bureau of the Census
   "2008 American Community Survey" (http://www.census.gov/acs/www/index.html)
*Population five years old and older.

Percent of Population Speaking Spanish at Home in 2008

National Percent = 12.2%*

ALPHA ORDER

RANK	STATE	PERCENT
39	Alabama	2.5
32	Alaska	3.6
4	Arizona	21.5
26	Arkansas	4.5
2	California	28.1
10	Colorado	12.0
12	Connecticut	9.7
24	Delaware	5.5
6	Florida	18.9
18	Georgia	7.2
38	Hawaii	2.6
15	Idaho	7.4
9	Illinois	12.8
28	Indiana	4.0
34	Iowa	3.5
19	Kansas	6.6
41	Kentucky	2.2
36	Louisiana	2.9
50	Maine	0.9
23	Maryland	5.6
16	Massachusetts	7.3
36	Michigan	2.9
32	Minnesota	3.6
42	Mississippi	2.1
39	Missouri	2.5
47	Montana	1.3
21	Nebraska	6.1
5	Nevada	20.1
43	New Hampshire	2.0
8	New Jersey	14.0
3	New Mexico	27.9
7	New York	14.2
19	North Carolina	6.6
46	North Dakota	1.4
43	Ohio	2.0
24	Oklahoma	5.5
14	Oregon	8.3
30	Pennsylvania	3.7
11	Rhode Island	9.8
30	South Carolina	3.7
45	South Dakota	1.9
35	Tennessee	3.2
1	Texas	29.0
13	Utah	9.2
48	Vermont	1.0
22	Virginia	5.9
16	Washington	7.3
48	West Virginia	1.0
27	Wisconsin	4.2
29	Wyoming	3.9

RANK ORDER

RANK	STATE	PERCENT
1	Texas	29.0
2	California	28.1
3	New Mexico	27.9
4	Arizona	21.5
5	Nevada	20.1
6	Florida	18.9
7	New York	14.2
8	New Jersey	14.0
9	Illinois	12.8
10	Colorado	12.0
11	Rhode Island	9.8
12	Connecticut	9.7
13	Utah	9.2
14	Oregon	8.3
15	Idaho	7.4
16	Massachusetts	7.3
16	Washington	7.3
18	Georgia	7.2
19	Kansas	6.6
19	North Carolina	6.6
21	Nebraska	6.1
22	Virginia	5.9
23	Maryland	5.6
24	Delaware	5.5
24	Oklahoma	5.5
26	Arkansas	4.5
27	Wisconsin	4.2
28	Indiana	4.0
29	Wyoming	3.9
30	Pennsylvania	3.7
30	South Carolina	3.7
32	Alaska	3.6
32	Minnesota	3.6
34	Iowa	3.5
35	Tennessee	3.2
36	Louisiana	2.9
36	Michigan	2.9
38	Hawaii	2.6
39	Alabama	2.5
39	Missouri	2.5
41	Kentucky	2.2
42	Mississippi	2.1
43	New Hampshire	2.0
43	Ohio	2.0
45	South Dakota	1.9
46	North Dakota	1.4
47	Montana	1.3
48	Vermont	1.0
48	West Virginia	1.0
50	Maine	0.9
	District of Columbia	6.9

Source: U.S. Bureau of the Census
"2008 American Community Survey" (http://www.census.gov/acs/www/index.html)
*Population five years old and older.

Marriages in 2008

National Total = 2,162,000 Marriages*

ALPHA ORDER

RANK	STATE	MARRIAGES	% of USA
18	Alabama	39,035	1.8%
46	Alaska	5,847	0.3%
20	Arizona	37,772	1.7%
26	Arkansas	30,961	1.4%
1	California	246,802	11.4%
19	Colorado	37,876	1.8%
34	Connecticut	19,105	0.9%
47	Delaware	5,391	0.2%
3	Florida	147,941	6.8%
11	Georgia	57,361	2.7%
30	Hawaii	25,068	1.2%
37	Idaho	14,536	0.7%
6	Illinois	75,882	3.5%
14	Indiana	50,671	2.3%
33	Iowa	19,564	0.9%
35	Kansas	18,693	0.9%
22	Kentucky	35,239	1.6%
21	Louisiana	36,276	1.7%
40	Maine	9,348	0.4%
24	Maryland	33,391	1.5%
23	Massachusetts	33,996	1.6%
13	Michigan	55,726	2.6%
27	Minnesota	28,820	1.3%
36	Mississippi	15,872	0.7%
17	Missouri	39,526	1.8%
43	Montana	7,267	0.3%
38	Nebraska	12,559	0.6%
5	Nevada	112,185	5.2%
41	New Hampshire	9,030	0.4%
15	New Jersey	45,682	2.1%
42	New Mexico	8,033	0.4%
4	New York	134,969	6.2%
10	North Carolina	58,994	2.7%
50	North Dakota	4,107	0.2%
7	Ohio	70,574	3.3%
31	Oklahoma	24,913	1.2%
29	Oregon	27,172	1.3%
8	Pennsylvania	69,538	3.2%
44	Rhode Island	6,487	0.3%
28	South Carolina	28,578	1.3%
45	South Dakota	6,196	0.3%
9	Tennessee	60,651	2.8%
2	Texas	179,451	8.3%
32	Utah	19,978	0.9%
49	Vermont	4,693	0.2%
12	Virginia	56,882	2.6%
16	Washington	42,133	1.9%
39	West Virginia	12,299	0.6%
25	Wisconsin	31,586	1.5%
48	Wyoming	4,722	0.2%

RANK ORDER

RANK	STATE	MARRIAGES	% of USA
1	California	246,802	11.4%
2	Texas	179,451	8.3%
3	Florida	147,941	6.8%
4	New York	134,969	6.2%
5	Nevada	112,185	5.2%
6	Illinois	75,882	3.5%
7	Ohio	70,574	3.3%
8	Pennsylvania	69,538	3.2%
9	Tennessee	60,651	2.8%
10	North Carolina	58,994	2.7%
11	Georgia	57,361	2.7%
12	Virginia	56,882	2.6%
13	Michigan	55,726	2.6%
14	Indiana	50,671	2.3%
15	New Jersey	45,682	2.1%
16	Washington	42,133	1.9%
17	Missouri	39,526	1.8%
18	Alabama	39,035	1.8%
19	Colorado	37,876	1.8%
20	Arizona	37,772	1.7%
21	Louisiana	36,276	1.7%
22	Kentucky	35,239	1.6%
23	Massachusetts	33,996	1.6%
24	Maryland	33,391	1.5%
25	Wisconsin	31,586	1.5%
26	Arkansas	30,961	1.4%
27	Minnesota	28,820	1.3%
28	South Carolina	28,578	1.3%
29	Oregon	27,172	1.3%
30	Hawaii	25,068	1.2%
31	Oklahoma	24,913	1.2%
32	Utah	19,978	0.9%
33	Iowa	19,564	0.9%
34	Connecticut	19,105	0.9%
35	Kansas	18,693	0.9%
36	Mississippi	15,872	0.7%
37	Idaho	14,536	0.7%
38	Nebraska	12,559	0.6%
39	West Virginia	12,299	0.6%
40	Maine	9,348	0.4%
41	New Hampshire	9,030	0.4%
42	New Mexico	8,033	0.4%
43	Montana	7,267	0.3%
44	Rhode Island	6,487	0.3%
45	South Dakota	6,196	0.3%
46	Alaska	5,847	0.3%
47	Delaware	5,391	0.2%
48	Wyoming	4,722	0.2%
49	Vermont	4,693	0.2%
50	North Dakota	4,107	0.2%
	District of Columbia	2,417	0.1%

Source: U.S. Department of Health and Human Services, National Center for Health Statistics
 "National Vital Statistics Reports" (Vol. 57, No. 19, July 29, 2009, http://www.cdc.gov/nchs/data/nvsr/nvsr57/nvsr57_19.pdf)
*Provisional data by state of occurrence.

Marriage Rate in 2008

National Rate = 7.1 Marriages per 1,000 Population*

ALPHA ORDER				RANK ORDER		
RANK	STATE	RATE		RANK	STATE	RATE
8	Alabama	8.4		1	Nevada	43.1
7	Alaska	8.5		2	Hawaii	19.5
41	Arizona	5.8		3	Arkansas	10.8
3	Arkansas	10.8		4	Tennessee	9.8
27	California	6.7		5	Idaho	9.5
13	Colorado	7.7		6	Wyoming	8.9
45	Connecticut	5.5		7	Alaska	8.5
35	Delaware	6.2		8	Alabama	8.4
11	Florida	8.1		9	Kentucky	8.3
38	Georgia	5.9		10	Louisiana	8.2
2	Hawaii	19.5		11	Florida	8.1
5	Idaho	9.5		12	Indiana	7.9
38	Illinois	5.9		13	Colorado	7.7
12	Indiana	7.9		13	South Dakota	7.7
30	Iowa	6.5		15	Vermont	7.6
27	Kansas	6.7		16	Montana	7.5
9	Kentucky	8.3		17	Texas	7.4
10	Louisiana	8.2		18	Utah	7.3
21	Maine	7.1		18	Virginia	7.3
38	Maryland	5.9		20	Oregon	7.2
49	Massachusetts	5.2		21	Maine	7.1
42	Michigan	5.6		22	Nebraska	7.0
45	Minnesota	5.5		23	New Hampshire	6.9
47	Mississippi	5.4		23	New York	6.9
27	Missouri	6.7		25	Oklahoma	6.8
16	Montana	7.5		25	West Virginia	6.8
22	Nebraska	7.0		27	California	6.7
1	Nevada	43.1		27	Kansas	6.7
23	New Hampshire	6.9		27	Missouri	6.7
48	New Jersey	5.3		30	Iowa	6.5
50	New Mexico	4.0		31	North Carolina	6.4
23	New York	6.9		31	North Dakota	6.4
31	North Carolina	6.4		31	South Carolina	6.4
31	North Dakota	6.4		31	Washington	6.4
37	Ohio	6.1		35	Delaware	6.2
25	Oklahoma	6.8		35	Rhode Island	6.2
20	Oregon	7.2		37	Ohio	6.1
42	Pennsylvania	5.6		38	Georgia	5.9
35	Rhode Island	6.2		38	Illinois	5.9
31	South Carolina	6.4		38	Maryland	5.9
13	South Dakota	7.7		41	Arizona	5.8
4	Tennessee	9.8		42	Michigan	5.6
17	Texas	7.4		42	Pennsylvania	5.6
18	Utah	7.3		42	Wisconsin	5.6
15	Vermont	7.6		45	Connecticut	5.5
18	Virginia	7.3		45	Minnesota	5.5
31	Washington	6.4		47	Mississippi	5.4
25	West Virginia	6.8		48	New Jersey	5.3
42	Wisconsin	5.6		49	Massachusetts	5.2
6	Wyoming	8.9		50	New Mexico	4.0
				District of Columbia		4.1

Source: CQ Press using data from U.S. Department of Health and Human Services, National Center for Health Statistics "National Vital Statistics Reports" (Vol. 57, No. 19, July 29, 2009, http://www.cdc.gov/nchs/data/nvsr/nvsr57/nvsr57_19.pdf)
*Provisional data by state of occurrence.

Estimated Median Age of Men at First Marriage: 2008

National Median = 28.0 Years*

RANK	STATE	AGE
35	Alabama	26.9
24	Alaska	27.6
20	Arizona	28.0
48	Arkansas	25.9
8	California	29.0
29	Colorado	27.4
5	Connecticut	29.4
14	Delaware	28.5
9	Florida	28.7
26	Georgia	27.5
14	Hawaii	28.5
50	Idaho	25.4
10	Illinois	28.6
35	Indiana	26.9
40	Iowa	26.8
46	Kansas	26.1
35	Kentucky	26.9
34	Louisiana	27.2
10	Maine	28.6
7	Maryland	29.2
3	Massachusetts	29.8
10	Michigan	28.6
29	Minnesota	27.4
44	Mississippi	26.4
35	Missouri	26.9
10	Montana	28.6
42	Nebraska	26.5
21	Nevada	27.9
6	New Hampshire	29.3
3	New Jersey	29.8
18	New Mexico	28.3
2	New York	30.0
33	North Carolina	27.3
23	North Dakota	27.7
29	Ohio	27.4
49	Oklahoma	25.7
24	Oregon	27.6
14	Pennsylvania	28.5
1	Rhode Island	30.3
22	South Carolina	27.8
45	South Dakota	26.3
41	Tennessee	26.7
35	Texas	26.9
46	Utah	26.1
17	Vermont	28.4
29	Virginia	27.4
26	Washington	27.5
42	West Virginia	26.5
26	Wisconsin	27.5
18	Wyoming	28.3

RANK	STATE	AGE
1	Rhode Island	30.3
2	New York	30.0
3	Massachusetts	29.8
3	New Jersey	29.8
5	Connecticut	29.4
6	New Hampshire	29.3
7	Maryland	29.2
8	California	29.0
9	Florida	28.7
10	Illinois	28.6
10	Maine	28.6
10	Michigan	28.6
10	Montana	28.6
14	Delaware	28.5
14	Hawaii	28.5
14	Pennsylvania	28.5
17	Vermont	28.4
18	New Mexico	28.3
18	Wyoming	28.3
20	Arizona	28.0
21	Nevada	27.9
22	South Carolina	27.8
23	North Dakota	27.7
24	Alaska	27.6
24	Oregon	27.6
26	Georgia	27.5
26	Washington	27.5
26	Wisconsin	27.5
29	Colorado	27.4
29	Minnesota	27.4
29	Ohio	27.4
29	Virginia	27.4
33	North Carolina	27.3
34	Louisiana	27.2
35	Alabama	26.9
35	Indiana	26.9
35	Kentucky	26.9
35	Missouri	26.9
35	Texas	26.9
40	Iowa	26.8
41	Tennessee	26.7
42	Nebraska	26.5
42	West Virginia	26.5
44	Mississippi	26.4
45	South Dakota	26.3
46	Kansas	26.1
46	Utah	26.1
48	Arkansas	25.9
49	Oklahoma	25.7
50	Idaho	25.4
	District of Columbia	31.5

Source: U.S. Bureau of the Census
   "2008 American Community Survey" (http://www.census.gov/acs/www/index.html)
*The median age at first marriage is calculated indirectly by estimating the proportion of young people who will marry during their lifetime, calculating one-half of this proportion, and determining the age (at the time of the survey) of people at this half-way mark. It does not represent the actual median age of the population who married during the calendar year.

Estimated Median Age of Women at First Marriage: 2008

National Median = 26.2 Years*

ALPHA ORDER				RANK ORDER		
RANK	STATE	AGE		RANK	STATE	AGE
41	Alabama	25.2		1	Connecticut	28.2
34	Alaska	25.5		1	Massachusetts	28.2
22	Arizona	26.0		3	New York	28.1
48	Arkansas	24.3		4	Rhode Island	27.8
11	California	26.7		5	New Jersey	27.6
31	Colorado	25.6		6	Maryland	27.3
1	Connecticut	28.2		7	Vermont	27.1
17	Delaware	26.3		8	Hawaii	26.8
16	Florida	26.4		8	Illinois	26.8
26	Georgia	25.9		8	Pennsylvania	26.8
8	Hawaii	26.8		11	California	26.7
49	Idaho	23.5		11	South Carolina	26.7
8	Illinois	26.8		13	Michigan	26.6
28	Indiana	25.8		14	Maine	26.5
34	Iowa	25.5		14	New Hampshire	26.5
44	Kansas	24.9		16	Florida	26.4
42	Kentucky	25.0		17	Delaware	26.3
31	Louisiana	25.6		17	Ohio	26.3
14	Maine	26.5		19	New Mexico	26.2
6	Maryland	27.3		19	North Carolina	26.2
1	Massachusetts	28.2		21	Wisconsin	26.1
13	Michigan	26.6		22	Arizona	26.0
22	Minnesota	26.0		22	Minnesota	26.0
22	Mississippi	26.0		22	Mississippi	26.0
31	Missouri	25.6		22	Virginia	26.0
34	Montana	25.5		26	Georgia	25.9
39	Nebraska	25.3		26	Oregon	25.9
29	Nevada	25.7		28	Indiana	25.8
14	New Hampshire	26.5		29	Nevada	25.7
5	New Jersey	27.6		29	Washington	25.7
19	New Mexico	26.2		31	Colorado	25.6
3	New York	28.1		31	Louisiana	25.6
19	North Carolina	26.2		31	Missouri	25.6
37	North Dakota	25.4		34	Alaska	25.5
17	Ohio	26.3		34	Iowa	25.5
47	Oklahoma	24.4		34	Montana	25.5
26	Oregon	25.9		37	North Dakota	25.4
8	Pennsylvania	26.8		37	South Dakota	25.4
4	Rhode Island	27.8		39	Nebraska	25.3
11	South Carolina	26.7		39	Texas	25.3
37	South Dakota	25.4		41	Alabama	25.2
42	Tennessee	25.0		42	Kentucky	25.0
39	Texas	25.3		42	Tennessee	25.0
49	Utah	23.5		44	Kansas	24.9
7	Vermont	27.1		45	West Virginia	24.6
22	Virginia	26.0		46	Wyoming	24.5
29	Washington	25.7		47	Oklahoma	24.4
45	West Virginia	24.6		48	Arkansas	24.3
21	Wisconsin	26.1		49	Idaho	23.5
46	Wyoming	24.5		49	Utah	23.5
					District of Columbia	29.7

Source: U.S. Bureau of the Census

 "2008 American Community Survey" (http://www.census.gov/acs/www/index.html)

*The median age at first marriage is calculated indirectly by estimating the proportion of young people who will marry during their lifetime, calculating one-half of this proportion, and determining the age (at the time of the survey) of people at this half-way mark. It does not represent the actual median age of the population who married during the calendar year.

Ratio of Unmarried Men to Unmarried Women: 2008

National Ratio = 112.8 Unmarried Men for Every 100 Unmarried Women*

ALPHA ORDER

RANK	STATE	RATIO
43	Alabama	107.9
1	Alaska	131.8
9	Arizona	118.6
33	Arkansas	109.4
11	California	117.9
5	Colorado	123.3
40	Connecticut	108.2
50	Delaware	103.7
13	Florida	117.2
37	Georgia	108.8
2	Hawaii	129.2
15	Idaho	116.7
30	Illinois	111.0
29	Indiana	111.4
16	Iowa	116.6
19	Kansas	116.0
25	Kentucky	112.1
45	Louisiana	106.5
37	Maine	108.8
48	Maryland	104.9
46	Massachusetts	106.0
32	Michigan	110.0
17	Minnesota	116.4
49	Mississippi	104.2
36	Missouri	109.0
7	Montana	121.4
14	Nebraska	117.0
4	Nevada	124.0
24	New Hampshire	112.7
28	New Jersey	111.6
27	New Mexico	111.9
44	New York	107.1
31	North Carolina	110.7
3	North Dakota	128.4
39	Ohio	108.5
12	Oklahoma	117.3
22	Oregon	114.6
34	Pennsylvania	109.3
47	Rhode Island	105.0
35	South Carolina	109.1
26	South Dakota	112.0
42	Tennessee	108.0
21	Texas	115.7
7	Utah	121.4
40	Vermont	108.2
23	Virginia	113.1
10	Washington	118.1
18	West Virginia	116.3
20	Wisconsin	115.8
6	Wyoming	121.7

RANK ORDER

RANK	STATE	RATIO
1	Alaska	131.8
2	Hawaii	129.2
3	North Dakota	128.4
4	Nevada	124.0
5	Colorado	123.3
6	Wyoming	121.7
7	Montana	121.4
7	Utah	121.4
9	Arizona	118.6
10	Washington	118.1
11	California	117.9
12	Oklahoma	117.3
13	Florida	117.2
14	Nebraska	117.0
15	Idaho	116.7
16	Iowa	116.6
17	Minnesota	116.4
18	West Virginia	116.3
19	Kansas	116.0
20	Wisconsin	115.8
21	Texas	115.7
22	Oregon	114.6
23	Virginia	113.1
24	New Hampshire	112.7
25	Kentucky	112.1
26	South Dakota	112.0
27	New Mexico	111.9
28	New Jersey	111.6
29	Indiana	111.4
30	Illinois	111.0
31	North Carolina	110.7
32	Michigan	110.0
33	Arkansas	109.4
34	Pennsylvania	109.3
35	South Carolina	109.1
36	Missouri	109.0
37	Georgia	108.8
37	Maine	108.8
39	Ohio	108.5
40	Connecticut	108.2
40	Vermont	108.2
42	Tennessee	108.0
43	Alabama	107.9
44	New York	107.1
45	Louisiana	106.5
46	Massachusetts	106.0
47	Rhode Island	105.0
48	Maryland	104.9
49	Mississippi	104.2
50	Delaware	103.7
	District of Columbia	94.0

Source: U.S. Bureau of the Census
"2008 American Community Survey" (http://www.census.gov/acs/www/index.html)
*Population 15 to 44 years old.

Divorces in 2008

Reporting States' Total = 838,088 Divorces*

ALPHA ORDER

RANK	STATE	DIVORCES	% of USA
17	Alabama	19,509	2.3%
39	Alaska	2,921	0.3%
13	Arizona	23,985	2.9%
22	Arkansas	15,908	1.9%
NA	California**	NA	NA
16	Colorado	20,992	2.5%
27	Connecticut	11,369	1.4%
38	Delaware	3,147	0.4%
1	Florida	82,055	9.8%
NA	Georgia**	NA	NA
NA	Hawaii**	NA	NA
33	Idaho	7,182	0.9%
8	Illinois	32,237	3.8%
NA	Indiana**	NA	NA
32	Iowa	7,269	0.9%
28	Kansas	9,971	1.2%
15	Kentucky	21,029	2.5%
NA	Louisiana**	NA	NA
36	Maine	4,709	0.6%
21	Maryland	16,210	1.9%
25	Massachusetts	12,992	1.6%
7	Michigan	33,812	4.0%
NA	Minnesota**	NA	NA
24	Mississippi	13,049	1.6%
14	Missouri	22,495	2.7%
37	Montana	3,449	0.4%
34	Nebraska	6,129	0.7%
20	Nevada	16,909	2.0%
35	New Hampshire	4,909	0.6%
11	New Jersey	25,766	3.1%
31	New Mexico	8,148	1.0%
3	New York	52,251	6.2%
5	North Carolina	35,086	4.2%
44	North Dakota	1,755	0.2%
4	Ohio	39,009	4.7%
18	Oklahoma	18,088	2.2%
23	Oregon	15,045	1.8%
6	Pennsylvania	34,089	4.1%
40	Rhode Island	2,825	0.3%
26	South Carolina	11,382	1.4%
42	South Dakota	2,473	0.3%
10	Tennessee	26,390	3.1%
2	Texas	77,649	9.3%
29	Utah	9,489	1.1%
43	Vermont	2,225	0.3%
9	Virginia	29,713	3.5%
12	Washington	24,558	2.9%
30	West Virginia	8,641	1.0%
19	Wisconsin	17,067	2.0%
41	Wyoming	2,727	0.3%

RANK ORDER

RANK	STATE	DIVORCES	% of USA
1	Florida	82,055	9.8%
2	Texas	77,649	9.3%
3	New York	52,251	6.2%
4	Ohio	39,009	4.7%
5	North Carolina	35,086	4.2%
6	Pennsylvania	34,089	4.1%
7	Michigan	33,812	4.0%
8	Illinois	32,237	3.8%
9	Virginia	29,713	3.5%
10	Tennessee	26,390	3.1%
11	New Jersey	25,766	3.1%
12	Washington	24,558	2.9%
13	Arizona	23,985	2.9%
14	Missouri	22,495	2.7%
15	Kentucky	21,029	2.5%
16	Colorado	20,992	2.5%
17	Alabama	19,509	2.3%
18	Oklahoma	18,088	2.2%
19	Wisconsin	17,067	2.0%
20	Nevada	16,909	2.0%
21	Maryland	16,210	1.9%
22	Arkansas	15,908	1.9%
23	Oregon	15,045	1.8%
24	Mississippi	13,049	1.6%
25	Massachusetts	12,992	1.6%
26	South Carolina	11,382	1.4%
27	Connecticut	11,369	1.4%
28	Kansas	9,971	1.2%
29	Utah	9,489	1.1%
30	West Virginia	8,641	1.0%
31	New Mexico	8,148	1.0%
32	Iowa	7,269	0.9%
33	Idaho	7,182	0.9%
34	Nebraska	6,129	0.7%
35	New Hampshire	4,909	0.6%
36	Maine	4,709	0.6%
37	Montana	3,449	0.4%
38	Delaware	3,147	0.4%
39	Alaska	2,921	0.3%
40	Rhode Island	2,825	0.3%
41	Wyoming	2,727	0.3%
42	South Dakota	2,473	0.3%
43	Vermont	2,225	0.3%
44	North Dakota	1,755	0.2%
NA	California**	NA	NA
NA	Georgia**	NA	NA
NA	Hawaii**	NA	NA
NA	Indiana**	NA	NA
NA	Louisiana**	NA	NA
NA	Minnesota**	NA	NA
	District of Columbia	1,475	0.2%

Source: U.S. Department of Health and Human Services, National Center for Health Statistics
   "National Vital Statistics Reports" (Vol. 57, No. 19, July 29, 2009, http://www.cdc.gov/nchs/data/nvsr/nvsr57/nvsr57_19.pdf)
*Provisional data by state of occurrence. National total is only for reporting states.
**Not available.

Divorce Rate in 2008

Reporting States' Rate = 3.5 Divorces per 1,000 Population*

ALPHA ORDER

RANK	STATE	RATE
11	Alabama	4.2
10	Alaska	4.3
19	Arizona	3.7
2	Arkansas	5.6
NA	California**	NA
11	Colorado	4.2
31	Connecticut	3.2
22	Delaware	3.6
8	Florida	4.5
NA	Georgia**	NA
NA	Hawaii**	NA
7	Idaho	4.7
41	Illinois	2.5
NA	Indiana**	NA
43	Iowa	2.4
22	Kansas	3.6
5	Kentucky	4.9
NA	Louisiana**	NA
22	Maine	3.6
36	Maryland	2.9
44	Massachusetts	2.0
28	Michigan	3.4
NA	Minnesota**	NA
9	Mississippi	4.4
16	Missouri	3.8
22	Montana	3.6
28	Nebraska	3.4
1	Nevada	6.5
19	New Hampshire	3.7
34	New Jersey	3.0
14	New Mexico	4.1
37	New York	2.7
16	North Carolina	3.8
37	North Dakota	2.7
28	Ohio	3.4
4	Oklahoma	5.0
15	Oregon	4.0
37	Pennsylvania	2.7
37	Rhode Island	2.7
41	South Carolina	2.5
33	South Dakota	3.1
11	Tennessee	4.2
31	Texas	3.2
27	Utah	3.5
22	Vermont	3.6
16	Virginia	3.8
19	Washington	3.7
6	West Virginia	4.8
34	Wisconsin	3.0
3	Wyoming	5.1

RANK ORDER

RANK	STATE	RATE
1	Nevada	6.5
2	Arkansas	5.6
3	Wyoming	5.1
4	Oklahoma	5.0
5	Kentucky	4.9
6	West Virginia	4.8
7	Idaho	4.7
8	Florida	4.5
9	Mississippi	4.4
10	Alaska	4.3
11	Alabama	4.2
11	Colorado	4.2
11	Tennessee	4.2
14	New Mexico	4.1
15	Oregon	4.0
16	Missouri	3.8
16	North Carolina	3.8
16	Virginia	3.8
19	Arizona	3.7
19	New Hampshire	3.7
19	Washington	3.7
22	Delaware	3.6
22	Kansas	3.6
22	Maine	3.6
22	Montana	3.6
22	Vermont	3.6
27	Utah	3.5
28	Michigan	3.4
28	Nebraska	3.4
28	Ohio	3.4
31	Connecticut	3.2
31	Texas	3.2
33	South Dakota	3.1
34	New Jersey	3.0
34	Wisconsin	3.0
36	Maryland	2.9
37	New York	2.7
37	North Dakota	2.7
37	Pennsylvania	2.7
37	Rhode Island	2.7
41	Illinois	2.5
41	South Carolina	2.5
43	Iowa	2.4
44	Massachusetts	2.0
NA	California**	NA
NA	Georgia**	NA
NA	Hawaii**	NA
NA	Indiana**	NA
NA	Louisiana**	NA
NA	Minnesota**	NA

	District of Columbia	2.5

Source: CQ Press using data from U.S. Department of Health and Human Services, National Center for Health Statistics
"National Vital Statistics Reports" (Vol. 57, No. 19, July 29, 2009, http://www.cdc.gov/nchs/data/nvsr/nvsr57/nvsr57_19.pdf)
*Provisional data by state of occurrence. National rate is only for reporting states.
**Not available.

Average Family Size in 2008

National Average = 3.22 Persons per Family

ALPHA ORDER

ALPHA ORDER

RANK ORDER

RANK	STATE	PERSONS		RANK	STATE	PERSONS
26	Alabama	3.10		1	Utah	3.67
6	Alaska	3.38		2	California	3.57
3	Arizona	3.46		3	Arizona	3.46
35	Arkansas	3.05		4	Hawaii	3.43
2	California	3.57		5	Texas	3.42
16	Colorado	3.17		6	Alaska	3.38
21	Connecticut	3.13		7	New York	3.33
20	Delaware	3.14		8	Nevada	3.32
21	Florida	3.13		9	Georgia	3.31
9	Georgia	3.31		10	Illinois	3.29
4	Hawaii	3.43		10	New Jersey	3.29
24	Idaho	3.12		12	New Mexico	3.26
10	Illinois	3.29		13	Louisiana	3.25
33	Indiana	3.06		14	Rhode Island	3.24
46	Iowa	2.92		15	Maryland	3.22
44	Kansas	3.00		16	Colorado	3.17
39	Kentucky	3.03		16	Massachusetts	3.17
13	Louisiana	3.25		18	Michigan	3.16
49	Maine	2.88		18	Mississippi	3.16
15	Maryland	3.22		20	Delaware	3.14
16	Massachusetts	3.17		21	Connecticut	3.13
18	Michigan	3.16		21	Florida	3.13
41	Minnesota	3.02		21	South Carolina	3.13
18	Mississippi	3.16		24	Idaho	3.12
37	Missouri	3.04		25	Montana	3.11
25	Montana	3.11		26	Alabama	3.10
37	Nebraska	3.04		27	Oklahoma	3.09
8	Nevada	3.32		27	Oregon	3.09
42	New Hampshire	3.01		27	Washington	3.09
10	New Jersey	3.29		30	Ohio	3.08
12	New Mexico	3.26		30	Virginia	3.08
7	New York	3.33		32	Tennessee	3.07
35	North Carolina	3.05		33	Indiana	3.06
50	North Dakota	2.82		33	Wyoming	3.06
30	Ohio	3.08		35	Arkansas	3.05
27	Oklahoma	3.09		35	North Carolina	3.05
27	Oregon	3.09		37	Missouri	3.04
39	Pennsylvania	3.03		37	Nebraska	3.04
14	Rhode Island	3.24		39	Kentucky	3.03
21	South Carolina	3.13		39	Pennsylvania	3.03
42	South Dakota	3.01		41	Minnesota	3.02
32	Tennessee	3.07		42	New Hampshire	3.01
5	Texas	3.42		42	South Dakota	3.01
1	Utah	3.67		44	Kansas	3.00
48	Vermont	2.90		45	Wisconsin	2.99
30	Virginia	3.08		46	Iowa	2.92
27	Washington	3.09		47	West Virginia	2.91
47	West Virginia	2.91		48	Vermont	2.90
45	Wisconsin	2.99		49	Maine	2.88
33	Wyoming	3.06		50	North Dakota	2.82
					District of Columbia	3.31

Source: U.S. Bureau of the Census
  "2008 American Community Survey" (http://www.census.gov/acs/www/index.html)

Seats in the U.S. House of Representatives in 2010

National Total = 435 Seats*

RANK	STATE	SEATS	% of USA
22	Alabama	7	1.6%
44	Alaska	1	0.2%
18	Arizona	8	1.8%
31	Arkansas	4	0.9%
1	California	53	12.2%
22	Colorado	7	1.6%
27	Connecticut	5	1.1%
44	Delaware	1	0.2%
4	Florida	25	5.7%
9	Georgia	13	3.0%
39	Hawaii	2	0.5%
39	Idaho	2	0.5%
5	Illinois	19	4.4%
14	Indiana	9	2.1%
27	Iowa	5	1.1%
31	Kansas	4	0.9%
25	Kentucky	6	1.4%
22	Louisiana	7	1.6%
39	Maine	2	0.5%
18	Maryland	8	1.8%
13	Massachusetts	10	2.3%
8	Michigan	15	3.4%
18	Minnesota	8	1.8%
31	Mississippi	4	0.9%
14	Missouri	9	2.1%
44	Montana	1	0.2%
34	Nebraska	3	0.7%
34	Nevada	3	0.7%
39	New Hampshire	2	0.5%
9	New Jersey	13	3.0%
34	New Mexico	3	0.7%
3	New York	29	6.7%
9	North Carolina	13	3.0%
44	North Dakota	1	0.2%
7	Ohio	18	4.1%
27	Oklahoma	5	1.1%
27	Oregon	5	1.1%
5	Pennsylvania	19	4.4%
39	Rhode Island	2	0.5%
25	South Carolina	6	1.4%
44	South Dakota	1	0.2%
14	Tennessee	9	2.1%
2	Texas	32	7.4%
34	Utah	3	0.7%
44	Vermont	1	0.2%
12	Virginia	11	2.5%
14	Washington	9	2.1%
34	West Virginia	3	0.7%
18	Wisconsin	8	1.8%
44	Wyoming	1	0.2%

RANK	STATE	SEATS	% of USA
1	California	53	12.2%
2	Texas	32	7.4%
3	New York	29	6.7%
4	Florida	25	5.7%
5	Illinois	19	4.4%
5	Pennsylvania	19	4.4%
7	Ohio	18	4.1%
8	Michigan	15	3.4%
9	Georgia	13	3.0%
9	New Jersey	13	3.0%
9	North Carolina	13	3.0%
12	Virginia	11	2.5%
13	Massachusetts	10	2.3%
14	Indiana	9	2.1%
14	Missouri	9	2.1%
14	Tennessee	9	2.1%
14	Washington	9	2.1%
18	Arizona	8	1.8%
18	Maryland	8	1.8%
18	Minnesota	8	1.8%
18	Wisconsin	8	1.8%
22	Alabama	7	1.6%
22	Colorado	7	1.6%
22	Louisiana	7	1.6%
25	Kentucky	6	1.4%
25	South Carolina	6	1.4%
27	Connecticut	5	1.1%
27	Iowa	5	1.1%
27	Oklahoma	5	1.1%
27	Oregon	5	1.1%
31	Arkansas	4	0.9%
31	Kansas	4	0.9%
31	Mississippi	4	0.9%
34	Nebraska	3	0.7%
34	Nevada	3	0.7%
34	New Mexico	3	0.7%
34	Utah	3	0.7%
34	West Virginia	3	0.7%
39	Hawaii	2	0.5%
39	Idaho	2	0.5%
39	Maine	2	0.5%
39	New Hampshire	2	0.5%
39	Rhode Island	2	0.5%
44	Alaska	1	0.2%
44	Delaware	1	0.2%
44	Montana	1	0.2%
44	North Dakota	1	0.2%
44	South Dakota	1	0.2%
44	Vermont	1	0.2%
44	Wyoming	1	0.2%
	District of Columbia**	0	0.0%

Source: U.S. Bureau of the Census

"Congressional Apportionment" (http://www.census.gov/population/www/censusdata/apportionment.html)

*This table shows the number of seats after reapportionment of the 2000 Census. This apportionment became effective with the Congress elected in November 2002 and that took office in January 2003.

**The District of Columbia has one non-voting delegate. Each state has two members in the U.S. Senate.

Estimated Population per U.S. House Seat in 2010

National Rate = 705,762 Persons per House Member*

ALPHA ORDER				RANK ORDER		
RANK	STATE	RATE		RANK	STATE	RATE
31	Alabama	672,673		1	Montana	974,989
27	Alaska	698,473		2	Utah	928,191
5	Arizona	824,472		3	Delaware	885,122
16	Arkansas	722,363		4	Nevada	881,028
28	California	697,390		5	Arizona	824,472
19	Colorado	717,821		6	South Dakota	812,383
25	Connecticut	703,658		7	Texas	774,447
3	Delaware	885,122		8	Idaho	772,901
12	Florida	741,519		9	Oregon	765,131
11	Georgia	756,093		10	South Carolina	760,207
41	Hawaii	647,589		11	Georgia	756,093
8	Idaho	772,901		12	Florida	741,519
29	Illinois	679,495		13	Washington	740,466
21	Indiana	713,679		14	Mississippi	737,999
47	Iowa	601,571		15	Oklahoma	737,410
24	Kansas	704,687		16	Arkansas	722,363
18	Kentucky	719,019		17	North Carolina	721,606
43	Louisiana	641,725		18	Kentucky	719,019
39	Maine	659,151		19	Colorado	717,821
22	Maryland	712,435		20	Virginia	716,599
38	Massachusetts	659,359		21	Indiana	713,679
35	Michigan	664,648		22	Maryland	712,435
40	Minnesota	658,277		23	Wisconsin	706,847
14	Mississippi	737,999		24	Kansas	704,687
34	Missouri	665,287		25	Connecticut	703,658
1	Montana	974,989		26	Tennessee	699,584
48	Nebraska	598,873		27	Alaska	698,473
4	Nevada	881,028		28	California	697,390
37	New Hampshire	662,288		29	Illinois	679,495
33	New Jersey	669,826		30	New York	673,843
32	New Mexico	669,890		31	Alabama	672,673
30	New York	673,843		32	New Mexico	669,890
17	North Carolina	721,606		33	New Jersey	669,826
42	North Dakota	646,844		34	Missouri	665,287
44	Ohio	641,258		35	Michigan	664,648
15	Oklahoma	737,410		36	Pennsylvania	663,409
9	Oregon	765,131		37	New Hampshire	662,288
36	Pennsylvania	663,409		38	Massachusetts	659,359
50	Rhode Island	526,605		39	Maine	659,151
10	South Carolina	760,207		40	Minnesota	658,277
6	South Dakota	812,383		41	Hawaii	647,589
26	Tennessee	699,584		42	North Dakota	646,844
7	Texas	774,447		43	Louisiana	641,725
2	Utah	928,191		44	Ohio	641,258
45	Vermont	621,760		45	Vermont	621,760
20	Virginia	716,599		46	West Virginia	606,592
13	Washington	740,466		47	Iowa	601,571
46	West Virginia	606,592		48	Nebraska	598,873
23	Wisconsin	706,847		49	Wyoming	544,270
49	Wyoming	544,270		50	Rhode Island	526,605
				District of Columbia**		NA

Source: CQ Press using data from U.S. Bureau of the Census
"Congressional Apportionment" (http://www.census.gov/population/www/censusdata/apportionment.html)
*National rate does not include population of the District of Columbia. D.C. has one non-voting delegate. Each state has two members in the U.S. Senate. This table is based only on U.S. Representatives and not U.S. Senate members. This table reflects reapportionment resulting from the 2000 census.
**Not applicable.

State Legislators in 2010

National Total = 7,382 Legislators*

ALPHA ORDER

RANK	STATE	LEGISLATORS	% of USA
27	Alabama	140	1.9%
49	Alaska	60	0.8%
43	Arizona	90	1.2%
30	Arkansas	135	1.8%
35	California	120	1.6%
42	Colorado	100	1.4%
9	Connecticut	187	2.5%
48	Delaware	62	0.8%
18	Florida	160	2.2%
3	Georgia	236	3.2%
46	Hawaii	76	1.0%
39	Idaho	105	1.4%
13	Illinois	177	2.4%
19	Indiana	150	2.0%
19	Iowa	150	2.0%
17	Kansas	165	2.2%
29	Kentucky	138	1.9%
25	Louisiana	144	2.0%
10	Maine	186	2.5%
8	Maryland	188	2.5%
6	Massachusetts	200	2.7%
23	Michigan	148	2.0%
5	Minnesota	201	2.7%
14	Mississippi	174	2.4%
7	Missouri	197	2.7%
19	Montana	150	2.0%
50	Nebraska	49	0.7%
47	Nevada	63	0.9%
1	New Hampshire	424	5.7%
35	New Jersey	120	1.6%
38	New Mexico	112	1.5%
4	New York	212	2.9%
15	North Carolina	170	2.3%
26	North Dakota	141	1.9%
32	Ohio	132	1.8%
22	Oklahoma	149	2.0%
43	Oregon	90	1.2%
2	Pennsylvania	253	3.4%
37	Rhode Island	113	1.5%
15	South Carolina	170	2.3%
39	South Dakota	105	1.4%
32	Tennessee	132	1.8%
11	Texas	181	2.5%
41	Utah	104	1.4%
12	Vermont	180	2.4%
27	Virginia	140	1.9%
24	Washington	147	2.0%
31	West Virginia	134	1.8%
32	Wisconsin	132	1.8%
43	Wyoming	90	1.2%

RANK ORDER

RANK	STATE	LEGISLATORS	% of USA
1	New Hampshire	424	5.7%
2	Pennsylvania	253	3.4%
3	Georgia	236	3.2%
4	New York	212	2.9%
5	Minnesota	201	2.7%
6	Massachusetts	200	2.7%
7	Missouri	197	2.7%
8	Maryland	188	2.5%
9	Connecticut	187	2.5%
10	Maine	186	2.5%
11	Texas	181	2.5%
12	Vermont	180	2.4%
13	Illinois	177	2.4%
14	Mississippi	174	2.4%
15	North Carolina	170	2.3%
15	South Carolina	170	2.3%
17	Kansas	165	2.2%
18	Florida	160	2.2%
19	Indiana	150	2.0%
19	Iowa	150	2.0%
19	Montana	150	2.0%
22	Oklahoma	149	2.0%
23	Michigan	148	2.0%
24	Washington	147	2.0%
25	Louisiana	144	2.0%
26	North Dakota	141	1.9%
27	Alabama	140	1.9%
27	Virginia	140	1.9%
29	Kentucky	138	1.9%
30	Arkansas	135	1.8%
31	West Virginia	134	1.8%
32	Ohio	132	1.8%
32	Tennessee	132	1.8%
32	Wisconsin	132	1.8%
35	California	120	1.6%
35	New Jersey	120	1.6%
37	Rhode Island	113	1.5%
38	New Mexico	112	1.5%
39	Idaho	105	1.4%
39	South Dakota	105	1.4%
41	Utah	104	1.4%
42	Colorado	100	1.4%
43	Arizona	90	1.2%
43	Oregon	90	1.2%
43	Wyoming	90	1.2%
46	Hawaii	76	1.0%
47	Nevada	63	0.9%
48	Delaware	62	0.8%
49	Alaska	60	0.8%
50	Nebraska	49	0.7%
	District of Columbia**	NA	NA

Source: National Conference of State Legislatures (Denver, CO)
   "2006 Post-Election Partisan Composition of State Legislatures"
   (http://www.ncsl.org/programs/legismgt/statevote/partycomptable2007.htm)
*There are 1,971 state senators (including Nebraska's 49 unicameral seats) and 5,411 state house members.
**Not applicable.

Population per State Legislator in 2010

National Rate = 41,589 Population per Legislator*

ALPHA ORDER

RANK	STATE	RATE
22	Alabama	33,634
42	Alaska	11,641
6	Arizona	73,286
32	Arkansas	21,403
1	California	308,014
12	Colorado	50,247
34	Connecticut	18,814
40	Delaware	14,276
3	Florida	115,862
20	Georgia	41,649
37	Hawaii	17,042
39	Idaho	14,722
7	Illinois	72,940
17	Indiana	42,821
33	Iowa	20,052
36	Kansas	17,083
24	Kentucky	31,262
25	Louisiana	31,195
45	Maine	7,088
27	Maryland	30,316
23	Massachusetts	32,968
9	Michigan	67,363
30	Minnesota	26,200
38	Mississippi	16,965
26	Missouri	30,394
46	Montana	6,500
21	Nebraska	36,666
19	Nevada	41,954
50	New Hampshire	3,124
8	New Jersey	72,564
35	New Mexico	17,943
4	New York	92,177
11	North Carolina	55,182
48	North Dakota	4,588
5	Ohio	87,444
31	Oklahoma	24,745
18	Oregon	42,507
13	Pennsylvania	49,821
43	Rhode Island	9,320
28	South Carolina	26,831
44	South Dakota	7,737
14	Tennessee	47,699
2	Texas	136,919
29	Utah	26,775
49	Vermont	3,454
10	Virginia	56,304
15	Washington	45,335
41	West Virginia	13,580
16	Wisconsin	42,839
47	Wyoming	6,047

RANK ORDER

RANK	STATE	RATE
1	California	308,014
2	Texas	136,919
3	Florida	115,862
4	New York	92,177
5	Ohio	87,444
6	Arizona	73,286
7	Illinois	72,940
8	New Jersey	72,564
9	Michigan	67,363
10	Virginia	56,304
11	North Carolina	55,182
12	Colorado	50,247
13	Pennsylvania	49,821
14	Tennessee	47,699
15	Washington	45,335
16	Wisconsin	42,839
17	Indiana	42,821
18	Oregon	42,507
19	Nevada	41,954
20	Georgia	41,649
21	Nebraska	36,666
22	Alabama	33,634
23	Massachusetts	32,968
24	Kentucky	31,262
25	Louisiana	31,195
26	Missouri	30,394
27	Maryland	30,316
28	South Carolina	26,831
29	Utah	26,775
30	Minnesota	26,200
31	Oklahoma	24,745
32	Arkansas	21,403
33	Iowa	20,052
34	Connecticut	18,814
35	New Mexico	17,943
36	Kansas	17,083
37	Hawaii	17,042
38	Mississippi	16,965
39	Idaho	14,722
40	Delaware	14,276
41	West Virginia	13,580
42	Alaska	11,641
43	Rhode Island	9,320
44	South Dakota	7,737
45	Maine	7,088
46	Montana	6,500
47	Wyoming	6,047
48	North Dakota	4,588
49	Vermont	3,454
50	New Hampshire	3,124
	District of Columbia**	NA

Source: CQ Press using data from National Conference of State Legislatures (Denver, CO)
"2006 Post-Election Partisan Composition of State Legislatures"
(http://www.ncsl.org/programs/legismgt/statevote/partycomptable2007.htm)
*There are 1,971 state senators (including Nebraska's 49 unicameral seats) and 5,411 state house members. National rate does not include population for the District of Columbia.
**Not applicable.

Registered Voters in 2008

National Total = 146,311,000

ALPHA ORDER

ALPHA ORDER

RANK	STATE	REGISTERED	% of USA
22	Alabama	2,438,000	1.7%
48	Alaska	345,000	0.2%
20	Arizona	2,874,000	2.0%
33	Arkansas	1,317,000	0.9%
1	California	14,885,000	10.2%
23	Colorado	2,437,000	1.7%
29	Connecticut	1,761,000	1.2%
45	Delaware	447,000	0.3%
3	Florida	8,774,000	6.0%
10	Georgia	4,624,000	3.2%
43	Hawaii	522,000	0.4%
41	Idaho	723,000	0.5%
6	Illinois	6,151,000	4.2%
16	Indiana	3,105,000	2.1%
30	Iowa	1,630,000	1.1%
32	Kansas	1,343,000	0.9%
26	Kentucky	2,259,000	1.5%
24	Louisiana	2,393,000	1.6%
39	Maine	801,000	0.5%
21	Maryland	2,828,000	1.9%
14	Massachusetts	3,293,000	2.3%
8	Michigan	5,531,000	3.8%
18	Minnesota	2,931,000	2.0%
31	Mississippi	1,589,000	1.1%
15	Missouri	3,224,000	2.2%
44	Montana	516,000	0.4%
36	Nebraska	939,000	0.6%
34	Nevada	1,147,000	0.8%
40	New Hampshire	756,000	0.5%
11	New Jersey	4,022,000	2.7%
37	New Mexico	937,000	0.6%
4	New York	8,458,000	5.8%
9	North Carolina	4,902,000	3.4%
47	North Dakota	399,000	0.3%
7	Ohio	6,108,000	4.2%
28	Oklahoma	1,798,000	1.2%
27	Oregon	1,961,000	1.3%
5	Pennsylvania	6,451,000	4.4%
42	Rhode Island	568,000	0.4%
25	South Carolina	2,385,000	1.6%
46	South Dakota	442,000	0.3%
19	Tennessee	2,921,000	2.0%
2	Texas	10,123,000	6.9%
35	Utah	1,056,000	0.7%
48	Vermont	345,000	0.2%
12	Virginia	3,950,000	2.7%
13	Washington	3,299,000	2.3%
38	West Virginia	917,000	0.6%
17	Wisconsin	3,095,000	2.1%
50	Wyoming	270,000	0.2%

RANK ORDER

RANK	STATE	REGISTERED	% of USA
1	California	14,885,000	10.2%
2	Texas	10,123,000	6.9%
3	Florida	8,774,000	6.0%
4	New York	8,458,000	5.8%
5	Pennsylvania	6,451,000	4.4%
6	Illinois	6,151,000	4.2%
7	Ohio	6,108,000	4.2%
8	Michigan	5,531,000	3.8%
9	North Carolina	4,902,000	3.4%
10	Georgia	4,624,000	3.2%
11	New Jersey	4,022,000	2.7%
12	Virginia	3,950,000	2.7%
13	Washington	3,299,000	2.3%
14	Massachusetts	3,293,000	2.3%
15	Missouri	3,224,000	2.2%
16	Indiana	3,105,000	2.1%
17	Wisconsin	3,095,000	2.1%
18	Minnesota	2,931,000	2.0%
19	Tennessee	2,921,000	2.0%
20	Arizona	2,874,000	2.0%
21	Maryland	2,828,000	1.9%
22	Alabama	2,438,000	1.7%
23	Colorado	2,437,000	1.7%
24	Louisiana	2,393,000	1.6%
25	South Carolina	2,385,000	1.6%
26	Kentucky	2,259,000	1.5%
27	Oregon	1,961,000	1.3%
28	Oklahoma	1,798,000	1.2%
29	Connecticut	1,761,000	1.2%
30	Iowa	1,630,000	1.1%
31	Mississippi	1,589,000	1.1%
32	Kansas	1,343,000	0.9%
33	Arkansas	1,317,000	0.9%
34	Nevada	1,147,000	0.8%
35	Utah	1,056,000	0.7%
36	Nebraska	939,000	0.6%
37	New Mexico	937,000	0.6%
38	West Virginia	917,000	0.6%
39	Maine	801,000	0.5%
40	New Hampshire	756,000	0.5%
41	Idaho	723,000	0.5%
42	Rhode Island	568,000	0.4%
43	Hawaii	522,000	0.4%
44	Montana	516,000	0.4%
45	Delaware	447,000	0.3%
46	South Dakota	442,000	0.3%
47	North Dakota	399,000	0.3%
48	Alaska	345,000	0.2%
48	Vermont	345,000	0.2%
50	Wyoming	270,000	0.2%
	District of Columbia	324,000	0.2%

Source: U.S. Bureau of the Census
"Voting and Registration" (Table 4a, http://www.census.gov/hhes/www/socdemo/voting/index.html)

Percent of Eligible Voters Reported Registered in 2008

National Percent = 71.0%*

ALPHA ORDER

RANK	STATE	PERCENT
28	Alabama	71.6
19	Alaska	73.7
39	Arizona	68.9
47	Arkansas	64.9
41	California	68.2
26	Colorado	72.2
20	Connecticut	73.5
18	Delaware	73.8
33	Florida	70.4
30	Georgia	71.0
50	Hawaii	59.1
39	Idaho	68.9
31	Illinois	70.9
42	Indiana	68.1
9	Iowa	76.3
36	Kansas	69.7
21	Kentucky	73.0
4	Louisiana	78.3
2	Maine	79.7
17	Maryland	73.9
24	Massachusetts	72.6
5	Michigan	77.1
2	Minnesota	79.7
6	Mississippi	77.0
14	Missouri	74.5
29	Montana	71.3
13	Nebraska	74.9
44	Nevada	66.9
10	New Hampshire	76.0
31	New Jersey	70.9
37	New Mexico	69.3
46	New York	65.8
11	North Carolina	75.7
1	North Dakota	83.7
21	Ohio	73.0
34	Oklahoma	70.1
21	Oregon	73.0
34	Pennsylvania	70.1
12	Rhode Island	75.5
14	South Carolina	74.5
7	South Dakota	76.9
48	Tennessee	64.5
43	Texas	67.3
49	Utah	59.7
25	Vermont	72.5
16	Virginia	74.3
27	Washington	71.7
45	West Virginia	66.1
8	Wisconsin	76.4
37	Wyoming	69.3

RANK ORDER

RANK	STATE	PERCENT
1	North Dakota	83.7
2	Maine	79.7
2	Minnesota	79.7
4	Louisiana	78.3
5	Michigan	77.1
6	Mississippi	77.0
7	South Dakota	76.9
8	Wisconsin	76.4
9	Iowa	76.3
10	New Hampshire	76.0
11	North Carolina	75.7
12	Rhode Island	75.5
13	Nebraska	74.9
14	Missouri	74.5
14	South Carolina	74.5
16	Virginia	74.3
17	Maryland	73.9
18	Delaware	73.8
19	Alaska	73.7
20	Connecticut	73.5
21	Kentucky	73.0
21	Ohio	73.0
21	Oregon	73.0
24	Massachusetts	72.6
25	Vermont	72.5
26	Colorado	72.2
27	Washington	71.7
28	Alabama	71.6
29	Montana	71.3
30	Georgia	71.0
31	Illinois	70.9
31	New Jersey	70.9
33	Florida	70.4
34	Oklahoma	70.1
34	Pennsylvania	70.1
36	Kansas	69.7
37	New Mexico	69.3
37	Wyoming	69.3
39	Arizona	68.9
39	Idaho	68.9
41	California	68.2
42	Indiana	68.1
43	Texas	67.3
44	Nevada	66.9
45	West Virginia	66.1
46	New York	65.8
47	Arkansas	64.9
48	Tennessee	64.5
49	Utah	59.7
50	Hawaii	59.1
	District of Columbia	78.3

Source: U.S. Bureau of the Census
   "Voting and Registration" (Table 4a, http://www.census.gov/hhes/www/socdemo/voting/index.html)
*As a percent of citizen population 18 and older.

Persons Voting in 2008

National Total = 131,144,000

ALPHA ORDER

RANK	STATE	VOTERS	% of USA
24	Alabama	2,126,000	1.6%
49	Alaska	304,000	0.2%
21	Arizona	2,497,000	1.9%
33	Arkansas	1,092,000	0.8%
1	California	13,828,000	10.5%
22	Colorado	2,308,000	1.8%
28	Connecticut	1,610,000	1.2%
45	Delaware	408,000	0.3%
3	Florida	7,951,000	6.1%
10	Georgia	4,183,000	3.2%
44	Hawaii	457,000	0.3%
41	Idaho	644,000	0.5%
7	Illinois	5,436,000	4.1%
18	Indiana	2,758,000	2.1%
30	Iowa	1,501,000	1.1%
32	Kansas	1,219,000	0.9%
26	Kentucky	1,952,000	1.5%
23	Louisiana	2,149,000	1.6%
39	Maine	716,000	0.5%
19	Maryland	2,611,000	2.0%
14	Massachusetts	3,044,000	2.3%
8	Michigan	4,865,000	3.7%
17	Minnesota	2,759,000	2.1%
31	Mississippi	1,439,000	1.1%
16	Missouri	2,846,000	2.2%
43	Montana	473,000	0.4%
37	Nebraska	844,000	0.6%
34	Nevada	1,027,000	0.8%
40	New Hampshire	708,000	0.5%
12	New Jersey	3,637,000	2.8%
36	New Mexico	846,000	0.6%
4	New York	7,559,000	5.8%
9	North Carolina	4,370,000	3.3%
47	North Dakota	321,000	0.2%
6	Ohio	5,483,000	4.2%
29	Oklahoma	1,507,000	1.1%
27	Oregon	1,818,000	1.4%
5	Pennsylvania	5,747,000	4.4%
42	Rhode Island	507,000	0.4%
25	South Carolina	2,100,000	1.6%
46	South Dakota	390,000	0.3%
20	Tennessee	2,516,000	1.9%
2	Texas	8,435,000	6.4%
35	Utah	939,000	0.7%
48	Vermont	308,000	0.2%
11	Virginia	3,650,000	2.8%
13	Washington	3,073,000	2.3%
38	West Virginia	741,000	0.6%
15	Wisconsin	2,887,000	2.2%
50	Wyoming	250,000	0.2%

RANK ORDER

RANK	STATE	VOTERS	% of USA
1	California	13,828,000	10.5%
2	Texas	8,435,000	6.4%
3	Florida	7,951,000	6.1%
4	New York	7,559,000	5.8%
5	Pennsylvania	5,747,000	4.4%
6	Ohio	5,483,000	4.2%
7	Illinois	5,436,000	4.1%
8	Michigan	4,865,000	3.7%
9	North Carolina	4,370,000	3.3%
10	Georgia	4,183,000	3.2%
11	Virginia	3,650,000	2.8%
12	New Jersey	3,637,000	2.8%
13	Washington	3,073,000	2.3%
14	Massachusetts	3,044,000	2.3%
15	Wisconsin	2,887,000	2.2%
16	Missouri	2,846,000	2.2%
17	Minnesota	2,759,000	2.1%
18	Indiana	2,758,000	2.1%
19	Maryland	2,611,000	2.0%
20	Tennessee	2,516,000	1.9%
21	Arizona	2,497,000	1.9%
22	Colorado	2,308,000	1.8%
23	Louisiana	2,149,000	1.6%
24	Alabama	2,126,000	1.6%
25	South Carolina	2,100,000	1.6%
26	Kentucky	1,952,000	1.5%
27	Oregon	1,818,000	1.4%
28	Connecticut	1,610,000	1.2%
29	Oklahoma	1,507,000	1.1%
30	Iowa	1,501,000	1.1%
31	Mississippi	1,439,000	1.1%
32	Kansas	1,219,000	0.9%
33	Arkansas	1,092,000	0.8%
34	Nevada	1,027,000	0.8%
35	Utah	939,000	0.7%
36	New Mexico	846,000	0.6%
37	Nebraska	844,000	0.6%
38	West Virginia	741,000	0.6%
39	Maine	716,000	0.5%
40	New Hampshire	708,000	0.5%
41	Idaho	644,000	0.5%
42	Rhode Island	507,000	0.4%
43	Montana	473,000	0.4%
44	Hawaii	457,000	0.3%
45	Delaware	408,000	0.3%
46	South Dakota	390,000	0.3%
47	North Dakota	321,000	0.2%
48	Vermont	308,000	0.2%
49	Alaska	304,000	0.2%
50	Wyoming	250,000	0.2%
	District of Columbia	306,000	0.2%

Source: U.S. Bureau of the Census
   "Voting and Registration" (Table 4a, http://www.census.gov/hhes/www/socdemo/voting/index.html)

Percent of Eligible Population Reported Voting in 2008

National Percent = 63.6%*

RANK	STATE (ALPHA ORDER)	PERCENT		RANK	STATE (RANK ORDER)	PERCENT
37	Alabama	62.4		1	Minnesota	75.0
26	Alaska	65.0		2	Maine	71.2
41	Arizona	59.9		2	New Hampshire	71.2
47	Arkansas	53.8		2	Wisconsin	71.2
32	California	63.4		5	Louisiana	70.3
9	Colorado	68.4		6	Iowa	70.2
19	Connecticut	67.2		7	Mississippi	69.7
17	Delaware	67.3		8	Virginia	68.7
31	Florida	63.8		9	Colorado	68.4
29	Georgia	64.2		10	Maryland	68.3
50	Hawaii	51.8		11	Michigan	67.8
39	Idaho	61.4		11	South Dakota	67.8
35	Illinois	62.6		13	Oregon	67.6
40	Indiana	60.5		14	North Carolina	67.5
6	Iowa	70.2		14	North Dakota	67.5
33	Kansas	63.3		16	Rhode Island	67.4
34	Kentucky	63.1		17	Delaware	67.3
5	Louisiana	70.3		17	Nebraska	67.3
2	Maine	71.2		19	Connecticut	67.2
10	Maryland	68.3		20	Massachusetts	67.1
20	Massachusetts	67.1		21	Washington	66.8
11	Michigan	67.8		22	Missouri	65.8
1	Minnesota	75.0		23	South Carolina	65.6
7	Mississippi	69.7		24	Ohio	65.5
22	Missouri	65.8		25	Montana	65.4
25	Montana	65.4		26	Alaska	65.0
17	Nebraska	67.3		27	Vermont	64.7
41	Nevada	59.9		28	Wyoming	64.3
2	New Hampshire	71.2		29	Georgia	64.2
30	New Jersey	64.1		30	New Jersey	64.1
35	New Mexico	62.6		31	Florida	63.8
43	New York	58.8		32	California	63.4
14	North Carolina	67.5		33	Kansas	63.3
14	North Dakota	67.5		34	Kentucky	63.1
24	Ohio	65.5		35	Illinois	62.6
44	Oklahoma	58.7		35	New Mexico	62.6
13	Oregon	67.6		37	Alabama	62.4
37	Pennsylvania	62.4		37	Pennsylvania	62.4
16	Rhode Island	67.4		39	Idaho	61.4
23	South Carolina	65.6		40	Indiana	60.5
11	South Dakota	67.8		41	Arizona	59.9
46	Tennessee	55.5		41	Nevada	59.9
45	Texas	56.1		43	New York	58.8
49	Utah	53.1		44	Oklahoma	58.7
27	Vermont	64.7		45	Texas	56.1
8	Virginia	68.7		46	Tennessee	55.5
21	Washington	66.8		47	Arkansas	53.8
48	West Virginia	53.4		48	West Virginia	53.4
2	Wisconsin	71.2		49	Utah	53.1
28	Wyoming	64.3		50	Hawaii	51.8
					District of Columbia	74.1

Source: U.S. Bureau of the Census
"Voting and Registration" (Table 4a, http://www.census.gov/hhes/www/socdemo/voting/index.html)
*As a percent of citizen population 18 and older.

Percent of Registered Population Reported Voting in 2008

National Percent = 89.6%*

ALPHA ORDER

RANK	STATE	PERCENT
42	Alabama	87.2
38	Alaska	88.1
43	Arizona	86.9
48	Arkansas	82.9
6	California	92.9
1	Colorado	94.7
14	Connecticut	91.4
15	Delaware	91.3
17	Florida	90.6
19	Georgia	90.5
41	Hawaii	87.5
30	Idaho	89.1
35	Illinois	88.4
34	Indiana	88.8
12	Iowa	92.1
16	Kansas	90.8
44	Kentucky	86.4
23	Louisiana	89.8
26	Maine	89.4
11	Maryland	92.3
9	Massachusetts	92.4
40	Michigan	88.0
2	Minnesota	94.1
17	Mississippi	90.6
36	Missouri	88.3
13	Montana	91.7
22	Nebraska	89.9
25	Nevada	89.5
3	New Hampshire	93.7
20	New Jersey	90.4
21	New Mexico	90.3
26	New York	89.4
30	North Carolina	89.1
50	North Dakota	80.5
23	Ohio	89.8
46	Oklahoma	83.8
7	Oregon	92.7
30	Pennsylvania	89.1
28	Rhode Island	89.3
38	South Carolina	88.1
37	South Dakota	88.2
45	Tennessee	86.1
47	Texas	83.3
33	Utah	88.9
28	Vermont	89.3
9	Virginia	92.4
5	Washington	93.1
49	West Virginia	80.8
4	Wisconsin	93.3
8	Wyoming	92.6

RANK ORDER

RANK	STATE	PERCENT
1	Colorado	94.7
2	Minnesota	94.1
3	New Hampshire	93.7
4	Wisconsin	93.3
5	Washington	93.1
6	California	92.9
7	Oregon	92.7
8	Wyoming	92.6
9	Massachusetts	92.4
9	Virginia	92.4
11	Maryland	92.3
12	Iowa	92.1
13	Montana	91.7
14	Connecticut	91.4
15	Delaware	91.3
16	Kansas	90.8
17	Florida	90.6
17	Mississippi	90.6
19	Georgia	90.5
20	New Jersey	90.4
21	New Mexico	90.3
22	Nebraska	89.9
23	Louisiana	89.8
23	Ohio	89.8
25	Nevada	89.5
26	Maine	89.4
26	New York	89.4
28	Rhode Island	89.3
28	Vermont	89.3
30	Idaho	89.1
30	North Carolina	89.1
30	Pennsylvania	89.1
33	Utah	88.9
34	Indiana	88.8
35	Illinois	88.4
36	Missouri	88.3
37	South Dakota	88.2
38	Alaska	88.1
38	South Carolina	88.1
40	Michigan	88.0
41	Hawaii	87.5
42	Alabama	87.2
43	Arizona	86.9
44	Kentucky	86.4
45	Tennessee	86.1
46	Oklahoma	83.8
47	Texas	83.3
48	Arkansas	82.9
49	West Virginia	80.8
50	North Dakota	80.5

	District of Columbia	94.4

Source: CQ Press using data from U.S. Bureau of the Census
"Voting and Registration" (Table 4a, http://www.census.gov/hhes/www/socdemo/voting/index.html)
*As a percent of citizen population 18 and older who are registered to vote.

XIV. Social Welfare

Poverty Rate in 2008

National Rate = 13.2% of Population in Poverty*

ALPHA ORDER

RANK	STATE	PERCENT
7	Alabama	16.4
44	Alaska	9.4
14	Arizona	14.4
4	Arkansas	17.5
22	California	12.9
30	Colorado	11.8
48	Connecticut	8.5
38	Delaware	10.5
24	Florida	12.6
12	Georgia	14.6
46	Hawaii	8.8
25	Idaho	12.4
27	Illinois	12.1
23	Indiana	12.7
34	Iowa	11.2
31	Kansas	11.6
5	Kentucky	17.2
2	Louisiana	18.3
26	Maine	12.4
49	Maryland	8.1
41	Massachusetts	9.9
16	Michigan	14.0
43	Minnesota	9.6
1	Mississippi	21.0
18	Missouri	13.3
15	Montana	14.2
34	Nebraska	11.2
36	Nevada	10.8
50	New Hampshire	7.6
47	New Jersey	8.7
3	New Mexico	17.9
17	New York	13.8
13	North Carolina	14.5
29	North Dakota	11.8
19	Ohio	13.3
9	Oklahoma	16.3
19	Oregon	13.3
28	Pennsylvania	11.9
32	Rhode Island	11.6
11	South Carolina	15.5
21	South Dakota	13.1
10	Tennessee	15.9
8	Texas	16.3
40	Utah	10.0
39	Vermont	10.3
42	Virginia	9.9
33	Washington	11.5
6	West Virginia	17.1
37	Wisconsin	10.7
45	Wyoming	9.2

RANK ORDER

RANK	STATE	PERCENT
1	Mississippi	21.0
2	Louisiana	18.3
3	New Mexico	17.9
4	Arkansas	17.5
5	Kentucky	17.2
6	West Virginia	17.1
7	Alabama	16.4
8	Texas	16.3
9	Oklahoma	16.3
10	Tennessee	15.9
11	South Carolina	15.5
12	Georgia	14.6
13	North Carolina	14.5
14	Arizona	14.4
15	Montana	14.2
16	Michigan	14.0
17	New York	13.8
18	Missouri	13.3
19	Ohio	13.3
19	Oregon	13.3
21	South Dakota	13.1
22	California	12.9
23	Indiana	12.7
24	Florida	12.6
25	Idaho	12.4
26	Maine	12.4
27	Illinois	12.1
28	Pennsylvania	11.9
29	North Dakota	11.8
30	Colorado	11.8
31	Kansas	11.6
32	Rhode Island	11.6
33	Washington	11.5
34	Iowa	11.2
34	Nebraska	11.2
36	Nevada	10.8
37	Wisconsin	10.7
38	Delaware	10.5
39	Vermont	10.3
40	Utah	10.0
41	Massachusetts	9.9
42	Virginia	9.9
43	Minnesota	9.6
44	Alaska	9.4
45	Wyoming	9.2
46	Hawaii	8.8
47	New Jersey	8.7
48	Connecticut	8.5
49	Maryland	8.1
50	New Hampshire	7.6

District of Columbia — 17.7

Source: CQ Press using data from U.S. Bureau of the Census
  "2008 American Community Survey" (http://www.census.gov/acs/www/index.html)
*Three-year average: 2006-2008. The poverty threshold for a family of four (two children) in 2008 was $21,234.

Percent of Senior Citizens Living in Poverty in 2008

National Percent = 9.9%*

RANK	STATE	PERCENT
6	Alabama	12.6
50	Alaska	4.2
41	Arizona	8.0
9	Arkansas	12.3
35	California	8.4
36	Colorado	8.3
48	Connecticut	6.1
46	Delaware	6.9
18	Florida	10.1
6	Georgia	12.6
24	Hawaii	9.1
31	Idaho	8.7
25	Illinois	9.0
44	Indiana	7.8
41	Iowa	8.0
26	Kansas	8.9
3	Kentucky	13.5
2	Louisiana	13.9
16	Maine	10.3
38	Maryland	8.2
22	Massachusetts	9.3
31	Michigan	8.7
40	Minnesota	8.1
1	Mississippi	15.7
16	Missouri	10.3
26	Montana	8.9
20	Nebraska	9.5
45	Nevada	7.2
43	New Hampshire	7.9
38	New Jersey	8.2
5	New Mexico	13.0
11	New York	12.1
13	North Carolina	11.2
14	North Dakota	11.0
33	Ohio	8.5
18	Oklahoma	10.1
33	Oregon	8.5
26	Pennsylvania	8.9
26	Rhode Island	8.9
12	South Carolina	12.0
8	South Dakota	12.5
4	Tennessee	13.4
9	Texas	12.3
47	Utah	6.7
21	Vermont	9.4
23	Virginia	9.2
30	Washington	8.8
15	West Virginia	10.5
36	Wisconsin	8.3
48	Wyoming	6.1

RANK	STATE	PERCENT
1	Mississippi	15.7
2	Louisiana	13.9
3	Kentucky	13.5
4	Tennessee	13.4
5	New Mexico	13.0
6	Alabama	12.6
6	Georgia	12.6
8	South Dakota	12.5
9	Arkansas	12.3
9	Texas	12.3
11	New York	12.1
12	South Carolina	12.0
13	North Carolina	11.2
14	North Dakota	11.0
15	West Virginia	10.5
16	Maine	10.3
16	Missouri	10.3
18	Florida	10.1
18	Oklahoma	10.1
20	Nebraska	9.5
21	Vermont	9.4
22	Massachusetts	9.3
23	Virginia	9.2
24	Hawaii	9.1
25	Illinois	9.0
26	Kansas	8.9
26	Montana	8.9
26	Pennsylvania	8.9
26	Rhode Island	8.9
30	Washington	8.8
31	Idaho	8.7
31	Michigan	8.7
33	Ohio	8.5
33	Oregon	8.5
35	California	8.4
36	Colorado	8.3
36	Wisconsin	8.3
38	Maryland	8.2
38	New Jersey	8.2
40	Minnesota	8.1
41	Arizona	8.0
41	Iowa	8.0
43	New Hampshire	7.9
44	Indiana	7.8
45	Nevada	7.2
46	Delaware	6.9
47	Utah	6.7
48	Connecticut	6.1
48	Wyoming	6.1
50	Alaska	4.2
	District of Columbia	15.2

Source: U.S. Bureau of the Census
"2008 American Community Survey" (http://www.census.gov/acs/www/index.html)
*People 65 years and older living with incomes below the poverty level.

Percent of Children Living in Poverty in 2008

National Percent = 18.2%*

ALPHA ORDER				RANK ORDER		
RANK	STATE	PERCENT		RANK	STATE	PERCENT
10	Alabama	21.7		1	Mississippi	30.4
46	Alaska	11.0		2	Arkansas	24.9
12	Arizona	20.8		3	Louisiana	24.7
2	Arkansas	24.9		4	New Mexico	24.2
19	California	18.5		5	Kentucky	23.5
31	Colorado	15.1		6	West Virginia	23.0
41	Connecticut	12.5		7	Oklahoma	22.6
37	Delaware	13.6		8	Texas	22.5
21	Florida	18.3		9	Tennessee	21.8
14	Georgia	20.1		10	Alabama	21.7
49	Hawaii	10.0		10	South Carolina	21.7
27	Idaho	15.8		12	Arizona	20.8
25	Illinois	17.0		13	Montana	20.6
21	Indiana	18.3		14	Georgia	20.1
34	Iowa	14.4		15	North Carolina	19.9
33	Kansas	14.5		16	Michigan	19.4
5	Kentucky	23.5		17	New York	19.1
3	Louisiana	24.7		18	Missouri	18.6
27	Maine	15.8		19	California	18.5
48	Maryland	10.2		19	Ohio	18.5
43	Massachusetts	12.0		21	Florida	18.3
16	Michigan	19.4		21	Indiana	18.3
45	Minnesota	11.4		23	Oregon	18.1
1	Mississippi	30.4		24	South Dakota	17.6
18	Missouri	18.6		25	Illinois	17.0
13	Montana	20.6		26	Pennsylvania	16.8
38	Nebraska	13.4		27	Idaho	15.8
32	Nevada	15.0		27	Maine	15.8
50	New Hampshire	9.0		29	Rhode Island	15.5
41	New Jersey	12.5		30	North Dakota	15.3
4	New Mexico	24.2		31	Colorado	15.1
17	New York	19.1		32	Nevada	15.0
15	North Carolina	19.9		33	Kansas	14.5
30	North Dakota	15.3		34	Iowa	14.4
19	Ohio	18.5		35	Washington	14.3
7	Oklahoma	22.6		36	Virginia	13.8
23	Oregon	18.1		37	Delaware	13.6
26	Pennsylvania	16.8		38	Nebraska	13.4
29	Rhode Island	15.5		39	Wisconsin	13.3
10	South Carolina	21.7		40	Vermont	13.2
24	South Dakota	17.6		41	Connecticut	12.5
9	Tennessee	21.8		41	New Jersey	12.5
8	Texas	22.5		43	Massachusetts	12.0
47	Utah	10.5		44	Wyoming	11.6
40	Vermont	13.2		45	Minnesota	11.4
36	Virginia	13.8		46	Alaska	11.0
35	Washington	14.3		47	Utah	10.5
6	West Virginia	23.0		48	Maryland	10.2
39	Wisconsin	13.3		49	Hawaii	10.0
44	Wyoming	11.6		50	New Hampshire	9.0
					District of Columbia	25.9

Source: U.S. Bureau of the Census
   "2008 American Community Survey" (http://www.census.gov/acs/www/index.html)
*Children 17 and under living in families with incomes below the poverty level.

Percent of Families Living in Poverty in 2008

National Percent = 9.7%*

<table>
<tr><td colspan="3"><u>ALPHA ORDER</u></td><td colspan="3"><u>RANK ORDER</u></td></tr>
<tr><td>RANK</td><td>STATE</td><td>PERCENT</td><td>RANK</td><td>STATE</td><td>PERCENT</td></tr>
<tr><td>8</td><td>Alabama</td><td>12.0</td><td>1</td><td>Mississippi</td><td>17.0</td></tr>
<tr><td>47</td><td>Alaska</td><td>5.7</td><td>2</td><td>Louisiana</td><td>13.4</td></tr>
<tr><td>15</td><td>Arizona</td><td>10.3</td><td>3</td><td>Kentucky</td><td>13.1</td></tr>
<tr><td>4</td><td>Arkansas</td><td>13.0</td><td>4</td><td>Arkansas</td><td>13.0</td></tr>
<tr><td>17</td><td>California</td><td>10.0</td><td>5</td><td>New Mexico</td><td>12.6</td></tr>
<tr><td>31</td><td>Colorado</td><td>7.8</td><td>6</td><td>Texas</td><td>12.4</td></tr>
<tr><td>40</td><td>Connecticut</td><td>6.7</td><td>6</td><td>West Virginia</td><td>12.4</td></tr>
<tr><td>38</td><td>Delaware</td><td>6.9</td><td>8</td><td>Alabama</td><td>12.0</td></tr>
<tr><td>23</td><td>Florida</td><td>9.5</td><td>9</td><td>Oklahoma</td><td>11.8</td></tr>
<tr><td>12</td><td>Georgia</td><td>11.1</td><td>10</td><td>South Carolina</td><td>11.6</td></tr>
<tr><td>46</td><td>Hawaii</td><td>6.0</td><td>10</td><td>Tennessee</td><td>11.6</td></tr>
<tr><td>24</td><td>Idaho</td><td>9.4</td><td>12</td><td>Georgia</td><td>11.1</td></tr>
<tr><td>25</td><td>Illinois</td><td>9.0</td><td>13</td><td>North Carolina</td><td>10.9</td></tr>
<tr><td>21</td><td>Indiana</td><td>9.6</td><td>14</td><td>Michigan</td><td>10.5</td></tr>
<tr><td>35</td><td>Iowa</td><td>7.3</td><td>15</td><td>Arizona</td><td>10.3</td></tr>
<tr><td>32</td><td>Kansas</td><td>7.7</td><td>15</td><td>New York</td><td>10.3</td></tr>
<tr><td>3</td><td>Kentucky</td><td>13.1</td><td>17</td><td>California</td><td>10.0</td></tr>
<tr><td>2</td><td>Louisiana</td><td>13.4</td><td>18</td><td>Ohio</td><td>9.8</td></tr>
<tr><td>26</td><td>Maine</td><td>8.6</td><td>19</td><td>Missouri</td><td>9.7</td></tr>
<tr><td>49</td><td>Maryland</td><td>5.4</td><td>19</td><td>Montana</td><td>9.7</td></tr>
<tr><td>37</td><td>Massachusetts</td><td>7.1</td><td>21</td><td>Indiana</td><td>9.6</td></tr>
<tr><td>14</td><td>Michigan</td><td>10.5</td><td>21</td><td>Oregon</td><td>9.6</td></tr>
<tr><td>44</td><td>Minnesota</td><td>6.2</td><td>23</td><td>Florida</td><td>9.5</td></tr>
<tr><td>1</td><td>Mississippi</td><td>17.0</td><td>24</td><td>Idaho</td><td>9.4</td></tr>
<tr><td>19</td><td>Missouri</td><td>9.7</td><td>25</td><td>Illinois</td><td>9.0</td></tr>
<tr><td>19</td><td>Montana</td><td>9.7</td><td>26</td><td>Maine</td><td>8.6</td></tr>
<tr><td>39</td><td>Nebraska</td><td>6.8</td><td>27</td><td>Pennsylvania</td><td>8.5</td></tr>
<tr><td>29</td><td>Nevada</td><td>7.9</td><td>28</td><td>South Dakota</td><td>8.2</td></tr>
<tr><td>50</td><td>New Hampshire</td><td>5.0</td><td>29</td><td>Nevada</td><td>7.9</td></tr>
<tr><td>44</td><td>New Jersey</td><td>6.2</td><td>29</td><td>North Dakota</td><td>7.9</td></tr>
<tr><td>5</td><td>New Mexico</td><td>12.6</td><td>31</td><td>Colorado</td><td>7.8</td></tr>
<tr><td>15</td><td>New York</td><td>10.3</td><td>32</td><td>Kansas</td><td>7.7</td></tr>
<tr><td>13</td><td>North Carolina</td><td>10.9</td><td>32</td><td>Rhode Island</td><td>7.7</td></tr>
<tr><td>29</td><td>North Dakota</td><td>7.9</td><td>32</td><td>Washington</td><td>7.7</td></tr>
<tr><td>18</td><td>Ohio</td><td>9.8</td><td>35</td><td>Iowa</td><td>7.3</td></tr>
<tr><td>9</td><td>Oklahoma</td><td>11.8</td><td>35</td><td>Virginia</td><td>7.3</td></tr>
<tr><td>21</td><td>Oregon</td><td>9.6</td><td>37</td><td>Massachusetts</td><td>7.1</td></tr>
<tr><td>27</td><td>Pennsylvania</td><td>8.5</td><td>38</td><td>Delaware</td><td>6.9</td></tr>
<tr><td>32</td><td>Rhode Island</td><td>7.7</td><td>39</td><td>Nebraska</td><td>6.8</td></tr>
<tr><td>10</td><td>South Carolina</td><td>11.6</td><td>40</td><td>Connecticut</td><td>6.7</td></tr>
<tr><td>28</td><td>South Dakota</td><td>8.2</td><td>40</td><td>Wisconsin</td><td>6.7</td></tr>
<tr><td>10</td><td>Tennessee</td><td>11.6</td><td>42</td><td>Utah</td><td>6.6</td></tr>
<tr><td>6</td><td>Texas</td><td>12.4</td><td>43</td><td>Vermont</td><td>6.5</td></tr>
<tr><td>42</td><td>Utah</td><td>6.6</td><td>44</td><td>Minnesota</td><td>6.2</td></tr>
<tr><td>43</td><td>Vermont</td><td>6.5</td><td>44</td><td>New Jersey</td><td>6.2</td></tr>
<tr><td>35</td><td>Virginia</td><td>7.3</td><td>46</td><td>Hawaii</td><td>6.0</td></tr>
<tr><td>32</td><td>Washington</td><td>7.7</td><td>47</td><td>Alaska</td><td>5.7</td></tr>
<tr><td>6</td><td>West Virginia</td><td>12.4</td><td>47</td><td>Wyoming</td><td>5.7</td></tr>
<tr><td>40</td><td>Wisconsin</td><td>6.7</td><td>49</td><td>Maryland</td><td>5.4</td></tr>
<tr><td>47</td><td>Wyoming</td><td>5.7</td><td>50</td><td>New Hampshire</td><td>5.0</td></tr>
<tr><td></td><td></td><td></td><td></td><td>District of Columbia</td><td>13.7</td></tr>
</table>

Source: CQ Press using data from U.S. Bureau of the Census
   "2008 American Community Survey" (http://www.census.gov/acs/www/index.html)
*Families living with incomes below the poverty level.

Percent of Female-Headed Families With Children Living in Poverty in 2008

National Percent = 36.3%*

ALPHA ORDER				RANK ORDER		
RANK	STATE	PERCENT		RANK	STATE	PERCENT
7	Alabama	43.5		1	Mississippi	50.5
49	Alaska	23.1		2	Arkansas	47.4
27	Arizona	36.1		3	West Virginia	46.8
2	Arkansas	47.4		4	Kentucky	46.2
36	California	32.0		5	Louisiana	44.9
42	Colorado	29.9		6	North Dakota	43.8
37	Connecticut	31.7		7	Alabama	43.5
47	Delaware	25.6		8	Oklahoma	43.1
34	Florida	32.1		9	Maine	42.2
25	Georgia	37.0		10	Montana	41.8
48	Hawaii	24.6		10	Tennessee	41.8
16	Idaho	40.6		12	South Carolina	41.2
26	Illinois	36.9		13	Ohio	41.1
24	Indiana	37.3		14	South Dakota	40.8
22	Iowa	38.1		15	Michigan	40.7
38	Kansas	31.6		16	Idaho	40.6
4	Kentucky	46.2		17	Missouri	40.3
5	Louisiana	44.9		18	North Carolina	39.7
9	Maine	42.2		19	Texas	39.4
50	Maryland	20.4		20	Oregon	39.0
40	Massachusetts	30.3		21	New Mexico	38.9
15	Michigan	40.7		22	Iowa	38.1
31	Minnesota	32.7		23	Pennsylvania	37.4
1	Mississippi	50.5		24	Indiana	37.3
17	Missouri	40.3		25	Georgia	37.0
10	Montana	41.8		26	Illinois	36.9
29	Nebraska	33.5		27	Arizona	36.1
45	Nevada	28.0		28	New York	35.3
41	New Hampshire	30.1		29	Nebraska	33.5
46	New Jersey	27.8		30	Washington	33.0
21	New Mexico	38.9		31	Minnesota	32.7
28	New York	35.3		32	Wisconsin	32.6
18	North Carolina	39.7		33	Rhode Island	32.5
6	North Dakota	43.8		34	Florida	32.1
13	Ohio	41.1		34	Wyoming	32.1
8	Oklahoma	43.1		36	California	32.0
20	Oregon	39.0		37	Connecticut	31.7
23	Pennsylvania	37.4		38	Kansas	31.6
33	Rhode Island	32.5		39	Virginia	30.6
12	South Carolina	41.2		40	Massachusetts	30.3
14	South Dakota	40.8		41	New Hampshire	30.1
10	Tennessee	41.8		42	Colorado	29.9
19	Texas	39.4		43	Vermont	29.8
44	Utah	29.5		44	Utah	29.5
43	Vermont	29.8		45	Nevada	28.0
39	Virginia	30.6		46	New Jersey	27.8
30	Washington	33.0		47	Delaware	25.6
3	West Virginia	46.8		48	Hawaii	24.6
32	Wisconsin	32.6		49	Alaska	23.1
34	Wyoming	32.1		50	Maryland	20.4
					District of Columbia	34.9

Source: CQ Press using data from U.S. Bureau of the Census
   "2008 American Community Survey" (http://www.census.gov/acs/www/index.html)
*Households headed by females with own children under 18 years living with them with incomes below the poverty level as a percent of all such female-headed households.

State and Local Government Expenditures for Public Welfare Programs in 2007

National Total = $384,497,731,000*

ALPHA ORDER

RANK	STATE	EXPENDITURES	% of USA
26	Alabama	$4,752,984,000	1.2%
44	Alaska	1,426,924,000	0.4%
20	Arizona	6,577,168,000	1.7%
31	Arkansas	3,639,171,000	0.9%
1	California	46,919,222,000	12.2%
29	Colorado	3,813,169,000	1.0%
25	Connecticut	4,764,593,000	1.2%
45	Delaware	1,315,824,000	0.3%
5	Florida	18,564,802,000	4.8%
13	Georgia	9,390,492,000	2.4%
42	Hawaii	1,526,193,000	0.4%
43	Idaho	1,512,541,000	0.4%
7	Illinois	14,546,962,000	3.8%
17	Indiana	7,112,951,000	1.8%
32	Iowa	3,609,501,000	0.9%
34	Kansas	3,000,137,000	0.8%
22	Kentucky	5,763,045,000	1.5%
24	Louisiana	4,855,672,000	1.3%
35	Maine	2,457,036,000	0.6%
19	Maryland	7,012,898,000	1.8%
9	Massachusetts	11,857,115,000	3.1%
10	Michigan	11,030,637,000	2.9%
12	Minnesota	9,405,245,000	2.4%
28	Mississippi	4,041,081,000	1.1%
21	Missouri	5,891,899,000	1.5%
47	Montana	852,975,000	0.2%
38	Nebraska	2,076,814,000	0.5%
40	Nevada	1,871,928,000	0.5%
41	New Hampshire	1,545,937,000	0.4%
8	New Jersey	12,038,199,000	3.1%
33	New Mexico	3,220,501,000	0.8%
2	New York	44,639,956,000	11.6%
11	North Carolina	9,799,491,000	2.5%
49	North Dakota	736,917,000	0.2%
6	Ohio	17,219,544,000	4.5%
27	Oklahoma	4,419,796,000	1.1%
30	Oregon	3,801,295,000	1.0%
3	Pennsylvania	20,537,934,000	5.3%
39	Rhode Island	2,059,800,000	0.5%
23	South Carolina	5,368,362,000	1.4%
48	South Dakota	768,059,000	0.2%
15	Tennessee	7,620,066,000	2.0%
4	Texas	20,358,931,000	5.3%
37	Utah	2,179,899,000	0.6%
46	Vermont	1,203,638,000	0.3%
14	Virginia	7,671,956,000	2.0%
18	Washington	7,096,773,000	1.8%
36	West Virginia	2,389,610,000	0.6%
16	Wisconsin	7,447,419,000	1.9%
50	Wyoming	623,366,000	0.2%

RANK ORDER

RANK	STATE	EXPENDITURES	% of USA
1	California	$46,919,222,000	12.2%
2	New York	44,639,956,000	11.6%
3	Pennsylvania	20,537,934,000	5.3%
4	Texas	20,358,931,000	5.3%
5	Florida	18,564,802,000	4.8%
6	Ohio	17,219,544,000	4.5%
7	Illinois	14,546,962,000	3.8%
8	New Jersey	12,038,199,000	3.1%
9	Massachusetts	11,857,115,000	3.1%
10	Michigan	11,030,637,000	2.9%
11	North Carolina	9,799,491,000	2.5%
12	Minnesota	9,405,245,000	2.4%
13	Georgia	9,390,492,000	2.4%
14	Virginia	7,671,956,000	2.0%
15	Tennessee	7,620,066,000	2.0%
16	Wisconsin	7,447,419,000	1.9%
17	Indiana	7,112,951,000	1.8%
18	Washington	7,096,773,000	1.8%
19	Maryland	7,012,898,000	1.8%
20	Arizona	6,577,168,000	1.7%
21	Missouri	5,891,899,000	1.5%
22	Kentucky	5,763,045,000	1.5%
23	South Carolina	5,368,362,000	1.4%
24	Louisiana	4,855,672,000	1.3%
25	Connecticut	4,764,593,000	1.2%
26	Alabama	4,752,984,000	1.2%
27	Oklahoma	4,419,796,000	1.1%
28	Mississippi	4,041,081,000	1.1%
29	Colorado	3,813,169,000	1.0%
30	Oregon	3,801,295,000	1.0%
31	Arkansas	3,639,171,000	0.9%
32	Iowa	3,609,501,000	0.9%
33	New Mexico	3,220,501,000	0.8%
34	Kansas	3,000,137,000	0.8%
35	Maine	2,457,036,000	0.6%
36	West Virginia	2,389,610,000	0.6%
37	Utah	2,179,899,000	0.6%
38	Nebraska	2,076,814,000	0.5%
39	Rhode Island	2,059,800,000	0.5%
40	Nevada	1,871,928,000	0.5%
41	New Hampshire	1,545,937,000	0.4%
42	Hawaii	1,526,193,000	0.4%
43	Idaho	1,512,541,000	0.4%
44	Alaska	1,426,924,000	0.4%
45	Delaware	1,315,824,000	0.3%
46	Vermont	1,203,638,000	0.3%
47	Montana	852,975,000	0.2%
48	South Dakota	768,059,000	0.2%
49	North Dakota	736,917,000	0.2%
50	Wyoming	623,366,000	0.2%
	District of Columbia	2,161,303,000	0.6%

Source: U.S. Bureau of the Census, Governments Division
   "State and Local Government Finances 2006-2007" (http://www.census.gov/govs/estimate/index.html)
*Direct general expenditures. Includes funds for cash assistance programs, medical and other vendor payments, welfare institutions, and other public welfare programs.

Per Capita State and Local Government Expenditures
for Public Welfare Programs in 2007
National Per Capita = $1,275*

ALPHA ORDER

RANK	STATE	PER CAPITA
38	Alabama	$1,025
2	Alaska	2,091
37	Arizona	1,034
19	Arkansas	1,280
18	California	1,295
49	Colorado	787
14	Connecticut	1,366
10	Delaware	1,521
40	Florida	1,016
44	Georgia	985
25	Hawaii	1,195
41	Idaho	1,009
30	Illinois	1,138
31	Indiana	1,121
24	Iowa	1,212
35	Kansas	1,081
15	Kentucky	1,354
32	Louisiana	1,110
5	Maine	1,865
20	Maryland	1,245
6	Massachusetts	1,824
34	Michigan	1,097
7	Minnesota	1,812
13	Mississippi	1,383
42	Missouri	997
46	Montana	891
28	Nebraska	1,173
50	Nevada	729
27	New Hampshire	1,174
12	New Jersey	1,394
9	New Mexico	1,636
1	New York	2,298
35	North Carolina	1,081
29	North Dakota	1,155
11	Ohio	1,495
22	Oklahoma	1,224
39	Oregon	1,018
8	Pennsylvania	1,640
3	Rhode Island	1,952
23	South Carolina	1,213
45	South Dakota	964
21	Tennessee	1,234
47	Texas	854
48	Utah	818
4	Vermont	1,940
43	Virginia	994
33	Washington	1,098
17	West Virginia	1,319
16	Wisconsin	1,330
26	Wyoming	1,191

RANK ORDER

RANK	STATE	PER CAPITA
1	New York	$2,298
2	Alaska	2,091
3	Rhode Island	1,952
4	Vermont	1,940
5	Maine	1,865
6	Massachusetts	1,824
7	Minnesota	1,812
8	Pennsylvania	1,640
9	New Mexico	1,636
10	Delaware	1,521
11	Ohio	1,495
12	New Jersey	1,394
13	Mississippi	1,383
14	Connecticut	1,366
15	Kentucky	1,354
16	Wisconsin	1,330
17	West Virginia	1,319
18	California	1,295
19	Arkansas	1,280
20	Maryland	1,245
21	Tennessee	1,234
22	Oklahoma	1,224
23	South Carolina	1,213
24	Iowa	1,212
25	Hawaii	1,195
26	Wyoming	1,191
27	New Hampshire	1,174
28	Nebraska	1,173
29	North Dakota	1,155
30	Illinois	1,138
31	Indiana	1,121
32	Louisiana	1,110
33	Washington	1,098
34	Michigan	1,097
35	Kansas	1,081
35	North Carolina	1,081
37	Arizona	1,034
38	Alabama	1,025
39	Oregon	1,018
40	Florida	1,016
41	Idaho	1,009
42	Missouri	997
43	Virginia	994
44	Georgia	985
45	South Dakota	964
46	Montana	891
47	Texas	854
48	Utah	818
49	Colorado	787
50	Nevada	729

District of Columbia 3,686

Source: CQ Press using data from U.S. Bureau of the Census, Governments Division
"State and Local Government Finances 2006-2007" (http://www.census.gov/govs/estimate/index.html)
*Direct general expenditures. Includes funds for cash assistance programs, medical and other vendor payments, welfare institutions, and other public welfare programs.

State and Local Government Spending for Public Welfare Programs as a Percent of All State and Local Government Expenditures in 2007
National Percent = 17.0%*

ALPHA ORDER

RANK	STATE	PERCENT
34	Alabama	15.5
44	Alaska	13.8
22	Arizona	16.7
8	Arkansas	21.3
36	California	14.9
48	Colorado	11.3
25	Connecticut	16.5
19	Delaware	17.0
40	Florida	14.2
37	Georgia	14.7
42	Hawaii	14.0
20	Idaho	16.9
30	Illinois	16.0
20	Indiana	16.9
22	Iowa	16.7
30	Kansas	16.0
9	Kentucky	21.2
42	Louisiana	14.0
1	Maine	24.5
25	Maryland	16.5
5	Massachusetts	22.0
32	Michigan	15.8
3	Minnesota	23.0
17	Mississippi	18.1
28	Missouri	16.1
47	Montana	12.8
24	Nebraska	16.6
49	Nevada	10.9
16	New Hampshire	18.3
28	New Jersey	16.1
13	New Mexico	19.9
7	New York	21.9
25	North Carolina	16.5
33	North Dakota	15.6
11	Ohio	20.3
14	Oklahoma	19.5
38	Oregon	14.4
5	Pennsylvania	22.0
2	Rhode Island	24.0
18	South Carolina	17.2
35	South Dakota	15.4
9	Tennessee	21.2
44	Texas	13.8
46	Utah	13.0
4	Vermont	22.8
38	Virginia	14.4
40	Washington	14.2
12	West Virginia	20.2
15	Wisconsin	18.4
50	Wyoming	10.3

RANK ORDER

RANK	STATE	PERCENT
1	Maine	24.5
2	Rhode Island	24.0
3	Minnesota	23.0
4	Vermont	22.8
5	Massachusetts	22.0
5	Pennsylvania	22.0
7	New York	21.9
8	Arkansas	21.3
9	Kentucky	21.2
9	Tennessee	21.2
11	Ohio	20.3
12	West Virginia	20.2
13	New Mexico	19.9
14	Oklahoma	19.5
15	Wisconsin	18.4
16	New Hampshire	18.3
17	Mississippi	18.1
18	South Carolina	17.2
19	Delaware	17.0
20	Idaho	16.9
20	Indiana	16.9
22	Arizona	16.7
22	Iowa	16.7
24	Nebraska	16.6
25	Connecticut	16.5
25	Maryland	16.5
25	North Carolina	16.5
28	Missouri	16.1
28	New Jersey	16.1
30	Illinois	16.0
30	Kansas	16.0
32	Michigan	15.8
33	North Dakota	15.6
34	Alabama	15.5
35	South Dakota	15.4
36	California	14.9
37	Georgia	14.7
38	Oregon	14.4
38	Virginia	14.4
40	Florida	14.2
40	Washington	14.2
42	Hawaii	14.0
42	Louisiana	14.0
44	Alaska	13.8
44	Texas	13.8
46	Utah	13.0
47	Montana	12.8
48	Colorado	11.3
49	Nevada	10.9
50	Wyoming	10.3

District of Columbia   25.5

Source: CQ Press using data from U.S. Bureau of the Census, Governments Division
"State and Local Government Finances 2006-2007" (http://www.census.gov/govs/estimate/index.html)
*As a percent of direct general expenditures. Includes funds for cash assistance programs, medical and other vendor payments, welfare institutions, and other public welfare programs.

Social Security (OASDI) Payments in 2007

National Total = $584,764,000,000*

ALPHA ORDER

RANK	STATE	PAYMENTS	% of USA
20	Alabama	$10,522,000,000	1.8%
50	Alaska	769,000,000	0.1%
19	Arizona	11,478,000,000	2.0%
31	Arkansas	6,445,000,000	1.1%
1	California	53,615,000,000	9.2%
29	Colorado	7,172,000,000	1.2%
27	Connecticut	7,638,000,000	1.3%
45	Delaware	1,960,000,000	0.3%
2	Florida	40,901,000,000	7.0%
11	Georgia	14,904,000,000	2.5%
42	Hawaii	2,422,000,000	0.4%
41	Idaho	2,750,000,000	0.5%
7	Illinois	23,549,000,000	4.0%
13	Indiana	13,502,000,000	2.3%
30	Iowa	6,604,000,000	1.1%
33	Kansas	5,521,000,000	0.9%
24	Kentucky	9,187,000,000	1.6%
25	Louisiana	8,086,000,000	1.4%
39	Maine	3,056,000,000	0.5%
22	Maryland	9,509,000,000	1.6%
15	Massachusetts	12,849,000,000	2.2%
8	Michigan	22,736,000,000	3.9%
21	Minnesota	9,705,000,000	1.7%
32	Mississippi	6,021,000,000	1.0%
16	Missouri	12,634,000,000	2.2%
44	Montana	1,993,000,000	0.3%
37	Nebraska	3,439,000,000	0.6%
35	Nevada	4,338,000,000	0.7%
40	New Hampshire	2,837,000,000	0.5%
10	New Jersey	18,102,000,000	3.1%
36	New Mexico	3,561,000,000	0.6%
3	New York	38,267,000,000	6.5%
9	North Carolina	18,316,000,000	3.1%
48	North Dakota	1,295,000,000	0.2%
6	Ohio	23,770,000,000	4.1%
28	Oklahoma	7,465,000,000	1.3%
26	Oregon	7,686,000,000	1.3%
5	Pennsylvania	29,918,000,000	5.1%
43	Rhode Island	2,289,000,000	0.4%
23	South Carolina	9,495,000,000	1.6%
46	South Dakota	1,585,000,000	0.3%
14	Tennessee	13,007,000,000	2.2%
4	Texas	35,232,000,000	6.0%
38	Utah	3,395,000,000	0.6%
47	Vermont	1,359,000,000	0.2%
12	Virginia	13,799,000,000	2.4%
17	Washington	12,005,000,000	2.1%
34	West Virginia	4,950,000,000	0.8%
18	Wisconsin	11,881,000,000	2.0%
49	Wyoming	994,000,000	0.2%

RANK ORDER

RANK	STATE	PAYMENTS	% of USA
1	California	$53,615,000,000	9.2%
2	Florida	40,901,000,000	7.0%
3	New York	38,267,000,000	6.5%
4	Texas	35,232,000,000	6.0%
5	Pennsylvania	29,918,000,000	5.1%
6	Ohio	23,770,000,000	4.1%
7	Illinois	23,549,000,000	4.0%
8	Michigan	22,736,000,000	3.9%
9	North Carolina	18,316,000,000	3.1%
10	New Jersey	18,102,000,000	3.1%
11	Georgia	14,904,000,000	2.5%
12	Virginia	13,799,000,000	2.4%
13	Indiana	13,502,000,000	2.3%
14	Tennessee	13,007,000,000	2.2%
15	Massachusetts	12,849,000,000	2.2%
16	Missouri	12,634,000,000	2.2%
17	Washington	12,005,000,000	2.1%
18	Wisconsin	11,881,000,000	2.0%
19	Arizona	11,478,000,000	2.0%
20	Alabama	10,522,000,000	1.8%
21	Minnesota	9,705,000,000	1.7%
22	Maryland	9,509,000,000	1.6%
23	South Carolina	9,495,000,000	1.6%
24	Kentucky	9,187,000,000	1.6%
25	Louisiana	8,086,000,000	1.4%
26	Oregon	7,686,000,000	1.3%
27	Connecticut	7,638,000,000	1.3%
28	Oklahoma	7,465,000,000	1.3%
29	Colorado	7,172,000,000	1.2%
30	Iowa	6,604,000,000	1.1%
31	Arkansas	6,445,000,000	1.1%
32	Mississippi	6,021,000,000	1.0%
33	Kansas	5,521,000,000	0.9%
34	West Virginia	4,950,000,000	0.8%
35	Nevada	4,338,000,000	0.7%
36	New Mexico	3,561,000,000	0.6%
37	Nebraska	3,439,000,000	0.6%
38	Utah	3,395,000,000	0.6%
39	Maine	3,056,000,000	0.5%
40	New Hampshire	2,837,000,000	0.5%
41	Idaho	2,750,000,000	0.5%
42	Hawaii	2,422,000,000	0.4%
43	Rhode Island	2,289,000,000	0.4%
44	Montana	1,993,000,000	0.3%
45	Delaware	1,960,000,000	0.3%
46	South Dakota	1,585,000,000	0.3%
47	Vermont	1,359,000,000	0.2%
48	North Dakota	1,295,000,000	0.2%
49	Wyoming	994,000,000	0.2%
50	Alaska	769,000,000	0.1%
	District of Columbia	744,000,000	0.1%

Source: Social Security Administration
   "Social Security Bulletin, Annual Statistical Supplement 2008" (http://www.ssa.gov/policy/docs/statcomps/supplement/2008/)
*"OASDI" is Old Age, Survivors and Disability Insurance. National total includes $9,486,000,000 in payments to recipients in
U.S. territories and foreign countries.

Per Capita Social Security (OASDI) Payments in 2007

National Per Capita = $1,907*

ALPHA ORDER

RANK	STATE	PER CAPITA
4	Alabama	$2,269
50	Alaska	1,127
41	Arizona	1,804
5	Arkansas	2,268
47	California	1,480
46	Colorado	1,481
11	Connecticut	2,189
6	Delaware	2,266
8	Florida	2,238
45	Georgia	1,563
34	Hawaii	1,897
39	Idaho	1,834
38	Illinois	1,843
17	Indiana	2,128
9	Iowa	2,217
28	Kansas	1,989
13	Kentucky	2,158
37	Louisiana	1,848
3	Maine	2,320
44	Maryland	1,688
30	Massachusetts	1,977
7	Michigan	2,262
35	Minnesota	1,870
24	Mississippi	2,061
16	Missouri	2,138
21	Montana	2,082
32	Nebraska	1,943
43	Nevada	1,689
14	New Hampshire	2,154
20	New Jersey	2,096
40	New Mexico	1,809
31	New York	1,970
27	North Carolina	2,021
26	North Dakota	2,029
23	Ohio	2,063
22	Oklahoma	2,067
25	Oregon	2,059
2	Pennsylvania	2,389
12	Rhode Island	2,170
15	South Carolina	2,146
28	South Dakota	1,989
19	Tennessee	2,107
48	Texas	1,478
49	Utah	1,274
10	Vermont	2,190
42	Virginia	1,787
36	Washington	1,857
1	West Virginia	2,733
18	Wisconsin	2,121
33	Wyoming	1,899

RANK ORDER

RANK	STATE	PER CAPITA
1	West Virginia	$2,733
2	Pennsylvania	2,389
3	Maine	2,320
4	Alabama	2,269
5	Arkansas	2,268
6	Delaware	2,266
7	Michigan	2,262
8	Florida	2,238
9	Iowa	2,217
10	Vermont	2,190
11	Connecticut	2,189
12	Rhode Island	2,170
13	Kentucky	2,158
14	New Hampshire	2,154
15	South Carolina	2,146
16	Missouri	2,138
17	Indiana	2,128
18	Wisconsin	2,121
19	Tennessee	2,107
20	New Jersey	2,096
21	Montana	2,082
22	Oklahoma	2,067
23	Ohio	2,063
24	Mississippi	2,061
25	Oregon	2,059
26	North Dakota	2,029
27	North Carolina	2,021
28	Kansas	1,989
28	South Dakota	1,989
30	Massachusetts	1,977
31	New York	1,970
32	Nebraska	1,943
33	Wyoming	1,899
34	Hawaii	1,897
35	Minnesota	1,870
36	Washington	1,857
37	Louisiana	1,848
38	Illinois	1,843
39	Idaho	1,834
40	New Mexico	1,809
41	Arizona	1,804
42	Virginia	1,787
43	Nevada	1,689
44	Maryland	1,688
45	Georgia	1,563
46	Colorado	1,481
47	California	1,480
48	Texas	1,478
49	Utah	1,274
50	Alaska	1,127
	District of Columbia	1,269

Source: CQ Press using data from Social Security Administration
"Social Security Bulletin, Annual Statistical Supplement 2008" (http://www.ssa.gov/policy/docs/statcomps/supplement/2008/)
*"OASDI" is Old Age, Survivors and Disability Insurance. National per capita does not include payments or population in U.S. territories and foreign countries.

Social Security (OASDI) Monthly Payments in 2007

National Total = $49,218,145,000*

ALPHA ORDER					RANK ORDER			
RANK	STATE	PAYMENTS	% of USA		RANK	STATE	PAYMENTS	% of USA
20	Alabama	$871,901,000	1.8%		1	California	$4,529,307,000	9.2%
50	Alaska	64,509,000	0.1%		2	Florida	3,476,594,000	7.1%
19	Arizona	975,362,000	2.0%		3	New York	3,231,745,000	6.6%
31	Arkansas	537,711,000	1.1%		4	Texas	2,947,003,000	6.0%
1	California	4,529,307,000	9.2%		5	Pennsylvania	2,512,443,000	5.1%
29	Colorado	608,090,000	1.2%		6	Ohio	1,982,811,000	4.0%
27	Connecticut	649,645,000	1.3%		7	Illinois	1,979,725,000	4.0%
45	Delaware	166,396,000	0.3%		8	Michigan	1,910,947,000	3.9%
2	Florida	3,476,594,000	7.1%		9	North Carolina	1,548,633,000	3.1%
11	Georgia	1,255,047,000	2.5%		10	New Jersey	1,535,998,000	3.1%
42	Hawaii	207,882,000	0.4%		11	Georgia	1,255,047,000	2.5%
41	Idaho	232,982,000	0.5%		12	Virginia	1,161,431,000	2.4%
7	Illinois	1,979,725,000	4.0%		13	Indiana	1,136,120,000	2.3%
13	Indiana	1,136,120,000	2.3%		14	Tennessee	1,089,862,000	2.2%
30	Iowa	556,787,000	1.1%		15	Massachusetts	1,083,680,000	2.2%
33	Kansas	465,619,000	0.9%		16	Missouri	1,059,868,000	2.2%
24	Kentucky	757,639,000	1.5%		17	Washington	1,019,168,000	2.1%
25	Louisiana	660,195,000	1.3%		18	Wisconsin	1,006,891,000	2.0%
39	Maine	257,085,000	0.5%		19	Arizona	975,362,000	2.0%
22	Maryland	802,360,000	1.6%		20	Alabama	871,901,000	1.8%
15	Massachusetts	1,083,680,000	2.2%		21	Minnesota	823,464,000	1.7%
8	Michigan	1,910,947,000	3.9%		22	Maryland	802,360,000	1.6%
21	Minnesota	823,464,000	1.7%		23	South Carolina	801,117,000	1.6%
32	Mississippi	497,947,000	1.0%		24	Kentucky	757,639,000	1.5%
16	Missouri	1,059,868,000	2.2%		25	Louisiana	660,195,000	1.3%
44	Montana	168,254,000	0.3%		26	Oregon	652,713,000	1.3%
37	Nebraska	290,108,000	0.6%		27	Connecticut	649,645,000	1.3%
35	Nevada	369,289,000	0.8%		28	Oklahoma	624,706,000	1.3%
40	New Hampshire	237,887,000	0.5%		29	Colorado	608,090,000	1.2%
10	New Jersey	1,535,998,000	3.1%		30	Iowa	556,787,000	1.1%
36	New Mexico	299,527,000	0.6%		31	Arkansas	537,711,000	1.1%
3	New York	3,231,745,000	6.6%		32	Mississippi	497,947,000	1.0%
9	North Carolina	1,548,633,000	3.1%		33	Kansas	465,619,000	0.9%
48	North Dakota	108,033,000	0.2%		34	West Virginia	405,337,000	0.8%
6	Ohio	1,982,811,000	4.0%		35	Nevada	369,289,000	0.8%
28	Oklahoma	624,706,000	1.3%		36	New Mexico	299,527,000	0.6%
26	Oregon	652,713,000	1.3%		37	Nebraska	290,108,000	0.6%
5	Pennsylvania	2,512,443,000	5.1%		38	Utah	288,039,000	0.6%
43	Rhode Island	193,843,000	0.4%		39	Maine	257,085,000	0.5%
23	South Carolina	801,117,000	1.6%		40	New Hampshire	237,887,000	0.5%
46	South Dakota	134,026,000	0.3%		41	Idaho	232,982,000	0.5%
14	Tennessee	1,089,862,000	2.2%		42	Hawaii	207,882,000	0.4%
4	Texas	2,947,003,000	6.0%		43	Rhode Island	193,843,000	0.4%
38	Utah	288,039,000	0.6%		44	Montana	168,254,000	0.3%
47	Vermont	115,179,000	0.2%		45	Delaware	166,396,000	0.3%
12	Virginia	1,161,431,000	2.4%		46	South Dakota	134,026,000	0.3%
17	Washington	1,019,168,000	2.1%		47	Vermont	115,179,000	0.2%
34	West Virginia	405,337,000	0.8%		48	North Dakota	108,033,000	0.2%
18	Wisconsin	1,006,891,000	2.0%		49	Wyoming	83,979,000	0.2%
49	Wyoming	83,979,000	0.2%		50	Alaska	64,509,000	0.1%
						District of Columbia	62,306,000	0.1%

Source: Social Security Administration
   "Social Security Bulletin, Annual Statistical Supplement 2008" (http://www.ssa.gov/policy/docs/statcomps/supplement/2008/)
*For December 2007. "OASDI" is Old Age, Survivors and Disability Insurance. National total includes $780,955,000 in payments
to recipients in U.S. territories and foreign countries.

Social Security (OASDI) Beneficiaries in 2007

National Total = 49,864,838*

ALPHA ORDER

RANK	STATE	BENEFICIARIES	% of USA
20	Alabama	934,770	1.9%
50	Alaska	68,853	0.1%
19	Arizona	959,520	1.9%
30	Arkansas	588,910	1.2%
1	California	4,571,486	9.2%
28	Colorado	616,232	1.2%
29	Connecticut	592,533	1.2%
45	Delaware	157,239	0.3%
2	Florida	3,477,190	7.0%
11	Georgia	1,305,181	2.6%
42	Hawaii	207,992	0.4%
40	Idaho	240,070	0.5%
7	Illinois	1,921,996	3.9%
14	Indiana	1,097,739	2.2%
32	Iowa	558,541	1.1%
33	Kansas	457,826	0.9%
21	Kentucky	827,346	1.7%
25	Louisiana	735,263	1.5%
39	Maine	280,342	0.6%
24	Maryland	786,407	1.6%
16	Massachusetts	1,080,847	2.2%
8	Michigan	1,802,700	3.6%
23	Minnesota	814,960	1.6%
31	Mississippi	559,344	1.1%
15	Missouri	1,089,782	2.2%
44	Montana	176,539	0.4%
37	Nebraska	295,459	0.6%
35	Nevada	362,534	0.7%
41	New Hampshire	231,819	0.5%
10	New Jersey	1,388,380	2.8%
36	New Mexico	327,219	0.7%
4	New York	3,097,330	6.2%
9	North Carolina	1,587,350	3.2%
48	North Dakota	116,418	0.2%
6	Ohio	1,992,152	4.0%
26	Oklahoma	657,878	1.3%
27	Oregon	643,251	1.3%
5	Pennsylvania	2,456,196	4.9%
43	Rhode Island	193,783	0.4%
22	South Carolina	822,377	1.6%
46	South Dakota	144,993	0.3%
13	Tennessee	1,139,632	2.3%
3	Texas	3,102,890	6.2%
38	Utah	290,128	0.6%
47	Vermont	117,296	0.2%
12	Virginia	1,180,114	2.4%
17	Washington	982,948	2.0%
34	West Virginia	424,614	0.9%
18	Wisconsin	980,454	2.0%
49	Wyoming	84,022	0.2%

RANK ORDER

RANK	STATE	BENEFICIARIES	% of USA
1	California	4,571,486	9.2%
2	Florida	3,477,190	7.0%
3	Texas	3,102,890	6.2%
4	New York	3,097,330	6.2%
5	Pennsylvania	2,456,196	4.9%
6	Ohio	1,992,152	4.0%
7	Illinois	1,921,996	3.9%
8	Michigan	1,802,700	3.6%
9	North Carolina	1,587,350	3.2%
10	New Jersey	1,388,380	2.8%
11	Georgia	1,305,181	2.6%
12	Virginia	1,180,114	2.4%
13	Tennessee	1,139,632	2.3%
14	Indiana	1,097,739	2.2%
15	Missouri	1,089,782	2.2%
16	Massachusetts	1,080,847	2.2%
17	Washington	982,948	2.0%
18	Wisconsin	980,454	2.0%
19	Arizona	959,520	1.9%
20	Alabama	934,770	1.9%
21	Kentucky	827,346	1.7%
22	South Carolina	822,377	1.6%
23	Minnesota	814,960	1.6%
24	Maryland	786,407	1.6%
25	Louisiana	735,263	1.5%
26	Oklahoma	657,878	1.3%
27	Oregon	643,251	1.3%
28	Colorado	616,232	1.2%
29	Connecticut	592,533	1.2%
30	Arkansas	588,910	1.2%
31	Mississippi	559,344	1.1%
32	Iowa	558,541	1.1%
33	Kansas	457,826	0.9%
34	West Virginia	424,614	0.9%
35	Nevada	362,534	0.7%
36	New Mexico	327,219	0.7%
37	Nebraska	295,459	0.6%
38	Utah	290,128	0.6%
39	Maine	280,342	0.6%
40	Idaho	240,070	0.5%
41	New Hampshire	231,819	0.5%
42	Hawaii	207,992	0.4%
43	Rhode Island	193,783	0.4%
44	Montana	176,539	0.4%
45	Delaware	157,239	0.3%
46	South Dakota	144,993	0.3%
47	Vermont	117,296	0.2%
48	North Dakota	116,418	0.2%
49	Wyoming	84,022	0.2%
50	Alaska	68,853	0.1%
	District of Columbia	71,215	0.1%

Source: Social Security Administration
"Social Security Bulletin, Annual Statistical Supplement 2008" (http://www.ssa.gov/policy/docs/statcomps/supplement/2008/)
*For December 2007. "OASDI" is Old Age, Survivors and Disability Insurance. National total includes 1,264,778 beneficiaries in U.S. territories and foreign countries.

Average Monthly Social Security (OASDI) Payment in 2007

National Average = $997 Each Month per Beneficiary*

ALPHA ORDER				RANK ORDER		
RANK	STATE	AVERAGE BENEFIT		RANK	STATE	AVERAGE BENEFIT
42	Alabama	$933		1	New Jersey	$1,106
41	Alaska	937		2	Connecticut	1,096
14	Arizona	1,017		3	Michigan	1,060
48	Arkansas	913		4	Delaware	1,058
26	California	991		5	New York	1,043
27	Colorado	987		6	Washington	1,037
2	Connecticut	1,096		7	Indiana	1,035
4	Delaware	1,058		8	Illinois	1,030
19	Florida	1,000		9	Wisconsin	1,027
35	Georgia	962		10	New Hampshire	1,026
21	Hawaii	999		11	Pennsylvania	1,023
34	Idaho	970		12	Maryland	1,020
8	Illinois	1,030		13	Nevada	1,019
7	Indiana	1,035		14	Arizona	1,017
23	Iowa	997		14	Kansas	1,017
14	Kansas	1,017		16	Oregon	1,015
46	Kentucky	916		17	Minnesota	1,010
49	Louisiana	898		18	Massachusetts	1,003
45	Maine	917		19	Florida	1,000
12	Maryland	1,020		19	Rhode Island	1,000
18	Massachusetts	1,003		21	Hawaii	999
3	Michigan	1,060		21	Wyoming	999
17	Minnesota	1,010		23	Iowa	997
50	Mississippi	890		24	Ohio	995
33	Missouri	973		25	Utah	993
38	Montana	953		26	California	991
29	Nebraska	982		27	Colorado	987
13	Nevada	1,019		28	Virginia	984
10	New Hampshire	1,026		29	Nebraska	982
1	New Jersey	1,106		29	Vermont	982
47	New Mexico	915		31	North Carolina	976
5	New York	1,043		32	South Carolina	974
31	North Carolina	976		33	Missouri	973
43	North Dakota	928		34	Idaho	970
24	Ohio	995		35	Georgia	962
39	Oklahoma	950		36	Tennessee	956
16	Oregon	1,015		37	West Virginia	955
11	Pennsylvania	1,023		38	Montana	953
19	Rhode Island	1,000		39	Oklahoma	950
32	South Carolina	974		39	Texas	950
44	South Dakota	924		41	Alaska	937
36	Tennessee	956		42	Alabama	933
39	Texas	950		43	North Dakota	928
25	Utah	993		44	South Dakota	924
29	Vermont	982		45	Maine	917
28	Virginia	984		46	Kentucky	916
6	Washington	1,037		47	New Mexico	915
37	West Virginia	955		48	Arkansas	913
9	Wisconsin	1,027		49	Louisiana	898
21	Wyoming	999		50	Mississippi	890
					District of Columbia	875

Source: CQ Press using data from Social Security Administration
"Social Security Bulletin, Annual Statistical Supplement 2008" (http://www.ssa.gov/policy/docs/statcomps/supplement/2008/)
*As of December 2007. "OASDI" is Old Age, Survivors and Disability Insurance. National average does not include beneficiaries or payments in U.S. territories or foreign countries.

Social Security Supplemental Security Income Beneficiaries in 2007

National Total = 7,359,525 Beneficiaries*

ALPHA ORDER

RANK	STATE	BENEFICIARIES	% of USA
13	Alabama	165,521	2.2%
48	Alaska	11,440	0.2%
23	Arizona	100,724	1.4%
26	Arkansas	95,802	1.3%
1	California	1,247,231	16.9%
31	Colorado	58,497	0.8%
33	Connecticut	54,197	0.7%
45	Delaware	14,401	0.2%
4	Florida	431,015	5.9%
9	Georgia	208,016	2.8%
41	Hawaii	23,262	0.3%
40	Idaho	23,697	0.3%
6	Illinois	261,901	3.6%
22	Indiana	104,366	1.4%
34	Iowa	44,659	0.6%
35	Kansas	40,405	0.5%
11	Kentucky	184,378	2.5%
15	Louisiana	162,271	2.2%
37	Maine	33,328	0.5%
24	Maryland	97,858	1.3%
12	Massachusetts	178,856	2.4%
8	Michigan	228,068	3.1%
29	Minnesota	78,401	1.1%
18	Mississippi	122,745	1.7%
19	Missouri	121,876	1.7%
43	Montana	15,629	0.2%
42	Nebraska	23,052	0.3%
36	Nevada	35,548	0.5%
44	New Hampshire	15,119	0.2%
16	New Jersey	156,374	2.1%
32	New Mexico	56,387	0.8%
2	New York	648,908	8.8%
10	North Carolina	205,604	2.8%
49	North Dakota	8,003	0.1%
7	Ohio	257,874	3.5%
27	Oklahoma	85,102	1.2%
30	Oregon	64,031	0.9%
5	Pennsylvania	333,531	4.5%
38	Rhode Island	31,101	0.4%
21	South Carolina	105,519	1.4%
47	South Dakota	12,961	0.2%
14	Tennessee	163,142	2.2%
3	Texas	544,605	7.4%
39	Utah	24,472	0.3%
46	Vermont	13,920	0.2%
17	Virginia	140,419	1.9%
20	Washington	121,577	1.7%
28	West Virginia	78,931	1.1%
25	Wisconsin	96,037	1.3%
50	Wyoming	5,832	0.1%

RANK ORDER

RANK	STATE	BENEFICIARIES	% of USA
1	California	1,247,231	16.9%
2	New York	648,908	8.8%
3	Texas	544,605	7.4%
4	Florida	431,015	5.9%
5	Pennsylvania	333,531	4.5%
6	Illinois	261,901	3.6%
7	Ohio	257,874	3.5%
8	Michigan	228,068	3.1%
9	Georgia	208,016	2.8%
10	North Carolina	205,604	2.8%
11	Kentucky	184,378	2.5%
12	Massachusetts	178,856	2.4%
13	Alabama	165,521	2.2%
14	Tennessee	163,142	2.2%
15	Louisiana	162,271	2.2%
16	New Jersey	156,374	2.1%
17	Virginia	140,419	1.9%
18	Mississippi	122,745	1.7%
19	Missouri	121,876	1.7%
20	Washington	121,577	1.7%
21	South Carolina	105,519	1.4%
22	Indiana	104,366	1.4%
23	Arizona	100,724	1.4%
24	Maryland	97,858	1.3%
25	Wisconsin	96,037	1.3%
26	Arkansas	95,802	1.3%
27	Oklahoma	85,102	1.2%
28	West Virginia	78,931	1.1%
29	Minnesota	78,401	1.1%
30	Oregon	64,031	0.9%
31	Colorado	58,497	0.8%
32	New Mexico	56,387	0.8%
33	Connecticut	54,197	0.7%
34	Iowa	44,659	0.6%
35	Kansas	40,405	0.5%
36	Nevada	35,548	0.5%
37	Maine	33,328	0.5%
38	Rhode Island	31,101	0.4%
39	Utah	24,472	0.3%
40	Idaho	23,697	0.3%
41	Hawaii	23,262	0.3%
42	Nebraska	23,052	0.3%
43	Montana	15,629	0.2%
44	New Hampshire	15,119	0.2%
45	Delaware	14,401	0.2%
46	Vermont	13,920	0.2%
47	South Dakota	12,961	0.2%
48	Alaska	11,440	0.2%
49	North Dakota	8,003	0.1%
50	Wyoming	5,832	0.1%
	District of Columbia	22,102	0.3%

Source: Social Security Administration
    "Social Security Bulletin, Annual Statistical Supplement 2008" (http://www.ssa.gov/policy/docs/statcomps/supplement/2008/)
*For December 2007. National total includes 827 beneficiaries in U.S. territories or otherwise not distributed by state. The SSI program provides income support to persons age 65 and older and blind or disabled adults and children.

Average Monthly Social Security Supplemental Security Income Payment: 2007

National Average = $437.05 Each Month per Beneficiary*

ALPHA ORDER

RANK	STATE	AVERAGE BENEFIT
36	Alabama	$418.48
29	Alaska	425.74
8	Arizona	446.94
39	Arkansas	413.07
11	California	443.79
31	Colorado	421.99
12	Connecticut	443.70
20	Delaware	434.54
22	Florida	434.19
37	Georgia	417.13
9	Hawaii	446.86
30	Idaho	425.09
1	Illinois	466.89
14	Indiana	442.68
44	Iowa	408.33
28	Kansas	426.34
19	Kentucky	435.04
23	Louisiana	432.53
43	Maine	408.78
7	Maryland	451.81
15	Massachusetts	439.55
2	Michigan	464.04
10	Minnesota	446.22
40	Mississippi	412.96
26	Missouri	428.03
38	Montana	416.44
45	Nebraska	407.37
21	Nevada	434.40
34	New Hampshire	420.46
27	New Jersey	426.81
33	New Mexico	420.47
6	New York	455.21
47	North Carolina	405.93
50	North Dakota	379.67
5	Ohio	460.41
25	Oklahoma	428.75
17	Oregon	438.08
4	Pennsylvania	462.57
16	Rhode Island	438.69
41	South Carolina	411.50
49	South Dakota	395.16
35	Tennessee	419.10
42	Texas	409.77
24	Utah	429.81
48	Vermont	405.21
32	Virginia	421.31
3	Washington	463.28
13	West Virginia	442.93
18	Wisconsin	435.48
46	Wyoming	406.27

RANK ORDER

RANK	STATE	AVERAGE BENEFIT
1	Illinois	$466.89
2	Michigan	464.04
3	Washington	463.28
4	Pennsylvania	462.57
5	Ohio	460.41
6	New York	455.21
7	Maryland	451.81
8	Arizona	446.94
9	Hawaii	446.86
10	Minnesota	446.22
11	California	443.79
12	Connecticut	443.70
13	West Virginia	442.93
14	Indiana	442.68
15	Massachusetts	439.55
16	Rhode Island	438.69
17	Oregon	438.08
18	Wisconsin	435.48
19	Kentucky	435.04
20	Delaware	434.54
21	Nevada	434.40
22	Florida	434.19
23	Louisiana	432.53
24	Utah	429.81
25	Oklahoma	428.75
26	Missouri	428.03
27	New Jersey	426.81
28	Kansas	426.34
29	Alaska	425.74
30	Idaho	425.09
31	Colorado	421.99
32	Virginia	421.31
33	New Mexico	420.47
34	New Hampshire	420.46
35	Tennessee	419.10
36	Alabama	418.48
37	Georgia	417.13
38	Montana	416.44
39	Arkansas	413.07
40	Mississippi	412.96
41	South Carolina	411.50
42	Texas	409.77
43	Maine	408.78
44	Iowa	408.33
45	Nebraska	407.37
46	Wyoming	406.27
47	North Carolina	405.93
48	Vermont	405.21
49	South Dakota	395.16
50	North Dakota	379.67
	District of Columbia	467.16

Source: Social Security Administration

"Social Security Bulletin, Annual Statistical Supplement 2008" (http://www.ssa.gov/policy/docs/statcomps/supplement/2008/)

*As of December 2007. National average includes payments to beneficiaries in U.S. territories and foreign countries. The SSI program provides income support to persons age 65 and older and blind or disabled adults and children.

Medicare Enrollees in 2008

National Total = 45,411,883 Enrollees*

ALPHA ORDER					RANK ORDER			
RANK	STATE	ENROLLEES	% of USA		RANK	STATE	ENROLLEES	% of USA
20	Alabama	809,193	1.8%		1	California	4,491,586	9.9%
50	Alaska	59,781	0.1%		2	Florida	3,211,813	7.1%
19	Arizona	869,591	1.9%		3	New York	2,891,085	6.4%
30	Arkansas	508,767	1.1%		4	Texas	2,801,840	6.2%
1	California	4,491,586	9.9%		5	Pennsylvania	2,221,376	4.9%
27	Colorado	579,322	1.3%		6	Ohio	1,840,714	4.1%
29	Connecticut	548,703	1.2%		7	Illinois	1,774,555	3.9%
45	Delaware	141,080	0.3%		8	Michigan	1,579,631	3.5%
2	Florida	3,211,813	7.1%		9	North Carolina	1,404,787	3.1%
11	Georgia	1,152,522	2.5%		10	New Jersey	1,282,636	2.8%
42	Hawaii	194,183	0.4%		11	Georgia	1,152,522	2.5%
40	Idaho	214,247	0.5%		12	Virginia	1,078,534	2.4%
7	Illinois	1,774,555	3.9%		13	Massachusetts	1,018,689	2.2%
16	Indiana	964,240	2.1%		14	Tennessee	1,004,176	2.2%
31	Iowa	506,152	1.1%		15	Missouri	966,061	2.1%
33	Kansas	417,996	0.9%		16	Indiana	964,240	2.1%
23	Kentucky	728,218	1.6%		17	Washington	903,249	2.0%
25	Louisiana	656,392	1.4%		18	Wisconsin	873,782	1.9%
39	Maine	253,188	0.6%		19	Arizona	869,591	1.9%
22	Maryland	744,564	1.6%		20	Alabama	809,193	1.8%
13	Massachusetts	1,018,689	2.2%		21	Minnesota	749,065	1.6%
8	Michigan	1,579,631	3.5%		22	Maryland	744,564	1.6%
21	Minnesota	749,065	1.6%		23	Kentucky	728,218	1.6%
32	Mississippi	479,231	1.1%		24	South Carolina	723,726	1.6%
15	Missouri	966,061	2.1%		25	Louisiana	656,392	1.4%
44	Montana	160,441	0.4%		26	Oregon	584,222	1.3%
37	Nebraska	271,368	0.6%		27	Colorado	579,322	1.3%
35	Nevada	330,003	0.7%		28	Oklahoma	578,488	1.3%
41	New Hampshire	211,657	0.5%		29	Connecticut	548,703	1.2%
10	New Jersey	1,282,636	2.8%		30	Arkansas	508,767	1.1%
36	New Mexico	294,269	0.6%		31	Iowa	506,152	1.1%
3	New York	2,891,085	6.4%		32	Mississippi	479,231	1.1%
9	North Carolina	1,404,787	3.1%		33	Kansas	417,996	0.9%
47	North Dakota	106,666	0.2%		34	West Virginia	372,995	0.8%
6	Ohio	1,840,714	4.1%		35	Nevada	330,003	0.7%
28	Oklahoma	578,488	1.3%		36	New Mexico	294,269	0.6%
26	Oregon	584,222	1.3%		37	Nebraska	271,368	0.6%
5	Pennsylvania	2,221,376	4.9%		38	Utah	264,086	0.6%
43	Rhode Island	177,874	0.4%		39	Maine	253,188	0.6%
24	South Carolina	723,726	1.6%		40	Idaho	214,247	0.5%
46	South Dakota	132,046	0.3%		41	New Hampshire	211,657	0.5%
14	Tennessee	1,004,176	2.2%		42	Hawaii	194,183	0.4%
4	Texas	2,801,840	6.2%		43	Rhode Island	177,874	0.4%
38	Utah	264,086	0.6%		44	Montana	160,441	0.4%
48	Vermont	104,917	0.2%		45	Delaware	141,080	0.3%
12	Virginia	1,078,534	2.4%		46	South Dakota	132,046	0.3%
17	Washington	903,249	2.0%		47	North Dakota	106,666	0.2%
34	West Virginia	372,995	0.8%		48	Vermont	104,917	0.2%
18	Wisconsin	873,782	1.9%		49	Wyoming	76,122	0.2%
49	Wyoming	76,122	0.2%		50	Alaska	59,781	0.1%
						District of Columbia	75,125	0.2%

Source: U.S. Department of Health and Human Services, Centers for Medicare and Medicaid Services
    "2009 Data Compendium" (http://www.cms.hhs.gov/DataCompendium/)
*Includes aged and disabled enrollees. Total includes 636,922 enrollees in Puerto Rico and other outlying areas, foreign countries, or whose address is unknown.

Percent of Population Enrolled in Medicare in 2008

National Percent = 14.6% of Population*

ALPHA ORDER

RANK	STATE	PERCENT
6	Alabama	17.4
50	Alaska	8.7
42	Arizona	13.4
3	Arkansas	17.8
45	California	12.2
47	Colorado	11.7
23	Connecticut	15.7
16	Delaware	16.2
5	Florida	17.5
46	Georgia	11.9
29	Hawaii	15.1
38	Idaho	14.1
40	Illinois	13.8
29	Indiana	15.1
8	Iowa	16.9
31	Kansas	14.9
7	Kentucky	17.1
31	Louisiana	14.9
2	Maine	19.2
43	Maryland	13.2
23	Massachusetts	15.7
22	Michigan	15.8
36	Minnesota	14.3
14	Mississippi	16.3
14	Missouri	16.3
11	Montana	16.6
27	Nebraska	15.2
44	Nevada	12.7
19	New Hampshire	16.1
33	New Jersey	14.8
33	New Mexico	14.8
33	New York	14.8
27	North Carolina	15.2
11	North Dakota	16.6
20	Ohio	16.0
21	Oklahoma	15.9
26	Oregon	15.4
3	Pennsylvania	17.8
8	Rhode Island	16.9
16	South Carolina	16.2
13	South Dakota	16.4
16	Tennessee	16.2
48	Texas	11.5
49	Utah	9.7
8	Vermont	16.9
39	Virginia	13.9
40	Washington	13.8
1	West Virginia	20.6
25	Wisconsin	15.5
36	Wyoming	14.3

RANK ORDER

RANK	STATE	PERCENT
1	West Virginia	20.6
2	Maine	19.2
3	Arkansas	17.8
3	Pennsylvania	17.8
5	Florida	17.5
6	Alabama	17.4
7	Kentucky	17.1
8	Iowa	16.9
8	Rhode Island	16.9
8	Vermont	16.9
11	Montana	16.6
11	North Dakota	16.6
13	South Dakota	16.4
14	Mississippi	16.3
14	Missouri	16.3
16	Delaware	16.2
16	South Carolina	16.2
16	Tennessee	16.2
19	New Hampshire	16.1
20	Ohio	16.0
21	Oklahoma	15.9
22	Michigan	15.8
23	Connecticut	15.7
23	Massachusetts	15.7
25	Wisconsin	15.5
26	Oregon	15.4
27	Nebraska	15.2
27	North Carolina	15.2
29	Hawaii	15.1
29	Indiana	15.1
31	Kansas	14.9
31	Louisiana	14.9
33	New Jersey	14.8
33	New Mexico	14.8
33	New York	14.8
36	Minnesota	14.3
36	Wyoming	14.3
38	Idaho	14.1
39	Virginia	13.9
40	Illinois	13.8
40	Washington	13.8
42	Arizona	13.4
43	Maryland	13.2
44	Nevada	12.7
45	California	12.2
46	Georgia	11.9
47	Colorado	11.7
48	Texas	11.5
49	Utah	9.7
50	Alaska	8.7
	District of Columbia	12.7

Source: U.S. Department of Health and Human Services, Centers for Medicare and Medicaid Services
    "2009 Data Compendium" (http://www.cms.hhs.gov/DataCompendium/)
*Includes aged and disabled enrollees. National rate includes only residents of the 50 states and the District of Columbia.

Medicare Program Payments in 2008

National Total = $300,045,000,000*

ALPHA ORDER

RANK	STATE	PAYMENTS	% of USA
18	Alabama	$5,429,000,000	1.8%
50	Alaska	413,000,000	0.1%
25	Arizona	4,381,000,000	1.5%
29	Arkansas	3,278,000,000	1.1%
1	California	26,290,000,000	8.8%
32	Colorado	2,956,000,000	1.0%
24	Connecticut	4,436,000,000	1.5%
41	Delaware	1,232,000,000	0.4%
2	Florida	24,025,000,000	8.0%
11	Georgia	7,932,000,000	2.6%
48	Hawaii	680,000,000	0.2%
42	Idaho	1,051,000,000	0.4%
5	Illinois	14,387,000,000	4.8%
15	Indiana	6,881,000,000	2.3%
30	Iowa	3,034,000,000	1.0%
31	Kansas	2,965,000,000	1.0%
20	Kentucky	5,077,000,000	1.7%
19	Louisiana	5,169,000,000	1.7%
37	Maine	1,657,000,000	0.6%
13	Maryland	7,002,000,000	2.3%
12	Massachusetts	7,597,000,000	2.5%
8	Michigan	11,680,000,000	3.9%
28	Minnesota	3,880,000,000	1.3%
27	Mississippi	3,973,000,000	1.3%
17	Missouri	6,395,000,000	2.1%
44	Montana	883,000,000	0.3%
36	Nebraska	1,825,000,000	0.6%
35	Nevada	1,931,000,000	0.6%
39	New Hampshire	1,484,000,000	0.5%
9	New Jersey	11,555,000,000	3.9%
38	New Mexico	1,527,000,000	0.5%
4	New York	20,158,000,000	6.7%
10	North Carolina	9,229,000,000	3.1%
47	North Dakota	723,000,000	0.2%
7	Ohio	12,146,000,000	4.0%
26	Oklahoma	4,247,000,000	1.4%
34	Oregon	2,171,000,000	0.7%
6	Pennsylvania	12,271,000,000	4.1%
43	Rhode Island	917,000,000	0.3%
21	South Carolina	4,952,000,000	1.7%
45	South Dakota	752,000,000	0.3%
16	Tennessee	6,491,000,000	2.2%
3	Texas	22,693,000,000	7.6%
40	Utah	1,349,000,000	0.4%
46	Vermont	740,000,000	0.2%
14	Virginia	6,959,000,000	2.3%
23	Washington	4,896,000,000	1.6%
33	West Virginia	2,248,000,000	0.7%
22	Wisconsin	4,926,000,000	1.6%
49	Wyoming	471,000,000	0.2%

RANK ORDER

RANK	STATE	PAYMENTS	% of USA
1	California	$26,290,000,000	8.8%
2	Florida	24,025,000,000	8.0%
3	Texas	22,693,000,000	7.6%
4	New York	20,158,000,000	6.7%
5	Illinois	14,387,000,000	4.8%
6	Pennsylvania	12,271,000,000	4.1%
7	Ohio	12,146,000,000	4.0%
8	Michigan	11,680,000,000	3.9%
9	New Jersey	11,555,000,000	3.9%
10	North Carolina	9,229,000,000	3.1%
11	Georgia	7,932,000,000	2.6%
12	Massachusetts	7,597,000,000	2.5%
13	Maryland	7,002,000,000	2.3%
14	Virginia	6,959,000,000	2.3%
15	Indiana	6,881,000,000	2.3%
16	Tennessee	6,491,000,000	2.2%
17	Missouri	6,395,000,000	2.1%
18	Alabama	5,429,000,000	1.8%
19	Louisiana	5,169,000,000	1.7%
20	Kentucky	5,077,000,000	1.7%
21	South Carolina	4,952,000,000	1.7%
22	Wisconsin	4,926,000,000	1.6%
23	Washington	4,896,000,000	1.6%
24	Connecticut	4,436,000,000	1.5%
25	Arizona	4,381,000,000	1.5%
26	Oklahoma	4,247,000,000	1.4%
27	Mississippi	3,973,000,000	1.3%
28	Minnesota	3,880,000,000	1.3%
29	Arkansas	3,278,000,000	1.1%
30	Iowa	3,034,000,000	1.0%
31	Kansas	2,965,000,000	1.0%
32	Colorado	2,956,000,000	1.0%
33	West Virginia	2,248,000,000	0.7%
34	Oregon	2,171,000,000	0.7%
35	Nevada	1,931,000,000	0.6%
36	Nebraska	1,825,000,000	0.6%
37	Maine	1,657,000,000	0.6%
38	New Mexico	1,527,000,000	0.5%
39	New Hampshire	1,484,000,000	0.5%
40	Utah	1,349,000,000	0.4%
41	Delaware	1,232,000,000	0.4%
42	Idaho	1,051,000,000	0.4%
43	Rhode Island	917,000,000	0.3%
44	Montana	883,000,000	0.3%
45	South Dakota	752,000,000	0.3%
46	Vermont	740,000,000	0.2%
47	North Dakota	723,000,000	0.2%
48	Hawaii	680,000,000	0.2%
49	Wyoming	471,000,000	0.2%
50	Alaska	413,000,000	0.1%
	District of Columbia	703,000,000	0.2%

Source: U.S. Department of Health and Human Services, Centers for Medicare and Medicaid Services
"Health Care Financing Review, 2009 Statistical Supplement" (http://cms.hhs.gov/MedicareMedicaidStatSupp)
*Figures for calendar year 2008. Includes payments to aged and disabled enrollees. Total does not include payments to beneficiaries in Puerto Rico and other outlying areas.

Medicare Program Payments per Enrollee in 2008

National Rate = $8,649*

ALPHA ORDER		
RANK	STATE	PER ENROLLEE
17	Alabama	$8,306
40	Alaska	7,043
25	Arizona	7,945
32	Arkansas	7,528
13	California	8,862
34	Colorado	7,496
8	Connecticut	9,419
11	Delaware	8,959
1	Florida	10,317
28	Georgia	7,857
50	Hawaii	5,531
45	Idaho	6,494
12	Illinois	8,893
19	Indiana	8,202
43	Iowa	6,842
27	Kansas	7,864
23	Kentucky	8,044
4	Louisiana	9,894
42	Maine	6,937
2	Maryland	10,092
9	Massachusetts	9,115
7	Michigan	9,448
26	Minnesota	7,895
10	Mississippi	9,089
22	Missouri	8,052
46	Montana	6,414
33	Nebraska	7,509
18	Nevada	8,249
35	New Hampshire	7,469
3	New Jersey	9,974
44	New Mexico	6,782
6	New York	9,545
29	North Carolina	7,853
37	North Dakota	7,152
14	Ohio	8,780
16	Oklahoma	8,498
49	Oregon	6,176
15	Pennsylvania	8,711
21	Rhode Island	8,086
24	South Carolina	7,972
48	South Dakota	6,307
20	Tennessee	8,103
5	Texas	9,769
39	Utah	7,059
38	Vermont	7,114
36	Virginia	7,320
41	Washington	6,958
30	West Virginia	7,659
31	Wisconsin	7,532
47	Wyoming	6,397

RANK ORDER		
RANK	STATE	PER ENROLLEE
1	Florida	$10,317
2	Maryland	10,092
3	New Jersey	9,974
4	Louisiana	9,894
5	Texas	9,769
6	New York	9,545
7	Michigan	9,448
8	Connecticut	9,419
9	Massachusetts	9,115
10	Mississippi	9,089
11	Delaware	8,959
12	Illinois	8,893
13	California	8,862
14	Ohio	8,780
15	Pennsylvania	8,711
16	Oklahoma	8,498
17	Alabama	8,306
18	Nevada	8,249
19	Indiana	8,202
20	Tennessee	8,103
21	Rhode Island	8,086
22	Missouri	8,052
23	Kentucky	8,044
24	South Carolina	7,972
25	Arizona	7,945
26	Minnesota	7,895
27	Kansas	7,864
28	Georgia	7,857
29	North Carolina	7,853
30	West Virginia	7,659
31	Wisconsin	7,532
32	Arkansas	7,528
33	Nebraska	7,509
34	Colorado	7,496
35	New Hampshire	7,469
36	Virginia	7,320
37	North Dakota	7,152
38	Vermont	7,114
39	Utah	7,059
40	Alaska	7,043
41	Washington	6,958
42	Maine	6,937
43	Iowa	6,842
44	New Mexico	6,782
45	Idaho	6,494
46	Montana	6,414
47	Wyoming	6,397
48	South Dakota	6,307
49	Oregon	6,176
50	Hawaii	5,531
	District of Columbia	10,215

Source: U.S. Department of Health and Human Services, Centers for Medicare and Medicaid Services
"Health Care Financing Review, 2009 Statistical Supplement" (http://cms.hhs.gov/MedicareMedicaidStatSupp)
*Figures for calendar year 2008. Includes payments to aged and disabled enrollees. National figure does not include enrollees in managed care plans in the denominator used to calculate average payments. National rate also does not include payments or enrollees in Puerto Rico and other outlying areas.

Medicaid Enrollment in 2008

National Total = 47,142,791 Enrollees*

ALPHA ORDER

RANK	STATE	ENROLLEES	% of USA
20	Alabama	764,914	1.6%
47	Alaska	96,807	0.2%
13	Arizona	1,048,635	2.2%
26	Arkansas	622,491	1.3%
1	California	6,606,893	14.0%
31	Colorado	429,895	0.9%
30	Connecticut	435,419	0.9%
43	Delaware	152,899	0.3%
4	Florida	2,276,014	4.8%
10	Georgia	1,271,355	2.7%
37	Hawaii	211,105	0.4%
41	Idaho	187,394	0.4%
5	Illinois	2,106,700	4.5%
18	Indiana	881,888	1.9%
33	Iowa	362,807	0.8%
35	Kansas	278,705	0.6%
22	Kentucky	731,911	1.6%
14	Louisiana	1,006,842	2.1%
36	Maine	258,751	0.5%
23	Maryland	710,790	1.5%
12	Massachusetts	1,155,134	2.5%
8	Michigan	1,547,246	3.3%
27	Minnesota	617,397	1.3%
25	Mississippi	669,690	1.4%
19	Missouri	833,112	1.8%
48	Montana	82,852	0.2%
39	Nebraska	202,297	0.4%
40	Nevada	188,831	0.4%
45	New Hampshire	113,496	0.2%
16	New Jersey	914,503	1.9%
29	New Mexico	472,629	1.0%
2	New York	4,147,101	8.8%
9	North Carolina	1,353,760	2.9%
50	North Dakota	53,556	0.1%
7	Ohio	1,783,993	3.8%
28	Oklahoma	583,057	1.2%
32	Oregon	417,946	0.9%
6	Pennsylvania	1,833,489	3.9%
42	Rhode Island	178,119	0.4%
24	South Carolina	689,338	1.5%
46	South Dakota	102,444	0.2%
11	Tennessee	1,207,136	2.6%
3	Texas	3,041,201	6.5%
38	Utah	208,009	0.4%
44	Vermont	141,260	0.3%
21	Virginia	753,714	1.6%
15	Washington	960,881	2.0%
34	West Virginia	311,064	0.7%
17	Wisconsin	907,455	1.9%
49	Wyoming	61,083	0.1%

RANK ORDER

RANK	STATE	ENROLLEES	% of USA
1	California	6,606,893	14.0%
2	New York	4,147,101	8.8%
3	Texas	3,041,201	6.5%
4	Florida	2,276,014	4.8%
5	Illinois	2,106,700	4.5%
6	Pennsylvania	1,833,489	3.9%
7	Ohio	1,783,993	3.8%
8	Michigan	1,547,246	3.3%
9	North Carolina	1,353,760	2.9%
10	Georgia	1,271,355	2.7%
11	Tennessee	1,207,136	2.6%
12	Massachusetts	1,155,134	2.5%
13	Arizona	1,048,635	2.2%
14	Louisiana	1,006,842	2.1%
15	Washington	960,881	2.0%
16	New Jersey	914,503	1.9%
17	Wisconsin	907,455	1.9%
18	Indiana	881,888	1.9%
19	Missouri	833,112	1.8%
20	Alabama	764,914	1.6%
21	Virginia	753,714	1.6%
22	Kentucky	731,911	1.6%
23	Maryland	710,790	1.5%
24	South Carolina	689,338	1.5%
25	Mississippi	669,690	1.4%
26	Arkansas	622,491	1.3%
27	Minnesota	617,397	1.3%
28	Oklahoma	583,057	1.2%
29	New Mexico	472,629	1.0%
30	Connecticut	435,419	0.9%
31	Colorado	429,895	0.9%
32	Oregon	417,946	0.9%
33	Iowa	362,807	0.8%
34	West Virginia	311,064	0.7%
35	Kansas	278,705	0.6%
36	Maine	258,751	0.5%
37	Hawaii	211,105	0.4%
38	Utah	208,009	0.4%
39	Nebraska	202,297	0.4%
40	Nevada	188,831	0.4%
41	Idaho	187,394	0.4%
42	Rhode Island	178,119	0.4%
43	Delaware	152,899	0.3%
44	Vermont	141,260	0.3%
45	New Hampshire	113,496	0.2%
46	South Dakota	102,444	0.2%
47	Alaska	96,807	0.2%
48	Montana	82,852	0.2%
49	Wyoming	61,083	0.1%
50	North Dakota	53,556	0.1%
	District of Columbia	146,072	0.3%

Source: U.S. Department of Health and Human Services, Centers for Medicare and Medicaid Services

"2008 Medicaid Managed Care Enrollment Report" (http://www.cms.hhs.gov/MedicaidDataSourcesGenInfo/)

*Unduplicated enrollment as of June 30, 2008. National total includes 1,022,711 Medicaid enrollees in Puerto Rico and the Virgin Islands.

Percent of Population Enrolled in Medicaid in 2008

National Percent = 15.2% of Population*

ALPHA ORDER				RANK ORDER		
RANK	STATE	PERCENT		RANK	STATE	PERCENT
15	Alabama	16.4		1	New Mexico	23.8
27	Alaska	14.1		2	Mississippi	22.8
18	Arizona	16.1		3	Vermont	22.7
5	Arkansas	21.7		4	Louisiana	22.6
9	California	18.1		5	Arkansas	21.7
45	Colorado	8.7		6	New York	21.3
34	Connecticut	12.4		7	Maine	19.6
11	Delaware	17.5		8	Tennessee	19.3
34	Florida	12.4		9	California	18.1
30	Georgia	13.1		10	Massachusetts	17.7
15	Hawaii	16.4		11	Delaware	17.5
36	Idaho	12.3		12	Kentucky	17.1
15	Illinois	16.4		12	West Virginia	17.1
29	Indiana	13.8		14	Rhode Island	16.9
37	Iowa	12.1		15	Alabama	16.4
43	Kansas	10.0		15	Hawaii	16.4
12	Kentucky	17.1		15	Illinois	16.4
4	Louisiana	22.6		18	Arizona	16.1
7	Maine	19.6		18	Wisconsin	16.1
32	Maryland	12.6		20	Oklahoma	16.0
10	Massachusetts	17.7		21	Michigan	15.5
21	Michigan	15.5		21	Ohio	15.5
38	Minnesota	11.8		23	South Carolina	15.3
2	Mississippi	22.8		24	North Carolina	14.6
28	Missouri	14.0		24	Pennsylvania	14.6
46	Montana	8.6		24	Washington	14.6
40	Nebraska	11.4		27	Alaska	14.1
50	Nevada	7.2		28	Missouri	14.0
46	New Hampshire	8.6		29	Indiana	13.8
42	New Jersey	10.6		30	Georgia	13.1
1	New Mexico	23.8		31	South Dakota	12.7
6	New York	21.3		32	Maryland	12.6
24	North Carolina	14.6		33	Texas	12.5
48	North Dakota	8.3		34	Connecticut	12.4
21	Ohio	15.5		34	Florida	12.4
20	Oklahoma	16.0		36	Idaho	12.3
41	Oregon	11.0		37	Iowa	12.1
24	Pennsylvania	14.6		38	Minnesota	11.8
14	Rhode Island	16.9		39	Wyoming	11.5
23	South Carolina	15.3		40	Nebraska	11.4
31	South Dakota	12.7		41	Oregon	11.0
8	Tennessee	19.3		42	New Jersey	10.6
33	Texas	12.5		43	Kansas	10.0
49	Utah	7.6		44	Virginia	9.7
3	Vermont	22.7		45	Colorado	8.7
44	Virginia	9.7		46	Montana	8.6
24	Washington	14.6		46	New Hampshire	8.6
12	West Virginia	17.1		48	North Dakota	8.3
18	Wisconsin	16.1		49	Utah	7.6
39	Wyoming	11.5		50	Nevada	7.2
					District of Columbia	24.8

Source: CQ Press using data from U.S. Department of Health and Human Services, Centers for Medicare and Medicaid Services "2008 Medicaid Managed Care Enrollment Report" (http://www.cms.hhs.gov/MedicaidDataSourcesGenInfo/)
*Unduplicated enrollment as of June 30, 2008. National percent does not include recipients or population in U.S. territories.

Estimated Medicaid Expenditures in 2009

National Total = $335,177,000,000*

RANK	STATE	EXPENDITURES	% of USA
24	Alabama	$4,871,000,000	1.5%
44	Alaska	1,201,000,000	0.4%
13	Arizona	7,972,000,000	2.4%
29	Arkansas	3,766,000,000	1.1%
1	California	39,903,000,000	11.9%
32	Colorado	3,114,000,000	0.9%
25	Connecticut	4,671,000,000	1.4%
46	Delaware	1,077,000,000	0.3%
4	Florida	16,119,000,000	4.8%
14	Georgia	7,615,000,000	2.3%
42	Hawaii	1,331,000,000	0.4%
40	Idaho	1,437,000,000	0.4%
5	Illinois	14,488,000,000	4.3%
22	Indiana	5,595,000,000	1.7%
33	Iowa	3,110,000,000	0.9%
34	Kansas	2,593,000,000	0.8%
23	Kentucky	5,509,000,000	1.6%
18	Louisiana	6,588,000,000	2.0%
36	Maine	2,462,000,000	0.7%
19	Maryland	6,353,000,000	1.9%
11	Massachusetts	8,688,000,000	2.6%
9	Michigan	10,551,000,000	3.1%
17	Minnesota	6,658,000,000	2.0%
27	Mississippi	4,203,000,000	1.3%
12	Missouri	8,619,000,000	2.6%
47	Montana	841,000,000	0.3%
39	Nebraska	1,629,000,000	0.5%
41	Nevada	1,332,000,000	0.4%
43	New Hampshire	1,316,000,000	0.4%
10	New Jersey	9,851,000,000	2.9%
31	New Mexico	3,401,000,000	1.0%
2	New York	32,428,000,000	9.7%
8	North Carolina	10,721,000,000	3.2%
50	North Dakota	549,000,000	0.2%
7	Ohio	14,051,000,000	4.2%
28	Oklahoma	3,968,000,000	1.2%
30	Oregon	3,532,000,000	1.1%
3	Pennsylvania	18,750,000,000	5.6%
37	Rhode Island	1,766,000,000	0.5%
26	South Carolina	4,562,000,000	1.4%
48	South Dakota	776,000,000	0.2%
15	Tennessee	7,389,000,000	2.2%
6	Texas	14,471,000,000	4.3%
38	Utah	1,720,000,000	0.5%
45	Vermont	1,088,000,000	0.3%
21	Virginia	6,079,000,000	1.8%
16	Washington	7,223,000,000	2.2%
35	West Virginia	2,467,000,000	0.7%
20	Wisconsin	6,198,000,000	1.8%
49	Wyoming	575,000,000	0.2%

RANK	STATE	EXPENDITURES	% of USA
1	California	$39,903,000,000	11.9%
2	New York	32,428,000,000	9.7%
3	Pennsylvania	18,750,000,000	5.6%
4	Florida	16,119,000,000	4.8%
5	Illinois	14,488,000,000	4.3%
6	Texas	14,471,000,000	4.3%
7	Ohio	14,051,000,000	4.2%
8	North Carolina	10,721,000,000	3.2%
9	Michigan	10,551,000,000	3.1%
10	New Jersey	9,851,000,000	2.9%
11	Massachusetts	8,688,000,000	2.6%
12	Missouri	8,619,000,000	2.6%
13	Arizona	7,972,000,000	2.4%
14	Georgia	7,615,000,000	2.3%
15	Tennessee	7,389,000,000	2.2%
16	Washington	7,223,000,000	2.2%
17	Minnesota	6,658,000,000	2.0%
18	Louisiana	6,588,000,000	2.0%
19	Maryland	6,353,000,000	1.9%
20	Wisconsin	6,198,000,000	1.8%
21	Virginia	6,079,000,000	1.8%
22	Indiana	5,595,000,000	1.7%
23	Kentucky	5,509,000,000	1.6%
24	Alabama	4,871,000,000	1.5%
25	Connecticut	4,671,000,000	1.4%
26	South Carolina	4,562,000,000	1.4%
27	Mississippi	4,203,000,000	1.3%
28	Oklahoma	3,968,000,000	1.2%
29	Arkansas	3,766,000,000	1.1%
30	Oregon	3,532,000,000	1.1%
31	New Mexico	3,401,000,000	1.0%
32	Colorado	3,114,000,000	0.9%
33	Iowa	3,110,000,000	0.9%
34	Kansas	2,593,000,000	0.8%
35	West Virginia	2,467,000,000	0.7%
36	Maine	2,462,000,000	0.7%
37	Rhode Island	1,766,000,000	0.5%
38	Utah	1,720,000,000	0.5%
39	Nebraska	1,629,000,000	0.5%
40	Idaho	1,437,000,000	0.4%
41	Nevada	1,332,000,000	0.4%
42	Hawaii	1,331,000,000	0.4%
43	New Hampshire	1,316,000,000	0.4%
44	Alaska	1,201,000,000	0.4%
45	Vermont	1,088,000,000	0.3%
46	Delaware	1,077,000,000	0.3%
47	Montana	841,000,000	0.3%
48	South Dakota	776,000,000	0.2%
49	Wyoming	575,000,000	0.2%
50	North Dakota	549,000,000	0.2%

District of Columbia**   NA   NA

Source: National Association of State Budget Officers
"2008 State Expenditure Report" (http://www.nasbo.org)
*Estimates for fiscal year 2009.
**Not available.

Percent Change in Medicaid Expenditures: 2008 to 2009

National Percent Change = 7.8% Increase*

<table>
<tr><td colspan="3">ALPHA ORDER</td><td colspan="3">RANK ORDER</td></tr>
<tr><td>RANK</td><td>STATE</td><td>PERCENT CHANGE</td><td>RANK</td><td>STATE</td><td>PERCENT CHANGE</td></tr>
<tr><td>18</td><td>Alabama</td><td>10.7</td><td>1</td><td>Arizona</td><td>41.2</td></tr>
<tr><td>7</td><td>Alaska</td><td>16.5</td><td>2</td><td>Wisconsin</td><td>27.1</td></tr>
<tr><td>1</td><td>Arizona</td><td>41.2</td><td>3</td><td>Mississippi</td><td>20.3</td></tr>
<tr><td>21</td><td>Arkansas</td><td>9.8</td><td>4</td><td>Missouri</td><td>17.9</td></tr>
<tr><td>42</td><td>California</td><td>4.2</td><td>5</td><td>Maine</td><td>17.7</td></tr>
<tr><td>15</td><td>Colorado</td><td>11.8</td><td>6</td><td>Nevada</td><td>16.9</td></tr>
<tr><td>22</td><td>Connecticut</td><td>9.5</td><td>7</td><td>Alaska</td><td>16.5</td></tr>
<tr><td>25</td><td>Delaware</td><td>8.7</td><td>8</td><td>Washington</td><td>16.1</td></tr>
<tr><td>28</td><td>Florida</td><td>8.0</td><td>9</td><td>Wyoming</td><td>14.1</td></tr>
<tr><td>35</td><td>Georgia</td><td>5.6</td><td>10</td><td>Louisiana</td><td>14.0</td></tr>
<tr><td>31</td><td>Hawaii</td><td>6.9</td><td>10</td><td>Oregon</td><td>14.0</td></tr>
<tr><td>20</td><td>Idaho</td><td>10.5</td><td>12</td><td>Virginia</td><td>13.8</td></tr>
<tr><td>40</td><td>Illinois</td><td>4.8</td><td>13</td><td>Maryland</td><td>13.1</td></tr>
<tr><td>34</td><td>Indiana</td><td>6.5</td><td>14</td><td>Kentucky</td><td>12.3</td></tr>
<tr><td>29</td><td>Iowa</td><td>7.5</td><td>15</td><td>Colorado</td><td>11.8</td></tr>
<tr><td>23</td><td>Kansas</td><td>9.3</td><td>16</td><td>Montana</td><td>11.7</td></tr>
<tr><td>14</td><td>Kentucky</td><td>12.3</td><td>17</td><td>New Mexico</td><td>10.8</td></tr>
<tr><td>10</td><td>Louisiana</td><td>14.0</td><td>18</td><td>Alabama</td><td>10.7</td></tr>
<tr><td>5</td><td>Maine</td><td>17.7</td><td>18</td><td>South Dakota</td><td>10.7</td></tr>
<tr><td>13</td><td>Maryland</td><td>13.1</td><td>20</td><td>Idaho</td><td>10.5</td></tr>
<tr><td>38</td><td>Massachusetts</td><td>5.3</td><td>21</td><td>Arkansas</td><td>9.8</td></tr>
<tr><td>27</td><td>Michigan</td><td>8.2</td><td>22</td><td>Connecticut</td><td>9.5</td></tr>
<tr><td>45</td><td>Minnesota</td><td>3.4</td><td>23</td><td>Kansas</td><td>9.3</td></tr>
<tr><td>3</td><td>Mississippi</td><td>20.3</td><td>24</td><td>West Virginia</td><td>9.1</td></tr>
<tr><td>4</td><td>Missouri</td><td>17.9</td><td>25</td><td>Delaware</td><td>8.7</td></tr>
<tr><td>16</td><td>Montana</td><td>11.7</td><td>26</td><td>Vermont</td><td>8.5</td></tr>
<tr><td>36</td><td>Nebraska</td><td>5.5</td><td>27</td><td>Michigan</td><td>8.2</td></tr>
<tr><td>6</td><td>Nevada</td><td>16.9</td><td>28</td><td>Florida</td><td>8.0</td></tr>
<tr><td>38</td><td>New Hampshire</td><td>5.3</td><td>29</td><td>Iowa</td><td>7.5</td></tr>
<tr><td>44</td><td>New Jersey</td><td>3.6</td><td>29</td><td>Texas</td><td>7.5</td></tr>
<tr><td>17</td><td>New Mexico</td><td>10.8</td><td>31</td><td>Hawaii</td><td>6.9</td></tr>
<tr><td>41</td><td>New York</td><td>4.5</td><td>32</td><td>Ohio</td><td>6.7</td></tr>
<tr><td>49</td><td>North Carolina</td><td>(2.5)</td><td>32</td><td>Oklahoma</td><td>6.7</td></tr>
<tr><td>47</td><td>North Dakota</td><td>1.1</td><td>34</td><td>Indiana</td><td>6.5</td></tr>
<tr><td>32</td><td>Ohio</td><td>6.7</td><td>35</td><td>Georgia</td><td>5.6</td></tr>
<tr><td>32</td><td>Oklahoma</td><td>6.7</td><td>36</td><td>Nebraska</td><td>5.5</td></tr>
<tr><td>10</td><td>Oregon</td><td>14.0</td><td>37</td><td>Pennsylvania</td><td>5.4</td></tr>
<tr><td>37</td><td>Pennsylvania</td><td>5.4</td><td>38</td><td>Massachusetts</td><td>5.3</td></tr>
<tr><td>50</td><td>Rhode Island</td><td>(3.9)</td><td>38</td><td>New Hampshire</td><td>5.3</td></tr>
<tr><td>43</td><td>South Carolina</td><td>4.1</td><td>40</td><td>Illinois</td><td>4.8</td></tr>
<tr><td>18</td><td>South Dakota</td><td>10.7</td><td>41</td><td>New York</td><td>4.5</td></tr>
<tr><td>48</td><td>Tennessee</td><td>(1.4)</td><td>42</td><td>California</td><td>4.2</td></tr>
<tr><td>29</td><td>Texas</td><td>7.5</td><td>43</td><td>South Carolina</td><td>4.1</td></tr>
<tr><td>46</td><td>Utah</td><td>1.5</td><td>44</td><td>New Jersey</td><td>3.6</td></tr>
<tr><td>26</td><td>Vermont</td><td>8.5</td><td>45</td><td>Minnesota</td><td>3.4</td></tr>
<tr><td>12</td><td>Virginia</td><td>13.8</td><td>46</td><td>Utah</td><td>1.5</td></tr>
<tr><td>8</td><td>Washington</td><td>16.1</td><td>47</td><td>North Dakota</td><td>1.1</td></tr>
<tr><td>24</td><td>West Virginia</td><td>9.1</td><td>48</td><td>Tennessee</td><td>(1.4)</td></tr>
<tr><td>2</td><td>Wisconsin</td><td>27.1</td><td>49</td><td>North Carolina</td><td>(2.5)</td></tr>
<tr><td>9</td><td>Wyoming</td><td>14.1</td><td>50</td><td>Rhode Island</td><td>(3.9)</td></tr>
<tr><td></td><td></td><td></td><td colspan="2">District of Columbia**</td><td>NA</td></tr>
</table>

Source: National Association of State Budget Officers
"2008 State Expenditure Report" (http://www.nasbo.org)
*Estimates for fiscal year 2009.
**Not available.

Percent of Population Receiving Public Aid in 2007

National Percent = 3.7% of Population*

ALPHA ORDER

RANK	STATE	PERCENT
8	Alabama	4.5
26	Alaska	2.8
26	Arizona	2.8
13	Arkansas	4.1
1	California	6.7
47	Colorado	1.7
32	Connecticut	2.7
21	Delaware	3.0
26	Florida	2.8
35	Georgia	2.6
22	Hawaii	2.9
47	Idaho	1.7
39	Illinois	2.5
22	Indiana	2.9
22	Iowa	2.9
35	Kansas	2.6
2	Kentucky	5.7
11	Louisiana	4.3
10	Maine	4.4
35	Maryland	2.6
12	Massachusetts	4.2
13	Michigan	4.1
32	Minnesota	2.7
4	Mississippi	5.0
19	Missouri	3.6
39	Montana	2.5
43	Nebraska	2.2
44	Nevada	2.1
46	New Hampshire	1.9
32	New Jersey	2.7
8	New Mexico	4.5
7	New York	4.7
26	North Carolina	2.8
44	North Dakota	2.1
16	Ohio	3.7
22	Oklahoma	2.9
26	Oregon	2.8
16	Pennsylvania	3.7
6	Rhode Island	4.8
20	South Carolina	3.1
41	South Dakota	2.4
5	Tennessee	4.9
26	Texas	2.8
49	Utah	1.4
15	Vermont	3.9
35	Virginia	2.6
16	Washington	3.7
3	West Virginia	5.4
41	Wisconsin	2.4
50	Wyoming	1.2

RANK ORDER

RANK	STATE	PERCENT
1	California	6.7
2	Kentucky	5.7
3	West Virginia	5.4
4	Mississippi	5.0
5	Tennessee	4.9
6	Rhode Island	4.8
7	New York	4.7
8	Alabama	4.5
8	New Mexico	4.5
10	Maine	4.4
11	Louisiana	4.3
12	Massachusetts	4.2
13	Arkansas	4.1
13	Michigan	4.1
15	Vermont	3.9
16	Ohio	3.7
16	Pennsylvania	3.7
16	Washington	3.7
19	Missouri	3.6
20	South Carolina	3.1
21	Delaware	3.0
22	Hawaii	2.9
22	Indiana	2.9
22	Iowa	2.9
22	Oklahoma	2.9
26	Alaska	2.8
26	Arizona	2.8
26	Florida	2.8
26	North Carolina	2.8
26	Oregon	2.8
26	Texas	2.8
32	Connecticut	2.7
32	Minnesota	2.7
32	New Jersey	2.7
35	Georgia	2.6
35	Kansas	2.6
35	Maryland	2.6
35	Virginia	2.6
39	Illinois	2.5
39	Montana	2.5
41	South Dakota	2.4
41	Wisconsin	2.4
43	Nebraska	2.2
44	Nevada	2.1
44	North Dakota	2.1
46	New Hampshire	1.9
47	Colorado	1.7
47	Idaho	1.7
49	Utah	1.4
50	Wyoming	1.2

| | District of Columbia | 5.8 |

Source: CQ Press using data from U.S. Social Security Administration and
U.S. Department of Health and Human Services

*As of December 2007. Includes recipients of Temporary Assistance to Needy Families (TANF) and/or Supplemental Security Income payments.

Recipients of Temporary Assistance to Needy Families (TANF) Payments: 2009

National Total = 4,084,494 Monthly Recipients*

ALPHA ORDER					RANK ORDER			
RANK	STATE	RECIPIENTS	% of USA		RANK	STATE	RECIPIENTS	% of USA
23	Alabama	43,523	1.1%		1	California	1,342,154	32.9%
44	Alaska	8,988	0.2%		2	New York	261,560	6.4%
13	Arizona	81,032	2.0%		3	Ohio	211,550	5.2%
38	Arkansas	19,190	0.5%		4	Michigan	161,354	4.0%
1	California	1,342,154	32.9%		5	Tennessee	152,361	3.7%
31	Colorado	24,075	0.6%		6	Washington	147,590	3.6%
29	Connecticut	32,574	0.8%		7	Pennsylvania	117,823	2.9%
42	Delaware	12,888	0.3%		8	Texas	103,720	2.5%
10	Florida	100,001	2.4%		9	Indiana	101,281	2.5%
26	Georgia	37,575	0.9%		10	Florida	100,001	2.4%
35	Hawaii	21,761	0.5%		11	Massachusetts	93,019	2.3%
49	Idaho	2,406	0.1%		12	Missouri	83,972	2.1%
18	Illinois	52,955	1.3%		13	Arizona	81,032	2.0%
9	Indiana	101,281	2.5%		14	New Jersey	76,021	1.9%
24	Iowa	41,104	1.0%		15	Virginia	75,059	1.8%
28	Kansas	34,740	0.9%		16	Kentucky	59,680	1.5%
16	Kentucky	59,680	1.5%		17	Maryland	54,524	1.3%
34	Louisiana	22,101	0.5%		18	Illinois	52,955	1.3%
30	Maine	24,554	0.6%		19	Oregon	51,895	1.3%
17	Maryland	54,524	1.3%		20	North Carolina	51,201	1.3%
11	Massachusetts	93,019	2.3%		21	Minnesota	48,435	1.2%
4	Michigan	161,354	4.0%		22	New Mexico	44,861	1.1%
21	Minnesota	48,435	1.2%		23	Alabama	43,523	1.1%
32	Mississippi	22,847	0.6%		24	Iowa	41,104	1.0%
12	Missouri	83,972	2.1%		25	Wisconsin	40,821	1.0%
45	Montana	8,782	0.2%		26	Georgia	37,575	0.9%
39	Nebraska	17,202	0.4%		27	South Carolina	37,497	0.9%
33	Nevada	22,267	0.5%		28	Kansas	34,740	0.9%
43	New Hampshire	12,639	0.3%		29	Connecticut	32,574	0.8%
14	New Jersey	76,021	1.9%		30	Maine	24,554	0.6%
22	New Mexico	44,861	1.1%		31	Colorado	24,075	0.6%
2	New York	261,560	6.4%		32	Mississippi	22,847	0.6%
20	North Carolina	51,201	1.3%		33	Nevada	22,267	0.5%
48	North Dakota	5,383	0.1%		34	Louisiana	22,101	0.5%
3	Ohio	211,550	5.2%		35	Hawaii	21,761	0.5%
37	Oklahoma	19,417	0.5%		36	West Virginia	20,379	0.5%
19	Oregon	51,895	1.3%		37	Oklahoma	19,417	0.5%
7	Pennsylvania	117,823	2.9%		38	Arkansas	19,190	0.5%
40	Rhode Island	16,414	0.4%		39	Nebraska	17,202	0.4%
27	South Carolina	37,497	0.9%		40	Rhode Island	16,414	0.4%
47	South Dakota	6,213	0.2%		41	Utah	15,807	0.4%
5	Tennessee	152,361	3.7%		42	Delaware	12,888	0.3%
8	Texas	103,720	2.5%		43	New Hampshire	12,639	0.3%
41	Utah	15,807	0.4%		44	Alaska	8,988	0.2%
46	Vermont	6,390	0.2%		45	Montana	8,782	0.2%
15	Virginia	75,059	1.8%		46	Vermont	6,390	0.2%
6	Washington	147,590	3.6%		47	South Dakota	6,213	0.2%
36	West Virginia	20,379	0.5%		48	North Dakota	5,383	0.1%
25	Wisconsin	40,821	1.0%		49	Idaho	2,406	0.1%
50	Wyoming	638	0.0%		50	Wyoming	638	0.0%
					District of Columbia**		NA	NA

Source: U.S. Department of Health and Human Services, Administration for Children and Families
"TANF Caseload Data" (http://www.acf.hhs.gov/programs/ofa/data-reports/index.htm)
*As of June 2009. Welfare reform replaced the Aid to Families with Dependent Children program (AFDC) with Temporary Assistance to Needy Families (TANF) as of July 1, 1997. National total includes 34,271 recipients in U.S. territories (32,897 in Puerto Rico).
**Not available.

Percent Change in TANF Recipients: 2008 to 2009

National Percent Change = 8.0% Increase*

ALPHA ORDER				RANK ORDER		
RANK	STATE	PERCENT CHANGE		RANK	STATE	PERCENT CHANGE
24	Alabama	10.5		1	Hawaii	73.1
20	Alaska	11.1		2	Delaware	51.8
27	Arizona	9.0		3	New Hampshire	49.1
34	Arkansas	3.2		4	Wyoming	42.7
21	California	11.0		5	Utah	39.4
15	Colorado	17.0		6	New Mexico	28.9
49	Connecticut	(15.7)		7	Maryland	25.5
2	Delaware	51.8		8	Florida	24.8
8	Florida	24.8		9	Washington	23.6
40	Georgia	0.3		10	Nevada	22.5
1	Hawaii	73.1		11	Ohio	22.1
22	Idaho	10.7		12	Montana	19.4
45	Illinois	(5.2)		13	Virginia	18.4
47	Indiana	(10.9)		14	Oklahoma	18.1
30	Iowa	7.9		15	Colorado	17.0
16	Kansas	15.8		16	Kansas	15.8
32	Kentucky	4.0		16	Tennessee	15.8
35	Louisiana	2.5		18	North Carolina	15.3
44	Maine	(3.9)		19	South Carolina	11.2
7	Maryland	25.5		20	Alaska	11.1
33	Massachusetts	3.3		21	California	11.0
42	Michigan	(2.9)		22	Idaho	10.7
37	Minnesota	2.2		22	Oregon	10.7
40	Mississippi	0.3		24	Alabama	10.5
38	Missouri	1.4		25	Wisconsin	9.9
12	Montana	19.4		26	South Dakota	9.3
29	Nebraska	8.3		27	Arizona	9.0
10	Nevada	22.5		27	North Dakota	9.0
3	New Hampshire	49.1		29	Nebraska	8.3
43	New Jersey	(3.8)		30	Iowa	7.9
6	New Mexico	28.9		31	West Virginia	5.3
36	New York	2.3		32	Kentucky	4.0
18	North Carolina	15.3		33	Massachusetts	3.3
27	North Dakota	9.0		34	Arkansas	3.2
11	Ohio	22.1		35	Louisiana	2.5
14	Oklahoma	18.1		36	New York	2.3
22	Oregon	10.7		37	Minnesota	2.2
39	Pennsylvania	1.1		38	Missouri	1.4
48	Rhode Island	(12.5)		39	Pennsylvania	1.1
19	South Carolina	11.2		40	Georgia	0.3
26	South Dakota	9.3		40	Mississippi	0.3
16	Tennessee	15.8		42	Michigan	(2.9)
46	Texas	(8.0)		43	New Jersey	(3.8)
5	Utah	39.4		44	Maine	(3.9)
50	Vermont	(27.4)		45	Illinois	(5.2)
13	Virginia	18.4		46	Texas	(8.0)
9	Washington	23.6		47	Indiana	(10.9)
31	West Virginia	5.3		48	Rhode Island	(12.5)
25	Wisconsin	9.9		49	Connecticut	(15.7)
4	Wyoming	42.7		50	Vermont	(27.4)

District of Columbia**   NA

Source: CQ Press using data from U.S. Department of Health and Human Services, Administration for Children and Families
    "TANF Caseload Data" (http://www.acf.hhs.gov/programs/ofa/data-reports/index.htm)
*June 2008 to June 2009. Welfare reform replaced the Aid to Families with Dependent Children program (AFDC) with Temporary
Assistance to Needy Families (TANF) as of July 1, 1997. National percent includes recipients in U.S. territories.
**Not available.

TANF Work Participation Rates in 2007

National Rate = 29.7%*

ALPHA ORDER				RANK ORDER		
RANK	STATE	PERCENT		RANK	STATE	PERCENT
27	Alabama	34.0		1	Wyoming	65.4
12	Alaska	46.8		2	Florida	64.2
32	Arizona	30.0		3	Mississippi	61.9
25	Arkansas	35.3		4	North Dakota	58.7
44	California	22.3		5	Illinois	55.5
38	Colorado	27.3		6	Georgia	54.2
33	Connecticut	28.8		7	South Dakota	53.5
30	Delaware	32.7		8	South Carolina	53.3
2	Florida	64.2		9	Idaho	53.0
6	Georgia	54.2		10	Utah	49.8
34	Hawaii	28.7		11	Pennsylvania	48.9
9	Idaho	53.0		12	Alaska	46.8
5	Illinois	55.5		13	Maryland	46.7
37	Indiana	27.5		14	Montana	46.4
19	Iowa	40.2		15	Tennessee	45.9
50	Kansas	12.8		16	Virginia	43.5
20	Kentucky	38.2		17	Louisiana	42.2
17	Louisiana	42.2		18	New Hampshire	42.0
45	Maine	21.9		19	Iowa	40.2
13	Maryland	46.7		20	Kentucky	38.2
46	Massachusetts	17.0		21	Oklahoma	38.1
36	Michigan	28.0		22	New York	38.0
35	Minnesota	28.1		23	Wisconsin	36.7
3	Mississippi	61.9		24	New Mexico	36.4
49	Missouri	14.0		25	Arkansas	35.3
14	Montana	46.4		26	Texas	34.6
42	Nebraska	23.0		27	Alabama	34.0
27	Nevada	34.0		27	Nevada	34.0
18	New Hampshire	42.0		29	New Jersey	33.0
29	New Jersey	33.0		30	Delaware	32.7
24	New Mexico	36.4		31	North Carolina	32.4
22	New York	38.0		32	Arizona	30.0
31	North Carolina	32.4		33	Connecticut	28.8
4	North Dakota	58.7		34	Hawaii	28.7
41	Ohio	23.7		35	Minnesota	28.1
21	Oklahoma	38.1		36	Michigan	28.0
48	Oregon	14.7		37	Indiana	27.5
11	Pennsylvania	48.9		38	Colorado	27.3
39	Rhode Island	26.8		39	Rhode Island	26.8
8	South Carolina	53.3		40	Washington	25.4
7	South Dakota	53.5		41	Ohio	23.7
15	Tennessee	45.9		42	Nebraska	23.0
26	Texas	34.6		43	Vermont	22.4
10	Utah	49.8		44	California	22.3
43	Vermont	22.4		45	Maine	21.9
16	Virginia	43.5		46	Massachusetts	17.0
40	Washington	25.4		47	West Virginia	15.4
47	West Virginia	15.4		48	Oregon	14.7
23	Wisconsin	36.7		49	Missouri	14.0
1	Wyoming	65.4		50	Kansas	12.8
					District of Columbia	35.0

Source: U.S. Department of Health and Human Services, Administration for Children and Families
    "Table 1A: TANF Work Participation Rates" (http://www.acf.hhs.gov/programs/ofa/particip/2007/tab1a.htm)
*For fiscal year 2007. Percent of parents in TANF families who work for at least 30 hours per week, or 20 hours per week if they
have children under age six. Welfare reform replaced the Aid to Families with Dependent Children program (AFDC) with
Temporary Assistance to Needy Families (TANF) as of July 1, 1997. National average includes recipients in U.S. territories.

Average Monthly TANF Assistance per Family in 2007

National Average = $376.62*

ALPHA ORDER				RANK ORDER		
RANK	STATE	PER FAMILY		RANK	STATE	PER FAMILY
42	Alabama	$209.23		1	Alaska	$601.33
1	Alaska	601.33		2	Hawaii	543.49
34	Arizona	266.97		3	California	527.66
50	Arkansas	151.28		4	New York	508.73
3	California	527.66		5	Vermont	496.26
31	Colorado	279.55		6	Massachusetts	479.39
10	Connecticut	421.40		7	Utah	474.51
37	Delaware	245.08		8	New Hampshire	467.25
36	Florida	253.95		9	Washington	431.11
45	Georgia	197.01		10	Connecticut	421.40
2	Hawaii	543.49		11	Wisconsin	412.92
28	Idaho	302.67		12	Rhode Island	411.79
38	Illinois	240.16		13	Maryland	411.29
43	Indiana	208.45		14	Oregon	395.62
23	Iowa	322.76		15	Montana	373.24
22	Kansas	324.33		16	Michigan	372.75
35	Kentucky	264.17		17	Maine	357.38
25	Louisiana	316.54		18	South Dakota	352.29
17	Maine	357.38		19	Nevada	344.39
13	Maryland	411.29		20	Minnesota	339.71
6	Massachusetts	479.39		21	Ohio	327.53
16	Michigan	372.75		22	Kansas	324.33
20	Minnesota	339.71		23	Iowa	322.76
46	Mississippi	186.14		24	North Dakota	319.38
39	Missouri	230.44		25	Louisiana	316.54
15	Montana	373.24		26	New Jersey	315.64
30	Nebraska	291.07		27	Pennsylvania	304.17
19	Nevada	344.39		28	Idaho	302.67
8	New Hampshire	467.25		29	New Mexico	292.61
26	New Jersey	315.64		30	Nebraska	291.07
29	New Mexico	292.61		31	Colorado	279.55
4	New York	508.73		32	West Virginia	273.30
40	North Carolina	213.10		33	Virginia	272.61
24	North Dakota	319.38		34	Arizona	266.97
21	Ohio	327.53		35	Kentucky	264.17
47	Oklahoma	182.71		36	Florida	253.95
14	Oregon	395.62		37	Delaware	245.08
27	Pennsylvania	304.17		38	Illinois	240.16
12	Rhode Island	411.79		39	Missouri	230.44
48	South Carolina	178.43		40	North Carolina	213.10
18	South Dakota	352.29		41	Wyoming	211.00
49	Tennessee	166.50		42	Alabama	209.23
44	Texas	200.63		43	Indiana	208.45
7	Utah	474.51		44	Texas	200.63
5	Vermont	496.26		45	Georgia	197.01
33	Virginia	272.61		46	Mississippi	186.14
9	Washington	431.11		47	Oklahoma	182.71
32	West Virginia	273.30		48	South Carolina	178.43
11	Wisconsin	412.92		49	Tennessee	166.50
41	Wyoming	211.00		50	Arkansas	151.28
					District of Columbia	329.80

Source: U.S. Department of Health and Human Services, Administration for Children and Families
"Average Monthly Amount of Assistance" (http://www.acf.hhs.gov/programs/ofa/character/FY2007/tab41.htm)
*For fiscal year 2007.   Welfare reform replaced the Aid to Families with Dependent Children program (AFDC) with Temporary Assistance to Needy Families (TANF) as of July 1, 1997. National average includes families in U.S. territories.

Percent of Households With Food Insecurity: 2008

National Percent = 12.2% of Households*

ALPHA ORDER

RANK	STATE	PERCENT
12	Alabama	13.3
25	Alaska	11.6
14	Arizona	13.2
3	Arkansas	15.9
21	California	12.0
25	Colorado	11.6
35	Connecticut	11.0
44	Delaware	9.4
19	Florida	12.2
4	Georgia	14.2
46	Hawaii	9.1
28	Idaho	11.4
33	Illinois	11.1
30	Indiana	11.2
25	Iowa	11.6
8	Kansas	13.8
17	Kentucky	12.6
35	Louisiana	11.0
9	Maine	13.7
43	Maryland	9.6
49	Massachusetts	8.3
21	Michigan	12.0
39	Minnesota	10.3
1	Mississippi	17.4
6	Missouri	14.0
37	Montana	10.9
38	Nebraska	10.4
18	Nevada	12.4
48	New Hampshire	8.5
39	New Jersey	10.3
5	New Mexico	14.1
29	New York	11.3
9	North Carolina	13.7
50	North Dakota	6.9
12	Ohio	13.3
6	Oklahoma	14.0
15	Oregon	13.1
30	Pennsylvania	11.2
24	Rhode Island	11.7
15	South Carolina	13.1
39	South Dakota	10.3
11	Tennessee	13.5
2	Texas	16.3
30	Utah	11.2
20	Vermont	12.1
47	Virginia	8.6
33	Washington	11.1
21	West Virginia	12.0
42	Wisconsin	10.1
45	Wyoming	9.2

RANK ORDER

RANK	STATE	PERCENT
1	Mississippi	17.4
2	Texas	16.3
3	Arkansas	15.9
4	Georgia	14.2
5	New Mexico	14.1
6	Missouri	14.0
6	Oklahoma	14.0
8	Kansas	13.8
9	Maine	13.7
9	North Carolina	13.7
11	Tennessee	13.5
12	Alabama	13.3
12	Ohio	13.3
14	Arizona	13.2
15	Oregon	13.1
15	South Carolina	13.1
17	Kentucky	12.6
18	Nevada	12.4
19	Florida	12.2
20	Vermont	12.1
21	California	12.0
21	Michigan	12.0
21	West Virginia	12.0
24	Rhode Island	11.7
25	Alaska	11.6
25	Colorado	11.6
25	Iowa	11.6
28	Idaho	11.4
29	New York	11.3
30	Indiana	11.2
30	Pennsylvania	11.2
30	Utah	11.2
33	Illinois	11.1
33	Washington	11.1
35	Connecticut	11.0
35	Louisiana	11.0
37	Montana	10.9
38	Nebraska	10.4
39	Minnesota	10.3
39	New Jersey	10.3
39	South Dakota	10.3
42	Wisconsin	10.1
43	Maryland	9.6
44	Delaware	9.4
45	Wyoming	9.2
46	Hawaii	9.1
47	Virginia	8.6
48	New Hampshire	8.5
49	Massachusetts	8.3
50	North Dakota	6.9
	District of Columbia	12.4

Source: U.S. Department of Agriculture, Economic Research Service
   "Household Food Security in the United States, 2008" (http://www.ers.usda.gov/Publications/ERR66/)
*Three-year average for 2006-2008. Refers to households for which access to enough food is limited by a lack of money and other resources. About one-third of food-insecure households have very low food security, meaning that at times the food intake of some household members is reduced and their normal eating patterns are disrupted.

Supplemental Nutrition Assistance Program Benefits in 2009

National Total = $50,361,309,546*

ALPHA ORDER

RANK	STATE	BENEFITS	% of USA
19	Alabama	$970,949,096	1.9%
44	Alaska	129,624,461	0.3%
12	Arizona	1,223,845,635	2.4%
28	Arkansas	569,987,431	1.1%
2	California	4,383,187,480	8.7%
29	Colorado	502,657,149	1.0%
32	Connecticut	417,158,566	0.8%
45	Delaware	129,098,106	0.3%
4	Florida	2,968,374,682	5.9%
8	Georgia	1,943,839,554	3.9%
38	Hawaii	273,683,509	0.5%
40	Idaho	200,937,001	0.4%
5	Illinois	2,322,771,336	4.6%
15	Indiana	1,071,248,747	2.1%
31	Iowa	419,857,396	0.8%
35	Kansas	301,563,664	0.6%
17	Kentucky	1,002,094,650	2.0%
14	Louisiana	1,119,136,582	2.2%
36	Maine	292,704,585	0.6%
26	Maryland	668,682,585	1.3%
20	Massachusetts	925,603,583	1.8%
7	Michigan	2,106,871,076	4.2%
30	Minnesota	472,798,561	0.9%
24	Mississippi	691,067,947	1.4%
13	Missouri	1,135,612,551	2.3%
43	Montana	134,564,381	0.3%
41	Nebraska	179,068,040	0.4%
37	Nevada	285,773,577	0.6%
46	New Hampshire	115,948,720	0.2%
23	New Jersey	750,159,374	1.5%
33	New Mexico	410,844,850	0.8%
3	New York	3,955,033,246	7.9%
10	North Carolina	1,625,497,467	3.2%
49	North Dakota	79,564,871	0.2%
6	Ohio	2,167,118,474	4.3%
27	Oklahoma	666,446,549	1.3%
22	Oregon	831,409,406	1.7%
9	Pennsylvania	1,900,787,569	3.8%
42	Rhode Island	170,463,595	0.3%
18	South Carolina	1,001,691,847	2.0%
47	South Dakota	111,278,093	0.2%
11	Tennessee	1,603,675,536	3.2%
1	Texas	4,399,125,072	8.7%
39	Utah	263,258,195	0.5%
48	Vermont	99,238,170	0.2%
21	Virginia	922,879,649	1.8%
16	Washington	1,046,740,870	2.1%
34	West Virginia	408,456,434	0.8%
25	Wisconsin	679,818,949	1.3%
50	Wyoming	37,074,837	0.1%

RANK ORDER

RANK	STATE	BENEFITS	% of USA
1	Texas	$4,399,125,072	8.7%
2	California	4,383,187,480	8.7%
3	New York	3,955,033,246	7.9%
4	Florida	2,968,374,682	5.9%
5	Illinois	2,322,771,336	4.6%
6	Ohio	2,167,118,474	4.3%
7	Michigan	2,106,871,076	4.2%
8	Georgia	1,943,839,554	3.9%
9	Pennsylvania	1,900,787,569	3.8%
10	North Carolina	1,625,497,467	3.2%
11	Tennessee	1,603,675,536	3.2%
12	Arizona	1,223,845,635	2.4%
13	Missouri	1,135,612,551	2.3%
14	Louisiana	1,119,136,582	2.2%
15	Indiana	1,071,248,747	2.1%
16	Washington	1,046,740,870	2.1%
17	Kentucky	1,002,094,650	2.0%
18	South Carolina	1,001,691,847	2.0%
19	Alabama	970,949,096	1.9%
20	Massachusetts	925,603,583	1.8%
21	Virginia	922,879,649	1.8%
22	Oregon	831,409,406	1.7%
23	New Jersey	750,159,374	1.5%
24	Mississippi	691,067,947	1.4%
25	Wisconsin	679,818,949	1.3%
26	Maryland	668,682,585	1.3%
27	Oklahoma	666,446,549	1.3%
28	Arkansas	569,987,431	1.1%
29	Colorado	502,657,149	1.0%
30	Minnesota	472,798,561	0.9%
31	Iowa	419,857,396	0.8%
32	Connecticut	417,158,566	0.8%
33	New Mexico	410,844,850	0.8%
34	West Virginia	408,456,434	0.8%
35	Kansas	301,563,664	0.6%
36	Maine	292,704,585	0.6%
37	Nevada	285,773,577	0.6%
38	Hawaii	273,683,509	0.5%
39	Utah	263,258,195	0.5%
40	Idaho	200,937,001	0.4%
41	Nebraska	179,068,040	0.4%
42	Rhode Island	170,463,595	0.3%
43	Montana	134,564,381	0.3%
44	Alaska	129,624,461	0.3%
45	Delaware	129,098,106	0.3%
46	New Hampshire	115,948,720	0.2%
47	South Dakota	111,278,093	0.2%
48	Vermont	99,238,170	0.2%
49	North Dakota	79,564,871	0.2%
50	Wyoming	37,074,837	0.1%
	District of Columbia	159,506,975	0.3%

Source: U.S. Department of Agriculture, Food, Nutrition and Consumer Services
    "Supplemental Nutrition Assistance Program" (http://www.fns.usda.gov/pd/snapmain.htm)
*Preliminary data. National total includes $112,528,867 to U.S. territories. Costs are for benefits only and exclude administrative expenditures. Program formerly called the Food Stamp Program.

Monthly Supplemental Nutrition Assistance Program Recipients in 2009

National Total = 33,722,293 Recipients*

ALPHA ORDER

RANK	STATE	RECIPIENTS	% of USA
19	Alabama	679,138	2.0%
48	Alaska	64,385	0.2%
13	Arizona	813,987	2.4%
28	Arkansas	411,153	1.2%
2	California	2,670,341	7.9%
30	Colorado	319,121	0.9%
34	Connecticut	258,165	0.8%
44	Delaware	90,933	0.3%
4	Florida	1,952,362	5.8%
9	Georgia	1,286,078	3.8%
41	Hawaii	114,599	0.3%
39	Idaho	136,243	0.4%
5	Illinois	1,462,421	4.3%
16	Indiana	706,695	2.1%
32	Iowa	295,106	0.9%
35	Kansas	219,265	0.7%
17	Kentucky	701,757	2.1%
15	Louisiana	723,738	2.1%
36	Maine	201,248	0.6%
27	Maryland	454,196	1.3%
21	Massachusetts	627,611	1.9%
6	Michigan	1,450,272	4.3%
29	Minnesota	344,972	1.0%
24	Mississippi	505,920	1.5%
12	Missouri	1,033,249	3.1%
43	Montana	92,453	0.3%
40	Nebraska	133,623	0.4%
37	Nevada	200,056	0.6%
45	New Hampshire	78,942	0.2%
25	New Jersey	499,853	1.5%
33	New Mexico	291,073	0.9%
3	New York	2,322,742	6.9%
10	North Carolina	1,137,294	3.4%
49	North Dakota	53,070	0.2%
7	Ohio	1,357,412	4.0%
26	Oklahoma	472,908	1.4%
22	Oregon	581,025	1.7%
8	Pennsylvania	1,337,803	4.0%
42	Rhode Island	102,303	0.3%
18	South Carolina	687,508	2.0%
46	South Dakota	73,981	0.2%
11	Tennessee	1,072,055	3.2%
1	Texas	3,003,156	8.9%
38	Utah	185,282	0.5%
47	Vermont	72,125	0.2%
20	Virginia	651,725	1.9%
14	Washington	761,220	2.3%
31	West Virginia	305,960	0.9%
23	Wisconsin	547,878	1.6%
50	Wyoming	26,762	0.1%

RANK ORDER

RANK	STATE	RECIPIENTS	% of USA
1	Texas	3,003,156	8.9%
2	California	2,670,341	7.9%
3	New York	2,322,742	6.9%
4	Florida	1,952,362	5.8%
5	Illinois	1,462,421	4.3%
6	Michigan	1,450,272	4.3%
7	Ohio	1,357,412	4.0%
8	Pennsylvania	1,337,803	4.0%
9	Georgia	1,286,078	3.8%
10	North Carolina	1,137,294	3.4%
11	Tennessee	1,072,055	3.2%
12	Missouri	1,033,249	3.1%
13	Arizona	813,987	2.4%
14	Washington	761,220	2.3%
15	Louisiana	723,738	2.1%
16	Indiana	706,695	2.1%
17	Kentucky	701,757	2.1%
18	South Carolina	687,508	2.0%
19	Alabama	679,138	2.0%
20	Virginia	651,725	1.9%
21	Massachusetts	627,611	1.9%
22	Oregon	581,025	1.7%
23	Wisconsin	547,878	1.6%
24	Mississippi	505,920	1.5%
25	New Jersey	499,853	1.5%
26	Oklahoma	472,908	1.4%
27	Maryland	454,196	1.3%
28	Arkansas	411,153	1.2%
29	Minnesota	344,972	1.0%
30	Colorado	319,121	0.9%
31	West Virginia	305,960	0.9%
32	Iowa	295,106	0.9%
33	New Mexico	291,073	0.9%
34	Connecticut	258,165	0.8%
35	Kansas	219,265	0.7%
36	Maine	201,248	0.6%
37	Nevada	200,056	0.6%
38	Utah	185,282	0.5%
39	Idaho	136,243	0.4%
40	Nebraska	133,623	0.4%
41	Hawaii	114,599	0.3%
42	Rhode Island	102,303	0.3%
43	Montana	92,453	0.3%
44	Delaware	90,933	0.3%
45	New Hampshire	78,942	0.2%
46	South Dakota	73,981	0.2%
47	Vermont	72,125	0.2%
48	Alaska	64,385	0.2%
49	North Dakota	53,070	0.2%
50	Wyoming	26,762	0.1%
	District of Columbia	103,311	0.3%

Source: U.S. Department of Agriculture, Food, Nutrition and Consumer Services
"Supplemental Nutrition Assistance Program" (http://www.fns.usda.gov/pd/snapmain.htm)
*Preliminary for fiscal year 2009. National total includes 47,818 recipients in U.S. territories. Program was formerly called the Food Stamp Program.

Average Monthly Supplemental Nutrition Assistance Program Benefit per Recipient in 2009
National Average = $124.45 per Recipient*

ALPHA ORDER

RANK	STATE	PER RECIPIENT
29	Alabama	$119.14
2	Alaska	167.77
15	Arizona	125.29
40	Arkansas	115.53
5	California	136.79
9	Colorado	131.26
6	Connecticut	134.65
36	Delaware	118.31
11	Florida	126.70
13	Georgia	125.95
1	Hawaii	199.02
19	Idaho	122.90
8	Illinois	132.36
12	Indiana	126.32
33	Iowa	118.56
43	Kansas	114.61
32	Kentucky	119.00
10	Louisiana	128.86
26	Maine	121.20
21	Maryland	122.69
19	Massachusetts	122.90
27	Michigan	121.06
45	Minnesota	114.21
46	Mississippi	113.83
50	Missouri	91.59
25	Montana	121.29
47	Nebraska	111.67
31	Nevada	119.04
22	New Hampshire	122.40
16	New Jersey	125.06
38	New Mexico	117.62
3	New York	141.90
30	North Carolina	119.11
17	North Dakota	124.94
7	Ohio	133.04
39	Oklahoma	117.44
28	Oregon	119.24
34	Pennsylvania	118.40
4	Rhode Island	138.85
24	South Carolina	121.42
14	South Dakota	125.34
18	Tennessee	124.66
23	Texas	122.07
34	Utah	118.40
42	Vermont	114.66
37	Virginia	118.00
44	Washington	114.59
48	West Virginia	111.25
49	Wisconsin	103.40
41	Wyoming	115.45

RANK ORDER

RANK	STATE	PER RECIPIENT
1	Hawaii	$199.02
2	Alaska	167.77
3	New York	141.90
4	Rhode Island	138.85
5	California	136.79
6	Connecticut	134.65
7	Ohio	133.04
8	Illinois	132.36
9	Colorado	131.26
10	Louisiana	128.86
11	Florida	126.70
12	Indiana	126.32
13	Georgia	125.95
14	South Dakota	125.34
15	Arizona	125.29
16	New Jersey	125.06
17	North Dakota	124.94
18	Tennessee	124.66
19	Idaho	122.90
19	Massachusetts	122.90
21	Maryland	122.69
22	New Hampshire	122.40
23	Texas	122.07
24	South Carolina	121.42
25	Montana	121.29
26	Maine	121.20
27	Michigan	121.06
28	Oregon	119.24
29	Alabama	119.14
30	North Carolina	119.11
31	Nevada	119.04
32	Kentucky	119.00
33	Iowa	118.56
34	Pennsylvania	118.40
34	Utah	118.40
36	Delaware	118.31
37	Virginia	118.00
38	New Mexico	117.62
39	Oklahoma	117.44
40	Arkansas	115.53
41	Wyoming	115.45
42	Vermont	114.66
43	Kansas	114.61
44	Washington	114.59
45	Minnesota	114.21
46	Mississippi	113.83
47	Nebraska	111.67
48	West Virginia	111.25
49	Wisconsin	103.40
50	Missouri	91.59

| | District of Columbia | 128.66 |

Source: U.S. Department of Agriculture, Food, Nutrition and Consumer Services
   "Supplemental Nutrition Assistance Program" (http://www.fns.usda.gov/pd/snapmain.htm)
*Preliminary for fiscal year 2009. National average includes recipients in U.S. territories. Program formerly called the Food Stamp Program.

Percent of Population Receiving
Supplemental Nutrition Assistance Program Benefits in 2009
National Percent = 11.0%*

ALPHA ORDER

ALPHA ORDER

RANK	STATE	PERCENT
12	Alabama	14.4
33	Alaska	9.2
16	Arizona	12.3
13	Arkansas	14.2
44	California	7.2
47	Colorado	6.4
43	Connecticut	7.3
27	Delaware	10.3
26	Florida	10.5
14	Georgia	13.1
35	Hawaii	8.8
35	Idaho	8.8
23	Illinois	11.3
24	Indiana	11.0
28	Iowa	9.8
40	Kansas	7.8
5	Kentucky	16.3
6	Louisiana	16.1
7	Maine	15.3
39	Maryland	8.0
31	Massachusetts	9.5
10	Michigan	14.5
46	Minnesota	6.6
2	Mississippi	17.1
1	Missouri	17.3
31	Montana	9.5
42	Nebraska	7.4
41	Nevada	7.6
48	New Hampshire	6.0
49	New Jersey	5.7
10	New Mexico	14.5
19	New York	11.9
17	North Carolina	12.1
38	North Dakota	8.2
20	Ohio	11.8
15	Oklahoma	12.8
8	Oregon	15.2
25	Pennsylvania	10.6
29	Rhode Island	9.7
9	South Carolina	15.1
34	South Dakota	9.1
3	Tennessee	17.0
17	Texas	12.1
45	Utah	6.7
21	Vermont	11.6
37	Virginia	8.3
22	Washington	11.4
4	West Virginia	16.8
29	Wisconsin	9.7
50	Wyoming	4.9

RANK ORDER

RANK	STATE	PERCENT
1	Missouri	17.3
2	Mississippi	17.1
3	Tennessee	17.0
4	West Virginia	16.8
5	Kentucky	16.3
6	Louisiana	16.1
7	Maine	15.3
8	Oregon	15.2
9	South Carolina	15.1
10	Michigan	14.5
10	New Mexico	14.5
12	Alabama	14.4
13	Arkansas	14.2
14	Georgia	13.1
15	Oklahoma	12.8
16	Arizona	12.3
17	North Carolina	12.1
17	Texas	12.1
19	New York	11.9
20	Ohio	11.8
21	Vermont	11.6
22	Washington	11.4
23	Illinois	11.3
24	Indiana	11.0
25	Pennsylvania	10.6
26	Florida	10.5
27	Delaware	10.3
28	Iowa	9.8
29	Rhode Island	9.7
29	Wisconsin	9.7
31	Massachusetts	9.5
31	Montana	9.5
33	Alaska	9.2
34	South Dakota	9.1
35	Hawaii	8.8
35	Idaho	8.8
37	Virginia	8.3
38	North Dakota	8.2
39	Maryland	8.0
40	Kansas	7.8
41	Nevada	7.6
42	Nebraska	7.4
43	Connecticut	7.3
44	California	7.2
45	Utah	6.7
46	Minnesota	6.6
47	Colorado	6.4
48	New Hampshire	6.0
49	New Jersey	5.7
50	Wyoming	4.9

| | District of Columbia | 17.2 |

Source: CQ Press using data from U.S. Department of Agriculture, Food, Nutrition and Consumer Services
   "Supplemental Nutrition Assistance Program" (http://www.fns.usda.gov/pd/snapmain.htm)
*Preliminary data for fiscal year 2009. National rate does not include recipients in U.S. territories. Program formerly called the Food Stamp Program.

Percent of Households Receiving
Supplemental Nutrition Assistance Program Benefits in 2009
National Percent = 13.5% of Households*

ALPHA ORDER

RANK	STATE	PERCENT
12	Alabama	15.5
33	Alaska	10.6
16	Arizona	15.0
12	Arkansas	15.5
41	California	9.2
49	Colorado	7.3
34	Connecticut	10.5
29	Delaware	12.2
18	Florida	14.2
14	Georgia	15.4
26	Hawaii	13.2
40	Idaho	9.6
18	Illinois	14.2
30	Indiana	12.1
31	Iowa	11.2
42	Kansas	9.0
4	Kentucky	18.7
4	Louisiana	18.7
6	Maine	18.4
36	Maryland	10.1
25	Massachusetts	13.6
8	Michigan	18.2
46	Minnesota	7.9
3	Mississippi	19.6
14	Missouri	15.4
32	Montana	10.9
45	Nebraska	8.2
38	Nevada	9.7
48	New Hampshire	7.6
47	New Jersey	7.7
11	New Mexico	16.1
10	New York	17.3
22	North Carolina	14.1
43	North Dakota	8.7
24	Ohio	13.9
18	Oklahoma	14.2
1	Oregon	20.5
27	Pennsylvania	12.9
27	Rhode Island	12.9
9	South Carolina	17.8
38	South Dakota	9.7
2	Tennessee	20.2
23	Texas	14.0
44	Utah	8.6
18	Vermont	14.2
37	Virginia	10.0
17	Washington	14.7
6	West Virginia	18.4
35	Wisconsin	10.4
50	Wyoming	5.4

RANK ORDER

RANK	STATE	PERCENT
1	Oregon	20.5
2	Tennessee	20.2
3	Mississippi	19.6
4	Kentucky	18.7
4	Louisiana	18.7
6	Maine	18.4
6	West Virginia	18.4
8	Michigan	18.2
9	South Carolina	17.8
10	New York	17.3
11	New Mexico	16.1
12	Alabama	15.5
12	Arkansas	15.5
14	Georgia	15.4
14	Missouri	15.4
16	Arizona	15.0
17	Washington	14.7
18	Florida	14.2
18	Illinois	14.2
18	Oklahoma	14.2
18	Vermont	14.2
22	North Carolina	14.1
23	Texas	14.0
24	Ohio	13.9
25	Massachusetts	13.6
26	Hawaii	13.2
27	Pennsylvania	12.9
27	Rhode Island	12.9
29	Delaware	12.2
30	Indiana	12.1
31	Iowa	11.2
32	Montana	10.9
33	Alaska	10.6
34	Connecticut	10.5
35	Wisconsin	10.4
36	Maryland	10.1
37	Virginia	10.0
38	Nevada	9.7
38	South Dakota	9.7
40	Idaho	9.6
41	California	9.2
42	Kansas	9.0
43	North Dakota	8.7
44	Utah	8.6
45	Nebraska	8.2
46	Minnesota	7.9
47	New Jersey	7.7
48	New Hampshire	7.6
49	Colorado	7.3
50	Wyoming	5.4
	District of Columbia	22.6

Source: CQ Press using data from U.S. Department of Agriculture, Food, Nutrition and Consumer Services
"Supplemental Nutrition Assistance Program" (http://www.fns.usda.gov/pd/snapmain.htm)
*Food stamp program households are preliminary data for fiscal year 2009. Percent calculated using 2008 estimated total households. National percent excludes households in U.S. territories. Program formerly called the Food Stamp Program.

Average Monthly Participants in Women, Infants and Children (WIC) Special Nutrition Program in 2009
National Total = 9,121,515 Participants*

RANK	STATE	PARTICIPANTS	% of USA
22	Alabama	140,810	1.5%
42	Alaska	25,813	0.3%
11	Arizona	208,846	2.3%
30	Arkansas	94,107	1.0%
1	California	1,438,941	15.8%
29	Colorado	107,930	1.2%
36	Connecticut	60,149	0.7%
44	Delaware	24,010	0.3%
4	Florida	505,673	5.5%
5	Georgia	499,193	5.5%
40	Hawaii	36,320	0.4%
38	Idaho	46,175	0.5%
6	Illinois	309,870	3.4%
14	Indiana	170,136	1.9%
32	Iowa	75,645	0.8%
31	Kansas	76,989	0.8%
20	Kentucky	141,785	1.6%
18	Louisiana	148,747	1.6%
41	Maine	26,662	0.3%
19	Maryland	146,411	1.6%
25	Massachusetts	128,139	1.4%
10	Michigan	243,275	2.7%
21	Minnesota	141,592	1.6%
28	Mississippi	111,478	1.2%
17	Missouri	150,256	1.6%
46	Montana	20,673	0.2%
39	Nebraska	45,585	0.5%
35	Nevada	67,829	0.7%
47	New Hampshire	18,362	0.2%
15	New Jersey	169,078	1.9%
34	New Mexico	70,157	0.8%
3	New York	518,961	5.7%
8	North Carolina	274,625	3.0%
49	North Dakota	14,578	0.2%
7	Ohio	303,651	3.3%
24	Oklahoma	130,064	1.4%
27	Oregon	113,248	1.2%
9	Pennsylvania	260,880	2.9%
43	Rhode Island	25,676	0.3%
23	South Carolina	134,753	1.5%
45	South Dakota	22,963	0.3%
13	Tennessee	174,832	1.9%
2	Texas	992,454	10.9%
33	Utah	72,539	0.8%
48	Vermont	17,496	0.2%
16	Virginia	160,150	1.8%
12	Washington	193,352	2.1%
37	West Virginia	53,060	0.6%
26	Wisconsin	127,891	1.4%
50	Wyoming	13,338	0.1%

RANK	STATE	PARTICIPANTS	% of USA
1	California	1,438,941	15.8%
2	Texas	992,454	10.9%
3	New York	518,961	5.7%
4	Florida	505,673	5.5%
5	Georgia	499,193	5.5%
6	Illinois	309,870	3.4%
7	Ohio	303,651	3.3%
8	North Carolina	274,625	3.0%
9	Pennsylvania	260,880	2.9%
10	Michigan	243,275	2.7%
11	Arizona	208,846	2.3%
12	Washington	193,352	2.1%
13	Tennessee	174,832	1.9%
14	Indiana	170,136	1.9%
15	New Jersey	169,078	1.9%
16	Virginia	160,150	1.8%
17	Missouri	150,256	1.6%
18	Louisiana	148,747	1.6%
19	Maryland	146,411	1.6%
20	Kentucky	141,785	1.6%
21	Minnesota	141,592	1.6%
22	Alabama	140,810	1.5%
23	South Carolina	134,753	1.5%
24	Oklahoma	130,064	1.4%
25	Massachusetts	128,139	1.4%
26	Wisconsin	127,891	1.4%
27	Oregon	113,248	1.2%
28	Mississippi	111,478	1.2%
29	Colorado	107,930	1.2%
30	Arkansas	94,107	1.0%
31	Kansas	76,989	0.8%
32	Iowa	75,645	0.8%
33	Utah	72,539	0.8%
34	New Mexico	70,157	0.8%
35	Nevada	67,829	0.7%
36	Connecticut	60,149	0.7%
37	West Virginia	53,060	0.6%
38	Idaho	46,175	0.5%
39	Nebraska	45,585	0.5%
40	Hawaii	36,320	0.4%
41	Maine	26,662	0.3%
42	Alaska	25,813	0.3%
43	Rhode Island	25,676	0.3%
44	Delaware	24,010	0.3%
45	South Dakota	22,963	0.3%
46	Montana	20,673	0.2%
47	New Hampshire	18,362	0.2%
48	Vermont	17,496	0.2%
49	North Dakota	14,578	0.2%
50	Wyoming	13,338	0.1%
	District of Columbia	17,473	0.2%

Source: U.S. Department of Agriculture, Food, Nutrition and Consumer Services "WIC Program (http://www.fns.usda.gov/pd/wicmain.htm)
*Preliminary data for fiscal year 2009. National total includes 224,737 participants in outlying areas not shown separately (Puerto Rico has 200,303 participants).

Average Monthly Benefit per Participant in Women, Infant and Children (WIC) Special Nutrition Program in 2009
National Average = $42.48*

ALPHA ORDER

RANK	STATE	AVERAGE BENEFIT
11	Alabama	$45.02
3	Alaska	53.50
23	Arizona	41.91
22	Arkansas	42.45
14	California	43.79
42	Colorado	35.61
6	Connecticut	49.05
36	Delaware	37.55
12	Florida	44.88
7	Georgia	48.13
2	Hawaii	54.18
39	Idaho	36.78
9	Illinois	45.65
32	Indiana	38.84
34	Iowa	38.03
44	Kansas	35.10
20	Kentucky	42.70
4	Louisiana	52.09
27	Maine	39.88
24	Maryland	41.34
26	Massachusetts	40.72
27	Michigan	39.88
25	Minnesota	40.97
1	Mississippi	54.93
49	Missouri	31.21
41	Montana	36.07
33	Nebraska	38.64
45	Nevada	33.21
31	New Hampshire	39.54
8	New Jersey	46.24
35	New Mexico	37.72
5	New York	50.07
21	North Carolina	42.47
13	North Dakota	44.75
40	Ohio	36.61
29	Oklahoma	39.78
38	Oregon	36.99
19	Pennsylvania	42.73
17	Rhode Island	43.21
15	South Carolina	43.70
43	South Dakota	35.55
37	Tennessee	37.35
48	Texas	31.47
47	Utah	32.26
10	Vermont	45.36
46	Virginia	32.67
16	Washington	43.22
18	West Virginia	42.92
30	Wisconsin	39.56
50	Wyoming	29.66

RANK ORDER

RANK	STATE	AVERAGE BENEFIT
1	Mississippi	$54.93
2	Hawaii	54.18
3	Alaska	53.50
4	Louisiana	52.09
5	New York	50.07
6	Connecticut	49.05
7	Georgia	48.13
8	New Jersey	46.24
9	Illinois	45.65
10	Vermont	45.36
11	Alabama	45.02
12	Florida	44.88
13	North Dakota	44.75
14	California	43.79
15	South Carolina	43.70
16	Washington	43.22
17	Rhode Island	43.21
18	West Virginia	42.92
19	Pennsylvania	42.73
20	Kentucky	42.70
21	North Carolina	42.47
22	Arkansas	42.45
23	Arizona	41.91
24	Maryland	41.34
25	Minnesota	40.97
26	Massachusetts	40.72
27	Maine	39.88
27	Michigan	39.88
29	Oklahoma	39.78
30	Wisconsin	39.56
31	New Hampshire	39.54
32	Indiana	38.84
33	Nebraska	38.64
34	Iowa	38.03
35	New Mexico	37.72
36	Delaware	37.55
37	Tennessee	37.35
38	Oregon	36.99
39	Idaho	36.78
40	Ohio	36.61
41	Montana	36.07
42	Colorado	35.61
43	South Dakota	35.55
44	Kansas	35.10
45	Nevada	33.21
46	Virginia	32.67
47	Utah	32.26
48	Texas	31.47
49	Missouri	31.21
50	Wyoming	29.66
	District of Columbia	44.25

Source: U.S. Department of Agriculture, Food, Nutrition and Consumer Services
"WIC Program (http://www.fns.usda.gov/pd/wicmain.htm)
*Preliminary data for fiscal year 2009. National average includes outlying areas and Indian reservations not shown separately.

Percent of Public Elementary and Secondary School Students Eligible for Free or Reduced-Price Meals in 2008
National Percent = 42.3%*

ALPHA ORDER

RANK	STATE	PERCENT
10	Alabama	50.7
33	Alaska	33.6
23	Arizona	37.9
4	Arkansas	56.2
7	California	51.1
32	Colorado	34.4
44	Connecticut	29.7
30	Delaware	36.0
14	Florida	45.6
9	Georgia	51.0
24	Hawaii	37.7
28	Idaho	37.2
21	Illinois	38.4
20	Indiana	39.2
34	Iowa	33.5
17	Kansas	39.9
7	Kentucky	51.1
2	Louisiana	63.2
29	Maine	36.1
35	Maryland	33.4
45	Massachusetts	29.5
24	Michigan	37.7
37	Minnesota	31.6
1	Mississippi	66.9
18	Missouri	39.5
31	Montana	35.7
26	Nebraska	37.4
19	Nevada	39.4
49	New Hampshire	18.1
47	New Jersey	28.1
3	New Mexico	60.8
15	New York	44.1
39	North Carolina	31.3
41	North Dakota	31.2
NA	Ohio**	NA
5	Oklahoma	55.2
16	Oregon	42.2
39	Pennsylvania	31.3
22	Rhode Island	38.0
6	South Carolina	51.5
46	South Dakota	28.5
11	Tennessee	49.3
13	Texas	47.7
43	Utah	29.9
47	Vermont	28.1
38	Virginia	31.4
27	Washington	37.3
12	West Virginia	49.2
36	Wisconsin	32.1
42	Wyoming	30.0

RANK ORDER

RANK	STATE	PERCENT
1	Mississippi	66.9
2	Louisiana	63.2
3	New Mexico	60.8
4	Arkansas	56.2
5	Oklahoma	55.2
6	South Carolina	51.5
7	California	51.1
7	Kentucky	51.1
9	Georgia	51.0
10	Alabama	50.7
11	Tennessee	49.3
12	West Virginia	49.2
13	Texas	47.7
14	Florida	45.6
15	New York	44.1
16	Oregon	42.2
17	Kansas	39.9
18	Missouri	39.5
19	Nevada	39.4
20	Indiana	39.2
21	Illinois	38.4
22	Rhode Island	38.0
23	Arizona	37.9
24	Hawaii	37.7
24	Michigan	37.7
26	Nebraska	37.4
27	Washington	37.3
28	Idaho	37.2
29	Maine	36.1
30	Delaware	36.0
31	Montana	35.7
32	Colorado	34.4
33	Alaska	33.6
34	Iowa	33.5
35	Maryland	33.4
36	Wisconsin	32.1
37	Minnesota	31.6
38	Virginia	31.4
39	North Carolina	31.3
39	Pennsylvania	31.3
41	North Dakota	31.2
42	Wyoming	30.0
43	Utah	29.9
44	Connecticut	29.7
45	Massachusetts	29.5
46	South Dakota	28.5
47	New Jersey	28.1
47	Vermont	28.1
49	New Hampshire	18.1
NA	Ohio**	NA
	District of Columbia	49.0

Source: CQ Press using data from U.S. Department of Education, National Center for Education Statistics
"Common Core of Data (CCD) Database" (http://nces.ed.gov/ccd/)
*Preliminary data for school year 2007-2008.
**Not available.

Child Support Collections in 2008

National Total = $26,220,681,928*

ALPHA ORDER

RANK	STATE	COLLECTIONS	% of USA
27	Alabama	$280,243,467	1.1%
40	Alaska	100,306,773	0.4%
25	Arizona	325,000,291	1.2%
32	Arkansas	197,538,510	0.8%
2	California	2,252,672,234	8.6%
26	Colorado	284,235,054	1.1%
28	Connecticut	262,954,575	1.0%
45	Delaware	74,167,622	0.3%
7	Florida	1,260,905,917	4.8%
16	Georgia	584,770,906	2.2%
41	Hawaii	99,363,991	0.4%
38	Idaho	141,131,617	0.5%
9	Illinois	769,531,768	2.9%
14	Indiana	595,184,963	2.3%
23	Iowa	336,575,027	1.3%
35	Kansas	181,804,296	0.7%
21	Kentucky	404,394,289	1.5%
24	Louisiana	331,300,847	1.3%
39	Maine	108,443,420	0.4%
20	Maryland	499,353,374	1.9%
18	Massachusetts	538,629,838	2.1%
6	Michigan	1,455,720,695	5.6%
13	Minnesota	614,573,014	2.3%
31	Mississippi	245,318,189	0.9%
17	Missouri	556,881,715	2.1%
49	Montana	56,954,973	0.2%
34	Nebraska	185,557,212	0.7%
37	Nevada	150,346,789	0.6%
43	New Hampshire	86,864,481	0.3%
8	New Jersey	1,060,194,751	4.0%
42	New Mexico	88,235,505	0.3%
4	New York	1,580,997,452	6.0%
11	North Carolina	663,167,601	2.5%
44	North Dakota	77,782,032	0.3%
3	Ohio	1,778,146,946	6.8%
29	Oklahoma	262,752,574	1.0%
22	Oregon	343,622,507	1.3%
5	Pennsylvania	1,480,151,351	5.6%
48	Rhode Island	60,919,775	0.2%
30	South Carolina	249,830,407	1.0%
46	South Dakota	74,123,877	0.3%
19	Tennessee	534,929,835	2.0%
1	Texas	2,558,700,378	9.8%
36	Utah	170,036,186	0.6%
50	Vermont	49,064,167	0.2%
15	Virginia	593,317,150	2.3%
10	Washington	674,403,645	2.6%
33	West Virginia	190,372,242	0.7%
12	Wisconsin	633,465,202	2.4%
47	Wyoming	62,367,134	0.2%

RANK ORDER

RANK	STATE	COLLECTIONS	% of USA
1	Texas	$2,558,700,378	9.8%
2	California	2,252,672,234	8.6%
3	Ohio	1,778,146,946	6.8%
4	New York	1,580,997,452	6.0%
5	Pennsylvania	1,480,151,351	5.6%
6	Michigan	1,455,720,695	5.6%
7	Florida	1,260,905,917	4.8%
8	New Jersey	1,060,194,751	4.0%
9	Illinois	769,531,768	2.9%
10	Washington	674,403,645	2.6%
11	North Carolina	663,167,601	2.5%
12	Wisconsin	633,465,202	2.4%
13	Minnesota	614,573,014	2.3%
14	Indiana	595,184,963	2.3%
15	Virginia	593,317,150	2.3%
16	Georgia	584,770,906	2.2%
17	Missouri	556,881,715	2.1%
18	Massachusetts	538,629,838	2.1%
19	Tennessee	534,929,835	2.0%
20	Maryland	499,353,374	1.9%
21	Kentucky	404,394,289	1.5%
22	Oregon	343,622,507	1.3%
23	Iowa	336,575,027	1.3%
24	Louisiana	331,300,847	1.3%
25	Arizona	325,000,291	1.2%
26	Colorado	284,235,054	1.1%
27	Alabama	280,243,467	1.1%
28	Connecticut	262,954,575	1.0%
29	Oklahoma	262,752,574	1.0%
30	South Carolina	249,830,407	1.0%
31	Mississippi	245,318,189	0.9%
32	Arkansas	197,538,510	0.8%
33	West Virginia	190,372,242	0.7%
34	Nebraska	185,557,212	0.7%
35	Kansas	181,804,296	0.7%
36	Utah	170,036,186	0.6%
37	Nevada	150,346,789	0.6%
38	Idaho	141,131,617	0.5%
39	Maine	108,443,420	0.4%
40	Alaska	100,306,773	0.4%
41	Hawaii	99,363,991	0.4%
42	New Mexico	88,235,505	0.3%
43	New Hampshire	86,864,481	0.3%
44	North Dakota	77,782,032	0.3%
45	Delaware	74,167,622	0.3%
46	South Dakota	74,123,877	0.3%
47	Wyoming	62,367,134	0.2%
48	Rhode Island	60,919,775	0.2%
49	Montana	56,954,973	0.2%
50	Vermont	49,064,167	0.2%
	District of Columbia	53,375,364	0.2%

Source: U.S. Department of Health and Human Services, Office of Child Support Enforcement
   "Child Support Enforcement Preliminary Data Report"
      (http://www.acf.hhs.gov/programs/cse/pubs/2009/preliminary_report_fy2008/)
*Fiscal year 2008. Total does not include $340,023,930 collected in U.S. territories.

XV. Transportation

Federal Highway Funding in 2009

National Total = $34,935,423,673*

ALPHA ORDER

RANK	STATE	FUNDS	% of USA
17	Alabama	$712,205,347	2.0%
37	Alaska	317,716,165	0.9%
16	Arizona	717,412,788	2.1%
29	Arkansas	441,748,761	1.3%
1	California	3,151,348,631	9.0%
27	Colorado	478,835,028	1.4%
28	Connecticut	460,155,029	1.3%
50	Delaware	138,995,962	0.4%
3	Florida	1,823,863,204	5.2%
6	Georgia	1,291,523,940	3.7%
48	Hawaii	146,376,665	0.4%
38	Idaho	264,363,453	0.8%
8	Illinois	1,188,411,298	3.4%
13	Indiana	924,749,746	2.6%
31	Iowa	399,296,237	1.1%
34	Kansas	352,290,620	1.0%
19	Kentucky	610,934,486	1.7%
26	Louisiana	536,890,674	1.5%
47	Maine	153,561,194	0.4%
23	Maryland	557,904,835	1.6%
22	Massachusetts	564,012,384	1.6%
9	Michigan	1,029,681,124	2.9%
24	Minnesota	546,241,868	1.6%
30	Mississippi	413,999,871	1.2%
14	Missouri	820,360,198	2.3%
35	Montana	341,548,074	1.0%
39	Nebraska	260,920,674	0.7%
40	Nevada	259,404,712	0.7%
46	New Hampshire	155,533,612	0.4%
12	New Jersey	926,756,832	2.7%
36	New Mexico	320,136,596	0.9%
4	New York	1,566,731,272	4.5%
10	North Carolina	1,005,184,153	2.9%
44	North Dakota	221,247,115	0.6%
7	Ohio	1,264,253,586	3.6%
25	Oklahoma	541,099,492	1.5%
32	Oregon	384,311,048	1.1%
5	Pennsylvania	1,561,543,705	4.5%
45	Rhode Island	172,384,360	0.5%
21	South Carolina	582,553,840	1.7%
42	South Dakota	233,274,850	0.7%
15	Tennessee	773,778,648	2.2%
2	Texas	2,958,430,854	8.5%
41	Utah	257,031,147	0.7%
49	Vermont	145,684,998	0.4%
11	Virginia	933,046,675	2.7%
20	Washington	582,783,226	1.7%
33	West Virginia	378,803,437	1.1%
18	Wisconsin	695,561,201	2.0%
43	Wyoming	230,887,178	0.7%

RANK ORDER

RANK	STATE	FUNDS	% of USA
1	California	$3,151,348,631	9.0%
2	Texas	2,958,430,854	8.5%
3	Florida	1,823,863,204	5.2%
4	New York	1,566,731,272	4.5%
5	Pennsylvania	1,561,543,705	4.5%
6	Georgia	1,291,523,940	3.7%
7	Ohio	1,264,253,586	3.6%
8	Illinois	1,188,411,298	3.4%
9	Michigan	1,029,681,124	2.9%
10	North Carolina	1,005,184,153	2.9%
11	Virginia	933,046,675	2.7%
12	New Jersey	926,756,832	2.7%
13	Indiana	924,749,746	2.6%
14	Missouri	820,360,198	2.3%
15	Tennessee	773,778,648	2.2%
16	Arizona	717,412,788	2.1%
17	Alabama	712,205,347	2.0%
18	Wisconsin	695,561,201	2.0%
19	Kentucky	610,934,486	1.7%
20	Washington	582,783,226	1.7%
21	South Carolina	582,553,840	1.7%
22	Massachusetts	564,012,384	1.6%
23	Maryland	557,904,835	1.6%
24	Minnesota	546,241,868	1.6%
25	Oklahoma	541,099,492	1.5%
26	Louisiana	536,890,674	1.5%
27	Colorado	478,835,028	1.4%
28	Connecticut	460,155,029	1.3%
29	Arkansas	441,748,761	1.3%
30	Mississippi	413,999,871	1.2%
31	Iowa	399,296,237	1.1%
32	Oregon	384,311,048	1.1%
33	West Virginia	378,803,437	1.1%
34	Kansas	352,290,620	1.0%
35	Montana	341,548,074	1.0%
36	New Mexico	320,136,596	0.9%
37	Alaska	317,716,165	0.9%
38	Idaho	264,363,453	0.8%
39	Nebraska	260,920,674	0.7%
40	Nevada	259,404,712	0.7%
41	Utah	257,031,147	0.7%
42	South Dakota	233,274,850	0.7%
43	Wyoming	230,887,178	0.7%
44	North Dakota	221,247,115	0.6%
45	Rhode Island	172,384,360	0.5%
46	New Hampshire	155,533,612	0.4%
47	Maine	153,561,194	0.4%
48	Hawaii	146,376,665	0.4%
49	Vermont	145,684,998	0.4%
50	Delaware	138,995,962	0.4%
	District of Columbia	139,652,880	0.4%

Source: U.S. Department of Transportation, Federal Highway Administration
"FHWA Apportionment" (http://www.fhwa.dot.gov/legsregs/directives/notices/n4510682.htm)
*Fiscal Year 2009 apportionments after penalty and after programmatic distribution.

Per Capita Federal Highway Funding in 2009

National Per Capita = $114*

ALPHA ORDER

RANK	STATE	PER CAPITA
13	Alabama	$151
1	Alaska	455
35	Arizona	109
12	Arkansas	153
49	California	85
44	Colorado	95
21	Connecticut	131
11	Delaware	157
41	Florida	98
21	Georgia	131
33	Hawaii	113
8	Idaho	171
45	Illinois	92
16	Indiana	144
20	Iowa	133
24	Kansas	125
17	Kentucky	142
28	Louisiana	120
32	Maine	116
41	Maryland	98
48	Massachusetts	86
39	Michigan	103
38	Minnesota	104
18	Mississippi	140
19	Missouri	137
3	Montana	350
15	Nebraska	145
41	Nevada	98
31	New Hampshire	117
37	New Jersey	106
10	New Mexico	159
50	New York	80
36	North Carolina	107
4	North Dakota	342
34	Ohio	110
14	Oklahoma	147
40	Oregon	100
25	Pennsylvania	124
9	Rhode Island	164
23	South Carolina	128
5	South Dakota	287
26	Tennessee	123
29	Texas	119
45	Utah	92
6	Vermont	234
30	Virginia	118
47	Washington	87
7	West Virginia	208
26	Wisconsin	123
2	Wyoming	424

RANK ORDER

RANK	STATE	PER CAPITA
1	Alaska	$455
2	Wyoming	424
3	Montana	350
4	North Dakota	342
5	South Dakota	287
6	Vermont	234
7	West Virginia	208
8	Idaho	171
9	Rhode Island	164
10	New Mexico	159
11	Delaware	157
12	Arkansas	153
13	Alabama	151
14	Oklahoma	147
15	Nebraska	145
16	Indiana	144
17	Kentucky	142
18	Mississippi	140
19	Missouri	137
20	Iowa	133
21	Connecticut	131
21	Georgia	131
23	South Carolina	128
24	Kansas	125
25	Pennsylvania	124
26	Tennessee	123
26	Wisconsin	123
28	Louisiana	120
29	Texas	119
30	Virginia	118
31	New Hampshire	117
32	Maine	116
33	Hawaii	113
34	Ohio	110
35	Arizona	109
36	North Carolina	107
37	New Jersey	106
38	Minnesota	104
39	Michigan	103
40	Oregon	100
41	Florida	98
41	Maryland	98
41	Nevada	98
44	Colorado	95
45	Illinois	92
45	Utah	92
47	Washington	87
48	Massachusetts	86
49	California	85
50	New York	80

District of Columbia   233

Source: CQ Press using data from U.S. Department of Transportation, Federal Highway Administration
"FHWA Apportionment" (http://www.fhwa.dot.gov/legsregs/directives/notices/n4510682.htm)
*Fiscal Year 2009 apportionments after penalty and after programmatic distribution. Calculated with 2009 population estimates.

Public Road and Street Mileage in 2008

National Total = 4,042,768 Miles*

ALPHA ORDER

RANK	STATE	MILES	% of USA
18	Alabama	97,325	2.4%
46	Alaska	15,328	0.4%
33	Arizona	60,439	1.5%
17	Arkansas	99,812	2.5%
2	California	172,512	4.3%
22	Colorado	88,266	2.2%
44	Connecticut	21,365	0.5%
49	Delaware	6,281	0.2%
11	Florida	121,386	3.0%
8	Georgia	121,875	3.0%
50	Hawaii	4,362	0.1%
35	Idaho	47,788	1.2%
4	Illinois	139,492	3.5%
19	Indiana	95,613	2.4%
14	Iowa	114,226	2.8%
3	Kansas	140,609	3.5%
26	Kentucky	78,749	1.9%
32	Louisiana	61,093	1.5%
43	Maine	22,829	0.6%
41	Maryland	31,385	0.8%
39	Massachusetts	36,104	0.9%
10	Michigan	121,666	3.0%
5	Minnesota	138,239	3.4%
27	Mississippi	74,886	1.9%
6	Missouri	129,717	3.2%
28	Montana	74,171	1.8%
20	Nebraska	93,615	2.3%
40	Nevada	33,907	0.8%
45	New Hampshire	16,006	0.4%
37	New Jersey	38,753	1.0%
30	New Mexico	68,384	1.7%
13	New York	114,473	2.8%
16	North Carolina	105,103	2.6%
23	North Dakota	86,842	2.1%
7	Ohio	122,973	3.0%
15	Oklahoma	113,325	2.8%
34	Oregon	59,250	1.5%
9	Pennsylvania	121,772	3.0%
48	Rhode Island	6,404	0.2%
31	South Carolina	66,254	1.6%
25	South Dakota	82,149	2.0%
21	Tennessee	92,173	2.3%
1	Texas	306,404	7.6%
36	Utah	44,705	1.1%
47	Vermont	14,423	0.4%
29	Virginia	73,903	1.8%
24	Washington	83,527	2.1%
38	West Virginia	38,452	1.0%
12	Wisconsin	114,843	2.8%
42	Wyoming	28,105	0.7%

RANK ORDER

RANK	STATE	MILES	% of USA
1	Texas	306,404	7.6%
2	California	172,512	4.3%
3	Kansas	140,609	3.5%
4	Illinois	139,492	3.5%
5	Minnesota	138,239	3.4%
6	Missouri	129,717	3.2%
7	Ohio	122,973	3.0%
8	Georgia	121,875	3.0%
9	Pennsylvania	121,772	3.0%
10	Michigan	121,666	3.0%
11	Florida	121,386	3.0%
12	Wisconsin	114,843	2.8%
13	New York	114,473	2.8%
14	Iowa	114,226	2.8%
15	Oklahoma	113,325	2.8%
16	North Carolina	105,103	2.6%
17	Arkansas	99,812	2.5%
18	Alabama	97,325	2.4%
19	Indiana	95,613	2.4%
20	Nebraska	93,615	2.3%
21	Tennessee	92,173	2.3%
22	Colorado	88,266	2.2%
23	North Dakota	86,842	2.1%
24	Washington	83,527	2.1%
25	South Dakota	82,149	2.0%
26	Kentucky	78,749	1.9%
27	Mississippi	74,886	1.9%
28	Montana	74,171	1.8%
29	Virginia	73,903	1.8%
30	New Mexico	68,384	1.7%
31	South Carolina	66,254	1.6%
32	Louisiana	61,093	1.5%
33	Arizona	60,439	1.5%
34	Oregon	59,250	1.5%
35	Idaho	47,788	1.2%
36	Utah	44,705	1.1%
37	New Jersey	38,753	1.0%
38	West Virginia	38,452	1.0%
39	Massachusetts	36,104	0.9%
40	Nevada	33,907	0.8%
41	Maryland	31,385	0.8%
42	Wyoming	28,105	0.7%
43	Maine	22,829	0.6%
44	Connecticut	21,365	0.5%
45	New Hampshire	16,006	0.4%
46	Alaska	15,328	0.4%
47	Vermont	14,423	0.4%
48	Rhode Island	6,404	0.2%
49	Delaware	6,281	0.2%
50	Hawaii	4,362	0.1%
	District of Columbia	1,505	0.0%

Source: U.S. Department of Transportation, Federal Highway Administration
"Highway Statistics 2008" (Table HM-10, http://www.fhwa.dot.gov/policyinformation/statistics/2008/index.cfm)
*Does not include 16,572 miles of roads and streets in Puerto Rico.

Percent of Public Road and Street Mileage Federally Funded in 2008

National Percent = 24.5% of Public Road and Street Mileage*

ALPHA ORDER

RANK	STATE	PERCENT
23	Alabama	24.7
10	Alaska	28.6
39	Arizona	21.5
38	Arkansas	21.8
2	California	32.0
44	Colorado	19.8
8	Connecticut	28.8
25	Delaware	24.4
40	Florida	21.4
19	Georgia	25.3
1	Hawaii	35.9
32	Idaho	23.5
20	Illinois	25.2
29	Indiana	23.6
35	Iowa	22.7
22	Kansas	24.8
49	Kentucky	17.6
37	Louisiana	21.9
13	Maine	27.7
21	Maryland	25.0
4	Massachusetts	30.8
6	Michigan	29.9
28	Minnesota	23.8
9	Mississippi	28.7
29	Missouri	23.6
45	Montana	19.7
36	Nebraska	22.0
48	Nevada	19.0
41	New Hampshire	21.3
18	New Jersey	26.6
50	New Mexico	16.8
27	New York	24.0
43	North Carolina	20.9
42	North Dakota	21.1
29	Ohio	23.6
12	Oklahoma	27.9
5	Oregon	30.5
34	Pennsylvania	23.1
14	Rhode Island	27.4
3	South Carolina	31.7
26	South Dakota	24.1
47	Tennessee	19.2
15	Texas	27.2
46	Utah	19.5
17	Vermont	26.8
7	Virginia	28.9
33	Washington	23.3
16	West Virginia	27.1
24	Wisconsin	24.6
11	Wyoming	28.1

RANK ORDER

RANK	STATE	PERCENT
1	Hawaii	35.9
2	California	32.0
3	South Carolina	31.7
4	Massachusetts	30.8
5	Oregon	30.5
6	Michigan	29.9
7	Virginia	28.9
8	Connecticut	28.8
9	Mississippi	28.7
10	Alaska	28.6
11	Wyoming	28.1
12	Oklahoma	27.9
13	Maine	27.7
14	Rhode Island	27.4
15	Texas	27.2
16	West Virginia	27.1
17	Vermont	26.8
18	New Jersey	26.6
19	Georgia	25.3
20	Illinois	25.2
21	Maryland	25.0
22	Kansas	24.8
23	Alabama	24.7
24	Wisconsin	24.6
25	Delaware	24.4
26	South Dakota	24.1
27	New York	24.0
28	Minnesota	23.8
29	Indiana	23.6
29	Missouri	23.6
29	Ohio	23.6
32	Idaho	23.5
33	Washington	23.3
34	Pennsylvania	23.1
35	Iowa	22.7
36	Nebraska	22.0
37	Louisiana	21.9
38	Arkansas	21.8
39	Arizona	21.5
40	Florida	21.4
41	New Hampshire	21.3
42	North Dakota	21.1
43	North Carolina	20.9
44	Colorado	19.8
45	Montana	19.7
46	Utah	19.5
47	Tennessee	19.2
48	Nevada	19.0
49	Kentucky	17.6
50	New Mexico	16.8

District of Columbia   30.2

Source: CQ Press using data from U.S. Department of Transportation, Federal Highway Administration
"Highway Statistics 2008" (Table HM-10, http://www.fhwa.dot.gov/policyinformation/statistics/2008/index.cfm)
*National percent does not include federally-funded highway miles in Puerto Rico.

Interstate Highway Mileage in 2008

National Total = 46,750 Miles*

ALPHA ORDER

RANK	STATE	MILES	% of USA
25	Alabama	905	1.9%
17	Alaska	1,082	2.3%
13	Arizona	1,168	2.5%
35	Arkansas	656	1.4%
2	California	2,460	5.3%
19	Colorado	953	2.0%
45	Connecticut	346	0.7%
50	Delaware	41	0.1%
7	Florida	1,471	3.1%
9	Georgia	1,242	2.7%
49	Hawaii	55	0.1%
36	Idaho	612	1.3%
3	Illinois	2,182	4.7%
12	Indiana	1,171	2.5%
28	Iowa	781	1.7%
26	Kansas	874	1.9%
30	Kentucky	762	1.6%
24	Louisiana	906	1.9%
44	Maine	366	0.8%
41	Maryland	481	1.0%
37	Massachusetts	573	1.2%
8	Michigan	1,243	2.7%
22	Minnesota	918	2.0%
33	Mississippi	698	1.5%
11	Missouri	1,181	2.5%
10	Montana	1,192	2.5%
41	Nebraska	481	1.0%
39	Nevada	570	1.2%
47	New Hampshire	225	0.5%
43	New Jersey	431	0.9%
18	New Mexico	1,000	2.1%
5	New York	1,705	3.6%
14	North Carolina	1,125	2.4%
38	North Dakota	571	1.2%
6	Ohio	1,574	3.4%
21	Oklahoma	933	2.0%
32	Oregon	729	1.6%
4	Pennsylvania	1,792	3.8%
48	Rhode Island	72	0.2%
27	South Carolina	843	1.8%
34	South Dakota	679	1.5%
16	Tennessee	1,105	2.4%
1	Texas	3,234	6.9%
20	Utah	936	2.0%
46	Vermont	320	0.7%
15	Virginia	1,119	2.4%
29	Washington	764	1.6%
40	West Virginia	554	1.2%
31	Wisconsin	743	1.6%
23	Wyoming	913	2.0%

RANK ORDER

RANK	STATE	MILES	% of USA
1	Texas	3,234	6.9%
2	California	2,460	5.3%
3	Illinois	2,182	4.7%
4	Pennsylvania	1,792	3.8%
5	New York	1,705	3.6%
6	Ohio	1,574	3.4%
7	Florida	1,471	3.1%
8	Michigan	1,243	2.7%
9	Georgia	1,242	2.7%
10	Montana	1,192	2.5%
11	Missouri	1,181	2.5%
12	Indiana	1,171	2.5%
13	Arizona	1,168	2.5%
14	North Carolina	1,125	2.4%
15	Virginia	1,119	2.4%
16	Tennessee	1,105	2.4%
17	Alaska	1,082	2.3%
18	New Mexico	1,000	2.1%
19	Colorado	953	2.0%
20	Utah	936	2.0%
21	Oklahoma	933	2.0%
22	Minnesota	918	2.0%
23	Wyoming	913	2.0%
24	Louisiana	906	1.9%
25	Alabama	905	1.9%
26	Kansas	874	1.9%
27	South Carolina	843	1.8%
28	Iowa	781	1.7%
29	Washington	764	1.6%
30	Kentucky	762	1.6%
31	Wisconsin	743	1.6%
32	Oregon	729	1.6%
33	Mississippi	698	1.5%
34	South Dakota	679	1.5%
35	Arkansas	656	1.4%
36	Idaho	612	1.3%
37	Massachusetts	573	1.2%
38	North Dakota	571	1.2%
39	Nevada	570	1.2%
40	West Virginia	554	1.2%
41	Maryland	481	1.0%
41	Nebraska	481	1.0%
43	New Jersey	431	0.9%
44	Maine	366	0.8%
45	Connecticut	346	0.7%
46	Vermont	320	0.7%
47	New Hampshire	225	0.5%
48	Rhode Island	72	0.2%
49	Hawaii	55	0.1%
50	Delaware	41	0.1%
	District of Columbia	13	0.0%

Source: U.S. Department of Transportation, Federal Highway Administration
"Highway Statistics 2008" (Table HM-15, http://www.fhwa.dot.gov/policyinformation/statistics/2008/index.cfm)
*Does not include 265 miles of highway in Puerto Rico that are part of the interstate system.

Toll Road Mileage in 2007

National Total = 4,791.0 Miles

RANK	STATE	MILES	% of USA
26	Alabama	0.7	0.0%
27	Alaska	0.0	0.0%
27	Arizona	0.0	0.0%
27	Arkansas	0.0	0.0%
14	California	95.8	2.0%
17	Colorado	64.6	1.3%
27	Connecticut	0.0	0.0%
19	Delaware	56.7	1.2%
1	Florida	685.8	14.3%
23	Georgia	6.2	0.1%
27	Hawaii	0.0	0.0%
27	Idaho	0.0	0.0%
7	Illinois	282.1	5.9%
10	Indiana	156.8	3.3%
27	Iowa	0.0	0.0%
9	Kansas	236.0	4.9%
15	Kentucky	93.6	2.0%
24	Louisiana	1.5	0.0%
12	Maine	106.2	2.2%
27	Maryland	0.0	0.0%
11	Massachusetts	138.2	2.9%
27	Michigan	0.0	0.0%
27	Minnesota	0.0	0.0%
27	Mississippi	0.0	0.0%
27	Missouri	0.0	0.0%
27	Montana	0.0	0.0%
27	Nebraska	0.0	0.0%
22	Nevada	6.4	0.1%
13	New Hampshire	97.1	2.0%
5	New Jersey	359.9	7.5%
27	New Mexico	0.0	0.0%
3	New York	567.6	11.8%
27	North Carolina	0.0	0.0%
27	North Dakota	0.0	0.0%
8	Ohio	241.2	5.0%
2	Oklahoma	596.7	12.5%
27	Oregon	0.0	0.0%
4	Pennsylvania	533.0	11.1%
27	Rhode Island	0.0	0.0%
20	South Carolina	23.5	0.5%
27	South Dakota	0.0	0.0%
27	Tennessee	0.0	0.0%
6	Texas	283.8	5.9%
25	Utah	1.0	0.0%
21	Vermont	11.9	0.2%
18	Virginia	57.9	1.2%
27	Washington	0.0	0.0%
16	West Virginia	86.8	1.8%
27	Wisconsin	0.0	0.0%
27	Wyoming	0.0	0.0%

RANK ORDER

RANK	STATE	MILES	% of USA
1	Florida	685.8	14.3%
2	Oklahoma	596.7	12.5%
3	New York	567.6	11.8%
4	Pennsylvania	533.0	11.1%
5	New Jersey	359.9	7.5%
6	Texas	283.8	5.9%
7	Illinois	282.1	5.9%
8	Ohio	241.2	5.0%
9	Kansas	236.0	4.9%
10	Indiana	156.8	3.3%
11	Massachusetts	138.2	2.9%
12	Maine	106.2	2.2%
13	New Hampshire	97.1	2.0%
14	California	95.8	2.0%
15	Kentucky	93.6	2.0%
16	West Virginia	86.8	1.8%
17	Colorado	64.6	1.3%
18	Virginia	57.9	1.2%
19	Delaware	56.7	1.2%
20	South Carolina	23.5	0.5%
21	Vermont	11.9	0.2%
22	Nevada	6.4	0.1%
23	Georgia	6.2	0.1%
24	Louisiana	1.5	0.0%
25	Utah	1.0	0.0%
26	Alabama	0.7	0.0%
27	Alaska	0.0	0.0%
27	Arizona	0.0	0.0%
27	Arkansas	0.0	0.0%
27	Connecticut	0.0	0.0%
27	Hawaii	0.0	0.0%
27	Idaho	0.0	0.0%
27	Iowa	0.0	0.0%
27	Maryland	0.0	0.0%
27	Michigan	0.0	0.0%
27	Minnesota	0.0	0.0%
27	Mississippi	0.0	0.0%
27	Missouri	0.0	0.0%
27	Montana	0.0	0.0%
27	Nebraska	0.0	0.0%
27	New Mexico	0.0	0.0%
27	North Carolina	0.0	0.0%
27	North Dakota	0.0	0.0%
27	Oregon	0.0	0.0%
27	Rhode Island	0.0	0.0%
27	South Dakota	0.0	0.0%
27	Tennessee	0.0	0.0%
27	Washington	0.0	0.0%
27	Wisconsin	0.0	0.0%
27	Wyoming	0.0	0.0%
	District of Columbia	0.0	0.0%

Source: U.S. Department of Transportation, Bureau of Transportation Statistics
"State Transportation Statistics 2008" (http://www.bts.gov/publications/state_transportation_statistics/)

Rural Road and Street Mileage in 2008

National Total = 2,977,228 Rural Miles*

ALPHA ORDER

RANK	STATE	MILES	% of USA
18	Alabama	75,390	2.5%
42	Alaska	12,987	0.4%
35	Arizona	37,522	1.3%
9	Arkansas	87,627	2.9%
13	California	83,483	2.8%
23	Colorado	68,921	2.3%
47	Connecticut	6,228	0.2%
48	Delaware	3,302	0.1%
34	Florida	40,366	1.4%
14	Georgia	83,261	2.8%
49	Hawaii	2,052	0.1%
33	Idaho	42,128	1.4%
6	Illinois	98,202	3.3%
20	Indiana	71,299	2.4%
5	Iowa	102,919	3.5%
2	Kansas	127,859	4.3%
24	Kentucky	66,213	2.2%
32	Louisiana	44,758	1.5%
40	Maine	19,837	0.7%
41	Maryland	14,051	0.5%
45	Massachusetts	7,978	0.3%
11	Michigan	85,853	2.9%
3	Minnesota	117,613	4.0%
26	Mississippi	63,929	2.1%
4	Missouri	106,765	3.6%
21	Montana	71,115	2.4%
10	Nebraska	87,297	2.9%
38	Nevada	26,741	0.9%
44	New Hampshire	11,098	0.4%
46	New Jersey	7,298	0.2%
28	New Mexico	60,386	2.0%
25	New York	66,071	2.2%
19	North Carolina	71,674	2.4%
12	North Dakota	84,945	2.9%
16	Ohio	78,260	2.6%
7	Oklahoma	97,268	3.3%
31	Oregon	46,260	1.6%
17	Pennsylvania	76,484	2.6%
50	Rhode Island	1,214	0.0%
30	South Carolina	49,833	1.7%
15	South Dakota	79,217	2.7%
22	Tennessee	69,719	2.3%
1	Texas	212,999	7.2%
36	Utah	33,632	1.1%
43	Vermont	12,965	0.4%
29	Virginia	50,334	1.7%
27	Washington	60,784	2.0%
37	West Virginia	33,092	1.1%
8	Wisconsin	92,572	3.1%
39	Wyoming	25,427	0.9%

RANK ORDER

RANK	STATE	MILES	% of USA
1	Texas	212,999	7.2%
2	Kansas	127,859	4.3%
3	Minnesota	117,613	4.0%
4	Missouri	106,765	3.6%
5	Iowa	102,919	3.5%
6	Illinois	98,202	3.3%
7	Oklahoma	97,268	3.3%
8	Wisconsin	92,572	3.1%
9	Arkansas	87,627	2.9%
10	Nebraska	87,297	2.9%
11	Michigan	85,853	2.9%
12	North Dakota	84,945	2.9%
13	California	83,483	2.8%
14	Georgia	83,261	2.8%
15	South Dakota	79,217	2.7%
16	Ohio	78,260	2.6%
17	Pennsylvania	76,484	2.6%
18	Alabama	75,390	2.5%
19	North Carolina	71,674	2.4%
20	Indiana	71,299	2.4%
21	Montana	71,115	2.4%
22	Tennessee	69,719	2.3%
23	Colorado	68,921	2.3%
24	Kentucky	66,213	2.2%
25	New York	66,071	2.2%
26	Mississippi	63,929	2.1%
27	Washington	60,784	2.0%
28	New Mexico	60,386	2.0%
29	Virginia	50,334	1.7%
30	South Carolina	49,833	1.7%
31	Oregon	46,260	1.6%
32	Louisiana	44,758	1.5%
33	Idaho	42,128	1.4%
34	Florida	40,366	1.4%
35	Arizona	37,522	1.3%
36	Utah	33,632	1.1%
37	West Virginia	33,092	1.1%
38	Nevada	26,741	0.9%
39	Wyoming	25,427	0.9%
40	Maine	19,837	0.7%
41	Maryland	14,051	0.5%
42	Alaska	12,987	0.4%
43	Vermont	12,965	0.4%
44	New Hampshire	11,098	0.4%
45	Massachusetts	7,978	0.3%
46	New Jersey	7,298	0.2%
47	Connecticut	6,228	0.2%
48	Delaware	3,302	0.1%
49	Hawaii	2,052	0.1%
50	Rhode Island	1,214	0.0%
	District of Columbia	0	0.0%

Source: U.S. Department of Transportation, Federal Highway Administration
    "Highway Statistics 2008" (Table HM-10, http://www.fhwa.dot.gov/policyinformation/statistics/2008/index.cfm)
*Does not include 3,105 miles of rural roads and streets in Puerto Rico.

Urban Road and Street Mileage in 2008

National Total = 1,065,540 Urban Miles*

<u>ALPHA ORDER</u>

RANK	STATE	MILES	% of USA
20	Alabama	21,935	2.1%
47	Alaska	2,341	0.2%
16	Arizona	22,917	2.2%
31	Arkansas	12,185	1.1%
2	California	89,029	8.4%
22	Colorado	19,345	1.8%
27	Connecticut	15,137	1.4%
44	Delaware	2,979	0.3%
3	Florida	81,020	7.6%
8	Georgia	38,614	3.6%
48	Hawaii	2,310	0.2%
38	Idaho	5,660	0.5%
7	Illinois	41,290	3.9%
13	Indiana	24,314	2.3%
32	Iowa	11,307	1.1%
29	Kansas	12,750	1.2%
30	Kentucky	12,536	1.2%
25	Louisiana	16,335	1.5%
43	Maine	2,992	0.3%
23	Maryland	17,334	1.6%
12	Massachusetts	28,126	2.6%
9	Michigan	35,813	3.4%
21	Minnesota	20,626	1.9%
34	Mississippi	10,957	1.0%
15	Missouri	22,952	2.2%
42	Montana	3,056	0.3%
37	Nebraska	6,318	0.6%
36	Nevada	7,166	0.7%
41	New Hampshire	4,908	0.5%
11	New Jersey	31,455	3.0%
35	New Mexico	7,998	0.8%
4	New York	48,402	4.5%
10	North Carolina	33,429	3.1%
49	North Dakota	1,897	0.2%
6	Ohio	44,713	4.2%
26	Oklahoma	16,057	1.5%
28	Oregon	12,990	1.2%
5	Pennsylvania	45,288	4.3%
40	Rhode Island	5,190	0.5%
24	South Carolina	16,421	1.5%
45	South Dakota	2,932	0.3%
18	Tennessee	22,454	2.1%
1	Texas	93,405	8.8%
33	Utah	11,073	1.0%
50	Vermont	1,458	0.1%
14	Virginia	23,569	2.2%
17	Washington	22,743	2.1%
39	West Virginia	5,360	0.5%
19	Wisconsin	22,271	2.1%
46	Wyoming	2,678	0.3%

<u>RANK ORDER</u>

RANK	STATE	MILES	% of USA
1	Texas	93,405	8.8%
2	California	89,029	8.4%
3	Florida	81,020	7.6%
4	New York	48,402	4.5%
5	Pennsylvania	45,288	4.3%
6	Ohio	44,713	4.2%
7	Illinois	41,290	3.9%
8	Georgia	38,614	3.6%
9	Michigan	35,813	3.4%
10	North Carolina	33,429	3.1%
11	New Jersey	31,455	3.0%
12	Massachusetts	28,126	2.6%
13	Indiana	24,314	2.3%
14	Virginia	23,569	2.2%
15	Missouri	22,952	2.2%
16	Arizona	22,917	2.2%
17	Washington	22,743	2.1%
18	Tennessee	22,454	2.1%
19	Wisconsin	22,271	2.1%
20	Alabama	21,935	2.1%
21	Minnesota	20,626	1.9%
22	Colorado	19,345	1.8%
23	Maryland	17,334	1.6%
24	South Carolina	16,421	1.5%
25	Louisiana	16,335	1.5%
26	Oklahoma	16,057	1.5%
27	Connecticut	15,137	1.4%
28	Oregon	12,990	1.2%
29	Kansas	12,750	1.2%
30	Kentucky	12,536	1.2%
31	Arkansas	12,185	1.1%
32	Iowa	11,307	1.1%
33	Utah	11,073	1.0%
34	Mississippi	10,957	1.0%
35	New Mexico	7,998	0.8%
36	Nevada	7,166	0.7%
37	Nebraska	6,318	0.6%
38	Idaho	5,660	0.5%
39	West Virginia	5,360	0.5%
40	Rhode Island	5,190	0.5%
41	New Hampshire	4,908	0.5%
42	Montana	3,056	0.3%
43	Maine	2,992	0.3%
44	Delaware	2,979	0.3%
45	South Dakota	2,932	0.3%
46	Wyoming	2,678	0.3%
47	Alaska	2,341	0.2%
48	Hawaii	2,310	0.2%
49	North Dakota	1,897	0.2%
50	Vermont	1,458	0.1%
	District of Columbia	1,505	0.1%

Source: U.S. Department of Transportation, Federal Highway Administration
"Highway Statistics 2008" (Table HM-10, http://www.fhwa.dot.gov/policyinformation/statistics/2008/index.cfm)
*Does not include 13,467 miles of urban roads and streets in Puerto Rico.

Percent of Roadways in Mediocre or Poor Condition: 2007

National Percent = 17.6%*

ALPHA ORDER			RANK ORDER		
RANK	STATE	PERCENT	RANK	STATE	PERCENT
38	Alabama	9.1	1	New Jersey	49.1
20	Alaska	19.2	2	Hawaii	43.3
35	Arizona	10.5	3	California	39.9
12	Arkansas	25.4	4	Idaho	35.6
3	California	39.9	5	Oklahoma	34.9
34	Colorado	10.9	6	Kansas	32.9
28	Connecticut	14.8	7	Maryland	32.8
25	Delaware	15.7	8	New Mexico	30.5
49	Florida	3.6	9	Rhode Island	29.8
44	Georgia	6.4	10	West Virginia	28.9
2	Hawaii	43.3	11	Louisiana	26.0
4	Idaho	35.6	12	Arkansas	25.4
21	Illinois	17.9	13	Pennsylvania	25.2
33	Indiana	11.5	14	Vermont	24.9
26	Iowa	15.3	15	Missouri	24.5
6	Kansas	32.9	16	New York	24.4
50	Kentucky	3.1	17	Michigan	21.1
11	Louisiana	26.0	18	Maine	21.0
18	Maine	21.0	19	New Hampshire	19.6
7	Maryland	32.8	20	Alaska	19.2
31	Massachusetts	12.4	21	Illinois	17.9
17	Michigan	21.1	22	Wisconsin	17.2
24	Minnesota	16.0	23	Mississippi	17.1
23	Mississippi	17.1	24	Minnesota	16.0
15	Missouri	24.5	25	Delaware	15.7
44	Montana	6.4	26	Iowa	15.3
36	Nebraska	10.1	27	South Dakota	14.9
37	Nevada	9.5	28	Connecticut	14.8
19	New Hampshire	19.6	29	South Carolina	14.1
1	New Jersey	49.1	30	Washington	12.7
8	New Mexico	30.5	31	Massachusetts	12.4
16	New York	24.4	32	Texas	11.6
40	North Carolina	8.6	33	Indiana	11.5
39	North Dakota	8.9	34	Colorado	10.9
48	Ohio	5.4	35	Arizona	10.5
5	Oklahoma	34.9	36	Nebraska	10.1
47	Oregon	6.0	37	Nevada	9.5
13	Pennsylvania	25.2	38	Alabama	9.1
9	Rhode Island	29.8	39	North Dakota	8.9
29	South Carolina	14.1	40	North Carolina	8.6
27	South Dakota	14.9	41	Wyoming	7.7
43	Tennessee	6.5	42	Virginia	7.2
32	Texas	11.6	43	Tennessee	6.5
46	Utah	6.3	44	Georgia	6.4
14	Vermont	24.9	44	Montana	6.4
42	Virginia	7.2	46	Utah	6.3
30	Washington	12.7	47	Oregon	6.0
10	West Virginia	28.9	48	Ohio	5.4
22	Wisconsin	17.2	49	Florida	3.6
41	Wyoming	7.7	50	Kentucky	3.1

District of Columbia 94.5

Source: CQ Press using data from U.S. Department of Transportation, Bureau of Transportation Statistics
"State Transportation Statistics 2008" (http://www.bts.gov/publications/state_transportation_statistics/)
*Does not include 3,564 miles for which the condition is not reported. Road condition ratings are derived from the International Roughness Index (IRI) and the Present Serviceability Rating (PSR). States are required to report to the Federal Highway Administration (FHWA) IRI data for the Interstate system, other principal arterials, rural minor arterials, and the National Highway System regardless of functional system.

Bridges in 2008

National Total = 599,241 Bridges*

RANK	STATE	BRIDGES	% of USA
15	Alabama	15,909	2.7%
47	Alaska	1,201	0.2%
29	Arizona	7,374	1.2%
23	Arkansas	12,539	2.1%
6	California	24,411	4.1%
27	Colorado	8,408	1.4%
38	Connecticut	4,180	0.7%
49	Delaware	857	0.1%
24	Florida	11,678	1.9%
17	Georgia	14,578	2.4%
48	Hawaii	1,120	0.2%
39	Idaho	4,125	0.7%
3	Illinois	26,102	4.4%
11	Indiana	18,543	3.1%
5	Iowa	24,798	4.1%
4	Kansas	25,514	4.3%
19	Kentucky	13,630	2.3%
21	Louisiana	13,320	2.2%
44	Maine	2,392	0.4%
34	Maryland	5,166	0.9%
35	Massachusetts	5,042	0.8%
25	Michigan	10,937	1.8%
22	Minnesota	13,125	2.2%
14	Mississippi	17,024	2.8%
7	Missouri	24,204	4.0%
36	Montana	4,968	0.8%
16	Nebraska	15,471	2.6%
46	Nevada	1,735	0.3%
45	New Hampshire	2,371	0.4%
32	New Jersey	6,474	1.1%
40	New Mexico	3,866	0.6%
13	New York	17,366	2.9%
12	North Carolina	17,889	3.0%
37	North Dakota	4,451	0.7%
2	Ohio	28,065	4.7%
8	Oklahoma	23,587	3.9%
30	Oregon	7,292	1.2%
9	Pennsylvania	22,349	3.7%
50	Rhode Island	741	0.1%
26	South Carolina	9,221	1.5%
33	South Dakota	5,920	1.0%
10	Tennessee	19,880	3.3%
1	Texas	50,599	8.4%
42	Utah	2,853	0.5%
43	Vermont	2,715	0.5%
20	Virginia	13,447	2.2%
28	Washington	7,656	1.3%
31	West Virginia	7,038	1.2%
18	Wisconsin	13,831	2.3%
41	Wyoming	3,036	0.5%

RANK	STATE	BRIDGES	% of USA
1	Texas	50,599	8.4%
2	Ohio	28,065	4.7%
3	Illinois	26,102	4.4%
4	Kansas	25,514	4.3%
5	Iowa	24,798	4.1%
6	California	24,411	4.1%
7	Missouri	24,204	4.0%
8	Oklahoma	23,587	3.9%
9	Pennsylvania	22,349	3.7%
10	Tennessee	19,880	3.3%
11	Indiana	18,543	3.1%
12	North Carolina	17,889	3.0%
13	New York	17,366	2.9%
14	Mississippi	17,024	2.8%
15	Alabama	15,909	2.7%
16	Nebraska	15,471	2.6%
17	Georgia	14,578	2.4%
18	Wisconsin	13,831	2.3%
19	Kentucky	13,630	2.3%
20	Virginia	13,447	2.2%
21	Louisiana	13,320	2.2%
22	Minnesota	13,125	2.2%
23	Arkansas	12,539	2.1%
24	Florida	11,678	1.9%
25	Michigan	10,937	1.8%
26	South Carolina	9,221	1.5%
27	Colorado	8,408	1.4%
28	Washington	7,656	1.3%
29	Arizona	7,374	1.2%
30	Oregon	7,292	1.2%
31	West Virginia	7,038	1.2%
32	New Jersey	6,474	1.1%
33	South Dakota	5,920	1.0%
34	Maryland	5,166	0.9%
35	Massachusetts	5,042	0.8%
36	Montana	4,968	0.8%
37	North Dakota	4,451	0.7%
38	Connecticut	4,180	0.7%
39	Idaho	4,125	0.7%
40	New Mexico	3,866	0.6%
41	Wyoming	3,036	0.5%
42	Utah	2,853	0.5%
43	Vermont	2,715	0.5%
44	Maine	2,392	0.4%
45	New Hampshire	2,371	0.4%
46	Nevada	1,735	0.3%
47	Alaska	1,201	0.2%
48	Hawaii	1,120	0.2%
49	Delaware	857	0.1%
50	Rhode Island	741	0.1%
	District of Columbia	243	0.0%

Source: U.S. Department of Transportation, Federal Highway Administration
"Deficient Bridges by State and Highway System, 2008" (http://www.fhwa.dot.gov/bridge/deficient.htm)
*As of December 2008. Includes federal-aid and nonfederal-aid system bridges. National total does not include 2,170 bridges in Puerto Rico.

Deficient Bridges in 2008

National Total = 150,320 Deficient Bridges*

ALPHA ORDER

RANK	STATE	BRIDGES	% of USA
16	Alabama	3,927	2.6%
48	Alaska	321	0.2%
39	Arizona	828	0.6%
21	Arkansas	2,846	1.9%
5	California	7,085	4.7%
33	Colorado	1,411	0.9%
34	Connecticut	1,409	0.9%
50	Delaware	133	0.1%
29	Florida	1,920	1.3%
20	Georgia	2,869	1.9%
45	Hawaii	487	0.3%
40	Idaho	792	0.5%
12	Illinois	4,269	2.8%
14	Indiana	4,177	2.8%
7	Iowa	6,545	4.4%
9	Kansas	5,196	3.5%
11	Kentucky	4,412	2.9%
17	Louisiana	3,909	2.6%
41	Maine	789	0.5%
35	Maryland	1,357	0.9%
24	Massachusetts	2,581	1.7%
22	Michigan	2,830	1.9%
31	Minnesota	1,568	1.0%
13	Mississippi	4,201	2.8%
3	Missouri	7,396	4.9%
38	Montana	942	0.6%
18	Nebraska	3,564	2.4%
49	Nevada	215	0.1%
42	New Hampshire	751	0.5%
25	New Jersey	2,172	1.4%
43	New Mexico	702	0.5%
8	New York	6,525	4.3%
10	North Carolina	5,131	3.4%
37	North Dakota	966	0.6%
6	Ohio	6,761	4.5%
4	Oklahoma	7,223	4.8%
30	Oregon	1,633	1.1%
1	Pennsylvania	10,403	6.9%
47	Rhode Island	397	0.3%
26	South Carolina	2,027	1.3%
32	South Dakota	1,473	1.0%
15	Tennessee	4,007	2.7%
2	Texas	9,819	6.5%
46	Utah	450	0.3%
36	Vermont	969	0.6%
19	Virginia	3,490	2.3%
27	Washington	2,024	1.3%
23	West Virginia	2,592	1.7%
28	Wisconsin	2,021	1.3%
44	Wyoming	658	0.4%

RANK ORDER

RANK	STATE	BRIDGES	% of USA
1	Pennsylvania	10,403	6.9%
2	Texas	9,819	6.5%
3	Missouri	7,396	4.9%
4	Oklahoma	7,223	4.8%
5	California	7,085	4.7%
6	Ohio	6,761	4.5%
7	Iowa	6,545	4.4%
8	New York	6,525	4.3%
9	Kansas	5,196	3.5%
10	North Carolina	5,131	3.4%
11	Kentucky	4,412	2.9%
12	Illinois	4,269	2.8%
13	Mississippi	4,201	2.8%
14	Indiana	4,177	2.8%
15	Tennessee	4,007	2.7%
16	Alabama	3,927	2.6%
17	Louisiana	3,909	2.6%
18	Nebraska	3,564	2.4%
19	Virginia	3,490	2.3%
20	Georgia	2,869	1.9%
21	Arkansas	2,846	1.9%
22	Michigan	2,830	1.9%
23	West Virginia	2,592	1.7%
24	Massachusetts	2,581	1.7%
25	New Jersey	2,172	1.4%
26	South Carolina	2,027	1.3%
27	Washington	2,024	1.3%
28	Wisconsin	2,021	1.3%
29	Florida	1,920	1.3%
30	Oregon	1,633	1.1%
31	Minnesota	1,568	1.0%
32	South Dakota	1,473	1.0%
33	Colorado	1,411	0.9%
34	Connecticut	1,409	0.9%
35	Maryland	1,357	0.9%
36	Vermont	969	0.6%
37	North Dakota	966	0.6%
38	Montana	942	0.6%
39	Arizona	828	0.6%
40	Idaho	792	0.5%
41	Maine	789	0.5%
42	New Hampshire	751	0.5%
43	New Mexico	702	0.5%
44	Wyoming	658	0.4%
45	Hawaii	487	0.3%
46	Utah	450	0.3%
47	Rhode Island	397	0.3%
48	Alaska	321	0.2%
49	Nevada	215	0.1%
50	Delaware	133	0.1%
	District of Columbia	147	0.1%

Source: U.S. Department of Transportation, Federal Highway Administration
   "Deficient Bridges by State and Highway System, 2008" (http://www.fhwa.dot.gov/bridge/deficient.htm)
*As of December 2008. Includes federal-aid and nonfederal-aid system bridges. National total does not include 1,071 deficient
bridges in Puerto Rico. Bridges classified as deficient are either functionally obsolete or structurally deficient and are not
necessarily unsafe.

Deficient Bridges as a Percent of Total Bridges in 2008

National Percent = 25.1% of Bridges are Deficient*

ALPHA ORDER

RANK	STATE	PERCENT
25	Alabama	24.7
18	Alaska	26.7
50	Arizona	11.2
29	Arkansas	22.7
16	California	29.0
42	Colorado	16.8
8	Connecticut	33.7
46	Delaware	15.5
43	Florida	16.4
37	Georgia	19.7
4	Hawaii	43.5
39	Idaho	19.2
43	Illinois	16.4
30	Indiana	22.5
19	Iowa	26.4
35	Kansas	20.4
11	Kentucky	32.4
15	Louisiana	29.3
10	Maine	33.0
21	Maryland	26.3
2	Massachusetts	51.2
23	Michigan	25.9
49	Minnesota	11.9
25	Mississippi	24.7
13	Missouri	30.6
40	Montana	19.0
28	Nebraska	23.0
48	Nevada	12.4
12	New Hampshire	31.7
9	New Jersey	33.5
41	New Mexico	18.2
5	New York	37.6
17	North Carolina	28.7
33	North Dakota	21.7
27	Ohio	24.1
13	Oklahoma	30.6
31	Oregon	22.4
3	Pennsylvania	46.5
1	Rhode Island	53.6
32	South Carolina	22.0
24	South Dakota	24.9
36	Tennessee	20.2
38	Texas	19.4
45	Utah	15.8
7	Vermont	35.7
22	Virginia	26.0
19	Washington	26.4
6	West Virginia	36.8
47	Wisconsin	14.6
33	Wyoming	21.7

RANK ORDER

RANK	STATE	PERCENT
1	Rhode Island	53.6
2	Massachusetts	51.2
3	Pennsylvania	46.5
4	Hawaii	43.5
5	New York	37.6
6	West Virginia	36.8
7	Vermont	35.7
8	Connecticut	33.7
9	New Jersey	33.5
10	Maine	33.0
11	Kentucky	32.4
12	New Hampshire	31.7
13	Missouri	30.6
13	Oklahoma	30.6
15	Louisiana	29.3
16	California	29.0
17	North Carolina	28.7
18	Alaska	26.7
19	Iowa	26.4
19	Washington	26.4
21	Maryland	26.3
22	Virginia	26.0
23	Michigan	25.9
24	South Dakota	24.9
25	Alabama	24.7
25	Mississippi	24.7
27	Ohio	24.1
28	Nebraska	23.0
29	Arkansas	22.7
30	Indiana	22.5
31	Oregon	22.4
32	South Carolina	22.0
33	North Dakota	21.7
33	Wyoming	21.7
35	Kansas	20.4
36	Tennessee	20.2
37	Georgia	19.7
38	Texas	19.4
39	Idaho	19.2
40	Montana	19.0
41	New Mexico	18.2
42	Colorado	16.8
43	Florida	16.4
43	Illinois	16.4
45	Utah	15.8
46	Delaware	15.5
47	Wisconsin	14.6
48	Nevada	12.4
49	Minnesota	11.9
50	Arizona	11.2

| | District of Columbia | 60.5 |

Source: CQ Press using data from U.S. Department of Transportation, Federal Highway Administration
   "Deficient Bridges by State and Highway System, 2008" (http://www.fhwa.dot.gov/bridge/deficient.htm)
*As of December 2008. Includes federal-aid and nonfederal-aid system bridges. National percent does not include bridges in Puerto Rico. Bridges classified as deficient are either functionally obsolete or structurally deficient and are not necessarily unsafe.

Vehicle-Miles of Travel in 2008

National Total = 2,973,509,000,000 Miles

ALPHA ORDER

RANK ORDER

RANK	STATE	MILES	% of USA	RANK	STATE	MILES	% of USA
17	Alabama	59,303,000,000	2.0%	1	California	327,286,000,000	11.0%
50	Alaska	4,865,000,000	0.2%	2	Texas	235,382,000,000	7.9%
16	Arizona	61,628,000,000	2.1%	3	Florida	198,616,000,000	6.7%
30	Arkansas	33,163,000,000	1.1%	4	New York	134,085,000,000	4.5%
1	California	327,286,000,000	11.0%	5	Georgia	109,057,000,000	3.7%
25	Colorado	47,860,000,000	1.6%	6	Ohio	108,302,000,000	3.6%
31	Connecticut	31,737,000,000	1.1%	7	Pennsylvania	107,848,000,000	3.6%
46	Delaware	8,976,000,000	0.3%	8	Illinois	106,079,000,000	3.6%
3	Florida	198,616,000,000	6.7%	9	Michigan	101,825,000,000	3.4%
5	Georgia	109,057,000,000	3.7%	10	North Carolina	101,712,000,000	3.4%
43	Hawaii	10,278,000,000	0.3%	11	Virginia	82,278,000,000	2.8%
39	Idaho	15,251,000,000	0.5%	12	New Jersey	73,629,000,000	2.5%
8	Illinois	106,079,000,000	3.6%	13	Indiana	70,973,000,000	2.4%
13	Indiana	70,973,000,000	2.4%	14	Tennessee	69,469,000,000	2.3%
32	Iowa	30,713,000,000	1.0%	15	Missouri	68,273,000,000	2.3%
33	Kansas	29,727,000,000	1.0%	16	Arizona	61,628,000,000	2.1%
26	Kentucky	47,534,000,000	1.6%	17	Alabama	59,303,000,000	2.0%
27	Louisiana	45,091,000,000	1.5%	18	Minnesota	57,995,000,000	2.0%
40	Maine	14,559,000,000	0.5%	19	Wisconsin	57,462,000,000	1.9%
21	Maryland	55,023,000,000	1.9%	20	Washington	55,558,000,000	1.9%
22	Massachusetts	54,505,000,000	1.8%	21	Maryland	55,023,000,000	1.9%
9	Michigan	101,825,000,000	3.4%	22	Massachusetts	54,505,000,000	1.8%
18	Minnesota	57,995,000,000	2.0%	23	South Carolina	49,597,000,000	1.7%
28	Mississippi	43,711,000,000	1.5%	24	Oklahoma	48,499,000,000	1.6%
15	Missouri	68,273,000,000	2.3%	25	Colorado	47,860,000,000	1.6%
42	Montana	10,812,000,000	0.4%	26	Kentucky	47,534,000,000	1.6%
38	Nebraska	19,170,000,000	0.6%	27	Louisiana	45,091,000,000	1.5%
36	Nevada	20,780,000,000	0.7%	28	Mississippi	43,711,000,000	1.5%
41	New Hampshire	13,040,000,000	0.4%	29	Oregon	33,468,000,000	1.1%
12	New Jersey	73,629,000,000	2.5%	30	Arkansas	33,163,000,000	1.1%
34	New Mexico	26,279,000,000	0.9%	31	Connecticut	31,737,000,000	1.1%
4	New York	134,085,000,000	4.5%	32	Iowa	30,713,000,000	1.0%
10	North Carolina	101,712,000,000	3.4%	33	Kansas	29,727,000,000	1.0%
48	North Dakota	7,820,000,000	0.3%	34	New Mexico	26,279,000,000	0.9%
6	Ohio	108,302,000,000	3.6%	35	Utah	25,974,000,000	0.9%
24	Oklahoma	48,499,000,000	1.6%	36	Nevada	20,780,000,000	0.7%
29	Oregon	33,468,000,000	1.1%	37	West Virginia	20,774,000,000	0.7%
7	Pennsylvania	107,848,000,000	3.6%	38	Nebraska	19,170,000,000	0.6%
47	Rhode Island	8,187,000,000	0.3%	39	Idaho	15,251,000,000	0.5%
23	South Carolina	49,597,000,000	1.7%	40	Maine	14,559,000,000	0.5%
45	South Dakota	8,986,000,000	0.3%	41	New Hampshire	13,040,000,000	0.4%
14	Tennessee	69,469,000,000	2.3%	42	Montana	10,812,000,000	0.4%
2	Texas	235,382,000,000	7.9%	43	Hawaii	10,278,000,000	0.3%
35	Utah	25,974,000,000	0.9%	44	Wyoming	9,447,000,000	0.3%
49	Vermont	7,312,000,000	0.2%	45	South Dakota	8,986,000,000	0.3%
11	Virginia	82,278,000,000	2.8%	46	Delaware	8,976,000,000	0.3%
20	Washington	55,558,000,000	1.9%	47	Rhode Island	8,187,000,000	0.3%
37	West Virginia	20,774,000,000	0.7%	48	North Dakota	7,820,000,000	0.3%
19	Wisconsin	57,462,000,000	1.9%	49	Vermont	7,312,000,000	0.2%
44	Wyoming	9,447,000,000	0.3%	50	Alaska	4,865,000,000	0.2%
					District of Columbia	3,611,000,000	0.1%

Source: U.S. Department of Transportation, Federal Highway Administration
"Highway Statistics 2008" (Table VM-2, http://www.fhwa.dot.gov/policyinformation/statistics/2008/index.cfm)

Highway Fatalities in 2008

National Total = 37,261 Fatalities

RANK	STATE	FATALITIES	% of USA
12	Alabama	966	2.6%
50	Alaska	62	0.2%
14	Arizona	937	2.5%
23	Arkansas	600	1.6%
1	California	3,434	9.2%
26	Colorado	548	1.5%
37	Connecticut	264	0.7%
44	Delaware	121	0.3%
3	Florida	2,978	8.0%
4	Georgia	1,493	4.0%
46	Hawaii	107	0.3%
38	Idaho	232	0.6%
9	Illinois	1,043	2.8%
19	Indiana	814	2.2%
30	Iowa	412	1.1%
31	Kansas	385	1.0%
17	Kentucky	826	2.2%
16	Louisiana	912	2.4%
42	Maine	155	0.4%
24	Maryland	591	1.6%
34	Massachusetts	363	1.0%
11	Michigan	980	2.6%
28	Minnesota	456	1.2%
20	Mississippi	783	2.1%
13	Missouri	960	2.6%
39	Montana	229	0.6%
40	Nebraska	208	0.6%
35	Nevada	324	0.9%
43	New Hampshire	139	0.4%
25	New Jersey	590	1.6%
33	New Mexico	366	1.0%
7	New York	1,231	3.3%
6	North Carolina	1,433	3.8%
47	North Dakota	104	0.3%
8	Ohio	1,190	3.2%
21	Oklahoma	749	2.0%
29	Oregon	416	1.1%
5	Pennsylvania	1,468	3.9%
49	Rhode Island	65	0.2%
15	South Carolina	920	2.5%
45	South Dakota	119	0.3%
10	Tennessee	1,035	2.8%
2	Texas	3,382	9.1%
36	Utah	275	0.7%
48	Vermont	73	0.2%
18	Virginia	824	2.2%
27	Washington	521	1.4%
32	West Virginia	380	1.0%
22	Wisconsin	605	1.6%
41	Wyoming	159	0.4%

RANK	STATE	FATALITIES	% of USA
1	California	3,434	9.2%
2	Texas	3,382	9.1%
3	Florida	2,978	8.0%
4	Georgia	1,493	4.0%
5	Pennsylvania	1,468	3.9%
6	North Carolina	1,433	3.8%
7	New York	1,231	3.3%
8	Ohio	1,190	3.2%
9	Illinois	1,043	2.8%
10	Tennessee	1,035	2.8%
11	Michigan	980	2.6%
12	Alabama	966	2.6%
13	Missouri	960	2.6%
14	Arizona	937	2.5%
15	South Carolina	920	2.5%
16	Louisiana	912	2.4%
17	Kentucky	826	2.2%
18	Virginia	824	2.2%
19	Indiana	814	2.2%
20	Mississippi	783	2.1%
21	Oklahoma	749	2.0%
22	Wisconsin	605	1.6%
23	Arkansas	600	1.6%
24	Maryland	591	1.6%
25	New Jersey	590	1.6%
26	Colorado	548	1.5%
27	Washington	521	1.4%
28	Minnesota	456	1.2%
29	Oregon	416	1.1%
30	Iowa	412	1.1%
31	Kansas	385	1.0%
32	West Virginia	380	1.0%
33	New Mexico	366	1.0%
34	Massachusetts	363	1.0%
35	Nevada	324	0.9%
36	Utah	275	0.7%
37	Connecticut	264	0.7%
38	Idaho	232	0.6%
39	Montana	229	0.6%
40	Nebraska	208	0.6%
41	Wyoming	159	0.4%
42	Maine	155	0.4%
43	New Hampshire	139	0.4%
44	Delaware	121	0.3%
45	South Dakota	119	0.3%
46	Hawaii	107	0.3%
47	North Dakota	104	0.3%
48	Vermont	73	0.2%
49	Rhode Island	65	0.2%
50	Alaska	62	0.2%
	District of Columbia	34	0.1%

Source: U.S. Department of Transportation, National Highway Traffic Safety Administration
"Traffic Safety Facts-Speeding" (http://www.nhtsa.dot.gov/portal/site/nhtsa/)

Highway Fatality Rate in 2008

National Rate = 1.25 Fatalities per 100 Million Vehicle-Miles of Travel

ALPHA ORDER

RANK	STATE	RATE
9	Alabama	1.63
27	Alaska	1.27
12	Arizona	1.52
5	Arkansas	1.81
37	California	1.05
29	Colorado	1.15
46	Connecticut	0.83
22	Delaware	1.35
14	Florida	1.50
20	Georgia	1.37
39	Hawaii	1.04
12	Idaho	1.52
42	Illinois	0.98
29	Indiana	1.15
23	Iowa	1.34
26	Kansas	1.30
7	Kentucky	1.74
2	Louisiana	2.02
35	Maine	1.06
33	Maryland	1.07
50	Massachusetts	0.67
43	Michigan	0.96
48	Minnesota	0.79
6	Mississippi	1.79
17	Missouri	1.41
1	Montana	2.12
32	Nebraska	1.09
10	Nevada	1.56
33	New Hampshire	1.07
47	New Jersey	0.80
19	New Mexico	1.39
45	New York	0.92
17	North Carolina	1.41
24	North Dakota	1.33
31	Ohio	1.10
11	Oklahoma	1.54
28	Oregon	1.24
21	Pennsylvania	1.36
48	Rhode Island	0.79
3	South Carolina	1.85
25	South Dakota	1.32
15	Tennessee	1.49
16	Texas	1.44
35	Utah	1.06
40	Vermont	1.00
40	Virginia	1.00
44	Washington	0.94
4	West Virginia	1.83
37	Wisconsin	1.05
8	Wyoming	1.68

RANK ORDER

RANK	STATE	RATE
1	Montana	2.12
2	Louisiana	2.02
3	South Carolina	1.85
4	West Virginia	1.83
5	Arkansas	1.81
6	Mississippi	1.79
7	Kentucky	1.74
8	Wyoming	1.68
9	Alabama	1.63
10	Nevada	1.56
11	Oklahoma	1.54
12	Arizona	1.52
12	Idaho	1.52
14	Florida	1.50
15	Tennessee	1.49
16	Texas	1.44
17	Missouri	1.41
17	North Carolina	1.41
19	New Mexico	1.39
20	Georgia	1.37
21	Pennsylvania	1.36
22	Delaware	1.35
23	Iowa	1.34
24	North Dakota	1.33
25	South Dakota	1.32
26	Kansas	1.30
27	Alaska	1.27
28	Oregon	1.24
29	Colorado	1.15
29	Indiana	1.15
31	Ohio	1.10
32	Nebraska	1.09
33	Maryland	1.07
33	New Hampshire	1.07
35	Maine	1.06
35	Utah	1.06
37	California	1.05
37	Wisconsin	1.05
39	Hawaii	1.04
40	Vermont	1.00
40	Virginia	1.00
42	Illinois	0.98
43	Michigan	0.96
44	Washington	0.94
45	New York	0.92
46	Connecticut	0.83
47	New Jersey	0.80
48	Minnesota	0.79
48	Rhode Island	0.79
50	Massachusetts	0.67

District of Columbia	0.94

Source: CQ Press using data from U.S. Department of Transportation, National Highway Traffic Safety Administration
"Traffic Safety Facts-Speeding" (http://www.nhtsa.dot.gov/portal/site/nhtsa/)
"Highway Statistics 2008" (Table VM-2, http://www.fhwa.dot.gov/policyinformation/statistics/2008/index.cfm)

Percent of Traffic Fatalities That Were Speeding-Related: 2008

National Percent = 31.3%*

RANK	STATE (ALPHA ORDER)	PERCENT		RANK	STATE (RANK ORDER)	PERCENT
4	Alabama	46.3		1	Alaska	53.2
1	Alaska	53.2		2	Pennsylvania	48.9
10	Arizona	39.8		3	Hawaii	46.7
49	Arkansas	10.5		4	Alabama	46.3
18	California	33.2		5	Missouri	45.9
11	Colorado	38.3		6	Texas	42.0
23	Connecticut	31.4		7	Mississippi	41.8
30	Delaware	29.8		8	Washington	41.5
45	Florida	18.6		8	Wyoming	41.5
43	Georgia	20.7		10	Arizona	39.8
3	Hawaii	46.7		11	Colorado	38.3
22	Idaho	31.9		12	South Carolina	38.2
13	Illinois	36.9		13	Illinois	36.9
28	Indiana	30.7		14	Utah	35.6
50	Iowa	10.0		15	Maine	34.2
39	Kansas	24.9		15	Vermont	34.2
45	Kentucky	18.6		17	New York	33.3
35	Louisiana	27.4		18	California	33.2
15	Maine	34.2		19	North Carolina	33.1
21	Maryland	32.3		20	Wisconsin	32.7
36	Massachusetts	26.7		21	Maryland	32.3
40	Michigan	23.7		22	Idaho	31.9
32	Minnesota	29.4		23	Connecticut	31.4
7	Mississippi	41.8		23	Montana	31.4
5	Missouri	45.9		25	South Dakota	31.1
23	Montana	31.4		26	Oregon	30.8
47	Nebraska	15.4		26	Rhode Island	30.8
34	Nevada	28.7		28	Indiana	30.7
33	New Hampshire	28.8		29	Virginia	29.9
48	New Jersey	11.0		30	Delaware	29.8
44	New Mexico	19.1		31	Oklahoma	29.5
17	New York	33.3		32	Minnesota	29.4
19	North Carolina	33.1		33	New Hampshire	28.8
37	North Dakota	26.0		34	Nevada	28.7
42	Ohio	22.6		35	Louisiana	27.4
31	Oklahoma	29.5		36	Massachusetts	26.7
26	Oregon	30.8		37	North Dakota	26.0
2	Pennsylvania	48.9		38	West Virginia	25.5
26	Rhode Island	30.8		39	Kansas	24.9
12	South Carolina	38.2		40	Michigan	23.7
25	South Dakota	31.1		41	Tennessee	23.5
41	Tennessee	23.5		42	Ohio	22.6
6	Texas	42.0		43	Georgia	20.7
14	Utah	35.6		44	New Mexico	19.1
15	Vermont	34.2		45	Florida	18.6
29	Virginia	29.9		45	Kentucky	18.6
8	Washington	41.5		47	Nebraska	15.4
38	West Virginia	25.5		48	New Jersey	11.0
20	Wisconsin	32.7		49	Arkansas	10.5
8	Wyoming	41.5		50	Iowa	10.0

District of Columbia 35.3

Source: CQ Press using data from U.S. Department of Transportation, National Highway Traffic Safety Administration
"Traffic Safety Facts-Speeding" (http://www.nhtsa.dot.gov/portal/site/nhtsa/)
*A speeding-related crash is if the driver was charged with a speeding-related offense or if an officer indicated that racing, driving too fast for conditions, or exceeding the posted speed limit was a contributing factor in the crash.

Percent of Vehicles Involved in Fatal Crashes That Were Large Trucks: 2008

National Percent = 8.1%*

ALPHA ORDER

RANK	STATE	PERCENT
12	Alabama	9.6
45	Alaska	5.5
27	Arizona	7.9
10	Arkansas	9.8
38	California	6.4
25	Colorado	8.1
32	Connecticut	7.2
47	Delaware	4.6
38	Florida	6.4
24	Georgia	8.6
49	Hawaii	4.3
8	Idaho	10.5
16	Illinois	9.5
5	Indiana	11.4
4	Iowa	12.1
5	Kansas	11.4
21	Kentucky	8.9
21	Louisiana	8.9
9	Maine	10.3
42	Maryland	6.1
48	Massachusetts	4.5
38	Michigan	6.4
11	Minnesota	9.7
33	Mississippi	7.1
18	Missouri	9.3
17	Montana	9.4
3	Nebraska	14.4
46	Nevada	4.7
41	New Hampshire	6.2
43	New Jersey	5.9
12	New Mexico	9.6
36	New York	6.6
29	North Carolina	7.6
1	North Dakota	15.3
25	Ohio	8.1
7	Oklahoma	10.7
31	Oregon	7.5
12	Pennsylvania	9.6
50	Rhode Island	2.5
34	South Carolina	7.0
23	South Dakota	8.8
35	Tennessee	6.7
19	Texas	9.1
19	Utah	9.1
43	Vermont	5.9
37	Virginia	6.5
29	Washington	7.6
12	West Virginia	9.6
28	Wisconsin	7.8
2	Wyoming	15.0

RANK ORDER

RANK	STATE	PERCENT
1	North Dakota	15.3
2	Wyoming	15.0
3	Nebraska	14.4
4	Iowa	12.1
5	Indiana	11.4
5	Kansas	11.4
7	Oklahoma	10.7
8	Idaho	10.5
9	Maine	10.3
10	Arkansas	9.8
11	Minnesota	9.7
12	Alabama	9.6
12	New Mexico	9.6
12	Pennsylvania	9.6
12	West Virginia	9.6
16	Illinois	9.5
17	Montana	9.4
18	Missouri	9.3
19	Texas	9.1
19	Utah	9.1
21	Kentucky	8.9
21	Louisiana	8.9
23	South Dakota	8.8
24	Georgia	8.6
25	Colorado	8.1
25	Ohio	8.1
27	Arizona	7.9
28	Wisconsin	7.8
29	North Carolina	7.6
29	Washington	7.6
31	Oregon	7.5
32	Connecticut	7.2
33	Mississippi	7.1
34	South Carolina	7.0
35	Tennessee	6.7
36	New York	6.6
37	Virginia	6.5
38	California	6.4
38	Florida	6.4
38	Michigan	6.4
41	New Hampshire	6.2
42	Maryland	6.1
43	New Jersey	5.9
43	Vermont	5.9
45	Alaska	5.5
46	Nevada	4.7
47	Delaware	4.6
48	Massachusetts	4.5
49	Hawaii	4.3
50	Rhode Island	2.5

| | District of Columbia | 4.5 |

Source: U.S. Department of Transportation, National Highway Traffic Safety Administration
   "Traffic Safety Facts-Large Trucks" (http://www.nhtsa.dot.gov/portal/site/nhtsa/)
*Large trucks are those with gross vehicle weight greater than 10,000 pounds. In 2008, 4,006 large trucks were involved in fatal crashes.

Lives Saved by Child Restraints, Seat Belts,
Air Bags and Motorcycle Helmets in 2008
National Total = 17,869 Lives

Source: CQ Press using data from U.S. Department of Transportation, National Highway Traffic Safety Administration
"Traffic Safety Facts-Lives Saved" (http://www.nhtsa.dot.gov/portal/site/nhtsa/)

Safety Belt Usage Rate in 2008

National Rate = 83.0% Use Safety Belts

ALPHA ORDER				RANK ORDER		
RANK	STATE	PERCENT		RANK	STATE	PERCENT
22	Alabama	86.1		1	Michigan	97.2
25	Alaska	84.9		2	Hawaii	97.0
35	Arizona	79.9		3	Washington	96.5
47	Arkansas	70.4		4	Oregon	96.3
5	California	95.7		5	California	95.7
30	Colorado	81.7		6	Maryland	93.3
19	Connecticut	88.0		7	Iowa	92.9
9	Delaware	91.3		8	New Jersey	91.8
30	Florida	81.7		9	Delaware	91.3
16	Georgia	89.6		10	Indiana	91.2
2	Hawaii	97.0		10	Texas	91.2
39	Idaho	76.9		12	New Mexico	91.1
14	Illinois	90.5		13	Nevada	90.9
10	Indiana	91.2		14	Illinois	90.5
7	Iowa	92.9		15	North Carolina	89.8
38	Kansas	77.4		16	Georgia	89.6
43	Kentucky	73.3		17	West Virginia	89.5
41	Louisiana	75.5		18	New York	89.1
27	Maine	83.0		19	Connecticut	88.0
6	Maryland	93.3		20	Vermont	87.3
50	Massachusetts	66.8		21	Minnesota	86.7
1	Michigan	97.2		22	Alabama	86.1
21	Minnesota	86.7		23	Utah	86.0
46	Mississippi	71.3		24	Pennsylvania	85.1
40	Missouri	75.8		25	Alaska	84.9
36	Montana	79.3		26	Oklahoma	84.3
29	Nebraska	82.6		27	Maine	83.0
13	Nevada	90.9		28	Ohio	82.7
48	New Hampshire	69.2		29	Nebraska	82.6
8	New Jersey	91.8		30	Colorado	81.7
12	New Mexico	91.1		30	Florida	81.7
18	New York	89.1		32	North Dakota	81.6
15	North Carolina	89.8		33	Tennessee	81.5
32	North Dakota	81.6		34	Virginia	80.6
28	Ohio	82.7		35	Arizona	79.9
26	Oklahoma	84.3		36	Montana	79.3
4	Oregon	96.3		37	South Carolina	79.0
24	Pennsylvania	85.1		38	Kansas	77.4
44	Rhode Island	72.0		39	Idaho	76.9
37	South Carolina	79.0		40	Missouri	75.8
45	South Dakota	71.8		41	Louisiana	75.5
33	Tennessee	81.5		42	Wisconsin	74.2
10	Texas	91.2		43	Kentucky	73.3
23	Utah	86.0		44	Rhode Island	72.0
20	Vermont	87.3		45	South Dakota	71.8
34	Virginia	80.6		46	Mississippi	71.3
3	Washington	96.5		47	Arkansas	70.4
17	West Virginia	89.5		48	New Hampshire	69.2
42	Wisconsin	74.2		49	Wyoming	68.6
49	Wyoming	68.6		50	Massachusetts	66.8
				District of Columbia		90.0

Source: U.S. Department of Transportation, National Highway Traffic Safety Administration
  "Occupant Protection" (http://www-nrd.nhtsa.dot.gov/Pubs/811160.PDF)

Percent of Passenger Car Occupant Fatalities
Where Victim Used a Seat Belt in 2008
National Percent = 42% of Passenger Car Occupant Fatalities*

ALPHA ORDER

RANK	STATE	PERCENT
30	Alabama	36
20	Alaska	44
34	Arizona	34
40	Arkansas	32
1	California	58
10	Colorado	49
22	Connecticut	42
6	Delaware	51
25	Florida	40
28	Georgia	37
20	Hawaii	44
28	Idaho	37
18	Illinois	45
18	Indiana	45
23	Iowa	41
40	Kansas	32
30	Kentucky	36
40	Louisiana	32
17	Maine	47
4	Maryland	55
43	Massachusetts	30
6	Michigan	51
13	Minnesota	48
34	Mississippi	34
45	Missouri	29
46	Montana	28
26	Nebraska	39
10	Nevada	49
48	New Hampshire	26
13	New Jersey	48
13	New Mexico	48
6	New York	51
13	North Carolina	48
50	North Dakota	23
23	Ohio	41
33	Oklahoma	35
1	Oregon	58
37	Pennsylvania	33
49	Rhode Island	25
37	South Carolina	33
43	South Dakota	30
34	Tennessee	34
9	Texas	50
5	Utah	54
10	Vermont	49
30	Virginia	36
3	Washington	56
37	West Virginia	33
27	Wisconsin	38
46	Wyoming	28

RANK ORDER

RANK	STATE	PERCENT
1	California	58
1	Oregon	58
3	Washington	56
4	Maryland	55
5	Utah	54
6	Delaware	51
6	Michigan	51
6	New York	51
9	Texas	50
10	Colorado	49
10	Nevada	49
10	Vermont	49
13	Minnesota	48
13	New Jersey	48
13	New Mexico	48
13	North Carolina	48
17	Maine	47
18	Illinois	45
18	Indiana	45
20	Alaska	44
20	Hawaii	44
22	Connecticut	42
23	Iowa	41
23	Ohio	41
25	Florida	40
26	Nebraska	39
27	Wisconsin	38
28	Georgia	37
28	Idaho	37
30	Alabama	36
30	Kentucky	36
30	Virginia	36
33	Oklahoma	35
34	Arizona	34
34	Mississippi	34
34	Tennessee	34
37	Pennsylvania	33
37	South Carolina	33
37	West Virginia	33
40	Arkansas	32
40	Kansas	32
40	Louisiana	32
43	Massachusetts	30
43	South Dakota	30
45	Missouri	29
46	Montana	28
46	Wyoming	28
48	New Hampshire	26
49	Rhode Island	25
50	North Dakota	23

District of Columbia	36

Source: U.S. Department of Transportation, National Highway Safety Administration
   "Traffic Safety Facts-Occupant Protection" (http://www.nhtsa.dot.gov/portal/site/nhtsa/)
*Only those fatalities where seat belts are known to have been used are counted.

Fatalities in Alcohol-Related Crashes in 2008

National Total = 13,846 Fatalities*

<u>ALPHA ORDER</u>

RANK	STATE	FATALITIES	% of USA
13	Alabama	367	2.7%
49	Alaska	24	0.2%
17	Arizona	329	2.4%
24	Arkansas	205	1.5%
2	California	1,198	8.7%
25	Colorado	202	1.5%
36	Connecticut	104	0.8%
45	Delaware	49	0.4%
3	Florida	1,041	7.5%
6	Georgia	489	3.5%
44	Hawaii	50	0.4%
38	Idaho	93	0.7%
8	Illinois	434	3.1%
20	Indiana	250	1.8%
35	Iowa	113	0.8%
30	Kansas	157	1.1%
22	Kentucky	226	1.6%
11	Louisiana	404	2.9%
46	Maine	47	0.3%
27	Maryland	186	1.3%
31	Massachusetts	151	1.1%
16	Michigan	331	2.4%
28	Minnesota	161	1.2%
18	Mississippi	297	2.1%
15	Missouri	364	2.6%
37	Montana	103	0.7%
39	Nebraska	75	0.5%
33	Nevada	121	0.9%
42	New Hampshire	53	0.4%
26	New Jersey	197	1.4%
34	New Mexico	118	0.9%
10	New York	409	3.0%
5	North Carolina	500	3.6%
43	North Dakota	52	0.4%
9	Ohio	415	3.0%
19	Oklahoma	274	2.0%
29	Oregon	159	1.1%
4	Pennsylvania	578	4.2%
48	Rhode Island	29	0.2%
7	South Carolina	463	3.3%
47	South Dakota	41	0.3%
12	Tennessee	386	2.8%
1	Texas	1,463	10.6%
41	Utah	55	0.4%
50	Vermont	15	0.1%
14	Virginia	365	2.6%
23	Washington	225	1.6%
32	West Virginia	142	1.0%
20	Wisconsin	250	1.8%
39	Wyoming	75	0.5%

<u>RANK ORDER</u>

RANK	STATE	FATALITIES	% of USA
1	Texas	1,463	10.6%
2	California	1,198	8.7%
3	Florida	1,041	7.5%
4	Pennsylvania	578	4.2%
5	North Carolina	500	3.6%
6	Georgia	489	3.5%
7	South Carolina	463	3.3%
8	Illinois	434	3.1%
9	Ohio	415	3.0%
10	New York	409	3.0%
11	Louisiana	404	2.9%
12	Tennessee	386	2.8%
13	Alabama	367	2.7%
14	Virginia	365	2.6%
15	Missouri	364	2.6%
16	Michigan	331	2.4%
17	Arizona	329	2.4%
18	Mississippi	297	2.1%
19	Oklahoma	274	2.0%
20	Indiana	250	1.8%
20	Wisconsin	250	1.8%
22	Kentucky	226	1.6%
23	Washington	225	1.6%
24	Arkansas	205	1.5%
25	Colorado	202	1.5%
26	New Jersey	197	1.4%
27	Maryland	186	1.3%
28	Minnesota	161	1.2%
29	Oregon	159	1.1%
30	Kansas	157	1.1%
31	Massachusetts	151	1.1%
32	West Virginia	142	1.0%
33	Nevada	121	0.9%
34	New Mexico	118	0.9%
35	Iowa	113	0.8%
36	Connecticut	104	0.8%
37	Montana	103	0.7%
38	Idaho	93	0.7%
39	Nebraska	75	0.5%
39	Wyoming	75	0.5%
41	Utah	55	0.4%
42	New Hampshire	53	0.4%
43	North Dakota	52	0.4%
44	Hawaii	50	0.4%
45	Delaware	49	0.4%
46	Maine	47	0.3%
47	South Dakota	41	0.3%
48	Rhode Island	29	0.2%
49	Alaska	24	0.2%
50	Vermont	15	0.1%
	District of Columbia	13	0.1%

Source: U.S. Department of Transportation, National Highway Traffic Safety Administration
   "Traffic Safety Facts-Alcohol" (http://www.nhtsa.dot.gov/portal/site/nhtsa/)
*Drivers with Blood Alcohol Content (BAC) of .01 or more. "Legally Drunk" BAC differs from state to state but is often .08 or higher.

Fatalities in Alcohol-Related Crashes
as a Percent of All Highway Fatalities in 2008
National Percent = 37% of Highway Fatalities*

ALPHA ORDER

RANK	STATE	PERCENT
19	Alabama	38
19	Alaska	38
31	Arizona	35
37	Arkansas	34
31	California	35
25	Colorado	37
15	Connecticut	40
15	Delaware	40
31	Florida	35
40	Georgia	33
4	Hawaii	46
15	Idaho	40
11	Illinois	42
44	Indiana	31
47	Iowa	27
13	Kansas	41
47	Kentucky	27
7	Louisiana	44
46	Maine	30
44	Maryland	31
11	Massachusetts	42
37	Michigan	34
31	Minnesota	35
19	Mississippi	38
19	Missouri	38
5	Montana	45
30	Nebraska	36
25	Nevada	37
19	New Hampshire	38
40	New Jersey	33
43	New Mexico	32
40	New York	33
31	North Carolina	35
1	North Dakota	50
31	Ohio	35
25	Oklahoma	37
19	Oregon	38
18	Pennsylvania	39
5	Rhode Island	45
1	South Carolina	50
37	South Dakota	34
25	Tennessee	37
9	Texas	43
50	Utah	20
49	Vermont	21
7	Virginia	44
9	Washington	43
25	West Virginia	37
13	Wisconsin	41
3	Wyoming	47

RANK ORDER

RANK	STATE	PERCENT
1	North Dakota	50
1	South Carolina	50
3	Wyoming	47
4	Hawaii	46
5	Montana	45
5	Rhode Island	45
7	Louisiana	44
7	Virginia	44
9	Texas	43
9	Washington	43
11	Illinois	42
11	Massachusetts	42
13	Kansas	41
13	Wisconsin	41
15	Connecticut	40
15	Delaware	40
15	Idaho	40
18	Pennsylvania	39
19	Alabama	38
19	Alaska	38
19	Mississippi	38
19	Missouri	38
19	New Hampshire	38
19	Oregon	38
25	Colorado	37
25	Nevada	37
25	Oklahoma	37
25	Tennessee	37
25	West Virginia	37
30	Nebraska	36
31	Arizona	35
31	California	35
31	Florida	35
31	Minnesota	35
31	North Carolina	35
31	Ohio	35
37	Arkansas	34
37	Michigan	34
37	South Dakota	34
40	Georgia	33
40	New Jersey	33
40	New York	33
43	New Mexico	32
44	Indiana	31
44	Maryland	31
46	Maine	30
47	Iowa	27
47	Kentucky	27
49	Vermont	21
50	Utah	20
	District of Columbia	39

Source: U.S. Department of Transportation, National Highway Traffic Safety Administration
"Traffic Safety Facts-Alcohol" (http://www.nhtsa.dot.gov/portal/site/nhtsa/)
*Drivers with Blood Alcohol Content (BAC) of .01 or more. "Legally Drunk" BAC differs from state to state but is often .08 or higher.

Percent of Fatal Traffic Accidents Involving Older Drivers in 2008

National Percent = 11.1%*

ALPHA ORDER

RANK	STATE	PERCENT
48	Alabama	8.6
47	Alaska	8.8
27	Arizona	11.2
24	Arkansas	11.4
45	California	9.0
27	Colorado	11.2
26	Connecticut	11.3
33	Delaware	10.5
27	Florida	11.2
31	Georgia	11.0
37	Hawaii	10.1
42	Idaho	9.3
24	Illinois	11.4
39	Indiana	9.6
4	Iowa	14.7
11	Kansas	13.3
32	Kentucky	10.6
50	Louisiana	7.9
4	Maine	14.7
34	Maryland	10.4
20	Massachusetts	12.0
7	Michigan	14.3
8	Minnesota	14.2
34	Mississippi	10.4
21	Missouri	11.9
36	Montana	10.2
3	Nebraska	16.0
43	Nevada	9.2
22	New Hampshire	11.8
12	New Jersey	13.0
45	New Mexico	9.0
10	New York	13.7
30	North Carolina	11.1
41	North Dakota	9.5
16	Ohio	12.6
15	Oklahoma	12.8
18	Oregon	12.5
16	Pennsylvania	12.6
2	Rhode Island	18.5
38	South Carolina	10.0
6	South Dakota	14.5
12	Tennessee	13.0
49	Texas	8.5
44	Utah	9.1
1	Vermont	18.6
23	Virginia	11.6
19	Washington	12.1
9	West Virginia	13.8
12	Wisconsin	13.0
39	Wyoming	9.6

RANK ORDER

RANK	STATE	PERCENT
1	Vermont	18.6
2	Rhode Island	18.5
3	Nebraska	16.0
4	Iowa	14.7
4	Maine	14.7
6	South Dakota	14.5
7	Michigan	14.3
8	Minnesota	14.2
9	West Virginia	13.8
10	New York	13.7
11	Kansas	13.3
12	New Jersey	13.0
12	Tennessee	13.0
12	Wisconsin	13.0
15	Oklahoma	12.8
16	Ohio	12.6
16	Pennsylvania	12.6
18	Oregon	12.5
19	Washington	12.1
20	Massachusetts	12.0
21	Missouri	11.9
22	New Hampshire	11.8
23	Virginia	11.6
24	Arkansas	11.4
24	Illinois	11.4
26	Connecticut	11.3
27	Arizona	11.2
27	Colorado	11.2
27	Florida	11.2
30	North Carolina	11.1
31	Georgia	11.0
32	Kentucky	10.6
33	Delaware	10.5
34	Maryland	10.4
34	Mississippi	10.4
36	Montana	10.2
37	Hawaii	10.1
38	South Carolina	10.0
39	Indiana	9.6
39	Wyoming	9.6
41	North Dakota	9.5
42	Idaho	9.3
43	Nevada	9.2
44	Utah	9.1
45	California	9.0
45	New Mexico	9.0
47	Alaska	8.8
48	Alabama	8.6
49	Texas	8.5
50	Louisiana	7.9

District of Columbia	13.6

Source: CQ Press using data from U.S. Department of Transportation, National Highway Traffic Safety Administration
   "Traffic Safety Facts-Older Population" (http://www.nhtsa.dot.gov/portal/site/nhtsa/)
*Drivers 65 years old and older. People 65 or older make up 13 percent of the total U.S. population.

Percent of Highway Fatalities Who Were Young Drivers: 2008

National Percent = 7.4% of Fatalities*

ALPHA ORDER

RANK	STATE	PERCENT
6	Alabama	9.6
17	Alaska	8.1
46	Arizona	5.1
10	Arkansas	8.8
43	California	6.3
25	Colorado	7.5
42	Connecticut	6.4
47	Delaware	5.0
38	Florida	6.5
38	Georgia	6.5
38	Hawaii	6.5
4	Idaho	9.9
19	Illinois	7.7
6	Indiana	9.6
29	Iowa	7.0
10	Kansas	8.8
32	Kentucky	6.9
34	Louisiana	6.8
14	Maine	8.4
27	Maryland	7.1
13	Massachusetts	8.5
29	Michigan	7.0
29	Minnesota	7.0
25	Mississippi	7.5
8	Missouri	9.2
15	Montana	8.3
1	Nebraska	12.0
50	Nevada	4.6
12	New Hampshire	8.6
44	New Jersey	6.1
36	New Mexico	6.6
47	New York	5.0
36	North Carolina	6.6
19	North Dakota	7.7
35	Ohio	6.7
3	Oklahoma	10.1
47	Oregon	5.0
23	Pennsylvania	7.6
19	Rhode Island	7.7
19	South Carolina	7.7
23	South Dakota	7.6
9	Tennessee	9.1
16	Texas	8.2
45	Utah	5.5
2	Vermont	11.0
5	Virginia	9.7
38	Washington	6.5
27	West Virginia	7.1
17	Wisconsin	8.1
32	Wyoming	6.9

RANK ORDER

RANK	STATE	PERCENT
1	Nebraska	12.0
2	Vermont	11.0
3	Oklahoma	10.1
4	Idaho	9.9
5	Virginia	9.7
6	Alabama	9.6
6	Indiana	9.6
8	Missouri	9.2
9	Tennessee	9.1
10	Arkansas	8.8
10	Kansas	8.8
12	New Hampshire	8.6
13	Massachusetts	8.5
14	Maine	8.4
15	Montana	8.3
16	Texas	8.2
17	Alaska	8.1
17	Wisconsin	8.1
19	Illinois	7.7
19	North Dakota	7.7
19	Rhode Island	7.7
19	South Carolina	7.7
23	Pennsylvania	7.6
23	South Dakota	7.6
25	Colorado	7.5
25	Mississippi	7.5
27	Maryland	7.1
27	West Virginia	7.1
29	Iowa	7.0
29	Michigan	7.0
29	Minnesota	7.0
32	Kentucky	6.9
32	Wyoming	6.9
34	Louisiana	6.8
35	Ohio	6.7
36	New Mexico	6.6
36	North Carolina	6.6
38	Florida	6.5
38	Georgia	6.5
38	Hawaii	6.5
38	Washington	6.5
42	Connecticut	6.4
43	California	6.3
44	New Jersey	6.1
45	Utah	5.5
46	Arizona	5.1
47	Delaware	5.0
47	New York	5.0
47	Oregon	5.0
50	Nevada	4.6

District of Columbia** NA

Source: CQ Press using data from U.S. Department of Transportation, National Highway Traffic Safety Administration
"Traffic Safety Facts-Young Drivers" (http://www.nhtsa.dot.gov/portal/site/nhtsa/)
*Drivers 15 to 20 years old. Based on 2,739 fatalities of young drivers. An additional 3,689 passengers and nonoccupants were killed in crashes involving young drivers. Young drivers accounted for 6.4 percent of all drivers.
**Not available.

Licensed Drivers in 2008

National Total = 208,320,601 Licensed Drivers

ALPHA ORDER				RANK ORDER			
RANK	STATE	DRIVERS	% of USA	RANK	STATE	DRIVERS	% of USA
21	Alabama	3,753,550	1.8%	1	California	23,697,667	11.4%
48	Alaska	503,162	0.2%	2	Texas	15,374,063	7.4%
17	Arizona	4,315,579	2.1%	3	Florida	14,033,844	6.7%
30	Arkansas	2,055,189	1.0%	4	New York	11,284,545	5.4%
1	California	23,697,667	11.4%	5	Pennsylvania	8,646,273	4.2%
22	Colorado	3,605,682	1.7%	6	Illinois	8,260,940	4.0%
27	Connecticut	2,883,324	1.4%	7	Ohio	7,962,266	3.8%
45	Delaware	651,877	0.3%	8	Michigan	7,118,378	3.4%
3	Florida	14,033,844	6.7%	9	North Carolina	6,457,000	3.1%
10	Georgia	6,257,484	3.0%	10	Georgia	6,257,484	3.0%
42	Hawaii	884,767	0.4%	11	New Jersey	5,782,155	2.8%
39	Idaho	1,038,314	0.5%	12	Indiana	5,550,469	2.7%
6	Illinois	8,260,940	4.0%	13	Virginia	5,301,182	2.5%
12	Indiana	5,550,469	2.7%	14	Washington	4,953,872	2.4%
32	Iowa	1,989,663	1.0%	15	Massachusetts	4,674,058	2.2%
31	Kansas	2,021,905	1.0%	16	Tennessee	4,450,644	2.1%
26	Kentucky	2,932,659	1.4%	17	Arizona	4,315,579	2.1%
25	Louisiana	2,998,162	1.4%	18	Missouri	4,196,682	2.0%
41	Maine	1,006,057	0.5%	19	Wisconsin	4,075,764	2.0%
20	Maryland	3,786,650	1.8%	20	Maryland	3,786,650	1.8%
15	Massachusetts	4,674,058	2.2%	21	Alabama	3,753,550	1.8%
8	Michigan	7,118,378	3.4%	22	Colorado	3,605,682	1.7%
23	Minnesota	3,190,183	1.5%	23	Minnesota	3,190,183	1.5%
33	Mississippi	1,935,764	0.9%	24	South Carolina	3,185,408	1.5%
18	Missouri	4,196,682	2.0%	25	Louisiana	2,998,162	1.4%
44	Montana	738,982	0.4%	26	Kentucky	2,932,659	1.4%
38	Nebraska	1,346,406	0.6%	27	Connecticut	2,883,324	1.4%
35	Nevada	1,678,550	0.8%	28	Oregon	2,856,085	1.4%
40	New Hampshire	1,031,158	0.5%	29	Oklahoma	2,301,848	1.1%
11	New Jersey	5,782,155	2.8%	30	Arkansas	2,055,189	1.0%
36	New Mexico	1,365,249	0.7%	31	Kansas	2,021,905	1.0%
4	New York	11,284,545	5.4%	32	Iowa	1,989,663	1.0%
9	North Carolina	6,457,000	3.1%	33	Mississippi	1,935,764	0.9%
49	North Dakota	473,019	0.2%	34	Utah	1,687,306	0.8%
7	Ohio	7,962,266	3.8%	35	Nevada	1,678,550	0.8%
29	Oklahoma	2,301,848	1.1%	36	New Mexico	1,365,249	0.7%
28	Oregon	2,856,085	1.4%	37	West Virginia	1,360,926	0.7%
5	Pennsylvania	8,646,273	4.2%	38	Nebraska	1,346,406	0.6%
43	Rhode Island	748,351	0.4%	39	Idaho	1,038,314	0.5%
24	South Carolina	3,185,408	1.5%	40	New Hampshire	1,031,158	0.5%
46	South Dakota	597,326	0.3%	41	Maine	1,006,057	0.5%
16	Tennessee	4,450,644	2.1%	42	Hawaii	884,767	0.4%
2	Texas	15,374,063	7.4%	43	Rhode Island	748,351	0.4%
34	Utah	1,687,306	0.8%	44	Montana	738,982	0.4%
47	Vermont	541,990	0.3%	45	Delaware	651,877	0.3%
13	Virginia	5,301,182	2.5%	46	South Dakota	597,326	0.3%
14	Washington	4,953,872	2.4%	47	Vermont	541,990	0.3%
37	West Virginia	1,360,926	0.7%	48	Alaska	503,162	0.2%
19	Wisconsin	4,075,764	2.0%	49	North Dakota	473,019	0.2%
50	Wyoming	404,489	0.2%	50	Wyoming	404,489	0.2%
					District of Columbia	373,735	0.2%

Source: U.S. Department of Transportation, Federal Highway Administration
   "Highway Statistics 2008" (Table DL-22, http://www.fhwa.dot.gov/policyinformation/statistics/2008/index.cfm)

Licensed Drivers per 1,000 Driving Age Population in 2008

National Ratio = 871 Licensed Drivers

<table>
<tr><th colspan="3">ALPHA ORDER</th><th colspan="3">RANK ORDER</th></tr>
<tr><th>RANK</th><th>STATE</th><th>RATIO</th><th>RANK</th><th>STATE</th><th>RATIO</th></tr>
<tr><td>4</td><td>Alabama</td><td>1,022</td><td>1</td><td>Indiana</td><td>1,116</td></tr>
<tr><td>10</td><td>Alaska</td><td>952</td><td>2</td><td>Vermont</td><td>1,063</td></tr>
<tr><td>34</td><td>Arizona</td><td>867</td><td>3</td><td>Connecticut</td><td>1,034</td></tr>
<tr><td>19</td><td>Arkansas</td><td>920</td><td>4</td><td>Alabama</td><td>1,022</td></tr>
<tr><td>46</td><td>California</td><td>832</td><td>5</td><td>New Hampshire</td><td>973</td></tr>
<tr><td>15</td><td>Colorado</td><td>933</td><td>6</td><td>Nebraska</td><td>970</td></tr>
<tr><td>3</td><td>Connecticut</td><td>1,034</td><td>7</td><td>Wyoming</td><td>965</td></tr>
<tr><td>14</td><td>Delaware</td><td>943</td><td>8</td><td>Montana</td><td>954</td></tr>
<tr><td>12</td><td>Florida</td><td>948</td><td>8</td><td>Washington</td><td>954</td></tr>
<tr><td>41</td><td>Georgia</td><td>844</td><td>10</td><td>Alaska</td><td>952</td></tr>
<tr><td>39</td><td>Hawaii</td><td>854</td><td>11</td><td>South Dakota</td><td>950</td></tr>
<tr><td>26</td><td>Idaho</td><td>898</td><td>12</td><td>Florida</td><td>948</td></tr>
<tr><td>47</td><td>Illinois</td><td>819</td><td>13</td><td>Oregon</td><td>944</td></tr>
<tr><td>1</td><td>Indiana</td><td>1,116</td><td>14</td><td>Delaware</td><td>943</td></tr>
<tr><td>44</td><td>Iowa</td><td>838</td><td>15</td><td>Colorado</td><td>933</td></tr>
<tr><td>17</td><td>Kansas</td><td>927</td><td>15</td><td>Maine</td><td>933</td></tr>
<tr><td>33</td><td>Kentucky</td><td>868</td><td>17</td><td>Kansas</td><td>927</td></tr>
<tr><td>32</td><td>Louisiana</td><td>873</td><td>18</td><td>West Virginia</td><td>923</td></tr>
<tr><td>15</td><td>Maine</td><td>933</td><td>19</td><td>Arkansas</td><td>920</td></tr>
<tr><td>40</td><td>Maryland</td><td>850</td><td>20</td><td>North Dakota</td><td>917</td></tr>
<tr><td>28</td><td>Massachusetts</td><td>891</td><td>21</td><td>Wisconsin</td><td>911</td></tr>
<tr><td>24</td><td>Michigan</td><td>900</td><td>22</td><td>Tennessee</td><td>907</td></tr>
<tr><td>49</td><td>Minnesota</td><td>776</td><td>23</td><td>Missouri</td><td>901</td></tr>
<tr><td>37</td><td>Mississippi</td><td>857</td><td>24</td><td>Michigan</td><td>900</td></tr>
<tr><td>23</td><td>Missouri</td><td>901</td><td>24</td><td>South Carolina</td><td>900</td></tr>
<tr><td>8</td><td>Montana</td><td>954</td><td>26</td><td>Idaho</td><td>898</td></tr>
<tr><td>6</td><td>Nebraska</td><td>970</td><td>27</td><td>North Carolina</td><td>893</td></tr>
<tr><td>44</td><td>Nevada</td><td>838</td><td>28</td><td>Massachusetts</td><td>891</td></tr>
<tr><td>5</td><td>New Hampshire</td><td>973</td><td>29</td><td>New Mexico</td><td>887</td></tr>
<tr><td>42</td><td>New Jersey</td><td>841</td><td>30</td><td>Rhode Island</td><td>879</td></tr>
<tr><td>29</td><td>New Mexico</td><td>887</td><td>31</td><td>Ohio</td><td>876</td></tr>
<tr><td>50</td><td>New York</td><td>722</td><td>32</td><td>Louisiana</td><td>873</td></tr>
<tr><td>27</td><td>North Carolina</td><td>893</td><td>33</td><td>Kentucky</td><td>868</td></tr>
<tr><td>20</td><td>North Dakota</td><td>917</td><td>34</td><td>Arizona</td><td>867</td></tr>
<tr><td>31</td><td>Ohio</td><td>876</td><td>35</td><td>Pennsylvania</td><td>862</td></tr>
<tr><td>48</td><td>Oklahoma</td><td>811</td><td>36</td><td>Virginia</td><td>861</td></tr>
<tr><td>13</td><td>Oregon</td><td>944</td><td>37</td><td>Mississippi</td><td>857</td></tr>
<tr><td>35</td><td>Pennsylvania</td><td>862</td><td>38</td><td>Utah</td><td>856</td></tr>
<tr><td>30</td><td>Rhode Island</td><td>879</td><td>39</td><td>Hawaii</td><td>854</td></tr>
<tr><td>24</td><td>South Carolina</td><td>900</td><td>40</td><td>Maryland</td><td>850</td></tr>
<tr><td>11</td><td>South Dakota</td><td>950</td><td>41</td><td>Georgia</td><td>844</td></tr>
<tr><td>22</td><td>Tennessee</td><td>907</td><td>42</td><td>New Jersey</td><td>841</td></tr>
<tr><td>43</td><td>Texas</td><td>839</td><td>43</td><td>Texas</td><td>839</td></tr>
<tr><td>38</td><td>Utah</td><td>856</td><td>44</td><td>Iowa</td><td>838</td></tr>
<tr><td>2</td><td>Vermont</td><td>1,063</td><td>44</td><td>Nevada</td><td>838</td></tr>
<tr><td>36</td><td>Virginia</td><td>861</td><td>46</td><td>California</td><td>832</td></tr>
<tr><td>8</td><td>Washington</td><td>954</td><td>47</td><td>Illinois</td><td>819</td></tr>
<tr><td>18</td><td>West Virginia</td><td>923</td><td>48</td><td>Oklahoma</td><td>811</td></tr>
<tr><td>21</td><td>Wisconsin</td><td>911</td><td>49</td><td>Minnesota</td><td>776</td></tr>
<tr><td>7</td><td>Wyoming</td><td>965</td><td>50</td><td>New York</td><td>722</td></tr>
<tr><td></td><td></td><td></td><td></td><td>District of Columbia</td><td>758</td></tr>
</table>

Source: CQ Press using data from U.S. Department of Transportation, Federal Highway Administration
"Highway Statistics 2008" (Table DL-22, http://www.fhwa.dot.gov/policyinformation/statistics/2008/index.cfm)

Motor Vehicle Registrations in 2008

National Total = 248,164,738 Motor Vehicles*

ALPHA ORDER

RANK	STATE	VEHICLES	% of USA
20	Alabama	4,729,791	1.9%
48	Alaska	690,756	0.3%
22	Arizona	4,373,232	1.8%
32	Arkansas	2,040,988	0.8%
1	California	33,483,061	13.5%
35	Colorado	1,618,219	0.7%
29	Connecticut	3,093,744	1.2%
45	Delaware	867,744	0.3%
3	Florida	16,461,925	6.6%
8	Georgia	8,569,625	3.5%
42	Hawaii	945,491	0.4%
39	Idaho	1,318,233	0.5%
7	Illinois	9,793,821	3.9%
14	Indiana	5,847,546	2.4%
26	Iowa	3,430,867	1.4%
30	Kansas	2,448,768	1.0%
24	Kentucky	3,604,048	1.5%
23	Louisiana	3,979,188	1.6%
41	Maine	1,074,465	0.4%
21	Maryland	4,525,233	1.8%
15	Massachusetts	5,328,349	2.1%
9	Michigan	7,945,471	3.2%
19	Minnesota	4,783,491	1.9%
33	Mississippi	2,034,907	0.8%
18	Missouri	4,865,776	2.0%
43	Montana	926,975	0.4%
34	Nebraska	1,756,628	0.7%
37	Nevada	1,417,214	0.6%
40	New Hampshire	1,213,955	0.5%
12	New Jersey	6,246,882	2.5%
36	New Mexico	1,569,771	0.6%
4	New York	11,088,903	4.5%
11	North Carolina	6,248,829	2.5%
47	North Dakota	717,221	0.3%
5	Ohio	10,933,169	4.4%
27	Oklahoma	3,291,970	1.3%
28	Oregon	3,105,673	1.3%
6	Pennsylvania	10,366,408	4.2%
46	Rhode Island	794,380	0.3%
25	South Carolina	3,603,960	1.5%
44	South Dakota	907,384	0.4%
16	Tennessee	5,098,147	2.1%
2	Texas	18,207,948	7.3%
31	Utah	2,438,685	1.0%
50	Vermont	581,466	0.2%
10	Virginia	6,525,948	2.6%
13	Washington	5,979,710	2.4%
38	West Virginia	1,402,030	0.6%
17	Wisconsin	4,998,903	2.0%
49	Wyoming	664,041	0.3%

RANK ORDER

RANK	STATE	VEHICLES	% of USA
1	California	33,483,061	13.5%
2	Texas	18,207,948	7.3%
3	Florida	16,461,925	6.6%
4	New York	11,088,903	4.5%
5	Ohio	10,933,169	4.4%
6	Pennsylvania	10,366,408	4.2%
7	Illinois	9,793,821	3.9%
8	Georgia	8,569,625	3.5%
9	Michigan	7,945,471	3.2%
10	Virginia	6,525,948	2.6%
11	North Carolina	6,248,829	2.5%
12	New Jersey	6,246,882	2.5%
13	Washington	5,979,710	2.4%
14	Indiana	5,847,546	2.4%
15	Massachusetts	5,328,349	2.1%
16	Tennessee	5,098,147	2.1%
17	Wisconsin	4,998,903	2.0%
18	Missouri	4,865,776	2.0%
19	Minnesota	4,783,491	1.9%
20	Alabama	4,729,791	1.9%
21	Maryland	4,525,233	1.8%
22	Arizona	4,373,232	1.8%
23	Louisiana	3,979,188	1.6%
24	Kentucky	3,604,048	1.5%
25	South Carolina	3,603,960	1.5%
26	Iowa	3,430,867	1.4%
27	Oklahoma	3,291,970	1.3%
28	Oregon	3,105,673	1.3%
29	Connecticut	3,093,744	1.2%
30	Kansas	2,448,768	1.0%
31	Utah	2,438,685	1.0%
32	Arkansas	2,040,988	0.8%
33	Mississippi	2,034,907	0.8%
34	Nebraska	1,756,628	0.7%
35	Colorado	1,618,219	0.7%
36	New Mexico	1,569,771	0.6%
37	Nevada	1,417,214	0.6%
38	West Virginia	1,402,030	0.6%
39	Idaho	1,318,233	0.5%
40	New Hampshire	1,213,955	0.5%
41	Maine	1,074,465	0.4%
42	Hawaii	945,491	0.4%
43	Montana	926,975	0.4%
44	South Dakota	907,384	0.4%
45	Delaware	867,744	0.3%
46	Rhode Island	794,380	0.3%
47	North Dakota	717,221	0.3%
48	Alaska	690,756	0.3%
49	Wyoming	664,041	0.3%
50	Vermont	581,466	0.2%
	District of Columbia	223,799	0.1%

Source: U.S. Department of Transportation, Federal Highway Administration
"Highway Statistics 2008" (Table MV-1, http://www.fhwa.dot.gov/policyinformation/statistics/2008/index.cfm)
*Includes automobiles, trucks and buses. Does not include motorcycles.

Motor Vehicles per Driving Age Population in 2008

National Rate = 1.04 Motor Vehicles*

ALPHA ORDER			RANK ORDER		
RANK	STATE	RATE	RANK	STATE	RATE
6	Alabama	1.29	1	Wyoming	1.58
5	Alaska	1.31	2	Iowa	1.44
46	Arizona	0.88	2	South Dakota	1.44
42	Arkansas	0.91	4	North Dakota	1.39
12	California	1.18	5	Alaska	1.31
50	Colorado	0.42	6	Alabama	1.29
24	Connecticut	1.11	7	Nebraska	1.27
8	Delaware	1.26	8	Delaware	1.26
24	Florida	1.11	9	Utah	1.24
14	Georgia	1.16	10	Montana	1.20
42	Hawaii	0.91	10	Ohio	1.20
19	Idaho	1.14	12	California	1.18
39	Illinois	0.97	12	Indiana	1.18
12	Indiana	1.18	14	Georgia	1.16
2	Iowa	1.44	14	Louisiana	1.16
22	Kansas	1.12	14	Minnesota	1.16
26	Kentucky	1.07	14	Oklahoma	1.16
14	Louisiana	1.16	18	Washington	1.15
36	Maine	1.00	19	Idaho	1.14
32	Maryland	1.02	19	New Hampshire	1.14
32	Massachusetts	1.02	19	Vermont	1.14
36	Michigan	1.00	22	Kansas	1.12
14	Minnesota	1.16	22	Wisconsin	1.12
45	Mississippi	0.90	24	Connecticut	1.11
28	Missouri	1.04	24	Florida	1.11
10	Montana	1.20	26	Kentucky	1.07
7	Nebraska	1.27	27	Virginia	1.06
48	Nevada	0.71	28	Missouri	1.04
19	New Hampshire	1.14	28	Tennessee	1.04
42	New Jersey	0.91	30	Oregon	1.03
32	New Mexico	1.02	30	Pennsylvania	1.03
48	New York	0.71	32	Maryland	1.02
47	North Carolina	0.86	32	Massachusetts	1.02
4	North Dakota	1.39	32	New Mexico	1.02
10	Ohio	1.20	32	South Carolina	1.02
14	Oklahoma	1.16	36	Maine	1.00
30	Oregon	1.03	36	Michigan	1.00
30	Pennsylvania	1.03	38	Texas	0.99
41	Rhode Island	0.93	39	Illinois	0.97
32	South Carolina	1.02	40	West Virginia	0.95
2	South Dakota	1.44	41	Rhode Island	0.93
28	Tennessee	1.04	42	Arkansas	0.91
38	Texas	0.99	42	Hawaii	0.91
9	Utah	1.24	42	New Jersey	0.91
19	Vermont	1.14	45	Mississippi	0.90
27	Virginia	1.06	46	Arizona	0.88
18	Washington	1.15	47	North Carolina	0.86
40	West Virginia	0.95	48	Nevada	0.71
22	Wisconsin	1.12	48	New York	0.71
1	Wyoming	1.58	50	Colorado	0.42
				District of Columbia	0.45

Source: CQ Press using data from U.S. Department of Transportation, Federal Highway Administration
"Highway Statistics 2008" (Table MV-1, http://www.fhwa.dot.gov/policyinformation/statistics/2008/index.cfm)
*Persons age 16 and older. Motor Vehicles include automobiles, trucks and buses. Motorcycles are not included.

Average Travel Time to Work in 2008

National Average = 25.5 Minutes*

ALPHA ORDER

RANK	STATE	MINUTES
22	Alabama	24.0
46	Alaska	18.4
18	Arizona	25.0
39	Arkansas	21.3
6	California	27.0
20	Colorado	24.6
16	Connecticut	25.1
18	Delaware	25.0
11	Florida	25.9
6	Georgia	27.0
9	Hawaii	26.1
42	Idaho	20.2
4	Illinois	28.5
30	Indiana	23.2
45	Iowa	18.5
43	Kansas	19.1
33	Kentucky	22.6
15	Louisiana	25.3
28	Maine	23.3
2	Maryland	31.5
5	Massachusetts	27.3
22	Michigan	24.0
33	Minnesota	22.6
21	Mississippi	24.1
26	Missouri	23.8
48	Montana	17.9
47	Nebraska	18.0
22	Nevada	24.0
10	New Hampshire	26.0
3	New Jersey	30.1
36	New Mexico	21.9
1	New York	31.6
27	North Carolina	23.4
50	North Dakota	16.0
32	Ohio	22.9
41	Oklahoma	21.2
35	Oregon	22.5
12	Pennsylvania	25.8
31	Rhode Island	23.1
28	South Carolina	23.3
49	South Dakota	16.4
22	Tennessee	24.0
16	Texas	25.1
39	Utah	21.3
36	Vermont	21.9
8	Virginia	26.9
13	Washington	25.4
13	West Virginia	25.4
38	Wisconsin	21.7
44	Wyoming	18.7

RANK ORDER

RANK	STATE	MINUTES
1	New York	31.6
2	Maryland	31.5
3	New Jersey	30.1
4	Illinois	28.5
5	Massachusetts	27.3
6	California	27.0
6	Georgia	27.0
8	Virginia	26.9
9	Hawaii	26.1
10	New Hampshire	26.0
11	Florida	25.9
12	Pennsylvania	25.8
13	Washington	25.4
13	West Virginia	25.4
15	Louisiana	25.3
16	Connecticut	25.1
16	Texas	25.1
18	Arizona	25.0
18	Delaware	25.0
20	Colorado	24.6
21	Mississippi	24.1
22	Alabama	24.0
22	Michigan	24.0
22	Nevada	24.0
22	Tennessee	24.0
26	Missouri	23.8
27	North Carolina	23.4
28	Maine	23.3
28	South Carolina	23.3
30	Indiana	23.2
31	Rhode Island	23.1
32	Ohio	22.9
33	Kentucky	22.6
33	Minnesota	22.6
35	Oregon	22.5
36	New Mexico	21.9
36	Vermont	21.9
38	Wisconsin	21.7
39	Arkansas	21.3
39	Utah	21.3
41	Oklahoma	21.2
42	Idaho	20.2
43	Kansas	19.1
44	Wyoming	18.7
45	Iowa	18.5
46	Alaska	18.4
47	Nebraska	18.0
48	Montana	17.9
49	South Dakota	16.4
50	North Dakota	16.0

| | District of Columbia | 29.5 |

Source: U.S. Bureau of the Census
   "2008 American Community Survey" (http://www.census.gov/acs/www/)
*Workers 16 and older not working at home.

Percent of Commuters Who Drive to Work Alone: 2008

National Percent = 75.5%*

RANK	STATE	PERCENT		RANK	STATE	PERCENT
1	Alabama	83.0		1	Alabama	83.0
48	Alaska	66.2		2	Tennessee	82.7
34	Arizona	75.3		3	Ohio	82.6
15	Arkansas	80.2		4	Michigan	82.2
43	California	72.7		5	Indiana	81.9
38	Colorado	73.7		6	Mississippi	81.7
21	Connecticut	78.7		7	Louisiana	81.5
22	Delaware	78.6		8	Kentucky	81.2
19	Florida	79.4		9	South Carolina	81.1
27	Georgia	77.7		10	New Hampshire	81.0
49	Hawaii	65.7		11	Kansas	80.9
37	Idaho	74.1		11	West Virginia	80.9
39	Illinois	73.3		13	Rhode Island	80.8
5	Indiana	81.9		14	Oklahoma	80.5
25	Iowa	77.9		15	Arkansas	80.2
11	Kansas	80.9		16	North Carolina	80.0
8	Kentucky	81.2		17	Missouri	79.8
7	Louisiana	81.5		18	Nebraska	79.7
29	Maine	77.3		19	Florida	79.4
41	Maryland	73.2		20	Wisconsin	79.3
44	Massachusetts	72.3		21	Connecticut	78.7
4	Michigan	82.2		22	Delaware	78.6
27	Minnesota	77.7		23	Texas	78.3
6	Mississippi	81.7		24	South Dakota	78.2
17	Missouri	79.8		25	Iowa	77.9
42	Montana	72.8		26	North Dakota	77.8
18	Nebraska	79.7		27	Georgia	77.7
30	Nevada	76.8		27	Minnesota	77.7
10	New Hampshire	81.0		29	Maine	77.3
45	New Jersey	71.7		30	Nevada	76.8
32	New Mexico	76.6		31	Virginia	76.7
50	New York	53.7		32	New Mexico	76.6
16	North Carolina	80.0		33	Pennsylvania	76.2
26	North Dakota	77.8		34	Arizona	75.3
3	Ohio	82.6		35	Utah	75.0
14	Oklahoma	80.5		36	Wyoming	74.9
45	Oregon	71.7		37	Idaho	74.1
33	Pennsylvania	76.2		38	Colorado	73.7
13	Rhode Island	80.8		39	Illinois	73.3
9	South Carolina	81.1		39	Vermont	73.3
24	South Dakota	78.2		41	Maryland	73.2
2	Tennessee	82.7		42	Montana	72.8
23	Texas	78.3		43	California	72.7
35	Utah	75.0		44	Massachusetts	72.3
39	Vermont	73.3		45	New Jersey	71.7
31	Virginia	76.7		45	Oregon	71.7
47	Washington	71.5		47	Washington	71.5
11	West Virginia	80.9		48	Alaska	66.2
20	Wisconsin	79.3		49	Hawaii	65.7
36	Wyoming	74.9		50	New York	53.7
				District of Columbia		37.2

Source: U.S. Bureau of the Census
"2008 American Community Survey" (http://www.census.gov/acs/www/)
*Workers 16 and older who traveled to work by car, truck or van.

Percent of Commuters Who Drive to Work in Carpools: 2008

National Percent = 10.7%*

ALPHA ORDER

RANK	STATE	PERCENT
16	Alabama	11.8
2	Alaska	14.4
3	Arizona	13.1
8	Arkansas	12.6
13	California	11.9
19	Colorado	11.3
46	Connecticut	8.8
31	Delaware	10.6
33	Florida	10.3
13	Georgia	11.9
1	Hawaii	16.2
5	Idaho	12.9
41	Illinois	9.4
36	Indiana	10.1
23	Iowa	11.0
33	Kansas	10.3
19	Kentucky	11.3
24	Louisiana	10.9
24	Maine	10.9
29	Maryland	10.8
47	Massachusetts	8.6
41	Michigan	9.4
41	Minnesota	9.4
10	Mississippi	12.3
21	Missouri	11.1
18	Montana	11.4
35	Nebraska	10.2
12	Nevada	12.1
48	New Hampshire	8.4
44	New Jersey	9.1
6	New Mexico	12.7
50	New York	7.7
17	North Carolina	11.5
37	North Dakota	10.0
45	Ohio	8.9
13	Oklahoma	11.9
29	Oregon	10.8
40	Pennsylvania	9.7
49	Rhode Island	8.0
24	South Carolina	10.9
38	South Dakota	9.8
31	Tennessee	10.6
9	Texas	12.4
3	Utah	13.1
21	Vermont	11.1
24	Virginia	10.9
11	Washington	12.2
24	West Virginia	10.9
38	Wisconsin	9.8
6	Wyoming	12.7

RANK ORDER

RANK	STATE	PERCENT
1	Hawaii	16.2
2	Alaska	14.4
3	Arizona	13.1
3	Utah	13.1
5	Idaho	12.9
6	New Mexico	12.7
6	Wyoming	12.7
8	Arkansas	12.6
9	Texas	12.4
10	Mississippi	12.3
11	Washington	12.2
12	Nevada	12.1
13	California	11.9
13	Georgia	11.9
13	Oklahoma	11.9
16	Alabama	11.8
17	North Carolina	11.5
18	Montana	11.4
19	Colorado	11.3
19	Kentucky	11.3
21	Missouri	11.1
21	Vermont	11.1
23	Iowa	11.0
24	Louisiana	10.9
24	Maine	10.9
24	South Carolina	10.9
24	Virginia	10.9
24	West Virginia	10.9
29	Maryland	10.8
29	Oregon	10.8
31	Delaware	10.6
31	Tennessee	10.6
33	Florida	10.3
33	Kansas	10.3
35	Nebraska	10.2
36	Indiana	10.1
37	North Dakota	10.0
38	South Dakota	9.8
38	Wisconsin	9.8
40	Pennsylvania	9.7
41	Illinois	9.4
41	Michigan	9.4
41	Minnesota	9.4
44	New Jersey	9.1
45	Ohio	8.9
46	Connecticut	8.8
47	Massachusetts	8.6
48	New Hampshire	8.4
49	Rhode Island	8.0
50	New York	7.7
	District of Columbia	6.6

Source: U.S. Bureau of the Census
"2008 American Community Survey" (http://www.census.gov/acs/www/)
*Workers 16 and older who traveled to work by car, truck or van.

Percent of Commuters Who Travel to Work by Public Transportation: 2008

National Percent = 5.0%*

ALPHA ORDER

RANK	STATE	PERCENT
45	Alabama	0.5
24	Alaska	1.7
20	Arizona	2.3
48	Arkansas	0.4
8	California	5.3
15	Colorado	3.4
11	Connecticut	4.4
13	Delaware	3.8
21	Florida	2.0
18	Georgia	2.4
6	Hawaii	5.9
36	Idaho	1.0
4	Illinois	8.7
33	Indiana	1.1
30	Iowa	1.2
45	Kansas	0.5
30	Kentucky	1.2
28	Louisiana	1.3
40	Maine	0.7
5	Maryland	8.5
3	Massachusetts	8.9
27	Michigan	1.4
15	Minnesota	3.4
48	Mississippi	0.4
26	Missouri	1.6
33	Montana	1.1
40	Nebraska	0.7
14	Nevada	3.7
38	New Hampshire	0.8
2	New Jersey	10.3
30	New Mexico	1.2
1	New York	26.7
33	North Carolina	1.1
44	North Dakota	0.6
22	Ohio	1.9
48	Oklahoma	0.4
10	Oregon	4.5
8	Pennsylvania	5.3
17	Rhode Island	2.7
40	South Carolina	0.7
45	South Dakota	0.5
40	Tennessee	0.7
24	Texas	1.7
18	Utah	2.4
37	Vermont	0.9
12	Virginia	4.3
7	Washington	5.5
38	West Virginia	0.8
22	Wisconsin	1.9
28	Wyoming	1.3

RANK ORDER

RANK	STATE	PERCENT
1	New York	26.7
2	New Jersey	10.3
3	Massachusetts	8.9
4	Illinois	8.7
5	Maryland	8.5
6	Hawaii	5.9
7	Washington	5.5
8	California	5.3
8	Pennsylvania	5.3
10	Oregon	4.5
11	Connecticut	4.4
12	Virginia	4.3
13	Delaware	3.8
14	Nevada	3.7
15	Colorado	3.4
15	Minnesota	3.4
17	Rhode Island	2.7
18	Georgia	2.4
18	Utah	2.4
20	Arizona	2.3
21	Florida	2.0
22	Ohio	1.9
22	Wisconsin	1.9
24	Alaska	1.7
24	Texas	1.7
26	Missouri	1.6
27	Michigan	1.4
28	Louisiana	1.3
28	Wyoming	1.3
30	Iowa	1.2
30	Kentucky	1.2
30	New Mexico	1.2
33	Indiana	1.1
33	Montana	1.1
33	North Carolina	1.1
36	Idaho	1.0
37	Vermont	0.9
38	New Hampshire	0.8
38	West Virginia	0.8
40	Maine	0.7
40	Nebraska	0.7
40	South Carolina	0.7
40	Tennessee	0.7
44	North Dakota	0.6
45	Alabama	0.5
45	Kansas	0.5
45	South Dakota	0.5
48	Arkansas	0.4
48	Mississippi	0.4
48	Oklahoma	0.4
	District of Columbia	35.7

Source: U.S. Bureau of the Census
   "2008 American Community Survey" (http://www.census.gov/acs/www/)
*Workers 16 and older.

Annual Miles per Vehicle in 2008

National Annual Average = 11,982 Miles*

ALPHA ORDER

RANK	STATE	MILES
21	Alabama	12,538
50	Alaska	7,043
10	Arizona	14,092
5	Arkansas	16,249
47	California	9,775
1	Colorado	29,576
43	Connecticut	10,258
41	Delaware	10,344
27	Florida	12,065
18	Georgia	12,726
35	Hawaii	10,871
30	Idaho	11,569
36	Illinois	10,831
24	Indiana	12,137
49	Iowa	8,952
23	Kansas	12,140
15	Kentucky	13,189
32	Louisiana	11,332
14	Maine	13,550
22	Maryland	12,159
44	Massachusetts	10,229
17	Michigan	12,815
25	Minnesota	12,124
2	Mississippi	21,481
11	Missouri	14,031
29	Montana	11,664
33	Nebraska	10,913
8	Nevada	14,663
38	New Hampshire	10,742
28	New Jersey	11,787
3	New Mexico	16,741
26	New York	12,092
4	North Carolina	16,277
34	North Dakota	10,903
45	Ohio	9,906
7	Oklahoma	14,733
37	Oregon	10,776
40	Pennsylvania	10,404
42	Rhode Island	10,306
12	South Carolina	13,762
46	South Dakota	9,903
13	Tennessee	13,626
16	Texas	12,927
39	Utah	10,651
20	Vermont	12,575
19	Virginia	12,608
48	Washington	9,291
6	West Virginia	14,817
31	Wisconsin	11,495
9	Wyoming	14,227

RANK ORDER

RANK	STATE	MILES
1	Colorado	29,576
2	Mississippi	21,481
3	New Mexico	16,741
4	North Carolina	16,277
5	Arkansas	16,249
6	West Virginia	14,817
7	Oklahoma	14,733
8	Nevada	14,663
9	Wyoming	14,227
10	Arizona	14,092
11	Missouri	14,031
12	South Carolina	13,762
13	Tennessee	13,626
14	Maine	13,550
15	Kentucky	13,189
16	Texas	12,927
17	Michigan	12,815
18	Georgia	12,726
19	Virginia	12,608
20	Vermont	12,575
21	Alabama	12,538
22	Maryland	12,159
23	Kansas	12,140
24	Indiana	12,137
25	Minnesota	12,124
26	New York	12,092
27	Florida	12,065
28	New Jersey	11,787
29	Montana	11,664
30	Idaho	11,569
31	Wisconsin	11,495
32	Louisiana	11,332
33	Nebraska	10,913
34	North Dakota	10,903
35	Hawaii	10,871
36	Illinois	10,831
37	Oregon	10,776
38	New Hampshire	10,742
39	Utah	10,651
40	Pennsylvania	10,404
41	Delaware	10,344
42	Rhode Island	10,306
43	Connecticut	10,258
44	Massachusetts	10,229
45	Ohio	9,906
46	South Dakota	9,903
47	California	9,775
48	Washington	9,291
49	Iowa	8,952
50	Alaska	7,043

District of Columbia   16,135

Source: CQ Press using data from U.S. Department of Transportation, Federal Highway Administration
"Highway Statistics 2008" (Tables MV-1 and VM-2, http://www.fhwa.dot.gov/policyinformation/statistics/2008/index.cfm)
*Includes automobiles, trucks, buses and motorcycles.

Average Miles per Gallon in 2008

National Average = 17.4 Miles per Gallon*

ALPHA ORDER				RANK ORDER		
RANK	STATE	MILES PER GALLON		RANK	STATE	MILES PER GALLON
17	Alabama	18.1		1	Florida	21.1
50	Alaska	9.6		1	Hawaii	21.1
20	Arizona	17.8		3	West Virginia	20.0
33	Arkansas	16.7		4	Mississippi	19.7
10	California	18.4		5	New York	19.4
12	Colorado	18.2		6	New Mexico	19.3
19	Connecticut	18.0		7	Michigan	19.2
9	Delaware	18.5		8	Vermont	19.1
1	Florida	21.1		9	Delaware	18.5
12	Georgia	18.2		10	California	18.4
1	Hawaii	21.1		10	Minnesota	18.4
20	Idaho	17.8		12	Colorado	18.2
31	Illinois	16.8		12	Georgia	18.2
33	Indiana	16.7		12	North Carolina	18.2
48	Iowa	14.3		12	Oklahoma	18.2
27	Kansas	17.2		12	Wisconsin	18.2
37	Kentucky	16.3		17	Alabama	18.1
37	Louisiana	16.3		17	Rhode Island	18.1
23	Maine	17.6		19	Connecticut	18.0
25	Maryland	17.4		20	Arizona	17.8
25	Massachusetts	17.4		20	Idaho	17.8
7	Michigan	19.2		20	Utah	17.8
10	Minnesota	18.4		23	Maine	17.6
4	Mississippi	19.7		23	Tennessee	17.6
33	Missouri	16.7		25	Maryland	17.4
42	Montana	15.2		25	Massachusetts	17.4
40	Nebraska	15.8		27	Kansas	17.2
46	Nevada	14.5		27	Washington	17.2
37	New Hampshire	16.3		29	Pennsylvania	17.0
47	New Jersey	14.4		30	Ohio	16.9
6	New Mexico	19.3		31	Illinois	16.8
5	New York	19.4		31	Virginia	16.8
12	North Carolina	18.2		33	Arkansas	16.7
45	North Dakota	14.6		33	Indiana	16.7
30	Ohio	16.9		33	Missouri	16.7
12	Oklahoma	18.2		33	Oregon	16.7
33	Oregon	16.7		37	Kentucky	16.3
29	Pennsylvania	17.0		37	Louisiana	16.3
17	Rhode Island	18.1		37	New Hampshire	16.3
41	South Carolina	15.6		40	Nebraska	15.8
43	South Dakota	14.9		41	South Carolina	15.6
23	Tennessee	17.6		42	Montana	15.2
44	Texas	14.8		43	South Dakota	14.9
20	Utah	17.8		44	Texas	14.8
8	Vermont	19.1		45	North Dakota	14.6
31	Virginia	16.8		46	Nevada	14.5
27	Washington	17.2		47	New Jersey	14.4
3	West Virginia	20.0		48	Iowa	14.3
12	Wisconsin	18.2		49	Wyoming	13.5
49	Wyoming	13.5		50	Alaska	9.6
					District of Columbia	28.3

Source: CQ Press using data from U.S. Department of Transportation, Federal Highway Administration
   "Highway Statistics 2008" (Table VM-2, http://www.fhwa.dot.gov/policyinformation/statistics/2008/index.cfm)
*Total vehicle-miles for 2008 divided by total highway motor-fuel use. Includes gasoline, gasohol, diesel, and other "special fuels."

Airports in 2007

National Total = 13,729 Airports*

ALPHA ORDER				RANK ORDER			
RANK	STATE	AIRPORTS	% of USA	RANK	STATE	AIRPORTS	% of USA
32	Alabama	189	1.4%	1	Texas	1,428	10.4%
2	Alaska	548	4.0%	2	Alaska	548	4.0%
31	Arizona	192	1.4%	3	Illinois	542	3.9%
26	Arkansas	228	1.7%	4	California	539	3.9%
4	California	539	3.9%	5	Florida	511	3.7%
22	Colorado	256	1.9%	6	Ohio	507	3.7%
46	Connecticut	55	0.4%	7	Indiana	477	3.5%
49	Delaware	33	0.2%	8	Pennsylvania	455	3.3%
5	Florida	511	3.7%	9	Wisconsin	445	3.2%
16	Georgia	348	2.5%	10	New York	402	2.9%
48	Hawaii	36	0.3%	11	Missouri	384	2.8%
27	Idaho	218	1.6%	12	Michigan	379	2.8%
3	Illinois	542	3.9%	13	Minnesota	374	2.7%
7	Indiana	477	3.5%	14	Kansas	364	2.7%
28	Iowa	213	1.6%	15	Washington	358	2.6%
14	Kansas	364	2.7%	16	Georgia	348	2.5%
34	Kentucky	159	1.2%	17	Oregon	343	2.5%
24	Louisiana	238	1.7%	18	North Carolina	322	2.3%
39	Maine	107	0.8%	19	Oklahoma	315	2.3%
36	Maryland	153	1.1%	20	Virginia	303	2.2%
43	Massachusetts	78	0.6%	21	North Dakota	286	2.1%
12	Michigan	379	2.8%	22	Colorado	256	1.9%
13	Minnesota	374	2.7%	23	Nebraska	240	1.7%
29	Mississippi	199	1.4%	24	Louisiana	238	1.7%
11	Missouri	384	2.8%	25	Montana	231	1.7%
25	Montana	231	1.7%	26	Arkansas	228	1.7%
23	Nebraska	240	1.7%	27	Idaho	218	1.6%
40	Nevada	99	0.7%	28	Iowa	213	1.6%
47	New Hampshire	53	0.4%	29	Mississippi	199	1.4%
38	New Jersey	116	0.8%	30	Tennessee	198	1.4%
37	New Mexico	150	1.1%	31	Arizona	192	1.4%
10	New York	402	2.9%	32	Alabama	189	1.4%
18	North Carolina	322	2.3%	33	South Carolina	165	1.2%
21	North Dakota	286	2.1%	34	Kentucky	159	1.2%
6	Ohio	507	3.7%	35	South Dakota	155	1.1%
19	Oklahoma	315	2.3%	36	Maryland	153	1.1%
17	Oregon	343	2.5%	37	New Mexico	150	1.1%
8	Pennsylvania	455	3.3%	38	New Jersey	116	0.8%
50	Rhode Island	10	0.1%	39	Maine	107	0.8%
33	South Carolina	165	1.2%	40	Nevada	99	0.7%
35	South Dakota	155	1.1%	40	Utah	99	0.7%
30	Tennessee	198	1.4%	42	Wyoming	91	0.7%
1	Texas	1,428	10.4%	43	Massachusetts	78	0.6%
40	Utah	99	0.7%	44	West Virginia	76	0.6%
45	Vermont	60	0.4%	45	Vermont	60	0.4%
20	Virginia	303	2.2%	46	Connecticut	55	0.4%
15	Washington	358	2.6%	47	New Hampshire	53	0.4%
44	West Virginia	76	0.6%	48	Hawaii	36	0.3%
9	Wisconsin	445	3.2%	49	Delaware	33	0.2%
42	Wyoming	91	0.7%	50	Rhode Island	10	0.1%
					District of Columbia	2	0.0%

Source: U.S. Department of Transportation, Bureau of Transportation Statistics
   "State Transportation Statistics 2007" (http://www.bts.gov/publications/state_transportation_statistics/)
*This table comprises all U.S. public use and private use airports. Public use facilities are open to the public with no prior authorization or permission required. Private use facilities are not open to the general public and include medical, law enforcement, corporate, and other such facilities.

Inland Waterway Mileage in 2007

National Total = 29,627 Miles*

ALPHA ORDER

RANK	STATE	MILES	% of USA
6	Alabama	1,270	4.3%
1	Alaska	5,497	18.6%
40	Arizona	0	0.0%
3	Arkansas	1,860	6.3%
26	California	286	1.0%
40	Colorado	0	0.0%
32	Connecticut	117	0.4%
34	Delaware	99	0.3%
5	Florida	1,540	5.2%
14	Georgia	721	2.4%
40	Hawaii	0	0.0%
33	Idaho	111	0.4%
8	Illinois	1,095	3.7%
24	Indiana	353	1.2%
19	Iowa	492	1.7%
31	Kansas	120	0.4%
4	Kentucky	1,591	5.4%
2	Louisiana	2,823	9.5%
37	Maine	73	0.2%
18	Maryland	532	1.8%
35	Massachusetts	90	0.3%
40	Michigan	0	0.0%
28	Minnesota	258	0.9%
12	Mississippi	873	2.9%
10	Missouri	1,033	3.5%
40	Montana	0	0.0%
25	Nebraska	318	1.1%
40	Nevada	0	0.0%
39	New Hampshire	8	0.0%
23	New Jersey	360	1.2%
40	New Mexico	0	0.0%
22	New York	394	1.3%
7	North Carolina	1,152	3.9%
40	North Dakota	0	0.0%
21	Ohio	444	1.5%
30	Oklahoma	150	0.5%
16	Oregon	681	2.3%
27	Pennsylvania	259	0.9%
38	Rhode Island	39	0.1%
20	South Carolina	482	1.6%
36	South Dakota	75	0.3%
11	Tennessee	946	3.2%
13	Texas	834	2.8%
40	Utah	0	0.0%
40	Vermont	0	0.0%
17	Virginia	674	2.3%
9	Washington	1,057	3.6%
15	West Virginia	682	2.3%
29	Wisconsin	231	0.8%
40	Wyoming	0	0.0%

RANK ORDER

RANK	STATE	MILES	% of USA
1	Alaska	5,497	18.6%
2	Louisiana	2,823	9.5%
3	Arkansas	1,860	6.3%
4	Kentucky	1,591	5.4%
5	Florida	1,540	5.2%
6	Alabama	1,270	4.3%
7	North Carolina	1,152	3.9%
8	Illinois	1,095	3.7%
9	Washington	1,057	3.6%
10	Missouri	1,033	3.5%
11	Tennessee	946	3.2%
12	Mississippi	873	2.9%
13	Texas	834	2.8%
14	Georgia	721	2.4%
15	West Virginia	682	2.3%
16	Oregon	681	2.3%
17	Virginia	674	2.3%
18	Maryland	532	1.8%
19	Iowa	492	1.7%
20	South Carolina	482	1.6%
21	Ohio	444	1.5%
22	New York	394	1.3%
23	New Jersey	360	1.2%
24	Indiana	353	1.2%
25	Nebraska	318	1.1%
26	California	286	1.0%
27	Pennsylvania	259	0.9%
28	Minnesota	258	0.9%
29	Wisconsin	231	0.8%
30	Oklahoma	150	0.5%
31	Kansas	120	0.4%
32	Connecticut	117	0.4%
33	Idaho	111	0.4%
34	Delaware	99	0.3%
35	Massachusetts	90	0.3%
36	South Dakota	75	0.3%
37	Maine	73	0.2%
38	Rhode Island	39	0.1%
39	New Hampshire	8	0.0%
40	Arizona	0	0.0%
40	Colorado	0	0.0%
40	Hawaii	0	0.0%
40	Michigan	0	0.0%
40	Montana	0	0.0%
40	Nevada	0	0.0%
40	New Mexico	0	0.0%
40	North Dakota	0	0.0%
40	Utah	0	0.0%
40	Vermont	0	0.0%
40	Wyoming	0	0.0%
	District of Columbia	7	0.0%

Source: U.S. Department of Transportation, Bureau of Transportation Statistics
    "State Transportation Statistics 2007" (http://www.bts.gov/publications/state_transportation_statistics/)
*Waterway mileage was determined by including the length of channels 1) with a controlling draft of nine feet or greater, 2) with commercial cargo traffic reported for 1998 and 1999, but 3) were not offshore. Channels within major bays are included (e.g., Chesapeake Bay, San Francisco Bay, Puget Sound, Long Island Sound, and major sounds and straits in southeastern Alaska). Channels in the Great Lakes are not included.

Percent of Recreational Boating Accidents Involving Alcohol: 2008

National Percent = 8.1% of Accidents*

ALPHA ORDER

RANK	STATE	PERCENT
16	Alabama	11.8
5	Alaska	15.9
28	Arizona	7.0
18	Arkansas	10.6
29	California	6.9
34	Colorado	5.1
17	Connecticut	11.3
2	Delaware	18.2
33	Florida	5.5
20	Georgia	10.0
46	Hawaii	0.0
9	Idaho	13.8
35	Illinois	5.0
45	Indiana	1.8
19	Iowa	10.5
46	Kansas	0.0
36	Kentucky	4.3
4	Louisiana	16.4
21	Maine	9.4
29	Maryland	6.9
42	Massachusetts	3.1
39	Michigan	3.7
6	Minnesota	15.1
14	Mississippi	12.5
11	Missouri	13.3
1	Montana	29.0
7	Nebraska	15.0
9	Nevada	13.8
40	New Hampshire	3.6
36	New Jersey	4.3
41	New Mexico	3.3
29	New York	6.9
13	North Carolina	12.8
32	North Dakota	6.7
27	Ohio	7.2
44	Oklahoma	1.9
25	Oregon	7.5
3	Pennsylvania	16.9
43	Rhode Island	2.9
24	South Carolina	8.4
14	South Dakota	12.5
12	Tennessee	13.1
26	Texas	7.3
46	Utah	0.0
46	Vermont	0.0
38	Virginia	4.2
22	Washington	9.2
23	West Virginia	9.1
8	Wisconsin	14.5
46	Wyoming	0.0

RANK ORDER

RANK	STATE	PERCENT
1	Montana	29.0
2	Delaware	18.2
3	Pennsylvania	16.9
4	Louisiana	16.4
5	Alaska	15.9
6	Minnesota	15.1
7	Nebraska	15.0
8	Wisconsin	14.5
9	Idaho	13.8
9	Nevada	13.8
11	Missouri	13.3
12	Tennessee	13.1
13	North Carolina	12.8
14	Mississippi	12.5
14	South Dakota	12.5
16	Alabama	11.8
17	Connecticut	11.3
18	Arkansas	10.6
19	Iowa	10.5
20	Georgia	10.0
21	Maine	9.4
22	Washington	9.2
23	West Virginia	9.1
24	South Carolina	8.4
25	Oregon	7.5
26	Texas	7.3
27	Ohio	7.2
28	Arizona	7.0
29	California	6.9
29	Maryland	6.9
29	New York	6.9
32	North Dakota	6.7
33	Florida	5.5
34	Colorado	5.1
35	Illinois	5.0
36	Kentucky	4.3
36	New Jersey	4.3
38	Virginia	4.2
39	Michigan	3.7
40	New Hampshire	3.6
41	New Mexico	3.3
42	Massachusetts	3.1
43	Rhode Island	2.9
44	Oklahoma	1.9
45	Indiana	1.8
46	Hawaii	0.0
46	Kansas	0.0
46	Utah	0.0
46	Vermont	0.0
46	Wyoming	0.0

District of Columbia   0.0

Source: CQ Press using data from United States Coast Guard
   "Boating Statistics 2008" (http://www.uscgboating.org/statistics/accident_statistics.aspx)
*Alcohol involvement in a boating accident includes any accident in which alcoholic beverages are consumed in the boat and the investigating official has determined that the operator was impaired or affected while operating the boat.

Railroad Accidents and Incidents in 2008

National Total = 12,648*

ALPHA ORDER					RANK ORDER			
RANK	STATE		ACCIDENTS	% of USA	RANK	STATE	ACCIDENTS	% of USA
19	Alabama		242	1.9%	1	Illinois	1,142	9.0%
41	Alaska		93	0.7%	2	New York	1,036	8.2%
30	Arizona		159	1.3%	3	Texas	952	7.5%
18	Arkansas		243	1.9%	4	California	819	6.5%
4	California		819	6.5%	5	Pennsylvania	752	5.9%
25	Colorado		198	1.6%	6	New Jersey	444	3.5%
37	Connecticut		95	0.8%	7	Indiana	350	2.8%
43	Delaware		61	0.5%	8	Ohio	333	2.6%
16	Florida		254	2.0%	9	Nebraska	311	2.5%
12	Georgia		280	2.2%	10	Louisiana	290	2.3%
50	Hawaii		0	0.0%	11	Missouri	286	2.3%
40	Idaho		94	0.7%	12	Georgia	280	2.2%
1	Illinois		1,142	9.0%	13	Minnesota	270	2.1%
7	Indiana		350	2.8%	14	Kansas	266	2.1%
15	Iowa		264	2.1%	15	Iowa	264	2.1%
14	Kansas		266	2.1%	16	Florida	254	2.0%
28	Kentucky		182	1.4%	16	Washington	254	2.0%
10	Louisiana		290	2.3%	18	Arkansas	243	1.9%
47	Maine		28	0.2%	19	Alabama	242	1.9%
32	Maryland		141	1.1%	20	Tennessee	236	1.9%
21	Massachusetts		222	1.8%	21	Massachusetts	222	1.8%
22	Michigan		213	1.7%	22	Michigan	213	1.7%
13	Minnesota		270	2.1%	23	North Carolina	202	1.6%
31	Mississippi		143	1.1%	23	Virginia	202	1.6%
11	Missouri		286	2.3%	25	Colorado	198	1.6%
27	Montana		193	1.5%	26	Wisconsin	195	1.5%
9	Nebraska		311	2.5%	27	Montana	193	1.5%
44	Nevada		53	0.4%	28	Kentucky	182	1.4%
49	New Hampshire		7	0.1%	29	Oklahoma	177	1.4%
6	New Jersey		444	3.5%	30	Arizona	159	1.3%
37	New Mexico		95	0.8%	31	Mississippi	143	1.1%
2	New York		1,036	8.2%	32	Maryland	141	1.1%
23	North Carolina		202	1.6%	33	Oregon	140	1.1%
36	North Dakota		107	0.8%	34	Wyoming	132	1.0%
8	Ohio		333	2.6%	35	South Carolina	122	1.0%
29	Oklahoma		177	1.4%	36	North Dakota	107	0.8%
33	Oregon		140	1.1%	37	Connecticut	95	0.8%
5	Pennsylvania		752	5.9%	37	New Mexico	95	0.8%
48	Rhode Island		19	0.2%	37	West Virginia	95	0.8%
35	South Carolina		122	1.0%	40	Idaho	94	0.7%
45	South Dakota		49	0.4%	41	Alaska	93	0.7%
20	Tennessee		236	1.9%	42	Utah	73	0.6%
3	Texas		952	7.5%	43	Delaware	61	0.5%
42	Utah		73	0.6%	44	Nevada	53	0.4%
46	Vermont		34	0.3%	45	South Dakota	49	0.4%
23	Virginia		202	1.6%	46	Vermont	34	0.3%
16	Washington		254	2.0%	47	Maine	28	0.2%
37	West Virginia		95	0.8%	48	Rhode Island	19	0.2%
26	Wisconsin		195	1.5%	49	New Hampshire	7	0.1%
34	Wyoming		132	1.0%	50	Hawaii	0	0.0%
						District of Columbia	100	0.8%

Source: U.S. Department of Transportation, Federal Railroad Administration
"Railroad Accidents and Incidents 2008" (http://safetydata.fra.dot.gov/officeofsafety/)
*Accidents or incidents include all events reportable to the U.S. Department of Transportation. These include train accidents causing damage above an established threshold; highway-rail grade crossing incidents involving impact between railroad equipment and highway users at crossings; and all other reportable incidents that cause a fatality or injury to any person or an occupational illness to a railroad employee.

Railroad Mileage Operated in 2007

National Total = 140,695 Miles of Railroad*

ALPHA ORDER

RANK	STATE	MILES	% of USA
16	Alabama	3,295	2.3%
45	Alaska	506	0.4%
35	Arizona	1,751	1.2%
25	Arkansas	2,776	2.0%
3	California	5,330	3.8%
27	Colorado	2,643	1.9%
47	Connecticut	330	0.2%
48	Delaware	218	0.2%
23	Florida	2,859	2.0%
7	Georgia	4,775	3.4%
50	Hawaii	0	0.0%
37	Idaho	1,591	1.1%
2	Illinois	7,336	5.2%
9	Indiana	4,446	3.2%
11	Iowa	3,929	2.8%
6	Kansas	4,851	3.4%
28	Kentucky	2,558	1.8%
24	Louisiana	2,855	2.0%
40	Maine	1,165	0.8%
43	Maryland	757	0.5%
41	Massachusetts	1,069	0.8%
12	Michigan	3,699	2.6%
8	Minnesota	4,546	3.2%
29	Mississippi	2,435	1.7%
10	Missouri	4,077	2.9%
19	Montana	3,224	2.3%
20	Nebraska	3,223	2.3%
39	Nevada	1,194	0.8%
46	New Hampshire	416	0.3%
42	New Jersey	990	0.7%
33	New Mexico	1,895	1.3%
13	New York	3,565	2.5%
18	North Carolina	3,248	2.3%
15	North Dakota	3,478	2.5%
4	Ohio	5,307	3.8%
17	Oklahoma	3,249	2.3%
30	Oregon	2,384	1.7%
5	Pennsylvania	5,184	3.7%
49	Rhode Island	87	0.1%
31	South Carolina	2,269	1.6%
36	South Dakota	1,679	1.2%
26	Tennessee	2,649	1.9%
1	Texas	10,804	7.7%
38	Utah	1,421	1.0%
44	Vermont	569	0.4%
20	Virginia	3,223	2.3%
22	Washington	3,210	2.3%
32	West Virginia	2,248	1.6%
14	Wisconsin	3,503	2.5%
34	Wyoming	1,856	1.3%

RANK ORDER

RANK	STATE	MILES	% of USA
1	Texas	10,804	7.7%
2	Illinois	7,336	5.2%
3	California	5,330	3.8%
4	Ohio	5,307	3.8%
5	Pennsylvania	5,184	3.7%
6	Kansas	4,851	3.4%
7	Georgia	4,775	3.4%
8	Minnesota	4,546	3.2%
9	Indiana	4,446	3.2%
10	Missouri	4,077	2.9%
11	Iowa	3,929	2.8%
12	Michigan	3,699	2.6%
13	New York	3,565	2.5%
14	Wisconsin	3,503	2.5%
15	North Dakota	3,478	2.5%
16	Alabama	3,295	2.3%
17	Oklahoma	3,249	2.3%
18	North Carolina	3,248	2.3%
19	Montana	3,224	2.3%
20	Nebraska	3,223	2.3%
20	Virginia	3,223	2.3%
22	Washington	3,210	2.3%
23	Florida	2,859	2.0%
24	Louisiana	2,855	2.0%
25	Arkansas	2,776	2.0%
26	Tennessee	2,649	1.9%
27	Colorado	2,643	1.9%
28	Kentucky	2,558	1.8%
29	Mississippi	2,435	1.7%
30	Oregon	2,384	1.7%
31	South Carolina	2,269	1.6%
32	West Virginia	2,248	1.6%
33	New Mexico	1,895	1.3%
34	Wyoming	1,856	1.3%
35	Arizona	1,751	1.2%
36	South Dakota	1,679	1.2%
37	Idaho	1,591	1.1%
38	Utah	1,421	1.0%
39	Nevada	1,194	0.8%
40	Maine	1,165	0.8%
41	Massachusetts	1,069	0.8%
42	New Jersey	990	0.7%
43	Maryland	757	0.5%
44	Vermont	569	0.4%
45	Alaska	506	0.4%
46	New Hampshire	416	0.3%
47	Connecticut	330	0.2%
48	Delaware	218	0.2%
49	Rhode Island	87	0.1%
50	Hawaii	0	0.0%
	District of Columbia	23	0.0%

Source: Association of American Railroads
   "Railroads and States 2007" (http://www.aar.org/Resources/RailroadsStates.aspx)
*Includes Class I and non-Class I miles. Excludes trackage rights. Synonymous with route-miles, so that a mile of single track
is counted the same as a mile of double track.

Sources

ACT, Inc.
500 ACT Drive, P.O. Box 168
Iowa City, IA 52243-0168
319-337-1000
www.act.org

Administration for Children and Families
U.S. Department of Health and Human Services
370 L'Enfant Promenade, SW
Washington, DC 20201
202-401-9215
www.acf.hhs.gov

American Cancer Society, Inc.
1599 Clifton Road, NE
Atlanta, GA 30329-4251
800-227-2345
www.cancer.org

American Dental Association
211 E. Chicago Ave.
Chicago, IL 60611-2678
312-440-2500
www.ada.org

American Hospital Association
One North Franklin
Chicago, IL 60606-3421
312-422-3000
www.aha.org

American Medical Association
515 North State Street
Chicago, IL 60610
800-621-8335
www.ama-assn.org

Association of American Railroads
425 Third Street, SW
Suite 1000
Washington, DC 20024
202-639-2100
www.aar.org

Bureau of the Census
4600 Silver Hill Road
Washington, DC 20233-0001
800-923-8282
www.census.gov

Bureau of Economic Analysis
U.S. Department of Commerce
1441 L Street, NW
Washington, DC 20230
202-606-9900
www.bea.gov

Bureau of Justice Statistics
U.S. Department of Justice
810 Seventh St., NW
Washington, DC 20531
202-307-0765
www.ojp.usdoj.gov/bjs/

Bureau of Labor Statistics
U.S. Department of Labor
2 Massachusetts Ave., NE.
Washington, DC 20212-0001
202-691-5200
www.bls.gov

Bureau of Transportation Statistics
1200 New Jersey Ave., SE
Washington DC 20590
800-853-1351
www.bts.gov

Centers for Disease Control and Prevention
1600 Clifton Road
Atlanta, GA 30333
800-232-4636
www.cdc.gov

Centers for Medicare and Medicaid Services
7500 Security Blvd.
Baltimore, MD 21244-1850
877-267-2323
www.cms.hhs.gov

College Board
45 Columbus Ave.
New York, NY 10023-6992
212-713-8000
www.collegeboard.com

Economic Research Service
U.S. Department of Agriculture
1800 M Street, NW
Washington, DC 20036-5831
202-694-5050
www.ers.usda.gov

Energy Information Administration
1000 Independence Ave., SW
Washington, DC 20585
202-586-8800
www.eia.doe.gov

Environmental Protection Agency
Ariel Rios Building
1200 Pennsylvania Ave, NW
Washington, DC 20464
202-272-0167
www.epa.gov

Federal Bureau of Investigation
935 Pennsylvania Ave., NW
Washington, DC 20535
202-324-3000
www.fbi.gov

Federal Highway Administration
1200 New Jersey Ave., SE
Washington, DC 20590
202-366-4000
www.fhwa.dot.gov

Federation of Tax Administrators
444 North Capitol St., NW, Suite 348
Washington, DC 20001
202-624-5890
www.taxadmin.org

Food and Nutrition Service
U.S. Department of Agriculture
3101 Park Center Drive
Alexandria, VA 22302
703-305-2281
www.fns.usda.gov/fns/

General Services Administration
1800 F Street, NW
Washington, DC 20405
202-501-1231
www.gsa.gov

Health Resources and Services Administration
Division of Practitioner Data Banks
5600 Fishers Lane
Rockville, MD 20857
800-767-6732
www.hrsa.gov

Internal Revenue Service
U.S. Department of the Treasury
1111 Constitution Ave., NW
Washington, DC 20224
800-829-1040
www.irs.gov

Medical Expenditure Panel Survey
Agency for Healthcare Research and Quality
540 Gaither Road
Rockville, MD 20850
301-427-1364
www.meps.ahrq.gov

National Agricultural Statistics Service
1400 Independence Ave., SW
Washington, DC 20250
800-727-9540
www.nass.usda.gov

National Assembly of State Arts Agencies
1029 Vermont Ave., NW, 2nd Fl
Washington, DC 20005
202-347-6352
www.nasaa-arts.org

National Association of Realtors
430 N. Michigan Ave.
Chicago, IL 60611
800-874-6500
www.realtor.org

National Association of State Park Directors
8829 Woodyhill Road
Raleigh, NC 27613
919-676-8365
www.naspd.org

National Center for Education Statistics
U.S. Department of Education
1990 K Street, NW
Washington, DC 20006
202-502-7300
http://nces.ed.gov

National Center for Health Statistics
U.S. Department of Health and Human Services
3311 Toledo Road
Hyattsville, MD 20782
800-232-4636
www.cdc.gov/nchs/

National Conference of State Legislatures
770 E. First Place
Denver, CO 80230
303-346-7700
www.ncsl.org

National Education Association
1201 16th Street, NW
Washington, DC 20036-3290
202-833-4000
www.nea.org

National Highway Traffic Safety Administration
1200 New Jersey Ave., SE
Washington, DC 20590
888-327-4236
www.nhtsa.dot.gov

National Institute on Alcohol Abuse and Alcoholism
5635 Fishers Lane, MSC 9304
Bethesda, MD 20892-9304
301-443-3860
www.niaaa.nih.gov/

National Oceanic & Atmospheric Administration
U.S. Department of Commerce
1401 Constitution Ave., NW, Rm 5128
Washington, DC 20230
202-482-6090
www.noaa.gov

National Weather Service
Storm Prediction Center
120 David Boren Blvd
Norman, OK 73072
405-579-0771
www.spc.noaa.gov

Social Security Administration
Windsor Park Building
6401 Security Blvd.
Baltimore, MD 21235
800-772-1213 (information)
www.ssa.gov

Tax Foundation
529 14th Street, NW
Suite 420
Washington, DC 20036
202-464-6200
www.taxfoundation.org

U.S. Department of Defense
Directorate for Public Inquiry and Analysis
Room 2E565, The Pentagon
1400 Defense Pentagon
Washington, DC 20301-1400
703-428-0711
www.defenselink.mil

U.S. Department of Veterans Affairs
810 Vermont Ave., NW
Washington, DC 20420
202-273-5700
www.va.gov

U.S. Geological Survey
12201 Sunrise Valley Drive
Reston, VA 20192
703-648-5953
www.usgs.gov

Index